The Oxford History of the Ancient Near East

The Oxford History of the Ancient Near East
Editors: Karen Radner, Nadine Moeller, and D. T. Potts

This groundbreaking, five-volume series offers a comprehensive, fully illustrated history of Egypt and Western Asia (the Levant, Anatolia, Mesopotamia, and Iran), from the emergence of complex states to the conquest of Alexander the Great. Written by a highly diverse, international team of leading scholars, whose expertise brings to life the people, places, and times of the remote past, the volumes in this series focus firmly on the political and social histories of the states and communities of the ancient Near East. Individual chapters present the key textual and material sources underpinning the historical reconstruction, paying particular attention to the most recent archaeological finds and their impact on our historical understanding of the periods surveyed.

Volume 1: From the Beginnings to Old Kingdom Egypt and the Dynasty of Akkad

Volume 2: From the End of the Third Millennium BC to the Fall of Babylon

The Oxford History of the Ancient Near East

Volume II: From the End of the Third Millennium BC *to the Fall of Babylon*

━━━━━━━◦⟨⦿⟩◦━━━━━━━

Edited by

KAREN RADNER
NADINE MOELLER
D. T. POTTS

OXFORD
UNIVERSITY PRESS

OXFORD
UNIVERSITY PRESS

Oxford University Press is a department of the University of Oxford. It furthers
the University's objective of excellence in research, scholarship, and education
by publishing worldwide. Oxford is a registered trade mark of Oxford University
Press in the UK and certain other countries.

Published in the United States of America by Oxford University Press
198 Madison Avenue, New York, NY 10016, United States of America.

© Oxford University Press 2022

Library of Congress Cataloging-in-Publication Data
Names: Radner, Karen, editor, author. | Moeller, Nadine, editor, author. |
Potts, Daniel T., editor, author.
Title: The Oxford history of the ancient Near East /
edited by Karen Radner, Nadine Moeller, and Daniel T. Potts.
Description: New York : Oxford University Press, 2022. |
Includes bibliographical references and index. |
Contents: Volume 2. From the end of the third millennium BC to the fall of Babylon
Identifiers: LCCN 2020002854 | ISBN 9780190687571 (v. 2: hardback) |
ISBN 9780190687595 (v. 2: epub) | ISBN 9780197601037 (v. 2: online)
Subjects: LCSH: Egypt—Civilization. | Egypt—Antiquities. |
Egypt—History—Sources. | Middle East—Civilization. |
Middle East—Antiquities. | Middle East—History—Sources.
Classification: LCC DT60 .O97 2020 | DDC 939.4—dc23
LC record available at https://lccn.loc.gov/2020002854

DOI: 10.1093/oso/9780190687571.001.0001

1 3 5 7 9 8 6 4 2
Printed by Sheridan Books, Inc., United States of America

Contents

Preface   vii

Time Chart   xi

The Contributors   xiii

Abbreviations   xix

11. Establishing an Absolute Chronology of the Middle Bronze Age (Felix Höflmayer)   1

12. Egypt in the First Intermediate Period (Juan Carlos Moreno García)   47

13. The Kingdom of Ur (Steven J. Garfinkle)   121

14. The Middle East after the Fall of Ur: Isin and Larsa (Klaus Wagensonner)   190

15. The Middle East after the Fall of Ur: From Assur to the Levant (Ilya Arkhipov)   310

16. The Middle East after the Fall of Ur: From Ešnunna and the Zagros to Susa (Katrien De Graef)   408

17. Before the Kingdom of the Hittites: Anatolia in the Middle Bronze Age (Gojko Barjamovic)   497

18. The Kingdom of Babylon and the Kingdom of the Sealand (Odette Boivin)   566

19. Egypt's Middle Kingdom: A View from Within (Harco Willems)   656

20. Middle Kingdom Egypt and Africa (Kathryn A. Bard)   728

21. Middle Kingdom Egypt and the Eastern Mediterranean (Ezra S. Marcus)   777

22. Egypt's Middle Kingdom: Perspectives on Culture and Society (Wolfram Grajetzki)   854

Index   925

Preface

THIS IS THE second volume of the *Oxford History of the Ancient Near East*, which covers Egypt and Nubia, the Levant, Anatolia, Mesopotamia, and Iran from the turn of the third to the second millennium BC and through the first half of that millennium, broadly corresponding to the Middle Bronze Age. The first volume (published in August 2020) closed with the end of the Old Kingdom in Egypt and of the Akkad state in Mesopotamia, and as we stated in its preface, future generations of scholars will hopefully establish whether we should have included Egypt's First Intermediate Period and/or the kingdom of the Third Dynasty of Ur in that volume. Their discussion opens the present volume, after a chapter devoted to the absolute chronology of the first half of the second millennium BC and the possibilities, problems, and priorities inherent in the different sources, including historical data, archaeological finds, and stratigraphies, and radiocarbon-dated, organic materials that need to be correlated and synchronized across a vast geographical region from the Nile to Iran.

In Egypt, the Middle Kingdom constituted a long-lived, and relatively well-documented, state that greatly influenced the neighboring regions in Nubia and the Levant. Further east, the political organization of Mesopotamia and Syria after the disintegration of the kingdom of Ur can be described as a mosaic of medium-sized, small, and single-city states, with quickly changing alliances and several short-lived attempts to establish larger political units; the most successful project loomed large in Iran from which the *Sukkalmah* Dynasty's power at times reached as far as northern Syria. The availability of sources for this "warring state period" is extremely uneven, with the events of some decades documented in great detail in certain places, while otherwise centuries can be sketched in rough outlines only. We therefore decided to organize this part of the volume geographically in four chapters, with a regional focus on southern Mesopotamia; on northern Mesopotamia and Syria; on the eastern Tigris region and Iran; and on Anatolia. The emergence of a kingdom centered on Babylon eventually led to a brief period of political unification under Hammurabi and his successors that came to an end with the "Fall of Babylon"; the relevant chapter covers also the rival southern state of the Sealand that outlived the kingdom of Babylon by centuries. The following Time Chart (pp. xi-xii) presents a concise overview of the chronological coverage of the volume, but note also the detailed chronological tables accompanying Chapters 11, 14, 16, and 18.

The cover of the present volume depicts, together with its modern impression on a strip of clay, an Old Syrian cylinder seal, which is today housed in the collection of the Morgan Library & Museum, New York (accession number 0967) and was acquired by Pierpont Morgan between 1885 and 1908. It shows the weather god standing on two mountains, facing a nude goddess. A suppliant goddess on the right, further female figures above, a tethered bull, and smaller symbols (bird, lion, celestial signs) add complexity to a scene that is typical of Old Syrian–style cylinder seals from the early second millennium BC. After the seal of the Old Kingdom ruler Sahura on the cover of the first volume of the *Oxford History of the Ancient Near East*, it is the second of the five cylinder seals from different parts of the Near East chosen to adorn the covers of the individual volumes in order to highlight the region's great cultural commonalities and divergences. The present seal epitomizes the universe of ideas, cultural practices, and diverse traditions that link the regions covered in this volume.

This book brings together another distinguished group of experts in the field, again a mix of established scholars and bright new talents from across the globe. We are very grateful to all of them for contributing the twelve chapters that make up this volume, covering the time "from the end of the third millennium BC to the fall of Babylon" and showcasing the very different approaches that the available sources necessitate, from the analysis of hugely diverse groups of texts to the close study of material culture such as pottery and coffin styles. Draft manuscripts were received between August 2018 and August 2020.

In transcribing Egyptian proper nouns, we follow the conventions of *The Oxford History of Ancient Egypt*, edited by Ian Shaw (OUP 2004, rev. ed.). While we use hyphenation to separate the components of Sumerian personal names with two constituent elements (e.g., Ur-Namma) we do not do this for longer names (e.g., Ninšatapada instead of Nin-šata-pada). We follow normal practice in marking the individual words within Akkadian proper nouns (e.g., Dur-Yasmah-Addu, Rim-Sin). We also mark the individual words within Elamite and Amorite names (e.g., Tan-Ruhurater, Samsi-Addu). Whenever a person or place is widely known by a conventional spelling, we use that (e.g., Hammurabi instead of Hammu-rapi, Cutha instead of Kutiu). We do not use any long vowels in proper nouns, including modern Arabic and Farsi place names.

Our work on the *Oxford History of the Ancient Near East* was greatly facilitated by the fellowships awarded by the Center for Advanced Studies of LMU Munich (CAS^{LMU}) to Nadine Moeller and Dan Potts, which allowed us to come together in Munich in July 2016, 2017, and 2018, when the groundwork for this volume was laid. Much of the joint editorial work on the chapters of the second volume was achieved in our 2019 meetings in Chicago, Penjwin (Kurdish Autonomous Region of Iraq), and Pouillon (Chalosse region, France). However, the global COVID-19 (Sars-CoV-2) pandemic and resultant travel restrictions made it impossible for us to meet in 2020. Our close collaboration continued, thanks to our joint GoogleDrive folders and especially the WhatsApp group "OHANE Editors," which came to be our most important communication tool.

As ever, we are greatly indebted to our editor at Oxford University Press, Stefan Vranka, who accompanied and facilitated our work on this volume at every step. The index was prepared by Luiza Osorio Guimarães da Silva (Chicago), who was also instrumental in harmonizing proper nouns across chapters and volumes. At LMU Munich, we are grateful to Denise Bolton, who language-edited several chapters; to Thomas Seidler, who checked and consolidated the chapter bibliographies; and to Dr Andrea

Squitieri, who created the cartography for the individual chapters. We also thank Philipp Seyr (Liège) for harmonizing the Egyptian names and spellings across the volume. Their work was funded by the Alexander von Humboldt Foundation via the International Award for Research in Germany 2015 to Karen Radner. We are very grateful for their speed and attention to detail as well as their patience and good humor, especially in the often difficult times of 2020 when libraries and offices were closed.

Time Chart

	Egypt	Syria	Mesopotamia — Iraq					Iran
		Lagaš / *Assur*	*Isin* (2019–1794)	*Larsa* (2025–1763)	*Ur* (2110–2003)	*Babylon* (1894–1595)	*Ešnunna* (c.2026–c.1760)	*Elam* Sukkalmah Dynasty
2150 BC	**First Intermediate Period** (2160–2055)	…			Ur-Namma			Ebarat I
	Ninth and Tenth Dynasties / **Eleventh Dynasty**	Gudea			Šulgi			Kindattu
	Herakleopolis / *Thebes*	…			Amar-Sin			Idattu I
	Khety (Nebkaura) — Mentuhotep I (fictious?)				Šu-Sin			Tan-Ruhurater
	Khety (Wahkara) — Intef I (Sehertawy)		Išbi-Erra	Naplanum	Ibbi-Sin		Bilalama	
	Khety (Meryibra) — Intef II (Wahankh)		Šu-ilišu	Yamsium			Išar-ramaši	Ebarat II
	Merykara — Intef III (Nakhtnebtepnefer)		Iddin-Dagan	Samium			Ušur-awassu	
2050 BC	**Middle Kingdom** (2055–1650)	**Assur**	Išme-Dagan	Zabaya			Azuzum	Šilhaha
	Eleventh Dynasty (all of Egypt)	Irišum I (1972–1933)	Lipit-Eštar	Gungunum			Ur-Ninmarki	
	Mentuhotep II (Nebhepetra)	…	Ur-Ninurta	Abi-sare			Ur-Ningišzida	Pala-išan
	Mentuhotep III (Sankhkara)		Bur-Sin	Sumu-El		Sumu-abum	Ipiq-Adad I	
	Mentuhotep IV (Nebtawyra)		Lipit-Enlil				Šarriya	
	Twelfth Dynasty		Erra-imitti	Nur-Adad		Sumu-la-El	Warassa	Temti-Agum I
	Amenemhat I (Sehetepibra)		Enlil-bani	Sin-iddinam			Belakum	
	Senusret I (Kheperkara)							

	Egypt	*Yamhad*	*Mari*	*Ekallatum*			Babylon	Ešnunna / *Sealand*	Elam
	Amenemhat II (Nubkaura)							Ibal-pi-El I	Kuk-našur I (?)
	Senusret II (Khakheperra)							Ipiq-Adad II	…
	Senusret III (Khakaura)							Naram-Sin	Širuktuh (c. 1785)
	Amenemhat III (Nimaatra)	Sumu-epuh	Yagid-Lim	Samsi-Addu (1833–1775)	Zambiya	Sin-iribam	Sabium	…	
			Yahdun-Lim		Iter-piša	Sin-iqišam	Apil-Sin	Daduša	
	Amenemhat IV (Maakherura)		Sumu-Yamam		Ur-dukuga	Ṣilli-Adad	Sin-muballiṭ	Ibal-pi-El II	Siwe-palar-huppak
	Queen Sobekneferu	Yarim-Lim I	Zimri-Lim (1774–1761)		Sin-magir	Warad-Sin		Šilli-Sin (1764–1760?)	Kudu-zuluš I (c. 1767–1765)
1800 BC	**Thirteenth Dynasty** (selection of kings, in chronological order)	Hammurabi I			Damiq-ilišu (1816–1794)	Rim-Sin I (1822–1763)	Hammurabi (1792–1750)		Kuter-Nahhunte
	Amenemhat Sobekhotep (Sekhemra-khuytawy)	Abba-El I							Temti-Agum II
	Ameny-Qemau	Yarim-Lim II							Atta-mera-halki
	Sobekhotep II (Khaankhra)	Niqmi-epuh					Samsu-iluna (1749–1712)	**Sealand** (c. 1720–c. 1480) / Ili-ma-ilu	Tatta
	Hor (Awibra)	Irkabtum							Kuk-našur II
	Wegaf (Khuytawyra)						Abi-ešuh (1711–1684)	Itti-ili-nibi	Kuter-Silhaka
	Khendjer (Userkara)								
	Sobekhotep III (Sekhemra-sewadjtawy)						Ammi-ditana (1683–1647)	Dam-(i)q-ilišu	Temti-raptaš
	Neferhotep I (Khasekhemra)								Kudu-zuluš II
	Sobekhotep IV (Khaneferra)							Iškibal	Sirtuh
1650 BC	Ay (Merneferra)	Hammurabi II					Ammi-ṣaduqa (1646–1626)	Šušši	
1600 BC		…					Samsu-ditana (1625–1595)	Gulkišar (c. 1595)	Tan-uli
		Hammurabi III						DIŠ+U-EN (?)	Temti-halki
		…						Pešgaladarameš	Kuk-našur III
								Ayadaragalama	
								Ekurduana	
								Melamkura	
1500 BC								Ea-gamil (c. 1480)	

The Contributors

Ilya Arkhipov (PhD, Institute of World History of the Russian Academy of Sciences in Moscow) is associate professor at the Institute of Oriental and Classical Studies of the HSE University, Moscow. His main fields of interest are the history of Old Babylonian Upper Mesopotamia, and Akkadian vocabulary and grammar. His publications include a volume of texts from the Mari archives (*Le vocabulaire de la métallurgie et la nomenclature des objets en métal dans les textes de Mari*; Peeters, 2012).

Kathryn A. Bard (PhD, University of Toronto) is professor of Archaeology and Classical Studies at Boston University, and fellow of the American Academy of Arts and Sciences. She directed excavations at the Predynastic sites of Hu-Semaineh in Upper Egypt (1989, 1991), but her research interests later expanded to the relationships between Egypt and the Horn of Africa. With Rodolfo Fattovich (University of Naples "L'Orientale"), she co-directed excavations at Aksum, Ethiopia (1993–2002), and Mersa/Wadi Gawasis, Egypt (2003–2011). Her most recent book, co-authored with Rodolfo Fattovich, is *Seafaring expeditions to Punt in the Middle Kingdom: excavations at Mersa/Wadi Gawasis, Egypt* (Brill, 2018).

Gojko Barjamovic (PhD, University of Copenhagen) is a senior lecturer on Assyriology at Harvard University. A member of the Royal Danish Academy of Sciences, his field of research is the social and economic history of Mesopotamia with focus on the study of trade and trans-regional interaction in the second millennium BC. He has written and edited several books, including *A historical geography of Anatolia in the Old*

Assyrian colony period (Museum Tusculanum, 2011), and *Libraries before Alexandria* (Oxford University Press, 2019).

Odette Boivin (PhD, University of Toronto) is a postdoctoral researcher in Ancient Near Eastern Studies at Westfälische Wilhelms-Universität Münster. Her research focuses on Babylonian history in the second and first millennia BC. She has published a number of studies on the mid-second millennium Kingdom of the Sealand, including *The First Dynasty of the Sealand in Mesopotamia* (De Gruyter, 2018). She is also editing and studying mid-first millennium BC cuneiform archives from central and southern Iraq.

Katrien De Graef (PhD, Ghent University) is associate professor of Assyriology and History of the Ancient Near East at Ghent University. Her research focuses on the relations between Babylonia and Elam in the third and second millennium BC on the one hand, and on the Old Babylonian period on the other hand, specifically on the cities of Sippar (Iraq) and Susa (Iran) as well as socioeconomic history, ancient topography, and questions of gender and sealing practices. The author of two monographs presenting some of the rich textual sources from Susa (*Les archives d'Igibuni: les documents Ur III du chantier B à Suse*, 2005; *De la dynastie Simaški au sukkalmahat: les documents fin PE II—début PE III du chantier B à Suse*, 2006), she co-edited with Jan Tavernier the volume *Susa and Elam: archaeological, philological, historical and geographical perspectives* (Brill, 2013).

Steven J. Garfinkle (PhD, Columbia University) is professor of Ancient History at Western Washington University, and editor of the *Journal of Ancient Near Eastern History* (De Gruyter). His research focuses on the society and economy of early Mesopotamia, with emphasis on the intersections between commerce, state formation, and violence. He is the author of numerous studies on the kingdom of Ur and the history of the late third millennium BC, including *Entrepreneurs and enterprise in early Mesopotamia* (CDL Press, 2012).

Wolfram Grajetzki (PhD, Humboldt-Universität zu Berlin) is an honorary research associate at the Institute of Archaeology of University College London. Having gained his PhD with a study on the highest

Middle Kingdom court officials, he has worked on field projects and excavations in Egypt and Pakistan and has taught in London and Berlin. His many books include *The Middle Kingdom of ancient Egypt: history, archaeology and society* (Duckworth, 2006), *Court officials of the Egyptian Middle Kingdom* (Duckworth, 2009), *The coffin of Zemathor and other rectangular coffins of the late Middle Kingdom and Second Intermediate Period* (Golden House, 2010), and *Tomb treasures in the late Middle Kingdom: the archaeology of female burials* (University of Pennsylvania Press, 2014).

Felix Höflmayer (PhD, University of Vienna) studied Egyptology and archaeology and specializes in the archaeology of the eastern Mediterranean, with a focus on interregional relations and absolute chronology. After holding postdoctoral fellowships at the German Archaeological Institute in Amman (Jordan) and Berlin and the Oriental Institute of the University of Chicago, he joined the Austrian Academy of Sciences in Vienna in 2015 and currently co-directs the Austrian excavations at Tel Lachish.

Ezra S. Marcus (D.Phil., University of Oxford) is an associate researcher at the Recanati Institute for Maritime Studies in the Leon Charney School for Marine Sciences at the University of Haifa, after previous appointments as a lecturer in Israel and the United States. A maritime and coastal archaeologist, he has worked both in Israel and in Turkey and is currently directing a number of legacy projects, all focused on the southern Levantine coast and the role of maritime trade in Middle Bronze Age coastal settlement and its subsequent history.

Nadine Moeller (PhD, University of Cambridge) is professor of Egyptian Archaeology at Yale University. Her research focuses on ancient Egyptian urbanism, on which she has published the monograph *The archaeology of urbanism in Ancient Egypt* (Cambridge University Press, 2016). She has participated in numerous fieldwork projects in Egypt and since 2001 has been directing excavations at Tell Edfu in southern Egypt.

Juan Carlos Moreno García (PhD, École Pratique des Hautes Études, Paris) is a CNRS senior researcher at the Sorbonne University in Paris, specializing in the study of ancient Egypt's socioeconomic history and the structure of the state. Recent publications include *The state in ancient Egypt: power, challenges and dynamics* (Bloomsbury, 2019), *Dynamics of production in the ancient Near East, 1300–500 BC* (Oxbow, 2016), and *Ancient Egyptian administration* (Brill, 2013). He is editor-in-chief of *The Journal of Egyptian History* (Brill).

Daniel T. Potts (PhD, Harvard University) is professor of Ancient Near Eastern Archaeology and History at the Institute for the Study of the Ancient World, New York University. A corresponding member of the German Archaeological Institute, he has worked in Iran, the United Arab Emirates, Saudi Arabia, Turkey, Armenia, and the Kurdish Autonomous Region of Iraq. His numerous books include *The archaeology of Elam: formation and transformation of an ancient Iranian state* (Cambridge University Press, 2nd ed., 2015) and *Nomadism in Iran: from antiquity to the modern era* (Oxford University Press, 2014).

Karen Radner (PhD, University of Vienna) holds the Alexander von Humboldt Chair of the Ancient History of the Near and Middle East at LMU Munich. A member of the German Archaeological Institute and the Bavarian Academy of Sciences and Humanities, her numerous books include *A short history of Babylon* (Bloomsbury, 2020) and *Ancient Assyria: a very short introduction* (Oxford University Press, 2015), as well as editions of cuneiform archives from Iraq, Syria, and Turkey.

Klaus Wagensonner (PhD, University of Vienna) is postdoctoral associate at the Department of Near Eastern Languages and Civilizations and the Babylonian Collection at Yale University. His research focuses on early scholarly traditions, in particular lexical texts from the late Uruk to Old Babylonian periods. He also investigated scribal families of Middle Assyrian Assur. Currently, he is preparing the publication of Sumerian literary texts in the Yale Babylonian Collection, as well as of Old Babylonian letters from Kiš in various British and US collections.

Harco Willems (PhD, Rijksuniversiteit Groningen) is full professor of Egyptology at the Department of Archaeology of KU Leuven. His research focuses on Old and Middle Kingdom Egypt, with social structure, landscape, and religion constituting major points of interest that resulted, for example, in the monograph *Historical and archaeological aspects of Egyptian funerary culture* (Brill, 2014). He has participated in archaeological fieldwork in the Dakhla oasis and Shanhur and is currently the director of the excavations at Deir el-Bersha.

Abbreviations

AAE	*Arabian Archaeology and Epigraphy*
AfO	*Archiv für Orientforschung*
AJA	*American Journal of Archaeology*
ÄL	*Ägypten & Levante*
AnSt	*Anatolian Studies*
AoF	*Altorientalische Forschungen*
ASAE	*Annales du Service des Antiquités de l'Égypte*
BaM	*Baghdader Mitteilungen*
BASOR	*Bulletin of the American Schools of Oriental Research*
BIFAO	*Bulletin de l'Institut Français d'Archéologie Orientale*
BiOr	*Bibliotheca Orientalis*
CAD	*The Assyrian Dictionary of the Oriental Institute of the University of Chicago*
CDLJ	*Cuneiform Digital Library Journal*
EA	*Egyptian Archaeology*
GM	*Göttinger Miszellen*
IEJ	*Israel Exploration Journal*
IrAnt	*Iranica Antiqua*
JA	*Journal Asiatique*
JAEI	*Journal of Ancient Egyptian Interconnections*
JANEH	*Journal of Ancient Near Eastern History*
JAOS	*Journal of the American Oriental Society*
JAR	*Journal of Archaeological Research*
JARCE	*Journal of the American Research Center in Egypt*
JAS	*Journal of Archaeological Science*
JCS	*Journal of Cuneiform Studies*

JEA	*Journal of Egyptian Archaeology*
JEH	*Journal of Egyptian History*
JEOL	*Jaarbericht "Ex Oriente Lux"*
JNES	*Journal of Near Eastern Studies*
JWP	*Journal of World Prehistory*
MARI	*Mari: Annales de recherches interdisciplinaires*
MDAIK	*Mitteilungen des Deutschen Archäologischen Instituts, Kairo*
MDOG	*Mitteilungen der Deutschen Orient-Gesellschaft*
NABU	*Nouvelles Assyriologiques Brèves et Utilitaires*
NEA	*Near Eastern Archaeology*
OJA	*Oxford Journal of Archaeology*
OLZ	*Orientalistische Literaturzeitung*
PEQ	*Palestine Exploration Quarterly*
QSR	*Quaternary Science Reviews*
RA	*Revue d'Assyriologie et d'archéologie orientale*
RdE	*Revue d'Égyptologie*
RlA	*Reallexikon der Assyriologie und Vorderasiatischen Archäologie*
SAK	*Studien zur altägyptischen Kultur*
SEL	*Studi Epigrafici e Linguistici sul Vicino Oriente Antico*
SMEA	*Studi Micenei ed Egeo Anatolici*
WdO	*Die Welt des Orients*
ZA	*Zeitschrift für Assyriologie und Vorderasiatische Archäologie*
ZAR	*Zeitschrift für Altorientalische und Biblische Rechtsgeschichte*
ZÄS	*Zeitschrift für Ägyptische Sprache und Altertumskunde*

11

Establishing an Absolute Chronology of the Middle Bronze Age

Felix Höflmayer

11.1. Chronological concepts: historical, archaeological, scientific chronologies

A sound chronological framework is the backbone of all history writing. Every historical argument stands or falls according to the relative or absolute chronology applied. The answer to the question *when* is the first prerequisite to raise questions about *how* and *why*.

For the ancient Near East in the Middle Bronze Age (ca. 2000–1500 BC; figure 11.1), three different methodological approaches to chronology are currently in use: historical (or political) chronologies for Egypt and Mesopotamia; archaeological (or relative) chronologies mainly for the Levant; and radiocarbon chronologies which have been generated for both historical chronologies and relative chronologies, but which are *independent* of both systems of dating.

Before the introduction of scientific dating methods, such as radiocarbon dating, scholars had to rely on other sources to construct a chronological framework that allowed an ordering of events relative to

Felix Höflmayer, *Establishing an Absolute Chronology of the Middle Bronze Age* In: *The Oxford History of the Ancient Near East*. Edited by: Karen Radner, Nadine Moeller, and D. T. Potts, Oxford University Press.
© Oxford University Press 2022. DOI: 10.1093/oso/9780190687571.003.0011

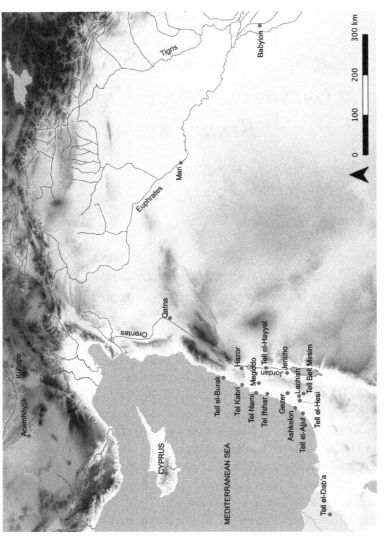

FIGURE 11.1. Sites mentioned in this chapter. Prepared by Andrea Squitieri (LMU Munich).

each other. Different chronological systems were established for different fields, e.g., Egypt, Mesopotamia, or the Levant, and the respective systems differed in the sources they used to construct their chronological framework, as well as in their results. In regions with an abundance of written sources and elaborate calendar systems, such as Egypt or Mesopotamia, our modern chronological models often followed and adapted ancient concepts for structuring time, such as the sequence of Egyptian kings and dynasties or the year-name or eponym lists of Mesopotamia. In regions where written sources were lacking, scholars based their chronological reconstructions on material culture, most often on the development of the shape and decoration of pottery, based on the stratigraphic sequences of so-called key-sites. Although these systems seem to be methodologically independent from each other, in fact several interdependencies exist between them, although these often lack systematic definition.

As long as a scholar's research questions remain within the limits of a given society or field employing a single chronological system, the subject of absolute dates is of marginal interest, if the relative sequence of events can be reconstructed to a satisfying degree of certainty. As soon as a research question touches upon interregional developments, a single chronological system might not suffice to order events and developments temporally, requiring one to find other means of structuring time and events related to different chronological systems. In particular, the analysis of long-term developments, such as questions of urbanization, the rise and fall of complex societies, migration, and/or the spread of technology and knowledge throughout the ancient Near East and beyond, makes an overarching absolute chronology necessary to track changes and to distinguish between cause and effect in human history. In order to relate events within (and the development of) different regions, such as Egypt, the Levant, Mesopotamia, and Anatolia, to each other, one needs to relatively synchronize the different chronological systems in use by establishing chronological links based on imported objects or dated textual references to identifiable historical events in other cultures. Using absolute calendrical dates derived from various sources (mostly from datable texts on astronomical observations) proved to be challenging before the advent of radiocarbon dating, as there were often several competing chronological models available based on the same set of evidence (e.g., the High, Middle, and Low Chronologies for Mesopotamia). Nevertheless, for a long time, absolute dates seemed to be less important than the relative synchronization of different chronological systems. Philip Betancourt, who published extensively on the subject of the Santorini eruption in the mid-second millennium BC and its relationship with Egyptian chronology, correctly pointed out that

> the problem is that the discovery of the absolute dates is not as important as the question of the relative chronology. For historical conclusions, moving an event a hundred years forward or back in time is not as important at our present level of knowledge as understanding its relevance to other events from approximately the same time.[1]

It was only with the advent of radiocarbon dating that a direct link between an organic object and a calendrical date could be established. Only then was the same yardstick employed to measure time in all regions and throughout all periods.

Chronology has been one of the most contested fields of research in ancient Near Eastern studies. The three seminal volumes *High, Middle, or Low*, edited by Paul Aström and published in 1987 and 1989, summarized the diverging chronologies of Mesopotamia, Egypt, the Middle Bronze Age of the Levant, Cyprus, the Aegean, and Anatolia that had been created by historians up to the late 1980s.[2] Later, the project "Synchronization of Civilizations in the Eastern Mediterranean in the Second Millennium BC" (SCIEM-2000), hosted by the Austrian Academy of Sciences and funded by the Austrian Research Fund, aimed to provide a synchronized chronology of the Middle and Late Bronze

1. Betancourt 1998: 295.

2. Åström 1987a; 1987b; 1989.

Ages for the entire eastern Mediterranean.[3] Although no final consensus could be reached, a substantial amount of new data enriched the chronological discussion and provided new arguments for consideration. Both of these projects aimed at synchronizing historical (political) and relative (archaeological) chronological systems with each other.

In this chapter, we will outline the different chronological systems relevant to the Middle Bronze Age ancient Near East, i.e., the historical chronology of Egypt during the Middle Kingdom and the Second Intermediate Period, the Middle Bronze Age phases of the Levant, and the different chronological options for the historical chronology of Mesopotamia. Then we will summarize prior chronological synchronizations for the ancient Near East. Finally, we will outline the method, potential, and limitations of radiocarbon dating for this period and produce an absolute, radiocarbon-based chronological framework for the entire Middle Bronze Age ancient Near East.

II.I.I. The Egyptian historical chronology

The Egyptian historical chronology is one of the most important chronological reference systems for the ancient Near East and the eastern Mediterranean.[4] Our current chronological system for Dynastic Egypt is, in itself, an interpretation of a complicated network of interlocking, mostly written, data. The basic system of grouping the reigns of multiple kings into thirty dynasties derives from the late Egyptian priest Manetho, who most likely compiled his major work *Aegyptiaca* in the third century BC.[5] Although this work has not been preserved, substantial quotations from it can be found in the works of other Greek and Roman authors, including Flavius Josephus, Sextus Julius Africanus, Eusebius of Caesarea, and Georgios Syncellus. Manetho's chronological system is surprisingly similar to contemporary sources, such as the Turin Canon; both refer

---

3. Bietak 2000; 2003; Bietak and Czerny 2007.

4. Beckerath 1997; Kitchen 2000; Hornung et al. 2006a.

5. Waddell 1940; Helck 1956; Hornung et al. 2006b.

to individual kings, both attribute a certain reign-length to them, and both form dynasties of several groups of individual kings.[6] Therefore, it is likely that Manetho both had access to firsthand sources and was able to verify his dates with contemporary sources (or, if not, to explain why certain parts of his chronology were corrupted).[7] Other contemporary sources such as king lists, dated monuments (mentioning a king's name and the respective year of reign), and genealogical data[8] helped to corroborate and to refine this chronological system.

It is important to stress that this chronological system is a *political* one. Time is structured by a sequence of individual reigns of kings (and then grouped into dynasties). This is similar to how we order time (in certain contexts) when we speak about "the Obama administration" or "the Trump administration."

The Egyptian historical chronology is, a priori, a floating chronology; it needs additional information to be placed absolutely in calendrical time. One important method for establishing absolute dates is the system of dead-reckoning, i.e., adding up the highest accounted individual regnal years from a point in time for which an absolute calendrical date has been agreed upon. One of these fixed dates in the field of Egyptology is the Persian conquest of Egypt under King Cambyses in 525 BC.[9] Of course, adding up the highest accounted regnal years is often hampered by fragmentary, or sometimes ambivalent, sources, which are particularly common in the so-called Intermediate Periods. One also has to take into account potential co-regencies between certain pharaohs.[10]

Another method for establishing absolute calendrical dates (often used in conjunction with dead-reckoning) is astrochronology, i.e., the calculation of absolute dates for astronomical observations mentioned in datable written sources. Especially for the Middle Kingdom, the

---

6. Gardiner 1959; Helck 1992; Ryholt 1997; 2004; Allen 2010.

7. Gundacker 2015; Hornung et al. 2006b.

8. Bennett 2002; Jansen-Winkeln 2006; Bierbrier 2006; Bennett 2006.

9. Depuydt 1996.

10. Kitchen 2000; 2007.

prediction of a Sothic rise mentioned in Papyrus Berlin 10012 is of key importance, and it has been used for establishing the chronology of the Middle Kingdom in absolute calendrical time.[11] Lunar dates have also been used to calculate the chronology of the Middle Kingdom, and Rolf Krauss and other colleagues have used this method to arrive at a chronological reconstruction that is significantly lower than the traditional Middle Kingdom chronology.[12]

The Middle Kingdom and the Second Intermediate Period (from the Twelfth to the Seventeenth Dynasties) is the period of Egyptian history relevant to the Middle Bronze Age of the ancient Near East.[13] While the attribution of individual kings to certain dynasties is generally established, the meaning of the terms "Middle Kingdom" and "Second Intermediate Period" vary. Some scholars regard only the Twelfth Dynasty as the Middle Kingdom; others include also the Thirteenth Dynasty. Open discussions also continue about the sequence of kings in the Second Intermediate Period (in particular regarding the position of the Hyksos king Khyan in the sequence of Fifteenth Dynasty rulers) or about potential overlap between certain dynasties (e.g., whether the end of the Thirteenth Dynasty overlaps with the beginning of the Fifteenth Dynasty).[14]

For the scope of this chapter, it is not necessary to outline in detail the different historical arguments for one or another chronological model of Middle Kingdom and Second Intermediate Period Egypt. It is important to stress that (a) the historical chronology of Egypt is a *political* one and is therefore, a priori, *independent* of the development of material culture in Egypt; and (b) before the application of radiocarbon dating and Bayesian analysis, absolute calendrical dates for the Egyptian Middle Kingdom and Second Intermediate Period derived from an interpretation of astronomical observations, resulting in a High and a Low Middle Kingdom Chronology (table 11.1).

---

11. Borchardt 1899; Luft 1992.

12. Krauss 1985; 2003; 2006.

13. Franke 1988a; 1988b; Schneider 2008.

14. Forstner-Müller and Moeller 2018.

Table 11.1. Different chronological models for the Egyptian historical chronology of the Middle Kingdom

Dynasties	Kings	Low Chronology (after Hornung, Krauss, and Warburton)	High Chronology (after Kitchen)	High Chronology (after von Beckerath)
Twelfth Dynasty	Amenemhat I	1939–1910	1973–1944	1976–1947
	Senusret I	1920–1875	1953–1908	1956–1911/10
	Amenemhat II	1878–1843	1911–1876	1914–1879/76
	Senusret II	1845–1837	1878–1872	1882–1872
	Senusret III	1837–1819	1872–1853	1872–1853/52
	Amenemhat III	1772–1764	1853–1808	1853–1806/05
	Amenemhat IV	1763–1760	1808–1799	1807/06–1798/97
	Sobekneferu	1763–1760	1799–1795	1798/97–1794/93
Thirteenth Dynasty		1759–1630	1795–1638	1794/93–1648/45
Fifteenth Dynasty (Hyksos)		?–1530	1638–1540	1648/45–1539/36
Start of Eighteenth Dynasty		1539	1540	1550

11.1.2. The Mesopotamian historical chronology

Within the chronological systems of the ancient Near East, the Mesopotamian system of historical chronology was not only in use in the land between the Euphrates and Tigris rivers, but was also partly employed within Syria and eastern Anatolia. For chronological discussions of the central and southern Levant, the Mesopotamian chronology has only rarely been taken into account. However, for the absolute chronology of the Middle Bronze Age Levant (and Egypt), absolute calendrical dates for the First Dynasty of Babylon (i.e., the Hammurabi dynasty; see chapter 18 in this volume), which ended approximately around the mid-second millennium BC, are indeed of interest. As with Egyptian historical chronology, our chronological system for First Dynasty Mesopotamia is essentially a *political* one, based on the interpretation of texts such as king lists, eponym lists, dated monuments, and royal inscriptions. This floating political chronology is, in itself, fairly well established and the internal order of political events is generally not disputed.[15]

Absolute evidence for dating the First Babylonian Dynasty is found, as in Egyptian historical chronology, in written sources containing astronomical observations, especially the Venus tablets of Ammi-ṣaduqa.[16] Astronomical calculations initially led to three competing chronological models, the so-called High, Middle, and Low Chronologies (HC, MC, and LC).

While the High Chronology, advocated by Peter Huber, placed the fall of Babylon (and the end of the First Dynasty of Babylon and the so-called Old Babylonian period) at 1651 BC, the more conventionally used Middle Chronology dated the same event to 1595 BC, and the Low Chronology to 1531 BC.[17] These three chronological models of the First Dynasty of Babylon already have a 120-year difference between them. Two additional chronological systems, suggesting even later dates, were published in the last two decades and complement the current

15. Pruzsinszky 2009.

16. Huber et al. 1982; Huber 2000.

17. Pruzsinszky 2009.

discussions around absolute dates for the First Dynasty of Babylon. The so-called New Chronology, advocated by Hermann Gasche, dates the fall of Babylon to 1499 BC and, more recently, Joachim Mebert suggested a date of 1522 BC.[18] Therefore, it is possible to date the same historical event (the fall of Babylon) across a span of more than 150 years, based on different interpretations of written sources and their respective astronomical calculations. After many discussions in the field, most scholars adopted the Middle Chronology. However, as Regine Pruzsinszky pointed out, this happened "for reasons of 'convenience,' not because the middle chronology has been 'proven.'"[19]

The so-called Revised Eponym List of Assyria (REL) is of crucial importance for linking the relative chronology of the Middle Bronze Age of the Levant (and subsequently Egypt) with the competing chronological models for the First Dynasty of Babylon (for details, cf. section 11.4). The REL is basically an annual timescale based on textual sources from Assur and the Mari Eponym Chronicles.[20] As with any politically based chronological framework, the REL is a priori floating in time. Relative years are designated by the prefix REL and a running number that ranges from REL 1 to REL 255. One can order political events relatively in time (based on the eponyms), but for evidence for absolute calendrical dating one needs to synchronize this floating chronology with other systems to establish absolute dates. In fact, it has been possible to synchronize the REL with the Babylonian chronology, as the northern Mesopotamian ruler Samsi-Addu (= "Šamši-Adad I" in the Assyrian King List; REL 165–197) died in the 18th year of Hammurabi.[21] Therefore, the death of Samsi-Addu in REL 197 could be dated either to 1830 BC (High Chronology), 1774 BC (Middle Chronology), 1710 BC (Low Chronology), 1701 BC (Mebert's chronology), or 1678 BC (New Chronology) (table 11.2).

---

18. Gasche et al. 1998; Mebert 2010.

19. Pruzsinszky 2009: 17.

20. Barjamovic et al. 2012.

21. Charpin and Ziegler 2003.

Table 11.2. Dates for selected reigns according to different models for the Mesopotamian historical chronology

	New Chronology	Mebert Chronology	Low Chronology	Middle Chronology	High Chronology
End of Babylon (First Dynasty)	1499	1522	1531	1595	1651
Reign of Ammi-ṣaduqa	1550–1530	1573–1553	1582–1562	1646–1626	1702–1682
Death of Samsi-Addu (REL 197)	1678	1701	1710	1774	1830
Reign of Hammurabi	1696–1654	1719–1677	1728–1686	1792–1750	1848–1806

11.1.3. The relative chronology of the Middle Bronze Age in the Levant

The relative chronological model for the Levant, and specifically for the southern Levant, differs significantly from both the Egyptian as well as the Mesopotamian historical chronologies. Relative chronological systems are mainly based on the development of material culture, the appearance and disappearance of so-called *fossils directeurs* which are regarded as characteristic for certain chronological periods. In societies without written historical sources (as with the Middle Bronze Age Levant), this typological method, originally developed for prehistoric Europe by Oscar Montelius,[22] remains the only possible method for structuring time. Ideally, the development of material culture can be reconstructed based on sites with long, overlapping stratigraphic sequences.

During the early twentieth century, many different chronological terminologies were in use for excavations in the Levant. Flinders Petrie differentiated between an Amorite, a Phoenician, and a Jewish period in his excavation of Tell el-Hesi; Stewart Macalister divided the stratigraphy of Gezer into Pre-, First, Second, Third, and Fourth Semitic Periods; and Ernst Sellin and Carl Watzinger subdivided their sequence in Jericho into prehistoric, Canaanite, Israelite, and Jewish phases.[23] In 1922, the leading archaeologists of the southern Levant met in Jerusalem and agreed upon a new terminology, which, with some modification, is still in use today.[24] William Foxwell Albright was one of the first to apply this new chronological terminology to his excavations at Tell Beit Mirsim.[25]

Our current relative chronological model for the Levant discriminates between an Early, a Middle, and a Late Bronze Age, followed by Iron Age phases. Relative archaeological terms for the Middle Bronze Age are unfortunately somewhat confusing (table 11.3). Today, we usually

---

22. Montelius 1903.

23. Petrie 1891; Macalister 1912; Sellin and Watzinger 1913.

24. Garstang et al. 1922.

25. Albright 1930–1931; 1931–1932; 1936–1937.

Table 11.3. Different terminologies for the relative chronology of the Middle Bronze Age

Early Bronze Age I–III			
Middle Bronze Age I	Early Bronze Age IV / Intermediate Bronze Age		
Middle Bronze Age IIA	Middle Bronze Age IIA	Middle Bronze Age I	Middle Bronze Age I
Middle Bronze Age IIB	Middle Bronze Age IIB	Middle Bronze Age II	Middle Bronze Age II
	Middle Bronze Age IIC		Middle Bronze Age III
Late Bronze Age			

employ the terms Middle Bronze Age I, II, and III, but at the same time, Middle Bronze Age IIA, IIB, and IIC are also in use (MB I = MB IIA; MB II = MB IIB; MB III = MB IIC). Some scholars prefer a bipartite structure as opposed to the tripartite version more commonly in use (Middle Bronze Age I and II or Middle Bronze Age IIA and IIB), in which case Middle Bronze Age II incorporates both Middle Bronze Age II and III (IIB and IIC, respectively). The reason for this confusing terminology goes back to William Foxwell Albright, who named the non-urbanized interlude between the first cities of the Early Bronze Age and the second urbanization of the Middle Bronze Age the "Middle Bronze Age I." This period was later referred to either as the "Early Bronze Age IV" or the "Intermediate Bronze Age." Consequently, what we today regard as the first phase of the Middle Bronze Age ended up being referred to as the "Middle Bronze Age IIA." Later, scholars adopted the more logical sequence of Middle Bronze I, II, and III, which we also employ in this chapter.[26]

---

26. Cohen 2002.

The relative chronological framework for the Middle Bronze Age Levant (see chapter 21 in this volume) is based on the development of material culture, most notably pottery, as observed on key sites in the Levant with adequate stratigraphic sequences.[27] It must be stressed that this system is mainly based on stratigraphic sequences from the southern Levant (modern Israel, the Palestinian Territories, and Jordan), due to much more intensive excavation and publication in this region during the last century. Because of this, the Middle Bronze Age sequence is a floating chronology. The terms Middle Bronze Age I, II, and III are applied to a certain package of material culture, and absolute dates for these phases (and synchronization with the Egyptian and/or Mesopotamian chronologies) may only be inferred via links to chronological systems that have other means of applying absolute calendrical dates.

11.2. *Previous synchronistic models for the Middle Bronze Age*

Several synchronistic models for the Middle Bronze Age ancient Near East were proposed prior to the systematic application of radiocarbon dating. Discussion surrounding these focused mainly on the synchronization (and subsequent absolute dating) of the Middle Bronze Age with the historical chronology of Egypt. Although the relative Middle Bronze Age chronology can be linked to Mesopotamia via Hazor and the Mari letters (see later discussion in this section), this connection has not been utilized to reconstruct absolute dates for the southern Levant, as

> any attempt at a direct synchronism with Mesopotamia [. . .] is bedeviled by the uncertainty among Assyriologists as to the most likely dates for the Old Babylonian period.[28]

---

27. Sharon 2014.

28. Dever 1992: 11.

Nevertheless, proponents of a Low Middle Bronze Age Chronology have attempted to link the Levantine chronological system with Mesopotamia, advocating for Mebert's chronology or the New Chronology.[29] In this section, we will summarize the traditional models for synchronizing the Middle Bronze Age Levant with Egypt (based on Dever and Weinstein) and contrast these with the Low Chronology proposed by Manfred Bietak (and others), who tried to establish a coherent chronology for the ancient Near East from Egypt to Mesopotamia, based on what critics view as insufficient evidence.

The Traditional Chronology has occasionally been based only on very general chronological associations with Egypt. The beginning of the Middle Bronze Age was traditionally dated to around 2000 BC, but this date was based on the assumption that the de-urbanized Early Bronze IV (or Intermediate Bronze Age) coincided with Egypt's First Intermediate Period, and that therefore Middle Bronze Age I should start at about the same time as the Egyptian Twelfth Dynasty.[30] The transition from Middle Bronze I to Middle Bronze II was placed at ca. 1800/1750 BC and thought to coincide with the transition from the Egyptian Twelfth to the Thirteenth Dynasty—a "convenient starting point."[31] Other scholars opted for a slightly later beginning, around 1725 BC, already in the early Thirteenth Dynasty.[32] The start of Middle Bronze III was traditionally dated to ca. 1650 BC and this period was thought to be

> exactly equivalent to the climax of the Hyksos or Asiatic occupation of Egypt and the rise of Semitic rulers to power under Dynasty 15.[33]

---

29. Ben-Tor 2004; Bietak 2013.

30. Dever 1992: 2.

31. Dever 1992: 10.

32. Weinstein 1992: 38.

33. Dever 1992: 12.

The end of the Middle Bronze Age and the beginning of the Late Bronze Age has been equated "with the Egyptian campaigns in Asia that were the apparent cause of at least partial destruction of nearly every site,"[34] beginning under Kamose and Ahmose, but lasting into the early Eighteenth Dynasty. The widespread destruction that marked the end of the Middle Bronze Age at many sites in the southern Levant was thus synchronized with the so-called expulsion of the Hyksos from Egypt and its aftermath.

It becomes clear that the traditional synchronization with the historical chronology of Egypt (making it the source for any absolute dates applied to relative chronological phases in the Levant) was not so much based on any detailed archaeological observation or correspondence between material cultures, but rather on historical assumptions that were accepted as given. Middle Bronze I would be equated with the Twelfth Dynasty, Middle Bronze II with the Thirteenth Dynasty, and Middle Bronze III with the Fifteenth Dynasty (the Hyksos Period). The start of the Late Bronze Age would coincide with the expulsion of the Hyksos and assumed military raids directly afterwards.[35]

In the 1980s and 1990s, Manfred Bietak proposed a new, earlier chronology for the Middle Bronze Age. He based his dates largely on the Austrian excavations at Tell el-Dab'a (ancient Avaris) in the eastern Nile delta.[36] This site was well integrated within the eastern Mediterranean exchange networks and, in addition to local Egyptian material culture, significant quantities of originally imported, and then locally produced, Levantine Middle Bronze Age pottery, as well as Cypriot material, were unearthed. This made possible a chronological synchronization between the stratigraphic phases at Tell el-Dab'a and the relative chronologies of the Levant, Cyprus, and the Aegean. Bietak based his synchronization on the first appearance of widely circulated pottery types:

---

34. Dever 1992: 13.

35. Dever 1992; Mumford 2014.

36. Bietak 1975; 1991b; 1996; 2013.

Especially significant was the repetitive pattern of the first appearances of Kamares ware and Middle and Late Cypriot wares in the stratigraphy of a series of sites [...]. This enabled the export of the Egyptian chronology to the Levant and Cyprus by establishing timelines.[37]

While the chronological synchronization between the Tell el-Dabʿa stratigraphy and the relative chronology of the Levant was based on material culture, according to the excavator the site's stratigraphy itself was dated in accordance with so-called datum-lines—secure links between the stratigraphic phases and Egyptian historical chronology.[38]

The Low Chronology dated the start of the Middle Bronze Age to ca. 1900 BC, based on the depictions of socket spearheads and a duckbill axe in the tomb of Khnumhotep II at Beni Hasan, datable to the 6th year of Senusret II. Earlier tombs at the same site still showed the fenestrated axes usually associated with Early Bronze IV (or Intermediate Bronze Age).[39] The transition from Middle Bronze I to Middle Bronze II was thought to be equivalent to Stratum F at Tell el-Dabʿa. While the preceding Stratum G/1–3 was still characterized by Middle Bronze I pottery and bronzes, in Stratum F, the earliest Middle Bronze II pottery and bronzes appear, while some Middle Bronze I material became obsolete. The following Stratum E/3, however, showed clear Middle Bronze II material culture. Stratum F was dated into the mid- to late Thirteenth Dynasty, to ca. 1710–1680 BC.[40] The transition from Middle Bronze II to Middle Bronze III was thought to coincide with early Stratum D/3 at Tell el-Dabʿa, falling into the mid-Fifteenth Dynasty or around ca. 1590 BC.[41] The end of the Middle and the beginning of the Late Bronze Age was linked to the first appearance of Cypriot White Slip I and Base Ring I

---

37. Bietak 2013: 81.

38. Bietak 2013; Höflmayer 2015: 268–269.

39. Bietak 2002: 40; Weinstein 1992: 33–34.

40. Bietak 1991a; 2013.

41. Bietak 1991a; 2013.

wares in Tell el-Dabʿa Stratum C/3, dated to ca. 1500/1450 BC. The start of the Late Bronze Age was thus equated with the early Eighteenth Dynasty down to the Thutmosid period.[42]

While the Traditional Chronology of the Middle Bronze Levant employed a very schematic synchronization based on general historical assumptions, the Low Chronology was based on the development of material culture within a single site, Tell el-Dabʿa (figure 11.2).

Sources for absolute dates were only available via dating the archaeological strata of Tell el-Dabʿa according to the Egyptian historical chronology. Tell el-Dabʿa thus served as the hinge (and the only hinge) between the historical chronology of Egypt and the Levantine relative chronological phases. Every problem within Egyptian historical chronology, or with the dating of the stratigraphic sequence at Tell el-Dabʿa, would therefore also be imposed on the relative chronology of the Middle Bronze Age Levant (figure 11.3).

The Low Chronology for the Middle Bronze Age southern Levant was also linked to Mesopotamia via Middle Bronze Age Hazor and the Mari letters.[43] Although Hazor is located in modern-day Israel, and is therefore treated as part of the southern Levant, its actual material culture finds closer parallels further north, and it should therefore be regarded as "the southernmost extension of the Syro-Mesopotamian world."[44] Hazor was well integrated into the Syro-Mesopotamian trade network and had commercial relations with Qatna, east of the Orontes, and Mari, on the west bank of the middle Euphrates (see chapter 15 in this volume). So far, more than fifteen cuneiform documents have been unearthed at Hazor, at least eight of them dating to the Middle Bronze Age and one of them containing an Old Babylonian letter mentioning Mari and Ekallatum.[45] On the other hand, Hazor is also mentioned several times in the Mari

---

42. Bietak 2013.

43. Ben-Tor 2004; Bietak 2013.

44. Maeir 2000: 38.

45. Horowitz and Wasserman 2000; Horowitz et al. 2018; Horowitz 2013.

FIGURE 11.2. Stratigraphical table for Tell el-Dab'a. After Bietak 2013: fig. 8.1.

MB-PHASES	B.C.	EGYPT RELATIVE CHRONOLOGY	TOWN CENTER (Middle Kingdom) Ezbet Rushdi R/I	NEW CENTER MB-Population F/I	PALACE DISTRICT F/II	EASTERN TOWN A/I-IV	NORTHEASTERN TOWN A/V	PALACE DISTRICT Ezbet Helmi H/I-VI	GENERAL STRATIGRAPHY
LB I	1410	Dyn. XVIII (TIII, TIII, TI, AII)						Amenhotep	C2
	1440								C3
	1470								D1
MB III (MB II C)	1500	AHMOSE							D1 · Ahmose — **DATUM LINE ± 1530 BC**
	1530							Thera Pumice c	D2
	1560	XV HYKSOS	DENUDED	a2	e1	D2	D2	Paintings d	D3 · Khyan
MB II (MB II B)	1590			b1	e2 CONFLAGRATION	D3	D3	e/1	E1
	1620	KINGDOM OF NAMES NEHESY	DENUDED PITS	b2	d	E1	E1	e/2–f	E2
	1650			b3 EPIDROMIC	e?	E2	E2	g	E3
MB I/II (MB II A–B)	1680	XIII	DENUDED STORAGE PITS	c HIATUS	unexcavated	E3			F
	1710			d1		F			G
	1740			d2 HIATUS		G/1-3			G/4 Tell el-Ashkelon
	1770		b1	d2a		G/4		UNOCCUPIED	H
MB I (MB II A)	1800	XII (So, SI, SII, AII, SI, AI)	b2	d2b		H			I
	1830		c1-2 Senusret III - year 5	HIATUS					K Senusret III - year 5 — **DATUM LINE ± 1868 BC**
	1860		e1-4	c1		EXPANSION OF THE SETTLEMENT →			L
?	1890	XI	f	c2-3					M HIATUS
	1920		?	?					N/1
	1950								N/2.3
EB IV (MB I)	1980	X	HERAKLEO-POLITAN FOUNDATION						
	2000								
	2050								

© M Bietak (2011)

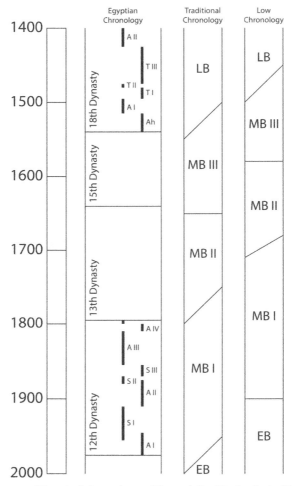

FIGURE 11.3. Historical chronology of Egypt (after Kitchen), the Traditional Chronology of the Levant (after Dever), and the Low Chronology of the Levant (after Bietak). Prepared by Felix Höflmayer.

correspondence; it is the southernmost site represented in this archive.[46] Since Mari was destroyed in the 32nd year of Hammurabi (HC: 1816; MC: 1760; LC: 1696; MebC: 1687; NC: 1664), the correspondence with Hazor must have taken place before this time.

The Hazor of the Mari correspondence was identified with Stratum XVI on the acropolis and Stratum 3 in the lower city ("Greater Hazor"), both datable to the Middle Bronze II period.[47] During Middle Bronze I, no significant settlement existed at the site, and initial fortifications were only erected during Stratum XVII of the acropolis and Stratum 4 of the lower city at the transitional Middle Bronze I/II period. Therefore, the transition from Middle Bronze I to Middle Bronze II must have happened before the fall of Mari in the 32nd year of Hammurabi.[48]

A detailed analysis of the development of the material culture at Hazor and Tell el-Dabʿa provided the possibility for stratigraphic synchronization. According to the excavators of these sites, Amnon Ben-Tor and Manfred Bietak, Hazor Stratum XVII of the acropolis and Stratum 4 of the lower city should be regarded as contemporary with Tell el-Dabʿa Stratum F, both datable to the transitional Middle Bronze Age I/II period.[49] Stratum F was dated to the mid/late-Thirteenth Dynasty (ca. 1710–1680 BC) and thus, Ben-Tor dated the rise of "Greater Hazor" to ca. 1700/1690 BC at the earliest. Since the rise of "Greater Hazor" provided a *terminus post quem* for the fall of Mari in the 32nd year of Hammurabi, both Bietak and Ben-Tor discarded the High Chronology (fall of Mari: 1816 BC) and the Middle Chronology (fall of Mari: 1760 BC). Although the Low Chronology (fall of Mari: 1696 BC) falls closer to the presumed rise of "Greater Hazor" around 1700 BC, both Bietak and Ben-Tor regarded either Mebert's chronology (fall of Mari: 1687 BC) or the New Chronology (fall of Mari: 1664 BC) as the only possible chronological matches with Mesopotamia.[50]

---

46. Bonechi 1992.

47. Ben-Tor 2004.

48. Ben-Tor 2004; Bietak 2013.

49. Ben-Tor 2004; Bietak 2013.

50. Ben-Tor 2004; Bietak 2013.

Prior to the systematic application of radiocarbon dating and Bayesian analysis, analysis of the historical and archaeological sources for the Middle Bronze Age Levant resulted in two competing models: the Traditional Chronology, based on general historical assumptions regarding synchronization with Egypt; and the Low Chronology, based on the stratigraphic sequence of a single site, Tell el-Dabʿa. While the authors favoring the Traditional Chronology did not opt for any particular one of the competing chronological models for Mesopotamia, the authors favoring the Low Chronology only regarded Mebert's chronology or the New Chronology as viable options.

11.3. Radiocarbon dating and dendrochronology

Although the method of radiocarbon dating had been developed by the mid-twentieth century AD and was initially applied in Egyptian and Near Eastern archaeology, archaeologists in these fields were reluctant to apply this method with any consistency. Only in recent decades has a more systematic approach to the application of radiocarbon dating (coupled with Bayesian analysis) been followed in the fields of ancient Near Eastern studies.

The method of radiocarbon dating has been described in detail in many papers and handbooks. For the scope of this chapter, we will focus on a brief overview in order to facilitate understanding of current issues in the field.[51]

The element carbon (C) exists in three different isotopes: ^{12}C and ^{13}C, which are both stable, and ^{14}C (radiocarbon), which is radioactive and decays according to a known half-life of approximately 5,730 years. Radiocarbon is produced in the upper atmosphere when atmospheric nitrogen (^{14}N) is bombarded by thermal neutrons. The resulting isotope, ^{14}C, quickly oxidizes into $^{14}CO_2$ (carbon dioxide). It then diffuses into the atmosphere and is absorbed by plants through photosynthesis, finally entering animals (including humans) via the ingestion of plants. As long

---

51. Bowman 1995; Bronk Ramsey 2008; Taylor and Bar-Yosef 2014; Kutschera 2018.

as any organism is alive, it is part of the global carbon cycle of acquiring "fresh" ^{14}C to constantly replace decaying radiocarbon. Once an organism ceases to acquire carbon and exits the global carbon cycle (i.e., dies), no more radiocarbon is absorbed, while the already existing ^{14}C continues to decay (the ^{12}C level in the organism remains constant). The lower the proportion of ^{14}C to ^{12}C is found in a given organic sample, the older it is, as more time has elapsed from the point when the sample stopped exchanging carbon with the environment.[52]

Unfortunately, the production of radiocarbon in the upper atmosphere has not been constant over time. Changes in the influx of cosmic rays, variations in the Earth's magnetic field, and other factors caused significant variations in the production of radiocarbon, resulting in varying ratios of $^{12}C/^{14}C$ in the atmosphere and consequently also in living organisms. In order to accommodate these variations, the respective atmospheric carbon isotope ratios of any given calendar year must be calculated, which has been done by measuring the carbon isotopic ratios in tree-ring sequences of known age. These measurements allow the radiocarbon date of a given organic sample to be calibrated, i.e., the radiocarbon age of a given sample is compared to the record of isotopic carbon ratios in tree-ring sequences of known age in order to determine the true calendar age of the sample.[53] These calibration curves are updated on a regular basis, which also can lead to shifts in calibrated dates from time to time. While most studies that are referenced in this chapter employed the calibration curve published in 2013 (IntCal13),[54] the recent publication of the new calibration curve (IntCal20) brought significant changes, especially for the mid-second millennium BC.[55] In the following, it will be noted where calibrated results employing IntCal20 differ from results employing IntCal13, and to what extent they affect Middle Bronze Age chronologies and synchronisms.

---

52. Bronk Ramsey 2008.

53. Stuiver and Suess 1966.

54. Reimer et al. 2013.

55. Reimer et al. 2020.

Due to the measuring process in the laboratory and the shape of the calibration curve, radiocarbon dates are expressed as probability distributions on the absolute calendrical timeline, sometimes ranging over a century or more. It is also important to stress that a radiocarbon date does not, per se, date the archaeological context it was found in, but only the point in time when the sample ceased to exchange carbon with its environment (i.e., its death). Depending on the context and the type of sample, the radiocarbon date can be regarded as a *terminus post quem* (e.g., charcoal from timber) or an approximate *terminus ad quem* (e.g., charred seeds found inside a storage jar from a destruction horizon).

Although the probability distribution of any individually calibrated radiocarbon date can span over a century or more, additional information can be employed to increase the precision of a given date or set of dates. Bayesian analysis of radiocarbon dates allows the consideration of additional information, such as the sequence of dates based on archaeological stratigraphy or other historical information. Such information is termed *prior information* as it is derived from sources other than, and prior to, radiocarbon dating in the laboratory.[56] Based on this prior information and the respective radiocarbon measurements, a *posterior probability* for each individual sample and any additional events in the model can be calculated. A Bayesian model is nothing else than the combination of archaeological (or historical) evidence and radiocarbon measurements, resulting in much more precise models than would be possible with single calibrated radiocarbon dates.

To develop an integrated radiocarbon-backed chronological model for the Middle Bronze Age ancient Near East, three different lines of evidence, often complementing each other, must be reviewed:

(1) Radiocarbon dates for Middle Kingdom Egypt;
(2) Radiocarbon dates for Middle Bronze Age archaeological sites in Egypt and the Levant;

---

56. Buck et al. 1991; Weninger et al. 2006; Bronk Ramsey 2009.

(3) Radiocarbon dates linkable to the REL and the Mesopotamian chronology.

11.3.1. Middle Kingdom Egypt and the Second Intermediate Period

The nature and characteristics of the Egyptian historical chronology have been outlined earlier, as well as absolute dating assessments based on various lines of evidence. In 2010, Christopher Bronk Ramsey, Michael W. Dee, and other colleagues published an important paper in the journal *Science*, which demonstrated that radiocarbon dating and Bayesian analysis, in fact, agreed with historic estimates for absolute dates established for Dynastic Egypt.[57] For their project, over 200 new measurements were conducted on short-lived material that were associated with archaeological contexts that could be dated in historical terms, such as botanical remains from kings' tombs.[58] Three individual Bayesian models were constructed for the Old, Middle, and New Kingdoms, using the known succession of kings and their respective reign-lengths (plus additional error) as prior information.

Based on their models, the Twelfth Dynasty should be dated approximately between ca. 1980 and ca. 1770 BC (1st year of Amenemhat I between 1991 and 1973 BC; 1st year of Wegaf between 1785 and 1758 BC, both at 68 percent probability).[59] The Second Intermediate Period (Thirteenth to Seventeenth Dynasties) was not modeled in detail due to lack of suitable samples and inherent problems in our understanding of the sequence and reign-lengths of individual kings (the new discussion around the placement of the Hyksos king Khyan in the sequence of Fifteenth Dynasty rulers and around a potential contemporaneity of the Thirteenth and the Fifteenth Dynasty might serve as an example for still

---

57. Bronk Ramsey et al. 2010; Shortland and Bronk Ramsey 2013.

58. Brock and Dee 2013.

59. Bronk Ramsey et al. 2010; Dee 2013a.

open questions in this period of Egyptian history).[60] These dates agree with estimates proposed by Kenneth Kitchen and Jürgen von Beckerath[61] and are slightly higher than the Low Middle Kingdom Chronology proposed by Erik Hornung, Rolf Krauss, and David A. Warburton and initially based on Krauss's interpretation of the lunar data.[62]

Additionally, the beginning of the New Kingdom (and therefore the end of the Second Intermediate Period) has been found to agree with historical estimates. According to their models, the New Kingdom started in the mid-sixteenth century BC (1st year of Ahmose between 1566 and 1552 BC at 68 percent probability).[63] Slightly higher dates for the beginning of the New Kingdom were calculated when employing longer reign lengths for certain Eighteenth Dynasty pharaohs, resulting in a date between 1578 and 1569 BC at 68 percent probability.[64]

11.3.2. Middle Bronze Age sites in Egypt and the Levant

In recent years, several radiocarbon sequences for Middle Bronze Age sites have been published.[65] Sites included (south to north): Tell el-Dabʿa (Egypt),[66] Tell el-Ajjul (Gaza strip),[67] Ashkelon (Israel),[68] Tel Lachish (Israel),[69] Jericho (Palestine),[70] Tell el-Hayyat

---

60. Moeller and Marouard 2011; Forstner-Müller and Moeller 2018.

61. Beckerath 1997; Kitchen 2000.

62. Hornung et al. 2006a; Krauss 1985; 2006.

63. Bronk Ramsey et al. 2010; Dee 2013b.

64. Manning 2014.

65. Höflmayer 2015; 2017.

66. Kutschera et al. 2012.

67. Fischer 2009.

68. Bruins and van der Plicht 2017.

69. Preliminary Late Bronze Age dates were published by Webster et al. 2019. For an assessment of the end of the Middle Bronze Age, see Webster 2020.

70. Bruins and van der Plicht 1995.

(Jordan),[71] Tel Ifshar (Israel),[72] Tel Nami (Israel),[73] Megiddo (Israel),[74] Tel Kabri (Israel),[75] and Tell el-Burak (Lebanon).[76] In the following, we will discuss the sites that provided key contributions to the new radiocarbon chronology of the Middle Bronze Age.

While the site of Tell el-Dabʿa served as a primary argument for the Low Chronology of the Middle Bronze Age Levant and was used to argue in favor of Mebert's chronology and the New Chronology of Mesopotamia, it also played a crucial role in a new assessment of Middle Bronze Age chronology based on radiocarbon data. In 2012, Walter Kutschera, Manfred Bietak, and other colleagues published the radiocarbon sequence for Tell el-Dabʿa, one of the most extensive sequences for a Bronze Age site in the eastern Mediterranean.[77] Their results at Tell el-Dabʿa seriously challenged both the excavator's historical/archaeological dates for the individual strata, as well as the entire Middle Bronze Age Low Chronology for which Tell el-Dabʿa served as a cornerstone. On average, the radiocarbon dates were about 120 years higher (older) than the dates proposed by the excavator. The excavator, Manfred Bietak, claimed that a so-far-unknown effect must have affected the samples and/or the dates and rejected their validity outright,[78] but other scholars have pointed out several weaknesses in the construction of the Tell

---

71. Falconer and Fall 2017; Fall et al. 2021.

72. Marcus 2013; Höflmayer 2017.

73. Radiocarbon dates for Tel Nami were reported in a preliminary way by Marcus 2003; Bronk Ramsey et al. 2002; Hedges et al. 1997. While there is no final publication of the site or the radiocarbon dates, see Höflmayer 2021 for a discussion of these dates based on the published information.

74. Toffolo et al. 2014; Martin et al. 2020.

75. Höflmayer et al. 2016b.

76. Höflmayer et al. 2016a.

77. Kutschera et al. 2012.

78. Bietak 2013.

el-Dabʿa chronology, especially in the links between the stratigraphic phases and the Egyptian historical chronology.[79]

Radiocarbon dates for the beginning of the Middle Bronze Age are currently only available at Tell el-Hayyat in the Jordan valley. Here, Phase 6 was dated to the Early Bronze IV (or Intermediate Bronze Age) and Phase 5 to the Middle Bronze I.[80] Radiocarbon dates for this transition suggest a date around ca. 1900 BC, or a little bit earlier.[81]

Dates for the transition from Middle Bronze Age I to Middle Bronze Age II come from several sites, such as Tell el-Dabʿa, Tel Ifshar, Tell el-Hayyat, and Tell el-Burak.

In Tell el-Dabʿa, the transition from Middle Bronze I to Middle Bronze II is equated with Stratum F. According to the radiocarbon model published for Tell el-Dabʿa, Stratum F begins in the mid-nineteenth century and ends around 1800 BC.[82]

In Tel Ifshar on the Sharon Plain, a Middle Bronze Age settlement with a detailed stratigraphic sequence, has been excavated. Phases A to G could be dated to the Middle Bronze Age I, while Phase H was dated to the transition from Middle Bronze I to Middle Bronze II.[83] A substantial set of radiocarbon dates from short-lived samples from secure contexts, such as containers, granaries, or floor levels, has been published.[84] An Egyptian Marl A3 jar, found in Phase C and datable to the first half of the Twelfth Dynasty, can be used as an additional constraint.[85] The transition from Middle Bronze I to Middle Bronze II (Phase H) could be dated to the mid/late-nineteenth century BC using the Egyptian import as additional chronological evidence, or to the mid- to late nineteenth or

---

79. Manning et al. 2014; Höflmayer 2015.

80. Falconer and Fall 2006.

81. Falconer and Fall 2017; Fall et al. 2021.

82. Kutschera et al. 2012.

83. Marcus et al. 2008a; Marcus 2013.

84. Marcus 2013; Höflmayer 2017.

85. Marcus et al. 2008b.

early eighteenth century BC by not including the Egyptian import as a chronological marker.[86]

At Tell el-Hayyat in the Jordan valley, the transition from Middle Bronze I to Middle Bronze II, falls into Phase 3.[87] According to the model published by Fall and colleagues, Phase 3 dates to the early to mid-eighteenth century BC (similarly to Stratum F at Tell el-Dab'a).[88]

In Tell el-Burak, a small site in coastal Lebanon, a monumental mudbrick structure datable to the late Middle Bronze I or Middle Bronze I/II transitional phase has been excavated.[89] Radiocarbon samples mostly come from its fill layers and also include charcoal samples, but carefully constructed Bayesian models that use charcoal dates only as a *terminus post quem* result in a nineteenth or early eighteenth century BC date for the end of this building.[90]

Radiocarbon dates for the Middle Bronze I/II transition are thus consistently higher than dates proposed by the Traditional (1800/1750 BC) or Low (ca. 1700 BC) Chronologies and point to a date sometime in the second half of the nineteenth century BC (ca. 1850/1800 BC).[91]

Radiocarbon data for the transition from Middle Bronze II to Middle Bronze III are less abundant than for the Middle Bronze I/II transition. Nevertheless, several sites provide evidence for this transition as well, such as Tell el-Dab'a, Tel Kabri, and Tell el-Hayyat in the Jordan valley.

In Tell el-Dab'a, the transition from Middle Bronze II to Middle Bronze III equates to the beginning of Stratum D/3. According to the radiocarbon model published by Walter Kutschera, Manfred Bietak,

---

86. Höflmayer 2017.

87. Falconer and Fall 2006; 2017.

88. Falconer and Fall 2017; Fall et al. 2021.

89. Kamlah and Sader 2019.

90. Höflmayer et al. 2016a; Höflmayer 2017.

91. Höflmayer 2017.

and others, the transition from Stratum E/1 to Stratum D/3 falls to the second half of the eighteenth century BC, most likely around 1700 BC.[92]

At Tell el-Hayyat, the transition from Middle Bronze II to Middle Bronze III occurred during Phase 2.[93] Based on their radiocarbon model, Phase 2 starts at some point in the first half of the eighteenth century BC and ends somewhere in the second half, or around 1700 BC.[94] A date for the Middle Bronze II/III transition sometime in the eighteenth century BC seems to be likely, although it must be pointed out that the younger phases at Tell el-Hayyat are represented by only a few radiocarbon dates. Additional measurements may therefore change this current assessment.[95]

In Tel Kabri in the Upper Galilee, a Middle Bronze Age palace has been excavated, which was in use approximately until the end of the Middle Bronze II period.[96] Radiocarbon samples, mainly short-lived, but also a few charcoal samples, were available for Phases V (transitional Middle Bronze I/II) through Phase III (late Middle Bronze II), but these are clustered mostly within Phase III—the point when the palace ended.[97] Radiocarbon dating suggests a date around 1700 BC for the end of the palace in Phase III and thus for Middle Bronze Age II.[98]

Radiocarbon dates for the Middle Bronze II/III transition are therefore also consistently higher than dates suggested by the Traditional (ca. 1650 BC) or the Low (ca. 1590 BC) Chronologies and give ca. 1700 BC as the transition date from Middle Bronze II to Middle Bronze III.

The end of the Middle Bronze Age and the beginning of the Late Bronze Age is more complicated to grasp from a radiocarbon point of

---

92. Kutschera et al. 2012; Höflmayer 2017.

93. Falconer and Fall 2006.

94. Falconer and Fall 2017.

95. Höflmayer 2017.

96. Kempinski 2002; Yasur-Landau et al. 2018; Yasur-Landau and Cline 2020.

97. Höflmayer et al. 2016b.

98. Höflmayer et al. 2016b; Höflmayer 2017.

view. Radiocarbon dates exist for Tell el-Dabʻa and Tell el-Ajjul; dates for the late Middle Bronze III period exist at Jericho, Tell el-Hayyat, and Tel Lachish. Circumstantial evidence can also be mentioned for the Minoan eruption of Santorini.

At Tell el-Dabʻa, the beginning of the Late Bronze Age is connected to the first appearance of White Slip I and Base Ring I wares in Stratum C/3.[99] According to the radiocarbon model published by Walter Kutschera, Manfred Bietak, and others, Strata C/3–2 fall to the late seventeenth century BC,[100] but employing the new calibration curve IntCal20, the same strata date to around 1600 BC or the early to mid-sixteenth century BC. It should be noted here that Stratum C/2 also produced pumice that can be traced to the Minoan eruption of Santorini (see later discussion in this section).[101]

At Tell el-Ajjul, Horizons 7–6 are dated to the Middle Bronze III, Horizon 5 to a transitional Middle Bronze/Late Bronze phase, and Horizons 4–3 solely to the Late Bronze Age I. Horizon 5 produced the first imports of Cypriot White Slip I and Base Ring I wares and the presence of pumice from the Minoan Santorini eruption.[102] Unfortunately, only a few radiocarbon dates are available for this site, and the results are ambiguous. Based on the dates published, the Late Bronze Age started sometime in the sixteenth century BC,[103] but when employing the new calibration curve IntCal20, Horizons 6, 5, and 4–3 all fall into the second half of the sixteenth century BC. At Tell el-Ajjul, the start of the Late Bronze Age now dates to the mid- to late sixteenth century BC, which would be well in agreement with the Traditional Chronology.

The stratigraphic sequence at Tell el-Hayyat ends with Phase 1, which is dated to the Middle Bronze III.[104] There is no Late Bronze Age phase

---

99. Bietak 2013.

100. Kutschera et al. 2012; Höflmayer 2017.

101. Sterba et al. 2009.

102. Fischer 2004.

103. Fischer 2009; Höflmayer 2017.

104. Falconer and Fall 2006.

at the site. The end of Phase 1 falls, according to the published radiocarbon dates, in the seventeenth century BC or maybe as early as the late eighteenth century BC.[105] However, as the younger phases at Tell el-Hayyat are not well represented, and since it is not entirely clear whether the ultimate end of Middle Bronze III is present at the site, one should regard this date with caution.[106]

For Jericho, in the 1990s Hendrik Bruins and Johannes van der Plicht published a set of radiocarbon dates for the end of the Middle Bronze Age based on Kathleen Kenyon's excavations.[107] These dates were recently recalibrated and fall at around 1600 BC;[108] when employing the new IntCal20 calibration curve, an end-date sometime during the sixteenth century BC would also be possible.

New dates for the late Middle Bronze III are also available from Tel Lachish. Here, Stratum P-4 and P-3 were dated to the late Middle Bronze III.[109] New radiocarbon dates for both of these phases fall into the early to mid-sixteenth century BC,[110] and when employing IntCal20, even later, into the late sixteenth century BC.

Circumstantial evidence from Santorini can also be mentioned. It is generally agreed that the appearance of White Slip I and Base Ring I is a key marker for the start of the Late Bronze Age in the Levant. White Slip I pottery was already present before the volcano of Santorini erupted in the mid-second millennium BC.[111] Radiocarbon dates for the eruption of Santorini fall consistently to the late seventeenth century BC, but employing the new IntCal20 calibration curve, also a date in the early sixteenth century BC would be possible (and are, therefore,

---

105. Falconer and Fall 2017; Höflmayer 2017; Fall et al. 2021.

106. Höflmayer 2017.

107. Bruins and van der Plicht 1995.

108. Höflmayer 2017.

109. Ussishkin 2004.

110. For the dates from Tel Lachish, see Webster 2020.

111. Merrillees 2001.

in agreement with radiocarbon dates for Strata C/3-2 at Tell el-Dabʿa, where White Slip I, Base Ring I, and Minoan pumice have also been found).[112]

Radiocarbon dates for the start of the Late Bronze Age seem to be rather ambiguous. Several sites point to ca. 1600 BC for the beginning of the Late Bronze Age (such as Tell el-Dabʿa or Santorini); other sites, such as Tel Lachish, have late Middle Bronze III phases still in the sixteenth century BC. Currently, it seems reasonable to allow a longer time span for the transition from the Middle to the Late Bronze Age and to suggest the period between 1600 and 1550 BC for the end of the Middle Bronze Age in the Levant. Future radiocarbon dates, however, may yet change this picture.

11.3.3. Revised Eponym List (REL)

Radiocarbon evidence from two sites in Anatolia, Kültepe and Acemhöyük, allow absolute calendrical dating of the REL and thus also for the Babylonian chronology.[113]

At Kültepe (see chapter 17 in this volume), the transition from Lower Town Level II to IB can be dated to between REL 138 and 142, based on the documents found in the respective phases.[114] Shortly before, around REL 125, the Waršama palace was erected to replace the Old Palace; it can be dated to ca. REL 80–110. From the Waršama palace, several samples of juniper were retrieved that still contained bark and were thus regarded as suitable samples for dating the felling of the trees and the construction of the palace.[115] According to the results, the erection of the Waršama palace fell within the period between 1855 and 1839 BC (95.4 percent probability). The only chronology that agrees with this result is the Middle Chronology, which places REL 125 to 1846 BC.

---

112. Manning et al. 2014; 2020.

113. Manning et al. 2016; 2017; 2020.

114. Barjamovic et al. 2012.

115. Manning et al. 2016.

Employing the High Chronology (REL 125 at 1902 BC), REL 125 would fall about half a century before the palace was actually erected; using the Low Chronology (1782 BC), Mebert's chronology (1773 BC), or the New Chronology (1750 BC), construction would have been significantly later than the radiocarbon dates for the outer tree rings and would move REL 80–110 of the Old Palace to after the construction of the Waršama Palace.

At Acemhöyük, the so-called Sarikaya Palace is also datable in terms of the REL, as a large number of bullae of the northern Mesopotamian ruler Samsi-Addu were found here. Samsi-Addu is datable to between REL 165 and 197. Additionally, other documents with dates from the REL 190s have been found in the Sarikaya Palace. A number of juniper samples, some of them containing bark, were retrieved from the Sarikaya Palace and provided information on the felling of the trees and the subsequent palace construction.[116] Based on these results, the earliest use of the Sarikaya Palace associated with Samsi-Addu can be dated to the early eighteenth century BC (1797–1781 BC at 95.4 percent probability). This result is also only compatible with the Middle Chronology, which would date the death of Samsi-Addu (REL 197) in the 18th year of Hammurabi to 1774 BC.[117] A High Chronology date of 1830 BC for the end of Samsi-Addu in REL 197 can be ruled out, as the palace would then have been erected a generation after Samsi-Addu's death. The Low Chronology (1710 BC), Mebert's chronology (1701 BC), and the New Chronology (1678 BC) are also unlikely, as according to these chronologies, the palace would have been erected between 80 and more than 100 years after Samsi-Addu's death, without any earlier (in terms of REL) documents being present in the palace.

Therefore, the radiocarbon data for both Acemhöyük and Kültepe are not only internally consistent, but also allow us to place the previously floating REL absolutely in time, and, through synchronization

---

116. Manning et al. 2016.

117. Manning et al. 2016; 2017.

with the Babylonian chronology, a decision between the competing chronological systems of Mesopotamia can be made favoring the Middle Chronology.

11.4. An integrated chronological model for the Middle Bronze Age Near East

Radiocarbon testing around the eastern Mediterranean provides consistent results for historical and archaeological chronological models from Egypt to Mesopotamia. Internal, relative synchronizations suggested by various scholars, such as between the Tell el-Dabʿa stratigraphic phases and the relative chronological periods in the Levant, or between the Levant and Mesopotamia, can be substantiated. The High Middle Kingdom Chronology for Egypt and the Middle Chronology for Mesopotamia also agree with the results of radiocarbon dating. Radiocarbon dates for the archaeological (relative) chronology of the Levant, however, produced results that are marginally higher than the Traditional Chronology (which was based on very general historical assumptions) and significantly higher than the Low Chronology (based on the single site of Tell el-Dabʿa with its disputed links to the Egyptian historical chronology).

According to radiocarbon data, the Egyptian Middle Kingdom began shortly after 2000 BC. Shortly after that, at some point in the twentieth century BC and no later than 1900 BC, the Middle Bronze I period in the Levant seems to have also begun. The transition from Middle Bronze I to Middle Bronze II occurred sometime in the nineteenth century (around 1800 BC at latest) contemporary with the mid- to late Twelfth Dynasty in Egypt. This transition also provides a *terminus post quem* for the fall of Mari in the 32nd year of Hammurabi, as Middle Bronze II Hazor is mentioned in the Mari letters. Based on the radiocarbon dates for Acemhöyük and Kültepe, it is possible to rule out the High, Low, and New Chronologies, as well as Mebert's chronology, for Mesopotamia, so that the end of Mari (and the 32nd year of Hammurabi) falls to 1760 BC. In Egypt, the Thirteenth Dynasty started also around that time, within the first half of the eighteenth century BC. The transition from Middle Bronze II to Middle Bronze III most likely happened around 1700 BC; the equivalent point in time in historic Egyptian terminology remains elusive for now, as the discussion regarding an overlap between the Thirteenth and Fifteenth Dynasties has not been ultimately settled. It seems likely, however, that this is also (at least roughly) the time period of the Hyksos ruler Khyan in Egypt. According to the latest radiocarbon results, the transition from the Middle to the Late Bronze Age may have spanned half a century, or perhaps even more. It would have started around (or shortly before) 1600 BC, although at some sites, strata dated to the beginning of the Late Bronze Age produced radiocarbon dates as late as the mid- to late sixteenth century BC. The transition from the Middle to the Late Bronze Age thus should be seen as more of a process than a single event. It seems to have started at some places earlier than the start of the New Kingdom in Egypt (and the so-called expulsion of the Hyksos; see chapter 23 in volume 3) around 1570 BC at the earliest, or (more conservatively) around 1550 BC. At some sites, the final phases of the Middle Bronze Age continued until the mid- to late sixteenth century BC, already contemporary with the early Egyptian New Kingdom.

Recent decades of radiocarbon dating and Bayesian analysis have succeeded in establishing a coherent scientific absolute calendrical chronology for the Middle Bronze Age Near East (figure 11.4). While the Egyptian High Middle Kingdom Chronology and the Middle Chronology for Mesopotamia have been corroborated by radiocarbon dating, both the Traditional and the Low Chronologies for the Middle Bronze Age Levant have not been likewise substantiated. Undoubtedly, future work will ultimately shift some of the transitions outlined here, as well as their synchronizations with other cultures of the ancient Near East. But it is hoped that this radiocarbon-backed chronological system may serve as a starting point for future endeavors in refining both historical and archaeological chronologies throughout the ancient Near East.

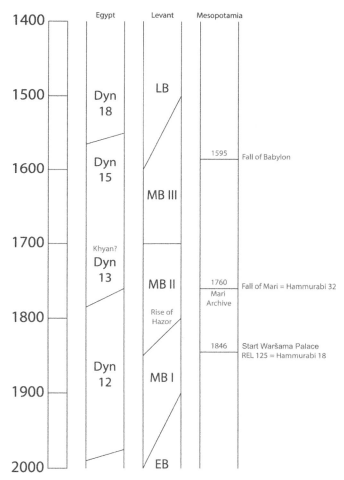

FIGURE 11.4. A radiocarbon-backed synchronized chronological framework for Egypt and the Levant, as well as some key events for Mesopotamia. Prepared by Felix Höflmayer.

REFERENCES

Albright, W.F. 1930–1931. *The excavation of Tell Beit Mirsim in Palestine, vol. I: the pottery of the first three campaigns.* New Haven, CT: Yale University Press.

Albright, W.F. 1931–1932. *The excavation of Tell Beit Mirsim, vol. IA: the Bronze Age pottery of the fourth campaign.* New Haven, CT: Yale University Press.

Albright, W.F. 1936–1937. *The excavation of Tell Beit Mirsim, vol. II: the Bronze Age.* New Haven, CT: Yale University Press.

Allen, J.P. 2010. The Second Intermediate Period in the Turin King List. In Marée, M. (ed.), *The Second Intermediate Period (Thirteenth-Seventeenth Dynasties): current research, future prospects.* Leuven: Peeters, 1–10.

Åström, P. (ed.) 1987a. *High, middle or low? Acts of an international colloquium on absolute chronology held at the University of Gothenburg 20th–22nd August 1987, part 1.* Gothenburg: Paul Åströms.

Åström, P. (ed.) 1987b. *High, middle or low? Acts of an international colloquium on absolute chronology held at the University of Gothenburg 20th–22nd August 1987, part 2.* Gothenburg: Paul Åströms.

Åström, P. (ed.) 1989. *High, middle or low? Acts of an international colloquium on absolute chronology held at the University of Gothenburg 20th–22nd August 1987, part 3.* Gothenburg: Paul Åströms.

Barjamovic, G., Hertel, T., and Larsen, M.T. 2012. *Ups and downs at Kanesh: chronology, history and society in the Old Assyrian period.* Leiden: NINO.

Beckerath, J. von. 1997. *Chronologie des pharaonischen Ägypten: die Zeitbestimmung der ägyptischen Geschichte von der Vorzeit bis 332 v. Chr.* Mainz: Zabern.

Bennett, C. 2002. A genealogical chronology of the Seventeenth Dynasty. *JARCE* 39: 123–155.

Bennett, C. 2006. Genealogy and the chronology of the Second Intermediate Period. *ÄL* 16: 231–243.

Ben-Tor, A. 2004. Hazor and chronology. *ÄL* 14: 45–67.

Betancourt, P.P. 1998. The chronology of the Aegean Late Bronze Age: unanswered questions. In Balmuth, M.S., and Tykot, R.H. (eds.), *Sardinian and Aegean chronology: towards the resolution of relative and absolute dating in the Mediterranean.* Oxford: Oxbow, 291–296.

Bierbrier, M. 2006. Genealogy and chronology. In Hornung, E., Krauss, R.K., and Warburton, D. A. (eds.), *Ancient Egyptian chronology.* Leiden: Brill, 37–44.

Bietak, M. 1975. *Tell el-Dabʿa, II: der Fundort im Rahmen einer archäologisch-geographischen Untersuchung über das ägyptische Ostdelta.* Vienna: Verlag der Österreichischen Akademie der Wissenschaften.

Bietak, M. 1991a. Egypt and Canaan during the Middle Bronze Age. *BASOR* 281: 27–72.

Bietak, M. 1991b. *Tell el-Dabʿa, V: ein Friedhofsbezirk der mittleren Bronzezeitkultur mit Totentempel und Siedlungsschichten, Teil 1.* Vienna: Verlag der Österreichischen Akademie der Wissenschaften.

Bietak, M. 1996. *Avaris, the capital of the Hyksos: recent excavations at Tell el-Dabʿa.* London: British Museum Press.

Bietak, M. (ed.) 2000. *The synchronisation of civilisations in the Eastern Mediterranean in the second millennium BC.* Vienna: Verlag der Österreichischen Akademie der Wissenschaften.

Bietak, M. 2002. Relative and absolute chronology of the Middle Bronze Age: comments on the present state of research. In Bietak, M. (ed.), *The Middle Bronze Age in the Levant.* Vienna: Verlag der Österreichischen Akademie der Wissenschaften, 29–42.

Bietak, M. (ed.). 2003. *The synchronisation of civilisations in the Eastern Mediterranean in the second millennium BC, vol. 2.* Vienna: Verlag der Österreichischen Akademie der Wissenschaften.

Bietak, M. 2013. Antagonisms in historical and radiocarbon chronology. In Shortland, A.J., and Bronk Ramsey, C. (eds.), *Radiocarbon and the chronologies of ancient Egypt.* Oxford: Oxbow, 76–109.

Bietak, M., and Czerny, E. (eds.). 2007. *The synchronisation of civilisations in the Eastern Mediterranean in the second millennium BC, vol. 3.* Vienna: Verlag der Österreichischen Akademie der Wissenschaften.

Bonechi, M. 1992. Relations amicales Syro-Palestiniennes: Mari et Hazor au XVIIIe siècle av. J.C. In Durand, J.-M. (ed.), *Florilegium Marianum: recueil d'études en l'honneur de Michel Fleury.* Paris: Société pour l'étude du Proche-Orient ancien, 9–22.

Borchardt, L. 1899. Der zweite Papyrusfund von Kahun und die zeitliche Festlegung des Mittleren Reiches der ägyptischen Geschichte. *ZÄS* 37: 89–103.

Bowman, S. 1995. *Radiocarbon dating.* London: British Museum Press. 2nd rev. ed.

Brock, F., and Dee, M.W. 2013. Sample selection for radiocarbon dating. In Shortland, A.J., and Bronk Ramsey, C. (eds.), *Radiocarbon and the chronologies of ancient Egypt.* Oxford: Oxbow, 40–47.

Bronk Ramsey, C. 2008. Radiocarbon dating: revolutions in understanding. *Archaeometry* 50: 249–275.

Bronk Ramsey, C. 2009. Bayesian analysis of radiocarbon dates. *Radiocarbon* 51: 337–360.

Bronk Ramsey, C., Dee, M.W., Rowland, J.M., Higham, T.F.G., Harris, S.A., Brock, F., Quiles, A., Wild, E.M., Marcus, E.S., and Shortland, A.J. 2010. Radiocarbon-based chronology for Dynastic Egypt. *Science* 328: 1554–1557.

Bronk Ramsey, C., Higham, T.F.G., Owen, D.C., Pike, A.W.G., and Hedges, R.E.M. 2002. Radiocarbon dates from the Oxford AMS system: archaeometry datelist 31. *Archaeometry* 44: 1–150.

Bruins, H.J., and van der Plicht, J. 1995. Tell es-Sultan (Jericho): radiocarbon results of short-lived cereal and multiyear charcoal samples from the end of the Middle Bronze Age. *Radiocarbon* 37: 213–220.

Bruins, H.J., and van der Plicht, J. 2017. The Minoan Santorini eruption and its ^{14}C position in archaeological strata: preliminary comparison between Ashkelon and Tell el-Dabʿa. *Radiocarbon* 59: 1295–1307.

Buck, C.E., Kenworthy, J.B., Litton, C.D., and Smith, A.F.M. 1991. Combining archaeological and radiocarbon information: a Bayesian approach to calibration. *Antiquity* 65: 808–821.

Charpin, D., and Ziegler, N. 2003. *Mari et le Proche-Orient à l'époque amorrite: essai d'histoire politique.* Paris: Société pour l'étude du Proche-Orient ancien.

Cohen, S.L. 2002. *Canaanites, chronologies, and connections: the relationship of Middle Bronze IIA Canaan to Middle Kingdom Egypt.* Winona Lake, IN: Eisenbrauns.

Dee, M.W. 2013a. A radiocarbon-based chronology for the Middle Kingdom. In Shortland, A.J., and Bronk Ramsey, C. (eds.), *Radiocarbon and the chronologies of ancient Egypt.* Oxford: Oxbow, 174–181.

Dee, M.W. 2013b. A radiocarbon-based chronology for the New Kingdom. In Shortland, A.J., and Bronk Ramsey, C. (eds.), *Radiocarbon and the chronologies of ancient Egypt.* Oxford: Oxbow, 65–75.

Depuydt, L. 1996. Egyptian regnal dating under Cambyses and the date of the Persian conquest. In Der Manuelian, P. (ed.), *Studies in honor of William Kelly Simpson, vol. I.* Boston: Museum of Fine Arts, 179–190.

Dever, W.G. 1992. The chronology of Syria-Palestine in the second millennium BCE: a review of current issues. *BASOR* 288: 1–25.

Falconer, S.E., and Fall, P.L. 2006. *Bronze Age rural ecology and village life at Tell el-Hayyat, Jordan.* Oxford: Archaeopress.

Falconer, S.E., and Fall, P.L. 2017. Radiocarbon evidence from Tell Abu en-Ni'aj and Tell el-Hayyat, Jordan, and its implications for Bronze Age Levantine and Egyptian chronologies. *JAEI* 13: 7–19.

Fall, P.L., Falconer, S.E. and Höflmayer, F. 2021. New Bayesian radiocarbon models for Early Bronze IV Tell Abu en-Ni'aj and Middle Bronze Age Tell el-Hayyat, Jordan. Radiocarbon 63: 41–76.

Fischer, P.M. 2004. Coast contra inland: Tell el-'Ajjul and Tell Abu al-Kharaz during the late Middle and Late Bronze Ages. *ÄL* 14: 249–264.

Fischer, P.M. 2009. The chronology of Tell el-Ajjul, Gaza: stratigraphy, Thera, pumice and radiocarbon dating. In Warburton, D.A. (ed.), *Time's up! Dating the Minoan eruption of Santorini*. Aarhus: Aarhus University Press, 253–265.

Forstner-Müller, I., and Moeller, N. (eds.) 2018. *The Hyksos ruler Khyan and the early Second Intermediate Period in Egypt: problems and priorities of current research*. Vienna: Holzhausen.

Franke, D. 1988a. Zur Chronologie des Mittleren Reiches, Teil II: die sogenannte 'Zweite Zwischenzeit' Altägyptens. *Orientalia* 57: 245–274.

Franke, D. 1988b. Zur Chronologie des Mittleren Reiches (12.–18. Dynastie), Teil 1: die 12. Dynastie. *Orientalia* 57: 113–138.

Gardiner, A.H. 1959. *The Royal Canon of Turin*. Oxford: Oxford University Press.

Garstang, J., Vincent, L., Albright, W.F., and Phythian-Adams, W.J.T. 1922. A new chronological classification of Palestinian archaeology. *BASOR* 7: 9.

Gasche, H., Armstrong, J.A., Cole, S.W., and Gurzadyan, V.G. 1998. *Dating the fall of Babylon*. Ghent: University of Ghent.

Gundacker, R. 2015. The chronology of the Third and Fourth Dynasties according to Manetho's Aegyptiaca. In Der Manuelian, P., and Schneider, T. (eds.), *Towards a new history of the Egyptian Old Kingdom: perspectives on the Pyramid Age*. Leiden: Brill, 76–199.

Hedges, R.E.M., Pettitt, P.B., Bronk Ramsey, C., and van Klinken, G. 1997. Radiocarbon dates from the Oxford AMS system: archaeometry datelist 23. *Archaeometry* 39: 247–262.

Helck, W. 1956. *Untersuchungen zu Manetho und den ägyptischen Königslisten*. Berlin: Akademie-Verlag.

Helck, W. 1992. Anmerkungen zum Turiner Königspapyrus. *SAK* 19: 151–216.

Höflmayer, F. 2015. Carbone-14 comparé: Middle Bronze Age I (IIA) chronology, Tell el-Dab'a and radiocarbon data. In Mynářová, J., Onderka, P., and

Pavúk, P. (eds.), *There and back again: the crossroads, II.* Prague: Charles University, 265–295.

Höflmayer, F. 2017. A radiocarbon chronology for the Middle Bronze Age southern Levant. *JAEI* 13: 20–33.

Höflmayer, F. 2021. Tel Nami, Cyprus, and Egypt: radiocarbon dates and early Middle Bronze Age chronology. *Palestine Exploration Quarterly.* Retrieved from https://doi.org/10.1080/00310328.2020.1866329 (last accessed April 21, 2021).

Höflmayer, F., Kamlah, J., Sader, H., Dee, M.W., Kutschera, W., Wild, E.M., and Riehl, S. 2016a. New evidence for Middle Bronze Age chronology and synchronisms in the Levant: radiocarbon dates from Tell el-Burak, Tell el-Dab'a, and Tel Ifshar compared. *BASOR* 375: 53–76.

Höflmayer, F., Yasur-Landau, A., Cline, E.H., Dee, M.W., Lorentzen, B., and Riehl, S. 2016b. New radiocarbon dates from Tel Kabri support a high Middle Bronze Age chronology. *Radiocarbon* 58: 599–613.

Hornung, E., Krauss, R.K., and Warburton, D.A. (eds.). 2006a. *Ancient Egyptian chronology.* Leiden: Brill.

Hornung, E., Krauss, R.K., and Warburton, D.A. 2006b. King-lists and Manetho's Aigyptiaka. In Hornung, E., Krauss, R.K., and Warburton, D.A. (eds.), *Ancient Egyptian chronology.* Leiden: Brill, 33–36.

Horowitz, W. 2013. Hazor: a cuneiform city in the west. *NEA* 76: 98–101.

Horowitz, W., Oshima, T., and Sanders, S.L. 2018. *Cuneiform in Canaan: the next generation.* University Park, PA: Eisenbrauns. 2nd rev. ed.

Horowitz, W., and Wasserman, N. 2000. An Old Babylonian letter from Hazor with mention of Mari and Ekallātum. *IEJ* 50: 169–174.

Huber, P.J. 2000. Astronomy and ancient chronology. *Akkadica* 119–120: 159–176.

Huber, P.J., Sachs, A., Stol, M., Whiting, R.M., Leichty, E., Walker, C.B.F., and van Driel, G. 1982. *Astronomical dating of Babylon I and Ur III.* Malibu, CA: Undena.

Jansen-Winkeln, K. 2006. The relevance of genealogical information for Egyptian chronology. *ÄL* 16: 257–273.

Kamlah, J., and Sader, H. (eds.) 2019. *Tell el-Burak I: the Middle Bronze Age, with chapters related to the site and to the late Medieval period.* Wiesbaden: Harrassowitz.

Kempinski, A. (ed.). 2002. *Tel Kabri: the 1986–1993 excavation seasons.* Tel Aviv: Emery and Claire Yass Publications in Archaeology.

Kitchen, K.A. 2000. The historical chronology of ancient Egypt, a current assessment. In Bietak, M. (ed.), *The synchronisation of civilisations in the Eastern Mediterranean in the second millennium BC*. Vienna: Verlag der Österreichischen Akademie der Wissenschaften, 39–52.

Kitchen, K.A. 2007. Egyptian and related chronologies: look, no sciences, no pots! In Bietak, M., and Czerny, E. (eds.), *The synchronisation of civilisations in the Eastern Mediterranean in the second millennium BC, vol. 3*. Vienna: Verlag der Österreichischen Akademie der Wissenschaften, 163–171.

Krauss, R.K. 1985. *Sothis- und Monddaten: Studien zur astronomischen und technischen Chronologie Altägyptens*. Hildesheim: Gerstenberg.

Krauss, R.K. 2003. Arguments in favor of a low chronology for the Middle and New Kingdom in Egypt. In Bietak, M. (ed.), *The synchronisation of civilisations in the Eastern Mediterranean in the second millennium BC, vol. 2*. Vienna: Verlag der Österreichischen Akademie der Wissenschaften, 175–197.

Krauss, R.K. 2006. Lunar dates. In Hornung, E., Krauss, R.K., and Warburton, D.A. (eds.), *Ancient Egyptian chronology*. Leiden: Brill, 395–431.

Kutschera, W. 2018. Applications of ^{14}C, the most versatile radionuclide to explore our world. In Scheidenberger, C., and Pfützner, M. (eds.), *The Euroschool on exotic beams, vol. 5*. Cham: Springer, 1–30.

Kutschera, W., Bietak, M., Wild, E.M., Bronk Ramsey, C., Dee, M.W., Golser, R., Kopetzky, K., Stadler, P., Steier, P., Thanheiser, U., and Weninger, F. 2012. The chronology of Tell el-Daba: a crucial meeting point of ^{14}C dating, archaeology, and Egyptology in the 2nd millennium BC. *Radiocarbon* 54: 407–422.

Luft, U. 1992. *Die chronologische Fixierung des ägyptischen Mittleren Reiches nach dem Tempelarchiv von Illahun*. Vienna: Verlag der Österreichischen Akademie der Wissenschaften.

Macalister, R.A.S. 1912. *The excavation of Gezer, 1902–1905 and 1907–1909*. London: John Murray.

Maeir, A.M. 2000. The political and economic status of MB II Hazor and MB II trade: an inter- and intra-regional view. *PEQ* 132: 37–58.

Manning, S.W. 2014. *A test of time and a test of time revisited: the volcano of Thera and the chronology and history of the Aegean and east Mediterranean in the mid-second millennium BC*. Oxford: Oxbow.

Manning, S.W., Barjamovic, G., and Lorentzen, B. 2017. The course of ^{14}C dating does not run smooth: tree-rings, radiocarbon, and potential impacts of a calibration curve wiggle on dating Mesopotamian chronology. *JAEI* 13: 70–81.

Manning, S.W., Griggs, C.B., Lorentzen, B., Barjamovic, G., Bronk Ramsey, C., Kromer, B., and Wild, E.M. 2016. Integrated tree-ring-radiocarbon high-resolution timeframe to resolve earlier second millennium BC Mesopotamian chronology. *PLOSOne* 11: e0157144.

Manning, S.W., Höflmayer, F., Moeller, N., Dee, M.W., Bronk Ramsey, C., Fleitmann, D., Higham, T.F.G., Kutschera, W., and Wild, E.M. 2014. Dating the Thera (Santorini) eruption: coherent archaeological and scientific evidence supporting a high chronology. *Antiquity* 88: 1164–1179.

Manning, S.W., Wacker, L., Büntgen, U., Bronk Ramsey, C., Dee, M.W., Kromer, B., Lorentzen, B., and Tegel, W. 2020. Radiocarbon offsets and Old World chronology as relevant to Mesopotamia, Egypt, Anatolia and Thera (Santorini). *Scientific Reports* 10, no. 13785. Available online at https://doi.org/10.1038/s41598-020-69287-2 (last accessed September 5, 2020).

Marcus, E.S. 2003. Dating the early Middle Bronze Age in the southern Levant: a preliminary comparison of radiocarbon and archaeo-historical synchronizations. In Bietak, M. (ed.), *The synchronisation of civilisations in the Eastern Mediterranean in the second millennium BC, vol. 2.* Vienna: Verlag der Österreichischen Akademie der Wissenschaften, 95–110.

Marcus, E.S. 2013. Correlating and combining Egyptian historical and southern Levantine radiocarbon chronologies at Middle Bronze Age IIa Tel Ifshar, Israel. In Shortland, A.J., and Bronk Ramsey, C. (eds.), *Radiocarbon and the chronologies of ancient Egypt.* Oxford: Oxbow, 182–208.

Marcus, E.S., Porath, Y., and Paley, S.M. 2008a. The early Middle Bronze Age IIa phases at Tel Ifshar and their external relations. *ÄL* 18: 221–244.

Marcus, E.S., Porath, Y., Schiestl, R., Seiler, A., and Paley, S.M. 2008b. The Middle Kingdom Egyptian pottery from Middle Bronze Age IIa Tel Ifshar. *ÄL* 18: 203–219.

Martin, M.A.S., Finkelstein, I., and Piasetzky, E. 2020. Radiocarbon-dating the Late Bronze Age: cultural and historical considerations on Megiddo and beyond. BASOR 384: 211–240.

Mebert, J. 2010. *Die Venustafeln des Ammi-ṣaduqa und ihre Bedeutung für die astronomische Datierung der altbabylonischen Zeit.* Vienna: Institut für Orientalistik der Universität Wien.

Merrillees, R.S. 2001. Some Cypriote White Slip pottery from the Aegean. In Karageorghis, V. (ed.), *The White Slip ware of Late Bronze Age Cyprus.* Vienna: Verlag der Österreichischen Akademie der Wissenschaften, 89–100.

Moeller, N., and Marouard, G. 2011. Discussion of late Middle Kingdom and early Second Intermediate Period history and chronology in relation to the Khayan sealings from Tell Edfu. *ÄL* 21: 87–121.

Montelius, O. 1903. *Die typologische Methode.* Stockholm: Selbstverlag des Verfassers.

Mumford, G.D. 2014. Egypt and the Levant. In Steiner, M.L., and Killebrew, A.E. (eds.), *The Oxford handbook of the archaeology of the Levant, c. 8000–332 BCE.* Oxford: Oxford University Press, 69–89.

Petrie, W.M.F. 1891. *Tell el Hesy (Lachish).* London: Committee of the Palestine Exploration Fund.

Pruzsinszky, R. 2009. *Mesopotamian chronology of the 2nd millennium BC: an introduction to the textual evidence and related chronological issues.* Vienna: Verlag der Österreichischen Akademie der Wissenschaften.

Reimer, P.J., Bard, E., Bayliss, A., Beck, J.W., Blackwell, P.G., Bronk Ramsey, C., Buck, C.E., Cheng, H., Edwards, R.L., Friedrich, M., Grootes, P.M., Guilderson, T.P., Haflidason, H., Hajdas, I., Hatté, C., Heaton, T.J., Hoffmann, D.L., Hogg, A.G., Hughen, K.A., Kaiser, K.F., Kromer, B., Manning, S.W., Niu, M., Reimer, R.W., Richards, D.A., Scott, E.M., Southon, J.R., Staff, R.A., Turney, C.S.M., and van der Plicht, J. 2013. Intcal13 and Marine13 radiocarbon age calibration curves 0–50,000 years cal BP. *Radiocarbon* 55: 1869–1887.

Reimer, P.J., Austin, W.E.N., Bard, E., Bayliss, A., Blackwell, P.G., Bronk Ramsey, C., Butzin, M., Cheng, H., Edwards, R.L., Friedrich, M., Grootes, P.M., Guilderson, T.P., Hajdas, I., Heaton, T.J., Hogg, A.G., Hughen, K.A., Kromer, B., Manning, S.W., Muscheler, R., Palmer, J.G., Pearson, C.L., van der Plicht, J., Reimer, R.W., Richards, D.A., Scott, E.M., Southon, J.R., Turney, C.S.M., Wacker, L., Adolphi, F., Büntgen, U., Capano, M., Fahrni, S.M., Fogtmann-Schulz, A., Friedrich, R., Köhler, P., Kudsk, S., Miyake, F., Olsen, J., Reinig, F., Sakamoto, M., Sookdeo, A., and Talamo, S. 2020. The IntCal20 northern hemisphere radiocarbon age calibration curve (0–55 Cal kBP). *Radiocarbon* 62: 725–757.

Ryholt, K.S.B. 1997. *The political situation in Egypt during the Second Intermediate Period, c. 1800–1550 BC.* Copenhagen: Museum Tusculanum Press.

Ryholt, K.S.B. 2004. The Turin King List. *ÄL* 14: 135–155.

Schneider, T. 2008. Das Ende der kurzen Chronologie: eine kritische Bilanz der Debatte zur absoluten Datierung des Mittleren Reiches und der Zweiten Zwischenzeit. *ÄL* 18: 275–313.

Sellin, E., and Watzinger, C. 1913. *Jericho: die Ergebnisse der Ausgrabungen.* Leipzig: Hinrichs.

Sharon, I. 2014. Levantine chronology. In Steiner, M.L., and Killebrew, A.E. (eds.), *The Oxford handbook of the archaeology of the Levant, c. 8000–332 BCE*. Oxford: Oxford University Press, 44–65.

Shortland, A.J., and Bronk Ramsey, C. (eds.) 2013. *Radiocarbon and the chronologies of ancient Egypt*. Oxford: Oxbow.

Sterba, J.H., Foster, K.P., Steinhauser, G., and Bichler, M. 2009. New light on old pumice: the origins of Mediterranean volcanic material from ancient Egypt. *JAS* 36: 1738–1744.

Stuiver, M., and Suess, H.E. 1966. On the relationship between radiocarbon dates and true sample ages. *Radiocarbon* 8: 534–540.

Taylor, R.E., and Bar-Yosef, O. 2014. *Radiocarbon dating: an archaeological perspective*. Walnut Creek, CA: Left Coast Press.

Toffolo, M.B., Arie, E., Martin, M.A.S., Boaretto, E., and Finkelstein, I. 2014. Absolute chronology of Megiddo, Israel, in the Late Bronze and Iron Ages: high-resolution radiocarbon dating. *Radiocarbon* 56: 221–244.

Ussishkin, D. (ed.) 2004. *The renewed archaeological excavations at Lachish (1973–1994)*. Tel Aviv: Emery and Claire Yass Publications in Archaeology.

Waddell, W.G. 1940. *Manetho (Loeb Classical Library 350)*. Cambridge, MA: Harvard University Press.

Webster, L. 2020. *Synchronising the chronologies of the Late Bronze Age Southern Levant and Egypt: a radiocarbon dating perspective*. PhD thesis. University of Vienna and Macquarie University, Sydney.

Webster, L., Streit, K., Dee, M.W., Hajdas, I., and Höflmayer, F. 2019. New radiocarbon-based assessment supports the prominence of Tel Lachish during the LB IB–IIA. *Radiocarbon* 61: 1711–1727.

Weinstein, J.M. 1992. The chronology of Palestine in the early second millennium BCE. *BASOR* 288: 27–46.

Weninger, F., Steier, P., Kutschera, W., and Wild, E.M. 2006. The principle of the Bayesian method. *ÄL* 16: 317–324.

Yasur-Landau, A., and Cline, E.H. (eds.), 2020. *Excavations at Tel Kabri: the 2005–2011 seasons*. Leiden: Brill.

Yasur-Landau, A., Cline, E.H., Koh, A.J., Ratzlaff, A., Goshen, N., Susnow, M., Waiman-Barak, P., and Crandall, A.M. 2018. The wine storage complexes at the Middle Bronze II palace of Tel Kabri: results of the 2013 and 2015 seasons. *AJA* 122: 309–338.

12

Egypt in the First Intermediate Period

Juan Carlos Moreno García

12.1. Introduction

When scholars of the late nineteenth and early twentieth centuries AD
developed the reconstruction of the pharaonic past, two types of periods—"Kingdoms" and "Intermediate Periods"—were thought to have
shaped Egyptian history, and this theory was generally accepted until
recently.[1] The former were characterized as times in which power was
centralized and exercised without restriction by powerful kings (pharaohs), when decisions were made within a well-delimited, hierarchical
structure of authority epitomized by different levels of scribes, dignitaries, and members of the royal court, and when the careful management
and distribution of the kingdom's resources guaranteed abundance for
everybody. The "Intermediate Periods," on the other hand, stood for
exactly the opposite: times of political division, economic crisis, intense
fragmentation of power ("regionalization"), and the collapse of administrative hierarchies together with the ability of kings and local rulers

---

1. The chapter was language-edited by Denise Bolton and Karen Radner.

Juan Carlos Moreno García, *Egypt in the First Intermediate Period* In: *The Oxford History of the
Ancient Near East.* Edited by: Karen Radner, Nadine Moeller, and D. T. Potts, Oxford University Press.
© Oxford University Press 2022. DOI: 10.1093/oso/9780190687571.003.0012

to levy taxes. Such interpretations should be understood in the light of the cultural concerns and popular historiographical themes of the period when they were formulated (history conceived as a succession of cycles of rise and downfall of states and empires, evolution of social organisms, etc.).

These influences are still present in current approaches to the history of these epochs. The powerful imagery derived from the available textual sources, their apparent internal logic, as well as the support they seemed to find in art history (as works of art produced in Egypt's Intermediate Periods are deemed to look poor and "primitive"; cf. figure 12.1), led to a seemingly self-evident narrative shaped by a sort of "historical common sense" that obscures the historical reality of the periods in question. They have been systematically interpreted as periods of chaos, misery,

FIGURE 12.1. Funerary stele of Nemtiui, overseer of fields of the Great House, probably from Akhmim. The inscription is a good example for the use of non-standard hieroglyphs. IN 1875. Roemer und Pelizaeus Museum, Hildesheim. Photo by Einsamer Schütze, via Wikimedia Commons (https://commons.wikimedia.org/w/index.php?curid=3466336), Creative Commons Attribution-ShareAlike 3.0 Generic (CC BY-SA 3.0) license.

and corruption of the "natural" social order, an approach for which the scarcity of written and archaeological sources for these periods held to some extent a certain appeal.[2]

The label "First Intermediate Period" (figures 12.2 a–c) is perhaps the most successful example of the persuasiveness of these prejudices, as they have severely distorted our interpretation of the end of the Old Kingdom and the historical developments that took place in the century and a half or so that followed.[3] The written sources from this period are relatively sparse, and their precise dating is problematic at best. They mostly derive from provincial rulers rather than from royal chancelleries, their geographical distribution is quite uneven (relatively abundant in southern Egypt and much rarer in the north), and the historical information they contain is limited. These circumstances are hardly encouraging and prompted modern researchers to turn to later literary texts and art historical sources to compensate for the dearth of contemporary textual data, and they found ample confirmation that the period following the Old Kingdom was dire and chaotic. Later literary texts that supposedly describe the events that occurred during the First Intermediate Period portray a world where the traditional order had been entirely subverted, where warfare dominated the relations between the local rulers who had replaced the unified monarchy of the Old Kingdom pharaohs, and where foreigners moved and settled wherever they pleased throughout the Nile valley, while the idea of a return to normality, with a single monarch again ruling all of Egypt, nourished the hopes of a population tired of fragmented power, war, and famine. As for art, its primitive, almost naive aspect, coupled with the use of unskilled writing on many monuments, only confirmed that the heights of artistic quality and excellence in craftsmanship prevalent in the Old Kingdom under the patronage of its kings were now lost.

Only very recently, archaeological research, a reassessment of both inscriptions and literary texts, and a better knowledge of the

---

2. Moreno García 2015b; 2016.

3. Mazé 2016.

international contexts at the end of the third millennium BC have caused researchers to question many of the previous assumptions, and this has led to more balanced interpretations of the First Intermediate Period. Far from being a period of crisis, it emerged as a time of innovation and of adjustments to the balance of power between rulers and subjects—a time when trade thrived, urban life flourished, and private economic activities expanded. This also prompted a reassessment of the Old Kingdom, particularly in its final two centuries, as its politics and

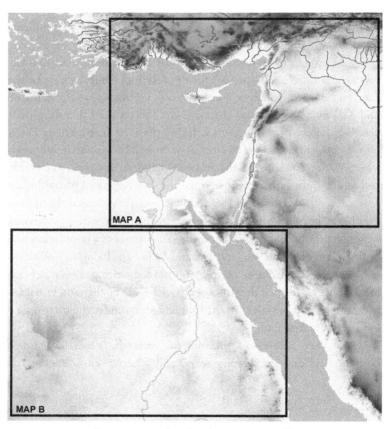

FIGURE 12.2A. Sites mentioned in this chapter. Prepared by Andrea Squitieri (LMU Munich).

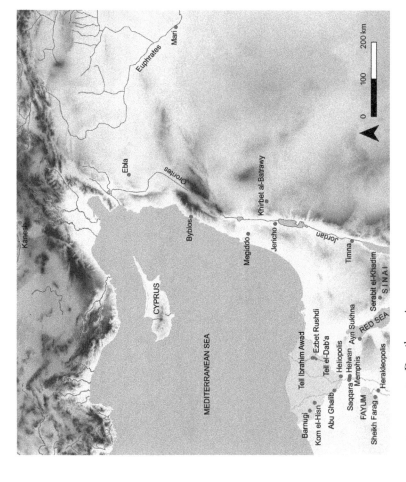

FIGURE 12.2B. Detail map A.

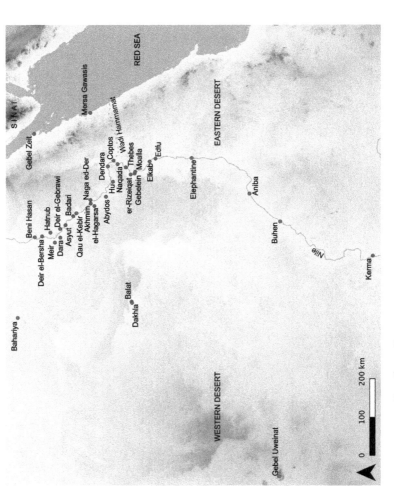

SINAI

Gebel Zeit

RED SEA

Mersa Gawasis

Beni Hasan

Deir el-Bersha
Meir   Hatnub
Dara   Deir el-Gebrawi
Asyut   Badari
Qau el-Kebir
Akhmim   Naga ed-Der
el-Hagarsa'
                Dendara
Abydos   Hu   Coptos
         er-Rizeiqat Wadi Hammamat
         Gebelein Thebes
                    Moalla
                 Elkab
                 Edfu

Elephantine

EASTERN DESERT

Aniba

Buhen

Nile

Kerma

Balat

Dakhla

Bahariya

WESTERN DESERT

Gebel Uweinat

0   100   200 km

N

FIGURE 12.2C. Detail map B.

attempts to control lucrative trade routes might better explain its collapse than merely blaming the climatic changes around 2200 BC,[4] alleged foreign invasions, or the sudden rise of provincial rulers who during the previous eight centuries had accepted the monarchy's authority (or at least not openly challenged it). Of course, many questions still remain unsolved, but they challenge researchers to approach and analyze the sources from new perspectives and to revisit assumptions that have been taken for granted even when supported only by surprisingly scarce and ambiguous evidence, and these questions also promote archaeological research in order to fill the many gaps of the written documentation. While simplistic "common sense" approaches to this period, typically concerned with a catastrophic event and the inevitable "collapse" that would result from it, are still popular, one of the effects of this historiographic renewal is that there is room for approaches that question the very nature, foundation, and scope of the Old Kingdom monarchy, as well as the dynamics underlying the balance of power that had sustained it.[5]

Powerful imagery is usually associated with the Egyptian monarchy and state, both in pharaonic culture and in modern Egyptological thought. This imagery promotes a view that sees the "natural" political condition of ancient Egypt as that of a united state under the rule of a single monarch, pharaoh himself (or very occasionally, herself), and that any other configuration of power is rejected as anomalous, with the (re)unification of Egypt at any cost attributed as their primary goal to rulers in periods of political fragmentation. The echoes of European nationalism, with the key concept that nation, state, and people are interchangeable, as prevailed in the late nineteenth century AD when the basic outlines of Egyptian history were reconstructed, are easily discernible behind interpretations that recreate ancient Egypt as

---

4. Bunbury 2010; Bárta 2015.

5. As demonstrated by the studies of, e.g., Müller-Wollermann 1986; Gestermann 1987; Seidlmayer 1987, 2000; Moeller 2005; Morris 2006; 2019; Morenz 2009; Römer 2011; Bussmann 2014; Willems 2014; Moreno García 2015b; 2016; 2018a; Schneider 2017; Bárta 2019.

a sort of nation-state *avant la lettre*.[6] But the implications of the easy acceptance of this idea have been profound, as it has caused researchers to largely ignore the importance of politics in Egyptian history, as if a pharaoh-to-be could simply and without discussion impose authority across Egypt; as if negotiations between competing authorities, alternative configurations of power, and political arrangements were simply oddities in a country that was meant to form a single political entity under the authority of a single ruler; or as if geopolitics and the influence of foreign actors pursuing their own interests and priorities could simply be ignored, particularly when such actors are based in less politically and culturally "developed" areas such as Nubia or the southern Levant.

There is no doubt that when regional rulers succeeded in reunifying Egypt they tried to legitimize their authority, and to embellish their pedigree, by stressing royal continuity and cultural traditions and by promoting the return to the "classic" models, thus rejecting the previous situation as abnormal.[7] However, there is equally no doubt that their ability to claim the crown of Egypt and to consolidate power required them to satisfy the interests of many political actors, including members of other branches of the royal family. We must stress that unification was just one possible configuration of power, and not an ineluctable pathway toward "normality"; when Egypt was unified it was because the kings and the other political actors had found a satisfactory compromise

---

6. The influence of nineteenth-century European historiography on the basic interpretation of ancient Egypt's past and the organization of the pharaonic state cannot be overstated, as the choice of themes and approaches inspired by distinctive "national" schools of historical thought (e.g., French or German) still shape modern interpretations. Medieval historiography provides a useful comparison, as since the nineteenth century, French and German historiography markedly differ in their basic assessment of the post-Carolingian world. The French school emphasizes the emergence of "territorial" powers and the disintegration of the Carolingian institutional order, while the German school sees this period as one of continuity, as power was based not on territorial domination but on interpersonal relationships between kings and aristocrats; cf. Bührer-Thierry, Patzold, and Schneider 2018.

7. Redford 1986: 259–275.

for their respective interests and agendas.[8] On the other hand, the monarchy collapsed when the king was no longer able to maintain his role as the primary mediator between all factions and when the interests of the monarchy could no longer be aligned with those of the state's other political powers, at court and in the provinces.[9] The end of the Old Kingdom and the events that followed might be best understood from this perspective.

12.2. *A period of change*

The last two centuries of the third millennium BC witnessed deep changes in the organization of power and in the very foundations of the political entities that then existed in the Nile valley. The preceding centuries were characterized by the centralization of authority under a single ruler, in particular under the Sixth Dynasty (cf. chapters 5 and 7 in volume 1). This took place in parallel to Mesopotamia under the Akkad Dynasty (cf. chapters 9 and 10 in volume 1) but in contrast to Nubia (cf. chapter 6), where no similar consolidation of power seems to have occurred.

12.2.1. Geographies of power and the circulation of wealth

In stark contrast to the centralized rule of the Sixth Dynasty kings, we now see dramatic changes in the exercise of power as Egypt entered a period of political division, crisis of the monarchy, military confrontations between provincial warlords, and finally the emergence of two rival kingdoms: Thebes in the south and Herakleopolis in the north. Conversely, Nubia and its wider region, which had formerly been divided into various smaller polities such as Yam, Setjau, and Irtjet that were ruled by "governors," now saw the consolidation

---

8. Moreno García 2018a.

9. Baines and Yoffee 1998.

of a large kingdom encompassing the area between the Second and Fourth Nile Cataracts and that later was known as "Kush," with its center at Kerma, just south of the Third Cataract.[10] If we look toward Mesopotamia, we find that the kingdom of Ur (cf. chapter 13 in this volume) that eventually succeeded the Akkad state only directly governed southern Iraq, with no permanent control over regions in Syria or Elam. The fragmentation of the large political entities that had dominated Egypt and Western Asia in the second half of the third millennium BC took place in the context of deep-rooted changes that affected regions extending far beyond the borders of the Nile valley to include not only Western Asia and the Mediterranean but also Central Asia and the lands bordering the northern coastline of the Indian Ocean.[11]

During this period, the emergence of new powers in Iran (Anšan and Šimaški) altered the long-distance routes that provided copper and other goods to Mesopotamia through Marhaši (a region east of Elam) and Makkan (Oman). As a result, Makkan lost its monopoly on the copper trade with Mesopotamia, while the trade economy of Dilmun (Bahrain) boomed. Strong relationships with the Harappan area, which encompassed the Indus valley and Gujarat, were of vital importance to Dilmun's socioeconomic development, which was now able to obtain copper not only from Oman but also from central and south-central Iran, Rajasthan, and Gujarat.[12] Tin arrived in Mesopotamia, Syria, and Anatolia from Central Asia at a time marked by a flourishing of bronze metallurgy and technical innovations in the Middle East[13] and the emergence of Cyprus as another major source of high-quality copper.[14] Contact between Egypt and the Aegean, especially Crete, intensified during this

---

10. For a useful summary, see Emberling 2014.

11. Warburton 2007; 2011; 2013; Wilkinson 2014.

12. Laursen 2009; Højlund 2013.

13. Lyonnet 2005; Wilkinson 2014.

14. Muhly and Kassianidou 2012: 128.

time:[15] given the characteristic counterclockwise currents in the Eastern Mediterranean, navigation between these two areas was easier through the western parts of the Nile delta, a region that flourished only after the end of the Old Kingdom. Our picture would be incomplete without stressing that beyond metal, high-quality manufactured goods such as textiles were popular merchandise of the long-distance trade, or without considering the role of pastoral populations as crucial agents in the circulation of commodities, ideas, and new metallurgical techniques over vast areas.[16]

The fact that the pharaohs of the Sixth Dynasty controlled Egypt while the contemporary kings of Akkad ruled over Mesopotamia, Elam, and parts of Syria meant that safety and ease of travel in the extensive areas under their combined authority greatly facilitated the circulation of commodities. The archives of Ebla (cf. chapter 8 in volume 1) mention a commercial partner called Dugurasu, which is likely to be identified with Egypt.[17] With the city of Byblos acting as intermediary, Dugurasu exported elephant tusks, linen, and gold and imported tin, lapis lazuli, and textiles. Iny, a dignitary who led several maritime commercial missions to Byblos and other locations in the Levant, reports that he brought silver, lead (or tin?), some kind of oil, and lapis lazuli, as well as Asiatic (*aamu*) men and women into Egypt during the reigns of Pepy I, Merenra, and Pepy II.[18] The Old Kingdom's influence was not restricted to Byblos, but can also be detected at Megiddo, Jericho, Ebla, and Khirbet al-Batrawy (in western Jordan).[19] This is likely related to the import of copper, not only from Sinai but also from Wadi Faynan and (probably)

---

15. Wiener 2013; Morero and Prévalet 2015.

16. Kepinski 2007; Gernez 2011.

17. Biga 2010; Biga and Roccati 2012; Biga and Steinkeller 2021; for a different view, see Archi 2016. Cf. also Matthiae 2017; Pinnock 2018.

18. Marcolin and Espinel 2011.

19. Adams 2017; Nigro 2014; Nigro, Montanari, Mura, Yasine, and Rinaldi 2018; Scandone-Matthiae 2003.

Timna through the Gulf of Aqaba and the Jordan valley,[20] thus bypassing Palestine and its nomadic populations. The Abusir papyri and later documents also mention "Asiatic copper," a term that apparently designated a different, more expensive type of copper. Precious and semi-precious stones (some of them from Egypt), minerals, and other goods traversed routes via the Red Sea, the Gulf of Aqaba, and the Arabian peninsula to reach Jordan, Palestine, and Syria.[21] This may explain why Old Kingdom Egypt launched several campaigns against the unruly nomadic population that lived in the southern Levant, why during this very same period nomadic populations in the Negev area extracted and transported copper toward Canaan and Egypt,[22] and why Egyptian prestige objects have been recovered at Ebla and Byblos (cf. chapter 6 in volume 1).

Trade considerations may also explain why Egypt tried to bypass the areas of the Nile controlled by Nubia (especially after the abandonment of the fortress of Buhen), most likely in an attempt to reach those regions that produced coveted commodities directly by sea or by desert routes. The maritime expeditions to Punt, the creation of a logistics center at Balat in the oasis of Dakhla, the early evidence of an Egyptian presence at the Red Sea harbor of Mersa Gawasis, and the importance of control over "gateways" and tribute from abroad, evoked in the inscriptions of many provincial officials, particularly at Coptos, Thebes, and Elephantine during the late Sixth Dynasty, all indicate a strong interest in promoting trade and in controlling the flow of wealth across northeastern Africa (cf. chapter 6). The royal decrees of Coptos testify that gold, copper, and other precious objects were taxed by Egyptian officials, and the involvement of officials from Elephantine in trade missions to Punt and Byblos, as well as the rise of Thebes, all point to an intensification of exchange activities through the Red Sea.[23]

---

20. Sowada 2009: 187; Nigro 2014.

21. Nigro 2014.

22. Jirásková 2011; Finkelstein, Adams, Dunseth, and Shahack-Gross 2018.

23. Moreno García 2019b; 2021.

It is probably too simplistic to consider foreign trade to be the one crucial factor in the events that unfolded during the Sixth Dynasty and that culminated in the collapse of the unified monarchy, but neither should its importance be underestimated. The recent discovery of pottery from the southern Red Sea region at the harbor of Ayn Sukhna suggests that the port's scope of activity was not limited to the Sinai and its copper and malachite ores, but extended into regions situated farther south. The late Old Kingdom materials at the Red Sea harbor at Mersa Gawasis are quite probably related to the rise of Thebes and Coptos to political prominence during this period. The discovery of temples built in a Levantine architectural style at Tell Ibrahim Awad in eastern Lower Egypt may indicate the presence of a community of Asiatics, perhaps involved in maritime and land trade operations in the service of the Egyptian crown.[24] According to all this evidence, Old Kingdom Egypt was deeply enmeshed in exchange networks in which Byblos, Ebla, Punt, and some Nubian political entities were essential partners.

The role of Byblos as an intermediary in trade between Egypt and other areas of the Near East sheds light on two matters that are otherwise inexplicable. On the one hand, Byblos' role explains why the lowest exchange ratio between silver and gold in Western Asia is attested at Ebla and Mari, where it oscillated between 6:1 and 2:1, quite close to the ratio of 2:1 prevailing in Egypt. On the other hand, it can account for the fact that the weight unit of 9.1–9.4 g became common in Egypt only at a relatively late date from the middle of the second millennium BC onward, while it had already been in use for more than a millennium in many regions of the eastern Mediterranean, especially in Syria.[25] As a major supplier of gold and exotic items, Egypt's position in the Eurasian economic sphere depended on its capacity to preserve its role as the indispensable intermediary and provider of gold and highly coveted goods, mainly obtained from Nubia and the southern reaches of the Red Sea.[26]

---

24. Bietak 2003; 2010.

25. Rahmstorf 2017: 194.

26. Warburton 2007; Moreno García 2017.

It is also possible that, as occurred in later periods, less prestigious items such as leather, natron, cereals, linen, and more were also part of this traffic.[27]

Support for the Old Kingdom's trade operations was provided by a logistical network of harbors, and production and administrative centers, with the institutions called *hut* being the most important among them. Their purpose was to produce and store foodstuffs and other goods for distribution to caravans and expeditions. This is stated clearly in a passage of the tomb inscription of Harkhuf, a caravan leader from Elephantine:

> Orders have been brought to the governor(s) of the new agricultural domains, the companion(s), and the overseer(s) of priests commanding that supplies be furnished from what is under the charge of each of them from every *hut* belonging to a processing centre and from every temple, with no exemption.[28]

The role played by the *hut*-centers in provisioning the king's agents is also exemplified by the inscriptions from Hatnub, which refer to the equipment delivered by the local *hut* to the teams of workers sent to the quarries, the organization of the expeditions by an overseer of a *hut*, and the close relationship between the *hut* and the agricultural estates of the crown.[29] An inscription from Dendara provides another example when Seneni, the overseer of a *hut*, claimed that he had delivered grain to the personnel of a *hut* in his position as "keeper of the provisions (*iri aqu*) of every day."[30] An inscription from Elephantine, dated to about 2000 BC, mentions deliveries of cereals, dates, and cattle from the overseer of a *hut* to several dignitaries, including a messenger who arrived in Elephantine on a mission for the king. Finally, an administrative document from the early second millennium BC enumerates

---

27. Moreno García 2016.

28. Strudwick 2005: 333.

29. Moreno García 2007; 2013.

30. Fischer 1968: 209–213.

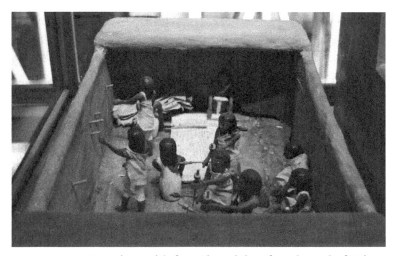

FIGURE 12.3. A wooden model of a textile workshop, from the tomb of Meketra in Thebes. Egyptian Museum, Cairo. Photo by Soutekh67, via Wikimedia Commons (https://commons.wikimedia.org/w/index.php?curid=32561917), Creative Commons Attribution-Share Alike 3.0 Generic (CC BY-SA 3.0) license.

various kinds of textiles delivered to an official: he received them from a warehouse, from a work camp (*kheneret*), and from a locality or royal center called *hut-Khety* "*hut* of [king] Khety." *Hut*-centers were crucial nodes in the geography of the Old Kingdom's tax system. They were established in almost every province and served as agricultural centers with their own fields, cattle, and workers. *Hut*-centers were also involved in the production of textiles (figure 12.3). They functioned as local warehouses where agricultural and manufactured products such as sandals, textiles, and ropes were stored for delivery to royal agents. Together with temples, the *hut* formed a network of royally controlled centers that enabled the collection of taxes and the mobilization of workforces along the Nile valley and placed these resources at the disposal of the crown.[31]

31. Moreno García 2007; 2013.

Because of the trade routes that crossed Upper Egypt both by land and along the Nile, this region became increasingly important for the Old Kingdom, and new structures were implemented in the area's administrative organization. One key development was the creation of the position of "overseer of Upper Egypt," who supervised and coordinated the activities of the officials of the crown in this region—a post often held by the vizier. Among the many duties of the overseer of Upper Egypt was the compilation of lists of people obliged to perform compulsory work for the king, the levying of transport duties, the procurement of metals, the organization of new agricultural domains, and record keeping. Weni is perhaps the best-known overseer of Upper Egypt, and he describes his responsibilities in these terms in his autobiographical tomb inscription:

> I acted for him [i.e., the king] as overseer of Upper Egypt in a satisfactory manner so that no one there did any harm to his fellow, I was doing every task, assessing everything due to the [royal] Residence in this Upper Egypt twice, every regular corvée due to the [royal] Residence in this Upper Egypt twice, carrying out my official duties so as to make my reputation in this Upper Egypt.[32]

The overseer of Upper Egypt also controlled foreign imports. In his autobiographical tomb inscription, Iny states that after the successful completion of a trade mission, he traveled to the court, together with the overseer of Upper Egypt, in order to inspect the produce (*inu*) he had brought from abroad.[33]

Additionally, local potentates were elevated to official positions and entrusted with administrative and managerial duties, mostly relating to temples and *hut*-centers. These potentates imitated the lavish lifestyle typical of the royal court and the palatial elites. They maintained huge retinues consisting of family members, followers, and subordinates, while their decorated tombs, and the luxurious goods buried within, reveal

---

32. Strudwick 2005: 355–356.

33. Marcolin and Diego Espinel 2011: 574.

that their collaboration with the monarchy was concomitant with the reinvestment of a substantial portion of the crown's revenue produced and circulating across Egypt in the provinces they ruled. The political consequences are obvious. In the long term, such localized accumulations of both wealth and political power posed a threat to the centralized state, including the emergence of local political agendas and alliances that did not necessarily align with those of the distant sovereign.

The end of the Old Kingdom did not interrupt the trade networks that had flourished previously. On the contrary, there is increasing evidence that these networks continued to operate during the First Intermediate Period and that at least in some cases, trade was controlled by nomadic population groups and non-institutional actors. In other words, international trade did not depend on expeditions and trade missions organized by the crown, and the existence of the Old Kingdom state was not essential for the continuation of trade contacts abroad. Perhaps the most important change was the development of a trade route that connected the Eastern Mediterranean with Nubia through the western delta, the Fayum region, and an area in Middle Egypt that included Asyut, Deir el-Bersha, and Beni Hasan.[34]

In the western delta, Kom el-Hisn emerged as an important center with clear evidence of foreign influence, in particular the presence of "warrior tombs." These graves are similar to Levantine burials, with battle axes, knives, and daggers, from the late third and early second millennium BC. The tombs also contain a remarkable abundance of jewelry, especially necklaces made of gold, silver, lapis lazuli, and semi-precious stones, objects made of gold sheets, amulets, and scarabs.[35] Lapis lazuli, gold, turquoise, and semi-precious stones were also discovered in tombs at Barnugi, an important center for the production of natron in the western Nile delta that flourished during this period.

In the Fayum region, where the city of Herakleopolis was located and which constituted the core of the Herakleopolitan kingdom of the

---

34. Moreno García 2016; 2017.

35. Wenke, Redding, and Cagle 2016: 348–350.

First Intermediate Period, Asiatic weapons were found.[36] The inscription of an official who lived around 2000 BC stresses that Herakleopolis was indeed a "great gateway" and that it played a role as a control point for goods arriving from abroad.[37] Myrrh and aromatic plants appear to have been extremely important among these commodities, as Herakleopolitan kings created separate administrative units to deal with them: a dignitary buried at Herakleopolis held the title of "great one of the department of myrrh," while another, Hetepwadjet, was "measurer of the department of unguents."[38] It is possible that copper arriving from Anatolia and the Aegean also played an important role in the trade. Contact between Egypt and Crete developed at this time, and geochemical analysis of sediments from Alexandria has revealed metal imports from Anatolia, Cyprus, and the Aegean into the western delta during the third millennium BC, in sharp contrast to the eastern delta, which imported copper from the Levant.[39] The use of Aegean-style textile motifs in the decoration of early second millennium tombs in Asyut and Meir in Middle Egypt may indicate the importance of textiles in the trade contacts between Egypt and the Aegean at that time.[40]

Upper Egypt was not excluded from the lucrative trade routes that passed through the Nile valley at the time. An inscription from Coptos shows that a local chief donated an astonishing number of precious items to the local temple, including forty gold and copper vessels, gold and silver pieces, lapis lazuli and turquoise, thirty-six collars decorated with lapis lazuli, and substantial quantities of incense and myrrh.[41] Sennedjesu, an official from Dendara, claimed that

36. Moreno García 2017: 113.

37. Lichtheim 1988: 50; Moreno García 2019b.

38. Willems 2007: 95.

39. Véron 2013.

40. Moreno García 2017: 120; 2019a: 63–64.

41. Strudwick 2005: 125.

[I surpassed everyone who was and] who will exist therein in people, Lower Egyptian grain and emmer, gold, copper, clothing, oil, [honey], . . . [cattle], goats, cargo ships and everything.[42]

Trade between Egypt and Nubia continued to flourish after the end of the Old Kingdom. The flow of large vessels (most likely filled with foodstuffs) from Egypt into Nubia increased during the First Intermediate Period,[43] while the inscription of Setka of Elephantine refers to his role as a provider of precious African goods to the Herakleopolitan kingdom: he imported myrrh from Byblos, gold and copper from Punt, and incense from Nubia (Yam) as well as ebony, ivory, and exotic animals from other locations and shipped all these goods northward to Herakleopolis.[44] Egyptian jewelry found in tombs at Aniba, located about 230 km south of Elephantine in Lower Nubia, is proof for the profitability of contacts with Egypt, either by trading or serving as a mercenary.[45] Finally, the recent discovery of First Intermediate Period Egyptian pottery at the Delta of Gash and at Mahal Teglinos in northeastern Sudan suggests that Egyptian materials arrived not only through the Nile valley, but also via the Eastern Desert and the Red Sea coast, thus crossing Nubia.[46] Nubia appears to have been well placed in the network of trade routes leading to Punt, the Red Sea, and the Mediterranean (cf. chapter 20). The presence of Nubian warriors at the service of Egyptian provincial warlords during the First Intermediate Period is probably a sign of the involvement of Nubian rulers in Egyptian affairs, for example as supporters of commercial partners based at Elephantine (where Nubian pottery is well attested), Asyut (the arrival point of caravans linking Nubia to the Nile valley through the oases of the Western Desert), and elsewhere.

---

42. Fischer 1968: 160.

43. Hafsaas-Tsakos 2010: 390–392.

44. Edel 2008: 1743–1744; cf. also the existence of a land route from Gebel Tingar (west of Elephantine) to Punt; see Darnell 2004: 27.

45. Hafsaas-Tsakos 2005: 140.

46. Manzo 2017: 50–51.

Limited as the available evidence is, it reveals nevertheless that precious metals and valuable imports such as lapis lazuli, myrrh, and ivory continued to arrive in Egypt in the First Intermediate Period. Together with other items that are largely invisible in the archaeological record (such as grain, fish, textiles, or metals), such merchandise fueled trade networks which benefited not only the elite but also wider parts of the population, judging from the precious items found in the tombs of ordinary people.[47] This may explain why control over "gateways" and foreign tribute became a major concern for localities well placed at strategic crossroads; why these localities became major political centers during the First Intermediate Period; and why they were not exclusively in the hands of Egyptian actors. Nubian and Asiatic populations were also active players and became involved in the politics and internal affairs of Egypt in the very late third millennium BC.[48]

12.2.2. Social transformations

The end of the centralized Egyptian state brought with it the decline of an institution that had played a major role in the organization of the Old Kingdom's territory: the *hut*, which provided the logistics for the circulation of goods and people along the Nile. This process was a gradual one, and the written sources of the First Intermediate Period still mention the *hut* as part of the political and administrative landscape. The kings of Herakleopolis in the north and Thebes in the south, as well as members of their families, continued to create *hut*-centers and to appoint *hut* overseers in areas that were administratively reorganized, such as Tell el-Dabʿa and Dendara, respectively. Even the "Teaching for Merykara," a literary composition set in the Herakleopolitan kingdom, still refers to the foundation of *hut* in border areas in order to protect and organize them. However, by the early second millennium BC there is a noticeable lack of objects inscribed by or belonging to *hut* overseers, and only "fossilized"

---

47. Dubiel 2012b.

48. Moreno García 2019b.

formulae used in monumental inscriptions and in literary texts still refer to these centers as a significant element in the Egyptian landscape.

It was during this period that another type of settlement emerges in the epigraphic record. For the first time, the term *demi* ("harbor") appears as a constitutive element in place names and as focal points of territorial organization and of social identity.[49] As a distinctive element of urban economic activity in the form of a market and exchange center, the term *demi* gradually became a synonym for "town; city." A *demi* could become a major target in military operations between competing regional powers, as recorded in the fragmentary autobiographical inscription from the tomb of Iti-ibi of Asyut.[50] In other instances, a *demi* was considered a kind of refuge: "a pleasant harbor for his clan" (*demi nedjem en wehytef*).[51] Not surprisingly, as harbors and quays were also marketplaces, terms such as *demi* ("city") and *meryt* ("quay") became synonymous with "market" in some cases. Thus Sarenput I, governor of the caravan and harbor city of Elephantine around 1950 BC, included control over river trade, harbors, markets, and foreign commodities arriving into Egypt among his duties. He was

> "overseer of all tribute at the entrance of the foreign countries in the form of royal ornaments, to whom the tribute of the *Medja*-country was brought as contribution of the rulers of the foreign countries," as well as "one who rejoices over the quay/marketplace, the overseer of the great ships of the Royal Domain, who supplies the Double Treasury, the superior of the harbors in the province of Elephantine (so that) what navigates and what moors was under his authority."[52]

---

49. The description of the transport of a colossal statue ended with its arrival at the harbor [*demi*] of a locality [*nut*]: Sethe 1935: 48; cf. also "Coffin Texts," Spell III 257: *waret tu net nutiu* ("this neighborhood of the citizens").

50. Brunner 1937: 18.

51. Anthes 1928: 28–31; Willems 2007: 43.

52. Obsomer 1995: 482.

As the old network of *hut*-centers was never re-established once the united monarchy of Egypt was restored around 2050 BC, it seems that *demi* ("harbor; city") replaced the *hut* as the focal point for storing and collecting taxes. In other words, settlements that had developed organically replaced centers founded by the crown, in what appears to have been a tendency toward a more autonomous organization of settlements born out of the circulation of goods and commodities in the Nile valley. Recent archaeological research confirms that cities thrived during the First Intermediate Period. This was the case in Abydos, which contains houses with identifiable storage facilities that do not appear to be elite dwellings and should probably be seen as "middle-class" residences.[53] In some of the buildings and their silos, seal impressions have been found that indicate domestic administrative activities. At the site of Elephantine, excavations have provided evidence for regular streets set at right angles to each other, as well as for the practice of sealing, especially at the governor's palace.[54] The surface area of Edfu and Dendara (figure 12.4) doubled during this period, while cities in the Fayum (Herakleopolis Magna) and Middle Egypt (Asyut and Deir el-Bersha) also flourished, as did settlements in the western Nile delta such as Kom el-Hisn, Barnugi, and Abu Ghalib; the latter two were apparently linked to "industrial" activities and a trade route that connected the Mediterranean to Middle Egypt through the western branch of the Nile.[55]

The First Intermediate Period seems to be an era when trade, economic prosperity, and urbanism went hand in hand. This was a time in which cities became ideologically relevant as a source of legitimation and identity, while the crisis of the monarchy deprived the king of this role. Thus, many inscriptions prominently mention the city's approval of an official's actions (e.g., "one beloved by his city," "one beloved by all his city"). The topos of protecting or enriching one's town figured prominently in the epigraphic record of this period, and similar expressions

---

53. Adams 2007.

54. von Pilgrim 1996; 2001.

55. Bagh 2002; 2004; Moeller 2016: 219–248; Moreno García 2017: 113.

FIGURE 12.4. Dendara is an example of the urban growth experienced by some cities during the First Intermediate Period. Aerial view of the extramural First Intermediate Period and early Middle Kingdom settlement area of Dendara; in the background, the temple of Hathor. Photo by Gregory Marouard.

continued to be later used in the inscriptions of the elite, especially in the provinces.[56] It is noteworthy that even ritual texts from the early second millennium BC recognize this situation when they describe the households of deceased people: they list not only the dead, their relatives, and their immediate social network, but also "citizens" (*nutiu*) and "people from the harbor/city" (*demiu*).[57] The "citizens" also figure prominently in biographical inscriptions of the First Intermediate Period, for example in Asyut.[58] Given the troubled political context of this period, the support of local armies and fellow citizens was crucial for the political

56. Moreno García 1997: 46–52.

57. "Coffin Texts," Spells II 151; 152; 154; 155; III 52, 91, 114, 257.

58. El-Khadragy 2008: 223; Edel 1984: 99, fig. 15.

ambitions of local potentates and warlords. Many contemporary inscriptions therefore mention the approval of one's actions by one's immediate social surroundings, such as the province or the city. City audiences were thus considered significant for the purposes of ideology and legitimacy, and they even entered the narratives of the literature of the Middle Kingdom, for instance in the "Teaching for Merykara": this text depicts demagogues and agitators who disturb the peace of cities through their speeches and who drive urban population groups to rebellion.[59] In the same vein, new expressions developed from the very concept of city, such as "townsman" (lit. "man of the city")[60] and "officer of the city troops" (lit. "the living one of the city").[61] This second term also points to the growing importance of towns and townsmen as the providers of military support to provincial leaders. Already from the Old Kingdom onward, the concept of the "local god" (lit. "city god") had begun to play a prominent role in forging individual and collective identities.[62] Thus, Neferiu from Dendara claimed that "it was (the god) Ique(r) who accomplished it for me: I being aggrandized beyond the great men and officials of all my town,"[63] while another official stated that "I nourished my brothers and sisters with my own property, (this) being what (the god) Onuris accomplished for me."[64]

It is likely that the use of urban troops during the troubled times that followed the Old Kingdom implied some kind of recognition (and approval?) of the urban population, as indicated by the testimony of the graffiti from Hatnub or the tomb autobiographies from Asyut, especially when the novel topos of the autonomous individual (*nedjes*, "the modest/humble one") is emphasized: the ability to earn his living, to build up a personal patrimony independent of the king or the administration and

---

59. Parkinson 1997: 217–218.

60. Quirke 1991.

61. Berlev 1971.

62. Moreno García 1997: 46–52.

63. Fischer 1968: 207.

64. Fischer 1968: 209.

to transfer it to his descendants.[65] Thus, although an official called Khety declared that he had been endowed by the king with an estate ("I was one bright of face, who gave gifts out of the possessions of the estate which the Majesty of my lord gave me"),[66] other officials, on the contrary, stress that part of their fortune came from their patrimonial wealth, as in the case of Intef, son of Myt:

> I acquired bulls, goats, cloths, ornaments (from the) treasury and grain, part thereof I obtained by my own effort (and another part) from what pharaoh Mentuhotep (II) made for me because he loved me.[67]

When people began to present themselves as *nedjes* on their monuments during the First Intermediate Period, the concept was based on two closely related qualities: the private acquisition of substantial wealth; and the autonomy of one's own actions ("to act by my own arm"). An excellent example is provided by the stele of Heqaib, an official who lived in the area of Thebes during the First Intermediate Period:

> I was an excellent *nedjes* speaking with his mouth and acting with his arm, who makes his town keep at a distance from him. I was a noble one in Thebes, a great pillar in the southern district. I surpassed every peer of mine in this city in respect of riches of every kind. So people said, when I was acting by my (own) arm: "[He is] one that is free from robbing another." I provided this whole city with Upper Egyptian barley for many (?) years, not to speak of the [...]. I gave bread to the hungry and clothes to the naked. I did not calumniate the great ones and I gave ease to the *nedjes*. I gave a loan of corn (?) to Upper Egypt and Upper Egyptian barley to this northern district. I also gave oil to the province of Elkab after

---

65. Moreno García 1997: 31–58; Franke 1998.

66. Landgráfová 2011: 54–58.

67. Landgráfová 2011: 32–34.

my town had been satisfied. I made a ship of forty (cubits) [i.e., about 20 m] and a barque, for transporting cattle and for ferrying him who had no boat in the season of inundation. I appointed a herdsman to (my) cattle and (further) herdsmen to (my) goats and to (my) asses. My people were more numerous and my precious goods were greater in number than those of any peer of mine. I was a (real) master of my heart in times of turmoil, while everybody else was shutting his door. When the ruler counted my cattle, he found that my possessions had increased. As for everyone who had to deal with me, I caused him to bend his arm.[68]

This inscription provides several clues about the desired qualities of a *nedjes*. First of all, he was to be a person who was proud of acting for himself, according to his own initiatives, needs, and expectations, and not merely as the agent of someone else (including the king). Second, he was to be capable of accumulating substantial wealth thanks to his own actions, unmatched by his peers. Finally, his prosperity and good sense were to benefit his neighbors and fellow citizens as well, especially in periods of turmoil and famine. It should be stressed that people who described themselves in this way were far from simple commoners, despite their claims to the contrary. In fact, their titles quite often reveal that they were officials. Nonetheless, it is clear that people of a certain status were eager to embrace new ideas that celebrated social and economic autonomy, as if they were ordinary people rather than officials and members of the elite. In fact, when inscriptions from this period evoke society as a whole, they use expressions formed by pairing the terms *aa* "the great one" and *nedjes* "the modest one": for example, "I made what the great ones loved and the modest ones praised."[69]

Evidence from Middle Egyptian provincial cemeteries such as Qau el-Kebir and Badari confirms that ordinary people had access to precious goods, including gold beads and other jewelry. Stamp seals are frequently

68. Polotski 1930; Morenz 2006.

69. Moreno García 1997: 32–33.

found with burials of women and children and show that they used these as ornaments in this period, whereas men's use of stamp seals as personal adornment is much less frequently attested. Seals were required in order to control property and to authenticate commercial transactions; although some authors claim that the growing number of seal owners does not reflect increasing wealth in rural populations,[70] I would argue for the opposite scenario. Not only have we found that ordinary people had access to gold items (thus revealing considerable wealth in their hands),[71] but there are two further arguments. First, seals and sealings started to be routinely employed in everyday legal transactions such as the purchase of land or houses or the hiring of specialized priests,[72] and the increased sealing practice left its mark in contemporary ritual texts, as references to sealing were much more frequent in the late third and early second millennium BC corpus of "Coffin Texts" than in the earlier Old Kingdom "Pyramid Texts."[73] Second, women began using the title of *nebet per* ("mistress of the house") during the First Intermediate Period. This title refers to an adult woman who either independently managed a household (with or without a male head) or who was otherwise engaged in business enterprises.[74] This is the most frequently attested female title, particularly on scarab seals, and several "mistresses of the house" possessed their own steles. The analysis of women's seals from Middle Egyptian cemeteries reveals traces of wear and usage, demonstrating that they were not created exclusively for funerary purposes.[75] This indicates that seals and sealings were widely used in society, not only by administrative officials and people of high status, but also by ordinary men and women. In turn, this suggests the existence of a wide scope of

70. Discussion: Seidlmayer 1987: 201–204; Dubiel 2012b: 70–72.

71. Seidlmayer 2007: 45–47; Dubiel 2012a.

72. Moreno García 2000: 125–126; Picardo 2015: 265–274.

73. "Pyramid Texts": Spell 214; "Coffin Texts": Spells 131, 134, 135, 137, 142, 398, 657, 992, 1080, and 1117.

74. Stefanović and Satzinger 2015.

75. Dubiel 2012b.

legal and economic transactions in which formal agreements and methods of authentication (i.e., sealing) were required.

The evidence from seals, contracts, houses,[76] and funerary equipment
provides support for the hypothesis that following the decline of the
Old Kingdom monarchy, conditions were favorable for the emergence
of a "middle class" of economically autonomous and relatively affluent
individuals, whose values influenced both contemporary scribal culture
and the terminology which officials used to present themselves in their
inscriptions. By the end of the third millennium BC, when a reunified
Egypt was once again ruled by a single centralized monarchy, this "middle class" had become a substantial component of Egyptian society; its
very existence highlights that simply returning to the social conditions
of the Old Kingdom, when such a "middle class" apparently did not
exist, would have been impossible. A new social and economic reality
had emerged during the First Intermediate Period, and the centralized
state had to cope with it.[77]

Our final thought in the present section concerns the role of the
nomadic populations who had entered the Nile valley and left their mark
on the settlement structure.[78] It is not by chance that starting from the
very late third millennium BC, the development of extensive pastoralism in Egypt was concomitant with the emergence of new terms such as
menmenet ("cattle on the move") and *wehyt* ("village clan; tribe"), particularly in Middle Egypt, a region frequented by Libyan herders. Also
the Fayum area was traversed by foreign populations whose distinctive
settlement forms are in some cases preserved in references to enclosures,
called *wenet* in texts from the early second millennium BC and *seger* in
texts from the Ramesside period. In the local economy of Middle Egypt,
Asiatics, Libyans, and perhaps also populations of Nubian origin appear
to have been notable actors, as nomadic herding, transhumance, and specialized uses of space that focused on pastoralism flourished in this region

---

76. Moeller 2016: 219–246.

77. Richards 2005; Vermeulen 2016; Mazé 2017.

78. Moreno García 2017.

at the turn of the third millennium BC; the reference to "cattle of *Retenu*" in the tombs of Meir and Deir el-Bersha and a late Old Kingdom burial of a Nubian woman close to Deir el-Bersha provide further evidence for the involvement of foreigners in the Middle Egyptian cattle economy. The inclusion of Libyans in the execration texts of the Middle Kingdom may be due to their prominent role in cattle husbandry and in the supply of desert minerals.[79]

12.3. Political conflict

One of the most striking aspects of the First Intermediate Period is that the exceptionally long and stable political order, which had prevailed for a thousand years, vanished. During this time, the monarchy seemed unable to fulfill its traditional role as the mediator between different factions and in particular as the keeper of the balance of power between its own interests and those of the members of the court and the regional rulers. It is quite significant that locally emerging potentates did not compete to establish themselves as pharaohs in Memphis but instead preferred to follow their own political agendas within their regional setting. Therefore, it appears that the monarchy had ultimately failed to harmonize regional interests with those of the crown.

That the monarchy proved unable to subdue rebels who controlled only tiny territories and limited agricultural resources in Upper Egypt (Coptos; Thebes) provides a salient clue about the realities of royal power in the preceding decades. There are two different sets of sources: the autobiographical inscription of Weni of Abydos and the royal decrees from the temple of the god Min at Coptos;[80] both suggest that the provincial administrative structure in Upper Egypt was rather loose, far from an alleged world of "provincial governors" acting as local deputies of the king, with well-defined duties and administrative tasks (although this conceptual framework is still frequently found

---

79. Moreno García 2018b: 164.

80. Strudwick 2005: 352–357 and 105–124, respectively.

in modern studies).[81] The passage in Weni's autobiography describing
the mobilization of soldiers and resources for an expedition into the
Levant shows that overseers of temples, leaders of royal production centers (*hut*, *ges-per*), "chiefs," leaders of foreigners, Nubians, and others
participated in the war effort, while the royal decrees of Coptos mention many offices and officials involved in the management of the workforce. It is striking that the "great chiefs" of provinces are conspicuously
absent from these texts and that the mobilization of resources took the
form of contributions provided by a mix of local potentates, temples,
royal centers, and other authorities under the administrative control
of the overseer of Upper Egypt. When the first rebellions against the
monarchy erupted at Coptos and Thebes, it was a local leader, Ankhtifi
of Moalla, who was entrusted with the mission of suppressing the insurrection; although Ankhtifi was subservient to an overseer of Upper
Egypt residing at Thinis (who is mentioned somewhat contemptuously
in Ankhtifi's inscription), he apparently used his own local resources to
stop the rebellion.[82]

12.3.1. Power dynamics and the rise of local identity

The last decades of the Old Kingdom do not exhibit any evidence for
political or economic disruption. As it is far from clear whether the
so-called 4.2 kiloyear megadrought had an impact on life in Egypt, the
causal relationship between this event and the societal collapse at the end
of the Old Kingdom, as has been repeatedly postulated in recent years,[83]
needs to be seriously called into question. In fact, the urban centers of
Egypt both thrived and declined over centuries, and it is likely that these
transformations related more to settlement changes, the expansion of

81. Moreno García 2013b.

82. Vandier 1950: 187.

83. Hassan 1997.

nomadic lifestyles, and the diffusion of new techniques, especially in metallurgy and in textile production.[84]

The collapse of the Old Kingdom monarchy seems to have been the result of a fairly smooth process in which the pharaohs lost control over provinces that began to act independently. The final decades of the Old Kingdom monarchy show no trace of disruption to Egypt's overall administrative organization and tax system.[85] A number of royal decrees found at Coptos demonstrate that the king was still founding agricultural domains for the local temple, that his authority was recognized there, and that local officials worked on his behalf, following his instructions regarding the extraction and transportation of blocks of stone. A letter found at Elephantine reveals that corrupt officials were still subject to the king's justice,[86] while Nenu of el-Hagarsa, elder son of Meryaa, claimed in the tomb of his father that he had buried him, embalmed him with unguents from the (royal) residence and with high-quality linen provided by the "House of Life," thus demonstrating that deliveries of precious goods were still markers of the king's favor and that these goods still were circulated between the capital and the provinces.[87]

What is more, provincial officials continued to use titles that celebrated their role as priests and officiants (*khenti-she*) in the funerary complexes of the pharaohs in the Memphite area. Furthermore, Ankhi, a royal official active in the twenty-third or twenty-second century BC, still could claim control over the entire country's production, as he was "overseer of every meal of the king that heaven gives and earth creates," "overseer of every meal of the king in all his places," and "overseer of the production of every desert," as well as "overseer of all vegetation."[88] Ankhi was no exception, as several contemporary officials boasted about similar administrative and fiscal responsibilities, often using metaphorical titles

---

84. Meller, Risch, Jung, and Arz 2015; Höflmayer 2017.

85. Moreno García 2013a: 146–151; 2015; 2021.

86. Strudwick 2005: 178–179.

87. Kanawati and McFarlane 1995: 33.

88. Altenmüller 2012.

closely related to provisioning the king's table and the treasury, such as "overseer of everything that heaven gives and earth creates" or "overseer of the abundance of the field of offerings of the king." In other cases, as was also true for Ankhi, these titles explicitly included deserts and marshland, for instance in the titles "overseer of every repast of the king that heaven gives and earth creates (and which comes) out of the production of every desert," "one who reckons up the production of the deserts, marshlands and heaven," or "overseer of the meal of the king who reckons up the production of the deserts, marshlands and heaven."[89] Hetepeni, an official who bore some of these titles, was also a "commander of the king's scribes who reckons the troops (of men and cattle) in the Double Domain"—all of Egypt, in other words. Control over people, territory, and resources continued to be a primary concern for the central administration, as it had been in previous centuries.

This was still a period of stability, in which the central role of the king enjoyed formal recognition. There was continuity in Egypt's administrative organization and in the chain of command, suggesting that the royal tax system continued to still be in effect during the very late Old Kingdom period. It is possible, however, that the increased frequency of terms concerning control over production and over border areas just prior to the collapse of the monarchy indicates problems underlying the organization of the kingdom, including the capacity of the king to control its resources.

Coptos emerged as a pivotal area, since the leaders of this province suddenly accumulated substantial power and wealth, married into the royal family, organized expeditions to the quarries, and were able to pass on their privileged position and authority to their descendants.[90] The textual documentation from the temple of Min suggests that the same family was in control of this institution for several generations, and that they used it as their main power base. Given the absence of evidence for royal centers (*hut*) and their overseers in this province, it is also possible that

---

89. Fischer 1996: 32–33, 40, pl. 6.

90. Strudwick 2005: 116–125; Mostafa 1984–1985; 1987; 2005.

the local temple of Coptos assumed functions usually reserved for the *hut*, such as providing supplies for expeditions and organizing the cultivation of land in the province. Situated at a strategic location, Coptos was close to the gold mines of the Eastern Desert, the route leading to Hu and the Western Desert, and the route that led to the Red Sea, especially during the period when the port of Mersa Gawasis was becoming an important center for trade with the land of Punt in the southern Red Sea region. What is more, the crown (temporarily?) exempted the temple of Min at Coptos from the payment of taxes, including metals and precious items.[91] The temple managed to accumulate substantial riches during the last decades of the Memphite monarchy, or shortly afterward, as is revealed by the inscription of a "king's son" who donated gold and copper vessels, gold and silver pieces, lapis lazuli, and turquoise, as well as considerable quantities of incense and myrrh, to the sanctuary.[92] Keeping in mind that some of these products were usually imported from the land of Punt, in the southern Red Sea,[93] Coptos emerged as a trade hub in Upper Egypt that probably tried to extend its influence toward the routes leading to the Western Desert.

The case of Thebes is less well documented. However, it is clear that this locality rose to prominence during the late Old Kingdom when its leaders were involved in the management of granaries and royal centers (*hut*), collecting information that arrived in the province,[94] leading expeditions (as indicated by the title *khetemu-netjer* ["treasurer of god"] held by expedition leaders and known from the fragmentary autobiography of Seniiqer), and perhaps also controlling the import of foreign products.[95] If the dating of the tomb of Seniiqer were finally confirmed, Thebes would have prominently participated in the organization of expeditions and in the import of goods from abroad at the very end

---

91. Strudwick 2005: 111–112.

92. Strudwick 2005: 125.

93. Strudwick 2005: 72; Edel 2008: 1743–1744.

94. Fábián 2011; Diego Espinel 2015–2016: 110.

95. Fábián 2011: 49, fig. 8; 2017: 61–66.

of the Old Kingdom. In this scenario, Thebes would have been one of several hitherto relatively obscure provinces whose leaders now became involved in activities that allowed them to control the circulation of goods and to create lavishly decorated tombs for themselves. This group of leaders certainly included Tjauty of Hu and Djaushemay and his son Djau of Deir el-Gebrawi.

During the early First Intermediate Period, Coptos and Thebes were considered rebellious and opposed to the authority of the pharaoh, who entrusted Ankhtifi of Moalla (see earlier mention, section 12.3) with the task of restoring order between Coptos and Elephantine, an area that included some of Egypt's main gateways toward Nubia and the Red Sea. Despite this, the leaders of Coptos and Thebes are attested as in control of the trade in foreign goods sometime later: Tjauty of Coptos was the "one who fills the heart of the king in the gateway of Upper Egypt" while Intef of Thebes claimed to be the "one who fills the heart of the king in the southern gateway."[96] It seems that the leaders of Coptos and Thebes had decided at some point that it was more profitable for their interests to act independently and no longer recognize the authority of the king in Memphis, despite their continued use of titles that referenced the term "king" and therefore the united monarchy. Coptos and Thebes became rivals for control over the routes leading to the Red Sea and to the Western Desert through Hu. In a desert inscription, Tjauty of Coptos claimed that "(I) made this for crossing this gebel, which the ruler of another province had closed. (I) fought with [his] province."[97] Whether or not this implies a conflict between Coptos and Thebes over a route leading to Hu, there is no doubt that Thebes eventually prevailed; but its undisputed control over the routes leading to the oases of the Western Desert, along with the tribute from these regions, was yet to come.

However, Thebes's rise to be the dominant power in southern Egypt was not inevitable. Judging from their preserved titles, its leaders and later its kings claimed descent from the lineage of a certain Mentuhotep

---

96. Somaglino 2010.

97. Darnell 2002: 30–37.

(I), about whom no historical information survives;[98] later Theban kings may simply have embellished their otherwise modest origins by inventing an ancient and noble pedigree. Other sources refer to the "House of Intef,"[99] possibly a designation for the early Theban kingdom, and it is quite likely that an official of this name (rather than the probably entirely fictitious Mentuhotep I) laid the basis for the later expansion of Thebes. At this early stage, Upper Egypt saw local dignitaries who bore the title *imi-ra mesha* ("overseer of troops," usually translated as "general") rise to prominence, signaling that the mobilization of armed forces and the ability to go to war were now considered important. The epigraphic sources from this period mention such military commanders in provinces including Edfu, Moalla, Gebelein, Thebes, Dendara, Naga ed-Der, Akhmim, el-Hagarsa, and Asyut, while elsewhere officials whose titles signal no apparent military function were nevertheless involved in warfare and in the raising of troops.

Sobeknakht of Dendara was one of these officials, and the brief inscription on his stele recalls the style of the aforementioned inscription of Ankhtifi:

> I prepared the vanguard of the troops (*hat djamu*) and I supplied it with all the strong *nedjes* at the time. I fought in the midst of the valiant troops and I did not go forth empty.[100]

In his autobiography, Ankhtifi describes a world (or, at least the Theban area) characterized by walled towns and fortresses, with local leaders at the head of their own armies. Ankhtifi emerges from this composition as the chief authority over the three southernmost provinces of Upper Egypt (Elephantine, Edfu, and Elkab), while also exercising some influence over Dendara and northern Nubia. Other regional leaders, too, managed to extend their control over several provinces. Such

---

98. Postel 2004.

99. Berlev and Hodjash 1998: 39–41.

100. Silverman 2008.

officials with supra-provincial authority seem to have been essential in the south just prior to the final consolidation of the Theban kingdom over the eight southernmost provinces of Egypt. Most prominent are Onurisnakht (nomes VIII and X),[101] Abihu of Dendara (nomes VI, VII, and VIII),[102] Ankhtifi and Hetepi (nomes I, II, and III),[103] an anonymous official from Coptos (nomes VI–IX),[104] and the "House of Khuu," that is, the area of Gebelein and Edfu, which was named after an ancient leader from Edfu. The combination of firm leadership and control over the armed forces in the hands of ambitious local rulers coincided with the weakening of royal authority. The last Old Kingdom pharaohs were obliged to rely on the support of loyal regional leaders in order to implement their authority locally and to suppress rebellion.

In these troubled times, literature as well as figurative art began to celebrate military roles, thus fostering the development of a heroic ethos that further stressed the abilities of the local rulers. Officials frequently had themselves depicted as archers on their monuments (figure 12.5). In a fragmentary First Intermediate Period inscription from el-Hagarsa, we encounter the term *djamu* for the first time in a military context, designating recruits and inexperienced soldiers[105] (contrasted with *ahautiu* "warriors" in Middle Kingdom texts[106]). Another expression with military connotations that goes back to the same period is *ankh en niut* ("soldier of the town militia").[107] Both Thebans and Herakleopolitans, as well as their respective allies, employed Nubian troops.[108]

101. Goedicke 1999: 149–152.

102. Fischer 1968: 203–205.

103. Gabra 1976.

104. Fischer 1964: 106–111.

105. Kanawati 1995: 15.

106. Stefanović 2007.

107. Berlev 1971.

108. Fischer 1961; Darnell 2003; El-Khadragy 2006; 2008.

FIGURE 12.5. Funerary stele of Semin, who is being represented as an archer, a new symbol of self-identity in the troubled political period that followed the end of the Old Kingdom monarchy. MMA 20.2.29. Courtesy of the Metropolitan Museum of Art, New York (www.metmuseum.org).

The centralized network of royal centers (*hut*) that used to facilitate the production and storage of agricultural goods throughout the realm was losing importance; however, Rediukhnum of Dendara, an official in the service of one of the first known Theban queens, claimed that officials (*seru*) and overseers of *hut* were being appointed by the Theban kings in the zones under their control during the early Eleventh Dynasty.[109] More generally, the crisis of pharaonic authority led to the disorganization of its institutions in the separatist areas around Thebes, as later officials were forced to restore the tax system in this region.

---

109. Landgráfová 2011: 74–78.

Given the uncertainties surrounding the exact dating of many monuments from the First Intermediate Period, reconstructing a chain of events cannot hope to be chronologically precise.[110] Nevertheless, it is possible to discern the gradual rise of Intef of Thebes to regional power. One of his subordinates, a "general" who was also called Intef, claimed in his stele that he had navigated downstream and upstream on a mission for the "great chief of Upper Egypt" Intef to the place (*bu*)

> to which the governors (*heqau*) of Upper and Lower Egypt (were going). Every governor, having arrived there, then rejoiced on meeting me, because I was good of speech.[111]

A similar statement appears in the inscription of yet another Intef (so assumed because of his wife's different name), as he was sent to "every secret place (*set nebet sesheta*)" and on "all kinds of mission (*wepet*)" for his lord,[112] while an official from Dendara whose name has not survived stated that he had accomplished a mission (*wepet*) for the "great chief of Upper Egypt" Intef the Great.[113]

It is very likely that the Theban leader Intef, who is referred to in these inscriptions, was the same dignitary whose funerary stele bears the titles of "great chief of the Theban province," "one who fills the heart of the king in the southern gateway" and "great pillar who makes his (i.e., the king's) two lands to live."[114] In this way, Intef portrayed himself as one of several powerful magnates who (at least formally) still recognized the authority of the king, sending his emissaries to meet other potentates in the north and the south and claiming the title of "one who fills the heart of the king in the southern gateway," as held also by Tjauty of Coptos.

---

110. Gomaà 1980; Morenz 2006.

111. Fischer 1996: 83–90.

112. Clère and Vandier 1948: 2.

113. Fischer 1968: 122 n. 532, and 129 n. 571.

114. CGC 20009: Clère and Vandier 1948: 8.

Intef's political initiatives probably marked the shift in the balance of power from Coptos to Thebes that led to the consolidation of Thebes as the dominant force in southern Egypt. The meetings and missions referred to by his subordinates suggest diplomatic efforts designed to cement his position. Ankhtifi clearly did not succeed in curbing the power of Intef. That a stele of one of Intef's subordinates was discovered at Dendara reveals that his influence eventually extended over even this province, replacing the power that Ankhtifi had previously exercised there. The fact that the tomb of Ankhtifi at Moalla was not destroyed may suggest that Intef and Ankhtifi (or one of his successors) had arrived at some kind of compromise. In any case, according to the inscription of Hetepi of Elkab, it was not until the reign of Intef II that the three southernmost provinces of Egypt were more or less firmly integrated into the Theban kingdom. At Elephantine, for instance, local leaders such as Setka still sent trade missions to Herakleopolis, Thebes's northern enemy, and found their cultural particularities recognized and respected by the Theban kings: Intef II, for instance, offered monuments in the memorial chapel dedicated to the deified local dignitary Heqaib at Elephantine.

It seems that despite the pro-military ethos displayed in the inscriptions and the iconography of the First Intermediate Period, negotiation and the use of "soft power" played a significant role in the gradual construction of the Theban polity, which sought to extend its influence over local leaders without needlessly expending brute force. The price paid for this was that the authority of the early Theban rulers was built on fragile ground, with compromises and concessions made to local notables in exchange for their support, a characteristic that continued in subsequent centuries. It is possible that later generations considered Intef the Great a king, despite the fact that nothing in his own monuments reveals any claim to royalty. His successor Intef II shows a similar reluctance to claim kingship. While he certainly used royal titles, he represented himself in the pose of a mere dignitary on his steles and other monuments—a far cry from the regalia and royal attitude expected from the customary depictions of pharaohs, as if he felt somewhat unsure of his royal status.

The northern state under Herakleopolitan rule shared key strategies with the Theban polity. The kings' efforts to create and to legitimize authority were marked by negotiations with local leaders with a high degree of autonomy (e.g., at Asyut, Deir el-Bersha, and Beni Hasan); by intense fighting for control over the Abydos region (figure 12.6), a cult center for the increasingly popular cult of Osiris with a royal ancestral burial ground that was situated in a crucial position along the desert route network; and very likely by the creative fabrication of an ancestry fit for a royal house (as archaeological and epigraphical evidence for the Herakleopolitan rulers preceding Merykara is largely lacking).

Such concerted efforts to gain and keep power were very reasonable when one considers that the end of the Old Kingdom monarchy was followed by the emergence of multiple regional candidates who could claim

FIGURE 12.6. Funerary stele from the Abydos region, probably from Naga ed-Der, depicting Indi and his wife Mutmuti, priestess of the goddess Hathor at Thinis. Indi bears the titles of "mayor, royal sealer, sole companion, lector priest, the revered," but mentions no king by name. MMA 25.2.3. Courtesy of the Metropolitan Museum of Art, New York (www.metmuseum.org).

royal status. Khui of Dara was one of them; the enormous mastaba, or step pyramid, and funerary temple that he built show how a local potentate in the area of Asyut had accumulated enough wealth and power to dare to claim kingship for himself. Closer to the Theban area, Imhotep and Iti are attested as kings in graffiti left by expeditions crossing Wadi Hammamat. While Imhotep may be identical with the "king's son" mentioned in another rock inscription in this area, nothing else is known about Imhotep and Iti, including their family connections, geographical context, or the extent of their authority.[115] As for the area south of Edfu, rock inscriptions found at Naga el-Shebaykah and at Shatt el-Rigal record two more kings, Isu and Hetep, also otherwise unknown.[116] Another three kings, called Kakara-Iny, Iyibkhentra, and Segerseni, are known from the inscriptions they left in Lower Nubia, but their chronological positions are discussed controversially.[117] The ability to mobilize considerable resources is only clear in Imhotep's case:

> I carried out works for king Imhotep with 1,000 men of the Great House and 100 stonemasons, 1,200 sailors and 50 specialists (?) from the Residence. His majesty had this large troop of men come from the Residence, and I carried out this work for grain payments and for all sorts of linen; his majesty gave 50 oxen and 200 goats for every day.[118]

All these sources reveal the instability prevailing in southernmost Egypt, where various local lords claimed royal status, led "houses" (such as the House of Khuu), and occasionally fought between themselves. This was a very fluid political environment, in which identities were transformed and rebuilt in reaction to new situations and opportunities, in which the rulers of Thebes only reluctantly claimed kingship on their own

---

115. Papazian 2015: 402–403.

116. Papazian 2015: 404–405.

117. Török 2009: 101–102; Williams 2013.

118. Strudwick 2005: 143.

monuments, and in which personal initiative and autonomy crystallized in the popular concept of *nedjes*.

The picture would be incomplete without highlighting the role of Nubians in the political events of the First Intermediate Period. Nubian soldiers were represented in figurines and the scenes decorating the walls of several tombs from Middle and Upper Egypt (Elephantine, Moalla, and Asyut), and Nubian burials have been discovered in the area of Gebelein and er-Rizeiqat.[119] This probably reflects that Nubian soldiers served in the armed forces of the pharaohs of Egypt and of local warlords and were well integrated in local communities.[120] The cowhide and cattle skull found beside the coffin in the tomb of Ini, the regional "great chief" of Gebelein, may testify to Nubian funerary customs.[121] The inscription on the stele of Qedes, one of the Nubian soldiers living at Gebelein, references the mixed population of Nubians and Egyptians of Gebelein when he claimed to have acquired property and "surpassed everyone in this entire town in swiftness, its Nubians as well as its Upper Egyptians."[122]

The nature of the Nubian military presence in Egypt is difficult to pinpoint. Perhaps it was the result of agreements between Nubian rulers and local Egyptian potentates that may have included stipulations to provide military assistance to the latter. The armed conflicts in various parts of Egypt certainly created employment opportunities for fighters. By this time, the Nubians had very likely become indispensable trade partners. Setka's inscription from Elephantine shows that local rulers were able to supply the Herakleopolitan kings with precious goods from Nubia, the Mediterranean, and the southern Red Sea. This means that Elephantine enjoyed some freedom of action but needed the support of Nubian mediators at a time when the monarchy could no longer organize caravans or provide the logistics necessary for leading expeditions into Nubia. Thebes only succeeded in the reign of Mentuhotep II with

---

119. Ejsmond 2017.

120. Fischer 1961.

121. Donadoni Roveri 1990.

122. Fischer 1961: 44–56.

the incorporation of northern Nubia, the oases, and the desert routes that linked them.

The inscription of Ankhtifi of Moalla offers a clue to the relationship between Nubians and Egyptians, as he claims to have delivered grain to Lower Nubia, an assertion that seems to be confirmed by the increased flow of large-scale Egyptian containers into Nubia, probably filled with foodstuffs, during the First Intermediate Period.[123] Moreover, Ankhtifi also boasted about delivering grain as far north as Abydos in exchange for precious goods. Keeping in mind that Abydos was the arrival point for routes from the Western Desert, the grand claims in his biographical inscription point to the importance of the exchange between Nubia and Upper Egypt, in which Moalla was a mediator. Asyut was another destination for routes from the desert, so the scenes of Nubian soldiers found in tombs there suggest the existence of agreements between Nubian and local rulers that kept these trade routes open, to the benefit of both parties.

Nubians may therefore have played an important role as providers of precious goods and supporters of local leaders in an increasingly fragmented Upper Egypt while continuing to use the routes of the Western Desert. It is not by chance that Mereri, the overseer of priests, an official from Dendara, claimed that he was beloved by the Nubians of the desert.[124] Other texts confirm the presence of Nubians in the desert: the contemporary inscription of Tjemerery, governor of Thinis, mentions an "overseer of the army [. . .] in repelling foreigners who came down from the southern foreign lands," indicating that the invaders presumably came via the oasis route connecting the Thinite province with Nubia.[125] Furthermore, a magical text mentions "the Nubian woman who has come from the desert."[126] Later, when Egypt was again reunified under the Middle Kingdom, inscriptions record that the royal tax system was being restored and that these measures included the oases, Lower Nubia,

123. Hafsaas-Tsakos 2010: 390–392.

124. Fischer 1968: 138, 140.

125. Fischer 1968: 141.

126. Koenig 1987: 104.

and the Thinite area: "Wawat and the oasis, I annexed them to Upper Egypt."[127]

Henenu, an official serving Mentuhotep II (cf. section 12.4), boasted about having taxed "Thinis of the Thinite province and the Aphroditopolite province" for his sovereign and about his position as "the treasurer of the [products?] of the oasis,"[128] as also Djemi had done: "I taxed the people of Wawat for any chief who appeared in this province in bringing taxes (also) from the Thinite province, and I was praised for it."[129]

The events that took place in the north of Egypt and that culminated in the emergence of the Herakleopolitan kingdom are obscure and difficult to ascertain. The city of Herakleopolis is located at the entrance of Fayum from the south and lies close both to the Nile and the Bahr Yusuf. In the First Intermediate Period, it became the nucleus of a northern kingdom about which little is known for lack of contemporary sources. There are later literary compositions such as the "Teaching for Merykara," a text which was inspired by the Herakleopolitan king of that name and which may draw on events that occurred during his reign but were recorded much later.[130] But crucial questions concerning the extent of the area controlled by the Herakleopolitan kings, the foundations of their authority, and the resources they managed remain unsolved.

Nevertheless, the available evidence clearly indicates that the rise of Herakleopolis was linked to the development of a western axis of trade that passed through the western Nile delta and through localities such as Barnugi and Kom el-Hisn; Barnugi is an important center for the production of natron, whose tombs contained gold, lapis lazuli, turquoise, and other semi-precious stones, while Kom el-Hisn served as a

---

127. Fischer 1964: 112–118.

128. Hayes 1949.

129. Goedicke 1960.

130. Stauder 2013: 175–199.

checkpoint for people entering from Libya.[131] Herakleopolis was therefore well integrated in the interregional economic network of the First
Intermediate Period, as also the inscription of Setka of Elephantine confirms. The Fayum was also the starting point for routes leading through
the desert to the oasis of Bahariya, where tombs from the Old Kingdom
have recently been found.[132] The titles of local administrators in the
Fayum area show that their duties included the control of pasture land,
herds of cattle, and the movement of people.[133]

Situated at a crossroads, the importance of Herakleopolis is emphasized by the inscription of an official who lived around 2000 BC, who
wrote that the city was a "great gateway" indeed, and that it served as a
control point for goods arriving from the desert and abroad.[134] We have
already emphasized that myrrh and aromatic plants were such important
commodities that the Herakleopolitan rulers had specific administrative
officials in order to deal with these aromatics (see section 12.2.1). In the
third millennium BC, copper from the Levant had entered Egypt through
the eastern Nile delta, drawing on collaboration with nomadic peoples
from the Negev and the Sinai, but this trade collapsed in the twenty-
second century BC.[135] At this time Cyprus became the main supplier of
copper for Western Asia, including the Levant, and contact between the
Aegean and Egypt intensified; due to the way the Eastern Mediterranean
and its currents are navigated, the western Nile delta would have been
easier to reach from Anatolia and the Aegean.[136]

The importance of trading activities may explain why many burials
at Kom el-Hisn feature eastern weapon types typical of the so-called
warrior tombs attested in the contemporary Levant. These weapons
were markers of masculinity, status, and wealth, and were associated

131. Moreno García 2015a; 2017.

132. Colin, Adam, Duvette, and Grazi 2013.

133. Grajetzki 2001; Moreno García 2015a: 78–79.

134. Lichtheim 1988: 50; Moreno García 2019b.

135. Finkelstein, Adams, Dunseth, and Shahack-Gross 2018.

136. Véron et al. 2013.

with traders and nomadic populations.[137] Similar weapons have also been discovered in areas under Herakleopolitan control, namely Sheikh Farag in the Fayum, Helwan, and perhaps Abydos. The epigraphic record confirms the importance of Asiatic traders and warriors in the Herakleopolitan kingdom, as several officials bore the title of "overseer of the Asiatic troops (*aamu*)."[138] The decline of the copper route that had linked formerly productive areas in the southern Levant to Egypt may also explain why in Lower Egypt, many settlements disappeared along the eastern branch of the Nile, whereas there is great prosperity observable in the western Nile delta and the cities in southern and Middle Egypt expanded.

As for the area under the authority of Herakleopolis, it seems that the kingdom was organized around four major axes: the northeastern Nile delta, where a king called Khety (a name used by several Herakleopolitan rulers) founded a production center (*hut*) at Ezbet Rushdi, a favorably positioned site that would later become part of Tell el-Dab'a (ancient Avaris);[139] Heliopolis[140] and Wadi Tumilat, a traditional gateway to Lower Egypt for Asiatic populations (where the name of an official in charge of the area incorporated the royal name Khety);[141] Middle Egypt, a region that flourished at that time and whose leaders provided crucial support to the Herakleopolitan kings against the ambitions of Thebes; and finally, perhaps also the oases of the Western Desert, as they maintained close connections to Middle Egypt and as the names of some officials attested there also reference the royal name Khety;[142] later, the Theban kings were forced to conquer the oases region, an important refuge for fugitives and rebels in the early second millennium BC.[143]

---

137. Wengrow 2009; Gernez 2011; Kletter and Levi 2016.

138. Moreno García 2017: 102–103.

139. Goedicke 2002.

140. Abd El-Gelil, Saadani, and Raue 1996.

141. Somaglino 2015–2016.

142. Baud, Collin, and Tallet 1999: 5–6, 11–12.

143. Darnell 2008: 100–101.

Little is known about the internal organization of the Herakleopolitan kingdom, although it appears to have been quite loose. Historical evidence for the kings of Herakleopolis is surprisingly scarce, even from the great necropoles surrounding Memphis or from personal names that incorporated Herakleopolitan royal names;[144] the only exception is King Merykara. The tombs of officials buried at Herakleopolis itself are quite modest[145] and sharply contrast with the burials at Asyut, Beni Hasan, or Deir el-Bersha, rich in decorations and inscriptions, as the noble families there seem to have amassed substantial wealth and to have retained considerable autonomy under Herakleopolitan rule. The inscription of one such noble at Asyut mentions:

> the whole land was with him: the "counts" (*hatiu-a*) of Upper Egypt and the magnates (*buau*) of Herakleopolis" and "the Council of the Great House (*qenebet en per-aa*) was in fear and the favorites of the majesty of Herakleopolis (*imiu-set-ibu en she-fyt net Nen-nesut*) (likewise) (?).[146]

This may point to a twofold power structure that was based, on the one hand, on members of the royal court and high officials residing at Herakleopolis and, on the other hand, on local nobles ("counts"). Mention of the king's council, the integration of young officials into the royal administration (according to a traditional formula in tomb autobiographies: "I was a youth who tied on the [fillet]"[147]), and the education of noble children from the provinces with the royal princes[148] reveal a formal continuity with the royal traditions of the Old Kingdom, while

---

144. Daoud 2005; Knoblauch 2012; Legros 2016.

145. Pérez-Die 2005.

146. El-Khadragy 2008: 223.

147. Abd El-Gelil, Saadani, and Raue 1996: 145–146.

148. Lichtheim 1988: 29.

references to new institutions (such as *at* and *akhenuty* ["chamber"], first attested at Herakleopolis)[149] also suggest administrative innovations.[150]

Our final point concerns Merykara, one of the last kings of the Herakleopolitan kingdom and by far the best-documented ruler of this dynasty.[151] It is possible that his prominence is owed to the resistance that he, possibly as the leader of some sort of northern confederacy, offered to the Theban attacks on the regions of Abydos and Asyut. If this were the case, the Herakleopolitan kingdom may actually have been a relatively late development in a politically divided northern Egypt, in which the exceptional circumstances of Thebes's expansionism prompted local rulers and regional leaders to group together under the banner of one of their number, Khety of Herakleopolis. Only later, Khety and his son and successor Merykara may then have rewritten the history of their clan, claiming royal ancestry for an otherwise modest provincial family, as their rivals in Thebes had done.[152] This could explain why it was Merykara who strengthened the links with the necropolis of Saqqara, the most important royal necropolis of the third millennium BC.[153] Assuming limited political insignificance for most of the Herakleopolitan rulers can also explain why the members of the Middle Egyptian nobility were so easily integrated into the Theban kingdom and, in some cases, attained prominent positions in the unified monarchy, as they had always enjoyed considerable autonomy to follow their own interests. From a cultural point of view, Harco Willems[154] noted the very close similarities in the execution of texts in the Asyut tombs, inscribed just before reunification under the Theban ruler Mentuhotep II, and the texts of Ahanakht I and his father Djehutinakht at Deir el-Bersha; these similarities suggest that a Herakleopolitan artistic style had developed immediately before

149. Pérez-Die and Vernus 1992; Willems 2007: 95.

150. Cf. also Demidchik 2013.

151. For a different opinion, see Demidchik 2016.

152. Redford 1986: 144–151.

153. Malek 1994; Theis 2010; Willems 2014: 168–171; Raue 2014.

154. Willems 2014: 81.

reunification and that this style remained in use afterward, as rather than suppressing this style, Mentuhotep II encouraged artists trained in the Herakleopolitan tradition to work in Thebes on his own monuments. This view may find support also in the popularity of images depicting attacks on fortresses in tombs at Beni Hasan and General Intef's tomb at Thebes[155] from the time of reunification (or slightly before).

12.3.2. Competing for sovereignty: Herakleopolis, Thebes, and Nubia

The modest local origins of the monarchies of Herakleopolis and Thebes underpin their designation as the "houses" of their respective founders: the "House of Khety" in the north and the "House of Intef" in the south.[156] But at a time when Egypt was prone to political division, Lower Nubia, on the other hand, saw the emergence of the kingdom of Kush, both rival to and commercial partner of Egypt during the first half of the second millennium BC. The relationship between Nubia, Thebes, and Herakleopolis as the major powers in the Nile valley was characterized by a mix of hostility and collaboration, and it would be wrong to think that the policy followed by the Theban kings sought the reunification of Egypt at any cost. Matters seem to have been pragmatic and opportunistic, especially as trade was a major consideration in the decisions and strategic goals of all these actors. Each sought to occupy an advantageous position in relation to the rivals, while at the same time avoiding major disturbances in the network of economic relations that benefited them all. This view may explain several issues: why the inscription of Djari, an official from Thebes, records both a campaign against the Herakleopolitans and the subsequent request made for food to those same Herakleopolitans when Thebes was starving;[157] how Setka of Elephantine could successfully conduct commercial missions for

---

155. Monnier 2014: 175–180, 196–197.

156. Berlev 1981.

157. Lichtheim 1988: 40–41.

Herakleopolis along the Nile, which required crossing Theban territory and was thus impossible without Thebes' consent;[158] why the tombs of Herakleopolitan nobles in Middle Egypt were not destroyed in revenge after the Theban conquest of this area; and why, according to the graffiti of Hatnub and the biography of Khnumhotep I of Beni Hasan, some of these nobles supported the Theban kings Mentuhotep II and Amenemhat I against their rivals in Middle Egypt (including Asiatics and Nubians).[159]

In this political environment, loyalties shifted and local leaders may have been tempted to look for support in rival polities. Rediukhnum, a "great chief" of Beni Hasan (then under Herakleopolitan rule), left a monument at Dendara (then part of the Theban kingdom),[160] while after the reunification of Egypt, some Herakleopolitan nobles attained important positions at the service of the Theban conqueror Mentuhotep II. Thus, Hasi, a palace overseer of linen buried at Naqada in the Coptite province, claimed to have served three local overseers of priests. As one of them was named Khety, he may have taken his name from a Herakleopolitan ruler, which could imply that local dignitaries visited the royal palace and were exposed to northern influences.[161] Other provincial leaders under Theban control played an ambiguous role in navigating between their own local interests and the authorities in Thebes. The royal seal-bearer Iti from Gebelein, for instance, boasted about his support for Thebes: "I was a great pillar in the Theban nome, a man of standing in the Southland," but at the same time, he enjoyed sufficient autonomy to be able to claim that he nourished Gebelein while Thebes was hungry, regarding the overlord with a certain ironic detachment: "Whether I served a great lord, or served a small lord, no fault of mine occurred."[162] The same is true of the Nubians. They appear in

---

158. Edel 2008: 1743–1744.

159. Mourad 2015: 84, 94.

160. Willems 2014: 47.

161. Fischer 1964: 65–67.

162. Lichtheim 1988: 31–32.

the service of both Theban and Herakleopolitan armies, and in the case of Thebes, Nubian soldiers were employed even in campaigns against Nubian territories.[163] All this suggests an unstable landscape of changing alliances, and this volatility must necessarily have underpinned any political decision. A combination of force and negotiation was needed to achieve political goals, perhaps at the price of preserving the well-established interests and agendas of local actors, with huge future consequences for the stability of the resultant monarchy.

The area of the Thinite and Aphroditopolite provinces was the main scenario for the battles between the northern and southern powers. Perhaps this was the result of efforts to control a locality with an increasingly significant symbolic importance due to the cult of Osiris, in addition to its economic importance as the starting point for the caravan route into the Western Desert. The area was fiercely disputed: occasionally the Thebans would advance as far north as Asyut, only to retreat again. Intef, son of Ka, a hunter in the service of the Theban kings Intef II, Intef III, and Mentuhotep II, records in his funerary stele the rebellion of Thinis "in Year 14," presumably of Mentuhotep II.[164] In any case, the Thinite province fell under Theban control during the reign of Intef II, along with the region of Elephantine,[165] where the Theban ruler presented offerings in the sanctuary of Heqaib and built chapels for the local deities. Inscriptions from his reign also point to the administrative reorganization of the kingdom of Thebes. Thus, Neferukayet, Intef II's spouse, claims to have improved the administration of the territories under Theban authority:

She has reorganized Upper Egypt, the foremost of people, from Elephantine to the Aphroditopolite province, with women

---

163. Darnell 2003; 2004.

164. Landgráfová 2011: 26.

165. Gabra 1976.

together with governors of *hut* and dignitaries from the whole land.[166]

An inscription of King Intef II, which is unfortunately rather fragmentarily preserved, mentions events that conclude with the consolidation of the southern frontier of an unknown province, the integration of its authorities (specifically, governors and chiefs of the army), and some measures relating to royal centers (*hut*) and fortresses.[167] It is quite possible that Intef II's campaigns in the Thinite and Aphroditopolite provinces were intended to consolidate the border of the Theban kingdom there and to reorganize the administrative and royal production centers in this area, from which desert routes (protected by forts?) led to the oases of the Western Desert. Another inscription states that Intef II conquered the Thinite province and established his northern frontier in the province of Aphroditopolis, after having opened all the fortresses there.[168] Several centuries earlier, an official called Nesutnefer had been in charge of the fortresses and the royal centers (*hut*) in the Thinite and Aphroditopolite provinces,[169] while an official from Dendara, the overseer of priests Mereri, claimed that he had built a fortress and that he was beloved by the Nubians of the desert,[170] as if such fortresses were intended to monitor the movement of desert populations. Intef II's takeover of Thinis was recorded a century later, when the scribe of the cadaster and overseer of fields Intefiqer wrote during the reign of the Middle Kingdom pharaoh Senusret I (1956–1911 BC):

There had served as scribe of the watered fields of Thinite Abydos my father and the father of my father since the time of Horus

---

166. Landgráfová 2011: 76.

167. Arnold 1976: 50–51, pl. 42, 52.

168. Arnold 1976: 52–53, pl. 53.

169. Strudwick 2005: 423.

170. Fischer 1968: 138, 140.

Wahankh, the king of Upper and Lower Egypt, the Son of Ra Intef (II).[171]

All these measures and the strategic position of the Thinite province on the routes of the oases of the Western Desert are mentioned explicitly in the inscription of the overseer of troops Djemi:

> I marched against Abydos, which was under the enemy. I caused him to go down to his realm from the center of the city, there was none who had the power to march against him. I taxed the people of Wawat for every [chief?] who had been in the area. I brought taxes from the Thinite province (and) I was praised for it.[172]

It was perhaps not by chance that the leaders of Asyut fiercely resisted Theban progress into the Thinite and the Aphroditopolite provinces because control of this region enabled Thebes to intercept or block commercial traffic between Nubia and Asyut through the oases of the Western Desert.

Control over resources, especially those from the desert routes, was crucial for the early Theban rulers, and this can provide some clues about their strategic priorities and their economic and taxation concerns. The inscriptions of the overseer of the seal Tjetji, who served under kings Intef II and Intef III, exemplify this:

> The treasury was in my hand under my seal, being the choicest of every good thing brought to the majesty of my lord from Upper and Lower Egypt; being everything that gladdens the heart as tribute of this entire land, through fear of him throughout this land; and what was brought to the majesty of my lord by the chiefs who rule the desert, through fear of him throughout the foreign lands. He gave these things to me, knowing the excellence

---

171. Lichtheim 1988: 73.

172. Darnell 2008: 99.

of my performance. I accounted for them to him without there ever being a fault of mine deserving punishment, because my competence was great.[173]

Of course, the scope of the managerial activities performed by Tjetji also included the reorganization of the administration and the evaluation of the wealth of the realm:

As for any royal department that the majesty of my lord entrusted to me, and for which he made me carry out a commission according to his *ka*'s desire, I did it for him. I improved all their procedures.

. . .

I built a barge for the city and a boat for all service: the accounting with the magnates, and every occasion of escorting or sending.[174]

Bringing precious foreign goods to Egypt appears as a major concern of the nascent Theban kingdom also in an inscription that probably dates to the reign of Intef II:

It was with beautiful southern goods, which he had brought back from his victories, that he built monuments for (the god) Montu and that he satisfied (the god) Amun.[175]

Such southern goods included myrrh and a precious unguent called *hek-enu*. Other activities of Intef II were the restoration of cults, the rebuilding of temples, and the provision of offerings, as he claimed in one of his steles.[176] This work concerned also what was later to become the temple

---

173. Lichtheim 1988: 46–48; Landgráfová 2011: 10–15.

174. Lichtheim 1988: 46–48; Landgráfová 2011: 10–15.

175. Mathieu 2008.

176. Arnold 1976: 52–53, pl. 53.

of the god Amun at Karnak, as a column in the area, inscribed by Intef II and dedicated to Amun-Ra, shows.[177]

12.4. *Mentuhotep II of Thebes and the reunification of Egypt*

12.4.1. Geopolitics and trade

The political situation along the Nile when Mentuhotep II (2055–2004 BC) ascended to power was not quite favorable to the Theban rulers. The desert areas east of Thebes were in hostile hands, according to an inscription from his reign.[178] As far as the Nile, the essential waterway, was concerned, the Theban kings controlled the area between Elephantine in the south and Qau in the north. Other sections were in the hands of the Herakleopolitan kingdom in the north and the Nubian kingdom of Kerma/Kush in the south. As recorded in the inscription of Setka, direct contact between Herakleopolis and Kush was possible via the Nile, but alternate routes, by land across the oasis of the Western Desert and by sea across the Red Sea, allowed one to circumvent a hostile Thebes, which sought to block traffic along the Nile.

From this perspective, Mentuhotep II's strategic goals seem to have been the elimination of any rival along the Nile (especially the Lower Nubian section, north of the Second Cataract) and the control of the flow of goods between northeast Africa and the Mediterranean.[179] The inscriptions from his reign record campaigns against the populations living east of Thebes in the mountainous desert areas between the Nile and the Red Sea. Other military interventions sought to secure control over the Western Desert trade routes and their oases, and an inscription recently found at Gebel Uweinat in the area of the modern border between Libya, Sudan, and Egypt records the import of incense

---

177. Le Saout, Ma'arouf, and Zimmer 1987: 294–297.

178. Darnell 2008.

179. Moreno García 2018a.

and other goods from the land of Yam (northwest Sudan? Ennedi?) and from other territories via the Western Desert and across the oasis of Dakhla.[180]Whereas alleged references to campaigns to the land of Qedem in the Levant are based on the misinterpretation of an Egyptian term,[181] several inscriptions from his reign record battles in Nubia.[182] His successor Mentuhotep III sent the first Middle Kingdom maritime expedition to the land of Punt,[183] while Mentuhotep IV sent expeditions to the mines in the Sinai from the Red Sea harbor of Ayn Sukhna.[184]

With the conquest and incorporation of the Herakleopolitan kingdom, Mentuhotep II finally succeeded in controlling the lower Nile, as well as the alternate routes leading to it by land and (at least partly) by sea. His realm, the nascent Middle Kingdom, became the unavoidable middleman in all trade between central Africa and the Mediterranean. However, the kingdom of Kush remained a formidable power; throughout the first half of the second millennium BC, it did not surrender control of strategic goods like gold or its close contact with the northern Indian Ocean sphere of exchange.[185]

The inscriptions of some of the dignitaries who served under Mentuhotep II, as well as the archaeological evidence, show how important long-distance trade was to the political decisions made by this sovereign. One of these dignitaries, Khety, was "overseer of the two treasuries," "overseer of silver and gold, overseer of lapis-lazuli and turquoise," and "overseer of horn, hoof, scale, and feather," a title apparently related to the control of herds and animal husbandry in Egypt. Another official, Dagi, was promoted to the rank of vizier sometime during the final decade of Mentuhotep II's reign and, as the chief steward in Year 8 of Mentuhotep III, he was "overseer of the double treasury" and "overseer of the double

---

180. Cooper 2012; Darnell 2008; Diego Espinel 2013; Moreno García 2015b.

181. Darnell 2008: 94–95.

182. Darnell 2003; 2004; 2008; Postel 2008.

183. Lichtheim 1998: 52–54.

184. Abd-el-Raziq et al. 2002: 40–41, fig. 10–11.

185. Boivin and Fuller 2009; Fuller et al. 2011; Manzo 2014; 2017.

house of gold."[186] Another official who was also called Khety listed the duties he performed for a king Mentuhotep in his Theban tomb, which included controlling (supplies of?) precious ointments, overseeing mining expeditions into Sinai and other regions, and importing precious minerals and stones (including lapis lazuli, native to the land of Tefreret according to this text and to later inscriptions).[187] Finally, the coffin of Queen Ashait mentions myrrh and depicts three foreign female servants, two of whom were Medjay from the southern Eastern Desert, while the third one was called Ibhatit, "the one from Ibhat," referring to a region in the Nubian Eastern Desert. All this evidence indicates a deep interest in precious metals, semi-precious stones, and aromatic plants.[188]

Other indirect indications for the relevance of long-distance trade come from a type of ritual object whose interpretation still raises many problems. These objects, called "paddle dolls," suddenly appear around the reign of Mentuhotep II and could be regarded as a manifestation of the newly reunified monarchy's involvement in exchange networks. They are flat, female figurines made of wood, usually with very stylized (or largely absent) arms, exuberant hairstyles, and markings that indicate the pubic triangle, shoulder straps, and tattoos representing protective creatures. However, their most distinctive characteristics are the colorful garments with distinctive patterns they wear. Especially when considering that Egyptian clothes were typically made of difficult-to-dye linen whose white color conveyed highly prized cultural values such as purity, prestige, and cleanliness, the colorful garments worn by the paddle dolls were likely meant to depict clothes made of wool, indicating "foreignness" and serving as a marker of cultural contrast to "Egyptianness." At the end of the third millennium BC, innovations in Western Asian wool textile technology resulted in considerable advances in dying wool and in weaving complex designs.[189] The resultant contrast in dress between

---

186. Allen 1996.

187. Landgráfová 2011: 54–58.

188. Diego Espinel 2011: 246–255; 2017; Moreno García 2017: 106–109.

189. Moreno García 2019a: 63–65.

Egypt and Western Asia is evident in Egyptian iconography, notably the Asiatics represented in the tomb of General Intef and the famous Asiatic caravan scene represented in the tomb of Khnumhotep II, governor of Beni Hasan, where the colorful clothes of Asiatic men and women stand in sharp contrast to the white kilts worn by Egyptians. Furthermore, textiles made of fine wool were the highly coveted object of intense international trade, as the Assyrian merchants' archives from the central Anatolian city of Kaneš (modern Kültepe) show (cf. chapter 17).[190]

So it is highly significant that during the late third and early second millennium, flat female figurines similar to the "paddle dolls" appeared across a vast geographic area from Central Asia and the Indus valley to the Aegean and Egypt, usually along the most important land routes,[191] as if these figurines (in their multiple local adaptations) conveyed basic notions about protection within a context of expanding interregional exchange and contact between cultures and peoples. In Tomb 88 of the extraordinarily rich, late third millennium BC necropolis of Qubbet el-Hawa, close to Elephantine, a "paddle doll" was discovered among other evidence for long-distance trade, such as an Aegean Kamares style vessel.[192] Other types of female figurines have been recovered in mining sites, where different population groups worked together, like Serabit el-Khadim on the Sinai and Gebel Zeit, close to the Red Sea.[193] Overall, the sudden appearance of "paddle dolls" in Egypt, especially in the Theban area and to a lesser extent in Middle Egypt, provides crucial, though indirect, evidence for the importance of mining, international trade, and the import of exotic goods during the reign of Mentuhotep II.

To conclude, geopolitics and trade undoubtedly played an important role in the political strategies that finally led to the reunification of Egypt. In a period of intensive international exchange, new trade routes were being developed across Western Asia and northeastern Africa,

---

190. Moreno García 2019a: 64.

191. Wilkinson 2014: 262–266.

192. Edel 2008: 993–994, 1044–1045.

193. Moreno García 2019a: 65–68.

and Egypt was part of this. Its rulers sought to profit from the flow of goods across, or near, their borders and control it whenever possible. The need to negotiate and collaborate with nomadic and foreign population groups resulted in a political system that was less rigidly centralized than in previous times, as also was the case with the contemporary states in Syria and Mesopotamia. There and in Egypt, regimes with a relatively short life span (when compared with other periods in Egyptian history), the absence of complex large-scale polities ("empires"), flexibility, and a certain fragility in royal authority seem to be the common characteristics of the states that emerged toward the end of the third and the beginning of the second millennium BC.

12.4.2. Unification: a costly political process?

Reunification was not the inevitable response to the political crisis that developed in Egypt at the end of the Old Kingdom. The policy of the Theban rulers, which was probably inspired by the desire to control the lucrative trade networks crossing the Nile valley, was to neutralize and contain their rivals operating in the lands on the Nile: Herakleopolis and Kush, respectively. While the ultimate outcome was the return to a formally unified country under the rule of a single monarch, crucial questions remain about how precisely this was achieved and to what extent this resolved the problems that led to the collapse of the Old Kingdom. Whereas we do not know the exact circumstances that led to Mentuhotep II becoming pharaoh of a reunified Egypt, the use of not only force, but also negotiation, seems to have played an important role in the integration of provincial leaders into the Theban power sphere. This view explains why the potentates of Middle Egypt remained by far the most powerful nobles in the new monarchy (at least judging from their lavish burials); why they managed to preserve their own interests in foreign trade; why the kings failed to implement an efficient tax system and to rebuild the network of royal centers that had characterized the Old Kingdom; and finally, why the intentional destruction of the tombs in the necropolis of Herakleopolis (if not immediately after the Theban conquest, then early in the Twelfth Dynasty) remained an isolated phenomenon, while the tombs of other former Theban rivals at places like Moalla, Asyut, and Beni Hasan were not harmed.[194] In short, the price that Thebes was willing to pay for political support and for the smooth acceptance of Theban authority over Middle and Lower Egypt was to preserve the autonomy of the local leaders in these regions.

A further clue to this process is that important officials of the recently incorporated Herakleopolitan kingdom collaborated with Mentuhotep II in the reorganization of his realm. Ahanakht of Deir el-Bersha was one of them. He became vizier, while several of his subordinates occupied important positions in the reunified monarchy. Ahanakht described himself as the one who judged between the provinces, the one who established the boundary cairns of the Hare province, under whose governance "the South was content while the Northland was under his command," and the one who unified the Hare province.[195] Various officials with the traditionally Herakleopolitan name Khety, or its composite forms such as Khetyankh or Khentikhety, probably originated in the north and were integrated in the administrative structure of the reunified kingdom,[196] where they held important managerial roles. Judging from the inscriptions from Mentuhotep II's reign, the main protagonists of the reconstruction of the fiscal foundations of the kingdom were seal bearers, chiefs of the treasury, and great stewards.[197]

Ultimately, the authority of the new pharaohs of the Middle Kingdom seems somewhat precarious, hardly capable of resolving the challenges previously encountered by their Old Kingdom predecessors. Among other details, the Middle Kingdom's introduction of a system of co-regencies, the murder of Amenemhat I, the conflicts described by Amenemhat I and Senusret I in their inscriptions, and the support offered by Nubians and Asiatics in Middle Egypt to the rivals of these sovereigns reveal that the First Intermediate Period was hardly an

---

194. Pérez Die 2005; 2015.

195. Brovarski 1981: 18.

196. Vernus 1970.

197. Allen 1996.

exceptional time in which the exercise of power took a strange, abnormal path. On the contrary, it appears to have been the consequence of the political, economic, and structural problems that had originally emerged two centuries earlier during the Sixth Dynasty, and the shock waves resulting therefrom still affected the New Kingdom, when a new and more stable configuration of power resulted in Egypt's transformation into an imperial power.[198]

REFERENCES

Abd el-Gelil, M., Saadani, A., and Raue, D. 1996. Some inscriptions and reliefs from Matariya. *MDAIK* 52: 143–156.

Adams, M.D. 2007. Household silos, granary models, and domestic economy in ancient Egypt. In Hawass, Z.A., and Richards, J. (eds.), *The archaeology and art of ancient Egypt: essays in honor of David B. O'Connor, vol. 1*. Cairo: Supreme Council of Antiquities, 1–23.

Adams, M.J. 2017. The Egyptianized pottery cache from Megiddo's Area J: a foundation deposit for Temple 4040. *Tel Aviv* 44: 141–164.

Allen, J.P. 1996. Some Theban officials of the early Middle Kingdom. In Der Manuelian, P. (ed.), *Studies in honor of William Kelly Simpson, vol. I*. Boston: Museum of Fine Arts, 1–26.

Altenmüller, H. 2012. Bemerkungen zum Architrav und zur Scheintür des Felsgrabes des Anchi unter der Südumfassung der Djoseranlage in Saqqara. *SAK* 41: 1–20.

Anthes, R. 1928. *Die Felseninschriften von Hatnub*. Leipzig: Hinrichs.

Archi, A. 2016. Egypt or Iran in the Ebla Texts? *Orientalia* 85: 1–49.

Arnold, D. 1976. *Gräber des Alten und Mittleren Reiches in El-Tarif*. Mainz: Zabern.

Bagh, T. 2002. Abu Ghâlib, an early Middle Kingdom town in the western Nile delta: renewed work on material excavated in the 1930s. *MDAIK* 55: 29–61.

Bagh, T. 2004. Early Middle Kingdom seals and sealings from Abu Ghâlib in the western Nile delta: observations. In Bietak, M., and Czerny, E. (eds.), *Scarabs of the second millennium BC from Egypt, Nubia, Crete and*

---

198. Moreno García 2018a.

the Levant: chronological and historical implications. Vienna: Verlag der Österreichischen Akademie der Wissenschaften, 13–25.

Baines, J., and Yoffee, N. 1998. Order, legitimacy, and wealth in ancient Egypt and Mesopotamia. In Feinman, G.M., and Marcus, J. (eds.), *Archaic states.* Santa Fe, NM: School of Advanced Research Press, 199–260.

Bárta, M. 2015. Long term or short term? Climate change and the demise of the Old Kingdom. In Kerner, S., Dann, R.J., and Bangsgaard, P. (eds.), *Climate and ancient societies.* Copenhagen: Museum Tusculanum Press, 177–195.

Bárta, M. 2019. *Analyzing collapse: the rise and fall of the Old Kingdom.* Cairo: American University in Cairo Press.

Baud, M., Collin, F., and Tallet, P. 1999. Les gouverneurs de l'oasis de Dakhla au Moyen Empire. *BIFAO* 99: 1–19.

Berlev, O.D. 1971. Les prétendus "citadins" au Moyen Empire. *RdE* 23: 23–48.

Berlev, O.D. 1981. The Eleventh Dynasty in the dynastic history of Egypt. In Young, D.W. (ed.), *Studies presented to Hans Jakob Polotsky.* East Gloucester, MA: Pirtle & Polson, 361–377.

Berlev, O.D., and Hodjash, S. 1998. *Catalogue of the monuments of ancient Egypt from the museums of the Russian Federation, Ukraine, Bielorussia, Caucasus, Middle Asia and the Baltic States.* Fribourg: Academic Press/ Göttingen: Vandenhoeck & Ruprecht.

Bietak, M. 2003. Two ancient Near Eastern temples with bent axis in the eastern Nile delta. *ÄL* 13: 13–38.

Bietak, M. 2010. The Early Bronze Age III temple at Tell Ibrahim Awad and its relevance to the Egyptian Old Kingdom. In Hawass, Z., Der Manuelian, P., and Hussein, R.B. (eds.), *Perspectives on ancient Egypt: studies in honor of Edward Brovarski.* Cairo: American University in Cairo Press, 65–77.

Biga, M.G. 2010. Tra Menfi e Ebla. In Associazione Amici collaboratori del Museo egizio di Torino (ed.), *L'Egitto tra storia e letteratura.* Turin: AdArte, 23–40.

Biga, M.G., and Roccati, A. 2012. Tra Egitto e Siria nel III millennio a.C. *Atti della Reale Accademia delle Scienze di Torino, classe di scienze morali, storiche e filologia* 146: 17–42.

Biga, G., and Steinkeller, P. 2021. In search of Dugurasu. *JCS* 73: 9–73.

Boivin, N., and Fuller, D.Q. 2009. Shell middens, ships and seeds: exploring coastal subsistence, maritime trade and the dispersal of domesticates in and around the ancient Arabian Peninsula. *JWP* 22: 113–180.

Brovarski, E. 1981. Ahanakht of Bersheh and the Hare Nome in the First Intermediate Period. In Simpson, W.K., and Davis, W.M. (eds.), *Studies* in ancient Egypt, the Aegean and the Sudan: essays in honour of Dows Dunham. Boston: Museum of Fine Arts, 14–30.

Brunner, H. 1937. *Die Texte aus den Gräbern der Herakleopolitenzeit von Siut.* Leipzig: Hinrichs.

Bührer-Thierry, G., Patzold, S., and Schneider, J. (eds.) 2018. *Genèse des espaces politiques (IXe-XIIe siècle): autour de la question spatiale dans les royaumes francs et post-carolingiens.* Turnhout: Brepols.

Bunbury, J. 2010. The development of the river Nile and the Egyptian civilisation: a water historical perspective with focus on the First Intermediate Period. In Tvedt, T., and Coopey, R. (eds.), *A history of water, vol. 2: rivers and society from early civilisations to modern times.* London: I.B. Tauris, 52–71.

Bussmann, R. 2014. Scaling the state: Egypt in the third millennium BC. *Archaeology International* 17: 79–93.

Clère, J.J., and Vandier, J. 1948. *Textes de la Première Période Intermédiaire et de la XIème dynastie.* Brussels: Fondation Égyptologique Reine Élisabeth.

Colin, F., Adam, F., Duvette, C., and Grazi, C. 2013. À la recherche des origines de Psôbthis: les premières tombes de la nécropole de Qaret el-Toub (fouilles de l'IFAO à Bahariya, état 2009). In Dospěl, M., and Suková, L. (eds.), *Bahriya oasis: recent research into the past of an Egyptian oasis.* Prague: Charles University, 185–226.

Cooper, J. 2012. Reconsidering the location of Yam. *JARCE* 48: 1–22.

Daoud, K.A. 2005. *Corpus of inscriptions of the Herakleopolitan period from the Memphite necropolis: translation, commentary and analyses.* Oxford: Archaeopress.

Darnell, J.C. 2002. *Theban desert road survey in the Egyptian Western Desert, vol. 1: Gebel Tjauti rock inscriptions 1-45 and Wadi el-Ḥôl rock inscriptions 1-45.* Chicago: The Oriental Institute of the University of Chicago.

Darnell, J.C. 2003. The rock inscriptions of Tjehemau at Abisko. *ZÄS* 130: 31–48.

Darnell, J.C. 2004. The route of Eleventh Dynasty expansion into Nubia: an interpretation based on the rock inscriptions of Tjehemau at Abisko. *ZÄS* 131: 23–37.

Darnell, J.C. 2008. The Eleventh Dynasty royal inscription from Deir el-Ballas. *RdE* 59: 81–110.

Demidchik, A. 2013. The history of the Herakleopolitan king's domain. In Fischer-Elfert, H.-W., and Parkinson, R.B. (eds.), *Studies on the Middle Kingdom in memory of Detlef Franke.* Wiesbaden: Harrassowitz, 93–106.

Demidchik, A. 2016. The sixth Heracleopolitan king Merikare Khety. *JEH* 9: 97–120.

Diego Espinel, A. 2011. *Abriendo los caminos de Punt: contactos entre Egipto y el ámbito afroárabe durante la Edad del Bronce (ca. 3000 a.C.–1065 a.C.).* Barcelona: Bellaterra.

Diego Espinel, A. 2013. The tribute from Tekhebeten (a brief note on the graffiti of Mentuhetep II at Jebel Uweinat). *GM* 237: 15–19.

Diego Espinel, A. 2015–2016. Bringing treasures and placing fears: Old Kingdom epithets and titles related to activities abroad. *Isimu* 18-19: 103–146.

Diego Espinel, A. 2017. The scents of Punt (and elsewhere): trade and functions of *sntr* and *'ntw* during the Old Kingdom. In Incordino, I., and Creasman, P.P. (eds.), *Flora trade between Egypt and Africa in antiquity.* Oxford: Oxbow, 21–47.

Donadoni Roveri, A.M. 1990. Gebelein. In Robins, G. (ed.), *Beyond the pyramids: Egyptian regional art from the Museo Egizio, Turin.* Atlanta, GA: Emory University Museum of Art and Archaeology, 23–29.

Dubiel, U. 2012a. "Dude looks like a lady…": der zurechtgemachte Mann. In Neunert, G., Gabler, K., and Verbovsek, A. (eds.), *Sozialisationen: Individuum—Gruppe—Gesellschaft.* Wiesbaden: Harrassowitz, 61–78.

Dubiel, U. 2012b. Protection, control and prestige: seals among the rural population of Qau-Matmar. In Regulski, I., Duistermaat, K., and Verkinderen, P. (eds.), *Seals and sealing practices in the Near East: developments in administration and magic from prehistory to the Islamic period.* Leuven: Peeters, 51–80.

Edel, E. 1984. *Die Inschriften der Grabfronten der Siut-Gräber in Mittelägypten aus der Herakleopolitenzeit.* Opladen: Westdeutscher Verlag.

Edel, E. 2008. *Die Felsgräbernekropole der Qubbet el-Hawa bei Assuan, I. Abteilung, vol. II.* Paderborn: Ferdinand Schöningh.

Ejsmond, W. 2017. The Nubian mercenaries of Gebelein during the First Intermediate Period in the light of recent field research. *JAEI* 14: 11–13.

El-Khadragy, M. 2006. The Northern Soldiers-Tomb at Asyut. *SAK* 35: 147–164.

El-Khadragy, M. 2008. The decoration of the rock-cut chapel of Khety II at Asyut. *SAK* 37: 219–241.

El-Raziq, M., Castel, G., Tallet, P., and Ghica, V. 2002. *Les inscriptions d'Ayn Soukhna.* Cairo: Institut français d'archéologie orientale.

Emberling, G. 2014. Pastoral states: toward a comparative archaeology of early Kush. *Origini* 36: 125–156.

Fábián, Z.I. 2011. News from Old Kingdom Thebes. In Bechtold, E., Gulyás, A., and Hasznos, A. (eds.), *From Illahun to Djeme: papers presented in honour of Ulrich Luft.* Oxford: Archaeopress.

Fábián, Z.I. 2017. Feltárás az el-Hoha domb déli oldalán a TT 184 számú sír (*Nefermenu*) körzetében, 2015. *Orpheus Noster Antiquity and Renaissance* 9: 7–77.

Finkelstein, I., Adams, M.J., Dunseth, Z.C., and Shahack-Gross, R. 2018. The archaeology and history of the Negev and neighbouring areas in the third millennium BCE: a new paradigm. *Tel Aviv* 45: 63–88.

Fischer, H.G. 1961. The Nubian mercenaries of Gebelein during the First Intermediate Period. *Kush* 9: 44–80.

Fischer, H.G. 1964. *Inscriptions from the Coptite Nome, Dynasties VI–XI.* Rome: Pontificium Institutum Biblicum.

Fischer, H.G. 1968. *Dendera in the third millennium BC, down to the Theban domination of Upper Egypt.* Locust Valley, NY: Augustin.

Fischer, H.G. 1996. *Varia Nova: Egyptian studies 3.* New York: Metropolitan Museum of Art.

Franke, D. 1998. Kleiner Mann (*nḏs*)—Was bist Du? *GM* 167: 33–48.

Fuller, D.Q., Boivin, N., Hoogervorst, T., and Allaby, R. 2011. Across the Indian Ocean: the prehistoric movement of plants and animals. *Antiquity* 85: 544–558.

Gabra, G. 1976. Preliminary report on the stela of *Ḥtpi* from el-Kab from the time of Wahankh Inyôtef, II. *MDAIK* 32: 45–56.

Gernez, G. 2011. The exchange of products and concepts between the Near East and the Mediterranean: the example of weapons during the Early and Middle Bronze Ages. In Duistermaat, K., and Regulski, I. (eds.), *Intercultural contacts in the ancient Mediterranean.* Leuven: Peeters, 327–341.

Gestermann, L. 1987. *Kontinuität und Wandel in Politik und Verwaltung des frühen Mittleren Reiches in Ägypten.* Wiesbaden: Harrassowitz.

Goedicke, H. 1960. The inscription of *Dmj. JNES* 19: 288–291.

Goedicke, H. 1999. Two inlaid inscriptions of the earliest Middle Kingdom. In Teeter, E., and Larson, J.A. (eds.), *Gold of praise: studies on ancient Egypt in honor of Edward F. Wente.* Chicago: The Oriental Institute of the University of Chicago, 149–157.

Goedicke, H. 2002. The building inscription from Tell el-Dabʿa of the time of Sesostris III. *ÄL* 12: 187–190.

Gomaà, F. 1980. *Ägypten während der Ersten Zwischenzeit*. Wiesbaden: Reichert.

Grajetzki, W. 2001. Die Nekropole von el-Harageh in der 1. Zwischenzeit. *SAK* 29: 55–60.

Hafsaas-Tsakos, H. 2005. *Cattle pastoralists in a multicultural setting: the C-Group people in Lower Nubia, 2500–1500 BCE*. Bergen: University of Bergen.

Hayes, W.C. 1949. Career of the great steward Henenu under Nebhepetrēʿ Mentuhotpe. *JEA* 35: 43–49.

Höflmayer, F. (ed.) 2017. *The late third millennium in the ancient Near East: chronology, C14, and climate change*. Chicago: The Oriental Institute of the University of Chicago.

Højlund, F. 2013. Dilmun: beyond the southern frontier of Mesopotamia. In Bergerbrant, S., and Sabatini, S. (eds.), *Counterpoint: essays in archaeology and heritage studies in honour of Professor Kristian Kristiansen*. Oxford: Archaeopress, 541–547.

Jirásková, L. 2011. Relations between Egypt and Syria-Palestine in the latter part of the Old Kingdom. In Duistermaat, K., and Regulski, I. (eds.), *Intercultural contacts in the ancient Mediterranean*. Leuven: Peeters, 539–568.

Kanawati, N., and McFarlane, A. 1995. *The tombs of el-Hagarsa, vol. III*. Sydney: Australian Centre for Egyptology.

Kepinski, C. 2007. Mémoires d'Euphrate et d'Arabie, les tombes à tumulus, marqueurs territoriaux de communautés en voie de sédentarisation. In Kepinski, C., Lecomte, O., and Tenu, A. (eds.), *Studia euphratica: le Moyen Euphrate iraquien révélé par les fouilles préventives de Haditha*. Paris: De Boccard, 87–128.

Kletter, R., and Levi, Y. 2016. Middle Bronze Age burials in the southern Levant: Spartan warriors or ordinary people? *OJA* 35: 5–27.

Knoblauch, C. 2012. The Memphite area in the late First Intermediate Period and the Middle Kingdom. In Evans, L. (ed.), *Ancient Memphis: "Enduring is the perfection."* Leuven: Peeters, 267–278.

Koenig, Y. 1987. La Nubie dans les textes magiques: "l'inquiétante étrangeté." *RdE* 38: 105–110.

Landgráfová, R. 2011. *It is my good name that you should remember: Egyptian biographical texts on Middle Kingdom stelae*. Prague: Charles University.

Laursen, S.T. 2009. The decline of Magan and the rise of Dilmun: Umm an-Nar ceramics from the burial mounds of Bahrain, c. 2250–2000 BC. *AAE* 20: 134–155.

Legros, R. 2016. *Stratégies mémorielles: les cultes funéraires privés en Égypte ancienne de la VIe à la XIIe dynastie.* Lyon: MOM Éditions.

Le Saout, F., Ma'arouf, A.H., and Zimmer, T. 1987. Le Moyen Empire à Karnak, varia 1. *Cahiers de Karnak* 8: 293–323.

Lyonnet, B. 2005. Another possible interpretation of the Bactrio-Margiana Culture (BMAC) of Central Asia: the tin trade. In Jarrige, C., and Lefèvre, V. (eds.), *South Asian archaeology 2001, vol. 1: prehistory.* Paris: Éditions Recherche sur les Civilisations, 191–200.

Malek, J. 1994. King Merykare and his pyramid. In Berger, C., Clerc, G., and Grimal, N. (eds.), *Hommages à Jean Leclant, vol. IV.* Cairo: Institut français d'archéologie orientale, 203–214.

Manzo, A. 2014. "... Nella tua terra l'oro è come polvere": la gestione del commercio nell'Africa nordorientale durante l'Età del Bronzo. In Genito, B., and Caterina, L. (eds.), *Archeologia delle "Vie della Seta": percorsi, immagini e cultura materiale.* Naples: Scienze e Lettere, 27–54.

Manzo, A. 2017. *Eastern Sudan in its setting: the archaeology of a region far from the Nile valley.* Oxford: Archaeopress.

Marcolin, M., and Diego Espinel, A. 2011. The Sixth Dynasty biographic inscriptions of Iny: more pieces to the puzzle. In Bárta, M., Coppens, F., and Krejčí, J. (eds.), *Abusir and Saqqara in the year 2010.* Prague: Czech Institute of Egyptology, 570–615.

Mathieu, B. 2008. Le lasso d'Hathor: relecture de la stèle Turin Suppl. 1310. *GM* 219: 65–72.

Matthiae, P. 2017. The Victory Panel of early Syrian Ebla: finding, structure, dating. *Studia Eblaitica* 3: 33–83.

Mazé, C. 2016. Quand les Égyptiens découpaient l'histoire en tranches: la Première Période Intermédiaire (2150–1980 av. J.-C.) dans la mémoire culturelle de l'Égypte ancienne et l'écriture de son passé. In Allard, P., Heintz, M., and Müller, C. (eds.), *Les transitions historiques: rythmes, crises, héritages.* Paris: De Boccard, 39–56.

Mazé, C. 2017. À la recherche des "classes moyennes": les espaces de la différenciation sociale dans l'Égypte du IIIe millénaire av. J.-C. *BIFAO* 116: 123–176.

Meller, H., Risch, R., Jung, R., and Arz, H.W. (eds.) 2015. *2200 BC: a climatic breakdown as a cause for the collapse of the Old World?* Halle: Landesamt für Denkmalpflege und Archäologie.

Moeller, N. 2005. The First Intermediate Period: a time of famine and climate change? *ÄL* 15: 153–167.

Moeller, N. 2016. *The archaeology of urbanism in ancient Egypt: from the Predynastic period to the end of the Middle Kingdom.* Cambridge: Cambridge University Press.

Monnier, F. 2014. Une iconographie égyptienne de l'architecture défensive. *Égypte Nilotique et Méditerranéenne* 7: 173–219.

Moreno García, J.C. 1997. *Études sur l'administration, le pouvoir et l'idéologie en Égypte, de l'Ancien au Moyen Empire.* Liège: Centre Informatique de Philosophie et Lettres.

Moreno García, J.C. 2000. Acquisition de serfs durant la Première Période Intermédiaire: une étude d'histoire sociale dans l'Égypte du IIIe millénaire. *RdE* 51: 123–139.

Moreno García, J.C. 2007. The state and the organization of the rural landscape in 3rd millennium BC pharaonic Egypt. In Bollig, M., Bubenzer, O., Vogelsang, R., and Wotzka, H.-P. (eds.), *Aridity, change and conflict in Africa.* Cologne: Heinrich-Barth-Institut, 313–330.

Moreno García, J.C. 2013a. Building the Pharaonic state: territory, elite, and power in ancient Egypt in the 3rd millennium BCE. In Hill, J.A., Jones, P.H., and Morales, A.J. (eds.), *Experiencing power, generating authority: cosmos, politics, and the ideology of kingship in ancient Egypt and Mesopotamia.* Philadelphia: University of Pennsylvania Museum of Archaeology and Anthropology, 185–217.

Moreno García, J.C. 2013b. The territorial administration of the kingdom in the 3rd millennium. In Moreno García, J.C. (ed.), *Ancient Egyptian administration.* Leiden: Brill, 85–151.

Moreno García, J.C. 2015a. Ḥwt jḥ(w)t, the administration of the western Delta and the "Libyan Question" in the 3rd millennium. *JEA* 101: 69–105.

Moreno García, J.C. 2015b. Climatic change or sociopolitical transformation? Reassessing late 3rd millennium Egypt. In Meller, H., Risch, R., Jung, R., and Arz, H.W. (eds.), *2200 BC: a climatic breakdown as a cause for the collapse of the Old World?* Halle: Landesamt für Denkmalpflege und Archäologie, 79–94.

Moreno García, J.C. 2016. Social inequality, private accumulation of wealth and new ideological values in late 3rd millennium BCE Egypt. In Meller, H., Hahn, H.P., Jung, R., and Risch, R. (eds.), *Arm und Reich: zur Ressourcenverteilung in prähistorischen Gesellschaften*. Halle: Landesamt für Denkmalpflege und Archäologie, 491–512.

Moreno García, J.C. 2017. Trade and power in ancient Egypt: Middle Egypt in the late third/early second millennium BC. *JAR* 25: 87–132.

Moreno García, J.C. 2018a. Divergent trajectories on the Nile: polities, wealth and power between 4000–1600 BCE. In Meller, H., Risch, R., and Gronenborn, D. (eds.), *Surplus without state: political forms in prehistory*. Halle: Landesamt für Denkmalpflege und Archäologie, 337–372.

Moreno García, J.C. 2018b. Elusive 'Libyans': identities, lifestyles and mobile populations in NE Africa (late 4th–early 2nd millennium BC). *JEH* 11: 145–182.

Moreno García, J.C. 2019a. Textile display in Middle Kingdom Egypt (late third–early second millennium BC): symbolism, social status and long-distance trade. In Gaspa, S., and Vigo, M. (eds.), *Textiles in ritual and cultic practices in the ancient Near East from the third to the first millennium BC*. Münster: Ugarit, 55–77.

Moreno García, J.C. 2019b. Marketplaces and hubs of trade in Egypt at the end of the 3rd millennium BC: Heracleopolis Magna in context. In Rahmstorf, L., and Stratford, E. (eds.), *Weights and marketplaces from the Bronze Age to the Early Modern Period*. Kiel: Wachholtz Verlag, 185–202.

Moreno García, J.C. 2021. Changes and limits of royal taxation in pharaonic Egypt (2300–2000 BCE). In Valk, J., Campbell, R., and Soto Marín, I. (eds.), *The mechanics of extraction: comparing principles of taxation and tax compliance in the ancient world*. New York: NYU Press, 290–324.

Morenz, L. 2006. Zwischen Kontext, Intermedialität, Intertextualität und Individualität: die Selbst-Präsentation eines Nedjes-iker (BM 1671). *Lingua Aegyptia* 14: 389–407.

Morenz, L. 2009. *Die Zeit der Regionen im Spiegel der Gebelein-Region: kulturgeschichtliche Re-Konstruktionen*. Leiden: Brill.

Morero, E., and Prévalet, R. 2015. Technological transfer of luxury craftsmanship between Crete and the Orient during the Bronze Age. In Mynářová, J., Onderka, P., and Pavúk, P. (eds.), *There and back again: the crossroads, II*. Prague: Charles University, 59–83.

Morris, E. 2006. "Lo, nobles lament, the poor rejoice": social order inverted in First Intermediate Period Egypt. In Schwartz, G., and Nichols, J. (eds.), *After collapse: the regeneration of complex societies*. Tucson, AZ: University of Arizona Press, 58–71.

Morris, E. 2019. Ancient Egyptian exceptionalism: fragility, flexibility and the art of not collapsing. In Yoffee, N. (ed.), *The evolution of fragility: setting the terms*. Cambridge: McDonald Institute for Archaeological Research, 61–87.

Mostafa, M.F. 1984–1985. Erster Vorbericht über einen Ersten Zwischenzeit-Text aus Kom el-Koffar, Teil I. *ASAE* 70: 419–429.

Mostafa, M.F. 1987. Kom el-Koffar, Teil II: Datierung und historische Interpretation des Textes B. *ASAE* 71: 169–184.

Mostafa, M.F. 2005. The Autobiography "A" and a related text (Block 52) from the tomb of Shemai at Kom el-Koffar/Qift. In Khaled A.D., Bedier, S., and Abd el-Fatah, S. (eds.), *Studies in honor of Ali Radwan, vol. II*. Cairo: Supreme Council of Antiquities, 161–195.

Mourad, A.-L. 2015. *Rise of the Hyksos: Egypt and the Levant from the Middle Kingdom to the early Second Intermediate Period*. Oxford: Archaeopress.

Muhly, J.D., and Kassianidou, V. 2012. Parallels and diversities in the production, trade and use of copper and iron in Crete and Cyprus from the Bronze Age to the Iron Age. In Cadogan, G., Iacovou, M., Kopaka, K., and Whitley, J. (eds.), *Parallel lives: ancient island societies in Crete and Cyprus*. London: British School at Athens, 119–140.

Müller-Wollermann, R. 1986. *Krisenfaktoren im ägyptischen Staat des ausgehenden Alten Reichs*. PhD dissertation, University of Tübingen.

Nigro, L. 2014. The copper route and the Egyptian connection in 3rd millennium BC Jordan seen from the caravan city of Khirbet al-Batrawy. *Vicino Oriente* 18: 39–64.

Nigro, L., Montanari, D., Mura, F., Yasine, J., and Rinaldi, T. 2018. A hoard of Nilotic nacreous shells from Egypt to Jericho (Early Bronze II, 3000–2800 BCE): their finding, content and historical archaeological implications. *PEQ* 150: 110–125.

Obsomer, C. 1995. *Sésostris Ier: étude chronologique et historique du règne*. Brussels: Connaissance de l'Égypte ancienne.

Papazian, H. 2015. The state of Egypt in the Eighth Dynasty. In Der Manuelian, P., and Schneider, T. (eds.), *Towards a new history for the Egyptian Old Kingdom: perspectives on the Pyramid Age*. Leiden: Brill, 393–428.

Parkinson, R.B. 1997. *The Tale of Sinuhe and other ancient Egyptian poems, 1940–1640 BC.* Oxford: Oxford University Press.

Pérez-Die, M.C. 2005. La nécropole de la Première Période Intermédiaire— début du Moyen Empire à Héracléopolis Magna: nouvelles découvertes et résultats récents (campagne 2001). In Pantalacci, L., and Berger-el-Naggar, C. (eds.), *Des Néferkarê aux Montouhotep: travaux archéologiques en cours sur la fin de la VIe dynastie et la première période intermédiaire.* Lyon: Maison de l'Orient et de la Méditerranée; Paris: De Boccard, 239–254.

Pérez-Die, M.C. 2015. Ehnasya el Medina (Herakleopolis Magna). Excavations 2004–2007 at the necropolis of the First Intermediate Period/Early Middle Kingdom. In Kousoulis, P., and Lazaridis, N. (eds.), *Proceedings of the tenth international congress of Egyptologists.* Leuven: Peeters, 393–409.

Pérez-Die, M.C., and Vernus, P. 1992. *Excavaciones en Ehnasya El Medina, Heracleópolis Magna.* Madrid: Ministerio de Cultura.

Picardo, N. 2015. Hybrid households: institutional affiliations and household identity in the town of Wah-sut (South Abydos). In Müller, M. (ed.), *Household studies in complex societies: (micro) archaeological and textual approaches.* Chicago: The Oriental Institute of the University of Chicago, 243–287.

Pinnock, F. 2018. Ancora sui rapporti tra Ebla e l'Egitto: nota a margine. In Vacca, A., Pizzimenti, S., and Micale, M.G. (eds.), *A oriente del Delta: scritti sull'Egitto ed il Vicino Oriente antico in onore di Gabriella Scandone Matthiae.* Roma: Scienze e lettere, 495–520.

Polotski, H.J. 1930. The stela of Heqa-Yeb. *JEA* 16: 194–199.

Postel, L. 2004. *Protocole des souverains égyptiens et dogme monarchique au début du Moyen Empire: des premiers Antef au début du règne d'Amenemhat Ier.* Turnhout: Brepols.

Postel, L. 2008. Une nouvelle mention des campagnes nubiennes de Montouhotep II à Karnak. In Gabolde, L. (ed.), *Hommages à Jean-Claude Goyon.* Cairo: Institut français d'archéologie orientale, 329–340.

Quirke, S. 1991. "Townsmen" in the Middle Kingdom: on the term *s n niwt tn* in the Lahun temple accounts. *ZÄS* 118: 141–149.

Rahmstorf, L. 2017. The use of bronze objects in the 3rd millennium BC: a survey between Atlantic and Indus. In Maran, J., and Stockhammer, P. (eds.), *Appropriating innovations: entangled knowledge in Eurasia, 5000–1500 BCE.* Oxford: Oxbow, 184–210.

Raue, D. 2014. Königsbekannte: Inschriften zur "anderen" Ersten Zwischenzeit im Norden Ägyptens. In Backes, B., and von Nicolai, C. (eds.), *Kulturelle Kohärenz durch Prestige*. Munich: Utz, 179–200.

Redford, D.B. 1986. *Pharaonic king-lists, annals and day-books: a contribution to the study of the Egyptian sense of history*. Mississauga: Benben Publications.

Richards, J. 2005. *Society and death in ancient Egypt: mortuary landscapes of the Middle Kingdom*. Cambridge: Cambridge University Press.

Römer, M. 2011. Was ist eine Krise? Oder: Wie ist das Alte Reich (nicht) untergegangen. *GM* 230: 83–101.

Scandone-Matthiae, G. 2003. Les rapports entre Ebla et l'Égypte à l'Ancien et au Moyen Empire. In Hawass, Z. (ed.), *Egyptology at the dawn of the twenty-first century, vol. 2: history, religion*. Cairo: American University in Cairo Press, 487–493.

Schneider, T. 2017. "What is the past but a once material existence now silenced": the First Intermediate Period from an epistemological perspective. In Höflmayer, F. (ed.), *The late third millennium in the ancient Near East: chronology, C14, and climate change*. Chicago: The Oriental Institute of the University of Chicago, 311–322.

Seidlmayer, S.J. 1987. Wirtschaftliche und gesellschaftliche Entwicklung im Übergang vom Alten zum Mittleren Reich: ein Beitrag zur Archäologie der Gräberfelder der Region Qau-Matmar in der Ersten Zwischenzeit. In Assmann, J., Davies, V., and Burkard, G. (eds.), *Problems and priorities in Egyptian archaeology*. London and New York: Kegan Paul International, 175–217.

Seidlmayer, S.J. 2000. The First Intermediate Period (c. 2160–2055 BC). In Shaw, I. (ed.), *The Oxford history of ancient Egypt*. Oxford: Oxford University Press, 108–136.

Seidlmayer, S.J. 2007. Gaben und Abgaben im Ägypten des Alten Reiches. In Klinkott, H., Kubisch, S., and Müller-Wollermann, R. (eds.), *Geschenke und Steuern, Zölle und Tribute: Antike Abgabenformen in Anspruch und Wirklichkeit*. Leiden: Brill, 31–63.

Sethe, K. 1935. *Urkunden des ägyptischen Altertums, vol. VII: historisch-biographische Urkunden des Mittleren Reiches*. Leipzig: Hinrichs.

Silverman, D.P. 2008. A reference to warfare at Dendereh, prior to the unification of Egypt in the Eleventh Dynasty. In Thompson, S.E., and Der Manuelian, P. (eds.), *Egypt and beyond: essays presented to Leonard H. Lesko*. Providence, RI: Brown University, 319–331.

Somaglino, C. 2010. Les "portes" de l'Égypte de l'Ancien Empire à l'époque Saïte. *Égypte, Afrique et Orient* 59: 3–16.

Somaglino, C. 2015–2016. La stèle de Héni et la géographie de la frange orientale du Delta à l'Ancien et au Moyen Empire. *Bulletin de la Société Française d'Égyptologie* 193-194: 29–51.

Sowada, K.N. 2009. *Egypt in the Eastern Mediterranean during the Old Kingdom: an archaeological perspective.* Fribourg: Academic Press/ Göttingen: Vandenhoeck & Ruprecht.

Stauder, A. 2013. *Linguistic dating of Middle Egyptian literary texts.* Hamburg: Widmaier.

Stefanović, D. 2007. *ḏȝmw* in the Middle Kingdom. *Lingua Aegyptia* 15: 217–229.

Stefanović, D., and Satzinger, H. 2015. I am a *Nbt-pr*, and I am independent. In Miniaci, G., and Grajetzki, W. (eds.), *The world of Middle Kingdom Egypt (2000–1550 BC): contributions on archaeology, art, religion, and written sources, vol. I.* London: Golden House, 333–338.

Theis, C. 2010. Die Pyramiden der Ersten Zwischenzeit nach philologischen und archäologischen Quellen. *SAK* 39: 321–339.

Török, L. 2009. *Between two worlds: the frontier region between ancient Nubia and Egypt, 3700 BC–AD 500.* Leiden: Brill.

Vandier, J. 1950. *Mo'alla: la tombe d'Ankhtifi et la tombe de Sébekhotep.* Cairo: Institut français d'archéologie orientale.

Vermeulen, T. 2016. Réflexions sur les couches intermédiaires de la société égyptienne. *Néhet* 4: 139–165.

Vernus, P. 1970. Sur une particularité de l'onomastique du Moyen Empire. *RdE* 22: 155–169.

Véron, A.J., et al. 2013. A 6000-year geochemical record of human activities from Alexandria (Egypt). *QSR* 81: 138–147.

von Pilgrim, C. 1996. *Elephantine XVIII: Untersuchungen in der Stadt des Mittleren Reiches und der Zweiten Zwischenzeit.* Mainz: Zabern.

von Pilgrim, C. 2001. The practice of sealing in the administration of the First Intermediate Period and the Middle Kingdom. In Gratien, B. (ed.), *Le sceau et l'administration dans la Vallée du Nil.* Villeneuve d'Ascq: Université Lille 3, 161–172.

Warburton, D. 2007. What happened in the Near East ca. 2000 BC? In Seland, E.H. (ed.), *The Indian Ocean in the ancient period: definite places, translocal exchange.* Oxford: Archaeopress, 9–22.

Warburton, D. 2011. What might the Bronze Age world system look like? In Wilkinson, T.C., Sherratt, S., and Bennet, J. (eds.), *Interweaving worlds: systemic interactions in Eurasia, 7th to 1st millennia BC*. Oxford: Oxbow, 120–134.

Warburton, D. 2013. Integration by price in the Bronze Age. In Frenez, D., and Tosi, M. (eds.), *South Asian archaeology 2007, vol. I: prehistoric periods*. Oxford: Archaeopress, 287–296.

Wengrow, D. 2009. The voyages of Europa: ritual and trade in the eastern Mediterranean circa 2300–1850 BC. In Parkinson, W.A., and Galaty, M.L. (eds.), *Archaic state interaction: the eastern Mediterranean in the Bronze Age*. Santa Fe, NM: School for Advanced Research Press, 141–160.

Wenke, R.J., Redding, R.W., and Cagle, A.J. (eds.) 2016. *Kom el-Hisn (ca. 2500–1900 BC): an ancient Egyptian settlement in the Nile delta*. Atlanta, GA: Lockwood Press.

Wiener, M.H. 2013. Contacts: Crete, Egypt, and the Near East circa 2000 B.C. In Aruz, J., Graff, S.B., and Rakic, Y. (eds.), *Cultures in contact from Mesopotamia to the Mediterranean in the second millennium BC*. New York: Metropolitan Museum of Art, 34–43.

Wilkinson, T.C. 2014. *Tying the threads of Eurasia: trans-regional routes and material flows in Transcaucasia, eastern Anatolia and western Central Asia, c. 3000–1500 BC*. Leiden: Sidestone.

Willems, H. 2007. *Dayr al-Barshā, vol. I: the rock tombs of Djehutinakht (no. 17K74/1), Khnumnakht (no. 17K74/2), and Iha (no. 17K74/3), with an essay on the history and nature of nomarchal rule in the early Middle Kingdom*. Leuven: Peeters.

Willems, H. 2014. *Historical and archaeological aspects of Egyptian funerary culture: religious ideas and ritual practice in Middle Kingdom elite cemeteries*. Leiden: Brill.

Williams, B. 2013. Three rulers in Nubia and the early Middle Kingdom in Egypt. *JNES* 72: 1–10.

13

The Kingdom of Ur

Steven J. Garfinkle

13.1. Introduction

To overturn the appointed times, to obliterate the divine plans,
the storms gather to strike like a flood. An, Enlil, Enki and
Ninhursag have decided its fate—to overturn the divine powers
of Sumer, to lock up the favorable reign in its home, to destroy
the city, to destroy the house, to destroy the cattle-pen, to level
the sheepfold . . . so as to obliterate the divine powers of Sumer, to
change its preordained plans, to alienate the divine powers of the
reign of kingship of Ur . . . to break up the unity of the people of
Nanna, numerous as ewes; . . . that Šimaški and Elam, the enemy,
should dwell in their place; that its shepherd, in his own palace,
should be captured by the enemy, that Ibbi-Sin should be taken to
the land Elam in fetters. . . .[1]

---

1. Translation after Black et al. 2004: 128–129; see also the Electronic Text Corpus of
Sumerian Literature, catalogue no. 2.2.3 (ETCSL; http://etcsl.orinst.ox.ac.uk/cgi-
bin/etcsl.cgi?text=t.2.2.3#; last accessed March 19, 2020) and Michalowski 1989.

Steven J. Garfinkle, *The Kingdom of Ur* In: *The Oxford History of the Ancient Near East*. Edited by: Karen
Radner, Nadine Moeller, and D. T. Potts, Oxford University Press. © Oxford University Press 2022.
DOI: 10.1093/oso/9780190687571.003.0013

These lines from a composition known today as "The Lament for Sumer and Ur" record the fall of one of the best-known, and best-documented, states in the history of ancient Mesopotamia, the kingdom of Ur. Ibbi-Sin, led off as a captive to Susa, was the last king of the Third Dynasty of Ur. His predecessors crafted a territorial kingdom in Sumer and Akkad, the ancient names for the two regions in southern Mesopotamia. In this chapter, I will use the terms Southern Mesopotamia and Babylonia interchangeably to describe the geographic and cultural area that was roughly contiguous with the states created by Ur-Namma's dynasty and later by the First Dynasty of Babylon (see chapter 18 in this volume). This area between and around the Tigris and Euphrates rivers runs from the point where the rivers are closest together in the north (roughly where we find the modern city of Baghdad) to the Persian Gulf in the south.

The kingdom of Ur (figures 13.1a–b) founded by Ur-Namma in the late third millennium BC, rose just as spectacularly as it fell, and it occupies a significant place both in our modern reconstructions of the history of the ancient Near East and in the ancient Mesopotamian conceptions of that same history. Ur-Namma's dynasty reunited the city-states of southern Mesopotamia and ruled over the region for about a hundred years. For ease of reference and the reader's guidance, this chapter uses the conventional Middle Chronology that dates the kingdom of Ur from 2110 to 2003 BC, although these dates are by no means certain and may need adjustment.[2]

This period is known as the Third Dynasty of Ur because it was the third dynasty from Ur to rule over southern Mesopotamia according to the Sumerian King List (SKL). Scholars frequently shorten the description of this Third Dynasty of Ur to Ur III, and that convention will be used here as well. In this chapter, I will use the kingdom of Ur and Third Dynasty of Ur interchangeably. Additionally, modern investigators often label this era as the Neo-Sumerian period. I reject the use of the term "Neo-Sumerian period" altogether because it conveys a renaissance of earlier Sumerian culture that, in my view, does not do justice to the rich

---

2. For the difficulties of establishing the absolute chronology of the period, see chapter 11 in this volume.

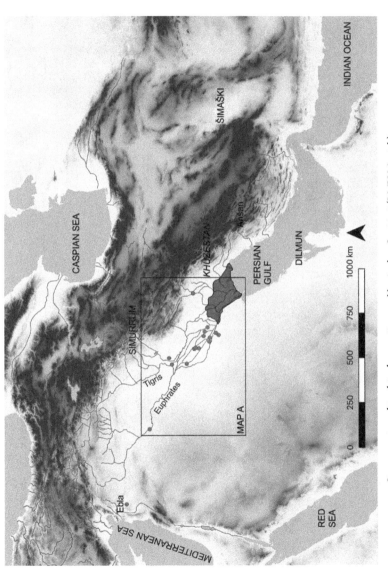

FIGURE 13.1A. Sites mentioned in this chapter. Prepared by Andrea Squitieri (LMU Munich).

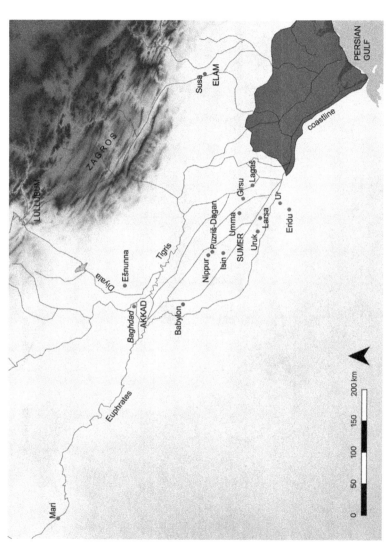

FIGURE 13.1B. Detail map A.

history and culture created at this time; this terminology also focuses us too narrowly on perceived ethnic differences among the Mesopotamian population, in particular between Akkadians and Sumerians, a previously popular view that finds little support among specialists today.

For modern observers, the era inaugurated by the kings of the Third Dynasty of Ur is one of the best-documented periods in all of the long history of the ancient Near East. Though the dynasty ruled for not much longer than a century, it left behind a vast record of its activities in the form of tens of thousands of cuneiform tablets. Approximately 100,000 texts from this period have been published, thousands more are sitting in the collections of museums, seminaries, universities, and libraries around the world, and countless tablets remain buried in sites across the modern Middle East.[3] These texts are overwhelmingly administrative in nature: the institutional archives from the provinces of Umma and Girsu alone comprise nearly 70 percent of the available text corpus of the period. Alongside these administrative texts, which record the crown's efforts to direct the state economy and its inhabitants, we have much smaller archives documenting economic life from a non-institutional perspective,[4] as well as a large sample of royal inscriptions (figure 13.2) and texts composed in honor of the kings of Ur.[5]

These extensive historical sources from this brief period allow for detailed study of the second experiment in secondary state formation in the history of southern Mesopotamia. The kings of Ur, roughly a century after the fall of the kingdom of Akkad, brought the ancient city-states of

---

3. The characteristics of this vast corpus are detailed in Molina 2008. The great majority of the published texts from this period are available online as the result of two digital text corpus projects, the Database of Neo-Sumerian Texts (BDTNS: http://bdtns.filol.csic.es) and the Cuneiform Digital Library Initiative (CDLI: https://cdli.ucla.edu); both last accessed March 19, 2020.

4. Most notable among these are collections from Nippur and from Iri-Sagrig; for the latter, see Owen 2013.

5. This includes the royal inscriptions (collected in Frayne 1997); the royal hymns and praise poems (accessible online on ETCSL: http://etcsl.orinst.ox.ac.uk; with the translations of selected compositions offered in Black et al. 2004); and the royal correspondence preserved in later copies from the Old Babylonian period (Michalowski 2011).

FIGURE 13.2. Stone foundation tablet of Šulgi of Ur recording the building of a temple in Ur. British Museum, Department of the Middle East, BM 118560. Courtesy of the Trustees of the British Museum.

Sumer and Akkad together again into a single political community. The vast administrative records documenting crown activity allow modern observers a unique window into the processes by which this larger state was created and maintained. These administrative texts were frequently dated, and the kings of Ur followed the practice of naming the years of their reigns after important events. The year names allow us to better follow the dynastic history of the kingdom, as well as many of their strategic endeavors and ritual practices. Indeed, Šulgi, the second king of the dynasty, is the first ruler in early Mesopotamia for whom we can reconstruct his entire reign through an unbroken and well-ordered series of year names. The years were named for events that royal authority considered significant, such as the building of temples and other infrastructure, the installation of priests and other cultic events, and, of course, military success. The first year of each king's reign recorded that fact: for example, "Year Šulgi became king."[6] The year names therefore provide us with tremendous additional evidence to reconstruct the histories and activities of the kings of Ur.

For the ancient Mesopotamians in the first half of the second millennium BC, the Third Dynasty of Ur was a critical part of their historical memory.[7] The kings of Ur may not have achieved the long-term mythic status of some of the Akkadian kings, like Sargon and Naram-Sin,[8] but succeeding dynasties copied and recopied the records of their accomplishments. The kings of Ur also connected themselves with the mythic Mesopotamian past. They were champions of Ur, but they shared a close connection with the city of Uruk, to which the dynastic family traced its origins. Ur-Namma and his successors consciously and continuously reinforced this link to one of Mesopotamia's oldest and grandest urban centers, and the home of the legendary king Gilgamesh. The kings of Ur styled themselves as the brethren of Gilgamesh and heirs to the

---

6. Many years had more than one name, since a year was often named after the previous year until the royal household had settled on a name for the new year. For example, Šulgi's 24th year was named: "Year Karhar was destroyed"; and his 25th year bore two names: "Year after the year Karhar was destroyed"; and "Year Simurrum was destroyed". On year names and calendars in the Ur III period, see Widell 2004; Dahl 2010. The most up-to-date catalog of the year names of early Mesopotamian rulers is available online at CDLI (http://cdli.ox.ac.uk/wiki/rulers_of_mesopotamia; last accessed March 19, 2020).

7. Michalowski 2016.

8. Mesopotamian literature down to the first millennium BC was full of heroic references to the dynasty of Akkad, and it is clear to a modern audience that many aspects of kingship were associated with the Sargonic kings who first brought all of southern Mesopotamia under their rule.

tradition of heroic kingship in which that epic partook.[9] Significantly, the Third Dynasty of Ur was looked to as a model during the early parts of the second millennium BC as the various successor states fought to re-establish unified control of the region. The hymns, prayers, and laments first authored during the reign of the kings of Ur, or written in the aftermath of the collapse of their dynasty, formed a critical part of the school curriculum in the Old Babylonian period. Hence, this era had a tremendous intellectual influence on the succeeding periods of ancient Mesopotamian history.

Modern scholars have not always been certain of how to handle this early state and its abundance of extant records. The explosion of so much administrative and literary productivity provides rich opportunities to explore early state formation and gain a clearer understanding of the political economy at that time. Yet this wealth has also proved discon-certing. How can we process and explain the sheer numbers of admin-istrative texts created over the course of the last century of the third millennium BC? Answering this question often has as much to do with the experience of our modern commentators as it does with the ancient evidence itself. This has given rise to images of the Ur III state as char-acterized by an overwhelming and highly bureaucratized central admin-istration that exercised absolute control of the kingdom's residents. Certainly, as we will find in the following discussion, the kingdom of Ur aspired to centralized control of much of the means of production, and both monitored and directed that control through a powerful literate administration. At the same time, the new dynasts had to accommodate regional power networks that could not simply be supplanted. We must, therefore, understand the extant administrative archives as evidence for the state's aspirations toward control, rather than as evidence of the gen-uine exercise of such authority.

As a case study in secondary state formation, the Third Dynasty of Ur gives us a remarkable opportunity to describe and assess this process.

---

9. The standard version of the epic was not composed until after the fall of the Third Dynasty of Ur, but the cycle of stories and poems on which that version was based must have been widely known to Mesopotamians in the late third millennium BC.

Paradoxically, however, the depth and breadth of the Ur III administrative record creates challenges to our ability to accurately describe life in this very active kingdom. First, the archives derive almost exclusively from administrative offices that directed state activity. The production of texts in early Mesopotamia has received extensive recent scholarly examination in an effort to determine why texts were created and preserved in cuneiform archives.[10] As a result of these analyses, we have a renewed understanding that many transactions in ancient Mesopotamia did not necessitate a written record. Texts were created most often to record the fulfillment of duties toward state institutions, to engage in state-level planning, and to note the participation of elites in important state functions. Therefore, the abundance of texts from institutional contexts makes sense, but it does not provide a global view of Mesopotamian society and economy at the end of the third millennium BC. We have to be very careful about the conclusions we draw from the abundance of state records, and match this with an awareness not only of what may not have been found, but also of what may not have been written down in the first place.

A second challenge that arises from the survival of so many Ur III texts is that the records to which we have access derive mostly from provincial settings and not from the central royal archives, presumably at Ur.[11] The city of Ur has been substantially excavated over the past century, but until recently, very little of that archaeological activity has exposed the Ur III levels of the site.[12] This means that our records document state power as exercised in important provincial centers, such as Umma and Girsu, and in significant locations connected with the royal

10. See Van de Mieroop 1997; Steinkeller 2003a; Garfinkle 2015. On the world beyond writing in the Ur III period, see Adams 2006.

11. At the time of writing (2020), the Database of Neo-Sumerian Texts (BDTNS: http://bdtns.filol.csic.es) lists slightly more than 4,000 extant texts from the city of Ur, as compared to nearly 30,000 from the city of Umma, more than 27,000 from Girsu, and over 15,000 from the royal distribution center at Puzriš-Dagan.

12. The recent investigations at Ur include new abilities to survey the site that show a much larger city than we had previously known; see Hammer 2019.

family, such as Puzriš-Dagan and Iri-Sagrig. These texts frequently document the assertion of power from above, as the kings of Ur sought to better incorporate the old city-states into their larger territorial kingdom. The success of these efforts is evident in the provincial archives, but the picture will remain incomplete until we have a more balanced record including a greater variety of royal archives.

Nowhere are the limitations of this vast corpus of Ur III texts more apparent than in the absence of the military archives. We get a significant view of the kingdom's military activities from the information recorded in the year names, which demonstrate the regularity of warfare in this period, and from the extant administrative records that record the proceeds of these campaigns.[13] Yet our view of this crucial institution is limited by the absence of archives detailing the day-to-day operations of the military and its logistical needs. As Bertrand Lafont noted,

> And yet very few documents, with little detail in them, are available on the armies that led these military conquests. Moreover, we know little about how these kings organized, from a military point of view, the defenses either at the center or at the outskirts of their kingdom. Although the military organization of this period is extremely important to the history of ancient Mesopotamia, the total evidence that we have to date is so sketchy and incomplete that it allows only minimal insight.[14]

The rich textual evidence is also not equally distributed across the century during which the Third Dynasty of Ur ruled over southern Mesopotamia. Examinations of the surviving corpora show that they primarily document the middle of the dynasty, from the third decade of Šulgi's reign down to the first decade of the reign of Ibbi-Sin. This means that our window into their world is restricted to a period of roughly fifty years that correlates with their greatest economic

---

13. See Garfinkle 2014.

14. Lafont 2009: 1.

and military successes. As we will see, this is no accident, since the expanded military adventures inaugurated midway through Šulgi's kingship created the need for increased documentation. The year names provide greater continuity in our ability to reconstruct the history of the Third Dynasty, and we have good sequences of year names for each king after Ur-Namma; but the year names cannot compensate for the absence of detailed records from the early days and waning moments of the kingdom.

Therefore, our abundant records most often provide a centralized and idealized view of the state and its power. This has led to hyperbolic descriptions of the Ur III state as totalitarian, and this view often pervades the secondary and textbook literature on the dynasty and its fortunes. As I will detail in this chapter, the kings of Ur had to negotiate with local and regional hierarchies, while also creating parallel, statewide institutions loyal directly to the crown (like the military and the statewide cults of the divine kings). Ultimately, these negotiations expose limits on royal authority and the efforts of the crown to confront them. This requires a more nuanced approach to this case study in which we are wary of the ways in which our modern vocabulary (replete with references to bureaucracy and modern totalitarian states) is often ill suited to accurately describe the ancient reality.

In this chapter, we will explore the historical background to the rise of the Third Dynasty of Ur, and undertake a survey of its development. Following this, we will use topical sections to examine the socioeconomic organization of this early state, the relationship between the kingdom and the broader Near East, and the development of military strategies and social networks to support the enlarged notion of kingship and community fostered by the dynasty's kings. Ultimately, we will find that the kingdom of Ur was a short-lived experiment in secondary state formation that foundered when the later kings could not live up to the expectations placed on them by the royal ideology pioneered by its early kings. The collapse of the Ur III state was precipitated, in part, by the failure of the dynasty to create a more enduring institutional basis for the power they had taken in southern Mesopotamia.

13.2. Background: the late third millennium
BC in southern Mesopotamia

The Third Dynasty of Ur came to power after a period of political crisis in southern Mesopotamia. The collapse of the kingdom of Akkad (conventionally dated to ca. 2200 BC) brought about a return to the norms of city-state living for urban residents in the south, but later records bemoan the absence of the newly established region-wide unity that Sargon had inaugurated. We need to allow that these claims arose in later times when the idea of a single state encompassing Babylonia had become normative. And yet, the fragmentation that followed the collapse of the Sargonic kingdom was real, and it allowed for the incursions of foreign rulers into southern Mesopotamia: the reviled Gutians and later the resurgent Elamite state under Puzur-Inšušinak.

The third millennium BC was both a tumultuous and formative era for Mesopotamian civilization and the broader ancient Near East. The invention of the cuneiform writing system in the late fourth millennium BC provides historians with unparalleled access to information about the process of early state formation in the region. By the time that writing appeared, the dominant form of political community in Mesopotamia was the independent city-state, consisting most often of a large urban center and its agricultural hinterland.[15] These city-states were densely populated independent political, social, and economic entities that dotted the landscape. This was especially true in southern Mesopotamia, where the fertile alluvial plain watered by the Tigris and Euphrates, along with the many canals associated with those rivers, allowed for intensive cultivation of cereal agriculture. The city-states had a long history of trading with each other and with neighboring regions where they sought resources not available locally, especially the luxury resources that Mesopotamian elites sought as material manifestations of their status and privilege.[16]

---

15. The nature of these city-states and their sociopolitical structure is effectively summarized in Steinkeller 2017: 117–119; Yoffee 2005: 53–59.

16. Van de Mieroop 2002.

The environment in ancient Mesopotamia allowed for the production of tremendous agricultural surpluses that formed the basis for the creation of wealth and supported ever more complex craft specialization. In spite of the increase in labor specialization, the majority of the ancient population in these cities worked in the agricultural sector in a form of dependent labor in which the workers received rations from the institutional households. Along with farming, animal husbandry was critical to the success of agrarian communities in city-states of early Mesopotamia, each of which controlled large herds of sheep and goats.[17] The importance of animal husbandry, and the byproducts manufactured from these animals in royal craft workshops, can hardly be overstated. This was the case not only due to the economic impact of these herds, but also because the desire to increase the herds under royal and institutional management, and to ensure that they had access to pastureland, had a profound impact on the military and strategic goals of the kingdom (see section 13.6).

This is a significant point, since the rapid territorial expansion of the state under the Third Dynasty of Ur, along with its frequent military adventures beyond its frontiers, have led many scholars to label this kingdom as an early empire. By contrast, in my view, the kings of Ur sought to recreate the core of the southern Mesopotamian state as envisioned by Sargon of Akkad, in which all of those who were part of the lands of Sumer and Akkad were brought together under one banner. And the Ur III state had clear cultural boundaries on which it did not seek to expand.[18] The frequent campaigning, described vividly in year names and royal inscriptions, should be seen not as an expression of imperial expansion, but rather as efforts undertaken by the kings of Ur to collect booty and express hegemony over an adjacent region that was home to the some of the best available pastureland, and the gateway to important trade routes. This hegemony never amounted to direct administrative control of the periphery across the Zagros Mountains. The four quarters,

---

17. Porter 2012.

18. For alternative views, see, for example, Steinkeller 1991; Lafont 2009.

over which the kings of the Third Dynasty of Ur would ultimately claim control, encompassed the space in the ancient Mesopotamian imagination that was populated by its great and ancient city-states dedicated to their common pantheon of gods.

The kings of third millennium BC Mesopotamia ruled their cities as representatives of a divine order that accounted for all the southern city-states and saw the kings as earthly representatives of the gods who lived in the temples at the center of their communities. Without their kings to guide them and to ensure that the rituals of their society were upheld, the urban population would be left at the mercy of their environment and neighboring groups. By the time the Akkadian kingdom had risen and fallen, the world with which the Mesopotamians were in contact included not only their immediate neighbors, but also a far-flung collection of growing polities from the Indus valley in the east to the Mediterranean coast in the west. The growing importance of the figure of the ruler to guide the people of the teeming Mesopotamian cities can be seen in the SKL. Piotr Steinkeller demonstrated that the text was first composed at the time of the Third Dynasty of Ur, and almost certainly during the reign of Šulgi.[19] The text solidifies and normalizes the relatively new idea of unified kingship over the four quarters of their world. The SKL in its Ur III form, and in the later versions of the early second millennium BC, reimagined the Mesopotamian past for the benefit of the era's royal ideology, going back to time immemorial when the gods first granted kingship to the world of men. The text outlines the boundaries of kingship as exercising dominion over their entire cultural world; indeed, the cities found in the text as past seats of kingship form a basic map of the territory of the kingdom of Ur.[20]

Returning to the earlier history recorded in the text, when the SKL reaches the collapse of the kingdom of Akkad, it proclaims, "Who was king? Who was not king?"[21] This lament notes the anxiety this situation

---

19. Steinkeller 2003b.

20. Wilcke 1989.

21. Jacobsen 1939: 113; available online as ETCSL no. 2.1.1 (http://etcsl.orinst.ox.ac.uk/cgi-bin/etcsl.cgi?text=t.2.1.1#; last accessed March 19, 2020).

caused for the later authors of the SKL, who, by the end of the third millennium BC, had become accustomed to the idea of a larger framework for kingship that included all of Babylonia, and it reflects the chaos that prevailed at the end of that dynasty with foreigners, the Gutians, invading southern Mesopotamia, and with the growing influence of the Elamites to the east, who came to dominate northern Babylonia. After the fall of Akkad, the SKL signaled the return of the older norm in the region: a divided world of city-states in which the Mesopotamian landscape was dotted with independent communities, each led by their own rulers. The reality was that the idea of unification among the southern city-states was even older than the kingdom of Akkad, and had its roots in the south in the ancient city of Uruk.[22] The most pressing problem introduced by the collapse of the Sargonic kingdom under Šar-kali-šarri was the disruption of Mesopotamian autonomy by outsiders. The literary texts, and later traditions, ascribed the fall of Akkad to the withdrawal of divine favor, the instrument of which was the Gutians who invaded from the Zagros and took control of prominent cities like Adab. The Gutians became the archetypal outsider whose lack of urban culture and sophistication provided an easy contrast with the ideal of settled, agrarian Mesopotamian life. To quote the composition today known as "The Curse of Akkad,"

> Not classed among people, not reckoned as part of the land, Gutium, a people who know no inhibitions, with human instincts, but canine intelligence, and monkey features, Enlil brought them out of the mountains. Like hordes of locusts they lie over the land.[23]

---

22. For a discussion of Uruk as the wellspring of a pan-Sumerian kingdom encompassing the four quarters of their world, see chapter 10 in volume 1. This is a critical observation considering how closely the kings of Ur connected themselves with the city of Uruk.

23. Cooper 1983: 58–59.

We find this image again and again in the cuneiform tradition, and it was a view that also broadly defined the Babylonian literary relationship with other arriving groups like the Amorites. And yet, we know that some Gutians had settled within the boundaries of southern Mesopotamia prior to the collapse of Akkad, and when they took control of eastern portions of Babylonia in the chaotic aftermath, they presented themselves as rulers according to Mesopotamian norms. Gutian kings used the same royal epithets, and styled themselves as the kings of the four quarters.

The fall of Akkad, the incursion of the Gutians, and the growing power of Elam all made for an uncertain geopolitical situation in southern Mesopotamia, while also allowing for a resurgence of the independent city-states in the heartland of Sumer. Strong local dynasties emerged again in Lagaš and Uruk in particular, and we are fairly well informed about their development through a rich series of surviving royal inscriptions. The most famous of these belonged to Gudea, the seventh ruler of the Second Dynasty of Lagaš (figure 13.3).[24] Gudea is today widely known from his statues and inscribed clay foundation cylinders, for which he commissioned long texts recording his achievements. The statues of Gudea are also among the most extraordinary artistic achievements of the period. These statues, all made from imported stone, bear witness not only to the wealth of his community and its craftsmanship, but also to the wide foreign trade connections on which the prestige economy in southern Mesopotamia thrived. Gudea's dynasty spans much of the confused period between the downfall of Akkad and the rise of the kingdom of Ur. Lagaš regained its independence and maintained it into the time of Ur-Namma, only being absorbed into that new state sometime after its founding.[25]

In his many inscriptions, Gudea focused on presenting his rule within clear and customary patterns that would have been familiar to southern Mesopotamian elites. He took the traditional title of governor or city

---

24. Edzard 1997: 3.

25. For the contemporaneity of Gudea with Ur-Namma, see Wilcke 2011.

FIGURE 13.3. Statue of Gudea of Lagaš, made of imported diorite. Metropolitan Museum of Art, New York. Accession number 59.2 (Harris Brisbane Dick Fund). Courtesy of the Metropolitan Museum of Art.

ruler (Sumerian *ensi*), rather than the grander title of king (Sumerian *lugal*) that had come to signal larger ambitions. He built and restored temples, and he took care of the gods on behalf of the community. This emphasis on building was reinforced in the iconography of his statues. Two surviving statues depicted him seated, with the architect's plan of a temple on his lap for consultation.

> When Ningirsu had directed his meaningful gaze on his city, had chosen Gudea as the legitimate shepherd in the land. . . . He built Ningirsu's House on ground that was as clean as Eridu. No one was lashed by the whip or hit by the goad, no mother would beat her child. . . . No hoe was used in the city cemetery,

no bodies were buried, no cult musician brought his harp, let no lamentation sound, and no wailing women sang a dirge. Within the boundaries of Lagaš no one took an accused person to the place of oath-taking, and no debt collector entered anyone's house. Gudea made things function as they should for his lord Ningirsu. . . . When he was about to build the House of Ningirsu, Ningirsu, his master who loves him, opened for him the roads leading from the Upper to the Lower Sea.[26]

Gudea's text here lays out the norms of rule in ancient Sumer. The ruler, chosen by the gods of his city, with the endorsement of the broader pantheon, brings idyllic conditions to his community: the proposed absence of both death and debt likely encompassing the greatest sources of anxiety felt by urban Mesopotamians. Gudea also asserts that all roads lay open to him through divine favor, and this is how the rich resources described in this and other texts were available to him in his construction of the temple for Ningirsu. The rulers of Lagaš did not lay claim to the broader dominion of the earlier Sargonic kings, but they asserted their complete management of the affairs of their city. Gudea also evinced a genuine concern for what we might call social justice, and this is a refrain to which the kings of Ur and their successors would regularly return.[27]

The absence of frequent references to conquest by Gudea suggests that the striking martial presentation of kingship familiar from the Sargonic period (see chapters 9 and 10 in volume 1) had not yet been fully absorbed into the royal literary tradition. At the same time, we know that Gudea's Lagaš was not an island of peace in the midst of a sea of conflict. During this interregnum, in which city-states like Lagaš regained their previous independence, the contests for power and access to resources continued and pitted native dynasties against their neighbors, and against the

---

26. Inscription of Gudea's Statue B; translation after Edzard 1997: 32–33. Note the emphasis on Gudea as the legitimate shepherd. This is an image of kingship to which I will return in section 13.6.

27. Note the similar language in the prologues to the so-called Law Codes of Ur-Namma and Hammurabi. For editions of both, see Roth 1997.

outside powers who intervened. Gudea himself campaigned in the east. On the same statue quoted earlier, he made his only surviving reference to this conflict: "He defeated the cities of Anšan and Elam and brought the booty therefrom to Ningirsu in his Eninnu."[28] The Susiana plain was the urban heartland of the neighboring region in modern Iran. Susa itself had become home to a growing kingdom contemporary with Gudea's Lagaš, and led most famously by its conquering king, Puzur-Inšušinak.[29]

Alongside Lagaš's return to independence and prosperity, the era after the fall of Akkad featured the return to regional prominence of the city of Uruk. As we saw earlier, Uruk may have begun the process of unifying Sumer even before the rise of Sargon, and this reflected both the size and importance of that city in the region. Therefore, we should not be surprised that Uruk once again took up the flag of southern Mesopotamian independence. The SKL records a series of kings ruling over Uruk in the wake of Akkad's defeat before that city too succumbed to the rule of the Gutians. The SKL may overstate the extent of Gutian interference at Uruk, but it fell to the last independent king of Uruk in this era, Utu-hegal, to uphold Urukean autonomy, and to drive the foreigners out of southern Mesopotamia. Royal inscriptions that survive in later copies recorded his victory:

> The god Enlil—as for the Gutium, the fanged serpent of the mountain, who acted with violence against the gods, who carried off the kingship of the land of Sumer to the mountain land, who filled the land of Sumer with wickedness . . . the god Enlil, lord of the foreign lands, commissioned Utu-hegal, the mighty man, the king of the four quarters, the king whose utterance cannot be countermanded, to destroy their name.[30]

---

28. Edzard 1997: 35. And for a date for the conquest of Susa to the reign of Ur-Namma, and contemporary with Gudea, see Marchesi 2012.

29. On Puzur-Inšušinak, see Steinkeller 2013.

30. Frayne 1993: 284–285.

The text goes on to describe Utu-hegal's decisive victory, and his capture of the last Gutian king, Tirigan, before ending with the note, "He brought back the kingship of the land of Sumer."[31] This notion of kingship (Sumerian nam-lugal) fits in well with texts, like the SKL, that were composed during the Third Dynasty of Ur. Kingship was seen as something at home in southern Mesopotamia, but also as something that could be taken away. And Utu-hegal's intent in the text is clear: kingship meant, in an aspirational sense, authority over all of southern Mesopotamia and its ancient city-states. With his defeat of Tirigan, Utu-hegal was poised to complete that aspiration, but his death left this work unfinished.

13.3. A brief history of the kingdom of Ur

The dynasty founded by Ur-Namma (whose rule is conventionally dated to 2110–2093 BC) survived for the reigns of five kings across three generations: his son Šulgi (2092–2045 BC); Šulgi's sons Amar-Sin (2044–2036 BC) and Šu-Sin (2035–2027 BC); and Šu-Sin's son Ibbi-Sin (2026–2003 BC).[32]

The founder Ur-Namma followed in the footsteps of the military success achieved by Utu-hegal over the Gutians. Ur-Namma consolidated his power at the city of Ur and gained control of most of the powerful city-states in southern Mesopotamia. This included Nippur, the city at the center of their pantheon.[33] For a time, Lagaš under Gudea remained independent and allied with the efforts of the kings of Ur, especially in the campaigns to expel the Elamites from northern Babylonia and the Diyala. Ur-Namma engaged in construction projects across his new state, and the creation of the kingdom of Ur inaugurated an enormous

---

31. Frayne 1993: 287.

32. For these dates, see Sallaberger and Schrakamp 2015: 131.

33. This moment is recorded in Ur-Namma's year names as: "Year: The king received kingship from Nippur." Unfortunately, we do not have a clear sense of the order of Ur-Namma's year names, so we cannot accurately place this event within the eighteen years of his reign. This legitimization of kingship over Sumer and Akkad through possession of Nippur, home to the head of their pantheon, became a pattern for succeeding dynasties in the second millennium BC.

statewide investment in building. This building activity focused on roads and canals, the economic sinews that allowed the cities to flourish and grow, as well as on temple building and maintenance. In this way, the dynasty sought to assure their subjects not only of freedom from the outside influence of Gutians and Elamites, but also of prosperity and stability. The kings of Ur used this building activity as a display of control as well as piety (figure 13.4). Ur-Namma founded his dynasty at Ur, but the

FIGURE 13.4. Copper foundation figurine of Ur-Namma, showing the king carrying a basket of earth for a building project. British Museum, Department of the Middle East, BM 113896. Courtesy of the Trustees of the British Museum.

royal family had strong ties to neighboring Uruk that they canonized in royal literature, identifying themselves as the kin of Gilgamesh, and under the direct protection of the gods of that city.[34]

Uruk remained an important center of power throughout the history of the kingdom of Ur, along with Nippur. We regard Ur as the seat of the kingdom, but this is too restricted and modern a notion of the seat of political power. The capital of the kingdom of Ur could rightly be regarded as wherever the royal household happened to be. We know that senior members of the royal household had estates throughout the kingdom and often maintained multiple residences in places like Ur and Nippur. The movement of the kings between these centers was likely related to religious festivals and local cultic obligations. Even peripheral towns, like Iri-Sagrig at the gateway to the Diyala region (exact location unknown), could be home to the royal residence, and the prominence of royal attendants at military staging towns also highlights the close connection in this era between dynastic success and military power.

Secure in his power at home, Ur-Namma challenged the growing authority of the Elamites and waged a campaign, in which Gudea of Lagaš likely participated, that defeated Puzur-Inšušinak. During his reign Ur-Namma's kingdom was forged on the battlefield, and his victory over the Elamites confirmed his control over southern Mesopotamia. At the same time, the evidence from the year names and royal inscriptions suggests a relatively peaceful era focused on the consolidation of political control of the heartland of Sumer and Akkad. As outlined earlier, in spite of the vast archives from this period, the earliest decades of the dynasty provide the fewest records, and we are more reliant on the year names and surviving royal inscriptions for our reconstructions of the early history of the Ur III period.

In reuniting the city-states of southern Mesopotamia, the kings of Ur followed in many ways in the footsteps of their Akkadian predecessors. This required imposing centralized authority over the traditional sociopolitical hierarchies in the urban centers of the region. This process

---

34. See Steinkeller 2017. The emphasis on the divine connections of the royal family at Ur grew decisively after Ur-Namma's death and the accession of Šulgi.

distanced the residents of these communities from the seat of royal authority; therefore, the kings of Ur had to create institutions on which to found this larger notion of power and community, while also paying deference to local traditions. This was the same project on which the Sargonic kings had commenced, though the frequent rebellions against their rule from within Babylonia show how hard it was to leave behind the older notion of political community. The kings placed members of their household in significant priestly offices throughout the kingdom, and often in the grand temples that the kings had built or renovated, in order to foster community and reinforce authority.

This larger notion of kingship and community placed great emphasis on the statewide role played by the king. Piotr Michalowski noted some time ago that this was achieved to a great extent through the charisma exercised by the kings.[35] Much of this work was left to Ur-Namma's successor Šulgi (see later discussion in this section) and it is from the latter's long reign that we get a clearer sense of how the dynasty sought to remake a divided political landscape into a coherent territorial kingdom. One critical area for these efforts was in the administration of justice. Perhaps the most famous document ascribed to the reign of the dynasty's first king is the so-called Law Code of Ur-Namma.[36] Like its more famous successor, the Law Code of Hammurabi, these texts were not law codes in the modern sense, but are best understood as statements about justice and royal authority. Ur-Namma's code provides direct insight into these traditions in early Mesopotamia. Indeed, this category of royal inscription can be seen as providing something of a social compact in early Mesopotamia. The kings acknowledged the need to provide justice, stability, and continuity with the past, and in exchange, they asserted genuine monarchic control over the community.

This continuity with the past is evident in the claims made in these texts. Ur-Namma's code promised a just reign, and the detailing of that justice in the body of the text was intended to reassure the larger audience

---

35. Michalowski 1991; 2013.

36. For publication and commentary, including the earliest exemplar of the text, see Civil 2011.

of this expanded kingdom that they could rely on the maintenance of previously agreed-upon juridical norms. Here too, we see the kings of Ur acknowledging that their expansion of the accepted notion of political community would distance most residents of their kingdom from the dynasty's home in Ur. After announcing the divine right of Ur-Namma to kingship and then highlighting his military prowess, the text turned to commercial matters. The king established standard weights and measures, and then he opened up and secured the rivers and roads for commerce.[37] Following this we get one of the characteristic statements about justice in early Mesopotamia:

> I did not deliver the orphan to the rich. I did not deliver the widow to the mighty. I did not deliver the man with but one shekel to the man with one mina. I did not deliver the man with but one sheep to the man with one ox. . . . I established justice in the land.[38]

Statements like this are often read for their value as royal propaganda, and the passage quoted here buttresses the common understanding of this era as one in which the crown asserted new, and authoritarian, control over the community. In this instance we see the king showing that his authority is so great that it can tame the interests of the "man of one mina." As an aside, let's be clear about one important point this particular passage raises. The king is articulating the protection of the elite from the super elite. The possession of even a shekel of silver worth of property was likely beyond the means of many of the dependent laborers who formed the backbone of the communities of southern Mesopotamia.[39]

---

37. The dynasty regarded commerce, and especially long-distance trade, as state priorities, going so far as to celebrate the return of the ships of Makkan (ancient Oman) to the ports of the god Nanna in a royal inscription: Frayne 1997: 39–42.

38. Roth 1997: 16–17.

39. A mina was equivalent to sixty shekels, and in modern terms a mina equates to approximately half a kilo of silver. For a sense of scale, unskilled slaves could be purchased at that time for between one and three shekels, and even the price of a skilled slave only rarely exceeded ten shekels. Draft animals frequently cost

The growth of the state in early Mesopotamia meant that the king was extending his coercive authority over a broader sociopolitical landscape, but this was also a cooperative process in which the elite, and especially the "men of one mina," sought out the protection of state regulation, and this allowed the kings of Ur to deepen the investment of regional elites in the success of their kingdom.

Some modern observers have noted that the Ur III kings championed legal centralism in which a uniform system of justice is seen as the prerogative of the state and to which social relations can be both defined and subordinated.[40] Certainly this is the gist of the prologue to Ur-Namma's laws. I will return later to the question of whether this centralism was achieved in practice; however, there is no doubt that the crown's allies in this endeavor were the commercial interests of the large non-institutional households of the elites. Claus Wilcke suggested that early territorial states, like the kingdom of Ur, were really composed of islands within larger territories.[41] These islands, as envisioned by Wilcke, were the urban centers connected to one another by roads and canals. The households, both individual and institutional, that controlled property and access to the means of production, were the social fabric of these islands. And here, I think that we can extend this metaphor of islands that I am borrowing.

The households themselves were the islands within the territory of southern Mesopotamia. The larger state formation of early dynasts, like the Ur III kings, consisted of binding these islands in distant towns more closely to each other and to the crown. To make this clear, we can use the terms recently employed by Seth Richardson and note that the crown

---

less than ten shekels. These price conditions prevailed in an agrarian economy in which bottlenecks formed around the availability of labor and draft animals, making them highly desired commodities.

40. Culbertson 2009: 152 provides an examination of this concept in broader legal history and in the scholarship on early Mesopotamian law. On the legal traditions of the Ur III period, see Lafont and Westbrook 2003.

41. Wilcke 2007: 16.

was in "political competition for constituencies."[42] The households of wealthy urban professionals were essential clients for the newly forming regional state. Much of this was accomplished through the extension of state power over the economy through the law. This is usually understood as a coercive process by which the royal sector appropriated control of the means of production across the state. My contention here is that this was not only a process that favored entrepreneurial activity, but one that was actively sought by the entrepreneurs who were the heads of many of these households. Ur-Namma placed his kingdom on a firm socio-economic basis through the construction of both physical and juridical infrastructure to bind the provinces more closely to the royal household. Ur-Namma's efforts were interrupted by his death on campaign.

We are best informed about the end of Ur-Namma's reign from the literary text "The Death of Ur-Namma." The king's death on the battle-field reminds us that this was a state born in violence and that its early history was of consolidation of its victories, both over neighboring states and over the peripheral peoples who threatened the alluvial plain from across the Zagros Mountains. The king's death also provoked something of an existential crisis for the dynasty. Throughout the early history of Mesopotamia, the success of kings and their cities was closely tied to their perceived relationships with the gods, and especially with the gods of their cities. A king falling in battle could indicate the withdrawal of divine favor, and it certainly threatened the charismatic control that kings exercised over their communities. I will return to this theme later, but in connection with the death of Ur-Namma we should highlight that the key metaphor for kingship in early Mesopotamia was that of the king as shepherd.[43] This idea encapsulated both the responsibilities and privi-leges of kingship. This image is prominent in the composition known today as "The Death of Ur-Namma": "Evil came upon Ur and made the trustworthy shepherd pass away. It made Ur-Namma, the trustworthy

---

42. Richardson 2012: 7–8.

43. This imagery was reinforced by the frequent association of the divine kings of the Third Dynasty with the shepherd Dumuzi, Inana's consort and an important god in his own right.

shepherd, pass away."[44] The text goes on to indicate how the founder of the dynasty responded to this terrible crisis. Ur-Namma, the good shepherd, finds himself in the netherworld among the gods and heroes claimed by the dynasty, such as Gilgamesh. The king laments the fate of Sumer as well as his own absence from the world of the living:

> My king's heart was full of tears, he . . . bitterly that he could not complete the wall of Ur; that he could no longer enjoy the new palace he had built; . . . that he could no longer bring pleasure to his wife with his embrace; that he could not bring up his sons on his knees; that he would never see in their prime the beauty of their little sisters who had not yet grown up.[45]

We can see here that the unfinished business of the king related directly to his societal responsibilities (here connected to building) as well as to his dynastic responsibilities (family and continuity in the royal household). The emphasis on the king's family likely reflects the anxieties of a young dynasty. As Steinkeller noted,

> In practice, however, the House of Ur was all about descent and kinship relations, in which, of course, it followed the Sargonic example. In fact, the Ur III kings outdid their Sargonic predecessors in that area, since their state was, for all practical purposes, a family affair, in that, like in the modern House of Saud, nearly everybody of importance was related by blood to the royal family.[46]

This is a theme to which we will return again and again. For the kings of Ur, their power was exercised in this patrimonial model, and this was one of the crucial ways in which they both expanded their power and created new sources of social power they could use to tie elites in their

---

44. Translation after Black et al. 2004: 57; see also ETCSL no. 2.4.1 (http://etcsl. orinst.ox.ac.uk/cgi-bin/etcsl.cgi?text=t.2.4.1.1#; last accessed March 19, 2020).

45. Translation after Black et al. 2004: 60; see also ETCSL no. 2.4.1 (http://etcsl. orinst.ox.ac.uk/cgi-bin/etcsl.cgi?text=t.2.4.1.1#; last accessed March 19, 2020).

46. Steinkeller 2017: 38.

community more directly to the royal household. This process included the regular practice of arranging diplomatic marriages with powerful ruling households in neighboring areas.[47]

Ur-Namma, once in the netherworld, reminded the gods that he had always taken care of them and provided abundance for his cities. He then undertook the appropriate rituals and made the correct offerings to the gods, fulfilling his role as king, even in death. As a result, Ur-Namma was rewarded with a place among the gods in the netherworld. The post mortem deification of the first king of the dynasty had a lasting impact on its self-representation, as this became the norm in life for Ur-Namma's successors. The building of temples to the kings of Ur and the celebration of festivals in their honor offered additional ways in which they were creating a common sense of community across the many urban centers of their kingdom.

Šulgi, Ur-Namma's son and successor, ruled over the kingdom for forty-eight years, and his reign is one of the longest and best documented in all of Mesopotamian history. Historians credit Šulgi with a number of statewide administrative reforms that built on the infrastructure created by his predecessor and established the basic outlines for rule over this enlarged political community.[48] The kings of Ur sought ways of creating statewide norms while acknowledging local elites. We see this, for example, in the calendars that appear in our administrative corpora. As independent city-states, each urban community had a long tradition of maintaining local practices, and this often included calendars, systems of weights and measures, and even scribal training based in these smaller communities. In response, the kings of Ur created a statewide calendar to make their administration both more efficient and more regular (which modern scholars often refer to by the German term *Reichskalender*). At the same time, the use of local calendars persisted alongside this statewide calendar for the entirety of the reign of the Third Dynasty of Ur. The survival of local practices in the face of these administrative reforms

47. Michalowski 1975; Steinkeller 2017.

48. Steinkeller 1991.

is a good reminder of how important local and regional identities were in the formerly independent city-states.

The early years of Šulgi's reign are less well documented, but during this period, his year names indicate a similar attention to statewide building that had characterized Ur-Namma's rule. Šulgi completed the division of the state into provinces that were more or less analogous to the boundaries of the formerly independent city-states. Governors (Sumerian *ensi*) ruled each of the provinces on behalf of the crown, and these governors controlled most of the significant institutions in their territories, including the temples. The core of the kingdom of Ur consisted of about twenty provinces under the control of such governors, and at times, the kings also appointed governors at places in neighboring areas, such as Ešnunna and Susa. This is an indication of the shifting nature of the kingdom's boundaries and highlights the difficulties in defining its periphery.

The position of governor was hereditary. The holders of this office were typically drawn from elite local families. The power of these families was subordinated to that of the royal household, but their survival again shows us how the kings of Ur negotiated with regional elites.[49] By contrast, the kings of Ur centralized the military command system, and generals (Sumerian *šagina*) served in the provinces alongside the governors. The generals were often senior members of the royal family and they reported directly to the kings. This division of authority nicely acknowledged the historical autonomy of the urban social networks while overlaying these regional hierarchies with a military hierarchy bound much more closely to the royal family.

From Šulgi's reign, we also have information about the second highest office in the kingdom, usually translated as "grand vizier" (Sumerian *sukkal-mah*).[50] A certain Aradmu held this title from late in the reign of Šulgi through the early years of Ibbi-Sin, and he served for a time simultaneously as governor of Girsu under Amar-Sin. As grand vizier,

---

49. Hallo 1972 and Zettler 1994 discuss the example of an elite household in Nippur whose local prominence both preceded and outlasted the dynasty.

50. On the long history of this position in southern Mesopotamia and its connection to the city of Lagaš, see Michalowski 2011: 64–70.

he exercised significant military and diplomatic responsibilities. He not only reported directly to the king, but he was also married into the royal household, and his daughter married a royal prince. Again, this shows the manner in which the kings leveraged ties to the royal family to build loyalty among important elite households.

Šulgi's year names show the attention he paid to the efforts started by his father. During his first two decades on the throne, he claimed to have built or restored numerous temples, as well as furnishing the gods with thrones and boats that were critical to their rituals and worship. It was also during this early period that Šulgi deified himself and became a direct part of this ritual and worship. This focus on building in the year names also found robust expression in the royal hymns composed in honor of the king.

> I, Šulgi, the mighty king, superior to all, strengthened the roads, put in order the highways of the Land. I marked out the double-hour distances, built there lodging houses. . . . Whichever direction one comes from, one can refresh oneself when the time is cool; and travellers and wayfarers who arrive at night can seek haven there as in a well-built city.[51]

These roadways allowed Šulgi famously to claim that he had run from Ur to Nippur and back in a single day, an event also memorialized in his seventh year name. This combination of the practical and the mythical was common to royal representation under the Third Dynasty of Ur. The kings were at once efficient administrators and heroic figures whose achievements highlighted their divine origins.

The continued emphasis on road and canal building was part of a larger effort to secure the economic foundation of the kingdom of Ur. These efforts are most apparent in the second half of Šulgi's reign and culminated in the construction of Puzriš-Dagan (modern Drehem) in

---

51. Translation after Black et al. 2004: 305; see also ETCSL no. 2.4.2.01 (http://etcsl.orinst.ox.ac.uk/cgi-bin/etcsl.cgi?text=t.2.4.2.01#; last accessed March 19, 2020).

the king's thirty-ninth year.[52] This center stood at the heart of the kingdom's redistributive economy. The kings of Ur used a system called *bala* in Sumerian, which ensured that local institutional surpluses would be transferred to the crown for its use.[53] The underlying meaning of the word *bala* is "rotation"; therefore, the *bala* system called for the provinces to take turns providing goods (most often in kind) and services to the crown. The amount expected from the provinces was based on the size of their local economies, with larger provinces, such as Girsu, providing greater *bala* contributions. As a result, the royal household again used the preexisting local networks to divert significant resources from the provincial agricultural economies for centralized use. The *bala* system was also used to account for and allocate some of the vast booty and tribute that flowed into state coffers from the growing level of military activity under Šulgi. This is where the kingdom's system of taxation intersected with Šulgi's building activity at Puzriš-Dagan, which served as a central collection point for the redistribution of livestock and animal products for the kingdom.

The construction of Puzriš-Dagan is indicative of the growing scale of economic centralization and military campaigning in the second half of Šulgi's reign. This site, adjacent to the city of Nippur, had already been in use by the royal household as a redistribution center, but the increased profile of the center and its growing roster of administrative personnel illustrate many of the successes of the dynasty.[54] This center provides us with the third largest corpus of administrative texts from the Third Dynasty of Ur, which documents the transfer of tens of thousands of animals, both those coming in as booty from peripheral areas, and those transferred internally to the crown by its dependents as tribute.

This movable wealth resulted from the regular campaigns that Šulgi and his successors launched across the eastern marches of their kingdom.

---

52. Sigrist 1992.

53. Sharlach 2004; and see section 13.4 in this chapter.

54. Tsouparopoulou 2008; 2013. For the increased distribution and administration of animal products in this era, see Allred 2006.

From the twentieth year of Šulgi until early in the reign of Ibbi-Sin, the armies of the Third Dynasty of Ur went to war virtually every year.[55] These campaigns served multiple purposes as the kings of Ur sought to make safe the eastern marches of the kingdom, to protect access to pasturage and herds, and to bind the military elite ever more closely to the royal household. This era of constant warfare directly impacts our view of the kingdom's administration, since the best-documented years of the Third Dynasty of Ur coincide with this period of intense military activity. We take Šulgi's twentieth year as the start of this era of constant warfare since that year name records that the men of Ur were conscripted as spearmen. Some scholars see this as evidence for the expansion and professionalization of the army of the kings of Ur.[56] Whether we see this as a formal step or not, it highlights the growing militarization of the community. Ultimately, this growing emphasis on armed conflict must be seen as part of the state-building projects of the kings of Ur (figure 13.5). The strategic goals of these efforts will be evaluated later, but the impact of the kingdom entering a state of near constant warfare can be seen in the administrative record.

Šulgi repeatedly campaigned outside the borders of his state against both urban and semi-nomadic groups living along the eastern and northeastern margins of the kingdom. These campaigns were part of a sustained effort to collect tribute and to control access to the kingdom while ensuring that the crown had access to the pasturelands to the east, and to the gateways to major trade networks. An example of the relentless nature of this military activity can be seen in the fact that Šulgi's forty-fourth year was named for the ninth time that the king defeated Simurrum.

Seven years earlier, and two years before the construction of Puzriš-Dagan, Šulgi's year names recorded the building of the "Wall of the Frontier" (Sumerian bad₃ ma-da). This potentially enormous construction project was a line of fortifications built to the north of Nippur, and

---

55. Garfinkle 2014.

56. Steinkeller 1991. For a discussion of this question, see also Sallaberger 1999: 148; Lafont 2009.

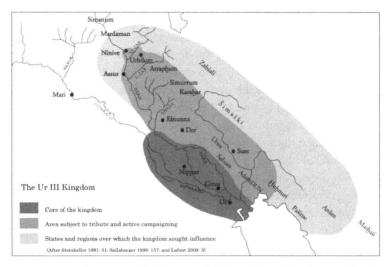

FIGURE 13.5. The areas of influence of the kingdom of Ur. Prepared by the author.

we should regard it as part of an effort to define the boundaries of the state, and to achieve control of territory in the liminal areas where the settled agrarian core of the state encountered potential resistance from outside groups.[57] The wall can be seen as evidence for tension along this boundary between the settled population within and the semi-nomads without; however, this suggested tension assumes that all such groups were hostile to the state-building enterprises of the kingdom of Ur, and it presumes that ethnic groups identified in our texts, such as the Amorites along this boundary, were viewed as enemies of this process. This is too reductionist an idea for what was really going on along the margins of the state. Amorites could be both insiders (trusted members of court) as well as outsiders (threatening the pasture lands to which the kingdom needed access), and this was true for other neighboring groups as well (such as the Elamites). This suggests that the wall building of the kings

---

57. Michalowski 2011: 122–169.

of Ur aimed to define the limits of state control on the ground, and to expand the concept of the state to include critical areas outside of the alluvial plain. The point of the wall on the frontier was not to create an impermeable barrier, but instead to move the locus of the state's strategic and military activity outside of the core of the kingdom.

For the Third Dynasty of Ur, these material efforts were wed to social measures to ensure the cooperation and the loyalty of neighboring peoples and states. Diplomatic marriages featuring members of Ur's royal household became a focal point of these efforts. Royal marriages provided the opportunity to bind elites from communities over which the kings desired hegemony more closely to the royal household. Šulgi first married the daughter of the ruler of Mari, but this was followed by a succession of marriages that connected important regions to the family of the king. The most famous of these wives was Šulgi-simti,[58] whose origins likely lay in the strategically critical area of the Diyala region, at or near Ešnunna. These marriages had diplomatic significance, but the many wives of Šulgi also became important players at court and had significant cultic functions. The wives received significant property and appear in our records as beneficiaries of their own significant institutional households.

Marriage into the royal family was not limited to interstate diplomacy. Elites throughout the kingdom, like Aradmu, were joined to the king's family to serve the dynasty's goals of ensuring a larger statewide community dependent on connections to the crown. The best evidence for this comes from the well-documented estate at Garšana, located within the Umma province, which belonged to a royal princess, Simat-Ištaran, and her husband, the general and doctor, Šu-Kabta.[59] Estates like this also attest to the contest for local authority between the growing royal and military sector and the traditional urban elites of southern Mesopotamia.[60] During periods of stability and prosperity, this process

---

58. Sharlach 2017.

59. Owen and Mayr 2007; Heimpel 2009; Owen 2011; Kleinerman 2011.

60. For an example of the tension between provincial authorities and crown properties (like the estate at Garšana), see Molina 2010: 210–211.

favored the expansion of royal authority. Major traditional centers, like Nippur, as well as important strategic towns, like Iri-Sagrig, hosted a "who's who" of the extended royal family and their marriage alliances.

Šulgi died in the eleventh month of his forty-eighth year on the throne, and his son Amar-Sin succeeded him. The death of Šulgi remains something of a mystery, and the fact that two of his wives, including Šulgi-simti, died shortly thereafter has led some to see a violent end to his rule. If the reigns of Ur-Namma and Šulgi represented the formative periods of expansion and consolidation of their new kingdom, then the reign of Amar-Sin illustrated the benefits of that consolidation. Little is known about Amar-Sin before he came to the throne, but his year names speak to the now expected mix of active campaigning outside the core of the state, along with frequent attention to his cultic responsibilities and the installation of priests and priestesses. The latter activity again shows the care that the kings of Ur took to install members of the royal family, and loyalists more broadly, in the most significant cultic positions in their community. The crown connected itself directly to the leadership of every critical statewide institution that formed the core of southern Mesopotamian notions of identity and power.

The success of these endeavors is clearest in the surviving administrative documents. Amar-Sin's reign sits at the likely apex of text production in the Ur III period. This era also witnessed the continuing documentation of the delivery of booty and tribute from the king's campaigns across the Zagros Mountains.[61] This stability apparently lasted until Amar-Sin's seventh year. At that point, in several major urban centers of the state, we find new governors installed and the ouster of the hereditary occupants.[62] This may have been an effort by the king to break some of the local bonds of community loyalty that impeded the goal of statewide allegiance, but in many of these cases, the original family soon resumed governorship. During that same year, Amar-Sin hosted a banquet at Ur where his generals swore an oath of loyalty to the king.[63] While such an

---

61. Garfinkle 2014.

62. Allred 2013; for governors and their families, see also Zettler 1994; Dahl 2007.

63. Steinkeller 2008.

event might not have been unusual, it is otherwise unattested in the Ur III archives.

The swearing of oaths in the name of the king, and enforced by the gods, became common in this period on legal and commercial documents. This points to the ways in which the community responded to the growth of royal authority and patronage. At the same time, it was unusual for the king's closest family members, who numbered prominently among the generals, to be asked to renew their loyalty to the monarch. The traditions of southern Mesopotamia emphasized the patrimonial organization of power: property and status were maintained within families and passed down in a patrilineal manner. In many cases this saw professions and offices passed down from father to son, but these were also shared laterally within a generation, and inheritance of office often fell to an individual's brother and not his son.[64] Indeed, the last three kings of the Third Dynasty of Ur were all likely brothers who ruled in turn. Therefore, this moment, when Amar-Sin's generals declared their loyalty, may hint at dynastic tensions within the family and the loyalty of some officials to his brother Šu-Sin. This is made more likely by the fact that Šu-Sin replaced many of the new governors appointed by his brother Amar-Sin, and returned the old families to power.

The last two kings of the Ur III period, Šu-Sin and Ibbi-Sin, oversaw the state's precipitous collapse. The beginning of Šu-Sin's reign witnessed an immediate reduction in the scale of military activity and its rewards. Only two of his nine years were named for victories abroad, and the focus is much more on cultic affairs. This picture is reinforced in the administrative archives, where the delivery of booty, especially livestock, was largely absent prior to his eighth year, which followed an extensive campaign against a restless periphery. The most significant strategic endeavor on which Šu-Sin engaged was his building of the wall in the west to hold back the Tidnum (the name of an Amorite group).[65] The building of the wall was documented in several of his year names, as well as in dedicatory

---

64. Dahl 2007.

65. Michalowski 2011: 122–169.

inscriptions, and in the corpus of royal letters from the Old Babylonian period that were ascribed to the kings of Ur.

In sum, these texts point to a growing concern with the incursions of Amorites into the northern parts of the kingdom's heartland. Šu-Sin's royal inscriptions label them as ravaging people who do not know grain. As we have already seen, Amorite identity was a shifting concept, and remains so in modern scholarship as well,[66] and Amorites found a prominent place at court as allies of the crown,[67] while also figuring in the imagination of the kingdom of Ur as an existential outside threat. The building of the wall commenced in his fourth year. The project involved a massive collection of resources and deployment of labor. The wall was not an unbroken line, but rather a string of fortifications stretching from the edge of the Euphrates up into the Zagros Mountains northwest of the Diyala region.[68] Šu-Sin clearly aimed to regularize the state's control of access to the pasture- and resource-rich lands adjacent to the kingdom. Earlier kings had achieved this through near constant military campaigns, but Šu-Sin appears not to have been able to mount the same robust and regular campaigns. By the time he came to power, however, both his own audience at home and the powers abroad subjected to tribute had come to expect these regular military excursions and the wealth and prestige that they brought into the center. By this time as well, some of these liminal groups had settled in the region now behind the wall and expected the state to make them safe.

These expectations formed the background to the most significant event in Šu-Sin's reign, his campaign to the lands of Šimaški and Zabšali in his seventh year that heralded the short-lived return of deliveries of booty and tribute to state centers like Puzriš-Dagan. His account of this conquest fills a long royal inscription and includes the usual muscular tale of destruction and heroic royal accomplishment, but it is also careful to account for the great variety of booty hauled away. The kingdom's

---

66. Michalowski 2011; 2016; Burke 2020.

67. For foreigners at the court of the kings, see Sharlach 2005.

68. For a sketch map, see Michalowski 2011: 158.

elites expected the transfer of resources from regions like Šimaški, and after the campaigns, the elites at home in southern Mesopotamia could expect continued tribute in the form of livestock, slaves, and foreign goods. The economy of the kingdom could function without this constant infusion of resources, but the prestige economy, on which so much of the power of the Ur kings relied, could not.

An additional, earlier, sign of trouble can be found in Šu-Sin's royal inscriptions documenting his other major campaign, which took place against Simanum in his third year, as a result of a local revolt against the ruler, who was allied by marriage with the royal house of Ur:

> He settled the enemy people, his booty, Simanum, for the god Enlil and the goddess Ninlil, on the frontier of Nippur, he built them a town. He set them apart for Enlil and Ninlil. The god of their town was Šu-Sin. Since the days of decreeing the fates, no king has established a town for the god Enlil and the goddess Ninlil on the frontier of Nippur, with the people he captured.[69]

These captives were not the typical slaves that formed part of the expected booty and who were often donated to royal workshops. This remarkable passage illustrates the difficulties that the kings of Ur encountered in enforcing their authority across the Zagros Mountains when the kings began to campaign less frequently and less successfully. Simanum was a critical foreign land whose native dynasty had been bound to the court at Ur through marriage. Šu-Sin's decision to deport some of the people of Simanum and settle them in the heartland of his kingdom almost certainly was an attempt to prop up the power of a local ruler allied to Ur's royal family,[70] and it may also have been part of the state project of providing allied communities with protection behind the kingdom's fortified marches.

---

69. Frayne 1997: 298.

70. Michalowski 1975.

Šu-Sin died in the tenth month of his ninth year on the throne, and this is recorded in administrative texts that highlighted arrangements for his funeral, as well as for the coronation of his successor, in the major cities of the kingdom: Ur, Uruk, and Nippur. The challenges facing the kingdom had become apparent during the difficult years of Šu-Sin; and Ibbi-Sin found himself unable to restore order. The situation continued to unravel during the first decade of his long reign. He ruled for twenty-four years, but his effective control of the kingdom waned from his third year onward. We find evidence for this in the fact that the archives from major provincial sites were disrupted around that time.[71] Ibbi-Sin's early year names portray no direct evidence of this crisis, and he recorded a successful campaign against Simurrum in his third year. His ninth and fourteenth years detailed campaigns in the east against the growing power of Elam, but there are no other campaigns recorded, and it is clear that the kingdom was on the defensive for most of his reign.

At the same time, the surviving records from the city of Ur continue to illustrate a wealthy society greatly concerned with matters at court. The royal workshops continued to produce luxury goods for the crown, and a rare later copy of one of Ibbi-Sin's royal inscriptions noted that he used booty from his campaign in Susa to commission a gold ceremonial vessel dedicated to Nanna.[72] The king may have had deep pockets, but there are also signs of economic stress in the administrative archives. Increases in prices early in Ibbi-Sin's reign suggest grain shortages at the capital that are astonishing in light of both the agricultural productivity of southern Mesopotamia,[73] and the organizational prowess of the kingdom's administrators. The strategic situation rapidly deteriorated, and all of the available evidence points to a shrinking kingdom that lost control of major urban centers throughout the heartland. In his sixth

---

71. Texts using Ibbi-Sin's year name formulae began to disappear rapidly in major urban centers across the kingdom. The last texts dated to his reign in Ešnunna come from his second year, in Susa from his third, in Girsu from his fifth year, in Umma from his sixth year, and in Nippur from his seventh year.

72. Frayne 1997: 370–371.

73. Gomi 1984.

year, Ibbi-Sin reinforced the walls of Ur and Nippur, but this did not stem the tide of fragmentation.

The letters of the kings of Ur, preserved in Old Babylonian copies, provide direct insight into this deterioration. The letters record Ibbi-Sin's negotiations with his governors to ensure the security of the kingdom and to relieve the food shortages at Ur. In this correspondence, the most significant figure to emerge is Išbi-Erra, the governor of Isin:

> Speak to Ibbi-Sin, my king, saying (the words of) Išbi-Erra, your servant: You gave me orders concerning an expedition from Isin to Kazallu to purchase grain. As the market price was equivalent to (one shekel) per *kor*, twenty talents of silver were invested in the purchase of grain. Word having reached me that hostile Amorites had entered your frontier territory, I proceeded to deliver all the grain . . . into the city of Isin. But now all the Amorites have entered the homeland, and have captured all of the great storehouses, one by one. Because of [these] Amorites, I cannot hand over the grain for threshing; they are too strong for me, and I am made to stay put.[74]

Ibbi-Sin never received the full measure of grain for which he had paid Išbi-Erra, and the latter set himself up as an independent ruler of Isin by the eighth year of Ibbi-Sin's reign. It is not clear at this distance whether Išbi-Erra's bid for independence was opportunistic, or whether he was complicit in allowing the frontier to further disintegrate and hasten the demise of the kingdom of Ur. In either case, by the early years of Ibbi-Sin, the deliveries of tribute from beyond the frontier had stopped, and the state was losing control of the most resource-rich provinces at home, from which it derived the lion's share of its subsistence. The *bala* system on which the kingdom's redistributive economy depended collapsed without the participation of the core cities in southern Mesopotamia, and many of the state's administrators were withdrawn to the city of Ur. Išbi-Erra compounded these problems by taking the city of Nippur

---

74. Michalowski 2011: 417–418.

and depriving the king in Ur of control of the religious center of their community.

Beyond the heartland and to the east, trouble continued to mount as the eastern states, from Šimaški to Anšan, united in their opposition to Ur and gained control of most of southwestern Iran. This development posed the immediate existential threat to Ibbi-Sin's kingdom. The measure of this threat is made clear in the fact that Ibbi-Sin's military campaigns were aimed eastward and not at resuscitating the failing fortunes of his kingdom at home. In spite of his claims of success, we can hear the drumbeat of the approaching Elamite army. His last year names record foreigners bringing war to Ur, and after twenty-four years on the throne, Ibbi-Sin was led away in chains to Susa. The easterners occupied the city after their capture of the king, but they were prevented from advancing further by Išbi-Erra and an Amorite coalition that eventually succeeded in expelling the Elamites from the Mesopotamian heartland. The kingdom of the Third Dynasty of Ur collapsed as a result of a mix of inside and outside pressures, similar in many ways to the fall of the kingdom of Akkad, but what was new were the apparent ambitions of the insiders. Instead of restoring the ancient independence of the city-states, rulers like Išbi-Erra sought to recreate southern Mesopotamian states on the model of the kingdom of Ur.

13.4. *Kings, merchants, and laborers: society and economy in the kingdom of Ur*

The kingdom of the Third Dynasty of Ur thrived as a result of the agricultural wealth of southern Mesopotamia. The political economy of early states in the region was redistributive in nature. The ancient Mesopotamians believed that most of the means of production were "owned" by the divine representatives of the pantheon in each of the urban centers. The evolution of kingship in these city-states saw rulers emerge as the earthly stewards of this divine wealth. This gave kings an enormous amount of control over both the labor and the productivity in each of the individual city-states, and enabled a social hierarchy to develop in which most of the ostensibly free people in these communities were, in reality, dependent laborers who relied on state institutions to provide rations for the support of their families. This pool of dependent laborers formed the foundation of a corvée system on which public works projects, from canals and temples to walls and roads, relied.[75]

This redistributive economy created the expectation that it was normative for the state to receive the lion's share of the agricultural produce. This was true for the earlier city-states, but the scale increased dramatically with the growth of a larger territorial kingdom. Moreover, the state had to address the problem of collection and storage of bulk agricultural commodities. Merchants (Sumerian dam-gar_3) provided some of the solutions to these challenges. Because the commerce in which they engaged frequently necessitated record keeping, the work of merchants is quite well documented, and they have long received significant scholarly attention.[76] They engaged in a wide range of activities, but trade was their primary professional responsibility. The merchants arranged for the purchase or sale of commodities on behalf of their clients.

Merchants provide us with crucial information for the investigation of the political economy in the Ur III period because of their role as intermediaries on behalf of the growing power of the state.[77] Merchants worked on behalf of the state, and they participated in tax collection as well; moreover, merchants and other traders facilitated the import of strategic materials, like copper. The reliance of the state on these individuals demonstrates the value of their specialized knowledge and the symbiotic relationship between their enterprise and the growth of the

---

75. On corvée labor in the Ur III period, see Steinkeller 2013. Many of the urban professionals in this era, such as merchants and smiths, were also subject to periodic corvée obligations alongside the dependent laborers.

76. The long bibliography on merchants in early Mesopotamia includes, for example, Curtis and Hallo 1959; Foster 1997; Powell 1977; Snell 1977; 1982; Neumann 1979; 1992; 1993; 1999; Englund 1990: 13–55; Zettler 1992: 220–226; Steinkeller 2002; 2004; Garfinkle 2004; 2008; 2010; 2012; Feuerherm 2010.

77. Scholars continue to debate the question of whether these merchants were themselves state dependents or whether they acted independently on behalf of their own households, and this is connected to broader debates concerning the nature of the ancient economy. For reviews of these debates, see Garfinkle 2012; Aubet 2013.

kingdoms of early Mesopotamia. Long-distance trade was a critical arena for commercial activity, but in spite of its cultural and even literary significance, the scale of such trade was always dwarfed by local exchange.[78]

The households of ancient Mesopotamia, especially those of the great institutions, had to be able to dispose of their surplus in exchange for necessary goods. Hence, merchants acted on behalf of fishermen, handling the sale of their catch and the payment of their taxes to the central authority, and merchants represented large institutions, such as the temples and the palace, selling their excess produce and acquiring necessary goods. Often, the institutions relied on the merchants for the continued operation of their workshops as well their agrarian endeavors. This was especially the case for workshops that required raw materials not locally available in Mesopotamia. The merchants were able to exercise a great deal of autonomy, despite growing centralization, because their hierarchies, like those of so many professions in early Mesopotamia, were the result of regional and traditional professional organizations that operated beyond the control of the crown.

The kings of Ur turned to the merchants not only to procure necessary trade goods, and to exchange products grown on their estates, but also to collect the taxes owed to the crown. This situation has long been recognized for the succeeding Old Babylonian period,[79] and I suggest that something similar was afoot under the Third Dynasty of Ur. The activities of the merchants on behalf of the palace can be described as tax farming. Tax farming is an arrangement in which the state sells the right to collect taxes to individuals or groups. Much of the evidence for this comes from the provincial archives at Umma and Girsu. The merchants were intimately involved with the *bala* system described earlier (section 13.3).[80] The produce delivered by the provinces in rotation frequently came in

---

78. Foster 1977; Van de Mieroop 2002.

79. Van de Mieroop 1992: 203.

80. Sharlach 2004.

the form of bulk commodities like barley, but it could include regionally specific products as well.[81]

Girsu, as a very large and prosperous region, was assigned two *bala* months. The merchants worked with the *bala* system at both the local and the state levels. At the local level, the merchants helped the provincial authorities arrange for their *bala* payments, and at the state level the merchants collected the *bala* resources and in some cases administered accounts on its behalf.[82] For the merchants of Girsu, there is direct evidence that they were involved in making collections for the *bala*. A group of Girsu documents lists transactions undertaken for the *bala* (Sumerian *bala-še₃*).[83] In these texts, merchants delivered silver for the *bala*, and other merchants most often made the collections. Those merchants then delivered the silver to the central administration. For the best-documented year from which we find these texts, Amar-Sin's Year 5, the merchants of Girsu appear to have provided a set amount that was due in the twelfth month of the year. The regularity of the payments made for the *bala* in Amar-Sin's Year 5 may indicate a negotiated fee owed by the merchants that corresponded to their tax-farming role. The size of the payments made by individual merchants paralleled their placement within the organization of merchants. Most of the merchants who delivered larger payments were elsewhere identified in texts as overseers (Sumerian *ugula*) supervising the work of other merchants.[84] The management of this system was in the hands of the merchants themselves within a professional hierarchy, most often organized along familial lines.

Unfortunately, the brevity of the *bala-še₃* texts makes it difficult for us to establish the precise nature of the transactions that they record, but the prosopographic connections in these texts allow us to draw some further conclusions. A prominent individual named Lu-Utu was a frequent

---

81. This regional specialization was already in place in the Sargonic period; see Foster 1977: 38–39.

82. This process is apparent, for example, in the archive of Turam-ili, a senior Ur III merchant; see Garfinkle 2002; 2008; 2012.

83. Sharlach 2004; Garfinkle 2010.

84. Garfinkle 2008b; 2010.

recipient of silver for the *bala* from the merchants. We encounter Lu-Utu in a number of additional texts that recorded significant deliveries of silver by merchants. The amounts of silver in these texts may indicate a consolidation of smaller deliveries or the results of larger transactions undertaken on his behalf by the merchants. Lu-Utu occupied a significant place in the provincial administration at Girsu, organizing the activity of the merchants on behalf of the governor. Numerous texts record Lu-Utu's receipt of significant amounts of grain from the governor and his transfer of that grain to merchants in exchange for silver.

The expertise and cooperation of these local professionals was required in order for the royal household to effectively collect resources from the local economies. This highlights the complex set of negotiations in which the kings of Ur had to engage in order to both broaden and deepen their management of the state's economy. The royal household used existing social networks to gain more efficient control of resources. In doing so, they afforded great opportunity to urban entrepreneurs, like merchants, and the households they represented. These opportunities worked in both directions, but the urban professionals also took on a great amount of responsibility toward the crown to meet royal demands. Hence, the leaders of professional organizations had liability on behalf of their socio-professional networks. This system also served to coordinate and deploy the vast labor resources of the state. The ability of the kings to carry out the diverse and monumental infrastructure projects described earlier depended on the elites across the kingdom who organized dependent laborers for tasks as varied as canal maintenance and warfare.

13.5. The Third Dynasty of Ur in the wider world: Mari and the west, Elam and the east

The vast administrative archives from the heartland of the kingdom focus our attention on the core of the state, but the evidence from the year names and royal inscriptions show us how important the lands beyond Ur's frontiers were to the kings of the Third Dynasty. We have a tendency to look east, both because that area received the most sustained military attention, and because we know that the final defeat of the kingdom came from that direction. The kings of Ur, however, looked in all directions, and their sustained engagement with upper Euphrates and the road to the upper sea deserves our attention, so we will begin in the west.

The west (Akkadian *Amurru*) was notably the land of the Amorites (Sumerian *kur mar-tu*). The Amorites played a great role in the imagination of the southern Mesopotamians, as their lifestyle was associated most closely with semi-nomadic pastoralism, and this was seen as living outside the norms of settled life in their urban centers. This stark contrast stands out most clearly as a trope in the literary texts and royal inscriptions, and the reality on the ground was much more complex. Amorites can be found among the generals of the Third Dynasty of Ur, as well as among the forces against which those generals deployed the armies of the kingdom. The region of the upper Euphrates and neighboring areas of Syria were also home to numerous cities and kingdoms. Urbanization in Syria may have been disrupted late in the third millennium BC, but there were still great states to contend with and to negotiate with for access to the lucrative trade routes connecting Mesopotamia to the Mediterranean coastline and beyond. The gateway to many of these trade routes was the city of Mari on the great bend of the Euphrates.

Mari was a significant city already before the time of the kings of Akkad, and had likely waged wars before that time with the city of Ebla for regional hegemony. Sargon, or perhaps his grandson Naram-Sin (see chapter 10 in volume 1), conquered Mari and installed military governors (Akkadian *šakkanakku*) there to enforce Akkadian hegemony. When the power of Sargon's kingdom waned, these military governors gained independence and created a dynasty that lasted down to the eighteenth century BC. This dynasty therefore ruled the city during the time of the Third Dynasty of Ur. In contrast to their warring tactics along the eastern frontier, the kings of Ur pursued a more diplomatic approach to the west, and they sought influence in places like Mari almost exclusively through marriage alliances. Ur-Namma set this tone by arranging for his son and heir to marry into the *šakkanakku* dynasty. The result was a period of Ur III domination, but Mari remained autonomous and provided the kings of Ur with access to the Middle Euphrates and its trade routes.

In the same manner that Mesopotamians labeled the west as the land of the Amorites (Sumerian *kur mar-tu*), when they looked east they described the various peoples living there as Elamites; the Sumerian term for a high, elevated place (*nim*) was used as a designation for the east and became a catch-all expression for the people from that region.[85] What is known about the complex political history of the Susiana plain in the modern Iranian province of Khuzestan and its neighboring areas is the subject of chapter 16 in this volume. In the present context, we must stress that our views of these eastern polities for the period in question come to us almost exclusively from a southern Mesopotamian perspective. In contrast to the west, the east remained a significant military focus for the Third Dynasty of Ur throughout its history. This likely stemmed both from the economic and strategic importance of the region, as well as the fact that it was home to peer polities with the Third Dynasty of Ur.

The year names and royal inscriptions of the time show the significance of Anšan and Susa as regional powers. The kings of Ur regarded their urbanized neighbors both as potential threats and as potential allies. Perhaps more importantly, they regarded the cities of Elam and neighboring areas as more familiar territory than the adjacent mountainous terrain in the Zagros toward which they directed so many of their military campaigns. Susa was included among those provinces of the state that received a governor, and both the textual and archaeological records demonstrate that people from Ur were resident in Susa at that time. Again, this highlights the contingent nature of our notions of the state's periphery. Similar to the situation at Mari, the kings of Ur devoted diplomatic attention to the east as well. The royal household secured dynastic marriages with the ruling families of states in the east beyond Susa, such as Anšan, Marhaši, and Simanum.[86] These states controlled access to some of the most important pathways, for both trade and armies, in the ancient Near East; hence, they were trading partners,

---

85. For a discussion of the term "Elam," see Potts 1999: 1–9.

86. Michalowski 1975; Laursen and Steinkeller 2017: 47–62, where they also note diplomatic connections with Makkan; and see later discussion in the present section.

but also potential strategic allies who could help the kings of Ur manage access to southern Mesopotamia and the neighboring Diyala Region. We should not, therefore, be surprised that the kingdom of Ur arose when its armies expelled Puzur-Inšušinak from northern Babylonia, and it collapsed when its armies could not prevent the Elamites from armed incursion into southern Babylonia.

The city of Lagaš occupied a crucial position as one of the principal ports of trade with the east, a portal to both the nearby sea routes in the Persian Gulf that gave access to Susiana, as well as the long-distance networks of the Gulf and beyond.[87] Susa's incorporation into the core of the kingdom of Ur solidified these trade and diplomatic arrangements between southern Mesopotamia and ancient Iran. In addition, some of our best evidence for understanding how texts were actually created and stored in non-institutional contexts during this era comes from the city of Susa. French excavations at Susa in the nineteenth century revealed a great deal of information about its twenty-first-century BC past, and provide us with some of the only Ur III–period texts that have been recovered as a result of controlled archaeological excavation.[88]

The importance of trade with the east is apparent in the emphasis placed on that overseas commerce in the royal inscriptions of Mesopotamia in the late third millennium BC.[89] Dilmun (modern Bahrain), Makkan (modern Oman), and Meluhha (associated in this era with the Indus valley) were critical entrepôts connecting Babylonia with the east going back into the Early Dynastic period (see chapter 8 in volume 1). Makkan was Ur's chief trading partner in the region, though the trade with Dilmun was revitalized during the middle of the twenty-first century BC. As Steffan Laursen and Piotr Steinkeller noted,

---

87. For the importance of the port of Lagaš, and the enormous scale of both trade and troops that transshipped there, see Laursen and Steinkeller 2017: 71–78, where they also highlight the scale of the weaving workshops that provided for much of the Babylonian exports.

88. De Graef 2005; 2008; and also chapter 16 in this volume.

89. For overviews of the economic and strategic relations with the Gulf region, see Potts 1994; Crawford 2013; Laursen and Steinkeller 2017.

As is indicated primarily by the archaeological record, in the Ur III period, Makkan became a major player in the Gulf trade, with a role second only to that of Babylonia. It is fair to say that these two partners monopolized commercial exchanges in the Gulf.[90]

The kingdom of Ur had a large fleet at its disposal, and there is evidence for the shipment of grain to the Gulf region as well. At times the grand vizier organized these transactions, which speaks to their strategic importance to the kingdom.

The kingdom of Ur was located at the nexus of many of the most important crossroads connecting the Indian Ocean world with the Near East and the Mediterranean. Diplomats and merchants moved between distant centers of commerce to advance the strategic goals of the kingdom. The kings of Ur saw threats and opportunities in both the east and the west, and their response to these challenges helped to determine the course of much of their state-building activities. Increasingly, this also meant that soldiers from Ur moved along these pathways as well.

13.6. Militarism and patronage: frontier strategy and the king as shepherd

The kingdom of Ur was an early experiment in larger state-building that relied at home on the charisma and patronage of its kings, and abroad on the ability of those kings to extract tribute and booty from the people who lived along its frontiers and from outlying communities well beyond the boundaries of their kingdom's provinces. The ability to undertake these mandates determined the success or failure of the kings of the Third Dynasty of Ur. As a result, the kings developed strategies to support their household and build a larger sense of community, and their activities along and beyond the frontier served these local and internal interests. The kings of Ur did not have a grand strategy to project their authority directly over outlying communities, but the importance

---

90. Laursen and Steinkeller 2017: 57. Also for Gudea of Lagaš, Makkan was a significant trading partner.

of their aggression toward peripheral groups was an outgrowth of the ideology of kingship that they developed. The frontier served as the new boundary of this larger state. The king's maintenance of this boundary required that he project strength beyond it, while taking care of everything within. This fits in very well with the frequent representation of the king as shepherd.

The concept of the frontier is equally critical to our historical reconstructions of ancient Mesopotamia. This is the place where we imagine both threats and opportunities lay for the growing states of southern Mesopotamia in the third and early second millennia BC. To quote Piotr Michalowski,

> The notion of the frontier is critical to our understanding of salient aspects of the Mesopotamian geographical imagination. A frontier is not a line in the sand but a liminal zone, an area of multifaceted interaction that can unite as much as it separates, and is often the place where new cultural and political orders can establish themselves and grow.[91]

As a result, we can see that the relationship with the frontier informed the development of Mesopotamian conceptions of community and political order, and the kings of Ur used this knowledge in their self-representation.

The frontier was also a wild place. In literature, the highland frontiers were the locus for the activity of mythical creatures, both divine and monstrous. We have already noted that the kings of Ur connected their dynasty to the legendary Gilgamesh of Uruk. Significantly, the *Epic of Gilgamesh* captured themes already present in Ur III society that contrasted the civilization of the urban space and its immediate hinterland with the dangerous places outside of that zone. And yet, it is important to be precise about where the boundaries were placed in the epic tradition between civilization and chaos. In the first tablet, Gilgamesh was

---

91. Michalowski 2011: 127.

reminded of his responsibility to protect the hunters who lived beyond the watered fields; and in his entry into Mesopotamian society, Enkidu took on the task of protecting the shepherds, whose mobile pastoralism often defies our traditional definitions of Mesopotamian space. This takes on added significance with the repeated declaration that the city of Uruk, where Enkidu can take his place among men, is "the Sheepfold."[92] This idea of the sheepfold brings us back to one most frequent epithets for kingship used by the Third Dynasty of Ur: the king as shepherd of the people.

We have already seen the prominent descriptions of the king as shepherd in the "Death of Ur-Namma" (see earlier discussion, section 13.3). This imagery was a rich part of the literary record associated with the Ur III kings. The Šulgi hymns make clear that the king was not only a shepherd of the people, but someone familiar with shepherding. He protected the sheepfold and was the killer of lions too numerous to count. And he was connected not just to shepherding, but also to Gilgamesh: "I am Šulgi, good shepherd of Sumer. Like my brother and friend Gilgamesh, I can recognize the virtuous and I can recognize the wicked."[93]

The king as shepherd also appeared in the royal correspondence that survives in Old Babylonian copies. One of Aradmu's letters to Šulgi names the latter as the "rightful shepherd of the people."[94] In the epilogue to the laws of Ur-Namma, the punishments for erasing the inscription include "may no one build a sheepfold."[95] This is another legacy of late third millennium kingship that informed the concepts common in the beginning of the second millennium BC. We find the king as shepherd highlighted among the royal epithets in the prologues to the

---

92. George 1999: 1.

93. Šulgi C; translation after ETCSL no. 2.4.2.03 (http://etcsl.orinst.ox.ac.uk/cgi-bin/etcsl.cgi?text=t.2.4.2.03#; last accessed March 19, 2020); see also Castellino 1972: 9–242.

94. Michalowski 2011: 341–342.

95. Civil 2011: 252.

so-called Law Codes of the early second millennium BC, issued by kings of Ešnunna and Babylon.[96]

The idea of the king as shepherd tied the deified kings of Ur to their legendary predecessors and to their gods. Nanna, the moon god of the city of Ur, was himself closely associated with livestock. The hymn today known as "Nanna A" ends with the following line:

> Your moonlight is holy and bright, and because like Utu you are
> a shepherd of the Land, Nanna, it shines forth for the king like
> the daylight.[97]

Another hymn to Nanna, today known as "The Herds of Nanna," depicts the god possessing enormous cattle pens, and the text numbers his penned and his wild cows in the hundreds of thousands. Near the end of the text, Nanna received the following praise: "He is ever able to increase the butter of abundance in the holy animal pens."[98] The kings of Ur had a divine mandate to increase the size of their herds, and to protect the pens and pasturelands in which this wealth was maintained.

Hence, the frontier strategy of the kings of Ur connected them directly to the act of being a good shepherd of Sumer. This imagery, and the idea of the king as patron and protector, directly influenced the development of community under the Third Dynasty of Ur. One of the most pressing problems that the Ur rulers faced in consolidating their kingdom was spatial, and here we need to think not only in terms of the physical space required to hand out royal estates, but also in terms of the larger social networks that had to be created to support the larger kingdom. The kings of Ur needed to create room for new constituencies bound to the larger idea of the kingdom, and they needed to find ways to reward those who carried the banner of the dynasty. The military

---

96. Roth 1997: 25, 77.

97. Translation after Black et al. 2004: 143; see also ETCSL no. 4.13.01 (http://etcsl.orinst.ox.ac.uk/cgi-bin/etcsl.cgi?text=t.4.13.01#; last accessed March 19, 2020).

98. Translation after Black et al. 2004: 146; see also ETCSL no. 4.13.06 (http://etcsl.orinst.ox.ac.uk/cgi-bin/etcsl.cgi?text=t.4.13.06#; last accessed March 19, 2020).

arena was the primary area for this royal activity and advancement. The traditional elites in the cities of the heartland, despite their political subordination, remained entrenched players in the local economies, but campaigns beyond the frontier offered opportunity for the new royal elite.[99] As the chronological distribution of their archives demonstrates, the kingdom of Ur, as we know it, was a consequence of the social and economic effects of a state of near constant warfare.

The world created by the dynasty's kings was a martial society engaged in annual campaigning, but the goals of these military forays did not include the outright conquest and administration of frontier zones. The most decisive evidence that we have that the kingdom of Ur was not imperial in nature comes from the most frequent and mundane historical evidence at hand: the year names. The year names demonstrate that frequent warfare was critical to the dynasty's measures of its own success and prowess, but the year names also show that these campaigns failed to achieve the permanency associated with conquest. The kings of Ur went to war virtually every year of the kingdom, or at least they went on campaigns annually, and these campaigns were frequently directed against the same places year after year.[100]

The campaigns of the kings, which became virtually annual midway through Šulgi's reign, allowed for the creation of new social networks and new sources of wealth. The latter was especially important both to the kings and the royal elite. Wealth from beyond the frontier provided new pathways to privilege through patronage in an agrarian environment that was already constrained in alluvial Mesopotamia. As Marc Van de Mieroop recently noted,

> In pre-industrial societies agriculture was the basis of the economy and most of it was subsistence agriculture in autarkic village communities and manors. There was very little surplus for trade

---

99. Garfinkle 2015: 157–160.

100. Michalowski 2011; Garfinkle 2014.

in foodstuffs and fibers and whenever such trade existed, it was under the auspices of central institutions.[101]

This is a crucial reminder that the fields of barley, which made urban life possible for the great cities of Mesopotamia, did not immediately translate into portable wealth.

The tremendous herds of sheep and goats provided a great measure of the wealth that drove commerce in early Mesopotamia. One of the most notable features of the surviving administrative archives is the prominence of livestock and their movement between households and institutions. The repeated military raids across the frontier, documented most clearly in the year names and administrative texts, brought in a great amount of livestock, as well as slaves. The former added to the enormous institutional herds of the kingdom, while the latter provided labor in the workshops that processed the wool and hair into textiles. The texts from Puzriš-Dagan frequently document this new wealth as booty, tribute, and offerings from groups of men associated with the royal and military sector.

These delivery lists show how the core constituents of the new state were brought together on these tablets in a system of patronage. The lists of notables offering animals to the crown at Puzriš-Dagan, which might bring together governors, merchants, and Amorite dignitaries, memorialized their participation in this reciprocal arrangement. The lists were acts of commemoration. In light of the deification of the kings of Ur, this language takes on added significance. Indeed, they were delivering actual sheep to their royal shepherd. This new wealth was founded on the activities of two significant groups that were central to the expanded notion of state and community: soldiers and shepherds. The soldiers carried out the raids that led to the acquisition of all of this booty and tribute. The shepherds were responsible for safeguarding all of this newfound bounty. And ultimately, the kings of the Third Dynasty of Ur presented themselves as patrons to both groups (figure 13.6).

---

101. Van de Mieroop 2015: 80.

FIGURE 13.6. Greenstone cylinder seal of Ur-Namma of Ur and its modern impression, showing a governor being presented before the king. British Museum, Department of the Middle East, BM 89126. Courtesy of the Trustees of the British Museum.

The frontier strategy of the kings of Ur consisted of the idea of the state as sheepfold. The building of the line of fortifications that composed Šulgi's wall of the frontier (Sumerian *bad₃ ma-da*) was about the expansion of the sheepfold.[102] The basic premise of the city-state as the normative, and largely self-sufficient, political community in southern Mesopotamia was cast aside now that the kings of Ur oversaw a much larger community that required an extensive hinterland and had to incorporate new groups, whether the Amorites who joined the kingdom, or those settled within it, as Šu-Sin had done with some of the people of Simanum. The kings of Ur expanded the size of their state community in many ways. The physical expansion of the kingdom envisioned here was not imperial conquest. Instead, the kingdom took on an expanded need to protect communities of mobile pastoralists and the different environmental zones to which they needed access: lowlands, steppe, and highlands. Significantly, the wealth that was in their care was central to the system of patronage on which Ur's royal power depended.

If we view Šulgi's engagements with locations like Simurrum as acts of conquest, then the repeated return to the same place smacks of failure,

---

102. Michalowski 2011: 122.

which was hardly a claim that Šulgi would have had inscribed on thousands of texts bearing the year named for his ninth defeat of Simurrum. If we see these campaigns as raids, then they take on significance as the boasts of a king who could repeatedly ravage the same countryside and bring home booty to be spread among the court's clients.

The kings of Ur and their elites had a great deal of their wealth in the care of shepherds. Anne Porter pointed out that for the vast herds accounted for in the Ur III administrative archives,

> [i]t is inconceivable that even a significant portion of the numbers of animals implied here would be herded as locally as the perimeters of the irrigated lands that constitute the locale of these city states, for several reasons. Contested land usage and issues of carrying capacity are but two.[103]

This highlights the dual problems that the kings of Ur sought to solve with their raids in the highlands. Within the old established heartland of Mesopotamia, there was less room for them to maneuver. They could not upset the traditional local and regional hierarchies and patterns of land use without undermining the local economies, and the principles of status on which their own power was based. So they needed new room for social networks bound directly to the crown. They also needed additional sources of wealth to support their royal endeavors and the new royal elites. The emphasis on military campaigning and booty solved both of these problems, but it not only relied on the success of the kings, it also created the problem of what to do to safeguard the animals. The areas to the east in which Šulgi campaigned "were, and still are, prime pastoralist territory."[104] Indeed, good pasturage can still be found in much of what we regard as the frontier zone.

Following Piotr Michalowski, it is no coincidence that the wall of the frontier was built in the years immediately preceding the construction

---

103. Porter 2012: 243.

104. Porter 2012: 296.

of Puzriš-Dagan.[105] The line of fortifications was designed to protect the expanded sheepfold that was the Ur III kingdom and to provide opportunities to collect and protect more tribute and booty. The expansion of the fortifications under Šu-Sin shows how important this idea was, but also how fragile. In this view, Iri-Sagrig, home to a dizzying array of soldiers, messengers, and merchants at the edge of the Diyala, became the prime city at the inner edge of this operational zone for organizing and staging the campaigns into the east, and for managing the wealth that these raids produced. The success of this enterprise became the fuel on which the kingdom ran, both practically and ideologically.

The walls built by both Šulgi and Šu-Sin served primarily to create a divider between land that was under the protection of the king, and the wild lands on the other side. In Šulgi's day, this was a successful venture, providing a staging ground for numerous raids into the lands beyond the frontier and providing protection for the growing flocks and their pasturelands. Šu-Sin's efforts, by contrast, were an ambitious failure. After all, it is clear that building walls and securing the sheepfold had tremendous symbolic value to the kings of Ur, and the successes of Šulgi and Amar-Sin created herds and allies, especially in the Diyala region, that needed to be secured. But the rest of the textual evidence from Šu-Sin's reign suggests that he did not secure this area, nor was he able as consistently as his predecessors to raid the lands beyond the frontier and bring back both the victories and the riches that the state and its elites required.

Michalowski and others have shown that for the late third millennium BC there was no Amorite phenomenon that we can regard in a monolithic manner.[106] Amorites were insiders and outsiders when viewed from the royal court of Ur, where individuals with this label occupied crucial positions. For Amorites in the Ur III period, their lived experiences ranged from being the expected mobile pastoralists to being settled and, in some cases, senior members of urban communities

---

105. Michalowski 2011: 133.

106. Michalowski 2011; 2016; Burke 2020.

in southern Mesopotamia. Significantly, many of them must have lived and worked in and behind the frontier, on the protected side of the fortifications.

We are left with the question of why Šu-Sin built his wall to hold back one of these Amorite groups, the Tidnum. Some modern observers envision this situation as the traditional conflict between the settled and the nomad, between the desert and the sown. In this way, the Tidnum have stood, in our minds, for a larger Amorite collective identity, and this is an idea we should challenge. The Tidnum may simply have been an unallied group of mobile pastoralists who needed to be kept out of the expanded sheepfold of the Ur III kingdom; and who were regarded quite separately from the Amorites who already served inside that kingdom. In my view, some allied pastoralists received shelter behind the fortifications, while others were kept at bay. And it makes sense that all of this was taking place within the Amorite lands along the frontier zone because of the herds and pasturelands there, the control of which had become embedded in notions of space and identity in the Ur III kingdom. Here we can return to the lamentation over the fall of Ur with which we began this chapter. When the gods broke up the power of the people of Nanna, the divine protector of the city of Ur, the text lamented the leveling of the sheepfold, and the breaking of the unity of those people, who were described as numerous as ewes. Further, Ibbi-Sin, their shepherd, was led away in bonds. This description of disruption and chaos was rooted in the imagery of the sheepfold that I have been examining.

Ultimately, to better understand the goals, military and otherwise, of the royal household in this early experimental state, we have to re-envision what the projection of state power meant to kings like Šulgi, Amar-Sin, and Šu-Sin. Instead of an expansive empire, seeking direct control of outlying peoples, places, and polities, I am arguing that the kings of Ur sought a larger notion of political community than the earlier city-states, in which they could create new space, both ideologically and on the ground, in which an expanded royal elite could operate and through which they could protect their divinely sanctioned positions and their property. This larger state was bounded by a notion of the frontier as both a physical and cultural boundary. This boundary was not impermeable, but the kings of Ur sought to control access to the frontier. Significantly, this means that as the kings of the four quarters, the rulers of Ur were not articulating a notion of limitless power over the whole world, but instead they were asserting complete power over their world, over the four quarters of southern Mesopotamia.

Therefore, the defense zone of the kingdom of Ur is transformed into an operational zone. The Third Dynasty of Ur moved the locus of conflict squarely to the edges of their kingdom, and used the resulting conflicts to reinforce their ideologies of kingship, and, as shepherds, to protect the resulting kingdom. This operational zone was also a place in which room was created for the royal military elite to exercise their new roles and to extract the resources that enriched the kingdom and allowed for patronage to be richly bestowed and rewarded.[107] These activities did not require the conquest and administration of established foreign polities, but they were underpinned by regular successful campaigns. These raids beyond the frontier filled the pastures of the sheepfold with animals, staffed the vast weaving establishments, and brought both wealth and renown to the kings of Ur. The shift in strategy in Šu-Sin's reign, the emphasis on building a larger wall, represents an attempt to safeguard this zone and its pasturelands in an environment of diminished resources combined with more established resistance in the east.

The focus of royal military activity in the operational zone of the frontier opened up new space, but also brought in new resources, herds, and people, all of which had to be carefully shepherded by the kings. The eventual fall of the kingdom resulted from failures inside the state as much as it did from outside intervention. Certainly, the frontier policies of the kings of Ur created resistance, but this came more from established polities across the Zagros and in modern Iran than from the Amorites to the west. Finally, Šu-Sin, and after him Ibbi-Sin, proved unable to carry on the required regular campaigning beyond the frontier and to maintain the greater sheepfold that their predecessors had created.

---

107. This notion of the frontier as an operational zone is consistent with earlier discussions of the Sumerian term *mada* by Michalowski 1978; 2011; Maeda 1992.

13.7. Conclusion and aftermath

The kings of Ur acknowledged no limit to their talents, to their martial ferocity, and to their relationship with the gods, but none of this implies that they understood their authority to be limitless on the ground. Indeed, the royal hymns bear this out. Certainly the kings were mighty warriors, and Šulgi claimed to have "placed a yoke on the neck of Elam,"[108] but for the most part the kings meted out destruction and came home with lapis lazuli, a particularly good metaphor for loot. The kings of Ur, and their armies of clients, went to war to protect their kingdom and to expand its coffers. The policies of the kings in maintaining dynastic alliances with powerful families in the periphery fit in nicely with the idea that they recognized the limits of their political reach.

The ephemeral nature of Ur's military presence in the periphery matched the temporary conditions of the tributary economy in the heartland. In spite of the claims made by our texts, both in their content and in their numbers, the kingdom of Ur was a short-lived state. Once the ability and charisma of the kings began to fade, they could no longer raid the periphery with impunity and feed the system of patronage they had established at home.

In a recent treatment of early Mesopotamia, Robert Adams stated, "Ur III was aggressively successful as an empire for a half-century or so."[109] While I obviously would prefer a different label for this success than "empire," I agree with his diagnosis that the failures of the state arose from this brief period of accomplishment. Both Adams and Norman Yoffee noted that the Third Dynasty of Ur was successful in spite of the absence of real centralized institutions of government, rather than because of them.[110] The crown in this era was good at extracting resources, at home and abroad, and at diverting those resources to the

---

108. This and the following quote are from Šulgi B; translation after ETCSL no. 2.4.2.02 (http://etcsl.orinst.ox.ac.uk/cgi-bin/etcsl.cgi?text=t.2.4.2.02#; last accessed March 19, 2020); see also Castellino 1972: 243–294.

109. Adams 2009: 3.

110. Yoffee 1995: 295–296.

growing royal family and its clients. In all of these endeavors, the kings relied on local and regional elites who could be co-opted by this system of patronage. A large scribal administration came into existence more to document these activities than to manage them. These administrators had to ensure that the resources were being registered and properly distributed. The vast extant archives are proof of the temporary success of the court and its clients, but the texts show us the limits of this power, rather than exemplifying the creation of new instruments of government administration.

Kings like Šulgi encouraged the development of statewide structures, but they did not create a firm institutional foundation to provide stability for those structures. Establishing more statewide institutions ran into both ideological and practical problems. It was one thing to assume greater control over the temple estates in the various cities, but it would have been impossible to dissociate them from the regional social networks in which they were embedded. There was also little room in the traditional hierarchies of the provinces to reward crown dependents. This encouraged the kings to look toward centralizing structures, but the prevailing incentives to retain hereditary privileges undermined the effectiveness of these efforts. The army was the only statewide institution to break entirely free of local control, but it was nonetheless characterized by the persistence of familial control of offices, and it was also dependent upon the continuation of past military successes. Adams envisioned the situation as follows:

> Here we see not the densely occupied landscape under overall royal management such as has sometimes been proposed, but the outward scattering of the royal progeny into model townships with royal largess (and hapless provincial support as well) but little evidence of the intended transfer of accompanying, more serious responsibilities. The suspicion thus lurks that Sumerian šagina may sometimes have signified a hereditary rank, like lord or marquess, and only secondarily (or not at all) as general.[111]

---

111. Adams 2009: 4.

We need only include the clients of the state alongside these royal progeny and we now have a clear view of both the successes of the kingdom of
the Third Dynasty of Ur, as well as a greater understanding of its limited
duration.

The image of kingship forged by the kings of Ur proved more durable
in Mesopotamian historical memory, at least into the first half of the second millennium BC. The kings of Isin, Larsa, Ešnunna, and Babylon (see
chapters 14, 16, and 18 in this volume), among others, fought to capture
this legacy and found new kingdoms in southern Mesopotamia based
on this new idea of a larger political community—the four quarters of
their world.

REFERENCES

Adams, R.McC. 2006. Shepherds at Umma in the Third Dynasty of Ur: inter-
locutors with a world beyond the scribal field of ordered vision. *Journal of
the Economic and Social History of the Orient* 49: 133–169.
Adams, R.McC. 2008. An interdisciplinary overview of a Mesopotamian city
and its hinterlands. *CDLJ* 2008: no. 1. Retrieved from https://cdli.ucla.
edu/pubs/cdlj/2008/cdlj2008_001.html (last accessed 29 May 2021).
Adams, R.McC. 2009. Old Babylonian networks of urban notables. *CDLJ*
2009: no. 7. Retrieved from https://cdli.ucla.edu/pubs/cdlj/2009/
cdlj2009_007.html (last accessed 29 May 2021).
Allred, L. 2006. *Cooks and kitchens: centralized food production in late third
millennium Mesopotamia.* PhD dissertation, Johns Hopkins University,
Baltimore, MD.
Allred, L. 2013. The tenure of provincial governors. In Garfinkle, S.J., and
Molina, M. (ed.), *From the 21st century BC to the 21st century AD: proceed-
ings of the international conference on Neo-Sumerian studies.* Winona Lake,
IN: Eisenbrauns, 115–121.
Aubet, M. 2013. *Commerce and colonization in the ancient Near East.*
Cambridge: Cambridge University Press.
Black, J., Cunningham, G., Robson, E., and Zolyomi, G. 2004. *The literature
of ancient Sumer.* Oxford: Oxford University Press.
Burke, A. 2020. *The Amorites and the Bronze Age Near East: the making of a
regional identity.* Cambridge: Cambridge University Press.

Castellino, G. 1972. *Two Šulgi hymns (BC)*. Rome: Istituto di studi del Vicino Oriente.

Civil, M. 2011. The law collection of Ur-Namma. In George, A.R. (ed.), *Cuneiform royal inscriptions and related texts in the Schøyen Collection*. Bethesda, MD: CDL Press: 221–286.

Cooper, J. 1983. *The curse of Agade*. Baltimore, MD: Johns Hopkins University Press.

Crawford, H. 2013. Trade in the Sumerian world. In Crawford, H. (ed.), *The Sumerian world*. London and New York: Routledge, 447–461.

Culbertson, L.E. 2009. *Dispute resolution in the provincial courts of the Third Dynasty of Ur*. PhD dissertation, University of Michigan, Ann Arbor.

Curtis, J., and Hallo, W.W. 1959. Money and merchants in Ur III. *Hebrew Union College Annual* 30: 103–139.

Dahl, J. 2007. *The ruling family of Ur III Umma: a prosopographical analysis of an elite family in southern Iraq 4000 years ago*. Leiden: NINO.

Dahl, J. 2010. Naming Ur III years. In Kleinerman, A., and Sasson, J.M. (eds.), *Why should someone who knows something conceal it? Cuneiform studies in honor of David I. Owen*. Bethesda, MD: CDL Press, 85–93.

De Graef, K. 2005. *Les archives d'Igibuni: les documents Ur III du chantier B à Suse*. Ghent: University of Ghent.

De Graef, K. 2008. Rest in pieces: the archive of Igibuni. In Garfinkle, S.J., and Johnson, C. (eds.), *The growth of an early state in Mesopotamia: studies in Ur III administration*. Madrid: Consejo Superior de Investigaciones Científicas: 225–234.

Edzard, D.O. 1997. *The royal inscriptions of Mesopotamia: early periods, vol. 3/1: Gudea and his dynasty*. Toronto: University of Toronto Press.

Englund, R.K. 1990. *Organisation und Verwaltung der Ur III-Fischerei*. Berlin: Reimer.

Feuerherm, K. 2010. The *tamkar* network from Ur III to Rim-Sîn. *Journal of the Canadian Society for Mesopotamian Studies* 5: 5–12.

Foster, B.R. 1977. "Commercial activity in Sargonic Mesopotamia." *Iraq* 39: 31–44.

Foster, B.R. 1997. A Sumerian merchant's account of the Dilmun trade. *Acta Sumerologica* 19: 53–62.

Frayne, D.R. 1993. *The royal inscriptions of Mesopotamia: early periods, vol. 2: Sargonic and Gutian periods (2234–2113 BC)*. Toronto: University of Toronto Press.

Frayne, D.R. 1997. *The royal inscriptions of Mesopotamia: early periods, vol. 3: Ur III period (2112–2004 BC)*. Toronto: University of Toronto Press.

Garfinkle, S.J. 2002. Turam-ili and the community of merchants in the Ur III period. *JCS* 54: 29–48.

Garfinkle, S.J. 2004. Shepherds, merchants, and credit: some observations on lending practices in Ur III Mesopotamia. *Journal of the Economic and Social History of the Orient* 47: 1–30.

Garfinkle, S.J. 2008. Silver and gold: merchants and the economy of the Ur III state. In Michalowski, P. (ed.), *On Ur III times: studies in honor of Marcel Sigrist*. Boston: The American Schools of Oriental Research, 63–70.

Garfinkle, S.J. 2010. Merchants and state formation in early Mesopotamia. In Slotsky, A., and Melville, S. (eds.), *Opening the tablet box: Near Eastern studies in honor of Benjamin R. Foster*. Leiden: Brill, 185–202.

Garfinkle, S.J. 2012. *Entrepreneurs and enterprise in early Mesopotamia: a study of three archives from the Third Dynasty of Ur*. Bethesda, MD: CDL Press.

Garfinkle, S.J. 2013. The Third Dynasty of Ur and the limits of state power. In Garfinkle, S.J., and Molina, M. (eds.), *From the 21st century BC to the 21st century AD: proceedings of the international conference on Neo-Sumerian studies*. Winona Lake, IN: Eisenbrauns, 153–167.

Garfinkle, S.J. 2014. The economy of warfare in southern Iraq at the end of the third millennium BC. In Neumann, H., et al. (eds.), *Krieg und Frieden im alten Vorderasien*. Münster: Ugarit-Verlag, 353–362.

Garfinkle, S.J. 2015. Ur III administrative texts: building blocks of state community. In Delnero, P., and Lauinger, J. (eds.), *Texts and contexts: the circulation and transmission of cuneiform texts in social space*. Berlin: De Gruyter: 143–165.

George, A.R. 1999. *The Epic of Gilgamesh*. London: Penguin.

Gomi, T. 1984. On the critical economic situation at Ur early in the reign of Ibbisin. *JCS* 36: 211–242.

Hallo, W.W. 1972. The house of Ur-Meme. *JNES* 31: 87–95.

Hammer, E. 2019. The city and landscape of Ur: aerial, satellite, and ground reassessment. *Iraq* 81: 173–206.

Heimpel, W. 2009. *Workers and construction work at Garšana*. Bethesda, MD: CDL Press.

Jacobsen, T. 1939. *The Sumerian King List*. Chicago: The Oriental Institute of the University of Chicago.

Kleinerman, A. 2011. Doctor Shu-Kabta's family practice. In Kleinerman, A., and Sasson, J.M. (eds.), *Why should someone who knows something conceal it? Cuneiform studies in honor of David I. Owen.* Bethesda, MD: CDL Press, 177–181.

Lafont, B. 2009. The army of the kings of Ur: the textual evidence. *CDLJ* 2009: no. 5. Retrieved from https://cdli.ucla.edu/file/publications/cdlj2009_005.pdf (last accessed 29 May 2021).

Lafont, B., and Westbrook, R. 2003. Neo-Sumerian period (Ur III). In Westbrook, R. (ed.), *A history of ancient Near Eastern law.* Leiden: Brill, 183–226.

Laursen, S., and Steinkeller, P. 2017. *Babylonia, the Gulf region, and the Indus: archaeological and textual evidence for contact in the third and early second millennia BC.* Winona Lake, IN: Eisenbrauns.

Maeda, T. 1992. The defense zone during the rule of the Ur III dynasty. *Acta Sumerologica* 14: 135–172.

Marchesi, G. 2012. Ur-Nammâ(k)'s conquest of Susa. In De Graef, K., and Tavernier, J. (eds.), *Susa and Elam: archaeological, philological, historical and geographical perspectives.* Leiden: Brill, 285–291.

Michalowski, P. 1975. The bride of Simanum. *JAOS* 95: 716–719.

Michalowski, P. 1978. Foreign tribute to Sumer in the Ur III period. *ZA* 68: 34–49.

Michalowski, P. 1989. *The lamentation over the destruction of Sumer and Ur.* Winona Lake, IN: Eisenbrauns.

Michalowski, P. 1991. Charisma and control: on continuity and change in early Mesopotamian bureaucratic systems. In Gibson, McG., and Biggs, R. (eds.), *The organization of power: aspects of bureaucracy in the ancient Near East.* Chicago: The Oriental Institute of the University of Chicago, 45–58.

Michalowski, P. 2011. *The correspondence of the kings of Ur: an epistolary history of an ancient Mesopotamian kingdom.* Winona Lake, IN: Eisenbrauns.

Michalowski, P. 2013. Networks of authority and power in Ur III times. In Garfinkle, S.J., and Molina, M. (eds.), *From the 21st century BC to the 21st century AD: proceedings of the international conference on Neo-Sumerian studies.* Winona Lake, IN: Eisenbrauns, 169–206.

Michalowski, P. 2016. The Ur III literary footprint and the historian. In Bartoloni, G., and Biga, G. (eds.), *Not only history: proceedings of a conference in honor of Mario Liverani.* Winona Lake, IN: Eisenbrauns.

Molina, M. 2008. The corpus of Neo-Sumerian tablets: an overview. In Garfinkle, S.J., and Johnson, C. (eds.), *The growth of an early state in*

Mesopotamia: studies in Ur III administration. Madrid: Consejo Superior de Investigaciones Científicas, 19–53.

Molina, M. 2010. Court records from Umma. In Kleinerman, A., and Sasson, J.M. (eds.), *Why should someone who knows something conceal it? Cuneiform studies in honor of David I. Owen*. Bethesda, MD: CDL Press, 201–217.

Neumann, H. 1979. Handel und Händler in der Zeit der III. Dynastie von Ur. *AoF* 6: 15–67.

Neumann, H. 1992. Zur privaten Geschäftstätigkeit in Nippur in der Ur III-Zeit. In de Jong Ellis, M. (ed.), *Nippur at the centennial*. Philadelphia: University of Pennsylvania Museum of Archaeology and Anthropology, 161–176.

Neumann, H. 1993. Zu den Geschäften des Kaufmanns Ur-Dumuzida aus Umma. *AoF* 20: 69–86.

Neumann, H. 1999. Ur-Dumuzida and Ur-Dun: reflections on the relationship between state-initiated foreign trade and private economic activity in Mesopotamia towards the end of the third millennium BC. In Dercksen, J.G. (ed.), *Trade and finance in ancient Mesopotamia*. Istanbul: Nederlands Historisch-Archeologisch Instituut, 43–53.

Owen, D.I. (ed.) 2011. *Garšana studies*. Bethesda, MD: CDL Press.

Owen, D.I. 2013. The archive of Iri-Saĝrig/Āl-Šarrākī: a brief survey. In Garfinkle, S.J., and Molina, M. (eds.), *From the 21st century BC to the 21st century AD: proceedings of the international conference on Neo-Sumerian studies*. Winona Lake, IN: Eisenbrauns, 89–104.

Owen, D.I., and Mayr, R.H. 2007. *The Garšana archives*. Bethesda, MD: CDL Press.

Porter, A. 2012. *Mobile pastoralism and the formation of Near Eastern civilizations: weaving together society*. Cambridge: Cambridge University Press.

Potts, D.T. 1999. *The archaeology of Elam: formation and transformation of an ancient Iranian state*. Cambridge: Cambridge University Press.

Potts, T.F. 1994. *Mesopotamia and the east: an archaeological and historical study of foreign relations c. 3400–2000 BC*. Oxford: Oxford University Committee for Archaeology.

Powell, M. 1977. Sumerian merchants and the problem of profit. *Iraq* 39: 23–30.

Richardson, S. 2012. Early Mesopotamia: the presumptive state. *Past & Present* 215: 3–49.

Roth, M.T. 1997. *Law collections from Mesopotamia and Asia Minor*. Atlanta, GA: Scholars Press.

Sallaberger, W. 1999. Ur III Zeit. In Attinger, P., and Wäfler, M. (eds.), *Mesopotamien: Akkade-Zeit und Ur III-Zeit*. Fribourg: Academic Press; Göttingen: Vandenhoeck & Ruprecht, 121–414.

Sallaberger, W., and Schrakamp, I. 2015. Philological data for a historical chronology of Mesopotamia of the third millennium. In Sallaberger, W., and Schrakamp, I. (eds.), *Associated regional chronologies for the ancient Near East and the Eastern Mediterranean, vol. 3: history & philology*. Turnhout: Brepols, 1–136.

Sharlach, T.M. 2004. *Provincial taxation and the Ur III state*. Leiden: Brill.

Sharlach, T.M. 2005. Diplomacy and the rituals of politics at the Ur III court. *JCS* 57: 17–29.

Sharlach, T.M. 2017. *An ox of one's own: royal wives and religion at the court of the Third Dynasty of Ur*. Berlin: De Gruyter.

Sigrist, M. 1992. *Drehem*. Bethesda, MD: CDL Press.

Snell, D. 1977. The activities of some merchants of Umma. *Iraq* 39: 45–50.

Snell, D. 1982. *Ledgers and prices: early Mesopotamian balanced accounts*. New Haven, CT: Yale University Press.

Steinkeller, P. 1991. The administrative and economic organization of the Ur III state: the core and the periphery. In Gibson, McG., and Biggs, R. (eds.), *The organization of power: aspects of bureaucracy in the ancient Near East*. Chicago: The Oriental Institute of the University of Chicago, 15–33.

Steinkeller, P. 2002. Money lending practices in Ur III Babylonia: the issue of economic motivation. In Hudson, M., and Van de Mieroop, M. (eds.), *Debt and economic renewal in the ancient Near East*. Bethesda, MD: CDL Press, 109–137.

Steinkeller, P. 2003a. Archival practices at Babylonia in the third millennium. In Brosius, M. (ed.), *Ancient archives and archival traditions: concepts of record-keeping in the ancient world*. Oxford: Oxford University Press, 37–56.

Steinkeller, P. 2003b. An Ur III manuscript of the Sumerian King List. In Sallaberger, W., Volk, K., and Zgoll, A. (eds.), *Literatur, Politik, und Recht in Mesopotamien: Festschrift für Claus Wilcke*. Wiesbaden: Harrassowitz, 267–292.

Steinkeller, P. 2004. Towards a definition of private economic activity in third millennium Babylonia. In Rollinger, R., and Ulf, C. (eds.), *Commerce and monetary systems in the ancient world*. Stuttgart: Steiner, 91–114.

Steinkeller, P. 2008. Joys of cooking in Ur III Babylonia. In Michalowski, P. (ed.), *On the Third Dynasty of Ur: studies in honor of Marcel Sigrist*. Boston: The American Schools of Oriental Research, 185–192.

Steinkeller, P. 2012. Puzur-Inšušinak at Susa: a pivotal episode of early Elamite history reconsidered. In De Graef, K., and Tavernier, J. (eds.), *Susa and Elam: archaeological, philological, historical and geographical perspectives*. Leiden: Brill, 293–317.

Steinkeller, P. 2013. Corvée labor in Ur III Times. In Garfinkle, S.J., and Molina, M. (eds.), *From the 21st century BC to the 21st century AD: proceedings of the international conference on Neo-Sumerian studies*. Winona Lake, IN: Eisenbrauns, 347–424.

Steinkeller, P. 2017. *History, texts and art in early Babylonia*. Berlin: De Gruyter.

Tsouparopoulou, C. 2008. *The material face of bureaucracy: writing, sealing, and archiving tablets for the Ur III state at Drehem*. PhD dissertation, University of Cambridge.

Tsouparopoulou, C. 2013. A reconstruction of the Puzrish-Dagan central livestock agency. *CDLJ* 2013: no. 2. Retrieved from https://cdli.ucla.edu/pubs/cdlj/2013/cdlj2013_002.html (last accessed 29 May 2021).

Van de Mieroop, M. 1992. *Society and enterprise in Old Babylonian Ur*. Berlin: Reimer.

Van de Mieroop, M. 1997. Why did they write on clay? *Klio* 79: 7–18.

Van de Mieroop, M. 2002. In search of prestige: foreign contacts and the rise of an elite in early dynastic Babylonia. In Ehrenberg, E. (ed.), *Essays on the ancient Near East and Egypt in honor of Donald P. Hansen*. Winona Lake, IN: Eisenbrauns, 125–138.

Van de Mieroop, M. 2015. Production and commerce in the Old Babylonian period. *Rivista di Storia Economica* 31: 79–96.

Widell, M. 2004. The calendar of Neo-Sumerian Ur and its political significance. *CDLJ* 2004: no. 2. Retrieved from https://cdli.ucla.edu/file/publications/cdlj2004_002.pdf (last accessed 29 May 2021).

Wilcke, C. 1989. Genealogical and geographical thought in the Sumerian King List. In Behrens, H., Loding, D., and Roth, M.T. (eds.), *dumu-e2-dub-ba-a: studies in honor of Åke W. Sjoberg*. Philadelphia: University of Pennsylvania Museum of Archaeology and Anthropology, 557–571.

Wilcke, C. 2007. *Early ancient Near Eastern law: a history of beginnings*. Winona Lake, IN: Eisenbrauns.

Wilcke, C. 2011. Eine Weihinschrift Gudeas von Lagaš mit altbabylonischer Übersetzung. In George, A.R. (ed.), *Cuneiform royal inscriptions and related texts in the Schøyen Collection*. Bethesda, MD: CDL Press, 29–47.

Yoffee, N. 1995. Political economy in early Mesopotamian states. *Annual Review of Anthropology* 24: 281–311.

Yoffee, N. 2005. *Myths of the archaic state*. Cambridge: Cambridge University Press.

Zettler, R.L. 1992. *The Ur III temple of Inanna at Nippur: the operation and organisation of urban religious institutions in Mesopotamia in the late third millennium BC*. Berlin: Reimer.

Zettler, R.L. 1994. The genealogy of the house of Ur-Me-me: a second look. *AfO* 31: 1–9.

14

The Middle East after the Fall of Ur

ISIN AND LARSA

Klaus Wagensonner

14.1. Introduction

The decline and subsequent collapse of the tightly bureaucratized and
centralized kingdom of Ur (ca. 2112–2004 BC; see chapter 13 in this
volume) made room for a number of opportunists to establish local
dynasties in the areas formerly held by Ur.[1] Already in the early phase of
Ibbi-Sin's reign we see territories and cities falling away from Ur's control.
Many of the events and causes that led to the end of the Third Dynasty
of Ur (Ur III) lie still in the shadows, which is to a certain degree due
to the scarcity of sources.[2] This chapter surveys the historical, political,
social, and economic changes in southern Mesopotamia after the decline
of the kingdom of Ur (figure 14.1). The fragmented political landscape

---

1. The following online resources are referenced in this chapter: CDLI = Cuneiform
Digital Library Initiative: http://cdli.ucla.edu; ETCSL = Electronic Text
Corpus of Sumerian Literature: http://etcsl.orinst.ox.ac.uk (last accessed August
25, 2020).

2. Michalowski 2011: 175.

Klaus Wagensonner, *The Middle East after the Fall of Ur* In: *The Oxford History of the Ancient Near East.*
Edited by: Karen Radner, Nadine Moeller, and D. T. Potts, Oxford University Press. © Oxford University
Press 2022. DOI: 10.1093/oso/9780190687571.003.0014

and ever-changing shifts in the territorial maps in the first two centuries of the second millennium BC resulted in a rather fluid historical period.

Two city-states, in particular, influenced the political landscape in this period: Isin and Larsa. Isin, the city of the goddess of healing, Gula, or Nin-Isina ("Lady of Isin"), was chosen to be the new power base by one of Ibbi-Sin's former generals. Larsa, the city of the sun god Utu, is probably best known for its last ruler Rim-Sin, the longest-ruling monarch in Mesopotamian history.

In this chapter, we will follow their successes, struggles, and conflicts until Hammurabi of Babylon conquered the kingdom of Larsa in 1763 BC. In doing so, we also encounter other states in the area that managed to exert some level of independence for shorter periods of time, such as Uruk, Kisurra, and later Babylon (for which, see chapter 18 in this volume). Before diving into the historical facts of this period, the present chapter will provide a general outline of the available textual sources, society, and the languages used.

14.1.1. The sources

While the preceding Ur III period is mainly characterized by an abundance of economic records—the number of other textual genres such as scholarly literature and even royal inscriptions pales in comparison—the early Old Babylonian period witnessed a steep increase in the variety of attested textual genres. Royal inscriptions, seal legends, year names, literature, letters, and of course administrative and legal texts all contribute to the reconstruction of historical facts and sometimes even tie together loose threads of information. The distribution of sources for the roughly 250 years that are being discussed here—this chapter understandably focuses on textual sources, in particular—is fairly uneven in terms of quantity and quality. Whereas, on occasion, sources allow for synchronisms between different kingdoms and thus offer a bird's eye view of historical developments, at other times fine-grained micro-history can be reconstructed, for instance, through an analysis of private archives.

Two types of sources form the foundation on which we can build a historical framework for the early Old Babylonian period: royal inscriptions and year names. The length of a ruler's reign is usually not an indication of the number of inscriptions he left for posterity. In the periods

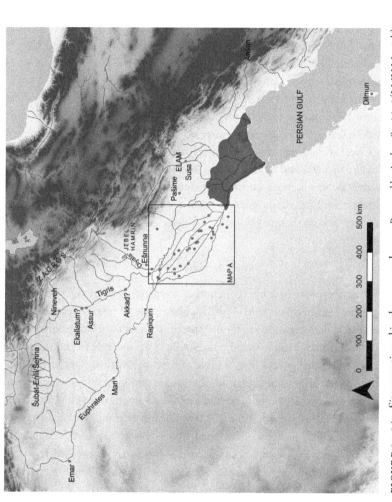

FIGURE 14.1A. Sites mentioned in the present chapter. Prepared by Andrea Squitieri (LMU Munich).

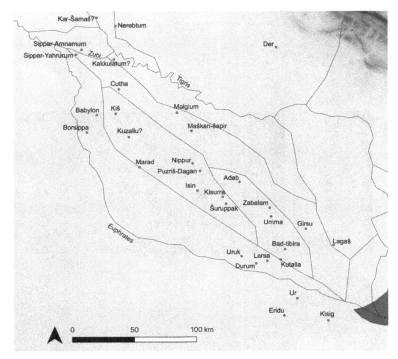

FIGURE 14.1B. Detail map A.

under investigation, rulers left inscriptions on building materials such as bricks (stamped and inscribed), on clay nails and cones,[3] clay cylinders, stone tablets, steles, statues, and other objects made of stone and metal. Cylinder seals (or their impressions on clay artifacts) belonging to members of the royal family or servants and officials of the king are important historical sources as well (figure 14.2), which may even inform us about marriage alliances.[4] When it comes to the materiality of the early Old Babylonian royal inscriptions, it should be noted that quite a

3. von Dassow 2009: 75–85.

4. Examples are the seal of Šallurtum, daughter of the Babylonian king Sumu-abum and wife of Sin-kašid of Uruk (see section 14.6), or the seal belonging to Šat-Sin, a princess from Kisurra, who was married to Sumu-El of Larsa (see section 14.4.2).

FIGURE 14.2. Carnelian seal belonging to Ili-iddinam, servant of ANam (NBC 1199). Author's photograph.

few of the extant inscriptions are only known from copies on clay tablets. Like the copies of royal inscriptions of Old Akkadian rulers in the Old Babylonian period, these copies undoubtedly represent authentic historical sources.[5] To a great extent, royal inscriptions of the early Old Babylonian period deal with pious deeds of the kings. The main topics are the construction of temples and shrines or other architecture related

5. George 2011: no. 53 is a clay tablet with a copy of a dedicatory inscription of one of Rim-Sin's queens, who also left an original inscription (Frayne 1990: no. 4.2.14.23); see section 14.9.3.

to places of worship; the consecration of statues, both royal and divine, or other cultic furniture; and the installation of priests and priestesses or building work associated with them. Building inscriptions are the most numerous among the extant texts.

They inform us about a plethora of construction and renovation projects undertaken by the kings. The two main types of construction are temples (including shrines and other religious architecture) and fortifications—the "great wall" of Larsa features in a number of inscriptions. One type of construction dealt with prominently in the year names, however, is widely absent from royal inscriptions of this period: digging canals. This can probably be explained by the very fact that a canal, in contrast to local architecture such as a temple or a votive object, lacks a suitable support on which to place an inscription.[6] Other pious acts sometimes commemorated in these inscriptions include the consecration of statues of both divinities and kings (see also section 14.1.3). A noteworthy difference from royal inscriptions of other periods is the relative lack of mention of military campaigns. The kings of Isin and Larsa fought many battles and textual sources provide ample evidence for that, but their commemoration in royal inscriptions is rare.[7]

Another important point to note, in inscriptions from the periods under discussion here, is the exceptional agency of women. While in all periods the ruler commemorates his building projects—royal inscriptions and year names are vivid testimonies of their deeds—we see with

---

6. For this problem, see Charpin 2002a: 549–550. E.g., Warad-Sin of Larsa claims in an inscription on bricks found at the site of Diqdiqqah just outside of Ur: "When I implored Nanna and Ningal, they supported me in my place of prayer that I dig the canal 'Nanna-Rejoices' (and) that I restore (its banks)" (Frayne 1990: no. 4.2.13.25: ll. 7–14); cf. also the inscription of Rim-Sin of Larsa that commemorates the digging of the Mami-šarrat canal (Frayne 1990: no. 4.2.14.15).

7. E.g., Nur-Adad of Larsa calls himself in his inscriptions "subduer of the foreign lands for Utu" (Frayne 1990: no. 4.2.8.4: ll. 17–18). A ruler's expansionist activities could also be encoded as the benevolent act of a god, such as in an inscription of Rim-Sin of Larsa dedicated to the goddess Ama-gula, about whom the king states: "when she entrusted into my hands Isin, the city of kingship" (Frayne 1990: no. 4.2.14.19: ll. 17–19). Some of the campaigns of Sin-iddinam of Larsa are described in the long inscription George 2011: no. 37; see section 14.5.1.

the dynasties of Isin and Larsa that also women, namely the daughters, sisters, and wives of kings, left behind building inscriptions which differ little in tone and intent from those of their male protagonists.[8] Thus it is no surprise that the high priestesses of the moon god at Ur left building inscriptions in their own name.

Since the publication of the monumental volume on Old Babylonian royal inscriptions by Douglas R. Frayne, many new texts have become known.[9] New texts—royal inscriptions are only one example—help to fill in gaps and confirm or disprove hypotheses. While some recently published texts are duplicates or new manuscripts of already known inscriptions, others add a great deal to our historical knowledge.[10]

As royal inscriptions of this period are not dated, the information included in them needs to be corroborated by other data such as the practice of naming a year after a major event that happened the preceding year. Year names are of considerable importance for the historian, not only because they provide a look at the events of a ruler's reign, but also because they allow us to establish when a king exerted power at a certain place, as local administrators adapted their dating systems to political circumstances. We see this, for instance, at Kisurra. When Kisurra was briefly under Babylon's control in the reign of Sumu-abum (1894–1881 BC), one of the year names used in documents from Kisurra reads, "Year: Sumu-abum returned to his city."[11]

Alongside royal inscriptions, the year names of this period add military campaigns to the repertoire of topics mentioned. Political events in the year names can also help tie together loose historical threads. Like royal inscriptions, year names may highlight important construction

---

8. Lion 2011: 94–95.

9. Frayne 1990. For new texts, see, e.g., Goodnick Westenholz and Westenholz 2006; von Dassow 2009; George 2011.

10. E.g., the clay barrel cylinder with a long inscription of Sin-iddinam of Larsa, published by Volk 2011.

11. Goddeeris 2009: 16.

projects (e.g., of temples or canals) or other pious acts of the king such as the consecration of a statue or the installation of an *en* priestess. The wording of year names is highly flexible, adapting often to local tradition or the idiosyncrasies of a particular scribe. Many year names have short versions and long versions. Longer year names occasionally mention multiple memorable events, while the shorter version may focus on only one of them. Additionally, it should be noted that a specific year may bear more than one name.

Date lists are a crucial tool in establishing a sequence for the year names of a particular king. The complete list of year names from the dynasty of Larsa is inscribed on a large, four-sided prism, written in the reign of Hammurabi of Babylon (see section 14.3.1). Other date lists may only concern the years of a specific ruler. For several of the kings discussed in this chapter the sequence of their regnal years has not yet been established with certainty. This is particularly true for the kings of Isin, as not enough information can be gathered from extant date lists.

Another source, of course not as fine-grained as lists of year names, is king lists. Here, we should differentiate two types. The Sumerian King List, with its incipit, "After kingship descended from heaven," represents in a strict sense a literary composition. It enumerates all Mesopotamian cities which served as seats of kingship and their respective kings from before the flood to historical periods. This text was long considered a creation of the Old Babylonian period, but a manuscript of the list dating to the preceding Ur III period shows that the composition already existed by that time.[12] The list ends with the First Dynasty of Isin, which shows that the Isin kings extended the list. This probably helped them to claim the role of rightful heirs to the Ur III kings.[13] As part of the literary corpus that was copied again and again in various places, the list cannot be taken at face value; the lengths of the reigns show a high degree

12. Steinkeller 2003.

13. Brisch 2011: 714.

of variation across the extant manuscripts.[14] The passage relevant to us reads as follows:

> Ur was defeated by weapon. Its kingship was brought to Isin. In Isin, Išbi-Erra was king. He ruled for thirty-three years [variant has thirty-two]. Šu-ilišu, son of Išbi-Erra, ruled for twenty years [variants have ten and fifteen]. Iddin-Dagan, son of Šu-ilišu, ruled for twenty-one years [variant has twenty-five]. Išme-Dagan, son of Iddin-Dagan, ruled for twenty years [variant has eighteen]. Lipit-Eštar, son of Išme-Dagan, ruled for eleven years. Ur-Ninurta [some manuscripts add: the son of Iškur—may he have years of abundance, a good reign, and a sweet life—] ruled for twenty-eight years. Bur-Sin, son of Ur-Ninurta, ruled for twenty-one years. Lipit-Enlil, son of Bur-Sin, ruled for five years. Erra-imitti ruled for eight years [variant has seven]. [One manuscript adds: . . . ruled for . . . six months.] Enlil-bani ruled for twenty-four years. Zambiya ruled for three years. Iter-piša ruled for four years. Urdukuga ruled for four years. Sin-magir ruled for eleven years. Damiq-ilišu, son of Sin-magir, ruled for twenty-three years. Fourteen kings: they ruled for 203 years [variant has 225 years and six months].[15]

Lists of reigns, as are available for the rulers of both Isin and Larsa, are more reliable historiographic texts. In the former, the rulers of Isin are preceded by the kings of the Third Dynasty of Ur. As with the Sumerian King List, the legitimizing aspect of this sequence is obvious (see section 14.2.2).

Due to the self-congratulatory tone of the royal inscriptions and the typical terseness of the year names, it is impossible to reconstruct a fuller picture of the period in question, as these sources do not talk

---

14. Jacobsen 1939. For the manuscripts, see Vincente 1995: 236–238 and George 2011: 202–205, with nos. 98–99.

15. Translation   after   ETCSL   (http://etcsl.orinst.ox.ac.uk/cgi-bin/etcsl. cgi?text=t.2.1.1; last accessed August 25, 2020).

about, e.g., the lack of resources, the loss of control over parts of the kingdom, or natural disasters. Occasionally year names deal with solutions to previous problems (e.g., a debt remission edict [*andurārum*] or cleaning the river from silt). Texts of the bureaucracy (such as administrative records and legal documents) may, on occasion, fill in gaps or highlight certain issues. One of the most important sources, however, is certainly correspondence. For the time period in question we are faced with two different data sets. On the one hand, original letters from royal, official, and private archives present us with facts at face value. They may detail construction projects or report an enemy closing in on settlements.[16] On the other hand, some of the early rulers in this period are attested in so-called literary letters. In the Old Babylonian period, correspondence purportedly dating to the preceding Ur III period and the Isin dynasty was copied as part of the instruction of future scribes.[17] The question of their "authenticity" has often been raised. I follow here Piotr Michalowski's recent assessment that in developing the contents for scribal training, "some elements of authentic Ur III letters were incorporated into the curriculum, but that it is impossible to discern the various levels of redaction that transformed them into the school texts we are familiar with."[18]

Furthermore, the period under discussion in this chapter is treated in a number of literary compositions, both in Sumerian and Akkadian. The kings of Isin and Išme-Dagan, in particular, followed in the footsteps of the kings of the Third Dynasty of Ur. Court poets composed a great number of royal hymns. Already the founder of the dynasty, Išbi-Erra, left eight texts. Four of them are divine hymns, the

---

16. The former aspect is highlighted in the letters belonging to the so-called Archive of Lu-igisa (see section 14.3.2). Information on political news comes, for instance, from the recently published letters of Sumu-El sent to his military officials, informing them e.g. about Erra-imitti's advances.

17. Michalowski 2011: 47, 216–224.

18. Michalowski 2011: 218. Cf. the composition known as the *Tribulations of Gimil-Marduk*, an Akkadian juridical document that appears to be based on actual court documents: George 2009: 146–148; Charpin 2020: 166–168.

remainder narrative poems. As will be discussed further, three of the four Sumerian compositions subsumed under the heading "Tetrad," i.e., literary texts that were studied after the elementary phases of Old Babylonian scribal instruction, pertain to kings of Isin. Allusions to this period also come from one of the city laments, the *Nippur Lament*, which glorifies king Išme-Dagan for restoring order to the religious center Nippur.

Last but not least, kings may be remembered in much later periods. Anecdotal information may appear in late chronicles.[19] The historical value of such data is, however, limited at best.

The picture presented in this chapter is of course the current state of our knowledge. The identification and publication of new sources, be it through analysis of excavated materials or the cataloguing and publication of hitherto unpublished materials in museum collections, will change and deepen our knowledge of the period under discussion. This chapter attempts to add information from recently published materials with the caveat that publication projects are still ongoing which may fill in gaps in our knowledge in the future.

14.1.2. Written languages

As implied in the preceding discussion of sources (section 14.1.1), Sumerian occupied an important position in the intellectual, religious, and economic life of the period. Administrative and legal documents were generally written in Sumerian. Official inscriptions, as we have seen, are chiefly composed in Sumerian,[20] as are ideological texts. Exceptions can be found in poetry that is less "mainstream" (e.g., love lyrics). The main exception, however, is the correspondence of this period. Letters

---

19. See, e.g., the information on Erra-imitti of Isin's succession in the *Chronicle of Early Kings* (see section 14.3) and, in the same text, on Rim-Sin of Larsa's capture by Hammurabi of Babylon. At least the latter matches information gleaned from contemporary letters (see section 14.9.4).

20. Although there are also Akkadian inscriptions, e.g. by Zabaya, one of the early rulers of Larsa: Frayne 1990: no. 4.2.4, or by Išme-Dagan: George 2011: no. 38.

were generally written in Akkadian. This is a significant change from the period of the preceding kingdom of Ur.

14.1.3. The deification of the ruler

The deification of rulers is nothing new in the period under discussion here, but it merits a few brief notes. As deification we understand the ascription of divine status to persons or objects and concepts.[21] Here we are concerned only with individuals who were accorded divine status. In texts, deified persons are marked by the sign DINGIR. Additionally, deification led to new cult practices. A cult of statues of previous kings placed in temples or parts of the palace as recipients of worship is fairly well documented for this period.[22] The kings of Larsa dedicated seventy statues to temples. This by far succeeds any dedications of the kings of Isin or of the preceding Ur III period.[23] The kings of Isin regularly deified their names. The situation was different at Larsa. Sumu-El was the first king of Larsa to have his name deified in his own inscriptions.[24] An inscription on a dog figurine dedicated by a priest at Girsu to Nin-Isina for the life of Sumu-El lacks the divine classifier.[25] He was also deified in an inscription of Warad-Sin that recounts earlier restoration works. His successor Nur-Adad appears deified once in his own inscriptions.[26] For the three subsequent kings, whose names all start with the theophoric element Sin, no judgment can be made. Warad-Sin was only once deified, namely in the aforementioned inscription. Rim-Sin's case is interesting. Early in his

21. Selz 2016 (with previous literature).

22. See section 14.5.1, for the case of Nur-Adad's statue, whose inscription is known from a copy only, but for which his successor Sin-iddinam left two letter-prayers. Year names and archival texts corroborate the worship of earlier rulers and the attempts to preserve their memory in this way.

23. Wasserman 2018: xxxvi, n. 21.

24. Frayne 1990: no. 4.2.7.1; no. 4.2.7.2.

25. Frayne 1990: no. 4.2.7.2001.

26. Frayne 1990: no. 4.2.8.2.

reign his name did not bear a divine marker. After he conquered Uruk, however, his name was regularly written with the divine classifier.

14.1.4. Population and society

The Amorites played a crucial role in the preceding Ur III period. Their language, Amorite, was a West Semitic language, and is predominantly attested in personal names.[27] The sources used in this chapter mention several Amorite tribes. These were affiliated with two major tribal groups, the Yaminites (*bānū jamīn*), the "sons of the right [i.e., south]," and the Sim'alites (*bānū sim'āl*), the "sons of the left [i.e., north]."[28] One of the tribes mentioned in this chapter is the Amnanum tribe which belonged to the Yaminite group. Tribal affiliation should not be underestimated, as it had an effect on political alliances. Sin-kašid of Uruk, himself "king of Amnanum," and his successors had friendly relationships with Babylon, whose kings belonged to the same tribe (see section 14.6). Emutbal (or Yamutbal), which is crucial for the dynasty Kudur-mabuk founded at Larsa, belonged to the Sim'alite tribal group, as did the kings of Mari and Aleppo.[29]

14.1.5. This chapter's structure

The early (and middle) Old Babylonian period exhibits a fairly complex historical structure. While Isin under Išbi-Erra exerted its control in southern Mesopotamia in the early years of the dynasty, Larsa soon expanded.

This chapter therefore follows the historical periods. Aspects of society, economy, literature, and so forth, are interwoven into each part. Our historical journey starts with Isin's slow rise to power under Išbi-Erra and his immediate successors (see section 14.2). The four parts

27. Streck 2000; Golinets 2020.

28. de Boer 2013b: 273–274.

29. Stol 2004: 647.

of this section deal with historical events and the reigns of Isin's first five rulers, before they were challenged by the advances of Larsa. In the subsequent section, we remain in the time frame of the late twentieth and early nineteenth centuries BC and examine the origins of the kingdom of Larsa (see section 14.3). The political landscape changed significantly after the reign of the sixth king Abi-sare. With Sumu-El and his urge to expand the territory of Larsa, the two kingdoms were increasingly at odds with each other (see section 14.4). While Isin continued to be independent, Larsa was able to consolidate its power under a new dynasty that was established in the reign of Nur-Adad (see section 14.5). Although the two kingdoms of Isin and Larsa are the main focal points of this chapter, another important city in the south, Uruk, must not be overlooked. In the course of the nineteenth century BC, the rulers of Uruk established a significant level of independence (see section 14.6). With section 14.7, we return to Isin to look at the reigns of Enlil-bani and Erra-imitti. Back at Larsa, Kudur-mabuk, the "father of Emutbal," established a new dynasty with his two sons, Warad-Sin and Rim-Sin (see section 14.8). The extraordinarily long reign of the latter warrants its own section, with the pivotal point in his reign, the capture of Isin, followed by slow decline in the second half of his reign and Hammurabi's conquest, which brought an end to the kingdom of Larsa (see section 14.9).

14.2. The political climate of southern Mesopotamia after Ibbi-Sin

According to the Sumerian King List, the last ruler of the Ur III state, Ibbi-Sin, ruled twenty-four years (2028–2004 BC). This is corroborated by the year names from his reign.[30] Ibbi-Sin's rule was anything but tranquil. Having inherited a weakened state from his father, Šu-Sin, he lost control over parts of the state early in his reign, as demonstrated by the relatively sudden decline of administrative archives at several sites in

---

30. See also the list of reigns of the kings of Ur and Isin published as George 2011: no. 100: l. 5 (see section 14.2.2 in this chapter).

southern Mesopotamia. At Umma (modern Tell Jokha), which yielded more than 30,000 economic records, the last text dates to Ibbi-Sin's fifth year.[31] A similar phenomenon occurred at Girsu, and Drehem followed immediately thereafter.[32] As territories, once under the umbrella of Ur's rule, slowly broke away, some cities established their own power base. Much of this history still lies in the shadows due to a scarcity of sources. Important clues to the decline of the Ur III state derive not from contemporary archives, but from the so-called *Correspondence of the Kings of Ur*, which is solely attested in Old Babylonian sources that likely were redacted.[33] Other sources of information, although literary and ideological, are compositions belonging to the genre of Sumerian City Laments. These texts concern the destruction of important cities in the Ur III state.[34] Examples include the *Lamentation over the Destruction of Sumer and Ur*[35] or the *Ur Lament*.[36] The former was probably composed in the early Old Babylonian period and aimed to legitimize the kings of Isin.[37] Many aspects of the decline of the Ur III state under Ibbi-Sin have been described in section 13.3 of chapter 13 in this volume and will therefore not be repeated here.

14.2.1. Isin's rise to power under Išbi-Erra

One of Ibbi-Sin's officials, a certain Išbi-Erra (ca. 2017–1985 BC), was able to establish his rule at Isin and Nippur in the eighth year of Ibbi-Sin's reign, while Ur's king continued to exert control over Ur and its hinterland. Almost everything we know about Išbi-Erra's background

---

31. Lafont 1995: 6.

32. Lafont 1995: 6–7; also Michalowski 2011: 178.

33. Michalowski 2011.

34. Samet 2014: 3, 6.

35. Michalowski 1989.

36. Michalowski 2011: 171.

37. Michalowski 2005: 199.

is derived from the aforementioned *Royal Correspondence of Ur*. Its historical accuracy, therefore, is suspect.[38] According to one letter, Išbi-Erra should have traveled to Kazallu to buy grain, but Amorites invaded the state, which caused Išbi-Erra to bring the grain to Isin:

> Should there be a shortage of grain, I will be the one who brings you grain. My king is troubled by the war with the Elamite, but his own grain rations are rapidly being depleted, so do not release your grip on power, do not rush to become his servant, and to follow him! There is (enough) grain in my city to provision your palace and all the people for fifteen years, so let the responsibility of guarding the cities of Isin and Nippur be mine![39]

This letter—we do not know how much of it is historically correct—shows Išbi-Erra (still) under the authority of the king of Ur. A document from the fourteenth year of Ibbi-Sin records rations for messengers of Išbi-Erra, who are men from Isin.[40] Išbi-Erra's origins, however, may be found at Mari.[41] Both the literary letters and hymns produced by the poets at Isin's court indicate this. In the royal correspondence, clearly dating later than the letter previously cited, Ibbi-Sin, conveying a decision of the god Enlil, writes to the governor of Kazallu:

> At some time in the past, Enlil had already come to hate Sumer, and had elevated a monkey descending from his mountain to the stewardship of the homeland. But now Enlil has given the kingship to a *peddler of exotic spices*, to Išbi-Erra, who is not even of Sumerian seed. (…) As long as an enemy is installed in

---

38. Questions about these letters' authenticity have often been raised; see the summaries of the debate in Michalowski 2011: 216–224; Huber Vulliet 2011: 504–505.

39. Michalowski 2011: 418: text *IšIb1*: ll. 21–29.

40. Legrain 1937: no. 1421: ll. 5–7.

41. Michalowski 1995: 182–183; 2005: 203–204.

Ur, Išbi-Erra, the man of Mari, will continue to rip out its foundations, and so Sumer will be measured out (like grain).[42]

Ibbi-Sin's rebuke serves here as a warning for the governor not to see
Išbi-Erra as an ally. The hymnal literature corroborates Išbi-Erra's Mari
origins. One hymn states:

[An] and Enlil restored the divine verdicts (concerning Sumer).
They cast their glance at the mountains where cedars are cut and
the true shepherd [...], divine Išbi-Erra they chose from Mari to
be the king of the land.[43]

In the Ur III period, Mari was not an alien entity, but was intimately
linked to the royal house of Ur through dynastic marriages.[44] Although
the events in the early years of Išbi-Erra and his rise to power remain
blurred, important data on the economic life of this period come from
the so-called Isin Craft Archive, which comprises more than nine hundred administrative texts. The texts cover about thirty-three years, from
Išbi-Erra's fourth to Šu-ilišu's third year.[45] The extant sources, which
derive from illicit excavations, form a reconstructed archive that attests
to the activities of a craft workshop (figure 14.3). This archive is representative of the economy of the First Dynasty of Isin, and its texts follow closely the administrative conventions of the Ur III period. The
consumers or recipients of the finished products were the palace and
the royal family, the temples, central storehouses, and other workshops.
Other products were sent abroad as official presents.[46] Several steps in
the workflow of the workshop can be observed through the lens of the

---

42. Michalowski 2011: 464: text *IbPu*1: ll. 13–16, 19–21.

43. *Išbi-Erra* G: ll. 9'–11'; translation after Michalowski 2005: 206–208. For the liter-
    ary compositions pertaining to the Isin kings, see table 14.1.

44. Sharlach 2001.

45. Van de Mieroop 1987a: 1.

46. Goddeeris 2007a: 200.

FIGURE 14.3. Administrative texts belonging to the so-called Isin Craft Archive. Author's photograph.

extant sources. A group of accounts records the delivery of raw materials. After this step follows the distribution of the raw materials to the various craftsmen. The third text type concerns the manufacture of furniture and other finished products. Only a few texts record the receipt of the finished products by the officials of the workshop. The best documented step, however, is the distribution of the finished goods. The following text is a noteworthy example of this last step, as it lists the furniture that was given as a present to the king's daughter for a wedding:

One woman's chair, (its) seat inlaid with silver, its glue is ten shekels; five shekels oxhide (for the) cushion, with two-thirds white sheepskin and one red sheepskin it is covered, two-thirds white sheepskin for its lining; one bed of *mes*-wood, ten shekels glue have been applied to it: the chair and the bed are from the workshop.

One waterproofed(?) covering, its waterproofed(?) *alum*-sheepskins are ten, its thread of ordinary wool is seven shekels;

one hinge(?) of a cover, its red oxhide is six shekels: Lu-Ninšubur
(was) conveyor.

One jar of five litres for good oil, four large oil-jars, their bitumen is one and a half litres, their sheepskin is seventy shekels, for
their lids: Libur-beli (was) conveyor.

Presents for Libur-ni'aš, the daughter of the king, the day she
was married by Šuruš-kin, the son of Huba-simti.

Issued by Šu-Ninkarrak, Day 3, Month II, Year Išbi-Erra 15.
Copy of (the tablet) in a bag.[47]

Politically, this account is important, as it may attest to a possible alliance by marriage with the son of a high-ranking official.[48] The accounts
belonging to this archive also attest to presents being sent to places such as
Mari and Ebla.[49] Other places that appear in these accounts are Borsippa,
Kiš, and also Dilmun in the Persian Gulf. The trade with Dilmun used
Ur as a hub. Despite the importance of this workshop at Isin, the extant
textual record represents only a fraction of Isin's economy.

Apart from the Isin archive, further economic records are known
from Nippur and Ur. To date, only one royal inscription of Išbi-Erra's
has been found, commemorating the production of a lyre for Enlil.[50]
A fragmentary text in the Iraq Museum preserves twenty-three of his
year names.[51] The name of his twenty-sixth year, which commemorates his victory over the Elamites and the recapture of Ur, is especially

---

47. Crawford 1954: no. 438; see Van de Mieroop 1987a: 108–109 and, for ll. 21–24,
Steinkeller 2008: n. 10.

48. The last sign in l. 23 of this text used to be read SUKKAL, but the sign is certainly
-ke₄, as Steinkeller 2008 notes.

49. Van de Mieroop 1987a: 116–117. A text mentions an official present to be sent
to Mari, as well as sandals and bags given to messengers from Mari (Crawford
1954: no. 384: ll. 2, 6–7), whereas another one records furniture as a present to a
certain Ilum-bani, a "man of Mari" (Van de Mieroop 1987b: no. 113: l. 4).

50. Frayne 1990: no. 4.1.1.1.

51. Baqir 1948. For a discussion of this text, see Van de Mieroop 1987a: 120–128.

noteworthy.[52] His last two year names concern the installation of a priestess for Lugalirra at Durum,[53] a settlement near Uruk, whose two patron deities were Meslamta'ea and Lugalirra (see section 14.6). Toward the end of Išbi-Erra's reign, Isin had exerted its power in the north as far as Marad, Apiak, Borsippa, and Kazallu, and in the south at Uruk, Ur, Eridu, and Larsa.[54]

Išbi-Erra is attested in a number of scholarly sources. He appears, for instance, in the *Tummal Chronicle*, an Old Babylonian composition which describes the restoration of Tummal outside Nippur for the goddess Ninlil by different rulers. The text ends with the king of Isin: "Išbi-Erra built the House-Mountain-Endowed-with-Sight, Enlil's storehouse."[55] Išbi-Erra also appears in omens of the first half of the second millennium as a historical figure. One Old Babylonian omen, for instance, reads: "If a large weapon mark is placed on the right and rides on the gall-bladder, it is the weapon of Išbi-Erra who overthrew Elam."[56] This latter omen finds confirmation in an inscribed liver model from Mari: "Omen of Išbi-Erra, against whom Elam fought, and who took Elam (in the end)."[57] Išbi-Erra also appears in a very late text from Uruk in the Seleucid period, the so-called *Uruk List of Kings and Sages*. The list states that "[in the time of Išbi]-Erra, the king, Sidu, (who was) also (known as) Enlil-ibni, was the chief-scholar."[58]

Sidu is also otherwise known in cuneiform culture in a list of literary works and their authors (known from the seventh-century library of

---

52. Sigrist 1988: 19–20.

53. Sigrist 1988: 21: Year 32 (and 33).

54. Frayne 1989: 19; Charpin 2004: 62.

55. *Tummal Chronicle*: ll. 32–33; see Kleinerman 2011: 142. An alternative translation is: "Išbi-Erra, who looks after the Ekur, built Enlil's storehouse"; see George 1993: 117.

56. Goetze 1947a: no. 46: v. 4–6; see Goetze 1947b: 262–263; Schaudig 2019: 295–297 (source 16).

57. Rutten 1938: 43, no. 9; with Schaudig 2019: 294 (source 15).

58. Lenzi 2008: 141; Frahm 2010: 175.

Ashurbanipal of Assyria) which identifies him as author of the "[Series of] Sidu" as well as a lamentation-priest and chief-scholar of Nippur.[59] The "series of Sidu," a collection of proverbs, was probably compiled long after Isbi-Erra's time. His inclusion in this list was possibly an attempt by late scholars to include the latest king who also appears in the Old Babylonian proverb tradition, with which the late series of Sidu shares some characteristics.[60]

Several Sumerian literary compositions of the Old Babylonian period deal with Isbi-Erra. The texts known as *Isbi-Erra* A and *Isbi-Erra* B concern his struggles with the Elamites.[61] The aims of the latter composition are to glorify and legitimize the king of Isin in standing against the Elamites and to highlight the fact that Ur's destruction was a decision of the gods.[62] Table 14.1 contains a list of all literary compositions (divine and royal hymns, poems, etc.) pertaining to the kings of Isin.

14.2.2. Isbi-Erra's successors

The Isin dynasty comprises a total of fifteen kings. A list of its kings with the number of years of their reigns is preserved on two nearly identical tablets. Both lists include the kings of the Third Dynasty of Ur, possibly to add credence to the legitimacy of Isin's rule.[63]

Isbi-Erra's son and successor, Šu-ilišu, used a new title in his own inscriptions, "king of Ur," which had particular prestige. According to one inscription, Šu-ilišu returned a looted statue of the moon god from

---

59. Frahm 2010: 172: K. 9717+: l. 13′; cf. the tablet's photograph in CDLI (https://cdli.ucla.edu/P398270; last accessed August 26, 2020).

60. Frahm 2010: 176.

61. Tinney 1996: 2. For *Isbi-Erra* A, see Sjöberg 1993; for *Isbi-Erra* B, see van Dijk 1978.

62. Vanstiphout 1989–1990: 58.

63. One of the two manuscripts was recently published as George 2011: no. 100. The other manuscript, now in an Italian private collection, was edited by Fales 1989: 144–145. A similar list also exists for the dynasty of Larsa; see section 14.3.1.

Table 14.1. The literary corpus pertaining to the kings of the Isin dynasty

King	Genre	Compositions
Išbi-Erra	Divine hymns	*tigi*-song of Nanaya (= Išbi-Erra C) Hymn to Nin-Isina (= Išbi-Erra D) Hymn to Nisaba (= Išbi-Erra E) Hymn to Nin-Šubur (= Išbi-Erra F)
	Narrative poems	Išbi-Erra A Išbi-Erra B Išbi-Erra G Išbi-Erra H
Šu-ilišu	Divine hymns	*adab*-song of Nergal (= Šu-ilišu A) *adab*-song of An (= Šu-ilišu B) *adab*-song (= Šu-ilišu C)
Iddin-Dagan	Divine hymns	Hymn to Inana (= Iddin-Dagan A) *adab*-song of Ningublaga (= Iddin-Dagan C)
	Royal hymns	Hymn to Iddin-Dagan (= Iddin-Dagan B) *namerima*-song for Iddin-Dagan (= Iddin-Dagan D)
Išme-Dagan	Divine hymns	*adab*-song of Bawu (= Išme-Dagan B) *adab*-song of Enki (= Išme-Dagan D) *balbale*-song of Enki (= Išme-Dagan E) *adab*-song of Enlil (= Išme-Dagan F) *adab*-song of Ninlil (= Išme-Dagan G) *adab*-song of Enlil (= Išme-Dagan H) *tigi*-song of Enlil (= Išme-Dagan I) *balbale*-song of Inana (= Išme-Dagan J) *Inana and Išme-Dagan* (= Išme-Dagan K)

(continued)

Table 14.1. *Continued*

King	Genre	Compositions
		adab-song of Inana (= Išme-Dagan L) *adab*-song of Nanna (= Išme-Dagan M) *adab*-song of Nergal (= Išme-Dagan N) Song of Ninurta (= Išme-Dagan O) Song of Ninurta (= Išme-Dagan P) *adab*-song of Nuska (= Išme-Dagan Q) Hymn to Damu (= Išme-Dagan R) *Dedication of a Statue by Išme-Dagan* (= Išme-Dagan S) *Nergal and Išme-Dagan* (= Išme-Dagan T) *adab*-song of Dagan (?) (= Išme-Dagan U) *tigi*-song of Inana (= Išme-Dagan Y)
	Royal hymns	Self-praise of Išme-Dagan (= Išme-Dagan A) Hymn to Nippur and Išme-Dagan (= Išme-Dagan C) Self-praise of Išme-Dagan (= Išme-Dagan V) Hymn to Nippur and Išme-Dagan (= Išme-Dagan W) Išme-Dagan Z Išme-Dagan A_1 Išme-Dagan B_1 Išme-Dagan C_1 Išme-Dagan D_1 Išme-Dagan E_1

Table 14.1. *Continued*

King	Genre	Compositions
	Prayers	Prayer of Išme-Dagan (= Išme-Dagan X)
Lipit-Eštar	Divine hymns	*adab*-song of An (= Lipit-Eštar C) *adab*-song of Ninurta (= Lipit-Eštar D) *namgala*-song of Nin-Isina (= Lipit-Eštar E) *adab*-song of Ninurta [?] (= Lipit-Eštar G) *Inana and Lipit-Eštar* (= Lipit-Eštar H)
	Royal hymns	Self-praise of Lipit-Eštar (= Lipit-Eštar A) Praise of Lipit-Eštar (= Lipit-Eštar B) *Lipit-Eštar and the Plow* (= Lipit-Eštar F) Lipit-Eštar I
Ur-Ninurta	Divine hymns	Song of Inana (= Ur-Ninurta A) *tigi*-song of Enki (= Ur-Ninurta B) *adab*-song of Ninurta (= Ur-Ninurta C) *adab*-song of Inana (= Ur-Ninurta D) *adab*-song of An (= Ur-Ninurta E) *adab*-song of Iškur (= Ur-Ninurta F)
	Wisdom literature	*Instructions of Ur-Ninurta* (= Ur-Ninurta G)
Bur-Sin	Divine hymns	*adab*-song of Ninurta (= Bur-Sin A) *adab*-song of Enlil (= Bur-Sin B) *sergida*-song of Sud (= Bur-Sin C)
Enlil-bani	Royal hymns	Praise of Enlil-bani (= Enlil-bani A)
Damiq-ilišu	Letter prayer	Damiq-ilišu A

Anšan to Ur.[64] The same inscription mentions his construction of the Dublamah, "the place of judgment," at Ur. His few inscriptions also indicate that he resettled scattered people in Ur and around Isin.[65] His doing so may reflect the Elamite invasion in Ibbi-Sin's twenty-fourth year, when the Elamites ransacked Ur, destroyed its sanctuaries, and massacred its inhabitants.[66] The lack of textual sources at Ur before Šu-ilišu's fifth year appears to corroborate his claims. The latest datable texts in the aforementioned Isin Craft Archive (see section 14.2.1) date to his third year.

Little is known about the reign of Iddin-Dagan (1976–1956 BC). According to an intriguing, unprovenanced inscription, preserved as a copy on a clay tablet kept at the University of Pennsylvania Museum, Iddin-Dagan commissioned two copper statues for the goddess Ninlil, but could not bring them to Nippur; this quite likely indicates that Iddin-Dagan had no control over this important religious center. In referring to the statues, the text claims that "from Iddin-Dagan until Enlil-bani, the king, they stood in Isin for 117 years."[67] Enlil-bani (1862–1839 BC) finally relocated these statues and brought them to Nippur. It is likely that Iddin-Dagan also lost control over Uruk in the south.[68] Iddin-Dagan's year names chiefly refer to pious acts, except for two of the year names, according to which he betrothed his daughter, Matum-niatum, to the king of Anšan and thus followed a diplomatic custom that was already efficiently used by some of the Ur III rulers before him.[69]

---

64. Frayne 1990: no. 4.1.2.1: ll. 8–11: "when he brought (back the statue of) the god Nanna from Anšan to Ur."

65. Frayne 1990: no. 4.1.2.2: ii 5–6; no. 4.1.2.3: ll. 6–8.

66. Van de Mieroop 1992: 49–50.

67. Frayne 1990: no. 4.1.10.11: ll. 6–9; see Loding 1973; Tinney 1996: 3. The manuscript is divided into two parts, which are separated by a single ruling. The first part (ll. 1–25) contains Enlil-bani's inscription, which ends in a curse formula. This text is followed by a short passage (ll. 26–37) that represents Iddin-Dagan's original inscription, ending with its own curse formula. A likely scenario is that Enlil-bani added his inscription to Iddin-Dagan's statue; see Tinney 1996: 3.

68. Frayne 1998: 21.

69. Sigrist 1988: 24: Years A and B.

The collection of short literary compositions known today as the *Sumerian Epistolary Miscellany* contains two letters concerning Iddin-Dagan. The first text, of twelve lines length, is a letter sent by the head of security (*rabi sikkatim*), Sin-tillati, to the king, in which he informs the king that Amorites attacked him when he went to Kakkulatum.[70] Sin-tillati was victorious and took prisoners, but was unsure about what to do with them. If they were to stay in the camp, the king should send provisions or put them into service elsewhere. The second letter contains the king's answer. He congratulates Sin-tillati:

> Thanks to you, my expeditionary force can (now) cross from one bank of the river to another inspiring fear and causing a blockade. When you went upstream to Kakkulatum, Lamma, Dagan, Kabta and Enlil caused the (enemy) troops to submit. My splendor covers the homeland, while you approached the enemy land with your heroism and your strength. You have been able to make prisoners of the enemy.[71]

From a historian's point of view, these two literary letters need to be taken with a grain of salt, as historical sources can neither prove nor disprove this intervention. In her discussion of this collection, Alexandra Kleinerman highlights the dichotomy between the two letters as part of Iddin-Dagan's correspondence and the set of letters pertaining to Lipit-Eštar (see section 14.2.4). While the first set portrays a successful military campaign, the second set has a completely different tone. Lipit-Eštar was very unhappy with his head of security, Nanna-ki'ag, who reported

---

70. *Sumerian Epistolary Miscellany* no. 2; see Kleinerman 2011: 116–117. Kakkulatum is located on the Zubi canal in the Diyala region; see Heimpel 2003: xxv, Map 5. This city is known from Mari sources, according to which Elamite troops crossed the Zubi canal in this area and destroyed Kakkulatum's defenses, and Ešnunna's king Ibal-pi-El II (1779–1766 BC) monitored the withdrawal of Elamite troops in this area; see Heimpel 2003: 614.

71. *Sumerian Epistolary Miscellany* no. 3: ll. 4–9; see Kleinerman 2011: 118–120.

to him that the settlement of Edana turned against the king and invited
Gungunum's army into it.[72]

The portrayal of Iddin-Dagan's success in these two literary letters is
by no means reflected in the literature of his successor, Išme-Dagan, who
contrasts his own achievements with the failures of his predecessor. In
the Sumerian composition known as the *Nippur Lament*, which glorifies
Išme-Dagan, we read:

> To Išme-Dagan, the sacral officiant, who daily serves, the joyous,
>   his reverent one,
> (Enlil) has given him the command to sanctify its food, to purify
> its water!
> He has commanded him to purify its defiled rituals!
> He has put in order its disordered and scattered rites,
> The most sacred (things), neglected and defiled, he has put back
>   in their place.[73]

Iddin-Dagan's court poets left a small number of hymns. Most notewor-
thy is the hymn detailing the rites performed for the so-called Sacred
Marriage between the king and the goddess of love and war, Inana (Iddin-
Dagan A).[74] Another hymn, an *adab* song of Ningublaga (Iddin-Dagan
C), asks that the "vigorous wild bull" (Sumerian *sumun₂ zi*) Ningublaga
be the "crusher of Iddin-Dagan's enemies."[75] Finally, one of his hymns
(Iddin-Dagan D) contains curses against the king's enemies.[76] While his
year names do not indicate any military actions in his reign, the literature
of the time, including the two literary letters mentioned earlier, portray
him in a different light.

---

72. Kleinerman 2011: 29–30 with nn. 53 and 54; and see section 14.2.4 in this chap-
    ter. For Gungunum, see section 14.3.2.

73. *Nippur Lament*, ll. 276–280; see Tinney 1996: 118–119.

74. Reisman 1973; Jones 2003; Attinger 2014; see also Brisch 2011: 713–714.

75. Iddin-Dagan C: l. 30; for an edition, see ETCSL (http://etcsl.orinst.ox.ac.uk/
    cgi-bin/etcsl.cgi?text=t.2.5.3.3; last accessed August 25, 2020).

76. Römer 2001: 37.

Before proceeding, it should be emphasized that three of the Isin kings are represented in a subset of curricular texts in the Old Babylonian "Eduba'a." The four compositions of the so-called *Tetrad* were copied by apprentice scribes after they completed the elementary phases of their education. The texts belonging to the *Tetrad* were the first literary texts, apart from proverbs, that students engaged with in their training. They were copied onto round school lentils, as instructor-student exercises and extracts, and finally complete manuscripts were inscribed onto larger (collective) tablets or prisms. Apart from a hymn to the goddess of writing, Nisaba, the other three texts of the *Tetrad* are hymns to Iddin-Dagan, Lipit-Eštar, and Enlil-bani.[77]

14.2.3. A time of prosperity under Išme-Dagan

We are slightly better informed about the reign of Iddin-Dagan's successor Išme-Dagan (reigned 1955–1937 BC), the fourth ruler who sat on Isin's throne. A greater number of royal inscriptions have survived from his reign (figure 14.4). His "standard inscription," found stamped on bricks from Isin and Ur, refers to him as "provider of Nippur, constant [attendant] of Ur, who is daily at the service of Eridu, *en* priest of Uruk, king of Isin, king of the land of Sumer and Akkad, beloved spouse of Inana."[78] In the course of his reign he built several walls, namely the fortifications of Isin and Durum.[79] The wall of Durum is particularly interesting, as Išme-Dagan described this settlement near Uruk as "city of military governorship and his [i.e., Išme-Dagan's] princeship."[80] Recently, Andrew George published the rare example of an Akkadian inscription recording the construction of a wall at a place

---

77. Tinney 1999; for a photograph of four, six-sided prisms covering the *Tetrad*, see Wagensonner 2019: 61, fig. 13. See also section 14.2.4 in this chapter.

78. Frayne 1990: no. 4.1.4.1: ll. 2–11; cf. no. 4.1.4.2, which adds "mighty king" (l. 8).

79. Isin's great wall is commemorated in Frayne 1990: no. 4.1.4.5 (to which add the exemplar George 2011: no. 39). The name of the wall was "By grace of Enlil, Išme-Dagan is powerful" (ll. 16–17).

80. See also section 14.6.

FIGURE 14.4. A number of clay cones bearing inscriptions of Isin rulers. Author's photograph.

called Naznannum (?). The king's titles in this inscription differ from the standard titulary known from other texts; among other things he is called "sun of Isin."[81]

Išme-Dagan appears to have regained power over Nippur, which was of great ideological importance. One inscription states, "when he canceled the tribute of Nippur, beloved city of Enlil, (and) relieved its men of military service."[82] Besides Nippur, Ur also came into greater focus at this time. Isin's king installed his daughter as *en* priestess of the moon god Nanna there, thus following a tradition that started with Sargon of Akkad and likely already earlier. Her name was Enanatuma. She left

81. George 2011: no. 38: l. 13.

82. Frayne 1990: no. 4.1.4.5: ll. 5–11.

a diorite statuette which was found in room C.22 of the Gipar-ku, the residence of the *en* priestesses. According to its inscription, Enanatuma dedicated the statue to Ningal for her own life and brought it into Ningal's bed chamber.[83] Later, Ur was conquered by the Larsa ruler Gungunum (1932–1906 BC),[84] who appears not to have interfered with Enanatuma's tenure as *en* priestess. Two building inscriptions were dedicated to Gungunum, in which Enanatuma did not conceal her patronage (see section 14.3.2).[85]

Year names of Išme-Dagan also indicate that he installed a priestess of Ninurta, and an *en* priest of Inana.[86] Judging from the year names and the royal inscriptions, Išme-Dagan's reign appears to have been one of prosperity. This is also reflected in the large number of literary works that concern him. No fewer than twenty-six hymns can be assigned to him alone. A particular feature of some of these hymns is the close parallel they show to those of the Ur III king Šulgi. It seems that the court poets of the king of Isin deliberately attempted to cast their hymns in the mold of the texts of the preceding ruler of Ur.[87] This is particularly obvious in hymns of both rulers that deal with the fashioning of cultic objects. While the hymn *Šulgi* R describes the construction of a barge for the goddess Ninlil including all its parts, the hymn *Išme-Dagan* I mimics the former in structure and describes the construction of a chariot for Enlil.

---

83. Frayne 1990: no. 4.1.4.14. For an image of the statue, see Stol 2016: 561, fig. 43, and also the online catalog of the University Museum of the University of Pennsylvania (https://www.penn.museum/collections/object/53090; last accessed August 25, 2020).

84. The first year mentioning Nanna, the patron deity of Ur, is Gungunum's tenth year; see also section 14.3.2.

85. Frayne 1990: no. 4.2.5.1: ll. 8–12; no. 4.2.5.2: ll. 12–17.

86. Sigrist 1988: 27: Years N and O.

87. Klein 1985; 1990; Brisch 2011: 713. For the hymns of Išme-Dagan, see also Ludwig 1990; Ludwig and Metcalf 2017.

14.2.4. The king who established justice: Lipit-Eštar

The fifth king of the Isin dynasty, Lipit-Eštar, ruled for eleven years
(1936–1926 BC).[88] He was a contemporary of the Larsa kings Zabaya and
Gungunum (see sections 14.3.1 and 14.3.2). According to one of his year
names, he established justice in the lands of Sumer and Akkad.[89] Bricks
have been found at Ur, Uruk, and Isin inscribed with a short inscription
that also alludes to this act.[90] Lipit-Eštar's construction of the "House of
Justice" (Sumerian e_2 nig_2-si-sa_2) is commemorated on a large number of
small, headless cones (figure 14.4).[91] This project was probably related to
Lipit-Eštar's establishment of a law code. Written in the Sumerian language, his laws are the earliest laws of the Old Babylonian period. They
were preceded by the *Law Collection of Ur-Namma*, from which they
differ significantly.[92] The later *Laws of Hammurabi*, composed in
Akkadian, build on these earlier law collections substantially.[93] Like
Hammurabi's law collection, the *Code of Lipit-Eštar* consists of a prologue, the actual provisions, and an epilogue. The composition is known
from sources, mainly from Nippur, and to a lesser extent from Kiš and
Sippar. Its prologue states:

> At that time, An and Enlil called Lipit-Eštar, the wise shepherd,
> whose name has been pronounced by the god Nunamnir—in
> order to establish justice in the land, to eliminate cries for justice,

88. We happen to know the name of Lipit-Eštar's mother, Lamassatum, as she commemorated the construction of a storehouse for the goddess Inana: Frayne
1990: no. 4.1.5.7.

89. Sigrist 1988: 28: Year A.

90. Frayne 1990: no. 4.1.5.1: ll. 14–16: "the king, who established justice in the land of
Sumer and Akkad." For the Akkadian version, see Frayne 1990: no. 4.1.5.3: ll. 30–35.

91. Frayne 1990: no. 4.1.5.4.

92. Roth 1997: 13–22; Civil 2011.

93. For a summary, see Charpin 2010b: 72–73.

to eradicate enmity and armed violence, to bring well-being to the lands of Sumer and Akkad.[94]

In the Epilogue, Lipit-Eštar refers to a stele, on which the laws are inscribed.[95] Two stone fragments from Nippur probably belonged to such a stele.[96] His law code, although composed in Sumerian, can be viewed as a prototype of the *Laws of Hammurabi*. In contrast to the latter, Lipit-Eštar's laws never entered a scholarly tradition that would outlive the Old Babylonian period. The provisions concern the free individual (Sumerian lu_2), wives, children, and slaves, as well as palace dependents.[97]

Apart from establishing justice in the land, another year name states that Lipit-Eštar "remitted the arrears of Sumer and Akkad"[98] and built a palace at Isin.[99] Among his other building projects was the digging of the Ninki canal.[100] This may have formed part of his restoration of Ur.[101] In a literary letter belonging to the so-called *Sumerian Epistolary Miscellany*, the head of security (*rabi sikkatim*), Nanna-ki'ag, informed Lipit-Eštar about a venture of Gungunum. The settlement of Edana turned their backs from Isin, so Gungunum's army could set up their

---

94. *Laws of Lipit-Eštar*: i 20–37; see Roth 1997: 25.

95. *Laws of Lipit-Eštar*: xxi 38; see Roth 1997: 34.

96. Legrain 1926: no. 47; and Buccellati and Biggs 1969: no. 49; see Roth 1997: 35, n. 1.

97. Roth 1997: 24.

98. Sigrist 1988: 28: Year E (and F).

99. Frayne 1990: no. 4.1.5.2: ll. 17–18: "'House-Suitable-for-Kingship,' my great abode." A related Akkadian inscription is found on a large number of headless cones from Isin and deals with the fashioning of a pair of pot stands at the palace gate (Frayne 1990: no. 4.1.5.3: ll. 20–26).

100. Sigrist 1988: 28: Year D.

101. Frayne 1990: no. 4.1.5.5: ll. 17–23: "By the degree of Enlil and Nanna I restored Ur (and) dug its moat." The name of his Year B offers a similar statement; see Sigrist 1988: 28.

camp there. Nanna-ki'ag continued, "that army came from the Amar-
Sin canal in order to build brick(works), fortify (the settlement)
Dunnum and dig a canal."[102] The next letter in this corpus is a letter
by Lipit-Eštar to Nanna-ki'ag, in which the king complained about
the inaction of his official and dispatched military forces in order to
remove the enemy troops from their positions.[103] These two literary
letters must be read cautiously, as their historical accuracy cannot be
proven.[104] Taken together, it seems that Gungunum's advances did not
yet harm Isin's control of Ur during the lifetime of Lipit-Eštar. Probably
late in his reign, the king of Isin chose his daughter Enninsunzi as *en*
priestess of Ningublaga by divination.[105] None of Lipit-Eštar's year
names refers to her consecration.[106] From the name of Gungunum's
thirteenth year, we will learn in section 14.3.2 that the king of Larsa
installed Enninsunzi into this high religious office, probably two
or three years later. A large number of cones from Ur commemorate the construction of the *gipar* by Lipit-Eštar as the residence
of Enninsunzi.[107]

Apart from his *Law Code* and a number of literary letters, Lipit-Eštar
is also remembered thanks to several royal and divine hymns (see table
14.1). Two of his hymns are of particular interest, as they are among the

---

102. *Sumerian Epistolary Miscellany* no. 4: ll. 9–11; see Kleinerman 2011: 121. A place
name Dunnum is mentioned in Gungunum's twenty-second year, but this
event must be placed historically later than the literary letter.

103. *Sumerian Epistolary Miscellany* no. 5; see Kleinerman 2011: 124–126.

104. Compare Kleinerman 2011: 30, n. 53.

105. Sigrist 1988: 28: Year G.

106. Compare Gungunum's Year 6, in which the *en* priestess of the sun god was chosen by divination, with also the names of Years 7 and 8 based on this event,
while the *en* priestess was consecrated only in his ninth year. For the time lag
between the selection and consecration of an *en* priest(ess), see Fitzgerald
2002: 56.

107. Frayne 1990: no. 4.1.5.6: ll. 14–23: "[Lipit-Eštar built] the *gipar* house for
Enninsunzi, the *en* priestess of the god Ningublaga in Ur, [. . .] his beloved
daughter." For the *gipar* of the *en* priestess of Ningublaga, the son of the moon
god, see Charpin 1986: 220–223; Richter 2004: 441–444.

most copied Sumerian literary texts known. As noted earlier (section 14.2.2), the short composition *Lipit-Eštar* B was part of the so-called *Tetrad*. Like the other three texts of this group, this composition is also attested on school tablets.[108] Learning these comparatively easy Sumerian texts not only had an ideological purpose, but also formed an apt transition from the elementary stages of scribal training to more advanced literature. In his hymn, Lipit-Eštar is praised for his intellect, which he owed to the goddess of writing, Nisaba:

> Nisaba, woman radiant with joy, righteous woman, scribe, lady who knows everything, guides your fingers on the clay. She makes the wedges beautiful on the tablet and adorns them with a golden stylus. Nisaba generously bestowed upon you the measuring rod, the surveyor's gleaming line, the yardstick and the tablets which confer wisdom.[109]

Not many kings in Mesopotamian history claimed to be literate: besides Šulgi of Ur and much later Ashurbanipal of Assyria (668–631 BC), Lipit-Eštar was one of the very few. The second praise poem that should be mentioned is *Lipit-Eštar* A, which belongs to a group of ten compositions referred to as the so-called *Decad*. These were Sumerian compositions learned and copied by advanced apprentices.[110] In contrast to the first hymn, this song of praise is written as a monologue; Lipit-Eštar speaks to the reader. As in the other text, Lipit-Eštar is here also referred to as Enlil's son. While his intellectual capabilities are less emphasized, the king praises his virtues as a strong and pious ruler.

Lipit-Eštar was still remembered in much later times, as a very fragmentary chronicle from the seventh-century-BC library of Ashurbanipal

---

108. For a partial bilingual version of the composition (ll. 1–4), see Volk 2012.

109. *Lipit-Eštar* B: ll. 18–24. For this composition, see Vanstiphout 1978.

110. Delnero 2012: 11–13.

of Assyria at Nineveh briefly refers to him: "[. . . k]ing of Isin, the *sukkalmah*, Lipit-Eštar."[111]

Lipit-Eštar was succeeded by Ur-Ninurta, who ruled for twenty-eight years (1925–1898 BC) but appears to have inherited a somewhat weakened kingdom. Isin could not counteract Gungunum's advances. Already at the beginning of his reign, Larsa was able to take over the important harbor of Ur, thereby depriving Isin of access to trading partners in the Persian Gulf, for which Ur was an important hub. Gungunum's presence at Ur is only indicated by the name of his tenth year, but we know from administrative texts found there that he had established himself in this important city several years earlier. Gungunum's advances even allowed him to take over Uruk, Adab, Zabalam, Nippur, and Kisurra.[112] Kisurra, in particular, was in close proximity to Isin.[113]

Roughly half of Ur-Ninurta's year names are known. Their sequence, however, cannot yet be established.[114] Probably in one of his early years he "freed the inhabitants of Nippur from corvée labor and remitted the arrears of royalty, which weighed on their necks."[115] According to this year name, Ur-Ninurta appears to have recaptured Nippur.[116] An important building project in his reign must have been the construction of the wall of Imgur-Sin.[117] This building project is not commemorated by one of his inscriptions. One inscription containing various epithets of

111. Edzard 1957: 98 with n. 475; Glassner 2004: 274–275. For the fragment K. 2973, see also CDLI (https://cdli.ucla.edu/P237122; last accessed August 25, 2020). The text continues with a description of Lipit-Eštar's worship in the Ekur temple.

112. Goddeeris 2016a.

113. For the checkered history of Kisurra, see section 14.4.2.

114. See Wilcke 1985: 309–311. Documents from Kisurra also attest to a year name that refers to Ur-Ninurta's death; see section 14.4.2.

115. Sigrist 1988: 29: Year A.

116. Ur-Ninurta is the earliest ruler of this period to be attested in documents from Nippur; see Goddeeris 2016c: 5.

117. Several consecutive years are named after this event; see Sigrist 1988: 29: Years B–E.

the king can be found on bricks predominantly from Nippur, Isin, and Uruk.[118] The second inscription is only known from a tablet copy from Nippur. In it, Ur-Ninurta dedicated a "[copper] image, whose form was endowed with my face, clasping a votive kid, standing to make supplications for me,"[119] which was set up in the main courtyard of the Gagiššua, Ninlil's temple.

Quite a number of literary texts are known in which Ur-Ninurta appears as the protagonist (see table 14.1). All but one of these literary works are different types of divine hymns with a prayer for the king. *Ur-Ninurta* B, for instance, is a *tigi* song of the god of wisdom, Enki, which ends in the following prayer:

> May Ur-Ninurta, the king in whom Enlil trusts, open up your [i.e., Enki's] house of wisdom in which you have gathered knowledge in plenty, and then be the great ruler of the black-headed. Make terrifying splendor befitting his godhead issue from him, the lion of kingship, in everything that he does, for as long as he lives. May you present him with weighty tribute from the upper and the lower seas, and let Ur-Ninurta bring it into the glorious Ekur. May Enlil look upon him joyously, and add to his period of rule blissful days and years of joy and life.[120]

One composition, however, must be highlighted here. The *Instructions of Ur-Ninurta* is a short wisdom text of seventy-one lines.[121] After the Flood, "in order to organize the plans of Sumer and to abolish wickedness, to implement righteousness,"[122] Ninurta installed the king for long days. Ur-Ninurta is praised as someone who performs his religious duties

---

118. Frayne 1990: no. 4.1.6.1.

119. Frayne 1990: no. 4.1.6.2: vi 6'–10'.

120. *Ur-Ninurta* B: ll. 36–44; translation based on ETCSL (http://etcsl.orinst. ox.ac.uk/cgi-bin/etcsl.cgi?text=c.2.5.6.2; last accessed August 25, 2020).

121. For an edition, see Alster 2005: 221–240.

122. *Instructions of Ur-Ninurta*, ll. 8–9.

diligently (ll. 19–24) and thus he is granted a long life of happiness. The king's righteousness is contrasted to those who do not fulfill their religious duties (ll. 30–36). The second part of the composition instructs his subjects to work diligently and hard on their fields and canals. The text ends with short expressions of humility and submission. With their focus on Nippur, the *Instructions* may have been composed after Ur-Ninurta recaptured the city.[123]

14.3. The kingdom of Larsa

The previous section was chiefly concerned with events as seen from the perspective of Isin and its first six rulers. The long reign of Ur-Ninurta of Isin ended in 1898 BC. Both under Lipit-Eštar and his successor, Ur-Ninurta, King Gungunum of Larsa became troublesome. It is therefore time to turn to the early periods of Larsa's political status at the end of the Ur III period and in the century thereafter.

The site of Larsa (modern Tell Senkereh) lies about 20 km east of Uruk and about 40 km north of Ur. The tell has an oval shape and extends approximately 1,800 m from east to west and 2,000 m from north to south. Its highest point stands 22 m above the plain. In his travel account, William Kennett Loftus, the first modern researcher to investigate the tell, refers to the sheer number of cuneiform tablets at the site.[124] Unfortunately, Loftus's aim was not to collect these records. The first scientific excavations at Larsa took place in 1933 under André Parrot.[125] But in the meantime, Larsa had fallen victim to illicit digging, which caused its rich store of textual records to spill onto the antiquities market.[126] The main religious structure of Larsa, the Ebabbar, is the temple of the sun god and features prominently in the inscriptions left by the kings of Larsa.

---

123. Goddeeris 2016a.

124. Loftus 1857: 252.

125. Huot 1983; Margueron 1983.

126. For a summary, see Middeke-Conlin 2020: 9–10.

14.3.1. The early years of the kingdom of Larsa: in the shadow of Isin's supremacy

Probably coinciding with the beginning of Ibbi-Sin's reign and six years earlier than a dynasty began to form at Isin, a dynasty of Amorite descent began consolidating its power at Larsa. Hardly anything is known about the reigns of the first four rulers of this dynasty.

An exercise tablet now kept in the Yale Babylonian Collection contains a list of all rulers of the Larsa dynasty and the number of years they ruled (figure 14.5). The list extends until Samsu-iluna of Babylon (chapter 18 in this volume), who is assigned a reign of just twelve years. It is therefore likely that the list was composed in his twelfth or the subsequent year.[127]

Another important source is a large, four-sided prism (now in the Louvre) that was compiled in the thirty-ninth regnal year of Hammurabi of Babylon. The text starts with the same four kings as the Yale text and thereafter lists all year-names from the reign of Gungunum up to Rim-Sin.[128] The first four rulers named in these lists are Naplanum (reigning 21 years), Yamṣium or Emṣium (reigning 28 years), Samium (reigning 35 years), and Zabaya (reigning 9 years). Given the fact that the date list from Larsa offers no year names and no economic records survive bearing year names that can be assigned to these rulers, it seems likely that these Amorite chiefs were not necessarily independent rulers but may have been dependent on Isin. Nor cannot it be ruled out that later generations "invented" the beginning of the dynasty which, according to the Yale text, preceded the emergence of Isin in Ibbi-Sin's sixth year.[129] An economic record from Puzriš-Dagan (modern Drehem), dating to

---

127. Clay 1915: no. 32. For an edition of the text, see Grayson 1983: 89. The sequence of the two sides should be switched; the flat obverse is rather damaged, and its content is repeated on the much better-preserved reverse.

128. Thureau-Dangin 1918: AO 7025 (CDLI P492501); side (b) of the prism is broken; for an edition see CDLI (https://cdli.ucla.edu/P492501; last accessed August 25, 2020).

129. Edzard 2001; Charpin 2004: 69 with n. 207.

FIGURE 14.5. A list of Larsa rulers. Yale Babylonian Collection, YBC 2142 (reverse). Author's photograph.

the second year of Ibbi-Sin, records deliveries for small cattle, among others, for the sun-god Utu at Larsa.[130] This text therefore indicates that, in Naplanum's reign, Larsa was not yet independent from Ur.[131] An Amorite named Naplanum occurs frequently in administrative records of the Ur III period, ranging in date from late in the reign of

---

130. Keiser 1971: no. 607: l. 6.

131. Fitzgerald 2002: 18–19.

Šulgi to Šu-Sin.[132] Following Piotr Steinkeller, Naplanum was the most important Amorite chieftain who interacted with the Ur III state.[133] In the seventh and eighth years of Amar-Sin, Naplanum resided at Kisig, thus in the central area of the (later) kingdom of Larsa.[134] Naplanum's original home appears to be the "land of Martu" (Sumerian *kur mar-tu*), which may be situated to the east of the Tigris in the area of the Jebel Hamrin.[135]

Very little can be said about Naplanum's two successors Emṣium and Samium. Like Naplanum, these chieftains did not leave any official inscriptions despite their long reigns. Samium, however, is invoked in the oath of a legal document from Girsu.[136] He thus appears to have exerted some power there.[137] Only Zabaya, the last of these early rulers and Samium's son, left inscriptions. From Larsa comes an Akkadian inscription on bricks commemorating the construction of the Ebabbar temple.[138] Another similar inscription was found in a settlement on the northern fringes of the kingdom of Larsa, about 14 km north of Nippur. This settlement, Maškan-šapir, rose to some significance in the periods under discussion. The documentary evidence suggests that, for most of this period, Maškan-šapir was linked to the kingdom of Larsa.[139]

---

132. Steinkeller 2004: 37, n. 56.

133. Steinkeller 2004: 38.

134. For the evidence of his presence in Kisig, see Steinkeller 2004: 38, n. 64. The site of Kisig (probably modern Tell al-Laḥm) is relatively close to Ur; see Beaulieu 1992. Naplanum's son Ili-babum did business in Ur in the second year of Ibbi-Sin.

135. Steinkeller 2004: 39.

136. De Genouillac 1936: pl. LIII: AO 13015: ll. 8–9. A contemporaneous letter from Ešnunna mentions a Samium, but this individual may be a different one: Whiting 1987: no. 30: l. 32 (with commentary on p. 87).

137. De Graef 2008.

138. Frayne 1990: no. 4.2.4.1.

139. Steinkeller 2004: 27.

Zabaya referred to himself as *rabiān Amurrim*, which can be translated as "Amorite chief."[140] Another dedicatory inscription to the goddess Nanše is known from a late first millennium BC copy in the so-called Sippar temple library.[141] An Old Babylonian letter from Girsu suggests that Maškan-šapir remained under control of Larsa in the reign of Zabaya.[142]

There is still much speculation concerning the extent to which these early chieftains of the Larsa dynasty fit into the historical fabric of the last decades of the Ur III period. The situation, however, becomes clearer as we move on to the subsequent rulers.

14.3.2. More light on Larsa: the reigns of Gungunum and Abi-sare

Samium had a second son called Gungunum (1932–1906 BC), who ascended the throne of Larsa after his brother Zabaya.[143] He was a contemporary of Lipit-Eštar and Ur-Ninurta of Isin. Despite the relative supremacy of Isin over southern Mesopotamia in the twentieth century BC, the kingdom of Larsa began to expand in Gungunum's reign.

---

140. Frayne 1990: no. 4.2.4.2 (AbD 88–286, not AbD 88–280); see Stone and Zimansky 2004: 146–147, 152, fig. 101. We find the title *rabiān Amurrim* also in an inscription from the reign of Larsa's sixth king Abi-sare (Frayne 1990: no. 4.2.6.I: i 27′) and in the seal impression of one of his servants (Simmons 1978: no. 207; see Frayne 1990: no. 4.2.6.2004: l. 4).

141. Al-Rawi 2002. It is difficult to say whether a copy of an inscription of Zabaya found at Sippar would indicate that Sippar was under Larsa's control in Zabaya's reign. The manuscript's colophon refers to a bronze buck, and as this was a movable object, the copy may have also been produced elsewhere.

142. Veenhof 2005: no. 10: ll. 10′–12′: "Since my lord Zabaya has ascended to the throne he has given all this [i.e., commodities accounted for before]." For an oath invoking Zabaya's predecessor Samium in a legal document from Girsu, see immediately preceding text in this section.

143. In a royal inscription found stamped on bricks from Larsa and Umm al-Wawiya, he refers to himself as "mighty heir of Samium" (Frayne 1990: no. 4.2.5.3: ll. 4–5).

The aforementioned date list in the Louvre, which was certainly drawn up at Larsa, assigns twenty-seven year names to Gungunum's reign.[144] Among the activities covered by his year names are also two campaigns to Iran during which Pašime (modern Tell Abu Sheeja) and Anšan were defeated in his third through fifth years.[145] We have seen that Iddin-Dagan forged an alliance with Anšan in his second year (see section 14.2.2). The names of his sixth to ninth years commemorate the choice of an *en* priestess of the sun god by divination and her installation.[146] This act is not reflected in any inscriptions so far.

The presence of dates as early as Gungunum's sixth year on administrative texts from Ur suggests that his rule extended there as well.[147] Up to this point, Ur was under the control of Isin. The loss of Ur had serious ramifications for the kingdom of Isin. As noted earlier (section 14.2.3), Išme-Dagan of Isin (1955–1937 BC) installed his daughter in the prestigious office of the moon god's *en* priestess there, before Gungunum took over control. She took the name Enanatuma. Gungunum, however, did not remove her. On the contrary, Enanatuma dedicated two of her inscriptions, commemorating building work, to the new king of Ur. In these she acknowledges her new patron, the "king of the land of Sumer and Akkad."[148]

The year name of Gungunum's thirteenth year commemorates the installation of Enninsunzi as *en* priestess of Ningublaga.[149] This

---

144. Thureau-Dangin 1918: AO 7025, side (a): ll. 5–33.

145. Gungunum may have exercised some control over Elam, as a text from Susa dates to his 16th regnal year; see Vallat 1996: 310–311; Charpin 2004: 73.

146. Sigrist 1990: 7–8: Years 6–8.

147. Figulla and Martin 1953: no. 617. The names of Years 20, 25, and 26 refer to building work and the consecration of a statue at Ur, while already Year 10 commemorates furniture brought into the temple of Nanna, the patron deity of Ur.

148. Frayne 1990: no. 4.2.5.1; no. 4.2.5.2.

149. Sigrist 1990: 8.

en priestess is not completely unknown. She was none other than the daughter of Lipit-Eštar, king of Isin (see section 14.2.4).

At Ur the archive of documents found in the temple of Ningal covers 120 years, from the ninth year of Gungunum to the nineteenth year of Rim-Sin.[150] This *long durée* of archives shows that temples and their economy were not necessarily vulnerable to changes in the political landscape.[151] The lack of a year name recording the takeover of Ur may suggest that Ur fell peacefully into Gungunum's hands and life went on as normal under the new ruler. The names of the subsequent years record more pious acts, as well as the digging of canals.[152]

Gungunum's nineteenth year name reports the defeat of the army of Malgium.[153] In his twenty-first year, Gungunum focused again on Larsa and built its great wall. Brick stamps from Larsa and nearby Umm al-Wawiya, as well as a recently published building inscription on a broken clay nail, commemorate this building project.[154] The conflicts between the two powers Isin and Larsa had ever so slightly intensified since Zabaya's reign, and Gungunum may have felt the need to tend to Larsa's fortifications.

Gungunum is remembered furthermore in a number of songs of praise, several of which are composed in Sumerian and one in Akkadian (table 14.2).

---

150. For these texts, see Figulla 1953; Black and Spada 2008.

151. Charpin 2004: 56.

152. E.g., Sigrist 1990: 9: Year 15: "Year: (Gungunum) filled the ditches (connected) to the banks of the Anepada canal (with water)." Year 17 reports on the Imgur-Sin canal; Year 19 concerns the opening of the intake for the mountain canal; Year 22 records the digging of the Išartum canal; and Years 27 and 28 report further canal works.

153. Based on textual evidence, the city of Malgium can be located somewhere between Der and Babylon, probably close to Maškan-šapir; see Charpin 2004: 31, n. 19.

154. For the brick inscription, see Frayne 1990: no. 4.2.5.3, for the clay nail, see George 2011: no. 44. The name of the wall was "Utu conquers the rebel lands." This inscription is also the earliest text that includes a royal statement of ideal market rates of commodities against silver; see George 2011: 96 and section 14.6.3 in this chapter.

Table 14.2. The literary corpus pertaining to the kings of the Larsa dynasty (see also Brisch 2007: 264–269; Peterson 2016)

King	Genre	Compositions
Gungunum	Divine hymns	*adab*-song of Nanna (= Gungunum A) Gungunum B[a]
	Akkadian hymn	van Dijk 1976: no. 41
Sin-iddinam	Divine hymns	Praise poem of Sin-iddinam (= Sin-iddinam A) Sin-iddinam B Sin-iddinam C Collection of four prayers for Sin-iddinam (= Sin-iddinam D) Sin-iddinam and Iškur (= Sin-iddinam E)
	Letter prayers	*Sin-iddinam to Nin-Isina* *Sin-iddinam to Utu*
Sin-iqišam	Divine hymns	Hymn to Numušda for Sin-iqišam (= Sin-iqišam A)
Warad-Sin	Hymns and prayers	Praise poem of Warad-Sin (Földi and Zólyomi 2020)
Rim-Sin	Hymns and prayers	Prayer to Enlil for Rim-Sin (= Rim-Sin A) Hymn to Haya for Rim-Sin (= Rim-Sin B) Prayer to An for Rim-Sin (= Rim-Sin C) Prayer to Nanna for Rim-Sin (= Rim-Sin D) Prayer to Nanna for Rim-Sin (= Rim-Sin E) Prayer to Nanna for Rim-Sin (= Rim-Sin F) Prayer to Nanna for Rim-Sin (= Rim-Sin G) *adab*-song to Inana for Rim-Sin (= Rim-Sin H)
	Letters of petition	*Letter of Ninšatapada to Rim-Sin* *Letter of Nanna-manšum to Rim-Sin*[?]
	Love lyrics	van Dijk, Goetze, and Hussey 1985: no. 24 Yale Babylonian Collection, MLC 1362[b]

[a] See Peterson 2016: 163; Sjöberg 1973: 24–31 (Text 4/B) had combined this fragmentary composition with *Gungunum* A.

[b] This text is unpublished; an edition by the present author is in preparation.

One of these hymns invokes the twin god(s) Enki-Nirah,[155] while an *adab* song of the moon god must have been composed after Gungunum's takeover of Ur for it ends with the following lines:

> In your Ur, the ancient city, the princely land, the city of the great divine powers, in your Ekišnugal which light does not enter, the house which never diminishes, may Gungunum whom you have chosen attain a life of many days.[156]

A rather fragmentary text, the "oldest known example of a royal hymn with a prayer in Akkadian,"[157] ends with the following passage:

> [The kingship] of Gungunum rose above the multitudes of rebels; it is strong![158]

Gungunum's successor Abi-sare reigned for eleven years (1905–1895 BC). The name of his third year commemorates the consecration of a silver statue for the moon god at Ur.[159] "No. 7 Quiet Street" at Ur yielded a large number of copies of royal inscriptions, including a copy of a long inscription that was once inscribed on the aforementioned silver statue. Abi-sare's royal titulary contains the title "king of Ur" and "Amorite chief."[160] The theme of the second extant royal inscription of Abi-sare, found stamped on two bricks from Larsa, is the strengthening of the great wall of Larsa and the construction of a palace. This wall was constructed by Abi-sare's predecessor, Gungunum, in his twenty-first

---

155. Cohen 2017: 11–21.

156. Sjöberg 1973: 52: rev. 11′–13′ (with Sjöberg 1973: 25, 28).

157. Wasserman 2018: xxix.

158. Wasserman 2018: xxxii.

159. Sigrist 1990: 12: Years 3 and 4.

160. Frayne 1990: no. 4.2.6.1: i 26′–27′.

year.[161] Neither of these two building projects features in Abi-sare's year names.

The control of water became crucial in Abi-sare's reign. An important strategic tool in southern Mesopotamia was to cut off the water supply of a rival by damming the river upstream. We have already noted that the digging of canals was commemorated in the repertoire of Gungunum's year names. Four of the nine year names of Abi-sare record canal works.[162] The canals mentioned in the year names are the Imgur-Inana-Zabalam (or Šega-Inana-Zabalam) canal, the Anepada canal,[163] and the Hiritum canal.[164]

Digging these canals and the construction work associated with them were part of a major project that continued into the reign of Abi-sare's successor, Sumu-El, who also commemorated the digging of canals in two of his year names.[165] Details of this major project also come from administrative texts consisting of approximately fifty letters and about sixty economic records, which are known as the "Archive of Lu-igisa," although in fact they are a group of archives probably originating in the region of Lagaš.[166] Among other things, these ephemeral texts provide information on the construction of a reservoir and a wall at the mouth of the canal of Isin.[167]

We shall cite here two texts that relate to this corpus, a letter and an administrative account. According to the letter, a certain Ikun-pi-Sin was

---

161. Frayne 1990: no. 4.2.6.2: ll. 6–11: "[Abi-sare . . .], in the course of one year strengthened the great wall of Larsa, the wall 'Utu-Conquers-the-Rebel-Lands' [and] built the palace of his settlement." For the inscription of Gungunum that mentions this wall, see earlier discussion in the present section.

162. Years 2 (and 3), 4 (and 5), 6 (and 7); see Charpin 2002a: 548, Table 1.

163. The Anepada canal is already mentioned in Gungunum's fifteenth year.

164. A variant of the name of his seventh year replaces the name of the canal by the designation "grand canal of Abi-sare"; see Sigrist 1990: 13.

165. Years 7 (and 8) and 20 (and 21–22); see Charpin 2002a: 548, Table 1.

166. For this archive, see Walters 1970 (with the review of Stol 1971); see further Charpin 2004: 78 with n. 258.

167. Charpin 2002a: 557.

arrested, probably because he neglected the maintenance of the canals, which was his responsibility. As in legal documents, several witnesses are mentioned at the end of the letter:

> Speak to Banum, thus Ikun-pi-Sin. As to what I wrote to you: if I really have answered in a fraudulent way, I will surely render an account to Sumu-El, my lord. (This is) the second month that I myself have been held in custody. My canals are dammed up, so call up the slaves! After the messenger of Nur-Sin had inspected, I myself came to open my canals, but me, he "killed" me and it is a grief to (my) heart. [List of witnesses][168]

The second text is a simple administrative account:

> Sixty liters barley (for) *miksu* tax, the first time; two *kor*, [the second] time: Delivery of Ibni-Dagan, a representative of the incantation priests, for the wages of the workers (who) dug the Etellum canal. Received by Erra-bani. The conveyor is Lu-igisa. Seal of Sin-talu and Šulgi-dan. Month II, Year Abi-sare 10.[169]

14.4. The fight for power between Isin and Larsa

14.4.1. The reign of Sumu-El

The reign of Abi-sare's successor, Sumu-El (1894–1866 BC), was characterized by ups and downs.[170] He was a contemporary of the Isin kings Bur-Sin, Lipit-Enlil, and Erra-imitti. At Babylon, Sumu-abum and Sumu-la-El were in power. Only a few inscriptions survive from his fairly long reign. One inscription on cones found at Ur commemorates the

---

168. Stol 1981: no. 227; see Rowton 1967: 274.

169. Alexander 1943: no. 99 (NBC 5469); see Walters 1970: 3–4 (text 2).

170. The seal of one of Sumu-El's servants whose impression is preserved on a number of tablets provides a syllabic spelling for his name; see Frayne 1990: no. 4.2.7.2003: [*su*]-*mu*-⌜*i-la*⌝.

construction of a storehouse for the goddess Inana.[171] A second inscription, also from Ur, deals with the construction of a temple for the goddess Nanaya.[172]

In addition to the information derived from Sumu-El's inscriptions, his year names record a number of events. His fourth year is named after his defeat of Akusum and the army of Kazallu. Only one year later, Sumu-El defeated the army of Uruk. Girsu appears to have remained under Sumu-El's control. The famous dog figurine excavated there contains a dedication to the goddess Nin-Isina for the life of Sumu-El.[173]

Juridical documents, particularly correspondence sent by the king to his generals (Akkadian *rabi sikkatim*), are an important source of political information. The extant letters, some of which were published only recently, show that, at the end of Sumu-El's reign, Isin exerted military pressure on Larsa. This comes through clearly in the following short messages, four of which are given here in translation:

> Speak to the heads of security, thus Sumu-El: Important, your watches must be strict! Why do you keep releasing troops from service so acquiescently? Just now, Erra-imitti is giving orders to march on Šayana. Make no mistake, as soon as your numbers have decreased, he will reach out against me and do some damage. Important, do not release troops from service![174]

> Speak to Beli-ay-annadi and the Heads of Security, thus Sumu-El: Important, your watches must be strict! Do not fail in your duties! Just now, Erra-imitti has come upstream to Uṣarpara. I don't know (whether) he will move toward you or go to Uruk.[175]

---

171. Frayne 1990: no. 4.2.7.1.

172. Frayne 1990: no. 4.2.7.2.

173. Frayne 1990: no. 4.2.7.2001.

174. George 2018: no. 1.

175. George 2018: no. 17.

> Speak to Beli-ay-annadi and the Heads of Security, thus Sumu-El: Important, your watches must be strict! Just now Erra-imitti has come upstream to Kisurra. Reinforce your outlying districts![176]

> Speak [to] the heads of security, thus Sumu-El: Important, your watches must be strict! Just now, Erra-imitti is going to plunder this river bank. The soldiers must [not] be able to cross over!"[177]

As Andrew George put it, Sumu-El "emerges as an anxious delegator with little confidence in his correspondents' competence."[178] Indeed, the end of Sumu-El's reign was probably characterized by political and military mishaps and a general weakness of the state. The letter-prayer of Sin-iddinam addressed to a statue of Nur-Adad refers to the economic and social problems preceding Nur-Adad's takeover of power at Larsa:

> No plants grew in its [i.e., of Larsa] steppe. Wheat did not lean in the furrow. In the city, all the stored grain was depleted. In all the streets there was disease. House was turned against house. Battle was waged in its public square. Murder was committed by means of weapons. In all the streets ruin set in. Brother consumed brother."[179]

Like Išme-Dagan in the *Nippur Lament* (see section 14.2.3), Sin-iddinam did not identify the king responsible for this dire situation, but Sumu-El is the only likely candidate.

---

176. George 2018: no. 18.

177. Chambon 2015.

178. George 2018: xi.

179. van Dijk 1971: no. 41: ll. 61–76; see Fitzgerald 2002: 84.

14.4.2. Isin under Bur-Sin and Erra-imitti

Bur-Sin (1897–1876 BC) followed Ur-Ninurta on Isin's throne. Two of his royal inscriptions are known. One of them, stamped on bricks from Nippur and Isin, contains various epithets of the king. Among other things, Bur-Sin refers to himself as "the one who restored the cultic ordinances of Eridu."[180] Another inscription is inscribed on the base of a fragment of an agate statuette, dedicated to the goddess Inana, the whereabouts of which are currently unknown.[181] It is noteworthy that "king of Isin" does not appear among Bur-Sin's titles here. Two other inscriptions appear on votive objects dedicated to the goddesses Nanaya and Nin-Isina for the life of Bur-Sin. Only a few of his year names have been identified to date. These mostly record pious acts. Two year names, however, refer to construction work on walls.[182]

From Uruk comes an inventory of literary letters, including one addressed to Bur-Sin.[183] Many of the incipits listed in this text coincide with literary letters also copied at Nippur. The latest king dealt with there, however, is Lipit-Eštar (1934–1924 BC). This may indicate that the production of literary letters stopped at Nippur earlier than in other places such as Uruk.[184]

The court poets of Bur-Sin also left three divine hymns, one of which is addressed to Sud, Enlil's spouse and the patron deity of the ancient city of Šuruppak. The reverence of this deity by a king of Isin is certainly noteworthy. An inscription of Enlil-bani (1862–1839 BC) commemorates the construction of the temple Edimgalana, which is identical to one of her shrines also mentioned in this hymn, which introduces Bur-Sin and the role he played in governing the land:

---

180. Frayne 1990: no. 4.1.7.1: l. 5; see also George 2011: no. 41.

181. Frayne 1990: no. 4.1.7.2; see also Weidner 1927.

182. Sigrist 1988: 30: Year A: "Year, when Bur-Sin built the great walls. . . ."

183. Cavigneaux 1996: 57–59, no. 112.

184. Huber Vulliet 2011: 499.

> Your vizier (. . .) has made the true crown radiantly manifest over
> Bur-Sin. Since you have placed your gleaming (crown) on his head,
> (the vizier) has bestowed upon (the king) [. . .] the scepter to guide
> the people. Bur-Sin—he is truly their shepherd and prince! Since
> you have given him the staff (to direct) the teeming peoples, may he
> govern the entirety of your settled lands for you![185]

Although Šuruppak (modern Fara) was a prominent site in the late Early
Dynastic period, it seems not unlikely that by the Isin period it still had
some religious significance for the kings of Isin.[186]

Bur-Sin was succeeded by Lipit-Enlil, who only ruled for five years
(1875–1871 BC). He was a contemporary of Sumu-El of Larsa and Sumu-
la-El of Babylon. His few year names indicate dedications for Enlil at
Nippur.[187] Sumu-El appears to have briefly lost control of Nippur in his
thirteenth and fourteenth years, likely to Bur-Sin of Isin.[188] So far, no
inscriptions of Lipit-Enlil have been identified. The offering lists from
the Ninurta temple (the Ešumeša) at Nippur, which were found during the fourth and fifth excavation seasons, are an important economic
source for the nineteenth century BC. The approximately four hundred
texts cover more than seventy-five years, beginning in the first year of
Lipit-Enlil. After listing offerings presented to the gods, the texts name
the individuals to whom the offerings were subsequently redistributed.[189]

Little is known about the reign of Isin's next king, Erra-imitti, who
reigned for eight years (1870–1863 BC). He left no royal inscriptions apart
from a seal belonging to one of his servants, found at Ur.[190] Anecdotal

---

185. Metcalf 2019: no. 1: ll. 17–23.

186. See the discussion in Metcalf 2019: 10–11. Richter 2004: 250–251 had previously argued that Sud's proximity to the goddess of healing may have triggered
her veneration in Isin, but the new hymn makes this hypothesis unlikely.

187. Sigrist 1988: 31.

188. Reculeau 2008.

189. For these records, see Sigrist 1984; also Goddeeris 2007a: 200.

190. Frayne 1990: no. 4.1.9.2001.

information, however, comes from a late chronicle. The *Chronicle of Early Kings*, known from two Late Babylonian manuscripts, deals with the transition of power from Erra-imitti to his successor Enlil-bani. In one section the document states:

> King Erra-imitti ordered Enlil-bani, the gardener, to sit on the throne as royal substitute and put the crown of kingship on his head. Erra-imitti died in his palace while swallowing hot soup in little sips. Enlil-bani, who sat on the throne, did not resign and was elevated to the royal office.[191]

This account may not be entirely fictional, as the custom of substitute kings may date back to the Old Babylonian period.[192] Erra-imitti's year names show that he conquered Kisurra,[193] a city in close proximity to Isin. By Erra-imitti's time, Kisurra could look back on a rather checkered past in the preceding century alone. Larsa had a hold on it as early as Gungunum's reign.[194] Isin's king Ur-Ninurta may have had control over Kisurra, at least briefly, but this was short-lived. Local rulers consolidated their power over Kisurra at the end of his reign.[195] In one of his year names, Kisurra's first ruler, Itur-Šamaš, recorded the construction of Kisurra's wall, probably to secure his reign and independence.[196]

---

191. Glassner 2004: 272–273: no. 20 (BM 26472): ll. 31–36.

192. Hunger and Pingree 1999: 25–26.

193. Sigrist 1988: 32: Year D.

194. According to Sommerfeld 1983: 206 with n. 8, Gungunum may have had control of the area already as early as his tenth year (based on a text published by van Dijk 1968: no. 23). Apart from Year 10, the texts from Kisurra also attest to his Years 23, a, b, and c. One text is dated to "Year: Gungunum died"; see Goddeeris 2009: 15.

195. Texts from Kisurra are attested up to Gungunum's Year 4, while four texts are dated to "Year: Ur-Ninurta died"; see Goddeeris 2009: 15.

196. Goddeeris 2009: 17: Year a: "Year: Itur-Šamaš built the wall of Kisurra (named) 'Ka-Hadi-El.'" Note that Sommerfeld 1983: 207–208 had assumed that Hadi-El was the name of the first ruler of Kisurra, but also gave the now accepted reading as an option.

Excavated family archives cover a period of about thirty years starting at the end of the twentieth century BC.[197] A number of bricks contain a short Akkadian inscription: "Itur-Šamaš, chief of the Rabbeans,[198] son of Iddin-Ilum, governor of Kisurra, beloved of Šamaš and Annunitum."[199] Most of Itur-Šamaš's year names commemorate pious acts.[200]

Itur-Šamaš was succeeded by a number of short-lived rulers: Ṣallum, Ubaya, and Zikru. Noteworthy are the last two independent rulers of Kisurra, Manna-balti-El and his son Ibni-šadum. None of these rulers left inscriptions, but their year names commemorate various building projects, including irrigation works.[201] In one of his year names, Ibni-šadum mentioned the building of the wall of Pi-naratim.[202] The Larsa king Sumu-El commemorated its destruction in his eighth year.[203] Two years later he undertook a campaign into northern Mesopotamia, which led to a significant expansion of the kingdom of Larsa. Kisurra's independence lasted around thirty years.[204] We know from the impressions of a seal that Sumu-El's daughter married the last king of Kisurra. The

---

197. Goddeeris 2007b.

198. The Rabbeans are a Yaminite tribe, according to the Mari sources. Part of this tribe was located in the area of the Middle Euphrates, the other in the area of Kisurra; see Charpin 2004: 74, n. 241. But according to Stol 2008, Rababu (as written in Itur-Šamaš's title) is not necessarily identical with the Yaminite tribe; see also Michel 2008; de Boer 2013b: 271.

199. Frayne 1990: no. 4.7.1.1.

200. Itur-Šamaš's Years f (and g), h (and i), k, and m commemorate various construction projects for temples for Annunitum, Enki, Adad and a deity in Akšak. According to the name of Year c, he fashioned a *tilimdu*-cup for Sud. In Years d (and e), he fashioned a bronze kettledrum for Annunitum. According to the name of Year j, he installed an *en* priestess of Nanna. The only other military endeavor is Year l with the seizure of Ibarum. For the year names, see Goddeeris 2009: 17–18.

201. E.g., Manna-balti-El's Year g: "Year: he dug a grand irrigation ditch (towards) the sea (called) 'Hill of Enlil'"; see Goddeeris 2009: 20.

202. Goddeeris 2009: 20: Year a.

203. Sigrist 1990: 17; see also section 14.5.2.

204. See the synchronistic table in Sommerfeld 1983: 228–229.

inscription reads: "Šat-Sin, daughter of Sumu-El, daughter-in-law of Manna-balti-El, the wife of Ibni-šadum."[205]

After losing its independence under Sumu-El, Kisurra was ruled by various overlords: Babylon, Uruk, and Isin. Sumu-abum of Babylon ruled briefly over Kisurra.[206] There is consensus that Uruk also exerted control over Kisurra. A number of year names related to Uruk are attested in documents from Kisurra. The only ruler mentioned in these is a certain Alila-hadum.[207] Oath formulae in the extant legal documents further attest to a second ruler named Sumu-binasa (or Sumu-kanasa).[208] None of these rulers is yet attested in inscriptions from Uruk (see section 14.6.1).[209]

Erra-imitti's takeover of Kisurra must have been directed against Larsa and its contemporary kings Sumu-El (until 1866 BC) and Nur-Adad.[210] Recently published letters sent by Sumu-El to his heads of security highlighting the precarious military situation of the time may be related to Erra-imitti's invasion of Larsa territory (see section 14.4.1).[211] Another year name of Erra-imitti records the destruction of the wall of Kazallu.[212] Some years earlier, Sumu-El was already victorious over Kazallu.[213]

Table 14.3 presents the dynasties of Isin, Larsa, Uruk, and Babylon in the twentieth and mid-nineteenth centuries BC.

---

205. Charpin 2002b; also Földi 2013: §6.10.

206. Sommerfeld 1983: 220–221. Sumu-abum's rule over Kisurra may fall into his twelfth or thirteenth year. One document from Kisurra is dated to the "Year in which Sumu-abum returned to his city"; see Goddeeris 2009: 16.

207. Goddeeris 2009: 16.

208. Kienast 1978: no. 19: rev. 9'.

209. Charpin 2004: 76, n. 248 refers to the mention of Sumu-binasa in the letter AO 21105: l. 18 (see Charpin and Durand 1981: 104–106).

210. Sommerfeld 1983: 226–227, referring to a sale contract from Kisurra dated to Year E of Erra-imitti (published as Simmons 1978: no. 319).

211. George 2018: 11 with n. 3. Some of these letters are cited in section 14.4.1.

212. Sigrist 1988: 32: Year E.

213. Defeats of Kazallu's army occur in Sumu-El's Years 4 and 15.

Table 14.3. The dynasties of Isin, Larsa, Uruk, and Babylon from the late twenty-first to the mid-nineteenth century BC.

Isin	Larsa	Uruk	Babylon
Išbi-Erra (2019–1987)	Naplanum (2025–2005)		
Šu-ilišu (1986–1977)	Yamsium (2004–1977)		
Iddin-Dagan (1976–1956)	Samium (1976–1942)		
Išme-Dagan (1955–1937)	Zabaya (1941–1933)		
Lipit-Eštar (1936–1926)	Gungunum (1932–1906)		
Ur-Ninurta (1925–1898)	Abi-sare (1905–1895)	Alila-hadum	
Bur-Sîn (1897–1876)	Sumu-El (1894–1866)	Sumu-binasa	Sumu-abum (1894–1881)
Lipit-Enlil (1875–1871)		Naram-Sîn	Sumu-la-El (1880–1845)
Erra-imitti (1870–1863)	Nur-Adad (1865–1850)	Sîn-kašid (ca. 1865/60–1833)	
Enlil-bani (1862–1839)			

14.5. The path to a unified state: Larsa's rise to power

We have seen that over a period of 150 years, Larsa was able to slowly assert its hold in southern Mesopotamia. The early rulers of Larsa, particularly those without recorded year names, were Amorite chiefs and probably did not enjoy independent rule in Larsa. The first signs of a strengthening of Larsa's rule occurred during the reign of the fourth king, Zabaya. The fate of Larsa changed dramatically in the mid-nineteenth century, however, when political power in Babylonia slowly shifted there, in the reign of Nur-Adad. This section deals with five kings, from Nur-Adad to Ṣilli-Adad, whose reigns cover just thirty years.

14.5.1. The reigns of Nur-Adad and Sin-iddinam

The origins of Nur-Adad, who ruled for sixteen years (1865–1850 BC), are unknown, and it is probable that he usurped Larsa's throne. A letter-prayer addressed by his successor to a statue of Nur-Adad recounts his rise to power:

> [Utu] was moved by his [artful] lot to restore his city-lordship and chose the righteous shepherd, Nur-Adad, the father who engendered me. He took him from amidst the countless people and elevated him to the kingship of the land.[214]

Nur-Adad left a number of inscriptions. In these, as well as those of his successors, including Ṣilli-Adad, all references to Amorites are omitted. Possibly the family of Nur-Adad was not of Amorite descent.[215] In his inscriptions he does not refer to himself as "king of Ur" any longer, but as

---

214. van Dijk 1971: no. 41: ll. 97–107. However, note that also Nur-Adad's son and successor Sin-iddinam is said to have been "rightfully chosen among the countless people by [the youth U]tu" (Wagensonner 2011: 19: YBC 4624: iii 13–15).

215. Fitzgerald 2002: 78.

"provider of Ur," which probably had cultic significance.[216] In one of his inscriptions Nur-Adad recognized himself as a native of Larsa,[217] perhaps to help legitimize himself as king there. Indications are that Nur-Adad or his family were possibly of Lagašite extraction.[218]

None of Nur-Adad's year names deal with military campaigns, except for one variant year name, which commemorates the (re)capture of Maškan-šapir.[219] There is too little information to tell in whose reign, after Zabaya, the important settlement of Maškan-šapir was lost to Larsa. Other than the recapture of this settlement, only pious acts are commemorated in Nur-Adad's year names. Two years were named after his consecration of a "throne with armrests finished in gold."[220] He also appointed an *en* priestess of the sun god.[221] Nur-Adad's piety extended toward other gods as well, such as Inana, Enki, and Nanna. Two of his year names commemorated the consecration of a copper statue of his predecessor Abi-sare.[222] As we shall see further in this section, his son Sin-iddinam also fashioned a statue of his predecessor.

Two of Nur-Adad's inscriptions deal with construction work in the moon god's sanctuary at Ur.[223] Nur-Adad also invested in the Gipar-ku, the residence of the *en* priestess at Ur,[224] although we do not know who held this position during his reign. One of Nur-Adad's year names refers to the construction of Enki's temple, which is also corroborated by

---

216. E.g., Frayne 1990: no. 4.2.8.1: l. 3.

217. Frayne 1990: no. 4.2.8.7: i 24–25: "He (i.e., Utu) bestowed upon me the shepherdship of my [city], in which I was born."

218. van Dijk 1965: 15; see also the discussion in Fitzgerald 2002: 78–79.

219. Sigrist 1990: 23: Year G; see also Steinkeller 2004: 27.

220. Sigrist 1990: 22: Years B and C.

221. Sigrist 1990: 22: Years C and D.

222. Sigrist 1990: 23: Years J and K.

223. Frayne 1990: no. 4.2.8.2 deals with the construction of the Ganunmah, a "proper house for butter and cheese," whereas Frayne 1990: no. 4.2.8.3 commemorates the construction of an oven and a cauldron for the moon god.

224. Frayne 1990: no. 4.2.8.4.

an inscription found at both Ur and Eridu.[225] The year name, according to which Nur-Adad built the great wall of Larsa called "Utu has achieved his triumph,"[226] is also corroborated by an inscription. Lastly, another year name records dredging the Euphrates, which was silting up.[227]

At Larsa, Nur-Adad also began but did not complete the construction of a palace, excavated in 1933, north of the Ebabbar temple. An anepigraphic ground plan on a clay tablet in the Schøyen Collection may depict this or a very similar palace.[228] The detailed plan shows rooms, halls, and antechambers situated around a central courtyard.

This fairly long list of pious acts and constructions initiated by Nur-Adad suggests a period of prosperity for Larsa. But there are indications of problems during his reign as well. There may have been a natural disaster, such as a change in the course of the Euphrates and maybe even the Tigris. The aforementioned year name recording the dredging of the Euphrates may imply a difficult environmental situation.[229] There may also have been enemy attacks on Larsa, possibly involving the well-established tactic of cutting off the city's water supply by blocking its

---

225. Sigrist 1990: 23: Year H ("G"). For the order of Years G to M, see Fitzgerald 2002: 90–96 and compare the inscriptions: Frayne 1990: nos. 4.2.8.5 and 4.2.8.6.

226. Frayne 1990: no. 4.2.8.7: ll. 74–75. The name of Year I is closely comparable; see Sigrist 1990: 23.

227. Sigrist 1990: 22: Year E. This year is also referred to by Sin-iddinam in his second letter-prayer to Nur-Adad's statue; see van Dijk 1971: no. 41: ll. 209–211. The second letter-prayer contains several references to year names of Nur-Adad, which help to put them into sequence.

228. Friberg 2007: 229 (MS 3031); for a photograph, see CDLI (https://cdli.ucla.edu/P252037; last accessed August 25, 2020).

229. The issue may also be implied by the following statement in one of his inscriptions: "when he had made Ur content, had removed evil [and the cause for any] complaint from it, had regathered its scattered people" (Frayne 1990: no. 4.2.8.3: ll. 26–32). Nur-Adad's successor Sin-iddinam may also refer to these problems when stating: "[The gods] instructed (me) [. . .] to dig the Tigris, to restore (its banks, and) to establish my name for a long life-span" (Frayne 1990: no. 4.2.9.2: ll. 27–32; see Edzard 1957: 144).

canals.[230] His successor Sin-iddinam left two letter-prayers which were addressed to a statue of Nur-Adad. We only have a copy of the inscription on the statue and the two letters.[231] The first letter addresses all the problems (diverted canals, enemy fortifications, insufficient crops, unrest, and so forth) that had accumulated before the sun god chose Nur-Adad to be Larsa's ruler (see section 14.5.1). Thereafter, Sin-iddinam recounts his father's restoration of peace and prosperity. The letter-prayer implies that all difficulties ended when Nur-Adad became king, but archival documents show that they continued to plague his reign.[232] According to his "standard inscription," found stamped on bricks from Larsa, Nur-Adad was "the one who has made the foundation of the throne of Larsa secure (and) regathered its scattered people."[233]

Nur-Adad's successor Sin-iddinam ruled for seven years (1849–1843 BC). Despite a relatively short reign, quite a substantial number of royal inscriptions and literary compositions from it have survived. Sin-iddinam already came to power during Nur-Adad's lifetime and served as co-regent at least until his fourth year.[234] Two legal texts from Lagaš invoke both Nur-Adad and Sin-iddinam in their oaths.[235]

According to a copy of one of his inscriptions, Sin-iddinam fashioned a statue of his father Nur-Adad:

---

230. Charpin 2002a: 556–558.

231. van Dijk 1971: no. 41. The royal inscription covers ll. 1–40 while the two letter-prayers cover ll. 41–163 and ll. 164–211. For this tablet, see also van Dijk 1965; Römer 1984: 320–325; Fitzgerald 2002: 83–89.

232. Only six of Nur-Adad's sixteen year names are attested in Ur; see Charpin 2004: 102.

233. Frayne 1990: no. 4.2.8.1: ll. 14–18.

234. One of Sin-iddinam's royal inscriptions mentions that after a battle, which included events that are recorded in the name of his fifth year, Sin-iddinam returned to his father Nur-Adad in Larsa: George 2011: no. 37: iii 63–65 (also discussed later in this section). One of his other inscriptions mentions that the dedication was for the life of his father and his own life: Frayne 1990: no. 4.2.9.10; compare also no. 4.2.9.1: ll. 34–35.

235. Biggs 1976: no. 38 (first year of Sin-iddinam); no. 39 (Year D of Nur-Adad); see also Stol 2011: 517.

(Sin-iddinam) fashioned for him [i.e., Utu] a silver standing statue (depicting) the father who engendered him, Nur-Adad, king of Larsa, endowed with beautiful inscribed limbs.[236]

The inscription further notes that the statue was set up in the main courtyard of the Ebabbar temple to receive offerings. The multi-column tablet on which this inscription was copied is a compilation tablet. As mentioned earlier, the royal inscription is followed by two letter-prayers of Sin-iddinam, addressed to the statue. It is likely that these prayers were indeed inscribed on tablets that were deposited near the statue.

According to the name of Sin-iddinam's second year, the Tigris was dug, i.e., dredged.[237] This was also commemorated in one of his inscriptions, in which Sin-iddinam states that it was done "in order to establish good water for my city (and) land."[238] It is likely that this was a consequence of a natural catastrophe that occurred during his father's reign.

Four of Sin-iddinam's inscriptions concern the construction of the Ebabbar temple at Larsa,[239] an event that is also commemorated in the name of his third regnal year.[240] For a long time, stamped bricks found at Ur were the only testimony to Sin-iddinam's construction of Ur's wall. According to the inscription on these bricks,

He made firm the foundation of the throne of Larsa for him [i.e., Nanna] and perfectly carried out a reign of order. After he smote with weapons the land that rebelled against him and smashed the weapon of his enemy, at that time, by the decree of

---

236. Frayne 1990: no. 4.2.9.1: ll. 28–33.

237. Sigrist 1990: 24.

238. Frayne 1990: no. 4.2.9.2: ll. 17–18.

239. Frayne 1990: nos. 4.2.9.3–6.

240. Sigrist 1990: 24.

the god Nanna and the goddess Ningal, he built the great wall of
Ur like a mountain in a pure place.[241]

A remarkable royal inscription that was recently published adds a plethora of new information on this construction project and other events in
his reign. The text is inscribed in four columns on a hollow clay barrel
cylinder, and recounts in great detail the construction of the wall and
other buildings in Ur.[242] In contrast to any other building inscription
of the early Old Babylonian period, the text also narrates three major
military campaigns against enemies of Larsa. The first campaign was
directed against an insurrection in the "Upper Land," which led to the
complete destruction of their fortifications (iii 19–34). The second campaign was directed against Ibrat and the city of Murub (?) (iii 42–53).
This campaign is recorded in the name of Sin-iddinam's fifth year.[243] The
third incident was an attack by enemy troops, probably from Malgium
(iii 54–75).[244] Sin-iddinam managed to fight off the enemy and take
its leader (Sumerian *lugal*) Warassa prisoner. Thereafter the remainder of the enemy troops were released and Sin-iddinam returned to
Larsa. "In order that my name is mentioned in Der in remote (days)"
was Sin-iddinam's justification for showing mercy to the enemy troops.
The enemy king was entrusted to Ištaran. The mention of Warassa,
Der, and its patron deity Ištaran, is noteworthy, suggesting the enemy
leader cannot be identified with a ruler (Sumerian *ensi₂*) of Ešnunna.[245]
Although we know of a Warassa, king of Der, who was a contemporary of Hammurabi of Babylon (1792–1750 BC), he lived much too late

---

241. Frayne 1990: no. 4.2.9.13: ll. 18–30.

242. George 2011: no. 37.

243. Sigrist 1990: 24.

244. Guichard 2014: 15–16, n. 17 suggested reading $ma\text{-}al_7(\text{AN})\text{-}gi_5(\text{KI})$ in iii 54,
     instead of the verbal form $ma\text{-}an\text{-}sa_2$.

245. Morello 2016: 644; for the historical considerations, see Volk 2011: 63–65.

to have been Sin-iddinam's foe.[246] As a ruler of Ešnunna seems to be excluded by the mention of Der, there may have been a different, otherwise unattested King Warassa in Sin-iddinam's reign. It has recently been suggested that Warassa was a king of Malgium.[247]

An unprovenanced tablet, recording that Ibal-pi-El of Ešnunna made a treaty with Sin-iddinam and Sin-kašid of Uruk, probably dates toward the end of Sin-iddinam's reign. This text allows us to establish a rare synchronism between five rulers:

> Ibal-pi-El swore to Sin from [heav]en and Išhara from Išur – (by) Tišpak and Adad:
>
> I swear that I will neither abandon Sin-iddinam the king of Larsa nor Sin-kašid the king of Uruk. I swear that I will not make peace with the enemy of Sin-iddinam the king of Larsa or Sin-kašid the king of Uruk. [If] Sin-iddinam the king of Larsa [or Sin]-kašid the king of Uruk send me message as follows: "Our enemy and adversary attacks (us)," when they have written to me, with all my [heart] I swear to call to account [without delay (?) at the head] of my whole army the enemy of Sin-iddinam the king of Larsa and Sin-kašid the king of Uruk. (...)
>
> That Sabium king of Babylon and Ikun-pi-Sin king of Nerebtum write to me to (obtain) an army, I swear that I will not give them an army and that my army will not fight with the army of Sin-iddinam and Sin-kašid. I swear that I will not oppose my army against them out of vileness. Until Sin-iddinam and

---

246. Heimpel 2003: 562, with reference to Charpin et al. 1988: no. 372, in which Warassa is expected to exchange messengers with Babylon; cf. also Morello 2016: 644–645, who does not refer to the present text.

247. Guichard 2014: 15–16, n. 17. For the poorly attested kings of Malgium, see de Boer 2013a. Note that de Boer 2014 emphasizes the mention of Der in this context, proposing that Warassa was a dynastic name in Der; due to the close proximity of Malgium and Der, he could have been king of Der and led troops of Malgium.

Sin-kašid have made peace with Sabium and Ikun-pi-Sin, I myself
swear not to make peace (with them)![248]

A small group of administrative texts from Larsa dating to the last two
years of Sin-iddinam's reign record expenditures of grain to various
individuals, many of whom are from cities outside Larsa. Different delegations from northern Mesopotamia and the Diyala region were present in Larsa this time around.[249] The name of Sin-iddinam's sixth year
records the destruction of the land of Ešnunna.[250] The grain accounts
state that people from Ešnunna were present at Larsa in his seventh year.
Sin-iddinam's victory over Ešnunna must have allowed him to secure an
alliance.

Sin-iddinam also left a sizable body of literary compositions. At
least four songs of praise can be assigned to him, most of which are
only preserved on a single manuscript. Exceptionally, *Sin-iddinam* A,
known from two manuscripts, is of particular interest, as it deals with
the cultic practice of Sumerian divine journeys. In the case of this short
composition, it seems that the king accompanied the moon god on his
journey to Nippur.[251] Also noteworthy is a composition referred to as
Sin-iddinam E, which is preserved on a two-column tablet in the Yale
Babylonian Collection and was written in an archaizing hand. This
tablet may not be literary at all, but rather a copy of a royal inscription
of Sin-iddinam. In this text, the king dedicates a throne to the storm
god Iškur.[252]

---

248. Guichard 2014: 11–13 (CUNES 49-04-176; for a photograph see
     CDLI: https://cdli.ucla.edu/P449459; last accessed October 1, 2020).

249. For these grain accounts, see Goetze 1950: 94–96; Guichard 2014: 17–19.

250. Sigrist 1990: 24.

251. For recent editions of this text, see Brisch 2007: 122–128; Wagensonner 2007.
     Note that the moon god traveled frequently from Ur to Nippur.

252. For a new edition and a discussion of the difficulties of assigning such a text to
     a specific text genre, see Wagensonner 2011.

Sin-iddinam also left a number of letter-prayers. His letter to the sun-god Utu, known from several Old Babylonian manuscripts,[253] also found its way into the seventh-century-BC library of Ashurbanipal of Assyria at Nineveh in an interlinear Sumerian-Akkadian version.[254] The second letter is addressed to Nin-Isina, the goddess of healing.[255] In this letter-prayer Sin-iddinam assures the goddess that he was never neglectful of his duties or in his worship of the gods. He mentions that Asalluhi, "the king of Babylon, son of Ilurugu" (l. 16), plotted against his city and sought evil against the king of Larsa. Sin-iddinam does not refer here to an actual historical figure, as his contemporaries in Babylon were Sumu-la-El (1880–1845 BC) and Sabium (1844–1831 BC), but the name of Sin-iddinam's fourth year refers to a defeat of the Babylonian army.[256] Sin-iddinam continues to recount a dream, where evil is cast onto him. He describes his sickness to the goddess:

> My sickness is like a darkness that never becomes light. No one can see it. The physician cannot diagnose it, no bandage can provide relief. No incantations can be recited. (…) My sickness, for which herbs grow neither in the steppe nor in the mountains, no one has had before.[257]

In the final part of the letter he asks the goddess for mercy.

Last but not least, an intriguing and frequently cited text deserves mention. A clay liver model dating to the Old Babylonian period is inscribed with the following historical omen:

---

253. Manuscripts are known from Nippur, Sippar, and Uruk, while two unprovenanced sources likely originate from Larsa: https://cdli.ucla.edu/P345806 and https://cdli.ucla.edu/P345400 (CDLI; last accessed August 25, 2020). The composition is also attested in Late Bronze Age Emar on the Middle Euphrates.

254. For an edition, see Brisch 2007: 158–178; cf. also Peterson 2016: 172–178.

255. Brisch 2007: 142–156; cf. also Peterson 2016: 167–172.

256. Sigrist 1990: 24.

257. Brisch 2007: 142–145 (ll. 25–28).

This (exact appearance of the) liver fell to king Sin-iddinam, when he offered a sacrifice in the Šamaš temple during the month of Elul; for the sheep's owner: he will throw back the enemy and control what is not his.[258]

14.5.2. Kings with short reigns: the years following Sin-iddinam

Between 1842 and 1835 BC, three kings briefly sat on Larsa's throne. The first was Sin-iribam (1842–1841 BC). Until recently, no royal inscriptions of his were known, apart from a stone weight belonging to his palace[259] and a number of seals belonging to his servants. His familial relationship, if any, with his predecessor Sin-iddinam was, therefore, unclear. These crucial questions have now finally been resolved, thanks to a recently published clay cone in the Schøyen Collection. The text of this inscription was already known from two other manuscripts, but due to their poor state of preservation one was wrongly assigned to Sin-iddinam and the other could not be assigned to a king at all. The new manuscript informs us that Sin-iribam was not a son of Sin-iddinam, but of an otherwise unknown individual named Ga'eš-rabi.[260] According to this inscription Sin-iribam constructed the Ebabbar temple. His second year name suggests that he consecrated a large copper statue in the temple of the moon god.[261] His year names were used at Nippur, indicating Larsa's control of the city during his reign.[262]

---

258. The text inscribed on this liver model has often been misinterpreted. The translation given here follows Winitzer 2017: 46 (ex. 2.45) with n. 62. Sin-iddinam is not the only ruler of this period to appear in the context of divination. Also Išbi-Erra of Isin is mentioned in omens and on liver models; see section 14.2.1.

259. Frayne 1990: no. 4.2.10.1.

260. George 2011: no. 50: l. 9. Ga'eš, the seat of the moon god Nanna's temple Karzida, is located just outside of Ur; see George 1993: 108. In one of Sin-iddinam's inscriptions, he refers to himself as "son, [born] in Ga'eš" (Frayne 1990: no. 4.2.9.7: l. 9).

261. Sigrist 1990: 26.

262. De Graef 2011a.

Sin-iribam was followed by his son Sin-iqišam (1840–1836 BC).[263] Like his predecessor, Sin-iqišam was a contemporary of Sabium of Babylon (1844–1831 BC), who claimed that he defeated the troops of Larsa in his fifth year.[264] This defeat must have happened early in his reign. Due to the short and probably weak reign of Sin-iqišam's predecessor, Sabium probably seized his opportunity. In his second year, the king of Larsa undertook a campaign against Pi-naratim and Naṣarum.[265] He also installed divine statues in Kazallu. For the remaining three years of his reign he refocused his attention on Larsa. His third year was named after construction work on the great wall of Larsa.[266] Sin-iqišam left two or three royal inscriptions, one of which reports on the construction of the temple of Ningišzida at Ur.[267] One rather long inscription, which may be an inscription of Sin-iqišam, is known from a later copy on a clay tablet from Nippur.[268] Curiously, the king's name (ii 6) is truncated as ᵈEN, suggesting that the inscription from which the text had been copied may have been damaged.[269]

Only one short song of praise is known for Sin-iqišam (Sin-iqišam A). This is addressed to Numušda,[270] the principal deity of Kazallu and Kiritab.[271] The text refers twice to the king, such as in the following passage:

---

263. Frayne 1990: no. 4.2.11.2: l. 5.

264. Horsnell 1999: II 67. For the possibility that this attack happened already in Sin-iribam's reign, see Charpin 2004: 106–107.

265. Sigrist 1990: 27–28. The settlement Pi-naratim is located near Cutha and Kiš and was repeatedly conquered by kings of Larsa; see Streck 2005.

266. In his third year, Sin-iqišam also installed eleven silver statues and one gold statue in the temple of the sun-god: Sigrist 1990: 27–28.

267. Frayne 1990: no. 4.2.11.2.

268. Frayne 1990: no. 4.2.11.1; for an RTI image of the tablet taken by the present author, see CDLI (https://cdli.ucla.edu/P262842; last accessed August 25, 2020).

269. To leave blank space where damage had occurred was one way to flag a break in an ancient manuscript when copying the text; see Cancik-Kirschbaum and Kahl 2018: 220.

270. Sin-iqišam A; for a summary, see Brisch 2007: 49–50.

271. Cavigneaux and Krebernik 2001: 613.

My god, hand over to the king the disobedient lands! Numušda, hand over to prince Sin-iqišam the disobedient lands![272]

Sin-iqišam's successor, Ṣilli-Adad (1835 BC), only ruled for a few months. This explains why his year name needed to be modified by administrators in the ninth month. We find two variants, "Year: Ṣilli-Adad was removed from kingship," and "Year: Ṣilli-Adad is no (longer) king."[273] In the capital Larsa, however, even after month IX the year name continued in use, referring to him as king. Despite his short reign, Ṣilli-Adad left two inscriptions in Ur. One, preserved on bricks and cones, commemorates the reinforcement of the Etemenniguru for the moon god.[274] The other, though badly damaged, may also date to his reign. In it, Ṣilli-Adad refers to himself not as king of Larsa, but as "city governor of Ur, Larsa, Lagaš, and the land of Kutalla," as well as "provider of Nippur."[275]

    An administrative text from Ur records "forty days of the *pāšišum*-prebend of the statue of Sin-iqišam." As this text is undated, it remains unclear whether this statue was fashioned by Ṣilli-Adad or one of his successors. Based on the remainder of this document, its location may

---

272. Sin-iqišam A: ll. 31–32.

273. See Sigrist 1990: 30. For the first variant, see, e.g., Grice 1919: no. 56: ll. 16–17 (dated to month XII), with several other documents dated with this specific year name published in Grice 1919. For the second variant, see Charpin 2004: 107, n. 432.

274. Frayne 1990: no. 4.2.12.1: ll. 11–12.

275. Frayne 1990: no. 4.2.12.1: ll. 4–10. Also two inscriptions of Warad-Sin, dating to his first year, employ the same titulary; see Frayne 1990: no. 4.2.13.1: ll. 6–10; no. 4.2.13.2: ll. 6–12. Kutalla is a small settlement near Larsa, and the name of Gungunum's eighteenth year commemorates his construction of a temple of the god Lugalkiduna, the principal deity of Kutalla; see Charpin 1980: 183; 2004: 236. Note the "double-headed ax of Lugalkiduna" that is mentioned in a lawsuit document from Kutalla: "Iddin-Enlil approached the judge of Larsa; in the presence of the mayor-*rabiānum* of Kutalla and the elders of the city, Iddin-Enlil made rounds in the garden [i.e., the object of dispute]—a double-headed ax of Lugalkiduna was carried. [Thus] he proved [his rights] and took [the garden] in his possession" (ll. 12–19); see Dombradi 1996: I 91.

have been the Nanna temple.[276] A few of the texts from the archive of Dumuzi-gamil from Ur, which date to the middle of Rim-Sin's reign, attest to similar cult activities. One records bread offerings for four silver statues of Sin-iqišam;[277] another mentions barley for a gold statue of the same king.[278]

Ṣilli-Adad's relationship to his predecessor is unclear. On the basis of a document from the Yale Babylonian Collection recording the rental of a field,[279] which mentions names reminiscent of members of the royal family (Sin-iddinam, Ṣilli-Adad, and Ahu-ṭab; the latter is known as a royal son from a receipt for sesame dating to Nur-Adad's reign[280]), Madeleine Fitzgerald thought that Ṣilli-Adad might have been one of Nur-Adad's sons;[281] but the fact that we now know from a royal inscription of Ṣilli-Adad's predecessor Sin-iribam that this king was not a son of Nur-Adad (as discussed earlier in this section) weakens this hypothesis.

Ṣilli-Adad's reign may have been a weak one and left a power vacuum that allowed Kudur-mabuk to establish a new dynasty as the ruling family in Larsa. Table 14.4 presents an overview of the dynasties of Isin, Larsa, Babylon, and Uruk from the mid-nineteenth to the eighteenth centuries BC.

14.6. Uruk in the early Old Babylonian period: the "dynasty" of Sin-kašid

One of the most commonly attested royal inscriptions from ancient Mesopotamia is a short text of King Sin-kašid of Uruk that commemorates his construction of a palace at Uruk and that is known from

---

276. Charpin 1980: no. 88: l. 13; also Charpin 2018.

277. Figulla and Martin 1953: no. 404: l. 7. The text dates to Year 32 of Rim-Sin.

278. Figulla and Martin 1953: no. 406: l. 2. For this and the previous text, see Charpin 1980: 52; 2018.

279. Fitzgerald 2002: 123 (YBC 8737).

280. Grice 1919: no. 153: l. 7.

281. Fitzgerald 2002: 123; De Graef 2011b.

Table 14.4. The dynasties of Isin, Larsa, Babylon, and Uruk from the mid-nineteenth to the eighteenth century BC.

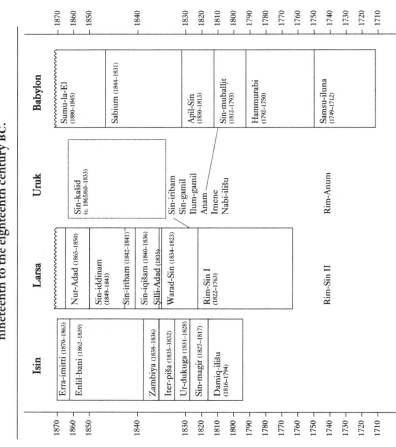

FIGURE 14.6. Building inscriptions of Sin-kašid of Uruk. Author's photograph.

small clay tablets and cones (figure 14.6). The known objects number in the hundreds and can be found in many collections of ancient Near Eastern artifacts. The composite translation of three variants of the text reads: "Sin-kašid, the strong man, the king of Uruk, the king of Amnanum, (the provider of Eanna,) (when he built Eanna,) built his royal palace."[282]

Sin-kašid called himself "king of Amnanum." The Amnanu were a tribe belonging to the tribal group of the Yaminites (see section 14.1.4). Outside of Uruk, the kings of Babylon also belonged to the Amnanum. At Kisurra, we encountered the Rabbu or Rabbeans, who were Yaminites

---

282. Frayne 1990: no. 4.4.1.2 is currently known from 175 exemplars (http://cdli.ucla.edu/Q002239); no. 4.4.1.3 from 425 exemplars (http://cdli.ucla.edu/Q002240); and no. 4.4.1.4 from 160 exemplars (http://cdli.ucla.edu/Q002241; all last accessed on CDLI on August 25, 2020).

as well. Itur-Šamaš refers to himself as "chief of the Rabbeans."[283] Both Amnanu and Rabbu were foes of Yahdun-Lim of Mari:

> In that same year, La'um, king of Samanum and the land of the Ubrabium, Bahlu-kullim, king of Tuttul and the land of the Amnanum, Ayalum, king of Abattum and the land of the Rabbum—these kings rebelled against him.[284]

Sin-kašid reigned around 1860 and was a contemporary of Babylon's king Sumu-la-El (1880–1845 BC), whose daughter Šallurtum was his wife. This matrimonial alliance is attested on three sealed clay bullae, found in Sin-kašid's palace at Uruk, with the inscription: "Šallurtum, daughter of King Sumu-la-El, wife of King Sin-kašid, his beloved."[285] Sumu-la-El expanded Babylon's control significantly, thus laying the foundation for Babylon's later hegemony in southern Mesopotamia.[286] This synchronism allows us to place Sin-kašid in context. Another synchronism with Sin-iddinam of Larsa is confirmed by a treaty between Ibal-pi-El, the king of Larsa and Sin-kašid. This document also refers to Sabium and a king of Nerebtum (see section 14.5.1). The mention of Sabium (1844–1831 BC) shows that the treaty must have been concluded rather late in Sin-kašid's reign, probably at the beginning of Sabium's reign.[287]

Literary sources tell us that Sin-kašid's daughter, Ninšatapada, was installed as high priestess of the temple of Meslamta'ea in the nearby city of Durum. Durum (modern Umm al-Wawiya) was fortified under the Isin ruler Išme-Dagan.[288] Because of Išme-Dagan's account and

---

283. See section 14.4.2.

284. Frayne 1990: no. 4.6.8.2: ll. 67–75.

285. Frayne 1990: no. 4.4.1.16; see Falkenstein 1963: pl. 7.

286. Charpin 2004: 94–95.

287. For a discussion of the synchronism, see Guichard 2014: 19–24.

288. Frayne 1990: no. 4.1.4.11. In this inscription, Durum is called the "city of military governorship and his (i.e., Išme-Dagan's) princeship." For the location of Durum, see Michalowski 1977; for other possible identifications, see De Graef 2007.

the fact that both Išme-Dagan and Sin-kašid, who never mentions his father, served as governors (Akkadian *šakkanakkum*) there, it has been suggested that Sin-kašid himself was of Isin descent.[289] One laconically short year name (probably one of Sin-kašid's) reads "Year: Durum."[290] Sin-kašid himself undertook extensive building projects there. A significant number of clay cones found in an oven in his palace at Uruk were prepared by scribes to be sent to Durum. These commemorate the construction of the temple of Lugalirra and Meslamta'ea, both city gods of Durum.[291] It is likely that Sin-kašid himself installed his daughter in the office of the high priestess there. According to one inscription he built a *gipar* residence for Niši-inišu, another daughter, who became *nin-diĝir* priestess of Lugalbanda.[292] Ninšatapada is known from a literary letter addressed to Rim-Sin of Larsa, written in a highly literate language. After addressing the king of Larsa with many epithets, the priestess introduces herself: "This is what Ninšatapada, the female scribe, priestess of Meslamta'ea, daughter of Sin-kašid, king of Uruk, your servant-girl says."[293] The priestess praises the king of Larsa for the mercy he showed when he took over Uruk and spared its population from a cruel fate. Its inhabitants live in peace and tranquility. But what about her? She was exiled from her town Durum, abandoned, without support, and in old age. Desperately she pleads with the king to let her return to her city, so she can sing his praises.[294]

Fact or fiction, the letter of Ninšatapada can be precisely dated. The name of Rim-Sin's twentieth year states that he "captured Kisurra and

---

289. Hallo 1991: 379–380; Charpin 2004: 108 with n. 435; 2011c: 519. Note also an inscription that commemorates the construction of a temple for Nin-Isina: Frayne 1990: no. 4.4.1.11.

290. Falkenstein 1963: 10 (Year "9").

291. Frayne 1990: nos. 4.4.1.13–14.

292. Frayne 1990: no. 4.4.1.9.

293. *Ninšatapada to Rim-Sin*: ll. 16–19; see Hallo 1991: 387.

294. A bilingual letter-prayer addressed to Zimri-Lim bears some striking similarities with the letter of Ninšatapada; see Charpin 1988; 2004: 519 with n. 519.

destroyed Durum by means of the strong weapon Enlil bestowed upon him."[295] The priestess herself says that she has already lived five years in exile (a variant has four years). Thus, her letter was written around 1800 BC.[296]

14.6.1. Rulers before Sin-kašid

Before looking at Sin-kašid's successors, it is appropriate to investigate his predecessors. For a long time Uruk lacked any inscriptions that could be assigned to a king prior to Sin-kašid. The documents from Kisurra, however, attest to two kings of Uruk in both year names and oath formulae, Alila-hadum and Sumu-binasa.[297] So far no inscriptions have been found at Uruk itself that can be assigned to these two rulers, who ruled around 1890 BC.

The gap between Sumu-binasa and Sin-kašid could not be closed until recently, when a hitherto unknown king of Uruk named Naram-Sin was identified thanks to three copies of a royal inscription.[298] This ruler refers to himself as "god of his land."[299] This title may intentionally recall the deification of his namesake, Naram-Sin of Akkad (see chapters 9 and 10 in volume 1).[300] It was recently proposed that one of the legends dealing with the kings of Akkad (known as *Erra and Naram-Sin*) may possibly

---

295. Sigrist 1990: 48–49.

296. Hallo 1991: 381.

297. Sumu-binasa occurs in an oath formula: Kienast 1978: no. 19: rev. 9'; see also section 14.4.2.

298. A clay cone housed at the University of Minnesota was published by von Dassow 2009, with a duplicate in the form of a fragmentary clay nail head from Uruk published by Eckart Frahm as an appendix (von Dassow 2009: 86–89). The third copy, another clay nail from Uruk, was published by Sanati-Müller 2011: 82–86; see Fiette 2014.

299. von Dassow 2009: 68: l. 4.

300. According to the famous Bassetki statue, the gods of various cities requested that the king be made the "god of their city" (Frayne 1993: no. 2.1.4.10: l. 49).

concern this ruler of Uruk, rather than the king of Akkad.[301] Be that as it may, the discovery of the inscription of Naram-Sin, king of Uruk, allows us to bridge the gap between the two kings attested in documents from Kisurra and Sin-kašid (see table 14.2).

14.6.2. The kings after Sin-kašid

Little is known about the kings who followed Sin-kašid on Uruk's throne. His successor Sin-iribam, a namesake of a king of Larsa (1842–1841 BC), who ruled more or less contemporaneously, can be linked to Warad-Sin of Larsa. A sale contract from Larsa concerning a slave sold by an inhabitant of Durum dates to the sixth year of Warad-Sin. The oath on this legal document reads: "He swore (by) Warad-Sin, king of Larsa, and Sin-iribam, king of Uruk."[302] Sin-iribam has not left any royal inscriptions. The archival texts found in the palace of Sin-kašid, who was probably also his father, only preserve three year names.[303]

Sin-iribam was succeeded by his son, Sin-gamil, who left an inscription commemorating his construction of Nanaya's temple at Uruk. Like his predecessor Sin-kašid, Sin-gamil also used the title "king of Amnanum."[304] Currently, only three year names can be assigned to his reign, but the summary of a fragmentary account from Sin-kašid's palace dealing with distributions of oil from the reign of Sin-iribam to the reign of IRnene shows that he must have reigned at least four years.[305] According to one of his year names, Sin-gamil brought three statues of his father into the temple of Inana.[306] We also know that a later king,

---

301. Goodnick Westenholz 1997: 189–201; for this suggestion, see Charpin 2015.

302. Grice 1919: no. 124 ll. 14–15; see Charpin 2004: 110 with n. 450.

303. For references, see Falkenstein 1963: 9 no. 2; 12 no. 24; 14 no. 30; also Charpin 2011a.

304. Frayne 1990: no. 4.4.3.1: l. 7.

305. Sanati-Müller 1993: 147–149, no. 201: rev. vi′ 2′–5′; see Charpin 2011b.

306. Falkenstein 1963: 10 no. 11.

ANam, left a building inscription commemorating the construction of Nergal's temple in Uṣarpara, "for the life of Sin-gamil."[307]

Sin-gamil was succeeded by his brother, Ilum-gamil. We know this family relationship from a clay cone, according to which a certain Ubar-Adad built the residence of the office of the *en* priest(ess) for the god Iškur "for the life of Ilum-gamil, king of Uruk, son of Sin-iribam."[308] From his reign we also have the meagre remains of a treaty between him and a king, whose name is not preserved: "With whom Ilum-gamil is at war, I swear to be at war; with whom Ilum-gamil is at peace, I swear to be at peace."[309]

Most of the administrative texts from Sin-kašid's palace at Uruk date to the reigns of Ilum-gamil's two successors, ANam and IRnene. The correct reading of the Sumerian names of both rulers is uncertain.[310] In his own inscriptions, ANam refers to himself as the son of a certain Ilan-šemea.[311] In a very important document, a long letter of ANam to the Babylonian king Sin-muballiṭ, the king of Uruk reminds his ally that both kingdoms belong to "one house" (Akkadian *bītum ištēn*).[312] As we have seen, the kings of Uruk and Babylon both belonged to the Yaminite tribe of Amnanum.[313] ANam describes the long-standing alliance that stretched back to his grandfather's time:

---

307. Frayne 1990: no. 4.4.3.2001: ll. 4–7. Another broken inscription of ANam (Frayne 1990: no. 4.4.3.2002), which concerns construction work for the goddess Kanisura, may have contained this same dedication.

308. Frayne 1990: no. 4.4.4.2001: ll. 4–7.

309. W 19900, 147: i 1′–6′; see Lafont 2001: 287; Charpin 2004: 110 with n. 454.

310. The name of ANam is always written AN-*am₃*, and could hence also be read as Dingiram. Alternative readings for his successor's name IRnene (written IR₃-*ne-ne*) are Urdunene and Irdanene; see Charpin 2004: 109.

311. Frayne 1990: no. 4.4.3.2001: ll. 7–8: "ANam, chief accountant, son of Ilan-šemea."

312. *Letter of ANam to Sin-muballiṭ*: ii 1–2; see Falkenstein 1963: 60. The letter may not be an archival document. Its length (150 lines), format (two columns per side), style, and also the fact that it was found at the place of its origin, all suggest that it is a literary letter. Nevertheless, it may well draw on historical facts; see Beaulieu 2018: 71–72.

313. Stol 2004: 647.

Ever since the kings of Uruk and Babylon are one house—except for the present moment when my heart and your heart were grieved—and, by what I have heard from the mouth of my father and my grandfather, whom I have known personally, ever since the time of Sin-kašid and since the time I witnessed myself until now, the army of Amnan-Yahrur has indeed arrived here two or three times for military assistance to this house.[314]

It is likely that his father Ilan-šemea was himself a son of Sin-iribam. According to one inscription, ANam built a temple of Nergal for the life of his brother Sin-gamil (see earlier discussion in this section), and according to another, he undertook renovation work on the Eanna temple at Uruk. Two inscriptions deal with the residence of the *en* priest:

When I renovated and restored the temple of An and Inana, the ancient work of Ur-Namma and Šulgi, I founded there the *gipar* of the *en* priest, his abode of rejoicing, suitable for her [i.e., Inana's] delight.[315]

ANam also renovated the wall of Uruk, the "ancient work of Gilgamesh," and "constructed it for him in baked bricks in order that water might roar in its surrounding."[316]

Although ANam's successor, a king named IRnene (written IR₃-*ne-ne*), did not leave any royal inscriptions, archival documents from the Sin-kašid palace fill in historical facts that are missing in official inscriptions. The

314. W 20473: iii 25–32; see Falkenstein 1963: 58. Translation after van Koppen 2006: 129. For Amnan-Yahrur as a collective term for the troops of Babylon, see chapter 18 in this volume.

315. Frayne 1990: no. 4.4.6.2: i 10–18. Two of his year names feature the gate of the *gipar*; see Falkenstein 1963: 14–15, no. 31.

316. Frayne 1990: no. 4.4.6.4: ll. 5–12. See also Frayne 1990: no. 4.4.6.5: l. 10, which mentions the wall's moat.

Urukean kings appear to have exchanged gifts with their counterparts at Larsa and Babylon. In the first year of IRnene, a silver spear was possibly sent as a diplomatic gift to Larsa.[317]

Nevertheless, the relationship between Uruk and Larsa degraded. IRnene joined a coalition against Larsa, but even the assembled forces could not topple Rim-Sin's kingdom. The name of his fourteenth year records their defeat: "The troops of Uruk, Isin, Babylon, Sutium, Rapiqum, and IRnene, king of Uruk, were defeated by weapon."[318] This event is also referred to in an inscription of Rim-Sin:

> When he smote with weapons the army of Uruk, Isin, Babylon, Rapiqum, and Sutium, captured IRnene, king of Uruk, in that battle, and laid his foot on his head as if he were a snake.[319]

The end of IRnene did not signal the end of the kingdom of Uruk. Between his capture and Rim-Sin's destruction of the city, as recorded in his twenty-first year name, a scarcely documented king named Nabi-ilišu reigned at Uruk.[320] According to his year names, Rim-Sin conquered Pi-naratim and Naṣarum in his fifteenth year, Imgur-Gibil and Zibnatum in his seventeenth, Bit-Šu-Sin and Uṣarpara in his eighteenth, and Kisurra and Durum in his twentieth. It is noteworthy that the summary accounts found in the Sin-kašid palace stop with IRnene, which indicates a disruption of administrative processes after his reign.[321]

---

317. According to the text published as Sanati-Müller 1990: no. 98 (for a possible reconstruction, see Charpin and Durand 1993: 369–370). The text published as Sanati-Müller 1990: no. 100 is comparable and may deal with a present for king Sabium of Babylon.

318. Sigrist 1990: 43–44.

319. Frayne 1990: no. 4.2.14.8: ll. 19–28; compare also no. 4.2.14.9: ll. 17–24; no. 4.2.14.10: ll. 15–19.

320. Charpin and Reculeau 2001; Charpin 2004: 113.

321. Charpin 2004: 113.

14.6.3. Market rates and wages in royal inscriptions from Larsa and Uruk

Having now dealt with inscriptions of the earlier kings of Larsa and those of Uruk, this brief excursus discusses a recurring motif in several of the extant inscriptions. Several of the inscriptions from Larsa and Uruk contain a statement by the king referring to the ideal market rates of commodities against silver. This motif has recently been discussed by Eva von Dassow as one of the criteria to date a previously unknown ruler of Uruk. This ruler, Naram-Sin, is now known through three manuscripts of an inscription (see section 14.6.1). The market rates he announces are identical to those found in inscriptions of king Sin-kašid.[322] The earliest examplar, however, can now be dated to the reign of Gungunum of Larsa (1932–1906 BC). The inscription commemorating the construction of the wall of Larsa, which is also referenced in the name of Gungunum's twenty-first year, must therefore date to late in his reign (see section 14.3.2). The relevant part of the text reads as follows:

> At that time, in the days of my reign, the market rate was set at three *kor* of barley, ten minas of wool, fifteen liters of oil for one shekel (of silver).[323]

Approximately half a century later, Nur-Adad (1865–1850 BC) was the next Larsa king to use this motif in one of his inscriptions (see section 14.5.1):

> During my good reign, according to the market value, which was in my land, thus one shekel of silver purchased two *kor* of barley, two *seah* of oil, ten minas of wool, (and) ten *kor* of dates.[324]

---

322. von Dassow 2009: 71–2.

323. George 2011: no. 44: ll. 29–33.

324. Frayne 1990: no. 4.2.8.7: ii 57–63.

In the same inscription, Nur-Adad also mentions the wages for his workers:

> At that time, I built the great wall of Larsa like a mountain in a pure place. The wages of each worker were three *seah* of barley, two liters of bread, two liters of beer, two shekels of oil; thus they received this in one day.[325]

His successor Sin-iddinam (1849–1843 BC) refers to the wages as well for irrigation work:

> When I dug the Tigris, the great river, the wages of each worker were: One *kor* of barley, two liters of bread, four liters of beer, two shekels of oil, in one day so they received this.[326]

In another of his inscriptions dealing with the construction of the Ebabbar temple, Sin-iddinam refers to both the wages and the market rates:

> [The wages of each (worker) were: x *kor* of grain], two liters of dates, two liters of cheese, two liters of sesame bran, two shekels of oil, not including food from the sheepfolds. In one day so they received this. In the days of my successful reign, which the god Utu, my lord gave to me, four *kor* of barley, twelve *kor* of dates, fifteen minas of wool, three *seah* of vegetable oil, five *seah* of lard, according to the market value in Ur, Larsa and my land, so much [was sold] per one shekel of silver.[327]

---

325. Frayne 1990: no. 4.2.8.7: ii 64–70.

326. Frayne 1990: no. 4.2.9.2: ll. 51–59; also George 2011: no. 49: ii 50–59.

327. Frayne 1990: no. 4.2.9.6: ll. 49–69. See also George 2011: no. 37: iv 2–13: "In the days of my successful reign, which Nanna and Utu bestowed upon me, four *kor* of barley, ten *kor* of dates, fifteen minas of wool, three liters of sesame oil, five liters of lard, according to the market value in Ur and Larsa, so much was sold per one shekel of silver."

Table 14.5. Ideal market rates according to royal inscriptions from Larsa and Uruk

Commodity	Larsa			Uruk	
	Gungunum	Nur-Adad	Sin-iddinam	Sin-kašid	Naram-Sin
Barley	3 *kor*	2 *kor*	4 *kor*	3 *kor*	3 *kor*
Wool	10 minas	10 minas	12 or 15 minas	12 minas	12 minas
Oil	15 litres	2 *seah*	3 *seah*	3 *seah*	3 *seah*
Dates		10 *kor*	12 *kor*		
Lard			5 *seah*		
Copper				10 minas	[10] minas

Around the same time, two rulers at Uruk, the scarcely attested Naram-Sin and Sin-kašid, used the same motif. The market rates are identical in the inscriptions of both kings:

> In his period of kingship, according to the market value of his land, three *kor* of barley, twelve minas of wool, ten minas of copper, three *seah* of vegetable oil cost one shekel of silver.[328]

Table 14.5 summarizes these quotes.[329] It is also possible to extrapolate market rates from the vast corpus of administrative texts, but little can be

---

328. Frayne 1990: no. 4.4.1.8: ll. 15–22. These values are duplicated in the following inscriptions: Frayne 1990: no. 4.4.1.10: ll. 13–20; no. 4.4.1.11: ll. 14–23; no. 4.4.1.12: ll. 10–17; no. 4.4.1.13: ll. 11–19; no. 4.4.1.14: ll. 11–19; no. 4.4.1.15: ll. 16–23.

329. The table is based on von Dassow 2009: 72, Table 1, but adds the recently published inscription from the reign of Gungunum.

said regarding these rates before the reign of Rim-Sin.[330] No later kings of Larsa or Uruk mention any market rates in their inscriptions.[331]

14.7 Back in Isin: Enlil-bani and his successors

We have seen earlier (section 14.4) that following the reign of Gungunum the kingdom of Isin came increasingly under the scrutiny of the Larsa kings. Recently published correspondence shows that the Larsa king Sumu-El clearly struggled with the military pushback of Erra-imitti, who eventually reconquered Nippur and Kisurra.[332] It also seems plausible that Sumu-El's reign did not receive high marks from his successors.[333] With Nur-Adad on Larsa's throne, a new era of growth set in. He came to power in the last two years of Erra-imitti.

The next ruler of Isin was Enlil-bani (1862–1839 BC), who left a sizable number of inscriptions. He ruled for twenty-four years and was a contemporary of Nur-Adad and Sin-iddinam of Larsa, both of whom paved the way to Larsa's prosperity and supremacy in the early second millennium. In his own inscriptions, Enlil-bani emphasized his close relationship with a number of important sanctuaries. According to several bricks from Isin, he was a "shepherd who makes everything abundant for Nippur," a "farmer (who grows) tall grain for Ur," "who purifies the divine ordinances of Eridu," and the "favorite *en* priest of Uruk."[334] Several inscriptions deal with the construction of Isin's wall, which was

---

330. Middeke-Conlin 2020: 408–415, Table 4A.

331. von Dassow 2009: 72 refers to an Akkadian inscription of Šamši-Adad I (= Samsi-Addu) that states: "When I built the temple of the god Enlil, my lord, the prices in my city, Assur, (were): two *kor* of barley could be purchased for one shekel of silver; fifteen minas of wool for one shekel of silver; and two *seah* of oil for one shekel of silver, according to the prices of my city Assur" (Grayson 1987: no. A.0.39.1: ll. 59–72).

332. Chambon 2015; Goddeeris 2016c: 5, n. 1.

333. See section 14.5.1.

334. Frayne 1990: no. 4.1.10.1.

given the name "Enlil-bani is firm as to foundation."[335] Enlil-bani was heavily involved in the building of religious structures. The divine beneficiaries included Nin-Isina with a temple known as the E'urgira, the "dog house,"[336] Ninibgal,[337] Nintinuga,[338] and Sud.[339] Enlil-bani also constructed a palace[340] that is mentioned in a poem of his. This song of praise, roughly 180 lines in length, is one of four hymns that form part of the so-called *Tetrad*, which was copied by scribal apprentices after fulfilling their elementary education (see section 14.2.2). Manuscripts of this text have survived from the capital Isin, as well as Nippur, Sippar, Ur, and unprovenanced locations. The text states:

> When you take your seat, you cause all the foreign lands to bow down. All sovereigns become allies with you and you soothe their quarrels. With numerous oxen and numerous sheep, with gold, carnelian and lapis lazuli they enter your palace. With their lips they kiss the ground before you.[341]

Remains of Enlil-bani's palace were found in the southeastern part of the city. This identification was possible thanks to personnel lists from the courtyard. Another part of the complex yielded administrative accounts from his reign dealing with grain and flour.[342] These record the delivery of fixed amounts of flour for a meal (Akkadian *naptanum*) and

---

335. Frayne 1990: no. 4.1.10.2: ll. 15–16; compare also Frayne 1990: no. 4.1.10.3, according to which the wall had become dilapidated.

336. Frayne 1990: no. 4.1.10.4.

337. Frayne 1990: no. 4.1.10.5.

338. Frayne 1990: no. 4.1.10.6.

339. Frayne 1990: no. 4.1.10.7. According to this inscription (an example of which was found near the site of Fara), Enlil-bani built the shrine Edimgalana (l. 6). For the recently published hymn to Sud, see section 14.4.2.

340. Frayne 1990: no. 4.1.10.9; no. 4.1.10.10.

341. *Enlil-bani* A: ll. 98–111.

342. Sallaberger 1996: 178–179.

therefore represent part of the palace administration. Since there is no date list (yet) for Enlil-bani's reign, dated texts such as the ones in the palace archive at Isin help to reconstruct a possible sequence of his regnal years.[343] It is likely that his edict exempting Isin's citizenry from debts can be dated to the beginning of his reign.[344]

While his predecessor Iddin-Dagan had no control over Nippur, Enlil-bani relocated two statues fashioned by Iddin-Dagan to Nippur 117 years later (see section 14.2.2).[345]

The next three kings of the Isin dynasty had rather short reigns. The first among them was a king named Zambiya (1838–1836 BC).[346] Sin-iqišam of Larsa claims in his fifth year to have defeated an army of Elamites, as well as Zambiya.[347] According to one of the few attested year names of Zambiya, he fashioned four statues for Inana and Nanaya.[348] His close relationship with the goddess of love is also expressed in a number of cones from Isin which commemorate the construction of Isin's wall, which was named "Zambiya is the beloved of Eštar."[349]

The few year names of Iter-piša, from whose reign no extant royal inscriptions are known thus far, commemorate pious acts such as the production of a bronze kettledrum for Inana-of-Zabalam, and ceremonial weapons for Enlil and Ninurta at Nippur.

The next king, Ur-dukuga, who bore a Sumerian name, reigned for only four years. He was a contemporary of the Larsa king Warad-Sin. Both clay cones and one of his year names commemorate the construction of

343. Sallaberger 1996: 188–191.

344. Sigrist 1988: 33: Year A; Sallaberger 1996: 187, 189.

345. Frayne 1990: no. 4.1.10.11.

346. van Koppen 2018.

347. Sigrist 1990: 29: Year 5.

348. Sigrist 1988: 35: Year A.

349. Frayne 1990: no. 4.1.11.1: ll. 16–22. For a hand drawing of the text, see Wilcke 2018: 120, no. 11.

a temple of Dagan at Isin.[350] The important religious center Nippur was briefly lost to Larsa, eventually regained, and lost again toward the end of Ur-dukuga's reign.

14.8. Emutbal (Yamutbal) and Larsa: Kudur-mabuk and his sons

As noted earlier, Maškan-šapir was under Larsa's control as early as the reign of Zabaya (see section 14.3.1). In his own inscriptions, Zabaya used the title *rabiān Amurrim*, "Amorite chief," but not king of Larsa. Maškan-šapir was also the center of the territory of the Emutbal (or Yamutbal), an Amorite tribe, possibly belonging to the Sim'alite branch.[351] Zabaya's title, which was also used by his successor Abi-sare, suggests that being head of the tribe was more significant than being ruler of Larsa.[352] Although sources are scarce, it is likely that Zabaya's three predecessors were Amorite sheikhs as well. The political landscape of southern Babylonia in the mid-nineteenth century BC has been likened to Samsi-Addu's state in Syria. The latter ruled an empire from his capital Šubat-Enlil (modern Tell Leilan) with his two sons, Išme-Dagan ruling in Ekallatum and Yasmah-Addu in Mari. It was proposed that a similar model existed in southern Mesopotamia. The main reason for suggesting a two-state model, with Maškan-šapir as the center of the Emutbal in the north and Larsa as a sovereign state in the south, lies in the fact that Kudur-mabuk never became king of Larsa, but successively placed his two sons Warad-Sin (see section 14.8.2) and Rim-Sin I (see section 14.9) on Larsa's throne. He regularly appears in the early inscriptions of both kings. This model, however, was challenged by Piotr Steinkeller, who suggested that the kingdom of Larsa was dimorphic in nature, combining

---

350. Frayne 1990: no. 4.1.13.1: ll. 21–24. The name of Year C provides the exact same information; see Sigrist 1988: 37; Goddeeris 2016b.

351. Edzard 1957: 105–106; Steinkeller 2004: 34–36. For the possibility that Emutbal belonged to the Sim'alites, see de Boer 2013b: 272 with n. 30.

352. Steinkeller 2004: 37.

two different entities, a tribal state of Emutbal and a sovereign state of Larsa. This hypothesis is further strengthened by the ethnic designation Emutbal itself, which was eventually used to designate a much broader area than originally intended due to population movements.[353]

14.8.1. The father of the Amorites: Kudur-mabuk

In the last third of the nineteenth century, Larsa witnessed the inception of a new dynasty, the founder of which was Kudur-mabuk. Inscriptions refer to Kudur-mabuk as "father of the Amorites" (Sumerian *ad-da kur mar-tu*)[354] or "father of Emutbal" (*ad-da e-mu-ut-ba-la*). Before he was able to install his son Warad-Sin at Larsa, he must have positioned himself in Maškan-šapir to gain enough strength in order to prepare for the takeover.[355] Despite his ample use of Amorite titulary, Kudur-mabuk's name and the name of his father Simti-Šilhak suggest a strong connection, by birth and upbringing, to Elam or at least the region east of the Tigris.[356] Both of Kudur-mabuk's sons bore Akkadian names. Kudur-mabuk never referred to himself as king. The only exception is in a caption preserved on a clay tablet, which describes a stele depicting "king" Kudur-mabuk smiting Ṣilli-Eštar, the king of Maškan-šapir.[357] The influence of Kudur-mabuk on the reign of his two sons is apparent in their royal inscriptions. Kudur-mabuk appears on his own in a longer Akkadian inscription, according to which he built a house made of baked bricks to accommodate a stele for regular offerings.[358]

---

353. Steinkeller 2004: 36.

354. See also section 14.1.4.

355. Steinkeller 2004: 32–33.

356. For discussions of the dynasty's origins, see Steinkeller 2004: 30–31; De Graef 2016: 643; Beaulieu 2018: 75.

357. Frayne 1990: no. 4.2.13a.1. The stele is said to have been set up in Ninlil's temple in Nippur.

358. Frayne 1990: no. 4.2.13a.2. Among his epithets is the statement: "He did no wrong to Larsa and Emutbal."

Kudur-mabuk's daughter was installed as *en* priestess of the moon god at Ur, where she took the name Enanedu. Her elevation to this office is recorded in the name of Warad-Sin's seventh year.[359] Leonard Woolley also discovered a badly damaged stone tablet at Ur which appears to deal with the events surrounding Enanedu's installation.[360] Later in Rim-Sin's reign, Enanedu undertook building activities in the Gipar, commemorated on a clay cone inscription[361] in which she states:

> When the gods Nanna and Ningal looked (at me) with their shining faces, gave to me life and a joyful expression, and made my name supreme in the shrine Ekišnugal, residence of their divinity, they placed a supplication of life in my pure mouth: that they take my extended hand in order to prolong the life-span of Rim-Sin, my twin brother, and that they deliver into his hands the foreign land, all his enemies.[362]

More than a millennium later, while re-establishing the custom of appointing a princess to the office of *en* priestess of the moon god, King Nabonidus (556–539 BC) referred to an inscription that he found in the foundations:

> I discovered an ancient inscribed object of Enanedu, *en* priestess of Ur, daughter of Kudur-mabuk, sister of Rim-Sin, king of Ur, who had renewed Egipar and restored it (and who) surrounded the burial ground of the ancient *en* priestesses near the boundary of Egipar with a wall.[363]

---

359. Sigrist 1990: 33; for the date list in the Moussaieff Collection: Abraham 2008: 29: l. 8.

360. Frayne 1990: no. 4.2.13.15.

361. Frayne 1990: no. 4.2.14.20. The text was first published by Gadd 1951.

362. Frayne 1990: no. 4.2.14.20: ll. 15–25. Rim-Sin's name is preceded by the divine classifier, which suggests a later stage in his reign.

363. Weiershäuser and Novotny 2020: no. 34: ii 1–5.

The similarities of information contained in the original inscription and the inscription claimed to have been found by Nabonidus one millennium later seem to suggest that Nabonidus's scribes were familiar with the text.[364]

14.8.2. Warad-Sin

Kudur-mabuk's son Warad-Sin sat on Larsa's throne for eleven years (1834–1823 BC), after having been installed there by his father, who, as noted earlier, founded a new dynasty there. It appears likely that Warad-Sin was not an entirely independent ruler during his reign. One indicator of his level of autonomy is provided by his extensive corpus of royal inscriptions (figure 14.7). Warad-Sin left more royal inscriptions than any other king of Larsa. Most of the deeds commemorated in these inscriptions also appear in the extant year names of his reign. There was some disagreement about the length of his rule in the past. Thus far we know of fourteen names which were used to indicate his twelve or thirteen regnal years. Apart from archival documents, we have a number of date lists at our disposal.[365] The Dynastic List of Larsa (figure 14.5) assigns twelve years to his reign. A date list in Chicago, however, assigns to him thirteen years.[366] Thanks to a recently published, unprovenanced date list, it is now clear that Warad-Sin indeed reigned twelve years and the additional year name in the Chicago date list represents a variant of his third year.[367]

In two of Warad-Sin's early inscriptions he is referred to not as king, but as "governor of Ur, Larsa, Lagaš, and the land of Kutalla." This title was also used by his predecessor, Ṣilli-Adad.[368] The name of his second year mentions

---

364. For a discussion, see Schaudig 2003: 482–485.

365. For references to the individual sources, see Abraham 2008: 27.

366. Stol 1976: 2–3 (Oriental Institute Museum, Chicago, A 7534).

367. The text is kept in the Moussaieff Collection and was published by Abraham 2008: 37–38.

368. See section 14.5.2. In the dedicatory inscription on an agate eye stone, Warad-Sin's only title is "governor of Utu" (Frayne 1990: no. 4.2.13.30: ll. 4–5).

FIGURE 14.7. A royal inscription of Warad-Sin of Larsa dedicated to the goddess Nin-Isina. Yale Babylonian Collection, YBC 12025 (obverse). Author's photograph.

the destruction of Kazallu.[369] In an inscription that probably refers to this campaign, Kudur-mabuk is portrayed as the active party:[370]

> Kudur-mabuk, father of the Amorite land, son of Simti-šilhak, the one who repaid a favor for the Ebabbar, who smote the army

---

369. Sigrist 1990: 31. The abbreviated version of this name is attested in the date list published by Abraham 2008: 27: l. 2.

370. De Graef 2016: 643–644.

of Kazallu and Muti-abal in Larsa and Emutbal, who by decree
of Nanna and Utu seized Kazallu, tore down its wall, and made
it submit.[371]

According to another fragmentary inscription, Warad-Sin smote the
army of Kazallu and defeated its king, Muti-abal.[372] This campaign
against Kazallu was probably undertaken in defense after Kazallu and
Maškan-šapir jointly attacked Larsa and ended Ṣilli-Adad's reign.[373]
A reflection of this attack may also be found in another inscription commemorating the construction of Nanna's temple, in which Kudur-mabuk
took an active role:

> I, Kudur-mabuk, (…) when the god Nanna agreed to my entreaty
> and delivered into my hands the enemies who had thrown down
> the top of the Ebabbar temple, he returned to Larsa Maškan-šapir
> and Kar-Šamaš.[374]

The second military campaign attested in Warad-Sin's year names was the
defeat of Malgium.[375] These are the only military campaigns recorded in
Warad-Sin's inscriptions and year names, most of which commemorate

---

371. Frayne 1990: no. 4.2.13.3: ll. 7–19. Kudur-mabuk built a temple of the god
     Nergal for his own life and the life of his son Warad-Sin. At least one of the
     two manuscripts of this inscription comes from Uruk. It has been suggested
     that Uruk may have been briefly under Larsa's control in Warad-Sin's reign, also
     because a legal document dating to Warad-Sin's sixth year features an oath that
     invokes both his name and that of Sin-iribam of Uruk. However, the mention
     of these two rulers is more likely due to the fact that the document's seller is an
     individual from Durum (which was under Uruk's control) and the purchaser a
     man from Larsa; see Charpin 2004: 118 and section 14.6.2.

372. Frayne 1990: no. 4.2.13.4.

373. Charpin 2004: 118.

374. Frayne 1990: no. 4.2.13.10: ll. 5–21. Kar-Šamaš is a settlement on the Tigris,
     slightly north of its confluence with the Diyala and the Zubi canal.

375. Sigrist 1990: 31–32; see also Abraham 2008: 37: l. 3. This year name is one of two
     variants, with the alternative name commemorating the consecration of a gold
     statue of Warad-Sin in the temple of the sun-god Utu.

building projects, such as the construction or renovation of temples and the consecration of statues and thrones.

Real estate documents bear oaths invoking both Warad-Sin and his father even later on.[376] Judging from the extensive corpus of royal inscriptions from Warad-Sin's reign, his father slowly disappeared from them after his sixth year.

Kudur-Mabuk's hold on Maškan-šapir appears not to have been of long duration, as his son Warad-Sin needed to recapture it already in his fourth regnal year. Only a few royal inscriptions survive in which Kudur-mabuk serves as sole actor. In most inscriptions in which he appears, he is commemorated together with his son Warad-Sin. Warad-Sin's reign in Larsa was fairly short. Nevertheless, he left a staggering number of royal inscriptions.

The name of Warad-Sin's sixth year commemorates the installation of fourteen copper statues at Nippur.[377] This, and the fact that Warad-Sin is attested in archival documents in Nippur from his seventh year onward, shows that Nippur was again under his authority. The name of Warad-Sin's ninth regnal year commemorates the installation of a statue of his father Kudur-mabuk in the temple of Šamaš.[378] As administrative texts show, such statues received offerings. We see this custom also with some of the later kings of Larsa. According to the name of the second year of Rim-Sin, the king brought a copper statue of Warad-Sin into the Egalbara.[379] One year later, he brought four copper statues of Kudur-mabuk to Nanna's temple.[380] Three years later, in Rim-Sin's fifth

---

376. E.g., Grice 1919: no. 127: l. 12, which dates to the twelfth year of Warad-Sin; see also De Graef 2016: 643.

377. Sigrist 1990: 33 (Year "7"): "Year, (Warad-Sin) brought fourteen copper statues to Nippur and three thrones whose august dais is covered with gold into the temple of Nanna, the temple of Ningal, and the temple of Utu."

378. Sigrist 1990: 34–35.

379. Sigrist 1990: 37.

380. Sigrist 1990: 38. A short version of this year name is attested in George 2011: no. 102: l. 3, in which Kudur-mabuk's name is written *ku-du-un-na-bu-ug*. According to this list, the statues were instead brought into Utu's temple.

year, the king brought to the same location two copper statues of his
father Kudur-mabuk and one stele.[381] The destination of these statues,
the Egalbara, was interpreted as the "outer palace,"[382] but Dominique
Charpin has proposed identifying it as a sort of vestibule to the palace
in Larsa, which is convincing considering the similar customs in Zimri-
Lim's palace at Mari.[383] According to the name of his sixth year, Rim-Sin
also fashioned a golden statue of Sin-iddinam (1849–1843 BC).[384]

14.9. The wild bull of the moon god: Rim-Sin of Larsa

The last king of the dynasty of Larsa was Rim-Sin (1822–1763 BC). With a
reign of sixty years, he was the longest-ruling monarch in Mesopotamian
history. Rim-Sin followed his brother Warad-Sin on the throne, and we can
assume that he was rather young when he became king. The sources about
his reign are abundant: royal inscriptions, year names, literary letters, and of
course ephemeral texts such as letters written by or addressed to Rim-Sin,
administrative and legal documents (see section 14.9.3), and political correspondence from the Mari archives informing Zimri-Lim of events taking
place in the south.[385] Larsa undoubtedly reached the apex of its power in the
course of his long reign. Rim-Sin's year names show an intriguing pattern.
The first twenty-nine years show the usual practice of naming years (see
later discussion). The name of his thirtieth year commemorates his defeat
and capture of Isin, the crowning achievement of his reign. The names of
all of the subsequent thirty years of his reign were modeled on this event.[386]

---

381. Sigrist 1990: 38–39: Year 5; also attested in the new date list published as George
    2011: no. 102: l. 5.

382. George 1993: 87.

383. Charpin 2018.

384. Sigrist 1990: 39–40.

385. Van de Mieroop 1993: 48–49.

386. The date list containing all year names of the Larsa dynasty shows the dif-
    ference between these two groups of year names quite vividly. Rim-Sin's

Thus year names of the second half of his reign became mute as they no longer reported on contemporary events (see section 14.9.3).

14.9.1. The first half of Rim-Sin's reign

When Rim-Sin came to power, his kingdom stretched from the Persian Gulf to the central part of Babylonia and included the cities of Eridu and Ur in the south; Larsa, Kutalla, Bad-tibira, Girsu, Zabalam, and Adab in the center; and Maškan-šapir and Nippur in the north. His neighbors were Uruk, Isin, and Babylon.[387] When assembling all known royal inscriptions of Rim-Sin,[388] Douglas Frayne established seven chronological groups. The earliest inscriptions from his reign are texts that still refer to his father Kudur-mabuk, either acting together with his son or for whose life a particular construction or votive offering was made. In contrast to Warad-Sin's inscriptions, however, Kudur-mabuk played a less prominent role in those of Rim-Sin, although he is still mentioned first, in cases where they built a temple together. Rim-Sin himself is referred to as "prince, who reveres Nippur,"[389] which shows that this city was under the control of the kingdom of Larsa. This epithet was omitted in later inscriptions. The early construction projects in Rim-Sin's reign centered on temples for Iškur,[390]

---

reign starts at the bottom of the broken side (b) of this four-sided prism. His first twenty-nine year names take up the space until the middle of side (d). Some of these year names take up six lines and more, whereas the remaining 31 years only need space of one line each. For a hand drawing of the prism, see Thureau-Dangin 1918.

387. Pientka-Hinz 2008: 368, §2.

388. There are now three texts from the Schøyen Collection that must be added to this corpus: George 2011: nos. 51–53.

389. Frayne 1990: no. 4.2.14.1: l. 10; no. 4.2.14.2: l. 10; no. 4.2.14.3: l. 10; no. 4.2.14.4: l. 8; no. 4.2.14.5: l. 8; no. 4.2.14.6: l. 14.

390. Frayne 1990: no. 4.2.14.1. Rim-Sin takes the active part, but dedicates the construction for his and the life of his father.

Inana,[391] Nanaya,[392] Dumuzi,[393] Nergal,[394] and Enki.[395] As the last of these inscriptions omits any reference to his father, it may be that Kudur-mabuk had passed away by then.

Several of Rim-Sin's year names commemorate the installation of royal statues in different temples and the palace. He dedicated one statue of his brother, six statues of his father, and one statue of Sin-iddinam in his second, third, fifth, and sixth years. In his eleventh year, he brought into Utu's temple two copper statues depicting himself praying.[396] One year name deals with the consecration of an *ugbabtum* priestess of the god Adad at Karkar.[397] These kinds of projects defined the early years of his reign.

This changed in his fourteenth year. According to the name of this year, and several of his royal inscriptions, Rim-Sin "defeated the armies of Uruk, Isin, Babylon, Sutium, Rapiqum, and IRnene, the king of Uruk."[398] Royal inscriptions dating to this period also show a change in the relationship to Nippur. While Rim-Sin had hitherto used the epithet "prince, who reveres Nippur," this now changed to "shepherd, who fervently prays for Nippur," as attested in a number of inscriptions that also refer to the events of his fourteenth year.[399]

---

391. Frayne 1990: no. 4.2.14.2. Kudur-mabuk and Rim-Sin act together. The construction of Inana's temple is also commemorated in the name of Rim-Sin's fourth year: "Year (Rim-Sin) built the temple of Inana, the temple of Nanna, and the temple of Enki in Larsa"; see Sigrist 1990: 38.

392. Frayne 1990: no. 4.2.14.3. Kudur-mabuk and Rim-Sin act together.

393. Frayne 1990: no. 4.2.14.4. Rim-Sin is the active party, but dedicates the construction for his and the life of his father.

394. Frayne 1990: no. 4.2.14.5. Rim-Sin is again the active party, but dedicates the construction for his and the life of his father.

395. Frayne 1990: no. 4.2.14.6.

396. Sigrist 1990: 42: Year 11.

397. Sigrist 1990: 42: Year 12.

398. Sigrist 1990: 43–44: Year 14; for the inscriptions: Frayne 1990: no. 4.2.14.8: ll. 19–28; no. 4.2.14.9: ll. 17–24; no. 4.2.14.10: ll. 15–19; see also section 14.6.2.

399. Frayne 1990: no. 4.2.14.8: l. 11; no. 4.2.14.9: l. 10; no. 4.2.14.10: l. 8.

In subsequent years, Rim-Sin continued his military endeavors, conquering Pi-naratim and Naṣarum in his fifteenth year; Imgur-Gibil and Zibnatum in his seventeenth year; Bit-Šu-Sin and Uṣarpara one year later; and Durum and Kisurra in his twentieth year. This latter year name shows that he fought on multiple fronts, as Kisurra is located near Isin and Durum near Uruk. Around this time, he must have also regained control of Nippur, as royal inscriptions from this date onward include the epithet "shepherd, who bears tribute for Nippur."[400] According to the name of his twenty-first year, he eventually succeeded in destroying Uruk, but spared its inhabitants.[401] This was also the point in his reign when the letter of a priestess to him claims to have been written (see section 14.6). According to two of his inscriptions, "An, Enlil, Enki and the great gods entrusted Uruk, the ancient city," into his hands.[402] From that point onward, he called himself the "righteous shepherd" (Sumerian sipa zi), a title which preceded his deified name.

Rim-Sin's later year names became longer, but military campaigns were less often mentioned. A focus on irrigation work in them is noteworthy. While the digging of canals was commemorated in his seventh and ninth years,[403] further canals were dug in his twenty-second to twenty-fourth, twenty-sixth, and his twenty-seventh years.[404] The reason for the silence on military achievements may be due to Babylon's interference in the region. Uruk was an ally of Babylon, as can be shown by ANam's letter to Sin-muballiṭ (1812–1793 BC) (see section 14.6.2). Rim-Sin's defeat of Uruk posed a significant threat to Babylon. The name of Sin-muballiṭ's eleventh year records the construction of the wall of Murum, which interrupted communications between the south and the north.[405] Several strategic Babylonian measures are attested at this time.

---

400. E.g., Frayne 1990: no. 4.2.14.11: l. 12.

401. Sigrist 1990: 49–50: Year 21.

402. Frayne 1990: no. 4.2.14.12: ll. 14–18; no. 4.2.14.13: ll. 23–26.

403. Rim-Sin dug a canal from Lagaš to the Persian Gulf; see Sigrist 1990: 41: Year 9.

404. For royal work projects concerning canals, see Charpin 2002a.

405. Charpin 2004: 121 with n. 521.

In a letter from Kiš, Sin-magir of Isin (1827–1817 BC) informed the governor of Kiš: "240 enemy ships are assembled in Maškan-šapir. It is in that direction, to the quay of Kiš, to you, that they are heading."[406]

The remaining military campaigns of Rim-Sin had one focus: Isin. The name of his twenty-fifth year records the capture of Al-Damiq-ilišu. Its allied inhabitants of Isin were taken as prisoners to Larsa.[407] As commemorated in his twenty-ninth regnal year, the next setback for Isin was Rim-Sin's capture of Dunnum, the "major stronghold of (the kingdom of) Isin."[408] One year later, Isin, "the city of kingship," fell.[409] From then on, the title "king of Isin" was added to Rim-Sin's titulary, as shown by the copy of an inscription, the original of which must have been composed around this time.[410]

14.9.2. The last kings of Isin

According to his royal inscriptions, Sin-magir (1827–1817 BC) built the great wall of Dunnum, whose name was "Sin-magir makes the foundation of the land firm."[411] One of his year names may also refer to this construction.[412] Sin-magir was a contemporary of the Larsa kings Warad-Sin and Rim-Sin. As noted earlier (section 14.9.1), Dunnum was later conquered

---

406. Kupper 1959: D 29 = AO 10788: ll. 4–10; see also Charpin 2004: 122 with n. 524. This armada must have used the Tigris; see Steinkeller 2001: 39 with n. 69.

407. Sigrist 1990: 53–54: Year 25.

408. Sigrist 1990: 58–59: Year 29.

409. Sigrist 1990: 59–60: Year 30.

410. Frayne 1990: no. 4.2.14.19: ll. 14–16: "king of Larsa, Uruk, (and) Isin, king of Sumer and Akkad." The subsequent passage (ll. 17–19) alludes to the capture of Isin: "when she [i.e., the goddess Ama-gula] gave Isin, the city of kingship, into my hands."

411. Frayne 1990: no. 4.1.14.1: ll. 18–23. For a hand drawing of this inscription, see Wilcke 2018: 122, no. 15.

412. Jean 1929: 112: AO 11151: l. 28; see also Richter 2011.

by Rim-Sin in his twenty-ninth year. An inscription that is known from three bricks from Isin names a palace of Sin-magir.[413]

The *lukur* priestess Nuṭuptum dedicated an inscription to the goddess Aktuppitum of Kiritab for Sin-magir's life on the occasion of the construction of a storehouse. The priestess called herself "[mother] of his [fir]stborn,"[414] and this was certainly Damiq-ilišu, Sin-magir's successor. As a contemporary of Rim-Sin's, it cannot be excluded that Sin-magir was also father of a future queen of the Larsa king named Rim-Sin-Šala-baštašu (see section 14.9.3).

Damiq-ilišu (1816–1794 BC), the last king of the dynasty of Isin, ruled for twenty-three years. His royal inscriptions commemorate building work on the wall of Isin,[415] the construction of a storehouse for the god Martu,[416] and the construction of the temple Ekitušbidu at Isin.[417] A fragmentary date list from Nippur, now kept in the University of Pennsylvania Museum, contains on its obverse the names of years four to twelve of Damiq-ilišu's reign.[418]

The name of Rim-Sin's twenty-fifth year refers to a defeat of Isin under Damiq-ilišu:

> The righteous shepherd Rim-Sin with the powerful help of An, Enlil, and Enki seized the city Al-Damiq-ilišu, brought its inhabitants who had helped Isin as prisoners to Larsa, and established his triumph greater than before.[419]

---

413. Frayne 1990: no. 4.1.14.3.

414. Frayne 1990: no. 4.1.14.2: l. 11.

415. The name of this wall is "Damiq-ilišu is the favorite of the god Ninurta" (Frayne 1990: no. 4.1.15.1: ll. 21–22).

416. Frayne 1990: no. 4.1.15.2: ll. 19–20: "the 'house of pure divine ordinances,' his beloved storehouse."

417. Frayne 1990: no. 4.1.15.3.

418. Lieberman 1982; for a photograph see CDLI (https://cdli.ucla.edu/P266202; last accessed August 25, 2020). After a break, the reverse of the tablet features Years 40 to 46 of Rim-Sin, while the text's colophon mentions a total of 27 years.

419. Sigrist 1990: 53–54: Year 25.

This weakening of Isin allowed Rim-Sin to take control of the city in 1794 BC. Although beyond the time frame of this chapter, it should be noted that, despite the brevity and political instability of his reign, Damiq-ilišu was remembered in later periods more than any of his predecessors. The so-called *Weidner Chronicle* (or *Esagila Chronicle*), for instance, a composition that only survives in manuscripts from the first millennium BC, is an apocryphal letter from Damiq-ilišu addressed to either Apil-Sin, king of Babylon, or Rim-Sin, king of Larsa, both of whom were contemporaries of the king of Isin.[420] The third king of the First Sealand Dynasty was named Dam(i)q-ilišu. Whether this name was in veneration of the earlier Isin king, however, remains unknown. According to the *Babylonian Royal Chronicle*, the founder of the Second Sealand Dynasty, Simbar-Šipak, was a "descendant of Eriba-Sin, a soldier who died in combat during the reign of Damiq-ilišu."[421]

14.9.3. After Isin was taken: the second half of Rim-Sin's reign

Taking the names of his last thirty years into consideration only, the defeat of Isin appears as the defining moment in Rim-Sin's reign. By 1794 BC, successful military campaigns had allowed Rim-Sin to extend his hegemony from the Persian Gulf to the border with Babylon.

The second half of Rim-Sin's reign is far less well-known than his first thirty years. One of the main reasons for this reduced level of knowledge is not the lack of sources, but the fact that the remaining year names of his reign refer repeatedly to the capture of Isin, thus for

---

420. Al-Rawi 1990: 1. The remainders of the signs in the first line allow for both possibilities. Alternatively, Glassner 2004: 263 proposes Rim-Sin as the addressee and Enlil-bani as the sender. Enlil-bani reigned until 1839 BC, i.e., seventeen years before Rim-Sin ascended Larsa's throne, and I therefore favor Damiq-ilišu. See also in the letter, Frankena 1974: no. 73: ll. 13–17: "(If) you detain him until I come, will you answer to Rim-Sin and Damiq-ilišu?"

421. Glassner 2004: 132–133: *Babylonian Royal Chronicle*: v 2′–3′.

example "the seventh year after [the year] Isin was captured by [means of] weapons."[422]

Although this choice of Rim-Sin's chancellery makes it much easier (also for the modern researcher) to identify years, it unfortunately also means that any deeds (building projects, canals, installation of priestesses, and so forth) and possible victories during these years went unmentioned. Additionally, using this type of year name severed the link between the dating system and royal inscriptions. As we have seen in many cases cited earlier, year names often corroborate information gleaned from contemporary inscriptions (see section 14.1.1). Furthermore, the standardization of the dating system across the kingdom led to difficulty in identifying the provenance of many illicitly found tablets claimed to come from Larsa. A rigorous study of a document's external and internal characteristics can often help identify the place of its composition.[423] A large lot of approximately three hundred tablets was found in the so-called *Scherbenloch* (German for "hole of potsherds") at Uruk.[424] Legal texts from scientific excavations also come from Girsu, Kisurra, Kutalla, Larsa, Nippur, and Ur.[425]

Although the capture of Isin was the crowning achievement of Rim-Sin's reign, after over two centuries of competition between Isin and Larsa for supremacy in southern Mesopotamia, the military successes and expansion of the first half of his reign were not permanent. Indeed, some were short-lived. The name of Hammurabi's seventh year (1787 BC) records the capture of Uruk and Isin.[426] Family archives from Isin, among them those of the family of Dada, show that Babylon did not hold the city for long, however.[427]

---

422. E.g., Van de Mieroop 2007: 32.

423. On this approach's potential, see Charpin 2010a: 68–114. Modern non-invasive analytical methods such as portable x-ray fluorescence (PXRF) analysis help to identify different places of origin, but they require a large enough sample.

424. Cavigneaux 1996.

425. Pientka-Hinz 2008: 368, §1.4.

426. Horsnell 1999: II 112–113.

427. Charpin 1992: 208–211; 2004: 124.

Among the inscriptions that cannot be dated precisely are those dedicated by his two queens. A third queen is known only from her cylinder seal. According to its legend, Beltani was the daughter of a certain Habannum, who is not otherwise attested as a member of a royal family.[428] His queen Simat-Eštar left two inscriptions, both of which concern the construction of the temple of Belet-ekallim (Nin-egal). Simat-Eštar calls herself "beloved spouse of Rim-Sin"[429] and "ornament befitting the king."[430] She may have been the principal wife of Rim-Sin around the time of Isin's capture.[431] Another of his queens, Rim-Sin-Šala-baštašu, also left two inscriptions. One was found on a basalt column, originally crowned by a water vessel. The inscription, which is masterfully carved into the stone, spans fifty lines and is dedicated to Inana, "the reliable deity, whose compassion is good, (with) patient mercy, who greatly knows how to take by the hand those in dire straits and the sick."[432] The queen dedicated the water vessel for the life of Rim-Sin and their daughter Liriš-gamlum. The purpose of the queen's precious gift to the goddess becomes clear later:

> In order to save Liriš-gamlum from the hand of evil-doers or bandits, to hand over the *asakku* and *ašbur* diseases that are in her body to (a demon) who does not know fear, to make the *šahal* disease leave her eyes, to banish the dangers of sickness.[433]

Rim-Sin-Šala-baštašu also dedicated nine bronze milk cups to An. Although the original of this inscription is lost, a later copy on a clay tablet

---

428. Frayne 1990: no. 4.2.14.22; see also Földi 2016.

429. Frayne 1990: no. 4.2.14.17: ll. 19–20; also no. 4.2.14.16: ll. 13–14. According to the latter inscription, Simat-Eštar was the daughter of a certain Warad-Nanna.

430. Frayne 1990: no. 4.2.14.17: l. 32.

431. Charpin 2019.

432. Frayne 1990: no. 4.2.14.23: ll. 5–7. For a photo of the column and its inscription, see Lassen and Wagensonner 2020: 89–91.

433. Frayne 1990: no. 4.2.14.23: ll. 30–35.

is preserved. The inscription has a very similar tone to the one cited here. Again, the purpose of the dedication is to find relief for the princess's frail health.[434] The queen refers to herself in both inscriptions as the daughter of a certain Sin-magir. No title is attached to her father's name, but it should be noted that a king of Isin bearing the same name was a contemporary of Rim-Sin and thus may very well be identical to her father (see section 14.9.2).

Turning now briefly to Larsa's economy in this period, the kingdom of Larsa enjoyed an age of prosperity in Rim-Sin's reign. Elite residences, reaching sizes of 500 to over 1,000 m², were concentrated in the north-eastern part of the city.[435] The second half of Rim-Sin's reign reveals a centralized state at work, aided by a number of reforms. The development toward a centralized economy with its focal point on the capital Larsa worked to the detriment of the previous temple economy.[436] During the reign of Warad-Sin, economic assets and the preparation of offerings were still managed directly by temple personnel.[437] With Rim-Sin and his reforms, the situation changed dramatically. The number of documents pertaining to temple administration diminished; private archives show that henceforth citizens played an important role in the income of temples. Certain temple offices were "monetized" and shares in them can be found in inheritance documents. Such shares could even be leased and sold. Attempts at centralization can also be seen in other branches of the economy such as trade. Ur, long an important hub for trade with the Persian Gulf, was no longer managed locally, but from Larsa.[438] The ephemeral texts of the Rim-Sin era, namely administrative and certain legal documents as well as letters, are often easy to recognize.

---

434. George 2011: no. 53.

435. On their architecture, see, e.g., Calvet 1996; Charpin 2004: 123–124.

436. As a notable example for the early reign of Rim-Sin, one can cite a large tablet from his second year detailing the offerings and rites in the temples of Larsa for a duration of ten days. See Goodnick Westenholz and Westenholz 2006: 3–81.

437. Goddeeris 2007a: 201.

438. Goddeeris 2007a: 201.

FIGURE 14.8. Administrative texts from the reign of Rim-Sin of Larsa. Author's photograph.

Letters of the chancellery of Rim-Sin tended to use a standardized tablet format. These tablets are usually rather elongated and, depending on the length of the letter, were only partially inscribed. It appears that scribes took down dictation, not knowing the length of the final message beforehand.[439] Extant letters are inscribed in a rather small script, which is sometimes referred to as "Rim-Sin script." Both letters and texts of the administration also exhibit other external features that distinguish them from earlier and later Old Babylonian archival texts. A striking external feature of these often elongated, rectangular tablets is their rather pointed corners (figure 14.8).

Another reform concerned the calendar. We have already seen that, after Isin's annexation, year names were counted consecutively. Up to this point, the administration used the traditional Nippur calendar of twelve months. In the middle of Rim-Sin's reign, however, his administrators

---

439. Charpin 2010a: 120.

began using a new system which introduced intercalary months at irregular intervals in order to adjust for discrepancies between solar and lunar years.[440] This new system is chiefly attested in texts from Nippur.[441]

Rim-Sin proclaimed several edicts of redress (Akkadian *mišarum*) in his reign. Probably the most influential businessman in this period was Balmunamhe, who amassed a huge amount of real estate during his career,[442] which spanned the reigns of Warad-Sin and Rim-Sin. Most of the records at our disposal are legal transactions (sale, lease, hire, loan, partnership, marriage, adoption, and the division of inheritance). Balmunamhe was also heavily involved in slave sales and most of the texts recording his activities involve slaves. Slaves often resulted from debts on loans that could not be paid off. Rim-Sin's edicts in his twenty-fifth, thirty-fourth, and forty-first years partially counteracted these developments, as the palace intervened in the economic affairs of private businessmen. As a result, private moneylenders were forced to forfeit profits from their loans. Rim-Sin's edicts also reduced the amount of debt slavery, and the enormous accumulation of real estate.[443] Balmunamhe is only one of several examples. Early in his career his acquisitions concentrated on small plots in the city. Later he also acquired larger properties in the countryside.[444] Rim-Sin was also the first Larsa king who proclaimed an *andurarum*, which represents a measure to bring balance and order in society annulling debts.[445] For a long time Rim-Sin's edicts were only known through legal documents containing expressions such as "according to the edict of the king" (Akkadian *ana ṣimdat šarrim*).[446] A small, elongated tablet in the Schøyen Collection contains what

---

440. Van de Mieroop 1993: 64; Charpin 2004: 125.

441. Kraus 1959; Robertson 1983.

442. Dyckhoff 1999.

443. Van de Mieroop 1993: 64.

444. Van de Mieroop 1987c: 19.

445. Van de Mieroop 1993: 64.

446. Kraus 1984.

appears to be the first extant royal edict of the kingdom of Larsa.[447] One of its paragraphs reads:

> A house, date plantation, field or riverside field that one man acquired fraudulently from another: he must return (it).
>   If a man buys a vacant plot and they order (its reversion) to the (original) estate, vacant plot shall be provided for vacant plot.[448]

No law collections survive from Rim-Sin's reign. The following royal letter addressed to a number of high-ranking officials, including Balmunamhe, can be seen in the context of capital punishment. The message itself is short:

> Speak to Lu-Ninurta, Balmunamhe, Ipqu-Erra, and Mannum-kima-Sin, thus Rim-Sin, your lord: Because he cast a boy into the oven, you, throw the slave into the kiln![449]

Rim-Sin also features in a number of Sumerian and Akkadian literary works. Currently, eight Sumerian songs of praise mentioning him are known, in addition to several more fragmentary texts. A novelty is the subscript "O Rim-Sin, my king." The majority of the extant manuscripts come from Ur.[450] Two literary letters are currently known. One, discussed earlier, is the letter of Sin-kašid's daughter, Ninšatapada, who wrote to Rim-Sin asking him for help (see section 14.6). Among the Akkadian literary works is a hymn to Amurru and Ašratum with prayers, possibly for Rim-Sin.[451] Akkadian love literature is also attested for the king of Larsa.

---

447. The tablet was first published as George 2009: no. 18. For the interpretation of this text as an edict, see Moore 2018. The text was republished with corrections as George and Spada 2019: no. 65.

448. George 2009: no. 18: ll. 12–18.

449. Stol 1981: no. 197.

450. Brisch 2007: 57–69.

451. Gurney 1989: no. 1.

One tablet in the Yale Babylonian Collection contains what appears to be a dialogue between a man and a woman, accompanied by a chorus. The text may have been composed in the context of the "Sacred Marriage rite" between the king and the goddess Nanaya.[452]

14.9.4. The fall of Larsa

The full name of the thirty-first year of Hammurabi of Babylon is as follows:

> Year, in which Hammurabi, the king, with the help of An and Enlil, went before the army and by the supreme power which the greatest gods had given to him, conquered the land of Emutbal and its king, Rim-Sin. He brought forth his life to its . . .; and caused . . . Sumer and Akkad to dwell at his command.[453]

For sixty years Rim-Sin remained on the throne of Larsa. As we have seen, Rim-Sin's year names from the second half of his long reign give little away as to events happening in this period. Political news about his last two or three years (1765–1763 BC) on Larsa's throne appears in the correspondence sent from Babylon to Mari on the Middle Euphrates. King Zimri-Lim had informants in Babylon who kept him apprised of the situation abroad. Information comes from letters sent by Yarim-Addu, Šarrum-andulli, Yasim-Addu, Yeškit-El, Ibal-El, and Zimri-Addu.[454] Zimri-Lim was informed that, on separate occasions, the ruler of Elam invited both Hammurabi of Babylon and Rim-Sin to enter into an alliance with him and assist him in attacking the other.[455] On several occasions when the eastern border of Hammurabi's kingdom was

---

452. Sigrist and Goodnick Westenholz 2008: 669–670. For a new edition, see Wasserman 2016: 169–174.

453. Horsnell 1999: II 141–143.

454. Van de Mieroop 1993: 58.

455. Charpin et al. 1988: no. 362; see Heimpel 2003: 318–319.

under attack, he requested help from Rim-Sin,[456] but Rim-Sin made only vague promises to join forces.[457] Nevertheless, without his assistance, Hammurabi still managed to defeat Elam in 1764 BC, as commemorated in his thirtieth year name. Once Elam was no longer a threat, Hammurabi could focus on Larsa. Zimri-Lim's informants said about Rim-Sin that he "is hostile to Hammurabi."[458] In a fragmentary letter, an informant quotes from Hammurabi's grievances against Rim-Sin.[459] In 1763 BC, Hammurabi marched together with troops from Mari against Larsa. In one fragmentary letter, Zimri-Addu informed the Mari king that Larsa was under siege and that Babylonian troops had entered the city, detaining Rim-Sin. The Larsa king was brought to Babylon, but we have no information on his fate.[460] By this time Rim-Sin was of an advanced age.[461] In another letter, Zimri-Addu responded to the need to buy lapis lazuli as follows:

> The land of Larsa, all of it, is sleepless. It is gripped by terror, and everybody keeps carrying his head. They brought their cattle and sheep into their houses and do not let them go out through the gate. Not only is there no silver for (buying) lapis lazuli to be seen in anybody's hand—who is there who would sell lapis lazuli?[462]

---

456. Charpin et al. 1988: nos. 363–364; nos. 366–367; see Heimpel 2003: 319–322.

457. Charpin et al. 1988: no. 368; see Heimpel 2003: 322.

458. Charpin et al. 1988: no. 372: l. 29; see Heimpel 2003: 326; Van de Mieroop 2007: 34.

459. Charpin et al. 1988: no. 385; see Heimpel 2003: 333–334; Van de Mieroop 2007: 34.

460. Birot 1993: no. 156: rev. 6'–7': "They brought Rim-Sin out alive"; see also Heimpel 2003: 465. According to a letter by Zimri-Addu and Menirum, Rim-Sin was brought to Babylon with his property: Birot 1993: no. 158: ll. 4–5: "They brought out Rim-Sin and his servants [or perhaps: sons?] together with his property to Babylon."

461. Van de Mieroop 1993: 61.

462. Birot 1993: no. 161: ll. 8–15; see Heimpel 2003: 466.

When Hammurabi took over the kingdom of Larsa and integrated it into his kingdom, the prosperous days of Rim-Sin's prime were long gone. The economy was spiraling downward. Within seventeen years, Rim-Sin proclaimed three edicts of redress.[463] It seems likely that a shortage of water had caused a decline in agricultural productivity.[464] The intensive care for canals seen in the first half of Rim-Sin's reign appears to have had no lasting effect.

For Larsa's populace, life continued under its new ruler, Hammurabi. The Babylonian king installed his own officials at Larsa, from which they administered the southern territories.[465] What eventually happened to Rim-Sin is unknown. The *Chronicle of Early Kings*, inscribed on two tablets of Late Babylonian date, contains a paragraph on Hammurabi's defeat of Rim-Sin and is the only reference to the king of Larsa from a later period:

> Hammurabi, king of Babylon, mustered his troops and marched on Rim-Sin, king of Ur. He conquered Ur and Larsa, took away their possessions to Babylon, and brought [Rim-Si]n there in a . . .[466]

More than two decades after the end of Rim-Sin's reign at Larsa, and well into the reign of Hammurabi's successor Samsu-iluna (1749–1712 BC), some southern cities revolted against the supremacy of Babylon. Based on year names and royal inscriptions, the beginning of Samsu-iluna's reign appears prosperous, but the Babylonian kingdom slowly but surely crumbled. The focus shifted and was limited to Babylon in

---

463. These date to his twenty-fifth, thirty-fourth, and forty-first years; see Charpin 2004: 126. For these edicts, see Kraus 1984.

464. van Koppen 2007: 217.

465. Van de Mieroop 2007: 37–38.

466. Glassner 2004: 272–273: Chronicle 20 (BM 96152): ll. 8–12. The king's name is written AM-^{d}30.

Samsu-iluna's sixth to eighth regnal years.[467] This ostensible neglect of the south resulted in a rebellion and the subsequent establishment of several small kingdoms, most notably one at Uruk under a certain Rim-Anum, and another at Larsa, under a second Rim-Sin.[468] The available sources for this rebellion come from Samsu-iluna's royal inscriptions, his year names, and the year names of his opponents (see chapter 18 in this volume).[469] According to an unprovenanced inscription of Samsu-iluna, Rim-Sin II moved his base to the city of Keš.[470]

14.10. Concluding remarks

From the last decades of the third millennium until the mid-eighteenth century BC, two cities and their territories acted on the political stage in southern Mesopotamia: Isin and Larsa. As we have seen, the political landscape was ever-changing in the space of just a few generations. While Isin and its rulers seem to have been the leading city in the earlier periods, Larsa, in particular, was able to gain power over several key areas in the course of the twentieth century BC. Let us end this chapter with a famous letter from the Mari archives, in which Itur-Asdu sums up the political stage quite aptly:

> There is no king, who by himself is strong. Hammurabi, the man of Babylon, follow ten or fifteen kings; Rim-Sin, the man of Larsa, equally; Ibal-pi-El, the man of Ešnunna, equally; Amut-pi-El, the man of Qatna, equally. Yarim-Lim, the man of Yamhad, follow twenty kings.[471]

---

467. Vedeler 2015: 3.

468. For a synchronism between the reigns of Samsu-iluna, Rim-Sin II, and Rim-Anum, see Seri 2013: 35, Table 5.

469. See Lambert and Weeden 2020. For the year names of Rim-Sin II, see Michalowski 2019.

470. Michalowski 2019: 10.

471. Dossin 1938: 117–118 (A. 482).

REFERENCES

Abraham, K. 2008. New evidence for Warad-Sîn's MU-MALGIUM-BASIG ("The Destruction of Malgium") year name. *RA* 102: 27–38.

Alexander, J.B. 1943. *Early Babylonian letters and economic texts*. New Haven, CT: Yale University Press.

Al-Rawi, F.N.H. 1990. Tablets from the Sippar Library, I: the "Weidner Chronicle," a supposititious royal letter concerning a vision. *Iraq* 52: 1–13.

Al-Rawi, F.N.H. 2002. Tablets from the Sippar Library, X: a dedication for Zabaya of Larsa. *Iraq* 64: 247–248.

Alster, B. 2005. *Wisdom of ancient Sumer*. Bethesda, MD: CDL Press.

Attinger, P. 2014. Iddin-Dagan A. In Koslova, N., Vizirova, E., and Zólyomi, G. (eds.), *Studies in Sumerian language and literature: Festschrift für Joachim Krecher*. Winona Lake, IN: Eisenbrauns, 11–82.

Baqir, T. 1948. A date-list of Ishbi-Irra from an unpublished text in the Iraq Museum. *Sumer* 4: 103–114.

Beaulieu, P.-A. 1992. Kissik, Dūru and Udannu. *Orientalia* 61: 400–424.

Beaulieu, P.-A. 2018. *A history of Babylon, 2200 BC–AD 75*. Hoboken, NJ: Wiley-Blackwell.

Biggs, R.D. 1976. *Inscriptions from al-Hiba-Lagash: the first and second seasons*. Malibu, CA: Undena.

Birot, M. 1993. *Correspondance des gouverneurs de Qaṭṭunân* (Archives royales de Mari 27). Paris: Éditions Recherche sur les Civilisations.

Black, J.A., and Spada, G. 2008. *Texts from Ur kept in the Iraq Museum and in the British Museum*. Messina: Dipartimento di Scienze dell'Antichità dell'Università degli Studi di Messina.

Brisch, N. 2007. *Tradition and the poetics of innovation: Sumerian court literature of the Larsa dynasty (c. 2003–1763 BCE)*. Münster: Ugarit-Verlag.

Brisch, N. 2011. Changing images of kingship in Sumerian literature. In Radner, K., and Robson, E. (eds.), *The Oxford handbook of cuneiform culture*. Oxford: Oxford University Press: 706–724.

Buccellati, G., and Biggs, R.D. 1969. *Cuneiform texts from Nippur: the eighth and ninth seasons*. Chicago: University of Chicago Press.

Calvet, Y. 1996. Maisons privées paléo-babyloniennes à Larsa: remarques d'architecture. In Veenhof, K.R. (ed.), *Houses and households in ancient Mesopotamia*. Leiden: NINO, 197–209.

Cancik-Kirschbaum, E., and Kahl, J. (with the collaboration of Wagensonner, K.) 2018. *Erste Philologien: Archäologie einer Disziplin vom Tigris bis zum Nil.* Tübingen: Mohr Siebeck.

Cavigneaux, A. 1996. *Uruk: altbabylonische Texte aus dem Planquadrat Pe XVI-4/5.* Mainz: Zabern.

Cavigneaux, A., and Krebernik, M. 2001. Numušda. *RlA* 9: 611–614.

Chambon, G. (with a note by Guichard, M.) 2015. "Il faut que vos gardes soient fortes!" Une lettre de Sūmu-El sur la guerre entre Isin et Larsa. *Semitica* 57: 33–42.

Charpin, D. 1980. *Archives familiales et propriété privée en Babylonie ancienne: étude des documents de "Tell Sifr."* Geneva: Droz.

Charpin, D. 1986. *Le clergé d'Ur au siècle d'Hammurabi (XIXe–XVIIIe siècles av. J.-C.).* Geneva: Droz.

Charpin, D. 1988. Les malheurs d'un scribe ou de l'inutilité du Sumérien loin de Nippur. In deJong Ellis, M. (ed.), *Nippur at the centennial.* Philadelphia: University of Pennsylvania Museum of Archaeology and Anthropology, 7–27.

Charpin, D. 1992. Immigrés, réfugiés et déportés en Babylonie sous Hammurabi et ses successeurs. In Charpin, D., and Joannès, F. (eds.), *La circulation des biens, des personnes et des idées dans le Proche-Orient ancien.* Paris: Éditions Recherche sur les Civilisations, 207–218.

Charpin, D. 2002a. La politique hydraulique des rois paléo-babyloniens. *Annales: Histoire, Sciences Sociales* 57: 545–559.

Charpin, D. 2002b. Ibni-šadûm, roi de Kisurra, fils de Manna-balti-El et gendre de Sûmû-El de Larsa. *NABU* 2002: 41–42 (no. 39).

Charpin, D. 2004. Histoire politique du Proche-Orient amorrite (2002–1595). In Charpin, D., Edzard, D.O., and Stol, M., *Mesopotamien: die altbabylonische Zeit.* Fribourg: Academic Press; Göttingen: Vandenhoeck & Ruprecht, 25–480.

Charpin, D. 2010a. *Reading and writing in Babylon.* Cambridge, MA: Harvard University Press.

Charpin, D. 2010b. *Writing, law, and kingship in Old Babylonian Mesopotamia.* Chicago: University of Chicago Press.

Charpin, D. 2011a. Sîn-erībam von Uruk. *RlA* 12: 516.

Charpin, D. 2011b. Sîn-gāmil von Uruk. *RlA* 12: 516.

Charpin, D. 2011c. Sîn-kāšid. *RlA* 12: 519–520.

Charpin, D. 2015. Histoire de la Mésopotamie. *Annuaire de l'École Pratique des Hautes Études: Section des sciences historiques et philologiques* 146: 8–10.

Charpin, D. 2018. En marge d'EcritUr, 1: un temple funéraire pour la famille royale de Larsa? *NABU* 2018: 14–16 (no. 11).

Charpin, D. 2019. En marge d'Archibab, 32: du nouveau sur la famille royale de Larsa du temps de Rim-Sin I. *NABU* 2019: 29–30 (no. 18).

Charpin, D. 2020. Un clergé en exil: le transfert des dieux de Nippur à Dur-Abi-ešuh. In Gabbay, U., and Pérennès, J.J. (eds.), *Des polythéismes aux monothéismes: mélanges d'Assyriologie offerts à Marcel Sigrist.* Leuven: Peeters, 149–187.

Charpin, D., and Durand, J.-M. 1981. Textes paléo-babyloniens divers du Musée du Louvre (suite). *RA* 75: 97–106.

Charpin, D., and Durand, J.-M. 1993. Notes de lecture: *Texte aus dem Sînkāšid Palast. MARI* 7: 367–375.

Charpin, D., and Reculeau, H. 2001. Nabi-ilišu, roi d'Uruk vaincu par Rīm-Sîn. *NABU* 2001: 72 (no. 75).

Charpin, D., Joannès, F., Lackenbacher, S., and Lafont, B. 1988. *Archives épistolaires de Mari, I/2* (Archives royales de Mari 26/2). Paris: Éditions Recherche sur les Civilisations.

Civil, M. 2011. The law collection of Ur-Namma. In George, A.R. (ed.), *Cuneiform royal inscriptions and related texts in the Schøyen Collection.* Bethesda, MD: CDL Press, 221–286.

Clay, A.T. 1915. *Miscellaneous inscriptions in the Yale Babylonian Collection.* New Haven, CT: Yale University Press.

Cohen, M.E. 2017. *New treasures of Sumerian literature: "When the Moon Fell from the Sky" and other works.* Bethesda, MD: CDL Press.

Crawford, V.E. 1954. *Sumerian economic texts from the First Dynasty of Isin.* New Haven, CT: Yale University Press.

de Boer, R. 2013a. An early Old Babylonian archive from the kingdom of Malgium? *JA* 301: 19–25.

de Boer, R. 2013b. Early Old Babylonian Amorite tribes and gatherings and the role of Sumu-abum. *Aram* 26: 269–284.

de Boer, R. 2014. Notes on an early OB treaty between Larsa, Uruk, and Ešnunna. *NABU* 2014: 124–127 (no. 76).

de Genouillac, H. 1936. *Époques d'Ur IIIe dynastie et de Larsa.* Paris: Geuthner.

De Graef, K. 2007. Another brick in the wall: *Dūrum* in the Old-Elamite Susa texts. *Akkadica* 128: 85–98.

De Graef, K. 2008. Samium. *RlA* 11: 625.

De Graef, K. 2011a. Sîn-erībam von Larsa. *RlA* 12: 515–516.

De Graef, K. 2011b. Ṣillī-Adad. *RlA* 12: 497.

De Graef, K. 2016. Warad-Sîn. *RlA* 14: 643–644.

Delnero, P. 2012. *The textual criticism of Sumerian literature*. Boston: American Schools of Oriental Research.

Dombradi, E. 1996. *Die Darstellung des Rechtsaustrags in den altbabylonischen Prozessurkunden*. Stuttgart: Steiner.

Dossin, G. 1938. Les archives épistolaires du palais de Mari. *Syria* 19: 105–126.

Dyckhoff, C. 1999. *Das Haushaltsbuch des Balamunamḫe*. PhD dissertation, Ludwig-Maximilians-Universität Munich.

Edzard, D.O. 1957. *Die "Zweite Zwischenzeit" Babyloniens*. Wiesbaden: Harrassowitz.

Edzard, D.O. 2001. Nablānum. *RlA* 9: 5.

Fales, F.M. 1989. *Prima dell'alfabeto: la storia della scrittura attraverso testi cuneiformi inediti*. Venice: Erizzo.

Falkenstein, A. 1963. Zu den Inschriftenfunden der Grabung in Uruk-Warka 1960–1961. *BaM* 2: 1–82.

Fiette, B. 2014. "Retour au sein maternel": une expression nouvelle pour les édits de restauration des rois amorrites. *NABU* 2013: 127–128 (no. 77).

Figulla, H.H. 1953. Accounts concerning allocation of provisions for offerings in the Ningal temple at Ur. *Iraq* 15: 88–122.

Figulla, H.H., and Martin, W.J. 1953. *Ur excavations texts, V: letters and documents of the Old Babylonian period*. London: British Museum Publications.

Fitzgerald, M.A. 2002. *The rulers of Larsa*. PhD dissertation, Yale University.

Földi, Z. 2013. Gleanings from the antiquities market: a contribution to the Electronic Text Corpus of Sumerian Royal Inscriptions. *Cuneiform Digital Library Bulletin* 2013/3. Retrieved from https://cdli.ucla.edu/pubs/cdlb/2013/cdlb2013_003.html (last accessed August 25, 2020).

Földi, Z. 2016. On the seal of Ayalatum and the dynasty of Larsa. *NABU* 2016: 65–66 (no. 37).

Földi, Z., and Zólyomi, G. 2020. A praise poem of Warad-Sîn, king of Larsa, to Nippur. *AoF* 47: 57–66.

Frahm, E. 2010. The latest Sumerian proverbs. In Melville, S.C., and Slotsky, A.L. (eds.), *Opening the tablet box: Near Eastern studies in honor of Benjamin R. Foster*. Leiden: Brill, 155–184.

Frankena, R. 1974. *Briefe aus dem Berliner Museum* (Altbabylonische Briefe 6). Leiden: Brill.

Frayne, D.R. 1989. A struggle for water: a case study from the historical records of the cities Isin and Larsa (1900–1800 BC). *Bulletin of the Canadian Society for Mesopotamian Studies* 17: 17–28.

Frayne, D.R. 1990. *The royal inscriptions of Mesopotamia: early periods, vol. 4: Old Babylonian period (2003–1595 BC)*. Toronto: University of Toronto Press.

Frayne, D.R. 1993. *The royal inscriptions of Mesopotamia: early periods, vol. 2: Sargonic and Gutian Periods (2334–2113 BC)*. Toronto: University of Toronto Press.

Frayne, D.R. 1998. New light on the reign of Išme-Dagān. *ZA* 88: 6–44.

Friberg, J. 2007. *A remarkable collection of Babylonian mathematical texts: manuscripts in the Schøyen Collection: cuneiform texts 1*. Berlin: Springer.

Gadd, C.J. 1951. En-an-e-du. *Iraq* 13: 27–39.

George, A.R. 1993. *House most high: the temples of ancient Mesopotamia*. Winona Lake, IN: Eisenbrauns.

George, A.R. 2009. *Babylonian literary texts in the Schøyen Collection*. Bethesda, MD: CDL Press.

George, A.R. (ed.) 2011. *Cuneiform royal inscriptions and related texts in the Schøyen Collection*. Bethesda, MD: CDL Press.

George, A.R. 2018. *Old Babylonian texts in the Schøyen Collection, part 1: selected letters*. Bethesda, MD: CDL Press.

George, A.R., and Spada, G. 2019. *Old Babylonian texts in the Schøyen Collection, part 2: school letters, model contracts, and related texts*. University Park, PA: Eisenbrauns.

Glassner, J.-J. 2004. *Mesopotamian chronicles*. Atlanta, GA: Society of Biblical Literature.

Goddeeris, A. 2007a. The Old Babylonian economy. In Leick, G. (ed.), *The Babylonian world*. London and New York: Routledge, 198–209.

Goddeeris, A. 2007b. The economic basis of the local palace of Kisurra. *ZA* 97: 47–85.

Goddeeris, A. 2009. *Tablets from Kisurra in the collections of the British Museum*. Wiesbaden: Harrassowitz.

Goddeeris, A. 2016a. Ur-Ninurta. *RlA* 14: 435–436.

Goddeeris, A. 2016b. Ur-dukuga. *RlA* 14: 411.

Goddeeris, A. 2016c. *The Old Babylonian legal and administrative texts in the Hilprecht Collection Jena*. Wiesbaden: Harrassowitz.

Goetze, A. 1947a. *Old Babylonian omen texts.* New Haven, CT: Yale University Press.

Goetze, A. 1947b. Historical allusions in Old Babylonian omen texts. *JCS* 1: 253–265.

Goetze, A. 1950. Sin-iddinam of Larsa: new tablets from his reign. *JCS* 4: 83–118.

Golinets, V. 2020. Amorite. In Hasselbach-Andee, R. (ed.), *A companion to ancient Near Eastern Languages.* Hoboken, NJ: Wiley Blackwell, 185–201.

Goodnick Westenholz, J. 1997. *Legends of the kings of Akkade.* Winona Lake, IN: Eisenbrauns.

Goodnick Westenholz, J., and Westenholz, A. 2006. *Cuneiform inscriptions in the collection of the Bible Lands Museum Jerusalem: the Old Babylonian inscriptions.* Leiden: Brill.

Grayson, A.K. 1983. Königslisten und Chroniken. B. Akkadisch. *RlA* 6: 86–135.

Grayson, A.K. 1987. *The royal inscriptions of Mesopotamia: Assyrian periods, vol. 1: Assyrian rulers of the third and second millennia BC (to 1115 BC).* Toronto: University of Toronto Press.

Grice, E.M. 1919. *Records from Ur and Larsa dated in the Larsa dynasty.* New Haven, CT: Yale University Press.

Guichard, M. 2014. Un traité d'alliance entre Larsa, Uruk et Ešnunna contre Sabium de Babylone. *Semitica* 56: 9–34.

Gurney, O.R. 1989. *Literary and miscellaneous texts in the Ashmolean Museum.* Oxford: Oxford University Press.

Hallo, W.W. 1991. The royal correspondence of Larsa, III: the princess and the plea. In Charpin, D., and Joannès, F. (eds.), *Marchands, diplomates et empereurs: études sur la civilisation mésopotamienne offertes à Paul Garelli.* Paris: Éditions Recherche sur les Civilisations, 377–388.

Heimpel, W. 2003. *Letters to the king of Mari: a new translation, with historical introduction, notes, and commentary.* Winona Lake, IN: Eisenbrauns.

Horsnell, M.J.A. 1999. *The year-names of the First Dynasty of Babylon.* Hamilton, ON: McMaster University Press.

Huber Vulliet, F. 2011. Letters as correspondence, letters as literature. In Radner, K., and Robson, E. (eds.), *The Oxford handbook of cuneiform culture.* Oxford: Oxford University Press, 486–507.

Hunger, H., and Pingree, D. 1999. *Astral sciences in Mesopotamia.* Leiden: Brill.

Huot, J.-L. 1983. *Larsa et 'Oueili. Travaux de 1978–1981.* Paris: Éditions Recherche sur les Civilisations.

Jacobsen, T. 1939. *The Sumerian King List.* Chicago: The Oriental Institute of the University of Chicago.

Jean, C.-F. 1929. Nouveaux contrats de Larsa. *RA* 26: 101–114.

Jones, P. 2003. Embracing Inana: legitimation and mediation in the ancient Mesopotamian sacred marriage hymn Iddin-Dagan A. *JAOS* 123: 291–302.

Keiser, C.E. 1971. *Neo-Sumerian account texts from Drehem.* New Haven, CT: Yale University Press.

Kienast, B. 1978. *Die altbabylonischen Briefe und Urkunden aus Kisurra.* Stuttgart: Steiner.

Klein, J. 1985. Šulgi and Išmedagan: runners in the service of the gods. *Beer-Sheva* 2: 7*–38*.

Klein, J. 1990. Šulgi and Išmedagan: originality and dependence in Sumerian royal hymnology. In Klein, J., and Skaist, A. (eds.), *Bar-Ilan studies in Assyriology dedicated to Pinḥas Artzi.* Ramat-Gan: Bar-Ilan University Press, 65–136.

Kleinerman, A. 2011. *Education in early 2nd millennium BC Babylonia: the Sumerian epistolary miscellany.* Leiden: Brill.

Kraus, F.R. 1959. Ungewöhnliche Datierungen aus der Zeit des Königs Rīm-Sin von Larsa. *ZA* 53: 138–167.

Kraus, F.R. 1984. *Königliche Verfügungen in altbabylonischer Zeit.* Leiden: Brill.

Kupper, J.-R. 1959. Lettres de Kiš. *RA* 53: 19–38.

Lafont, B. 1995. La chute des rois d'Ur et la fin des archives dans les grands centres administratifs de leur empire. *RA* 89: 3–13.

Lafont, B. 2001. Relations internationales, alliances et diplomatie au temps des royaumes amorrites: essai de synthèse. In Durand, J.-M. and Charpin, D. (eds.), *Mari, Ébla et les Hourrites, vol. 2.* Paris: Éditions Recherche sur les Civilisations, 213–326.

Lambert, W.G., and Weeden, M. 2020. A statue inscription of Samsuiluna from the papers of W.G. Lambert. *RA* 114: 15–62.

Lassen, A., and Wagensonner, K. 2020. *Women at the dawn of history.* New Haven, CT: Yale Babylonian Collection.

Legrain, L. 1926. *Royal inscriptions and fragments from Nippur and Babylon.* Philadelphia: University of Pennsylvania Museum of Archaeology and Anthropology.

Legrain, L. 1937. *Ur excavations texts, III: business documents of the Third Dynasty of Ur.* London: British Museum Publications.

Lenzi, A. 2008. The Uruk list of kings and sages and late Mesopotamian scholarship. *Journal of Ancient Near Eastern Religions* 8: 137–169.

Lieberman, S.J. 1982. The years of Damiqilishu, king of Isin. *RA* 76: 97–117.

Lion, B. 2011. Literacy and gender. In Radner, K., and Robson, E. (eds.), *The Oxford handbook of cuneiform culture*. Oxford: Oxford University Press: 90–112.

Loding, D. 1973. A new chronological source for the Isin-Larsa period. *AfO* 24: 47–50.

Loftus, W.K. 1857. *Travels and researches in Chaldaea and Susiana with an account of excavations at Warka, the "Erech" of Nimrod, and Shush, "Shushan the Palace" of Esther, in 1849–52*. New York: Robert Carter & Brothers.

Ludwig, M.-C. 1990. *Untersuchungen zu den Hymnen des Išme-Dagan von Isin*. Wiesbaden: Harrassowitz.

Ludwig, M.-C., and Metcalf, C. 2017. The song of Inanna and Išme-Dagan: an edition of BM 23820+23831. *ZA* 107: 1–21.

Margueron, J. 1983. Larsa. B. Archäologisch. *RlA* 6: 500–503.

Metcalf, C. 2019. *Sumerian literary texts in the Schøyen Collection, vol. I: literary sources on Old Babylonian religion*. University Park, PA: Eisenbrauns.

Michalowski, P. 1977. Dūrum and Uruk during the Ur III period. *Mesopotamia* 12: 83–96.

Michalowski, P. 1989. *The lamentation over the destruction of Sumer and Ur*. Winona Lake, IN: Eisenbrauns.

Michalowski, P. 1995. The men from Mari. In Van Lerberghe, K., and Schoors, A. (eds.), *Immigration and emigration within the ancient Near East: Festschrift E. Lipiński*. Leuven: Peeters, 181–188.

Michalowski, P. 2005. Literary works from the court of king Ishbi-Erra of Isin. In Sefati, Y., Artzi, P., Cohen, C., Eichler, B.L., and Hurowitz, V.A. (eds.), *"An experienced scribe who neglects nothing": ancient Near Eastern studies in honor of Jacob Klein*. Bethesda, MD: CDL Press, 199–212.

Michalowski, P. 2011. *The correspondence of the kings of Ur: an epistolary history of an ancient Mesopotamian kingdom*. Winona Lake, IN: Eisenbrauns.

Michalowski, P. 2019. Memories of Rim-Sin II. In Chambon, G., Guichard, M., and Langlois, A.-I. (eds.), *De l'argile au numérique: mélanges Assyriologiques en l'honneur de Dominique Charpin*. Leuven: Peeters, 669–692.

Michel, C. 2008. Rabbû. *RlA* 11: 209–210.

Middeke-Conlin, R. 2020. *The making of a scribe: errors, mistakes and rounding numbers in the Old Babylonian kingdom of Larsa*. Berlin: Springer.

Moore, S.A. 2018. An edict of Rīm-Sîn I of Larsa. *NABU* 2018: 112 (no. 67).

Morello, N. 2016. Warassa. *RlA* 14: 644–645.

Peterson, J. 2016. The literary corpus of the Old Babylonian Larsa dynasties: new texts, new readings, and commentary. *Studia Mesopotamica: Jahrbuch für altorientalische Geschichte und Kultur* 3: 125–213.

Pientka-Hinz, R. 2008. Rīm-Sîn I. und II. *RlA* 11: 367–371.

Reculeau, H. 2008. Roi temporaire de Sumer et d'Akkad: Sumu-El de Larsa à Nippur. *NABU* 2008: 29–30 (no. 22).

Reisman, D. 1973. Iddin-Dagan's sacred marriage hymn. *JCS* 25: 185–202.

Richter, T. 2004. *Untersuchungen zu den lokalen Panthea Süd- und Mittelbabyloniens in altbabylonischer Zeit.* Münster: Ugarit-Verlag. 2nd rev. ed.

Richter, T. 2011. Sîn-māgir. *RlA* 12: 521.

Robertson, J.F. 1983. An unusual dating system from Isin-Larsa period Nippur: new evidence. *Acta Sumerica Japonica* 5: 147–161.

Römer, W.H.P. 1984. Historische Texte in sumerischer Sprache. In Kaiser, O. (ed.), *Historisch-chronologische Texte, I* (Texte aus der Umwelt des Alten Testaments I/4). Gütersloh: Gütersloher Verlagshaus: 289–353.

Römer, W.H.P. 2001. *Hymnen und Klagelieder in sumerischer Sprache.* Münster: Ugarit-Verlag.

Roth, M.T. 1997. *Law collections from Mesopotamia and Asia Minor.* Atlanta, GA: Scholars Press.

Rowton, M.B. 1967. Watercourses and water rights in the official correspondence from Larsa and Isin. *JCS* 21: 267–274.

Rutten, M. 1938. Trente-deux modèles de foies en argile inscrits provenant de Tell-Hariri (Mari). *RA* 35: 36–52.

Sallaberger, W. 1996. Zu einigen Jahresdaten Enlil-bānis von Isin. *ZA* 86: 177–191.

Samet, N. 2014. *The lamentation over the destruction of Ur.* Winona Lake, IN: Eisenbrauns.

Sanati-Müller, S. 1990. Texte aus dem Sîn-kāšid-Palast, dritter Teil: Metalltexte. *BaM* 21: 133–213.

Sanati-Müller, S. 1993. Texte aus dem Sîn-kāšid-Palast, sechster Teil: Texte verschiedenen Inhalts, III. *BaM* 24: 137–184.

Sanati-Müller, S. 2011. Zwei altbabylonische Tonkegelfragmente aus der Heidelberger Uruk-Warka-Tontafelsammlung. *Zeitschrift für Orient-Archäologie* 4: 82–91.

Schaudig, H. 2003. Nabonid, der "Archäologe auf dem Königsthron": zum Geschichtsbild des ausgehenden neubabylonischen Reiches. In Selz, G.J.

(ed.), *Festschrift für Burkhart Kienast zu seinem 70. Geburtstage dargebracht von Freunden, Schülern und Kollegen*. Münster: Ugarit-Verlag, 447–497.

Schaudig, H. 2019. *Explaining disaster: tradition and transformation of the "Catastrophe of Ibbi-Sîn" in Babylonian literature*. Münster: Zaphon.

Selz, G.J. 2016. Vergöttlichung. A. In Mesopotamien. *RlA* 14: 545–548.

Seri, A. 2013. *The house of prisoners: slavery and state in Uruk during the revolt against Samsu-iluna*. Berlin: De Gruyter.

Sharlach, T. 2001. Beyond chronology: the Šakkanakkus of Mari and the kings of Ur. In Hallo, W.W., and Winter, I.J. (eds.), *Seals and seal impressions*. Bethesda, MD: CDL Press, 59–70.

Sigrist, M. 1984. *Les* sattukku *dans l'Ešumeša durant la période d'Isin et Larsa*. Malibu, CA: Undena.

Sigrist, M. 1988. *Isin year names*. Berrien Springs, MI: Andrews University Press.

Sigrist, M. 1990. *Larsa year names*. Berrien Springs, MI: Andrews University Press.

Sigrist, M., and Goodnick Westenholz, J. 2008. The love poem of Rīm-Sîn and Nanaya. In Cohen, C., et al. (eds.), *Birkat Shalom: studies in the Bible, ancient Near Eastern literature, and postbiblical Judaism presented to Shalom M. Paul*. Winona Lake, IN: Eisenbrauns, 667–704.

Simmons, S.D. 1978. *Early Old Babylonian documents*. New Haven, CT: Yale University Press.

Sjöberg, Å.W. 1973. Miscellaneous Sumerian hymns. *ZA* 63: 1–55.

Sjöberg, Å. W. 1993. The ape from the mountain who became the king of Isin. In Cohen, M.E., Snell, D.C., and Weisberg, D.B. (eds.), *The tablet and the scroll: Near Eastern studies in honor of William W. Hallo*. Bethesda, MD: CDL Press, 211–220.

Sommerfeld, W. 1983. Untersuchungen zur Geschichte von Kisurra. *ZA* 73: 204–231.

Steinkeller, P. 2001. New light on the hydrology and topography of southern Babylonia in the third millennium. *ZA* 91: 22–84.

Steinkeller, P. 2003. An Ur III manuscript of the Sumerian King List. In Sallaberger, W., Volk, K., and Zgoll, A. (eds.), *Literatur, Politik und Recht in Mesopotamien: Festschrift für Claus Wilcke*. Wiesbaden: Harrassowitz, 267–292.

Steinkeller, P. 2004. A history of Mashkan-shapir and its role in the kingdom of Larsa. In Stone, E.C., and Zimansky, P. (eds.), *The anatomy of a*

Mesopotamian city: survey and soundings at Mashkan-shapir. Winona Lake, IN: Eisenbrauns, 26–42.

Steinkeller, P. 2008. On Birbirrum, the alleged earliest-documented *rabiānum* official, and on the end of Ibbi-Suen's Reign. *NABU* 2008: 3–5 (no. 3).

Stol, M. 1971. Review of Walters, S.D. 1970. *BiOr* 28: 365–369.

Stol, M. 1976. *Studies in Old Babylonian history.* Leiden: NINO.

Stol, M. 1981. *Letters from Yale, transliterated and translated* (Altbabylonische Briefe 9). Leiden: Brill.

Stol, M. 2004. Wirtschaft und Gesellschaft in altbabylonischer Zeit. In Charpin, D., Edzard, D.O., and Stol, M., *Mesopotamien: die altbabylonische Zeit.* Fribourg: Academic Press; Göttingen: Vandenhoeck & Ruprecht, 643–975.

Stol, M. 2008. Rababu. *RlA* 11: 209.

Stol, M. 2011. Sîn-iddinam. *RlA* 12: 517–518.

Stol, M. 2016. *Women in the ancient Near East.* Berlin: De Gruyter.

Stone, E.C., and Zimansky, P. 2004. *The anatomy of a Mesopotamian city: survey and soundings at Mashkan-shapir.* Winona Lake, IN: Eisenbrauns.

Streck, M.P. 2000. *Das amurritische Onomastikon der altbabylonischen Zeit, Band 1: die Amurriter, die onomastische Forschung, Orthographie und Phonologie, Nominalmorphologie.* Münster: Ugarit-Verlag.

Streck, M.P. 2005. Pī-nārātim. *RlA* 10: 566–567.

Thureau-Dangin, F. 1918. La chronologie de la dynastie de Larsa. *RA* 15: 1–57.

Tinney, S. 1996. *The Nippur lament: royal rhetoric and divine legitimation in the reign of Išme-Dagan of Isin (1953–1935 BC).* Philadelphia: University of Pennsylvania Museum of Archaeology and Anthropology.

Tinney, S. 1999. On the curricular setting of Sumerian literature. *Iraq* 61: 159–172.

Vallat, F. 1996. L'Élam à l'époque paléo-babylonienne et ses relations avec la Mésopotamie. In Durand, J.-M. (ed.), *Mari, Ébla et les Hourrites: dix ans de travaux, vol. 1.* Paris: Éditions Recherche sur les Civilisations: 297–319.

Van de Mieroop, M. 1987a. *Crafts in the early Isin period: a study of the Isin craft archive from the reigns of Išbi-Erra and Šu-ilišu.* Leuven: Peeters.

Van de Mieroop, M. 1987b. *Sumerian administrative documents from the reigns of Išbi-Erra and Šu-ilišu.* New Haven, CT: Yale University Press.

Van de Mieroop, M. 1987c. The archive of Balmunamḫe. *AfO* 34: 1–29.

Van de Mieroop, M. 1992. *Society and enterprise in Old Babylonian Ur.* Berlin: Reimer.

Van de Mieroop, M. 1993. The reign of Rim-Sin. *RA* 87: 47–69.

Van de Mieroop, M. 2007. *King Hammurabi of Babylon: a biography*. Malden, MA: Wiley-Blackwell.

van Dijk, J.J. 1965. Une insurrection générale au pays de Larša avant l'avénement de Nūradad. *JCS* 19: 1–25.

van Dijk, J.J. 1968. *Cuneiform texts: Old Babylonian contracts and related material* (Texts in the Iraq Museum 5). Wiesbaden: Harrassowitz.

van Dijk, J.J. 1971. *Nicht-kanonische Beschwörungen und sonstige literarische Texte*. Berlin: Akademie-Verlag.

van Dijk, J.J. 1976. *Texts of varying content* (Texts in the Iraq Museum 9). Wiesbaden: Harrassowitz.

van Dijk, J.J. 1978. Išbi'erra, Kindattu, l'homme d'Elam, et la chute de la ville d'Ur. *JCS* 4: 189–208.

van Dijk, J.J., Goetze, A., and Hussey, M.I. 1985. *Early Mesopotamian incantations and rituals*. New Haven, CT: Yale University Press.

van Koppen, F. 2006. Miscellaneous Old Babylonian period documents. In Chavalas, M.W. (ed.), *The ancient Near East: historical sources in translation*. Malden, MA: Wiley-Blackwell, 107–133.

van Koppen, F. 2007. Aspects of society and economy in the later Old Babylonian period. In Leick, G. (ed.), *The Babylonian world*. London and New York: Routledge, 210–223.

van Koppen, F. 2018. Zambīja. *RlA* 15: 202.

Vanstiphout, H.L.J. 1978. Lipit-Eštar's praise in the Edubba. *JCS* 30: 33–61.

Vanstiphout, H.L.J. 1989–1990. The man from Elam: a reconsideration of Išbi-Erra "Hymn B." *JEOL* 31: 53–62.

Vedeler, H.T. 2015. The ideology of Rim-Sin II of Larsa. *JANEH* 2: 1–17.

Veenhof, K.R. 2005. *Letters in the Louvre* (Altbabylonische Briefe 14). Leiden: Brill.

Vincente, C.-A. 1995. The Tall Leilān recension of the Sumerian King List. *ZA* 85: 234–270.

Volk, K. 2011. Eine neue Inschrift des Königs Sîn-iddinam von Larsa. In George, A.R. (ed.), *Cuneiform royal inscriptions and related texts in the Schøyen Collection*. Bethesda, MD: CDL Press, 59–88.

Volk, K. 2012. Ein zweisprachiger Übungstext zu Lipit-Eštar B. In Mittermayer, C., and Ecklin, S. (eds.), *Altorientalische Studien zu Ehren von Pascal Attinger: mu-ni u₄ ul-li₂-a-aš ĝa₂-ĝa₂-de₃*. Fribourg: Academic Press; Göttingen: Vandenhoeck & Ruprecht, 359–368.

von Dassow, E. 2009. Narām-Sîn of Uruk: a new king in an old shoebox. *JCS* 61: 63–91.

Wagensonner, K. 2007. Götterreise oder Herrscherreise oder vielleicht beides? *Wiener Zeitschrift für die Kunde des Morgenlandes* 97: 541–559.

Wagensonner, K. 2011. New light on "Sîn-iddinam and Iškur." *KASKAL: Rivista di storia, ambiente e culture del Vicino Antico* 8: 11–41.

Wagensonner, K. 2019. Larsa schools: a palaeographic journey. In Devecchi, E., Mynářová, J., and Müller, G.G.W. (eds.), *Current research in cuneiform palaeography, vol. 2*. Gladbeck: PeWe-Verlag, 41–86.

Walters, S.D. 1970. *Water for Larsa: an Old Babylonian archive dealing with irrigation*. New Haven, CT: Yale University Press.

Wasserman, N. 2016. *Akkadian love literature of the third and second millennium BCE*. Wiesbaden: Harrassowitz.

Wasserman, N. 2018. A forgotten hymn in praise of Gungunum, king of Larsa: TIM 9, 41 and its historical context. In Cogan, M. (ed.), *In the Lands of Sumer and Akkad*. Jerusalem: The Israel Academy of Sciences and Humanities, xix–xliv.

Weidner, E.F. 1927. Eine Statuette des Königs Pûr-Sin von Isin. *AfO* 4: 133–134.

Weiershäuser, F., and Novotny, J. 2020. *The royal inscriptions of Amēl-Marduk (561–560 BC), Neriglissar (559–556 BC), and Nabonidus (555–539 BC), kings of Babylon*. University Park, PA: Eisenbrauns.

Whiting, R.M. 1987. *Old Babylonian letters from Tell Asmar*. Chicago: The Oriental Institute of the University of Chicago.

Wilcke, C. 1985. Neue Quellen aus Isin zur Geschichte der Ur-III-Zeit und der I. Dynastie von Isin. *Orientalia* 54: 299–318.

Wilcke, C. (ed.) 2018. *Keilschrifttexte aus Isin – Išān Baḥrīyāt: Ergebnisse der Ausgrabungen der Deutschen Forschungsgemeinschaft unter der Schirmherrschaft der Bayerischen Akademie der Wissenschaften*. Munich: Verlag der Bayerischen Akademie der Wissenschaften.

Winitzer, A. 2017. *Early Mesopotamian divination literature: its organizational framework and generative and paradigmatic characteristics*. Leiden: Brill.

15

The Middle East after the Fall of Ur

FROM ASSUR TO THE LEVANT

Ilya Arkhipov

THIS CHAPTER DEALS with the history of the territory extending from the Zagros foothills through Upper Mesopotamia to the Levant (figure 15.1), in the period beginning in the late twenty-first century BC, when the kingdom of Ur (see chapter 13 in this volume) lost its connections with Upper Mesopotamia, and ending at the turn of the sixteenth century BC, when Hittite troops seized Aleppo (see chapter 30 in volume 3).[1] The majority of the written records for this period come from the

---

1. My work has been greatly facilitated by the Archibab database project ("Archives babyloniennes: XXe–XVIIe siècles av. J.-C.": www.archibab.fr; last accessed August 15, 2020) directed by Dominique Charpin. Jack Sasson and Nele Ziegler read drafts of this chapter and offered me valuable comments, while Denis Lacambre advised me on the eponym chronology and Elisa Roßberger provided helpful suggestions for archaeological literature. The English style of my translations of Mari letters owes much to that of Jack Sasson. Sergey Loesov helped me improve the English of this chapter, which was then language-edited by Denise Bolton. The chapter systematically covers the literature up to 2018, with selected later references. The following abbreviations are used for text editions: AbB 7 = Kraus 1977; AbB 8 = Cagni 1980; AbB 12 = van Soldt 1990; AbB 13 = van Soldt 1994; ARM

Ilya Arkhipov, *The Middle East after the Fall of Ur* In: *The Oxford History of the Ancient Near East*. Edited by: Karen Radner, Nadine Moeller, and D. T. Potts, Oxford University Press. © Oxford University Press 2022.
DOI: 10.1093/oso/9780190687571.003.0015

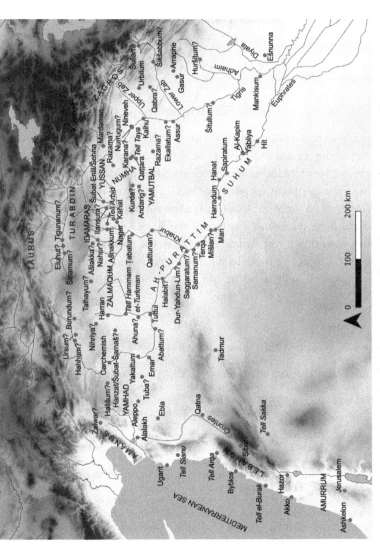

FIGURE 15.1. Sites mentioned in this chapter. Prepared by Andrea Squitieri (LMU Munich).

archives from the city of Mari, which cover a period dating to ca. 1805–1761 BC,[2] and therefore these four decades are treated in far more detail than the preceding two centuries and the following 160 years. Moreover, the Mari sources also set the agenda for the subjects favored in our narrative.

15.1. Thriving cities with an unrecorded history, ca. 2000 to ca. 1805 BC

15.1.1. The written sources

For a historian working mainly with written records, the first two centuries of the second millennium BC are a dark age for the region, since there are very few indigenous texts from this period. The most important of the pertinent corpora are the Old Assyrian texts. In the city of Assur itself (see section 15.1.4), only a few royal inscriptions were found, but the huge Anatolian archives of the Assyrian trade colonies of the nineteenth century BC tell us about both the metropolis and the caravan stations on the route to Anatolia. Other synchronic local sources are limited to a handful of concise and controversially dated royal

---

1 = Dossin 1950; ARM 2 = Jean 1950; ARM 4 = Dossin 1951; ARM 5 = Dossin 1952; ARM 6 = Kupper 1954; ARM 13 = Dossin et al. 1964; ARM 14 = Birot 1974; ARM 22 = Kupper 1983; ARM 26/1 = Durand 1988; ARM 26/2 = Charpin et al. 1988; ARM 27 = Birot 1993; ARM 28 = Kupper 1998; FM 2 = Charpin and Durand (ed.) 1994; FM 3 = Charpin and Durand (ed.) 1997; FM 5 = Charpin and Ziegler 2003; FM 6 = Charpin and Durand (ed.) 2002.

2. For the dates based on Assyrian eponyms, I conventionally follow the Revised Eponym List (REL) of Barjamovic et al. 2012. However, two alternative reconstructions have been proposed for REL 193 (Charpin and Ziegler 2003: 164–165) and for REL 180 and 181 (Kryszat 2008: 214). Arguments in favor of both were recently provided by Charpin and Ziegler 2014 and Lacambre 2019, respectively. If these apply, all dates prior to 1779 BC need to be lowered by three years. For the dates based on the year names of Zimri-Lim, I follow Charpin and Ziegler 2003 unless noted otherwise. For the events that are datable within the accuracy of a lunar month, I have used a rough and conventional conversion based on the fact that the eponym years began in autumn and Zimri-Lim's years began in spring. For example, a date such as "the first month of the first year of Zimri-Lim's reign" has been converted to "the spring of 1774 BC," etc.

inscriptions and seal legends mentioning the rulers of Mari[3] and of Ebla.[4] Some references to this period are also found in later chronological and commemorative compositions: seven Kültepe lists of Assyrian year eponyms (*līmum*),[5] two Mari fragments containing lists of early rulers,[6] the Mari Eponym Chronicle (a very fragmentary composition that contains accounts of historic events for each year),[7] and the Assyrian King List.[8] Lower Mesopotamian texts of this period pay virtually no attention to the north. A Sippar letter datable to the early nineteenth century bc mentions the trade factories of Sippar merchants in Mari and Mišlan.[9] A number of Levantine cities, from Jerusalem to Byblos, are mentioned, with their rulers, in Egyptian texts of the Twelfth Dynasty.[10]

Yet the paucity of textual data does not mean that the region was deserted or transformed into pasture lands. The archaeological record provides a glimpse into its urban life in the early second millennium, giving us a taste of the world that would be revealed by the Mari archives.

---

3. The rulers bearing the title *šakkanakku* ("governor") reigned in Mari in the late third and the early second millennium. The inscriptions and seal legends referring to the "*Šakkanakku* dynasty" are collected in Gelb and Kienast 1990: 355–367, but they contain little more than the names of the rulers.

4. For the one royal inscription of this period found in Ebla, see Gelb and Kienast 1990: 370. Two unpublished cuneiform tablets from Ebla may date to the same period: Durand 2018: 360.

5. See most recently Barjamovic et al. 2012 (with references to the text editions).

6. Durand 1985: 152–159. The two fragments contain only the names of rulers, their affiliations and their reign lengths. For the date of the last *Šakkanakku*, see the discussion in Durand 2008a, Otto 2008, and Marchetti 2008. For a previously unknown *Šakkanakku* ruler who may date to the early second millennium BC, see Mayr 2015. The so-called *Šakkanakku* documents from Mari, Terqa, and Tuttul belong to the late nineteenth century BC. Though some of them are earlier than 1805, all these documents, for the sake of convenience, are described in section 15.2.1.

7. Birot 1985; for a review of the literature, see Koliński 2015: 61–62.

8. Grayson 1983: 101–116. The list of the kings prior to 1808 contains only their names, affiliations, and reign lengths.

9. Charpin 1989b.

10. Helck 1971: 38–67; Hikade 2012: 837–839.

15.1.2. The archaeological evidence

The late third millennium crisis did not uniformly affect the entire territory from Assur on the Tigris to the coastal areas of the Levant; while many cities were abandoned or shrank in size, other centers prospered as before, or even boomed. The transition from the Early Bronze Age to the Middle Bronze Age, at the turn of the second millennium BC, was marked by an impressive re-urbanization, or by continuing urban development, in various parts of the region: cities were increasing in number and size, new palaces and temples were built, burials were rich, and long-distance trade was thriving.

Surveys undertaken in the areas east of the Tigris and in the Middle Tigris region show that settlements became more numerous.[11] Excavations in Assur revealed an uninterrupted occupation of the site.[12] The northern Jezirah never returned to the prosperity it enjoyed in the third millennium BC, yet continuous or renewed settlement is attested on many sites.[13] Old Assyrian itineraries of the nineteenth century BC mention several Jezirah localities which appear as important cities in the later sources.[14] On the Middle Euphrates, major construction works took place at the turn of the millennia in the old cities of Tuttul and Mari; in particular, it is then that the Great Palace of Mari was built.[15] Inland in western Syria, the beginning of the Middle Bronze Age saw a quick recovery and a new expansion of its urban centers.[16] Impressive new fortifications and palaces were built in Ebla around 2000 BC, following the city's destruction in the twenty-first century BC. Alalakh

---

11. For now, see Battini 2011 and Mühl 2013: 152–171; relevant work is currently conducted by the "Land of Nineveh Archaeological Project," the "Erbil Plain Archaeological Survey" project, the "Upper Greater Zab Archaeological Reconnaissance" project, and the University of Tübingen's archaeological mission at Bassetki (ancient Mardaman).

12. Veenhof 2008a: 38–41.

13. Matney 2012: 565–567; Laneri et al. (ed.) 2012.

14. Most recently, see Koliński 2014: 14–17.

15. Akkermans and Schwartz 2003: 286–287; Butterlin 2007.

16. Akkermans and Schwartz 2003: 291–296; Genz 2012: 621–626; Morandi Bonacossi 2014: 414–420.

FIGURE 15.2. Pendant with the inscription "Yapa-šemu-abi, prince of Byblos" in Egyptian hieroglyphs, from Tomb 2 of the Royal Necropolis of Byblos. Early second millennium BC. National Museum Beirut (Lebanon). Photo by Jona Lendering (www.livius.org), Creative Commons Attribution-Share Alike 4.0 International (CC BY-NC 4.0) license.

was founded at the same time, while Qatna experienced unprecedented growth. On the Mediterranean coast of Syria and Lebanon, significant remains dating to the early second millennium were found in Ugarit, Tell Arqa (ancient Irqata), and Byblos. The earliest royal tombs and the famous Temple of Obelisks in Byblos may date to the nineteenth century BC (figure 15.2). In the southern Levant, the Middle Bronze Age re-urbanization was marked by the construction of massive fortifications, in particular in Ashkelon and Akko.[17]

17. Burke 2008: 80–81; Harrison 2012: 641–644.

Egyptian imports were found both at the coastal sites of Ugarit and Byblos and in inland Syria as far as Qatna and Aleppo. These imports include jewelry, scarabs, and statues dating to the Twelfth Dynasty.[18] North Syrian cities were involved in the Old Assyrian commerce connecting Anatolia and Iran (see section 15.1.4).

In the virtual absence of written sources, little can be said about the political organization of the region, but the most natural assumption is that there existed the same patchwork of city-states as in the later period, and this is indirectly confirmed by Old Assyrian and Egyptian sources. We can only speculate why no archives of this period have been discovered as yet in the region. Perhaps the blame lies, paradoxically, with its peaceful development; there were no catastrophic events to bury intact archives under the ruins of buildings, as happened in other periods in Ebla, Kaneš, Mari, or Nineveh.

15.1.3. A change in the population

Attested by texts found in Mari, Nabada, and Ebla, East Semitic language varieties similar to Akkadian were spoken on the Middle Euphrates, in Upper Mesopotamia, and in northwest Syria in the late third millennium BC (see chapter 8 in volume 1). In the course of the Amorite migrations, they may have been replaced by West Semitic by the turn of the millennium (cf. chapter 13 in this volume). However, the date and the circumstances of the population change remain murky. The last known survivor of the Syrian East Semitic language varieties, the so-called *Šakkanakku* dialect, was used in Mari, Tuttul, and Terqa as a written language until the end of the nineteenth century BC (see section 15.3.2). The extant royal names from Ebla of the early second millennium BC may still belong to

---

18. For references, see Genz 2012: 626; Hikade 2012: 839–840. See also chapter 21 in this volume.

the East Semitic onomasticon of the third millennium BC,[19] but part of the royal names of the *Šakkanakku* dynasty in Mari are West Semitic.[20] Old Assyrian texts found in Anatolia contain virtually no Amorite names,[21] but most people they mention were natives of either Assur or Anatolia, where there had never been an important West Semitic population. By contrast, these texts refer to some Upper Mesopotamian toponyms of West Semitic origin.[22]

In the southern Levant and on the Mediterranean coast of Syria and Lebanon, West Semitic was probably spoken as early as the third millennium and throughout the second millennium, as we can extrapolate forward from the Eblaite–West Semitic language contact, and backward from the situation in the late second millennium BC. We may even speculate that the language(s) spoken here in the early second millennium BC must have been the Northwest Semitic ancestor(s) of Ugaritic (on the Syrian coast), Aramaic (somewhere in the mainland Syria), and Canaanite (in the rest of the Levant).[23]

15.1.4. Assur in the twentieth and nineteenth centuries BC

Around 2025 BC, Assur gained independence from the rule of the Third Dynasty of Ur and became a city-state with a characteristic political structure. The city was ruled by an assembly that acted in concert with

19. Bonechi 1997. Note that the inscription of Ibbiṭ-Lim of Ebla, which is conventionally dated to ca. 1900, contains a blend of Old Assyrian and unidentified (possibly West Semitic) linguistic features.

20. Streck 2000: 39 n. 1.

21. Veenhof 2008a: 22–23.

22. Charpin 2003: 15–18 (part of the West Semitic toponyms discussed by Charpin appear in Old Assyrian texts).

23. The Egyptian sources of the early second millennium BC may contain specifically Northwest Semitic personal names (Leonid Kogan, personal communication; for the evidence, see Helck 1971: 44–67).

a hereditary prince who was the caretaker of the god Aššur; it was the god, and not the prince, who was considered the city's king. In addition, public finance and commerce were the responsibility of the "City Hall" (*bēt ālim*) which was presided over by a magistrate appointed for a year (*līmum*, often translated as "year eponym").[24]

Nothing is known about Assur's political relations with its neighboring cities. The inscriptions of the rulers of Assur mention only construction works and economic measures aimed at abolishing debts and fostering long-distance trade.[25] At least from the time of Irišum I (1972–1933 BC), Assur was the pivot in the long-distance trade connecting Elam and Babylonia with Anatolia and the Levant (see chapter 17 in this volume). Though texts mainly reveal the Anatolian part of the trade network, a few documents and archaeological finds illustrate interactions with Mari and Ebla.[26] No later than in the twentieth century BC, Assur developed its own cuneiform syllabary for the local kind of Akkadian that we call Old Assyrian, at the time when most of Lower Mesopotamia still wrote Sumerian. The conquests of Samsi-Addu brought an end to Assur's independence.

15.1.5. Key events of the mid- and late nineteenth century BC

In the mid-nineteenth century, a process of political consolidation began in the Diyala valley, on the Middle Tigris, and on the Middle Euphrates. A certain Ila-kabkabu (1846–1832 BC)[27] ruled somewhere either in the

---

24. For a summary of Assur's political organization, see Veenhof 2017: 70–73.

25. Grayson 1987: 11–46. All cuneiform tablets found at Assur date to later periods (see sections 15.2.2 and 15.5.6).

26. Bär 2005; Peyronel 2017; Durand 2018: 352.

27. These dates are based on the Mari Eponym Chronicle, with two assumptions: first, that Aminum, Ila-kabkabu, and Samsi-Addu ruled in sequence in the same city; and second, that the death of Aminum is mentioned in a fragmentary passage (manuscript A, line 26′); see the discussion in Janssen 2015.

Diyala valley or on the Middle Tigris, in a kingdom whose name and location is debated.[28] At about the same time (exact dates unknown), Yagid-Lim rose to power in Ṣuprum, a town in the vicinity of Mari.[29] Both Yagid-Lim and Ila-kabkabu successfully expanded their territories. A later text describes them as the lords of the banks of the Euphrates and the Tigris, respectively.[30] They waged war against each other in the Jezirah. What happened to Mari during this conflict is unknown. *Šakkanakku* texts mention both Yagid-Lim and Ila-kabkabu, but both of them appear to have been foreigners from the Mari point of view.[31] Yagid-Lim outlived Ila-kabkabu and was succeeded by his son Yahdun-Lim.

At the same time, a king of Ešnunna called Ipiq-Adad unified most of the Diyala valley under his authority.[32] In 1828–1827 BC, he also conquered Arraphe and Gasur in the Trans-Tigris region. Late in his reign, he seized the Middle Euphrates valley up to Yabliya.[33]

If we believe the Mari Eponym Chronicle, Samsi-Addu, son of Ila-kabkabu, was born in 1847 BC and inherited his father's throne in 1832 BC. The first twenty years of his reign are not documented. It was perhaps during this period that Samsi-Addu avowed himself a servant of the king of Ešnunna.[34] The later events are known only from the Assyrian

28. For a recent summary, see Ziegler 2014: 184–185.

29. For a summary of Yagid-Lim's rule, see Charpin and Ziegler 2003: 33–35.

30. Charpin and Ziegler 2003: 33 (M. 5037⁺: ll. 1′–5′).

31. Charpin and Ziegler 2003: 33; Cavigneaux and Colonna d'Istria 2009: 54, 62–64. The documents mention visits by envoys of Yagid-Lim and Ila-kabkabu. As for the ruler of Mari, the texts refer to him by his title *šakkanakku*, while his name is unknown.

32. Charpin 2004b: 129–131. For the identification of that ruler of Ešnunna as Ipiq-Adad III (rather than Ipiq-Adad II), see Guichard 2014c: 22–23; this is not universally accepted; see chapter 16 in this volume for an alternative view.

33. The reconstruction of the conquests of Ipiq-Adad (III?) is based on his year names. Note in particular an isolated contract from Al-Kapim dated by a year name of Ipiq-Adad (Mohammad 2002: no. 1; cf. van Koppen and Lacambre 2008–2009: 158–162).

34. According to the retrospective account in ARM 2: no. 49: ll. 8–13 (from Zimri-Lim's time).

King List, whose reliability in this respect is questionable.[35] Naram-Sin, the new king of Ešnunna (ca. 1810–1801 BC), ousted Samsi-Addu from his home city.[36] After a brief exile in Babylon, Samsi-Addu managed to seize Ekallatum.[37] Three years later, he conquered Assur (ca. 1808 BC). His home city must have remained under Ešnunna's control, while Ekallatum became the first capital of his growing realm.

15.2. The age of Mari, ca. 1805–1761 BC: the sources

15.2.1. The Mari archives

About 19,000 cuneiform tablets and fragments dating to the early second millennium have been unearthed in Mari (modern Tell Hariri).[38] Over 17,000 of them were discovered in the Great Palace.[39] Almost all of these texts come from the archives of the kings of Mari.[40] The palace

---

35. The respective part of the Assyrian King List does not square with the Assyrian Eponym Lists. For a recent attempt to overcome the contradiction, see Bloch 2014.

36. Naram-Sin also invaded the Khabur triangle all the way up to Ašnakkum (Charpin 2004b: 131), but this raid must have remained without consequences, as the following events show.

37. For a tentative reconstruction of this city's early history, see Ziegler 2002: 211–213.

38. For overviews of the Mari archives from different viewpoints, see Durand 1997–2000: I 25–40; Durand and Guichard 1997: 19–23 (for literary texts); Charpin and Ziegler 2003: 1–20; and Charpin 2014c: 39–46.

39. Outside the palace, some 1,500 school tablets and fragments were found in the so-called *Maison aux tablettes*, datable to Zimri-Lim's reign. In particular, they contain copies of Yahdun-Lim's royal inscriptions, Sumerian literary compositions, and model accounting documents; see Nicolet 2016 and the summary in Cavigneaux and Colonna d'Istria 2009: 52. Besides, over 300 accounting documents from the time of Yasmah-Addu and Zimri-Lim were discovered in the Small Eastern Palace (Charpin 1985a: 267–268; 1985b). Most of them remain unpublished.

40. For the archaeological context and archival attribution of the epigraphic finds from the palace, see Arkhipov 2019. A few hundred texts come from the archives of officials and queens rather than the kings themselves.

archives fall into two large groups depending on their date, language, and script.

The first group comprises about 1,500 accounting documents of the so-called *Šakkanakku* type, with only a few texts of other genres, including one contract and no letters.[41] Their script and language are close to those that had been used in Mari during the Ur III period. However, all *Šakkanakku* documents date to the late nineteenth century BC. These texts are not dated by year names or eponyms, but fortunately their contents provide several synchronisms. The earliest datable documents mention Ila-kabkabu, who died in 1832 BC, while the latest datable documents are of Yahdun-Lim's time.[42] While they remain an underexploited source of data for research into material culture and economic history,[43] with the exception of a few terse mentions of foreign rulers and messengers they contain no information about political history.

The rest of the palace archives, almost 16,000 tablets and fragments, constitute the second group. Chronologically, they range from ca. 1805 to 1761 BC, coinciding with the reigns of the last four rulers of Mari, Yahdun-Lim (?–1791 BC), Sumu-Yamam (1791–1790 BC), Samsi-Addu (1790–1775 BC), and Zimri-Lim (1774–1761 BC).[44] As is typical for cuneiform archives, the number of texts increases toward the end of their lifetime and reaches its peak during the reign of Zimri-Lim, with an average of three texts per day.[45] The texts are written in the classical Old Babylonian script and language, with the exception of a handful of Sumerian and Hurrian compositions (cf. section 15.3.2). The archives comprise accounting documents and letters in roughly equal amounts,

---

41. Less than a third of the *Šakkanakku* texts have currently been published; for the references, see Durand 2008b: 562–563 and Colonna d'Istria 2014: 169–171.

42. Durand 1985: 160–171.

43. Cf. Durand 2009 and Colonna d'Istria 2014.

44. A handful of texts belong to the time of the Babylonian occupation (1761–1759 BC); for the references, see Charpin and Ziegler 2003: 244–245.

45. As Dominique Charpin noted, "this reign of a little more than thirteen years is by far the best known period in the history of Syria of the whole second millennium" (Charpin and Ziegler 2003: 169, translation mine).

while texts of other genres are exceptional.[46] Slightly more than half of the texts in this group have been published.[47]

As Wolfgang Heimpel once wrote about his encounter with the Mari letters:

> In these lines, the mere beginning of a letter, there was more history than I had found and taught in my years as instructor of Mesopotamian history. I was shocked, ashamed, and hooked.[48]

Most students of the Mari texts have felt something similar. Why is Mari so special? First, the Mari archives are the largest royal archive ever discovered in the ancient Near East. In addition, unlike many other large cuneiform archives, they comprise a huge number of letters. Royal archives are a gold mine for historians, because they contain records of seminal events, political struggles, public administration, and foreign affairs, while private archives rarely shed light on matters outside the limited world of their owners. Moreover, the kings of Mari were among the most powerful rulers of the period, and the geographical range of their archives is the entire cuneiform world, rather than only a few nearby cities. The horizon of the Mari archives is demarcated by Anšan in Elam, Dilmun in the Persian Gulf, Kumme in northwestern Zagros, Hattusa in Anatolia, Hazor in Palestine, Alašiya on Cyprus, and Crete (where some goods and merchants originated).[49] An additional treat for the modern reader are the direct, first-person quotes from sayings of major historical figures of the period, such as Samsi-Addu of Ekallatum, Zimri-Lim of

---

46. They include about 200 private contracts and some thirty scholarly and literary compositions, including royal inscriptions. Among the literary compositions, an original royal hymn today known as Epic of Zimri-Lim is of particular interest: Guichard 2014a.

47. The latest printed bibliography of editions and studies of Mari texts is provided in Charpin 2004b: 453–475. A continuously updated Mari bibliography is published online by the project Archibab (www.archibab.fr; last accessed August 15, 2020).

48. Heimpel 2003: xi.

49. Charpin and Ziegler 2003: 26–27.

Mari, Ibal-pi-El II of Ešnunna, Yarim-Lim I of Aleppo, and Hammurabi of Babylon, creating a very personal encounter. Finally, most texts in royal archives were penned by learned and broad-minded royal scribes who were capable of providing both subtle analyses and wider generalizations on specific historical events as well as their social milieu.[50] The extracts from Mari letters cited in this chapter are intended to provide a glimpse of both their informative and literary value, although they represent only a tiny part of the corpus.

Juxtaposing accounting texts and letters makes it possible to write a detailed monthly, and sometimes even daily, chronicle of political history. Accounting texts indirectly refer to political events when, for example, they record gifts for foreign messengers, dowries of Mari princesses marrying foreign rulers, weapons for military campaigns, or the king's presence in conquered cities. These references are concise but precisely dated; therefore accounting texts constitute the chronological frame for the events that letters, undated, describe in great detail.[51] As for economic, social, and cultural history, narrative accounts of the letters, supplemented by quantitative data of the accounting texts, shed light on almost any aspect of life in Western Asia of that time.

15.2.2. The sources contemporary with the Mari archives

For the period between ca. 1805–1761 BC, the Mari texts constitute about 90 percent of the epigraphic finds made in Upper Mesopotamia and the Levant. However, the remaining 10 percent include some large and important corpora. Six Upper Mesopotamian cities have yielded considerable numbers of cuneiform texts contemporary to the Mari archives. The following section describes only the texts that can be dated to 1805–1761 BC. Terqa, Šubat-Enlil, and Qaṭṭara have also yielded important archives of a later date, for which see sections 15.5.2–4.

---

50. On the narrative quality of Mari letters, see Sasson 2015: 5–7.

51. For the method and its limitations, see Charpin and Ziegler 2003: 14–18; Sasson 2015: 7–9.

In **Šušarra** (modern Tell Shemshara), the archive of a local ruler was found, containing about a hundred letters and one hundred fifty accounting documents.[52] All of them date to a few years before 1778 BC. The archive provides a valuable addition to the Mari data, particularly regarding the geography and history of the Trans-Tigris area during Samsi-Addu's time.

In **Qaṭṭara** (modern Tell al-Rimah), the reign of Samsi-Addu is represented by a few seal impressions and a handful of accounting documents.[53] Sixteen letters from the local king's archive, as well as a building inscription brought from the nearby city of Razama, belong to Zimri-Lim's time.[54] These letters contain supplementary information about events also referred to in the Mari letters, such as the invasion of Ešnunna in 1771 BC.

In **Šehna/Šubat-Enlil** (modern Tell Leilan), the epigraphic finds that can be dated to Samsi-Addu's reign are limited to seal impressions and a few stray accounting tablets; Zimri-Lim's time is represented by over 700 accounting documents, one diplomatic treaty, and one letter.[55] The accounting documents from both periods do not mention historical events, but their dates and prosopography are crucial for reconstructing the chronology of events for the city and its region.

In **Ašnakkum** (modern Chagar Bazar), over 450 accounting documents that can be dated to 1784–1776 BC have been discovered in administrative buildings.[56] They are an important source of information

---

52. Published in Eidem 1992; Eidem and Laessøe 2001.

53. Dalley et al. 1976: 249–250 and nos. 244–248.

54. Dalley et al. 1976: nos. 1–16; Frayne 1990: no. 26.1.

55. Most of the texts remain unpublished; see the references in Charpin and Ziegler 2003: 22–23; and cf. Ristvet and Weiss *apud* Eidem 2011: xvii–lii, and Lacambre 2019. The majority of the accounting documents come from the archive of a legate of Andarig, a neighboring city that controlled Šubat-Enlil in the 1760s (see section 15.4.3).

56. Talon and Hammade 1997; Lacambre and Millet Albà 2008. About a third of the texts remain unpublished (Denis Lacambre, personal communication).

about the administration of the city and the political order under Samsi-Addu's reign.

Terqa (modern Tell Ashara) has yielded an inscription of Samsi-Addu,[57] about thirty *Šakkanakku* documents, and almost 200 classic Old Babylonian tablets and fragments, including letters, legal and administrative documents, school tablets, and literary fragments.[58] When they can be dated, the texts belong to the reigns of Yahdun-Lim and Zimri-Lim. Most of them are fragmentary and come from private archives, but some documents may have belonged to the archive of a provincial governor of Zimri-Lim's time.

In **Tuttul** (modern Tell Bi'a), almost 400 tablets from this period have been found.[59] Of the ca. fifty tablets of the *Šakkanakku* type, datable to Yahdun-Lim's time, all are accounting documents, with the sole exception of a letter (the only known of the *Šakkanakku* type). The classic Old Babylonian texts are letters, school texts, and accounting documents from Yasmah-Addu's and Zimri-Lim's time. Most of the texts were found in the palace archives owned by the city's rulers and governors. They mainly concern local affairs, but some of the documents provide important chronological anchors for political events.

In addition, small lots of one to eight cuneiform tablets have been found in Assur,[60] in Al-Kapim,[61] at Tell Taya,[62] at Kazane Höyük (perhaps Nihriya),[63] at Tell Sianu (unpublished), and in Hazor in modern-day

---

57. Grayson 1987: no. 39.8.

58. Only about a third of tablets in each group have been published; see the overview and the references in Masetti-Rouault and Rouault 2013: 599–600.

59. Published by Krebernik 2001.

60. Most Old Assyrian and Old Babylonian archival documents from Assur cannot be dated or belong to a later period (see section 15.5.6), but at least one accounting text belongs to Samsi-Addu's time: Lacambre 2019: 514–518.

61. Mohammad 2002: nos. 2–4, 6–7.

62. Postgate 1973.

63. Michalowski and Mısır 1998.

Israel.[64] Samsi-Addu's inscriptions have been discovered in Assur,[65] in Nineveh,[66] in the vicinity of Mardin,[67] and at an unknown site in Upper Mesopotamia.[68] Stamped bricks from the vicinity of Tuz Khurmatu mention a local ruler.[69] Numerous cylinder seals and a few inscribed beads, most of them unprovenanced, can be added to the list. Based on prosopographical evidence, most of the texts can be dated to Samsi-Addu's time, except for the stamped bricks from Tuz Khurmatu and the tablets from Al-Kapim, which belong to the reign of Zimri-Lim. The texts from Gasur,[70] Tell al-Hawa (perhaps ancient Razama),[71] Tell Arbid,[72] the vicinity of Nusaybin,[73] Tell Hammam et-Turkman,[74] Hazor, and other sites in the southern Levant[75] have generally been dated to the Middle Bronze Age and may belong to later periods than we are concerned with here.

The period of ca. 1805–1761 BC corresponds to the first half of Level Ib in the periodization of the Kültepe archives. Level Ib texts are almost exclusively concerned with Anatolian matters. However, some of the documents point to political and commercial contacts with northwestern

---

64. For the Hazor tablets datable to this period, see the references in Charpin and Ziegler 2003: 25 and Durand 2006. For undatable or later Middle Bronze Age texts from Hazor, see further discussion later in this section.

65. Grayson 1987: nos. 39.1, 39.9, and 39.11.

66. Grayson 1987: nos. 39.2 and 39.3. The cuneiform tablets from Nineveh belong to later periods (see section 15.5.1).

67. Grayson 1987: no. 39.1001.

68. Waetzoldt 2000.

69. Frayne 1990: no. 20.1.

70. Six Old Assyrian letters and fragments; see the references in Veenhof 2008a: 39.

71. George 1990.

72. Eidem 2008b: 40 (note that the tablet fragment is in Old Assyrian).

73. Donbaz 1999.

74. van Soldt 1995.

75. Horowitz et al. 2006, to which add the references in Horowitz et al. 2012, including the fragments of cuneiform laws found in Hazor.

Syria and Upper Mesopotamia.[76] In addition to references to Syrian cities in Old Assyrian documents, the evidence includes several texts written in Old Babylonian, in particular the letter of Anum-Hirbi, a king
who ruled in Mamma, Zalwar, and Haššum during the reigns of Samsi-
Addu and Zimri-Lim.[77] There are also a few Kültepe letters written in
the Hurrian milieus of Syria, or possibly even the Trans-Tigris region,
but they are difficult to date and may be later than 1761 BC.[78] Seals of the
servants of Yahdun-Lim and Samsi-Addu were found in Acemhöyük in
Anatolia (for which see chapter 17 in this volume).[79]

Lower Mesopotamian texts that refer to Upper Mesopotamia are
not rare in this period,[80] but their interpretation is sometimes open to
debate[81] and their importance is secondary to the abundance of indigenous sources. Yet some of the inscriptions and date formulas of the kings
of Ešnunna and Babylon provide indispensable pieces of information
about their conquests in Upper Mesopotamia and the Trans-Tigris area.

The wealth of written records overshadows the archaeological evidence for this period. However, several important monuments shed light
on the "Age of Mari."[82] The most important is the final incarnation of
the grand architectural complex that contains the Great Palace of Mari
at its center. Excavations there also brought to light some of its inventory (figure 15.3).[83] Other palaces have been discovered, in particular in

---

76. Veenhof 2008: 59.

77. Anum-Hirbi is also mentioned in Mari texts, in other contemporary Anatolian
sources, and in various texts from later periods; see Miller 2001. See also
chapter 17 in this volume.

78. Most recently, see Veenhof 2008b: 10–21; Michel 2010: 71–76.

79. Frayne 1990: no. 6.8.6; Grayson 1987: no. 39.10.

80. For the mention of Upper Mesopotamian toponyms in Lower Mesopotamian
sources, see Ziegler and Langlois 2017.

81. An example is AbB 8: no. 15; cf. Charpin and Ziegler 2003: 140, n. 530.

82. For overviews, see Akkermans and Schwartz 2003: 298–324, Genz 2012: 622–
626, Morandi Bonacossi 2014: 420–428.

83. Margueron 2004: 459–523.

FIGURE 15.3. Goddess with Flowing Vase, from the Great Palace of Mari, Room 64 / Court 106. Early second millennium BC. National Museum of Aleppo, Syria. Photo by Virginia Verardi, reproduced with permission.

Ebla, Šubat-Enlil, Qaṭṭara, Tell Sakka, and Tell el-Burak. Temples of this period are known from Ebla, Qaṭṭara, Šubat-Enlil, and Assur. Some of the public edifices unearthed in the northern Jezirah were built by order of Samsi-Addu. Rich burials, such as the latest royal tombs of Byblos and the earliest royal tombs of Ebla, may also coincide with the "Age of Mari." Despite the decline under the late Twelfth and the Thirteenth Dynasties, Egyptian imports and influences, including the appearance of Egyptian motifs in Syro-Palestinian glyptic art, reveal the continuing contact between the lands on the Nile and the northern Levant.[84]

15.2.3. Too much data?

Given the huge amount of historical information available for this period, a brief synthesis like the one that follows can only be very selective. To create an outline of political history, one must first ask "the political history of what"? The Mari archives and contemporary sources mention approximately eighty states that existed in Upper Mesopotamia and the Levant during this period, ranging from the large-scale state ruled by Samsi-Addu to obscure towns whose ephemeral chiefs proclaimed themselves "kings." For most of these states, more or less detailed historical narratives can be written, and for many of them such outlines are already available.[85] Whereas the history of large kingdoms such as Yamhad and Qatna is often far too sparsely documented, political events in some of the petty states in the northern Jezirah are described in great detail. As Jesper Eidem notes,

> indeed certain Mari letters with reports on events in the region read like Machiavellian nightmares with kings concluding conflicting alliances, competing for control of the same town with any number of colleagues—and suddenly facing decapitation and an ignominious end.[86]

---

84. Some of the imports, although manufactured in the time of the Twelfth and Thirteenth Dynasties, may have been brought to the Levant in later periods when contact between these regions intensified; see Genz 2012: 626.

85. See the bibliography in Charpin and Ziegler 2003: 263–268, to which add Chambon 2014; Charpin 2015a; Charpin and Durand 2004b; Guichard 2007; 2009b; 2011; 2014b; Jacquet 2014; Sasson 2010; van Koppen 2015; Ziegler 2004; 2015b.

86. Eidem 2000: 257.

It is not possible to discuss several dozen of these states in the present chapter. Therefore, this chapter focuses on the history of the Mari kingdom, including the vice-kingdom of Mari within Samsi-Addu's realm. Mari is the source for the bulk of the written records, and therefore its history is by far the best known. Other states are documented primarily in the context of their relationships to Mari. Their histories will be addressed *en passant* when dealing with the history of Mari.

As for the fields beyond political history, this chapter will only contain an overview of issues crucial for understanding the historical narrative, in particular the ethnolinguistic setting, historical geography, and state and international relations. A reader interested in other subjects is advised to consult the recent introductory works on the world of Mari,[87] and surveys of individual aspects of its economy, society, and culture. To mention only monographs, state-of-the-art syntheses are available for various aspects of material culture,[88] for religion in general,[89] divination, prophecy, and medicine,[90] cult,[91] palace staff,[92] collective governing bodies,[93] and taxes.[94]

---

87. For a comprehensive encyclopedia entry on Mari, see Durand et al. 2008; for anthologies of Mari letters in translation, accompanied by introductions covering historical and social questions, see Durand 1997–2000; Heimpel 2003; Sasson 2015.

88. Tableware: Guichard 2005; textiles and leatherwork: Durand 2009; viticulture: Chambon 2009; metallurgy and jewelry: Arkhipov 2012; irrigation: Reculeau 2018; grain management: Chambon 2018.

89. Durand 2008b.

90. Durand 1988.

91. Jacquet 2012.

92. Ziegler 1999; 2007.

93. Fleming 2004.

94. Marti 2008.

15.3. The age of Mari, ca. 1805–1761 BC: the geographic and political setting

15.3.1. Elements of a historical geography

The territory extending from the Zagros foothills to the Levant divides into several geographic zones.[95] The valleys of the eastern tributaries of the Tigris, from the Adhaim in the south to the Lesser Khabur (or Iraqi Khabur) in the north, form a geographical unit which is sometimes called the Trans-Tigris region. This region was divided between a few city-states of which Qabra was the most powerful. Šušarra (Tell Shemshara) has yielded archives that are of crucial importance for the history of the Trans-Tigris region during this period. Gasur (Yorghan Tepe; later known as Nuzi), Arraphe (modern Kirkuk), and Urbilum (Arbela; modern Erbil), major regional centers of earlier or later periods, are mentioned in the texts, but their importance in the early second millennium seems to have been secondary.

The Middle Tigris valley was dominated by Assur (Qal'at Sherqat), the commercial and religious center, and Ekallatum, the seat of power. Nineveh (Kuyunjik) and Kalhu (Nimrud), the future capitals of Assyria, were provincial towns. Nurrugum was a major political center in the vicinity of Nineveh. Further upstream were the city-states of Širwun, Haburatum, Burullum, and Mardaman (modern Bassetki). The Upper Tigris valley between Tur Abdin and Taurus was divided into the kingdoms of Tigunanum, Eluhut, and Šinamum.

The northern Jezirah, whose ancient name was Subartu, was organized into dozens of city-states. To quote the so-called Epic of Zimri-Lim, "Subartu is scattered like sheep on a pasture."[96] Only the most

---

95. For a comprehensive handbook of the historical geography of Upper Mesopotamia in the Old Babylonian period, see Ziegler and Langlois 2017; the accompanying maps are published in Fink 2017. For the Levant and the area east of the Tigris, see the references in Charpin and Ziegler 2003: 272–276. Only a few of the toponyms have been identified with specific sites, and with various degrees of certainty. In what follows, names of tells will be indicated only for excavated sites. The following discussion reflects the situation during Zimri-Lim's time.

96. Guichard 2014a: ii 43.

important cities can be mentioned here. The easternmost part of Subartu was called Yussan (or Yassan); its major political center was Razama-in-Yussan. The Ishkaft and Sinjar mountains divided Yussan and the Sinjar plain. Numhâ and Yamutbal, two names of regions originating from the names of Amorite tribes, were the ancient terms for the northern and the southern parts of the Sinjar plain. The principal city-states of Numhâ were Kurda and the dual kingdom of Karana and Qaṭṭara (Tell al-Rimah). Yamutbal was dominated by Andarig in the west and Razama-in-Yamutbal in the east.

To the west of Yussan, Šubat-Enlil (Tell Leilan), also known as Šehna, was the capital of the land of Apum. The central part of the Khabur triangle was called Idamaraṣ. The most politically important cities of the region were Ilanṣura, Kahat (Tell Barri), Ašnakkum (Chagar Bazar), and Ašlakka. The west of the Khabur triangle was known as Yapṭurum; its principal city was Talhayum. The kingdom of Burundum, between Karaca Dağ and the Euphrates, often mingled in the affairs of its southeastern neighbors. The region of the Upper Balikh was occupied by the tetrapolis of Zalmaqum, comprising the city-states of Šuda, Šubat-Šamaš (also known as Hanzat), Harran, and Nihriya (perhaps Kazane Höyük).

The Upper Euphrates valley and the adjacent plains were dominated by Emar (Tell Meskene), Yakaltum (Tell al-Munbaqa), Carchemish (Jarablus), Zalwar (perhaps Tilmen Höyük), Haššum, Ursum, and Hahhum (perhaps Lidar Höyük). From the viewpoint of its contemporaries, the Middle Euphrates valley was divided into two parts: Suhum, downstream of Mari; and Ah-Purattim ("The Banks-of-the-Euphrates"), from Mari upstream to Tuttul (Tell Bi'a). The principal cities of Suhum were Rapiqum, Hit, Yabliya, Al-Kapim (Tell Shishin), Hanat (later Anat), Sapiratum, Harradum (Khirbet ed-Diniyeh), and Puzurran. Between Mari and Tuttul, an important urban center was Terqa (Tell Ashara). On the Lower and Middle Khabur, there were cities such as Saggaratum, Qattunan, and Ṭabatum (Tell Ṭaban).

Northwestern Syria was referred to as the "Land of Yamhad," after the kingdom whose capital was Halab (Aleppo). Among the references to the cities of Yamhad in Mari texts, one finds the earliest mentions of Alalakh (Tell Atchana), then known as Alahtum, and Ugarit (Ras

Shamra). Southwestern Syria was called the "Land of Qatna," after the realm whose capital of the same name was situated at Tell al-Mishrifeh. The boundary regions of the kingdom of Qatna were the Beqaa plain and the oasis of Apum (later Damascus). On the route from Mari to Qatna, Tadmur (Palmyra) was already established as the main caravan stop. On the coast of Lebanon, Byblos was an independent kingdom. The southern Levant was referred to as Amurrum.[97] There were at least four kingdoms in this region, but we know of only one of its capitals, Haṣura (Hazor).

15.3.2. Languages and peoples

At the time of the Mari archives, the entire territory from the Trans-Tigris region to the Levant, wrote Akkadian, represented by three varieties: Old Assyrian, *Šakkanakku*, and Old Babylonian. Old Assyrian was written in Assur and its Anatolian trade colonies throughout the early second millennium BC (cf. chapter 17 in this volume). The handful of Old Assyrian texts discovered outside Assur and Anatolia must have been left behind by traveling Assyrian merchants.[98] Texts in the previously discussed *Šakkanakku* script and dialect were composed in Mari, Terqa, and Tuttul in the late nineteenth century BC. Old Babylonian was written everywhere from the Zagros mountains to Palestine starting from ca. 1805 BC.

The Old Babylonian script and written language were borrowed from Lower Mesopotamia. The chancellery of Yahdun-Lim, king of Mari, abolished the use of *Šakkanakku* for writing texts in ca. 1805 and introduced the Old Babylonian that had been in use in the Diyala region.[99] This "reform" spread to other cities within the kingdom, in particular Terqa. At the same time, Samsi-Addu began his expansion into Upper

---

97. Durand 1997–2000: I 574; 2004: 120–122.

98. The texts are from Gasur and Tell Arbid (see section 15.2.2). There is also a mid-eighteenth-century Old Assyrian treaty from Šehna (see section 15.5.3).

99. Charpin 2012a; cf. Nicolet 2016: I 337–346.

Mesopotamia and brought with him a slightly different variety of Old Babylonian, which had been used in his home city. When Samsi-Addu conquered most of Upper Mesopotamia, this Old Babylonian variety was introduced throughout his sphere of control,[100] including in Mari, where the type of Old Babylonian used by Samsi-Addu replaced the one introduced by Yahdun-Lim in ca. 1783 BC.[101] After the disintegration of Samsi-Addu's large-scale state, "his" Old Babylonian remained the written *lingua franca* in all of Upper Mesopotamia and the Levant, including in the Mari kingdom under Zimri-Lim.[102]

Texts in other languages are exceptional. People capable of writing Sumerian were hard to find,[103] yet Mari has yielded a few Sumerian school texts and canonical literary compositions.[104] The corpus in the Hurrian language consists of five incantations and a letter (?) fragment from Mari,[105] as well as one incantation from Tuttul.[106] Egyptian was written in Byblos, but the extant corpus is also tiny.[107]

---

100. Durand and Marti 2004: 123.

101. On this transition from a paleographic viewpoint, see Charpin 1985a: 267–268.

102. Most of the letters that were sent to Mari from appreciable distances are surprisingly uniform in their writing and language across Samsi-Addu's and Zimri-Lim's times; however, a systematic study that would establish whether some of them used differing varieties of Old Babylonian is currently lacking. Note that a group of letters from Ilansura combine Old Babylonian, Old Assyrian, and other features; see Charpin 1989a. For the characteristics of the texts found in Mari but written in the Levant, see Durand 2018: 347–350. Beyond that, over thirty letters found in Mari were penned by natives of Babylonia and Ešnunna and, as to be expected, were written in the Old Babylonian varieties of Babylonia and Ešnunna.

103. Ziegler and Charpin 2007: 69–72. The Sumerian names borne by a few Mari scribes reflect the cultural prestige of Sumerian rather than the mother tongue of their bearers.

104. Durand and Guichard 1997: 21–23; Guichard 2015; Nicolet 2016: II 211–238.

105. For references, see Durand and Guichard 1997: 22.

106. Krebernik 2001: no. 379. For the possibility of a more widespread Hurrian literacy, see Veenhof 2008b: 17.

107. For references, see Hikade 2012: 839.

The regional divisions for spoken languages did not coincide with the written ones. In the eighteenth century, few people in this region used the same language for writing as they used for speaking. As a spoken language, the *Šakkannakku* dialect went extinct long before the last text using it was written.[108] Old Assyrian was the vernacular of Assur and its colonies. The language and writing of some Old Babylonian texts from Upper Mesopotamia betray an Old Assyrian influence. This means that the area of this dialect was not limited to Assur, but we can say nothing more definitive than that. At least two other languages, or language groups, were widely spoken in the region. The language of personal names may hint at the mother tongue of their bearers, though the match is far from perfect. People with Hurrian names, including local kinglets, mainly lived in the Trans-Tigris area and the northernmost part of the Jezirah.[109] West Semitic names were borne by the majority of the population of Upper Mesopotamia and the Levant.[110] Also, letters written in these regions contain numerous lexical and syntactic loans from West Semitic.[111] A few Old Babylonian and Old Assyrian texts explicitly mention speakers of "Subarean" and "Amorite" (see further discussion later in this section), that is, Hurrian and West Semitic in modern terms.

We do not know how many people outside Lower Mesopotamia spoke Old Babylonian as their first language. Many people from the Trans-Tigris region to the Levant were given Akkadian names, but we do not know if their parents actually spoke Old Babylonian or merely followed an onomastic fashion; sometimes West Semitic names are simply rendered in writing via their Akkadian translations. Anyway, every

---

108. The most recent if somewhat outdated analysis of the *Šakkanakku* dialect is Gelb 1992.

109. Richter 2004.

110. For an analysis of the West Semitic personal names and lexical borrowings found in Old Babylonian texts, see Streck 2000, whose study provides, in particular, data on the percentage of West Semitic, Akkadian, and Hurrian names in Upper Mesopotamia; cf. the review of Charpin 2005–2006 and see also Golinets 2018.

111. For a recent summary, see Arkhipov and Loesov 2013: 5–7.

literate man or woman, whatever his or her mother tongue, could write in Old Babylonian and probably speak it to some extent. Even natives of Assur, those with their own written language, resorted to Old Babylonian for their international correspondence.[112]

Just as in other times and places, a complex relationship existed between the linguistic picture presented here and the various demonyms that were in use in that period. A good starting point for a discussion of this is the list of "ethnics" from an Old Assyrian letter quoting a statute from the city of Assur:

> The rule concerning gold is the same as previously: people may sell it among each other, but in accordance with the stele, no son of Assur whatever shall sell gold to any Akkadian, Amorite, or Subarean. Whoever does so will not remain alive.[113]

This reference to the "sons of Assur" (*mer'ū Aššur*) is the simplest one: the term refers to the natives of Assur, who spoke what we call Old Assyrian. They were called "Assyrians" (*aššurûm*) in Old Babylonian texts.[114] "Akkadian" (*akkidium* in Old Assyrian and *akkadûm* in Old Babylonian) mainly described the inhabitants of Lower Mesopotamia, who were native speakers of Old Babylonian.[115] However, the word was also applied to a part of the population of the Mari kingdom (see later discussion). "Subarean" (*šubirīum/šubarûm*) could mean speakers of

---

112. Charpin 2012a: 134–135.

113. Quoted after Dercksen 2004: 81.

114. In the present section, I use quotation marks to distinguish the renderings of ancient terms from the modern scholarly terms of the same origin. E.g., "Akkadian" is the rendering of *akkadûm*, and its meaning is different from what modern scholarship calls Akkadian.

115. Ziegler 2014: 180–181. As a language name, *akkadûm* appears in a Mari text: Durand 1992: 125 (A.109). It refers to what we call Old Babylonian, while *aššurûm* for the Assyrian language is not attested until later periods.

Hurrian,[116] but more frequently this notion included all the inhabitants of Subartu (the northern Jezirah), whatever their language.[117]

"Amorite" (*amurrīum/amurrûm*) represents the more complex case of the four. The word was used as a language name, which could only refer to a West Semitic variety.[118] However, not all "Amorites" spoke "Amorite." To understand why, we have to go back to the early second millennium BC. At that time, Mesopotamians used the designation "Amorites" to refer to the people who had West Semitic names, spoke West Semitic language(s), were nomads (or merely migrants), and came to Mesopotamia from the northwest (cf. chapters 13 and 14 in this volume). As was the case with many other nomads, they divided themselves into tribes and clans. The four major tribes were the Sim'alites ("Northerners" or "West Bankers"), the Yaminites ("Southerners" or "East Bankers"), the Numhâ, and the Yamutbal.[119] If they ever had a single, indigenous self-designation, it was "Hana."[120] When they called themselves "Amorites," it was the result of Mesopotamian influence.

By the eighteenth century, one group of "Amorites" had lost both their nomadic way of life and their language. This was particularly the case for the "Amorites" who had settled in Lower Mesopotamia. They were now sedentary and spoke Old Babylonian, yet they preserved their West Semitic personal names and the memory of their "Amorite" origin.

---

116. The language name *šubirīum/šubarûm* mainly refers to Hurrian: Durand 1992: 125 (A.109); Veenhof 2008b: 12–16 (kt 91/k 539: 30). See, however, Prechel and Richter 2001: 346–347.

117. For a bibliography on Subartu and Subareans in Old Babylonian sources, see Ziegler and Langlois 2017: 341–342.

118. Ziegler and Charpin 2007.

119. The two latter tribes were named after legendary ancestors. For the division of the Sim'alites and the Yaminites into clans, see Durand 2004: 157–184.

120. In Mari texts, the elusive term Hana can mean "nomads" whatever the tribe, but sometimes it was synonymous to Sim'alite and opposed to the names of other tribes. Moreover, sometimes the nomadic Hana and the sedentary Hana were distinguished from each other. In addition, the four "Amorite" tribes were perceived as "subdivisions of the Hana." For an overview of the suggested interpretations of the term, see Heimpel 2003: 34–36.

Samsi-Addu and his sons are a good example. The king's name was of West Semitic construction, but it also had the Akkadianized version Šamši-Adad. He venerated both Sargonic kings and "Amorite" forefathers as his ancestors.[121] His son Yasmah-Addu had a West Semitic name, but did not understand "Amorite,"[122] as his native language was Old Babylonian. Samsi-Addu's other son had the Akkadian name Išme-Dagan.

Other "Amorites" settled down in Upper Mesopotamia. They kept their West Semitic names, but the fate of their language is unknown.[123] Did they assimilate the earlier East Semitic population of the region, or did the opposite happen? A segment of the inhabitants of the Mari kingdom were considered "Akkadians." In some Mari letters, Zimri-Lim's officials reminded their lord of the following:

> First, you are the king of Hana, and second, you are the king of Akkadians.[124]

> My lord is the king of Akkadians and Amorites.[125]

However, it is possible to interpret this evidence in a number of ways.[126] Apart from that, we know that the sedentary population of the Euphrates valley between Mari and Tuttul was Amorite of the Yaminite kind.[127] Little is known of the Semitic language varieies spoken in the northern Jezirah.[128]

---

121. FM 3: no. 4.

122. Ziegler and Charpin 2007: 61–63.

123. For a discussion, see Charpin 2016b: 14–19.

124. ARM 6: no. 76: ll. 20–21.

125. A.489; unpublished, quoted by Durand 1992: 113. This opposition between "Akkadian and Amorite" is curiously identical to the way the *mīšarum* edicts refer to Babylonian citizens (see chapter 18 in this volume).

126. Rather than an indigenous East Semitic population, these "Akkadians" may have been Lower Mesopotamian expatriates who had been serving in the administration of Mari since Yasmah-Addu's time: Durand 1997–2000: II 481–482; cf. Ziegler 2014: 188.

127. Most recently, see Durand 2010b.

128. Cf. Durand 1992: 123–126.

A third population of "Amorites" forfeited neither their language nor their nomadic mode of subsistence. All or most of them were either Sim'alites or Yaminites. A letter written by a Yaminite nomad advocates the way of life that the Sumerian poem called "Marriage of Amurru"[129] had derided:

> Before leaving I told you: "You shall go with me. Zimri-Lim has ordered to come." You know how to eat, to drink and to lie around, but you do not know how to go with me! Staying and sleeping do not make you blush! As for me, if I remain one day in the house, my throat is closed up until I get out and draw a breath. [...] Or has hot and cold wind never hit your face? Are your traits not of your family? At the same place where your father and mother looked at your face when you fell out of the vulva, the vulva got you back![130]

The "Amorite" nomads roamed Syria and the northern Jezirah with their flocks,[131] as the following letter reports:

> Just as the lands of Yamhad, Qatna and Amurrum are the rangeland of the Yaminites where the Yaminites can get enough grain and graze their flocks, so, since times immemorial, the rangeland of the Hana is Idamaraṣ.[132]

The sedentary farmers of Idamaraṣ (the Khabur triangle) paid a particular kind of grain tribute (*šepatum*) to the nomads. An official of Zimri-Lim reminded the kings of Idamaraṣ:

---

129. Most recently, see Charpin 2015b.

130. Durand 1997–2000: no. 38: ll. 11–19, 32–37.

131. Durand 2004: 118–133.

132. Durand 2004: 120 (A.2730: ll. 33–38).

> Since ever and forever, the Hana are your shepherds, and you are their farmers. Now why are you detaining the grain of *šepatum* for the Hana?[133]

Yahdun-Lim and Zimri-Lim were of a nomadic Sim'alite origin and ruled over territories with both sedentary populations and nomads who grazed their flocks in the northern Jezirah (see the next paragraph).

And finally, the last group of "Amorites" had never left the Levant. We do not know if they have ever been nomadic, and they must have always spoken West Semitic. It is important to remember that in Mari texts, "Amurrum" in its narrow geographic sense refers to the southern Levant.

A few "ethnic" groups living outside the region appear in texts as raiders, mercenaries, or captives. In northwestern Iran, the Lullu (cf. chapter 16 in this volume) and the Gutians were powers to be reckoned with, both in the third millennium BC and in the age of Mari. The Gutians had a kingdom in the mountains; its capital city was perhaps called Kakmum.[134] The Turukkeans were a Hurrian-speaking group whose kingdom, called Itapalhum, was situated in the Zagros to the east of the Trans-Tigris.[135] Suteans roamed the Syrian desert.[136] They had West Semitic names, but were not another tribe of "Amorites" or "Hana." "Sutean" and "Amorite" were considered to be different languages.

15.3.3. The concepts of state and king

The political order and the ideology of kingship in most Upper Mesopotamian states, including Mari, mainly followed traditional

---

133. FM 6: no. 9: ll. 17′–20′.

134. For Gutians in the Old Babylonian period, see Ziegler 2015a.

135. For a recent summary on the Turukkeans, see Ziegler 2016b.

136. Most recently, see Ziegler and Reculeau 2014.

Mesopotamian patterns.[137] The kings of Mari strove to fulfill the agenda of a model Mesopotamian ruler. They led troops to battle, acted as supreme judges, proclaimed the abolition of debts, dug canals, built temples, and fortified cities. They claimed to have been appointed by gods, played a key role in temple rituals, and relied upon the judgments of their diviners in both peace and war. Titles of their highest officials, such as *šukkallum* ("vizier") or *šandabakkum* ("chief accountant"), were of Sumerian origin. However, several aspects of the state were either specific to Upper Mesopotamia, or documented only in Mari texts. Here are but a few examples.

The idiosyncrasy that is most commonly discussed is the so-called dimorphic state, in which the king was both the ruler of a well-defined territory with a sedentary population and the tribal leader of nomadic pastoralists.[138] This duality is particularly reflected in the titles of Yahdun-Lim and Zimri-Lim, who were the kings of Mari as well as of the Amorite nomads of the Sim'alite branch. The nomadic subjects of the Mari kings grazed their flocks outside the territory of the Mari kingdom, mainly in the northern Jezirah, under the lead of the officials called *merhûm* ("chief of pasture"). They had the right to cross state lines on the condition that their tribe was at peace with the country they wanted to enter. They paid taxes to the king of Mari and constituted the bulk of his troops. The Yaminite kingdoms of the Middle Euphrates, though less well-documented, must have had a similar political order.[139] More surprisingly, the Kingdom of Upper Mesopotamia, a large-scale territorial state built by a king with no particular connection to nomads or any Amorite tribe, also had nomadic subjects and a special official to supervise them.[140]

---

137. For the political order of Old Babylonian states, see Charpin 2004b: 232–316 (for both Lower and Upper Mesopotamia); Durand 2010a and Sasson 2015: 21–81, 119–180 (for Upper Mesopotamia).

138. The problem has been extensively studied; see the recent overviews by Durand 2004 and Fleming 2009.

139. Durand 2004: 160–177.

140. Villard 2001: 78–79.

Another characteristic of Upper Mesopotamia was the role of popular assemblies in some city-states.[141] The case of Assur is well known,
but the Mari texts have revealed that at least two other cities, Tuttul and
Emar, were also governed by assemblies. It is notable that Assur and Emar
were merchant cities. It is common knowledge that the Elders played a
decisive part in city administration throughout the ancient Near East,
but Mariote texts have showed that at least in some of the kingdoms in
northern Jezirah, the Elders may have wielded even more power than the
king.[142]

Texts from Mari also document the role of the queen much better
than contemporary Lower Mesopotamian sources.[143] Perhaps the most
striking piece of information so far gleaned is that the queen of Andarig
governed the city and negotiated with foreign rulers during the absence
of her husband.[144]

Furthermore, the Mari letters elucidate (or perhaps further muddle)
the old question regarding the ownership of private versus state land in
the ancient Near East. Late in his reign, Zimri-Lim of Mari obtained the
city of Alahtum (Alalakh) from the king of Yamhad, probably with the
goal of ensuring a constant supply of wine and olive oil.[145] In exchange,
Zimri-Lim promised to restore the settlement's infrastructure. This
unusual transaction revealed how entangled property rights were with
political power. Zimri-Lim was to become the tenant-in-chief of the
settlement's arable land, while previous tenants-in-chief were forced to
leave. Commoners native to the city could keep or recover their plots. Yet
things turned out to be more complicated; in order to redeem the land
within the city that had been granted to him, Zimri-Lim was ultimately

---

141. Most recently, see Fleming 2004: 211–216.

142. See FM 2: no. 117 (quoted section 15.4.3).

143. For letters shedding light on the position of female members of royal families,
see Durand 1997–2000: III 259–504; cf. also Ziegler 2016a.

144. In particular, see ARM 26/2: nos. 433 and 435. For the historical context, see
section 15.4.3.

145. For this episode, see Durand 2002; Sasson 2009; Lauinger 2015: 113–132.

FIGURE 15.4. Wall painting known as "The Investiture of Zimri-Lim," from Court 106 of the Great Palace of Mari. Early second millennium BC. Louvre, Paris. Photo by Marie-Lan Nguyen, via Wikimedia Commons (https://commons.wikimedia.org/w/index.php?curid=22761889; public domain).

compelled to reimburse the tenants (probably through the mediation of the king of Yamhad). In particular, the queen-mother did not want to cede the fields she held in Alahtum, demonstrating that her land was distinct from that of the king or the palace. An imminent abolition of debts (*andurārum*) in Yamhad also threatened Zimri-Lim's rights as the buyer because it entailed the restitution of land to its previous holders. The natives of Alalakh were forced to cultivate Zimri-Lim's fields as corvée workers, yet Zimri-Lim failed to obtain an exemption from mandatory military service in the Yamhad troops for them.

The Mari archives, combined with the archaeological record from the Great Palace, provide an exceptional insight into life in a Mesopotamian palace (figure 15.4).[146] The palace simultaneously housed the private

---

146. E.g., see Durand 1997: I 60–110.

apartments of the king with his harem,[147] and the administrative offices of his high officials. It was also the economic heart of the kingdom and the legal body constituting the closest match to our concept of "the state." The palace's architectural features and functional spaces have been revealed to us through texts as much as they have been through excavation.[148] Thousands of administrative documents reflect the internal accounts of the palace, from the distribution of rations to its staff, through inventories of its treasuries, to deliveries of raw materials for its workshops.[149] Administrative law is represented in particular by the records of the oaths of allegiance that the palace staff took on different occasions.[150] Letters describe the various aspects of palace life in the greatest detail. To give only one example, the following report by a Mari official to the king may contain the earliest ever description of administrative buck-passing:

> I have investigated the matter of the palace menials. Among the staff of 400 menials, 100 are provided with garments and 300 are not. I interrogated Mukannišum and Bali-Erah about the staff who have no garments, and Mukannišum answered me: "It is not my job! It is Bali-Erah who must provide them with garments!" Bali-Erah, however, answered me: "I have supplied 100 persons among the artisans. My job was only 100. Mukannišum must provide garments for the rest." This is what they answered me.[151]

---

147. For a study of Zimri-Lim's harem, see Ziegler 1999.

148. Durand 1987a.

149. For preliminary studies of the organization of accounting and bookkeeping in the palace, see Arkhipov and Chambon 2015; Arkhipov 2019.

150. Durand 1991.

151. ARM 6: no. 39: ll. 6–22.

15.3.4. International relations

In the age of Mari, international relations complied with unwritten yet sophisticated rules.[152] The basic principle was that of "brotherhood," with all kings being members of a large family, in which "peace and good relations" (*salīmum u damqātum*) were the default condition, while war was abnormal. This "family" was not entirely a metaphor, since the Amorite rulers claimed to have common ancestors.[153] In practice, this same principle was applied all over the cuneiform world, whatever the ethnic background of a given dynasty.

Hierarchical relations between rulers were described in kinship terms. In the diplomatic language of the period, kings of equal status addressed each other as "brothers," while a difference in status was perceived as the relation of "father" and "son." A "son's son" was referred to as a "servant," a "father's father" amounted to a "lord." This terminology reflected a position in a universal hierarchy, rather than personal ties between a "suzerain" and a "vassal." For example, Hammurabi of Babylon wrote to one of his "sons:" "To the kings who write me as sons, you must write as a brother. To Zimri-Lim, who writes me as a brother, you must write as a son."[154] However, being a servant of two masters was rarely possible in practice. In particular, a "son" had to carefully choose which of his "fathers" he would follow when war broke out between them.

This hierarchical positioning was neither stable nor hereditary. When an influential king died, his inexperienced successor might be downgraded. Relative status changed quite often due to circumstances, which sometimes led to diplomatic blunders:

> Messengers of Atamrum came here. In delivering their message, one time they said, "Thus says Atamrum, you servant." A second

---

152. This section is based on Lafont 2001; Charpin 2014b; 2016a; 2019; and Sasson 2015: 82–118.

153. In particular, Samsi-Addu and Hammurabi worshipped the same ancestors; see most recently Durand 2012.

154. ARM 26/2: no. 384: ll. 63'–65'.

time they said, "Thus says Atamrum, your son." They are able to make such a mess when they deliver a message.[155]

During the greater part of Zimri-Lim's reign, the summit of the hierarchy was occupied by the emperor of Elam, who was perceived as the overlord of all Western Asia.[156] He was followed by a few great (literally "powerful") kings (*šarrū dannūtum*). A letter enumerates the great powers of the time:

> There is no king who is powerful just on his own. Ten to fifteen kings follow Hammurabi of Babylon, as many follow Rim-Sin of Larsa, as many follow Ibal-pi-El of Ešnunna, and as many follow Amud-pi-El of Qatna. Twenty kings follow Yarim-Lim of Yamhad.[157]

Mari's status among these great powers is not entirely clear. Zimri-Lim was a "son" of Yarim-Lim and Ibal-pi-El, but a "brother" of Hammurabi and Amud-pi-El. In general, the greater the distance between any two kingdoms, the more likely were their kings to be on equal terms. The rulers of the northern Jezirah were sometimes "sons" and at other times "brothers" of Zimri-Lim, depending on their ongoing successes or failures. At the same time, the remote city-states of the Upper Tigris could usually afford "brotherly" relations with Zimri-Lim because he would hardly go so far north to claim lordship.

---

155. ARM 27: no. 162: ll. 30–35.

156. This situation changed at the end of Zimri-Lim's reign, when Elam was defeated by Babylon and Mari; see the discussion in the following and also chapter 18 in this volume. During this same war, Ešnunna lost its status as a great power (see chapter 16 in this volume).

157. Charpin and Ziegler 2003: 206, n. 330 (A.482: ll. 22–27). As for the clients of the great kings, we are mainly informed of those who ruled in the northern Jezirah and were subordinate to Mari, Ešnunna, and Babylon. For the Syrian vassals of Yamhad, see Charpin and Ziegler 2003: 206, n. 331.

The kings who were at peace exchanged visits, emissaries (rather than permanently posted ambassadors), trade agents,[158] diplomatic gifts, and daughters or sisters for marrying. They often asked each other for various forms of aid, from grain to troops, and it was not appropriate to refuse. "Write me for anything you need" was a set phrase in diplomatic letters. The helpfulness of a "son" could be reinforced by a garrison and a legate his "father" would place in his capital; a "father" also granted his "son" royal insignia and might formally install him on the throne. Between equals, the exchange of presents was subject to strict reciprocity, and an inadvertent slight could cause a row. The king of Qatna wrote to Yasmah-Addu:

> This matter ought not be discussed, yet I must say it now and get it off my chest. You are a great king. When you requested from me two horses, I had them conveyed to you. Yet you, you sent me 20 minas of tin! You do not need to be insincere to me. Rather than this paltry amount of tin, you should have sent nothing at all and—by the god of my father—I would not have been displeased! Here in Qatna, the value of such horses is 600 shekels of silver. But you sent me 20 minas of tin! What would anyone hearing this say? Will he not mock us? This house is your house.[159]

During times of war, communication never ceased completely. Letters were written to enemies, but the addresses such as "my brother" or "my son" were omitted. For example, the king of Yamhad once sent congratulations to Yasmah-Addu for having crushed a mutiny, though the two countries were in permanent conflict.[160] Asylum was easily granted to yesterday's enemies in distress. Nomads and merchants from third

---

158. For long-distance trade in the light of Mari texts, see Michel 1996.

159. ARM 5: no. 20: ll. 4–25.

160. ARM 5: no. 21. For the correspondence between officials of warring countries regarding the release of captive women, see Guichard and Ziegler 2004; Charpin 2012b.

countries could cross the boundaries of warring states: "Much as a merchant who journeys through war and peace, the Hana range on foot through war and peace."[161]

To conclude a peace or a formal alliance, mutual oaths of loyalty were the standard practice. In this period, alliances were made between kings rather than countries. When a king died, his agreements lost force and his successor had to renew all existing covenants. Mari texts describe two kinds of oath ceremonies, "donkey-killing" and "life-touching." When the rulers met in person, they pronounced the oaths and sacrificed an animal, preferably a donkey foal.[162] When an alliance was concluded by correspondence, the parties exchanged written texts of the oaths they were going to take in order to verify its provisions. Several drafts of such oaths have been found in Mari and Šubat-Enlil. They are traditionally, and incorrectly, referred to as "international treaties." Having agreed on the terms, both kings pronounced their oath, perhaps also touching a small quantity of the other's blood ("life") that had been brought to him. The preparation of the oath for an alliance between Mari and Babylon is reported in a letter that quotes the words of Hammurabi:

> The curse formula of this tablet is very harsh! It is not fit for [. . .] nor for proclamation by mouth. Now [. . .] since Sumu-la-El and Sin-muballiṭ, my father, and since I ascended the throne of my father, I have taken sacred oaths with Samsi-Addu and many other kings. I have those tablets and none of them is as harsh as this one. I have now sent my gods and my servants to your lord to administer the sacred oath. Once your lord takes oath by my gods, he must write me back so that I take oath for my part.[163]

---

161. Durand 1997–2000: no. 333: ll. 5–8.

162. E.g., see ARM 2: no. 37 (quoted in section 15.4.3).

163. Guichard 2004: 16–25 (A. 2968⁺: ll. 74–81).

15.4. *The age of Mari, ca. 1805–1761 BC: a historical overview*

15.4.1. The kingdom of Mari under Yahdun-Lim (?–1791 BC) and Sumu-Yamam (1791–1790 BC)

We do not yet know how and when Yahdun-Lim became the king of Mari, but it happened sometime between 1832 and 1805 BC.[164] Before that, he may have ruled in Ṣuprum like his father Yagid-Lim had before him (see earlier discussion in section 15.1.5).

The bulk of Mari *Šakkanakku* texts belong within this span of time, but they say little about political history. A reconstruction of events is feasible only from the year 1805 BC, when Yahdun-Lim introduced the Ešnunnean variety of Old Babylonian as the written language of his administration, together with the genres that describe events, such as letters, commemorative inscriptions, and year names. The order of his year names has not yet been established, so the relative chronology of the events described in the following is unknown.[165]

One of Yahdun-Lim's titles, perhaps the earliest one we know, was "the king of Mari and the land of the Sim'alites"; that is, he ruled over both the region of Mari and the nomads of the Amorite tribal confederation of Sim'alites. Other texts show that his kingdom also included Terqa and the banks of the lower and middle Khabur. Up the Euphrates, he eventually conquered the cities of Samanum, Tuttul, and Abattum, which had been ruled by Amorite dynasties of the Yaminite branch. After his victory, Yahdun-Lim proclaimed himself "king of Mari, Tuttul and the land of Hana, mighty king, gatherer of the Banks-of-the-Euphrates." In the same year, he went to Mount Lebanon and the Mediterranean coast, and boasted of having subdued a territory on the shore. Down the Euphrates,

---

164. In 1832 BC, his father Yagid-Lim was still alive (see section 15.1.5). Fifteen year names of Yahdun-Lim are known, and since he reigned until 1791 BC, the earliest year name must correspond to ca. 1805 BC. This date, however, may be lower, if we admit that for some years more than one name was used, as was the case during Zimri-Lim's reign.

165. The following is based on Charpin and Ziegler 2003: 35–73.

all of Suhum belonged to Ešnunna, and the boundary passed very close to the city of Mari. The relations between the two countries were friendly, and Yahdun-Lim accepted Ešnunna's patronage. Yahdun-Lim went on several successful campaigns up the Khabur and the Balikh. By that time, the northern Jezirah was divided into numerous petty kingdoms. Rather than annex territories, Yahdun-Lim imposed vassal status on several cities of Idamaraṣ and Yapṭurum; this particularly ensured the safe pasture for Yahdun-Lim's flocks in the Khabur triangle.[166] Even Tigunanum on the Upper Tigris seems to have acknowledged Yahdun-Lim's suzerainty. The city-states of Zalmaqum, as well as Kurda in the Sinjar plain, were on equal terms with Yahdun-Lim's Mari. In northwestern Syria, Yamhad was hostile to Mari, while Apišal had "brotherly" relations with Yahdun-Lim.

In the eastern part of the Khabur triangle, Yahdun-Lim was able to keep in check the steadily growing influence of Samsi-Addu, claiming victory in several battles and successfully establishing a boundary between Nagar and Šubat-Enlil that separated the two zones of influence. When Yahdun-Lim was dethroned by his son Sumu-Yamam in 1791 BC, the new king attempted to come to terms with Yamhad. But his efforts were not enough to prevent Samsi-Addu from seizing Mari less than two years later. Samsi-Addu's son Yasmah-Addu became the next king of Mari.

Yasmah-Addu's later letter to a god sums up Yahdun-Lim's and Sumu-Yamam's reigns within the traditional framework of sacrilege and divine punishment:

> Because of the transgressions that he committed against Samsi-Addu and [. . .] that the god is holding, Sumu-Yamam, his son, drove Yahdun-Lim from Mari. But Sumu-Yamam began to act like his father Yahdun-Lim and imitated him in wrongdoing: he destroyed your temple that former kings had built and built there his wife's house. You came to bring him to task, and his own servants killed him.[167]

---

166. Charpin and Ziegler 2003: 51, n. 195 (A.1098).

167. ARM 1: no. 3: ll. 1′–11′.

15.4.2. Samsi-Addu's Kingdom of Upper Mesopotamia, ca. 1810–1775 BC

The twenty years of Samsi-Addu's reign following his conquest of Assur are still poorly known.[168] During this period, he subdued cities between the Tigris and the Sinjar and gained a foothold in the eastern part of the northern Jezirah, where he established an outpost at Šehna, renamed Šubat-Enlil ("Enlil's Abode").[169] There is one murky reference to his early conquests made much farther west in the Upper Euphrates area.[170] In the central Jezirah, Samsi-Addu confronted Yahdun-Lim of Mari, who successfully resisted his expansionary effort. Yet in 1790 BC, less than two years after Yahdun-Lim's son Sumu-Yamam took power in Mari, Samsi-Addu was able to conquer the city (figure 15.5).[171] The details of this event are not known, but most likely the entire Mari kingdom was annexed quickly.[172] Samsi-Addu became the ruler of the largest Mesopotamian state since the Third Dynasty of Ur.

Scholars once considered Samsi-Addu's kingdom to be the earliest stage of the Assyrian Empire, but this view has long been abandoned.[173] Recent scholarship refers to his state as "the Kingdom of Upper Mesopotamia." Samsi-Addu's own titles, all of which appear in texts postdating the conquest of Mari, often point to his mission as the world leader: his inscriptions describe him as "the king of the universe," "the appointee of Enlil," and "the king of Akkad," on the pattern of Sargonic rulers. Samsi-Addu also claimed to possess "the land between the Tigris

---

168. Charpin 2004b: 152.

169. This may have happened at about 1803 BC: Lacambre 2019. Tell Taya may have been under Samsi-Addu's rule no later than in 1798 BC; see Durand and Ziegler 2014: 51, n. 11.

170. ARM 1: no. 1: ll. 2′–9′.

171. Charpin and Ziegler 2003: 78–79.

172. The earliest evidence for Samsi-Addu's control over Şuprum dates to 1790 BC (ARM 22: no. 306). Tuttul was under his authority no later than in 1786 BC; see Krebernik 2001: no. 72.

173. For an overview of the discussion, see Charpin 2004b: 128–129.

FIGURE 15.5. Statue of a lion from the temple of the "King of the Land" at Mari. Early second millennium BC. Louvre, Paris. A Mari text contains the name for a different but probably contemporary lion statue: "Drinker of the blood of Samsi-Addu's enemies by Ištar's command" (Grayson 1987, no. 39.2002). Photo by Rama, via Wikimedia Commons (https://commons.wikimedia.org/w/index.php?curid=59397714), Creative Commons Attribution-Share Alike 3.0 France (CC BY-SA 3.0 fr) license.

and the Euphrates." Apart from that, he had titles with a more precise local reference, of which the most frequent was "the vicar of (the god) Aššur."[174] We know of only one inscription in which Samsi-Addu calls

---

174. In particular, this is the only title Samsi-Addu used on his cylinder seal; see Patrier 2015.

himself "the king of Ekallatum."[175] Yet, to the rest of the world, Samsi-Addu was first and foremost the king of Ekallatum: he is called such in the inscription of a king of Ešnunna,[176] and his realm is retrospectively referred to as "Ekallatum" in a Mari letter from Zimri-Lim's time.[177]

Samsi-Addu's relationship to the city of Assur was ambivalent.[178] The god Aššur was prominent in Samsi-Addu's royal titles; Samsi-Addu had himself included in the list of kings of Assur;[179] he called Assur "the City" in his letters;[180] he took care of its temples, but as far as we know he never lived there. Throughout his realm, Samsi-Addu introduced the calendrical system followed in Assur, but disregarded its language and writing. Even the building inscriptions that he installed in Assur itself were composed in Old Babylonian rather than Old Assyrian. The attitude held by the city toward Samsi-Addu was ambivalent too: for a seventeenth-century BC king of Assur, he was a foreign usurper (see section 15.5.6), yet a few centuries later he would be integrated into the Assyrian historical myth as a great early king of Assyria.

For 1790–1784 BC, the sources are still very scarce.[181] In 1787 BC, Samsi-Addu conquered the eastern part of the Upper Tigris valley[182] and founded fortresses on the Euphrates at the boundary of Yamhad, which

175. Grayson 1987: no. 39.7.

176. Charpin 2004a: 151–166 (IM 95200: ix 9–10).

177. ARM 26/1: no. 196: l. 38.

178. Cf. Ziegler 2002: 213–220, 237.

179. That is, a forerunner of the Assyrian King List: Yamada 1994.

180. Ziegler 2002: 213–217.

181. In Mari, only a few stray accounting documents date to this period, and they say nothing about political history, while the Mari Eponym Chronicle is well preserved only for 1787 BC.

182. According to the Mari Eponym Chronicle, the northernmost of the conquered cities is Haburatum. The western part of the region, including Tigunanum, had been conquered, or at least raided, by Samsi-Addu as early as 1797 BC; see Lacambre 2019.

means that he already controlled the whole of Jezirah.[183] It was probably in the same year that Samsi-Addu went to war with Ešnunna and extended his southern possessions as far as Mankisum on the Tigris and Rapiqum on the Euphrates.[184] In 1784 BC, Samsi-Addu peacefully ceded Rapiqum to Hammurabi of Babylon,[185] but the rest of Suhum, which was under Ešnunna's control during Yahdun-Lim's reign, remained part of the Kingdom of Upper Mesopotamia.

In 1783 BC, Samsi-Addu's younger son, Yasmah-Addu, installed himself in the palace of Mari.[186] Starting from this year, the letters he received were deposited in the palace archive, and a number of them have survived to this day. Thus our documentation of both the political events and the organization of the Kingdom of Upper Mesopotamia increases immensely from this point onward.

Since the period for which the evidence is available, the kingdom appears to have been divided into three parts.[187] Samsi-Addu, who was called the "great king," resided in Šubat-Enlil and governed the eastern part of the northern Jezirah. Samsi-Addu's sons had received the eastern and western parts of the realm. The elder son, Išme-Dagan, resided in Ekallatum. His status was superior to Yasmah-Addu's. The latter resided in Mari; his domain first included the former kingdom of Yahdun-Lim

---

183. The city-states of the Upper Euphrates from Emar to Ursum kept their independence. For details, see Ziegler 2009.

184. This reconstruction follows the interpretation of Charpin and Ziegler 2003: 88–90 of a fragmentary line in the Mari Eponym Chronicle that is supported by historical references in later texts.

185. Charpin and Ziegler 2003: 85.

186. The situation of Yasmah-Addu in 1790-1784 BC is poorly known, but it is perhaps during this period that he held the title "king of Dur-Yasmah-Addu" (previously known as Dur-Yahdun-Lim). Since 1788 BC, the Eastern Palace in Mari had been the residence of an important person, perhaps Yasmah-Addu himself. In 1786 BC, Samsi-Addu's wife was in Mari with their "children," one of which may have been Yasmah-Addu. The "king" is mentioned in Mari and Tuttul texts dated to 1785 and 1784 BC, but we do not know if they refer to Yasmah-Addu or rather to Samsi-Addu's occasional visits. For the details, see Charpin and Ziegler 2003: 79–84.

187. Villard 2001: 14–17.

and Suhum, but later it was enlarged with parts of the northern Jezirah.[188] Both Išme-Dagan and Yasmah-Addu had the title "king" and behaved on equal terms with foreign sovereigns, including Hammurabi of Babylon. However, they always remained under their father's supervision. None of Samsi-Addu's letters to Išme-Dagan have been found, but his letters to Yasmah-Addu are full of lectures and finicky instructions, as in the following examples:

> Now you, how long must we keep on guiding you? Are you still a child and not an adult? Is there no hair on your cheeks? How much longer will you not take charge of your house? Do not you look at your brother who commands vast armies? You too take charge of your palace, your house![189]
>
> As for gathering ice, it's a good idea. When porters will be bringing ice from ten or twenty double leagues, instruct competent [?] cupbearers, your servants who are with you, to gather the ice. While [. . .] they must thoroughly clean it from dung and urine. So much for [. . .] and cleaning. When ice has been cleaned properly, it has to be covered with water.[190]

The governors of important cities constituted a lower level of local administration.[191] The local dynasties that had ruled in these cities were eliminated, and their surviving members escaped to allied kingdoms in the Levant and Lower Mesopotamia, as the family of Yahdun-Lim of Mari, whom we discuss in the next paragraph, illustrates. In a letter written during Zimri-Lim's era, a prince of Kurda remembered his days of exile:

---

188. For details about Išme-Dagan's and Yasmah-Addu's domains, see Villard 2001: 69–100, with additions by Charpin and Ziegler 2003: 126; Durand and Ziegler 2014: 53.

189. ARM 1: no. 108: ll. 5–10.

190. ARM 1: no. 21: ll. 8′–17′.

191. Villard 2001: 62–100; Lacambre 2019.

When a while back I lived in Zalwar, Samsi-Addu wrote to the king of Zalwar for my return. The king of Zalwar contrived to give instead of me a worthless man who had been kept on hand, saying, "Here he is." Aminum took this man as if he were me, and Samsi-Addu executed him.[192]

However, a few territories within Samsi-Addu's realm were ruled by vassal kinglets. The kings of Karana and Andarig in the Sinjar plain kept their thrones, as vassals of Samsi-Addu, while he was in the course of expanding his kingdom.[193] A local dynasty also remained in power in Yakaltum on the Euphrates,[194] while in the Trans-Tigris area "kings" for the newly conquered cities were appointed from among Samsi-Addu's local allies.[195]

In 1782 BC, Yasmah-Addu married a daughter of the king of Qatna.[196] The princess was very young, as is clear from a letter sent by a palace official to Yasmah-Addu, who was on a journey:

If there are four or five matrons under Mubalsaga's control who know the customs of the palace and are fit to serve the lady, my lord should have them sent here so that they can serve her. They could give her advice and cherish (?) her as it suits the occasion. As for the lady's nurse who came from Qatna, it was believed that this woman had been bringing up the lady since her childhood and knows her ways. But they simply picked up this woman the very day of the lady's departure from Qatna and sent her to Mari

192. Charpin and Durand 2004a (A.1215: ll. 15–22).

193. Samu-Addu, the vassal king of Karana, was replaced by a governor at around 1784 BC: Durand and Ziegler 2014: 50–52. Note that Samu-Addu was the father of the lady Iltani, whose archive (dating to a later period) was found in Qaṭṭara (see section 15.5.4). Andarig may have remained a vassal kingdom until the end of Samsi-Addu's reign; see Ziegler 2002: 258.

194. Ziegler 2009: 189–192.

195. Charpin and Ziegler 2003: 100.

196. Charpin and Ziegler 2003: 86–88.

with the lady, so she knows nothing about the customs of the palace. Because of this unreliable woman who now serves my lady, during the siesta, when the palace's bolts were set, she had her bring out songstresses to the temple of Ištar for *šurārum*.[197] The Lady suffered a sunstroke when she was in the Painted Court and she has been ill ever since.[198]

Both Qatna and Samsi-Addu's realm were on hostile terms with Yamhad. In the late 1781 BC, Yasmah-Addu sent an army to the Levant, ostensibly to help Qatna in its war against Yamhad. However, the battleground was not situated on the Yamhad frontier but on the southwestern boundary of Qatna. Mari troops helped Išhi-Addu to conquer a few cities in the Beqaa valley.[199] Another expedition went from Mari to Qatna at the end of 1778 BC.[200] The expeditionary corps took part in a campaign in the oasis of Damascus (the city itself is not mentioned).

During the greater part of his reign, Samsi-Addu was on bad terms with the kings of Ešnunna. In late 1783, Ešnunna attempted to regain the territories that Samsi-Addu had annexed in 1787 BC.[201] After Ešnunna's powerful foray into the regions of both the Tigris and Euphrates, Samsi-Addu and Daduša of Ešnunna concluded peace. Samsi-Addu may have ceded some territories, in particular Mankisum. From that moment onward, Šitullum was the southernmost city of Samsi-Addu's realm (and of the later kingdom of Ekallatum). On the same occasion, Samsi-Addu

---

197. The meaning of the term *šurārum* is unknown. It may be a ritual, a dance, or a game; see most recently Jacquet 2012: 63–64.

198. ARM 26/2: no. 298: ll. 18–48.

199. Some of them, e.g., Zobah (Ṣibat, later Ṣubutu), appear in the written record for the first time; see Charpin 1998.

200. For the expeditions to Qatna, see Charpin and Ziegler 2003: 101–103, 124–125.

201. The dating of this conflict, and the peace that followed, is conjectural; see Charpin and Ziegler 2003: 88–91.

and Daduša concluded a military alliance in order to conquer petty king-doms of the Trans-Tigris area.[202]

In the region of the two Zab rivers, sizable power had been amassed by a certain Bunu-Ištar, "king of Qabra and the land of Urbilum," who had a few vassals among his neighboring kinglets. In 1781 BC, the allied armies of Daduša and Samsi-Addu devastated the territory from Arraphe to Urbilum and seized the capital city of Qabra. In the inscriptions com-memorating this campaign, each of the two kings describes the victory as his exclusive achievement alone:

Samsi-Addu: On the 20th day of the 8th month, I crossed the Zab, intruded the land of Qabra and destroyed the harvest of this land, I took the fortified cities of the whole land of Arbela in the 9th month and installed my garrisons all over them. Only Qabra. . . .[203]

Daduša: After I transformed his (Bunu-Ištar's) neighborhoods into pas-ture and ruined his vast country, I grandly approached Qabra, his capital city [. . .]. I took this city in ten days [. . .]. I gave this city, its vast territory and its settlements (?) as a gift to Samsi-Addu, king of Ekallatum.[204]

Territories further up the Lower Zab, in the Zagros foothills, were inte-grated into Samsi-Addu's realm in 1780 BC. The kingdom of Ahazum was annexed, along with its capital Šikšabbum, while Šušarra became a vassal state. In this region, Samsi-Addu's interests collided with those of the Turukkeans. At that time, Išme-Dagan headed campaigns up the

---

202. The reconstruction of events is based on Ziegler and Charpin 2003: 91–101, with additions by Charpin 2004a: 163–166.

203. Grayson 1987: no. 39.1001: ii′ 12–iv′ 1 (cf. Charpin 2004a: 163). The preserved part of the inscription does not mention Daduša.

204. Charpin 2004a: 154 (IM 95200: viii 1–4, 8–9, ix 6–11). This is the only men-tion of Samsi-Addu in the lengthy inscription. Daduša also claims to have "sub-dued" the territory from Burundum and Eluhut to the Zagros, but in reality he would merely have sent troops to Samsi-Addu, who was suppressing the revolt in this region soon after the campaigns in the Trans-Tigris area; see most recently Jacquet 2014: 133–136.

Tigris against Nurrugum. The kingdom with its principal cities, including Nineveh, was conquered.

In the same year, the Kingdom of Upper Mesopotamia entered its first crisis.[205] In the summer of 1780, wars developed on three fronts. A rebellion broke out in Zalmaqum, when a local prince attempted to take power over the region. In the piedmont region of the Zagros, Turukkeans rose in upheaval. The insurgent cities were destroyed and their inhabitants deported. The upper reaches of the Lower Zab were devastated and abandoned. The city of Šušarra was destroyed during the rebellion and its archives abandoned. In Suhum, the inhabitants of Samsi-Addu's kingdom found their access to the city of Hit, where they procured essential bitumen and asphalt, blocked by the Babylonians. The poorly documented conflict ended with a status quo peace. Additionally, a plague decimated the Middle Euphrates in the same year. Late in 1780 BC, a legion of Turrukkean prisoners of war in a town within the Khabur triangle revolted. The local population supported the insurgents, and the mutiny was not crushed until the spring of 1778 BC. Yamhad took advantage of this situation and invaded the left bank of the Upper Euphrates with the support of Yaminite nomads. The sudden death of the king of Yamhad interrupted this offensive in the summer of 1778 BC.

The following three years were relatively untroubled. Late in 1777 BC, Samsi-Addu's troops assisted Ešnunna and Babylon in a siege of Malgium. In 1776 BC, Samsi-Addu's ambassadors even went to Dilmun, seeking to establish diplomatic relations with the Gulf region on the pattern of Sargonic kings. The same year, a general census was undertaken. A letter written by the king to his son at the moment of the census sheds light on the delicate relationship between the nomads and the royal administration:

> You wrote me about enrolling the Yaminites. The Yaminites are
> not suitable for enrolling. Should you do so, when their kin of the
> Rabbean clan who now are on the other bank of the river, in the
> land of Yamhad, hear about that, they will give them grief and will

---

205. For the following events, see Charpin and Ziegler 2003: 103–144.

not come back here to their land. Do not enroll them, but give them a strict order. This is the order you should give them: "The king is going on a campaign. All must assemble down to every last one. Any sheikh whose troop is not complete, omitting even one man, will have committed an offense against the king."[206]

However, in the second half of 1776 BC, disorder regained momentum in the northern Jezirah. The archives of Ašnakkum stopped recording events in the late summer when the city must have been lost to insurgents. In 1775 BC, turmoil continued all over the kingdom. Self-proclaimed kings seized power in several cities. These crises must have been at least partly due to Samsi-Addu's illness. The septuagenarian king died in the late summer or early autumn of 1775 BC.

15.4.3. Mari under Zimri-Lim, 1774–1761 BC

Zimri-Lim was the son of Hadni-Addu, a close relative of Yahdun-Lim. Zimri-Lim was never mentioned in any texts from Yahdun-Lim's and Sumu-Yamam's reigns, yet he must have been a teenager or even older when Samsi-Addu conquered Mari: some fifteen years later, Zimri-Lim was the father of several daughters of marriageable age.

During the fifteen years of Samsi-Addu's control of Mari, Zimri-Lim lived in exile. We do not know where exactly he had taken refuge. However, his ties with Yamhad shortly before and after his accession suggest that he lived in either Yamhad or in one of its vassal states. When the Kingdom of Upper Mesopotamia was falling apart, joint troops of Mari emigrants, Sim'alite nomads, and Yamhad began an offensive to install Zimri-Lim on the throne of Mari.[207] In the summer of 1775 BC, Zimri-Lim's troops entered Tuttul. Dur-Yasmah-Addu fell in the early autumn. Yasmah-Addu's letters report sieges of Saggaratum, Terqa,

---

206. ARM 1: no. 6: ll. 6–19.

207. The reconstruction of Zimri-Lim's rise to power is based on Charpin and Ziegler 2003: 175–186, with updates in Guichard and Ziegler 2004; Charpin 2012b; Guichard 2014a: 107–122; 2017.

Ṣuprum, and finally Mari itself. These letters must have been intercepted by Zimri-Lim's troops and brought back to Mari after its seizure. In the east, Išme-Dagan had renewed his father's alliances with Ešnunna and Babylon and planned to send troops to rescue his brother. However, Ešnunna switched sides almost immediately, when Babylon's aid proved insufficient. Late in 1775 BC, a few months after Samsi-Addu's death, Zimri-Lim's vanguards seized Mari. Yasmah-Addu did not have time to evacuate his treasury, harem, or archives. As to his own fate, several texts state that Yasmah-Addu "went out of Mari." He must have died in the course of these events or soon thereafter, as he ceased to be mentioned in any sources.

Following his vanguards by a few weeks, Zimri-Lim entered Mari in early 1774 BC. A couple of weeks later, he was enthroned as the king of Mari in Terqa, the city of Dagan.[208] A Sim'alite nomad called Bannum played a decisive role in the seizure of Mari for Zimri-Lim, allowing him to add the title "restorer of Yahdun-Lim's offspring" to his seal.[209] At the same time, Zimri-Lim's troops defeated Išme-Dagan in the Sinjar plain. Further east, Ešnunna was besieging Išme-Dagan's southernmost fortress Šitullum. Babylonians fought in Suhum on Išme-Dagan's side, but soon Suhum was conquered by Zimri-Lim's troops. In contrast to his brother Yasmah-Addu, we will encounter Išme-Dagan again.

When Mari was seized, a number of Yasmah-Addu's servants fled to the east, while others were taken captive. Some kept the offices they had held under Yasmah-Addu, or even made careers. This situation provoked Bannum to address some invective toward Zimri-Lim, as in the following:

> Asqudum, my captive, conceived untoward things in his heart and appointed to offices servants who will not strain themselves for my lord and the Sim'alites. I know that this man's mind is set

---

208. On the importance of Terqa for the royal ideology of Yahdun-Lim and Zimri-Lim, see Charpin and Ziegler 2003: 179.

209. Frayne 1990: no. 6.8.2004. On Bannum, who died a year after the seizure of Mari, see Charpin and Ziegler 2003: 144, 176.

to evil and he talks to my lord about untoward things with evil intentions. It is former servants of Išme-Dagan that he appointed to offices. When Išme-Dagan learns this, he will be very glad, thinking: "My former servants hold offices, they will provide for the reversion of this country and this will not cost me a piece of bread."[210]

Zimri-Lim's rise to power fits into the larger context of the restoration of local dynasties throughout the territory of Samsi-Addu's now disintegrating realm. In early 1774 BC, Išme-Dagan controlled only Ekallatum and its environs, while his servants defended enclaves in the Khabur triangle, such as Šubat-Enlil and Kahat. A number of new petty kingdoms, some of them ruled by heirs of local dynasties and some by usurpers, emerged in the North Jezirah. The kings of Andarig, Burundum, and Hanzat defeated Samsi-Addu's local governors in the Sinjar plain, Idamaraṣ, and Zalmaqum. Chieftains of the Yaminites living on the Middle Euphrates also claimed a royal status. Shortly after his accession to the throne of Mari, Zimri-Lim sent a circular letter to several kings of the northern Jezirah:[211]

The whole land returned to my side,[212] and everybody ascended to the throne of his father's house. I heard it said, "The whole land of Idamaraṣ, whoever is holding fortresses, heeds only to Zimri-Lim." Now then, write me and I will come to take a sacred oath for you. Hand over a city to me and I shall give it to its owner. You with your belongings, I will set you up wherever you say.

---

210. ARM 26/1: no. 5: ll. 28–42.

211. Two unsent copies of the letter have survived in the Mari archives: Durand 1997–2000: no. 247 (of which ll. 4–20 are quoted here) and ARM 28: no. 148 (badly damaged). The other copies of the letter must have been sent to their recipients.

212. ARM 28: no. 148 has "to its (hereditary) allotments" instead of "to my side."

Zimri-Lim did help some local rulers gain power,[213] partly in exchange for their military support of his own accession. Ibal-Addu, an aspirant to the throne of Ašlakka, was among those who fought on Zimri-Lim's side in 1775 BC, and Zimri-Lim helped him to acquire power in Ašlakka, but only four years later (see further discussion later in this section). However, at that time Zimri-Lim was a *primus inter pares* rather than the suzerain of petty kings. The new rulers of the northern Jezirah and the Middle Euphrates were considered Zimri-Lim's "brothers." Two of them, the king of Burundum and the chieftain of Mišlan, married Zimri-Lim's sisters. The kings of Yamhad and Ešnunna had the status of Zimri-Lim's "fathers."

After Zimri-Lim's position in Mari had been secured, he made the unheard-of move of changing his patronym to "the son of Yahdun-Lim," most likely in order to claim continuity between the two kingdoms. Indeed, Zimri-Lim's reign looks like a reiteration of that of Yahdun-Lim. Thus, Zimri-Lim's title was "the king of Mari and the land of Hana," while in letters he was often referred to as the king of the Sim'alites. This means that he, like Yahdun-Lim, wanted to emphasize his power over both a territory, Mari, and a nomad people, the Sim'alites. The heartland of Zimri-Lim's kingdom consisted of Mari, Terqa, and the banks of the lower and middle Khabur, similar to Yahdun-Lim's country. While the administrative structure of Yahdun-Lim's state is poorly understood, we know that Zimri-Lim's kingdom was divided into four provinces: Mari, Terqa, Saggaratum, and Qattunan.[214] The Sim'alite nomads were led by two chiefs-of-pasture (*merhûm*).

The most important difference between the two kingdoms was in their relationships to their powerful neighbor states, Yamhad and Ešnunna. In contrast to Yahdun-Lim, Zimri-Lim relied on an alliance with Yamhad. Aleppo's loyalty cost Mari territorial concessions in the west; while Yahdun-Lim and later Yasmah-Addu controlled the left bank of the Euphrates up to the boundary of Carchemish, Zimri-Lim's territory

213. Durand 1997–2000: no. 281: iii 8–9.

214. For a detailed description of Zimri-Lim's provincial administration, see Lion 2001, with updates in Ziegler 2011.

reached only as far as Halabit. Tuttul, Emar, and Abattum became buf-
fer states. Tuttul was a vassal of Mari, while Emar "paid tribute to three
kings."[215] Further up the Euphrates, between Abattum and Carchemish,
Yamhad controlled the two riverbanks, Ahuna on the Balikh being its
eastern outpost.[216] The alliance between Mari and Yamhad was consolidated by Zimri-Lim's marriage to an Aleppo princess.[217]

Ibal-pi-El II of Ešnunna helped Zimri-Lim defeat Išme-Dagan, and
Zimri-Lim acknowledged himself as Ibal-pi-El's "son." However, discord
emerged between Mari and Ešnunna concerning the region of Suhum.
At Yahdun-Lim's time, Ešnunna controlled Suhum, but later the region
was annexed by Samsi-Addu. Zimri-Lim conquered Suhum down to
Rapiqum and refused to restore the status quo ante by ceding the region
to Ešnunna. Nevertheless, relations between Mari and Ešnunna would
remain peaceful for another four years.[218] The status of Suhum within
the Mari kingdom is poorly documented, but it is clear that it was not a
province.[219]

In the spring of 1774 BC, Zimri-Lim went on campaign to the Khabur
triangle.[220] His principal target was Kahat, defended by a garrison faith-
ful to Išme-Dagan. What remained of Samsi-Addu's harem also stayed in
the city. Bannum advised the king before the expedition:

> Previously, Yahdun-Lim, when he would go to that land, would
> give gifts to rulers of Idamaraṣ, and his flocks were secure, there

---

215. Durand 1990: 52 (A.885: ll. 9–10). This probably refers to Mari, Yamhad, and
Carchemish.

216. Charpin and Ziegler 2003: 182.

217. Charpin and Ziegler 2003: 191–193.

218. See also Guichard 2002.

219. There may have been vassal kings in cities of Suhum such as Puzurran, Yabliya,
and Sapiratum: Charpin and Ziegler 2003: 181–182, n. 87.

220. For the events of 1774 and 1773 BC, see Charpin and Ziegler 2003: 186–193.

was neither deception nor transgression. Now then, act in the same way as your father.[221]

For securing the transhumance rights for his flocks in this region, Zimri-Lim had to either buy or to force local rulers into obedience, as Yahdun-Lim had done. Indeed, the kings of Idamaraṣ had been Yahdun-Lim's vassals. When Zimri-Lim seized Kahat, its newly installed king was the first ruler to acknowledge his vassal status toward Zimri-Lim.[222]

In early 1773 BC, Zimri-Lim came to terms with Hammurabi of Babylon. In particular, they jointly decided to install a new king of Kurda (a capital of Numhâ), who was expected to become a vassal of them both. However, upon his accession, the king of Kurda was unwilling to acknowledge Zimri-Lim as his suzerain. The case is related in a letter giving a sense both of diplomatic practices of the time and the political order of petty kingdoms:

> When together with our lord [. . .] we arrived at Mari, we approached our lord with the proposal concerning Simah-ilane: "Our lord should make an effort to bring out Simah-ilane from where he is now [i.e., from Babylonian exile], so that our lord could restore the Sim'alites and the Numha to one single finger that is not liable to splitting. Until our lord brings out Simah-ilane, he should write to Hammurabi as a son." My lord listened to the appeal of his servants, wrote to Hammurabi as a son and brought out Simah-ilane. [. . .] The sheikhs and elders of Numha went and told Simah-ilane: "Why would you write to Zimri-Lim as a son? You should always write to Zimri-Lim as a brother, just as Aštamar-Addu used to write to Yahdun-Lim as a brother." It was at the instigation of the sheikhs and elders of Numha that Simah-ilane wrote to Zimri-Lim as a brother.[223]

221. Charpin and Ziegler 2003: 51, n. 195 (A.1098: ll. 27–30).

222. ARM 28: no. 131.

223. FM 2: no. 117: ll. 5–21, 30–41.

Moreover, the installation of Simah-ilane outraged the king of Ešnunna, who already had a grudge against Zimri-Lim because of Suhum. By that time, a quarrel had arisen between Zimri-Lim and the Yaminite chieftains. Zimri-Lim no longer wished to be on equal terms with them, while they had proven unwilling to accept his superiority.[224] Inspired by Ešnunna's promise of support, the Yaminites rose in revolt. However, Ešnunna's aid never arrived, and Zimri-Lim's troops, assisted by the Sim'alite nomads and his northern Jezirah allies, defeated the rebels in the late spring of 1773 BC. The Yaminite chiefs took refuge in Qatna and Carchemish. The victory over the Yaminites was celebrated in the year name "Zimri-Lim brought in order the Banks-of-the-Euphrates." It was perhaps at that moment that Zimri-Lim took the title "gatherer of the Banks-of-the-Euphrates,"[225] once more following Yahdun-Lim's example.

Early in 1772 BC, Zimri-Lim went on campaign against Šubat-Enlil. The city, in which Samsi-Addu's treasury was allegedly stored, was held by a former high official of Samsi-Addu's state. Seizing Šubat-Enlil was the ambition of both Zimri-Lim and the rulers of surrounding petty kingdoms such as Ilanṣura, Apum, Razama-in-Yussan, Kurda, and Andarig. But the governor of Šubat-Enlil kept these potential usurpers at bay through the payment of ransoms, and the city remained intact.

In the middle of 1772 BC, a new Yaminite mutiny broke out, this time supported by the kingdoms of Zalmaqum.[226] Zimri-Lim was victorious again, and this time the year name celebrating the victory was more explicit: "When Zimri-Lim defeated the Yaminites." Its wording was identical to a year name from Yahdun-Lim's reign.

At the turn from 1772 to 1771 BC, Zimri-Lim received embassies from all over Western Asia, including the "great powers" of Qatna,

---

224. Guichard 2002: 127–132 (A.3274⁺).

225. Frayne 1990: no. 6.12.4.

226. For the period of 1772–1770 BC, our overview is based on Charpin and Ziegler 2003: 193–206, with additions in Guichard 2004; 2017: 92–103. However, the chronology of the events takes into account the suggestions of Arkhipov 2010 and of the edited volume "Nouvelles recherches sur la chronologie des archives royales de Mari," currently prepared by Dominique Charpin.

Yamhad, Babylon, and Ešnunna, dozens of petty kingdoms of the northern Jezirah, and remote lands such as Hazor in the Levant or Huršitum in the southern Trans-Tigris region. When six new rulers of city-states of the Khabur triangle visited Mari, Zimri-Lim inaugurated them as kings, which indicates that his position as the suzerain of Idamaraṣ was now unquestioned.

The city-state of Ašlakka must not have been loyal enough. In the summer of 1771 BC, Zimri-Lim seized the city and installed Ibal-Addu, whom we have encountered before, as the new king. At the same moment, the smoldering conflict between Ešnunna and Mari finally developed into a large-scale war in the northern Jezirah. The beginning of Ešnunna's offensive on the Tigris is described by one of Zimri-Lim's officials:

> My lord knows how full of deceit that house is. I fear that until it captures Andarig, it will keep my lord completely duped. But as soon as it seizes Andarig, it will aim for Kurda. Subsequently, it will cross Mount Saggar [i.e., Sinjar], and the whole land of Subartu will shout "hail, my lord" to it. This house began to behave as did Samsi-Addu: it keeps resetting its frontiers. It seized Ekallatum and moved toward Qaṭṭara and Allahad. Once it seizes a town, it forces it under its control. This house is indeed full of deceit. Now before the burden becomes too heavy to bear and time is up, we must attack it. The Haneans are eager for battle; the rulers of Idamaraṣ are gathered with their armies and are waiting only for my lord.[227]

At this point, Išme-Dagan was no longer in Ekallatum, as he had left the city under the advice of his generals and had taken refuge in Babylon at some point between 1773 BC and the invasion of Ešnunna.[228] After the troops of Ešnunna had seized Aššur, Ekallatum, and Qaṭṭara, the king of

227. Durand 1997–2000: no. 442: ll. 5–28.

228. FM 6: no. 21; cf. Charpin and Ziegler 2003: 198.

Andarig and the rulers of Yussan submitted to Ibal-pi-El II of Ešnunna. Only Karana and Kurda continued to resist. Further north, Ešnunna occupied Šubat-Enlil[229] and invaded a part of Idamaraṣ. In the autumn of 1771 BC, Ešnunna opened a second front in Suhum and was able to advance along the Euphrates up to Hanat. Ešnunna's army included a Yaminite chieftain in its ranks, and the Yaminites attempted to open a third front in the west of the Khabur triangle.

During the first months of the conflict, Zimri-Lim remained in Ašlakka. He was never overtly hostile toward Ešnunna. Zimri-Lim's envoy was able to remain safely in Šubat-Enil while it was occupied by Ešnunneans. The rulers of Idamaraṣ complained to one of Zimri-Lim's generals:

> We had accepted Zimri-Lim as our lord, but now he is at peace with our friends and at peace with our enemies, so we do not understand our lord Zimri-Lim's approach to peace and war.[230]

The kings of the northern Jezirah divided into two hostile camps: those who submitted to Ešnunna and those who had not. Both parties pleaded with Zimri-Lim for help. The king of Mari kept sending messengers to reconcile them, as if their conflict had nothing to do with Ešnunna. Finally, he forced Andarig to join the anti-Enšunna coalition. Soon thereafter, Zimri-Lim's army arrived at the Sinjar plain. No battle took place, but the stand-down of the two armies at Andarig was later perceived as Zimri-Lim's victory. As one Mari general reminded a vassal:

> Do you not know that my lord, without allied troops, ousted the ruler of Ešnunna, a powerful king, from the gate of Andarig? Why do you keep insulting my lord? Do you not know that the

229. Note that before the invasion, the governor of Šubat-Enlil sought help from Ešnunna; see Ziegler 2002: 233; Charpin and Ziegler 2003: 198.

230. Guichard 2017: 93–96 (A.2047: ll. 7–12).

spear of Zimri-Lim and the Hana is stronger than that of all this land?[231]

Most likely, it was the sudden attack on the eastern boundaries of Ešnunna that forced a withdrawal of troops from the northern Jezirah. In early 1770 BC, Ešnunna's troops evacuated Suhum as well. Hammurabi of Babylon seized the opportunity to annex Rapiqum, which had belonged to Mari before the war. In late 1770 BC, after long negotiations, a treaty was concluded between Ešnunna and Mari. The status quo was restored between the two parties: Ešnunna abandoned its territorial claims, but Ibal-pi-El II kept his status as Zimri-Lim's "father." A peace agreement was also concluded between Zimri-Lim and the Yaminites, who finally acknowledged the king's suzerainty and did not revolt for the remainder of his reign.

In the eastern part of the northern Jezirah, Ešnunna's retreat caused a violent settling of scores.[232] Šubat-Enlil was finally plundered. A new generation of kinglets rose to power, and a new local hierarchy was established. The king of Razama headed a suite of several rulers in Yussan. The king of Andarig controlled most of the Sinjar plain and installed a proxy ruler in Šubat-Enlil, supervised by a legate from Andarig whose archive, dating to 1769–1765 BC, was unearthed during the excavations at Tell Leilan (see section 15.2.2). Both of these kings enjoyed the status of Zimri-Lim's "brothers."

Early in 1769 BC, a census was held in the Mari kingdom, as was customary after major crises. Incredible as it may seem, the lists of its entire adult male population, settlement by settlement, have survived almost completely.[233] Together with other data, they make it possible to evaluate the number of Zimri-Lim's subjects at 30,000–50,000 men, women, and children.[234]

231. ARM 26: no. 303: ll. 26′–33′.

232. For the events of 1769–1766 BC, see Charpin and Ziegler 2003: 206–214.

233. The census lists have not yet been published; cf. Charpin and Ziegler 2003: 205.

234. Charpin 2005.

In 1769 BC, Nahur in Idamaraṣ was occupied by Mari troops and was transformed into a military outpost, to ensure dominance over the central and western parts of the Jezirah. Zimri-Lim's main proxy in this strategic region was Ilanṣura, whose king Haya-Sumu accepted his status as Zimri-Lim's "son." A letter from this period says:

> All the kings gathered together in Nahur before Haya-Sumu and spoke in their assembly as follows: "Besides Zimri-Lim and Haya-Sumu, there is no other lord and father. We shall do only what Zimri-Lim our lord will order us."[235]

Ultimately, the hierarchic order established in the Jezirah did not prevent a number of local conflicts, annexations, and coups.[236] In the second part of 1767 BC, Zimri-Lim made a long journey through the Khabur triangle up to the town of Hušla in Yussan. Stabilizing the region must have been one of his objectives, as he deposed a turbulent petty king and exchanged gifts with many local rulers while traveling.

In the summer of 1767 BC, messengers began shuttling between Mari and Elam with an unprecedented intensity. At that time, a conflict was looming between Elam and Ešnunna (cf. chapter 16 in this volume). In the spring of 1766 BC, Mari sent reinforcements to the Elamites and Babylonians who were already besieging the capital of Ešnunna. The city fell a few weeks later.[237]

In the spring of 1765 BC, Zimri-Lim went on a journey to the kingdom of Yamhad.[238] With a company of over 4,000 men, he planned to help Yarim-Lim crush the mutiny of a local king in northwestern Syria. Troops sent by vassals from the northern Jezirah joined the expedition. The journey was also a pilgrimage to Adad of Aleppo. On his

---

235. ARM 26: no. 347: ll. 5–15.

236. Charpin and Ziegler 2003: 208–210.

237. The chronological solution "b" of Charpin and Ziegler 2003: 213 is preferred here.

238. For the events of 1765–1764 BC, see Charpin and Ziegler 2003: 214–228.

way, Zimri-Lim exchanged gifts with several northwestern Syrian kings, including the ruler of Byblos. The farthest point on his route was Ugarit, where the Mari mission met with Cretan merchants.

While Zimri-Lim was staying in Yamhad, seminal events were unfolding in the east. After Ešnunna had been seized by the armies of Elam, Mari, and Babylon, Elam turned against its allies and started an offensive on two fronts: in Babylonia, and north along the Tigris.

The official in charge of Mari during Zimri-Lim's absence received alarming letters from the kings of Babylon and Ilanṣura. The message from Ilanṣura was as follows: "The army of Elam and Ešnunna in its full strength went up to Zimri-Lim's land, into Idamaraṣ. There is nobody to save the land of Idamaraṣ."[239] The invading army included both Elamites and soldiers from occupied Ešnunna. A segment of the troops was headed by an exiled prince called Atamrum, whose home city in the Sinjar plain had been annexed by Andarig. Atamrum began by seizing Andarig, one of the two city-states that dominated the eastern part of northern Jezirah in 1769–1766 BC. The city's ruler fled, and Atamrum was proclaimed king. Then he campaigned against Razama, the region's second political center.[240]

To the northwest, the invasion reached as far as Šubat-Enlil, where an Elamite governor was appointed.[241] Just as in 1771 BC, the northern Jezirah divided into two camps: some local rulers submitted to the Elamites, while others tried to organize a resistance.[242] One of the

---

239. ARM 6: no. 66: ll. 4–8.

240. Several letters contain detailed descriptions of Atamrum's long siege of Razama: ARM 26/2: no. 318; ARM 27: no. 132; Durand 1997–2000: no. 548. While they are an important source for the methods of siege warfare, understanding their technical vocabulary is a challenge for modern scholars.

241. The letters quoting this man's speeches provide a lively idea of his character; some of them insinuate that he was a drunkard: ARM 14: no. 102; ARM 26/2: nos. 305, 306, 310, 311; ARM 28: no. 57.

242. The letters sent to Mari by Zimri-Lim's envoys to Ilanṣura are a particularly good source for these events. They also reveal its king's ambivalence toward both Elam and Mari, his opportunist assaults on neighboring kingdoms, and the mutual hatred shared by his two wives, both daughters of Zimri-Lim: ARM 26/2: no. 301–356; Durand 1997–2000: no. 1226–1230.

Elamite proxies, the new ruler of Ašnakkum, wrote to the neighboring king of Ašlakka with extraordinary hubris:

> I acceded to my father's throne but having been very busy, I have not sent you my news. Now you are my brother, and besides you, I have no brother. I will make peace with any city or king that you take under control. You must not worry. Your throne is yours to keep. Just as I hold in hand Adad and Šamaš, I also hold Elamites and Ešnunneans behind my back.[243]

The division led to violent clashes between the two parties and ended with another generational change among the kinglets of the region. The king of Ašlakka, in response to Zimri-Lim's official who had promised protection against the Elamites and their allies, wrote:

> Sabbuganni of Amaz grasped the hem of your lord, but […] and he did not find a savior. Why did your lord Zimri-Lim not save him? Sammetar of Ašnakkum who had married Zimri-Lim's sister, people from […] packed him in a skin and delivered him to the Elamites. Why did your lord Zimri-Lim not save him? When Zimri-Lim set Yawi-ila for kingship in Talhayum, […] ended him in his own house. Why did your lord not save him? Šubram with his people, who grasped the hem of your lord, Samsi-Erah, a commoner, plundered his house and goods! Why did your lord Zimri-Lim not save him? As for me, you will save me in the same way one of these days. Who has grasped your hem and saved himself?[244]

Zimri-Lim's stance toward the Elamites was similar to his maneuvering during the invasion of Ešnunna. Zimri-Lim acknowledged himself a "son" of the Elamite ruler, while the Elamite governor of Šubat-Enlil returned

---

243. ARM 4: no. 20: 5–16; cf. Durand 1997–2000: I 632–633.

244. Charpin and Ziegler 2003: 222 (A.3194: ll. 11–24).

the compliment by answering as a "son" to Zimri-Lim. Atamrum asked Zimri-Lim for reinforcements for his siege of Razama, while the king of Razama pleaded with Zimri-Lim for rescue from Atamrum. Zimri-Lim eventually chose to help Razama; shortly after his return from Yamhad in the late summer of 1765 BC, he went on campaign to the northern Jezirah. The expedition's details are not documented, but three months later the kinglets in the Khabur triangle had concluded an alliance with Zimri-Lim. A Mari official reported to the king:

> I went to Ašlakka and they fetched for me a puppy-dog and a goat for the donkey-foal killing among the Hana and Idamaraṣ. But I respected my lord: I did not give permission for the puppy-dog or goat. Instead, I myself had them slaughter a foal, the young one of a she-ass, and in this way established peace between the Hana and Idamaraṣ. As far as Hurra—all over Idamaraṣ—the Hana will be sated, and sated people lack belligerence.[245]

Throughout this time, Zimri-Lim had never been overtly hostile to Elam. His disposition changed in late 1765 BC, when long negotiations between Mari and Babylon finally resulted in an anti-Elamite treaty. The alliance was joined by Yamhad and several kingdoms from Zalmaqum and the Sinjar plain. Atamrum also abandoned the Elamite cause, after much maneuvering, having married Zimri-Lim's daughter in the early summer of 1764 BC.[246] Only Qatna and Larsa refused to take part in the alliance, probably due to their traditional rivalry with Yamhad and Babylon. Marshaling his vassals' forces, Zimri-Lim appealed to a Yaminite chieftain to forget about tribal differences, as the Sim'alite Mari ("downstream") and the Yaminite cities ("upstream") were being equally menaced by the Elamites.

---

245. ARM 2: no. 37: ll. 5–18. In this letter, "the Hana" refers to the Sim'alite subjects of Zimri-Lim. The ritual of killing a donkey-foal as part of making a treaty is discussed in section 15.3.4.

246. Charpin 2008.

> May god not bring the wicked enemy to the Banks-of-the-
> Euphrates! May your god and Dagan, lord of the land, shatter the
> weapons of the Elamites! If they do come to the Banks-of-the-
> Euphrates, they will not act as if they were telling the beads of a
> necklace, one white and one black, saying, "That city is Sim'alite,
> and that city is Yaminite." Are they not like a flood on a river that
> evens out the upstream with the downstream?[247]

Meanwhile, the main forces of the Elamites withdrew from the Jezirah,
having left a small garrison in Šubat-Enlil. The decisive battle was being
prepared in the south. All countries included in the anti-Elamite coalition sent troops to Babylonia. In the summer of 1764 BC, the Elamites
were defeated at a locality called Hiritum (see chapter 16 in this volume). Upon their retreat, the Elamites devastated the Tigris valley as far
as Ekallatum. The war ended, and Elam lost its traditional status of the
suzerain of all Mesopotamia.[248]

The Šubat-Enlil garrison was doomed. A letter transmits the words
of its commander:

> "I guard the city for my lord. I will not open the city to anybody.
> If a reinforcement from my lord arrives, I am saved. If not, I will
> be put to death on top of [. . .]. If a hand is laid on me, my lord
> will weep for me." This man does not know that the Elamites
> retreated from Hiritum and left for their country.[249]

It was at the time of the Elamite invasion that Išme-Dagan, son of Samsi-
Addu, reappeared on the scene in a series of events whose chronological
order is difficult to establish. Now he appears as the new-old ruler of
Ekallatum, now as a captive of the Elamites, now as a traitor to Babylon's

---

247. Durand 1997–2000: no. 733: ll. 8–24.

248. A distorted allusion to the Elamite invasion may be preserved in the Bible
(Gen. 14); see Charpin and Ziegler 2003: 226 (with previous literature).

249. ARM 26/2: no. 328: ll. 15–22. Soon thereafter, the city was seized by Atamrum's
troops.

cause, now as Hammurabi's ally at Hiritum, and now as a powerful counselor at Hammurabi's court. We definitely know that soon after the defeat of the Elamites, Išme-Dagan was back in Ekallatum.

Just as happened during their advance, the retreat of the Elamites provoked a wave of coups and annexations in the petty kingdoms of the northern Jezirah.[250] Only rarely could the rulers hold on to power. The king of Šubat-Enlil, who had been obliged to accept Elamite patronage, was killed, and the city came under the direct rule of Andarig. Before the war, Qaṭṭara possessed Karana, while Razama-in-Yamutbal controlled Ekallatum. Now, the new ruler of Karana subdued Qaṭṭara, while Išme-Dagan of Ekallatum conquered Razama. On the other hand, Išme-Addu, the Elamite minion who had seized power in Ašnakkum, did not survive the retreat of the invaders. The new king of Ašnakkum made a pun especially for the occasion in a letter to a Mari official: "Since I cut off the head of Išme-Addu, my lord's enemy, and sent it to my lord, people from Hurra and Šinah came and cut down my gardens."[251]

In the second part of 1764 and in 1763 BC, the Sinjar plain was a battleground between two hostile alliances, Andarig and Karana versus Kurda and Ekallatum.[252] First, all four kings acknowledged themselves to be Zimri-Lim's "sons." Išme-Dagan wrote submissive letters to the king of Mari, who had once been his most bitter enemy. Zimri-Lim's influence in the region had reached a peak, creating a source of worry for Babylon and Ešnunna. An envoy from Mari, sending a report from a large meeting of kings and representatives in a town on the Sinjar plain, wrote:

> Before the donkey-killing and during their negotiation, in front of representatives from Babylon, Ešnunna, and the Turukkeans, in front of the seven kings at his back and all his allied troops, Atamrum forthrightly spoke these words, "Aside from Zimri-Lim,

250. For the events of 1763–1761 BC, see Charpin and Ziegler 2003: 228–245.

251. ARM 2: no. 33: ll. 5'–7'.

252. Letters from Zimri-Lim's envoys to Andarig, Kurda, and Karana describe the events in great detail but may give an inflated sense of the region's importance for Mari: ARM 26/2: nos. 387–442, 510–529.

our father, our elder brother and our guide, there is no other king." As Atamrum was speaking forthrightly in this way, the delegates of Babylon and Ešnunna were irritated and moved away to the side.[253]

However, the Turukkeans raided Išme-Dagan's kingdom from the east. Išme-Dagan asked for help from the kingdom of Ešnunna, which had only partially recovered after the Elamite invasion. Their alliance was concluded in the spring of 1763 BC. With Ešnunna's support, Išme-Dagan not only repelled the attacks in the east, but also became a more powerful threat to Karana and Andarig. The alliance between Ekallatum and Ešnunna outraged both Mari and Babylon. In the summer of 1763 BC, Zimri-Lim set off with an army "to rescue Andarig," as one of his year names says. Išme-Dagan's troops refused to enter the battle. At the same moment, Ešnunna concluded an alliance with Babylon, and Ešnunna's troops were recalled from Ekallatum. In the autumn of 1763 BC, after renewed onslaughts by the Turukkeans and the troops of Andarig and Karana, Išme-Dagan left Ekallatum and fled to Babylon, as he had done at least twice before. Despite his earlier quarrel with Hammurabi, he was welcomed at the Babylonian court and may even have been appointed governor of a city.

In 1763 BC, Mari and Andarig sent reinforcements to Hammurabi who was besieging Larsa (cf. chapter 18 in this volume). The city fell in the autumn of that same year. In the late 1763 BC, Atamrum returned from Babylonia to Andarig with a large Babylonian army, much to Zimri-Lim's annoyance. When, a few months later, Atamrum suddenly died, the king of Mari wrote to an official:

> Atamrum, who offended me when I granted him favors, who kept repaying me evil for good and was planning further evil deeds,— the god has called him to task. Rejoice![254]

---

253. ARM 26/2: no. 404: ll. 13–20.

254. ARM 13: no. 97: ll. 4–12.

Under Atamrum's successors, the kingdom of Andarig grew increasingly subject to Babylon's overt control.

In the Khabur triangle, the year 1762 BC was marked by two military campaigns under Zimri-Lim. In early 1762 BC, Zimri-Lim campaigned against Ašlakka. Its king, Ibal-Addu, had been installed by Zimri-Lim himself eight years earlier and had married Zimri-Lim's daughter.[255] Ibal-Addu's ill treatment of his wife may have been one of the reasons for Zimri-Lim's expedition. Ašlakka was seized in the spring, Ibal-Addu's harem and archives were brought to Mari as trophies, and a king loyal to Mari was installed in the city-state. Eluhut had supported Ašlakka in the war against Zimri-Lim, and later enticed several cities away from the new king of Ašlakka. In mid-1762 BC, Zimri-Lim traveled north again, where he defeated Eluhut.

In the western part of Upper Mesopotamia, Mari's influence reached previously unknown heights. Prior to his death in 1764 BC, the previous king of Carchemish had been on equal terms with Zimri-Lim, while the new king professed himself to be a "son" of the king of Mari. In 1762 BC, the royal court of Carchemish were shaken by fratricide and a palace coup.[256] A letter reports Hammurabi of Babylon's fury at these events:

> A messenger from the son of Aplahanda of Carchemish arrived, asking for songstresses. But Hammurabi answered: "Songstresses are all he needs! He is not a nobleman! Why did he lay hand on a blood-kin?" Hammurabi is very angry about the murder of Aplahanda's son.[257]

In early 1761 BC, Mari was conquered by Babylonian troops. Little of what we know about the earlier relationship between Mari and Babylon foreshadowed this catastrophe. The last overt conflict between them

---

255. The letters of Ibal-Addu's wife to her father Zimri-Lim are full of complaints: Durand 1997–2000: nos. 1242–1250; see also Guichard 2009a.

256. Charpin and Durand 2004b.

257. ARM 27: no. 162: ll. 41–47.

dated to 1774 BC, when Babylon unsuccessfully supported Išme-Dagan against Zimri-Lim, who had just taken power in Mari. Later, the two powers were on good terms, despite a slightly heated territorial dispute in Suhum. On several occasions, Hammurabi addressed the issue of the city of Hit, which then belonged to Mari.[258] A letter reports his "macro-economic" reasoning in the debate:

> The strength of your land is in donkeys and wagons, but the strength of this land is in boats. It is only for its bitumen and asphalt that I desire this city. Were it not so, why would I desire it? I will listen to whatever Zimri-Lim writes in exchange for Hit.[259]

Zimri-Lim never ceded Hit, but the dispute did not prevent Mari and Babylon from making a military alliance against Elam in 1765 BC and against Larsa in 1763 BC. In 1762 BC, Hammurabi put an end to Ešnunna's independence (cf. chapter 18 in this volume). Zimri-Lim may have supported Ešnunna at this time, to himself avoid a one-on-one conflict with Babylon. However, this was exactly what happened; Mari inevitably became Hammurabi's next target.

The Mari archives end abruptly in the early spring of 1761 BC. Mari texts contain no mention whatsoever of the Babylonian onslaught, nor do they have any information regarding Zimri-Lim's fate.[260] We learn about the seizure of Mari from one of Hammurabi's year names:

> Hammurabi [. . .] overthrew in battle the army of Mari and Malgium, subjugated Mari and its settlements and the various cities of the mountainous land of Subartu, such as Ekallatum, all of Burundum and the land of Zalmaqum, from the Euphrates up

---

258. Charpin and Ziegler 2003: 202, 208, 221.

259. ARM 26/2: no. 468: ll. 21′–26′.

260. For possible scenarios, see Sasson 1998: 460–461; cf. most recently Rutz and Michalowski 2016.

to the banks of the Tigris, and made them dwell under his command in friendship.[261]

This year name indicates that during the same campaign, Hammurabi defeated the troops from several city-states of the northern Jezirah, some of which might have come to rescue Mari.

The Babylonian military remained in the palace of Mari for a year and a half. They left behind a few lists of soldiers and several clay labels inscribed "letters of Samsi-Addu's servants" and "letters of Zimri-Lim's servants."[262] The labels had been attached to coffers containing thousands of letters. As was customary at that time, the invaders intended to bring the tablets back to Babylon as trophies. We do not know why these coffers remained in Mari. Many other letters may have been taken away.[263] In 1759 BC, the palace was set on fire and abandoned for good.

15.5. Local histories between Babylon and Aleppo, 1761–ca. 1600 BC

15.5.1. The sources

For the period between 1761 and ca. 1600 BC, we do not have a text corpus that would give us a panoramic view of the entirety of Upper Mesopotamia and the Levant, as the Mari archives have done for the previous forty years. However, several medium-size royal and private archives, as well as archaeological evidence, give us insight into the history of several kingdoms of this time. The sources also shed light on the region's relations with Babylonia and Yamhad, the two great powers that, after 1761 BC, divided the cuneiform world into their zones of influence.

---

261. Horsnell 1999: 146–149.

262. For the references, see Charpin and Ziegler 2003: 244–245. The site of Mari also yielded a private legal text postdating Zimri-Lim (FM 5: no. 3), but its exact date and place of discovery are unknown.

263. This is deduced from the fact that the Mari archives do not contain letters that we would expect to have found, such as correspondence with Babylon, Yamhad, and Ešnunna from the final years of Zimri-Lim's reign (Charpin 1995).

Some of these archives were either discovered or (re)published only in the past ten years, and this has led to modifications of earlier reconstructions of the history of this period.

In addition to the archives mentioned in the following, isolated tablets dated to this period have also been found at Nineveh,[264] Yakaltum,[265] Al-Kapim,[266] Qal'at al-Hadi (perhaps ancient Šurnat),[267] Lidar Höyük (perhaps ancient Hahhum),[268] al-'Usiya,[269] Oylum Höyük,[270] and Tell Sakka.[271] A couple of year names of Hammurabi of Babylon celebrate his victories in the north after 1761 BC,[272] while his Code provides a glimpse into the extent of Babylonian possessions in Upper Mesopotamia. The clauses of the *mišarum* edicts that refer to Numhâ, Yamutbal, and Idamaraṣ as parts of the kingdom of Babylon must also date back to the reign of Hammurabi.[273] Several year names of his successor, Samsu-iluna, are crucial for the chronology of events in the Middle Euphrates region and in the northern Jezirah.[274] Apart from these, only a few letters shed light on the lands to the north and northwest of Babylonia, in particular the small archive of a Babylonian merchant comprising letters sent from cities such as Emar, Haššum, and Assur.[275] During that time,

---

264. Dalley 2001.

265. von Soden 1982.

266. Mohammad 2002: no. 5.

267. Durand 1987b.

268. Müller 2008.

269. Cavigneaux and Ismail 1990: 405.

270. Donbaz 2014.

271. Durand and Abdallah 2014: no. 1.

272. Horsnell 1999: 155, 159. Hammurabi's expedition against the Turukkeans and the Gutians is mentioned both in a year name and in a few archival texts from Babylonia; see Ziegler 2015a.

273. Charpin 1987: 41–44.

274. Horsnell 1999: 211–212, 220–221, 226.

275. AbB 12: nos. 51–58.

Upper Mesopotamia was the homeland of numerous slaves sold in the Kingdom of Babylon.[276]

15.5.2 Hana: the successor of Mari

We do not know what happened in the Middle Euphrates region during the decade following Hammurabi's campaign of 1761 BC. The entire area must have remained under Babylon's control, since the *Laws of Hammurabi*, composed in the late 1750s BC (see chapter 18 in this volume), mentions both Mari and Tuttul as places in the Kingdom of Babylon. The region is better documented starting from Samsu-iluna's time, in particular by texts found in Terqa.[277]

The Middle Bronze Age levels of Terqa have yielded a few dozen tablets postdating 1761 BC, mainly private contracts and accounting documents, but also a few letters and school tablets.[278] The texts do not mention historical events, but many of them are dated by the year names of six local kings who ruled in succession: Yapah-Sumu-abum,[279] Iṣi-Sumu-abum, Yadih-abum, Kaštiliaš,[280] Šunuhru-Ammu, and Ammi-madar.[281] For

---

276. van Koppen 2004.

277. The following is based on Charpin 2004b: 356–364; 2011.

278. About fifty documents have been published. For the texts from recent regular excavations, see the overview and the references in Masetti-Rouault and Rouault 2013: 600. For the texts from early undocumented excavations, see Podany 2002: nos. 1–9. There are also about 200 unpublished texts dating to the late Middle Bronze or the early Late Bronze Age; see Masetti-Rouault and Rouault 2013: 600–601.

279. A "chief of Hana" named Yapah-Sumu-abum appears in a document from the Alalakh archives: Lauinger 2015: 325–329 (AlT 56: r. 20). He may have been a nomad chief who had stayed in Yamhad before he came to power in the kingdom of Hana; see Podany 2002: 32. His career may well have resembled that of Zimri-Lim a few decades earlier.

280. Note the Kassite name; this Kaštiliaš may be the author of the letter found in Tell Sakka near Damascus that is addressed to a Zimri-Lim, probably the local king: Abdallah and Durand 2014: no. 1.

281. Their sequence has been established by prosopographic data. One or more other kings may have ruled between the reigns of Yadih-abum and Kaštiliaš.

the dating of this dynasty, the main anchor is Samsu-iluna's year name reporting the events of 1723 BC, which mentions a victory over Yadih-abum, the third king of the dynasty.[282] We do not know if Terqa was the capital of the kingdom. The titles of the kings do not appear in texts, but their successors who ruled in the Late Bronze age called themselves "the kings of Hana." The texts from Terqa show that there was no break in the local dynasty at the end of the Old Babylonian period. For convenience, scholars use the term "Hana kingdom" for the earlier period as well.

The territorial extent of the "Hana kingdom" had been another mystery until recently, when twenty-six tablets and fragments were excavated in Ṭabatum on the Middle Khabur.[283] Some of them mention Iṣi-Sumu-abum and Yadih-abum in a context which makes clear that the kings of Hana controlled the city.[284] Additionally, a tablet dated with a year name of Iṣi-Sumu-abum was discovered in Harradum, in the region of Suhum.[285] It means that, at least during the reign of Iṣi-Sumu-abum, the kingdom ranged across approximately the same territory as Zimri-Lim's Mari, comprising a large section of the Middle Euphrates and the banks of the lower and middle Khabur. As well, the continuity between Mari and the "Hana kingdom" was manifest in their shared administrative terminology, contract formulae, units of measurement, and calendar. Moreover, several later "kings of Hana" were named after Yahdun-Lim dynasty rulers, and there are reasons to believe that the capital of the "Hana kingdom" was nothing other than Mari.[286]

---

282. Horsnell 1999: 220–221.

283. Only four of them have been published: Yamada 2008; 2011; 2016. The edition of the entire corpus is in preparation.

284. In the early 1740s BC, Ṭabatum was an independent kingdom: Eidem 2008a: 295. Therefore, the tablets from Ṭabatum must date between 1747 and 1723 BC.

285. Joannès et al. 2006: no. 16.

286. As suggested by Charpin 2011: 51. The archaeological levels of Mari dating to the time after 1759 BC have been destroyed by wind erosion.

After Samsu-iluna's victory over Yadih-abum, Babylonian rule may have been established on the Middle Euphrates for a few years,[287] but eventually the local dynasty returned to power for several decades. A Lower Mesopotamian letter suggests that, at the time of Ammi-ditana, Suhum was under the control of Babylon, while an independent "land of Mari" (that is, the "Hana kingdom"?) was situated upstream.[288] A few unpublished documents from Terqa are dated by the year names of two later Babylonian kings, Ammi-ṣaduqa and Samsu-ditana. This may mean that the region fell back under the control of Babylon, but the details will become clear only when those documents are published.

15.5.3. Šehna: continuity and change in the northern Jezirah

After 1761 BC, Šubat-Enlil is more frequently mentioned by its erstwhile name Šehna. In the "Lower Town Palace East" of the city, royal archives have been unearthed that postdate 1761 BC and coincide with the late reign of Mutiya and the early reign of Till-abnu.[289] One archive is clearly earlier than the other, with a fifteen-year gap dividing them. The earlier archive comprises more than 200 letters, seven international treaties, and over 500 accounting documents, including fragments, dating to the period from 1750–1747 BC. The archive also contains a copy of the Sumerian King List, a surprising discovery.

In the letters, Šehna appears as the center of an independent kingdom called Apum, although the city came under the control of Andarig toward the end of the reign of Zimri-Lim of Mari (see section 15.4.3). The correspondence of the kings Mutiya and Till-abnu reveals a world very similar to that seen in the Mari archives. The

---

287. A year name of Samsu-iluna celebrates building works in Saggaratum on the Khabur in 1718: Horsnell 1999: 226–227.

288. AbB 13: no. 60; see the commentary in Charpin 2004b: 369–370.

289. For comprehensive studies of the archives and references to the text editions, see Eidem 2008a; 2011. The following is based on these works, with the additions of Charpin 2014a: 141–160; 2016a: 148–186.

northern Jezirah had again been divided into dozens of warring kingdoms. In Eluhut and Alilanum, the kings had even survived since
Zimri-Lim's era. The same rules of international relations remained
in force, with a hierarchy of "fathers," "brothers," and "sons"; mutual
oaths of allegiance; and the exchange of messengers and goods. A few
cities in the vicinity of Šehna were either its vassals or its directly governed possessions. Its western neighbor Ilanṣura, which from 1775 to
1761 BC had been the "regional power" dominating the central part of
the Khabur triangle, was the appanage of the crown prince of Šehna.
Kahat further west, Kurda, Andarig and Karana in the Sinjar plain,
and Razama in Yussan were on equal terms with Šehna. A peace
"treaty" between Šehna and Razama has survived. Another "treaty,"
in Old Assyrian, was concluded between Šehna and Assur. The text is
very damaged, but the preserved lines concern the rights of Assyrian
merchants.

The geographic range of the Šehna archives is much smaller than
that of Mari texts and is almost entirely limited to the eastern and
central parts of the northern Jezirah. Among the regions that are not
covered by the documents, the Middle Euphrates is the most con-
spicuous. Apart from the kingdoms of the northern Jezirah, the only
country that is prominent in the texts is Yamhad. During this period,
the kings of Yamhad had emerged as the overlords of the northern
Jezirah. Aleppo's status was similar to that of Mari under Zimri-Lim
some twenty years earlier: the envoys of the king of Yamhad had considerable influence in the courts of the smaller kingdoms, reconciling
warring city-states, and when necessary, calling in troops from their
homeland.

The later archive comprises over fifty accounting documents and
fragments datable to the 1730s BC. At this time, Yakun-Ašar was the
king of Šehna. The texts are mainly records of wine expenditures, but
some of them refer to Šehna's diplomatic contacts with other countries,
Babylon in particular. Their negotiations must have failed because in
1728 BC the army of Samsu-iluna of Babylon devastated the northern
Jezirah and destroyed Šehna. From that time onward, the city was
abandoned.

15.5.4. Qaṭṭara: on the outskirts of the super power

Over 300 tablets datable to the period after 1761 BC were found in Qaṭṭara from various locations in the palace and the temple.[290] About 200 texts, three-quarters of them letters, belong to the palace archives of Iltani. She was the sister of the king of Karana, who had come to power during the time of Zimri-Lim of Mari. In 1765 BC, Qaṭṭara became a provincial city of the kingdom of Karana, and Iltani installed herself in the former royal palace of Qaṭṭara shortly thereafter. Iltani's husband, who was referred to in the Mari texts as the royal diviner of Karana, appears in the Qaṭṭara texts as a high official. The dated documents of the archive belong to 1759–1755 BC, but other texts may be slightly earlier or later.

The texts speak mainly of private affairs, but they also clearly indicate that the city was under the control of a Babylonian general. Karana was the capital of a large district extending from the southeast piedmonts of Sinjar to the Tigris. It may have retained its status as a vassal kingdom for a few years after 1761 BC, but would have become a Babylonian province no later than in 1757 BC. The Qaṭṭara texts also confirm that Babylonians controlled Assur and Andarig. The only independent state in Upper Mesopotamia mentioned in the archives is Širwun in the region east of the Tigris.[291] According to texts from Šehna, by the early 1740s BC, Karana (or Qaṭṭara) may again have been an independent kingdom.[292]

The largest archive found in the temple included 36 letters and some 20 accounting texts, the bulk of which are datable to the 1730s BC. The striking fact about this archive is that its most prominent figure, a certain Ili-Samas, referred to himself as a servant of Pithana, the famous

---

290. Published in Dalley et al. 1976. For a comprehensive study of these archives whose texts are of considerable interest for economic and social history, see Langlois 2017, on which the present section is based.

291. The king of Širwun visited Qaṭṭara (Dalley et al. 1976: no. 82), but later (?) the country was conquered by Qaṭṭara troops (Dalley et al. 1976: no. 72).

292. Eidem 2011: 36–37.

Anatolian ruler.[293] The latest texts from this group date to 1729 BC, the eve of Samsu-iluna of Babylon's devastating northern campaign.

15.5.5. Harradum: a Babylonian outpost

Over a hundred documents were discovered at the site of Harradum in Suhum.[294] Nearly a third of them are letters, and the rest consist of legal texts, including a peculiar contract between the city and its mayor,[295] and a redress (*mīšarum*) decree sealed by Ammi-ditana.[296] The documents were collected in private archives and pay little attention to political events.

However, information from these documents can be used by modern historians to reconstruct the city's history in the period following 1761 BC.[297] Harradum had belonged to Mari during Zimri-Lim's reign and must have been conquered by Hammurabi together with the rest of the Middle Euphrates. A text dated by a year name of Samsu-iluna shows that Harradum was still under Babylon's control in 1744 BC.[298] Another text, bearing a year name of Iṣi-Sumu-abum, indicates that at some moment between 1744 and 1724 BC, Harradum belonged to the "Hana kingdom."[299] Both texts are composed in accordance with Middle Euphrates literary practices and are similar to contemporary texts from Terqa. In 1724 BC, Samsu-iluna reconquered the city and transformed it into a Babylonian military outpost. The bulk of the texts found in Harradum date from 1724 to 1629 BC and are typically Babylonian in form.

---

293. Lacambre and Nahm 2015.

294. Published in Joannès et al. 2006.

295. Charpin 2010a.

296. Charpin 2010b.

297. For an overview of the city's history, see Charpin 2013.

298. Joannès et al. 2006: no. 23.

299. Joannès et al. 2006: no. 16.

15.5.6. Assur: the dawn of Assyria

In the period of the Mari archives (see sections 15.4.2 and 15.4.3), the city of Assur belonged to the rulers of Ekallatum, that is, Samsi-Addu and his son Išme-Dagan. During the reign of Zimri-Lim of Mari, Išme-Dagan's status changed several times from that of ruler of Ekallatum to refugee in Babylon, and back again. We do not know for certain who controlled Ekallatum and Assur around 1761 BC. Hammurabi mentions Ekallatum among his defeated enemies after his victory over Mari. According to the Assyrian King List, a source whose reliability is often challenged, Išme-Dagan reigned in Assur during forty years,[300] and if this is accepted, then Išme-Dagan would certainly have been king at the time of Hammurabi's conquest. Ekallatum may then have been a vassal kingdom of Babylon, as the Code of Hammurabi claims control over Assur and Nineveh. That Išme-Dagan was indeed the king in Assur after the fall of Mari is confirmed by the fact that his son, Mut-Aškur, was included in a non-canonical list of Assyrian rulers as Išme-Dagan's successor.

The two lists of rulers, which are often contradictory, are almost the only sources for the history of Assur and its region during the second half of the eighteenth century and the entire seventeenth century BC. The Assyrian King List affirms that Išme-Dagan was succeeded by several "sons of nobody." Then a native of Nineveh came to power. However, the following rulers were named after Samsi-Addu and Išme-Dagan, their real or ideological ancestors. The kings of the next dynasty were natives of Assur, as their names show. Apart from that, we have an inscription of Puzur-Sin, a ruler of Assur who claimed to have put an end to Samsi-Addu's dynasty, which was "not of the flesh of the city of Assur."[301] As Puzur-Sin is not mentioned in any king list, his regnal dates cannot be determined. Only a few cuneiform tablets from Assur can be dated to this period; they are legal documents that had been kept in later archives dating to the Middle Assyrian period.[302]

---

300. The following outline is based on Yamada 2017.

301. Grayson 1987: no. 40.1001.

302. Veenhof 2008a: 37.

15.5.7. Tigunanum: Babylonian classics in a Hurrian city

Somewhere in the area of the town of Bismil on the Upper Tigris in modern-day Turkey, illicit excavations over the last few decades have yielded a few hundred tablets which once constituted the archive of Tunib-Teššub, the king of Tigunanum.[303] The city of Tigunanum had previously been known from texts from Mari and Šehna. Among the tablets that have been published there are a few letters, including one from the Hittite king Hattusili I. The archive can thus be dated to the last decades of the seventeenth century BC. The accounting tablets that have been published indicate that the majority of the kingdom's population was Hurrian.

Surprisingly, the finds also include a number of literary and scholarly compositions, of which only a few divinatory compendia and reports have been published until now.[304] This demonstrates a demand for the output of cuneiform culture, far away from Babylon in the Hurrian milieu of the Upper Tigris valley. In this way, the finds from Tigunanum can be connected with the interest in the same cuneiform traditions in Hattusa, Emar, and Ugarit in the Late Bronze Age.

15.5.8. Alalakh: a city in Yamhad

For the early and mid-eighteenth century BC, the great kingdom of Yamhad is well documented by the many texts found in Mari and Šehna (see sections 15.4.1–3 and 15.5.3), but no texts from this period have been found within the territory of the kingdom itself. However, we do have an indigenous corpus from later in time.

The excavations of Alalakh have revealed an impressive palace with Minoan-inspired frescoes.[305] "Level VII" of the palace and the nearby

---

303. For a summary on Tigunanum and its archives, see Charpin 2016c, to which add George et al. 2017: nos. 59–63 and the "Lambert folio" texts published on pp. 98–99.

304. George 2013: nos. 17–21, I–XVII.

305. Akkermans and Schwartz 2003: 304–305.

temple have yielded about 300 tablets from several archives. They date from the second half of the eighteenth century to the late seventeenth century BC.[306] Over half of them are accounting texts, while the rest are mainly legal documents. There are also three letters, but they are damaged and of modest interest. The archives belonged to the vice-kings of Alalakh, who were members of the royal family of Aleppo. Though the texts are valuable mainly as sources for economic and legal history, they have allowed scholars to reconstruct the dynastic chronology of both Alalakh and Yamhad, as well as a few historical events.

The Alalakh archives are contemporary with the reigns of six or seven kings of Yamhad: Abba-El, Yarim-Lim II, Niqmi-epuh, Irkabtum, Hammurabi II, Yarim-Lim III, and possibly Abba-El II (the order of the last three has not yet been determined). Abba-El was the son of Hammurabi I, the king of Yamhad mentioned in late texts from the Mari archives and in the Šehna archives.[307] A letter from Samsu-iluna to Abba-El was found in Sippar.[308] This means that Abba-El reigned in the 1740s BC (and possibly later), while the other five kings ruled from the late eighteenth century to the seventeenth century BC. Alalakh was destroyed in the late seventeenth century, perhaps in the context of the Hittite expansion, but the details are unknown.

After a war of succession, Abba-El was acknowledged as the king. He granted Alalakh to his brother and ally Yarim-Lim. After Yarim-Lim's death, Alalakh was inherited by his son and was turned into a vassal kingdom ruled by a cadet branch of the dynasty, whose suzerain was the "great king" of Aleppo. Another vassal kingdom appearing in the Alalakh archives is Tuba, where the crown princes of Aleppo ruled before the accession.

---

306. For an exhaustive study of the Middle Bronze Age texts from Alalakh, see Lauinger 2015 (with references to the previous text editions). For the political history of Yamhad in this period, see also Charpin 2004b: 351–354, 375–381.

307. Two earlier kings of Yamhad, Sumu-epuh and Yarim-Lim I, appear in the Mari archives; see Charpin and Ziegler 2003: 263.

308. AbB 7: no. 1. How this letter ended up in Sippar is not known.

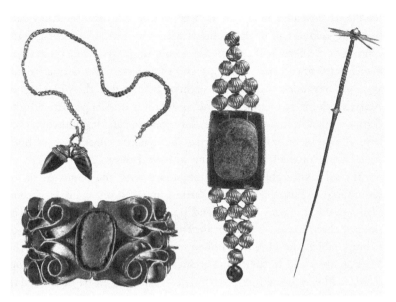

FIGURE 15.6. Funerary objects from the royal tombs of Ebla (Tomb of the Princess and Tomb of the Lord of Goats). Early second millennium BC. National Museum of Aleppo, Syria. Reproduced from Matthiae, Pinnock, and Scandone Matthiae 1995: figs. 387, 392–393, 398, with the kind permission of Frances Pinnock.

15.5.9. Ebla: a last revival

Ebla must have been an important kingdom in the early second millennium BC.[309] Therefore it is surprising that the city is never mentioned in any Mari texts. However, it does appear in the Alalakh archives, which record the marriage of an unnamed king of Ebla and a princess from Aleppo.[310]

The few stray texts found in Ebla itself are roughly contemporary with the Alalakh archives.[311] The archaeological finds from this period include extremely rich royal tombs (figure 15.6) which have yielded, in

309. Morandi Bonacossi 2014: 421.

310. Durand 2018: 356.

311. For the references, see Charpin 2004b: 376, adding Durand 2018: 360–370.

particular, an Egyptian mace inscribed with the name of a Thirteenth Dynasty pharaoh.[312] Tablets, inscriptions, and seal legends from Ebla may mention a few local kings, but the attempts to reconstruct a dynasty have caused controversy.[313] In the late seventeenth century BC, the city was destroyed. The event may have merited a mention, in fictionalized form, in the Hittite-Hurrian Epic of Release.[314]

15.5.10. The Hittite expansion

The history of northern Syria in the last decades of the seventeenth century BC is recorded mainly by Hittite sources,[315] which documented the Anatolian kingdom's growing interest in the regions south of the Taurus mountains (cf. chapter 31 in volume 3). The Annals of Hattusili I report the seizure of Zalwar, the siege of Ursum, the conquest of Haššum, the first clash with Yamhad, and the seizure of Hahhum. Finally, the raids of the following Hittite king, Mursili I, put an end to both Yamhad and Babylon, the two powers that had dominated the cuneiform world for one and a half centuries.

15.6. In conclusion

In terms of universal cultural heritage, the excavations of the Middle Bronze Age layers at Mari, Ebla, and Byblos yielded spectacular architecture and pieces of art, while some of the letters from the Mari correspondence belong to the finest epistolary texts ever written in cuneiform.

For Upper Mesopotamia and the northern Levant, the first half of the second millennium BC can be seen as the first truly "historical" period. Unprecedentedly, the entire territory from the Zagros mountains to

---

312. For the references, see Hikade 2012: 840.

313. Durand 2018: 363–368 (with previous literature).

314. Neu 1996: 479–483; Durand 2018: 357–360.

315. Charpin 2004b: 377–381.

the Mediterranean coast was now occupied by urban, state-level, literate societies that locally produced abundant written records. This made the region an integral part of the wider cuneiform world for centuries to come. The local scribal schools of the early second millennium BC in particular played a key role in facilitating the further spread of cuneiform culture, as it came to flourish in the Late Bronze Age in Emar, Ugarit, Hattusa, and the centers of the "Amarna Age."

REFERENCES

Akkermans, P.M.M.G., and Schwartz, G.M. 2003. *The archaeology of Syria: from complex hunter-gatherers to early urban societies, c. 16,000–300 BC*. Cambridge: Cambridge University Press.

Arkhipov, I. 2010. La chronologie de la guerre d'Ešnunna. *NABU* 2010: 84–85 (no. 73).

Arkhipov, I. 2012. *Le vocabulaire de la métallurgie et la nomenclature des objets en métal dans les textes de Mari*. Leuven: Peeters.

Arkhipov, I. 2019. Who kept records in the palace of Mari, and why? In Wicke, D. (ed.), *Der Palast im antiken und islamischen Orient*. Wiesbaden: Harrassowitz, 35–42.

Arkhipov, I., and Chambon, G. 2015. Pratiques comptables dans le palais de Mari au Proche-Orient ancien (début du IIe millénaire av. J.-C.). In Mattéoni, O., and Beck, P. (eds.), *Classer, dire, compter: discipline du chiffre et fabrique d'une norme comptable à la fin du Moyen Âge*. Paris: Comité pour l'histoire économique et financière de la France, 361–374.

Arkhipov, I., and Loesov, S. 2013. A retrospective review of the letters by Yaqqim-Addu, governor of Saggaratum under Zimri-Lim. *Babel und Bibel* 7: 5–50.

Bär, J. 2005. Die Beziehungen zwischen Mari und Assur während der Šakkanakku-Periode. In Kalvelagen, R., Katz, D., and van Soldt, W.H. (eds.), *Ethnicity in ancient Mesopotamia*. Leiden: NINO, 11–30.

Barjamovic, G., Hertel, T., and Larsen, M.T. 2012. *Ups and downs at Kanesh: chronology, history and society in the Old Assyrian period*. Leiden: NINO.

Battini, L. 2011. The Eastern Tigris region in the first half of the 2nd millennium BC. In Miglus, P.A., and Mühl, S. (eds.), *Between the cultures: the Central Tigris region from the 3rd to the 1st millennium BC.* Heidelberg: Heidelberger Orientverlag, 111–141.

Birot, M. 1974. *Lettres de Yaqqim-Addu, gouverneur de Sagarâtum* (Archives royales de Mari 14). Paris: Geuthner.

Birot, M. 1985. Les chroniques "assyriennes" de Mari. *MARI* 4: 219–242.

Birot, M. 1993. *Correspondance des gouverneurs de Qaṭṭunân* (Archives royales de Mari 27). Paris: Éditions Recherche sur les Civilisations.

Bloch, Y. 2014. The conquest eponyms of Šamšī-Adad I and the Kaneš Eponym List. *JNES* 73: 191–210.

Bonechi, M. 1997. II millennium Ebla kings. *RA* 91: 33–38.

Burke, A.A. 2008. *"Walled up to Heaven": the evolution of Middle Bronze Age fortification strategies in the Levant.* Winona Lake, IN: Eisenbrauns.

Butterlin, P. 2007. Mari, les *Šakkanakku* et la crise de la fin du troisième millénaire. In Kuzucuoğlu, C., and Marro, C. (eds.), *Sociétés humaines et changement climatique à la fin du troisième millénaire: une crise a-t-elle eu lieu en haute Mésopotamie?* Istanbul: Institut Français d'Études Anatoliennes-Georges Dumézil, 227–245.

Cagni, L. 1980. *Briefe aus dem Iraq Museum* (Altbabylonische Briefe 8). Leiden: Brill.

Cavigneaux, A., and Colonna d'Istria, L. 2009. Les découvertes épigraphiques des fouilles récentes de Mari: état des recherches en janvier 2009. *Studia Orontica* 6: 51–67.

Cavigneaux, A., and Ismail, B.K. 1990. Die Statthalter von Suḫu und Mari im 8. Jh. v. Chr. *BaM* 21: 321–456.

Chambon, G. 2009. *Les archives du vin à Mari.* Paris: Société pour l'étude du Proche-Orient ancien.

Chambon, G. 2014. Apišal, un royaume du Nord-Ouest. In Ziegler, N., and Cancik-Kirschbaum, E. (eds.), *Entre les fleuves, II: d'Aššur à Mari et au-delà.* Gladbeck: PeWe-Verlag, 233–238.

Chambon, G. 2018. *Les archives d'Ilu-kân: gestion et comptabilité du grain dans le palais de Mari.* Paris: Société pour l'étude du Proche-Orient ancien.

Charpin, D. 1985a. Les archives d'époque 'assyrienne' dans le palais de Mari. *MARI* 4: 243–268.

Charpin, D. 1985b. Les archives du devin Asqudum dans la résidence du chantier A. *MARI* 4: 453–462.

Charpin, D. 1987. Les décrets royaux à l'époque paléo-babylonienne, à propos d'un ouvrage récent. *AfO* 34: 36–44.

Charpin, D. 1989a. L'akkadien des lettres d'Ilân-ṣurâ. In Lebeau, M., and Talon, P. (eds.), *Reflets de deux fleuves: volume de mélanges offerts à A. Finet*. Leuven: Peeters, 31–40.

Charpin, D. 1989b. Mari et Mišlân au temps de Sumula-El. *NABU* 1989: 76–77 (no. 102).

Charpin, D. 1995. La fin des archives dans le palais de Mari. *RA* 89: 29–40.

Charpin, D. 1998. Toponymie amorrite et toponymie biblique: la ville de Ṣîbat/Ṣobah. *RA* 92: 79–92.

Charpin, D. 2003. La "toponymie en miroir" dans le Proche-Orient amorrite. *RA* 97: 3–34.

Charpin, D. 2004a. Données nouvelles sur la région du Petit Zab au XVIIIᵉ siècle av. J.C. *RA* 98: 151–178.

Charpin, D. 2004b. Histoire politique du Proche-Orient amorrite. In Charpin, D., Edzard, D.O., and Stol, M., *Mesopotamien: die altbabylonische Zeit*. Fribourg: Academic Press; Göttingen: Vandenhoeck & Ruprecht, 25–480.

Charpin, D. 2005. Pour une estimation de la population du royaume de Mari. *NABU* 2005: IV 19–20 (no. 96).

Charpin, D. 2005–2006. Review of M. Streck, Das amurritische Onomastikon der altbabylonischen Zeit. *AfO* 51: 282–292.

Charpin, D. 2008. La dot de la princesse mariote Inbatum. In Tarhan, T., Tibet, A., and Konyar, E. (eds.), *Muhibbe Darga armağanı*. Istanbul: Sadberk Hanım Müzesi, 159–172.

Charpin, D. 2010a. Les pouvoirs locaux à l'époque paléo-babylonienne: le cas du maire et des anciens de Harrâdum. In Dönmez, Ş. (ed.), *DUB.SAR E.DUB.BA.A: studies presented in honour of Veysel Donbaz*. Istanbul: Ege, 41–54.

Charpin, D. 2010b. Un édit du roi Ammi-ditana de Babylone. In Shehata, D., Weiershäuser, F., and Zand, K.V. (eds.), *Von Göttern und Menschen - Beiträge zu Literatur und Geschichte des Alten Orients. Festschrift für Brigitte Groneberg*. Leiden: Brill, 17–46.

Charpin, D. 2011. Le "pays de Mari et des bédouins" à l'époque de Samsu-iluna de Babylone. *RA* 105: 41–59.

Charpin, D. 2012a. Mari à l'école d'Ešnunna: écriture, langue, formulaires. In Mittermayer, C., and Ecklin, S. (eds.), *Altorientalische Studien zu Ehren von Pascal Attinger: mu-ni u₄ ul-li₂-a-aš ĝa₂-ĝa₂-de₃*. Fribourg: Academic Press; Göttingen: Vandenhoeck & Ruprecht, 119–137.

Charpin, D. 2012b. Une lettre d'un roi inconnu: nouvelles données sur le début du règne de Zimri-Lim. In Boiy, T., Bretschneider, J., Goddeeris, A., Hameeuw, H., Jans, G., and Tavernier, J. (eds.), *The ancient Near East, a life! Festschrift Karel Van Lerberghe.* Leuven: Peeters, 91–103.

Charpin, D. 2013. Harrâdum, entre Babylone et le "pays de Mari." In Cancik-Kirschbaum, E., Klinger, J., and Müller, G.G.W. (eds.), *Diversity and standardization: perspectives on ancient Near Eastern cultural history.* Berlin: De Gruyter, 27–48.

Charpin, D. 2014a. Chroniques bibliographiques, 15. le royaume d'Uruk et le pays d'Apum, deux voisins de Babylone vaincus par Samsu-iluna. *RA* 108: 121–160.

Charpin, D. 2014b. Guerre et paix dans le monde amorrite et post-amorrite. In Neumann, H., Dittmann, R., Paulus, S., Neumann, G., and Schuster-Brandis, A. (eds.), *Krieg und Frieden im Alten Vorderasien.* Münster: Ugarit-Verlag, 189–214.

Charpin, D. 2014c. The historian and the Old Babylonian archives. In Baker, H.D., and Jursa, M. (eds.), *Documentary sources in ancient Near Eastern and Greco-Roman economic history: methodology and practice.* Oxford: Oxbow, 24–58.

Charpin, D. 2015a. Le mariage d'une princesse de Qabra avec un prince de Qaṭna. In Marti, L., Nicolle, C., and Shawaly, K. (eds.), *Recherches en Haute-Mésopotamie, II: mission archéologique de Bash Tapa (campagnes 2012–2013) et les enjeux de la recherche dans la région d'Erbil.* Paris: Société pour l'étude du Proche-Orient ancien, 5–12.

Charpin, D. 2015b. Les "barbares amorrites": clichés littéraires et réalités. In Durand, J.-M., Guichard, M., and Römer, T. (eds.), *Tabou et transgressions.* Fribourg: Academic Press; Göttingen: Vandenhoeck & Ruprecht, 31–46.

Charpin, D. 2016a. Les débuts des relations diplomatiques au Proche-Orient ancien. *RA* 110: 127–186.

Charpin, D. 2016b. Quelques aspects du multilinguisme dans la Mésopotamie antique. In Fournet, J.-L., Mouton, J.-M., and Paviot, J. (eds.), *Civilisations en transition, II: sociétés multilingues à travers l'histoire du Proche-Orient.* Byblos: Centre International des Sciences de l'Homme, 11–36.

Charpin, D. 2016c. Tigunani. *RlA* 14: 30–31.

Charpin, D. 2019. *"Tu es de mon sang": les alliances dans le Proche-Orient ancien.* Paris: Les belles lettres.

Charpin, D., and Durand, J.-M. (eds.) 1994. *Recueil d'études à la mémoire de Maurice Birot* (Florilegium Marianum 2). Paris: Société pour l'étude du Proche-Orient ancien.

Charpin, D., and Durand, J.-M. (eds.) 1997. *Recueil d'études à la mémoire de Marie-Thérèse Barrelet* (Florilegium Marianum 3). Paris: Société pour l'étude du Proche-Orient ancien.

Charpin, D., and Durand, J.-M. (eds.) 2002. *Recueil d'études à la mémoire d'André Parrot* (Florilegium Marianum 6). Paris: Société pour l'étude du Proche-Orient ancien.

Charpin, D., and Durand, J.-M. 2004a. Prétendants au trône dans le Proche-Orient amorrite. In Dercksen, J.G. (ed.), *Assyria and beyond: studies presented to Mogens Trolle Larsen*. Leiden: NINO, 99–115.

Charpin, D., and Durand, J.-M. 2004b. "Qu'as-tu fait de ton frère?": un meurtre à la cour de Karkemiš. *NABU* 2004: 32 (no. 34).

Charpin, D., Joannès, F., Lackenbacher, S., and Lafont, B. 1988. *Archives épistolaires de Mari, vol. I/2* (Archives royales de Mari 26/2). Paris: Éditions Recherche sur les Civilisations.

Charpin, D., and Ziegler, N. 2003. *Mari et le Proche-Orient à l'époque amorrite: essai d'histoire politique* (Florilegium Marianum 5). Paris: Société pour l'étude du Proche-Orient ancien.

Charpin, D., and Ziegler, N. 2014. En marge d'Archibab, 14: la séquence des éponymes. *NABU* 2014: 21–22 (no. 12).

Colonna d'Istria, L. 2014. Wool economy in the royal archive of Mari during the Šakkanakku period. In Breniquet, C., and Michel, C. (eds.), *Wool economy in the ancient Near East and the Aegean: from the beginnings of sheep husbandry to institutional textile industry*. Oxford: Oxbow, 167–201.

Dalley, S. 2001. Old Babylonian tablets from Nineveh; and possible pieces of early Gilgamesh Epic. *Iraq* 63: 155–167.

Dalley, S., Walker, C.B.F., and Hawkins, J.D. 1976. *The Old Babylonian tablets from Tell al Rimah*. London: British School of Archaeology in Iraq.

Dercksen, J.G. 2004. *Old Assyrian institutions*. Leiden: NINO.

Donbaz, V. 1999. One Old Babylonian text in the vicinity of Nusaybin. *NABU* 1999: 58–59 (no. 58).

Donbaz, V. 2014. A tiny late "Old Babylonian" tablet found at Oylum Höyük. In Engin, A., Helwing, B., and Uysal, B. (eds.), *Armizzi: studies in honor of Engin Özgen*. Ankara: Asa, 109–111.

Dossin, G. 1950. *Correspondance de Šamši-Addu et de ses fils* (Archives royales de Mari 1). Paris: Imprimerie nationale.

Dossin, G. 1951. *Correspondance de Šamši-Addu et de ses fils (suite)* (Archives royales de Mari 4). Paris: Imprimerie nationale.

Dossin, G. 1952. *Correspondance de Iasmaḫ-Addu* (Archives royales de Mari 5). Paris: Imprimerie nationale.

Dossin, G., Bottéro, J., Birot, M., Burke, M.L., Kupper, J.-R., and Finet, A. 1964. *Textes divers* (Archives royales de Mari 13). Paris: Geuthner.

Durand, J.-M. 1985. La situation historique des *Šakkanakku*: nouvelle approche. *MARI* 4: 147–172.

Durand, J.-M. 1987a. L'organisation de l'espace dans le palais de Mari. In Lévy, É. (ed.), *Le système palatial en Orient, en Grèce et à Rome.* Strasbourg: Université des sciences humaines, 39–110.

Durand, J.-M. 1987b. Tell Qala'at al Hādī. *NABU* 1987: 20–21 (no. 37).

Durand, J.-M. 1988. *Archives épistolaires de Mari, vol. I/1* (Archives royales de Mari 26/1). Paris: Éditions Recherche sur les Civilisations.

Durand, J.-M. 1990. La cité-état d'Imâr à l'époque des rois de Mari. *MARI* 6: 39–92.

Durand, J.-M. 1991. Précurseurs syriens aux protocoles néo-assyriens. In Charpin, D., and Joannès, F. (eds.), *Marchands, diplomates et empereurs: études sur la civilisation mésopotamienne offerts à P. Garelli.* Paris: Éditions Recherche sur les Civilisations, 13–71.

Durand, J.-M. 1992. Unité et diversités au Proche-Orient à l'époque amorrite. In Charpin, D., and Joannès, F. (eds.), *La circulation des biens, des personnes et des idées dans le Proche-Orient ancien.* Paris: Éditions Recherche sur les Civilisations, 97–128.

Durand, J.-M. 1997–2000. *Les documents épistolaires du palais de Mari, vol. I–III.* Paris: Les éditions du Cerf.

Durand, J.-M. 2004. Peuplement et sociétés à l'époque amorrite, I: les clans bensim'alites. In Nicolle, C. (ed.), *Nomades et sédentaires dans le Proche-Orient ancien.* Paris: Éditions Recherche sur les Civilisations, 111–197.

Durand, J.-M. 2006. La date des textes de Hazor. *NABU* 2006: 88–89 (no. 86).

Durand, J.-M. 2008a. *Šakkanakku*, A: Philologisch. *RlA* 11: 560–563.

Durand, J.-M. 2008b. La religion amorrite en Syrie à l'époque des archives de Mari. In del Olmo Lete, G. (ed.), *Mythologie et religion des sémites occidentaux, vol. I: Ébla, Mari.* Leuven: Peeters, 161–703.

Durand, J.-M. 2009. *La nomenclature des habits et des textiles dans les textes de Mari*. Paris: CNRS Éditions.

Durand, J.-M. 2010a. Être chef d'un état amorrite. In Kogan, L., Koslova, N., Loesov, S., and Tishchenko, S. (eds.), *City administration in the ancient Near East*. Winona Lake, IN: Eisenbrauns, 31–58.

Durand, J.-M. 2010b. Un centre benjaminite aux portes de Mari: réflexions sur le caractère mixte de la population du royaume de Mari. In Dönmez, Ş. (ed.), *DUB.SAR E.DUB.BA.A: studies presented in honour of Veysel Donbaz*. Istanbul: Ege, 109–114.

Durand, J.-M. 2012. Le *kispum* dans les traditions amorrites. In Durand, J.-M., Römer, T., and Hutzli, J. (eds.), *Les vivants et leurs morts*. Fribourg: Academic Press; Göttingen: Vandenhoeck & Ruprecht, 33–51.

Durand, J.-M. 2018. Les textes d'Ébla "paléobabylonienne." In Matthiae, P., Pinnock, F., and D'Andrea, M. (eds.), *Ebla and beyond: ancient Near Eastern studies after fifty years of discoveries at Tell Mardikh*. Wiesbaden: Harrassowitz, 345–378.

Durand, J.-M., and Abdallah, F. 2014. Deux documents cunéiformes retrouvés au Tell Sakka. In Ziegler, N., and Cancik-Kirschbaum, E. (eds.), *Entre les fleuves, II: d'Aššur à Mari et au-delà*. Gladbeck: PeWe-Verlag, 233–248.

Durand, J.-M., Charpin, D., Chambon, G., Jacquet, A., Marti, L., and Reculeau, H. 2008. Tell Hariri/Mari: textes. In Briend, J., and Tassin, C. (eds.), *Supplément au dictionnaire de la Bible, fasc. 77–78*. Paris: Letouzey & Ané, 213–455.

Durand, J.-M., and Guichard, M. 1997. Les rituels de Mari. In Charpin, D., and Durand, J.-M. (eds.), *Recueil d'études à la mémoire de Marie-Thérèse Barrelet*. Paris: Société pour l'étude du Proche-Orient ancien, 19–78.

Durand, J.-M., and Marti, L. 2004. Chroniques du Moyen-Euphrate, 3: les documents du Tell Bi'a. *RA* 98: 121–150.

Durand, J.-M., and Ziegler, N. 2014. Les soldats perdus de Karanâ. In Ziegler, N., and Cancik-Kirschbaum, E. (eds.), *Entre les fleuves, II: d'Aššur à Mari et au-delà*. Gladbeck: PeWe-Verlag, 49–64.

Eidem, J. 1992. *The Shemshara archives, 2: the administrative texts*. Copenhagen: The Royal Danish Academy of Sciences and Letters.

Eidem, J. 2000. Northern Jezira in the 18th century BC: aspects of geo-political patterns. In Rouault, O., and Wäfler, M. (eds.), *La Djéziré et l'Euphrate syriens de la protohistoire à la fin du IIe millénaire av. J.-C.: tendances dans l'interprétation historique des données nouvelles.* Turnhout: Brepols, 255–264.

Eidem, J. 2008a. Apum: a kingdom on the Old Assyrian route. In Wäfler, M. (ed.), *Mesopotamia: the Old Assyrian period.* Fribourg: Academic Press; Göttingen: Vandenhoeck & Ruprecht, 267–352.

Eidem, J. 2008b. Old Assyrian trade in northern Syria: the evidence from Tell Leilan. In Dercksen, J.G. (ed.), *Anatolia and the Jazira during the Old Assyrian period.* Leiden: NINO, 31–41.

Eidem, J. 2011. *The royal archives from Tell Leilan: Old Babylonian letters and treaties from the Lower Town Palace East.* Leiden: NINO.

Eidem, J., and Laessøe, J. 2001. *The Shemshara archives, 1: the letters.* Copenhagen: Royal Danish Academy of Sciences and Letters.

Fink, C. 2017. *Obermesopotamien im 2. Jt. v. Chr.: Fundorte und Karten.* Paris: Collège de France; Société pour l'étude du Proche-Orient ancien.

Fleming, D.E. 2004. *Democracy's ancient ancestors: Mari and early collective governance.* Cambridge: Cambridge University Press.

Fleming, D.E. 2009. Kingship of city and tribe conjoined. In Szuchman, J. (ed.), *Nomads, tribes and the state in the ancient Near East: cross-disciplinary perspectives.* Chicago: The Oriental Institute of the University of Chicago, 227–240.

Frayne, D.R. 1990. *The royal inscriptions of Mesopotamia: early periods, vol. 4: Old Babylonian period (2003–1595 BC).* Toronto: University of Toronto Press.

Gelb, I. 1992. Mari and the Kish civilization. In Young, G.D. (ed.), *Mari in retrospect: fifty years of Mari and Mari studies.* Winona Lake, IN: Eisenbrauns, 121–202.

Gelb, I., and Kienast, B. 1990. *Die altakkadischen Königsinschriften des dritten Jahrtausends v. Chr.* Stuttgart: Steiner.

Genz, H. 2012. The northern Levant. In Potts, D.T. (ed.), *A companion to the archaeology of the ancient Near East.* Malden, MA: Wiley-Blackwell, 607–628.

George, A.R. 1990. Inscriptions from Tell al-Hawa 1987–88. *Iraq* 52: 41–46.

George, A.R. 2013. *Babylonian divinatory texts chiefly in the Schøyen Collection, with an appendix of material from the papers of W. G. Lambert.* Bethesda, MD: CDL Press.

George, A.R., Hertel, T., Llop-Raduà, J., Radner, K., and van Soldt, W.H. 2017. *Assyrian archival documents in the Schøyen Collection and other documents from North Mesopotamia and Syria*. Bethesda, MD: CDL Press.

Golinets, V. 2018. *Das amurritische Onomastikon der altbabylonischen Zeit, 2: Verbalmorphologie des Amurritischen und Glossar der Verbalwurzeln*. Münster: Ugarit-Verlag.

Grayson, A.K. 1983. Königslisten und Chroniken, B: Akkadisch. *RlA* 6: 86–135.

Grayson, A.K. 1987. *The royal inscriptions of Mesopotamia: Assyrian periods, vol. 1: Assyrian rulers of the third and second millennia BC (to 1115 BC)*. Toronto: University of Toronto Press.

Guichard, M. 2002. Les relations diplomatiques entre Ibal-pi-El II et Zimri-Lim: deux étapes vers la discorde. *RA* 96: 109–142.

Guichard, M. 2004. "La malédiction de cette tablette est très dure!" Sur l'ambassade d'Itûr-Asdû à Babylone en l'an 4 de Zimri-Lîm. *RA* 98: 13–32.

Guichard, M. 2005. *La vaisselle de luxe des rois de Mari*. Paris: Éditions Recherche sur les Civilisations.

Guichard, M. 2007. Les rois de Tarmanni(we). *NABU* 2007: 72 (no. 57).

Guichard, M. 2009a. Le remariage d'une princesse et la politique de Zimri-Lîm dans la région du Haut Habur. *RA* 103: 19–30.

Guichard, M. 2009b. Šuduhum, un royaume d'Ida-Maraṣ et ses rois Yatâr-malik, Hammi-kun et Amud-pa-El. In Cancik-Kirschbaum, E., and Ziegler, N. (eds.), *Entre les fleuves, I: Untersuchungen zur historischen Geographie Obermesopotamiens im 2. Jahrtausend v. Chr*. Gladbeck: PeWe-Verlag, 75–120.

Guichard, M. 2011. Un David raté ou une histoire de *habiru* à l'époque amorrite: vie et mort de Samsi-Erah, chef de guerre et homme du peuple. In Durand, J.-M., Römer, T., and Langlois, M. (eds.), *Le jeune héros: recherches sur la formation et la diffusion d'un thème littéraire au Proche-Orient ancien*. Fribourg: Academic Press; Göttingen: Vandenhoeck & Ruprecht, 29–93.

Guichard, M. 2014a. *L'épopée de Zimri-Lîm*. Paris: Société pour l'étude du Proche-Orient ancien.

Guichard, M. 2014b. Nouvelles données sur Zalluhān, un petit royaume des bords du Habur d'après les archives de Mari. In Ziegler, N., and Cancik-Kirschbaum, E. (eds.), *Entre les fleuves, II: d'Aššur à Mari et au-delà*. Gladbeck: PeWe-Verlag, 77–108.

Guichard, M. 2014c. Un traité d'alliance entre Larsa, Uruk et Ešnunna contre Sabium de Babylone. *Semitica* 56: 9–34.

Guichard, M. 2015. Une prière bilingue inédite de Mari: l'art d'amadouer son dieu et seigneur, de la littérature à la pratique. In Durand, J.-M., Marti, L., and Römer, T. (eds.), *Colères et repentirs divins*. Fribourg: Academic Press; Göttingen: Vandenhoeck & Ruprecht, 343–375.

Guichard, M. 2017. Chroniques de l'Ida-Maraṣ et autres pays des environs. *Semitica* 59: 87–108.

Guichard, M., and Ziegler, N. 2004. Yanûh-Samar et les Ekallatéens en détresse. In Dercksen, J.G. (ed.), *Assyria and beyond: studies presented to Mogens Trolle Larsen*. Leiden: NINO, 229–247.

Harrison, T.P. 2012. The southern Levant. In Potts, D.T. (ed.), *A companion to the archaeology of the ancient Near East*. Malden, MA: Wiley-Blackwell, 629–646.

Heimpel, W. 2003. *Letters to the kings of Mari: a new translation, with historical introduction, notes, and commentary*. Winona Lake, IN: Eisenbrauns.

Helck, W. 1971. *Die Beziehungen Ägyptens zu Vorderasien*. Wiesbaden: Harrassowitz.

Hikade, T. 2012. Egypt and the Near East. In Potts, D.T. (ed.), *A companion to the archaeology of the ancient Near East*. Malden, MA: Wiley-Blackwell, 833–850.

Horowitz, W., Oshima, T., and Sanders, S. 2006. *Cuneiform in Canaan: cuneiform sources from the land of Israel in ancient times*. Jerusalem: Israel Exploration Society.

Horowitz, W. Oshima, T., and Vukosavović, F. 2012. Hazor 18: fragments of a cuneiform law collection from Hazor. *IEJ* 62: 158–176.

Horsnell, M.J.A. 1999. *The year-names of the first dynasty of Babylon*. Hamilton, ON: McMaster University Press.

Jacquet, A. 2011. *Documents relatifs aux dépenses pour le culte*. Paris: Société pour l'étude du Proche-Orient ancien.

Jacquet, A. 2014. Eluhut, un royaume du Haut Pays: une exploitation des données textuelles paléo-babyloniennes de la base HIGEOMES. In Ziegler, N., and Cancik-Kirschbaum, E. (eds.), *Entre les fleuves, II: d'Aššur à Mari et au-delà*. Gladbeck: PeWe-Verlag, 109–144.

Janssen, T. 2015. Aminum in AKL, MEC und auf den Siegeln seiner Diener. *NABU* 2015: 41–45 (no. 30).

Jean, C.-F. 1950. *Lettres diverses* (Archives royales de Mari 2). Paris: Imprimerie nationale.

Joannès, F., Kepinski-Lecompte, C., and Colbow, G. 2006. *Haradum II: les textes de la période paléo-babylonienne (Samsu-iluna — Ammi-ṣaduqa).* Paris: Éditions Recherche sur les Civilisations.

Koliński, R. 2014. 20th century BC in the Khabur Triangle region and the advent of the Old Assyrian trade with Anatolia. In Bonatz, D. (ed.), *The archaeology of political spaces: the Upper Mesopotamian piedmont in the second millennium BC.* Berlin: De Gruyter, 11–34.

Koliński, R. 2015. The Mari Eponym Chronicle: reconstruction of the lay-out of the text and the placement of fragment C. *Anatolica* 41: 61–86.

Kraus, F. R. 1977. *Briefe aus dem British Museum (CT 52)* (Altbabylonische Briefe 7). Leiden: Brill.

Krebernik, M. 2001. *Tall Bi'a/Tuttul, II: die altorientalischen Schriftfunde.* Saarbrücken: Saarbrücker Druckerei und Verlag.

Kryszat, G. 2008. Herrscher, Kult und Kulttradition in Anatolien nach den Quellen aus den altassyrischen Handelskolonien, Teil 3/2: Grundlagen für eine neue Rekonstruktion der Geschichte Anatoliens und der assyrischen Handelskolonien in spätaltassyrischer Zeit, II. *AoF* 35: 195–219.

Kupper, J.-R. 1954. *Correspondance de Baḫdi-Lim* (Archives royales de Mari 6). Paris: Imprimerie nationale.

Kupper, J.-R. 1983. *Documents administratifs de la salle 135 du palais de Mari* (Archives royales de Mari 22). Paris: Éditions Recherche sur les Civilisations.

Kupper, J.-R. 1998. *Lettres royales du temps de Zimri-Lim* (Archives royales de Mari 28). Paris: Éditions Recherche sur les Civilisations.

Lacambre, D. 2019. Samsi-Addu et la constitution de son empire: nouvelles données. In Chambon, G., Guichard, M., and Langlois, A.-I. (eds.), *De l'argile au numérique: mélanges assyriologiques en l'honneur de Dominique Charpin.* Leuven: Peeters, 513–544.

Lacambre, D., and Millet Albà, A. 2008. Textes administratifs. In Tunca, Ö., and Baghdo, A. (eds.), *Chagar Bazar (Syrie), III: les trouvailles épigraphiques et sigillographiques du chantier I (2000–2002).* Leuven: Peeters, 19–140.

Lacambre, D., and Nahm, W. 2015. Pithana, an Anatolian ruler in the time of Samsuiluna of Babylon: new data from Tell Rimah (Iraq). *RA* 109: 17–28.

Lafont, B. 2001. Relations internationales, alliances et diplomatie au temps des royaumes amorrites. In Durand, J.-M., and Charpin, D. (eds.), *Mari, Ebla et les Hourrites: dix ans de travaux, vol. 2.* Paris: Éditions Recherche sur les Civilisations, 213–328.

Laneri, N., Pfälzner, P., and Valentini, S. (eds.) 2012. *Looking north: the socio-economic dynamics of northern Mesopotamian and Anatolian regions during the late third and early second millennium BC.* Wiesbaden: Harrassowitz.

Langlois, A.-I. 2017. *Les archives de la princesse Iltani découvertes à Tell al-Rimah (XVIIIᵉ siècle avant J.-C.) et l'histoire du royaume de Karana/Qaṭṭara.* Paris: Société pour l'étude du Proche-Orient ancien.

Lauinger, J. 2015. *Following the man of Yamḫad: settlement and territory at Old Babylonian Alalah.* Leiden: Brill.

Lion, B. 2001. Les administrateurs provinciaux du royaume de Mari à l'époque de Zimri-Lîm. In Durand, J.-M., and Charpin, D. (eds.), *Mari, Ebla et les Hourrites: dix ans de travaux, vol. 2.* Paris: Éditions Recherche sur les Civilisations, 141–209.

Marchetti, N. 2008. On the reconstruction of the dynasty of the *šakkanakku* of Mari. *NABU* 2008: 15–17 (no. 10).

Margueron, J.-C. 2004. *Mari: métropole de l'Euphrate au IIIe et au début du IIe millénaire av. J.-C.* Paris: Picard.

Marti, L. 2008. *Nomades et sédentaires à Mari: la perception de la taxe-sugâgûtum.* Paris: Société pour l'étude du Proche-Orient ancien.

Masetti-Rouault, M.G., and Rouault, O. 2013. Terqa. *RlA* 13: 596–603.

Matney, T.P. 2012. Northern Mesopotamia. In Potts, D.T. (ed.), *A companion to the archaeology of the ancient Near East.* Malden, MA: Wiley-Blackwell, 556–574.

Matthiae, P., Pinnock, F., and Scandone Matthiae, G. (eds.) 1995. *Ebla: Alle origini della civiltà urbana: Trent'anni di scavi in Siria dell'Università di Roma "La Sapienza."* Milan: Mondadori Electa.

Mayr, R.H. 2015. A seal naming Hanun-Erra, shakkanakku of Mari. *NABU* 2015: 155 (no. 92).

Michalowski, P., and Mısır, A. 1998. Cuneiform texts from Kazane Höyük. *JCS* 50: 53–58.

Michel, C. 1996. Le commerce dans les textes de Mari. In Durand, J.-M. (ed.), *Mari, Ébla et les Hourrites: dix ans de travaux, vol. 1.* Paris: Éditions Recherche sur les Civilisations, 385–426.

Michel, C. 2010. Deux textes atypiques découverts à Kültepe. *JCS* 62: 71–80.

Miller, J. 2001. Anum-Hirbi and his kingdom. *AoF* 28: 65–101.

Mohammad, A.K. 2002. Texts from Šišîn. *Akkadica* 123: 1–10.

Morandi Bonacossi, D. 2014. The northern Levant (Syria) during the Middle Bronze Age. In Steiner, M.L., and Killebrew, A.E. (eds.), *The Oxford handbook of the archaeology of the Levant, c. 8000–332 BCE*. Oxford: Oxford University Press, 414–433.

Mühl, S. 2013. *Siedlungsgeschichte des mittleren Osttigrisgebietes: vom Neolithikum bis in die neuassyrische Zeit*. Wiesbaden: Harrassowitz.

Müller, G.G.W. 2008. Eine Tontafel vom Lidar Höyük. *AoF* 35: 312–317.

Neu, E. 1996. *Das hurritische Epos der Freilassung*. Mainz: Akademie der Wissenschaften und der Literatur.

Nicolet, G. 2016. *La 'Maison aux tablettes' et l'enseignement à Mari à l'époque paléo-babylonienne* (ca. 1800 av. J.-C.). PhD dissertation, University of Geneva.

Otto, A. 2008. *Šakkanakku*, B: Archäologisch. *RlA* 11: 563–565.

Patrier, J. 2015. Le sceau de Samsî-Addu. *RA* 109: 1–10.

Peyronel, L. 2017. From Ebla to Kanesh and vice versa: reflections on commercial interactions and exchanges between northern Syria and Anatolia during the Middle Bronze Age. In Kulakoğlu, F., and Barjamovic, G. (eds.), *Movement, resources, interaction: studies dedicated to Klaas Veenhof*. Turnhout: Brepols, 197–215.

Podany, A. 2002. *The land of Hana: kings, chronology, and scribal tradition*. Bethesda, MD: CDL Press.

Postgate, J.N. 1973. Tell Taya tablets, 1972–73. *Iraq* 35: 173–175.

Prechel, D., and Richter, T. 2001. Abrakadabra oder Althurritisch: Betrachtungen zu einigen altbabylonischen Beschwörungstexten. In Richter, T., Prechel, D., and Klinger, J. (eds.), *Kulturgeschichten: altorientalische Studien für V. Haas*. Saarbrücken: Saarbrücker Druckerei und Verlag, 333–372.

Reculeau, H. 2018. *L'agriculture irriguée à Mari: essai d'histoire des techniques*. Paris: Société pour l'étude du Proche-Orient ancien.

Richter, T. 2004. Die Ausbreitung der Hurriter bis zur altbabylonischen Zeit: eine kurze Zwischenbilanz. In Meyer, J.-W., and Sommerfeld, W. (eds.), *2000 v. Chr.: politische, wirtschaftliche und kulturelle Entwicklung im Zeichen einer Jahrtausendwende*. Saarbrücken: Saarbrücker Druckerei und Verlag, 263–311.

Rutz, M., and Michalowski, P. 2016. The flooding of Ešnunna, the fall of Mari: Hammurabi's deeds in Babylonian literature and history. *JCS* 68: 15–43.

Sasson, J.M. 1998. The king and I: a Mari king in changing perceptions. *JAOS* 118: 453–470.

Sasson, J.M. 2009. The trouble with Nur-Sin: Zimri-Lim's purchase of Alaḫtum. In Barreyra Fracaroli, D., and del Olmo Lete, G. (eds.), *Reconstruyendo el pasado remoto: estudios sobre el P.O.A. en homenaje a J. R. Silva Castillo*. Sabadell: AUSA, 191–201.

Sasson, J.M. 2010. On the "Išḫi-Addu" seal from Qatna, with comments on Qatna personal names in the OB period. In Dönmez, Ş. (ed.), *DUB.SAR E.DUB.BA.A: studies presented in honour of Veysel Donbaz*. Istanbul: Ege, 243–250.

Sasson, J.M. 2015. *From the Mari archives: an anthology of Old Babylonian letters*. Winona Lake, IN: Eisenbrauns.

Streck, M.P. 2000. *Das amurritische Onomastikon der altbabylonischen Zeit*, 1. Münster: Ugarit-Verlag.

Talon, P., and Hammade, H. 1997. *Old Babylonian texts from Chagar Bazar*. Brussels: Fondation Assyriologique George Dossin.

van Koppen, F. 2004. The geography of the slave trade and northern Mesopotamia in the late Old Babylonian period. In Hunger, H., and Pruzsinszky, R. (eds.), *Mesopotamian dark age revisited*. Vienna: Verlag der Österreichischen Akademie der Wissenschaften, 9–33.

van Koppen, F. 2015. Qaṭna in altsyrischer Zeit. In Pfälzner, P., and al-Maqdissi, M. (eds.), *Qaṭna and the networks of Bronze Age globalism*. Wiesbaden: Harrassowitz, 81–94.

van Koppen, F., and Lacambre, D. 2008–2009. Sippar and the frontier between Ešnunna and Babylon: new sources for the history of Ešnunna in the Old Babylonian period. *JEOL* 41: 151–177.

van Soldt, W.H. 1990. *Letters in the British Museum, part 1* (Altbabylonische Briefe 12). Leiden: Brill.

van Soldt, W.H. 1994. *Letters in the British Museum, part 2* (Altbabylonische Briefe 13). Leiden: Brill.

van Soldt, W.H. 1995. Three tablets from Tell Hammām et-Turkmān. In van den Hout, T.P.J., and De Roos, J. (eds.), *Studio historiae ardens: ancient Near Eastern studies presented to Philo H.J. Houwink ten Cate*. Leiden: NINO, 275–291.

von Soden, W. 1982. Eine altbabylonische Urkunde (79 MQB 15) aus Tall Munbāqa. *MDOG* 114: 71–78.

Veenhof, K.R. 2008a. The Old Assyrian period. In Eidem, J., and Veenhof, K.R., *Mesopotamia: the Old Assyrian period*. Fribourg: Academic Press / Göttingen: Vandenhoeck & Ruprecht, 13–264.

Veenhof, K.R. 2008b. Some displaced tablets from Kārum Kanesh (Kültepe). *AoF* 35: 10–27.

Veenhof, K.R. 2017. The Old Assyrian period (20th–18th century BCE). In Frahm, E. (ed.), *A companion to Assyria*. Malden, MA: Wiley-Blackwell, 57–79.

Villard, P. 2001. Les administrateurs de l'époque de Yasmaḫ-Addu. In Durand, J.-M., and Charpin, D. (eds.), *Mari, Ebla et les Hourrites: dix ans de travaux, vol.* 2. Paris: Éditions Recherche sur les Civilisations, 9–140.

Waetzoldt, H. 2000. Die Eroberung Eluhuts durch Šamši-Adad I. und der Krieg gegen Zalmaqu. In Marzahn, J., and Neumann, H. (eds.), *Assyriologica et Semitica: Festschrift für Joachim Oelsner*. Münster: Ugarit-Verlag, 523–537.

Yamada, S. 1994. The editorial history of the Assyrian King List. *ZA* 84: 11–37.

Yamada, S. 2001. An adoption contract from Tell Taban, the kings of the land of Hana, and the Hana-style scribal tradition. *RA* 105: 61–84.

Yamada, S. 2008. A preliminary report on Old Babylonian texts from the excavation of Tell Taban in the 2005 and 2006 seasons: the Middle Euphrates and the Habur areas in the post-Hammurabi period. *Al-Rafidan* 29: 47–62.

Yamada, S. 2016. Old Babylonian school exercises from Tell Taban. In Yamada, S., and Shibata, D. (eds.), *Cultures and societies in the Middle Euphrates and Habur areas in the second millennium BC, 1: scribal education and scribal traditions*. Wiesbaden: Harrassowitz, 45–68.

Yamada, S. 2017. The transition period (17th to 15th century BCE). In Frahm, E. (ed.), *A companion to Assyria*. Malden, MA: Wiley-Blackwell, 108–116.

Ziegler, N. 1999. *Le harem de Zimri-Lîm*. Paris: Société pour l'étude du Proche-Orient ancien.

Ziegler, N. 2002. Le royaume d'Ekallâtum et son horizon géopolitique. In Charpin, D., and Durand, J.-M. (eds.), *Recueil d'études à la mémoire d'André Parrot*. Paris: Société pour l'étude du Proche-Orient ancien, 211–274.

Ziegler, N. 2004. The conquest of the holy city of Nineveh and the kingdom of Nurrugûm by Samsî-Addu. *Iraq* 66: 19–26.

Ziegler, N. 2007. *Les musiciens et la musique d'après les archives de Mari*. Paris: Société pour l'étude du Proche-Orient ancien.

Ziegler, N. 2009. Die Westgrenze des Reichs Samsi-Addus. In Cancik-Kirschbaum, E., and Ziegler, N. (eds.), *Entre les fleuves, I: Untersuchungen zur historischen Geographie Obermesopotamiens im 2. Jahrtausend v. Chr.* Gladbeck: PeWe-Verlag, 181–209.

Ziegler, N. 2011. La province de Qaṭṭunân à l'époque de Zimri-Lîm. *RA* 105: 5–16.

Ziegler, N. 2014. Akkade à l'époque paléo-babylonienne. In Ziegler, N., and Cancik-Kirschbaum, E. (eds.), *Entre les fleuves, II: d'Aššur à Mari et au-delà.* Gladbeck: PeWe-Verlag, 273–289.

Ziegler, N. 2015a. Kakmum et le Gutium. In Marti, L., Nicolle, C., and Shawaly, K. (eds.), *Recherches en Haute-Mésopotamie, II: mission archéologique de Bash Tapa (campagnes 2012–2013) et les enjeux de la recherche dans la région d'Erbil.* Paris: Société pour l'étude du Proche-Orient ancien, 23–36.

Ziegler, N. 2015b. Qaṭna at the time of Samsi-Addu. In Pfälzner, P., and al-Maqdissi, M. (eds.), *Qaṭna and the networks of Bronze Age globalism.* Wiesbaden: Harrassowitz, 139–147.

Ziegler, N. 2016a. Economic activities of women according to Mari texts (18th century BC). In Lion, B., and Michel, C. (eds.), *The role of women in work and society in the ancient Near East.* Berlin: De Gruyter, 296–309.

Ziegler, N. 2016b. Turukkû, Turukkäer. *RlA* 14: 209–212.

Ziegler, N., and Charpin, D. 2007. Amurritisch lernen. *Wiener Zeitschrift für die Kunde des Morgenlandes* 97: 55–77.

Ziegler, N., and Langlois, A.-I. 2017. *Les toponymes paléo-babyloniens de la Haute-Mésopotamie.* Paris: Société pour l'étude du Proche-Orient ancien.

Ziegler, N., and Reculeau, H. 2014. The Sutean nomads in the Mari period. In Morandi Bonacossi, D. (ed.), *Settlement dynamics and human-landscape interaction in the dry steppes of Syria.* Wiesbaden: Harrassowitz, 209–226.

16

The Middle East after the Fall of Ur

FROM EŠNUNNA AND THE ZAGROS TO SUSA

Katrien De Graef

16.1. Introduction

Throughout the Ur III period (chapter 13 in this volume), interactions between lowland Mesopotamia and the highlands to its east were frequent: both violent, through raids, and diplomatic, through royal marriages.[1] In the second half of his reign, Šulgi of Ur besieged various

---

1. The following abbreviations are used for text editions: ARM 2 = Jean 1950; ARM 3 = Kupper 1950; ARM 21 = Durand 1983; ARM 22 = Kupper 1983; ARM 23 = Bardet 1984; ARM 26/2 = Durand and Charpin 1988; ARM 28 = Kupper 1998; ARM 31 = Guichard 2005; MDP 6 = Scheil 1905; MDP 10 = Scheil 1908; MDP 14 = Scheil 1913; MDP 18 = Dossin 1927; MDP 22 = Scheil 1930; MDP 23 = Scheil 1932a; MDP 24 = Scheil 1933; MDP 28 = Scheil 1939; MDP 43 = Amiet 1972; MDP 54 = De Graef 2005; MDP 55 = De Graef 2006; TS.XIII = Textes de Suse, level XIII: from Roman Ghirshman's excavations in Chantier A, Ville Royale, Susa (unpublished); YOS 5 = Grice 1919; and YOS 14 = Simmons 1978. The abbreviation CDLI refers to the Cuneiform Digital Library Initiative online resource: http://cdli.ucla.edu (last accessed October 20, 2019) while the abbreviation ZL refers to a regnal year of Zimri-Lim of Mari (e.g., ZL 9-vii-8 stands for the eighth day of the seventh month of Zimri-Lim's ninth regnal year).

Katrien De Graef, *The Middle East after the Fall of Ur* In: *The Oxford History of the Ancient Near East.* Edited by: Karen Radner, Nadine Moeller, and D. T. Potts, Oxford University Press. © Oxford University Press 2022. DOI: 10.1093/oso/9780190687571.003.0016

eastern territories in the western flanks of the Zagros Mountains, among them Simurrum and Lullubum, which eventually became part of the periphery of his realm.[2] The same goes for cities in the eastern plains such as Ešnunna in the Diyala valley and Susa in the Susiana plain: these were fully integrated into the kingdom of Ur, as shown by the use of Ur III year names in local contracts and the building activities in both cities of the rulers of Ur.[3] This chapter deals with these regions once they eschewed Ur's control.

Ešnunna, Simurrum, Lullubum, and Susa regained their independence well before the final collapse of the kingdom of Ur. At Ešnunna and Susa, this happened around the third year of the reign of Ibbi-Sin of Ur, or shortly thereafter, where the last Ur III year names used are Ibbi-Sin's Year 2 and 3, respectively.[4] The same seems to apply for Simurrum and Lullubum. Simurrum may already have declared its independence under Šu-Sin and Ibbi-Sin's campaign, mentioned in his third year name,[5] might have been Ur's final but unsuccessful attempt to regain control of this area,[6] the failure of which eventually resulted in the loss of Ur's northeastern provinces. A similar pattern can be observed for Lullubum. Later copies of the inscriptions on three statues of Šu-Sin of Ur show that Lullubum was in some way involved in the Šimaškian revolt against Šu-Sin at the end of his reign, as one of the governors taken captive by Šu-Sin was Waburtum, governor of Lullubum.[7] A tablet dated to Ibbi-Sin's reign found at Tell Brusti near Tell Shemshara reveals that Bitwata, located in what is generally believed to have been the Lullubum

---

2. Biggs 1997; Sallaberger 1999: 142–143; Frayne 2011: 509–510.

3. Steinkeller 1991; 1999: 151, 157, 170, 208–210.

4. Wu 1994: 2; Sallaberger 1999: 208–210; De Graef 2015: 293.

5. "Year: Ibbi-Sin the king destroyed Simurrum" (mu ^{d}*i-bi-*^{d}EN.ZU lugal uri$_2^{ki}$-ma-ke$_4$ *si-mu-ru-um*^{ki} mu-hul).

6. Walker 1985: 225.

7. Frayne 1990: 312.

homeland, was still under Ur III administration in the early years of that ruler's rule.[8]

The disintegration of the kingdom of Ur under its last king Ibbi-Sin gave way to the emergence and expansion of local powers in the region east of the Tigris, leading to the formation of rival polities (figure 16.1 a–c). This world of inter-Zagros conflicts remains largely undocumented, as our texts primarily deal with lowland-highland encounters. However, a few royal inscriptions have been preserved belonging to two of these rival kingdoms, Simurrum and Lullubum—sporadically attested at Mari, Ešnunna, and in other texts from lowland states—which provide some insight into the development and also interrelationships between these mountain polities.

The subjects of the present chapter are, on the one hand, the two Zagros kingdoms Simurrum and Lullubum and, on the other hand, the great cities of Ešnunna and Susa, both centers of very influential states of the early second millennium BC. In this chapter, we will follow the course of the Diyala upstream to first reach Ešnunna (section 16.2) and then, further up in the increasingly higher altitudes of the western flanks of the Zagros Mountains, the rival kingdoms of Simurrum (section 16.3) and Lullubum (section 16.4), before we change our location to reach the lowlands of southwestern Iran and to visit the ancient city of Susa at the heart of the vast Susiana plain (section 16.5).

16.2. The kingdom of Ešnunna

Located in the lower Diyala valley, Ešnunna was the capital of a province of the kingdom of Ur under Šu-Sin, whose governor, Ituriya, built a temple adjacent to his palace there.[9] The city regained its independence in the third year of Šu-Sin's successor, Ibbi-Sin.[10] Apart from the fifty-five

---

8. Shaffer and Wasserman 2003: 39.

9. Reichel 2001a; 2001b; 2008; 2018.

10. The latest Ur III text excavated at Ešnunna dates to the ninth month of the third year of Ibbi-Sin (= As. 30: T. 290; Whiting 1987b: 33, n. 3; Reichel 2018: 37–38); the texts mentioning Abilulu, who continued to work as a temple administrator

letters published by Robert Whiting,[11] most of the ca. 1,400 tablets
found in Ešnunna's palace and Šu-Sin's temple during the American excavations of the 1930s[12] remain still unpublished. Nevertheless, thanks to
synchronisms with Babylonian and/or Upper Mesopotamian rulers (cf.
chapters 14 and 15 in this volume), a relative chronology of the rulers of
Ešnunna can be pieced together.[13]

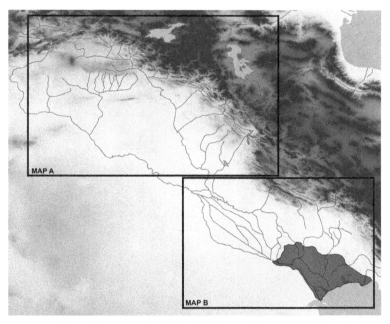

FIGURE 16.1A. Sites mentioned in this chapter. Prepared by Andrea Squitieri
(LMU Munich).

---

after Ešnunna gained its independence, show that the cult of Šu-Sin was defunct
by the ninth month of the third year of Ibbi-Sin: Reichel 2018: 37–38.

11. Whiting 1987a.

12. Frankfort, Lloyd, and Jacobsen 1940: 1.

13. Frankfort, Lloyd, and Jacobsen 1940: 159–200; Frayne 1990: 484–592;
1997b: 433–438; Reichel 2001a: 16.

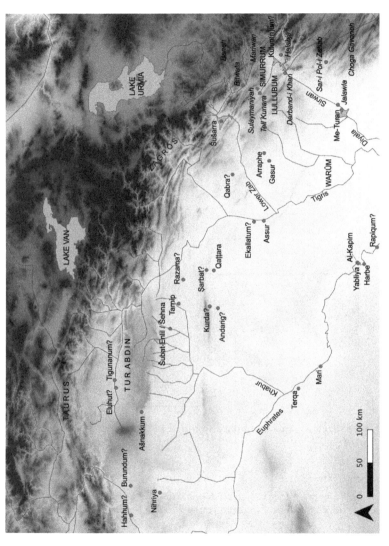

FIGURE 16.1B. Detail map A.

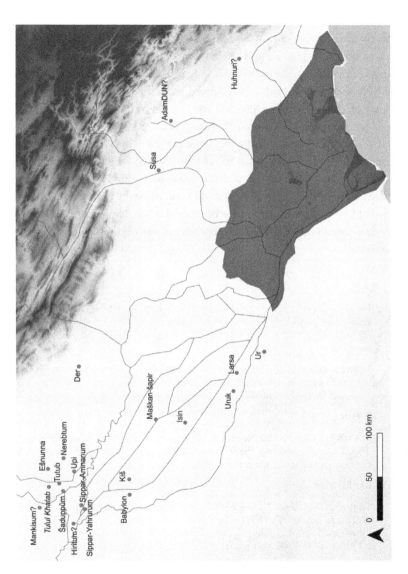

FIGURE 16.1C. Detail map B.

16.2.1. The transitional phase after the end of the kingdom of Ur (ca. 2026–1980 BC)

Early in the reign of Ibbi-Sin, the kingdom of Ur was already showing signs of disintegration, and at that time, Šu-iliya, son of the local governor Ituriya, proclaimed himself king of Ešnunna.[14] In the inscriptions on his seal and the seals of his subordinates, he is called "Mighty king, king of the land of Warûm, and son [or beloved] of the god Tišpak," the patron deity of Ešnunna.[15] Šu-iliya's name is always written with the divine determinative,[16] implying some continuity with the royal ideology of the Ur III period,[17] notwithstanding the switch from Sumerian to Akkadian, both as an administrative language and in personal names. The cult in honor of the new ruler of Ešnunna locally replaced that of Šu-Sin of Ur.[18] Five year names have been attributed to Šu-iliya,[19] who seems to have maintained good relations with his southern neighbor Išbi-Erra of Isin.[20]

---

14. For an in-depth study of the transition between the Ur III dynasty and the Old Babylonian period, see Reichel 2001a; 2001b; 2003; 2008; 2018, who integrated the archaeological and textual data of the sealings found in the palace and temple complex.

15. Frayne 1997b: 435–437; but see also Reichel 2001b; 2008; 2018. Note the Elamite names of two of his subordinates, Šilha and Attaya. For the god Tišpak, see Stol 2016, and for the land of Warûm, see Schrakamp 2016.

16. Whiting 1977.

17. Wu 1994: 2 suggests that Šu-iliya might have been deified as "son" of the deity Tišpak when he took over the governing of Ešnunna from his elderly father while the city was still under the control of the kingdom of Ur.

18. Reichel 2018: 38–39.

19. Saporetti 2013: 46–50 (I1A–I1E). Wu 1994: 5 lists six year names (Years a–f), but his Year f is attributed to Kirikiri by Saporetti 2013: 71 (I4B), following Frankfort, Lloyd, and Jacobsen 1940: 173. Note, however, that Saporetti 2013: 51–58 (I2A–I2E) lists another five year names that belong either to Šu-iliya or his successor Nur-ahum.

20. The unpublished tablet 1931-T148, with a year name attributed to Šu-iliya, mentions a gift from Išbi-Erra: Whiting 1987a: 115. Note that Wu 1994: 5 interpreted it as a gift to Išbi-Erra.

It is possible that a "Subarean" invasion, i.e., incursions by vaguely defined forces from the North Jezirah, ended Šu-iliya's reign, after which Išbi-Erra defeated these enemy troops and installed one Nur-ahum on the throne.[21] This intervention would have marked a decrease in Ešnunna's political power. From then on, the city god Tišpak was considered king, and Ešnunna's rulers merely his governors.[22] At the same time, Ešnunna entered into a series of diplomatic marriages with the Amorites: Nur-ahum married his daughter to Ušašum, son of the Amorite chief Abda-el,[23] and Abda-el married his daughter to Bilalama, son of Nur-ahum's successor, Kirikiri.[24] Kirikiri had a seal, originally belonging to a previous governor of Ešnunna (possibly Nur-ahum), recut for his son Bilalama.[25]

The end of Nur-ahum's reign is linked to a fire that destroyed the northwestern wing of the Šu-Sin temple.[26] This strongly suggests that the transition of power from Nur-ahum to Kirikiri was not smooth.

---

21. Both the defeat of the Subareans and the (re)installation of Nur-ahum are mentioned in a literary letter by Puzur-Numušda to Ibbi-Sin: Michalowski 2011: 439–462. The defeat of the Subareans is also commemorated in two year names known from the Ešnunna tablets. These have been attributed to Nur-ahum by Frankfort, Lloyd, and Jacobsen 1940: 170–171, no. 42–43. Nur-ahum could have been ousted by the Subareans and reinstalled by Išbi-Erra of Isin: Reichel 2003: 359. For "Subartu" and "Subareans" in the Old Babylonian sources, see Ziegler and Langlois 2017: 341–342.

22. E.g., "Nur-ahum, beloved of Tišpak, governor of Ešnunna"; see Frayne 1990: 485–488. An institutional evolution parallel to that of Ešnunna can also be observed at the city of Assur, where the local deity Aššur delegated his power to the local ruler, and at Der, whose patron deity Ištaran was represented by a governor: Charpin 2004: 64–68.

23. Nur-ahum granted a seal to his son-in-law on this occasion: Frayne 1990: 485–486.

24. This supposed "daughter exchange" led some scholars to assume that Nur-ahum and Kirikiri were brothers: Whiting 1987a: 27, followed by Charpin 2004: 64–68. However, Reichel 2003: 360–364 has shown this to be improbable.

25. Reichel 2003: 357; the seal's inscription reads: ^{d}*Tišpak* lugal *da-núm* lugal *ma-at wa-ri-im ki-ri-ki-ri* ensí áš-nun-na^{ki} *a-na bi-la-la-ma* dumu.ni-*šu i-qi₄-iš.*

26. Reichel 2003: 364–368.

Even more indicative of a dynastic break is the fact that the names of Kirikiri and his son Bilalama are Elamite.[27] However, the alliance with the Amorites was continued by Kirikiri, who married his son to Abda-el's daughter. Moreover, Ušašum, son-in-law of his predecessor Nur-ahum, wrote a letter to Kirikiri, in which Ušašum refers to Kirikiri as his "brother," viz. his (political) equal.[28]

Whereas Kirikiri's reign was probably short-lived,[29] his son and successor Bilalama reigned for at least twenty years.[30] His reign overlapped in part with those of Išbi-Erra and Šu-ilišu of Isin, and Tan-Ruhurater of Susa. Two royal inscriptions and the seals of five of his servants are known.[31] His reign was characterized by swiftly changing relations with the Amorites, but his rapport with Elam was good. At Ešnunna, he rebuilt the Esikil temple of Tišpak and added a new wing to the palace, as commemorated in a royal inscription.[32] The cella of the old temple dedicated to the cult of Šu-Sin, the deified king of Ur, however, became

---

27. It is not clear how long Nur-ahum reigned before Kirikiri took power and established a new dynasty. Saporetti 2013: 61–67 (I3A–I3D) attributed four year names to him, as does Wu 1994: 7 (a–c, h) who, however, adds a further four year names possibly to be attributed to Nur-ahum (d–g), resulting in a total of eight year names; these four years are attributed to Bilalama by Saporetti 2013: 96–100 (I6A–I6D). Note, however, that Saporetti 2013: 51–58 (I2A–I2E) listed another five year names as belonging to either Nur-ahum or his predecessor Šu-iliya.

28. Whiting 1987a: no. 11. Although Whiting 1987a: 48 suggested that the term *ahum* here signified "kinsman" rather than "brother" or "political equal," this is unlikely.

29. Saporetti 2013: 69–72 (I4A–I4B) attributed two year names to Kirikiri. Wu 1994: 12 lists only one year name with certainty (a = Saporetti's I4A) but adds another eight year names as possibly attributable to Kirikiri (b–i).

30. Frayne 1990: 491; Charpin 2004: 66. Saporetti 2013: 78–95 (I5A–I5K) attributed eleven year names to Bilalama, but added fifteen more to be placed around the reign of Bilalama: Saporetti 2013: 96–118 (I6A–I6O). Wu 1994: 18–19 attributed nine year names to Bilalama with certainty (a–h and j), adding two year names as possibly to be attributed to him (i and k) and listing another seven year names to be placed during the reigns from Bilalama to Urninmarki.

31. Frayne 1990: 491–492, 495–498.

32. Frayne 1990: 492.

a palace chancellery.[33] It was probably his brother-in-law Ušašum, son of Abda-el,[34] who informed him of the death of his father, the chief of the Amorites, and asked him for support, stressing the importance of having a relative in this role.[35]

One letter,[36] probably written by Išbi-Erra or Šu-ilišu of Isin, shows that the relationship between Ešnunna and Isin was problematic. Bilalama is accused of writing disrespectfully about the sender to Ilum-muttabbil, the ruler of Der. Wu Yuhong notes three other letters mentioning the war against the Amorites, two of which are sent to "my lord," who might have been Bilalama.[37]

Two children of Bilalama are known: Me-Kubi, his daughter, to whom he granted a seal, and Šalil-la-miklum, mentioned in an inscription on a duck weight.[38] In order to consolidate his relationship with the Šimaškians, now a major power in the east, Bilalama married his daughter[39] to Tan-Ruhurater, son of the Šimaškian king Idattu I and governor of Susa.

Bilalama's position seems to have been rather delicate. He consolidated his bond with the Šimaškians, but at the same time maintained good relations with Ilum-muttabbil of Der, who claimed to have defeated Elam, Anšan, and Šimaški.[40] He had strong ties to the new chief of the

---

33. Reichel 2018: 41. Known as "Bilalama's Building," it was destroyed in a violent conflagration, probably during the reign of Uṣur-awassu.

34. Whiting 1987a: no. 11 and 17.

35. Whiting 1987a: 50.

36. Whiting 1987a: no. 13.

37. Wu 1994: 20; Whiting 1987a: no. 6–7 and 9.

38. Frayne 1990: 493–494.

39. A royal inscription of Me-Kubi concerning the building of a temple for Inana, as well as a large tag bearing the seal impression of a servant of Me-Kubi, were found in Susa: Frayne 1990: 493–494. The tag was found in Level VI *ancien* of Chantier B by Ghirshman; see MDP 43: no. 1676, and Amiet *apud* Steve, Gasche, and De Meyer 1980: 135, pl. V, no. 3.

40. Frayne 1990: 677–678.

Amorites, who was his brother-in-law, but had a troubled relationship with the ruler of Isin.

16.2.2. Ešnunna's political rise (ca. 1980–1860 BC)

Bilalama was succeeded by Išar-ramašu, known only from a standard royal inscription on bricks.[41] Of his successor, Uṣur-awassu, only seals (his own and four of his servants)[42] and two year names have been preserved.[43] Whiting believed Uṣur-awassu to have been a son of Bilalama.[44] A synchronism between Uṣur-awassu and Šu-ilišu of Isin has been suggested.[45] It is possible that he was appointed ruler of Ešnunna by Ilum-muttabbil of Der who, in his campaign against Elam, Anšan, and Šimaški would have taken Ešnunna, destroyed its palace, and replaced Išar-ramašu by Uṣur-awassu, keeping Ešnunna under his influence for a while.[46] If this was indeed the case, the ruler of Der may have been seeking to break up the alliance between Ešnunna and Elam/ Šimaški, as Wu suggested.[47] Ušašum, now chief of the Amorites, calls Bilalama "my son" in a letter,[48] which is indicative of their relative positions.[49] Ušašum was a very important and powerful political player.[50]

---

41. Frayne 1990: 500.

42. Frayne 1990: 501–504; for the seals, see Reichel 2001b; 2008; 2018.

43. Saporetti 2013: 121–123, I7A–I7B.

44. Whiting 1987a: 28, 77.

45. Reichel 2001a: 88; 2018: 40, fig. 16.

46. Frankfort, Lloyd, and Jacobsen 1940: 5, 46, 199.

47. Wu 1994: 23.

48. Whiting 1987a: no. 24.

49. Whiting 1987a saw this as a reflection of the fact that Ušašum was Bilalama's brother-in-law, not as an indication of superiority.

50. Abda-el and Ušašum received gifts not only from Bilalama of Ešnunna but also from Išbi-Erra of Isin, showing the extent of Abda-el's (and later Ušašum's) influence: de Boer 2014a: 176.

Uṣur-awassu was succeeded by Azuzum, of whom only one year name,[51] a standard royal inscription, two seals, and the seals of two servants have been preserved.[52]Azuzum was succeeded by two rulers with Sumerian names, Ur-Ninmarki and Ur-Ningišzida,[53] during whose reigns, around 1950 BC, much of the palace at Ešnunna was rebuilt.[54] Ur-Ninmarki is known from three year names,[55] his standard inscription on bricks, his seal, the seal he donated to his son Ipiq-Adad, and the seals of five servants.[56] He is also mentioned on the seal of his father, whose name is unfortunately broken,[57] but which might have been Azuzum.[58] Ur-Ningišzida is known from four year names,[59] his standard inscription on bricks, the seal he presented to his son Erra-bani, and the seals of four servants.[60] He is also mentioned in the inscription on a statue which once stood in the temple of Tišpak,[61] later taken as booty by Šutruk-Nahhunte to Susa. The reigns of Azuzum, Ur-Ninmarki, and Ur-Ningišzida were a period of relative peace and stability, as their year

---

51. Saporetti 2013: 127 I9A.

52. Frayne 1990: 505–508. For the seals, see Reichel 2001b; 2008; 2018.

53. Wende 2016a; 2016b.

54. Reichel 2018: 44.

55. Saporetti 2013: 131–133 (I10A–I10C) and Wu 1994: 25 a–c attribute three year names to Ur-Ninmarki, and Saporetti 2013: 134–136 (I11A–I11B) lists another two year names to be placed around the reign of Ur-Ninmarki.

56. Frayne 1990: 509–515. For the seals, see also Reichel 2001b; 2008; 2018. Three letters were addressed to him (Whiting 1987a: no. 31–33) and a further three were addressed to either him or Ur-Ningišzida (Whiting 1987a: no. 34–36).

57. Frayne 1990: 511.

58. Whiting 1987b: 35.

59. Saporetti 2013: 139–144 (I12A–I12D).

60. Frayne 1990: 516–521. For the seals, see also Reichel 2001b; 2008; 2018.

61. Frayne 1990: 517.

names are almost entirely devoted to religious or building activities, and their letters concern trivial affairs.[62]

Ur-Ningiszida was succeeded by Ipiq-Adad, Ur-Ninmarki's son. He was the first of two rulers of Ešnunna to bear that name. Three (or more) year names can be attributed to him.[63] His standard royal inscription on bricks, his seal, and the seals of eight of his servants have survived.[64] In one letter, Abdi-Erah and Šiqlanum address Ipiq-Adad I as "father," acknowledging his political superiority. The letter concerns the Amorite assembly and mentions other Amorite rulers such as Mašparum and Išme-bala.[65] Four other letters with similar content, three of which were addressed "to the prince," were probably also sent to Ipiq-Adad I.[66]

Of Ipiq-Adad I's successor, Šarriya, only two year names and a standard inscription on bricks have been preserved.[67] Šarriya was succeeded by Warassa, possibly his son. We have the seals of two of his servants.[68] Seven year names are attributed to him. These show that he captured Nerebtum, Išur, and Tutub.[69] Warassa was succeeded by Belakum, son of Šarriya (and possibly his brother). Eight year names,[70] his standard

---

62. Whiting 1987a: 29.

63. Saporetti 2013: 148–152 (I13A–I13C); de Boer 2014a: 201–202. Saporetti 2013: 154–168 (I14A–I14K) lists another eleven year names to be placed around the reign of Ipiq-Adad I. Wu 1994: 26 attributes five year names (a–e) with certainty to Ipiq-Adad I, with a further nine more considered possible (f–o).

64. Frayne 1990: 522–529. For the seals, see Reichel 2001b; 2008; 2018.

65. Whiting 1987a: no. 40. For Abdi-Erah, Šiqlanum, Mašparum, and Išme-bala, see Whiting 1987a: 30–33; Wu 1994: 41–43; de Boer 2014a: 202–204.

66. Whiting 1987a: no. 41–44. There is no link with similar letters from Sippar-Amnanum, as proposed by Wu 1994: 28–36; see de Boer 2014b: 278–279 for the chronological arguments against Wu's suggestion.

67. Saporetti 2013: 170–171 (I15A–I15B); Frayne 1990: 531.

68. Frayne 1990: 532–533. For the seals, see Reichel 2001b; 2008; 2018.

69. Saporetti 2013: 323–334 (I25A–I25G). Wu 1994: 37–38 attributed only four certain (a–c, e) and two possible (d, f) year names to Warassa.

70. Saporetti 2013: 310–321 (I24A–I24H). Wu 1994: 38 (a–g) attributed seven year names to Belakum.

inscription on bricks, and the seals of six of his servants have been preserved.[71] We have a treaty between Belakum and an unknown ruler, which includes an assistance clause in case of attack by Akkad, Yamutbal, Numhium, and Idamaraṣ.[72]

Political fragmentation in the lower Diyala valley in the twentieth and early nineteenth centuries is reflected in the sequence of short-lived rulers at Ešnunna, who probably represent multiple dynastic lines. We note the important role of the chief of the Amorites. On the other hand, internal palatial administration at Ešnunna shows continuity.[73]

16.2.3. Ešnunna's expansion (ca. 1860–1770 BC)

Belakum was succeeded by Ibal-pi-El, the first of two rulers of Ešnunna to bear that name. In contrast to his later namesake, who always appeared as king, Ibal-pi-El I was governor. His standard inscription on bricks, a seal granted to his wife, and the seals of four of his servants are known.[74] Four year names can be attributed to him.[75] The end of his reign is usually dated around 1860 BC,[76] when he was succeeded by his son Ipiq-Adad II. There is a chronological problem, however. According to the so-called Mari Eponym Chronicle,[77] Ipiq-Adad II was active from 1860 BC, but a treaty between Ešnunna, Larsa, and Uruk against Babylon[78] shows that

71. Frayne 1990: 534–538. For the seals, see Reichel 2001b; 2008; 2018.

72. The text 1930-T575 is unfortunately not published, but is referenced in Frankfort, Lloyd, and Jacobsen 1940: 198, n. 97; CAD N/2 s.v. *nukurtu* a.1′; CAD Q s.v. *qâpu* C.

73. Reichel 2018: 45–47.

74. Frayne 1990: 539–543. For the seals, see Reichel 2001b; 2008; 2018.

75. Saporetti 2013: 336–342 (I26A–I26D). Wu 1994: 39 attributed seven year names to Ibal-pi-El I.

76. Charpin 2004: 389.

77. Originally published by Birot 1985, the most recent edition is Glassner 2004: 160–164.

78. Guichard 2014.

his father, Ibal-pi-El of Ešnunna, concluded this treaty in 1843 BC.[79] It has been suggested that the Mari Eponym Chronicle is incorrect, and that Ipiq-Adad II's activities have been dated too early.[80] Indeed, the treaty is a contemporary document, whereas the Mari Eponym Chronicle was written some seventy years later. If this is correct, then the Ibal-pi-El of the treaty is Ibal-pi-El I, who would then have been succeeded by his son Ipiq-Adad II around 1842 BC. Such an explanation would shorten the reign of Ipiq-Adad II from almost forty-six years to a more reasonable twenty-seven years.[81]

Only nine year names have been attributed to Ipiq-Adad II,[82] but the importance of his reign is highlighted by the Mari Eponym Chronicle and his own royal inscriptions.[83] He called himself king of Ešnunna and put the divine determinative in front of his name, something which had not been done since the reign of Šu-iliya. His expansion of Ešnunna's territory is reflected in his titles "mighty king, king who enlarged the kingdom of Ešnunna" and "king of the world" (*šar kiššatim*). According to the Mari Eponym Chronicle, early in his reign, Ipiq-Adad II defeated Aminum of Aššur. In the east he was defeated by the "man of Elam," possibly Širuktuh (1835/1834 BC).[84] In the northeast he captured Arraphe and Gasur around 1830–1828 BC, then turned south, defeating Nerebtum

---

79. The second Ibal-pi-El does not provide a solution since he reigned from 1778 to 1765 BC; see Charpin 2004: 390.

80. de Boer 2014c.

81. Guichard 2014: 22–24 proposed that an (otherwise unattested) Ibal-pi-El briefly interrupted the reign of Ipiq-Adad II (around 1843 BC), perhaps after the invasion of the territory of Ešnunna by Sin-iddinam around 1845. Cf. Sigrist 1990: 24.

82. Saporetti 2013: 355–364 (III₁A–III₁E) attributed five year names to him. Saporetti and Repiccioli 2013: 34–35 (III₁F–III₁A) added three year names to this list. Ipiq-Adad II's year names on a tablet in Tell Shishin (cf. the following discussion) should be added to this, making a total of nine year names. Wu 1994: 75–76 lists five certain (a–b1/2, e–g) and four possible (h–k) year names.

83. Glassner 2004: 160–163; Frayne 1990: 544–552.

84. Vallat 1996: 313.

in the eponymy of Abu-šalim (1825/1824 BC).[85] Ipiq-Adad II unified the entire Diyala valley, as is apparent from his year names and seals of his servants.[86] In the west, he conquered Rapiqum on the Euphrates[87] and pushed his conquests upstream, as shown by a tablet from Tell Shishin (ancient Al-Kapim), ca. 50 km north of Hit, which is dated by one of his year names.[88] As a result, the northern Mesopotamian flood plain was effectively divided between Ešnunna and Babylon. The border between the two zones lay somewhere northeast of Sippar-Amnanum, but was subject to change.[89]

Ipiq-Adad II was succeeded by his son Naram-Sin. His name was also written with the divine determinative. Naram-Sin bore the titles of king of Ešnunna and king of the world.[90] Thirteen (or more) year names are attributed to him. These occur mostly on tablets from Nerebtum and Šaduppûm,[91] implying that he retained firm control of the Diyala

---

85. Frayne 1990: 545–546.

86. Frayne 1990: 547–549.

87. As shown by the year name of Ipiq-Adad II on a tablet written in the territory of the kingdom of Ešnunna (possibly Yabliya) and brought to Sippar in antiquity where it was excavated. A shorter form is attested on tablets from Šaduppûm: Saporetti 2013: 363 (II1Eb/c). This indicates it should be situated in the last part of his reign; cf. van Koppen and Lacambre 2008–2009: 158–162. For Rapiqum, see Ziegler and Langlois 2017: 280–282.

88. Mohammad 2002: 1–2 no. 1. For the identification of Tell Shishin with ancient Al-Kapim, see Ziegler and Langlois 2017: 294. For the year name, see Saporetti and Repiccioli 2013: 34 (II1F).

89. van Koppen and Lacambre 2008–2009: 151–152.

90. Frayne 1990: 553–556.

91. Saporetti 2013: 368–396 (II2A–II2K) attributed eleven year names to Naram-Sin. Saporetti and Repiccioli 2013: 39 (II2L–II2M) added another two. Saporetti 2013: 397–406 (II3A–II3G) also listed another seven year names to be dated around the reign of Naram-Sin. However, the year name in the heading of Manuscript A of the "Laws of Ešnunna," attributed by Saporetti 2013: 452–453 (II6E) to Daduša, is likely to have been Naram-Sin's first year name.

valley, up to Me-Turan.[92] After having crossed the Tigris, Naram-Sin
seized Kakkulatum,[93] forcing Samsi-Addu of Ekallatum to take refuge
in Babylon, and pursued his campaign to the northwest, subduing the
entire Khabur triangle, and conquering Ašnakkum and Tarnip.[94] Naram-
Sin also marched his troops to the Middle Euphrates, annexing the territory of Suhum up to the city of Puzurran, ca. 10 km downstream from
Mari.[95] Later, Yahdun-Lim, king of Mari, bought back Puzurran from
the Ešnunnaean king,[96] whom he recognized as his protector and with
whom he concluded an alliance.[97] The military and political influence
of Ešnunna was coupled with considerable cultural influence. During
the reign of Yahdun-Lim, Mari adopted the writing system of the scribal
school of Ešnunna.[98] It was probably during Naram-Sin's reign[99] that the
so-called Laws of Ešnunna were compiled, the first law collection to be
composed in Akkadian. Two small objects with inscriptions referring to

---

92. As a tablet sealed by one of Naram-Sin's servants was found there; see Frayne
    1990: 556.

93. Commemorated in two of his year names: Saporetti 2013: 392–395 (II2I–II2J).
    For Kakkulatum, see Röllig 1980.

94. Saporetti 2013: 397–399 (II3A), who, however, places this year name around
    the time of Naram-Sin. Cf. Charpin 2004: 131 n. 569, who noted that this year
    name is only attributed to Naram-Sin based on prosopography. For Ašnakkum
    and Tarnip, see Ziegler and Langlois 2017: 42–43, 361.

95. Ziegler and Langlois 2017: 268–269. The conquest is documented in a year
    name: van Koppen and Lacambre 2008–2009: 162–164.

96. Charpin 1992.

97. Charpin 1991.

98. Charpin 2012.

99. The heading of Manuscript A mentions a fragmentary year name that has been
    attributed to Daduša: Saporetti 2013: 452–453 (II6E). Goetze 1951–1952: 16
    had dated the two manuscripts on the basis of textual analysis, attributing
    Manuscript B to the reign of Daduša while judging Manuscript A to be some-
    what older. Both texts are copies and Goetze considered the original source
    to be earlier than the reigns of Daduša and Naram-Sin. Yaron 1988: 20 dated
    both manuscripts to the time of Daduša or an immediate predecessor. It is more
    likely, as suggested by van Koppen and Lacambre 2008–2009: 152–153 n. 12,
    that the year name is the first one of Naram-Sin's reign.

Naram-Sin have been found far away from the kingdom of Ešnunna: on the island of Cythera in the Aegean Sea[100] and on Cyprus.[101]

After Naram-Sin's death, three rulers reigned in Ešnunna in rapid succession: Iqiš-Tišpak, Ibbi-Sin, and Dannum-tahaz.[102] Iqiš-Tišpak, "governor of Ešnunna," son of Ibni-Erra and unrelated to Ipiq-Adad II, ruled briefly.[103] He might have been a usurper.[104] Ibbi-Sin ruled for only one year.[105] Of Dannum-tahaz, we only have five (?) year names.[106]

With the advent of Daduša, son of Ipiq-Adad II and brother of Naram-Sin, Ešnunna became a first-rank power again. He, too, had his name deified and called himself king of Ešnunna.[107] Eight or nine year names can be attributed to him,[108] implying that he reigned at least eight years. More than twenty seals of his subordinates on tablets

100. Frayne 1990: 554; Repercioli 1999.

101. Frayne 1990: 554–555

102. van Koppen and Lacambre 2008–2009: 171–175.

103. One brick inscription and a seal impression of a servant, both from Ešnunna: Frayne 1990: 560–561. Two year names on tablets from Nerebtum and Šaduppum: Saporetti 2013: 346–348 (I28A–I28B). For evidence for him in the Nerebtum texts, see Wu 1994: 91.

104. Frayne 1990: 560; Wu 1994: 87.

105. Saporetti 2013: 431–432 (II5A).

106. Wu 1994: 89–90 (a–e) and Saporetti 2013: 408–430 (II4A–II4F) attribute six year names to Dannum-tahaz. However, van Koppen and Lacambre 2008–2009: 174 n. 88 note that Wu's year names b and c (= Saporetti's year names II4D–II4E) may have been extracts from one and the same year name, implying that Dannum-tahaz would have reigned for only four years.

107. Frayne 1990: 563.

108. Wu 1994: 159–160 attributed eight certain (1–g, i) year names and one possible one (h) to Daduša. Saporetti 2013: 436–462 (II6A–II6H) attributed eight year names to Daduša, adding another year name (II7A) to be placed around the reign of Daduša. Van Koppen and Lacambre 2008–2009: 164–167 identified a tablet from Sippar with a year name of Daduša (Saporetti's II6B = Wu's b). For additions and corrections to the year names of Daduša listed by Saporetti and Wu, see van Koppen and Lacambre 2008–2009: 164 n. 52, 56–57, 174 n. 88–89.

from Nerebtum, Šaduppûm, and Me-Turan[109] attest to his firm control over the Diyala valley. In 1782 BC (eponymy of Ikuppiya), Daduša successfully launched a campaign to reclaim the region of Suhum from Samsi-Addu.[110] With the Lower Suhum area back under its control, Ešnunna now directly threatened the kingdom of Mari, then part of the dominions of Samsi-Addu. Eventually a peace treaty was concluded, after which Daduša and Samsi-Addu allied in war against Qabra.[111] According to the Ešnunnean account of this war, as commemorated on the stele of Daduša (figure 16.2),[112] he invaded the land of Qabra in the autumn of 1779 BC and took the city of Qabra in ten days,[113] but then made a gift of it and the surrounding villages to his ally Samsi-Addu. The so-called Mardin Stele,[114] as well as letters from Mari and Tell Shemshara,[115] preserve accounts that reflect Samsi-Addu's point of view.

Daduša died the year after taking Qabra and was succeeded by his son Ibal-pi-El II who, like his father, called himself king, but did not deify his name.[116] He reigned for about seventeen years.[117] His

---

109. Frayne 1990: 563–572. The recapture of Me-Turan by Daduša is also mentioned in the Mari Eponym Chronicle: Glassner 2004: 165.

110. For a detailed description of this reconquest (including textual and other references), see Charpin and Ziegler 2003: 88–91; Charpin 2004: 161–163.

111. MacGinnis 2013.

112. Ismail 2003. For the identification of the figures depicted, see Rollinger 2017. The capture of Qabra is also mentioned in a year name: Saporetti 2013: 458–462 (II6H); Wu 1994: 160 i'; Charpin 2004: 169; MacGinnis 2013: 8.

113. Wu 1994: 178–181; Charpin and Ziegler 2003: 91–95; Charpin 2004: 166–168.

114. Börker-Klähn 1982: II 11 1b; Grayson 1987: 63–65.

115. An overview is given in MacGinnis 2013: 5–8.

116. Frayne 1990: 573–575.

117. Saporetti 2013: 477–602 (III1F–III1W) attributed seventeen year names to Ibal-pi-El II, the sequence of twelve of which is known thanks to five (partially) preserved date lists: Saporetti 2013: 472–476 (III1A–III1F). Saporetti and Repiccioli 2013: 66–67 (III1Z–III1ZA) added two more to the list, bringing the total to nineteen year names.

FIGURE 16.2. The stele of Daduša of Ešnunna. Iraq Museum, Baghdad (accession number IM 95200). Photograph by Karen Radner.

royal seal and the seals of twenty-five servants, some of whom already served under his father, have been found, mostly on tablets from Nerebtum, Šaduppûm, and Me-Turan,[118] implying that Ešnunna's continued control over the Diyala valley. However, relations with Upper Mesopotamia, weakened by revolts, remained difficult in the

---

118. Frayne 1990: 574–586.

following years. After the death of Samsi-Addu in his fourth year,[119] Ibal-pi-El II attacked the Middle Euphrates in 1772 BC and sent an ultimatum to Mari.[120] Zimri-Lim called on the rulers of Kurda, Razama, and Qaṭṭara for help. The Ešnunnaean troops, together with their Benjaminite allies, went up the Tigris, settled first in Aššur and then in Ekallatum, advanced and eventually settled in Šubat-Enlil/Šehna. In the second half of 1771 BC, Ešnunna was attacked by the kingdom of Halman, and the Ešnunnaean troops had to vacate Šubat-Enlil/Šehna. Moreover, the Benjaminites threatened the Euphrates valley, causing Zimri-Lim to leave the Sinjar plain and to return to Mari. Toward the end of 1771 BC, peace seems to have returned. Shortly after Ešnunna retreated from Suhum, tensions rose between Mari and Babylon over their joint border on the Euphrates. When negotiations failed, Zimri-Lim reconciled with the Benjaminites and started negotiations with Ešnunna. He accepted a treaty which recognized Ibal-pi-El II's superiority. In return, Ešnunna renounced its territorial ambitions in Suhum and Sinjar, a vacuum filled by Babylon settling in Rapiqum on the one side, and Mari recovering Yabliya and Harbe on the other.[121] Both Mari and Babylon gladly complied with the request of Elam to send soldiers to the siege of Ešnunna, which fell into the hands of the Elamites, somewhere between the ninth and tenth year of Zimri-Lim's reign.[122] This led to an Elamite conquest in Babylonia and Upper Mesopotamia.

---

119. Charpin and Ziegler 2003: 112–118, 134–138; Charpin 2004: 178. Samsi-Addu's death is commemorated in Ibal-pi-El II's fifth year name: Saporetti 2023: 503–507 (III₁K).

120. Charpin and Ziegler 2003: 194–195; Charpin 2004: 197.

121. Charpin and Ziegler 2003: 201–204; Charpin 2004: 204–206. For Andarig, see Ziegler and Langlois 2017: 24–26.

122. Charpin and Ziegler 2003: 212–213; Charpin 2004: 210.

16.2.4. Ešnunna's decline and final years (ca. 1770–1695 BC)

Hammurabi of Babylon planned to seize power in Ešnunna, with Zimri-Lim's blessing. However, after about two years of Elamite domination,[123] the Ešnunnaeans chose a new ruler: Ṣilli-Sin, an army officer of common origin, who called himself "governor of Ešnunna."[124] A seal of one of his servants was found on tablets of Me-Turan,[125] implying that he controlled the Diyala valley. This is also apparent from his year names, which are attested on tablets from Nerebtum, Tulul Khatab, and Me-Turan. His reign probably did not last very long, as only five year names can be attributed to him.[126] Indeed, as Hammurabi re-established diplomatic relations with Elam, tensions rose with Ešnunna. Hammurabi was eager to retrieve Mankisum and Upi (Opis) on the banks of the Tigris and proposed peace to Ṣilli-Sin in exchange for these territories. A treaty was being negotiated and a daughter of Hammurabi was given in marriage to Ṣilli-Sin,[127] but relations soured and Ešnunna was defeated by Babylon in 1762 BC.[128] Little is known about Ešnunna after this. Six years later, Hammurabi commemorated the destruction of Ešnunna by a great flood in his thirty-eighth year name.[129]

---

123. Evidence includes texts from Ešnunna impressed with seals of servants of Kuduzuluš, one of which has an oath by Tišpak and the *sukkalmah*: van Dijk 1970: 63–65.

124. Frayne 1990: 587.

125. Frayne 1990: 588–598.

126. Saporetti 2013: 634–639 (III4A–III4C) attributed three year names to him, and Saporetti and Repiccioli 2013: 68–69 (III4AA, III4D) added two more, for a total of five year names.

127. This is hinted at in one of Ṣilli-Sin's year names: Saporetti 2013: 635–637 (III4B).

128. Charpin and Ziegler 2003: 227–228 and 241; Charpin 2004: 226–227 and 326; Richardson 2005. The victory over Ešnunna is commemorated in Hammurabi's thirty-second year name.

129. Horsnell 1999: 157–159. Note the alternative interpretation of Charpin 2004: 332–333 n. 1735 that Hammurabi saved the city destroyed by water. Neither Hammurabi's royal inscriptions nor the Mari letters mention a flooding. See Rutz and Michalowski 2016: 31–32 for a possible reference in a literary text, which is, however, rejected by Ziegler 2016, according to whom there is no mention of water in the relevant passage.

Shortly thereafter, Hammurabi's son and successor Samsu-iluna collided with Iluni, king of Ešnunna, in his seventh year.[130] A few years later, Samsu-iluna claims to have murdered twenty-six rebellious kings, including Iluni,[131] probably in his tenth year.[132] The start date and length of Iluni's reign are uncertain. Guichard recently proposed that Iluni must have reigned at least six years.[133] Letters reveal that he ruled over an area extending from the mouth of the Diyala to Zab(b)an (likely a later name for the region of Simurrum; cf. section 16.3), possibly as far as Terqa,[134] and maintained close relations with Samsu-iluna before rebelling against Babylon.

Approximately thirty years later, Samsu-iluna's successor Abi-ešuḫ once more clashed with a ruler of Ešnunna, as his shown by his seventeenth (?) year name.[135] No inscriptions of Ahušina of Ešnunna have been preserved. Notwithstanding gaps and uncertainties, it is clear that Ešnunna was a major power, in part due to its location in the Diyala valley on the eastern border of the Babylonian/Amorite world, to the west of the Trans-Tigris and Inter-Zagros kingdoms and the vast Elamite/ Šimaškian state (cf. section 16.5). Ešnunna controlled the Diyala valley and, at times, large parts of Upper Mesopotamia. The Elamite conquest of Babylonia and Upper Mesopotamia, however, put an end to its independence and importance, although it bounced back as a local force embroiled in constant conflict with the then dominant geopolitical power Babylon (cf. chapter 18).

---

130. Charpin 2004: 337–339 (with references); Seri 2013: 47–50.

131. Frayne 1990: 387.

132. Vedeler 2016: 3–4; Guichard 2016: 18. Another possibility is that Iluni was killed a decade later, when Samsu-iluna collided again with the Ešnunnaeans, as is shown in his twentieth year name. See Horsnell 1999: 207–209.

133. On the basis of year names on tablets from Me-Turan: Saporetti 2013: 640– 641 (III5A–III5B); and one from Ur and on the seal of a servant: Charpin 1986a: 127, 175–175; Frayne 1990: 591.

134. Guichard 2016.

135. Horsnell 1999: 258–259.

16.3. *The kingdom of Simurrum*

Simurrum (or Šimurrum)[136] was an important kingdom, with its central city bearing the same name, in the so-called Hurrian frontier zone,[137] the belt of small polities led typically by Hurrian rulers on the eastern and northeastern periphery of Mesopotamia. Located in the western fringes of the Zagros Mountains along the upper reaches of the Diyala River and its tributaries, Simurrum is attested during the Sargonic, Ur III, and early Old Babylonian periods, but disappears from the records at some time during the Old Babylonian period. According to Frayne, the name Simurrum was replaced by Zab(b)an during the reign of Ṣilli-Sin of Ešnunna in the mid-eighteenth century BC.[138]

The location of the city of Simurrum is not known. Frayne suggested locating the city at the settlement mound at Kelar that is today occupied by the eighteenth-century AD castle of Qal'at Širwana (also Qalay Širwana),[139] situated northeast of modern Jalawla at the pass formed by the junction of its tributary, the Pungla River, with the Sirwan, as the upper course of the Diyala is known locally; Ahmed supported this hypothesis, adding that Qal'at Širwana is located on the strategic route

---

136. Written with *si-* and *ši-* and with double and single "r" in texts of the Old Babylonian period. See Ahmed 2012: 230–231 for the different spellings.

137. Hallo 1978.

138. Frayne 1997: 260. This hypothesis is based on the equation of Simurrum with Zab(b)an in lexical lists and the fact that in the texts from Me-Turan, from the time of Ṣilli-Sin of Ešnunna, only Zab(b)an appears but Simurrum is never mentioned. A text from Sippar dated to the twelfth year of the reign of Apil-Sin of Babylon (Pinches 1898: no. 47a; Weidner 1945–1951: 77; for the date, see Horsnell 1999: 84) mentions Simurrum and Zab(b)an. The geographical name Simurrum was still in use in the second half of the eighteenth century BC, as shown by a text dated to the twenty-seventh year of the reign of Samsu-iluna of Babylon mentioning a slave girl from Simurrum (Nies 1920: no. 80). Simurrum also seems to have been famous for its millstones; see YOS 8: 98 (Ur, Rim-Sin I of Larsa, Year 28) and YOS 12: 120 (Larsa, Samsu-iluna of Babylon, Year 4) and the discussion of Radner 2014: 576–577.

139. Frayne 1997a: 104; 1997b: 264–266; 1999: 151.

linking the south to the north even today.[140] However, Frayne subsequently changed his mind and favored instead identification with modern Šamiran, 14 km west of the modern city of Halabja in the Shahrizor region.[141] As Radner stressed, for geographical, geopolitical, and economic reasons this area just beyond the narrow gorge where the Sirwan pushes through the mountains at Darband-i Khan, in the southeastern part of the fertile and easily defendable Shahrizor, would indeed seem the most probable general location of the city.[142]

While the city's exact location remains unclear, various monuments of the kings of Simurrum in the form of rock reliefs and steles, which we will discuss in the following section, mark the extent of their military campaigns and provide hints to the location of their realm's core region. The examples found in the region of Bitwata in a valley off the Raniya Plain and in the area of Sar-i Pol-i Zohab, respectively, indicate the northern and southern reaches of Simurrum's control, whereas the inscribed stele found at the entrance to the valley of Zewiya (or Zayway) in the Pira Magrun range ("Haladiny Inscription") and the rock relief of Darband-i Gawr in the Qara Dagh range are both situated in the mountainous regions stretching alongside the Shahrizor Plain, within easy reach of modern Sulaymaniyah; all this indicates that the Shahrizor was a part, and most probably the center, of the kingdom of Simurrum.[143]

Two kings of Simurrum are known from their royal inscriptions: Iddi(n)-Sin and his son ANzabazuna,[144] whose reigns are to be dated

---

140. Ahmed 2012: 297–302.

141. Frayne 2011: 511.

142. Radner in Altaweel et al. 2012: 10.

143. Radner in Altaweel et al. 2012: 9–11.

144. It is not clear how to read the name of Iddi(n)-Sin's son: ᵈZabazuna or ANzabazuna. Since Iddi(n)-Sin's name is always deified (ᵈi-di-ᵈEN.ZU) it was probably ᵈZabazuna. Contrary to his father's typical Mesopotamian name, ANzabazuna is clearly non-Semitic. Frayne 1990: 707 believed the Z/Sabaz/sinum mentioned in a letter from Ešnunna to Bilalama (Whiting 1987a: no. 13: 10′) might be Iddi(n)-Sin's son, in which case his name too is to

at the end of the Ur III period[145] and in the early Old Babylonian period. Later, Simurrum is attested in texts from Mari, Šušarra (Tell Shemshara), Qaṭṭara (Tell al-Rimah), and Šubat-Enlil / Šehna (Tell Leilan).

16.3.1. Iddi(n)-Sin and his son ANzabazuna

Presently, six royal inscriptions are known of Iddi(n)-Sin and his son. The earliest is probably the rock relief in Sar-i Pol-i Zahab, testifying to the conflict of Simurrum with the neighboring kingdom of Lullubum for control of one of the main trade routes leading from Mesopotamia toward the east.[146] The text mentions the gods Ninsianna and Nišba, the personal god of the king and the patron deity of Simurrum, respectively.[147] According to the inscription, Iddi(n)-Sin defeated an enemy and set up an image on Mount Batir.[148] The relief depicts the beardless king with round cap trampling the defeated enemy. Two other reliefs at Sar-i-Pol-i Zahab are without inscriptions and show a similar beardless king with round cap facing a goddess. Seidl believes they all depict Iddi(n)-Sin and date to the time between the Ur III and

---

be read ᵈZabazuna (Z/Sabaz/sinum being an "Akkanianized" variant). Ahmed 2012: 203 n. 430 suggests that the name might have been linked with Zab(b)an, the geographical name used for Simurrum from the mid-eighteenth century BC onward, implying that ᵈZabazuna changed the name of the city from Simurrum to Zab(b)an when he rose to power. In this case the name should be read ᵈZab(b)a(n)-zuna. However, it seems that the reign of ANzabazuna is to be dated well before the mid-eighteenth century BC, which does not alter the fact that his name is related to the toponym.

145. It seems likely that Simurrum already had become the seat of an independent dynasty well before the end of the Ur III state, after the third year of Ibbi-Sin or even earlier.

146. This was attributed originally to ANnubanini of Lullubum (cf. section 16.4.1), but can now be attributed with certainty to Iddi(n)-Sin of Simurrum, based on the orthography, the curse formula, and the mention of the divine couple Ninsianna and Nišba. Ninsianna is always written in the typical Ur III way as ᵈnin-ᵈsi₄-an-na. See Richter 2004: 31, 415. For Nišba, see Cavigneaux and Krebernik 2001; Radner in Altaweel et al. 2012: 10.

147. Shaffer and Wasserman 2003: 20–22; Radner in Altaweel et al. 2012: 10.

148. Frayne 1990: 712–714.

Isin-Larsa periods at the end of the third and the beginning of the second millennium BC.[149]

The so-called Haladiny Inscription was found in the 1980s in a field south of the village of Qara Chatan at the foot of Pira Magrun, northwest of Sulaymaniyah,[150] and is linked to the Sar-i Pol-i Zahab reliefs. The inscription commemorates Iddi(n)-Sin's devastation of regions from Sar-i Pol-i Zahab northward to the Raniya plain. After having campaigned in the north, Iddi(n)-Sin turned to the south and east, seizing the lands of Halman (the region of Sar-i Pol-i Zahab) and Bel (possibly north of Sar-i Pol-i Zahab).[151] The next part of the text mentions ANnubanini, king of Lull(ub)bum. The inscription ends by stating that Nišba heard his words, destroyed the lands, and slayed the Amorites and Šimaškians, after which Iddi(n)-Sin overcame them and made the rebels build a temple for the god Nišba. This suggests that lands originally belonging to the kingdom of Simurrum had rebelled under the influence of the Amorites and Šimaškians but were conquered. The Haladiny Inscription was probably installed in a temple dedicated to the patron deity of Simurrum. Ahmed suggests this was located near the village of Qara Chatan where the inscription was found.[152] If Simurrum is located on the Sirwan River, then this temple was built far from its center. A possible explanation of this might be that a "second" capital was founded in the north where Iddi(n)-Sin's son ruled as governor, as the Bitwata inscriptions seem to imply.

The so-called Jerusalem Inscription deals with the campaign in the region of the Raniya plain.[153] It is on three pieces of rock, said to

---

149. Seidl *apud* Shaffer and Wasserman 2003: 50–51.

150. Ahmed 2012: 255–273, 311–317. Due to the political instability at the time, it was only given to the Museum of Sulaymaniyah in 1993 by a former Peshmerga fighter, Mr Haladiny, and was named after him.

151. The land of Bel is otherwise unknown, but Mirghaderi and Alibaigi 2018 locate it north of Sar-i Pol-i Zahab, near modern Lake Bel, north-northwest of Paveh in Iran's Kermanshah province.

152. Ahmed 2012: 293–295, 329–338.

153. Most recent edition: Shaffer and Wasserman 2003.

have been found in Bard-i Sanjian in Bitwata, and since 1971 in the Israel Museum in Jerusalem. According to the text, the rebellious city of Kulun(n)um, where Aurnahuš had seized power, was retaken by Iddi(n)-Sin. To commemorate this, Iddi(n)-Sin ordered that an image of himself be set up in Kulun(n)um. The inscription is accompanied by a relief (figure 16.3) depicting the beardless king with round cap, trampling a defeated enemy, no doubt the rebel Aurnahuš. The king faces a goddess, Ninhursag or Ninsianna, his personal goddess.[154]

Three other inscriptions on rectangular stones, the so-called Bitwata Inscriptions,[155] are said to have been found in Bard-i Sanjian. These also commemorate Iddi(n)-Sin's victory over Kulun(n)um[156] and mention his son ANzabazuna:[157]

> Iddi(n)-Sin, mighty king, king of Simurrum, ANzabazuna (is) his son; Kulun(n)um turned spiteful toward ANzabazuna. The gods Adad, Ištar and Nišba heard the word of ANzabazuna; he destroyed the city and consecrated it to these gods.

The reference to ANzabazuna in his father's royal titles stresses that he is the designated heir. This is a typical practice in the kingdoms of the Zagros foothills and reflects the influence of Hurrian traditions and

---

154. Seidl *apud* Shaffer and Wasserman 2003: 39–54.

155. Originally published in Al-Fouadi 1978; most recent edition: Frayne 1990: 708–711.

156. The inscriptions further state that he who should remove the [handi]work or erase the inscription will be cursed, which made Ahmed 2012: 282–286 suspect that the [handi]work mentioned refers to the tables and throne set up for the deities, mentioned in the text. As such, he suggests that the throne of Nišba might have been the large rock at the Bitwata that overlooks the entire region as far as the Raniya plain and is shaped like a throne or altar (locally known today as the "Throne of the Eastern Sun").

157. Frayne 1990: 708–711: ll. 1–21; but cf. also Farber 1998 for a new interpretation and translation of ll. 6–11.

FIGURE 16.3. The rock relief and inscription of Iddi(n)-Sin of Simurrum. Israel Museum, Jerusalem (accession number 71.073.0248). Photograph by Gary Todd, via Wikimedia Commons (https://commons.wikimedia.org/w/index. php?curid=77448701), Creative Commons Attribution-ShareAlike 2.0 (CC BY-SA 2.0) license.

political ideology.[158] Two seals, belonging to the scribe Teheš-atal[159] and one Ṣilli-ibri,[160] mention ANzabazuna as king.

An early Old Babylonian text from Isin, dated to the twenty-fifth year of the reign of Išbi-Erra of Isin (2019–1987 BC), mentions an unnamed king

---

158. Ahmed 2012: 295–296.

159. Frayne 1990: 715.

160. Frayne 1990: 716, who interprets ⌜zi⌝-li-⌜ib⌝-ri as Zili-ewri, with ibri as a rendering of Hurrian ewri ("lord"). However, Reichel 2001b: 120 interprets this name as Ṣilli-ibri, which is much more likely.

of Simurrum.[161] In a letter from Ešnunna,[162] possibly sent by Išbi-Erra[163] to Bilalama of Ešnunna (dated between 2000 and 1980 BC),[164] a Z/Sabaz/sinum appears who must be identical with ANzabazuna.[165] The seal impression of Ṣilli-ibri found in the phase of the Šu-Sin temple at Ešnunna attributed to Nur-ahum[166] implies that ANzabazuna succeeded his father to the throne of Simurrum before the reigns of Kirikiri and Bilalama at Ešnunna. The reigns of Iddi(n)-Sin and ANzabazuna of Simurrum are therefore roughly contemporary with the reigns of ANnubanini of Lullubum, Bilalama of Ešnunna, and Išbi-Erra of Isin (see chapter 14 in this volume).

16.3.2. Simurrum in the eighteenth century BC

After the reigns of Iddi(n)-Sin and ANzabazuna, we lose track of Simurrum for a century or two until it reappears in the eighteenth century BC in texts from Mari, Šušarra (Tell Shemshara), Qaṭṭara (Tell al-Rimah), and Šubat-Enlil/Šehna (Tell Leilan).

Two letters from Tell Shemshara mentioning Simurrum also refer to the Elamites. In the first one,[167] Šepratu quotes a letter from the Elamite king Šuruhtuh, and in the second,[168] Pišenden refers to a plan to secure help from the father, the great overseer (*abum waklum rabûm*), which may be a local rendering of the Elamite title *sukkalmah*.[169] This reflects the prestige and influence of the Elamites in international relations at

161. Crawford 1954: no. 421.

162. Whiting 1987a: no. 13.

163. Whiting 1987a: 56–57.

164. Reichel 2018: 40.

165. Frayne 1990: 707.

166. Reichel 2001b: 120.

167. Eidem and Læssøe 2001: no. 64.

168. Eidem and Læssøe 2001: no. 69.

169. Eidem and Læssøe 2001: 145.

that time. Simurrum is also mentioned in a number of Mari letters.[170] Noteworthy is a report received by Zimri-Lim of Mari that the king of Simurrum, who served the Gutian king Zazum, fled to Zaziya, who extradited him to the Gutian ruler.[171] A letter from Qaṭṭara[172] mentions troops from Simurrum. In a letter to Till-abnu, Inganum, king of Šehna (or Šubat-Enlil; modern Tell Leilan),[173] reports that Simurrean mercenaries in the service of King Halu-rabi have entered Nihru.[174] These texts depict quickly changing alliances between various kingdoms and city-states, both within the Zagros Mountains and between the highlands and lowlands, confirming that Simurrum was party to various conflicts.

16.4. The mountain region of Lullubum and its inhabitants

Lullubum, spelled Lul(l)ubu(m)$^{(ki)}$ and Lullu(m) in the texts of the early second millennium BC, refers to a mountainous territory and its inhabitants. Located in the headwater regions of the Diyala River in the Zagros Mountains, the territory controlled by Lullubum may at times have included the Shahrizor plain between the modern cities of Sulaymaniyah and Darband-i Khan in the Kurdish Autonomous Region of Iraq, extending to Mariwan and Baneh in Iranian Kurdistan, and possibly northward toward Lake Urmia. According to Radner,

> Lullubum is best identified with the high plateau between the
> Qara Dagh and the Binzird and Beranan ranges, stretching along

---

170. ARM 3: no. 81; ARM 21: no. 367; ARM 26/2: no. 491.

171. ARM 26/2: no. 491.

172. Dalley, Walker and Hawkins 1976: no. 11.

173. Eidem 2011: no. 134; for Šehna / Šubat-Enlil, see Ziegler and Langlois 2017: 242–245.

174. Ziegler and Langlois 2017: 253–254.

the southwestern perimeter of the Shahrizor from the Lower Zab to the Diyala.[175]

It has been argued that whereas in the third millennium BC, the term Lull(ub)um denoted a specific area, in the early second millennium BC it came to mean "(barbarous) mountain dweller."[176] Eidem suggested that the Lull(ub)eans attested in texts from Mari, Qaṭṭara, and Tigunanum were western "highlanders" whereas the "real" Lull(ub)eans are in the east, as mentioned in the texts of Tell Shemshara.[177] Ahmed, however, convincingly disagrees with this generic extension of the term.[178]

Only one royal inscription of a ruler identifying himself as Lull(ub)ean has been preserved, giving us a rare Lull(ub)ean or "domestic," point of view, in contrast to the more frequent sources from other states. Predating the attestations of Lullu(bum) and Lull(ub)eans in the Mari and Shemshara texts, this inscription can be dated to the early eighteenth century BC, roughly contemporary with the reigns of Samsi-Addu of Ekallatum and Zimri-Lim of Mari (see chapter 15 in this volume).

16.4.1. ANnubanini, king of Lullubum

The inscription and relief of a local ruler are carved into a rock outcrop at Sar-i Pol-i Zahab (figure 16.4), in Iran's Kermanshah province, close to the modern border with Iraq.[179] In the inscription, he calls himself mighty king and king of Lullubum[180] and states that he had made an image of himself and the goddess Ištar on Mount Batir, thus apparently

---

175. Radner in Altaweel et al. 2012: 10.

176. Klengel 1990; Eidem 1992.

177. Eidem 1992: 50–54.

178. Ahmed 2012: 75–80.

179. Most recent editions: Frayne 1990: 705–706; Mofidi-Nasrabadi 2004 (with additions and corrections).

180. Mofidi-Nasrabadi 2004: 296 fig. 5: (1) AN-*nu-ba-ni-ni* (2) lugal *da-núm* (3) lugal *lu-lu-bí-im*[ki].

FIGURE 16.4. The rock relief and inscription of ANnubanini of Lullubum from Sar-i Pol-i Zahab. Photograph by Koorosh Nozad Tehrani, via Wikimedia Commons (https://commons.wikimedia.org/w/index.php?curid=77395008), Creative Commons Attribution-ShareAlike 2.0 (CC BY-SA 2.0) license.

the ancient name of the peak at Sar-i Pol-i Zahab. Regardless of whether we are to read the initial AN as the first syllable of the ruler's name or instead as a divine determinative (that is, as Annubanini or ᵈNubanini), it is probable that this name is Lull(ub)ean, as Ahmed points to the frequent attestation of the suffix -ni in Lull(ub)ean personal names.[181] Other scholars nevertheless favor an Elamite interpretation.[182] In this

---

181. Ahmed 2012: 79; e.g., Sabini, Tar-dunni, Satuni, and the Lull(ub)ean named Ebi-unni mentioned in a list of barley rations from Shemshara: Eidem and Læssøe 2001: no. 11: (20) 0.1 še *e-bi-ú-un-ni* (21) *lu-ul-lu.*

182. Hüsing 1908: 17 links it to the Elamite deity Humban (Hanubani), which seems a bit far-fetched. Zadok 1983 considers many of the names with redupli-cated final syllable connected to Elamite verbal and nominal roots, but there is no consensus on this: cf., e.g., Foster 1982; Emberling 1995; Blažek 1999.

chapter, we follow modern convention and transliterate the name as ANnubanini.

The inscription is accompanied by a relief depicting ANnubanini as a victorious, bearded king with round cap, holding a bow and battle-axe, standing on a defeated enemy. He faces the goddess Ištar, who holds two naked, kneeling captives tied to each other by ropes. Below the king and goddess stand six other prisoners of war in a row.[183] Ahmed believes the enemy to have been the kingdom of Simurrum, which is very plausible.[184]

A letter from Ešnunna[185] deals with a conflict being fought in the mountainous area northwest of Ešnunna (cf. section 16.2), more specifically in the area of Halman and Niqqum, identified respectively with Sar-i Pol-i Zahab[186] and Khanaqin.[187] A person named Iddi(n)-Sin, probably the king of Simurrum (see section 16.3), is mentioned twice in this letter; this would seem to locate the conflict in the vicinity of Sar-i Pol-i Zahab, as confirmed also by another rock relief and its inscription at Sar-i Pol-i Zahab. Originally attributed to ANnubanini, the monument is now with certainty attributed to Iddi(n)-Sin of Simurrum.[188] Furthermore, the Haladiny Inscription (see section 16.3.1) shows that ANnubanini of Lullubum and Iddi(n)-Sin of Simurrum were contemporaries.[189]

According to Ahmed, the two reliefs are evidence for the long-lasting, bitter conflict between these two regional powers over the control of the strategically important region of Sar-i Pol-i Zahab, the

---

183. For recent photos of the relief, see Mofidi-Nasrabadi 2004.

184. Ahmed 2012: 246–249.

185. Whiting 1987a: 37–38.

186. Borger 1970; Frayne 1997a: 256, 258–259.

187. Frayne 1999: 151; Röllig 2001. Note also Guichard 2016, who suggests the possibility of identifying Niqqum with Choga Gavaneh, a site located in Shahabad-e Gharb, ca. 60 km west of Kermanshah in Iran. Cf. Abdi and Beckman 2007.

188. Walker 1985: 189; Frayne 1990: 712; Shaffer and Wasserman 2003: 20–22.

189. Ahmed 2012: 255–273.

gateway to one of the main trade routes to the east, the so-called Great Khorasan Road. As Iddi(n)-Sin of Simurrum was probably also a contemporary of Išbi-Erra of Isin and Nur-ahum of Ešnunna—and might have been already in power during the final years of Ibbi-Sin of Ur—ANnubanini, too, can be dated to the transitional period after the end of the Ur III state in the late third and early second millennium BC. The fact that these local powers fought for, and controlled, access to this crucial trade route may have played a role in the final downfall of the kingdom of Ur.

ANnubanini's inscription is written in Akkadian cuneiform. This is not surprising, as cuneiform was *scriptura administrativa* for various non-literate societies in contact with Mesopotamia. The language of the inscription is similar to that used in the inscriptions of Iddi(n)-Sin of Simurrum and also the Ešnunna letters.[190] One hundred sixteen cuneiform tablets, also written in Akkadian and provisionally dated to 2200–2000 BC,[191] were only recently excavated at Tell Kunara near Sulaymaniyah, likely a political and economic center of Lullubum.[192] The mention of the title $ensi_2$ "governor" and possibly also of a *sukkal* named Erib-eli (?) would seem to imply a dating to the time of the kingdom of Ur, although none of the tablets mentions Ur III year names.

16.4.2. Lullubum and its inhabitants in the eighteenth century BC

After the reign of ANnubanini at the turn of the second millennium BC, we lose track of the Lull(ub)eans for a century or two until they reappear in the texts from Mari and Šušarra (modern Tell Shemshara)

---

190. The language represents an intermediary stage between Old Akkadian and Old Babylonian or very early Old Babylonian: Edzard 1973: 74; Shaffer and Wasserman 2003: 35–39.

191. Tenu et al. 2019: 53–65.

192. Kepinski et al. 2015: 55–58; Tenu et al. 2019: 66–67.

in the early eighteenth century BC.[193] Letters excavated at Tell
Shemshara suggest that Kuwari, the Turrukean viceroy in Šušarra,
was mostly at odds with the nearby Lull(ub)ean kingdoms, but nevertheless needed them as allies in times of conflict.[194] When Kuwari
became a vassal of Samsi-Addu of Ekallatum (cf. chapter 15 in this
volume),[195] he was asked to ally himself with the king of Lull(ub)um and to
attack a rebel ruler, and even to make preparations for a treaty with
the king of Lull(ub)um. Lull(ub)eans are also mentioned in seven
administrative documents from Tell Shemshara,[196] which show that,
in addition to hostile encounters, Šušarra also maintained diplomatic
relations and the exchange of gifts with one (or more) Lull(ub)ean
kingdom(s).

Lull(ub)eans are also mentioned in documents from Qaṭṭara
(modern Tell al-Rimah)[197] on the Sinjar Plain and from Mari on the
middle Euphrates, but the Qaṭṭara texts are not very informative:[198]
they mention the escorting of a Lull(ub)ean to Ṣarbat,[199] and shoes
given to some Lull(ub)eans. Some of the Mari texts, however, give us
more information. In a letter to Yasmah-Addu (son of Samsi-Addu and
for a time his regent in Mari), his brother Išme-Dagan demands more
information on a recent defeat inflicted on Ešnunna by the Lull(ub)
eans,[200] while another text records that Yasmah-Addu received bronze

193. Lull(ub)um is mentioned in the Mari Eponym Chronicle (Glassner
2004: 163): in the eponymy of Aššur-imitti, Lullum has defeated the king in
Lazapatum, located in the vicinity of Šubat-Enlil / Šehna (Ziegler and Langlois
2017: 203). The eponymy of Aššur-imitti is dated 1832/1831 BC.

194. Eidem 1992: 50–54; Eidem and Læssøe 2001: 33–38.

195. Eidem and Læssøe 2001: no. 3, 12, 39, 42.

196. Eidem 1992 no. 11, 116, 128, 133, 140, 145–146.

197. Ziegler and Langlois 2017: 271–272.

198. Langlois 2017: 95–96, 183.

199. Ziegler and Langlois 2017: 318–319.

200. Ziegler 1997: 145–157.

weights from the Lull(ub)ean ruler.[201] Some time later, Adal-šenni, king of Burundum in the Tur Abdin mountains,[202] begs Zimri-Lim of Mari in a letter to send him presents for the king of the Lull(ub)eans who is passing through his kingdom,[203] whereas Ibal-Addu, king of Ašlakka, reports to Zimri-Lim on receiving news from Eluhut, the ruler of Lull(ub)um, Hahhum, the land of Zalmaqum, Burundum, and Talyahum in another letter to Zimri-Lim.[204] A messenger of the ruler of Lull(ub)um is mentioned in a list of envoys from kingdoms located on or near the upper course of the Tigris, and elsewhere.[205] An undated Old Babylonian text concerns a shipment of horses from the land of Lull(ub)um to Ebla via the city of Nihriya,[206] with three of the animals belonging to an Elamite.

These texts show that the Lull(ub)ean rulers were not only involved in local politics in the Zagros Mountains but also in highland-lowland relationships and conflicts, which is not surprising given their probable alliance with the Elamites.

16.5. The city of Susa and the Iranian powers Šimaški and Elam

Under the control of the kingdom of Ur since the state had been founded by Ur-Namma (see chapter 13 in this volume), Susa regained its independence early in the reign of Ibbi-Sin.[207] Already during the time of

---

201. ARM 22: no. 192.

202. Ziegler and Langlois 2017: 69–70.

203. ARM 28: no. 43.

204. ARM 28: no. 60; cf. Ziegler and Langlois 2017: 69–70, 96–98, 108–109, 357–358, 418–419.

205. ARM 23: no. 343; cf. Ziegler and Langlois 2017: 96–98, 179–181, 287–289.

206. Tsukimoto 1997. For Nihrija, see Ziegler and Langlois 2017: 252–253.

207. Marchesi 2013.

Ur's rule in the Susiana plain,[208] a new political power arose in central Iran: Šimaški was founded by Ebarat I,[209] a contemporary of Amar-Sin and Šu-Sin of Ur, and his son and successor Kindattu would play a major role in the final downfall of the Ur III state. Ur lost control over Susa after Ibbi-Sin's third year.[210] His fifth and sixth year names commemorate the marriage of his daughter to the governor of Zabšali, the largest principality of Šimaški, located somewhere north of Anšan, perhaps toward the Caspian Sea (or Lake Urmia),[211] implying that Ibbi-Sin attempted to (re-)confirm a political alliance with Susa's hinterland. The attacks on Huhnuri (modern Tepe Bormi[212]) and Anšan (modern Tell-e Malyan), commemorated in his ninth year name, and on Susa, AdamDUN, and Awan[213] in his fourteenth year name, show the ultimate convulsions

---

208. Cf. Steinkeller 1991 for the territorial extent of the core and periphery of the Ur III state.

209. The location of Ebarat I's original kingdom is as yet unknown. As Ebarat I is not mentioned in connection with any of the Šimaškian lands that were the object of the campaigns of Šu-Sin of Ur, Steinkeller 2007: 223 concludes that his domain must have been located in the eastern-most part of the Šimaškian territories, or even within the territory of Anšan itself. Before conquering Susa and Susiana, he must have annexed Anšan and other Šimaškian territories; see Steinkeller 2007: 229.

210. MDP 18: no. 79; cf. De Graef 2005: 91–92; 2015.

211. Schrakamp 2018.

212. Mofidi-Nasrabadi 2005 identified Huhnuri with Tepe Bormi near Ram Hormuz in Iran's Khuzestan province on the basis of an inscription found there. Alizadeh 2013 thinks this impossible, as he argues that surveys conducted in this region would indicate that it was not occupied between 2800 and 1900 BC, also casting doubt on the provenance of the inscription on which Mofidi-Nasrabadi's identification was based. In turn, Mofidi-Nasrabadi 2018: 115 n. 5 cited the testimony of two officials of the Iranian Cultural Heritage Organization who confirm that the inscription was found at Tepe Bormi, having interviewed the local residents who originally found it. For Ibbi-Sin's year names, cf. the corresponding CDLI wiki entry (cdli.ox.ac.uk/wiki/doku.php?id=year_names_ibbi-suen; last accessed October 20, 2019).

213. Steve 2001 proposed identifying AdamDUN with Tepe Surkhegan near Shushtar in Khuzestan province, but Potts 2010: 247 cast doubts on this identification. Michalowski 2008: 115 suggested that AdamDUN was the main city

of Ur's declining control over Susa and the Elamite periphery. Tablets
found at Susa (Ville Royale, Chantier B, Level VII) feature Ur III year
names from Šu-Sin's fourth year to Ibbi-Sin's first year, overlaid by traces
of violent destruction, linked to the conquest of the city by the Šimaškian
Ebarat I. This must have happened between the fourth and eighth year of
the reign of Ibbi-Sin.[214]

16.5.1. The transition from the Ur III to the *Sukkalmah* period (ca. 2025–1985 BC)

Ebarat I, third ruler in the so-called Šimaški King List,[215] father of
Kindattu and grandfather of Idattu I,[216] reigned at Susa for at least three
years.[217] Moreover, some Susa tablets have year names that can probably be attributed to (unnamed) Šimaškian kings.[218] This must mean
that Ebarat I (ca. Ibbi-Sin years 4–8?) was succeeded by his descendants
Kindattu, Idattu I, and Tan-Ruhurater, although their reigns might have
been interrupted by the repeated attempts of Ibbi-Sin to recapture the
city in his eighth and thirteenth years. A royal seal has been attributed to
Ebarat I[219] in which his name is deified, just as in one of his year names,[220]
probably a remainder of Ur III influence.

---

in the land of Awan, implying that Awan can be located in the southeastern
part of what is today Iran's Khuzestan province, not far from Susa. Cf. also
Steinkeller 2013: 297; De Graef 2018b: 294.

214. De Graef 2005: 1–14; 2008b; 2015 (with references).

215. Scheil 1931.

216. Steinkeller 2007: 221–222.

217. De Graef 2004; 2005: 99; 2015 (with references). Earlier, Steve, Vallat, and
Gasche 2002: 434–435 had proposed that Ebarat I ruled for only two years
at Susa, corresponding to the fifth and sixth regal years of Šu-Sin of Ur. This
hypothesis has now been refuted: De Graef 2005: 105–112; 2015: 294–296
(with references); Steinkeller 2007.

218. De Graef 2008a; 2015: 296 (with references).

219. Steinkeller 2007: 229 n. 51; see also Neumann 2013: 91.

220. MDP 23: no. 292; cf. De Graef 2004; 2005: 99; 2015.

Kindattu, sixth ruler of Šimaški in the Šimaški King List,[221] and son of Ebarat I,[222] bore the title "king of Anšan," according to the seal of his son Imazu,[223] who is otherwise unattested. He played a part in the final collapse of the Ur III state, as is shown by the literary composition known as "Išbi-Erra and Kindattu" or "Išbi-Erra B."[224] Its second verse probably describes the first, unsuccessful, invasion headed by Kindattu and repelled by Išbi-Erra.[225] In the third verse Kindattu withdraws the Elamite and Šimaškian forces.[226] Išbi-Erra's victory is commemorated in his sixteenth year name.[227] However, the Elamites and Šimaškians attacked a second time, conquered Ur, and took away Ibbi-Sin as a captive to Anšan.[228] Eventually, in his twenty-fifth year (commemorated in his twenty-sixth and twenty-seventh year names), Išbi-Erra was able to oust from Ur "the Elamite," either Kindattu or his son and successor Idattu I. A text from Isin dated to Išbi-Erra's nineteenth year mentions Kindattu and Idattu I,[229] indicating a possible co-regency. This text also

---

221. Scheil 1931.

222. Steinkeller 2007: 221–222. According to the so-called Genealogy of Šilhak-Inšušinak (König 1965: 110–115, no. 48 §2, no. 48a §3, and no. 48b §3), a twelfth-century BC royal inscription listing the rulers who restored or embellished the temple of Inšušinak, Kindattu was the son (*šak*) of Tan-Ruhurater. This is either a mistake—which is not inconceivable as the Genealogy was written about 800 years after Kindattu's reign—or it concerns another ruler of that name.

223. MDP 43: no. 1679 = Mofidi-Nasrabadi 2009: no. 30: Imazu, son of Kindattu, king of Anšan.

224. Originally published by Van Dijk 1978; cf. also Vanstiphout 1989–1990.

225. Van Dijk 1978: 193–196.

226. Van Dijk 1978: 199–200.

227. For this and all other year names of Išbi-Erra of Isin, see the corresponding CDLI wiki entry (cdli.ox.ac.uk/wiki/doku.php?id=year_names_ishbi-erra; last accessed October 20, 2019).

228. Described in the composition dubbed "Lamentation over the destruction of Sumer and Ur," see especially Michalowski 1989: ll. 33–37.

229. Crawford 1954: no. 382: ll. 6–8, 12–14.

bears testament to the existence of diplomatic relations between Isin and
Anšan despite having stood on opposite sides during the disintegration
of the kingdom of Ur. These relations dated back to at least Išbi-Erra's
fourteenth year, as shown by another text from Isin mentioning sealed
letters from Anšan.[230]

Idattu I, the seventh ruler in the Šimaški King List[231] and the son of
Kindattu, was "king of Anšan" and "king of Šimaški and Elam."[232] One
brick inscription is preserved,[233] mentioning Tan-Ruhurater as his son.
This is corroborated by the so-called Genealogy of Šilhak-Inšušinak.[234]
This text mentions an Idattu, sister's son (*ruhu šak*) of Hutran-
tem/pti. Mentioned right before Tan-Ruhurater, son of Idattu, this may
be Idattu I. There is no agreement among scholars regarding the meaning
of "sister's son." As Potts noted,[235] from the end of the third millennium
through the mid-second millennium BC the pattern of Elamite succession is inconsistent: there is both patrilineal succession (from father to
son, as was usual in Mesopotamian) and avuncular succession (from
father to nephew, as was typically Elamite). Applied to Idattu I, this may
mean he was the son of Kindattu and Hutran-tem/pti's sister. Whereas
his patrilineal descent is stressed in the contemporaneous inscription,[236]
his matrilineal/avuncular descent is stressed in the much later Genealogy
of Šilhak-Inšušinak, possibly because this was considered more important by then.

One of the year names that can probably be attributed to a Šimaškian
king mentions the making of a copper statue of Hutran-tem/pti.[237] This
king must be Idattu I (Idattu II's grandfather) or his successor Ebarat

230. Crawford 1954: no. 302.

231. Scheil 1931.

232. Steinkeller 2007; 2011.

233. Malbran-Labat 1995: 29 no. 9.

234. König 1965: 110–115, no. 48 §2, no. 48a §3, and no. 48b §3.

235. Potts 2018: 541.

236. Steinkeller 2007; 2011.

237. MDP 24: no. 385: ll. 8–10. Previously, the present author—unaware of the inscrip-
       tion published by Steinkeller—suggested attributing this year name to Idattu I,

II (who might have been Idattu I's son and thus Idattu II's uncle). Hutran-tem/pti, otherwise unattested, may have been the ruler of a central Iranian territory which was either conquered by Ebarat I and/or Kindattu or added to their realm through marriage.

Kiten-rakittapi, *sukkalmah* of Elam and *teppir*,[238] calls himself a servant of King Idattu I, implying that the *sukkalmah* of Elam was a deputy of the Šimaškian king[239] and it is likely that this also was the case for later *sukkalmah*s, as already suggested by Steinkeller.[240] In fact there was a stratified power system with the Šimaškian king as the highest authority, under whom two *sukkalmah*s each ruled over a part of the vast territory; further down, local officials and administrators, such as *sukkal*s and *teppir*s, supervised smaller territories or cities, under the authority of their *sukkalmah* and the king.[241] This stratified power system can be fully reconstructed from Idattu I's successor Ebarat II onward. Some of the other rulers known from the Šimaški King List, however, seem to have been sidelined once the stratified power system reached its full extent.

Tan-Ruhurater,[242] eighth ruler in the Šimaški King List, and probably Idattu I's son, did not succeed him as king. He was governor (*énsi*) of Susa.[243]

---

based on the mention of Pundudu, who is likely to be identified with Pududu, a servant of Idattu according to his seal: De Graef 2008a: 78–79. But it is now clear that the Idattu mentioned in the seal legend of Pududu is not Idattu I, the king of Šimaški, but Idattu II, governor (*énsi*) of Susa and son of Tan-Ruhurater.

238. A high judicial official: Tavernier 2007: 59–60.

239. Steinkeller 2007: 221–222; 2011: 21–22.

240. Steinkeller 2007: 222 n. 29.

241. De Graef 2012; 2013b.

242. De Graef 2013a.

243. His title on a brick, see Malbran-Labat 1995: 24–25, no. 4; and on his seal, see MDP 43: no. 1675 = MDP 55: no. 77: [*tan*-ᵈ]*ru-hu-[ra-te-er*] / énsi ⌈mùš. eren⌉[ki] / [...] ⌈x x⌉ [...] / ⌈dumu⌉ *i-da-*⌈*du*⌉ "Tan-Ruhurater, governor of Susa, [...], son of Idattu." The third line of the seal legend being unfortunately illegible, it is hard to interpret the fourth line, as it might refer to a personal name in line 3, although it is likely to refer to Tan-Ruhurater, corroborating the fact that he was the son of Idattu I.

A seal of one of his servants is preserved.[244] Tan-Ruhurater was married to Me-Kubi, daughter of Bilalama of Ešnunna, a sign of good relations between Šimaškian and Ešnunnaean kings at the time. The "house[hold]" (é) of Tan-Ruhurater is mentioned in a receipt of sesame,[245] dated by an otherwise unknown year name,[246] in all probability of a Šimaškian king, perhaps Idattu I, under whose authority Tan-Ruhurater was governor of Susa.[247] Surprisingly, there is no reference in the Elamite texts to the war with Ilum-muttabbil of Der, a contemporary and ally of Bilalama of Ešnunna (Tan-Ruhurater's father-in-law), who claimed to have defeated the armies of Anšan, Elam and Šimaški.[248] However, there are two year names, probably of a Šimaškian king, commemorating the destruction of Zidanum.[249] These may refer to the conflict between the Šimaškians and Zagros principalities involving the kingdom of Der under Ilum-muttabbil.

Idattu II, the tenth ruler in the Šimaški King List and the son of Tan-Ruhurater, succeeded his father as governor (énsi) of Susa. Three brick inscriptions of his,[250] as well as six (or possibly nine) seals of his subordinates,[251] are also known.

---

244. MDP 43: no. 1674.

245. MDP 28: no. 505.

246. The tablet is sealed by a subordinate of Ibbi-Sin, the last king of Ur: De Graef 2008a: 80–81. Unfortunately, this tablet could not be located for study either at the Louvre nor at the National Museum of Iran. This tablet does not necessarily have chronological implications since the seal may have been reused or recut, just like Kirikiri had an Ur III-period seal recut for his son Bilalama. According to the published line drawing, the legend of the seal is damaged.

247. Steve, Vallat, and Gasche 2002: 436–437 believed this to be another Tan-Ruhurater, a high official during the Ur III period, linking him to the Tan-Ruhurater who is mentioned as the father of Kindattu in the Genealogy of Šilhak-Inšušinak. But this must be another Kindattu since we know that Kindattu's father was Ebarat I.

248. Frayne 1990: 677–678.

249. De Graef 2008a: 74–76.

250. Malbran-Labat 1995: 26–29, no. 6–8.

251. Six of the seals include "governor" among Idattu II's titles: (1) MDP 14: no. 28 = Mofidi-Nasrabadi 2009: no. 18; (2) MDP

Another governor (*énsi*) of Susa by the name of Idattu-Inšušinak is known from his inscription on the edge of a stone basin.[252] According to this, he was the son of Pepi and also bore the title of military governor (*gìr.níta*) of Elam. It is not easy to situate this Idattu-Inšušinak. His titles (*énsi* and *gìr.níta*) suggest an early (possibly even Ur III?) date, but we know that the title *énsi* was still in use when the new power structure with king, *sukkalmah*s, and *sukkal*s was implemented.

Two more rulers are mentioned in the Šimaški King List: Idattu-napir (in eleventh position) and Idattu-temti (in twelfth position). Their title or function is unknown as they are otherwise unattested. In general, it is clear that after Ebarat II succeeded Idattu I as king of Anšan, Idattu I's (other?) descendants mentioned in the Šimaški King List were sidelined.

16.5.2. The early years of the *sukkalmah* regime (ca. 1980–1850? BC)

Ebarat II, the ninth ruler in the Šimaški King List, although never attested as *sukkalmah*, has long been assumed to be the founder of the so-called *sukkalmah* dynasty. According to this reconstruction, the short reign of the Šimaškian kings would have been followed by the rule of the *sukkalmah*s early in the second millennium BC, lasting about 500 years.[253] This is no longer tenable since we know that the Šimaškian kings instituted a stratified, three-level power structure, consisting of the Šimaškian

---

14: no. 29 = Mofidi-Nasrabadi 2009: no. 16; (3) MDP 18: no. 123–124; (4) MDP 28: no. 44 = Mofidi-Nasrabadi 2009: no. 34; (5) MDP 28: no. 548 = MDP 43: no. 1679; (6) MDP 43: no. 1677 = Mofidi-Nasrabadi 2009: no 32. Another seal (MDP 43: no. 2326 = Mofidi-Nasrabadi 2009: no. 34) names Idattu "shepherd of Šamaš, beloved of Inšušinak, mighty. . . ." Two other seals do not mention the title of governor, and it is therefore uncertain whether they refer to Idattu I or Idattu II: MDP 4:3 2325 = Mofidi-Nasrabadi 2009 no. 17; Amiet 1973: no. 43 = Mofidi-Nasrabadi 2009: no 25.

252. MDP 6: no. 16–19.

253. Cf., among many others, Stolper 1982; De Meyer 1982; Grillot and Glassner 1991; Glassner 1994; 2013; Steve, Vallat, and Gasche 2002: 440–452; Vallat 1994; 1996; 1997a; 2007; Potts 2016: 148–175.

king, two *sukkalmah*s, and various local officials and administrators. The system was probably implemented by Ebarat I, the first Šimaškian king who added Susa and Susiana to his vast kingdom, covering Šimaški in the northeast, Anšan in the southeast, Susa and Susiana in the southwest, and Elam in the northwest. Ebarat II, mentioned in the Genealogy of Šilhak-Inšušinak, without affiliation, was king of Anšan and Susa.[254] As he is listed in the Šimaški King List between Tan-Ruhurater (8) and Idattu II (10), he might have been a son of Idattu I and the (possibly younger) brother of Tan-Ruhurater, or a son of Tan-Ruhurater and (elder) brother of Idattu II. The fact that Ebarat II succeeded Idattu I as king favors the former possibility. The (elder?) Tan-Ruhurater did not succeed Idattu I as king. He was sidelined, perhaps as the result of an internecine struggle. No royal inscriptions of Ebarat II have been preserved, only three seals of his servants.[255]

We can reconstruct the following schema. Three *sukkalmah*s served under Ebarat II: Temti-Agun I, *sukkalmah* of Elam and Šimaški; Šilhaha, *sukkalmah* of Anšan and Susa,[256] who later succeeded Ebarat II as king; and Pala-iššan. As he was the older brother of Temti-Agun I, who started out as *sukkal* and *teppir* of Susa but rose to be *sukkalmah* of Elam and Šimaški,[257] it is probable that Temti-Agun I succeeded his elder brother Pala-iššan, who must have been *sukkalmah* of Elam and Šimaški before

---

254. According to the so-called Cylindroid of Atta-hušu: MDP 28: no. 4: ll. 1–2.

255. MDP 43: no. 1680 = Mofidi-Nasrabadi 2009: no. 14; MDP 43: no. 1686 = Mofidi-Nasrabadi 2009: no. 15; and a seal impressed on MDP 10: no. 4, 6, 7, 9, 13, 30, 40, 44: cf. De Graef 2012: 532–533.

256. As some rulers are attested with both titles (*sukkalmah* of Elam and Šimaški and *sukkalmah* of Susa and Anšan), Mofidi-Nasrabadi 2010 proposed seeing them as variants of one and the same title, considering Susa to be the capital of Elam and Anšan that of Šimaški. This is improbable, not only for geographical reasons, but also because we know that rulers often started out as *sukkal*, before first rising to *sukkalmah* of Elam and Šimaški, then to *sukkalmah* of Anšan and Susa (hence they could have these two titles successively) and eventually to king.

257. Mahboubian 2004: 40; Vallat 2008: 76; Glassner 2013: 326.

him. It seems even likely that Pala-iššan first was *sukkalmah* of Elam and Šimaški and then became *sukkalmah* of Anšan and Susa when Šilhaha became king and that his younger brother Temti-Agun I succeeded him as *sukkalmah* of Elam and Šimaški.[258] This would imply that the office of *sukkalmah* of Anšan and Susa was more prestigious than that of *sukkalmah* of Elam and Šimaški.

During Ebarat II's reign, both Atta-hušu[259] and Temti-Agun I[260] are attested as *sukkal* and *teppir* of Susa. It seems very likely that Temti-Agun I succeeded Atta-ḫušu. This is especially likely as Temti-Agun I later rose to be *sukkalmah* whereas Atta-hušu did not, implying that he must have died or fallen out of favor before he could be promoted. Since most of our sources come from Susa, its *sukkal* Atta-hušu is well known. Three brick inscriptions attest to his building activities.[261] In these inscriptions he is not called *sukkal* and *teppir*, but rather "shepherd of the people of Susa" (*sipa (šà) éren Susa*) and "shepherd of Inšušinak" (*sipa Inšušinak*). On a bronze *gunagi* vessel and bronze axe he is called "the one who holds the ŠA.DU.DAM of the people of Susa."[262] These are certainly traditional local Susian titles or epithets.[263] Similarly, Šilhaha was called "father of the land of Anšan and Susa" next to his title *sukkalmah*. A vice-*teppir* of Atta-hušu might have been Tebadda, who is mentioned in the Ašiši dossier.[264] Three seals of his servants are known.[265]

---

258. De Graef 2019.

259. Glassner 2013: 319–322.

260. Glassner 2013: 325.

261. Malbran-Labat 1995: 30–33 no. 10–13; Matsushima and Teramura 2012: 16–18 no. BK 7–9.

262. Sollberger 1968; De Graef 2012: 531–532.

263. The epithet "shepherd of Susa" is also found in the legend of the seal of Tetep²-mada, who claims to be the son of a sister of Šilhaha but is otherwise unattested: MDP 43: no. 2016 = Mofidi-Nasrabadi 2009: no. 36.

264. MDP 55: no. 26.

265. MDP 43: no. 1682 = no. 1683 = Mofidi-Nasrabadi 2009: no. 22; MDP 43: no. 2327 = Mofidi-Nasrabadi 2009: no. 24 and a seal impressed on MDP 10: no. 2, 11, and 21: cf. De Graef 2009; 2012: 532–533.

In his inscriptions, Atta-hušu claims to be the son of the sister of Šilhaha,[266] the first in a long line of rulers up to the twelfth century BC. While it seems likely that Atta-hušu, and also his contemporaries Pala-iššan and Temti-Agun I, were indeed the biological sons of one (or more) sister(s) of Šilhaha, this cannot reflect a biological reality for the later rulers, as we shall see.

The fact that, from now on, rulers declared their legitimacy by claiming avuncular descent from Šilhaha implies that this ruler must have been a key figure in the implementation of the stratified power system. This may even have involved some sort of dynastic break, as Šilhaha is the first ruler not included in the Šimaški King List to have become king, whereas the other Šimaškian rulers mentioned in this composition were sidelined. Šilhaha is described as the beloved son (*šak hatik*) of Ebarat II in the Genealogy of Šilhak-Inšušinak, but it is not certain that he was of Šimaškian descent. As for Atta-hušu, he might have been a transitional figure, not only because of his use of local or older titles and epithets ("shepherd") and new ones (*sukkal*, *teppir*), but also because of his descent. Indeed, an oath formula seems to imply that Atta-hušu was the son of Kindattu.[267] This might have been the Kindattu listed in the Genealogy of Šilhak-Inšušinak as a son of Tan-Ruhurater.[268] This is a perfect chronological match and would link the old Šimaškian dynastic line, which was put aside since the time of Tan-Ruhurater, to the new dynastic line of Šilhaha in the person of Atta-hušu.

---

266. This seems to be corroborated in the Genealogy of Šilhak-Inšušinak, where an Atta-hušu, son of a sister of Šilhaha, is mentioned: König 1965: 110–115, no. 48 §2, no. 48a §3, no. 48b §3. However, since he was listed after Širuktuh, Siwe-palar-huppak, and Kuk-kirwaš, it is not certain whether this is the same Atta-hušu altogether, as Širuktuh and Siwe-palar-huppak can be dated two centuries later thanks to synchronisms with Mesopotamian rulers. So, this is either a mistake or it concerns another ruler with that name.

267. MDP 55: no. 20.

268. Earlier, the present author argued that this could have been the Šimaškian king Kindattu (De Graef 2006: 23–24, 104–104; 2012: 537–543) but this view is no longer tenable.

FIGURE 16.5. Fragmentary silver *gunagu* vessel whose inscription states that it was made by Ukal, governor of Susa, for "Pala-iššan, beloved brother of Temti-Agun." Reproduced from http://mahboubiancollection.com/images/elam/6.jpg, with kind permission of the Mahboubian Collection.

Less is known of the brothers Pala-iššan and Temti-Agun I (figure 16.5).[269] Both claim to be the sister's son of Šilhaha, and once Šilhaha had succeeded Ebarat II as king,[270] Pala-iššan was promoted to *sukkalmah* of Anšan and Susa, and Temti-Agun I to *sukkalmah* of Elam and Šimaški[271] while a third brother, Kuk-sanit, succeeded Temti-Agun I as (*sukkal* and)

269. One seal of a servant of Pala-iššan is known: Scheil 1926: 36 = Mofidi-Nasrabadi 2009: no. 27, cf. De Graef 2012: 531–532.

270. Šilhaha bears the title of king (*lugal*) in MDP 28: no. 455: ll. 3–4.

271. Pala-iššan and Temti-Agun are mentioned in the inscription on the silver *gunagi* vessel: Mahboubian 2004: 40; Vallat 2008: 76; Glassner 2013: 326. Temti-Agun I succeeded his brother as *sukkalmah* of Elam and Šimaški, as is shown by the inscription on the silver *gunagi* vessel he offered to the god Napiriša for King Ebarat II and his own life, published by Glassner 2013: 325.

teppir of Susa.[272] The fact that Pala-iššan has a year name implies that he must have succeeded Šilhaha as king, although we have no attestation of him with this title. Pala-iššan is also attested with a Kuk-kirwaš[273] who started his career as *sukkal*, probably under Šilhaha, and was promoted to *sukkalmah* under Pala-iššan. In one inscription he calls himself *sukkalmah*, (former) *sukkal* of Elam, Šimaški, and Susa, son of a sister of Šilhaha.[274] The "Genealogy of Šilhak-Inšušinak" mentions a Kuk-kirwaš son of Lankuku.[275] Four seals of servants of Kuk-kirwaš are known.[276] Kuk-kirwaš is also mentioned alone in an oath,[277] and once each with Tem-sanit[278] and with Kuk-Nahhunte:[279] both Tem-sanit and Kuk-Nahhunte must have been co-rulers of Kuk-kirwaš at the time, but their titles are not mentioned.

The name Kuk-našur is attested in more than twenty oaths, but as there were at least three and maybe four rulers by that name,[280] it

272. Glassner 1996; 2013: 325. In turn, Kuk-sanit had a vice (*egir*) *sukkal* named Atta-puni under his authority (Glassner 2013: 324), which implies that he combined the offices of *sukkal* and *teppir*. He is mentioned together with Pala-iššan in an oath: MDP 28: no. 399: ll. 16–17.

273. In an oath: MDP 24: no. 348: ll. 11'-12', 14'-15'; MDP 24: no. 349: ll. 31–33. In a year name: De Graef 2008a: 68–70.

274. Malbran-Labat 1995: 40–42, no. 18 = Matsushima and Teramura 2012: 15, 19–25, no. 6, 10–16.

275. König 1965: 110–115, no. 48 §2, no. 48a §3, no. 48b §3. It is, however, not certain whether this is the same Kuk-kirwaš, as he is listed after Širuktuh and Şiwe-palar-huppak, who were contemporaries of Samsi-Addu of Ekallatum and Zimri-Lim of Mari and thus must have reigned at least a century later. So, this is either a mistake or else concerns another ruler of that name.

276. MDP 43: no. 1684 = Mofidi-Nasrabadi 2009: no. 28; Scheil 1926: no. 2 = Mofidi-Nasrabadi 2009: no. 29; Vallat 2004: no. 1 = Mofidi-Nasrabadi 2009: no. 35; and a seal on MDP 28: no. 531.

277. MDP 24: no. 350: ll. 10'–11'.

278. MDP 24: no. 351: ll. 32–34.

279. MDP 24: no. 352: ll. 27–29. Kuk-Nahhunte may also have been the father of Hute-kazan, one of the servants of Kuk-kirwaš, cf. earlier in this paragraph.

280. Three rulers called Kuk-našur according to Vallat 1997b; Steve, Vallat, and Gasche 2002: 381–384; and four rulers by this name according to Potts 2016: 151–153. Cf. section 16.5.5.2.

is hard to know which is which. However, twice a Kuk-našur is mentioned together with Kuk-Nahhunte,[281] who served under Kuk-kirwaš, which provides a chronological reference for this Kuk-našur I. This could be the Kuk-našur claiming to be the son of a sister of Šilhaha in a brick inscription, with the titles *sukkalmah*, (former) *sukkal* of Elam, Šimaški, and Susa.[282] If this is correct, it is possible that he was *sukkal* under Temti-Agun I (*sukkalmah* of Anšan and Susa), and rose to be *sukkalmah* of Elam and Šimaški when Temti-Agun I was promoted to king (unattested), and Kuk-kirwaš was promoted to *sukkalmah* of Anšan and Susa.

Many rulers in this period are attested mostly in oaths, often without their full title, which makes it impossible to situate them,[283] especially since the texts have no year names or eponyms.[284] We only have royal inscriptions from a small number of rulers, with their titles, and, moreover, several rulers are homonymous. Unfortunately, Mesopotamian sources show that Elamite rulers, generally unnamed, were involved internationally, both on a diplomatic and military level.

16.5.3. The beginnings of Elam's interventions in Mesopotamian politics (ca. 1850–1785 BC)

Let's begin with an attempt to assess Elam's role in the history of the kingdoms of Larsa and Ešnunna, ca. 1843–1834 BC. "The man of Elam" is mentioned in the Mari Eponym Chronicle as having defeated

---

281. MDP 24: no. 329–330.

282. Malbran-Labat 1995: 39–40, no. 18; see also Scheil 1932b.

283. Many attempts have been made to reconstruct the sequence of the rulers of the *sukkalmah* period, the most recent ones being those of Steve, Vallat, and Gasche 2002: 381–384; Vallat 2008; and Potts 2016: 151–153. However, they all adhere to the traditional interpretation that the *sukkalmah* was the highest authority and do not take the new (earlier) dating of Atta-hušu into consideration.

284. Apart from a few year names, the most recent of which is that of Pala-iššan and Kuk-kirwaš. See De Graef 2008a.

Ipiq-Adad II of Ešnunna in 1835/1834 BC (the eponym year of Šarrum-Adad, when Samsi-Addu succeeded his father). Vallat suggested that this ruler was Širuktuh,[285] who is mentioned by name in a letter from Tell Shemshara,[286] and also linked him to the defeat of the Elamite forces by Sin-iqišam of Larsa in 1837 BC.[287] However, Eidem argued that the letter in question is to be dated around 1785 BC, which would require Širuktuh to have reigned for over fifty years.[288] While this is not impossible, it is still improbable, especially as there is no evidence linking the defeat against Larsa or the victory against Ešnunna three or four years later to Širuktuh.

Around that time, a ruler with an Elamite name and arguably Elamite roots conquered Larsa and established a new ruling dynasty there: this was Kudur-mabuk, the son of Simti-Šilhak, whose exact origins and early career both remain tantalizingly unclear.[289] While his title "Father of the Amorites/Emutbal"[290] has sometimes been wrongly interpreted as proof of Amorite descent, both his and his father's names are clearly Elamite,[291] as is the name of Kudur-mabuk's daughter, Manzi-wartaš,[292]

---

285. Vallat 1996: 313.

286. Eidem and Læssøe 2001: no. 64.

287. In Sin-iqišam's fifth year name; see the corresponding CDLI wiki entry (http://cdli.ox.ac.uk/wiki/doku.php?id=year_names_sin-iqisham; last accessed October 21, 2019).

288. Eidem 1992: 16.

289. He is attested in three documentary texts from Larsa dating from the reigns of Sin-iddinam and Sin-iqišam: YOS 5: 167 (Sîn-iqišam 4); YOS 5: 216 (Sin-iddinam 7); YOS 14: 333 (undated). In this last text, he is described as "the Elamite who entered." Steinkeller *apud* Stone and Zimansky 2004: 31–32 n. 21 dated this text to the reign of Sin-iddinam.

290. Cf. the royal inscriptions of Warad-Sin and Kudur-mabuk in Frayne 1990: 206–211, 213–216, 219–222, 224–231, 236–240, 246–248, 250–251, 254–256, and 267–268.

291. Steinkeller *apud* Stone and Zimansky 2004: 30–34.

292. Manzi-wartaš is mentioned in a text from Uruk: Falkenstein 1963: 50. She may be identical with Kudur-mabuk's daughter who was ordained as *entu* priestess of Nanna under the cultic name of Enanedu; cf. Frayne 1990: 257, 315–316.

and there are many Elamites among the entourage of Kudur-mabuk and his sons.[293] But neither Kudur-mabuk nor his father, who must have been in some way connected to the Elamite ruling classes, are mentioned in any Elamite sources.[294]

When he first appears in the available sources, Kudur-mabuk already controlled the Emutbal tribes and was in contact with Larsa, as attested in the last year of its king Sin-iddinam (1843 BC), after which he conquered the city of Maškan-šapir. Seven years later, during the short reign of Sin-iqišam's successor Ṣilli-Adad, which lasted for less than a year (1835 BC), Kudur-mabuk also took the city of Larsa and established a new royal house with his sons Warad-Sin and Rim-Sin.

The question arises whether Sin-iqišam's defeat of Kazallu and the "Elamite army" in 1837 BC was not in some way linked to Kudur-mabuk, then already firmly established in nearby Maškan-šapir. Also, the almost simultaneous conquest of Larsa by Kudur-mabuk and the attack on Ešnunna by another (unnamed and unknown) Elamite leader must in some way have been coordinated, which may imply that Kudur-mabuk was still in close contact with his Elamite motherland.

If we now turn our attention to the rulers attested in Elam at that time, on the basis of the prosopographic study of legal documents from Susa, we are able to group them into two large clusters,[295] which we will discuss in the following sections.

---

293. Frayne 1990: 269 (Lahuratil-[...] son of Abili-[...] servant of Kudur-mabuk), 313–314 (Igmil-Sin son of Kuk-šigat, servant of Rim-Sin) and 315 (Šašim son of Nippi, servant of Rim-Sin).

294. A Šemti-šilhaki is mentioned in MDP 55: no. 10, but as this tablet was excavated in Level B VI ancien of the Ville Royale at Susa, which can be dated 2000–1950 BC, it is impossible that this would have been Kudur-mabuk's father.

295. A first attempt has been made by Jalilvand Sadafi 2013. The present author is currently preparing a prosopographical study of all administrative, economic, and legal texts from Susa (published and unpublished), on the basis of which dossiers and/or parts of archives can be reconstructed, and networks of members of the Susian urban elite can be established, which will no doubt shed more light on the order and succession of the rulers of various levels.

16.5.4. The earlier cluster of Elamite rulers: Širuktuh to Kuk-našur II (ca. 1785–1685 BC)

A first cluster consists of Širuktuh, Ṣiwe-palar-huppak, Kudu-zuluš I, Kuter-Nahhunte, Temti-Agun II, and Kuk-našur II. Širuktuḫ is mentioned in one letter from Shemshara, and Ṣiwe-palar-huppak and Kudu-zuluš I are mentioned in the Mari letters. This shows their wider territorial involvement and allows us to date their reigns approximately. The cluster is based on a letter[296] in which the sender writes that he, his grandfather, and his father were active during the reigns of the *sukkals*[297] Širuktuh, Ṣiwe-palar-huppak, Kudu-zuluš I, Kuter-Nahhunte, and Temti-Agun II. In the same letter, the sender claims to have been captured by the army of Kuk-našur II. In other words, at the time of writing, Kuk-našur II ruled, although at what rank is not clear. Most of these rulers appear elsewhere together with one (or two) other ruler(s), unfortunately mostly without title, which precludes reconstruction of the three-level structure. It is possible, though, to reconstruct a "chain" of contemporary rulers.

16.5.4.1. The rulers Širuktuh, Ṣiwe-palar-huppak, and Kudu-zuluš I
Širuktuh and Ṣiwe-palar-huppak are mentioned together in three oaths, one of which also includes Simut-wartaš, who in turn is mentioned together with Kudu-zuluš I.[298] Širuktuh, Ṣiwe-palar-huppak, and Kudu-zuluš I are mentioned together in a curse formula.[299] Širuktuh is also mentioned in an oath together with *amma haštuk*, and in the same text the oath is repeated, but now by the king (*lugal*), which might imply that Širuktuh became king at the time.[300] The epithet *amma haštuk* has

---

296. MDP 28: no. 14.

297. Only Širuktuh is designated *sukkal* but it is probable that all of them bore this title.

298. MDP 22: no. 62 and 134 (oath of Širuktuh and Ṣiwe-palar-ḫuppak), MDP 24: no. 346 (oath of Širuktuh, Simut-wartaš, and Ṣiwe-palar-ḫuppak, MDP 28: no. 420 (oath of Simut-wartaš and Kudu-zuluš I).

299. MDP 28: no. 397: ll. 14–17.

300. MDP 24: no. 328.

been interpreted in various ways,[301] but is likely to have been the "queen mother." Her appearance in an oath together with Širuktuh might imply that she had replaced (as queen regent?) a ruler who at the time was too young. Both Ṣiwe-palar-huppak and Temti-Agun II refer to the *amma haštuk* in their inscriptions. In a royal inscription in Elamite, which is exceptional as most *sukkalmah* period rulers use Sumerian and/or Akkadian for their inscriptions,[302] Ṣiwe-palar-huppak calls himself *ligawe rišakki* and *merrik hatamtik* (= *sukkalmah* and *sukkal Elam*?)[303] and son of the sister of Širuktuh and claims to have done something (broken) for the life of *amma haštuk*.[304] Temti-Agun II calls himself *sukkal* of Susa and son of the sister of Širuktuh and claims to have built a temple for Išme-karab for his own life, and the lives of Kuter-Nahhunte, Lila-irtaš, Temti-hiša-haneš, and W/Pelkiša the *amma-haštuk*.[305] Both Ṣiwe-palar-huppak and Temti-Agun II claim to be sons of a sister of Širuktuh and were thus (half-)brothers. As such, it seems logical that they would refer to the same queen mother, W/Pelkiša, who would then be Širuktuh's

---

301. "Founding mother" (König 1965: 34–35 n. 13), "mother par excellence" (Grillot 1988: 68), and "late or regretted mother" (Zadok 1984: 10). Glassner 2013: 326 n. 43 considered Amma-haštuk to be a personal name, in this case of the sister of Širuktuh. Cf. also Grillot and Glassner 1991, who originally believed that Amma-haštuk was the daughter of Šilhaha and the sister-wife of Širuktuh. This is chronologically impossible, and moreover the hypothesis of incestuous marriage between a ruler and his sister (originally put forward by Vallat 1994; 1997a) is outdated.

302. De Graef 2013c: 269–272; 2019: 94–95.

303. *ligawe rišakki* might well be the Elamite title behind the logogram *sukkalmah*, as already suggested by Quintana 1999, who translates, "I am the magnifier of the kingdom." Anthonioz and Malbran-Labat 2013 translate, "I (am) the great (one) for/upon the kingdom." *Merrik Hatamtik* means "I (am) the ruler/governor of Elam." Cf. Hinz and Koch 1987, vol. II s.v. me-ir-ri-ik. In other words, the combination *ligawe rišakki merrik Hatamtik* might be the Elamite rendering of *sukkalmah sukkal Elam* "*sukkalmah*, [former] *sukkal* of Elam," which would imply that Ṣiwe-palar-huppak started his career as *sukkal* but rose to be *sukkalmah* later, as we would expect.

304. König 1965: 34–36 (3 A+B I–II).

305. A brick inscription: Malbran-Labat 1995: 34–35, no. 14.

sister. If she acted as queen regent, she could have been Širuktuh's sister, temporarily replacing one of her sons.

Ṣiwe-palar-huppak and Kudu-zuluš I are mentioned together in three oaths.[306] Širuktuh is listed as son of the sister of Šilhaha in the Genealogy of Šilhak-Inšušinak after Šilhaha and before Ṣiwe-palar-huppak. Chronologically it is impossible that Širuktuh, situated around 1785 BC, was the son of a sister of Šilhaha, dated roughly around 1950 BC. Son of the sister of Šilhaha is thus to be interpreted here as a kind of epithet.[307] Širuktuh is mentioned in letters from Shemshara, which dates his reign to around 1785 BC.[308] One of these[309] concerns an allied attack of Assyrians, Ešnunnaeans, and Turukkeans on the Gutian *indaššu*.[310] The same Gutian ruler is probably mentioned in an Elamite inscription on an alabaster stele listing a series of conquests, probably by Širuktuh.[311] The stele gives the titles *ligawe rišakki* and *merrik hatamtik*,[312] implying that he was still *sukkalmah*, whereas in the letter he is king. The letter also shows he played a key role in the conflict involving Upper Mesopotamia, Ešnunna, and the Trans-Tigris and Zagros entities. Another Shemshara letter refers to the "father (and) great overseer" (*abum waklum rabûm*), maybe a local or Akkadian variant of the Elamite title *sukkalmah*.[313] Which Elamite ruler is implied, however, remains an open question.

---

306. MDP 22: no. 63–64; MDP 23: no. 200.

307. Was Širuktuh not the legitimate heir to the throne and might the fictitious link with the illustrious ancestor be an attempt to legitimate his position? Another possibility is that there were multiple rulers called Šilhaha.

308. The letters from Tell Shemshara cover a period of about two to three years corresponding to the twenty-eighth to thirtieth years of the reign of Samsi-Addu: Eidem 1992: 16.

309. Eidem and Læssøe 2001: no. 64. Cf. Potts 2016: 156–157.

310. According to Pongratz-Leisten 2015: 66 n. 111, the Hurrian title *endan* is used in the Tell Shemshara letters in the sense of "his royalty" in the following variants: *indušše, indaššu, endušše,* and *endaššu.*

311. Farber 1975: 84 iii 18′; Eidem 1985: 91 n. 43; Wu 1994: 186; Potts 2016: 157.

312. Farber 1975: 77.

313. Eidem and Læssøe 2001: 145.

Both Ṣiwe-palar-huppak and Kudu-zuluš I call themselves *sukkal* of Susa and son of the sister of Širuktuh in their royal charters.[314] Ṣiwe-palar-huppak might have started as *sukkal* of Susa, risen to *sukkal* of Elam[315]— and might have been succeeded as *sukkal* of Susa by Kudu-zuluš I?—and next to *sukkalmah*. Both Ṣiwe-palar-huppak and Kudu-zuluš I appear in the Mari texts, as Šeplarpak, *sukkal* of Elam and Kudušuluš, and *sukkal* of Susa.[316] Ṣiwe-palar-huppak is mentioned in seven other Mari texts,[317] in four of which he appears together with Kudu-zuluš I. Remarkably, though, in these texts they are called, respectively, king of Anšan and king of Susa. One text mentions Šeplarpak, king of Anšan, on the occasion of his conquest of Ešnunna.[318] Ṣiwe-palar-huppak is mentioned four times without a title in a draft of a treaty between Zimri-Lim of Mari and Hammurabi of Babylon against Ṣiwe-palar-ḫuppak, in which the latter's name is not adapted to the Mariote version but is correctly written.[319]

As these texts are dated to between the eighth and tenth years of Zimri-Lim (corresponding to the twenty-sixth to twenty-eighth years of Hammurabi), the reigns of Ṣiwe-palar-huppak and Kudu-zuluš I can be dated around 1767–1765 BC. Both were *sukkal* in the first month of Zimri-Lim's eighth year, whereas they were both kings (*lugal*) from the second month of the same year onward. Clearly, there is some mix-up here. For Kudu-zuluš I, the Mariotes could have confused *sukkal* (as local ruler) with *lugal*. Ṣiwe-palar-huppak could have been *sukkal*

314. MDP 28: no. 297, 396.

315. Mentioned in a fragmentary brick inscription from Anšan: Stolper 1982: 60 (M-693).

316. ARM 23: no. 355 (ZL 8-i-8); cf. Chambon 2009: 87.

317. ARM 31: no. 125–127 (ZL 8-ii-8), partial duplicates; in ARM 31: no. 127, the scribe wrote the name of Kudu-zuluš erroneously as Šulši-kudur (*šu-ul-⌈ši?⌉-ku-du-ur*); cf. Guichard 1994; ARM 31: no. 139 and 141 (ZL 9-i-11), partial duplicates; ARM 31: no. 147 (ZL 9-viii-2); ARM 31: no. 164 (ZL 10-iv) Cf. also Durand 1986: 119–120.

318. M.8806, cf. Dossin 1970: 97 and Durand 1986: 121–122. According to Heimpel 2003: 58, this fragment can be dated to ZL 10-ii.

319. Durand 1986: 111–115; 1997: 452–453.

of Elam until the beginning of the eighth year of Zimri-Lim (ZL 8-i-8) and might have become king (of Anšan, not of Elam) shortly after this, in 1767 BC. This would mean he would have skipped the rank of *sukkalmah*, which is improbable or at least exceptional. In one text, beside Ṣiwe-palar-ḫuppak, the *teppir* of Anšan is mentioned,[320] and since the rank of *teppir* was linked to that of *sukkal*,[321] this implies that he must have had a higher rank, which is also corroborated by the fact that he received three vases and the *teppir* of Anšan only one. His mention in the draft for the treaty between Zimri-Lim and Hammurabi of Babylon as representative of hostile Elam might also indicate he was king at that time.

There are numerous Mari texts in which one or more unnamed Elamites are mentioned as soldiers (*erén/ṣabum*), messengers (*dumu. meš šipri*), but mostly as *sukkal*, most frequently *sukkal* of Elam,[322] sometimes *sukkal* without specification, and rarely as *sukkal* of Susa.[323] In various texts "the Elamite man" (*lú elam*) appears. Given the relatively small chronological span of the attestations that all fall into the period from the third to the tenth years of the reign of Zimri-Lim of Mari, it is possible that all mentions of the *sukkal* of Elam refer to Ṣiwe-palar-ḫuppak, and that the unnamed *sukkal* of Susa is Kudu-zuluš I.[324] Charpin is convinced that by *sukkal* of Elam, *sukkalmah* is meant, as he believes this to be Ṣiwe-palar-huppak's title, although he is never attested as such.[325] An unnamed *sukkalmah* is attested twice in the

---

320. ARM 31: no. 139.

321. At least earlier, when Atta-ḫušu, Temti-Agun I, and Kuk-sanit combined the titles of *sukkal* and *teppir*, cf. supra.

322. Written in many variant spellings: *(lú) sukkal elam(.ma)^(ki)*, *(lú) sukkal elam. ma-tim*, *lú sukkal elam.meš*, *sukkal e-la-am-tim^(ki)*. Retrieved from the website Archibab ("Archives babyloniènnes, XXᵉ–XVIIᵉ siècles av. J.-C.": www. archibab.fr; last accessed October 20, 2019).

323. *sukkal šušim* and *sukkal šušim ša elam.ma^ki*. Retrieved from Archibab (www. archibab.fr; last accessed October 20, 2019).

324. Charpin 2004: 210; Durand 2013: 334.

325. Charpin 2004: 210 n. 1040. He is only once called *ligawe rišakki*, which might be the Elamite title *sukkalmah* written logographically.

Mari letters.[326] In one of them the *sukkal* of Elam and the *sukkal* of Susa
are also mentioned, showing that the difference between the titles *sukkal* and *sukkalmah* was recognized. Notwithstanding this one example,
there was some confusion in the use of these foreign titles, which is
not surprising at all: each of these *sukkal*s and *sukkalmah*s ruled over a
part of the vast Šimaškian territory and as such could be considered a
"king" by the Mesopotamians, all the more as *sukkal* and *sukkalmah* are
logograms concealing Elamite titles, making it even more complicated,
then and now.

The "*sukkal* of Elam" in the Mari letters could be the ruler of the
region of Elam, the northwestern part of the Šimaškian state closest to
Upper Mesopotamia, under the authority of a *sukkalmah* of Elam and
Šimaški. However, the term "Elamite" clearly also had a *pars pro toto*
sense in the Mesopotamian sources,[327] referring to the entirety of their
eastern neighboring state, implying that the *sukkal* or man of Elam or
the Elamite could refer to the head of the Šimaškian state, the king. This
would explain why Siwe-palar-huppak is called both *sukkal* of Elam and
king of Anšan.

Most importantly, though, the Mari texts inform us about the important role the Elamite rulers (on various levels) played in the wider region.
In this light it is remarkable that the Elamite sources do not refer to these
events, apart from the one stele listing a series of conquests which can
probably be attributed to Širuktuh.

16.5.4.2. *The sukkal of Elam as arbitrator between Mari and Babylon* (*1771 BC*)

The prestige of Elam is illustrated by the *sukkal* of Elam's role as arbitrator
between Mari and Babylon in the matter of the division of the territory

---

326. ARM 28: no. 181, an intercepted letter written by a *sukkalmah* to the rulers of
Subartu, and Charpin 1993: 176–177.

327. Note in this context the mention of a *sukkal* of Susa of Elam in ARM 2: no. 121
(*sukkal šušim ša elam.ma^ki*). Here Elam clearly refers to the Šimaškian state, as
Susa and Elam were different regions within this state from a Šimaškian point
of view.

of Suhum upon Ešnunna's withdrawal. From two letters,[328] we learn that
Zimri-Lim demanded that Hammurabi limit himself to the cities that
the *sukkal* of Elam gave to him. As these negotiations started in the fifth
year of Zimri-Lim, this *sukkal* of Elam was probably Ṣiwe-palar-huppak.
Apparently, the *sukkal* of Elam, addressed as "father" by both Zimri-Lim
and Hammurabi, was in a position to assign cities along the Euphrates to
a particular ruler. According to Charpin and Durand, the suzerainty of
the Elamites vis-à-vis the Amorites can be explained by the huge territory
controlled by the *sukkalmah*, in contrast to the small territories of the
Amorite rulers.[329] This might also imply that "*sukkal* of Elam" referred
to the Šimaškian king. On the other hand, if it were indeed the *sukkal*
of Elam, the proximity of his territory and his strong (military) influence in the Zagros and Trans-Tigris region could justify his authority. In
that case, the powerful omnipresence of the *sukkal* of Elam in the Mari
letters would show that the *sukkal*s were to a large extent autonomous
within the executive power of their rule. The Šimaškian state would then
be some sort of federal state in which the king had a merely symbolic
function, while actual executive power was in the hands of the *sukkal*s
and *sukkalmah*s.

16.5.4.3. *The war against Ešnunna, Babylon, and Upper Mesopotamia: 1765–1763 BC*

During the eighth and ninth years of the reign of Zimri-Lim of Mari,
diplomatic relations between Mari and the Šimaškian state intensified,
as precious gifts were sent to Ṣiwe-palar-huppak, *sukkal* of Elam (and
perhaps also king); Kudu-zuluš, *sukkal* of Susa; and an unnamed *teppir*
of Anšan. Moreover, a direct trade in tin between Susa and Mari was
established.[330] Apart from these diplomatic and commercial relations,
Mari, together with Babylon, supported the Elamites militarily in their
conquest of Ešnunna, probably in the beginning of Zimri-Lim's tenth

---

328. ARM 26/2: no. 449 and 450.

329. Charpin and Durand 1991: 64.

330. Joannès 1991.

year (1765 BC).[331] Zimri-Lim sent a present to "the king of Anšan," and in a report from Babylon it is said that "the *sukkal* of Elam" was still staying in Ešnunna and had not yet returned to his lands.[332] It is not clear whether Ṣiwe-palar-huppak is meant in both instances.

Two texts from Ešnunna are sealed by subordinates of Kudu-zuluš I.[333] In one of these, the oath is sworn by Tišpak and the *sukkal* or *sukkalmah*,[334] who might be Kudu-zuluš I and, if so, would then be the "*sukkal* of Elam" residing in Ešnunna. This could mean he had risen from *sukkal* of Susa to *sukkal* of Elam (or *sukkalmah*) by then, or that he was designated as (temporary) governor/ruler of Ešnunna by virtue of his position as *sukkal* of Susa. A letter to Zimri-Lim mentions the *sukkal* of Susa of Elam "whom they have killed."[335] This might refer to Kudu-zuluš I, but there is no way to confirm this.[336]

The dismantling of the Ešnunnaean power led to Hammurabi of Babylon's recovery of both Mankisum and Upi, riverside towns on the Tigris that had once been Babylon's but had been lost to Ešnunna. However, the Elamites were preparing for a grand conquest of both Upper Mesopotamia and Babylonia.

At the end of Zimri-Lim's ninth and the beginning of his tenth regnal year, Atamrum, whom the Elamites had put in charge of Ešnunna, seized

---

331. Charpin and Ziegler 2003: 212–213; Heimpel 2003: 57–58; Charpin 2004: 210. Note in this regard also Saporetti 2013: 605 on a letter from Me-Turan, published by Mustafa 1983: 234–236, no. 141, which might point to a threat by the Elamites and their Amorite allies.

332. ARM 26/2: no. 361.

333. van Dijk 1967: no. 33 and 34. Van Dijk 1970: 64 believed these texts to be from Malgium, but Charpin 1985: 52 correctly concluded they are from Ešnunna.

334. van Dijk 1967: no. 34. Van Dijk 1970: 64 read *sukkal.⌈mah⌉* but according to the hand copy the line is severely damaged, so this reading, while possible, is uncertain.

335. ARM 2: no. 121, ll. 5–6a. Durand 1997: 631 translated "whom they beat" rather than "whom they killed."

336. Heimpel 2003: 57 believes that this alludes to the death of Kudu-zuluš I.

Andarig and then Razama. Two months later, Zimri-Lim attempted to free Razama. The *sukkal* ordered Atamrum to leave Razama and to make a foray into Idamaraṣ.[337]

Meanwhile, a second Elamite army that had been marching up the Tigris seized Ekallatum, veered westward, and invaded the Khabur triangle. There, an Elamite named Kun(n)am(an) was installed in Šubat-Enlil, where he enjoyed complete authority as the "man of Šubat-Enlil," and the city was now considered to be "the city of the *sukkal*."[338] Elamite supremacy was now recognized throughout the region. Local rulers submitted to Kun(n)am(an), alliances were formed under his protection, and he acted as the arbitrator in conflicts between local potentates.[339]

Elam hoped to use the manpower of Idamaraṣ for its assault on Babylon. However, the rapid advance of the Elamites caused a wave of panic among Zimri-Lim's clients, who split into pro- and anti-Elamite factions. At the instigation of the Elamites, some local rulers were replaced by pro-Elamite candidates, while others were murdered.[340] Not only some of the clients, but even Hammurabi urged Zimri-Lim to intervene.

Immediately after their conquest of Ešnunna, the Elamites turned against Hammurabi. This seemed feasible, as the Babylonians and Mariotes had been unable to overcome Ešnunna's defenses, leaving the city to be seized by the Elamites.[341] Following Hammurabi's conquest of the riverside towns of the Tigris, the *sukkal* of Elam attacked Mankisum and gave Hammurabi an ultimatum: "Are not the cities of Ešnunna that

337. Charpin and Ziegler 2003: 221; Heimpel 2003: 65–75; Charpin 2004: 216–217. It is not known whether Zimri-Lim reached Razama in time to prevent the fall of the city to Atamrum; Charpin believes he did so, but Heimpel thinks he arrived too late.

338. Charpin 1986b; Charpin and Ziegler 2003: 217; Heimpel 2003: 69–71; Charpin 2004: 215–216. *Ku, kuna/i, ma,* and *man* are elements known from Elamite names: Zadok 1984: 21, 23, 27. No official or ruler known from the Elamite sources has a name that might have been corrupted to Kun(n)am(an).

339. Charpin 1986b.

340. Charpin 1990; Guichard 1999; Charpin and Ziegler 2003: 222–223; Charpin 2004: 220–222.

341. Heimpel 2003: 58.

you hold mine? Evacuate them and submit to my yoke! Otherwise, I will invade your country."[342] When Hammurabi refused to obey, the Elamite forces took Mankisum, advanced along the Tigris, and besieged Upi, which was occupied by the Babylonians. Hammurabi tried to negotiate a defensive alliance with Larsa. Initially, Rim-Sin agreed, but in the end Larsa did not live up to its promise, although its relations with Babylon were good. They had exchanged the parallel letters they received from the *sukkal* of Elam in which he asked Hammurabi for troops to attack Larsa and at the same time asked Rim-Sin for troops to attack Babylon.[343] Either Elam convinced Larsa of the benefits of a weak Babylon, or Elam occupied a part of Larsa's territory, prohibiting them from assisting the Babylonians.[344] A third possibility is that the Elamite roots of the Larsa dynasty played a role in Rim-Sin's ambiguous attitude and inaction. In reality, the Elamites did not prepare to leave, but on the contrary opened another front in Hammurabi's hinterland. Hammurabi had to evacuate Upi, after which the Elamites installed a garrison there and returned to Ešnunna.[345] It was certainly Elam's goal to penetrate into the heart of Hammurabi's kingdom and lay siege to Babylon itself. Mari dispatched troops to Babylon, and Babylon dispatched troops to Mari to help control Idamaraṣ. Babylon feared the troop concentration under Mari command, but still sent additional troops, fearing that the *sukkal* would attack from the north, its aim being to keep the two parts of the Elamite army separate.

Zimri-Lim of Mari tried to forge an anti-Elamite alliance with the western kingdoms and, in his tenth regnal year, simultaneously made an agreement with Hammurabi and the king of Aleppo not to make a separate peace with Elam.[346] The Elamite supremacy, hitherto unchallenged, would now be met with unprecedented opposition.

---

342. Unpublished Mari letter A.3618 cited in Charpin 2013: 344–345.

343. Charpin 2013: 345–346. Heimpel 2003: 63 dated the sending of the parallel letters to the winter of ZL 9, when Elam was preparing its spring campaign of ZL 10 in Mesopotamia.

344. Heimpel 2003: 61.

345. Charpin and Ziegler 2003: 220; Heimpel 2003: 59–61; Charpin 2004: 214–215.

346. Heimpel 2003: 512–513; cf. Durand 1986; Charpin 1990; Charpin and Ziegler 2003: 220–222; Charpin 2004: 217–219.

The luck of the Elamites ran out, thanks to the cohesion of the Amorite kingdoms and the defection of Atamrum, who rallied to Zimri-Lim. As an alliance with the Turukkeans did not work out, Kun(n)am(an)'s power in Idamaraṣ waned. He then tried to establish an alliance between Mari and Elam to attack Babylon, but this also failed.

Early in Zimri-Lim's eleventh regnal year, Babylonian and Mariote troops marched toward the Irnina canal, where the Elamites had unsuccessfully besieged Hiritum.[347] Hammurabi issued an order to "close" the Irnina (against the Elamites) and troops were stationed in Sippar-Yahrurum. The *sukkal* of Elam crossed the Tigris and launched an expedition against Subartu. Zimri-Lim managed to counter this with his anti-Elamite coalition in northern Mesopotamia, and the Elamites tasted defeat. Eventually, they ravaged the territory of Ešnunna and finally returned to their homeland.[348] Although there were plenty of competitors, Atamrum eventually took Šubat-Enlil.

Despite its relatively short duration, the Elamite invasion was traumatic, not only for those whose territory was directly invaded, i.e., the Babylonians and the kingdoms of Upper Mesopotamia, but also for their allies. Victory over the Elamites is commemorated in Hammurabi's thirtieth year name.[349] However, he did not wait long to renew relations with Elam. Even before the retreating Elamites had reached their homeland, Hammurabi sent a messenger to the *sukkal*. After all, Elam had tin, and the possible rise of a new Ešnunnaean kingdom made an alliance with Elam desirable.

At the end of his eleventh regnal year, Zimri-Lim was informed of the death of the *sukkal* of Elam,[350] possibly Ṣiwe-palar-huppak. Although Elamite intervention in the Zagros and Trans-Tigris territories, as well as in the Mesopotamian lowland, was certainly not new, it seems likely that their latest attempted expansion was motivated by the control of

---

347. For the location of Hiritum, see Cole and Gasche 1998: 21–23; Charpin and Ziegler 2003: 220 n. 463. For the battle of Hiritum, see Lacambre 1997; 2002; Heimpel 2003: 101–106.

348. Charpin and Ziegler 2003: 224–227; Charpin 2004: 222–226.

349. Horsnell 1999: 139–140.

350. ARM 26/2: no. 383.

the so-called road of tin, a route used by the Assyrian merchants to Cappadocia that ran through the region of Šehna/Šubat-Enlil.[351]

16.5.4.4. The rulers Kuter-Nahhunte, Temti-Agun II and Kuk-našur II
Kudu-zuluš I and Kuter-Nahhunte are mentioned together in an oath.[352] The same goes for Kuter-Nahhunte and Temti-Agun II, who appear together in twelve oaths and one curse formula.[353] Temti-Agun II and Kuk-našur II appear together in five oaths.[354] We do not know what title(s) Kuter-Nahhunte had. He calls himself son of the sister of Ṣiwe-palar-huppak in his royal charters.[355] In the curse formula of these charters, Ṣiwe-palar-huppak, Kudu-zuluš I, and Kuter-Nahhunte are always mentioned in the same order, implying that they were in office at least partly at the same time but on different levels, possibly (from high to low) as king, *sukkalmah*, and *sukkal*.

Recently, the first contemporary evidence of a second episode of warfare between Babylon and Elam was uncovered in the abbreviated fifth or sixth year name (year "f") of Abi-ešuh mentioning the army of Elam.[356] The attacker "Kudur-Nanhundi, the Elamite" and the date of the attack "1,635 years ago" are mentioned in a building inscription of

---

351. Charpin and Ziegler 2003: 217–218; Charpin 2004: 216.

352. MDP 23: no. 201.

353. Oaths: MDP 23: no. 202–203; MDP 24: no. 347, 368, 375–378, 382bis, 392; MDP 28: no. 408–409, 426. In MDP 24: no. 374, Kuter-Nahhunte and Temti-Agun II are mentioned together in a curse formula where the oath is sworn by the king (*lugal*). This might imply that one of the rulers was king at the time.

354. MDP 23: no. 167, 204–205, 325; MDP 28: no. 406. In the oath in MDP 23: no. 167, Temti-Agun bears the title *sukkalmah*.

355. Steve, Gasche, and De Meyer 1980: 88–89 mention nine royal charters of Kuter-Nahhunte found in Level 15 of Chantier A in the Ville Royale at Susa. In reality, some of these are fragments that can be joined, resulting in a maximum of only six royal charters. It is remarkable that Kuter-Nahhunte's title is never mentioned in these royal charters.

356. van Koppen 2013.

Ashurbanipal.[357] The Elamites crossed the Tigris and Irnina canal and threatened the cities of northern Babylonia, resulting in famine and distress, as shown by a Sippar tablet dated in Abi-ešuh year "e" (his fourth year).[358] Beaulieu suggested that the Elamites raided Kiš in the heartland of Babylonia.[359] Unfortunately, the full year name of Abi-ešuh's year "f" is not known, but it is clear that the Babylonians were able to repulse the Elamite attack.

This has some implications for Elamite history.[360] Kuter-Nahhunte calls himself son of the sister of Ṣiwe-palar-huppak, implying that he belonged to the next generation. However, Ṣiwe-palar-huppak was certainly involved in the Elamite invasion of 1767 and 1765 BC, whereas his nephew Kuter-Nahhunte waged war on Babylon ca. sixty years later, around 1706 BC. This is rather unlikely, unless Ṣiwe-palar-huppak was very young at the time and Kuter-Nahhunte was very old at the time of his encounter with Abi-ešuh. It is true that Kuter-Nahhunte lived a long life, as shown by an oath together with Kuter-Šilhaha, who belongs to the next cluster. Furthermore, the curse formula in Kuter-Nahhunte's royal charters implies that he was at least partly contemporaneous with Ṣiwe-palar-huppak and Kudu-zuluš I, in which case he must have been in his seventies or eighties when he clashed with Abi-ešuh.

Kuter-Nahhunte is often mentioned in oaths together with Temti-Agun II, where he comes first and Temti-Agun II second, implying that Kuter-Nahhunte was higher in rank and/or that Temti-Agun II ruled after him. Remarkably, though, Temti-Agun II calls himself son of the sister of Širuktuh, just like Ṣiwe-palar-huppak, Kudu-zuluš I, and Temti-Agun II, who would thus belong roughly to the same generation, whereas Kuter-Nahhunte (son of the sister of

---

357. van Koppen 2013: 380.

358. Van Lerberghe and Voet 1997.

359. Beaulieu 2003: 185. For the at least partial abandonment of age-old urban centers such as Ur, Uruk, Larsa, and Nippur, see Gasche 1989.

360. van Koppen 2013: 384–385.

Šiwe-palar-huppak) belonged to the next generation. It is possible that this epithet in fact refers to different dynastic lines of matrilineal descent, which explains why various rulers claimed descent from one and the same "forefather."

Temti-Agun II started out as *sukkal* of Susa, as stated in his royal charter,[361] but was promoted to *sukkalmah*, as attested by an oath in which he is mentioned together with Kuk-našur II.[362] He is also mentioned together with other contemporary rulers, namely Tatta (*sukkal* in one oath) and Atta-mera-halki (no title given) in oaths[363] and Lila-irtaš (no title) in the curse formula of his royal charter; the same Lila-irtaš is also mentioned in his royal inscription.[364]

Kuk-našur II calls himself *sukkal* of Susa and son of the sister of Temti-Agun II in his royal charter and seal inscription.[365] In the curse formula of the same royal charter he is mentioned after Temti-Agun II, implying that they ruled contemporaneously (possibly Temti-Agun II as *sukkalmah* and Kuk-našur II as *sukkal* under his authority). He is mentioned in ten oaths together with Kudu-zuluš II,[366] in one of which he is called *sukkal* of Elam, followed by Kudu-zuluš II, who is king of Susa.[367] Kuk-našur II was believed to have been a contemporary of Ammi-ṣaduqa of Babylon (1646–1626 BC).[368] This synchronism is based on a royal deed from Dilbat dated in the first year of Ammi-ṣaduqa, in which Kuk-našur II granted privileges to two of his servants. However, a closer look at this

---

361. MDP 28: no. 398.

362. MDP 23: no. 167.

363. Oaths with Tatta: MDP 23: no. 321–322; MDP 24: no. 383 and 391; MDP 28: no. 429; oath with Atta-mera-halki: MDP 24: no. 379. Tatta bears the title *sukkal* in the oath MDP 24: no. 391.

364. Malbran 1995: 34–35 no. 14.

365. MDP 23: no. 283; MDP 43: no. 2015.

366. MDP 22: no. 32, 36–38, 67, 86, 160; MDP 23: no. 195, 215; MDP 24: no. 340.

367. MDP 22: no. 160: 15–26: mu *ku-uk-na-šu-úr* sukkal elam.ma-⌜*tim*⌝ *ù ku-du-zu-lu-uš* lugal *šu-ší-im*.

368. Vallat 1993; 1997b.

text reveals that it was Kukka-^{d}našer, (now) *sukkalmah*, (former) *sukkal* of Elam and Šimaški, son of the sister of Šilhaha, who granted these privileges.[369] Neither the titles nor the descent of this Kukka-^{d}našer match those of the ruler generally identified as Kuk-našur II. It is clear that these are two different rulers named Kuk-našur, one *sukkalmah*, former *sukkal* of Elam and Šimaški, son of the sister of Šilhaha, and the other *sukkal* of Susa and son of the sister of Temti-Agun II. As noted by van Koppen,[370] the text is a copy of an original Elamite/Susian document,[371] which itself might have been much older than the copy made in Dilbat in the first year of Ammi-ṣaduqa. It might even be the exercise of an apprentice scribe considering the doodle at the bottom of the reverse. In short, a synchronism between Ammi-ṣaduqa and an Elamite ruler named Kuk-našur cannot be proven on this basis.

16.5.5. The later cluster of rulers: Kuter-Šilhaha to Kuk-našur III/IV (ca. 1685–1585 BC)

The second cluster consists of Kuter-Šilhaha, Temti-raptaš, (Kuk-našur "III"?), Kudu-zuluš II, Tan-uli, Temti-halki, and Kuk-našur III (or IV[372]). Two rulers of the second cluster (Kuter-Šilhaha and Kudu-zuluš II) are attested together with two rulers of the first cluster (Kuter-Nahhunte and Kuk-našur II or "III"). On the basis of the study of the so-called Anih-Šušim family, which can be reconstructed for six generations,[373] a tentative sequence of rulers can be reconstructed (table 16.1).[374]

---

369. Ungnad 1909: no. 67.

370. van Koppen 2013: 385.

371. Van Lerberghe 1986: 152 already noted that this tablet is clearly a copy of an Elamite/Susian document made by a Babylonian, who adapted some of the spellings (such as Kuk-našur's name) and used *ša* instead of the typical *šà* of the Susa tablets.

372. If there was a Kuk-našur "III" who ruled shortly after Kuk-našur II, cf. section 16.5.5.2.

373. De Meyer 1961; Vallat 2000.

374. On the basis of her reconstruction of the Inšušinak-šemi family tree, Jalilvand Sadafi 2013 suggested a different sequence of rulers.

*16.5.5.1. The rulers Kuter-Šilhaha, Temti-raptaš, Širtuh, and
Kudu-zuluš II*

Kuter-Šilhaha is present in the first and second cluster. In one oath, he is
mentioned together with Kuter-Nahhunte, and in two oaths with Kuk-
našur II.[375] In all other oaths, he is mentioned before Temti-raptaš or
Širtuh.[376] In one oath he bears the title of *sukkal*, in four others the title
of *sukkalmah*,[377] implying that he began his career as *sukkal*, and was promoted to *sukkalmah*, but we do not know over which area(s) or city(ies)
he ruled. On three occasions, his co-rulers Temti-raptaš and Širtuh are
called "king of Susa" (*šar šuši*), but are mentioned after the *sukkalmah*
Kuter-Šilhaha.

De Meyer considered the titles "*sukkal* of Susa," "king of Susa," and
"mayor of Susa" to be interchangeable, since Kudu-zuluš II is called king
of Susa and probably mayor.[378] Although the title of mayor (*rabianum*)
is attested only once in the Susa texts,[379] the equation seems logical, as
all were local rulers of a city. However, Kudu-zuluš II is never attested as
sukkal. The title "king of Susa" may in fact be an abbreviation of "king of
Susa and Anšan" (commonly used from the Kidinuid dynasty onward;
see chapter 34 in volume 3). In that case, both Temti-raptaš and Širtuh
would have been king. The fact that they are mentioned after the *sukkalmah* in the oaths may reflect the fact that the king mentions his

---

375. MDP 28: no. 409 (oath of Kuter-Nahhunte and Kuter-Šilhaha); MDP
22: no. 65 and MDP 23: no. 210 (oath of Kuter-Šilhaha and Kuk-našur II). In
the last two oaths, it might have been Kuk-našur "III" instead of Kuk-našur II;
cf. section 16.5.4.4.

376. MDP 22: no. 10, 117, 133; MDP 23: no. 169, 212–214 (oath of Kuter-Šilhaha and
Temti-raptaš); and MDP 22: no. 18; MDP 23: no. 211 (oath of Kuter-Šilhaha
and Širtuh).

377. MDP 23: no. 212 (*sukkal*); and MDP 22: no. 10, 18, 133; MDP 23: 169
(*sukkalmah*).

378. De Meyer 1982: 92. He is king in MDP 22: no. 160 and mayor (?) in MDP
24: no. 393: (2) Kudu-zuluš *ra-bi-[a-nu]* (as restored by V. Scheil).

379. An unnamed *rabânu* mentioned together with an unnamed *hamdagar* in MDP
28: no. 541. For the Old Elamite title *hamdagar*, cf. Hinz and Koch 1987, vol.
I s.v. ha-am-da-ga-ar "elamischer Würdenträger in Susa, vielleicht *Finanzchef*."

Table 16.1. Tentative chronological overview of rulers from Lullubum, Simurrum, Ešnunna, and Susa and synchronisms with Mesopotamian rulers

MESOPOTAMIA				LULLUBUM	SIMURRUM	EŠNUNNA	SUSA
Ur III	Babylonia		Upper Mesopotamia				
	Isin	Babylon					
Šu-Sin (2035–2027)						Ituriya	Ebarat I
Ibbi-Sin (2026–2003)				ANnubanini	Iddi(n)-Sin	Šu-iliya	Kindattu
	Išbi-Erra (2019–1987)				ANzabazuna	Nur-ahum	
						Kirikiri	Idattu I
						Bilalama (c. 2000–1980)	Tan-Ruhurater
	Šu-ilišu (1986–1977)					Išar-ramaši	Ebarat II *Šilhaha* *Atta-hušu*
						Ušur-awassu	*Pala-iššan Temti-Agun I*
	Larsa					Azuzum	*Šilhaha Pala-iššan*
						Ur-Ninmarki (c. 1950)	*Kuk-sanit* *Temti-Agun I Kuk-kirwaš*

MESOPOTAMIA	LULLUBUM	SIMURRUM	EŠNUNNA	SUSA
			Ur-Ningišzida (c. 1950)	Pala-iššan *Temti-Agun I Kuk-našur I Kuk-kirwaš Kuk-nahhunte*
			Ipiq-Adad I	
			Šarriya	Temti-Agun I *Kuk-kirwaš Kuk-našur I*
Sumu-la-El (1880-1845)			Warassa	Kuk-našur I ? [...]
Sabium (1844-1831)			Belakum	
Sin-iddinam (1849-1843)			Ibal-pi-El I (?-1842?)	
Sin-eribam (1842-1841)				
Sin-iqišam (1840-1836)			Ipiq-Adad II (1842?-1815)	
Šilli-Adad				
[Kudur-Mabuk] Warad-Sin (1834-1823)				
Samsi-Addu (1833-1775)				Širuktuh (c. 1785)

Table 16.1. *Continued*

MESOPOTAMIA	LULLUBUM	SIMURRUM	EŠNUNNA	SUSA
Apil-Sin (1830-1813)			Naram-Sin / Iqiš-Tišpak / Ibbi-Sin / Dannum-tahaz	
Rim-Sin I (1822-1763) / Sin-muballiṭ (1812-1793)			Daduša (? - 1779)	
Hammurabi (1792-1750) / Zimri-Lim (1775-1762)			Ibal-pi-El II (1779-1766) / [Elam]	Šiwe-palar-huppak / Kudu-zuluš I (c. 1767-1765)
			Ṣilli-Sin (1764-1760?)	Kuter-Nahhunte
Samsu-iluna (1749-1712)				Temti-Agun II / Atta-mera-halki / Tatta
Abi-ešuh (1711-1684)			Iluni	Kuk-našur II / Kuter-Šilhaha

MESOPOTAMIA	LULLUBUM	SIMURRUM	EŠNUNNA	SUSA
Ammi-ditana (1683–1647)				Temti-raptaš Kudu-zuluš II Sirtuh
Ammi-ṣaduqa (1646–1626) Samsu-ditana (1625–1595)				Tan-uli Temti-halki Kuk-našur III

addressee first in his letters.[380] As for the oaths, this might imply that the first ruler has the lower rank and the last one the higher, which would explain why a *sukkal* is sometimes mentioned first and another (higher ranked) ruler is mentioned second.[381] As the local ruler, it is not illogical for the *sukkal* to be mentioned first in oaths.

Temti-raptaš is only known from oaths, in two of which he bears the title "king of Susa." In seven oaths he is mentioned after Kuter-Šilhaha (first *sukkal*, later *sukkalmah*, cf. earlier in this section), and in six oaths he is mentioned before Kudu-zuluš II,[382] who bears the title "king of Susa" in another text, implying that Temti-raptaš might have succeeded Kudu-zuluš II as king.

Apart from the oath mentioned earlier, Širtuh is known from a royal charter in which he calls himself king of Susa, son of the sister of Kuk-našur II (or "III"), and beloved son of a woman whose name is unfortunately broken.[383] Like Kuter-Šilhaha, Kudu-zuluš II is mentioned in oaths with rulers from the first and second cluster. In ten oaths he is mentioned after Kuk-našur II and in six oaths he is mentioned after Temti-raptaš.

16.5.5.2. The rulers Tan-uli, Temti-halki, and Kuk-našur III/IV

Tan-uli is mentioned in the oaths of twenty-eight texts, nineteen times together with Temti-halki, twice with Kuk-našur III (or IV), and seven times alone.[384] In seven texts, he bears the title of *sukkal* (before Kuk-našur

---

380. De Meyer 1982: 97.

381. E.g., MDP 22: no. 160 (oath of Kuk-našur II, *sukkal* of Elam, and Kudu-zuluš, king of Susa); MDP 23: no. 212 (oath of Kuter-Šilhaha, *sukkal*, and Temti-raptaš who is known to have been king); MDP 24: no. 391 (oath of Tatta, *sukkal*, and Temti-Agun II who may have been *sukkalmah* by then).

382. MDP 22: no. 8, 116; MDP 23: no. 183; MDP 24: no. 341, 345, 393. If Kudu-zuluš II was king at the time, the title *ra-bi* [. . .] in MDP 24: no. 393 must refer to another term. Temti-raptaš is also attested alone in six oaths: MDP 22: no. 101; MDP 23: no. 216, 217, 218, 219, 220.

383. MDP 23: no. 284.

384. MDP 22: no. 7, 9, 20, 113; MDP 23: no. 171, 173, 177–178, 186, 247; MDP 24: no. 335–339, 353, 369; MDP 28: no. 416–417 (oath of Tan-uli and Temti-halki); MDP 22: no. 102; MDP 23: no. 206 (oath of Tan-uli and Kuk-našur

III or IV, Temti-halki, and alone), in four texts that of *sukkalmah* (before Temti-halki), implying he started as *sukkal* under the authority of (first?) Temti-halki and (then?) Kuk-našur but was promoted to *sukkalmah* during the reign of Temti-halki. Tan-uli is mentioned as *sukkal gal* (an error for *sukkalmah*?) in the oath of a sales contract found in Level XIII of Susa's Ville Royale,[385] which is dated by Gasche and De Meyer to between ca. 1665 and 1600 BC.[386] In his seal, Tan-uli calls himself *sukkalmah*, (former) *sukkal* of Elam and Šimaški, and son of the sister of Šilhaha.[387] Unless there are as yet unattested Šilhahas, it is impossible for Tan-uli to have been the nephew of Šilhaha who lived ca. 300 years earlier. Again, it is most probable that this epithet is a legitimation device, as might have been the case with Širuktuh (Kuk-našur "III"?).

Temti-halki is mentioned in the oaths of twenty-one texts, on nineteen occasions in second position after Tan-uli and twice in first position, before Kuk-našur III (or IV), on one occasion of which he bears the title of *sukkal*. As expected, he was promoted later to *sukkalmah*, as shown in two royal inscriptions in which he calls himself (now) *sukkalmah*, (former) *sukkal* of Elam, Šimaški, and Susa, son of the sister of Šilhaha, and beloved brother of Kurigugu.[388] His descent is corroborated by the Genealogy of Šilhak-Inšušinak, where he is listed as *ruhu šak Šilhaha*.[389] An administrative document bears the impression of a seal mentioning Temti-halki in its legend of four (or five) lines.[390] He is also mentioned

---

III or IV); MDP 22: no. 11, 60; MDP 23: no. 188, 196, 324; MDP 24: no. 370; TS.XIII.20 (oath of Tan-uli).

385. Steve, Gasche, and De Meyer 1980: 122.

386. Gasche and De Meyer 2006.

387. MDP 43: no. 2330. Amiet 1972: 297 restored the third line of the legend as "*sukkal* of Susa," but this must be "*sukkal* of Elam and Šimaški," as already corrected by Vallat 1989.

388. Malbran-Labat 1995: 36–38, no. 15–16.

389. König 1965: 110–115, no. 48 §2, no. 48a §3, no. 48b §3.

390. MDP 24: no. 386: (1′) [PN] (2′) ⌈*dumu*?⌉ x x x x x⌉ (3′) *ir* ⌈*šà*? *te*⌉-*em-ti-hal-ki* (4′) *DINGIR PI-il-*⌈x-*hu*?⌉-*ut* "PN, son of PN₂, servant of Temti-halki, . . ."; the

in relation to two *kubussûm* decrees that he issued with Kuk-našur III, or that were issued by him and later renewed by Kuk-našur III.[391] Four letters from Temti-halki were found in a group of 139 tablets and fragments found between two adjacent walls at Susa.[392] Being an intrusion from Level XIII, the letters can be dated between ca. 1665 and 1600 BC.

Kuk-našur III is only mentioned in the oaths of four texts, twice after Tan-uli and twice after Temti-halki. Contrary to his contemporaries, he did not claim descent from Šilhaha, but was the son of the sister of Tan-uli, as is shown by the Genealogy of Šilhak-Inšušinak.[393] No attestation of Kuk-našur's title has been preserved. In Level XII of the Ville Royale at Susa, a fragment of a letter by a *sukkalmah* to the king of Susa is impressed with a seal of Kuk-našur (now) *sukkalmah*, (former) *sukkal* of Elam and Šimaški.[394] Considering the date of Level XII (post 1600 BC), this might have been Kuk-našur III, in which case he completed the expected career of *sukkal* and *sukkalmah*.

In contrast to Mesopotamia, where a so-called dark age followed the fall of the Old Babylonian dynasty, there was no interruption at Susa, where the so-called *sukkalmah* dynasty was followed seamlessly by the Kidinuid dynasty (see chapter 34 in volume 3).

Our knowledge of the history of Susa and the Šimaškian state is still incomplete and to a great extent uncertain. We only have a small group of royal inscriptions and a larger group of economic, juridical, and administrative texts, with a few exceptions all undated and for the most part lacking archaeological context. Moreover, the majority of these texts come

---

meaning of the last line is unclear. Whereas the right impression shows clear traces of the name of the protective deity Lamma under the fourth line, the left impression shows traces of the sign IB, implying there might have been a fifth line, but this might have been the result of the seal having been impressed in a sloppy manner. A possible candidate for the owner or user of the seal is Temti-Rappa, the responsible administrator (*gìr*). Scheil 1933: 85 reads only two lines.

391. MDP 22: no. 85; MDP 23: no. 208. For *kubussûm*, see De Graef 2019: 102–109.

392. Steve, Gasche, and De Meyer 1980: 89; De Meyer 1982.

393. König 1965: 110–115, no. 48 §2, no. 48a §3, and no. 48b §3.

394. Steve, Gasche, and De Meyer 1980: 90.

from Susa, which gives us a limited view of the vast Šimaškian/Elamite kingdom. Although unattested in the Susa and/or Elamite sources, this vast eastern kingdom was extensively involved in the wider region, both on a diplomatic and a military level. The Mari letters provide rich and detailed evidence for the Elamite conquest of both Upper Mesopotamia and Babylonia ca. 1765–1763 BC, but the Elamites were certainly also involved in inter-Zagros (and in all probability also eastern) matters on various other occasions.

16.6. Concluding remarks

The disintegration of the Ur III state early in Ibbi-Sin's reign facilitated the emergence, or re-emergence, of various small polities east of the Tigris in the western flanks of the Zagros Mountains, on the one hand, and a large power block in the Iranian highlands, on the other. This world remains largely undocumented. Only on rare occasions is the "eastern" veil lifted by external sources such as the letters from Mari and Tell Shemshara. Apart from diplomatic exchanges and violent encounters, these texts primarily attest to the continuously changing pattern of alliances both within the Zagros Mountains and between highland and lowland polities.

REFERENCES

Abdi, K., and Beckman, G. 2007. An early second-millennium cuneiform archive from Choga Gavaneh, western Iran. *JCS* 59: 39–91.

Ahmed, K.M. 2012. *The beginnings of ancient Kurdistan (ca. 2500–1500 BC): a historical and cultural synthesis.* PhD dissertation, Leiden University.

Al-Fouadi, A.-H. 1978. Inscriptions and reliefs from Bitwata. *Sumer* 34: 122–129.

Alizadeh, A. 2013. The problem of locating ancient Huhnuri in the Ram Hormuz region. *NABU* 2013: 65 (no. 37).

Altaweel, M., Marsh, A., Mühl, S., Nieuwenhuyse, O., Radner, K., Rasheed, K., and Ahmed, S.A. 2012. New investigations in the environment, history, and archaeology of the Iraqi Hilly Flanks: Shahrizor Survey Project 2009–2011. *Iraq* 74: 1–35.

Amiet, P. 1972. *Glyptique Susienne des origins à l'époque des perses achéménides. Cachets, sceaux-cylindres et empreintes antiques découverts à Suse de 1913 à 1967* (Mémoires de la mission archéologique de Perse 43). Paris: Geuthner.

Amiet, P. 1973. Glyptique élamite, à propos de nouveaux documents. *Arts Asiatiques* 26: 3–45.

Anthonioz, S., and Malbran-Labat, F. 2013. Approche historique et philologique du titre royal "likame/we rišakke." In De Graef, K., and Tavernier, J. (eds.) 2013: 417–428.

Bardet, G. 1984. *Archives administratives de Mari, vol. 1* (Archives royales de Mari 23). Paris: Éditions Recherche sur les Civilisations.

Beaulieu, P.-A. 2003. *The pantheon of Uruk during the Neo-Babylonian period.* Leiden: Brill.

Biggs, R.D. 1997. Šulgi in Simurrum. In Young, G.D., Chavalas, M.W., Averback, R.E., and Danti, K.L. (eds.), *Crossing boundaries and linking horizons: studies in honor of Michael C. Astour.* Bethesda, MD: CDL Press, 169–178.

Birot, M. 1985. Les chroniques "assyriennes" de Mari. *MARI* 4: 219–242.

Blažek, V. 1999. Elam: a bridge between ancient Near East and Dravidian India? In Blench, R., and Spriggs, M. (eds.), *Archaeology and language, IV: language change and cultural transformation.* London and New York: Routledge, 48–78.

Borger, R. 1970. Vier Grenzsteinurkunden Merodachbaladans I. von Babylonian: der Teheran-Kudurru, SB 33, SB 169 und SB 26. *AfO* 23: 1–26.

Börker-Klähn, J. 1982. *Altvorderasiatischen Bildstelen und vergleichbarer Felsreliefs.* Mainz: Zabern.

Cavigneaux, A., and Krebernik, M. 2001. Nišba. *RlA* 9: 584–585.

Chambon, G. 2009. *Les archives du vin à Mari.* Paris: Société pour l'étude du Proche-Orient ancien.

Charpin, D. 1985. Données nouvelles sur la chronologie des souverains d'Ešnunna. In Durand, J.-M., and Kupper, J.-R. (eds.), *Miscellanea babylonica: mélanges offerts à Maurice Birot.* Paris: Éditions Recherche sur les Civilisations, 51–66.

Charpin, D. 1986a. *Le clergé d'Ur au siècle d'Hammurabi (XIXe–XVIIIe siècles av. J.-C.).* Geneva: Droz.

Charpin, D. 1986b. Les Élamites à Šubat-Enlil. In De Meyer, L., Gasche, H., and Vallat, F. (eds.), *Fragmenta historiae Elamicae: mélanges offerts à M.J. Steve.* Paris: Éditions Recherche sur les Civilisations, 129–137.

Charpin, D. 1990. Une alliance contre l'Élam et le rituel du *lipit napištim*. In Vallat, F. (ed.), *Contribution à l'histoire de l'Iran: mélanges offerts à Jean Perrot*. Paris: Éditions Recherche sur les Civilisations, 109–118.

Charpin, D. 1991. Un traité entre Zimri-Lim de Mari et Ibâl-pî-El II d'Ešnunna. In Charpin, D., and Joannès, F. (eds.), *Marchands, diplomats et empereurs: études sur la civilisation mésopotamienne offertes à Paul Garelli*. Paris: Éditions Recherche sur les Civilisations, 139–166.

Charpin, D. 1992. Les champions, la meule et le fleuve, ou le rachat du terroir de Puzzurân au roi d'Ešnunna par le roi de Mari Yahdun-Lim. In Durand, J.-M. (ed.), *Recueil d'études en l'honneur de Michel Fleury*. Paris: Société pour l'étude du Proche-Orient ancien, 29–38.

Charpin, D. 1993. Un souverain éphémère en Ida-Maraṣ: Išme-Addu d'Ašnakkum. *MARI* 7: 165–192.

Charpin, D. 2004. Histoire politique du Proche-Orient amorrite (2002–1595). In Charpin, D., Edzard, D.O., and Stol, M., *Mesopotamien: die altbabylonische Zeit*. Fribourg: Academic Press; Göttingen: Vandenhoeck & Ruprecht, 25–480.

Charpin, D. 2012. Mari à l'école d'Ešnunna: écriture, langue, formulaires. In Mittermayer, C., and Ecklin, S. (eds.), *Altorientalische Studien zu Ehren von Pascal Attinger: mu-ni u$_4$ ul-li$_2$-a-aš ǧa$_2$-ǧa$_2$-de$_3$*. Fribourg: Academic Press; Göttingen: Vandenhoeck & Ruprecht, 119–138.

Charpin, D. 2013. "Ainsi parle l'empereur": à propos de la correspondance des *sukkal-mah*. In De Graef, K., and Tavernier, J. (eds.) 2013: 341–353.

Charpin, D., and Durand, J.-M. 1991. La suzeraineté de l'empereur (sukkalmah) d'Elam sur la Mésopotamie et le "nationalisme" amorrite. In De Meyer, L., and Gasche, H. (eds.), *Mésopotamie et Elam*. Ghent: University of Ghent, 59–66.

Charpin, D., and Ziegler, N. 2003. *Mari et le Proche-Orient à l'époque amorrite: essai d'histoire politique*. Paris: Société pour l'étude du Proche-Orient ancien.

Cole, S.W., and Gasche, H. 1998. Second and first millennium BC rivers in northern Babylonia. In Gasche, H., and Tanret, M. (eds.), *Changing watercourses in Babylonia: towards a reconstruction of the ancient environment in Lower Mesopotamia*. Ghent: University of Ghent; Chicago: The Oriental Institute of the University of Chicago.

Crawford, V.E. 1954. *Sumerian economic texts from the First Dynasty of Isin*. New Haven, CT: Yale University Press.

Dalley, S., Walker, C.B.F., and Hawkins, J.D. 1976. *The Old Babylonian tablets from Tell al Rimah*. London: British School of Archaeology in Iraq.

de Boer, R. 2014a. *Amorites in the early Old Babylonian period*. PhD dissertation, Leiden University.

de Boer, R. 2014b. Early Old Babylonian Amorite tribes and gatherings and the role of Sulu-abum. *Aram* 26: 269–284.

de Boer, R. 2014c. Notes on an early OB treaty between Larsa, Uruk, and Ešnunna. *NABU* 2014: 124–127 (no. 76).

De Graef, K. 2004. Les noms d'année du roi simaškéen Ebarat I. *Akkadica* 125: 107–108.

De Graef, K. 2005. *Les archives d'Igibuni: les documents Ur III du chantier B à Suse*. Ghent: University of Ghent.

De Graef, K. 2006. *De la dynastie Simaški au sukkalmaḫat: les documents fin PE II — début PE III du chantier B à Suse*. Ghent: University of Ghent.

De Graef, K. 2008a. Annus simaškensis: l'usage des noms d'année pendant la période simaškéenne (ca. 1930–1880 av. notre ère) à Suse. *IrAnt* 43: 67–87.

De Graef, K. 2008b. Rest in pieces: the archive of Igibuni. In Garfinkle, S.J., and Johnson, J.C. (eds.), *The growth of an early state in Mesopotamia: studies in Ur III administration*. Madrid: Consejo Superior de Investigaciones Científicas, 225–234.

De Graef, K. 2009. Count your sheep! Doings and dealings of Kûyâ, trader in small stock during the early Sukkalmaḫat. *RA* 103: 5–18.

De Graef, K. 2012. Dual power in Susa: chronicle of a transitional period: from Ur III via Šimaški to the Sukkalmahs. *Bulletin of the School of Oriental and African Studies* 75: 525–546.

De Graef, K. 2013a. Tan-Ruhurate/ir. *RlA* 13: 443–444.

De Graef, K. 2013b. Elamite kings: Sukkalmah period. In Bagnall, R.S., Brodersen, K., Champion, C.B., Erskine, A., and Huebner, S.R. (eds.), *The encyclopedia of ancient history*. Malden, MA: Wiley-Blackwell, 2352–2353.

De Graef, K. 2013c. The use of Akkadian in Iran. In Potts, D.T. (ed.), *The Oxford handbook of ancient Iran*. Oxford: Oxford University Press, 263–282.

De Graef, K. 2015. Susa in the later IIIrd millennium: from Mesopotamian colony to independent state (MC 2210–1980). In Sallaberger, W., and Schrakamp, I. (eds.), *Associated regional chronologies for the ancient Near East and the Eastern Mediterranean, vol. 3: history & philology*. Turnhout: Brepols, 281–288.

De Graef, K. 2018a. The seal of an official or an official seal? The use of court seals in Old Babylonian Susa and Heft Tepe. *JAOS* 138: 121–142.

De Graef, K. 2018b. In Susa's fields: on the topography of fields in Old Babylonian administrative documents from Susa. In Tavernier, J., Gorris, E., Abraham, K., and Boschloos, V. (eds.), *Topography and toponymy in the ancient Near East: perspectives and prospects*. Peeters: Leuven, 267–311.

De Graef, K. 2019. It is you, my love, you, who are the stranger: Akkadian and Elamite at the crossroads of language and writing. In Mynářová, J., Kilani, M., and Alivernini, S. (eds.), *A stranger in the house — the cross-roads, III: proceedings of an international conference on foreigners in ancient Egyptian and Near Eastern societies of the Bronze Age*. Prague: Charles University, 91–120.

De Graef, K., and Tavernier, J. (eds.) 2013. *Susa and Elam: archaeological, philological, historical and geographical perspectives*. Leiden: Brill.

De Meyer, L. 1961. Une famille susienne du temps des *sukkalmahhu*. *IrAnt* 1: 8–19.

De Meyer, L. 1973. Epart sukkalmaḫ? In Beek, M.A. (ed.), *Symbolae biblicae et mesopotamicae Francisco Mario Theodoro de Liagre Böhl dedicatae*. Leiden: Brill, 293–294.

De Meyer, L. 1982. Les structures politiques en Susiane à l'époque des Sukkalmaḫ. In Finet, A. (ed.), *Le pouvoir local en Mésopotamie et dans les régions adjacentes*. Brussels: Institut des hautes études de Belgique, 92–97.

Dossin, G. 1927. *Autres textes sumériens et accadiens* (Mémoires de la mission archéologique de Perse 18). Paris: Geuthner.

Durand, J.-M. 1983. *Textes administratifs des salles 134 et 160 du palais de Mari* (Archives royales de Mari 21). Paris: Imprimerie nationale.

Durand, J.-M. 1986. Fragments rejoints pour une histoire élamite. In Gasche, H., and De Meyer, L. (eds.), *Fragmenta historiae elamicae: mélanges offerts à M.-J. Steve*, Paris: Éditions Recherche sur les Civilisations, 111–128.

Durand, J.-M. 1997. *Les documents épistolaires du palais de Mari, vol. I*. Paris: Les éditions du Cerf.

Durand, J.-M. 2013. La "suprématie élamite" sur les Amorrites: réexamen, vingt ans après la XXXVIᵉ RAI (1989). In De Graef, K., and Tavernier, J. (eds.) 2013: 329–339.

Durand, J.-M., and Charpin, D. 1988. *Archives épistolaires de Mari* (Archives royales de Mari 26). Paris: Éditions Recherche sur les Civilisations.

Edzard, D.O. 1973. Zwei Inschriften am Felsen von Sar-i-Pūl-i-Zohāb: Anubanini 1 und 2. *AfO* 24: 73–77.

Eidem, J. 1985. News from the Eastern front: the evidence from Tell Shemshāra. *Iraq* 47: 83–107.

Eidem, J. 1992. *The Shemshāra archives, 2: the administrative texts.* Copenhagen: The Royal Danish Academy of Sciences and Letters.

Eidem, J. 2011. *The royal archives from Tell Leilan: Old Babylonian letters and treaties from the Lower Town Palace East.* Leiden: NINO.

Eidem, J., and Læssøe, J. 2001. *The Shemshara archives, 1: the letters.* Copenhagen: The Royal Danish Academy of Sciences and Letters.

Emberling, G. 1995. *Ethnicity and the state in early third millennium Mesopotamia.* PhD dissertation, University of Michigan.

Falkenstein, A. 1963. Zu den Inschriftfunden der Grabung in Uruk-Warka 1960–1961. *BaM* 2: 1–82.

Farber, W. 1975. Eine elamische Inschrift aus der 1. Hälfte des 2. Jahrtausends. *ZA* 64: 74–86.

Farber, W. 1998. Did Kulunnum "carry a campaign" against Anzabazuna of Simurrum? *NABU* 1998: 121–122 (no. 129).

Foster, B.R. 1982. Ethnicity and onomastics in Sargonic Mesopotamia. *Orientalia* 51: 297–354.

Frankfort, H., Lloyd, S., and Jacobsen, T. 1940. *The Gimilsin temple and the palace of the rulers at Tell Asmar.* Chicago: The Oriental Institute of the University of Chicago.

Frayne, D.R. 1990. *The royal inscriptions of Mesopotamia: early periods, vol. 4: Old Babylonian period (2003–1595 BC).* Toronto: University of Toronto Press.

Frayne, D.R. 1997a. On the location of Simurrum. In Young, G.D., Chavalas, M.W., Averback, R.E., and Danti, K.L. (eds.), *Crossing boundaries and linking horizons: studies in honor of Michael C. Astour.* Bethesda, MD: CDL Press, 243–269.

Frayne, D.R. 1997b. The *royal inscriptions of Mesopotamia: early periods, vol. 3: Ur III period (2112–2004 BC).* Toronto: University of Toronto Press.

Frayne, D.R. 1999. The Zagros campaigns of Šulgi and Amar-Suena. In Owen, D.I., and Wilhelm, G. (eds.), *Nuzi at seventy-five.* Bethesda, MD: CDL Press, 141–201.

Frayne, D.R. 2011. Simurrum. *RlA* 12: 508–511.

Gasche, H. 1989. *La Babylonie au 17e siècle avant notre ère: approche archéologique, problèmes et perspectives*. Ghent: University of Ghent.

Gasche, H., and De Meyer, L. 2006. Lieu d'enseignement ou atelier de recyclage de terre à tablettes? In Butterlin, P., Lebeau, M., Monchambert, J.-Y., Montero Fenollós, J.L., and Muller, B. (eds.), *Les espaces Syro-Mésopotamiens: dimensions de l'expérience humaine au Proche-Orient ancien. Volume d'hommage offert à Jean-Claude Margueron*. Turnhout: Brepols, 361–373.

Glassner, J.-J. 1994. *ruḫušak — mār aḫatim*: la transmission du pouvoir en Élam. *JA* 282: 219–236.

Glassner, J.-J. 1996. Kuk-kirwaš, sukkalmah. *NABU* 1996: 29–30 (no. 35).

Glassner, J.-J. 2004. *Mesopotamian chronicles*. Atlanta, GA: Society of Biblical Literature.

Glassner, J.-J. 2013. Les premiers sukkalmaḫ et les derniers rois de Simaški. In De Graef, K., and Tavernier, J. (eds.) 2013: 319–328.

Goetze, A. 1951. The laws of Eshnunna. *Annual of the American Schools of Oriental Research* 31: 1–197.

Grayson, A.K. 1987. *The royal inscriptions of Mesopotamia: Assyrian periods, vol. 1: Assyrian rulers of the third and second millennia BC (to 1115 BC)*. Toronto: University of Toronto Press.

Grice, E.M. 1919. *Records from Ur and Larsa dated in the Larsa dynasty*. New Haven, CT: Yale University Press.

Grillot, F. 1988. À propos d'un cas de "lévirat" élamite. *JA* 276: 61–70.

Grillot, F., and Glassner, J.-J. 1991. Problèmes de succession et cumuls de pouvoirs: une querelle de famille chez les premiers sukkalmaḫ? *IrAnt* 26: 85–99.

Guichard, M. 1994. Résurrection d'un souverain élamite fantôme? *NABU* 1994: 92–93 (no. 102).

Guichard, M. 1999. Les aspects religieux de la guerre à Mari. *RA* 93: 27–48.

Guichard, M. 2005. *La vaisselle de luxe des rois de Mari* (Archives royales de Mari 31). Paris: Éditions Recherche sur les Civilisations.

Guichard, M. 2014. Un traité d'alliance entre Larsa, Uruk et Ešnunna contre Sabium de Babylone. *Semitica* 56: 9–34.

Guichard, M. 2016. Guerre et diplomatie: lettres d'Iluni roi d'Ešnunna d'une collection privée. *Semitica* 58: 17–59.

Hallo, W.W. 1978. Simurrum and the Hurrian frontier. *Revue Hittite et Asianique* 36: 71–83.

Heimpel, W. 2003. *Letters to the king of Mari: a new translation, with historical introduction, notes and commentary*. Winona Lake, IN: Eisenbrauns.

Hinz, W., and Koch, H. 1987. *Elamisches Wörterbuch*. Berlin: Reimer.

Horsnell, M.J.A. 1999. *The year-names of the First Dynasty of Babylon*. Hamilton, ON: McMaster University Press.

Ismail, B.K. 2003. Dādušas Siegestele IM 95200 aus Ešnunna: die Inschrift. *BaM* 34: 129–156.

Jalilvand Sadafi, S. 2013. Prosopographische Untersuchungen anhand der Rechtsurkunden aus Susa. In De Graef, K., and Tavernier, J. (eds.) 2013: 355–364.

Jean, C.-F. 1950. *Lettres diverses* (Archives royales de Mari 2). Paris: Geuthner.

Joannès, F. 1991. L'étain, de l'Élam à Mari. In De Meyer, L., and Gasche, H. (eds.), *Mésopotamie et Elam*. Ghent: University of Ghent, 67–76.

Kepinski, C., Tenu, A., Benech, C., Clancier, P., Hollemaert, B., Ouraghi, N., and Verdellet, C. 2015. Kunara, petite ville des piedmonts du Zagros à l'âge du Bronze: rapport préliminaire sur la première campagne de fouilles, 2012 (Kurdistan Irakien). *Akkadica* 136: 51–88.

Klengel, H. 1990. Lullu(bum). *RlA* 7: 164–168.

König, F.W. 1965. *Die elamischen Königsinschriften*. Graz: Selbstverlag E.F. Weidner.

Kupper, J.-R. 1950. *Correspondance de Kibri-Dagan* (Archives royales de Mari 3). Paris: Geuthner.

Kupper, J.-R. 1983. *Documents administratifs de la salle 135 du palais de Mari* (Archives royales de Mari 22). Paris: Éditions Recherche sur les Civilisations.

Kupper, J.-R. 1998. *Lettres royales du temps de Zimri-Lim* (Archives royales de Mari 28). Paris: Éditions Recherche sur les Civilisations.

Lacambre, D. 1997. La bataille de Hiritum. *MARI* 8: 431–454.

Lacambre, D. 2002. Études sur le règne de Zimrî-Lîm de Mari. *RA* 96: 1–21.

Langlois, A.-I. 2017. *Les archives de la princesse Iltani découvertes à Tell al-Rimah (XVIIIe siècle avant J.-C.) et l'histoire du royaume de Karana/ Qaṭṭara*. Paris: Société pour l'étude du Proche-Orient ancien.

MacGinnis, J. 2013. Qabra in the cuneiform sources. *Subartu: Journal of the Syndicate of Kurdish Archaeologists* 6/7: 3–10.

Mahboubian, H. 2004. *Elam: art and civilization of ancient Iran, 3000–2000 BC*. London: Mahboubian Gallery.

Malbran-Labat, F. 1995. *Les inscriptions royales de Susa: briques de l'époque paléo-élamite à l'empire néo-élamite*. Paris: Éditions de la Réunion des musées nationaux.

Marchesi, G. 2013. Ur-Nammâ(k)'s conquest of Susa. In De Graef, K., and Tavernier, J. (eds.) 2013: 285–292.

Matsushima, E., and Teramura, H. 2012. *Brick inscriptions in the National Museum of Iran: a catalogue*. Kyoto: Nakanishi.

Michalowski, P. 1989. *The lamentation over the destruction of Sumer and Ur*. Winona Lake, IN: Eisenbrauns.

Michalowski, P. 2008. Observations on "Elamites" and "Elam" in Ur III times. In Michalowski, P. (ed.), *On the Third Dynasty of Ur: studies in honor of Marcel Sigrist*. Boston: American Society of Oriental Research, 109–124.

Michalowski, P. 2011. *The correspondence of the kings of Ur: an epistolary history of an ancient Mesopotamian kingdom*. Winona Lake, IN: Eisenbrauns.

Mirghaderi, M.A., and Alibaigi, S. 2018. The toponym "land of Bel" in the Haladiny Inscription. *NABU* 2018: 106–108 (no. 62).

Mohammad, A.K. 2002. Texts from Šišin. *Akkadica* 123: 1–10.

Mofidi-Nasrabadi, B. 2004. Beobachtungen zum Felsrelief Anubaninis. *ZA* 94: 291–303.

Mofidi-Nasrabadi, B. 2005. Eine Steininschrift des Amar-Suena aus Tape Bormi (Iran). *ZA* 95: 161–171.

Mofidi-Nasrabadi, B. 2008. Two cylinder seals of Kuk-našur III and his title "DUMU.NIN9-šu šà Ší-il-ha-ha." *NABU* 2008: 40–41 (no. 31).

Mofidi-Nasrabadi, B. 2009. *Aspekte des Herrschaft und der Herrscherdarstellungen in Elam im 2. Jt. v. Chr.* Münster: Ugarit-Verlag.

Mofidi-Nasrabadi, B. 2010. Herrschaftstitulatur des Könige von Susa und Anšan. *Akkadica* 131: 109–120.

Mofidi-Nasrabadi, B. 2018. Who was "ᵈMÙŠ.EREN.EŠŠANA.DINGIR. MEŠ"? *Elamica* 8: 113–126.

Mustafa, A.-K.A.-J. 1983. *The Old Babylonian tablets from Me-Turan (Tell al-Sib and Tell Haddad)*. PhD dissertation, University of Glasgow.

Neumann, G. 2013. Elams Kulturkontakte mit seinen Nachbarn im Spiegel der Glyptik des 2. Jahrtausends v. Chr. In De Graef, K., and Tavernier, J. (eds.) 2013: 83–128.

Nies, J.B. 1920. *Historical, religious, and economic texts and antiquities*. New Haven, CT: AMS Press.

Quintana, E. 1999. "Yo soy el engrandecedor del reino": un titulo real elamita. *NABU* 1999: 96–97 (no. 97).

Pinches, T.G. 1898. *Cuneiform texts from Babylonian tablets in the British Museum, part IV*. London: Trustees of the British Museum.

Pongratz-Leisten, B. 2015. *Religion and ideology in Assyria*. Berlin: De Gruyter.

Potts, D.T. 2010. Adamšah, Kimaš and the miners of Lagaš. In Baker, H.D., Robson, E., and Zólyomi, G. (eds.), *Your praise is sweet: a memorial volume for Jeremy Black*. London: British Institute for the Study of Iraq, 245–254.

Potts, D.T. 2016. *The archaeology of Elam: formation and transformation of an ancient Iranian state*. Cambridge: Cambridge University Press. 2nd rev. ed.

Potts, D.T. 2018. The epithet "sister's son" in ancient Elam: aspects of the avunculate in cross-cultural perspective. In Kleber, K., Neumann, G., and Paulus, S. (eds.), *Grenzüberschreitungen - Studien zur Kulturgeschichte des Alten Orients: Festschrift für Hans Neumann*. Münster: Zaphon, 523–555.

Radner, K. 2014. Zagros spice mills: the Simurrean and the Hašimur grindstones. In Gaspa, S., et al. (eds.), *From source to history: studies on ancient Near Eastern worlds and beyond dedicated to Giovanni Battista Lanfranchi*. Münster: Ugarit-Verlag, 573–580.

Reichel, C. 2001a. *Political changes and cultural continuity in the palace of the rulers at Eshnunna (Tell Asmar) from the Ur III period to the Isin-Larsa period (ca. 2070–1850 B.C.)*. PhD dissertation, University of Chicago.

Reichel, C. 2001b. Seals and sealings at Tell Asmar: a new look at an Ur III to early Old Babylonian palace. In Hallo, W.W., and Winter, I.J. (eds.), *Seals and seal impressions*. Bethesda, MD: CDL Press, 101–131.

Reichel, C. 2003. A modern crime and an ancient mystery: the seal of Bilalama. In Selz, G.J. (ed.), *Festschrift für Burkhart Kienast zu seinem 70. Geburtstage dargebracht von Freunden, Schülern und Kollegen*. Münster: Ugarit-Verlag, 355–398.

Reichel, C. 2008. The king is dead, long live the king: the last days of the Šu-Sîn cult at Ešnunna and its aftermath. In Brisch, N. (ed.), *Religion and power: divine kingship in the ancient world and beyond*. Chicago: The Oriental Institute of the University of Chicago, 133–155.

Reichel, C. 2018. Centre and periphery: the role of the "palace of the rulers" at Tell Asmar in the history of Ešnunna (2,100–1,750 BCE). *Canadian Society for Mesopotamian Studies Journal 11/12*: 29–53.

Repiccioli, M. 1999. Una nuova interpretation dell'iscrizione cuneiforme di Citera a 150 anni al suo ritrovamento. *NABU* 1999: 19–20 (no. 18).

Richardson, S. 2005. Axes against Ešnunna. *Orientalia* 74: 42–50.

Richter, T. 2004. *Untersuchungen zu den lokalen Panthea Süd- und Mittelbabyloniens in altbabylonischer Zeit.* Münster: Ugarit-Verlag.

Röllig, W. 1980. Kakkulātum, Kār-Kakkulāti(m). *RlA* 5: 288–289.

Röllig, W. 2001. Niqqum. *RlA* 9: 569–570.

Rollinger, R. 2017. Dāduša's stela and the vexed question of identifying the main actors on the relief. *Iraq* 79: 203–212.

Rutz, M., and Michalowski, P. 2016. The flooding of Ešnunna, the fall of Mari: Hammurabi's deeds in Babylonian literature and history. *JCS* 68: 15–43.

Sallaberger, W. 1999. Ur III Zeit. In Attinger, P., and Wäfler, M. (eds.), *Mesopotamien: Akkade-Zeit und Ur III-Zeit.* Fribourg: Fribourg: Academic Press; Göttingen: Vandenhoeck & Ruprecht, 121–414.

Saporetti, C. 2013. *Formule dalla Diyāla nel periodo paleobabilonese, I: trascrizioni e commenti.* Rome: Informatica Applicata.

Saporetti, C., and Repiccioli, M. 2013. *Formule dalla Diyāla nel periodo paleobabilonese, supplemento 1.* Rome: Informatica Applicata.

Scheil, V. 1905. *Textes élamites-sémitiques, troisième série* (Mémoires de la mission archéologique de Perse 6). Paris: Ernest Leroux.

Scheil, V. 1908. *Textes élamites-sémitiques, quatrième série* (Mémoires de la mission archéologique de Perse 10). Paris: Ernest Leroux.

Scheil, V. 1913. *Textes élamites-sémitiques, cinquième série* (Mémoires de la mission archéologique de Perse 14). Paris: Ernest Leroux.

Scheil, V. 1926. Raptim. *RA* 23: 35–48.

Scheil, V. 1930. *Actes juridiques susiens* (Mémoires de la mission archéologique de Perse 22). Paris: Geuthner.

Scheil, V. 1931. Dynasties élamites d'Awan et de Simaš. *RA* 28: 1–8.

Scheil, V. 1932a. *Actes juridiques susiens (Suite: n° 166 à n° 327)* (Mémoires de la mission archéologique de Perse 23). Paris: Geuthner.

Scheil, V. 1932b. Kuter Nahhunte I. *RA* 29: 67–76.

Scheil, V. 1933. *Actes juridiques susiens (Suite: n° 328 à n° 395)* (Mémoires de la mission archéologique de Perse 24). Paris: Geuthner.

Schrakamp, I. 2016. Warīum, Warûm. *RlA* 14: 645–647.

Schrakamp, I. 2018. Zabšali. *RlA* 15: 174–175.

Seri, A. 2013. *The house of prisoners: slavery and state in Uruk during the revolt against Samsu-iluna.* Berlin: De Gruyter.

Shaffer, A., and Wasserman, N. 2003. Iddi(n)-Sîn, king of Simurrum: a new rock-relief inscription and a reverential seal. *ZA* 93: 1–52.

Sigrist, M. 1990. *Larsa year names*. Berrien Springs, MI: Andrews University Press.

Simmons, S.D. 1978. *Early Old Babylonian documents*. New Haven, CT: Yale University Press.

Sollberger, E. 1968. A tankard for Atta-hušu. *JCS* 22: 30–33.

Steinkeller, P. 1991. The administration and economic organization of the Ur III state: the core and the periphery. In Gibson, McG., and Biggs, R. (eds.), *The organization of power*. Chicago: The Oriental Institute of the University of Chicago, 15–33. 2nd rev. ed.

Steinkeller, P. 2007. New light on Šimaški and its rulers. *ZA* 97: 215–235.

Steinkeller, P. 2011. Idattu I of Šimaški. In George, A.R. (ed.), *Cuneiform royal inscriptions and related texts in the Schøyen Collection*. Bethesda, MD: CDL Press, 21–22.

Steinkeller, P. 2013. Puzur-Inšušinak at Susa: a pivotal episode of early Elamite history reconsidered. In De Graef, K., and Tavernier, J. (eds.) 2013: 293–317.

Steve, M.-J. 1989. Des sceaux-cylindres de Simaški? *RA* 83: 13–26.

Steve, M.-J. 2001. La tablette sumérienne de Šūštar (T. MK 203). *Akkadica* 121: 5–21.

Steve, M.-J., Gasche, H., and De Meyer, L. 1980. La Susiane au deuxième millénaire: à propos d'une interprétation des fouilles de Suse. *IrAnt* 15: 49–154.

Steve, M.-J., Vallat, F., and Gasche, H. 2002. Suse. *Supplément au Dictionnaire de la Bible* 73: 250–512.

Stol, M. 2016. Tišpak. *RlA* 14: 64–66.

Stolper, M.W. 1982. On the dynasty of Šimaški and the early sukkalmaḫs. *ZA* 72: 42–67.

Stolper, M.W. 2001. Nahhunte. *RlA* 9: 82–84.

Stone, E.C., and Zimansky, P.E. 2004. *The anatomy of a Mesopotamian city: survey and soundings at Mashkan-shapir*. Winona Lake, IN: Eisenbrauns.

Tavernier, J. 2007. The case of Elamite *tep-/tip-* and Akkadian *ṭuppu*. *Iran* 45: 57–69.

Tenu, A., Clancier, P., Marchand, F., Monerie, J., Sarmiento-Castillo, D., and Verdellet, C. 2019. Kunara: rapport préliminaire sur la cinquième campagne de fouilles (2017). *Akkadica* 140: 5–71.

Tsukimoto, A. 1997. From Lullû to Ebla: an Old Babylonian document concerning a shipment of horses. In Pongratz-Leisten, B., Kühne, H., and Xella,

P. (eds.), *Ana šadî Labnāni lū allik: Beiträge zu altorientalischen und mittelmeerischen Kulturen: Festschrift für Wolfgang Röllig.* Kevelaer: Butzon und Bercker / Neukirchen-Vluyn: Neukirchener Verlag, 407–412.

Ungnad, A. 1909. *Altbabylonische Urkunden.* Leipzig: Hinrichs.

Vallat, F. 1989. L'inscription de sceau-cylindre du sukkal-mah Tan-Uli. *NABU* 1989: 92 (no. 117).

Vallat, F. 1993. Kuk-našur et Ammiṣaduqa. *NABU* 1993: 30 (no. 39).

Vallat, F. 1994. Succession royale en Élam au IIème millénaire. In Gasche, H., Tanret, M., Janssen, C., and Degraeve, A. (eds.), *Cinquante-deux réflexions sur le Proche-Orient ancien offertes en hommage à Léon De Meyer.* Leuven: Peeters, 1–14.

Vallat, F. 1996. L'Élam à l'époque paléo-babylonienne et ses relations avec la Mésopotamie. In Durand, J.-M. (ed.), *Mari, Ebla et les Hourrites: dix ans de travaux.* Paris: Éditions Recherche sur les Civilisations, 297–319.

Vallat, F. 1997a. Nouveaux problèmes de succession en Elam. *IrAnt* 32: 53–70.

Vallat, F. 1997b. Les trois Kuk-Našur, *NABU* 1997: 102–103 (no. 110).

Vallat, F. 2000. L'Elam du IIe millénaire et la chronologie courte. *Akkadica* 119/120: 7–17.

Vallat, F. 2004. Le cylindre de Hute-kazan et la chronologie des premiers sukkalmah. *Akkadica* 125: 135–140.

Vallat, F. 2008. Temti-Agun I. Un nouveau Sukkalmaḫ. *Akkadica* 128: 73–84.

van Dijk, J.J. 1967. *Cuneiform texts: Old Babylonian contracts and juridical texts.* Wiesbaden: Harrassowitz.

van Dijk, J.J. 1970. Remarques sur l'histoire d'Élam et d'Ešnunna. *AfO* 23: 63–71.

van Dijk, J.J. 1978. Išbi'erra, Kindattu, l'homme d'Elam, et la chute de la ville d'Ur. *JCS* 4: 189–208.

van Koppen, F. 2013. Abiešuh, Elam and Ashurbanipal: new evidence from Old Babylonian Sippar. In De Graef, K., and Tavernier, J. (eds.) 2013: 377–397.

van Koppen, F., and Lacambre, D. 2008–2009. Sippar and the frontier between Ešnunna and Babylon: new sources for the history of Ešnunna in the Old Babylonian period. *JEOL* 41: 151–177.

Van Lerberghe, K. 1986. Un "Elamite" à Sippar-Amnānum. In De Meyer, L., Gasche, H., and Vallat, F. (eds.), *Fragmenta historiae elamicae: mélanges offerts à M.J. Steve.* Paris: Éditions Recherche sur les Civilisations, 151–155.

Van Lerberghe, K., and Voet, G. 1997. A poor man of Sippar. *AoF* 24: 148–157.

Vanstiphout, H.L.J. 1989–90. The man from Elam: a reconsideration of Išbi-Erra "Hymn B." *JEOL* 31: 53–62.

Vedeler, H.T. 2015. The ideology of Rim-Sin II of Larsa. *JANEH* 2: 1–17.

Walker, M.F. 1985. *The Tigris frontier from Sargon to Hammurabi: a philologic and historical synthesis*. PhD dissertation, Yale University.

Weidner, E.F. 1945–1951. Simurrum und Zaban. *AfO* 15: 77–78.

Wende, J. 2016a. Ur-Ninmarki. *RlA* 14: 435.

Wende, J. 2016b. Ur-Ningišzida. *RlA* 14: 435.

Whiting, R.M. 1977. The reading of the name DINGIR-šu-ì-lí-a. *JAOS* 97: 171–177.

Whiting, R.M. 1987a. *Old Babylonian letters from Tell Asmar*. Chicago: The Oriental Institute of the University of Chicago.

Whiting, R.M. 1987b. Four seal impressions from Tell Asmar. *AfO* 34: 30–35.

Wu, Y. 1994. *A political history of Eshnunna, Mari and Assyria during the early Old Babylonian period (from the end of Ur III to the death of Šamši-Adad)*. Changchun: Institute of History of Ancient Civilizations, Northeast Normal University.

Yaron, R. 1988. *The laws of Eshnunna*. Jerusalem: Magnes Press. 2nd rev. ed.

Zadok, R. 1983. A tentative structural analysis of Elamite hypocoristica. *Beiträge zur Namenforschung* 18: 93–120.

Zadok, R. 1984. *The Elamite onomasticon*. Naples: Universitá degli Studi di Napoli "L'Orientale."

Ziegler, N. 1997. L'armée—quel monstre! In Charpin, D., and Durand, J.-M. (eds.), *Recueil d'études à la mémoire de Marie-Thérèse Barrelet*. Paris: Société pour l'étude du Proche-Orient ancien, 145–152.

Ziegler, N. 2016. The flooding of Ešnunna. *NABU* 2016: 70–71 (no. 41).

Ziegler, N., and Langlois, A.-I. 2017. *Les toponymes paléo-babyloniens de la Haute-Mésopotamie*. Paris: Collège de France / Société pour l'étude du Proche-Orient ancien.

17

Before the Kingdom of the Hittites

ANATOLIA IN THE MIDDLE BRONZE AGE

Gojko Barjamovic

17.1. Topography and sources

Anatolia is commonly defined as the Asian portion of the Republic of Turkey that stretches between the Bosporus Strait and the mountains of the Caucasus.[1] It is bound by the seas of Marmara and the Mediterranean in the west and the Black Sea in the north; its eastern and southeastern frontier follows the modern political borders of Georgia, Armenia, Azerbaijan, Iran, Iraq, and Syria. It covers ca. 780,000 square kilometers (300,000 square miles) of mountainous terrain, broken by coastal plains, valleys, and broad highland plateaus with lakes and rivers.

The diversity in landscape, plant, and animal life is such that even neighboring biotopes can offer highly dissimilar conditions for human

---

1. The following abbreviations are used for text editions: AKT 1 = Bilgiç et al. 1990; CCT 1 = Smith 1921; CCT 4 = Smith 1927; ICK 3 = Matouš and Matoušová-Rajmová 1984; KTH = Lewy 1930; KTP = Stephens 1927; KTS 1 = Lewy 1926; TC 3 = Lewy 1935. Numbers starting with Kt refer to unedited texts from the excavations in the lower town of the site of Kültepe. REL followed by a number refers to year dates used by Assyrian traders (see below, section 17.2) according to the reconstructed sequence of Barjamovic et al. 2012.

Gojko Barjamovic, *Before the Kingdom of the Hittites* In: *The Oxford History of the Ancient Near East.* Edited by: Karen Radner, Nadine Moeller, and D. T. Potts, Oxford University Press. © Oxford University Press 2022. DOI: 10.1093/oso/9780190687571.003.0017

life. Coastal areas have a Mediterranean climate with cool, rainy winters, and hot, moderately dry summers. The interior plateau of Central Anatolia, which is shielded from the seas by mountains, sees wider daily and seasonal temperature variation, with cold winters, and dry, hot summers. The eastern mountainous area has the most inhospitable climate, with warm, dry summers and bitterly cold winters. Precipitation varies greatly between annual averages of more than 2,000 mm on the mountainous slopes toward the Black Sea to less than 250 mm in parts of the Konya Plain.

This distinctive topography set the early history of Central Anatolia apart from the alluvial plains of Egypt and Mesopotamia where the first states emerged. The Anatolian mountains, rich in metal, timber, and minerals, locked the region into a dynamic relationship of production and exchange with its more densely populated neighbors from the fourth millennium BC onward.[2]

The period after 3500 BC in particular saw an explosive economic growth in Iraq that led to the rise of statehood, urbanization, new technologies of communication, and a restructuring of social, political, and commercial institutions. A number of settlements sprang up along the main rivers of Western Asia and the foothills of the mountainous arch stretching from southwestern Iran into southeastern Turkey that shared their material and visual culture with the Mesopotamian cities. These settlements seem to have constituted a network of trading posts that functioned as dependable conduits of timber, stone, metal, and possibly workers for the urban south.[3] Some Anatolian sites, such as Arslantepe on the Upper Euphrates, acted as interstitial nodes in this intraregional network, connecting the urban centers to production sites located as far away as the Caucasus.[4] The system appears to have lasted a few centuries, after which the far-flung network of the early Mesopotamian cities

---

2. Sagona 2011.

3. Algaze 1993; 2008: 63–64.

4. Frangipane 1997; 2001; Palumbi 2011; Sagona 2014.

receded or transformed and the regions of Eastern Anatolia and the Caucasus were in diminished contact with the south.[5]

The extraction and processing of raw materials in Anatolia predates state formation, and dense urban sites formed centuries later than in Mesopotamia and seemingly at a slower pace. The concentration of population into urban settlements was probably coeval with notions of statehood and led to the gradual formation of a system of hundreds of micro-polities across the Anatolian plateau during the Early Bronze Age, ca. 3000–2100 BC (figure 17.1).[6] During the last phase of the Early Bronze Age, larger urban sites emerge with fortified acropoleis and major public buildings.[7]

The dynamics behind this demographic conglomeration and political consolidation are unknown, but seem to relate to both internal competition and interregional trade.[8] For this reason, demographic and social developments toward state formation were concentrated in the central and southern parts of Anatolia, with sites and populations in the areas east and west of it being smaller, and the areas politically less integrated.

Records from twenty-fourth-century BC Ebla in modern-day Syria report on extensive commercial contacts with a state called Armi,[9] probably located in Cilicia or in the Amuq.[10] Armi appears to have acted as a primary conduit for a voluminous trade with the Anatolian highlands. Texts refer to large amounts of silver and copper transported via Armi into Syria[11] and mention a network of diplomats and merchant settlements that facilitated the flow of raw materials and finished products between the two regions.[12]

---

5. Smith 2015.

6. Steadman 2011: 231–233.

7. Çevik 2007; Bachhuber 2012; 2015.

8. Wilkinson 2014; Massa and Palmisano 2018.

9. Archi 2011.

10. Bonechi 1990; 2016; Kroonen et al. 2018; Barjamovic 2019a.

11. Archi 2017.

12. Winters 2018; Biga and Steinkeller 2021.

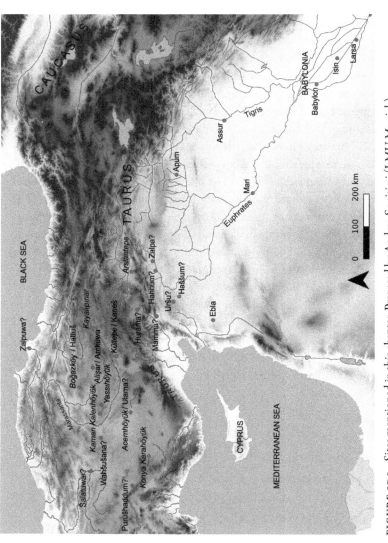

FIGURE 17.1. Sites mentioned in this chapter. Prepared by Andrea Squitieri (LMU Munich).

The apparent link between the emergence of grand public buildings in Central Anatolia and the development of political centralization and expanding long-distance trade finds support in a growing corpus of archaeological research in Turkey.[13] Archaeologists have been able to track deep qualitative changes in settlement structure, routes, and exchange patterns between the Euphrates Valley and Western Anatolia during the last half of the Early Bronze Age,[14] and have reconstructed networks of settlements, production sites, and polities capable of managing the manufacture, processing, and transportation of large volumes of goods out of the region.[15]

By the Middle Bronze Age, ca. 2050–1500 BC, populations consolidated into a hundred or so larger states, each focused on a single urban center surrounded by agricultural hinterland, villages, orchards, pastures, and production sites.[16] The mineral wealth of Anatolia continued to attract traders from Syria and Mesopotamia to settle permanently in the region and manage the traffic.[17] Among them, merchants from the city of Assur (see chapter 15 in this volume) in present-day Iraq play a particular role for our understanding of political and historical developments during the first half of the second millennium BC, since they brought with them the technology of cuneiform writing, and their business documents thus offer the first detailed records written locally in Anatolia.[18]

The Assyrian traders imported tin and luxury textiles to Anatolia and brought back silver and gold to Assur. They also worked as neutral commercial mediators between the politically competitive Anatolian states in a local circuit of copper and wool.[19] By 1850 BC, they had formed

---

13. Sagona and Zimansky 2009; McMahon and Steadman (eds.) 2011.

14. Efe 2007; Erarslan 2009; Kulakoğlu 2017; Şahoğlu 2005.

15. Yener 2000; Wilkinson 2014; Massa 2016.

16. Barjamovic 2011.

17. Larsen 1967; Veenhof 1972.

18. Veenhof 2008a; 2017a; Larsen 2015; Michel 2017.

19. Dercksen 1996; Lassen 2010.

enclaves in some forty major settlements on the territory of modern-day Turkey and Syria (figure 17.2).[20]

In time, several local Anatolian polities adopted the Assyrian cuneiform script for their own management.[21] In addition, the first possible forerunners of a local Anatolian hieroglyphic script appear around this time, parallel to, and perhaps driven by, the interaction with a cuneiform tradition.[22] In general, however, our understanding of Middle Bronze Age Anatolia is characterized by an absence of a written indigenous historiography and by very sparse historical sources in general. Almost the entirety of the written documentation was filtered through the eyes of outsiders whose main preoccupation was the management and recording of commercial ventures. The nearly 23,000 clay tablets left behind by the Assyrians provide information about the region and its social and political institutions in a tangential fashion and only hint at what was clearly a complex political interaction between states and their leaders.

In addition to the written sources, an extensive archaeological and pictorial record, especially from the site of Kültepe, ancient Kaneš,[23] provides information on architecture, ceramics, furniture, and dress, and provides some pictorial renditions of the mythology and spiritual life of the period. New components have been added to the picture in recent decades, using new scientific approaches that include environmental analyses,[24] topographical surveys, detailed material studies,

---

20. Barjamovic 2011; 2017.

21. Yoshida 2002.

22. For a careful review of the limited evidence, see Hawkins 2010. For more speculative statements, see Waal 2012; Poetto 2018.

23. Özgüç 2003; Kulakoğlu 2011; 2017; Kulakoğlu and Kangal 2010.

24. Cf. e.g., Kashima et al. 2005; Kashima 2011. In terms of paleoclimate variation, our current knowledge of Anatolia ca. 2500–1500 BC is primarily based on a triangulation between Mavri Trypa (Peloponnese, Greece), Jeita Cave (Beirut, Lebanon), and Gol-e Zard (central West Iran), with Nar Lake as confirmation; see Weiss 2019.

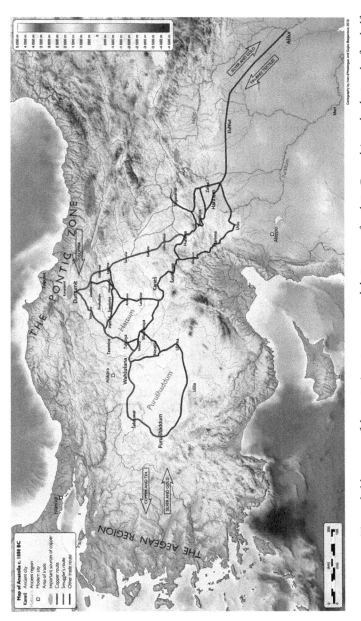

FIGURE 17.2. The probable course of the main Assyrian routes and their ports of trade in Central Anatolia during the first half of the nineteenth century BC. The exact location of most settlements discussed is this chapter are unknown and the historical geography of Bronze Age Turkey continues to be a source of much debate; see Forlanini 2008; Barjamovic 2017. Reproduced from Barjamovic 2011.

archaeozoological, archaeobotanical, archaeogenetical, and paleopatho-
logical work.[25] This has brought new material to a variety of topics,
including the environment, chronology, production, mobility, food-
ways, and public health.

Good fortune led Kaneš to be abandoned during the late Hellenistic
period in favor of a newly founded regional capital at Kayseri in eastern Cappadocia.[26] This spared the site of the older Bronze Age city of
much recent occupation. Unlike most other settlements dated to this
period, archaeologists have therefore had almost unrestricted access to
the remains of the Assyrian community and its Anatolian neighbors. In
addition, a conflagration in Kaneš around 1840 BC led to a generation
of homes and public buildings collapsing into ruin, thereby sealing and
preserving a snapshot of daily life and activities at the site for posterity
(figure 17.3).[27]

The absence of any coherent information on societal leaders or
local tradition of historiography in Anatolia during this period is to
some extent compensated by this rich material record. But its very
nature does preclude the writing of a political history in a traditional
sense, and instead lends itself well to micro-historical inquiries of
individuals and procedures.[28] The serious limitations imposed by the
sources on the writing of a political history of events in Anatolia are
alleviated by recent advances in the understanding of the internal
chronology and the geography of the period, which allow historians
to trace broad political and social development as structure and process instead.

---

25. Collected in Atici et al. (eds.) 2014; Kulakoğlu and Michel (eds.) 2015; Kulakoğlu
and Barjamovic (ed.), 2017.

26. Barjamovic 2015a.

27. Özgüç 2003; Barjamovic et al. 2012.

28. Stratford 2017.

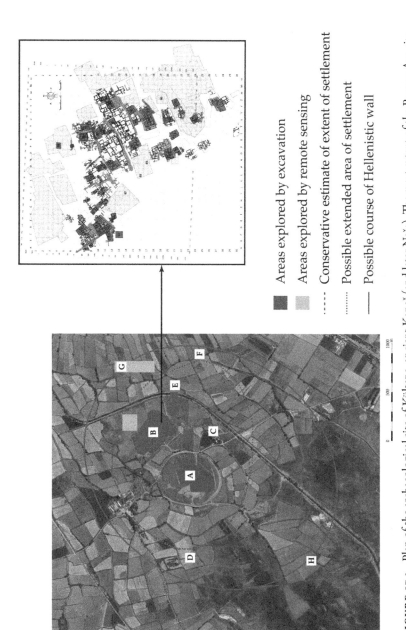

FIGURE 17.3. Plan of the archaeological site of Kültepe, ancient Kaneš (and later Neša). The exact extent of the Bronze Age site has not been established, but current data indicate that Kaneš covered an area of at least 170 ha; see Barjamovic 2014; 2015a. Twenty thousand people may have lived in and around the city, making it one of the largest urban settlements in existence at this time. Reproduced from Lassen et al. (ed.) 2019.

Areas explored by excavation

Areas explored by remote sensing

· · · · · Conservative estimate of extent of settlement

· · · · · Possible extended area of settlement

——— Possible course of Hellenistic wall

17.2. *Chronology and trade*

The conflagration that destroyed Kaneš sealed more than 22,000 of the ca. 23,000 clay tablets found at the site under a thick residue of burned debris. In archaeological terms, these texts belong to the "Lower Town Level II" at Kültepe and document the period between ca. 1925 and 1840 BC. However, the great majority of the records relate to just thirty years, or a single generation of the foreign traders and their interactions with Anatolian society ca. 1895–1865 BC. Less than 400 texts date to the period following the fire in ca. 1840 BC.[29]

The tablets dated after 1840 BC at Kültepe come from the archaeological stratum "Lower Town Level Ib" and the occupation that followed the fire. The city appears to have flourished for a period of at least a century and a half, with larger houses and more elaborate tombs than previously.[30] But poor preservation and deep changes in the way the Assyrians conducted their trade leave us with much fewer records to study from this period at the site.[31]

The smaller number of texts available from Kültepe is to some extent ameliorated by a major geographical broadening of sources. After 1810 BC, the formation of large transitory states in Iraq and northern Syria under Samsi-Addu, Zimri-Lim of Mari, and Hammurabi of Babylon (see chapters 15 and 18 in this volume) led to an explosion in documentary records from the region passed by the Assyrian traders.[32] At the same time, written evidence from other sites within Anatolia picks up during this period. Tablets written in the Old Assyrian version of the cuneiform script turn up at the sites of Alişar,[33] Boğazköy,[34] Kaman

---

29. Barjamovic et al. 2012: 3–28, 77–86.

30. See, e.g., T. Özgüç 1986: 17 (Kültepe); N. Özgüç 1966; (Acemhöyük); Alp 1968 (Konya Karahöyük).

31. Barjamovic et al. 2012: 61–68.

32. For a useful overview of the history and sources, see Charpin 2004; cf. chapter 15 in this volume.

33. Gelb 1935.

34. Otten 1957.

Kalehöyük,[35] Kayalıpınar,[36] and Acemhöyük.[37] This geographical extension provides a trickle of historical data and frames political developments in Anatolia in a new and broader scope. Most importantly, places, individuals, and dates known from later Hittite historiography appear during this last century and a half of Assyrian records in Anatolia,[38] with a shift in the nature of the sources that allows us to identify some local rulers and political events.

The chronology of the period is built around the fact that Assyrian traders named each new year after the individual who held the highest public office in their home city: the *limmum* of the City Assembly in Assur.[39] Traders settled in Kaneš did not date their commercial records as such,[40] but some 10 percent of their texts contain references to dated events that allow us to place them within a recently established relative chronological sequence provided by a compiled set of lists of such officials.[41] Due to a few breaks and inconsistencies in the manuscripts, our modern-day reconstruction of the sequence, known as the Revised Eponym List (REL), has an uncertainty of just one or two years for the first 138 years of the period, slightly more for the century that follows.[42] The entire list of officials corresponds to the years ca. 1970–1720 BC by modern reckoning. It provides scholars of the period with a powerful tool to place individuals and events in relative sequence to one another and to relate local developments to occurrences outside Anatolia itself.[43]

---

35. Yoshida 2002.

36. Sommerfeld 2006.

37. Kuzuoğlu 2016.

38. Beal 2003; Forlanini 1999; 2004a; 2004b; 2010; Miller 2001; Kloekhorst 2019.

39. Veenhof 2003.

40. Stratford 2015.

41. Cf. Veenhof 2003; Günbattı 2008.

42. Barjamovic et al. 2012; Roaf 2012; de Jong 2012–2013; 2016–2017; Nahm 2013; Bloch 2013; Koliński 2013; Lacambre and Nahm 2015.

43. Charpin and Durand 1997; Charpin and Ziegler 2003.

The period ca. 1895–1865 BC to which the majority of the commercial records belongs corresponds chronologically to the zenith of the ruling dynasties in Isin and Larsa in southern Babylonia (cf. chapter 14 in this volume). Surprisingly little is known about the political history of Syria and southeastern Turkey during this so-called *Šakkanakku* period,[44] but it seems to have been a time of political reorganization and decentralization across the region. The Assyrian records from Kültepe show that the entire territory was divided into a multitude of micro-states which taxed the transit trade and defended their borders.[45] The question remains to what extent the same routes were in use in earlier periods and whether they would have played a role in the political dynamics of expansion and dominion under the kingdoms of Akkad and Ur of the late third millennium BC.[46] Large palatial buildings that have recently come to light in excavations at Kültepe and Yassıhöyük, near Kırşehir, certainly imply that the trade was ancient and dates back centuries before the Assyrian records.[47]

Two early Assyrian rulers left inscriptions, which provide hints as to how and why this city in particular came to gain its prominent role in commerce after 1970 BC.[48] Their existence suggests that Assur may have been a relative latecomer to the Anatolian trade. Neither of the two inscriptions mention Anatolia, but they do refer to tax exemptions made on various commodities on the market of Assur, seemingly in an attempt to attract business.[49] In one possible scenario, the traders of Assur became providers to Anatolia of reliable deliveries of strategically important tin at a low cost,[50] and took advantage of the political fragmentation in Syria

44. Charpin 2004; Bär 2005.

45. Barjamovic 2018.

46. Steinkeller 2021.

47. Şahoğlu 2005; Efe 2007; Kulakoğlu 2017; Massa and Palmisano 2018.

48. Grayson 1987: 17–18, 22–23.

49. Larsen 1976: 76–77.

50. For the idea that Assyrian caravans were compelled to carry tin, see Veenhof 2008a: 212–215.

to build new routes and access a market in Anatolia that had previously been dominated by other parties.[51] Hints are offered in some of the earliest dated records from Kültepe, suggesting that the commercial system as we know it from the period ca. 1895–1865 BC had not been in existence for very long.[52] It seems that Assyrian merchants a generation or two earlier were itinerant, and that they had not yet established any permanent agency at Kaneš or beyond. It appears that their commercial expansion was a gradual process by which the first Assyrian families set up footholds in Hahhum on the Euphrates. Only later did they expand to Kaneš to build the full-fledged Anatolian system of ports and stations that we see reflected in the main generation of texts.

The evidence for this process is scant and other scenarios are possible. But a gradual and incremental expansion seems to be the most likely process by which the mature trading system could come into place. This raises important questions about what went on before the Assyrian merchants came to Kaneš. Who traded with Kültepe and the other Anatolian cities in the region a century earlier during the late Early Bronze Age? To what extent were political and commercial shifts related to the onset of a phase of intense aridity after ca. 2200 BC?[53] Were other networks in place that carried goods from the Euphrates to Anatolia before 2200 BC?[54] How did the Assyrians succeed in taking over any forerunners?[55] And was trade managed in entirely different ways in the earlier period—for instance, through state agents?[56]

These are all questions that cannot be answered at the moment, but to which continued archaeological attention may provide some answers. Our evidence for the political history of Anatolia in the early Middle

---

51. Barjamovic 2018.

52. Larsen 2010; Barjamovic et al. 2012: 45–51.

53. Weiss et al. 1993; Cullen et al. 2000; Riehl 2008; Weiss (ed.) 2012.

54. Winters 2018; Barjamovic 2019a.

55. Larsen 2015: 146–148.

56. Steinkeller 2021.

Bronze Age, ca. 2100–1500 BC, is more tangible, and the interpretations that one may offer are correspondingly less tentative. We can follow a process of continued territorial and political centralization, beginning with the urban conglomeration of the late Early Bronze Age and culminating in the unification of Central Anatolia under Hattusili I after 1650 BC. Our sources do not distinguish an "early phase" and a "late phase" in this development that would correspond, e.g., to the archaeological strata II and Ib at Kültepe, and the gradual social change visible in our sources appears unrelated to the fire that destroyed Kaneš after 1840 BC. Instead, one can trace a general trend in the political landscape of Anatolia within the period and show how the records from Kültepe Lower Town level II reflect a different reality from the texts dated a century later.

The records from Anatolia in the Middle Bronze Age document part of the broader political and social developments that took place within the region of Western Asia during the three centuries after the disintegration of the kingdom of Ur ca. 2020 BC and prior to the conquests of Babylon under Hammurabi and his successors. This was a period of flourishing for hundreds of micro-states across the Fertile Crescent in a decentralized state system that probably formed a root cause for the emergence of commercial systems based on political adaptation and private capital, like the one at Assur.

17.3. An international society

The micro-polities of Anatolia in the first half of the Middle Bronze Age (ca. 2100–1800 BC) each centered on a single major urban center that gave its name to the state. These states shared cultural and linguistic traditions on a regional scale and seemingly held customs and religious beliefs in mutual recognition. In addition, they seem to have had numerous administrative and economic features in common. Regional similarities in pottery style are also discernible.[57] The political scene was one

---

57. di Nocera and Forlanini 1992.

of rapidly changing alliances between leagues of cities. The commercial letters regularly refer to disruptions in trade due to conflict.[58]

The names of locals appearing in the records give a sense of a mixed linguistic environment, but there is no sign that language was a defining element of ethnic identity. The Assyrian texts refer to all Anatolians under a single term, *nuwā'um*. Present scholarship has sorted personal names into categories of "Hattian," "Hittite," "Luwian," and "Hurrian," following current linguistic criteria. Such definitions are then often woven into complex historical narratives of origin, population, and migration.[59] But the Assyrian texts distinguish only the latter group and portray a society in which a seemingly free combination of personal names derived from all four linguistic groups appears in the local population. Parents and children sometimes bore names derived from different languages, or names that combined cultural elements from two languages.[60] Dominant in Kaneš was the language that we call "Hittite" and which its native speakers later in history referred to as *neš(um)nili*, which means "the language of (the) Kaneš(ites)." Judging from the personal names of its population, it seems society was multilingual and to some extent polyglot.

Rather than language, locals were defined and self-identified according to political identity or citizenship. The ancient records use terms such as "the Kanešite," or list someone as "a man of Hattuš (Hattusa)." The apparent exception to this pattern is the use of the term "Subarean," which texts apply both to one particular individual,[61] and as a language

---

58. Barjamovic 2011: 26–33.

59. Forlanini 1995; 2004b; Kloekhorst 2019.

60. Take as an example the name Inar, which is likely a short form of a group of names, all with Hittite etymology; see Zehnder 2010: 40, Kloekhorst 2019: §5.3.58. In the document Kt 87/k 259, an Inar appears in filiation (*I-na-ar me-er-i-šu Ha-pu-wa-ah-šu-ša-ar*) with the (linguistic) Hittite Hapuahšušar (cf. Kloekhorst 2019: §5.3.34). In the document Kt 87/k 303, a man with the same name appears with the (linguistic) Hurrian patronym Arku-atal. And in the document Kt 94/k 1527, a man named Inar appears with the (linguistic) Assyrian patronym Elali. Language and ethnicity do not appear to converge in any simple way in local naming practices.

61. For references to the "Subarean" at Kaneš, see Barjamovic 2011: 11; but note CAD S, p. 341, on the similarly named object and the proposal that it may represent a

with its associated speakers, defined along ethnic and/or geographical lines.[62] The term probably overlaps with what modern scholars refer to as "Hurrian."[63]

Populations outside of Anatolia are occasionally distinguished in commercial letters and treaties. Such distinctions must therefore have been operative within the given contexts. In addition to "Subarean," a letter sent to the Assyrian port in Kaneš distinguishes "Akkadians" (i.e., people from southern Iraq) and "Amorites" (presumably the predominantly Semitic-speaking kinship groups of the Jezirah).[64] But it is not known whether language played a prominent role in such categorizations, or whether it was tangential to notions of territory and/or modes of social organization.[65]

The Assyrian merchants lived alongside the locals in Anatolia; they mingled, traded, and intermarried with the native population.[66] They negotiated rights that allowed them to retain internal legal and fiscal autonomy and maintain political and legal institutions separate from

---

personal name. With the publication of Erol 2018 no. 81 (see the following footnote), it seems clear that both spellings "Subarum" and "Šubarum" were used.

62. For Subarum as a geographical entity, see, e.g., Erol 2018: no. 81: ll. 27–32, 36–38: "I myself sued Šu-Ištar in Subarum . . . why would you repeatedly sue Šu-Ištar in Subarum?" (*a-na-ku Šu-Ištar i-na Sú-ba-ri-im a-šé-e-šu . . . mì-nam Šu-Ištar a-dí ma-lá ù ší-ni-šu i-na Sú-ba-ri-im ta-šé-e-šu*). For Subarean as a language, see Veenhof 2017b: no. 271 ll. 29–31: "Give the tablet to a scribe who reads Subarean and let him read it" (*ṭup-pá-am a-na* DUB.SAR *ša šu-bi₄-ri-a-ta-am i-ša-me-ú dí-ma li-iš-ta-sí*). For Subarum as an ethnic or geographical identity, see immediately following in this section.

63. Veenhof 2008b; Wilhelm 2008.

64. Cf. Sever 1990: ll. 16–25, in which the ruler of Assur in his function as president of the Assembly (*walkum*) quotes a law stating that: "In accordance with the words of the stele, a citizen of Assur may not pay any gold to an Akkadian, an Amorite, or a Subarean. The one who does shall not live" (*ki-ma : a-wa-at na-ru-a-im* DUMU *A-šùr šu-um-šu* KÙ.GI *a-na A-ki-dí-im a-mu-ri-im ù šu-bi-ri-im ma-ma-an la i-da-an ša i-du-nu ú-lá i-ba-la-aṭ*); cf. also Veenhof 1995: 1733–1734.

65. Highcock 2018a.

66. Larsen 2015: 133–145.

FIGURE 17.4. Drawing of a sealing on a clay tablet made by a cylinder that was carved locally in an Anatolian artistic style but that combined mythological symbols drawn from local and Mesopotamian traditions. Such imagery is common at Kültepe and signals the degree to which cultures merged and new hybrids developed in a highly cosmopolitan society. Reproduced from Larsen and Lassen 2014.

its host community.[67] But the Assyrian traders brought few possessions with them when they settled in Anatolia and they lived in a material world that was almost entirely foreign to them.[68] Apart from the introduction of cuneiform tablets and cylindrical seals by the Assyrians, local culture dominates the archaeological record (figure 17.4). There may have been differences observed in burial custom, weaving traditions, and food preferences between the two groups, but excavations have failed to reveal any consistent patterns.[69]

Instead, texts and imagery point to areas of cultural differences between Assyrians and locals. This is particularly pronounced in the political organization of the two communities,[70] and in the negotiation

67. Hertel 2013.

68. Larsen and Lassen 2014.

69. Lassen 2012; Atıcı 2014; Ricetti 2017; Hancock 2018b; 2019.

70. Larsen 1976: 155–156.

of gender roles between them.[71] Over time, we see an intermingling of cultural traditions between the two groups, e.g., in legal negotiations, economic activities, and mixed marriages.[72] In some cases, entirely new hybrids would emerge, as seen, e.g., in the pictorial carvings used on seals, which play with conventions and combine elements from both Anatolia and Mesopotamia to create a new style characteristic of the commercial community. Studies show that this fusion was not limited to Assyrian households,[73] but that the new style also made its way onto the personal seals of local Anatolians.[74]

Another example of such hybrid culture is reflected in the ceramic assemblage at Kültepe, which is exceptionally varied and shows a characteristic enthusiasm in daring shapes and elegant features that were not replicated elsewhere in Anatolia. Some designs were clearly meant to be humorous; others point to religious, probably ritual, use in their form. It is interesting that many of the most spectacular examples of this local pottery were found in graves under the floors of houses known to have been inhabited by Assyrian traders and their families. Perhaps this playful art is a reflection of the intellectual ferment in a particularly cosmopolitan society in which people spoke a variety of languages and may have marked ethnic origins and their fusion in food, dress, hairstyle, and jewelry.

Emphasis in the Assyrian community was given to protect their special legal standing as residents of local Anatolian society. Texts repeatedly underline citizenship (*mēr'a Aššur*) as a way to retain and justify extraterritorial status. The Assyrians ranked their expatriate settlements based on their size and role in the trade network. Towns that were home to a sufficient number of traders to form a judicial assembly with an upper and a lower chamber were known as "ports" (*kārum*) in Assyrian. Smaller communities with a permanent settlement of Assyrian households adequate

---

71. Larsen 2015: 243–259.

72. Lumsden 2008.

73. Larsen and Lassen 2014.

74. Lassen 2012; 2014.

only for a single chamber were known as "stations" (*wabartum*, literally "guest house"). Merchants who had taken up residence in towns with too few Assyrian households to form a permanent assembly were known simply as the "residents" (*wašbūtum*) of that place.

This three-tiered system formed a judicial hierarchy in which ports stood above stations, and the port at Kaneš stood above them all. The *kārum* in Kaneš answered directly to the governing City Assembly (*puhrum/ālum ṣaher rabi*) of Assur. A few commercial treaties survive to illustrate the specificities of the interactions between local authorities and the Assyrian commercial institutions.[75] An early draft of a treaty between Assyrian traders and an Anatolian prince opens up with the statement that: "No loss should befall a citizen of Assur in your land . . . should a loss occur in your land, you are to investigate and recompense us."[76] It goes on to specify that culprits are to be extradited to the Assyrian community in case of bloodshed. The agreement specifies an embargo on other foreign groups "coming up" and "crossing your land" on the pain of extradition and death. In return, the local ruler collects twelve shekels of tin per ascending caravan and 1¼ shekels of silver per descending donkey. He is also guaranteed a minimum (probably seasonal) income of five pounds of tin in case the trade closes down due to conflict. The agreement is brief, and the Assyrians were apparently in a position to dictate its conditions.

Longer and more detailed treaties regulated commercial interaction between the City Assembly in Assur and the rulers of more powerful states at Kaneš, Hahhum, and Apum.[77] Those texts are of a balanced nature and suggest that traders were negotiating from a position of limited authority. But the principal conditions remain the same: local authorities guarantee local jurisdiction and the safety of passage in exchange for taxes on transit.

---

75. Veenhof 2013.

76. Çeçen and Hecker 1995: ll. 1–7: *i-na ma-tí-kà : eb-lu-um sí-kà-tum mì-ma hu-lu-qá-e ša* DUMU *A-šùr lá i-ba-ší-ú šu-ma hu-lu-qá-ú-um i-na ma-tí-kà : i-ta-áb-ší lu ta-šé-e-ú-ma : lu tù-ta-ru-ni-a-tí-ni.*

77. Eidem 2011: 417–426; Veenhof 2013.

17.4. Trade and infrastructure

The trade system based on mercantilist principles of geographical monopoly and strong political protectionism guaranteed by treaty was one of parity and mutual benefit. Local rulers and traders both took profit from a system of protection-for-taxation. A small dossier of letters from Syria records a local ruler's anxious attempts to regain part of the Assyrian trade transiting his region,[78] pointing to its perceived importance for the local economy. This system appears to have led to a competition between states to attract commercial traffic, visible to us indirectly through the development of a sizable supporting physical infrastructure.[79]

One key element in the network of routes were bridges and ferries crossing the numerous watercourses of Anatolia. Bridges are generally the weakest link in a transportation network and cannot be built or efficiently sustained without skilled labor. They are expensive to construct and maintain and can function as gateways for enemies as well as traders. It must have been both an economic and technological challenge for the Anatolian micro-states to construct and guard them. With references to at least a dozen different bridges in Anatolia, such structures were nevertheless a common sight in the landscape and must relate to attempts by the individual states to attract trade and traffic.[80]

References to guards and guard-posts at the bridges or along the roads traveled by the Assyrians are also common in the commercial records (figure 17.5).[81] Their primary function was presumably to patrol the countryside and to apprehend smugglers and protect traders and travelers from misfortune, as required by the commercial treaties. It may also be that garrisons were responsible for keeping a designated stretch of a road or mountain pass clear and in good repair. Again, their presence

---

78. Guichard 2008.

79. Barjamovic 2018.

80. Barjamovic 2008; 2011: 22–24.

81. Barjamovic 2011: 25–26, 48–51.

FIGURE 17.5. Wheel ruts leading down to the site of Kültepe from the soft volcanic limestone ridges two kilometers to the south. Such remains bear witness to the complex infrastructure that was developed for the benefit of a voluminous circulation in raw materials and luxury goods within Anatolia during the Middle Bronze Age. It supports references in the commercial records to an extensive network of roads, fortifications, bridges, and inns connecting the competitive political landscape of the micro-states on the Anatolian Plateau. Author's photograph (taken in 2010).

across the Anatolian landscape points to some of the political and economic processes behind the trade.

Finally, a recurring feature in the texts from Anatolia in the Middle Bronze Age is the reference to inns or caravanserais that the Assyrian traders used as they passed through the region with heavy cargos.[82] Inns were key points along the road and were vital to the way in which people and goods would move. Some inns are known to have offered stabling facilities and long-term storage. One could buy livestock there, or take on guides and packers. A caravan consisting of hundreds of donkeys and a comparable number of men would obviously have required precise organization: the animals alone would consume around three tons of water per day, and the challenge of feeding them would have required significant accommodations in local agriculture.[83] It is difficult to determine exactly how common inns were, but more than thirty different inns are attested in the records, and even small and rarely mentioned settlements in Anatolia had them. This implies that a constant and lively traffic was the rule rather than the exception.

Services provided by inns were paid for in cash metal, and we may extrapolate from their frequency in the sources how the revenue the traders generated transformed the economy of the region. Southeast of Kaneš, where hundreds of Assyrians and their donkeys passed each year, the food consumption of an inn catering to the large caravans would have equaled that of a village. Its presence must have had notable consequences for local agricultural production and distribution. Manufacture had to be restructured to accommodate consumption, and the inns would have tied down part of the available local workforce (on a seasonal basis at least), with a lasting effect on the economy of the roadside communities and the polities that controlled them.

---

82. Barjamovic 2011: 34–37.

83. Barjamovic 2018.

17.5. Power and display

Executive and legislative power in the Anatolian states centered on a type of large public buildings called "grand residences" (*ekallum*) by the Assyrian traders. These were home to a ruling couple and a central locus of state officials in charge of overseeing and administering state affairs. The buildings offered extensive storage capacity in a local economy that was based on a combination of gifts, state service tied to land tenure, and the taxation of market trade.

Excavations at Kültepe and Acemhöyük have unearthed the basement levels of several such structures containing rows of rooms of vast storage capacity.[84] At Kaneš, dendrochronological analysis allows us to date the best-preserved example to immediately after the conflagration in ca. 1840 BC that destroyed the Lower Town Level II.[85] This building, called "Waršama Palace" by its excavator, covered more than a hectare of land (figure 17.6).[86] A dense plan of partially subterranean rooms with high walls surrounded a courtyard; a grand staircase led to the upper chambers with residential and public functions.[87]

Textual references to commercial transactions with the *ekallum*s of Anatolia are sometimes measured in volumes of double-digit tons.[88] Alongside records of a multitude of officials bearing titles related to storage and the supervision of labor and resources, this points to an economy in which storage of wealth was a central mechanism by which states would finance building projects, warfare, and the theatrics of power.

An early study of the Kanešite state conducted by Paul Garelli essentially remains accurate to this day,[89] with some elaboration possible

---

84. T. Özgüç 1999; N. Özgüç 2015.

85. Manning et al. 2017; Veenhof 2017c.

86. T. Özgüç 1999; Michel 2019.

87. Barjamovic 2019b.

88. Cf. Dercksen 1996: 202; Larsen 2010: 21.

89. Garelli 1963: 205–230.

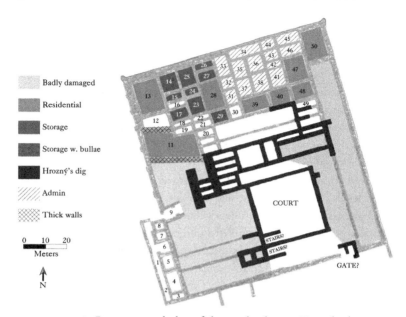

FIGURE 17.6. Reconstructed plan of the royal palace at Kaneš built ca. 1835 BC. Only the outline of the doorless basements is preserved, but it reveals the main features of a structure centered on a large courtyard and surrounded by more than one hundred storerooms. One or more grand staircases lead to an upper level, presumably dedicated to habitation and reception. The magnitude of the royal household as reflected in the surviving written record is mirrored in the architecture of this building, which occupied more than one hectare. Room numbers refer to T. Özgüç 1999. Reproduced from Barjamovic 2019b.

after half a century of excavations and access to a much larger written record.[90] Large royal residences are attested for more than a dozen cities in Anatolia, including Hahhum, Šamuha, Luhuzattiya, Kuššara, and Wahšušana.[91] Male rulers (*rubā'um*) are attested for even more states, with a "great ruler" (*rubā'um rabium*) ruling Purušhaddum.[92]

---

90. Veenhof 2008a: 147–179.

91. Michel 2019: 131–132.

92. Garelli 1963: 205–206.

Most of our sources on political leadership pertain to the state of Kaneš, but there are some signs of local variation across the region. Limited evidence means that it is difficult to give names to the individual particular political structures, but it seems likely that there was in fact a great variety of them existing at the same time, conditioned by local issues and traditions. A dossier of letters reporting on a violent uprising in Hahhum refers to the overthrow of its ruler by members of his own retinue.[93] A treaty between Assur and Hahhum[94] dated about a century later suggests that a trio of officials governed the state at that time: the *mūṣium* (perhaps "[head of] export"), the *hātunum* (lit. "the son in law"), and the *šinahilum* ("deputy").[95] A century later, texts from the reign of Hattusili I show that the city was back under traditional monarchic rule.[96] In the western city of Šalatuwar, executive power may have been shared between the ruler and some type of assembly.[97]

The later Hittite *panku-* (lit. "multitude, the people, the masses; assembly")[98] has sometimes been presented by contemporary scholarship as such as an assembly or advisory board to the ruler.[99] However, the exact function (and even existence) of the *panku-* as a formal body has been called into question. The narratives of the early Hittite Palace Chronicles portray members of the royal court as seated around a dinner, with everyone assigned to a particular place.[100] Such a scene may be closer to the political constitution of the *panku-* as an assembled body, where elites congregate to feast and provide royal counsel.

---

93. Larsen 1976: 271.

94. Günbattı 2004.

95. Veenhof 2013: 30–31.

96. Salvini 1994; Miller 1999; Barjamovic 2011: 106–107.

97. Barjamovic 2011: 355; Schwemer and Barjamovic 2019.

98. Kloekhorst 2008: 624–625.

99. Cf. the discussion in Beckman 1982.

100. Cammarosano 2006.

The smaller size of the states during the early Middle Bronze Age would allow for a closer integration of the high officials surrounding the *ekallum* and for them to take part in its daily ceremonial and administrative activities, so it seems feasible that the extended families of the elite would hold more direct access to state policy. This may be what is expressed in relation to the events at Šalatuwar, but in essence, the overall workings of the Anatolian states remain almost completely unknown to us.

Instead, in all Anatolian states where any degree of detailed information is available, production and storage were managed by an extensive corps of officials whose titles presumably relate in some way to their portfolio.[101] At Kaneš, where most of our evidence comes from, this included a group of supervisors whose titles in Akkadian translation are formed as a compound of the word "chief" (*rabi*) and a noun in the genitive (i.e., "chief of X").[102] The titles at Kaneš by themselves reveal little about relative hierarchy and mandate.[103] In most cases, we lack meaningful contexts to provide us with concrete information about their tasks and affiliation. The officials mostly appear in lists of witnesses, with little additional information about their duties. There is also a clear chronological bias of sources mentioning officials toward the later period of documentation contemporary with Lower Town Level Ib at Kaneš, when the use of cuneiform records in local administration seemingly grew more common. This may obscure important diachronic variation.

---

101. Garelli 1963: 205–239; Erol 2007; Veenhof 2008a: 219–233; Barjamovic 2021.

102. These could correspond to the GAL-level officials in the Hittite state, who formed its highest echelon; see Bilgin 2018: 97.

103. Most Anatolian titles were rendered in Akkadian, and we do not know the local words for these offices; see, e.g., Bilgiç 1954. The reasoning behind this habit of translating all local titles is unknown, since most of them held no direct cognate in state administration in the home city of the traders. Influence from states in the Syro-Mesopotamian region cannot be ruled out; see Larsen 2015: 244. The extensive list of officials at Kaneš may be compared to the top level of officials in the later Hittite administration; see Bilgin 2018: 446. A systematic investigation of possible parallels between the Kanešite state and the later Hittite administrative hierarchy is a desideratum.

Nevertheless, the comprehensive list of titles does provide a suggestive view of the economy and administration found in the state. Officials recorded include "chiefs" (*rabi*) of structures, livestock, and commodities;[104] other "chiefs" oversaw the management of the urban settlement, its hinterland, and state territory.[105] Several titles refer to the administration of personnel, craft specialists, and various institutions.[106] Commercial interactions were probably overseen by the "chief of the market" (*mahīrim*), the "(head) of export" (*mūṣium*),[107] and perhaps the "chief of translators" (*targumannē*). This upper level of officials was assisted by various specialists within and beyond city limits. They included "guides," bridge keepers, guards,[108] and perhaps the "protector of the city (Kaneš)."[109] No judges (*dayyānū*) occur in local contexts. Legal authority was seemingly held directly by the ruling couple in what were effectively face-to-face communities. Records show the rulers involved in legal proceedings with the Assyrians[110] and certain types of real estate transactions.[111]

---

104. Including the "house" (*bētim*), the "storerooms" (*huršātim*), "weapons" (*kakki*), "wagons" (*eriqqātim*), "tables" (*paššurē*), "cattle" (*alpātim*), "the mule" (*perdim*), "horses" (*sisē*), "kennels" (*kalbātim*), "bronze" (*siparrim*), "linens" (*kitātim*), "wood" (*eṣṣe*), "wine" (*karānim*), "oil" (*šamnim*), "urine" (*šinātē*), "onions[?]" (*šugatinnē*), and "greens" (*wa/urqē*).

105. E.g., the "chief" of the "gates" (*abullātim*), "gatekeepers" (*ūtu'ē*), "the countryside" (*ṣērim*), "borders" (*pattē*), "guard posts" (*maṣṣarātim*), "gardens" (*kiriātim*), and "threshing floor" (*adrim*).

106. E.g., the "chiefs" of "men" (*awīlim*), "workers" (*qaqqidē*), "soldiers" (*ṣābē*), "troops" (*ummanātē*), "slaves" (*urdē*), "ladies" (*bēlāte*), "cupbearers" (*šaqē / šaqiātim*), "couriers" (*dayyālim*), "runners" (*lāsimim*), "heralds" (*nāgirē*), "blacksmiths" (*nappāhē*), "fullers" (*ašlakē*), "gardeners" (*nukiribbē*), and "shepherds" (*rā'ē*).

107. For this translation cf. Veenhof 2016: 14 n. 6. For his key position in Purušhaddum, see Larsen 2017 and note also the text CCT 4 4a.

108. Barjamovic 2011: 22, 38–41.

109. The *nāṣir ālim/Kaneš*. There are also occasional mentions of a "town prefect" (*bēl ālim*) and a "land prefect" (*bēl mātim*), and texts refer to "bowmen" (*ša qašti*), "envoys" (*šāpirū*), and a "major domo" (*bēl bētim*).

110. Michel and Garelli 1996.

111. Kryszat 2008; Veenhof 2008a: 169–171.

Additional titles found in the Assyrian commercial records hint at the extensive nature of local production and economic life. They include references to occupations, such as fullers, leatherworkers, barbers, pluckers of wool, weavers, builders, carpenters, smiths, victuallers, cooks, potters, male and female alehouse keepers, and boatmen or skippers. Lower dignitaries may have been under the authority of the chief of "court officials" (*rabi šukkallim*) and have belonged to one of the two categories "those with a scepter" (*ša haṭṭim*)[112] or "those with sword" (*ša paṭrim*). Both terms appear to relate to an elite or managerial class, but sources do not allow us to distinguish them in any meaningful way.[113]

There are indications that members of the elite could act as a collective in certain situations, but insufficient evidence to trace any internal variation.[114] We know nothing about the relationship between the different officials and what it was that defined them as a group. In early Hittite history, high officials were in many cases related by blood (cf. chapter 31 in volume 3), and we may presume that also the states of early Middle Bronze Age Anatolia were ruled by extended families with substantial claims on land and great wealth. But earlier patrimonial models outlined for both Kaneš and the early Hittite state that focused on the role of the male ruler and the "bureaucratic features" of the court downplay the integrative and consensual elements of statehood that appear in the records from Kaneš.

---

112. For the LÚ.MEŠ ᴳᴵˢGIDRU of the Old Hittite state, see Pecchioli Daddi 1982: 172–180 and Bilgin 2018: 302–303.

113. The generic term for an "official" in the Old Assyrian records was *kaššum*. The spelling of this word is conventional for the lack of a clear etymology; see Balkan 1965: 173 n. 34; Larsen 1976: 359–360; Kryszat 2004a: 162–163; Veenhof 2008a: 226–227; and CAD K, p. 293.

114. The letter discussed in Dercksen 1996: 202 talks of a substantial debt in copper incurred by "the grand residence and its officers" (Kt a/k 583b, ll. 7–9: 24 *li-me* URUDU *é-kal-lúm ù té-ra-tù-šu i-hi-bi-lu-nim-ma*). Veenhof 2008a: 149 translates "the grand residence and its officials" as a collective. Klaas Veenhof in CAD T: 362 *s.v.* translates "the grand residence and its offices," which likewise suggests a notion of collective mandate or institutional ownership.

References to chiefs of "tables" and "cupbearers" point to a society that placed great emphasis on court ceremonial. This is supported by both the written and material record, which suggests that local elites maintained coherence and legitimized social differentiation through frequent festive display and cultic re-enactment. Their activities involved considerable consumption of food and wine;[115] and in one case, the archaeological remains from a single feast suggest that a major portion of the population participated in the festive event.[116] Its hundreds of participants could represent the totality of the leaders of the extended households that led the state.

The Assyrian commercial presence in Anatolia appears to have been predicated upon a great local demand for luxury textiles. Such textiles could cost more than a slave,[117] and although the exact number imported into Anatolia by the Assyrian commercial circuit remains unknown,[118] it is clear that hundreds, perhaps thousands, of pieces of fabric were traded each year. The value of such cargoes speaks to the wealth of the local elites and presumably also to the use of dress as a marker of social class.[119] Alongside a distinct group of locally produced stamp seals with standardized motifs of double-headed eagles and encircling guilloches, they point to what was probably a wider set of visual tropes embodying elite identity.[120]

---

115. Atıcı 2014; Fairbairn 2014; Barjamovic and Fairbairn 2019.

116. Note especially Fairbairn et al. 2019, which presents the remains from a single such feast that may have included up to 5 percent of the population in the state.

117. Garelli 1963: 315; cf. also Michel and Veenhof 2010 for the price of various textiles.

118. Barjamovic 2011: 11–15; Larsen 2015: 189–201; Stratford 2017: 291–315; Barjamovic 2018: 137–139.

119. Lassen 2010; cf. also Bachhuber 2016 for the Early Bronze Age. For an example of the importance of textiles as part of a ceremonial gift exchange between Assyrian traders and local rulers, see Barjamovic 2011: 310.

120. Lumsden 1990; Weingarten 1990; N. Özgüç 1996. Note the seal impressions found on documents notarized by the ruler of Kaneš; insofar as those are published in photograph, see the list in Günbattı 2014.

The large group of state officials seemingly constituted a single managerial elite managed by a small group of key stewards.[121] These included the "chief of the stairway" (*rabi simmiltim*), the "chief of battle" (*rabi sikkitim*), and perhaps also the "chief miller" (*rabi allahhinnim*). The first title appears to have been reserved for the royal heir; the reference to a stairway could be linked to the control of access to the audience chamber of the ruling couple by a grand staircase.[122] The second was likely the highest military officer of the state. The third official may have been a steward or overseer of the agricultural production.[123] Above them stood the royal couple. Their mutual division of power and obligations is poorly understood, and all extant commercial treaties and letters dealing with treaties and political alliances in Anatolia are linked to the male ruler.[124] The female ruler appears mainly in legal and some diplomatic functions.[125] Characteristically, the dozen or so names of Anatolian rulers known from the period are all male. However, there are at least three

---

121. Veenhof 2008a.

122. Cf. Barjamovic 2019b and note, e.g., the translation of *rabi simmiltim* as "*chef de la citadelle*" in Garelli 1963: 215.

123. The two letters from a high-ranking Anatolian in Veenhof 1989 offer an example of interactions among the Anatolian elite. The author is Huharimataku; his location is unknown, but cannot have been Kaneš, since the letters were sent there. He states that the ruler (*rubā'um*) offered him two offices (*allahhinnutum* and *šinahilutum*) and that he owed the ruler a gift (*erbum*). He craves an appropriate mount (*perdum*) to participate in battle (*sikkātum*). The high-ranking *šinahilum* (Dercksen 2007: 38) is so far linked mainly with the region of the Upper Euphrates; cf. the treaty with Hahhum edited in Günbatti 2004, and the text TC 3 75, which refers to the settlement of Naduhtum. The title also appears in an unpublished *waklum*-letter reported by M. Krebernik about a delegation traveling to Aššur from that area. There is no sign at present that the office existed at Kaneš. Similarly, the high-ranking "principal" (*barullum*) also seems to have been associated primarily with the political organization of the Upper Euphrates; cf. KTH 3 (Badna); Kt r/k 1 (Tiburziya); CCT 1 29 (Pahatima).

124. Cf., e.g., Kt f/k 183 (ruler of Tawiniya), Kt m/k 134 (ruler of Hurama), Balkan 1957 (Kt g/t 35 from the ruler of Mamma to ruler of Kaneš), KTP 14 (ruler of Wašhaniya), AKT 1 78 (Ruler and *mūṣium* of Purušhaddum with the ruler of Wahšušana).

125. Kuzuoğlu 2007.

examples of anonymous ruling queens, and it may be that an Assyrian gender bias in the sources masks or emphasizes gender divisions. Women like Tawananna of Hattuš and the Lady of Hurma later played a central role in the early Hittite state (cf. chapter 31 in volume 3), where kingship in several cases appears to have passed to maternal nephews.[126] It seems possible that an originally matrilocal order of succession in Anatolia was in the process of being dismantled during the first half of the second millennium BC and that this is reflected both in the Assyrian commercial records and in the early Hittite texts.

A comparison between the official titles found at Kültepe and those in later Hittite texts suggests a number of apparent similarities in the managerial hierarchy.[127] Whether this is due to structural coincidence, caused by direct genetic relationship,[128] or rooted in common traditions of governance, the comparison also accentuates notable exceptions. Out of some fifty titles, fifteen of the offices seem to be directly related, at least by name.[129] A noticeable difference between the two hierarchies is the lack at Kaneš of the cadre of scribes, diviners, and healers present at the Hittite court. The introduction of a Syro-Mesopotamian scholarly tradition and its associated scribal culture were clearly a cause of important adjustments to the institution in Anatolia during the early Hittite state.[130] But another smaller group of titles appear to have direct cognates across the two corpora. One group, which includes the chief (*rabi*/GAL) cupbearer, the chief herald, the chief of tables, and the chief of wine, appears to relate to court ceremonial. A second group of titles

---

126. Pecchioli Daddi 1994; Beal 2003.

127. For a recent compilation and detailed discussion of the Hittite official hierarchy, see Bilgin 2018.

128. Based on a linguistic analysis, Kloekhorst 2019 argues in favor of a direct genetic relationship between the (Kuššarite) court at Kaneš and its relocation to Hattuš (Hattusa) under Huzziya.

129. The Hittite material was compiled recently by Bilgin 2018. Scribal conventions may obscure further distinctions. Titles at Kaneš were translated into Akkadian, but typically were written with logograms at Hattuš.

130. Dardano 1997; van den Hout 2008; 2009. For the Assyrian tradition during the early Middle Bronze Age, see Barjamovic 2015b with further references.

relates to military command. It includes the lord or chief of watchtowers, the lord of battle, the land prefect (*bēl mātim*),[131] the town prefect (*bēl ālim*), and perhaps also the chief of infantry and the chief of the countryside (*rabi ṣērim*).

Any assertions based on a diachronic comparison of titles without actual knowledge of mandate is of course problematic, and the discussion here is meant only to illustrate some apparent continuities in the management of statehood between Kaneš and the growing land of Hatti. Some elements are inarguably universal; others are probably culturally embedded. This includes displays of power and prestige through dress, the use of visual tropes on seals, and extravagant feasting. Hints from the surviving architecture at Kaneš, archaeological assemblages, and the official titles themselves all point at the centrality of such displays and their function as vehicles to reify political order through spatial hierarchies. Some of the blueprints of court culture developed at Kaneš appear to have continued in the Hittite state,[132] with the difference primarily being one of scale. The small polities of the nineteenth century BC were effectively face-to-face communities where rule by social consensus in the elite was presumably more important than in the later territorial state with strong local courts and traditions.

17.6. Universal orders

The ruling couples in Anatolia of the early Middle Bronze Age held a monopoly of force inside their state and in dealings with the resident community of foreign traders. The legal authority of the male ruler is mainly attested in the sources through his ratification of certain legal documents (*iqqāte*) and last wills, while the royal couple appear in cases where Assyrians were in violation of local regulations, e.g., when

---

131. This official is attested only late in the Hittite Empire, suggesting either imperfect coverage of our records or an unrelated development.

132. For the use of spatial hierarchies as a token of power at the early Hittite court, see Cammarosano 2006.

smuggling contraband or caught in espionage.[133] There were permanent installations for the incarceration of convicts (*kišeršum*), and informants (*enātum*) were posted in the countryside to report on breaches of regulation.

Assyrian letters and loan clauses occasionally make reference to rulers of the Anatolian states leading soldiers into battle, conducting state visits, or participating in cultic and agricultural activities.[134] But in general, local affairs are not the concern of the Assyrian commercial records, and the topics of local documents mainly fall outside the domain of governance. Exceptions are a handful of administrative texts, a few dozen letters sent from local rulers or magnates to Assyrian traders or their institutions, and a few diplomatic letters exchanged between Anatolian rulers. The records offer very little information by themselves but are important for demonstrating an embryonic phase of writing introduced into the toolkit of a local administration that had functioned exclusively on oral command chains supported by the use of sealings (figure 17.7). The dispersal of the Assyrian ductus and its scribal conventions is reflected through the fact that records come not only from Kaneš with its major foreign settlement, but also from much smaller local centers, such as Ališar by Yozgat and Kaman Kalehöyük.

More direct information about the political scene is gained from the diplomatic correspondence of the Anatolian rulers. A well-preserved letter from the ruler of Mamma to his colleague in Kaneš refers to siege warfare, uncontrolled plunder, unruly client states, broken assurances, and the exchange of gifts and envoys. A second unpublished text from the Waršama Palace at Kaneš mentions smuggling, the taking of an oath,

---

133. Landsberger 1950; Michel and Garelli 1996; Larsen 2007.

134. For battles cf., e.g., Balkan 1957: 60 n. 98 (Kt g/k 185, Wašhaniya); Günbattı 1996: 30–35 (Kt n/k 388, Tawyinia); Kt 87/k 384 (Kaneš); Çeçen 2002 (Kt 92/k 526, location unknown); Balkan 1957 (Kt g/t 35, Kaneš). For cult cf., e.g., Kt j/k 9 (Çeçen 1998: 121): "When the ruler enters the *kaššum* in the temple of Anna"; Bayram 1990: 461 (Kt n/k 1716): "When the ruler exits the temple of Nepaš" (mentions the date REL 98); Günbattı 2016: no. 29a/b: "When the ruler enters the temple of Nepaš."

FIGURE 17.7. Clay tablet written in Assyrian language and cuneiform script. Members of the local population in Central Anatolia appropriated the technology of writing brought to the region by the traders for their own purpose. The contract shown here (Kt k/k 1) records a divorce settlement between a man with an Assyrian name and his wife, who bears a local Anatolian name. Both the front and back of the tablet are shown. It is written in a poor hand and contains grammatical errors that suggest that a native Anatolian may have written it. The three legal witnesses who sealed the tablet all bear local names. Two of them are priests. The front is sealed by two different stamps, whose use was exclusive to the native Anatolians. Sealing the tablet on the high middle ridge of the tablet became the standard way to authorize legal records in the later Hittite state. Reproduced courtesy of Fikri Kulakoğlu; see Kulakoğlu and Kangal 2010: no. 441.

the presence of the Assyrian community, and wine.[135] And finally, a diplomatic letter recently excavated at Hattuš (modern Boğazköy) sent by its last local ruler to one of his clients mentions *ašium*-metal (usually a contraband), a complex network of alliances, and the exchange of envoys, presumably during the period leading up to Anitta's conquests in western and northern Central Anatolia.[136] The fact that the Akkadian

---

135. Michel 2019: 130 takes it to be a contract, but its contents points toward it being a (diplomatic) letter.

136. Schwemer and Barjamovic 2019.

language and the cuneiform script served both as a tool of administration and as a lingua franca of Anatolian state interaction suggests some degree of local competence with its conventions.

The states in Anatolia were tied to each other by shifting alliances into a hierarchical network of major and minor powers.[137] Rulers of superior rank styled themselves as *rubāʾum*. The term is commonly translated into English as "prince," but is in reality a direct Akkadian rendering of the Sumerian term "big man" (*lugal*). In southern Babylonia, the word *lugal* was equated with Akkadian *šarrum* and used as the principal royal title. In the Old Assyrian texts, the word *šarrum* is instead used almost exclusively in reference to lower-ranking rulers. For example, the aforementioned letter from Mamma to Kaneš shows that the two *rubāʾum*s each controlled dependent *šarrum*s and that such clients were expected to behave in accordance with strict rules of interaction, which prohibited them from pursuing an independent foreign policy.[138]

This hierarchical system of rulers came under increasing pressure during the late nineteenth and early eighteenth centuries BC as some states began to annex others.[139] The resulting aggregates had larger territories and multiple urban centers. One can follow the process intermittently, beginning with a series of wars during the second half of the nineteenth century BC and culminating in the territorial integration of Central Anatolia under the royal family of Kuššara[140] and its potential move to Hattuš, as discussed in the following.[141]

The administrative records and local and Assyrian legal documents provide only limited insight into the organization of land tenure, ownership, and labor tax. Dercksen summarized a complex quadripartite

137. Larsen 1972; Barjamovic 2011: 175, 177, 230, 289, 295; Barjamovic et al. 2012: 49–50.

138. Galtung 1971; Liverani 1990.

139. Cf. e.g., Barjamovic 2011: 294–295 for two texts referring to a conflict involving the city of Hattuš, probably to be dated between 1870 BC and the destruction of the Level II of the Lower Town at Kültepe, ca. 1840 BC.

140. Barjamovic et al. 2012: 33–40.

141. Kloekhorst 2019.

structure of local property rights at Kaneš, which tied real estate to corvée and other state service.[142] Four key terms were in operation, two of them being Hittite words (*tuzzinum, ubadinnum*) and two Hurrian (*arhalum, unuššum*). This may point to a hybrid of two formerly separate traditions. Bilgiç related *tuzzinum* to the later Hittite word *tuzzi-* ("army") and linked it to the term *ubadinnum*,[143] which, according to Dercksen, designates a donation of real estate given to high-level officials by the ruler. Although it remains unclear what a *tuzzinum* was, it appears in some cases to act as a collective body which held some authority in the alienation of land.[144] The system may be ancestral to the organization of land tenure in the early Hittite state, where records of several royal land donations to high-ranking officials survive. A continuous practice in land management seems feasible now that the chronological gap between the late Assyrian trade at Kaneš and the rise of the Hittite state has recently been closed,[145] but where ownership at Kaneš was managed through the *tuzzinum*, later Hittite land donations suggest that land by that time was managed mainly through direct royal grants. Whether this is due to a bias of sources is unclear.

Although its exact nature is debated, the term LÚ ^{GIŠ}TUKUL (lit. "man of weapon") found in early Hittite texts appears to refer to state dependents, who were assigned the usufruct of a parcel in exchange for the services they were obliged to provide. A similar system may have been in place at Kaneš, although its actual mechanics are unclear except for the fact that a transfer of ownership of land or houses would be attached to the transfer of state service. Both individuals and corporate entities at Kaneš could hold control of agricultural land. Stipulations in the Assyrian commercial treaties absolve

142. Dercksen 2004; Barjamovic 2020.

143. Bilgiç 1954: 47–48.

144. Cf., e.g., ICK 3 21: "If anyone lays claim against PN$_1$ and PN$_2$, be it the *tuzinnum* or a creditor."

145. Barjamovic et al. 2012.

the foreign traders from such obligations,[146] suggesting that they were otherwise universal.[147]

The landscape around the city was organized into food-producing villages in a variety of different ways. Some villages were seemingly under alienable ownership and run by absentee landlords who were members of the managerial class.[148] Others would consist of households whose "heads" (*qaqqadātum*) would "follow" (*urki*) different officials.[149] And some villages were collectively owned by and self-organized in a hierarchy of status and gender.[150] More than thirty villages are currently known to have been located within the territory of Kaneš.[151] The village of Tumliya alone appears in more than a dozen different records, reflecting an agreement between a village representative called "the man of Tumliya" and an Assyrian trader to provide his family with flour.[152]

---

146. Veenhof 2013: 44–45.

147. The two key stipulations of a treaty with Kaneš (Günbattı 2004: Kt oo/k 6, ll. 78–86) protect Assyrians against conscription (*lapātum*) by the ruler for performing corvée (*unuššum*) and state that when a local decree orders the manumission (*addurārum*) of slaves, it does not apply to those belonging to the sons of Assur; see Veenhof 2013: 44.

148. Albayrak 2006: 98 (Kt c/k 1641) reports on a purchase of the village Tahišra by a man named Talia from the married couple Kulia and Wanuzal for five pounds of silver. A certain Šihišnuman is listed among the witnesses to the transaction as "the lord of" (*be-el-šu ša*) Talia. It suggests that Talia, in spite of being a purchaser of an entire village, was not himself of highest social rank.

149. Cf., e.g., Günbattı 1987; Barjamovic 2020: 115–116: "Fifteen [family] heads in Duruduruwa [of] Hadudu follow Hapuwaššu. Two heads follow Ikarum, the Chief of Battle. Five heads in the village of Armamana [under] Nkiliet [cf. Kloekhorst 2019: 227–231 for this name] and their overseers. Three heads follow the Chief of the Gate." (Kt g/t 42+, ll. 1–4: 15 *qá-qá-da-tum i-na Du-r[u-d]u-ru-wa Ha-du-du ur-ki Ha-pu-wa-šu* 2 *qá-qá-da-tum ur-ki : I-kà-ri-im* [GAL *sí-k]i-tim* 5 *qá-qá-da-tum i-n[a a-lim*ᵏⁱ] *Ar-ma-ma-na : Ni-ki-l[i-it]* ú *ša-pì-sú-nu :* 3 *qá-qá-da-tum ur-ki : GAL a-bu-lá-tim*).

150. For an example, see Shi 2015.

151. Forlanini 1992; Barjamovic 2011: 232–236.

152. Barjamovic 2011: 234 n. 886.

Whereas the commercially-focused Assyrians reckoned the passage of time according to an elaborate system of weeks, months, and years,[153] the locals at Kaneš used a calendar based on agricultural events. Their calendar points to an economy that revolved around the seasons ("spring" and "summer") and agricultural activities,[154] such as plowing, sowing, sprouting, grain harvest, grape harvest, olive harvest, threshing, wool plucking. Finally, records refer to at least four major religious festivals, perhaps one for each season.[155] If there was a way of counting years, we never hear about it.

Agricultural staples included cereals, fruits, vegetables, garden greens, and spice plants. The broad range of local food production has become apparent in recent archaeozoological[156] and archaeobotanical studies,[157] as well as in detailed studies of the textual record.[158] The discovery of workshops belonging to local craftspeople in the lower town,[159] as well as mine shafts and ore processing sites close to Kültepe,[160] shows the importance of production and the processing of raw materials beyond the basic level of a staple economy.

Occasional references to local traders in salt,[161] and the discovery of archives belonging to locals engaged in commerce, such as the Lady Madawada,[162] or credit trade, like Enišra, son of Kunsat,[163] hint at a local market that is otherwise hard to detect in the data. High-ranking officials would operate as independent agents, both in relation to the foreign

153. Stratford 2015.

154. Landsberger 1949.

155. Veenhof 2008a: 238–246.

156. Atıcı 2014.

157. Fairbairn 2014; Fairbairn et al. 2019.

158. Dercksen 2008a; 2008b.

159. T. Özgüç 1986: 39–41.

160. Yener et al. 2015.

161. Çayır 2013.

162. Cf. Albayrak 1998; Michel 2011.

163. Cf. Veenhof 1978; Michel 2011.

traders and as local creditors. A case in point was the "Chief Shepherd" Peruwa son of Šuppi-ibra, whose archive dating to the mid-nineteenth century BC was excavated at Kültepe between 1951 and 1954.[164] Peruwa was one of the highest officials in the state of Kaneš, but the records he kept at home do not contain any references to royal grants or interference from the *ekallum*.[165] Instead, the texts show that Peruwa functioned in the credit business, that he sold and bought slaves,[166] and that he had a special relationship to a village known as Talwahšušara.[167] Many texts refer to loans of money and grain to persons from this village, often to be repaid at harvest time. Peruwa used a cylinder seal cut in Assyrian style and occupied a large house in the southern part of the Lower Town.[168] The area surrounding his house was only partially excavated and never published, so we cannot identify his immediate neighbors. Close by were the three Anatolian households of Šarapunuwa son of Dalaš, Galulu, and Šakdunuwa.[169] All three were involved in the credit business and dealt with the agricultural hinterland of the city.

The Assyrian traders purchased most items required for their upkeep locally, including food, fuel, and household utensils. But a partially monetized local economy based on silver bullion as currency is also suggested by the agricultural loan contracts made between local Anatolians. When

164. Albayrak 2006; Günbattı 2016; Hertel 2014: no. 102. Note that Lassen 2012: 78 with n. 225, 496 no. 459, classifies Peruwa's seal as an "OA2"-style cylinder. This style appears to originate from a workshop located in Kaneš and is almost exclusively attested in records dated between REL 80 and 120. In Günbattı 2016: no. 64b: l. 11, he appears with the title "Chief Shepherd."

165. Larsen 2015: 140.

166. Günbattı 2016: 10–11.

167. Shi 2015.

168. Hertel 2014: no. 192. The ground floor measured more than 224 square meters (2,400 square ft.) and had at least fourteen rooms. At least seventy records come from the house; see N. Özgüç 1953a: 123; 1953b: 298–305; 2006: 23–32 (plan 1); Michel 2011: 99–100, 102–103, figs. 1 and 4; Günbattı 2016: 9–11. The problematic excavation season of 1952 when most of the house was excavated is discussed in Barjamovic 2019b.

169. Hertel 2014: nos. 97, 99 and 100.

such loans default around grain harvest, they typically are to be paid in kind.[170] Instead, loans defaulting after grape harvest were usually paid in silver.[171] This pattern suggests that some mechanism for converting the cash crop into silver was available locally.

Sacred and cultic practices in the Anatolian states are even less well documented than political and economic undertakings. An official hierarchy is reflected in the local titles, including the "chief of oblates" and "chief of offerings."[172] Priests of various deities and the celebration of their religious festivals are also sporadically attested.[173] Known gods include Anna, who was probably the chief deity of Kaneš,[174] Harihari, Higiša, Ilaliyanda, Kubaba(t), Nepaš, Parka, Peruwa, Tuhtuhan(n)um, Usumu, "The Lord" (*bēlum*), "the Lord of Battle" (*bēl qablim*), "the God of Kaneš" (*il Kaniš*), "the City Goddess" (*ilat ālim*), "the Sun" (logographic spelling [d]UTU), "the River" (*id/nārum*), and "the Storm" (logographic spellings [d]IM and [d]IO). Names and epithets are often impossible to disambiguate. It seems likely that several names in the list could refer to the same god. For instance, Nepaš, meaning "the Sky" or "Heavens,"[175] could be identical with the deity written with the logogram [d]IM. Anna, meaning "Mother" in Hittite,[176] could be the same as [d]UTU, the sun typically being female in Anatolian tradition, and/or "the City Goddess" (*ilat ālim*).

Local religious festivals are mostly recorded in documents as the term by which loans would default. Festivals for Anna, Nepaš, and Parka are

170. Veenhof 2008a: 238–239.

171. Barjamovic and Fairbairn 2019: 256, 265.

172. Cf. *rabi šariqē* and *rabi niqē*, respectively.

173. The word for priest is *kumrum*/UH.ME. For a discussion of their roles and festivals, see Kryszat 2004b; 2006; 2008a; 2008b; Veenhof 2008a: 235–237.

174. N. Özgüç 1965: 69–70 for a discussion of the chief goddess; but note Veenhof 2008a: 236–237, who takes Anna to be a male deity based on a separate reference to the "God of Kaneš" (*il Kaniš*) as part of an oath.

175. Cf. Kryszat 2006: 113; Kloekhorst 2008: 602–603.

176. Kloekhorst 2008: 174, 765.

particularly common, and may represent the core pantheon at Kaneš,[177] but Tuhtuhan(n)um, Parka, and Harihari also had festivals celebrated in their name.[178] Lead figurines showing deities and the molds used to produce them are ubiquitous at the site (figure 17.8).[179] They often show a family of gods: the divine couple and their children. Anna and Nepaš could represent the adult members of one such family, but several other readings are possible.[180]

Temples to Anna and Nepaš are attested in the texts, with two loan documents suggesting that the ruler of Kaneš would enter before the chief official of the temple of Anna once a year.[181] Votive offerings to the ruling family could be made in the temples.[182] Two major buildings of a similar layout located on the mound of Kültepe were identified by their excavator as temples.[183] They were linked to the claim found in the *Res Gestae* of Anitta that he constructed two new temples,[184] one "for the Weather God of the Heavens" and one "for our god" (*šiu(na)š-šummiš*), after the exile of the latter in the city of Zalpuwa.[185] The passage could therefore refer to the divine couple of Nepaš and Anna and the

---

177. Matouš 1965.

178. Veenhof 2008a: 243–245. For Tuhtuhan(n)um as a (personified, deified) object, see Dercksen 2007: 38.

179. Emre 1971; 1993.

180. Balkan 1992.

181. The texts Kt n/k 306 and Kt j/k 9 (Çeçen 1998) state that loans are due "when the ruler enters before the *kaššum*," with Kt j/k 9 adding "in the temple of Anna." The text Kt n/k 1716b: ll. 8–11 (Bayram 1990: 461) refers to a payment due "in one year, when the king exits the temple of Nepaš" (*a-na ša-na-at i-nu-mi ru-ba-um i-na* É *Ni-pá-as ú-ṣí-a-ni*). The text Kt 88/k 1090 refers to a priest (*kumrum*) of Nepaš named *Šu-li-li* (an individual by that name is otherwise unattested).

182. The text Kt a/k 852b (Balkan 1992: 23) refers to gold "which the *rabi ṣābim* donated to the son of his lord in the temple of Nepaš" (*ša a-na me-ra [b]e-li-šu i-na* É *Ni-pá-as i-qí-šu*).

183. Tahsin Özgüç 1999: 117–120.

184. Neu 1974; Carruba 2003.

185. Singer 1990.

FIGURE 17.8. Stone mold (left) of Kanešite gods and a modern imprint in white polymer (right). The mold was used to make thin lead plaques (cf. Emre 1971). It shows what appears to be a divine family. All four face the viewer in identical garments. The bearded male deity wears an elaborate horned crown and a wide belt clasped in front. He holds a fenestrated axe and a type of saber that ends in a spear point across his chest. The adult woman holds an infant girl in her arms. An older daughter stands between them. All females wear a necklace or pectoral. Their hair appears to be braided. The adult goddess also wears jewelry in her hair. In other molds, one child is male, and wears a crown like his father. The divinities portrayed in the Anatolian lead molds are not directly identifiable in the corpus of locally carved seal glyptic and seem to represent a distinct creative tradition. Reproduced courtesy of Fikri Kulakoğlu; see Kulakoğlu and Kangal 2010: no. 240.

reconstruction of their temples at Kaneš. If that were the case, the city would have been without its patron deity for about a century between the alleged sack of Kaneš by Uhna of Zalpuwa around 1840 BC and the conquests of Anitta nearly a century later.

As in later Anatolian tradition, festival processions would have left the city through the city gates in order to reach sacred localities in the countryside. One text lists the witness "Peruwa, gatekeeper of the Addahšum Gate,"[186] suggesting that Kaneš celebrated an *antahsum*-festival

---

186. Günbattı 2014: 116–118.

comparable to the one that held a central position in the later Hittite cultic calendar.[187] Other sacred points in the landscape include the Divine River, which occurs in records of legal proceedings,[188] and which could be identical to the Marassanta river (modern Kızılırmak). Also attested is the divine mountain Aškašepa, which occurs in the list of deities witnessing the treaty between the ruler of Kaneš and the City Assembly of Assur.[189] The name is probably to be understood as the "Goddess of the Gate" from Hittite *āška-* plus the element *-ze/ipa- / -še/ipa-*, which seems to function as a suffix that makes female deifications of the basic word.[190] It may refer to the volcanic cone of Erciyes, or perhaps to a high point above the passes across the Taurus ranges that led the Assyrian caravans into Kanešite territory.[191]

17.7. Conflict and unification

References to several of the political conflicts taking place in Central Anatolia during the second half of the early Middle Bronze Age appear in the records of the Assyrian merchants as a barely visible backdrop to their commercial activities. The merchant records produce a consistent image of a competitive political landscape of interdependent states in which alien traders could function as impartial middlemen and offer services that no embedded local agent could hope to provide.

One term in particular occurs regularly in relation to unrest and the cessation of trade; the exact translation of this word, *sikkātum*, remains disputed, but is taken here to signify "war," "army," and "conflict."[192] It

---

187. Cornelius 1970.

188. Written *i-id* in legal contexts, see, e.g., Larsen 2010: nos. 197, 221–222; Günbattı 2000 (Kt n/k 504); and written *nārum* in relation to priests, see Kt f/k 80b: ll. 2–5: KIŠIB *Apuna kumrim ša nārim*, KIŠIB *Labarša kumrim ša nārim*.

189. Veenhof 2013.

190. Kloekhorst 2008: 812.

191. Barjamovic 2011: 239–240 with map 15.

192. Cf. the discussion with reference to alternative translations in Barjamovic 2011: 30–33.

is important to emphasize that, in spite of its relative frequency in the sources compared to less ambiguous terms, such as *sihītum* ("revolt") and *sukkurtum* ("blockade"), the following discussion is not strictly dependent upon this particular translation of *sikkātum*. All of the conflicts examined in the following occur in contexts that use other expressions as well.

The western part of the Assyrian trade network in particular produces a consistent image of conflict and warfare, which can be used to illustrate the process of territorial centralization in Central Anatolia over time. The main antagonists were the states of Šalatuwar, Ulama, Wahšušana, and Purušhaddum. Although details are lacking, it seems that by the end of the nineteenth century BC, the result of these wars was a gradual shift in the political balance of power in favor of the latter. Sources pertaining to the three conflicts can be assigned to one of three fairly precisely dated groups, ca. 1895 BC, ca. 1873 BC, and some point after 1843 BC. So far, we know these western wars through roughly twenty texts. As always, the purpose of these records was not to inform posterity of political events; they are the product of an attempt to run a trade through times of crisis. Nevertheless, they provide an image of events that may be used to propose a model for the processes at play.

Sources can be assigned to the three chronological groups using prosopographical and archival analysis.[193] The earliest of the three conflicts is attested mainly through texts belonging to the archive of a trader named Aššur-re'i. The main antagonists seem to have been Purušhaddum and Wahšušana, with Šalatuwar perhaps being caught in the middle. One letter reports that trade is difficult because "the *rabi sikkitim* of Wahšušana is taking part in the *sikkātum*." In turn, another letter notifies Aššur-re'i that an Assyrian station has been relocated to Wahšušana, apparently as a safety measure against the approaching hostilities. Finally, a letter informs Aššur-re'i that "we have been relocated to Wahšušana." One may perhaps link this early evidence for hostilities involving Wahšušana and its unnamed neighbor to the events portrayed in a letter from the Assyrian

---

193. For full primary source references and further details see Barjamovic et al. 2012: 33–40.

station in Šalatuwar to the colony of Wahšušana, which refers to an ultimatum given to the city by the ruler of Purušhaddum. Šalatuwar is told to side with him in the impending attack on Wahšušana, or else he will consider the city his enemy. Regrettably, the messengers delivering the letter are difficult to track with certainty, and the text cannot be firmly dated on prosopographical grounds. However, if the events referred to in the archive of Aššur-re'i and in this letter are linked, then it would seem that the Assyrian community at Šalatuwar was transferred to safety in Wahšušana in anticipation of a coming attack from Purušhaddum.

A second conflict took place around the year 1873 BC and seems to have involved all four major states located on the Assyrian trade routes west of the Kızılırmak. It is of course possible that the evidence covers a series of individual skirmishes, but their apparent chronological proximity suggests that they were all related. One important group of sources for this "great western war" comes from the archive of the trader Šalim-Aššur,[194] in which a number of texts dating to the active career of Ennam-Aššur son of Šalim-Aššur refer to the conflict. The fact that Ennam-Aššur died around REL 107 gives us a *terminus ante quem* for the events. A letter reports on travelers from Wahšušana being held back from going to Šalatuwar in connection with the activities of a certain Wušunalam. The latter held office as *mūṣium* in Purušhaddum around REL 90, and may later have risen to become crown prince or even ruler of that city. Another related letter refers to combat and a revolt taking place in Šalatuwar, and a third missive reports on the armies' return in a reference to Šalatuwar. One also finds two letters from the archive of the trader Uṣur-ša-Ištar referring to hostilities taking place around Wahšušana. They refer to the army of Wahšušana being in "disarray" and mention that unnamed adversaries "have fallen upon the land of Wahšušana," causing "a state of revolt." The archive to which these letters belong remains unpublished, and it is difficult to establish a precise date for the events. However, the individuals appearing in the connected letter are known to have been active during the period REL 99–107, and it seems feasible to link the

---

194. For the archive of Šalim-Aššur, see Larsen 2010.

episode to the same conflict as the one recorded in the texts from the house of Šalim-Aššur.

A letter to Aššur-nada helps to further narrow down the date of the western conflicts. Its author refers to a cessation of trade, and declares that both the lands of Purušhaddum and Wahšušana are in a state of revolt. The end of Aššur-nada's active career falls around REL 103, and so in combination with the evidence from the houses of Šalim-Aššur and Uṣur-ša-Ištar, it seems reasonable to suggest that a war involving Wahšušana, Šalatuwar, and Purušhaddum took place between REL 100 and 103, corresponding to ca. 1870 BC in the Middle Chronology.

A dossier of some fifty texts involving the traders Buzazu, Ili-wedaku, and Puzur-Aššur son of Išar-kitti-Aššur, which can be dated to activities between the years REL 101–109, contains a number of additional references to unrest and the suspension of trade that also draws in the participation of the state of Ulama. An internal analysis of the dossier shows that most, if not all, of these references relate to events in the western part of central Anatolia. One letter sent to Buzazu mentions a conflict in Šalatuwar, a second message refers to the return of the army, and in a third letter Buzazu informs Puzur-Aššur that he was caught in a blockade. From the same dossier, a letter to Puzur-Aššur states that there is now peace in Purušhaddum and that Ulama and Purušhaddum have taken an oath.

The outcome of the conflict is unknown, except for the reference to the oath, which suggests that Ulama and Purušhaddum had previously been antagonists. One record refers to "guard posts" or "fortresses" (*maṣṣarātum*) located between Wahšušana and Ulama, and a letter suggests that a high official from Ulama held jurisdiction in the palace at Wahšušana. Together this may be taken as circumstantial evidence that also Wahšušana and Ulama had stood on opposite sides in the conflict, and that an additional consequence had been a victory of Ulama over Wahšušana.

The third and final possible conflict in the west is mentioned in two texts dated shortly before the destruction of the Lower Town Level II at Kültepe. One is a letter that refers to the Assyrian community abandoning the city of Wahšušana; another is a royal letter that mentions the destruction of the Assyrian settlement there. The two texts mention no other place besides Waḥšušana, and it is of course possible that some other disaster had hit the city.

Armed conflicts further east are less well documented, but include the well-known sack of Kaneš by Uhna of Zalpuwa reported in Anitta's *Res Gestae* that may have led to the destruction of Kaneš after 1840 BC. We also hear of "hostilities in Kaneš" as early as ca. 1890 BC, and a war between Kaneš and Tawiniya took place around 1864 BC that possibly also involved the participation of Wašhaniya as a client state or ally of Kaneš. Confrontations between cities seem to have been as common within the bend of the Kızılırmak as they were further west. An apparent difference between them and the western lands is that military alliances between several states and their clients appear more often. This supports the notion that state territories in this region were smaller.

The largest alliance attested in the records from Kültepe refers to states mostly located within the bend of the Kızılırmak River. This was a coalition mounted against Hattuš that was entered between the rulers of Šinahuttum, Amkuwa, Kapitra, and a man named Kuku, who may have been the ruler of Kaneš.[195] Perhaps this event can be related to a reference found in a text from the late archive of the merchant Kuliya,[196] which mentions that "the man of Hattuš went up against Wašhaniya and Baniharzum." The latter place-name is not attested elsewhere and probably belongs among the new political formations appearing during the last two decades of the period contemporary with the Lower Town Level II at Kültepe.

The numerous references to political turmoil in Anatolia seemingly reflect an ongoing process that resulted in the formation of a few major states at the expense of their neighbors. Sources allow us to follow this process from at least 1890 BC according to the Middle Chronology. In the east, Kuššara took control over Luhuzattiya at some point after 1870 BC, and in the central region of the Kızılırmak, Amkuwa controlled the

195. Cf., e.g., Larsen 1972; Barjamovic 2011: 294–295; Barjamovic et al. 2012: 49–50.

196. Veenhof 2010: no. 6.

town of Lakimišša[197] and entered the military alliance against Hattuš mentioned earlier, before it itself fell under Kanešite rule shortly before or after the conflagration that ravaged Kültepe around 1840 BC.[198]

Comparable events took place south of the Taurus during the first half of the eighteenth century BC as the state of Mamma gradually expanded its territory to include the former states of Zalwar, Uršu, and Haššum.[199] These conflicts gradually changed the political face of Anatolia from a multitude of micro-states among which the Assyrian traders could peddle their wares to a transformed landscape of sizable territorial states tied into opposed alliances. By the time that Pithana and Anitta unified the southern half of Central Anatolia under the rule of Kuššara, battles took them to places as far apart as Zalpuwa on the Black Sea and Šalatiwara (Šalatuwar) beyond the Hulana River.[200]

The acknowledgment of Anitta by the ruler of Purušhaddum[201] at some point before 1725 BC indicates that Central Anatolia had effectively become divided into an eastern and a western half. In historical hindsight, this may have been the end result of the series of confrontations between Purušhaddum and its eastern neighbors that we can follow for almost two centuries through the Old Assyrian evidence. Although the development cannot stand alone as an explanation for the transformation of the Assyrian trade network, it surely played some role in the structural changes that took place in the late period of trade at Kaneš.[202]

At the outset, it seems that the Assyrian ports and stations were established on the principle of "one settlement in each state," but as time went by, this system came to be based on convention as well as general considerations of infrastructure. The Assyrian station in Amkuwa did not cease

197. Barjamovic 2011: 315.

198. Barjamovic et al. 2012: 50.

199. Miller 2001; Miller and Corti 2018.

200. Barjamovic 2017.

201. Dercksen 2010.

202. Barjamovic et al. 2012: 37–38, 61–68.

to exist when Kaneš took over political control of the city, and Kaneš itself remained the center of Assyrian trade long after its conquest by the rulers of Kuššara. Instead of urban centrality, the emerging Anatolian states came to be based on new notions of territoriality. Zuzu as the last known ruler to have been based at Kaneš styled himself as the "Great Ruler of Alahzina," and the appearance on the scene of hitherto unknown players, most notably Harsamna (before 1775 BC)[203] and Harkiuna (after 1740 BC), shows that fundamental changes were taking place in the political landscape across the region.

Especially in the northeast, however, the system of smaller units may have prevailed for some time. The earliest rulers in Hattuš were still involved in battles with sovereign cities, such as Zalpuwa and perhaps Šinahuttum/Šanahwitta, and even within the Hittite state, the old city-states clearly preserved a large measure of political integrity and local authority (cf. chapter 30 in volume 3). Early accounts from the Hittite state claim that a character known as "the grandfather of the king" was in a position to give the former state of Hurama as a fiefdom to "the father of the old king," and Purušhaddum and Hurama were principal participants in a revolt against Hattuš (Hattusa) as late as the reigns of Hattusili I or his nephew Mursili I.[204]

Recent advances in our understanding of the chronology of the late Assyrian settlement at Kültepe have all but closed the chronological gap between the end of the reign of Zuzu and the expansion of the early rulers of Hattuš.[205] Zuzu may have reigned at least half a decade past 1715 BC and the last datable records from the Assyrian settlement in Kaneš, and with a conventional accession date of Hattusili I around 1650 BC, it is feasible that the reigns of his uncle Labarna (I) and his predecessor Huzziya would account for the intervening years.

---

203. Günbattı 2005: 450; Forlanini 2008: 76–77; Barjamovic 2011: 121, 230; Barjamovic et al. 2012: 38–40; Günbattı 2014; Schwemer and Barjamovic 2019.

204. Kempinski and Košak 1982.

205. Barjamovic et al. 2012.

It seems entirely possible that Huzziya was the ruler who rebuilt Hattuš after Anitta's victory over its ruler Wiyušti and its resulting destruction,[206] and that he or his successor either conquered the region around Kaneš,[207] or even hailed from there, but chose to move his political center to Hattuš.[208] Our evidence is limited, but the fact that the individual referred to as the "grandfather of the king" also held control over Hurama implies that the territory between Hurama and Hattuš, which includes Kaneš, was under his control.

If Kloekhorst is correct in suggesting that the family who rebuilt Hattuš and made it their capital were in fact successors of the dynastic line of Pithana,[209] then this would explain why the territory of the early rulers of Hattuš seemingly from the outset included several of the formerly independent cities that had gradually coalesced into larger units: Kuššara with Luhuzattiya and probably also Hurama, Kaneš with Amkuwa and Lakimišša, and their subsequent unification and expansion under Pithana and Anita to cover the eastern half of Central Anatolia.[210] It would also explain why the Hittite dialect of Hattuš diverged from that of Kaneš by in fact being the dialect that the ruling family spoke in Kuššara.[211]

The date of the destruction of the main palace on the acropolis of Kültepe and the end of the Level Ib settlement in the Lower Town was presumably the result of conflict, but if Kloekhorst is correct, this would not be due to a struggle with Hattuš, and the cause of the dramatic fire that destroyed the so-called Waršama Palace remains unknown.[212] It seems significant that no major governmental building

---

206. Schwemer and Barjamovic 2019.

207. Barjamovic et al. 2012.

208. Kloekhorst 2019.

209. Kloekhorst 2019.

210. Barjamovic et al. 2012: 49–52.

211. Kloekhorst 2019.

212. *Contra* Barjamovic et al. 2012.

at Kültepe appears to be contemporary with the later Ia stratum. Recent geophysical surveys of the plain surrounding Kültepe suggest that the site could have been abandoned during the Late Bronze Age due to a rising water table,[213] but the occupational remains of the latest phase in the Lower Town at Kültepe are too poorly preserved to draw any firm conclusions. On the mound, later occupation and the activities of local agriculturalists and early excavators have all but obliterated the remains of later occupation.[214] The scanty remains of the lower town show some indications of a decreasing level of prosperity, likely the result of Kaneš having become a provincial town in the expanding Hittite kingdom. However, although no cuneiform tablets have so far been recovered from the Ia houses, the continued presence of so-called Syrian Bottles and Pilgrim Flasks, and even a Mesopotamian cylinder seal, should be taken as an indication that at least some foreign travelers continued to make their way to the city.

This notion of a continuation of the long-distance trade with Mesopotamia is supported by a recently published letter written by a ruler of Assur to the ruler of the kingdom of Tigunani in northern Syria after 1640 BC.[215] The letter is concerned specifically with Assyrian access to the city of Šimalā, a city that controlled the main Assyrian crossing point of the Euphrates river toward Anatolia in the nineteenth century BC.[216] It is difficult to think of any reason other than trade for the apparent plea for free passage through northern Syria made by the ruler of Assur in this letter.

Whether the ruling family at Kaneš were conquered by Hattuš, or whether the court simply relocated to Hattuš under Huzziya at some point shortly before or after 1700 BC, the close relation between the two cities explains why Kanešite court culture, including a particular style of

---

213. Kulakoğlu 2014.

214. Hrozný 1927; Özgüç 1999; Barjamovic 2015a; 2019a.

215. George 2017: 97–100.

216. Barjamovic 2011: 213–217.

music associated with "Nešite singers" (i.e., "singers from Kaneš") and a specific type of Nešite dress continued to be found at Hattuš during its later stages. The move does not by itself explain the historical interest in the Anitta Text at Hattuš,[217] or his possible later veneration in the Hittite capital;[218] but the fact that the language we call "Hittite" was associated with Kaneš by its speakers does perhaps favor the interpretation that the court simply relocated there.

17.8. Ends and new beginnings

The texts from Kültepe allow us to trace a historical and political development and follow several commercial and social transformations in Assyrian society over the course of more than two centuries. But while we have tens of thousands of records covering just thirty years of history, 1895–1865 BC, in great detail, only a few hundred records inform us of

---

217. The interest in or veneration of outside kings would by no means be without parallels; note, e.g., the special position given in later Hittite literature to Anum-Hirbi as the archetypal shepherd boy turned conqueror. He rivals Anitta in the collective memory of the dynasty in Boğazköy; see Helck 1983; Ünal 1995: 272; Miller 2001: 97–101; Haas 2006: 18–19. The early Hittite fascination with Anum-Hirbi led to a wealth of literature surrounding this ruler, comparable to the treatment of two other foreign kings, Sargon and Naram-Sin of Akkad. The Anum-Hirbi legends were explored by later authors at a time when the Hittite state was preoccupied with an expansion in southeast Anatolia; see Miller 2001: 97–101, who discusses the fragmentary reference to a battle between Anum-Hirbi and the city of Zalpa as well as the later traditions concerning his war against Zalpa, Uršu, and Haššum and his death (possibly by suicide).

218. Ünal 1995: 274 connected the "Man of Kuššara" in a Hittite ritual text to the cult of the deified dynastic father Anitta. An earlier passage in that text deals with the city of Šanahwitta, which led Ünal to suggest that the tablet represents a compendium of rituals related to the earliest history of the Hittite state, connecting it also to another ritual text that mentions the dressing of the king of Kuššara (perhaps his cult statue?) and the "place of rest" (*mayyalu*, perhaps his bed). It is of course possible that this "Man of Kuššara" refers to Anitta, but it is perhaps more likely a reference to the Hittite king Hattusili I, who also had dealings with Šanahwitta and who himself died in Kuššara.

the following century and a half. Developments can therefore only be described in a very general fashion.

It seems that a distinct community of hybrid Assyrian-Anatolian households grew gradually more prominent after a few generations. There were now mixed families engaged mainly in local Anatolian trade and agriculture. They existed alongside what appears to have been a small Assyrian elite settled in Anatolia who guarded their Assyrian identity as a way to retain extraterritorial status. A distinctive group of traveling merchants continued to engage in the caravan trade and to connect the Anatolian colonies to the mother city of Assur.

Although it is manifest elsewhere, changes in the overland trade means that the exchange left only vague traces in the material from Kaneš itself. Those who actually carried the goods from Assur to Kaneš were now specialized transporters who did not produce the same kind of written record between merchants in Assur, caravan leaders en route, and agents in Kaneš and beyond. Instead, these three functions had been taken over by distinct members of a segmented society maintaining the trade circuit. The trail of texts simply trickles out.

There is no reason to assume that the later period of trade after the conflagration around 1840 BC was less intensive in terms of the trade than the thirty years that produced most of the surviving records. Rather, it constitutes an instructive case in how a particular situation could generate a huge amount of records for a short period and document a trade that is otherwise almost always indirect and invisible in ancient sources.

It seems likely that the trade with Anatolia ended around the turn of the sixteenth century BC as the large new centralized states of Hatti and Mitanni extended their dominion over Turkey and Syria, respectively. The Hittite Laws dating to this period do mention merchants, but they could all be of local Anatolian origin. As the larger states formed, there was less use for the politically neutral outsiders to run the commerce. The city of Assur itself re-emerged from the fog of history after 1360 BC as a reconstituted militaristic and aggressively expanding state of Assyria in which political power no longer belonged to its people, but was shared between the ruler and a relatively small number of noble families.[219] It is not inconceivable that the ruling families in this new state were descendants of the merchants who had once traveled the roads of Anatolia, but such a link would be very difficult to establish. Most of the history of the Assyrian trade system in Anatolia before and after the thirty years of dense textual documentation coming from Kültepe can be written thorough inference only.

REFERENCES

Albayrak, İ. 1998. Koloni çağında yeni bir bayan "Madawada." In Alp, S., et al. (eds.), *III. Uluslararası Hititoloji Kongresi bildirileri / Acts of the IIIrd International Congress of Hittitology*. Ankara: Uyum Ajans, 1–14.

Albayrak, İ. 2005. Fünf Urkunden aus dem Archiv von Peruwa, Sohn von Šuppibra. *JEOL* 39: 95–105.

Algaze, G. 1993. *The Uruk world system: the dynamics of expansion of early Mesopotamian civilization*. Chicago: University of Chicago Press.

Algaze, G. 2008. *Ancient Mesopotamia at the dawn of civilization: the evolution of an urban landscape*. Chicago: University of Chicago Press.

Alp, S. 1968. *Zylinder und Stempelsiegel aus Karahöyük bei Konya*. Ankara: Türk Tarih Kurumu.

Archi, A. 2011. In search of Armi. *JCS* 63: 5–34.

Archi, A. 2017. Metals in third millennium BC: standpoint Ebla. In Kulakoğlu, F., and Barjamovic, G. (eds.) 2017: 163–172.

Atici, L. 2014. Food and ethnicity at Kültepe-Kanesh: preliminary zooarchaeological evidence. In Atici, L., et al. (eds.) 2014: 193–209.

Atici, L., Kulakoğlu, F., Barjamovic, G., and Fairbairn, A. (eds.) 2014. *Current research in Kültepe/Kanesh: an interdisciplinary and integrative approach to trade networks, internationalism, and identity during the Middle Bronze Age*. Atlanta, GA: Lockwood Press.

Bachhuber, C. 2012. The Anatolian plateau. In Potts, D.T. (ed.), *A companion to the archaeology of the ancient Near East*. Malden, MA: Wiley-Blackwell, 575–595.

Bachhuber, C. 2015. *Citadel and cemetery in Early Bronze Age Anatolia*. Sheffield, UK: Equinox.

---

219. Jakob 2003; Postgate 2013.

Bachhuber, C. 2016. The industry and display of textiles in Early Bronze Age western Anatolia. In Pernicka, E., Ünlüsöy, S., and Blum, S.W.E. (eds.), *Early Bronze Age Troy: chronology, cultural development and interregional contacts.* Bonn: Habelt, 339–363.

Balkan, K. 1957. *Letter of king Anum-Hirbi of Mama to king Warshama of Kanish.* Ankara: Türk Tarih Kurumu.

Balkan, K. 1965. The Old Assyrian week. In Güterbock, H.G., and Jacobsen, T. (eds.), *Studies in honor of Benno Landseberger.* Chicago: University of Chicago Press, 159–174.

Balkan, K. 1992. The conception of trinity in the tablets from Kültepe. In Otten, H., et al. (eds.), *Hittite and other Anatolian and Near Eastern studies in honor of Sedat Alp.* Ankara: Türk Tarih Kurumu, 15–44.

Bär, J. 2005. Die Beziehungen zwischen Mari und Assur während der Šakkanakku-Periode. In van Soldt, W.H., Kalvelagen, R., and Katz, D. (eds.), *Ethnicity in ancient Mesopotamia.* Leiden: NINO, 11–30.

Barjamovic, G. 2008. The geography of trade: Assyrian colonies in Anatolia c. 1975–1725 BC and the study of early interregional networks of exchange. In Dercksen, J.G. (ed.) 2008c: 87–100.

Barjamovic, G. 2011. *A historical geography of Anatolia in the Old Assyrian colony period.* Copenhagen: Museum Tusculanum Press.

Barjamovic, G. 2014. The size of Kanesh and the demography of early Middle Bronze Age Anatolia. In Atici, L., et al. (eds.) 2014: 55–68.

Barjamovic, G. 2015a. Kültepe after Kaneš. In Kulakoğlu, F., and Michel, C. (eds.) 2015: 233–242.

Barjamovic, G. 2015b. Contextualizing tradition: incantations, writing and domestic life in Old Assyrian Kanesh. In Delnero, P., and Lauinger, J. (eds.), *Texts and contexts: approaches to textual transmission in the cuneiform world.* Berlin: De Gruyter, 48–86.

Barjamovic, G. 2017. A commercial geography of Anatolia: integrating Hittite and Assyrian texts, archaeology and topography. In Ullmann, L., and Weeden, M. (eds.), *Hittite landscape and geography.* Leiden: Brill, 311–318.

Barjamovic, G. 2018. Interlocking commercial networks and the infrastructure of trade in Western Asia during the Bronze Age. In Kristiansen, K., Lindkvist, T., and Myrdal, J. (eds.), *Trade and civilisation: economic networks and cultural ties from prehistory to the Early Modern era.* Cambridge: Cambridge University Press, 113–142.

Barjamovic, G. 2019a. Silver, markets and long-distance trade in the Konya region, 2400–1700 BCE. In Maner, Ç. (ed.), *Crossroads / Kavşaklar: the plain of Konya from prehistory to the Byzantine period*. Istanbul: Ege, 71–81.

Barjamovic, G. 2019b. Hrozný's excavations at Kültepe and the resurrection of a Bronze Age palace. In Kim, R.I., Mynářová, J., and Pavúk, P. (eds.), *Hrozný and Hittite: the first hundred years*. Leiden: Brill, 5–31.

Barjamovic, G. 2020. Extraction and inequality in Bronze Age Anatolia. In Mynářová, J., and Alivernini, S. (eds.), *Economic complexity in the ancient Near East: management of resources and taxation*. Prague: Charles University, 87–126.

Barjamovic, G., and Fairbairn, A. 2018. Anatolian wine in the Middle Bronze Age. *WdO* 48: 249–284.

Barjamovic, G., Hertel, T., and Larsen, M.T. 2012. *Ups and downs at Kanesh: observations on chronology, history and society in the Old Assyrian period*. Leiden: NINO.

Bayram, S. 1990. Kültepe tabletlerinde geçen yeni bir vâde ifâdesin ve çıkan neticeler. In Anonymous (ed.), *X. Türk Tarih Kongresi: kongreye sunulan bildiriler, vol. 2*. Ankara: Türk Tarih Kurumu Basimevi, 453–462.

Beal, R.H. 2003. The predecessors of Hattusili I. In Beckman, G., Beal, R.H., and McMahon, G. (eds.), *Hittite studies in honor of Harry A. Hoffner Jr*. Winona Lake, IN: Eisenbrauns, 13–36.

Beckman, G. 1982: The Hittite assembly. *JAOS* 102: 435–442.

Biga, G., and Steinkeller, P. 2021. In search of Dugurasu. *JCS* 73: 9–73.

Bilgiç, E. 1954. *Die einheimischen Appellativa der kappadokischen Texte und ihre Bedeutung für die anatolischen Sprachen*. Ankara: Türk Tarih Kurumu.

Bilgiç, E., Sever, H., Günbattı, C., and Bayram, S. 1990. *Ankara Kültepe tabletleri (Ankara Kültepe-Tafeln), vol. 1*. Ankara: Türk Tarih Kurumu.

Bilgin, T. 2018. *Officials and administration in the Hittite world*. Berlin: De Gruyter.

Bloch, Y. 2014. The conquest eponyms of Šamši-Adad I and the Kaneš Eponym List. *JNES* 73: 191–210.

Bonechi, M. 1990. Aleppo in età arcaica: a proposito di un'opera recente. *SEL* 7: 15–37.

Bonechi, M. 2016. Thorny geopolitical problems in the Palace G archives: the Ebla southern horizon, Part one: the Middle Orontes Basin. In Parayre, D. (ed.), *Le fleuve rebelle: géographie historique du moyen Oronte d'Ebla à l'époque médié*. Beirut: Presses de l'IFPO, 29–88.

Cammarosano, M. 2006. *Il decreto antico-ittita di Pimpira*. Florence: LoGisma.

Carruba, O. 2003. *Anittae Res Gestae*. Pavia: Italian University Press.

Çayır, M. 2013. Kültepe tabletlerinde geçen bir unvan, *rabi ṭābātim* "tuzcular âmiri." *Ankara Üniversitesi Dil ve Tarih-Coğrafya Fakultesi Dergisi* 53/1: 303–314.

Çeçen, S. 1998. Yerli kralların mabetleri ziyareti ve çıkan neticeler. In Alp, S., et al. (eds.), *III. Uluslararası Hititoloji Kongresi bildirileri / Acts of the IIIrd International Congress of Hittitology*. Ankara: Uyum Ajans, 119–124.

Çeçen, S. 2002. Kültepe belgelerine göre Anadolu şehir devletlerinde ayaklanma. *Archivum Anatolicum* 5: 65–68.

Çeçen, S., and Hecker, K. 1995. *Ina mātīka eblum*: zu einem neuen Text zum Wegerecht in der Kültepe-Zeit. In Dietrich, M., and Lorenz, O. (eds.), *Festschrift für Wolfram Freiherrn von Soden*. Münster: Ugarit-Verlag, 31–41.

Çevik, Ö. 2007. The emergence of different social systems in Early Bronze Age Anatolia: urbanisation versus centralisation. *AnSt* 57: 131–140.

Charpin, D. 2004. Histoire Politique du Proche-Orient amorrite (2002–1595). In Charpin, D., Edzard, D.O., and Stol, M., *Mesopotamien: die altbabylonische Zeit*. Fribourg: Academic Press; Göttingen: Vandenhoeck & Ruprecht, 25–480.

Charpin, D., and Durand, J.-M. 1997. Aššur avant l'Assyrie. *MARI* 8: 367–391.

Charpin, D., and Ziegler, N. 2003. *Mari et le Proche-Orient à l'époque amorrite: essai d'histoire politique*. Paris: Société pour l'étude du Proche-Orient ancien.

Cornelius, F. 1970. Das hethitische ANTAHŠUM(ŠAR)-Fest. In Finet, A. (ed.), *Actes de la XVIIe Rencontre Assyriologique Internationale*. Ham-sur-Heure: Comité Belge de Recherches en Mésopotamie, 171–174.

Cullen, H.M., de Menocal, P.B., Hemming, S., Hemming, G., Brown, F.H., Guilderson, T., and Sirocko, F. 2000. Climate change and the collapse of the Akkadian Empire: evidence from the deep sea. *Geology* 28: 379–382.

Dardano, P. 1997. *L'aneddoto e il racconto in età antico-hittita: la cosiddetta "Cronaca di Palazzo."* Rome: Il Calamo.

de Jong, T. 2012–2013. Astronomical fine-tuning of the chronology of the Hammurabi age. *JEOL* 44: 147–167.

de Jong, T. 2016–2017. Further astronomical fine-tuning of the Old Assyrian and Old Babylonian chronologies. *JEOL* 46: 123–139.

Dercksen, J.G. 1996. *The Old Assyrian copper trade in Anatolia*. Leiden: NINO.

Dercksen, J.G. 2004. Some elements of Old Anatolian society in Kaniš. In Dercksen, J.G. (ed.), *Assyria and beyond: studies presented to Mogens Trolle Larsen*. Leiden: NINO, 137–177.

Dercksen, J.G. 2007. On Anatolian loanwords in Akkadian texts from Kültepe. *ZA* 97: 26–46.

Dercksen, J.G. 2008a. Observations on land use and agriculture in Kaneš. In Michel, C. (ed.), *Old Assyrian studies in memory of Paul Garelli*. Leiden: NINO, 139–157.

Dercksen, J.G. 2008b. Subsistence, surplus and the market for grain and meat at ancient Kanesh. *AoF* 35: 86–102.

Dercksen, J.G. (ed.) 2008c. *Anatolia and the Jazira during the Old Assyrian period*. Leiden: NINO.

Dercksen, J.G. 2010. Anitta and the man of Purušhanda. In Dönmez, Ş. (ed.), *DUB.SAR É.DUB.BA.A: studies presented in honour of Veysel Donbaz*. Istanbul: Ege, 71–75.

Di Nocera, G.M., and Forlanini, M. 1992. *Atlante storico del Vicino Oriente antico, fasc. 4.2: Anatolia: la prima metà del II millennio AC*. Rome: Herder.

Efe, T. 2007. The theories of the "Great Caravan Route" between Cilicia and Troy: the Early Bronze Age III period in inland western Anatolia. *AnSt* 57: 47–64.

Eidem, J. 2011. *The royal archives from Tell Leilan: Old Babylonian letters and treaties from the Lower Town Palace East*. Leiden: NINO.

Emre, K. 1971. *Anadolu kurşun figürinleri ve taş kalıpları / Anatolian lead figurines and their stone moulds*. Ankara: Türk Tarih Kurumu.

Emre, K. 1993. New lead figurines and moulds from Kültepe and Kızılhamza. In Mellink, M., et al. (eds.), *Aspects of art and iconography, Anatolia and its neighbors: studies in honor of Nimet Özgüç*. Ankara: Türk Tarih Kurumu, 169–177.

Erarslan, A. 2009. Trade contacts of early urban societies in the eastern and southeastern Anatolian regions (5500–2000 BC). In Oniz, H. (ed.), *SOMA 2008: proceedings of the XII symposium on Mediterranean archaeology*. Oxford: Archaeopress, 8–17.

Erol, H. 2007. *Eski Asurca metinlerde meslek adları ve unvanlarla geçen şahıs isimleri*. MA thesis, University of Ankara.

Erol, H. 2018. *Kültepe tabletleri XI-a. I. cilt: Šu-Ištar'a ait belgeler*. Ankara: Türk Tarih Kurumu.

Fairbairn, A. 2014. Archaeobotanical investigations of plant consumption and trade at Middle Bronze Age Kültepe/Kanesh. In Atici, L., et al. (eds.) 2014: 175–192.

Fairbairn, A., Wright, N., Weeden, M., Barjamovic, G., Matsumura, K., and Rasch, R. 2019. Ceremonial plant consumption at Middle Bronze Age Büklükale, Kırıkkale Province, central Turkey. *Vegetation History and Archaeobotany* 28: 327–346.

Forlanini, M. 1992. Am mittleren Kızılırmak. In Otten, H., et al. (eds.), *Hittite and other Anatolian and Near Eastern studies in honor of Sedat Alp*. Ankara: Türk Tarih Kurumu, 171–179.

Forlanini, M. 1995. The kings of Kaniš. In Carruba, O., et al. (eds.), *Atti del II congresso internazionale di Hittitologia*. Pavia: Gianni Iuculano, 123–132.

Forlanini, M. 1999. Remarques sur la dynastie hittite: avant et après Boğazköy. *Hethitica* 14: 19–26.

Forlanini, M. 2004a. La nascita di un impero considerazioni sulla prima fase della storia hittita: da Kaniš a Hattuša. *Orientalia* 73: 363–389.

Forlanini, M. 2004b. Considerazioni sullo spostamento del centro del potere nel periodo della formazione dello stato hittita. In Mazoyer, M., and Casabonne, O. (eds.), *Antiquus oriens: mélanges offerts au professeur René Lebrun*. Louvain-Neuve: L'Harmattan, 249–269.

Forlanini, M. 2008. The historical geography of Anatolia and the transition from the *kārum* period to the Early Hittite Empire. In Dercksen, J.G. (ed.) 2008c: 57–86.

Forlanini, M. 2010. An attempt at reconstructing the branches of the Hittite royal family of the Early Kingdom period. In Cohen, Y., Gilan, A., and Miller, J.L. (eds.), *Pax hethitica: studies on the Hittites and their neighbours in honour of Itamar Singer*. Wiesbaden: Harrassowitz, 115–135.

Frangipane, M. 1997. A 4th millennium temple/palace complex at Arslantepe-Malatya: North-South relations and the formation of early state societies in the northern regions of Greater Mesopotamia. *Paléorient* 23: 45–73.

Frangipane, M. 2001. Centralization processes in Greater Mesopotamia: Uruk "expansion" as the climax of systemic interactions among areas of the Greater Mesopotamian region. In Rothman, M. (ed.), *Uruk, Mesopotamia and its neighbors*. Santa Fe, NM: School of Advanced Research Press, 307–348.

Galtung, J. 1971. A structural theory of imperialism. *Journal of Peace Research* 2: 81–117.

Garelli, P. 1963. *Les Assyriens en Cappadoce*. Paris: Maisonneuve.

Gelb, I.J. 1935. *Inscriptions from Alishar and vicinity*. Chicago: University of Chicago Press.

George, A. 2017. Babylonian documents from north Mesopotamia. In George, A.R. (ed.), *Assyrian archival documents in the Schøyen Collection and other documents from north Mesopotamia and Syria.* Bethesda, MD: CDL Press, 95–133.

Grayson, A.K. 1987. *Assyrian rulers of the third and second millennia BC (to 1115 BC).* Toronto: University of Toronto Press.

Guichard, M. 2008. Nahur et la route des marchands assyriens à l'époque de Zimrî-Lîm. In Dercksen, J.G. (ed.) 2008c: 43–56.

Günbattı, C. 1987. Yeniden işlenen bir Kültepe tableti. *Türk Tarih Kurumu Belleten* 199: 1–10.

Günbattı, C. 1996. Two new tablets throwing light on the relations between Anatolian kings and Assyrian merchants in the period of the Assyrian colonies. *Archivum Anatolicum* 2: 25–37.

Günbattı, C. 2000. Eski Anadolu'da "su ordali." *Archivum Anatolicum* 4: 73–88.

Günbattı, C. 2004. Two treaty texts found at Kültepe. In Dercksen, J.G. (ed.), *Assyria and beyond: studies presented to Mogens Trolle Larsen.* Leiden: NINO, 249–268.

Günbattı, C. 2005. 2000 ve 2001 yılı Kültepe kazılarında ele geçen bazı Ib tableteri. In Hazırlayan, Y., and Süel, A. (eds.), *Acts of the Vth international congress of hittitology / V. uluslararası hititoloji kongresi bildirileri.* Ankara: Çorum İl Özel İdaresi, 445–451.

Günbattı, C. 2008. An eponym list (KEL G) from Kültepe. *AoF* 35: 103–132.

Günbattı, C. 2014. *Harsamna kralı Hurmeli'ye gönderilen mektup ve Kaniš kralları / The letter sent to Hurmeli king of Harsamna and the kings of Kaniš.* Ankara: Türk Tarih Kurumu.

Günbattı, C. 2016. *Kültepe tabletleri X: Anadolu tüccarlar Šarabunuwa ve Peruwa-nin arşivleri.* Ankara: Türk Tarih Kurumu.

Haas, V. 2006. *Die hethitische Literatur: Texte, Stilistik, Motive.* Berlin: De Gruyter.

Hawkins, J.D. 2010. Early recognisable hieroglyphic signs (?) in Anatolia. In Kulakoğlu, F., and Kangal, S. (eds.) 2010: 96–97.

Helck, W. 1983. Zur ältesten Geschichte des Hatti-Reiches. In Boehmer, R.M., and Hauptmann, H. (eds.), *Beiträge zur Altertumskunde Kleinasiens: Festschrift für Kurt Bittel.* Mainz: Zabern, 271–282.

Hertel, T. 2013. *Old Assyrian legal practices: law and dispute in the ancient Near East.* Leiden: NINO.

Hertel, T. 2014. The lower town at Kültepe/Kanesh: the urban layout and the population. In Atici, L., et al. (eds.) 2014: 25–54.

Highcock, N.A. 2018a. *Community across distance: the forging of identity between Aššur and Anatolia*. PhD dissertation, New York University.

Highcock, N.A. 2018b. Assyrians abroad: expanding borders through mobile identities in the Middle Bronze Age. *JANEH* 4: 61–93.

Highcock, N.A. 2019. To toggle back and forth: clothing pins and portable identities in the Old Assyrian period. In Cifarelli, M. (ed.), *Fashioned selves: dress and identity in antiquity*. Oxford: Oxbow, 27–40.

Hrozný, F. 1927. Rapport préliminaire sur les fouilles tchécoslovaques du Kultépé. *Syria* 8: 1–12.

Jakob, S. 2003. *Mittelassyrische Verwaltung und Sozialstruktur: Untersuchungen*. Leiden: Brill.

Kashima, K. 2011. Climatic changes and their influences for the archaeological events during the Holocene in central Turkey and northern Syria. *Transactions: Japanese Geomorphological Union* 32: 108–114.

Kashima, K., Hirose, K., Yamaguchi, M., and Fujiki, T. 2005. Palaeoenvironmental change at Kültepe, the capital city of the Middle Bronze Age, central Anatolia, Turkey. *Kaman-Kalehöyük* 14: 137–146.

Kempinski, A., and Košak, S. 1982. CTH 13: the extensive annals of Hattušili I (?). *Tel Aviv* 9: 87–116.

Kloekhorst, A. 2008. *Etymological dictionary of the Hittite inherited lexicon*. Leiden: Brill.

Kloekhorst, A. 2019. *Kanišite Hittite: the earliest attested record of Indo-European*. Leiden: Brill.

Koliński, R. 2013. Review of Barjamovic et al. 2012. *BiOr* 70: 736–742.

Kroonen, G., Barjamovic, G., and Peyrot, M. 2018. *Linguistic supplement to Damgaard et al. 2018: Early Indo-European languages, Anatolian, Tocharian and Indo-Iranian*. Retrieved from http://doi.org/10.5281/zenodo.1240524 (last accessed August 1, 2021).

Kryszat, G. 2004a. *Zur Chronologie der Kaufmannsarchive aus der Schicht des Kārum* Kaneš: Studien *und Materialien*. Leiden: NINO.

Kryszat, G. 2004b. Herrscher, Herrschaft und Kulttradition in Anatolien nach den Quellen aus den altassyrischen Handelskolonien, Teil 1: die *sikkātum* und der *rabi sikkitim*. *AoF* 31: 15–45.

Kryszat, G. 2006. Herrschaft und Kulttradition in Anatolien nach den Quellen aus den assyrischen Handelskolonien, Teil 2: Götter, Priester und Feste Altanatoliens. *AoF* 33: 102–124.

Kryszat, G. 2008a. Herrscher, Kult und Kulttradition in Anatolien nach den Quellen aus den altassyrischen Handelskolonien, Teil 3/1: Grundlagen für eine neue Rekonstruktion der Geschichte Anatoliens und der assyrischen Handelskolonien in spätaltassyrischer Zeit. *AoF* 35: 156–189.

Kryszat, G. 2008b. Herrscher, Kult und Kulttradition in Anatolien nach den Quellen aus den altassyrischen Handelskolonien, Teil 3/2: Grundlagen für eine neue Rekonstruktion der Geschichte Anatoliens und der assyrischen Handelskolonien in spätaltassyrischer Zeit, II. *AoF* 35: 195–219.

Kulakoğlu, F. 2011. Kültepe–Kaneš: a second millennium BCE trading center on the central plateau. In Steadman, S., and MacMahon, G. (eds.) 2011: 1012–1030.

Kulakoğlu, F. 2014. Kanesh after the Assyrian colony period: current research at Kültepe and the question of the end of the Bronze Age settlement. In Atici, L., et al. (eds.) 2014: 85–94.

Kulakoğlu, F. 2017. Early Bronze Age monumental structures at Kültepe. In Kulakoğlu, F., and Barjamovic, G. (eds.) 2017: 217–226.

Kulakoğlu, F., and Barjamovic, G. (eds.) 2017. *Proceedings of the 2nd Kültepe international meeting: studies dedicated to Klaas Veenhof.* Turnhout: Brepols.

Kulakoğlu, F., and Kangal, S. (eds.) 2010. *Anatolia's prologue – Kültepe Kanesh Karum: Assyrians in Istanbul.* Kayseri: Kayseri Metropolitan Municipality.

Kulakoğlu, F., and Michel, C. (eds.) 2015. *Proceedings of the 1st Kültepe international meeting: studies dedicated to Kutlu Emre.* Turnhout: Brepols.

Kuzuoğlu, R. 2007. Asur ticaret kolonileri çağında Anadolu kraliçeleri. *Türk Tarih Kurumu Belleten* 262: 795–809.

Kuzuoğlu, R. 2016. Two cuneiform texts found in Acemhöyük from the Old Assyrian period. *Türk Tarih Kurumu Belleten* 289: 685–699.

Lacambre, D., and Nahm, W. 2015. Pithana, an Anatolian ruler in the time of Samsuiluna of Babylon: new data from Tell Rimah (Iraq). *RA* 109: 17–28.

Landsberger, B. 1949. Jahreszeiten im Sumerisch-Akkadischen. *JNES* 8: 248–272.

Landsberger, B. 1950. Kommt Hattum, "Hettiterland" und Hattī'um, "Hettiter" in den Kültepe-Tafeln vor? *Archiv Orientální* 18: 321–329.

Larsen, M.T. 1967. *Old Assyrian caravan procedures.* Leiden: NINO.

Larsen, M.T. 1972. A revolt against Hattuša. *JCS* 25: 100–101.

Larsen, M.T. 1976. *The Old Assyrian city-state and its colonies.* Copenhagen: Akademisk Forlag.

Larsen, M.T. 2007. Going to the river. In Roth, M.T., et al. (eds.), *Studies presented to Robert D. Biggs*. Chicago: The Oriental Institute of the University of Chicago, 173–188.

Larsen, M.T. 2010. *Kültepe tabletleri VI-a: the archive of the Šalim-Aššur family, vol. 1: the first two generations*. Ankara: Türk Tarih Kurumu.

Larsen, M.T. 2015. *Ancient Kanesh: a merchant colony in Bronze Age Anatolia*. Cambridge: Cambridge University Press.

Larsen, M.T. 2017. A complex business transaction with diplomatic repercussions: the conflict with Ušinalam. In Kulakoğlu, F., and Barjamovic, G. (eds.) 2017: 173–188.

Larsen, M.T., and Lassen, A.W. 2014. Cultural exchange at Kültepe. In Kozuh, M., et al. (ed.), *Extraction and control: studies in honor of Matthew W. Stolper*. Chicago: The Oriental Institute of the University of Chicago, 171–188.

Lassen, A.W. 2010. The trade in wool in Old Assyrian Anatolia. *JEOL* 42: 159–179.

Lassen, A.W. 2012. *Glyptic encounters: a stylistic and prosopographical study of seals in the Old Assyrian period: chronology, ownership and identity*. PhD dissertation, University of Copenhagen.

Lassen, A.W. 2014. The old Assyrian glyptic style: an investigation of a seal style, its owners and place of production. In Atici, L., et al. (ed.) 2014: 107–121.

Lassen, A.W., Frahm, E., and Wagensonner, K. (eds.) 2019. *Ancient Mesopotamia speaks: highlights from the Yale Babylonian Collection*. New Haven, CT: Yale University Press.

Lewy, J. 1926. *Die altassyrischen Texte vom Kültepe bei Kaisarije*. Constantinople: Selbstverlag der Antikenmuseen.

Lewy, J. 1930. *Die Kültepetexte aus der Sammlung Frida Hahn, Berlin*. Leipzig: Hinrichs.

Lewy, J. 1935. *Tablettes cappadociennes: troisième série, vol. 1*. Paris: Geuthner.

Liverani, M. 1990. *Prestige and interest: international relations in the Near East ca. 1600–1100 BC*. Padova: Sargon.

Lumsden, S. 1990. *Symbols of power: Hittite royal iconography in seals*. PhD dissertation, University of California, Berkeley.

Lumsden, S. 2008. Material culture and the middle ground in the Old Assyrian colony period. In Michel, C. (ed.), *Old Assyrian studies in memory of Paul Garelli*. Leiden: NINO, 21–43.

Manning, S.W., Barjamovic, G., and Lorenzen, B. 2017. The course of C14 dating does not run smooth: tree rings, radiocarbon, and potential impacts of a calibration curve wiggle on dating Mesopotamian chronology. *JAEI* 13: 70–81.

Massa, M. 2016. *Networks before empires: cultural transfers in Anatolia during the Early Bronze Age*. PhD dissertation, University College London.

Massa, M., and Palmisano, A. 2018. Change and continuity in the long-distance exchange networks between western/central Anatolia, northern Levant and northern Mesopotamia, c. 3200–1600 BCE. *Journal of Anthropological Archaeology* 49: 65–87.

Matouš, L. 1965. Anatolische Feste nach "Kappadokischen" Tafeln. In Güterbock, H.G., and Jacobsen, T. (eds.), *Studies in honor of Benno Landsberger*. Chicago: University of Chicago Press, 175–181.

Matouš, L., and Matoušová-Rajmová, M. 1984. *Kappadokische Keilschrifttafeln mit Siegeln aus den Sammlungen der Karlsuniversität in Prag*. Prague: Charles University.

Michel, C. 2011. The private archives from Kaniš belonging to Anatolians. *AoF* 38: 94–115.

Michel, C. 2017. Economy, society, and daily life in the Old Assyrian period. In Frahm, E. (ed.), *A companion to Assyria*. Malden, MA: Wiley-Blackwell, 80–107.

Michel, C. 2019. Palaces at Kaneš during the Old Assyrian period. In Wicke, D. (ed.), *Der Palast im antiken und islamischen Orient*. Wiesbaden: Harrassowitz, 121–138.

Michel, C., and Garelli, P. 1996. Heurts avec une principauté anatolienne. *Wiener Zeitschrift für die Kunde des Morgenlandes* 86: 277–290.

Michel, C., and Veenhof, K.R. 2010. The textiles traded by the Assyrians in Anatolia (19th–18th centuries BC). In Michel, C., and Nosch, M.L. (eds.), *Textile terminologies in the 3rd to 1st millennium BC in the ancient Near East and Eastern Mediterranean*. Oxford: Oxbow: 209–269.

Miller, J.L. 1999. *The expeditions of Hattušili I to the eastern frontiers: a study in the historical geography and internal chronology of the great king's campaigns*. MA thesis, Tel Aviv University.

Miller, J.L. 2001. Anum-Hirbi and his kingdom. *AoF* 28: 65–101.

Miller, J.L., and Corti, C. 2018. Zalpa. *RlA* 15: 193–202.

Nahm, W. 2013. The case for the Lower Middle Chronology. *AoF* 40: 350–372.

Neu, E. 1974. *Der Anitta-Text*. Wiesbaden: Harrassowitz.

Otten, H. 1957. Die altassyrischen Texte aus Boğazköy. *MDOG* 89: 68–80.

Özgüç, N. 1953a. Vorbericht über die Siegel und Siegelabdrücke. *Türk Tarih Kurumu Belleten* 17: 123–127.

Özgüç, N. 1953b. Preliminary report on the 1951 excavations at Kültepe. *Türk Tarih Kurumu Belleten* 17: 289–297.

Özgüç, N. 1965. *Kültepe mühür baskılarında Anadolu grubu / The Anatolian group of cylinder seal impressions from Kültepe.* Ankara: Türk Tarih Kurumu.

Özgüç, N. 1966. Excavations at Acemhöyük. *Anadolu* 10: 29–52.

Özgüç, N. 1996. Seal impressions on Kültepe documents notarized by native rulers. In Gasche, H., and Hrouda, B. (eds.), *Collectanea orientalia: histoire, arts de l'espace et industrie de la terre: études offertes en hommage à Agnès Spycket.* Neuchâtel: Recherches et publications, 267–277.

Özgüç, N. 2006. *Seal impressions on the clay envelopes from the archives of the native Peruwa and Assyrian trader Uṣur-ša-Ištar son of Aššur-imittī.* Ankara: Türk Tarih Kurumu.

Özgüç, N. 2015. *Acemhöyük–Burušhaddum I: cylinder seals and bullae with cylinder seal impressions.* Ankara: Türk Tarih Kurumu.

Özgüç, T. 1986. *Kültepe–Kaniš II: new researches at the trading center of the ancient Near East.* Ankara: Türk Tarih Kurumu.

Özgüç, T. 1999. *The palaces and temples of Kültepe—Kaniš/Neša.* Ankara: Türk Tarih Kurumu.

Özgüç, T. 2003. *Kültepe–Kaniš/Neša: the earliest international trade center and the oldest capital city of the Hittites.* Tokyo: Middle Eastern Culture Center in Japan.

Özgüç, T., and Özgüç, N. 1953. *Türk Tarih Kurumu tarafından yapılan Kültepe kazısı raporu 1949 / Bericht über die in Kültepe im Auftrage der Türkischen Historischen Gesellschaft in 1949 durchgeführten Ausgrabungen.* Ankara: Türk Tarih Kurumu.

Palumbi, G. 2011. The Arslantepe royal tomb and the "manipulation" of the kurgan ideology in eastern Anatolia at the beginning of the third millennium. In Borgna, E., and Celka, S.M. (eds.), *Ancestral landscapes.* Lyon: Maison de l'Orient et de la Méditerranée, 47–59.

Pecchioli Daddi, F. 1982. *Mestieri, professioni e dignità nell'Anatolia ittita.* Rome: Edizione dell'Ateneo.

Pecchioli Daddi, F. 1994. Il re, il padre del re, il nonno del re. *Orientis Antiqui Miscellanea* 1: 75–91.

Poetto, M. 2018. A hieroglyphic graffito on a pitcher from Kültepe. *News from the Lands of the Hittites: Scientific Journal for Anatolian Research* 2: 17–25.

Postgate, J.N. 2014. *Bronze Age bureaucracy: writing and the practice of government in Assyria*. Cambridge: Cambridge University Press.

Ricetti, M. 2017. Sealing without a seal: alternative sealing media at Kültepe during the Old Assyrian period. In Kulakoğlu, F., and Barjamovic, G. (eds.) 2017: 131–162.

Riehl, S. 2008. Changing growing conditions for crops during the Near Eastern Bronze Age (3000–1200 BC): the stable carbon isotope evidence. *JAS* 35: 1011–1022.

Roaf, M. 2012. The fall of Babylon in 1499 NC or 1595 MC. *Akkadica* 133: 147–174.

Sagona, A. 2011. Anatolia and the Trans-Caucasus: themes and variations (ca. 6400–1500 BC). In Steadman, S., and MacMahon, G. (eds.) 2011: 683–703.

Sagona, A. 2014. Rethinking the Kura-Araxes genesis. *Paléorient* 40: 23–46.

Sagona, A., and Zimansky, P. 2009. *Ancient Turkey*. London and New York: Routledge.

Şahoğlu, V. 2005. The Anatolian trade network and the Izmir region during the Early Bronze Age. *OJA* 24: 339–360.

Salvini, M. 1994. Una lettera di Hattušili I relativa alla spedizione contro Hahhum. *SMEA* 34: 61–80.

Schwemer, D., and Barjamovic, G. 2019. Textfunde der Kampagne 2018 (pp. 85–89). In Schachner, A. (ed.), Die Ausgrabungen in Boğazköy-Hattuša 2018. *Archäologischer Anzeiger* 2019: 43–117.

Sever, H. 1990. Yeni Kültepe tableterinde geçen *"kima awāt naruāim"* tabiri ve değerlendirilmesi. *Ankara Üniversitesi Dil ve Tarih-Coğrafya Fakültesi Dergisi* 34: 251–265.

Shi, X. 2015. Village life in ancient Anatolia: the case of Talwahšušara. In Kulakoğlu, F., and Michel, C. (ed.) 2015: 147–154.

Singer, I. 1990. "Our god" and "their god" in the Anitta Text. In Carruba, O., et al. (eds.), *Atti del II congresso internazionale di hittitologia*. Pavia: Gianni Iuculano, 343–349.

Smith, A.T. 2015. *The political machine: assembling sovereignty in the Bronze Age Caucasus*. Princeton, NJ: Princeton University Press.

Smith, S. 1921. *Cuneiform texts from the Cappadocian tablets in the British Museum*, part 1. London: British Museum.

Smith, S. 1927. *Cuneiform texts from the Cappadocian tablets in the British Museum,* part 4. London: British Museum.

Sommerfeld, W. 2006. Ein altassyrisches Tafelfragment aus Kayalıpınar. *MDOG* 138: 231–233.

Steadman, S. 2011. The Early Bronze Age on the plateau. In Steadman, S., and MacMahon, G. (eds.) 2011: 229–259.

Steadman, S., and MacMahon, G. (eds.) 2011. *The Oxford handbook of ancient Anatolia (10,000–323 BCE).* Oxford: Oxford University Press.

Steinkeller, P. 2021. The Sargonic and Ur III empires. In Bang, P.F., Bayly, C.A., and Scheidel, W. (eds.), *The Oxford world history of empire, vol. 2: the history of empires.* Oxford: Oxford University Press, 43–72.

Stephens, F.J. 1927. The Cappadocian tablets in the University Museum of Pennsylvania. *Journal of the Society of Oriental Research* 11: 101–136.

Stratford, E. 2015. Successor eponyms, debt notes, intercalation, and the Old Assyrian calendar during Kültepe Level II: a critical reappraisal. *JNES* 74: 301–324.

Stratford, E. 2017. *A year of vengeance, vol. 1: time, narrative, and the Old Assyrian trade.* Berlin: De Gruyter.

Ünal, A. 1995. Reminiszenzen an die Zeit der altassyrischen Handelskolonien in hethitischen Texten. *AoF* 22: 269–276.

van den Hout, T.P.J. 2008. A classified past: classification of knowledge in the Hittite empire. In Biggs, R.D., et al. (eds.), *Proceedings of the 51st Rencontre Assyriologique Internationale.* Chicago: The Oriental Institute of the University of Chicago, 211–219.

van den Hout, T.P.J. 2009. Reflections on the origins and development of the Hittite tablet collections in Hattuša and their consequences for the rise of Hittite literacy. In Pecchioli Daddi, F., et al. (eds.), *Central-north Anatolia in the Hittite period: new perspectives in light of recent research.* Rome: Herder, 71–96.

Veenhof, K.R. 1972. *Aspects of Old Assyrian trade and its terminology.* Leiden: Brill.

Veenhof, K.R. 1978. An ancient Anatolian money-lender: his loans, securities, and debt-slaves. In Hruška, B., and Komoróczy, G. (eds.), *Festschrift Lubor Matouš, vol. 2.* Budapest: Eötvös Loránd Tudományegyetem, Ókori Történeti Tanszék, 279–311.

Veenhof, K.R. 1989. Status and offices of an Anatolian gentleman: two unpublished letters of Huharimataku from Karum Kanish. In Emre, K., et al. (eds.), *Anatolia and the ancient Near East: studies in honor of Tahsin Özgüç*. Ankara: Türk Tarik Kurumu, 515–525.

Veenhof, K.R. 1995. "In accordance with the words of the stele": evidence for Old Assyrian legislation. *Chicago-Kent Law Review* 70: 181–184.

Veenhof, K.R. 2003. *The Old Assyrian list of year eponyms from Karum Kanish and its chronological implications*. Ankara: Türk Tarih Kurumu.

Veenhof, K.R. 2008a. The Old Assyrian period. In Veenhof, K.R., and Eidem, J., *Mesopotamia: the Old Assyrian period*. Fribourg: Academic Press; Göttingen: Vandenhoeck & Ruprecht, 13–264.

Veenhof, K.R. 2008b. Some displaced tablets from Karum Kanesh (Kültepe) (kt 86/k 48, kt 86/k 204 and kt 91/k 539). *AoF* 35: 10–27.

Veenhof, K.R. 2010. *Ankara Kültepe tabletleri V: the archive of Kuliya, son of Ali-Abum (Kt. 92/k 188)*. Ankara: Türk Tarih Kurumu.

Veenhof, K.R. 2013. New Mesopotamian treaties from the early second millennium BC from kārum Kanesh and Tell Leilan (Šehna). *ZAR* 19: 23–58.

Veenhof, K.R. 2016. A difficult Old Assyrian business venture: Mannum-kī-Aššur tries his luck with iron. *BiOr* 73: 13–39.

Veenhof, K.R. 2017a. The Old Assyrian period (20th–18th century BCE). In Frahm, E. (ed.), *A companion to Assyria*. Malden, MA: Wiley-Blackwell, 57–79.

Veenhof, K.R. 2017b. *Ankara Kültepe tabletleri VIII: the archive of Elamma, son of Iddin-Suen, and his family (Kt. 91/k 285–268 and Kt. 92/k 94–187)*. Ankara: Türk Tarih Kurumu.

Veenhof, K.R. 2017c. Acemhöyük: seals, chronology and history. In Kulakoğlu, F., and Barjamovic, G. (eds.) 2017: 243–257.

Waal, W. 2012. Writing in Anatolia: the origins of Anatolian hieroglyphs and the introductions of the cuneiform script. *AoF* 39: 287–315.

Weingarten, J. 1990. The sealing structure of Karahöyük and some administrative links with Phaistos on Crete. *Oriens Antiquus* 29: 63–95.

Weiss, H. (ed.) 2012. *Seven generations since the fall of Akkad*. Wiesbaden: Harrassowitz.

Weiss, H. 2019. Karl Popper, Imre Lakatos, and the 4.2 ka BP event in the northern North Atlantic, Anatolia and the Indus. *Climate of the Past Discussions* 2019. Retrieved from https://doi.org/10.5194/cp-2018-162-RC3 (last accessed August 1, 2021).

Weiss, H., Courty, M.A., Wetterstrom, W. Meadow, R. Guichard, F. Senior, L., and Curnow, A. 1993. The genesis and collapse of north Mesopotamian civilization. *Science* 261: 995–1004.

Wilhelm, G. 2008. Hurrians in the Kültepe texts. In Dercksen, J.G. (ed.) 2008c: 181–194.

Wilkinson, T.C. 2014. *Tying the threads of Eurasia: trans-regional routes and material flows in Transcaucasia, eastern Anatolia and western Central Asia, c. 3000–1500 BC*. Leiden: Sidestone.

Winters, R. 2018. *Negotiating exchange: Ebla and the international system of the Early Bronze Age*. PhD dissertation, Harvard University.

Yazıcıoğlu-Santamaria, G.B. 2017. Locals, immigrants, and marriage ties at Kültepe: results of strontium isotope analysis on human teeth from lower town graves. In Kulakoğlu, F., and Barjamovic, G. (eds.) 2017: 61–81.

Yener, K.A. 2000. *The domestication of metals: the rise of complex metal industries in Anatolia (c. 4500–2000 BC)*. Leiden: Brill.

Yoshida, D. 2002. Ein altassyrischer Text aus Kaman-Kalehüyük. *Kaman-Kalehöyük* 11: 133–137.

Zehnder, T. 2010. *Die hethitischen Frauennamen*. Wiesbaden: Harrassowitz.

18

The Kingdom of Babylon and the Kingdom of the Sealand

Odette Boivin

18.1. Introduction and definitions

Through the Bible and Greek historiography, Babylon achieved lasting—if equivocal—fame in the Judeo-Christian world as an imperial capital in the first millennium BC.[1] The city, however, had first risen to prominence over a millennium earlier, during the aptly named Old Babylonian period. From a mere city-state competing against others after the demise of the Ur III kingdom at the turn of the second millennium, it reached its zenith in the eighteenth century BC under Hammurabi[2] and his son Samsu-iluna. For about a generation, Babylon controlled the better

---

1. In this chapter, Archibab refers to the online database of Old Babylonian archival texts (http://www.archibab.fr/), and ETCSL to the Electronic Text Corpus of Sumerian Literature (http://etcsl.orinst.ox.ac.uk/). The following abbreviations are museum numbers: A (Louvre, Paris), BM (British Museum, London), IM (Iraq Museum, Baghdad), Sem (Kunsthistorisches Museum, Vienna), YBC (Yale Babylonian Collection).

2. The conventional English orthography "Hammurabi" is used here. Note that the current consensus is that this Amorite name was probably realized in speech as "Hammurapi." For a recent discussion of its etymology and morphology, see Michalowski and Streck 2018: 384–385.

Odette Boivin, *The Kingdom of Babylon and the Kingdom of the Sealand* In: *The Oxford History of the Ancient Near East.* Edited by: Karen Radner, Nadine Moeller, and D. T. Potts, Oxford University Press.
© Oxford University Press 2022. DOI: 10.1093/oso/9780190687571.003.0018

part of what is now Iraq and a small portion of Syria (figure 18.1 a–b). After this short-lived territorial apex, the kingdom endured another long century in relative stability, before collapsing at the beginning of the sixteenth century BC as a result of the combined effects of internal rebellion and foreign attacks.[3] Nevertheless, Babylon maintained its royal status, through several ups and downs, until the short reign of Alexander the Great, who made it his eastern capital in the fourth century BC.

Babylon's hegemonic power has influenced the modern nomenclature used to discuss ancient geography, history, and languages. The alluvial plain of Southern Mesopotamia, between the Tigris and the Euphrates, roughly from the area of Baghdad down to the shore of the Persian Gulf, is often called Babylonia. This was the core of Hammurabi's kingdom at the end of his reign. It also reflects an emic concept of territory, that of "Sumer and Akkad." Akkad refers to northern Babylonia, home to the speakers of the East Semitic language Akkadian, while Sumer refers to southern and central Babylonia, up to the area of Nippur, where speakers of Sumerian lived before gradually adopting Akkadian, a process completed around the turn of the second millennium. From the second millennium onward, two main regional dialects of Akkadian are recognizable in the sources: Babylonian in the area defined as Babylonia, and Assyrian further north. The historical period lasting from the fall of the Ur III kingdom until the fall of Babylon in 1595 BC is called the Old Babylonian period, as is this phase in the evolution of the Babylonian language. The first two centuries are referred to as Early Old Babylonian; the reigns of Hammurabi and Samsu-iluna—the better part of the eighteenth century BC—are the Middle Old Babylonian period; the remaining long century is called Late Old Babylonian. In both material culture and language, the end of the Old Babylonian period is often difficult to differentiate from the beginning of the Middle Babylonian (or Kassite) period, making it sometimes hardly possible to date artifacts, archaeological levels, and texts with precision.

---

3. The absolute dates used in this chapter follow the conventional Middle Chronology, but they are by no means certain; on the problems plaguing the reconstruction of Middle Bronze Age chronology, see chapter 11 in this volume.

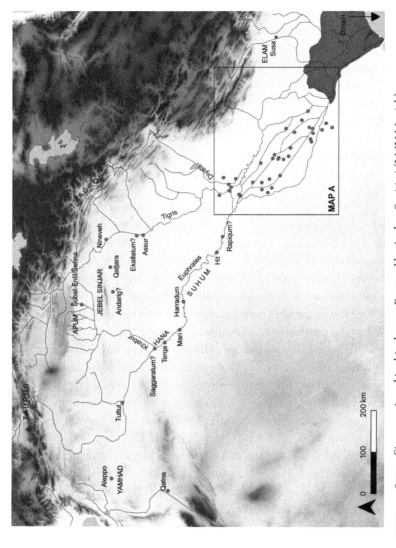

FIGURE 18.1A. Sites mentioned in this chapter. Prepared by Andrea Squitieri (LMU Munich).

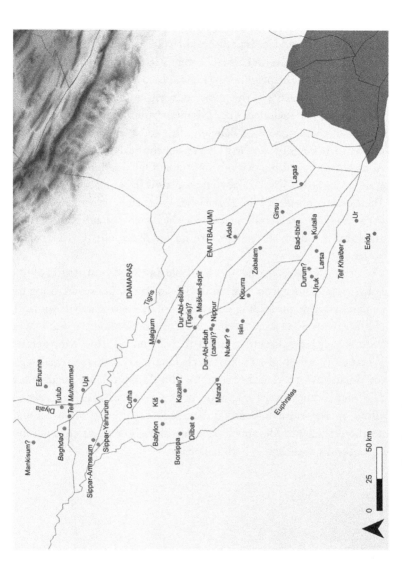

FIGURE 18.1B. Detail map A.

This chapter centers principally on the kingdom of Babylon, i.e., on the kingdom ruled by the First Dynasty of the kings of Babylon, as per the later King List A (see later discussion).[4] Its beginnings are coeval with the kingdoms of Isin and Larsa (chapter 14 in this volume); the contemporary history of the neighboring regions is covered in chapters 15–17 in this volume. Elements of the poorly understood history of the Sealand kingdom are also included, since it is intertwined with much of the later history of the kingdom of Babylon. This southern Babylonian polity, ruled by the kings of the First Dynasty of the Sealand, as per King List A, emerged toward the end of the Middle Old Babylonian period and endured into the Middle Babylonian period (chapter 33 in volume 3). The sequence of rulers of both dynasties and their approximative relative chronology are presented in table 18.1; the names of Early Kassite rulers are added to situate chronologically the end of the First Dynasty of the Sealand.

Although the textual sources available for the reconstruction of Old Babylonian history were written in Babylonian or Sumerian, using the cuneiform script, the leading royal houses of that period in Mesopotamia and northern Syria were of Amorite extraction. Amorite was a West Semitic language, distantly related to Babylonian. This West Semitic penetration of the highest political echelons in city-states and small territorial states as far east as the foothills of the Zagros follows a widespread east- and southeastward migration of Amorite speakers that is plainly visible in late third millennium sources.[5] Their progression through northern Syria into Mesopotamia is probably also reflected in a number of toponyms occurring in both regions.[6]

---

4. Recent studies include the volume with the contributions of Charpin 2004 (on the political history, including of neighboring kingdoms), Edzard 2004 (on literature and religion), and Stol 2004 (on economy and society), as well as Pecha 2018.

5. Burke 2020; also chapter 13 in this volume.

6. Charpin 2003; 2004: 59.

Table 18.1. Rulers of the kingdoms of Babylon and of the Sealand

Babylon I	Sealand I	Kassite	
Sumu-la-El (1880–1845)			
Sabium (1844–1831)			
Apil-Sin (1830–1813)			
Sin-muballiṭ (1812–1793)			
Hammurabi (1792–1750)			
Samsu-iluna (1749–1712)	Ili-ma-ilu (~1720–?)		
Abi-ešuh (1711–1684)	Itti-ili-nibi		
	Dam(i)q-ilišu		
Ammi-ṣaduqa (1646–1626)	Iškibal		
	Šušši		
Samsu-ditana (1625–1595)	Gulkišar (~1595)		
	DIŠ+U-EN?		
	Pešgaladarameš (~1575?)	:	
	Ayadaragalama (~1550?)	:	
	Ekurduana	Agum II	
	Melamkura	Burna-Buriaš	
	Ea-gamil (~1480)	Ulam-Buriaš	Kaštiliaš III
		Agum III	

The gentilic *Amurrû* (Sumerian Martu) is a Babylonian term reflecting the Amorites' migratory background, which simply means "from the West." Although Amorite groups had a sedentary component, they often appear in sources as (semi-)nomadic pastoralists.[7] Friction between local populations and newcomers found expression in a recurrent *topos* of Mesopotamian literature, the opposition between the sedentary/urban/civilized and the nomadic/uncivilized,[8] but this did not impede the Amorites' rapid integration into Mesopotamian society and their later accession to significant political power. The Amorites adopted the local language and customs to the point that rulers of Amorite ancestry eventually became sponsors and guardians of the Sumerian and Babylonian heritage with which they came to identify. Perhaps one composition reflects this process of integration best: *The Marriage of Martu*, which deals with the "Amorite god," a Mesopotamian deity created to represent this ethno-linguistic group on the divine plane.[9] In this poem, the divine bridegroom Martu is described as non-sedentary, uncouth, and ignorant of proper ritual customs. He is nonetheless accepted, laconically but wholeheartedly, by his bride, the daughter of a Sumerian god, probably embodying local southern Mesopotamian society.[10]

The palatial archives found at Mari, an important city on the Middle Euphrates, provide the richest information on Amorite political and social customs, as well as on their tribal structure—to be understood as a fluid concept. The term Hana is sometimes used as a general, cross-tribal demonym.[11] The main, broad confederations are (Ben)sim'alites, (Ben)yaminites, Yamutbal, and Numhâ. The first two are, respectively, the

---

7. E.g., Durand 2004: 114–115, §0.2.3 (on the methodological pitfalls in characterizing Amorite nomadism), 195–196 (for a summary of his own interpretation).

8. Michalowski 2011: 84.

9. Beaulieu 2005: 34–35.

10. Vanstiphout 1999: 470–474 (including remarks on a possible "late," i.e., Old Babylonian, date of the composition).

11. Durand 1992: 113–116 (who translates Hana as "bédouin").

"[sons] of the left" (northern tribes) and "[sons] of the right" (southern tribes), while the latter two terms were apparently derived from ancestors' names.[12] The Yaminites were subdivided into at least five tribes—the Yahrurum, Yarîh, Amnanum, Rabbûm, and Uprapûm[13]—while twelve Sim'alite tribes are attested.[14]

Nearly all kings of the First Dynasty of Babylon bear Amorite names. We do not have sources that reveal unambiguously exactly which tribe(s) they identified with, but a Yaminite affiliation appears most likely. Indeed, in a text pertaining to a ritual commemorating the dead (*kispum*), the Yaminite tribes Amnanum and Yahrurum, as well as the Numhâ group, appear among the "oldest" ancestors of Ammi-ṣaduqa, in his idealized genealogy reaching back twenty-eight generations.[15] In addition, in a royal letter discussed in more detail later, Babylonian troops are called Amnan-Yahrur,[16] a composite of the names of the two Yaminite tribes mentioned in the *kispum*-tablet. The presence of these tribes in northern Babylonia is reflected in the names of the twin cities Sippar-Amnanum and Sippar-Yahrurum.[17] Kings of the kingdom of the Sealand bore Akkadian or Sumerian names;[18] if they were related to an earlier Amorite royal house of southern Babylonia, they did not claim this ancestry in their names.

Another ethno-linguistic group gradually entered the history of the kingdom of Babylon: the Kassites. Two, perhaps tribal, affiliations are loosely associated with them: the Bimatites and the Samharites. They seem to have migrated, probably from the Zagros Mountains, into the Mesopotamian plains over several decades, possibly in three main

---

12. Durand 2004: 115, 133–134.

13. With further subdivisions: e.g., Muti-abal was a sub-clan of the Rabbûm; see Durand 2004: 158.

14. Durand 2004: 179.

15. Finkelstein 1966: 95–97 (BM 80328: ll. 8–10); Charpin and Durand 1986: 159–170.

16. Letter of ANam to Sin-muballiṭ; see Charpin 2004: 83–84, and later in this section.

17. Groneberg 1980: 208–209, s.v. Sip(p)ir-amnānum and Sip(p)ir-jaḫrurum.

18. Boivin 2018: 33–36.

waves.[19] And, just as the Amorites had begun forming royal houses in their new homelands at the turn of the second millennium, Kassite dynasties appeared around the middle of the millennium in the Diyala,[20] along the Middle Euphrates,[21] and at Babylon, after the demise of the First Dynasty. From the moment they appear in the cuneiform record, Kassites are often described as "soldiers" or "troops" and are sometimes clearly associated with the military. Their economic and social integration into Babylonian society may have been largely driven by several of them enlisting as mercenaries.[22]

18.2. Sources and some methodological considerations

Textual sources from the Old Babylonian period are varied and relatively abundant. They include letters, economic, legal, literary, divinatory, mathematical, and school texts. There is no contemporary full-fledged historiography, but royal inscriptions, usually commemorating the building of a temple, city wall, or hydraulic structure, occasionally mention military events. These were usually engraved on stone objects, but much later copies on clay tablets are also known.[23] At present, no royal inscriptions are extant for this dynasty prior to the reign of Hammurabi.[24] Year names, normally written in Sumerian, constitute another important

19. van Koppen 2017: 53–54, 78–79. For a succinct overview of the Kassite presence in that period, also outside Babylonia, see Brinkman 2017: 4–5; also 6–8 (for later evidence).

20. van Koppen 2017: 59–61.

21. Podany 2002: 10 (identifying the relevant texts); van Koppen 2017: 54; Brinkman 2017: 4–5.

22. Recently, van Koppen 2017: 53.

23. For instance, Frayne 1990: no. 4.3.6.3, copied by a mid-first millennium scribe who added in a colophon that he presented his copy as a votive gift.

24. The known inscriptions of the dynasty are published in Frayne 1990: 323–438.

source of information.[25] These often took the form of statements commemorating a major deed of the king in the past year, e.g., "Year in which Sabium, the king, built the Esagil temple."[26]

Year names usually record military events (invariably victories) or the royal patronage of cults. Keeping in mind that they can be somewhat hyperbolic, year names provide crucial information for the reconstruction of political and religious history. Some year names are known to us only in commonly used, abbreviated versions. Lists of year names were compiled in antiquity, a necessity given a dating system without a year count, and several such date lists have survived.[27] As a result, only a few lacunae remain in the internal chronology of some of the reigns of the kings of Babylon.[28] For the kings of the Sealand, by contrast, we are still largely in the dark, owing to the much smaller number of sources and their uneven distribution. The kings of this dynasty used a system referring to regnal year, apparently concurrently with year names in the Old Babylonian style.[29]

The use of a year name of a given king in the date formulae of tablets found at a particular town or city offers a means of determining whose rule was recognized there at the time. However, one should bear in mind that this is not always infallible. Indeed, in the formative period of the kingdom, and outside the Babylonian core area throughout the kingdom's existence, Babylon's "rule" often meant that a local ruler accepted *a certain level* of political control from Babylon. This finds expression in the fact that sometimes two rulers appear in the oath "sworn by (the name of the king)" normally used in legal texts, or in the fact that the oath and the year name refer to different kings. Such juxtapositions of rulers'

---

25. "Promulgation documents" establishing the year name were in Sumerian and Akkadian; the Sumerian version was normally used to date documents: Horsnell 1999: I 149.

26. After Horsnell 1999: II 70 (Sb 10).

27. Horsnell 1999: I 219–229.

28. Horsnell 1999: I 3–119.

29. Dalley 2009: 10–13; Boivin 2018: 248–250.

names are usually thought to reflect vassalage or co-regency.[30] However, unexpected variations in the recording of the names of the "local" rulers at Early Old Babylonian Sippar, after it came under Babylon's control, suggest that administrative and scribal practices must also be taken into account.[31] This is a stark reminder that there are multiple factors to consider when drawing a mental map of the political ascendancy of Babylon, a polity which emerged in a context of strong local powers.

Besides date lists, the main chronographic sources of relevance are of much later date (from the first millennium BC) and must therefore be used with some caution.[32] These include two dynastic king lists, commonly called King List A and King List B;[33] another dynastic king list with a prologue, sometimes called the Dynastic Chronicle;[34] and the so-called Synchronistic King List,[35] in which contemporary Assyrian and Babylonian rulers are presented side by side. All of them include both the kings of Babylon and of the Sealand. While the internal chronology of the First Dynasty of Babylon is fairly well established, we know only the general sequence of kings of the First Dynasty of the Sealand, and very little of the lengths of their reigns.[36] A chronicle, also from a first millennium scriptorium, is equally relevant for the history of both kingdoms. Here it will be called the *Chronicle of Early Kings B*. The main subject matter of the text appears to be political power in southern Babylonia in the first half of the second millennium BC.[37]

---

30. Goddeeris 2002: 27; 2005: 139.

31. Goddeeris 2005: 143.

32. E.g., reign lengths recorded in King Lists A and B are frequently incorrect; see Grayson 1980–1983: 100; Boivin 2018: 73–78.

33. Grayson 1980–1983: 90–96, §3.3 (King List A), 100, §3.7 (King List B).

34. Glassner 2004: 126–135, no. 3 = Grayson 1975: 139–144, no. 18.

35. Grayson 1980–1983: 116–121, §3.12.

36. Boivin 2018: 34–37, 73–78.

37. Glassner 2004: 270–273, no. 40 = Grayson 1975: 155–156, no. 20B (note that Grayson considered it the second part of another *Chronicle of Early Kings*); Boivin 2018: 46–49.

Without question, archival texts—epistolary, administrative, and legal—stemming from private or institutional contexts constitute the largest corpus of Old Babylonian documents. A recent count puts the number of published archival tablets at nearly 33,500,[38] and the corpus keeps growing. This, however, also includes archival texts from other polities contemporary with the kingdom of Babylon. Based on a previous inventory, about 60 percent of these clay tablets have a secure provenance and came from scientific excavations at roughly forty sites, mainly in Iraq and Syria. In fact, most of them come from outside the realm of the Babylonian kings, since the palace of Mari, on the Middle Euphrates, accounts for about 45 percent of the provenanced texts, dating to the time preceding the city's conquest by Babylon.[39] This does not mean that they are of little relevance for Babylonian history. On the contrary, the diplomatic letters from Mari are one of our main sources of information for that period, partly because no palace archive from the capital Babylon is extant.[40] As for the Sealand, the count of known archival texts, from at least four locations, is below 600 tablets.[41] Nearly all of these are excluded from the inventories of Old Babylonian texts cited earlier because they are of slightly later date.

Not all archival documents can be dated to a specific reign. For the kings of Babylon, the texts for which a date can be determined show that the Middle and Late Old Babylonian periods are best documented. For the Sealand kings, we have archival texts only for a few kings, nearly all

---

38. Based on the Archibab database; see Charpin 2018: 178.

39. Based on Jacquet 2013: 64–67.

40. The Old Babylonian levels are below the water table. Only two residential areas in the Eastern half of the city could be excavated, following a dam failure in the early years of the twentieth century. Sternitzke 2016 offers a useful summary of the textual finds in their archaeological context. Two bronze mace heads bearing the inscription "Palace of Hammurabi" were found at Tell Muhammad near Baghdad (Curtis 2004; Frayne 1990: no. 4.3.6.18). There is no evidence that he built a palace there; they may have been brought there from Babylon.

41. Boivin 2018: 10–11 (with references; MS 5009 is now published as George 2018: no. 221), also 61–61, 69; add Campbell et al. 2017: 28.

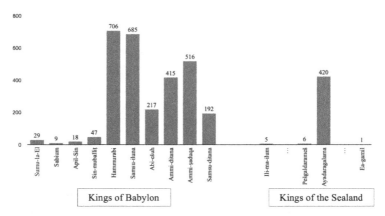

FIGURE 18.2. Estimate of number of (published) archival texts with a secure date, by reign; based on information retrieved from the Archibab database (as of July 20, 2020) and Boivin 2018: 248–250. Prepared by the author.

of which come from a palatial archive and date to a short period of little over a decade (figure 18.2).[42]

As for literary compositions and scholarly texts, including medical and divinatory literature, more than 7,300 Old Babylonian tablets are known. This includes texts that were written in the kingdoms of Isin and Larsa, during the Early Old Babylonian period.[43]

18.3. Two traditions concerning the beginnings of the dynasty

The First Dynasty of Babylon emerged in the very fragmented political landscape that followed the demise of the Third Dynasty of Ur in

42. For the kings of Babylon, this is based on the texts entered in the Archibab online database (as consulted on July 20, 2020), for the texts from the Sealand, on Boivin 2018: 248–250. The numbers should be used only to visualize the general temporal distribution of archival texts.

43. Tinney 2011: 578.

2004 BC (see chapter 13 in this volume), and which saw the rise of several Amorite royal houses. For the first century after these dramatic events, sources are lacking in northern Babylonia, unlike further south, where the kings of the First Dynasty of Isin maintained the institutions of their predecessors (see chapter 14 in this volume), allowing scribal activity to continue with fewer disruptions. In the north, textual sources reappeared at several sites around 1900, mainly in the form of letters and legal documents recording transfers of property.[44]

An examination of chronographic sources pertaining to this period reveals an important contradiction. Whereas Date List A and King List B present Sumu-abum as the first king and founder of the dynasty, before Sumu-la-El,[45] the Synchronistic King List assigns these roles to Sumu-la-El. Although earlier scholars accepted the primacy of Sumu-abum, this view has now been convincingly refuted.[46] The arguments for this include the facts that Sumu-abum and Sumu-la-El were in fact contemporaries; that some of their year names in Date List A look suspiciously alike (suggesting that the compiler reused Sumu-la-El's year names for his purported predecessor);[47] and that, in official inscriptions, some kings of the dynasty referred to Sumu-la-El as their ancestor.

Based on epistolary evidence from Tell ed-Der, Sumu-abum was apparently the leader, or one of the leaders, of a confederation called the "Amorite assembly,"[48] to which Sumu-la-El also belonged.[49] Indeed, a

---

44. Goddeeris 2002: 14–23.

45. Probably also King List A and the *Dynastic Chronicle*; this section is broken off in both documents, but the total of eleven kings suggests that Sumu-abum was included. For the *Dynastic Chronicle*, this is based on Glassner's (2004: 130, no. 3) reconstruction of line iv 12′ and his opinion that there was enough space for an additional line (iv 2′) between lines iv 1 and 2 of Grayson's edition (1975: 141 no. 18).

46. Charpin 2004: 82–85; Goddeeris 2005: 139–140; de Boer 2018: 55.

47. Compiled in Goddeeris 2005: 146; see, however, de Boer 2018: 63–64.

48. On this assembly, see de Boer 2014b.

49. From the Ikun-pîša archive, whose tablets are housed in the Iraq Museum. Only a few letters have been published or discussed; see, e.g., Wu 1994: 28 (on IM 49341); de Boer 2018: 60 (who is preparing an edition of the archive).

number of these letters suggest that Sumu-abum held a high position in the Amorite hierarchy, receiving larger audience gifts than other Amorite rulers, including Sumu-la-El.[50] He is also called a leader "of armies/troops,"[51] which could be another way of referring to the Amorite assembly. Between ca. 1890 and 1863/1862 (?) BC,[52] his influence extended over a fairly large area, as indicated by the fact that his name is associated with a number of places and Amorite local rulers in northern Babylonia, the lower Diyala, Nippur, and Kisurra further south.[53]

Hence, claiming Sumu-abum as the founder of the dynasty was probably a claim of tribal kinship and ancestry because of his prestigious role in the Amorite assembly. At the same time, it was a political statement, perhaps a territorial claim of sorts, since Sumu-abum's authority had been recognized in a large area that was later to fall under the sway of Babylon.[54] Date List A was compiled in the reign of Ammi-ṣaduqa,[55] which suggests that the process of reinterpreting the dynasty's origin may have begun at a time when the kingdom was disintegrating; this is also consistent with Sumu-abum's inclusion in Ammi-ṣaduqa's idealized ancestry in a tablet recording a funerary ritual (*kispum*).[56] This rewriting of the past was apparently successful since it was adopted in several later historiographic texts. However, Sumu-abum's absence from the Synchronistic King List shows that two traditions on the dynasty's beginnings were transmitted in the sources.

---

50. In particular, IM 49222 (edited in Wu 1994: 30) and IM 50425; see also de Boer 2018: 60; Charpin 2004: 83.

51. YBC 9955, edited in de Boer 2018: 57–59.

52. de Boer 2014a: 248–256; 2018: 66.

53. Charpin 2004: 82–83; Goddeeris 2011–2013a; de Boer 2018: 54–66; Farber and Wilent 2018.

54. This may have been an oblique way of resurrecting former glories, when the kingdom was shrinking, which began in Samsu-iluna's reign. But we do not know when Sumu-abum was included in date lists; it was perhaps at an even earlier date.

55. Horsnell 1999: I 176.

56. As discussed earlier in this section; Finkelstein 1966: 96 (BM 80328: 20).

18.4. Babylon's first bid for regional control

It thus appears that the First Dynasty of Babylon was founded by the Amorite leader Sumu-la-El in what was then a small city-state, one node in an unstable, pan-tribal confederation of Amorite leaders. The Amorite assembly, led for a few decades by Sumu-abum and acting perhaps mainly in military matters,[57] probably derived its authority from kinship ties rather than territorial domination, although we do not yet understand this institution very well. Concurrently, Sumu-la-El assumed the trappings of Mesopotamian kingship, including the sponsoring of ancient urban cults, in the two-tier leadership structure (Amorite assembly and local king) at Babylon.[58]

We do now know how Sumu-la-El (1880–1845 BC) came to rule over Babylon, and whether Sumu-abum had a hand in it. As his first year name does not celebrate his accession to the throne,[59] Sumu-la-El's transition to kingship and a more organized administration may have been a gradual process.[60] The first twenty years of his reign were mainly dedicated to territorial expansion in northern Babylonia, often through the annexation of cities whose rulers sometimes remained in place.[61] The latter part of his reign saw reforms and a shift toward palace-centered administration.[62] Sumu-la-El's year names suggest that, early in his reign (1877 BC), he fortified the capital Babylon; cities closer to his border,

---

57. War and peace were discussed in the assembly, according to the text IM 49341 (edited in Wu 1994: 28); see Charpin 2004: 87–88 n. 311.

58. Largely in agreement with Charpin 2004: 83–85 and de Boer 2018. In contrast, Wu and Dalley 1990 suggested that separate authorities ruled over the sedentary and non-sedentary populations.

59. For Sumu-la-El's year names, as quoted in this section, see Horsnell 1999: II 49–63; de Boer 2018: 75–80.

60. Yaminite clans had their own internal structures to elect a king among certain noble families; see Durand 2004: 158. Sumu-la-El's recognition as king of Babylon may have resulted from a gradual (?) transposition of a tribal to a more geographical concept of kingship.

61. Goddeeris 2011–2013b: 305.

62. Goddeeris 2002: 347–349.

e.g., Cutha (1855 BC) and Sippar (1853 BC) in the northeast, were forti-fied in the latter years of his rule.[63]

After coming to power Sumu-la-El first turned his military atten-tion to the south. His first confrontation, in 1879 BC, was with Halun-pi-umu,[64] king of Marad, who also controlled Kazallu,[65] and may have previously been an ally. This campaign, however, did not result in a last-ing conquest. His victory over Kiš, east of Babylon, ten years later was probably deemed of great significance to the young monarchy if we can derive any significance from the commemoration of this event over a lon-ger period of time. Indeed, it is attested in no fewer than five year names based on a formula of the type "the xth year after. . . ."[66] According to year name 19, the walls of Kiš were dismantled (in 1863 BC); the same fate awaited the walls of Kazallu the following year,[67] perhaps in a joint effort of Sumu-la-El and Sumu-abum, since both of them celebrated this deed in a year name.[68]

As for the political control of Sippar, the sources do not allude to a violent conquest. Sipparean scribes rarely used Sumu-la-El's year names to date texts,[69] scribal usage apparently giving precedence to the year names of the local ruler, but Sumu-la-El's name appeared often in oaths, as did Sumu-abum's.[70] Sumu-la-El also performed building work at

---

63. Year names 5 and 6, 27 and 29.

64. As per Sumu-la-El's year names 3 and 4.

65. Charpin 2004: 87–88; de Boer 2013; 2018: 67; on the location of Kazallu on a branch of the Euphrates between Kiš and Marad, see Cole and Gasche 1998: 27–29 (in particular n. 134 and n. 150).

66. Year names 13 to 17.

67. According to year names 20 and 21. The conquest of Kazallu is also commemo-rated in more than one year name, although not consecutive ones (year names 20, 21, and 25); in addition, year name 18 mentions an intervention to oust a ruler from Kazallu.

68. Sumu-abum's year name 13 (Horsnell 1999: II 47); Charpin 2004: 86. For an alternative chronology of events, see de Boer 2018: 63–64.

69. For a compilation of attestations, see de Boer 2018: 75–80.

70. Charpin 2004: 93; Goddeeris 2002: 41.

Sippar (year name 29), where a royal edict that he promulgated in the latter years of his reign was applied.[71] It seems thus that Sippar was an ally gradually absorbed into Babylon's expanding sphere of influence.

Sumu-la-El's daughters were instrumental in both internal and external diplomacy. At Sippar, Sumu-la-El dedicated his daughter Ayalatum as a *nadītum*-nun of the sun god Šamaš. This was a potent, pious gesture and acknowledgment of the ideological importance of the city in the young kingdom.[72] He gave his daughter Šallurtum in marriage to Sin-kašid, the king of Uruk, in southern Babylonia, a city which lay outside his sphere of political control.[73] The then newly founded kingdom of Uruk had succeeded in escaping from Larsa's overlordship.[74] For Sumu-la-El, having a southern Babylonian ally was certainly a desirable safeguard against the hegemonic ambitions of Larsa at that time. Indeed, year names of Sin-iddinam of Larsa commemorate a victory against "the army of Babylon" in 1847, followed by fortification work at Larsa's northeastern stronghold Maškan-šapir.[75] Clearly, Babylon and Larsa, both territorial states with expanding ambitions, had grown too close for comfort in that area.

By the end of his reign, Sumu-la-El had unified an area in northern Babylonia that ran across the Euphrates basin, from Sippar in the north to Marad in the south.[76] It cannot be considered a stable kingdom, however. Control of Kazallu, for instance, was disputed with Larsa, and the

---

71. Debt cancellation (*mīšarum*), discussed in section 18.8, and see Goddeeris 2011–2013b: 305; 2002: 331–334. The edict is commemorated in a year name used concurrently with another, but which one is not clear; see Horsnell 1999: II 62; Goddeeris 2002: 318.

72. See section 18.7; also de Boer 2014a: 262.

73. This marriage is attested by seal impressions of her seal that were found in the palace of Sin-kašid: Frayne 1990: no. 4.4.1.16.

74. Perhaps the deed of one Naram-Sin; see von Dassow 2009: 73–74.

75. Year names 4 and 7: http://cdli.ox.ac.uk/wiki/doku.php?id=year_names_sin-iddinam (last accessed August 10, 2020).

76. The main cities under his control, besides Babylon, Sippar, and Marad, were Cutha, Kiš, Lagaba, Borsippa, Kazallu, Dilbat, and Damrum; see Charpin 2004: 95.

city may have regained its independence for a time.[77] The political control exercised by Babylon was probably disjointed and unstable, and it must have varied widely between cities taken in battle or won over by diplomacy, let alone in rural areas.[78] Nevertheless, Sumu-la-El laid the administrative foundations of a territorial state. A few legal and administrative texts, probably concentrated in the later years of his reign, suggest an embryonic system of land taxation, centralized management of palace resources, and marketing of surpluses.[79]

The trend was clearly toward the amalgamation of a larger territory, and greater control over it, by subjugating or weakening more localized powers. But the rulers of Babylon were not alone in harboring such ambitions. Babylon's modest trend of expansion in the half century leading up to Hammurabi's accession in 1792 took place against the backdrop of neighboring states pursuing a more aggressive and successful course of conquest and consolidation: Upper Mesopotamia in the north, Ešnunna in the east, and Larsa in the south.

18.5. Consolidation: modest growth amid more successful neighbors

The period of transition from Sumu-la-El to his son Sabium (1844–1831) on the throne of Babylon is reflected in an oath formula naming them both—the father first—in a text from Sippar.[80] This suggests that Sabium was probably involved in state affairs at the end of his father's reign. The year name that marked Sabium's accession to the throne reads: "The year when Sabium entered the house of his father,"[81] an unusual formula

77. Charpin 2004: 107, 113–114.

78. Richardson 2012: 18–24, 45. Earlier, I called this a mental map of political ascendancy, while Richardson 2012: 22 speaks of "spectrum of legitimacy."

79. See Goddeeris 2002: 348–349 for a discussion of the relevant, admittedly few sources.

80. Ranke 1906: no. 9: 20; see also Goddeeris 2002: 323.

81. For Sabium's year names, see Horsnell 1999: II 65–74.

emulated by the next two generations of rulers before being abandoned. Sabium's son Apil-Sin used it alongside "the year when Apil-Sin washed himself" and "the year when Apil-Sin shaved,"[82] paralleling three of the steps of a priestly inauguration ritual (washing, shaving, entering the temple),[83] and thus emphasizing the sacred character attached to his royal dignity.

Sabium's southern and eastern neighbors were clearly wary of him early in his reign, since Sin-iddinam of Larsa, Sin-kašid of Uruk (Sabium's brother-in-law), and Ibal-pi-El (I?) of Ešnunna concluded a treaty against him in 1843 BC.[84] As it turned out, Larsa had the most cause for worry. Indeed, one of Sabium's year names commemorates a victory over Larsa (perhaps in 1839 BC),[85] and another victory (in 1835 BC) is attested over Nippur,[86] which had been under Larsa's control and pious patronage.[87] Seizing Nippur, an ancient and important cult center of the god Enlil, could be interpreted as a sign that Babylon was seeking to take on the role enjoyed at one time by Sumu-abum, who was recognized as king there. At any rate, it certainly marks Babylon's first bid to encroach into "the land of Sumer." But Sabium may not have controlled the city long, as its conquest is not commemorated in a year name.

In a curious, short Babylonian narrative of the chronicle type from the first millennium, Sabium is remembered as a king whose reign was marked by a huge loss of life due to seven years of plague and famine

---

82. For Apil-Sin's year names, see Horsnell 1999: II 75–90. Interestingly, the three unusual "enthronization year names" are attested only in Akkadian, perhaps because they did not stem from the local, Mesopotamian year name tradition that used primarily the Sumerian language.

83. The shaving is more explicit in a first millennium BC ritual: see Löhnert 2008: 185–186 (incantations I–VII and XII). But direct parallels can be established with a ritual from the second millennium BC: see Farber and Farber 2003: 101–107 (incantations 1, 4, and 6).

84. Guichard 2014; see also chapter 16 in this volume.

85. Year name "5?": Charpin 2004: 107 (with n. 424).

86. A text found there was dated to his year name 9; see Charpin 2004: 114.

87. Charpin 2004: 107.

FIGURE 18.3. The "Queen of the Night." Plaque of fired clay likely representing the goddess Ereškigal, the mistress of the dead and the queen of the netherworld where they resided (49.5 × 37 cm), ca. nineteenth/eighteenth century BC,
unprovenanced. British Museum, BM 2003,0718.1. © The Trustees of the British
Museum.

(figure 18.3), perhaps followed by an irregular succession.[88] In tone, this is somewhat reminiscent of the story of Sabium's near-contemporary, Erra-imitti of Isin, dying from eating hot soup, which entered two chronicles, including the *Chronicle of Early Kings B*. It seems thus that southern Mesopotamian rulers of that unstable period became the stuff of tales that eventually entered historiography.[89]

Sabium's son Apil-Sin (1830–1813 BC) followed in the footsteps of his father in trying to extend the border of the Babylonian kingdom, this time in the east, to the Tigris. He appears to have laid great emphasis on protecting both that border and his core cities. Indeed, several of Apil-Sin's year names commemorate the building of fortresses and city walls along the Tigris and near Babylon itself.

The next king, Sin-muballiṭ (1812–1793 BC), Hammurabi's father, shifted the target of Babylon's military efforts mainly toward the south. In a series of campaigns around the middle of his reign, he (took and) forti-fied Murum (1802 BC) and Marad (1801 BC), and defeated Larsa (1800 BC). His victory over Larsa seems to have granted him control of an area near Nippur since he fortified Ereš (1799 BC). He may have raided Isin (1797 BC) without deposing its king.[90] A letter informs us that the new king of Larsa, Rim-Sin (I), penetrated into Babylonian territory as far as Kiš with boats, apparently without success.[91]

Sin-muballiṭ apparently respected the alliance formed by his pre-decessors with Uruk, since he received a letter from its king, ANam, in which ANam apologized for the difficulties encountered by troops

---

88. Leichty and Walker 2004: 205–211 (edition of BM 29440); Waerzeggers 2015 (copy and comments).

89. The chroniclers may have had access to date lists or king lists because the sequence of rulers is correct in both stories; in the Sabium passage, it covers three generations.

90. For Sin-muballiṭ's year names, see Horsnell 1999: 91–104; these events are com-memorated in year names 11 (Murum), 12 (Marad), 14 (Larsa), 15 (Ereš), and 17 (Isin).

91. Charpin 2004: 121–122.

sent to him by his Babylonian ally as reinforcements against Larsa.[92] Although its style suggests the letter may be a fictitious, literary composition, it probably reflects the general political situation.[93] In it, the alliance between Babylon and Uruk is expressed as the two "being one house,"[94] and ANam evokes its past history.[95] However, Uruk fell to Larsa in 1802 BC,[96] leaving Babylon without a southern ally.

Sabium, Apil-Sin, and Sin-muballiṭ consolidated and expanded the small kingdom amalgamated by Sumu-la-El, and fortified several of its towns, both in its core area and on its eastern and southern borders. The corpus of their year names, together with those of Sumu-la-El, is the only official communication that we have from this formative period of the kingdom. These early year names contain the same elements found in the year names of later kings of Babylon and other rulers of that period. They constitute a terse, telegraphic narrative of kingship, retaining only what was deemed worthy of commemoration. Judging by the year names, royal authority expressed itself mainly in campaigning against foes and rebels; dismantling or building defensive infrastructure; building and repairing temples; dedicating votive objects; improving access to water by constructing various earthworks; and alleviating economic stress by canceling certain types of debt.[97] Babylon and Sippar received much of

---

92. Falkenstein 1963: 56–71 (text W 20473).

93. Beaulieu 2018: 72.

94. Letter of ANam to Sin-muballiṭ, lines ii 1–2 and iii 25. The family metaphor (allied kings of equal rank are "brothers," and "father and son" when of unequal rank) was common among Amorite rulers. It seems likely that this is what is expressed by the term house, i.e., family, here. In this case, it had also been cemented by a diplomatic marriage three generations earlier. See also Michalowski 2011: 86 (with literature on the interpretation of that passage).

95. Letter of ANam to Sin-muballiṭ, lines iii 25–37.

96. This is known from year name 14 of Rim-Sin I of Larsa and from a number of royal inscriptions; see Charpin 2004: 112 and chapter 14 in this volume.

97. However, the latter type of event, commemorating a debt cancellation edict, appears only in documents in which it was relevant, alongside another year name formula; Goddeeris 2002: 330–334; Horsnell 1999: I 8–9. This type of

the attention of the early rulers of Babylon.[98] Particularly noteworthy is the first mention of the Esagil temple of Marduk in Babylon (built by Sabium in 1834 BC),[99] which remained an important center of cult and learning until the end of Babylonian and cuneiform culture. But other temples were also built in Babylon, as well as its wall and city gates, shaping the city to reflect its status as a royal capital.

Because the early years of Hammurabi's reign (1792–1750 BC) are poorly documented, we do not know how the new king began navigating the complex and rapidly evolving political landscape which he inherited from his father.[100] By the year of his accession, in 1792 BC, Babylon was ensconced between three powerful territorial states: Samsi-Addu's Upper Mesopotamia to the north, which annexed Mari, on the middle Euphrates, probably in that same year; Ešnunna to the northeast, which had extended its influence well outside the Diyala river basin into the Suhum region on the Euphrates, upstream from Babylon; and Rim-Sin's Larsa to the south, at the height of its power following Isin's conquest in 1794 BC.[101] Samsi-Addu, who controlled the Upper Tigris around Assur, the Khabur triangle, and Mari, installed his two sons as kings, Išme-Dagan at Ekallatum and Yasmah-Addu at Mari, while he himself reigned as "great king" at Šubat-Enlil.[102] From the early days of Samsi-Addu's reign in the last third of the nineteenth century, Upper Mesopotamia and Ešnunna waged a protracted war against one another, fueled by their respective expansionist policies. With Babylon, Samsi-Addu maintained

---

event became part of the "official" year name terminology during the reign of Hammurabi in the early eighteenth century BC.

98. Babylon (or its temples) is the beneficiary of deeds commemorated at least in the year names: Sumu-la-El 5, 22, 23, 24; Sabium 10; Apil-Sin 2, 8, 10, 13, 15, 16, 17; as for Sippar: Sumu-la-El 1(?), 29; Sabium 8, 11; Apil-Sin 3; Sin-muballiṭ 3, 8.

99. Year name 10.

100. Hammurabi has been the object of the recent, dedicated studies of Van de Mieroop 2005 and Charpin 2012; and, for a concise overview, see Michalowski and Streck 2018.

101. See chapters 14, 15, and 16 in this volume.

102. Charpin 2004: 153, 157–158.

generally good relations, and both he and later his son Išme-Dagan sought refuge there in times of crisis.[103]

However, no international concerns appear in Hammurabi's early year names,[104] which all focus on internal affairs. He seems to have broken with the dynastic tradition of commemorating his accession with the formula that he "entered his father's house," opting instead for the simple "Hammurabi is king,"[105] in the Mesopotamian tradition of other second and third millennium dynasties. This was followed by the commemoration of a debt cancellation edict (year name 2). As an "official" year name, presented as the first royal deed in the reign, it inaugurated a pattern emulated by his successors. In these early instances of official communication, Hammurabi appears as the just and benevolent ruler of an existing kingdom, whose legitimacy was not based solely on his lineage. We learn from a few royal inscriptions that can be dated to the earlier part of his reign that he used at that time, and for several years to come, the relatively simple titles "mighty king, king of Babylon."[106] The surviving text corpus issued from Hammurabi's state offices is larger than that of his predecessors. In addition to the collection of laws discussed in section 18.8, as many as nineteen royal inscriptions are extant,[107] the earliest of the dynasty. The vast majority, dating to the latter part of this reign, were written on the occasion of a building project, although some pertain to military events.[108]

In addition, the epistolary corpus of the palace archives of Mari sheds light on the political history of the first three quarters of Hammurabi's

---

103. Charpin 2004: 150–151.

104. Horsnell 1999: II 105–174.

105. A longer version is not attested; it seems thus likely that it is not an abbreviated version. Of course, we cannot be certain that a formula of the type "he entered his father's house" was never used, marginally, at the same time.

106. Frayne 1990: no. 4.3.6.1: ll. 1–3 (heavily reconstructed); no. 4.3.6.2: ll. 29–31 (Akkadian version); no. 4.3.6.3: ll. 11–12.

107. Frayne 1990: no. 4.3.6.

108. Also, long versions of several of his year names were preserved in Date list O; see Horsnell 1999: I 202–203; 275–277.

reign. In fact, his destruction of Mari's palace in 1759 (?) BC ensured the preservation of these texts. The archaeological context of clay tags found in the palace bearing a year name of Hammurabi shows that, after his conquest of Mari, Babylonian troops packed diplomatic letters from the chancellery for later transport to Babylon, although, for unknown reasons, this never took place.[109] The absence of letters between Mari and the great powers,[110] like Elam, suggests that these were taken to Babylon, and thus are lost to us. Nevertheless, the tablets left behind and retrieved by the excavators provide precious insights into the intricacies of war and peace viewed through the lens of Mari's interests. For Babylon's history, they offer a welcome, outside counterpart to the official discourse conveyed by Hammurabi's scribes, as well as an inside view into Hammurabi's court, since letters from diplomatic envoys describe vividly what happened there.

One famous example is a long report by an envoy of Zimri-Lim's sojourning in Babylon with a delegation of allies, in order to conclude a treaty against Ešnunna. No doubt eager to display his finesse, he related a pointed verbal joust with a Babylonian court official about Mari's international rank. To the latter's somewhat disparaging remarks expressed in the usual terms of family relationships ("brother-to-brother" vs. "son-to-father"), the envoy countered by ridiculing the importance of these words, stating that he would enter the palace only if he was given precedence during the audience.[111] The most-cited passage from this missive, however, is a verbatim quotation of Hammurabi's reaction to the curse formula in the treaty laid out by Mari. Although he did agree to it, he complained that "the curse of this tablet (was) very hard!"[112]

According to the year names, the first three decades of Hammurabi's reign were largely dedicated to pious building work—beginning in

---

109. Charpin 1995: 35–36; Charpin and Ziegler 2003: 13.

110. Charpin 1995: 38–39.

111. Guichard 2004: 16–23 (text 1.2: ll. 8–17).

112. Guichard 2004: 16–23 (text 1.2: ll. 73–78).

Babylon and Sippar,[113] certainly the main urban pillars of his kingship—
and hydraulic projects. The first three military successes recorded in
this fashion, none of which led to lasting occupation, were probably all
against Babylon's southern rival, Larsa. Hammurabi's troops penetrated
into Larsean territory, reaching Uruk and Isin in 1787/1786 BC. In 1784
BC, campaigning eastward, Hammurabi captured Malgium on the Tigris,
upstream of the northeastern portion of the Larsean kingdom.[114] The
conquest of Malgium was apparently not perceived as a threat by Daduša,
the king of Ešnunna, whose attention was directed further upstream
toward Mankisum, on his border with Upper Mesopotamia. In preparation for a northern campaign Daduša sought, but was denied, Babylon's
support. An undated letter from Mari, probably from this period, shows
that the rulers of Upper Mesopotamia were following events closely:

> The "man" [= ruler] of Ešnunna (. . .) has written repeatedly to
> the "man" of Babylon (asking him) to join him to take Mankisum.
> (But) the "man" of Babylon did not agree.[115]

In fact, confirmation of an alliance between Hammurabi and Samsi-
Addu around this time is provided by an oath formula in which both
kings appear. Since this was in a document written at Babylon (in 1783
BC),[116] the Babylonian king was presumably very much the "junior
partner."[117] Earlier in the same year, Hammurabi had captured

---

113. Year names 3 and 4.

114. The conquests are commemorated in the year names 7 and 10; Charpin
2012: 27–28. Malgium can now safely be identified with Tell Yassir; see Jawad
et al. 2020.

115. In a letter between Samsi-Addu's sons, first published in Dossin 1951: no. 26: 9,
14–20; for a more recent translation, Durand 1998: 132–135: no. 534.

116. First published in Ranke 1906: no. 26; see Charpin 2004: 155–156, with notes
713–714.

117. There is no indication for downright vassalage, but Samsi-Addu clearly had
some political ascendancy over his smaller neighbor at the time.

Rapiqum,[118] presumably thereby dealing a blow to Ešnunna, since it was probably under its control at the time. This must have found favor with Samsi-Addu. At any rate, peace was eventually concluded between Upper Mesopotamia and Ešnunna.[119] As a result, Samsi-Addu retraced the border in the Suhum area, leaving Hit (later Itu) and Rapiqum to Babylon, and retaining the region further upstream for himself.[120]

In subsequent years, Hammurabi largely maintained peace with both Ešnunna and Upper Mesopotamia,[121] participating in a joint effort by these three powers against Malgium (1777 BC),[122] and hosting a Dilmunite (i.e., from Bahrain) delegation traveling back to the Persian Gulf after having visited the court of Samsi-Addu at Ekallatum.[123]

18.6. Expansion and imperial aspirations

Samsi-Addu died in 1775 BC and was succeeded on the throne of Upper Mesopotamia by his son Išme-Dagan,[124] who could not, however, contain widespread revolts, leading to the rapid disintegration of his kingdom, thus depriving Babylon of a powerful ally. At Mari, the Sim'alite prince in exile, Zimri-Lim, reclaimed the throne that had been usurped by Samsi-Addu.[125] Hammurabi eventually established diplomatic relations with Zimri-Lim, even providing him with military assistance.[126]

---

118. Year name 11.

119. Charpin and Ziegler 2003: 88–91.

120. Charpin 2004: 161–163 (with references); on the fact that Samsi-Addu apparently took his share of the spoils from Rapiqum, before leaving it to Hammurabi, see Durand 1992: 103.

121. However, see Charpin and Ziegler 2003: 110–111.

122. Charpin and Ziegler 2003: 126–127.

123. Charpin and Ziegler 2003: 141–143; Ziegler 2008.

124. Charpin and Ziegler 2003: 136–138.

125. Charpin and Ziegler 2003: 44–45.

126. Charpin 2004: 193–194, 197–198.

A letter from Mari suggests that, by then, Hammurabi, perhaps taking advantage of the reduced influence of Upper Mesopotamia, had begun positioning himself strategically on the international scene. This apparently included closer ties with the mighty Elamite ruler. Indeed, Zimri-Lim's envoys spoke to Hammurabi about: "[. . .] the kings, your allies, whose words you convey and whose compliments you transmit incessantly to the emperor of Elam [. . .]."[127]

A short period of stability followed. This is reflected in another diplomatic letter from Mari, which states that "no king is powerful on his own" and that "ten or fifteen kings follow Hammurabi of Babylon," among a few other powerful kings.[128] However, this fragile equilibrium was soon disrupted by Elam in a bid for more direct involvement in the lower plains, which would prove, in the long run, a springboard for Hammurabi's political ambitions. With the support of Babylon and Mari, Elam occupied Ešnunna.[129] But Hammurabi, taking advantage of the ensuing uncertainty in the Tigris area, formerly controlled by Ešnunna, seized Mankisum and Upi (Opis).[130] Elam countered with a threat of invasion,[131] and soon followed this up with action. It backed local rebellions, and its armies marched along the Tigris and the Euphrates, menacing the kingdoms of Mari, Babylon, and what remained of Upper Mesopotamia. The conflict inflamed the entire region, up to the Khabur area, then largely under Mari's control, and resonated as far west as the kingdom of Yamhad, in Syria, where Aleppo and Qatna chose opposing camps, Aleppo ranging itself with Zimri-Lim against Elam.[132]

---

127. Charpin et al. 1988: no. 449: ll. 30–32; a more recent edition and bibliography is available on Archibab. The Elamite king is described as "father" of Hammurabi in the letter (l. 49).

128. Charpin and Ziegler 2003: 206 n. 330 (letter A. 482: ll. 24–27), with a transliteration of the passage.

129. The exact date is uncertain; see Charpin and Ziegler 2003: 212–214.

130. Charpin and Ziegler 2003: 214.

131. According to the unpublished letter A. 3618, cited in Charpin 2012: 44; 2004: 214.

132. Charpin 2004: 213–222; Charpin and Ziegler 2003: 216–223.

In Babylon, Hammurabi tried to obtain Larsa's help, without success, as Rim-Sin I remained neutral.[133] Hammurabi found the ally he needed in Zimri-Lim. A treaty was concluded in 1765, but this appears to have been perceived as an alliance of necessity in these volatile circumstances, accompanied by grave misgivings on both sides.[134]

The Elamite troops were finally pushed back by the combined efforts of several Amorite kingdoms,[135] a feat celebrated by Hammurabi in his thirtieth year name. In accordance with the boastful rhetoric of official communication, the greater role played by Zimri-Lim and his allies was not mentioned. The year name ends with the statement that Hammurabi "made firm the foundations of Sumer and Akkad," foreshadowing his next, decidedly offensive, military step:[136] the conquest of the kingdom of Larsa, corresponding by and large to ancient Sumer.

A claim to sovereignty over "Sumer and Akkad" appears in Hammurabi's official communication with his defeat of Rim-Sin I, e.g., in his inscription commemorating the digging of a canal that provided water to several cities in the newly conquered south, where the phrase appears no fewer than four times.[137] In fact, operations against the kingdom of Larsa may already have been ongoing when year name 30 was proclaimed early in the year. Hammurabi first laid siege to Rim-Sin I's

---

133. The sources on that episode are quoted in detail by Charpin 2012: 44–45.

134. Charpin 2004: 216–219; the alliance also included Aleppo.

135. Charpin 2004: 222–226.

136. He claimed that Larsa was raiding towns in Babylon's territory when he asked Zimri-Lim for help, which may or may not have been true; see Charpin 2004: 317–318.

137. Frayne 1990: no. 4.3.6.7. It is also present in his royal titulature in later years, as "king of Sumer and Akkad" (first attested in Frayne 1990: no. 4.3.6.8, and then frequently thereafter), a title which goes back to the Ur III king Ur-Namma (e.g., Frayne 1997: no. E3/2.1.1.12: l. 9). The reference to the "four quarters," i.e. "the totality," may have appeared in his titulature around the same time, first in the formula that he "makes the four quarters be at peace," (e.g., in the inscription Frayne 1990: no. 4.3.6.4: ll. 4–6, with commentary), later in "king of the four quarters" (e.g., Frayne 1990: no. 4.3.6.12: l. 4), an ancient title attested since the Sargonic period (see chapter 9 in volume 1).

northern stronghold Maškan-šapir, which apparently fell without battle. This change of allegiance cascaded down throughout the northern portion of the kingdom, as reflected in the year names used in documents. Then, at the head of an army including troops from Mari, Hammurabi marched south and besieged the heavily fortified city of Larsa, probably for six months, apparently longer than expected, before it surrendered in 1763 BC.[138]

Recent excavations at Ur have uncovered the house of a Babylonian general stationed there following Babylon's conquest of Rim-Sin I's kingdom. The archive found in it shows that a local priest granted the general a private loan, suggesting that local elites were not disinclined to do business with Babylonian officers.[139] In the same vein, there is evidence that the family of a royal administrator retained their office through two changes on the throne some years later.[140] This suggests a fair level of dispassionate pragmatism in conducting everyday local affairs throughout periods of shifting political circumstances. Hammurabi's name was also recorded in a local king list compiled at Larsa.[141] In it, he follows Rim-Sin I and is accorded a reign of thirteen years, corresponding to the actual length of his rule there.

With the conquest of the kingdom of Larsa, Babylon became a major power, harkening back to the kingdoms of Akkad and Ur (see chapters 9–10 in volume 1 and chapter 13 in this volume). The king of Ešnunna Ṣilli-Sin, who had filled the void left by the retreating Elamites, prudently made peace with Hammurabi, who sealed the agreement by giving him his daughter in marriage.[142] However, this did not stop the Babylonian king from attacking Ešnunna the following year, perhaps

---

138. Charpin 2004: 319–323.

139. Charpin 2019a: 26–28.

140. The same family served under the Babylonian king Samsu-iluna, and two rebel kings; see Seri 2013: 50.

141. Grayson 1980–1983: 89, §3.1: 15.

142. We do not know her name, but the marriage was the object of a year name of Ṣilli-Sin; see Saporetti 2013: 635–636 (III4B).

with the main aim of controlling a portion of the riverine region along the Tigris.[143] The fate of Ešnunna itself remains uncertain, leaving us without a political context in which to interpret later events commemorated in Hammurabi's year name 38, which is only partially preserved. The formula references the destruction of Ešnunna and a flood, and it is generally assumed that Hammurabi flooded the city in order to destroy it.[144]

A sign that relations between Mari and Babylon were also souring, Zimri-Lim apparently sided with Ṣilli-Sin in the 1762 conflict, sending him gifts.[145] This is surprising, given the fact that, only a few months earlier, Ṣilli-Sin had backed Išme-Dagan in the latter's campaigns in the Jebel Sinjar, where both Mari and Babylon intervened against him.[146] It seems that, in the process, Hammurabi strengthened his influence over Atamrum, the king of Andarig, to the detriment of Mari, leading a general of Zimri-Lim's to complain:

> And the Babylonians who, every day before dark, continually enter into his [= Atamrum's] presence and keep one another informed—they do not let me in for their report and their deliberation, I do not hear their decision.[147]

Moreover, Babylon's involvement in the region meant sending numerous troops to the northwest, an act that was perceived as a direct threat in Mari.[148] Clearly, Hammurabi was now flexing his muscles well outside

---

143. Year name 32.

144. Charpin 2004: 332–333. This could have found an echo in a literary composition; see Rutz and Michalowski 2016: 24–28, 31–32 (especially l. 8′); for a different reading, see Ziegler 2016.

145. Charpin and Ziegler 2003: 241.

146. Charpin 2004: 325; Charpin and Ziegler 2003: 234–235, 237–238.

147. Charpin et al. 1988: no. 438: ll. 16′–19′; a more recent edition is available on Archibab.

148. Charpin and Ziegler 2003: 234–238, 242; the pressing oracular question asked by Zimri-Lim's wife on his behalf in that period (Charpin and Ziegler

his kingdom, in an area uncomfortably close to Mari, where Zimri-Lim had sought to maintain a strong if fluctuating supremacy.[149]

Worsening relations between Babylon and Mari were but a short prelude to open war. After gaining control over Mankisum, Hammurabi marched on the Tigris, taking Malgium and Ekallatum, and on the Euphrates, taking Mari in 1761 BC.[150] Two years later, the walls of Malgium and Mari were dismantled.[151] In the latter case, this apparently referred to the palace as well, since the archaeological excavations showed that, after it was looted, the palace was destroyed.[152] This marks the end of the rich documentation provided by the Mari royal correspondence. In a royal inscription, Hammurabi's defeat of Mari was commemorated as the occasion for a pious dedication to deities associated with war.[153]

The last years of Hammurabi's reign are poorly documented. Besides the ambiguous flooding event at Ešnunna (year name 38), year names 37 and 39 show that he campaigned in the upper Tigris and Trans-Tigris regions. An archive found in the palace of Qaṭṭara (Tell al-Rimah), between the Tigris and the Khabur, confirms that Hammurabi was recognized there. The archive belonged to Iltani, a local princess and wife of one Aqba-Hammu, a diviner who may or may not have taken the title of king, but was a "servant of Hammurabi," as per the legend of his seal.[154]

2003: 242, n. 691) is revealing: "This man [= Hammurabi] [. . .], will he campaign with hostility against us?" Edition: Durand 1988: no. 185-bis: ll. 19–21; a more recent edition is available on Archibab.

149. Charpin and Ziegler 2003: 186–229.

150. Year name 33; see Charpin 2004: 327–328.

151. Year name 35.

152. Charpin 2004: 328–329. The selection of tablets by the Babylonian troops was briefly discussed earlier.

153. Frayne 1990: no. 4.3.6.11: 27–30; on the gods Meslamta'ea and Lugal-gudua as war and pestilence deities, Wiggermann 2001. It also entered a literary composition: Rutz and Michalowski 2016: 31–32: rev. 12′–22′.

154. The texts probably date to the five or six years after the conquest of Mari; see Eidem 1989.

The fulfillment of Hammurabi's hegemonic ambitions is reflected in the novel title "king of all the Amorite land,"[155] which he adopted alongside the titles borrowed from the Mesopotamian tradition; in his late years, he also called himself "eternal seed of kingship."[156] The extent of his kingdom, at the time of his death, is probably largely reflected in the enumeration of cities found in the prologue of his collection of "laws," notwithstanding the theological principles that likely underpinned the structure of the text.[157] Judging by this, Hammurabi's kingdom encompassed Sumer, Akkad, the Diyala valley, the middle Tigris region, large stretches of the Upper Tigris, the middle Euphrates, and presumably the area north of it, including the Khabur triangle.

After Sabium, Hammurabi was the second king of the dynasty who found his way into first millennium chronicles. The *Chronicle of Early Kings B* recounts his conquest of the kingdom of Larsa in a short passage focusing on the cities of Ur and Larsa and his capture of Rim-Sin I.[158] One of his building inscriptions, apparently written on an alabaster tablet, is mentioned in an inscription of the Neo-Babylonian king Nabonidus (556–539 BC), who claimed that the tablet, "an inscription of Hammurabi, a king of the past, who came before me,"[159] was found and

155. Possibly from his thirty-fifth year; see Frayne 1990: no. 4.3.6.8: l. 4; no. 4.3.6.11: l. 25; and later inscriptions. Because of the ambiguity in the orthography of Amorite/Amorite land (e.g., Charpin 2004: 83 n. 289), the title has also been interpreted as referring to the king's ancestry.

156. Charpin 2004: 234–235.

157. E.g., Charpin 2004: 333–334. The cities enumerated are: Nippur, Eridu, Babylon, Ur, Sippar, Larsa, Uruk, Isin, Kiš, Cutha, Borsippa, Dilbat, Keš, Lagaš, Girsu, Zabalam, Karkara, Adab, Maškan-šapir, Malgium, Mari, Tuttul, (Ešnunna, represented only through its city-god), Akkad, Assur, and Nineveh. See Roth 1995: 77–80, i 50–iv 63.

158. *Chronicle of Early Kings B*, lines 8–12. He appears also in a chronicle of market prices, Glassner 2004: 294–297, no. 50 = Grayson 1975: 178–179, no. 23: 7.

159. Schaudig 2001: 445–466, no. 2.14: i 74′–ii 1; also 397–409, no. 2.11: ii 20–26.

re-deposited alongside his own during building work on the temple of the sun god at Larsa.[160]

18.7. The kings and the cults

Throughout the history of the First Dynasty of Babylon, pious dedications and building work on temples reflect the kings' patronage of a multiplicity of cults in the towns and cities they controlled. Three cities and their main deities stand out as the central religious axis of the dynasty: the god Marduk in Babylon, Šamaš in Sippar, and Enlil in Nippur. A comparison of the frequency with which deities appear in year names shows indeed that the Babylonian kings dedicated most of their attention to and claimed most often the patronage of this triad.[161]

From the beginning, the ancient cult center of Sippar was sponsored by the kings of Babylon, who were perhaps eager to associate their kingship with it at a time when the cult of Marduk had not yet attained supra-regional importance. Beyond pious deeds for Šamaš and claims of his patronage in official communications, evidence suggests the increasing involvement of Babylon in the affairs of the Ebabbar, the temple of the sun god Šamaš at Sippar, where a "junior" temple administrator from Babylon was installed alongside the local chief administrator. Eventually, the temple was placed under semi-direct royal administration by Hammurabi.[162]

Another religious institution that contributed to Sippar's reputation was the cloister of *nadītum*-nuns of Šamaš, a prestigious establishment with close links to the Ebabbar. It attracted upper-class women from several cities who lived in separate houses within the cloister enclosure, spending their time in prayer, interceding for family members.[163] The

---

160. Schaudig 2001: 397–409, no. 2.11: iii 27–31. We know of one foundation deposit of Hammurabi for that temple, a limestone tablet: Frayne 1990: no. 4.3.6.14.

161. Myers 2007: 193–196; Horsnell 1999 (volume II).

162. Myers 2007: 197–198.

163. Stol 2016: 597–600.

kings of Babylon patronized the cloister, at least three of them sending a daughter there, beginning with Sumu-la-El.[164] Although they could adopt children, these nuns symbolically married Šamaš and remained celibate in civil life.[165]

Nippur, where the Ekur temple of the god Enlil was located, was the most important religious center in ancient Sumer. Hammurabi's annexation of the kingdom of Larsa brought the city under Babylon's control. Not only Enlil, but the three great gods at the head of the Sumerian pantheon—An, Enlil, and Enki—were then duly acknowledged in official communications, especially An and Enlil.[166] The later Babylonian kings expended a great deal of effort and resources to keep the cult at Nippur active, as long as they possibly could.

Meanwhile, the pious deeds recorded in year names show that the Babylonian kings also sponsored cults in their capital Babylon, including the cult of the city-god Marduk. His later promotion to the position of head of the pantheon was still a few centuries away, but his close association with Babylonian kingship was already reflected on a theological level. Indeed, in a Sumerian hymnic prayer for Hammurabi, *Hammurabi D*,[167] Marduk acts, on behalf of the king, as his interlocutor with the great gods who bestow kingship on Hammurabi.

18.8. The administration of justice

The *Laws of Hammurabi* (LH), often called a code, constitute one of the most famous cuneiform documents of all periods. The best-preserved exemplar is a stele of black basalt found at Susa (figure 18.4), in southwestern Iran, to which it had been brought from an undetermined

---

164. Stol 2016: 589, 594.

165. Stemming from a different tradition, *naditum*-nuns of Marduk were allowed to marry; see Stol 2016: 587, 600–601, 605–606.

166. Boivin 2018: 193–195. Enki (Ea in Akkadian) appears in hymnic compositions, see especially ETCSL 2.8.2.2–2.8.2.4 (last accessed August 11, 2020).

167. ETCSL 2.8.2.4 (last accessed August 11, 2020).

FIGURE 18.4. *Laws of Hammurabi*. Diorite stele (2.25 × 0.65 m; Musée du Louvre, SB 8), mid-eighteenth century BC, found at Susa. © RMN-Grand Palais / Art Resource, NY.

Babylonian city as booty in antiquity.[168] It depicts the king standing before Šamaš, the supreme god of justice, who is said in the text to have "endowed him [= Hammurabi] with [a knowledge of] righteousness."[169]

The text entered the Babylonian scribal curriculum,[170] a status regained in contemporary cuneiform studies, in which the "laws" are a typical first-year reading exercise. The general organization of the text is tripartite. The prologue and epilogue were composed in a literary speech register of Babylonian, while the main body of the text, comprising at least 282 articles called "just pronouncements," used the standard Old Babylonian dialect. These articles deal mainly with family and inheritance, theft, voluntary and involuntary bodily harm, the status of slaves, false accusations and testimony, and commercial and agricultural questions.[171] Both the form and contents of LH were influenced by the earlier law collections of Ur-Namma and of Lipit-Eštar—several articles are similar, the later version in LH being often more complex and detailed.[172]

The prologue and epilogue express an ideology of kingship in which the king, as legitimate ruler, governs a large kingdom endowed to him by the gods, with a divine mandate to be its guardian of justice and righteousness.[173] While Hammurabi appears elsewhere as a warrior, a builder, and a pious king, the emphasis here is on his magnanimity and justness, as one who ensures that "the mighty (do) not wrong the weak."[174]

---

168. Fragments show that more than one exemplar of the stele were brought there; Maul 2012: 77 n. 2.

169. Roth 1995: 135 (passage beginning on line xlviii 95).

170. This is attested by a number of excerpts in "school copies"; see e.g., Maul 2012: 81 n. 32 and 98.

171. For a list of topics with the corresponding article, e.g., Sallaberger 2010: 50–51.

172. Démare-Lafont 2013: 73; the three texts are edited in Roth 1995. Ur-Namma was the founder of the Third Dynasty of Ur (see chapter 13 in this volume), and Lipit-Eštar a king of Isin (see chapter 14 in this volume).

173. E.g., Wilcke 2007: 210 and *passim*.

174. Roth 1995: 133 (passage beginning with line xlvii 59).

While the very long body of the text—the list of articles—was originally interpreted as a normative law code, applied in court,[175] this view was soon challenged by historians who viewed the LH either as a royal commemorative inscription or as the product of a learned scribal tradition. The latter interpretation is based largely upon the format of the articles, which are presented in casuistic form, e.g.: "If a man commits a robbery and is then seized, that man shall be killed."[176] The protasis describes the crime or situation which needs resolution, and the apodosis presents the judgment. This is strongly reminiscent of the structure used in omen collections, in which the protasis describes the *exta* (entrails) or portentous event, and the apodosis its interpretation. Medical texts present the same phraseology.

The rejection of a legislative function for the LH has found less acceptance among jurists, who contend that it had a normative, albeit subsidiary character in its application, i.e., it was not applied where a local legal norm sufficed. A too rigid generic approach was also criticized, since the LH can be viewed as *both* commemorative *and* legislative. Nowadays positions are converging toward a middle ground, as most scholars consider that the LH has legislative content expressed in "examples" or "model decisions."[177] The casuistic form and the grouping of variants may reflect the combination of empiricism and theory that characterizes the Mesopotamian "science of lists."

Hammurabi's role as a legislator was probably the corollary of his political function as king, and not specifically directed at weakening local structures.[178] Indeed, most conflicts were resolved locally. The city mayor (*rabiānum*), city elders (*šībūt ālim*), and assembly (*puḫrum*) were often called upon in local judicial proceedings.[179] In some cases, it was deemed

---

175. The following history of interpretation of the LH is largely based on Démare-Lafont 2000; 2013; Wilcke 2007; Neumann 2011.

176. Roth 1995: 85, §22 (lines ix 22–27).

177. The concept of "model decisions" was also accepted by proponents of the non-legislative nature of the LH; see Kraus 1960: 286, 289–291.

178. Démare-Lafont 2000; Wilcke 2007; Sallaberger 2010: 47, 56–57.

179. Seri 2006: 85–91, 127–134, 174–176.

necessary to inform a regional administrative authority.[180] Regional land administrators (*šāpir mātim/nārim*) and land managers (*šassukkum*) also had judicial functions, as did the province governor, whether dealing with cases at the provincial level or acting on behalf of the king.[181] The judiciary thus permeated several levels of state administration. Cases could be referred to another local jurisdiction, or a higher authority, especially if a litigant was appealing a decision.[182] The highest instance, the king, appears mainly in that context.[183] A letter sent by Hammurabi to the governor of the newly conquered province of Larsa instructs him to adjudicate a specific case according to the legal practice "now" in force there,[184] showing that royal law was relevant in legal proceedings at the provincial level. There is, however, no evidence of the direct application of the LH in any recorded judicial proceedings.[185]

Other evidence points to royal involvement in specific cases, perhaps leading to "codification." A letter to the city authorities of Sippar from Hammurabi's successor, Samsu-iluna, contains his judgments in answer to questions on two specific cases concerning the *nadītum*-nuns of Šamaš. Samsu-iluna formulated the first in a casuistic manner, and answered the second by broadening the scope of applicability to include variations in the case's circumstances. As the situations involved were not included in the LH, the letter can be considered a kind of addendum to it.[186] The procedure behind this missive also suggests that the LH

---

180. As in a letter sent "for information," probably to a regional land administrator (published by Kraus 1985: no. 171).

181. This is best attested for the Larsa province; Fiette 2018: 36–48 (governor); 63–65, 80 (administrators); 212–232 (managers).

182. Seri 2006: 131 (with examples).

183. Charpin 2000a: 83–84.

184. For the letter, see van Soldt 1994: no. 10; further discussed, e.g., in Charpin 2000a: 86, no. 42; Fiette 2018: 15.

185. Some decisions go against it; see Démare-Lafont 2013: 75.

186. Janssen 1991: 4–9: 16–31, 43–55. See also Charpin 2000a: 86–88, no. 43; Démare-Lafont 2013: 76–77.

may have originated as a collection of royal judgments. Royal edicts are another possible source for articles of the LH, e.g., those dealing with the inalienability of certain types of fields.[187]

Attested throughout the dynasty, royal edicts of economic redress (*mīšarum*), mainly aimed at canceling arrears owed to the palace and non-commercial private debts, became a typical inaugural gesture in the reign of Hammurabi. Our main source of information is the almost entirely preserved text of an edict dated to the tenth year of Ammi-ṣaduqa[188] which contains a series of articles, some in casuistic form, some formulated as general principles, and some as a combination of both:

> [§6, last clause] A creditor may not sue for payment against the household of any Akkadian or Amorite to whom he had extended credit; should he sue for payment, he shall die.[189]

Such edicts were periodic relief measures, not systemic correctives, and were thus probably ineffective in the long run, as their multiplication in the Late Old Babylonian period shows.

18.9.   Aspects of society and economy

The LH differentiates between three classes of people: the slave (*war-dum*) and two free-born classes, the "commoner" (*muškēnum*) and the "nobleman" (*awīlum*).[190] A number of articles are very specific about these status differences, for the gravity of the offense and the severity of the punishment/reparation depended on them. For instance, if an *awīlum*-man blinds the eye of his social equal, his eye shall be blinded;

---

187. For a possible forerunner of §§ 36, 37, and 41, see the letter published in Kraus 1968: no. 56, which is discussed in Fiette 2018: 232–233; Veenhof 1997–2000.

188. It was reconstructed from three manuscripts; see Finkelstein 1969 and Kraus 1958.

189. Finkelstein 1969: 49–50, 55–58.

190. Charpin 2012: 161–162.

if he blinds the eye of a commoner, he shall pay ca. 500 g of silver; in the case of a slave, he shall pay half the slave's value.[191]

Slaves were either house-born, temporarily reduced to servitude because of indebtedness, or captives—usually from abroad—sold by traders. A person once enslaved could be freed, i.e., returned to his/her original status, by a royal edict. House-born slaves could be manumitted by their owners. The relatively modest attestation of slaves in Old Babylonian sources suggests that they were not present in every household.[192] The other two classes are more nebulous, largely because the terms *awīlum* and *muškēnum* do not occur often in everyday documents. Free men and women were either identified by their name, administrative title, or by a more specific social/marital/professional designation, such as a certain type of soldier or a type of consecrated woman attached to a temple. While some of these terms seem clearly associated with specific strata in society, we do not know whether they followed the same social fault lines as the tripartite system reflected in the LH. The term *muškēnum* (commoner) comes from the root "to prostrate oneself," which suggests subordination; it later acquired the meaning "pauper," but it probably had no such connotation in the Old Babylonian period. The term appears in a number of texts from Mari in opposition to "the palace," used metonymically either to refer to officials or, more generally, to people integrated into its economic system.[193] Hence, depending on how one interprets the evidence, the *awīlum* (nobleman) may have been the holder of a plot of land (subsistence field) in return for service (*ilkum*) to the palace. The "commoner" may have had to render occasional service, perhaps a type of corvée labor, remunerated by rations. He has also been described as a homesteader.[194]

The Old Babylonian economy was mainly based on agriculture, especially barley and dates, and animal husbandry, in particular small livestock. Administrative and legal texts, even though they document

---

191. Roth 1995: 121, §196, §§198–199.

192. Charpin 2012: 162–163, 166.

193. Stol 1997; Charpin 2012: 164.

194. Stol 1997; 2004: 747–751 (on the types of service).

primarily the management of palace-controlled land, paint the picture of a fairly fragmented land tenure situation, perhaps partly the result of a transition toward a tributary and entrepreneurial economy. Private ownership of arable land, defined by the possibility to alienate it, is attested only in northern Babylonia.[195] Individual landholders worked small land plots encumbered with rent owed to the palace (tenancy field; *eqel biltim*), or a service obligation, which could be military or other skilled work (subsistence field; *šukūsum*). Holders of such land could also lease it out to a tenant. Palace reserve fields were exploited by agricultural entrepreneurs (*iššakkum*). The management of palace-controlled land, including irrigation, is best documented in the province of Larsa shortly after its conquest, in the letter archives of the governor Sin-iddinam and of the land manager Šamaš-hazir, whose correspondence also reflects aspects of the management of palace herds.[196] The palace marketed its surpluses of cereals, dates, wool, and other resources through merchants, thereby acquiring silver.[197]

Professions were often passed down within the family. We know that the family of a lamentation singer, Ur-Utu, held priestly functions for at least six generations.[198] Trades were learned from the parents or in apprenticeship. A collection of model contracts contains, for instance, a contract for a two-year apprenticeship as a cook.[199]

Outside the household, women were much less visible in public and economic life than men. Much of the evidence that we have pertains to women in exceptional situations, like the nuns of the cloister of Sippar, who were probably overwhelmingly of high social rank. From their correspondence and various contracts, we learn that they

---

195. Summarized, e.g., in Renger 2002: 140–141.

196. Fiette 2018.

197. Renger 2000; Stol 2004: 919–944; on the debate between substantivists and formalists about the presence or absence of "market forces," see, e.g., Stol 2004: 904–908.

198. Tanret 2011: 271.

199. Wilcke 1987: 106: col. ii′ (text); Charpin 2012: 167–168.

loaned silver and owned property, including fields and orchards, that produced revenue. The cloister was generally a milieu in which women took on roles that were otherwise the preserve of men, such as acting as scribes or witnesses.[200] However, a number of court decisions and contracts show that other women could own property and act in legal proceedings as well.[201] Women were normally economically dependent on their fathers or husbands. If they were orphaned or widowed, a relative usually stepped into the role of the deceased.[202] A number of articles of the LH pertain to the situation of a woman who finds herself in an unclear situation because her husband is held captive. For instance, if she was destitute, she was allowed to enter another man's household.[203]

Marriages involved several steps that gradually bound the families of the spouses-to-be by an exchange of gifts.[204] The bride received a dowry (*šeriktum, nudunnûm*) from her family, who in turn received a bridal gift (*terḫatum*) from the bridegroom's family,[205] apparently the step sealing the betrothal. The dowry remained the wife's property and constituted what her family passed down to her children. Divorce was possible, although some marriage contracts included penalty clauses, making it more difficult for the woman to instigate the procedure.[206]

---

200. Stol 2016: 594–595.

201. Charpin 2000a: 89–90, no. 45; Stol 2016: 302 (including Old Babylonian examples).

202. E.g., Roth 1995: 119, §184; Steele 2007: 306–307; Stol 2016: 287.

203. Roth 1995: 106, §134.

204. Steele 2007: 301–302; Charpin 2012: 165.

205. Stol 2016: 117–118, 134–138. Note that "bridal gift" is often translated as "bride price."

206. Steele 2007: 302 and 312 n.9.

18.10. Literature and scribal learning

The Old Babylonian period appears to us as a golden age of cuneiform literature and scholarly texts in Sumerian and Akkadian, both in terms of numbers of tablets preserved and in terms of innovation that took place in that period. Over 7,300 literary, lexical, medical, and divinatory tablets, and about 750 mathematical tablets, were recovered in a number of cities across the Babylonian kingdom, including Nippur, Ur, Kiš, and Sippar, as well as in areas that were not or not continuously part of it, for instance the Diyala.[207] The corpus of Sumerian literature, by far the best represented with ca. 80 percent of the literary tablets, comprised at least around 550 different compositions. By then a dead language, Sumerian was kept alive by scribes as an important component of their training. The diglossic setting in which scribal schooling took place found expression in a few compositions, including in the satirical depiction that a student makes of his life, recounting ruefully: "The Sumerian monitor (said): 'You spoke Akkadian!' He beat me."[208]

A great number of Sumerian literary compositions, including myths, epics, proverbs, lamentations, and hymns, are known to us through copies made by Old Babylonian learner scribes. These unbaked tablets were not intended to last, and the clay of which they were made would have been recycled by moistening it in a recycling bin, had these places of learning not been abandoned. Indeed, the large demographic movement that nearly emptied ancient urban centers, beginning in the reign of Samsu-iluna in the south and later affecting the northern plain,[209] led to a radical diminution of textual sources available to us, but this also accounts for the accidental preservation of an important segment of Sumerian literature.

Our reconstruction and understanding of the corpus of Sumerian literature is biased by the overrepresentation of tablets from Nippur— over 80 percent of Sumerian literary tablets come from this site. The

---

207. Tinney 2011: 578.

208. The passage comes from a composition called *Schooldays*; see George 2005: 127–129 (with previous literature).

209. For an overview, see Gasche et al. 1998: 25.

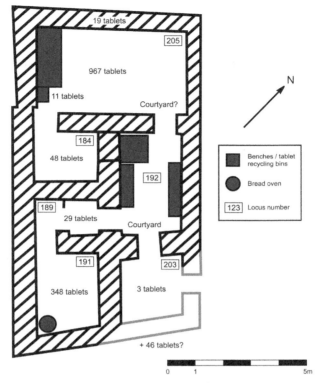

FIGURE 18.5. House "F" in Nippur. Simplified, composite plan. Drawing by Philippe Eldag and Odette Boivin, based on Robson 2001: 41 fig. 3. and Stone 1987: pls. 17–19.

largest find by far comes from "House F," which yielded about 1,400 tablets (figure 18.5).[210] Nippur's prominence, however, is probably not entirely an accident of discovery since, alongside Ur, which ranks second for the number of Old Babylonian school and literary tablets it has yielded,[211] Nippur was a leading center of scribal learning in the

---

210. Robson 2001; Tinney 2011: 578–579.

211. George 2005: 133–134; Tinney 2011: 579.

Ur III period before the turn of the millennium. This confirms continuity in learned scribal activity from the late third to the early second millennium.

Most Old Babylonian literary texts in Sumerian were based on older compositions, in some cases going back to forerunners from the Early Dynastic period.[212] The active preservation of the Sumerian literary heritage may have been a way of establishing a shared history and culture based on a (partly fictitious) common Sumerian past, especially at Nippur, where the curriculum appears to have been more conservative.[213] Some Sumerian compositions belonged to a standard curriculum, while others were less widely copied.[214] The formalizing of relatively fixed literary corpora seems to have taken place in this period.[215] A short letter published recently shows clearly that scribes, at least within certain circles, had a common understanding of what belonged to a standard group of works. In it, the sender listed the titles of seven ritual laments, adding that those are the ones he has, and asking the recipient of the letter to send to him "the ones I do not have."[216] Clearly, these correspondents shared an understanding of what constituted a complete collection of ritual laments.

The extent of control exercised by the state over scribal training is a matter of debate. It is generally acknowledged that it was lower than in the earlier Ur III scribal academies. Old Babylonian scribal training normally took place in private houses, and the compositions copied there are generally less centered on the person of the king than in the Ur III corpus.[217] There were local differences, however, and

---

212. Edzard 2004: 555–557; Tinney 2011: 592.

213. Delnero 2016: 30–31.

214. Tinney 2011: 584–585. For instance, based on the sources listed on the ETCSL website (last accessed August 11, 2020), 92 manuscripts of the composition *Gilgamesh and Huwawa* (ETCSL 1.8.1.5) are known, while only two manuscripts are extant for *The marriage of Martu* (ETCSL 1.7.1). On the Nippur scribal curriculum, see Robson 2001; Veldhuis 1997: 40–67.

215. Tinney 2011: 582–583.

216. Gadotti and Kleinerman 2011: 73.

217. George 2005: 130, 135; Charpin 2010: 25–46.

institutional control may have been greater at Nippur than at Ur. This is suggested by the greater mastery of the Sumerian language achieved by students at Nippur, and by the lower degree of diversity in the Nippurite curriculum, which comprised standard compositions also attested elsewhere.[218]

Scribal learning and literary activity in the Old Babylonian period may also have been influenced by a greater penetration of literacy into professional activity, for instance by diviners compiling, for the first time, large collections of omens. It has also been surmised that, more generally, an emerging urban elite comprising merchants and scholars, more or less independent from royal circles, fostered scribal activity.[219] Indeed, most scholars now consider that literacy was more widespread than previously assumed, when it was even surmised that members of the clergy were largely illiterate. In the Old Babylonian period we have evidence of scribal training in the family of a lamentation singer, for instance, and, based on circumstantial evidence, it has been suggested that administrators and even members of the military were literate.[220]

Be that as it may, the Old Babylonian period was not only a period of preservation and transmission of an existing scribal tradition, it was also a time of innovation. A number of Sumerian compositions, some of which are known principally from tablets that came presumably from Sippar, were probably composed in the last century of the First Dynasty of Babylon. Hence, Sumerian was also kept alive in the northern part of the kingdom, where it had never been the main spoken language.[221]

This is also the period in which Akkadian literature rose to prominence. Although they constitute only a small fraction of Old Babylonian literary tablets, Akkadian compositions survived about a thousand years,

---

218. Delnero 2016: 27–30, 41–44.

219. Veldhuis 2014: 30–32; on omen collections, also Glassner 2019: 424–425.

220. Tanret 2011: 276–278; Charpin 2010: 53–62.

221. Tinney 2011: 586; and Richardson 2018: 172–176 who suggested that it was also actively encouraged by the Babylonian kings, who tried to position themselves as the legitimate heirs of the Sumerian tradition, after the loss of the south.

while only a limited number of Sumerian texts were still copied after the
mid-second millennium. Some Akkadian works integrated Sumerian
forerunners. For instance, the Old Babylonian version of the Epic of
Gilgamesh (figure 18.6), an Akkadian composition about a legendary
king of the past, was partly based on Sumerian poems about Gilgamesh,

FIGURE 18.6. A manuscript of the Epic of Gilgamesh. Reverse side of an
unprovenanced clay tablet probably dating to the eighteenth century BC.
Yale Peabody Museum, YPM-BC-016806 = YBC 2178. Courtesy of the Yale
Babylonian Collection. Photograph by Klaus Wagensonner.

but it has a tone of its own and is by no means a translation and stitching together of existing components.[222]

In a completely different register, the burlesque dialogue *At the Cleaners* probably owes its form partly to the genre of Sumerian debate poems but has, as far as we know, no forerunner. It comes from Ur, where scribal training seems to have included more local elements and to have been anchored in a lived tradition.[223] Its humor still works today, like a modern skit on work in the service sector would. It opens with a pedantic customer giving his cleaner detailed and at times preposterous instructions, leading the cleaner—with whom the reader or listener feels compelled to identify—to retort: "Nobody but a creditor or tax collector would have the gall to talk the way you do!"[224]

18.11. From a short-lived empire to two kingdoms

For a brief period prior to Hammurabi's death, his son Samsu-iluna (1749–1712 BC) acted for him, apparently because of his father's illness. Indeed, a tablet written in the summer of 1750 BC bears a double date formula,[225] and Samsu-iluna refers directly to his regency in a letter: "The king, my father, is ill. In order to keep the land in good order, I have seated myself on my father's throne."[226]

No notable events are known during the early years of Samsu-iluna's reign.[227] In the sources available to us, the eighth year (1742/1741 BC) appears as a watershed moment in the history of the dynasty. It marked the beginning of the kingdom's disintegration, and a brief survey of

---

222. George 2003: 17–22; see also, e.g., Edzard 2004: 491–492; Tinney 2011: 588–589.

223. Delnero 2016: 39, 47 and *passim*.

224. Edzard 2004: 485, 558; Foster 2005: 151–152 (no. II.14: ll. 28–29).

225. Charpin 2004: 333.

226. Based on the letter published by Veenhof 2005: no. 130: ll. 4–7 (the passage is partly reconstructed).

227. For Samsu-iluna's year names, see Horsnell 1999: II 175–239.

events of that year suggests a combination of factors—economic, political, demographic, and perhaps environmental. In that year, hence less than a decade after the inaugural debt cancellation, a second one was proclaimed, which suggests serious economic problems, probably caused in part by recurring droughts.[228] Meanwhile, two rebel kings were recognized in southern cities, where scribes ceased to use Samsu-iluna's year names: Rim-Sin—the second ruler by that name—who probably began his conquests from Larsa, and Rim-Anum in Uruk.[229] Rim-Sin II's rule was acknowledged in several other southern and central Babylonian cities apart from Larsa, including Nippur, Bad-tibira, Lagaš, Kutalla, and Ur.[230] The relative chronology of these revolts is not certain but, by the autumn, both Rim-Sin II and Rim-Anum had established themselves as kings.[231] Elam may have supported the rebellion, since an overseer of the Elamites is attested at Uruk.[232] Around the same time, the Kassites, who had begun migrating onto the Mesopotamian plain, began causing problems. Samsu-iluna intervened militarily against them at Kikalla, probably near Kiš, an operation commemorated in his year name 9.[233]

Hence, by the beginning of his ninth year (1741 BC), Samsu-iluna found himself trying to retain or reassemble the pieces of his crumbling empire, one that owed its existence principally to the sweeping conquests made during the last third of Hammurabi's reign. It had existed a mere

---

228. Charpin 2000b: 190–197; Van Lerberghe et al. 2017.

229. Charpin 2004: 337–338; for a list of towns probably controlled by Rim-Anum, see Charpin 2014: 136.

230. Stol 1976: 56–57. Based on a reinterpretation of his year name "a," he may not have used the title "King of Ur" as generally assumed (Charpin 2019b). There is also evidence for the brief presence of another king at Ur, Iluni, perhaps the ruler of Ešnunna; see Guichard 2016: 28 n. 40, commenting on Seri 2013: 50–51 and *passim*.

231. The relative chronology of Rim-Anum's reign is uncertain; see Seri 2013: 29–36; Charpin 2004: 336–339; 2014: 129.

232. The text published by Rositani 2003: II.3 is discussed in Seri 2013: 240, 384.

233. The intervention took place either in the eighth or early in the ninth year; see Stol 1976: 44–45; Charpin 2004: 340; Seri 2013: 238.

generation, and the memory of local rule was undoubtedly still vivid in cities like Larsa and Uruk.[234]

The administrative archive of a "House of Prisoners" in Uruk yields precious insight into the shifting alliances among rebels. This institution received prisoners temporarily, allocating them as unfree workers to various other institutions, for instance as weavers.[235] Though sometimes ambiguous, the evidence from administrative records, including disbursements of food supplies to diplomatic messengers and prisoners of war, suggests episodes of cooperation between rebellious factions.[236] Isin was apparently either independent or allied with Babylon in the early stages of the rebellion.[237]

In his ninth year Samsu-iluna launched a counterattack, claiming victory over Idamaraṣ/Ešnunna, Emutbalum (i.e., the former kingdom of Larsa), Uruk, and Isin. The mention of the Idamaraṣ region/Ešnunna shows that the rebellion also affected areas east of the kingdom. Samsu-iluna's campaign did not, however, dislodge the southern rebels from their seats of power. Rim-Anum's third and last year name may commemorate an early episode in the same sequence of events. In it he claims to have defeated Emutbalum, Ešnunna, Isin, and Kazallu, whose armies had marched on Uruk.[238] Depending on the relative chronology of the reigns of Rim-Anum and Samsu-iluna, the similarity in the list of their foes *could* indicate a short-lived alliance between them.[239] At any rate, division among the rebels worked against them, and in the course of 1740/

---

234. Both Rim-Anum's and Rim-Sin II's secessionist coups could be viewed as attempts to rebuild the defunct kingdoms of Uruk (e.g., Charpin 2014: 136) and Larsa, respectively. For the latter, Rim-Sin II's throne name can probably be seen as programmatic; see Stol 1976: 55; Vedeler 2015.

235. Seri 2013: 252–258; for parallels with a similar institution in contemporary Larsa, see Charpin 2014: 131–133.

236. E.g., flour allocated to messengers and probably allied military leaders, as summarized in Seri 2013: 78–79.

237. Seri 2013: 46.

238. Michalowski and Beckman 2012: 427.

239. Most scholars consider that both year names were coeval; see Charpin 2004: 341; Seri 2013: 35–36; for a brief summary of the positions, see Boivin

1739 BC Samsu-iluna was able to reclaim control over the major southern centers. Scribes gradually reverted to using his year names beginning at Larsa, followed by Ur, then Nippur, and Kutalla. At Uruk, where Rim-Anum probably made a last stand against the Babylonian army, the palace was destroyed.[240] Samsu-iluna celebrated his victory in his eleventh year name, claiming that he dismantled the walls of Ur, Larsa, and Uruk.

The gradual change in date formulae in southern and central Babylonia suggests that the Babylonian army campaigned almost continuously throughout the year, even during the harvest seasons, both for barley (spring) and sesame (fall), the main staples of the Babylonian economy and diet. Considering that the troubles had started two years earlier, in a time of economic duress, the mobilization of resources for the war in the following years probably exacerbated the economic crisis.[241] Moreover, Samsu-iluna's counteroffensive lasted for another three years as he apparently sought to quell multiple rebellions. In his year name 12, Samsu-iluna claimed victory over the army of "Sumer and Akkad," which certainly suggests widespread revolts. At the same time, written records ceased in all southern Babylonian urban centers.[242] These only began to reappear, marginally, more than a century and a half later, during the reigns of the kings of the First Dynasty of the Sealand. The archaeological record largely confirms widespread abandonment

2018: 87 n. 7. However, prisoners from Babylon are attested at Uruk early in the last year of Rim-Anum; see Seri 2013: 223.

240. Charpin 2004: 342.

241. The archive of the House of Prisoners of Uruk shows that prisoners of war were used also for agricultural work (Seri 2013: 256–257), but their availability must have been difficult to predict.

242. At present, the latest known text with a date formula of Samsu-iluna in southern Babylonia comes from Ur and dates to the eighth month of his twelfth year (Figulla and Martin 1953: no. 868). Recent excavations at Ur have not, to my knowledge, produced later texts with his year names; but more details on that period will soon be available in Charpin 2020. Samsu-iluna also appears with a reign length of twelve years in a local Larsean king list that ends with him (Grayson 1980–1983: 89, §3.1: 16).

or near-abandonment of cities.[243] This probably resulted from a combination of causes: environmental factors, i.e., reduced access to water, perhaps resulting from a westward shift of branches of the Euphrates;[244] the destruction of significant elements of infrastructure during the counteroffensive; and the migration of segments of the population, perhaps mainly elites, toward areas still under Babylonian control (discussed later). This rapid de-urbanization also entailed a demographic shift toward small sites that have not been excavated, and where there was probably less scribal activity.

After his reconquest of Sumer and Akkad, Samsu-iluna apparently addressed his efforts to retaining central Babylonia. In his following two year names (13 and 14), he celebrated a victory over Kisurra and Sabum, and over "rebellious kings who caused Akkad to revolt" (the land of Sumer is no longer mentioned), after which he rebuilt the wall of Isin "which had been destroyed" (year name 15). Thus, between 1738 and 1736/1735 BC, Samsu-iluna restored Babylon's control over a diminished kingdom, and again fortified Isin, which was now located in his southern border area.

Samsu-iluna may have also fortified Nippur, which he had previously recaptured from Rim-Sin II.[245] This building work is commemorated in an inscription referring to previous work there by his grandfather, Sin-muballiṭ, and concluding with the unusual claim that he made his ancestor's name "eminent in the lands."[246] An appeal to the memory of an illustrious ancestor is also found in an inscription concerning the rebuilding of fortresses erected by Sumu-la-El.[247] This fortification program encompassed Maškan-šapir in 1734 BC (year name 17),[248] and extended north, to Sippar, where he also rebuilt the Ebabbar temple in

---

243. Gasche 1989: 127–132.

244. Cole and Gasche 1998: 27; for fuller secondary literature, see Boivin 2018: 92.

245. On the chronology of events in Nippur, see Boivin 2018: 102 (with references).

246. Frayne 1990: no. 4.3.7.2: 47–50.

247. Frayne 1990: no. 4.3.7.5: 47–54.

248. Samsu-iluna calls the area Emutbalum.

1733 BC (year names 16 and 18). A commemorative inscription about the entire project shows that, after his loss of southern Babylonia, Samsu-iluna appealed not only to his dynastic past to reassert his legitimacy, but also to divine favor, boasting that the god Šamaš granted him "everlasting happiness (and) kingship which has no rival."[249]

However, a third debt cancellation promulgated in the midst of his fortification program, perhaps to deal with the economic aftermath of the war, shows that all was not well in the remaining territory controlled by Babylon.[250] Rebellion had also re-emerged in the Diyala, since Samsu-iluna defeated, yet again, Ešnunna in 1731 BC (year name 20). A much-cited inscription commemorating building work at Kiš, and thus probably written in his twenty-third or twenty-fourth year,[251] celebrates Samsu-iluna's quelling of rebellions:

> The year was not half over that he killed Rim-Sin (II), the agitator of Emutbal who had been elevated to the kingship of Larsa, and in the land of Kiš he heaped up a burial mound over him. He killed twenty-six rebel kings, his foes; he annihilated all of them. He captured Iluni, king of Ešnunna who had disregarded his commands, he led him off in a neck-stock and had his throat cut.[252]

While the defeat of Rim-Sin certainly refers to events dating back to over a decade, the case of Iluni of Ešnunna is less clear because the chronology of his reign in relation to that of Samsu-iluna remains uncertain. He may have been the king defeated in 1731 BC (year name 20), or else ten

---

249. Frayne 1990: no. 4.3.7.3: ll. 110–114 (the line numbering follows the Akkadian version).

250. It is attested in a document from Sippar; see Charpin 2004: 347.

251. The building of the wall of Kiš is commemorated in his twenty-fourth year name.

252. Frayne 1990: no. 4.3.7.7: ll. 92–110. The narrative may have been modeled on the trope of the "great rebellion" found in Old Akkadian inscriptions that were still copied in the Old Babylonian period; see most recently Beaulieu 2018: 102–103; Glassner 2019: 490.

years earlier (year name 10), alongside the southern rebels.[253] Recently published tablets from Iluni's royal correspondence show that he had entertained diplomatic relations with Babylon and areas further east, in the Zagros, where he conducted his own diplomatic and military affairs.[254] His level of independence from Babylon at the time is thus unclear.[255] Iluni acted as an intermediary between his eastern neighbors and Babylon in the matter of the Suteans—who appear as marauders in the sources—who kidnapped people in the Diyala and the Zagros and sold them as slaves in Babylonia. The correspondence shows that Samsu-iluna acquiesced to Iluni's (unspecified) request in this matter, a fact which may explain Samsu-iluna's decree forbidding the purchase of slaves from these regions.[256] What led to war between the kings is unclear. At any rate, following his second victory over Ešnunna (in 1731 BC), Samsu-iluna established a military presence in the Diyala valley by rebuilding destroyed fortresses and building a new one to which he gave his name. This fortress, excavated at the site of Khafajah, was identified by its building inscription.[257] A number of tablets found there attest to

253. Guichard 2016: 26–29. The inscription names him last, which makes it possible that he was slayed later. Another commemorative inscription of Samsu-iluna, recently published by Lambert and Weeden 2020, confirms this impression. It contains a military narrative in which Rim-Sin figures as the main leader of rebels; Iluni appears later in the text (col. iv) and the theater of events is then in the Diyala.

254. Guichard 2016: 29–38.

255. One letter suggests that he proposed peace to Samsu-iluna, which would imply a high level of independence, but the passage is heavily reconstructed (Guichard 2016: 47–48 no. 4: ll. 12–14). Samsu-iluna's inscription cited earlier suggests that he considered him a vassal since he was expected to heed his commands.

256. For the piecing together of the evidence, see Guichard 2016: 36–38.

257. The building of the fortress bearing his name is commemorated in his year name 24 and in the inscription found in it (Frayne 1990: no. 4.3.7.8), which also mentions the rebuilding of other fortresses.

the administration of its garrison.[258] According to Samsu-iluna's year name 32 concerning hydraulic work in the area, Babylon's active involvement in the region lasted at least until 1719 BC.

In 1728 BC, while fortification work was probably underway or in preparation in the Diyala, Samsu-iluna campaigned to the northwest in the Khabur region. For some time this area had been coming under the growing power of the kings of Yamhad, based in Aleppo, who eclipsed Babylon's position there. This is clear from documents found in the Lower Town Palace of Šehna/Šubat-Enlil (Tell Leilan), once the capital of Samsi-Addu, which reveal the presence of envoys from Yamhad and diplomatic contact at the highest level.[259] The local kings on the throne of Šehna at the time used the title "king of the land of Apum."[260] We do not know what triggered Samsu-iluna's decision to campaign in the region (the death of king Hammurabi of Yamhad has been suggested as a possibility),[261] but his twenty-third year name states that he destroyed a number of cities including Šehna. Samsu-iluna's claim is confirmed by clear signs of destruction found by excavators in the palace at Tell Leilan.[262] Thereafter the city was largely abandoned.[263]

The Khabur raid was apparently just the first chapter in military operations aimed at reasserting Babylon's supremacy and weakening local powers in the west. Another target was a new Amorite dynasty that had installed itself in the middle Euphrates in the preceding years. Their capital was possibly Terqa, between Mari and the confluence of the Khabur and the Euphrates, where most texts documenting their

---

258. Charpin 2004: 348.

259. Eidem 2011: 16–18.

260. Eidem 2011: 6.

261. Eidem 2011: 16.

262. Including sealings bearing the name of the king defeated by Samsu-iluna, Yakun-Ašar, identified in his year name 23; see Charpin 2014: 143; Eidem 2011: 6.

263. Eidem 2011: 3–4.

rule were found.[264] Terqa had been a provincial capital of the kingdom of Mari, and the kingdom of the rulers of Terqa shows signs of continuity with the earlier state.[265] The name of this kingdom in that period is unknown. Later it was called "the land of Hana," in continuity with Zimi-Lim's kingdom of "Mari and the land of Hana."[266] For this reason its kings will be called kings of Hana in what follows.[267]

We do not know what form or level of administrative and political control was exercised by Babylon in the region when the dynasty of Hana emerged. If a parallel with Šehna is admissible, it may have been very low.[268] Texts from Harradum, in Suhum, show that the rulers of Hana extended their rule downstream well beyond Mari for a time.[269] This corpus also provides a chronology of the shifting border between the areas claimed by Babylon and Hana on the Euphrates. Indeed, one text is dated to Samsu-iluna's Year 6 (1744 BC), while one bears a date formula of the second king of Hana. The bulk of the archive covers nearly a century beginning in Samsu-iluna's Year 26 (1724 BC), in which all tablets bear year names of kings of Babylon.[270] Thus, around the time of the raid in the Khabur region, Samsu-iluna was also active in Suhum,[271] either campaigning or pursuing diplomatic efforts to counter the growing influence of the kings of Hana. At the latest by 1724 BC, Samsu-iluna had regained control over Harradum. A more decisive victory over Hana occurred the

---

264. Podany 2002: 20; Mari, where some signs of occupation were found after Hammurabi's destruction, was recently suggested as another possibility; see Charpin 2011: 47–53.

265. Charpin 2011: 42–45, 48–51, 53–56.

266. Podany 2002: 20.

267. Podany 2002: 9–12; this usage has been widely accepted. See also Charpin 2011: 46–47 on the question of the meaning of Hana, as a geographical or ethno-linguistic designation.

268. Note, however, that the city of Harradum seems to have been re-settled perhaps early in the reign of Samsu-iluna; see Joannès 2006: 18.

269. The following is largely based on the summary in Charpin 2011: 43–44.

270. The 116 texts were published in Joannès 2006: 35–156.

271. See also Charpin 2011: 59.

following year, when Samsu-iluna claimed to have "crushed" two "hostile kings" (year name 28), one of whom was Yadih-abum, the third king of Hana. Babylon appears to have invested in the region in the following years since year name 33 of Samsu-iluna records that he undertook extensive building work at Saggaratum, probably located in the heart of the kingdom of Hana.[272] This did not mark the end of the dynasty of Hana, however, which endured, with varying degrees of independence, into the Kassite period (chapter 33 in volume 3), long after the demise of the kings of Babylon.[273]

While Samsu-iluna was reasserting Babylon's hegemony to the east and west, a new dynasty, the kings of the Sealand, was forming in southern Babylonia. Like the kings of Hana, the First Dynasty of the Sealand survived the fall of Babylon by several generations. Largely owing to the lack of textual evidence in that period in southern Babylonia, where life took place for the most part outside the well-excavated urban centers, the origins of this dynasty are nebulous.[274] The original power base of the kings of the Sealand is unknown, but the founder of the dynasty, Ili-ma-ilu, was able to conquer Nippur in the twenty-ninth year of Samsu-iluna (1721/1720 BC) or shortly thereafter. Indeed, a few documents show that, for at least about a year and a half, scribes at Nippur used his year names.[275] This conquest may be the event recorded in the *Chronicle of Early Kings B*, in which Ili-ma-ilu is opposed to Samsu-iluna, but the passage is damaged and what is left of it contains no city name.[276] At any rate, from this point on in the *Chronicle*, the kings of Babylon appear on the losing side.

272. Charpin 2011: 59 n. 112 (with references).

273. On the kingdom of Hana, see chapter 15 in this volume.

274. For possible earlier attestations of the Sealand and of Ili-ma-ilu, see Boivin 2018: 30–31, 89–90 (with references). Interpreting early attestations is complicated by the fact that the term "Sealand" is based on the word "sea, lake" (A.AB. BA in Sumerian, *tâmtu(m)* in Babylonian), which could also have functioned as a nonspecific designation for an area near a lake; see Boivin 2018: 29–32.

275. Boivin 2018: 91, 102. On the date of the conquest of Nippur, see Boivin 2018: 241–244.

276. *Chronicle of Early Kings B*, rev. 1'–7'. It could even be a second victory of Ili-ma-ilu over Samsu-iluna: Boivin 2018: 91.

Although there was no notable destruction in Nippur, written documentation there largely stopped with the texts dated to Ili-ma-ilu, around the same time as it stopped in other central Babylonian cities, like Isin and Lagaba. Whether the diminution of texts outside Nippur was also linked to the Sealand king's northward thrust is impossible to say.[277] Central Babylonia simply appears to have fallen victim to the same wave of near-abandonment of urban centers that affected southern cities nearly two decades earlier.[278] An archive from a fortress built by Samsu-iluna's son, Abi-ešuh, shows that Babylon soon intervened to regain and retain control over Nippur and central Babylonia in conditions that remained difficult. Nonetheless, from the moment of Ili-ma-ilu's conquest of Nippur—however transient its occupation—the history of the core land of Babylonia became a history of two kingdoms: the Sealand in the southernmost area and Babylon to the north of it.

After these events, Samsu-iluna's year names commemorate mainly pious dedications and building work, including some in the Diyala and the Khabur, as well as the construction of a new palace.[279] Building a palace seems at odds with signs that the later years of his reign were marked, yet again, by economic difficulties. A fourth debt cancellation was probably promulgated in Year 28,[280] perhaps in an attempt to alleviate the consequences of recurring agricultural shortages. Indeed, a document dated early in the reign of Abi-ešuh shows how a citizen of Sippar had fled the city because of famine toward the end of Samsu-iluna's reign.[281]

---

277. Boivin 2018: 93. In Isin, signs of destruction were found.

278. Gasche 1989: 124–127.

279. Charpin 2004: 361–364.

280. Charpin 2000b: 198–202.

281. Briefly discussed in Charpin 2004: 359 (with n. 1875). We know also of Sipparean families bringing their daughters to the cloister without endowing them with means of subsistence, perhaps because of strained economic conditions; this cannot, however, be dated more precisely within Samsu-iluna's reign; see Janssen 1991.

18.12.   *Stalemate and the fortification of central Babylonia*

Samsu-iluna's efforts to counter secessionist trends having yielded mixed results, his son Abi-ešuh (1711–1684 BC) inherited a diminished kingdom. Babylon now had to share hegemony over the lower Mesopotamian plain with the Sealand kings. By the time Abi-ešuh ascended the throne, the Babylonian kings had also been plagued by recurring economic difficulties for several decades. In addition, two demographic phenomena were probably remodeling, to a certain extent, the socioeconomic fabric of some areas of the heartland. These were the continued migration of Kassites and the fairly recent, and perhaps still ongoing, arrival of refugees from the south. At first, the increasing presence of Kassites may have been most noticeable outside urban areas, while the influx of southern and central Babylonian migrants also, and perhaps mainly, affected the cities. We can trace the presence of members of southern clergies in northern cities by the occurrence of their titles there. The names of a number of deities whose city of origin was appended to their name, e.g., "Ištar-of-Uruk," also reflect the transfer of their cults. In addition, southern personal names appear in northern Babylonia in this period. Most refugees identified in the records belonged to priestly circles, but gardeners and merchants are also attested. We do not understand this demographic movement very well, but it seems fair to assume that the transfer of important cults took place with some level of central planning from Babylon. This included the relocation of cults from Larsa to Babylon and from Uruk to Kiš.[282]

We have fewer sources for the political history of Abi-ešuh's reign than for those of his two predecessors, a trend that continues and worsens down to the end of the dynasty. Only two short inscriptions of Abi-ešuh's are known, one of which concerns building work in a town north

---

282. Pientka 1998: 179–195, with additions in Charpin 1999–2000: 323–324 and Richardson 2018 (in particular Tables 4a and 4b).

of Babylon, in which he called himself the descendant of Sumu-la-El.[283] Abi-ešuh's year names are mostly about pious deeds, mainly the dedication of statues or emblems in temples.[284] In addition to a lack of informative year names, the internal chronology of Abi-ešuh's reign is not fully established, making it difficult to reconstruct its political history.[285] His second year name records a debt cancellation edict, by then a conventional inaugural practice. Anecdotally, it finds an echo in a court record about a woman, thus freed from jail where she had been put presumably for indebtedness, who found that her husband had remarried in her absence (!).[286]

Abi-ešuh militarized his southern border, striving to maintain Babylon's presence and sustain cultic activity in central Babylonia, e.g., at Nippur. By his fourth (?) year at the latest (1708 BC), Babylon had probably regained control over the city since a document mentions Babylonian troops attached to a "fortress of Nippur."[287] This text belongs to an archive that became available recently and has added significantly to our knowledge of Late Old Babylonian history.[288] The ca. 300 tablets are unprovenanced, but, from text-internal evidence, they can be shown to come from another fortress located nearby. It bears Abi-ešuh's name, Dur-Abi-ešuh, and must thus have been built very early in his reign. This fortress, whose complete name indicates that it stood at the outflow

283. Frayne 1990: no. 4.3.8.1: ll. 1′–2′ (in the Sumerian text); the other inscription (Frayne 1990: no. 4.3.8.2) pertains to a votive offering.

284. Hornsell 1999: II 241–272.

285. This is due to the poor state of preservation of the relevant date lists; see Horsnell 1999: I 51–81.

286. Charpin 2000a: 93–95 no. 49; 2004: 344–345, with previous literature. The record is also of particular interest because it takes place among the community of Larsean refugees in northern Babylonia.

287. This is the text published by Abraham and Van Lerberghe 2017: no. 41, dated to his year name "e," either Abi-ešuh's fourth or possibly fifth year. For a summary of the issue, see van Koppen 2013: 378–379.

288. Most texts were published in Van Lerberghe and Voet 2009 and Abraham and Van Lerberghe 2017.

of a canal called "Hammurabi Is the Abundance of the People,"[289] was part of a string of fortifications and military garrisons that was still to be completed. As administrative texts about their maintenance and work assignments attest, some of these garrisons sent detachments of soldiers to Dur-Abi-ešuh.[290] Some soldiers are simply identified by place of origin, without specifying whether or not it was a fortress. Therefore, it is not always possible to determine whether they were mercenaries, allied forces, or, as in the case of soldiers from Uruk, refugees. The network to which Dur-Abi-ešuh belonged included, at a minimum, the following fortresses in the Nippur area: the fortress of Nippur itself, Dur-Abi-ešuh at the outflow of the canal, Baganna, Nukar, and Dur-Sin-muballiṭ (which had been rebuilt by Samsu-iluna).[291] Another fortress also named Dur-Abi-ešuh was later built on the Tigris, around 1692 BC. It could be reached by boat from its namesake and was thus probably located near the mouth of the canal called "Hammurabi Is the Abundance of the People."[292]

This system of fortification, or part of it, remained in operation during the reigns of Abi-ešuh's successors, probably until at least the fifteenth year of Samsu-ditana (1611 BC), the last king of the dynasty. By this time, however, we do not know whether more than one fortress was still functioning and in Babylon's hands. The latest text from Dur-Abi-ešuh

---

289. This fortress is called Dur-Abi-ešuh[(canal)] in Boivin 2018 and Béranger 2019, to differentiate it from Dur-Abi-ešuh[(Tigris)] built later in the reign of Abi-ešuh; see Boivin 2018: 97–98 and later in this section. Until recently, these fortresses were thought to be one and the same, and they are thus often conflated in older publications.

290. In particular, Abraham and Van Lerberghe 2017: nos. 1–40. Soldiers from various origins appear in other texts; see Charpin 2018: 192–193.

291. Abraham and Van Lerberghe 2017: 4, who consider that there were Babylonian fortresses as far south as Durum and Uruk on the Euphrates; on Uruk, specifically, see also Boivin 2018: 97 n. 45. For a more circumspect interpretation of the data, see Charpin 2018: 192–194 (in particular n. 72) and also Béranger 2019: 116.

292. The reference to travel by boat between the fortresses appears in Abraham and Van Lerberghe 2017: no. 27: 4–9; also, Boivin 2018: 97–99 including n. 46 (on the location).

pertains to Nippurite cults and clergy operating at the fortress.[293] Indeed, Dur-Abi-ešuh was more than a military garrison. Its walls also offered protection to displaced temple personnel from Nippur. The geographic proximity to Nippur was probably the reason behind their relocation there. Indeed, the earlier records, from the reign of Ammi-ditana, show that sacrificial animals were brought from Dur-Abi-ešuh to Nippur,[294] where at least some residual cultic activity still occurred in its primary setting. The best attestation of displaced temple personnel at Dur-Abi-ešuh concerns Enlil-mansum, a priest of Enlil who oversaw, at the fortress, cultic activities of the Ekur, Enlil's temple at Nippur.[295] Early in the reign of Ammi-ṣaduqa, it apparently became impossible to perform sacrifices at Nippur. Consequently, these took place instead at Dur-Abi-ešuh.[296]

Construction of the second Dur-Abi-ešuh fortress, on the Tigris, was completed around Abi-ešuh's twentieth year (ca. 1692 BC) and was commemorated in a year name that indicates its location as "upstream from the barrage/weir."[297] This probably refers to an earthwork built about two years earlier, since Abi-ešuh claimed, in his nineteenth (?) year name, that he dammed the Tigris,[298] an achievement which entered both the divinatory and the historiographic traditions. Indeed, the detailed oracular question about the project, which the king's diviners used to ensure that it could go forward in auspicious circumstances, was still

---

293. The latest text known to the present author is dated to the fifteenth year of Samsu-ditana and was published in Sigrist et al. 2017: 311 no. 5.

294. E.g., Abraham and Van Lerberghe 2017: no. 45, dated to the eleventh year of Ammi-ditana (1672 BC). Some of Nippur's cult activity had probably been relocated or replicated in Babylon; see Gabbay and Boivin 2018: 36–38; Pientka 1998: 190–195; Charpin 1999–2000: 324.

295. Beginning with Van Lerberghe and Voet 2009: no. 2.

296. For a tentative reconstruction of the sequence of events, see Boivin 2018: 102–103 (with sources).

297. In the year name "m," perhaps his twenty-first year. On the reading "barrage/weir," see George 2009: 138–139.

298. Year name "o."

copied by scribes centuries later.[299] This stunning undertaking also won Abi-ešuh a place in the *Chronicle of Early Kings B*. The chronicle adds an intriguing explanation for it, noting that the damming of the Tigris was part of an unsuccessful bid to capture the Sealand king Ili-ma-ilu.[300] The primary reason, however, may have been to divert water into the canal leading to the other Dur-Abi-ešuh fortress and to the Nippur area, perhaps in an attempt to salvage Nippur. But there is no doubt that the corollary to such a measure was a reduction in water downstream, probably to the detriment of Ili-ma-ilu's kingdom.[301] We have no other evidence to corroborate this, but the report from a diviner practicing at Dur-Abi-ešuh (at the outflow of the canal) shows that he inquired about the well-being of the troops stationed at the dam and about the "intentions of the enemy,"[302] who may have been the Sealand, although this remains conjectural. Indeed the few year names of Abi-ešuh with military content suggest that he also faced other threats. These included Elam, against which he had fought early in his reign,[303] and Ešnunna, which he defeated probably only a few years before the diviner inquired about "the enemy" menacing the dam.[304] Still, judging by the presence of troops from Aleppo at Dur-Abi-ešuh in that period, Abi-ešuh apparently maintained strong alliances with states to the west of his realm.[305]

---

299. It is known from first millennium copies, see Lambert 2007: 54–57, no. 3c: ll. 22–47; no. 3d: ll. 1–3.

300. *Chronicle of Early Kings B*, rev. 8–10; see Boivin 2018: 51–55 on the possible interconnections between the relevant sources.

301. Boivin 2018: 95–96.

302. George 2013: no. 4: rev. 23′–25′, dated just after the construction of the fortress on the Tigris; see Boivin 2018: 99.

303. This was commemorated respectively in year name "d," probably his third year, and in year name "f," probably his fifth year; see van Koppen 2013: 377–379.

304. Abi-ešuh claims to have taken Ešnunna's king, Ahušina, captive; year name "dd," perhaps his seventeenth year.

305. In Abraham and Van Lerberghe 2017: no. 5: 4, dated in the nineteenth (?) year of Abi-ešuh, and in Abraham and Van Lerberghe 2017: no. 40: 17–19, dated two (?) years later. Troops from Aleppo, as well as from Qatna, are also attested in a few documents of uncertain date or dating to the reign of Ammi-ditana.

Whether or not the enemy threatening the troops near the Tigris dam was the Sealand, relations between the young southern polity and Babylon may have evolved rapidly. Indeed, messengers and soldiers from what could be read as the Sealand—or else an area near a lake—were present at Dur-Abi-ešuh (at the outflow of the canal), probably both shortly before (?) and after the construction of the dam.[306] At some point, probably late in the reign of Abi-ešuh, Ili-ma-ilu must have been replaced on the Sealand throne by his successor Itti-ili-nibi, of whom nothing is known apart from his name in king lists.

Ammi-ditana (1683–1647 BC), Abi-ešuh's son, also enjoyed a long reign which began, conventionally, with a debt cancellation edict.[307] According to his twenty-first year name, he issued another one twenty years later, assuredly a sign of renewed economic problems.[308] Like his father, his year names mostly commemorate pious dedications. By his second decade on the throne, Ammi-ditana began a program of fortifications. Indeed, his only two known official inscriptions and three of his year names pertain to these undertakings. His sixteenth, thirty-second, and thirty-fifth year names record the building of fortresses, the first of which bore his name, Dur-Ammi-ditana, and may be the fortress by the same name that was the subject of a royal inscription.[309] Since these fortresses do not appear explicitly in the Dur-Abi-ešuh archive and their

---

On the reading "Aleppo," see Charpin 2018: 193, 198–199 (comment to no. 39). A receipt from Harradum (first published by Joannès 2006: no. 18) shows also how regions under Babylon's control had to contribute to funding the upkeep of the fortresses. In this text (lines 1–3), two shekels of silver were received specifically as an *ilkum*-payment associated with the fortress of Dur-Abi-ešuh on the Tigris; see Charpin 2015: 146.

306. The messengers in Abraham and Van Lerberghe 2017: no. 3: ll. 9–10, and the soldiers in Földi 2014: 33 (text Sem 1278: l. 20); see Boivin 2018: 100 for a discussion.

307. For Ammi-ditana's year names, see Hornsell 1999: II 273–324.

308. It has been suggested that the second decade of Ammi-ditana was a period of crisis, visible, e.g., in disruptions in archives and real estate transactions (Richardson 2010: 15); the matter would require systematic investigation (Charpin 2015: 169).

309. Frayne 1990: no. 4.3.9.2.

exact locations are unknown, it is unclear whether they were part of the defense system of the southern/eastern border area that had been actively developed by Abi-ešuh. At any rate, Ammi-ditana also worked on improving the defenses of the capital Babylon, since the other inscription known from his reign pertains to construction work on its wall. In it, he called himself the descendant of Sumu-la-El,[310] following in the footsteps of his recent predecessors.

A volatile political situation was certainly the reason for continued, or renewed, investments in a defensive infrastructure that had previously proven insufficient. Indeed, a letter from the Dur-Abi-ešuh archive reveals that an unidentified enemy, with horses and hundreds of men, was able to briefly enter Nippur and loot the Ekur in Ammi-ditana's eleventh year (1672 BC), causing what was probably an already reduced population to flee and seek refuge in a fortress.[311] The enemy was repelled, but apparently not in a manner convincing enough to be commemorated in a year name. Sacrifices at Nippur continued into the reign of Ammi-ṣaduqa, largely managed from Dur-Abi-ešuh. However, records of animals distributed to diviners at the fortress show that travel to and from Nippur was a risky enterprise. Indeed, extispicy rituals were performed, e.g., to inquire about the safety of a man "traveling to Nippur along with a troop of conscripts in order to perform the sacrifice before the 15th day."[312]

As in the case of the enemy threatening the dam on the Tigris during Abi-ešuh's reign, there is more than one candidate for the attackers of Nippur. Whether acting alone or as part of a coalition, the most obvious one is probably the Sealand which, under its founder Ili-ma-ilu, had briefly controlled the city in the reign of Samsu-iluna. One can also infer continued interest in the ancient cultic center since sources dated to later kings of the Sealand dynasty show that Nippur deities were very

310. Frayne 1990: no. 4.3.9.1: i 7–8.

311. Abraham and Van Lerberghe 2017: no. 205; see also Boivin 2018: 101, 103 for the sequence of events; on the fortress where Nippurites sought refuge, see Béranger 2019: 111–112.

312. Abraham and Van Lerberghe 2017: no. 59: ll. 5–8.

prominent in what appears to be their "state pantheon."[313] However, the intended purpose of the assailants—whether it went beyond a looting expedition—is unclear. To complicate matters, a letter dated nearly four years later shows that Elamite soldiers and soldiers from the Sealand (?)[314] were present at Dur-Abi-ešuh. They are listed after prisoners, but were apparently distinct from them.[315] However one interprets this—whether these soldiers were mercenaries or allied troops at the time, toward the end of his reign, Ammi-ditana campaigned into Sealand territory, leading in 1648 BC to the destruction of the city wall of Udannu, probably located somewhere between Uruk and Larsa.[316] Ammi-ditana's thirty-seventh and last year name celebrated this event and added that the wall had been built by Damiq-ilišu who, according to king lists, was the third king on the Sealand throne. As far as we know, this was Babylon's last attempt to intervene militarily in the south and, in fact, the last military campaign commemorated in a year name of that dynasty.

18.13. *The final disintegration of the kingdom of Babylon*

Ammi-ditana left to his son Ammi-ṣaduqa (1646–1626 BC) a kingdom that was presumably roughly comparable to the one he had inherited, but we do not know to what extent Babylon was trying to reverse the disintegration that continued to spread to other parts of its realm. The year names of the later kings of the dynasty are generally silent on this, and only one official inscription of Ammi-ṣaduqa puts the occasion of a votive offering in the context of an unspecific military victory.[317]

---

313. Boivin 2018: 232–235; Gabbay and Boivin 2018.

314. The term used for Sea(land?) in this document is the same as in earlier texts from the archive, without an explicit toponymic marker.

315. Béranger 2019: 104–106 (Letter 3: l. 25).

316. On the reading of the toponym and the fact that the town was later again under the control of Sealand kings, see Boivin 2018: 62 (with previous literature).

317. Frayne 1990: no. 4.3.10.1.

Babylon was still in control of Suhum, as attested by year names at
Harradum. However, troubles were looming in the area, and the city
was abandoned late in Ammi-ṣaduqa's reign.[318] Further upstream, Terqa
probably remained under Babylon's control a little longer, into Samsu-
ditana's reign.[319] We do not know exactly when Babylon lost control
over the Diyala valley, but texts from the site of Tell Muhammad,
the oldest of which are almost certainly of Late Old Babylonian
date, make no reference to the rulers of Babylon. Rather, the Kassite
names of the local rulers there suggest that political control over the
region had begun shifting.[320] However, commercial relations remained
active. Indeed, contracts recording the sale of slaves in Ammi-ṣaduqa's
reign show that the Diyala was one of the sources of slaves traded in
Babylonia.[321]

Beside the occasional digging of canals, nearly all year names of
Ammi-ṣaduqa, as well as the other royal inscription extant—in addition to the one mentioned earlier—commemorate pious dedications,[322]
sometimes of statues of himself, for instance:

The year in which Ammi-ṣaduqa, the king, brought into the
Enamtila temple (for) the god Enlil, the great ruler who had
announced his name, a statue of himself in which he held a lamb
as a gift and a statue of himself offering prayer.[323]

---

318. The latest text with a secure date in the last layer of occupation before abandonment is dated to Year 18? (= Year 17 + b), hence 1629 BC; see Joannès 2006: 19.

319. Podany 2014: 54; 2002: 202.

320. For a summary of the evidence, see Boivin 2018: 80–84. See also chapter 33 in
volume 3.

321. They came from areas southeast, east, north, and northwest of the kingdom; see
van Koppen 2004; Charpin 2015: 154.

322. For his year names, see Horsnell 1999: II 325–358; the royal inscriptions are
Frayne 1990: no. 4.3.10.1–2.

323. Year name 5.

We know of two edicts cancelling debts, one at the beginning of his reign (year name 1), and one from his tenth year (see section 18.8). Ammi-ṣaduqa's eleventh year name informs us that he built a fortress on the Euphrates in 1637 BC. As discussed earlier, texts from Dur-Abi-ešuh demonstrate that the system of central Babylonian fortresses was still in operation, and that there was residual cultic activity in Nippur until at least 1638 BC.

An undated letter sent by Ammi-ṣaduqa to officials at Sippar(-Yahrurum) makes clear that fortified settlements against raiders were also a necessity further north. The text urged the officials to take preventive measures because of Samharite groups which roamed the environs, turning the city almost into a de facto fortress:

> (They) have already crossed over into the heart of the country in order to attack the herds, flocks, and troops (. . .). The city gate should not be opened until the sun has risen (. . .). Be on your guard![324]

Roaming looters probably contributed to a worsening of the economic situation, disrupting normal agricultural activity. And indeed, there is archaeological evidence that all was not well in the twin city of Sippar(-Amnanum). Under the house of the cultic singer Ur-Utu, nine children were buried during a period of five months,[325] which suggests hardship and famine even among the elite, after which the house was destroyed by fire, probably in 1629 BC.[326] While an impressive library was found stored in three rooms, around fifty clay tablets were scattered in another room, toward the only exit in that part of the house. These texts were mainly the most recent real estate deeds, which the fleeing family attempted to

---

324. Kraus 1977: no. 47: ll. 7–16, 10′; the passage concerning the city gate was partly reconstructed by the editor on the basis of parallels. Several letters of warning are attested; see Richardson 2005: 273–274 (for a compilation of the sources).

325. Gasche 1989: 64 Table III: "Maison d'Ur-Utu (Phase IIIb)"; Tanret 2011: 272.

326. According to the latest texts found there, dated to the eighteenth year of Ammi-ṣaduqa.

salvage but dropped on their way out.[327] The cause of the fire cannot be determined, but the general circumstances certainly suggest an attack on the city as a possibility.

We do not know whether the areas controlled by the Sealand kings were also affected by marauders, including Kassite groups. Some Kassites penetrated further south (they had caused some problems for Rim-Sin II of Larsa in the eighteenth century),[328] and they are marginally attested in later Sealand texts, but not as a threat. We have, in fact, no sources from the Sealand during the reign of Ammi-ṣaduqa, and the Babylonian sources do not record any relations, whether peaceful or belligerent, between these kingdoms.[329] This may have been a period of peace, following what seems to have ended in a stalemate between them, after the Sealand's brief thrust (or thrusts?) into central Babylonia and Babylon's destructive raid on Udannu. Pragmatic considerations may have prevailed for a time. After all, the Sealand was dependent on its neighbor upstream for its water supply, and Babylon may have wanted access to the Persian Gulf trade. Besides, launching a war must have been increasingly difficult given Babylon's ailing economy.

From what we know of Ammi-ṣaduqa's reign, it seems clear that his ill-fated successor, Samsu-ditana (1625–1595 BC), the last king of the dynasty, inherited a disintegrating kingdom. The extant sources, however, are silent on any measures he may have taken to stabilize the situation. His year names are not all preserved, the last four having been left blank after "the year (when)" in the only date list extant, and others are attested only in a very abbreviated form.[330] Moreover, no royal inscriptions from his reign have survived. Perhaps symptomatic of the waning authority of the king, Samsu-ditana multiplied the invocations of divine favor for his rule in his early year names, for instance, Marduk

---

327. Gasche 1989: 28; Tanret 2011: 280.

328. According to his second year name ("b"), see Stol 1976: 54.

329. The ideas presented in this paragraph are more fully developed in Boivin 2018: 107–111, 115–117 (with references).

330. Date list N's layout appears to confirm the reign length of thirty-one years recorded in King List B; see Horsnell 1999: I 93–94, 272–275, II 359–383.

"established his reign," An and Enlil "spoke their true word" to him, and Utu and Iškur "raised (his) head on high."[331] Royal communication being typically impervious to negative developments, his year names largely concern pious dedications, as far as we can judge from the abbreviated formulae. However, they seem to mirror the shrinking of the kingdom since, when the place of a votive offering is identified, it is always a temple in Babylon or Sippar.[332] This is also reflected in the gradual disappearance of textual documentation in central and northern Babylonia between his fourteenth year (Kiš and Dilbat) and twenty-sixth (?) year (Babylon).[333] Samsu-ditana was remembered mainly in association with the fall of Babylon, but his memory was not vilified in later tradition. In fact, the way in which he entered the *Chronicle of Early Kings B* speaks volumes about his insignificant place in Babylonian historiography. He is used in it as a mere marker of time, in a line referring to the fall of Babylon, written in smaller script between two regular entries: "At the time of Samsu-ditana, the Hittites marched against Akkad."[334]

The period leading up to and following the demise of the last Babylonian king is the time when relevant evidence has to be sought also, or mainly, on the side of the victors. Indeed, the raid of the Hittite king Mursili I on Babylon entered Hittite historiography, and Samsu-ditana is, to date, the only ruler of the First Dynasty of Babylon who is mentioned in a Sealand source, as a defeated opponent. The latter composition, only partly preserved, is an epic celebrating the victory of Gulkišar, the sixth king of the Sealand. There Samsu-ditana appears, without a title, in a portion of the text in which either Gulkišar or the goddess Ištar foretells his imminent, utter defeat: "I will darken the day of the troops of Samsu-ditana!"[335] We do not know whether this Sealand victory

---

331. Until his seventh year name; the examples cited are from year names 1, 3, and 4.

332. On the temples appearing in the year names, see George 1993.

333. Richardson 2005: 285.

334. *Chronicle of Early Kings B*, rev. 11′; see Boivin 2018: 49–50 (including a discussion of the form and layout).

335. Zomer 2019: 28–37 no. 1: obv. 7′.

preceded Babylon's final demise, or was part of it, or in fact whether the Sealand participated in the final onslaught on Babylon at all. As noted earlier, later chroniclers considered the Hittites solely responsible for it. The Hittite kingdom, in Anatolia, was on an expansive, southeastward trajectory at the time. The raid on Babylon by Mursili I, probably aimed at removing a power that still had some influence in Syria, is mentioned in a text from the reign of Telepinu, several decades later: "Now, later, he (Mursili I) marched to Babylon, and he destroyed Babylon and fought the Hurrian troops."[336]

The Hurrians were an ethno-linguistic group inhabiting parts of northern Mesopotamia, northern Syria, and eastern Anatolia (chapter 29 in volume 3). While they are presented in the Hittite account of events as another opponent, they appear in a Babylonian oracular question as a potential threat to Babylon. The question, known from a later copy, mentions Samsu-ditana, assuring a date in his reign. It was posed by diviners who inquired about the fate of an unnamed city besieged by multiple enemies, including the armies of Elam, the Kassites, Idamaraṣ, Hanigalbat (= probably the Hurrian core land), the Samharites, and Edaštušu.[337] Several assailants or potential assailants belonged to ethno-linguistic groups that were well represented in the Babylonian fortresses, where they probably served as mercenaries. For many of them, the balance of their loyalties may have been moving increasingly toward a tipping point as Babylon's fortunes deteriorated.[338] And indeed, in the oracular question, the enemy is described as having "rebelled against the god Marduk and Samsu-ditana."[339] The severity of the siege and the ensuing atmosphere of suspicion are palpable in it:

---

336. van den Hout 2003: 195, no. 1.76: §9. See also chapter 30 in volume 3.

337. Lambert 2007: 24–27, no. 1: ll. 31–40. The Edaštušu are unattested in other sources.

338. On the deleterious political impact of the multiplication of fortresses for Babylon, see Richardson 2005; 2019 (with an updated list of fortresses).

339. Lambert 2007: 26–27, no. 1: ll. 42–44.

Or, the resident senior man who lives in that city, will not go out of his mind, will not lose his reason, will not confer with the enemy army, will not open the bridge of the city gate (. . .) will he?[340]

The fall of Babylon appears thus to have been the result of attacks by several opposing forces, whether coordinated or not: the Hittite raid by Mursili I; possibly an attack by other powers, which may have included the Sealand and Elam; and a revolt of mercenaries once in the employ of Babylon, the latter probably fostered by difficult economic conditions. Later sources suggest that Hittite troops removed from the Esagil temple the images of Marduk and his consort—later returned to it by a Kassite king;[341] but signs of violent destruction in residential areas show that the attackers did not confine their looting to the palace and temples.[342]

18.14. The Sealand kingdom after the fall of Babylon

The Sealand endured in southern Babylonia over a century after Babylon's demise. Our best source of information for the later history of the Sealand is a palace archive and a smaller one, probably belonging to a satellite administrative institution of the palace. These date (at least partly) to a few decades after the fall of Babylon, late in the reign of Pešgaldarameš and early in the reign of Ayadaragalama. The smaller, as yet unpublished, archive comes from Tell Khaiber, between Ur and Larsa.[343] The largest corpus is without archaeological provenance, but comes almost certainly from the same general area on the southern

---

340. Lambert 2007: 26–29, no. 1: ll. 78–84.

341. An inscription of Agum-kakrime and the *Marduk Prophecy*; for a recent discussion, see van Koppen 2017: 73–74.

342. Sternitzke 2016; Gasche 1989: 120.

343. Sixty-eight tablets were found, and year names of Ayadaragalama appear on some of them; see Campbell et al. 2017: 28–33.

Euphrates, where the Sealand kings probably had their capital, as yet unidentified.[344] Text-internal evidence shows that the archive was the product of a palatial administration. The capital may have been called Urukug, a name associated with the dynasty in three contemporary sources and in later king lists.[345] These archives mainly provide evidence of the cultic and palatial economy, but also include data relevant to political history, in the form of administrative attestations of diplomatic contacts. In addition, the state pantheon promoted by the kings can be partially reconstructed from these texts.

At the latest by the reign of Gulkišar, the Sealand kings—who had borne only or mostly Akkadian names in the first half of the dynasty—assumed unusual, creative Sumerian names, perhaps in a conscious reference to the southern Sumerian past. Gulkišar's name sounds programmatic politically, since it probably means "Raider-of-the-totality,"[346] and could be a throne name assumed after his victory over Samsu-ditana. It remains unclear whether the Sealand kings occupied cities in central and northern Babylonia after the fall of Babylon. A Sealand occupation of Babylon itself was surmised by earlier scholars, but Gulkišar, the most obvious candidate for it, did not enter the *Chronicle of Early Kings B*. In addition, the palace archive suggests that the god Marduk was only of modest importance in the Sealand,[347] rendering this hypothesis unlikely. To judge from the importance of Nippurite deities in the state pantheon,[348] Nippur was certainly of religious and ideological interest to the Sealand kings, but the city may have been nearly impossible to occupy and rituals difficult to perform there at the time, due to insufficient access to water.

---

344. Boivin 2018: 12–13, 69–72. The larger part of the archive was published (474 texts) in Dalley 2009, with numerous references to thirty-two additional unpublished tablets.

345. Boivin 2018: 22–29; Gabbay and Boivin 2018: 35–36 n. 25, 40.

346. Boivin 2018: 37–42.

347. Boivin 2018: 46, 118–121, 225–226.

348. Boivin 2018: 234–235; Gabbay and Boivin 2018: 35–40.

Even if Gulkišar does not appear in the *Chronicle of Early Kings B*, his rule, at least over southern Babylonia, was remembered well after the demise of the Sealand Kingdom. Near the turn of the first millennium BC, the scribe of a royal land grant which renewed an endowment of land to a temple in the southern Tigris area and identified Gulkišar as the original grantor, referred to him as "King of the Sealand."[349] Somewhat earlier, a scribe used Gulkišar's name to confer antiquity on the purported original of the glass-making treatise he was copying, which shows that his memory was by then associated with ancient knowledge and a scribal tradition.[350]

A number of Sealand divinatory and literary texts have been published, some of which certainly date to the reigns of Gulkišar's successors.[351] Unusual spellings throughout the corpus suggest that Sealand scribes learned and worked in an atmosphere of innovation, which is perhaps to be expected after the preceding major disruptions.[352] As yet, it remains difficult to assess to what extent Sealand scribes contributed to the preservation of the scribal tradition, and to what tradition(s) they owed their own. Indeed, the texts they wrote seem to reflect multiple influences. A version of the Epic of Gilgamesh that is probably of Sealand date contains variants relocating the story in the city of Ur instead of Uruk, which could point to the influence of the Ur literary tradition.[353] A hymn of the Sealand king Ayadaragalama and a ritual lament probably of Sealand date both feature the gods of Nippur prominently, perhaps

---

349. The text also states a (wrong) duration of validity of that endowment; see Paulus 2014: 521 (ENAp 1: obv. 1–8) and the discussion in Boivin 2018: 120–121.

350. Boivin 2018: 119–120 (with previous literature).

351. George 2013: nos. 22–32 (omens); George 2007 (Gilgamesh); Gabbay 2014 (ritual lament); Gabbay and Boivin 2018 (hymn); this is in addition to the epic discussed earlier (Zomer 2019: no. 1); also, school texts, as yet unpublished, were found at Tell Khaiber, including excerpts of a lexical list: see Campbell et al. 2017: 30–32.

352. Boivin 2018: 183–185.

353. The tablet was published in George 2007; see also the discussion in Boivin 2018: 26–27, 184–185.

pointing toward the Nippurite tradition. However, the lament includes, unexpectedly, northern Babylonian cities in its list of cult places, which could reflect a more northerly influence.[354] Divinatory texts dated to the time of the Sealand dynasty share common features with texts from Susa, the capital of Elam, with which the Sealand entertained good relations, although the direction of influence may have been mainly from the Sealand to Susa, rather than the other way around.[355]

We do not know when a central political authority emerged again in northern Babylonia, this time under a Kassite dynasty, and whether this led initially to friction with the southern polity. One way or the other, the Sealand kings must have been interested in ensuring a sufficient water supply downstream and access to long-distance trade along the Euphrates—the latter is in fact evidenced by the presence of aromatics from the northern Levant at the Sealand palace.[356] The very few year names of Ayadaragalama that are not in the regnal year system commemorate mostly pious dedications; one shows, however, that he had to face rebellion.[357] During the reign of Ayadaragalama, the Sealand kingdom had diplomatic relations with Elam and at least one Kassite leader, unattested elsewhere. We have no diplomatic letters, hence no detail about the nature of these alliances, but administrative documents record the disbursement of foodstuffs to diplomatic envoys at the Sealand palace. Also, a few records suggest that the palace administration had commercial relations with Kassite groups, trading copper and textiles. What was received in exchange is unknown.[358]

From the extant documentation, it is difficult to determine the extent of the territory controlled by the Sealand kings, but it seems to have stretched from the lower Tigris to the lower Euphrates, and, from the Persian Gulf shore in the south, it may have reached part of central

---

354. Gabbay and Boivin 2018: 23, 26; Gabbay 2014: 151–153.

355. George 2013: 139–141; Boivin 2018: 104–107, 183–184.

356. Boivin 2018: 141–142.

357. Dalley 2009: 12 (year name "O").

358. Boivin 2018: 104–111.

Babylonia in the north.[359] As most of the extant documents concern local affairs, it is impossible to gauge the level of political control exercised by the Sealand kings over their territory, or to assess economic conditions in the kingdom. Agricultural taxes were paid to the palace; individuals performing various tasks for the palace received remuneration either as a field, a ration/salary, or a combination of both. Therefore, at the conceptual level, there are no fundamental differences with the Old Babylonian agricultural economy, although the merchandising of surpluses by the palace is, so far, not attested in the Sealand period.

At least by the time of Ea-gamil, the last king of the dynasty, the Sealand kingdom had gained political control over Dilmun (modern Bahrain and the adjacent portion of eastern Saudi Arabia) as attested by the fact that one text found at Qal'at al-Bahrain was dated to the fourth year of Ea-gamil (using the regnal year count).[360] This means that the Sealand had become an important stakeholder in the Persian Gulf trade. This involvement of the Sealand had probably begun earlier and may be reflected in the availability of the copper traded by the palace during the reign of Ayadaragalama. Other texts from the same building at Qal'at al-Bahrain, perhaps a palace, bear year formulae of rulers with Kassite names that are not attested elsewhere, and may reflect either a local dynasty or governors installed there. Their sequence cannot be established, leaving the circumstances of the Sealand conquest, and also of the subsequent conquest of Dilmun by the Kassite kings of Babylon, largely unclear. However, similar administrative practices throughout the corpus suggest smooth transitions.

At the time of Ea-gamil, the Sealand became a military target of the Kassite kings installed in Babylon. The *Chronicle of Early Kings B* ends with its conquest, presented as the result of two campaigns, one by Ulam-buriaš and one by Agum (III).[361] The first episode begins with the statement that Ea-gamil fled to Elam, while no Sealand king is named as

---

359. Boivin 2018: 61.

360. Boivin 2018: 122.

361. *Chronicle of Early Kings B*: rev. 12–18.

the opponent of Agum in the second. Therefore it is not clear whether Ea-gamil had returned in the interval. If another leader took over the Sealand throne, he did not enter any of the king lists known to us. The chronicle describes Agum's campaign as the conquest of the town of Dur-Enlile, of unknown location, where he destroyed a temple of Enlil that may be attested in a year name of Ayadaragalama.[362] This victory sealed the fate of the First Dynasty of the Sealand and reunified all of Babylonia after about two and a half centuries of divided history.

18.15.   Concluding remarks

The memory of the Old Babylonian kingdom of Babylon and of the Sealand Kingdom was transmitted in scribal circles, as is most notably manifest in king lists and chronicles. Their rise and fall did not capture the imagination of later scribes as vividly as that of earlier territorial states, however. Indeed, unlike the Akkad and Ur III dynasties, none of their kings was cast as an archetypal ruler in literature, neither as a heroic founder nor as a calamitous king. Still, the divinatory tradition did retain the names of Sumu-la-El and Hammurabi as successful kings, associating the latter in historical omens with "govern(ing) totality."[363] The end of both kingdoms occurred in a dark age characterized by a hiatus in textual evidence and discontinuous stratigraphies in the Mesopotamian plain, precluding a clear understanding of most aspects of the material conditions under which the transition to the Middle Babylonian period took place. Urban centers that had been gradually abandoned during the Old Babylonian period were then revived and temples rebuilt by Kassite rulers throughout a once again reunified Babylonia.

---

362. Boivin 2018: 123–124.

363. Glassner 2019: 367–369.

REFERENCES

Abraham, K., and Van Lerberghe, K. 2017. *A late Old Babylonian temple archive from Dūr-Abiešuḫ: the sequel*. Bethesda, MA: CDL Press.

Beaulieu, P.-A. 2005. The god Amurru as emblem of ethnic and cultural identity. In van Soldt, W.H. (ed.), *Ethnicity in ancient Mesopotamia*. Leiden: NINO, 31–46.

Beaulieu, P.-A. 2018. *A history of Babylon: 2200 BC–AD 75*. Hoboken, NJ: Wiley-Blackwell.

Béranger, M. 2019. Dur-Abi-ešuh and the aftermath of the attack on Nippur: new evidence from three unpublished letters. *RA* 113: 99–122.

Boivin, O. 2018. *The First Dynasty of the Sealand in Mesopotamia*. Berlin: De Gruyter.

Brinkman, J.A. 2017. Babylonia under the Kassites: some aspects for consideration. In Bartelmus, A., and Sternitzke, K. (eds.), *Karduniaš: Babylonia under the Kassites*. Berlin: De Gruyter, 1–44.

Burke, A. 2020. *The Amorites and the Bronze Age Near East: the making of a regional identity*. Cambridge: Cambridge University Press.

Campbell, S., Moon, J., Killick, R., Calderbank, D., Robson, E., Shepperson, M., and Slater, F. 2017. Tell Khaiber: an administrative centre of the Sealand period. *Iraq* 79: 21–46.

Charpin, D. 1995. La fin des archives du palais de Mari. *RA* 89: 29–40.

Charpin, D. 1999–2000. Review of R. Pientka, *Die spätaltbabylonische Zeit*. *AfO* 46/47: 322–324.

Charpin, D. 2000a. Lettres et procès paléo-babyloniens. In Joannès, F. (ed.), *Rendre la justice en Mésopotamie: archives judiciaires du Proche-Orient ancien (IIIe-Ier millénaires avant J.-C.)*. Saint-Denis: Presses Universitaires de Vincennes, 69–250.

Charpin, D. 2000b. Les prêteurs et le palais: les édits de *mîšarum*. In Bongenaar, A.C.V.M. (ed.), *Interdependency of institutions and private entrepreneurs*. Leiden: NINO, 185–211.

Charpin, D. 2003. La "toponymie en miroir" dans le Proche-Orient amorrite. *RA* 97: 3–34.

Charpin, D. 2004. Histoire politique du Proche-Orient amorrite (2002–1595). In Charpin, D., Edzard, D.O., and Stol, M., *Mesopotamien: die altbabylonische Zeit*. Fribourg: Academic Press; Göttingen: Vandenhoeck & Ruprecht, 25–480.

Charpin, D. 2010. *Reading and writing in Babylon*. Cambridge, MA: Harvard University Press.

Charpin, D. 2011. Le "pays de Mari et des bédouins" à l'époque de Samsu-iluna de Babylone. *RA* 105: 41–59.

Charpin, D. 2012. *Hammurabi of Babylon*. London: I.B. Tauris.

Charpin, D. 2014. Chroniques bibliographiques, 15: le royaume d'Uruk et le pays d'Apum, deux voisins de Babylone vaincus par Samsu-iluna. *RA* 108: 121–160.

Charpin, D. 2015. Chroniques bibliographiques, 17: six nouveaux recueils de documents paléo-babyloniens. *RA* 109: 143–196.

Charpin, D. 2018. Chroniques bibliographiques, 21: à l'occasion des dix ans du projet Archibab. *RA* 112: 177–208.

Charpin, D. 2019a. Priest of Ur in the Old Babylonian period: a reappraisal in light of the 2017 discoveries at Ur/Tell Muqayyar. *Journal of Ancient Near Eastern Religions* 19: 18–34.

Charpin, D. 2019b. En marge d'EcritUr, 4: Rim-Sin II, roi d'Ur? *NABU* 2019: 30–31 (no. 19).

Charpin, D. 2020. Le pillage d'Ur et la protection du temple de Ningal en l'an 12 the Samsu-iluna. In Charpin, D. (ed.), *Nouvelles recherches sur la ville d'Ur à l'époque paléo-babylonienne*. Paris: Société pour l'étude du Proche-Orient ancien.

Charpin, D., and Durand, J.-M. 1986. "Fils de Sim'al": les origines tribales des rois de Mari. *RA* 80: 141–183.

Charpin, D., and Ziegler, N. 2003. *Mari et le Proche-Orient à l'époque amorrite: essai d'histoire politique*. Paris: Société pour l'étude du Proche-Orient ancien.

Charpin, D., Joannès, F., Lackenbacher, S., and Lafont, B. 1988. *Archives épistolaires de Mari I/2* (Archives royales de Mari 26/2). Paris: Éditions Recherche sur les Civilisations.

Cole, S.W., and Gasche, H. 1998. Second and first millennium BC rivers in northern Babylonia. In Gasche, H., and Tanret, M. (eds.), *Changing watercourses in Babylonia: towards a reconstruction of the ancient environment in Lower Mesopotamia*. Ghent: University of Ghent; Chicago: The Oriental Institute of the University of Chicago.

Curtis, J. 2004. Maceheads from Tell Mohammed in the British Museum. In Frame, G. (ed.), *From the Upper Sea to the Lower Sea*. Leiden: NINO, 57–66.

Dalley, S. 2009. *Babylonian tablets from the First Sealand Dynasty in the Schøyen collection*. Bethesda, MA: CDL Press.

de Boer, R. 2013. Marad in the early Old Babylonian period: its kings, chronology, and Isin's influence. *JCS* 65: 73–90.

de Boer, R. 2014a. *Amorites in the early Old Babylonian period*. PhD dissertation, Leiden University.

de Boer, R. 2014b. Early Old Babylonian Amorite tribes and gatherings and the role of Sumu-abum. *Aram* 26: 269–284.

de Boer, R. 2018. Beginnings of Old Babylonian Babylon: Sumu-abum and Sumu-la-el. *JCS* 70: 53–86.

Delnero, P. 2016. Literature and identity in Mesopotamia during the Old Babylonian period. In Ryholt, K., and Barjamovic, G. (eds.), *Problems of canonicity and identity formation in ancient Egypt and Mesopotamia*. Copenhagen: Museum Tusculanum Press, 19–50.

Démare-Lafont, S. 2000. Codification et subsidiarité dans les droits du Proche-Orient ancien. In Lévy, E. (ed.), *La codification des lois dans l'antiquité*. Paris: De Boccard, 49–64.

Démare-Lafont, S. 2013. L'écriture du droit en Mésopotamie. In Artus, O. (ed.), *Loi et justice dans la littérature du Proche-Orient ancien*. Wiesbaden: Harrassowitz, 69–83.

Dossin, G. 1951. *Correspondance de Šamši-Addu et de ses fils (suite)* (Archives royales de Mari 4). Paris: Imprimerie nationale.

Durand, J.-M. 1988. *Archives épistolaires de Mari I/1* (Archives royales de Mari 26/1). Paris: Éditions Recherche sur les Civilisations.

Durand, J.-M. 1992. Unité et diversités au Proche-Orient à l'époque amorrite. In Charpin, D., and Joannès, F. (eds.), *La circulation des biens, des personnes et des idées dans le Proche-Orient ancien*. Paris: Éditions Recherche sur les Civilisations, 97–128.

Durand, J.-M. 1998. *Les documents épistolaires du palais de Mari, vol. II*. Paris: Les éditions du Cerf.

Durand, J.-M. 2004. Peuplement et sociétés à l'époque amorrite, I: les clans bensim'alites. In Nicolle, C. (ed.), *Nomades et sédentaires dans le Proche-Orient ancien*. Paris: Éditions Recherche sur les Civilisations, 111–197.

Edzard, D.O. 2004. Altbabylonische Literatur und Religion. In Charpin, D., Edzard, D.O., and Stol, M., *Mesopotamien: die altbabylonische Zeit*. Fribourg: Academic Press; Göttingen: Vandenhoeck & Ruprecht, 481–640.

Eidem, J. 1989. Some remarks on the Iltani archive from Tell al Rimah. *Iraq* 51: 67–78.

Eidem, J. 2011. *The royal archives from Tell Leilan: Old Babylonian letters and treaties from the Lower Town Palace East*. Leiden: NINO.

Falkenstein, A. 1963. Zu den Inschriftfunden der Grabung in Uruk-Warka 1960–1961. *BaM* 2: 1–82.

Farber, G., and Farber, W. 2003. Von einem, der auszog, ein gudu₄ zu werden. In Sallaberger, W., Volk, K., and Zgoll, A. (eds.), *Literatur, Politik und Recht in Mesopotamien: Festschrift für Claus Wilcke*. Wiesbaden: Harrassowitz, 99–114.

Farber, H., and Wilent, A. 2018. Sumu-abum at Nippur. *NABU* 2018: 75–76 (no. 44).

Fiette, B. 2018. *Le palais, la terre et les hommes: la gestion du domaine royal de Larsa d'après les archives de Šamaš-hazir*. Paris: Société pour l'Étude du Proche-Orient Ancien.

Figulla, H.H., and Martin, W.J. 1953. *Letters and documents of the Old Babylonian period* (Ur Excavation Texts 5). London: British Museum Publications.

Finkelstein, J.J. 1966. The genealogy of the Hammurapi dynasty. *JCS*: 95–118.

Finkelstein, J.J. 1969. The edict of Ammiṣaduqa: a new text. *RA* 63: 45–64.

Földi, Z. 2014. Cuneiform texts in the Kunsthistorisches Museum Wien, part IV: a new text from Dūr-Abī-ēšuḫ. *Wiener Zeitschrift für die Kunde des Morgenlandes* 104: 31–55.

Foster, B.R. 2005. *Before the muses: an anthology of Akkadian literature*. Bethesda, MD: CDL Press.

Frayne, D.R. 1990. *The royal inscriptions of Mesopotamia: early periods, vol. 4: Old Babylonian period (2003–1595 BC)*. Toronto: University of Toronto Press.

Frayne, D.R. 1997. *The royal inscriptions of Mesopotamia: early periods, vol. 3: Ur III period (2112–2004 BC)*. Toronto: University of Toronto Press.

Gabbay, U. 2014. A balaĝ to Enlil from the first Sealand dynasty. *ZA* 104: 146–170.

Gabbay, U., and Boivin, O. 2018. A hymn of Ayadaragalama, king of the First Sealand Dynasty, to the gods of Nippur: the fate of Nippur and its cults during the First Sealand Dynasty. *ZA* 108: 22–42.

Gadotti, A., and Kleinerman, A. 2011. "Here is what I have. Send me what I am missing": exchange of syllabi in ancient Mesopotamia. *ZA* 101: 72–77.

Gasche, H. 1989. *La Babylonie au 17e siècle avant notre ère: approche archéologique, problèmes et perspectives.* Ghent: University of Ghent.

Gasche, H., Armstrong, J.A., Cole, S.W., and Gurzadyan, V.G. 1998. *Dating the fall of Babylon: a reappraisal of second-millennium chronology.* Ghent: University of Ghent; Chicago: The Oriental Institute of the University of Chicago.

George, A.R. 1993. *House most high: the temples of ancient Mesopotamia.* Winona Lake, IN: Eisenbrauns.

George, A.R. 2003. *The Babylonian Gilgamesh epic.* Oxford: Oxford University Press.

George, A.R. 2005. In search of the É.DUB.BA.A: the ancient Mesopotamian school in literature and reality. In Sefati, Y., Artzi, P., Cohen, C., Eichler, B.L., and Hurowitz, V.A. (eds.), *"An experienced scribe who neglects nothing": ancient Near Eastern studies in honor of Jacob Klein.* Bethesda, MD: CDL Press, 127–137.

George, A.R. 2007. The civilizing of Ea-Enkidu: an unusual tablet of the Babylonian Gilgameš epic. *RA* 101: 59–80.

George, A.R. 2009. *Babylonian literary texts in the Schøyen collection.* Bethesda, MD: CDL Press.

George, A.R. 2013. *Babylonian divinatory texts chiefly in the Schøyen Collection.* Bethesda, MD: CDL Press.

George, A.R. 2018. *Old Babylonian texts in the Schøyen Collection, part 1: selected letters.* Bethesda, MA: CDL Press.

Glassner, J.-J. 2004. *Mesopotamian chronicles.* Atlanta, GA: Society of Biblical Literature.

Glassner, J.-J. 2019. *Le devin historien en Mésopotamie.* Leiden: Brill.

Goddeeris, A. 2002. *Economy and society in northern Babylonia in the early Old Babylonian period ca. (2000–1800 BC).* Leuven: Peeters.

Goddeeris, A. 2005. The emergence of Amorite dynasties in northern Babylonia during the early Old Babylonian period. In van Soldt, W.H., Kalvelagen, R., and Katz, D. (eds.), *Ethnicity in ancient Mesopotamia.* Leiden: NINO, 138–146.

Goddeeris, A. 2013a. Sumu-abum. *RlA* 13: 300–301.

Goddeeris, A. 2013b. Sumu-la-el. *RlA* 13: 304–305.

Grayson, A.K. 1975. *Assyrian and Babylonian chronicles.* Locust Valley, NY: Augustin.

Grayson, A.K. 1983. Königslisten und Chroniken. *RlA* 6: 77–135.

Groneberg, B. 1980. *Die Orts- und Gewässernamen der altbabylonischen Zeit.* Wiesbaden: Reichert.

Guichard, M. 2004. "La malédiction de cette tablette est très dure!" Sur l'ambassade d'Itûr-Asdû à Babylone en l'an 4 de Zimrî-Lim. *RA* 98: 13–32.

Guichard, M. 2014. Un traité d'alliance entre Larsa, Uruk et Ešnunna contre Sabium de Babylone. *Semitica* 56: 9–34.

Guichard, M. 2016. Guerre et diplomatie: lettres d'Iluni roi d'Ešnunna d'une collection privée. *Semitica* 56: 17–59.

Horsnell, M.J.A. 1999. *The year-names of the First Dynasty of Babylon.* Hamilton, ON: McMaster University Press.

Jacquet, A. 2013. Family archives in Mesopotamia during the Old Babylonian period. In Faraguna, M. (ed.), *Archives and archival documents in ancient societies.* Trieste: Edizioni Università di Trieste, 63–85.

Janssen, C. 1991. Samsu-iluna and the hungry *nadītums. Northern Akkad Project Reports* 5: 3–40.

Jawad, A.A., Abd Al-Reza, N., Nasir, A.J., As'id, A.A., and de Boer, R. 2020. The discovery of the location of Malgium (Tell Yassir). *JCS* 72: 65–86.

Joannès, F. 2006. *Haradum II: les textes de la période paléo-babylonienne (Samsu-iluna—Ammi-ṣaduqa).* Paris: Éditions Recherche sur les Civilisations.

Kraus, F.R. 1958. *Ein Edikt des Königs Ammi-ṣaduqa von Babylon.* Leiden: Brill.

Kraus, F.R. 1960. Ein zentrales Problem des altmesopotamischen Rechtes: was ist der Codex Hammu-rabi? *Genava NS* 8: 283–296.

Kraus, F.R. 1968. *Briefe aus dem Archive des Šamaš-ḫāzir* (Altbabylonische Briefe 4). Leiden: Brill.

Kraus, F.R. 1977. *Briefe aus dem British Museum* (Altbabylonische Briefe 7). Leiden: Brill.

Kraus, F.R. 1985. *Briefe aus kleineren westeuropäischen Sammlungen* (Altbabylonische Briefe 10). Leiden: Brill.

Lambert, W.G. 2007. *Babylonian oracle questions.* Winona Lake, IN: Eisenbrauns.

Lambert, W.G., and Weeden, M. 2020. A statue inscription of Samsuiluna from the papers of W.G. Lambert. *RA* 114: 15–62.

Leichty, E., and Walker, C. 2004. Three Babylonian chronicle and scientific texts. In Frame, G. (ed.), *From the Upper Sea to the Lower Sea: studies on the history of Assyria and Babylonia in honour of A.K. Grayson.* Leiden: NINO, 203–212.

Löhnert, A. 2010. Reconsidering the consecration of priests in ancient Mesopotamia. In Baker, H.D., Robson, E., and Zólyomi, G. (eds.), *Your praise is sweet: a memorial volume for Jeremy Black from students, colleagues and friends*. London: British Institute for the Study of Iraq, 183–191.

Maul, S. 2012. Tontafelabschriften des "Kodex Hammurapi" in altbabylonischer Monumentalschrift. *ZA* 102: 76–99.

Michalowski, P. 2011. *The correspondence of the kings of Ur: an epistolary history of an ancient Mesopotamian kingdom*. Winona Lake, IN: Eisenbrauns.

Michalowski, P., and Beckman, G. 2012. The promulgation of the name of the third year of Rim-Anum of Uruk. In Boiy, T., Bretschneider, J., Goddeeris, A., Hameeuw, H., Jans, G., and Tavernier, J. (eds.), *The ancient Near East, a life! Festschrift Karel Van Lerberghe*. Leuven: Peeters, 425–433.

Michalowski, P., and Streck, M. 2018. Hammurapi. *RlA* 15: 380–390.

Myers, J. 2007. Šamaš of Sippar and the First Dynasty of Babylon. In Roth, M.T., Farber, W., Stolper, M.W., and von Bechtolsheim, P. (eds.), *Studies presented to Robert D. Biggs*. Chicago: The Oriental Institute of the University of Chicago, 193–199.

Neumann, H. 2011. Bemerkungen zu einigen Aspekten babylonischen Rechtsdenkens im Spannungsfeld von Theorie und Praxis. In Cancik-Kirschbaum, E., van Ess, M., and Marzahn, J. (eds.), *Babylon: Wissenskultur in Orient und Okzident*. Berlin: De Gruyter, 159–170.

Paulus, S. 2014. *Die babylonischen Kudurru-Inschriften von der kassitischen bis zur frühneubabylonischen Zeit*. Münster: Ugarit-Verlag.

Pecha, L. 2018. *The material and ideological base of the Old Babylonian state*. Lanham, MA: Lexington Books.

Pientka, R. 1998. *Die spätaltbabylonische Zeit, Abiešuḫ bis Samsuditana: Quellen, Jahresdaten, Geschichte*. Münster: Rhema.

Podany, A.H. 2002. *The Land of Hana: kings, chronology, and scribal tradition*. Bethesda, MD: CDL Press.

Podany, A.H. 2014. Hana and the Low Chronology. *JNES* 73: 51–73.

Ranke, H. 1906. *Babylonian legal and business documents from the time of the First Dynasty of Babylon chiefly from Sippar*. Philadelphia: Department of Archaeology, University of Pennsylvania.

Renger, J. 2000. Das Palastgeschäft in der altbabylonischen Zeit. In Bongenaar, A.C.V.M. (ed.), *Interdependency of institutions and private entrepreneurs*. Leiden: NINO, 153–183.

Renger, J. 2002. Royal edicts of the Old Babylonian period: structural background. In Hudson, M., and Van de Mieroop, M. (eds.), *Debt and economic renewal in the ancient Near East*. Bethesda, MA: CDL Press, 139–162.

Richardson, S. 2005. Trouble in the countryside *ana tarṣi* Samsuditana: militarism, Kassites, and the fall of Babylon. In van Soldt, W.H. (ed.), *Ethnicity in ancient Mesopotamia*. Leiden: NINO, 273–289.

Richardson, S. 2010. *Texts from the late Old Babylonian period*. Boston: The American Schools of Oriental Research.

Richardson, S. 2012. Early Mesopotamia: the presumptive state. *Past & Present* 215: 3–49.

Richardson, S. 2018. Sumer and stereotype: re-forging "Sumerian" kingship in the late Old Babylonian period. In Fink, S., and Rollinger, R. (eds.), *Conceptualizing past, present and future*. Münster: Ugarit-Verlag, 145–186.

Richardson, S. 2019. Updating the list of late OB Babylonian fortresses. *NABU* 2019: 32 (no. 21).

Robson, E. 2001. The tablet house: a scribal school in Old Babylonian Nippur. *RA* 95: 39–66.

Rositani, A. 2003. *Rīm-Anum texts in the British Museum*. Messina: Dipartimento di Scienze dell'Antichità dell'Università degli Studi di Messina.

Roth, M.T. 1995. *Law collections from Mesopotamia and Asia Minor*. Atlanta, GA: Scholars Press.

Rutz, M., and Michalowski, P. 2016. The flooding of Ešnunna, the fall of Mari: Hammurabi's deeds in Babylonian literature and history. *JCS* 68: 15–43.

Sallaberger, W. 2010. König Ḫammurapi und die Babylonier: wem übertrug der Kodex Ḫammurapi die Rechtspflege? In Charvát, P., and Vlčková, P.M. (eds.), *Who was king? Who was not king?* Prague: Institute of Archaeology of the Academy of Sciences of the Czech Republic, 46–58.

Saporetti, C. 2013. *Formule dalla Diyāla nel periodo paleobabilonese, I: trascrizioni e commenti*. Rome: Informatica Applicata.

Schaudig, H. 2001. *Die Inschriften Nabonids von Babylon und Kyros' des Großen*. Münster: Ugarit-Verlag.

Seri, A. 2006. *Local power in Old Babylonian Mesopotamia*. Sheffield, UK: Equinox.

Seri, A. 2013. *The house of prisoners: slavery and state in Uruk during the revolt against Samsu-iluna*. Berlin: De Gruyter.

Sigrist, M. 1990. *Larsa year names*. Berrien Springs, MI: Andrews University Press.

Sigrist, M., Gabbay, U., and Avila, M. 2017. Cuneiform tablets and other inscribed objects from collections in Jerusalem. In Feliu, L., Karahashi, F., and Rubio, G. (eds.), *The first ninety years: a Sumerian celebration in honor of Miguel Civil*. Berlin: De Gruyter, 311–336.

Steele, L.D. 2007. Women and gender in Babylonia. In Leick, G. (ed.), *The Babylonian world*. London and New York: Routledge, 299–316.

Sternitzke, K. 2016. Der Kontext der altbabylonischen Archive aus Babylon. *MDOG* 148: 179–197.

Stol, M. 1976. *Studies in Old Babylonian history*. Leiden: NINO.

Stol, M. 1997. Muškēnu. *RlA* 8: 492–493.

Stol, M. 2004. Wirtschaft und Gesellschaft in altbabylonischer Zeit. In Charpin, D., Edzard, D.O., and Stol, M., *Mesopotamien: die altbabylonische Zeit*. Fribourg: Academic Press; Göttingen: Vandenhoeck & Ruprecht, 641–975.

Stol, M. 2016. *Women in the ancient Near East*. Berlin: De Gruyter.

Stone, E.C. 1987. *Nippur neighborhoods*. Chicago: The Oriental Institute of the University of Chicago.

Tanret, M. 2011. Learned, rich, famous, and unhappy: Ur-Utu of Sippar. In Radner, K., and Robson, E. (eds.), *The Oxford handbook of cuneiform culture*. Oxford: Oxford University Press, 270–287.

Tinney, S. 2011. Tablets of schools and scholars: a portrait of the Old Babylonian corpus. In Radner, K., and Robson, E. (eds.), *The Oxford handbook of cuneiform culture*. Oxford: Oxford University Press, 577–596.

Van de Mieroop, M. 2005. *King Hammurabi of Babylon*. Malden, MA: Wiley-Blackwell.

van den Hout, T.P.J. 2003. The proclamation of Telipinu. In Hallo, W.W., and Younger, K.L. (eds.), *The context of scripture, vol. 1: canonical compositions from the Biblical World*. Leiden: Brill, 194–198.

van Koppen, F. 2004. The geography of the slave trade and northern Mesopotamia in the late Old Babylonian period. In Hunger, H., and Pruzsinszky, R. (eds.), *Mesopotamian Dark Age revisited*. Vienna: Verlag der Österreichischen Akademie der Wissenschaften, 9–33.

van Koppen, F. 2013. Abiešuh, Elam and Ashurbanipal: new evidence from Old Babylonian Sippar. In De Graef, K., and Tavernier, J. (eds.), *Susa and*

Elam: archaeological, philological, historical and geographical perspectives. Leiden: Brill, 377–397.

van Koppen, F. 2017. The early Kassite period. In Bartelmus, A., and Sternitzke, K. (eds.), *Karduniaš: Babylonia under the Kassites*. Berlin: De Gruyter, 45–92.

Van Lerberghe, K., Kaniewski, D., Abraham, K., Guiot, J., and Van Campo, E. 2017. Water deprivation as military strategy in the Middle East, 3.700 years ago. *Méditerranée*. Retrieved from https://journals.openedition.org/mediterranee/8000 (last accessed August 15, 2020).

Van Lerberghe, K., and Voet, G. 2009. *A late Old Babylonian temple archive from Dūr-Abieśuḫ*. Bethesda, MA: CDL Press.

van Soldt, W.H. 1994. *Letters in the British Museum, part 2* (Altbabylonische Briefe 13). Leiden: Brill.

Vanstiphout, H.I.J. 1999. A meeting of cultures? Rethinking the "Marriage of Martu." In Van Lerberghe, K., and Voet, G. (eds.), *Languages and cultures in contact: the crossroads of civilizations in the Syro-Mesopotamian realm.* Leuven: Peeters, 461–474.

Vedeler, H.T. 2015. The ideology of Rim-Sin II of Larsa. *JANEH* 2: 1–17.

Veenhof, K.R. 1997–2000. The relation between royal decrees and "law codes" in the Old Babylonian period. *JEOL* 35/36: 49–83.

Veenhof, K.R. 2005. *Letters in the Louvre* (Altbabylonische Briefe 14). Leiden: Brill.

Veldhuis, N.C. 1997. *Elementary education at Nippur: the lists of trees and wooden objects*. PhD dissertation, Rijksuniversiteit Groningen.

Veldhuis, N.C. 2014. Intellectual history and Assyriology. *JANEH* 1: 21–36.

von Dassow, E. 2009. Narām-Sîn of Uruk: a new king in an old shoebox. *JCS* 61: 63–91.

Waerzeggers, C. 2015. The Neo-Babylonian chronicle about Sabium and Apil-Sîn: a copy of the text (BM 29440). *NABU* 2015: 85 (no. 54).

Wiggermann, F.A.M. 2001. Nergal. *RlA* 9: 215–226.

Wilcke, C. 1987. Die Inschriften der 7. und 8. Kampagnen (1983 und 1984). In Hrouda, B. (ed.), *Isin—Išān Baḥrīyāt, III*. Munich: Verlag der Bayerischen Akademie der Wissenschaften, 83–120.

Wilcke, C. 2007. Das Recht: Grundlage des sozialen und politischen Diskurses im Alten Orient. In Wilcke, C. (ed.), *Das geistige Erfassen der Welt im Alten Orient: Sprache, Religion, Kultur und Gesellschaft*. Wiesbaden: Harrassowitz, 209–244.

Wu, Y. 1994. *A political history of Eshnunna, Mari and Assyria during the early Old Babylonian period (from the end of Ur III to the death of Šamši-Adad).* Changchun: Institute of History of Ancient Civilizations, Northeast Normal University.

Wu, Y., and Dalley, S. 1990. The origins of the Manana dynasty at Kish, and the Assyrian King List. *Iraq* 52: 159–165.

Ziegler, N. 2008. Tilmuniter im Königreich Samsî-Addus. In Olijdam, E., and Spoor, R.H. (eds.), *Intercultural relations between south and southwest Asia.* Oxford: BAR, 253–259.

Ziegler, N. 2016. The flooding of Ešnunna? *NABU* 2016: 70–71 (no. 41).

Zomer, E. 2019. *Middle Babylonian literary texts from the Frau Professor Hilprecht Collection, Jena.* Wiesbaden: Harrassowitz.

19

Egypt's Middle Kingdom

A VIEW FROM WITHIN

Harco Willems

19.1. Introduction

The expression "a view from within" may suggest to the reader that the objective of this chapter is to describe historical processes from the perspective of those directly involved: Middle Kingdom Egyptians (figure 19.1 a–c); in other words, an emic view.[1] But of course, a concept like "Middle Kingdom" does not reflect the sensibilities of individuals living in the past, but rather the attempts of modern scholars to subdivide history into periods. Periodization reflects the way modern researchers define the past, and this is undeniably an etic approach.[2]

This kind of problem does not pose itself only to Egyptologists. It is an issue that affects the study of the past of any part of the world. Historians have produced an impressive amount of literature about the theoretical problem of how periodization affects our view of the past,

---

1. The chapter was language-edited by Denise Bolton.

2. For the terms "emic" and "etic" and their application to Egyptian material, see, e.g., Nyord 2019: 4–20.

Harco Willems, *Egypt's Middle Kingdom* In: *The Oxford History of the Ancient Near East.* Edited by: Karen Radner, Nadine Moeller, and D. T. Potts, Oxford University Press. © Oxford University Press 2022. DOI: 10.1093/oso/9780190687571.003.0019

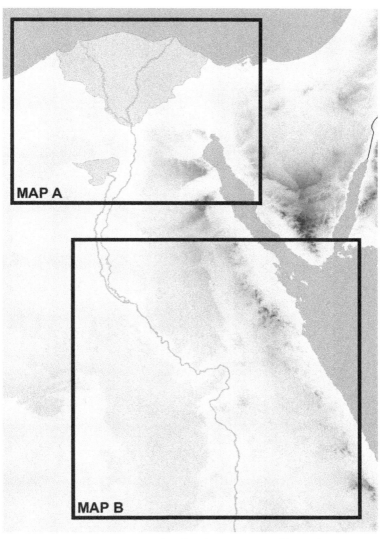

FIGURE 19.1A. Sites mentioned in this chapter. Prepared by Andrea Squitieri (LMU Munich).

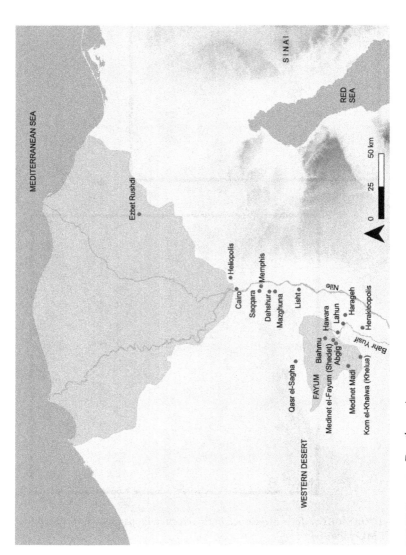

FIGURE 19.1B. Detail map A.

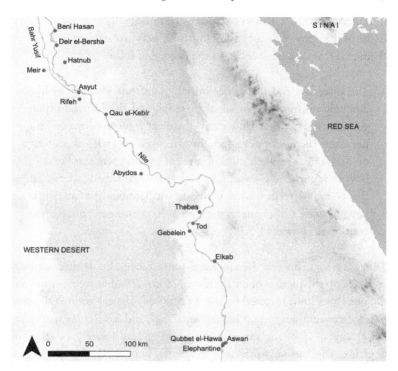

FIGURE 19.1C. Detail map B.

leading eventually to Jacques Le Goff's pertinent question: "Is it really necessary to cut history into slices?"[3]

Although Le Goff ultimately concluded that periodization is unavoidable, he demonstrated, using the period of the Renaissance as a specific example, that such chronological blanket terms, often developed in the context of academic teaching, lead to designations that not only serve as neutral references to slices of time, but simultaneously charge the eras

---

3. In the original French, "Faut-il vraiment découper l'histoire en tranches?"; Le Goff 2014.

thus distinguished with sets of conceptual notions. This process, known in the philosophy of history as "colligation," was first studied in depth by William H. Walsh, who describes the process as follows:

> The historian and his reader initially confront what looks like a largely unconnected mass of material, and the historian then goes on to show that sense can be made of it by revealing certain pervasive themes or developments. In specifying what was going on at the time he both sums up the individual events and tells us how to take them. Or again, he picks out what was significant in the events he relates, what is significant here being what points beyond itself and connects with other happenings as phases in a continuous process.[4]

The colligatory concept "Renaissance," for instance, almost automatically conjures up the picture of an artistic and intellectual movement spreading out from Italy, inspired by the writings of classical authors, leading to a greater emphasis on individual capacities, and from there to a rational examination of the surrounding world and, ultimately, of religious doctrine. The period is therefore frequently conceived of as the beginning of modernity. Such conceptual amalgams make it easier to present overall pictures of the past, for instance in teaching. But no medieval European would have had a sense that he or she was living in the Middle Ages; that entire concept arrived much later. As Le Goff demonstrates, many characteristics often considered to be "medieval" still prevailed in the Renaissance and much later; and many alleged Renaissance innovations emerged much earlier. In his view, periodization that leads to the assignation of characteristic traits to one era, which could with equal justice be attributed to others, obscures rather than clarifies historical processes. For Le Goff, the Renaissance was just one of many renaissances that took place over the course of "the long Middle Ages," which started after the fall of the Roman Empire and continued into the eighteenth

---

4. Walsh 1974: 136.

century. Many elements usually understood under the colligatory concept "Renaissance" characterize earlier and later eras as well.

The Egyptian "Middle Kingdom" (regarded by some as a "renaissance") is a similar colligatory concept.[5] In the scholarship of the nineteenth century AD, no Middle Kingdom was initially recognized. Richard Lepsius, for instance, distinguished between an Old Kingdom and a New Kingdom; what we would today call the Middle Kingdom was to him part of the Old.[6] This only changed when Alfred Wiedemann wrote his seminal history of ancient Egypt. He introduced the term "Middle Kingdom," but he used it to refer to the period between the beginning of the Twelfth Dynasty and the end of the Nineteenth Dynasty.[7] Only with the course of time did the Middle Kingdom come to be recognized as the period beginning after the First Intermediate Period and ending before the Hyksos Period. But even here, there is no consensus on when the era began and when it ended. The reunification of Egypt by Mentuhotep II is regarded as the starting point of the Middle Kingdom by most. However, Ludwig Morenz starts the Middle Kingdom with the ascent of the first Twelfth Dynasty king Amenemhat I to the throne.[8] On the other hand, Wolfgang Schenkel introduced the term "frühes Mittleres Reich" (i.e., Early Middle Kingdom) to refer to an only vaguely defined period covering both the late First Intermediate Period and the late Eleventh and early Twelfth Dynasties, and this expression is widely used.[9]

A similar ambiguity surrounds the end of the period. It has long been customary to situate this in the second half of the Thirteenth Dynasty, at the moment the royal court abandoned the capital at Itj-tawy under pressure from the Hyksos.[10] However, the proceedings of a recent international symposium dedicated to the Second Intermediate Period takes

---

5. Callender 2000 is among those who explicitly use the term "Renaissance."

6. Lepsius 1853: 1

7. Wiedemann 1884: 231–486

8. Morenz 2010.

9. Schenkel 1962.

10. E.g., Bourriau 2000.

the disintegration of the unified state of Egypt at the end of the Twelfth Dynasty as marking the beginning of the Second Intermediate Period. Following this view, the end of the Twelfth Dynasty is simultaneously the end of the Middle Kingdom.[11] Yet, in a recent monograph on the Thirteenth Dynasty, Julien Siesse again includes this era in the Middle Kingdom.[12] These varying chronological borders are significant, as they show that the decision about when the Middle Kingdom began or ended depends on the choice of researchers rather than on solid historical boundaries. In this, scholars are driven by what, in their view, are the general characteristics of the period.

Different nuances are possible here, but Gae Callender offers a portrait of the Middle Kingdom that would probably still be acceptable to many. Features she deems crucial are: peak achievements in art, architecture, and religion; "confidence in writing," leading to the production of literary masterpieces; an expanding bureaucracy resulting in the emergence of a "middle class"; and a generally more humane outlook. Egypt had an eye open to the surrounding world, and the Middle Kingdom was an "age of invention, great vision, and colossal projects." To Callender,

> [n]either Sinuhe nor the "shipwrecked sailor" could ever have been central characters in any Old Kingdom tale, but these individuals sit comfortably in the literature of the Middle Kingdom, which was an age of greater humanity.[13]

The stress placed here on the increase in opportunities for "middle-class" Egyptians probably echoes some (until recently) widespread ideas about the development of Egyptian society following the collapse of the Old Kingdom. In this context, central power would have weakened, leading to non-royals taking their lives in their own hands. This led to what has been dubbed a "democratization of the afterlife," with Egyptians of lower

---

11. Marée 2010: xi.

12. Siesse 2019.

13. Callender 2000: 183. Note that no Old Kingdom tales survive.

status adopting an elite style of funerary culture. It would also have led to social upheavals.[14]

According to other scholars, the social insecurity that allegedly prevailed during the First Intermediate Period led to Egyptians questioning the traditional values of the Old Kingdom, to existential doubts, and to new moral values resting on a reformulation of the age-old *maat* concept. In Jan Assmann's view, this system, while remaining hierarchical in nature, served to connect those in charge with society as a whole. He speaks of "connective justice: reciprocity and solidarity."[15]

Acceptance of the idea of the growing importance of sub-elite Egyptians, interpreted as an emergent "middle class," has also been used in attempts to interpret the social networks underlying the archaeological remains of cemetery populations.[16]

These paragraphs offer an overview of the concepts many Egyptologists would regard as colligations of the Middle Kingdom. But in fact, many of these ("peak achievements in art, religion and literature," "middle class," "increased sense of humanity") are certainly not categories we find mentioned in the Egyptian record itself, and others can be applied equally well to earlier or later periods (growing emphasis on writing; expansion on bureaucracy; colossal projects). What we are offered in these studies is not an inside view. It is an outside view that reflects Egyptologists' readings of the sources.

It is in fact illusory to pretend it is possible to write such an inside view, as we simply cannot ask Middle Kingdom Egyptians about their experiences. The closest possible alternative, which we will attempt in this chapter, is to stay close to the categories the Egyptians used themselves, or to try to isolate these even where they are not made explicit in

---

14. This theoretical model emerged in the first decades of the twentieth century, being formulated most persuasively after the First World War by scholars such as H. Kees. For an overview and criticism of the debate, see Willems 2014: 124–229. This issue will not be pursued in this chapter but cf. chapter 22 in this volume.

15. In the original German, "konnektive Gerechtigkeit: Gegenseitigkeit und Solidarität"; Assmann 1990: 58.

16. Richards 2005.

texts. I will borrow the historical approach of the *longue durée*, advocated by Le Goff (who himself was following in Fernand Braudel's footsteps), by assuming that the Egyptian Middle Kingdom is not a clearly distinct era in its own right, but merely part of an epoch of far longer duration for which Egyptology never coined a specific term. It could perhaps be called the nomarchal era. Nomarchs—provincial governors heading large groups of regional dependents—came to the fore toward the end of the Old Kingdom and dominated large parts of Egypt until the late Twelfth Dynasty. This system of rural regionalization remained characteristic of Egypt over half a millennium, and was only partly affected when the Old Kingdom gave way to the First Intermediate Period, and the First Intermediate Period to the Middle Kingdom. But since the nomarchs disappeared before the end of the Middle Kingdom, this definition generates its own problems.

19.2. Chronological issues

In the intense debate over Middle Kingdom chronology, a key role has been played by the astronomical date in Papyrus Berlin 10012 from Lahun. This source announces the so-called heliacal rising of the star Sothis (i.e., Sirius) on the sixteenth day of the fourth month of the *peret*-season in the civil year 7 of Senusret III. Since the New Year in the civil and Julian calendars are known to have coincided in AD 139, and since there is an offset of one day every four years between these calendars, in principle it is possible to calculate when the event mentioned in the Berlin papyrus took place. Lunar dates have been used to refine the result. This could provide an anchor point in the absolute chronology of the Middle Kingdom.

The debate over the Sothic date has concentrated on where the heliacal rising of Sirius was observed, which has a considerable impact on the result of the calculation. This has led to long and short chronologies, for each of which there are different versions (cf. chapter 11). Recent comparisons between radiocarbon dates and these chronologies indicate that the long chronology used by Ian Shaw (based on an assumed observation point near Memphis) is in very close agreement with the radiocarbon results.[17] This suggests that Senusret III's Year 1 should be set within a four-year interval around 1870 BC.[18] The rest of the Twelfth Dynasty can be calculated from this point. The answer to the hotly debated question of whether co-regencies occurred, and how long they lasted if they did, has only limited impact on the absolute dates arrived at.

19.3. Literature and politics

In 1956, Georges Posener published an influential book entitled *Littérature et politique dans l'Égypte de la XIIe dynastie*.[19] It argued that the rise of the Twelfth Dynasty (and the demise of the Eleventh) raised issues of legitimacy for the new royal house that were addressed, among other methods, by a conscious effort to produce literary works in which representatives of the new royal line were presented in a positive light. Posener did not hesitate to use the term "political propaganda" for these works, among them some of the most famous literary compositions surviving from ancient Egypt. The first was the "Prophecy of Neferti," a historical romance which suggests that the beneficial rule of the first Twelfth Dynasty king, Amenemhat I, had been anticipated as early as during the reign of King Sneferu, more than 600 years earlier. The second was the "Teaching of Amenemhat I," in which the murdered king posthumously instructs his son and successor, Senusret I, on how to deal severely, but justly, with his subjects. The third was the "Story of Sinuhe," an Egyptian official who, after overhearing a conversation about the death of Amenemhat I, flees Egypt, but is eventually persuaded by the merciful king Senusret I to return home. These and other propagandistic documents served a political purpose, but they were also literary masterpieces, which continued to be used as part of the teaching curriculum throughout the New Kingdom and even later. Regarded as the "classics"

---

17. Shaw 2002; Dee 2013.

18. Gautschy 2011 calculates 1872 BC as a possible date.

19. Posener 1956.

of Egyptian literature, these texts were part of the cultural background of every educated Egyptian.

For over half a century, Posener's views were central to mainstream Egyptology, and new "propagandistic" sources were occasionally added to his list. Wolfgang Schenkel, for instance, drew attention to a newly discovered temple inscription from Elephantine dating to the reign of Senusret I, which could be justly claimed to be of a propagandistic nature.[20] He contextualized this text by referring to the so-called Berlin Leather Roll, a copy of a building inscription from the temple of Heliopolis,[21] and to an inscription in the temple of Tod, which displays Senusret I as a pious king driving illegal occupants out of the temple and restoring its cult.[22] An impressive collection of texts concerning political aspects of the first two reigns of the Twelfth Dynasty could thus be singled out, and Posener's interpretation of these as political propaganda presented a brilliantly argued interpretative model for them. This model has served as a key to the interpretation of the history of the early Twelfth Dynasty.[23]

Since the turn of the century, however, researchers have been voicing growing opposition to Posener's approach. One line of thought, advocated in Richard B. Parkinson's study of Middle Kingdom literature, was to focus on the literary qualities of the texts rather than their alleged political messages.[24] As a result the texts were no longer used in a direct sense as historical sources. Another important consideration in the current debate is that many literary works traditionally attributed to the Middle Kingdom are not actually attested in that period, and only appear (and then frequently) in the Eighteenth Dynasty. Because of this, Andrea Gnirs has argued that texts like the "Prophecy of Neferti," the

20. Schenkel 1975; 1999.

21. Schenkel 1975: 110.

22. Barbotin and Clère 1991.

23. E.g., Obsomer 1995.

24. Parkinson 2002.

"Teaching of Amenemhat I," and other texts, were composed in the early Eighteenth Dynasty.[25]

A sophisticated contribution to this debate is Andreas Stauder's attempt to define linguistic dating criteria for the text corpus of Middle Egyptian literature.[26] Explicitly distancing himself from a unilinear model of linguistic development, he has developed an impressive approach to historical linguistics. His argument leads in the same direction as Gnirs' studies. Most importantly for the present chapter, he hypothesizes that texts like the "Prophecy of Neferti" and the "Teaching of Amenemhat I" probably date to the early Eighteenth Dynasty (see chapter 26 in volume 3). However, based on a strict application of his linguistic criteria, the *terminus ante quem non* for the first of these texts is more cautiously set in the mid-Thirteenth Dynasty and for the latter in the late Twelfth Dynasty.[27] Even so, the implication is that these texts were written long after they could have been relevant as early Middle Kingdom royal propaganda.

Gnirs has argued in detail why authors writing in the early New Kingdom drew so much inspiration from the reigns of Amenemhat I and Senusret I. In a first step, she pointed out that many of the concerns expressed in early Eighteenth Dynasty royal inscriptions are remarkably similar (even down to the use of specific vocabulary) to texts like the "Teaching of Amenemhat I." This text would accordingly have been written roughly contemporarily with the royal inscriptions referred to. She bases this on the problematic royal succession in the early Eighteenth Dynasty. The intention of the inscriptions was to convey the impression that the royal family pursued sensible policies to warrant a stable succession. In the words of Gnirs,

> The Teaching of King Amenemhat ... originated in the same frame of mind. This literary work shows to which dire consequences

25. E.g., Gnirs 2013a; 2013b.

26. Stauder 2013.

27. Stauder 2013: 337–497; 508; 511.

renouncement of this process of governance might lead, and at the same time it expresses a warning against the claims to power to which this might lead on the part of the court and administrative elites and even of members of the royal family.[28]

Although Gnirs avoids using the term, it is clear she means to say that the early Twelfth Dynasty royal succession is here presented in a discourse of Eighteenth Dynasty political propaganda.

This is of course a conceivable alternative to Posener's propaganda model, but the use of the "Teaching of Amenemhat I" for this purpose could only have been successful if the intended audience was well-informed about events that had occurred almost five centuries earlier, which would imply that traditions about early Twelfth Dynasty politics were still kept alive. Of course the "Story of Sinuhe" was known, and it mentions the death of Amenemhat I, but this text can hardly be taken as the sole source of inspiration for the authors of the conspiracy discourse. This leads to an important point. Posener's hypothesis implies that a number of well-known literary texts already existed long before they made their first appearance in the record. While this is a weak spot in his reasoning, Gnirs' interpretation also assumes that Egyptians of the early Eighteenth Dynasty had an awareness of early Twelfth Dynasty politics. If this was not based on the kind of early text transmission that Posener considered likely, what was their source of information? This point is not addressed by Gnirs.

A further issue is that Gnirs and Stauder emphasize the extent to which the "Teaching of Amenemhat I" is thematically similar to early Eighteenth Dynasty royal inscriptions. Although these similarities are in some cases undeniable, the surviving number of Middle Kingdom royal temple inscriptions is vanishingly small. There is no way to rule out the possibility that early Twelfth Dynasty royal inscriptions reflected the same themes, and that these were taken up again in the early New Kingdom.

Moreover, in the case of the "Teaching of Amenemhat I," Stauder's linguistic dating evidence is fairly restricted. His main point concerns

---

28. Gnirs 2013a: 168.

a grammatical phenomenon which occurs in only one passage (and may reflect a later adaptation of just that passage). Additionally, the chronological importance he attributes to it can be challenged.[29] This does not imply that the early dating of the "Teaching of Amenemhat I" is a fact; it is only a hypothesis I consider likely. It cannot explain why attestations of the "Teaching" only start to appear in the early Eighteenth Dynasty, but it sustains Posener's explanation of why this particular text was written in the first place, which is more convincing to me than the one proposed by Gnirs and implicitly followed by Stauder.

That strong efforts were made to disseminate a positive image of Senusret I in literary form is supported by inscriptions on contemporary temple walls. The first example is a text in the Satet temple at Elephantine. Formally, this building takes the form of a "divine booth," of which the outer walls were inscribed with text columns presenting a positive account of this king in connection with the cult of the goddess (figure 19.2).[30] According to a recent architectural reconstruction, the Montu temple built at Tod during the reign of Senusret I had a form closely similar to that of the Satet temple (figure 19.3).[31] The text columns on the outside of this temple describe protective measures made to ensure its cult, as well as a punitive action against illegal settlers there.[32] A large temple with the same form was erected by Senusret I at Karnak. A fragment of an inscription from this temple records a meeting

---

29. It concerns the use of the passive morpheme *.tu* with verbs expressing non-agentive, non-dynamic events in the "Teaching of Amenemhat I", § 11c–d (Adrom 2006: 65–66), for instance *en heqertu em renputi* ("People did not hunger in my years"). Fundamental criticism against Stauder's interpretation of this grammatical form as a dating criterion, as well as against the redating of many literary texts to the early New Kingdom, was recently voiced by Jansen-Winkeln 2017.

30. Schenkel 1975; 1999: 68–74. For the building, see Larché 2018: pl. 23.

31. Larché 2018: pl. 22.

32. Barbotin and Clère 1991. Buchberger 2006 dated the text to the reign of Sety I, (1290–1279 BC) but his criteria are unconvincing and do not consider the architecture and archaeology of the temples at Elephantine, Tod, and Karnak; see also Gabolde 2018: 224–233.

FIGURE 19.2. Reconstruction of the façade of the Satet temple on Elephantine island, reign of Senusret I. Adapted from Larché 2018: pl. 21.

text's upper limit

cut doorframe with
incised Ptolemaic
decoration

protruding surface of doorframe, covered by Ptolemaic pavement

final column of text

text in columns

procession of the Nile deities

0   1   2   3   4   5 m

FIGURE 19.3.   Reconstruction of the façade of the Montu temple at Tod of the reign of Senusret I. Adapted from Larché 2018: pl. 22.

between Senusret I and his courtiers; one may assume that some benefits for the temple of Amun were dealt with in the now missing part of the text.[33] The scant remains of the annals of Senusret I from the temple of Heliopolis stipulate that he also refurbished that temple during at least five successive years; these works included the erection of two obelisks, of which one is still standing today.[34]

The inscriptions from Elephantine, Tod, Karnak, and Heliopolis must reflect a conscious policy on Senusret I's part to refurbish temples across Egypt. The Heliopolitan building program is probably also hinted at in the Berlin Leather Roll.[35] Although this document is explicitly dated to the reign of Amenhotep II, it contains a text that purports to be a building inscription from the reign of Senusret I. It had always been accepted as an Eighteenth Dynasty copy of a Middle Kingdom original until Philippe Derchain proposed that effectively it had been composed in the early Eighteenth Dynasty.[36] However, we have just seen that Twelfth Dynasty sources document a large building project by Senusret I at Heliopolis, just like the Berlin Leather Roll. Moreover, the relief fragments from Karnak contain *exact* parallels to the opening passage of the Berlin Leather Roll. Both texts refer to the same kind of court session in connection with the building of a temple. The most straightforward explanation is that a general format for building inscriptions was used under Senusret I, and that the New Kingdom scribe composing the Berlin Leather Roll copied an original inscription of Senusret I that was still visible at that time. The Berlin Leather Roll must therefore be very close to an early Middle Kingdom original.[37] That such copying took place is clear from Luc Gabolde's recent study of the early Karnak temple. Here there is no doubt that

---

33. Habachi 1985: 352–359; Gabolde 2018: 224–233.

34. Postel and Régen 2005; Díaz Hernandez 2019.

35. de Buck 1938; Goedicke 1994 (including photographs).

36. Derchain 1992.

37. Similarly Piccato 1997.

inscriptions from the time of Senusret I were carefully copied during the early New Kingdom.[38]

From the perspective of a "view from within" the Middle Kingdom, an important preliminary question is how these texts were used. Who wrote them, for which audience, and for what context? These questions also have ramifications for what the communication was intended to achieve.

As Richard B. Parkinson has pointed out, literary texts were probably meant for public recitation. The fact that extant Middle Kingdom manuscripts of the stories of the Eloquent Peasant and Sinuhe probably derived from the personal libraries of members of the administrative class supports his idea that these compositions were recited in private contexts.[39] However, the fact that such texts ended up in private archives in the course of the Middle Kingdom cannot be taken as implying that the original author had this use in mind. Focusing first on the "Story of Sinuhe," an interesting feature of this text is that it adopts the model of tomb autobiographies. Most scholars have interpreted the text as a fictional autobiography,[40] but Posener felt less certain on this point. He explicitly leaves open the possibility that Sinuhe may have really existed, that he had a tomb at Lisht, and that a version of the story was inscribed there as his autobiography.[41] This suggestion has never played a major role in interpreting Sinuhe, perhaps because of the extremely original formulation of the text, which makes it stand out as an exception among tomb autobiographies. However, the outer walls of the mastaba of a man called Khnumhotep at Dahshur were inscribed with a text, which according to James P. Allen was not a normal funerary autobiography, but "was composed as a literary work, with grammatical constructions such as are characteristic of Middle

---

38. Gabolde 2018: 224–233. For early Eighteenth Dynasty "citations" of Middle Kingdom art, see Laboury 2013.

39. Parkinson 2002: 66–81.

40. E.g., Parkinson 1997: 21–26.

41. Posener 1956: 91–92.

Kingdom literary stories like the story of Sinuhe."[42] Here we have a real tomb of a courtier in a royal necropolis, of exactly the kind Sinuhe would have had if he really existed. This example suggests two things. In the first place, funerary autobiographies in the highest court circles could employ literary formats. Second, the "Story of Sinuhe" used this very form, arguably (although this cannot be proven) because it was a real tomb autobiography.

This raises the question of what funerary autobiographies were for in the first place. It is commonly assumed that such texts had the aim of "profiling" the tomb owner, but how did they achieve this purpose? Although this topic urgently needs more study, their location in tomb chapels suggests they were meant for cultic recitation. Parkinson suggested this originally, although only in passing.[43] The so-called *appels aux vivants* ("addresses to the living") in tomb chapels imply that passersby should recite the offering formulae on the tomb walls—a cult act.[44] Occasional passages in autobiographies point in the same direction. An example from the stele of Montuuser says this about the funerary autobiography:

> As regards anyone who shall *hear* this stele which is among the living, they shall say: "It is the truth!" (. . .) Moreover, as regards any scribe who will *recite* this stele, all people will approach him. . . .[45]

Likewise, Julie Stauder-Porchet has plausibly argued that one of the Old Kingdom precursors of Middle Kingdom autobiographies was systematically associated with the false door, an argument which induced the present author to argue that such biographies could have been recited

---

42. Allen 2009, citation from p. 18.

43. Parkinson 2002: 79.

44. For an overview of Middle Kingdom *appels aux vivants*, see Ilin-Tomich 2015.

45. Sethe 1928: 80, 1–4. Italics by the present author.

as part of the offering cult in tomb chapels.[46] Alexandra von Lieven has also suggested, albeit for a later period, that autobiographies may have been used in ritual performances at the tombs.[47] To sum up, the content of funerary autobiographies may well have been communicated through recitation during public celebrations at the tomb. Therefore, the themes raised would be of a nature that would be considered relevant to this context. In the case of the "Story of Sinuhe," it is likely that a similar theme was embedded in the narrative, even if it was not a real funerary autobiography.

Temple inscriptions were also applied in a context intended for ritual display, and therefore it could be argued that the examples from the time of Senusret I mentioned earlier derive from a recitative temple context. The text from the Berlin Leather Roll, in fact, describes a session in which the king addresses his courtiers and shares with them his intention to build a temple in Heliopolis. The fragmentary text from Karnak probably had the same format. In these cases the text may record for posterity how the king communicated about his temple building policy to the elite. The damaged nature of the texts from Elephantine and Tod makes their interpretation more hazardous, but it is at least conceivable that a similar communicative pattern prevailed. By recording such texts on walls, however, they could serve more than one purpose. As was the case with the autobiographical text of Khnumhotep at Dahshur, these temple texts were applied to the outer walls of buildings and were therefore available to the general public (to the extent they were able to read). They could be read (recited?) again, or could be copied (as evidently happened in the case of the Berlin Leather Roll), and this may have led to alternative means of circulating the information they contained. There was clearly a significant collection of such documents dating to the reign of Senusret I, and it is conceivable that this material served as a source of inspiration in later periods, either by copying these texts or by the composition of new texts inspired by the lore of the early Middle Kingdom.

---

46. Stauder-Porchet 2017: 179–183, 311–316; Willems 2019: 220–221.

47. von Lieven 2010: 66–67.

19.4. From nomarchs to monarchs: the Eleventh Dynasty

The previous section has concentrated considerably on the extent to which the two first pharaohs of the Twelfth Dynasty still stirred the imagination of the early Eighteenth Dynasty. However, outside of literary discourse, an earlier king enjoyed the even greater distinction of being venerated as a "saint."[48] This was Mentuhotep II Nebhepetra, who for example heads a listing of kings in the Ramesseum together with Meni (Menes in the Greek tradition), who had united Egypt for the first time, and Ahmose, the first pharaoh of the Eighteenth Dynasty, who had defeated the Hyksos.[49] Mentuhotep II's reputation obviously rested on his role in reuniting the Theban and the Herakleopolitan realms after what is today called the First Intermediate Period.

Mentuhotep was a descendant of a line of nomarchs who were in charge of the fourth nome of Upper Egypt in the early First Intermediate Period, but who, in the course of time, conquered several adjoining nomes and adopted the royal style. From this point onward, they are referred to as the Eleventh Dynasty.[50] It is historically relevant to briefly dwell on this background. The Eleventh Dynasty was not of royal stock, and its realm covered only the southern half of Egypt, the northern part being held for a long time by a royal family whose origins Manetho attributed to the town of Herakleopolis, and which he designated as the Ninth and Tenth Dynasties.[51] This contrast between the "royal" Ninth and Tenth Dynasties and the "nomarchal" Eleventh Dynasty may explain some of the differences between the two realms.

---

48. El-Enany 2003.

49. El-Enany 2003: 173–174 (doc. 13).

50. For the First Intermediate Period, see chapter 12 in this volume. For some of the achievements of Mentuhotep II, see Gestermann 1987 and cf. chapter 22.

51. Waddell 1948: 61–65.

Late Old Kingdom and First Intermediate Period local rulers (like "nomarchs") were often buried in tombs designed with a hierarchical structure: within one building, the ruler and his (mostly male) retinue were buried together. The architecture of the different burials seems to reflect the rank of their occupants: the ruler had the largest tomb shaft, his dependents had burial places of different sizes commensurate with their relative status.[52] The *saff* tomb complexes of the first Theban kings of the Eleventh Dynasty display the same arrangement, but on a gigantic scale.[53]

Before continuing our historical account, it is interesting to dwell on the social realities underlying these hierarchically structured tombs. The size difference in the burial apartments they contain must have reflected a difference in status, but the fact that differently sized tombs formed part of one complex betrays something more important than the trivial fact that hierarchical differences existed in Egyptian society. It suggests that the tomb complexes brought together members of one social group, which was internally characterized by differences in status. According to a prominent model in sociological interpretation, this must reflect a modular organization of Egyptian society in units of similar structure but of progressively larger size and more complex composition as the rank of the head of the unit increased. An interesting account of this was put forward by Mark Lehner, who argues that the social units in question are "households," in Egyptian called *per*.[54] The title of Lehner's paper, "The Fractal House of Pharaoh," captures the essence of his idea. According to Lehner, Egypt as a whole could be considered the pharaoh's *per*. His highest officials would have had their own *per*s, which on the one hand were part of pharaoh's *per*, but which on the other encompassed the *per*s of their subordinate officials, who, in turn, were at the head of a number of still smaller *per*s. Egyptian society as a whole, in the Old and Middle Kingdoms, would have been a network of such nested

---

52. Seidlmayer 1990: 403–405.

53. Di. Arnold 1976: 19–44.

54. Lehner 2000.

households.[55] In his view, *pers* had a "fractal" form: they differed in size and complexity, but were (like fractals in mathematics) governed by the same formal principles.

In Lehner's view, this model pairs morphological consistency with social dynamism. Although all *pers*, in his terminology, are formally consistent, their development would have been highly dynamic, and dependent on the degree to which a particular *per* would be successful in realizing its objectives. The heads of some *pers* would, under changing political, economic, or environmental conditions, react more adequately than others, leading to an expansion of some *pers* to the detriment of others, and this occurred at all social levels simultaneously. Successful high-range *pers* could in the course of time gain regional supremacy, and very successful heads could even attain royal status. According to Lehner, this is precisely what happened in the "Qena Bend" of southern Upper Egypt before the Theban Eleventh Dynasty rose to power.

This model seems to a large extent to do justice to early Egyptian realities, except in one point. The term "household" normally designates a dwelling unit.[56] Richer residential compounds consisting of different living units within one surrounding wall may also have been conceived of as a *per*. The "mansions" in the town of Lahun are of this kind.[57] It is easy to interpret such compounds in terms of Lehner's model.

However, besides the mansions, the town of Lahun, which was founded under Senusret II, displays numerous smaller houses of different types, which are neatly grouped together in different areas (cf. chapter 22 in this volume). As Barry Kemp has demonstrated, a significant difference between mansions and smaller townhouses is that only the former are provided with granaries. The smaller houses only rarely have a small silo. In view of this lack of storage for what was, in Egypt,

---

55. Similar conceptions lie at the root of Rainer Nutz's model of Egypt's Middle Kingdom economy; Nutz 2014.

56. For a discussion of the anthropological term applied to Egyptian contexts, see Willems 2015: 464–470.

57. For a recent discussion, see Moeller 2016: 271–290.

the most basic means of subsistence, Kemp argues that the inhabitants of the small houses were regularly provided with small quantities of cereals by the inhabitants of the mansions.[58] Even though the inhabitants of the smaller houses may have participated in agricultural tasks,[59] the fact that their houses did not contain storage facilities suggests that Kemp was probably right. Nadine Moeller suggests that the occupants of the smaller houses may have been part of the "households" of the heads of the mansions. However, their houses do not lie within the mansions, it is not clear which small houses belonged to which mansions, and moreover it is conceivable that the occupants of the smaller houses were linked to the heads of more than one mansion. This makes it unrealistic to assign them to the same "household." In my view, a more realistic interpretation would be that the small houses (*per*) constitute households in their own right, but that they are also linked to the mansions by bonds of patronage.

The hierarchical tombs discussed by Stefan Seidlmayer offer strong confirmation that the lower-status clientèle buried there had not always lived in their master's households during life. This is suggested by the archaeology of First Intermediate Period rural cemeteries in the regions of Aswan and Qau-Matmar. Here, the hierarchical tombs of the masters seem to have included the burials of their male staff; away from the monumental tombs of the masters, in smaller rural cemeteries, on the other hand, the largest tombs display a surprising lack of older male occupants. Here, females predominate. Seidlmayer's convincing explanation is that older males worked for their masters, and, upon their deaths, were not buried with the members of their own households, but in their master's tomb.[60]

This reinterpretation slightly adapts Lehner's model: not all smaller-size households are parts of higher-order households. Moreover, for this reason it may be incorrect to interpret the Egyptian state as a whole

58. Kemp 2006: 211–221.

59. Moeller 2015: 285.

60. Seidlmayer 1987.

as the king's "household." Many smaller *pers* were distinct households. The example of Lahun may suggest that their heads were tied by bonds of patronage to the heads of the larger households. Nevertheless, the dynamic interplay between the households of patrons and clients that Lehner's model implies seems to offer an adequate account of how Egyptian society functioned from the late Old Kingdom to the Middle Kingdom. Autobiographical texts from Middle Kingdom tombs reflect this social network profoundly.

Clientelist relationships of the kind just discussed have a strong economic dimension: the clients work for the patron, the patron cares for the clients. However, these relationships are often underpinned by symbolic notions which make the exceptional position of the patron seem self-evident and inescapable.[61] This can operate at different levels at the same time. Royals may deploy procedures that create connections between themselves and society at large (and particularly with the highest administrators); high officials like nomarchs may act in a similar fashion in their own local environment. Public manifestations of different kinds can be instrumental in creating and perpetualizing such social bonds. Such phenomena are very characteristic of the Middle Kingdom in general, and also of the Eleventh Dynasty, which we are now discussing. Before proceeding, it should be pointed out that, within clientelist networks, the wealth of different households can vary considerably. However, it is doubtful whether it is correct to designate the economic middle range as a "middle class," as has been proposed.[62] This concept, which is rooted in modern Western society, conjures up notions that seem alien to the social patterns discussed here.[63]

Let us now turn to the late First Intermediate Period *saff* tombs at el-Tarif. These huge structures encompass the burials of not only members of the royal family, but also dozens of members of the royal court. These

---

61. E.g., Bourdieu 1977: 178–180.

62. Richards 2005.

63. For a similarly cautious attitude, see chapter 22 in this volume.

are hierarchical tomb complexes. However, in addition to the secondary graves within the royal *saff* tombs, there are a large number of secondary *saff* tombs in the empty spaces between the royal ones. These latter are considerably smaller than those of the kings, but much larger than the secondary burials in the royal *saff* tombs. This distribution may reveal something significant about the composition of the cemetery population. It would seem likely that the royal *saff* tombs included the burials of a large number of palace servants. By contrast, the second-rank *saff* tombs may have belonged to the higher administrative echelons of the Theban state.

The emergence of the large burial ground of el-Tarif, situated on the Theban West Bank, for both kings and elite administrators, is remarkable since, as with the rise of the Eleventh Dynasty to royal status, nomarchal cemeteries seem to disappear in the rest of the Theban realm, that is, the Upper Egyptian nomes I–IX. Although there are occasional exceptions such as Hetepi, who was buried in el-Kab, his tomb stele explains that he was in charge under King Intef II of not just one nome, but the seven southernmost nomes of Egypt.[64] Put together, the evidence suggests that nome rule had given way to a centralized Theban administration whose officials were mostly buried in el-Tarif. A nome-style of rule seems to have encompassed the entire Theban realm as one administrative district. Within the nomes, lower-ranking officials designated as *heqa hut* ("administrator of a domain") were instituted.[65]

The upstart Eleventh Dynasty kings' rise to power seems to have gone hand in hand with a remarkable degree of public display. Old Kingdom pyramid complexes had been highly secluded places. The valley and pyramid temples, and the causeways connecting these, were surrounded by high walls. Accordingly, the rituals that took place inside could not be observed by outsiders. By contrast, the great First Intermediate Period *saff* tomb complexes were mostly open-air structures, and it has been

---

64. Gabra 1976.

65. Willems 2014: 33–53.

argued that the "dikes" surrounding them may have served as tribunes for the population to attend what was taking place inside.[66] Moreover, at the same time, the cult of Amun was instituted in the new temple at Karnak, opposite el-Tarif on the east bank of the Nile.[67] Perhaps the temple and the royal cemetery were built where they were on purpose. In this way, processions could link the temple cult with the cult of the dead kings in el-Tarif.[68] This happened at other locations as well: the processional cult of Osiris at Abydos, which has a distinct royal aspect, emerged around the same time.[69] But these processions did not have a solely royal dimension. The processions at Thebes went to the royal cemetery, but this was also the cemetery where the administrative class was buried. What we see emerging was a royal and divine festivity which was, at the same time, a funerary festivity for the higher echelons of society. The layout of such cemeteries unmistakably bears the imprint of a clientelist society.

We have just seen how, in the Theban realm, the administrative rank of the nomarchs seems to have been suppressed in the late First Intermediate Period. In the Herakleopolitan realm, nothing similar happened. These kings seem to have considered the nomarchs to be allies. Those at Asyut even played a key role in defending the Herakleopolitan kingdom against the Thebans.[70]

This was the power balance when Mentuhotep II ascended the throne. Meanwhile, the Thebans had gained power in all of southern Egypt and in large parts of Middle Egypt south of Asyut. Probably shortly before his thirteenth regnal year, Mentuhotep II finally succeeded in taking over power in the north as well.[71] Egypt was reunited. This

---

66. Willems 2020.

67. For the early temple at Karnak, see Gabolde 2018.

68. Rummel 2013.

69. Willems 2020.

70. Inscriptions in Tombs II, III, and particularly IV: Franke 1987; El-Khadragy 2012; Willems 2014: 44–45 n. 135.

71. Gestermann 2008; Willems 2014: 87.

resounding political feat has often been attributed to a military victory. There is nothing unlikely about such a scenario, but no incontrovertible evidence supports this hypothesis. It is also possible that the nomarchs in the Herakleopolitan realm simply changed their political allegiance in the context of growing pressure from Thebes. This at least would explain why, in contrast to the situation in southern Egypt, a nomarchal type of rule remained in place in Middle Egypt. Here, we witness a rapid growth of nomarchal cemeteries in places like Asyut, Meir,[72] Deir el-Bersha, and Beni Hasan. Also, recent work on the tomb inscriptions of the nomarch Ahanakht I at Deir el-Bersha suggests that this official not only held regional responsibilities, but was also appointed vizier, probably in addition to a vizier who simultaneously held office at Thebes. A biographical inscription in Ahanakht I's tomb suggests that the rationale underlying this policy was that a former Herakleopolitan nomarch was integrated within the Theban administration to keep the nomarchs of northern Egypt in check.[73]

Few historical inscriptions remain from the reign of Mentuhotep II. The most eloquent testimony of his policy is his building activity, which almost exclusively concerned temples in the southern part of Egypt. On Elephantine, the already ancient, pre-formal Satet temple was completely rebuilt in formal style, an operation which also led to significant adaptations in the surrounding area.[74] A new temple was built at Gebelein,[75] and another at Abydos; the inscriptions found there make clear that in the process, the landscape in which the Osiris processions were staged was adapted in its entirety.[76] But the greatest of all was the religious project at Thebes itself, where the existing processional landscape between

---

72. Vogt 2019 demonstrates that a number of undecorated but large rock tombs exist at Meir that probably predate the well-known decorated rock tombs, of which the earliest probably dates to the reign of Amenemhat I.

73. Willems 2007: 83–113; 2014: 76–98.

74. Kaiser 1993: 151–152.

75. Fiore Marochetti 2010.

76. Damarany, Abd el-Raziq, Okasha, Wegner, Cahail, and Wegner 2015.

Karnak and el-Tarif was expanded by a new processional tract to Deir el-Bahri, where Mentuhotep built his huge funerary temple (cf. chapter 22). In this way, he created the processional axis between Karnak and Deir el-Bahri, which was used for the Valley Festival.[77] From the outset, this festival had a funerary dimension, because, in addition to being dedicated to Hathor and Amun, the temple of Deir el-Bahri stood on top of the royal tomb. This means that the Amun procession to the west linked the god to the king. Moreover, monumental tombs for the highest political elite were carved into the desert slopes overlooking the processional road. This suggests that the divine procession was not only conceived of as a feature of the king's funerary cult. The Valley Festival was simultaneously an occasion from which private individuals could benefit.[78]

It has long been considered likely that all or most of the private tombs built in this area belonged to the highest officials of the court of Mentuhotep II and his immediate Eleventh Dynasty successors.[79] In this, a crucial role was played by Winlock's discovery of an unfinished temple in the valley immediately to the south of Deir el-Bahri (figure 19.4). Herbert Winlock argued that this building would have had a similar form to that of the temple of Mentuhotep II at Deir el-Bahri. Moreover, beneath it, Sir Robert Mond had earlier discovered a tomb of royal dimensions.[80] This led to the idea that this was an unfinished funerary temple for that king's immediate successor, Mentuhotep III Sankhkara.

A powerful support for this argument is the tomb of Meketra (TT 280). This tomb was oriented toward the temple, so he must have been a contemporary of the king who built this newly discovered temple. Since Meketra is referred to in inscriptions from late in the reign of Mentuhotep II, Winlock hypothesized that he survived Mentuhotep

---

77. Winlock 1947: 85–88 argued that the Valley Festival only started in the reign of Amenemhat I, but the temple of Mentuhotep II in Deir el-Bahri already features a depiction of it; see Di. Arnold 1974: pl. 22–23.

78. Willems 2020.

79. E.g., Di. Arnold 1971: 39–48. This dating was accepted by Willems 1988: 109–114.

80. Mond 1905: 77–79.

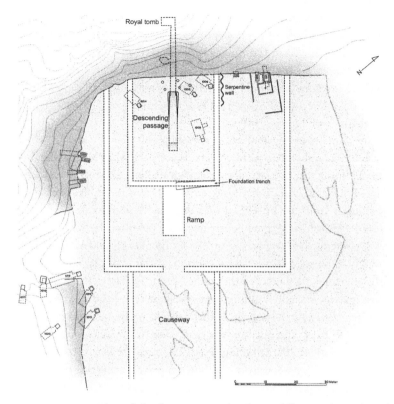

FIGURE 19.4. Plan of the funerary temple of a Middle Kingdom pharaoh (Mentuhotep III Sankhkara or Amenemhat I?) in the valley to the south of Deir el-Bahri. Adapted from Di. Arnold 2014: 25 fig. 9.

II and remained in service under Mentuhotep III, to whom the newly discovered temple would belong.[81] This reasoning was long accepted, and it offered a model for dating the early Middle Kingdom Theban officials. Broadly speaking, Meketra's term of office was assigned to the later years of Mentuhotep II and to Mentuhotep III; most officials

---

81. Winlock 1947: 51–53; 77–90.

buried in Deir el-Bahri can only be dated to the reign of Mentuhotep II, with some remaining in office later. Subsequently, there was the brief reign of Mentuhotep IV and (perhaps) a seven-year period of unrest, hinted at in the Turin Canon.[82] Then came the rule of Amenemhat I, who is known to have replaced the national capital at Thebes by the newly created one at Itj-tawy (Lisht). By this reasoning, all early Middle Kingdom court officials from Thebes automatically came to be regarded as late Eleventh Dynasty officials.

In 1991, however, Dorothea Arnold published an article which exerted great influence over interpretations of early Middle Kingdom history. Pointing to a number of archaeological and art-historical clues, she argued that the attribution of the temple to Mentuhotep III Sankhkara was highly unlikely. Instead, it was built by Amenemhat I before he moved to Lisht, where he constructed his pyramid. Accordingly, the royal court would have stayed in Thebes much longer than previously thought.[83] This led to a redating of some of the high officials who had formerly been attributed to the late Eleventh Dynasty. These included Meketra (whose tomb was oriented toward the temple now attributed to Amenemhat I), but also several other officials in Thebes, and indirectly also in Saqqara.[84] Included in this group was the vizier Ipi, in the forecourt of whose tomb the famous Heqanakht papyri were discovered. In the process, their dates were re-attributed from the late Eleventh Dynasty to the early reign of Senusret I.[85] Others have used Arnold's dating as a solid criterion for an early Middle Kingdom pottery chronology.[86] In view of the impact that Arnold's article had on perceptions of the early Middle Kingdom, her work can be justifiably called a game-changer.

---

82. Reconstructions in this tradition are Gestermann 1987: 30–31, 145–222; Willems 1988: 109–114.

83. Do. Arnold 1991.

84. Allen 1996; 2003.

85. Allen 2002.

86. Seiler 2012: 300–307.

However, the soundness of the arguments that led to the redating of the unfinished Theban temple has been questioned.[87] The problem with Arnold's analysis is that she nowhere provides a complete overview of the evidence. She only presents apodictic statements on the dating of various classes of objects, but only a small sample of these has been analyzed. Only a few cases are shown, for instance, of the pottery, and none in any detail. Remarkably, the information she provides on the so-called hemispherical cups does not allow the reader to apply the useful dating system based on vessel indices developed by Arnold herself.[88] She devised a similar proportion index system for comparing the body parts of funerary models, but this was based on only two pieces, the proportions of one of which contain an error.[89] The most damaging argument, however, was offered by Winlock. He noted that the graffiti of early Middle Kingdom priests involved in the celebrations of the Valley Festival were carved high in the hills separating Deir el-Bahri and the valley to its south. Most of these priests were involved not only in the cult of Mentuhotep II, but also in that of Mentuhotep III. Winlock argued that the priests sat on their high promontory on the lookout for the festival procession to arrive at the cult places of the two kings, and this supported his belief that the unfinished temple must have belonged to Mentuhotep III (figure 19.4).[90] Arnold rejected this conclusion, noting that since the temple was unfinished, it was unlikely a cult was ever celebrated there.[91] However, a completely finished, contemporary offering table was found at the site, which can only mean that some form of cult did indeed take place there. In view of the information provided by the graffiti, Winlock's suggestion that this must have been for Mentuhotep

---

87. Grajetzki 2003: 242; 2006: 29–30; Willems 1996: 23 n. 58; 2014: 169.

88. Do. Arnold 1988: 140–142 for dating by vessel indices; Do. Arnold 1991: 9–10 for the pottery.

89. Do. Arnold 1991: 25 and fig. 34. Arnold claims she bases her conclusions on "all extant wooden models of the late First Intermediate Period to the early Middle Kingdom," but she does not present any verifiable overview.

90. Winlock 1947: 77–90.

91. Do. Arnold 1991: 7–8.

III seems attractive.[92] Summing up the evidence, the unfinished temple must in all probability be assigned to a successor of Mentuhotep II, who could have been either Mentuhotep III, Mentuhotep IV, or the early Amenemhat I. Since this covers a period of only about twenty years, reliable archaeological dating criteria within this brief time frame must be deemed shaky, but the explicit reference to priests of Mentuhotep III in nearby graffiti tilts the balance in favor of Winlock's interpretation. Nothing points to Amenemhat I having undertaken activities here.

This has the effect that Meketra and a number of other high officials can be pushed back into the late Eleventh Dynasty again. James Allen has offered two important overviews of the early Middle Kingdom administration, also addressing the persons involved here. According to him, the most important government offices were three: the vizier, the steward (*imi-ra per*), and the royal treasurer (*imi-ra khetemet*).[93] Compressing the known officials in the shorter period advocated here is somewhat problematic as long as one assumes, with Allen, that only one vizier was in office at any particular moment. However, in this time period it is likely that the office was shared by different officials. The earliest case has already been referred to. This was Ahanakht I, nomarch of the Hare nome in Middle Egypt, who according to his tomb inscriptions was also appointed to the office of vizier. Arguably, he primarily had vizieral tasks in Middle and Lower Egypt, the area that Mentuhotep II had just taken over from the Herakleopolitans. Simultaneously, another vizier was probably in office in Thebes.[94]

Ahanakht I was probably followed as "northern" vizier by his successors in the Hare nome. This is certain in the case of the nomarch Nehri I and his son Kay.[95] What is interesting here is that Nehri and

92. A study with a full reassessment of the alleged funerary temple of Amenemhat I in western Thebes is under preparation by David Dujardin and the present author.

93. Allen 1996; 2003.

94. Willems 2007: 100–113; 2014: 96–98.

95. Hatnub Graffiti 16 and 24.

Kay, at least for a while, seem to have been viziers simultaneously.[96] This exceptional situation must be related to the equally exceptional political conditions prevailing in their time, about which more will be said later. In any case, since in the late Eleventh Dynasty there seem to have been parallel lines of viziers, it becomes easy to attribute the first six or seven viziers to the period between the unification of Egypt and the beginning of the Twelfth Dynasty.[97] The only problem surrounds the seventh vizier, Ipi. He owned the Theban Tomb 315 and was obviously a Theban vizier. It is known that another late Eleventh Dynasty vizier was Amenemhat, who is mentioned in texts dated to King Mentuhotep IV's second regnal year. If Ipi succeeded Amenemhat in office, as is often assumed, then it is likely that his tenure continued into the early reign of Amenemhat I.[98] But it cannot be ruled out that he preceded Amenemhat as vizier.

19.5. Amenemhat I

Despite a wealth of documentation dating back to the first king of the Twelfth Dynasty, very little is known with certainty about his reign. Textual evidence proves he had a father named Senusret and a mother called Neferet, and that he did not derive from the same family as the kings of the Eleventh Dynasty.[99] He is usually assumed to be the same person as the vizier Amenemhat, who we know to have been on an expedition to the Wadi Hammamat in the second year of Mentuhotep IV.[100] It has never become fully clear if this identification is correct, but it is

---

96. Willems 2007: 104–105.

97. Following the list drafted in Allen 2003: 21–25.

98. Thus already Allen 2003: 23; Grajetzki 2003: 242–244. In this case, the Heqanakht papers, which were found in a subsidiary tomb to that of Ipi, *must* postdate the late Eleventh Dynasty. However, Ipi's tomb was unfinished and he may have been in office for only a short time preceding the vizier Amenemhat, in which case the chronological debate is open again.

99. Di. Arnold 2015: 31 (with bibliography).

100. Couyat and Montet 1913: 77–78 (no. 110); 79–80 (no. 113); 98–100 (no. 192); 103 (no. 205).

Table 19.1. The two variants of Amenemhat's royal protocol

Royal Protocol	Version 1	Version 2
Horus name	*Sehetepibtawy* Who brings to peace the heart of the Two Lands	*Wehem-mesut* Repeater of births
Two Ladies name	*Sehetepibtawy* Who bring to peace the heart of the Two Lands	*Wehem-mesut* Repeater of births
Golden Horus name	*Sema* Unifier	*Wehem-mesut* Repeater of births
Prenomen	*Sehetepibra* Who brings to peace the heart of Ra	*Sehetepibra* Who brings to peace the heart of Ra
Nomen	*Amenemhat* Amun is at the forefront	*Amenemhat* Amun is at the forefront

not unlikely. The other main accomplishment of his reign was the move of his residence to Itj-tawy (Lisht), which would remain Egypt's capital until after the end of the Thirteenth Dynasty.[101] It was in the desert west of Lisht that he built his pyramid.[102]

Amenemhat's protocol was changed at least once, and since royal name strings often define a political program, this offers a first glimpse of the historical context. The two variants of his protocol are shown in table 19.1.[103]

The first version of the protocol, which emphasizes the need to pacify and unite the two lands, hints at a conflictual situation. The second, which was probably declared at a time after the country had been

---

101. Simpson 1963; Di. Arnold 1988: 14–15; Siesse 2019: 108–109.

102. Di. Arnold 2015; Jánosi 2016.

103. Postel 2004: 278–289.

reintegrated, presents the king as inaugurating a new era.[104] The king's "great names" clearly express the claim that Amenemhat overcame a period of political fragmentation. This may also underlie the text of the "Prophecy of Neferti," even if it was composed in the early Eighteenth Dynasty (see section 19.3).

The clearest indication of how we should conceive the political fragmentation faced by Amenemhat is provided by the autobiography in the tomb of the nomarch Khnumhotep I at Beni Hasan (Tomb 14). The text is barely legible, but it clearly concerns a conflict in the Nile valley. In tandem with Amenemhat I, Khnumhotep sailed southward to face the enemy troops, which consisted of "Asiatics" and Nubians. The king defeated the enemy and appointed Khnumhotep ruler of the town of Menat-Khufu as a reward. Later, he appointed him nomarch of the entire 16th Upper Egyptian nome. Khnumhotep's tomb depicts an Egyptian town being besieged by other Egyptians, clearly illustrating a situation described in the text.[105] Similar battle scenes are found in Tombs 15 and 17 at Beni Hasan, which probably also date to early in the reign of Amenemhat I.[106] The much later autobiography of Khnumhotep II affords more information about this period. It is here stated that Amenemhat I came to the 16th nome to reorganize the district administration by re-establishing the boundaries between the nomes.[107] This might also refer to regional conflicts, but since the text later says that subsequent kings did the same thing, this episode may instead describe a ritualized affirmation of state control.

Conditions very similar to those depicted in the biography of Khnumhotep I are described in Hatnub graffiti 14–32, written on the walls of the Hatnub alabaster quarries under Nehri I, a nomarch of the 15th Upper Egyptian nome.[108] Nehri refers to hostile incursions by Nubians, bedouins, and Upper and Lower Egyptians, forcing the

---

104. His name "Repeater of Births" has been linked to the instigation of a Renaissance, e.g. by Callender 2000.

105. Newberry 1893a: 85 and pl. XLV.

106. Newberry 1893b: pls. IV, XIII, XVI; for the date, see Willems 1985: 92–93

107. Newberry 1893a: pl. XXV, ll. 26–53; Kanawati and Evans 2014: pl. 110–111.

108. Anthes 1928: 32–68; Willems 1985; 2014: 79–87.

population of the town of Khemenu to seek refuge in a marsh area close to the city. Nehri relates these events to a "terrible fear of/for the royal palace" and claims to be fighting for the king. It has recently been plausibly argued that the regnal years 4, 5, 6, and 8 in the Nehri graffiti point to the reign of Amenemhat I.[109] These accounts therefore add detail to the allusions to conflict in Amenemhat's first royal protocol and to Khnumhotep I's autobiography. Hints at the involvement of Upper and Lower Egyptians, Nubians, Asiatics, and bedouins moreover indicate that the conflict must have been massive. Amenemhat I, the vizier Nehri, and the local big man Khnumhotep were probably part of a larger alliance of Egyptian administrators. Whom they were facing is less easy to tell. The texts only refer anonymously to a "he," and a still unpublished fragment from Nehri's tomb autobiography may also refer to an anonymous female opponent. Neither do we know when the conflict erupted. It may have been caused by Amenemhat I's aspirations to kingship; it may also be that the conflict had already started before that, during the last reigns of the Eleventh Dynasty.

It has been argued that two graffiti in Nubia mentioning the royal names Qakara-In(tef) and Iyibkhentra may refer to some of Amenemhat's opponents, although the matter is far from clear.[110] Another rival to Amenemhat I, either before or just after the latter's coronation, may be the ephemeral king "the Horus Sankhibtawy the king of Upper and Lower Egypt Sankhibra" mentioned on an architrave from a tomb at Heliopolis, but this might also be part of an otherwise unattested early protocol of Amenemhat I.[111]

The conflicts with Asiatics and bedouins hinted at in the texts from Beni Hasan and Hatnub seem to have stirred a protective measure: the construction of the "Walls of the Ruler" mentioned in the "Story of Sinuhe" and the "Prophecy of Neferti." According to the "Story of Sinuhe" (B15–17), these walls were "built to repel the Asiatics"; they probably

---

109. Gestermann 2008.

110. Postel 2004: 379–384; Grajetzki 2006: 26–28.

111. Ilin-Tomich 2015.

consisted of a string of watchtowers barring access from Palestine into the eastern Nile delta. One of the establishments in the hinterland of this defensive system has recently been excavated in Ezbet Rushdi, at a place where Senusret III later built a *ka*-house for Amenemhat I.[112]

We will now turn to the issue of Amenemhat I's activities at Itj-tawy. We have seen earlier that the hypothesis that he started to build a funerary temple at Thebes is not supported by concrete evidence, and we favor Winlock's idea that this building actually dates to the reign of Mentuhotep III. It is certain, however, that he built a pyramid complex at Itj-tawy (Lisht), which has recently been published.[113] This structure includes numerous reused blocks from earlier pyramids, dating to both the Old and Middle Kingdoms.[114] Surprisingly, the Middle Kingdom blocks incorporate part of a huge false door of Amenemhat I himself. This has led to Dieter Arnold's remarkable suggestion that Amenemhat I built an earlier pyramid but had it dismantled almost immediately upon completion.[115] The inscriptions from this building already refer to Amenemhat I as Wehem-mesut, and so must have been carved after Amenemhat's second protocol was introduced.

The building history of Amenemhat I's pyramid has played a significant role in interpreting the transfer of power from Amenemhat I to Senusret I. The "Story of Sinuhe" (R5) dates the demise of Amenemhat I to his thirtieth regnal year. Also, the lunette of Stele Cairo CG 20516 seems to directly associate two different year dates: Amenemhat I's Year 30 and Senusret I's Year 10. This has led to the assumption that a ten-year co-regency existed between the two kings.[116] It has even been assumed that co-regency was the characteristic mode of power transfer in the

---

112. Czerny 2015: 446 and *passim*.

113. Di. Arnold 2015; Jánosi 2016.

114. Jánosi 2016.

115. Di. Arnold 2015: 1, 7–9, pl. 16–17.

116. Murnane 1977: 1–5.

Middle Kingdom, and that the case of Amenemhat I and Senusret I was the first example.[117]

This idea was generally accepted when Robert Delia published a reassessment of the evidence, which, in his view, justified serious doubts regarding all Middle Kingdom examples. In the present case, the fact that Stele Cairo CG 20516 does not use the word for "regnal year" (*renpet-sep*), but instead the word for "year" (*renpet*), suggested to Delia that it indicates the number of years the stele owner lived under the two kings.[118] From the moment of publication, this issue has been hotly debated, with many authors supporting Delia's point of view and others decidedly rejecting it.[119] In fairness, it must be said that both sides have mustered strong arguments.

The strongest arguments favoring the co-regency derive from the pyramids of Amenemhat I and Senusret I. None of the control notes on building blocks in Senusret I's pyramid predates his Year 10.[120] In contrast, early evidence of Senusret I was found in his father's pyramid. One piece of evidence often referred to in this connection is a control note in Amenemhat's pyramid that contains a reference to a Year 1. This could not refer to Amenemhat's first regnal year, since this date would have been too early in his reign to have begun setting the building blocks of the pyramid's superstructure. Therefore, it would most likely refer to Year 1 of Senusret I, who would have taken responsibility for the construction of his father's pyramid from the start of their joint rule.[121] Moreover, the pyramid temple of Amenemhat saw two building phases. In the later Building Phase B, blocks were used from an earlier temple (Building Phase A) whose inscriptions mention Amenemhat I and Senusret I together. There is no indication that Building Phase B postdated the construction of the rest of Amenemhat I's pyramid. This suggests that

---

117. Murnane 1977: 244.

118. Delia 1982.

119. Pro, e.g., Obsomer 1995; contra, e.g., Jansen-Winkeln 1997.

120. F. Arnold 1990: 30–32.

121. E.g., Di. Arnold 2015: 1–2.

Building Phase A was completed during Amenemhat's and Senusret's co-regency, that in the final years of their co-regency, the temple of Building Phase A was torn down, and that the blocks were reused in the temple of Building Phase B. This theory is based on the assumption that, during the co-regency, the junior partner was responsible for finishing his father's pyramid complex and that, as a result of this, work on his own pyramid could not begin until his Year 10, when the co-regency was over.[122]

These arguments are tempting, but not conclusive. Senusret I's major temple building projects at Karnak and Heliopolis date from early in his reign, so he did have a sizable workforce available in his first ten years which could have been, but was not, assigned to his pyramid. The argument based on the Year 1 control note found within the superstructure of the pyramid of Amenemhat I is not compelling either. Since this pyramid contains many blocks taken from earlier buildings, the control note mentioning Year 1 could have come from any one of them. The third argument, based on the building history of the pyramid temple, is currently the strongest, but it is not compelling, and equally strong evidence favors the hypothesis that no co-regency occurred. For instance, the "Teaching of Amenemhat I" does not suggest a co-regency had started when the king died. We can only conclude that the debate is currently undecided.

19.6. Senusret I

Like his father, Senusret I chose Lisht as the site for his pyramid, and, with a forty-five-year reign, he had ample time to finish this monument. In a historical chapter, architectural history is not a major concern, but one aspect of his funerary complex deserves to be highlighted. By returning to the pyramid form, Amenemhat I had already revived the traditional shape of Old Kingdom royal funerary monuments. This may have been one of the ways in which he gave material expression to the pretension of his name "Repeater of Births." But Senusret I pushed the same

---

122. Most comprehensively Jánosi 2016: 4–7.

policy a step farther. Not only did he build a pyramid, the surrounding complex had exactly the same layout as late Old Kingdom pyramids, to such an extent that the pyramid temple could "without the evidence of the inscriptions, [. . .] be dated to the Sixth Dynasty."[123] The structure clearly intended to stand firmly within the Old Kingdom tradition.

Much has already been said about Senusret I, and not all needs repeating here. We have argued that he pursued an extensive temple building program, which was already in full swing long before work on his pyramid had begun. As we have seen, this included the composition of accomplished texts which may have been recited as part of the temple cult, but were also publicly displayed on the outer walls of the temples. Many literary texts were also composed for display and use outside the temple, and some of these, like the "Story of Sinuhe" and the "Teaching of Amenemhat I," clearly betray an effort to promote royal ideology.

The royal pyramid complex came to be surrounded by an impressive cemetery for the most eminent courtiers. Many of the tombs are enormous in size, and take the form of mastabas with exterior decorations of recessed paneling that reference the traditional palace façade motif. Although little of these superstructures has survived, they share the same design as the mastaba of Khnumhotep III discussed earlier, which displays an autobiography of ambitious literary quality on its exterior walls (see section 19.3).[124] That the "Story of Sinuhe" could have been created in this cultural context is credible.

Compared to both earlier and later Twelfth Dynasty cemeteries, one is struck by the extent of the terrain and the size and wealth of the private tombs. The same holds true in the provinces. Monumental tombs continued to be built at the old nomarchal centers of Rifeh,[125] Asyut,[126]

---

123. Di. Arnold 1988: 57.

124. Di. Arnold 2007.

125. Montet 1936.

126. Most notably, the tomb of Djefaihapy I; see Kahl 2016 (with references to further literature).

Meir,[127] Deir el-Bersha,[128] and Beni Hasan.[129] All these sites lie in the heartland of the nomarchy, which had survived the Theban assumption of power in northern Egypt. Up to that point in time, there had been no evidence for the existence of nomarchs in the southernmost nomes, but in Aswan, the local ruler Sarenput I is now also invested with this rank.[130]

This was undoubtedly related to developments in Nubia. Mentuhotep II had already displayed some activity in that area, but starting late in the reign of Amenemhat I, the colonization of Nubia was intensified, according to inscriptions from the fortress of Buhen and elsewhere. Under Senusret I's lone rule, the process continued, and it would expand later in the Twelfth Dynasty, with an intensive building program of fortresses through Lower Nubia (see chapter 20 in this volume). Aswan was an important hub on the route from the Egyptian heartland to Nubia, and it seems that this had a strong impact on the growing power of Sarenput I and his successors. The extensive rock tombs built by these people at Qubbet el-Hawa and the refurbishment of the Heqaib chapel in the village center of Elephantine provide evidence for this.

Heqaib had been an expedition leader toward the end of the Old Kingdom. The funerary cult at his tomb probably remained operational throughout the First Intermediate Period and Middle Kingdom. In addition, a chapel dedicated to him emerged within the settlement at Elephantine in the First Intermediate Period. This seems to have been the result of an initiative by the earliest Eleventh Dynasty kings. Under Senusret I, however, Sarenput I (whose tomb inscriptions leave no doubt about his close links with the king) reconstructed the Heqaib chapel, converting it into a *ka*-house destined not only for the cult of Heqaib, but also for the Sarenput family. Later in the Twelfth Dynasty and in

---

127. Blackman 1914; Blackman and Apted 1953.

128. Newberry 1895: 18–26 (Djehutinakht VI); 26–27 (Amenemhat); 37 (Nehri II). For the tomb of Amenemhat, see also Willems et al. 2009: 392–393.

129. Newberry 1893: 11–38; Kanawati and Evans 2016.

130. Sethe 1935: 6, 5, 17.

the Thirteenth, the place was regularly visited not only by locals, but also by Egyptian officials from elsewhere, who were on their way to the Nubian fortresses or back home.[131] Similar cult centers for the local elite also existed in other parts of Egypt.[132] It is clear that the kings supported such cults, which through their rituals established a link between the local population and its ruler. The clientelist system continued to prevail.

The increasing spread and the occasionally excessive size of private funerary monuments throughout Egypt is echoed at a smaller scale by the sharp increase in the number of private funerary steles. Most derive from Abydos, where they once formed part of small funerary chapels (called *mahat* in Egyptian) erected alongside the processional roads for the Osiris mysteries (see section 19.4). The original context of most of these steles is now lost, but by analyzing their textual content and decorative styles, William Kelly Simpson and Detlef Franke managed to reassemble groups of steles that must have once adorned different chapels. These chapels were concentrated in the Abydos North Cemetery (ANOC), and the groups originating from the chapels are commonly referred to as "ANOC-groups."[133] The first great outburst of this private building activity at Abydos dates to the reign of Senusret I. Several dozen steles are explicitly dated to his reign, but since many of these have been linked to sometimes large groups of undated steles, the cumulative number of sources is impressive.

In review, one observes an unprecedented spread of private funerary monuments, linked on the one hand to court and provincial cemeteries, and on the other to the expanding cult of Osiris at Abydos, where the king built temple structures and non-royals constructed tombs and cenotaphs in the processional landscape. All this gives the impression of wealth and stability. But not all was well in the state of Egypt.

This has already been hinted at in our discussion of the Tod stele of Senusret I, which mentions civil unrest at Tod, during which the temple

---

131. For the Heqaib chapel, see Habachi 1985; Franke 1994; Dorn 2015.

132. For an overview, see Willems 2014: 98–123.

133. Simpson 1974; Franke 1984.

of Montu was occupied by settlers. The inscription makes clear that this involved violent military action. Perhaps this event is related to the battle described in Stele Louvre C1: early in Senusret I's reign (so perhaps during his co-regency), this battle raged in the Theban region, not far from Tod.[134] Other evidence for military conflict near Thebes is afforded by a tomb in Deir el-Bahri which contained the remains of sixty men who apparently died on a nearby battlefield.[135] Judging from their names, it is likely that they were born in the early Twelfth Dynasty, so they could easily have served Senusret I.[136] It is not certain that the three sources relate to a single conflict. If they do, they testify to what must have been a significant one; if they do not, then they testify to fairly regular outbursts of violence in the Theban region.

At least one other problematic era is referred to in the tomb of nomarch Amenemhat at Beni Hasan. It relates a military campaign by Senusret I to Nubia to overthrow "enemies in the miserable land of Kush." This may have occurred in regnal year 18.[137]

Finally, there is evidence for political opposition to Senusret I at the highest level. In the first decades of his reign, a man called Intefiqer served him as vizier, and his (second) tomb, built at that time, may have been the "grand mastaba du nord" at Lisht.[138] However, his image was hacked out of his mother's tomb at Thebes, and very remarkably, execration texts written late in the reign of Senusret I list him among the foreign and Egyptian enemies who were to be magically destroyed. Clearly there must have been some palace intrigue in the latter part of Senusret I's reign.[139] It may have been events like this that induced Senusret I to

---

134. For the stele, see Obsomer 1993. For its attribution to the co-regency, see Jansen-Winkeln 1997: 123–125.

135. Winlock 1945.

136. Vogel 2003.

137. Simpson 2001.

138. Willems 2011: 290.

139. Posener 1988.

share the throne with his successor, Amenemhat II. This co-regency lasted only three years.[140]

19.7. *Amenemhat II and Senusret II*

In historical terms, there is a relative dearth of evidence pertaining to these two kings, and therefore few fundamental historical developments can be discussed. The nomarchy continued to flourish in Middle Egypt and Aswan, and the kings continued to be buried in pyramids. Amenemhat II selected a new building plot at Dahshur for his pyramid, but it has not been excavated very well. For this reason, the surrounding cemetery of the court officials, which certainly exists there, is not well known.[141] More or less the same can be said about the pyramid of Senusret II at Lahun.[142] These two kings were also co-regents: a graffito near Aswan mentions the Year 35 of Amenemhat II "corresponding to" (*khefet*) the Year 3 of Senusret II.[143]

The most important historical sources for Amenemhat II's reign are the remains of his annals, which probably derive from the temple of Atum at Heliopolis.[144] Certainly all Middle Kingdom kings had such annals, but few of these are preserved. Besides those of Amenemhat II, some fragments of Senusret I's annals survive (see section 19.3), but these are only very small. For this reason, the annals of Amenemhat II have a far wider importance beyond the historical interpretation of the few years they describe. They also offer us a glimpse at the kinds of policies that were considered worthy of recording for posterity. In a way, therefore, they provide us with an image of what a king's rule was expected to achieve.

---

140. Stele Leiden V4, mentioning Senusret's Year 44 in conjunction with Amenemhat II's second regnal year.

141. Lehner 1997: 174.

142. Petrie 1891; Brunton 1920; Petrie, Brunton, and Murray 1923.

143. Franke 1988: 117.

144. On the annals, see Altenmüller 2015 and the comments by Willems 2017.

Only parts of the annals are preserved. Hartwig Altenmüller argued that each text column was about 2 m high and that for each year there would have been a width of about 1.5 m; for the whole reign, he calculates that the annals would have amounted to a width of 52 m of running text! The fact that the largest fragment has a length of less than 2.5 m gives an impression of the amount of data missing even in this best-preserved case.

The annals refer to a few types of royal policies, arranged by regnal year. The first are royal rituals, like the king operating ten bird-nets, something that is known from earlier descriptions referring to, e.g., the *sed*-festival. Second, several entries refer to the king adding building elements to temples for deities, but also to a temple of Senusret I, perhaps in the eastern Nile delta. There are very frequent references to the supply of costly donations to divine temples across Egypt. Frequent mention is also made of the king presenting statues of his highest officials to temples; here again, we see the clientelist system of the Egyptian state in operation.

While the preceding remarks all concern the activity of the king in a religious context, some entries concern aspects of international politics. There are hints to expeditions into the Sinai, and to the children of "rulers of Kush" bringing gifts. This must reflect the effects of the Egyptian occupation of Nubia. Even more remarkable is that the text also refers to booty brought home from military encounters in the northern Levant, something that was not known before the discovery of the annals.

Finally, some of the ritual activities seem to have taken place in the southern Fayum, close to Abgig, where Senusret I had earlier built a monumental structure. This reflects a growing interest in this part of Egypt (see section 19.9).

19.8. Senusret III

There are no clear indications of a co-regency between Senusret II and Senusret III.[145] However, the question of whether one existed between

---

145. For general overviews, see Tallet 2005; Morfoisse and Andreu-Lanoë 2014.

Senusret III and Amenemhat III is hotly debated. Papyrus Berlin 10055 contains entries from Senusret's nineteenth regnal year, continuing uninterruptedly into a Year 1, which can only refer to Amenemhat III. This can be interpreted as meaning that Senusret III ruled for nineteen years and was succeeded by Amenemhat III, or alternatively that a co-regency with Amenemhat III started in Year 19. Supporting evidence for this second option has been found in a control note on a block from the Abydene mortuary temple of Senusret III, which mentions a Year 39, close to the thirty traditionally attributed to Senusret III.[146] Yet even Wegner, who discovered the control note, is extremely cautious in accepting a co-regency on this basis.[147]

Senusret III built two funerary monuments. The first, his pyramid at Dahshur, was clearly inspired by the Djoser complex. It is surrounded by the pyramids of numerous queens and princesses.[148] The second complex is located at Abydos South. It comprises a vast underground tomb,[149] a mortuary temple,[150] and the town of Wah-sut, which is reminiscent of the one at Lahun.[151] No evidence of a burial has been found within Senusret's pyramid at Dahshur, but there are indications that the tomb at Abydos was effectively used.[152] This suggests that Senusret III chose Abydos as his last resting place, and therefore that the royal funerary cult aimed to associate the king's afterlife explicitly with the Abydene cult of Osiris.

Other activity at Abydos is hinted at in contemporary private inscriptions, of which the stele of Iykhernofret (Berlin 1204) is the most explicit. It relates how Iykhernofret was sent by Senusret III to Abydos

---

146. Wegner 1996; 2007: 35–40.

147. Saladino Haney 2018 favors the co-regency hypothesis, but her arguments are not convincing.

148. For the pyramid complex, see Di. Arnold 2002a.

149. Wegner 2007: 365–393.

150. Wegner 2007.

151. Wegner 2001.

152. Di. Arnold 2002a: 33–45; Wegner 2007: 365–393.

to fashion a cult statue for Osiris and to build a new processional barque. Iykhernofret successfully accomplished this and directed the Osiris mysteries. Also, he must have erected his own tomb or cenotaph at Abydos, from which the steles of ANOC-group 1 derive. A very large number of other Abydene steles likewise date to the reign of Senusret III and Amenemhat III.

The royal complexes both at Dahshur and Abydos are surrounded by those of the courtiers. Those in Dahshur are documented best, and they were of a size and quality not unlike those at Lisht.[153] These include the mastaba of Khnumhotep, already cited.

Likewise, the nomarch cemeteries continue to exist. These include the well-known examples of Asyut, Meir, Deir el-Bersha, and Beni Hasan, but sometime during the mid-Twelfth Dynasty, new ones also emerged: a cemetery with vast nomarch tombs at Qau el-Kebir, in Kom el-Khalwa in the Fayum, and possibly at Rifeh as well. In cases like Qau, the size of the tombs is staggering; but on the whole, the nomarchal tombs gradually assume a less ambitious scale.[154] It has been suggested that this went hand in hand with a decrease in status of the provincial rulers. In most places the nomarch title *hery-tep aa en* NOME is no longer found. And then, in some places under Senusret III and in others under Amenemhat III, the construction of governors' tombs apparently ceased in the cemeteries listed here.[155] From this point forward, funerary remains began to concentrate at other burial sites, and nowhere on the monumental scale familiar from the nomarchal cemeteries. This went hand in hand with a fundamental change in funerary culture, which is manifested most noticeably in the almost complete disappearance of "Coffin Texts" and funerary models. Simultaneously, new forms of funerary equipment, which seem to be singularly devoid of theological background, came to the fore.[156]

---

153. Di. Arnold 2002b.

154. Overviews of the evidence are given by Tallet 2005.

155. Willems 2014: 177–181 describes the process in detail.

156. Bourriau 1991; Willems 2014: 219–225; cf. also chapter 22 in this volume.

This development occurred simultaneously with a momentous administrative reform that took place on a national scale. This process may have already started under Senusret III, but was certainly accomplished under Amenemhat III (cf. section 19.9).

A final point worth mentioning is Senusret III's foreign policy. Thus far, Egypt had been most active in Nubia, where it established a network of fortresses to monitor local populations and counter the ascent of a new power to the south: Kerma. This policy was vigorously pursued under Senusret III (cf. chapter 20 in this volume).

Early references to military endeavors in the Levant occur in the annals of Amenemhat II. The Egyptian army is said to have been engaged near the fortified towns of Iua and Iasy, which have been tentatively identified with Ura in southern Anatolia and with Cyprus, respectively.[157] Of slightly later date (Year 6 of Senusret II), the tomb of Khnumhotep II in Beni Hasan depicts a caravan of bedouins delivering galena to the tomb owner.[158] Intriguingly, the caravan leader, Abishai, is designated *heqa khasut* ("Ruler of Foreign Lands"). This is the first reference to the Hyksos (see chapter 23 in volume 3).

In the scene depicting this peaceful trade encounter, Khnumhotep II's son Khnumhotep III is standing behind his father's back, and he was responsible for the delivery.[159] No tomb of his is known at Beni Hasan. However, the tomb of Khnumhotep at Dahshur, already referred to several times, certainly belonged to him. This intriguing case has been interpreted as an indication that, when the nomarchy in Middle Egypt disappeared, some representatives of the old provincial elites received new jobs at the royal court. This was also the case with Khnumhotep III.

The inscriptions in his tomb describe how an army leader (probably Khnumhotep III himself) traveled to the Lebanon Mountains to collect cedar wood. On his way, he got involved in a conflict between the king (*malku*) of Byblos and his counterpart at Ullaza. Following an exchange of letters with the royal court in Egypt, Senusret III sent an army to

---

157. Altenmüller 2015: 297–312.

158. Newberry 1893: pl. XXX; Kanawati and Evans 2014: pl. 124, 128–129.

159. Franke 1991.

the Levant, which seems to have engaged with the king of Byblos. The same military campaign may also be described in the stele of Khusobek (Manchester 3306).[160]

Khnumhotep's tomb inscription demonstrates that Senusret III did not shrink from realizing trade objectives through military means, and in this case it had significant consequences. Later in the Twelfth Dynasty, the ruler of Byblos is no longer designated "king" (*malku*), but as "mayor of Byblos" (*hati-a en Kepeny*).[161] Titles of the same structure were borne at the time by mayors in Egypt.[162] This suggests that Byblos had been colonized and was now fully incorporated into Egypt. At roughly the same time, large numbers of foreigners dwelling in Egypt began to appear in administrative sources, suggesting that it had become easy for immigration into Egypt to occur.[163] This influx of foreigners from the northern Levant would continue and, particularly in the eastern Nile delta, would later lead to the demographic change that brought the Hyksos to power.[164]

19.9. The end of the Twelfth Dynasty: Amenemhat III, Amenemhat IV, and Sobekneferu

We have seen earlier that Amenemhat III's reign, lasting at least into his Year 46, may have begun with a long co-regency with his predecessor, but that the evidence for this is inconclusive. On the other hand, a one-year co-regency with Amenemhat IV is likely.[165] He reigned into his tenth regnal year, being succeeded by the female pharaoh Sobekneferu.

---

160. Allen 2009.

161. Ryholt 1997: 87–90.

162. Willems 2013: 360–381. For a full list of these officials, see Siesse, 2019: 259–261.

163. Schneider 2003: 235–290.

164. Bietak 2010.

165. Franke 1988: 120; Pignattari 2018.

Her highest-known date is Year 3, but the Turin Canon attributes five years to her.[166]

As was already pointed out, Amenemhat III's reign saw the ultimate abolishment of the nomarchy, overall changes to the administrative system, and various religious changes. The "nomarchal era," which had begun in the second half of the Old Kingdom, was now over. The idea that the Middle Kingdom ended at this point (or more generally at the end of the Twelfth Dynasty) would accordingly not be unreasonable. Since the Thirteenth Dynasty is usually considered to be part of the Middle Kingdom, however, we will do the same here, but not without underscoring that with Amenemhat III we are entering a very different Middle Kingdom. In fairness, it would be best to consider it as a transitory phase.

Amenemhat III built two pyramids: one at Dahshur, which for reasons of stability may have been replaced by a second pyramid at Hawara.[167] The latter complex included a pyramid temple of considerable size which, in the classical era, became renowned as the "labyrinth."[168]

Amenemhat III is often associated with large-scale irrigation projects adding the Fayum to Egypt's agricultural land reservoir. This tradition, which goes back to the classical authors, receives support from the abundant remains from Amenemhat's time that survive in the Fayum. He undertook building activities in the Sobek temple of *Shedet* (modern Medinet el-Fayum).[169] This temple may have been linked to Lake Qarun by a road, at the end of which stood two colossal seated statues of the king. Their pedestals can still be seen near the village of Biahmu.[170] A temple built by both Amenemhat III and IV survives at Medinet Madi.[171] North

---

166. Franke 1988: 121.

167. Dahshur: Di. Arnold 1987; Hawara: Petrie 1889; 1891; Petrie, Wainwright and Mackay 1912; cf. chapter 22 in this volume.

168. Petrie 1889; Blom-Böer 2006.

169. Di. Arnold 1992: 185–186, with bibliography.

170. Habachi 1940.

171. Di. Arnold 1992: 186–187.

of the Fayum, a late Twelfth Dynasty temple exists at Qasr el-Sagha.[172] And of course the location of his pyramid and the "labyrinth" at Hawara, close to *Shedet*, is suggestive. There is no room to doubt that the Fayum played a significant part in Amenemhat III's policy.

However, the evidence from Abgig of the time of Senusret I (discussed in section 19.7) and from the annals of Amenemhat II indicates a much earlier Twelfth Dynasty interest in the Fayum.[173] The location chosen by Senusret II for his pyramid, at Lahun, at the entrance to the Fayum and far from the building places for any earlier pyramids, is intriguing, since etymologically, the toponym Lahun goes back to the Middle Kingdom name *Ra-henet* ("The Opening of the Channel"). This refers to the place where the Bahr Yusif enters the Fayum. Lahun lies at a point where two dikes, which are known to be ancient, meet. It is here that water entering the Fayum depression could be controlled. During the Middle Ages, and possibly already much earlier than that, a third dike ran east from Lahun to a hill called the Gebel Abusir, and at the end point of the latter lies the major Middle Kingdom site of Harageh.[174] These three dikes allowed the administration to fine-tune the floodwater supply in the Nile valley and the Fayum. Evidence from archaeology and historical toponymy suggests that an early form of this complex control system was first installed during the course of the Twelfth Dynasty, with the location of the pyramid of Senusret II suggesting major operations in his day. The construction of the town beside the valley temple of Senusret II, an administrative center far surpassing what was customary for pyramid towns, points in the same direction. Moreover, Middle Kingdom administrative titles subdivide the Fayum into a "Northern Lake" and "Southern Lake," which must be Lake Qarun in the north and the Mala'a Basin in the south. The latter

---

172. Di. Arnold 1979.

173. For an overview of Twelfth Dynasty evidence in the Fayum, see Tallet 2005: 98–108.

174. Engelbach 1923.

probably played a crucial part in the large-scale hydrological infrastructure of the Fayum as a whole.[175]

In this connection it is worth mentioning a series of exceptionally high Nile flood records at the Nubian fortresses of Semna and Kumma, spanning a period of about ninety years starting early in the reign of Amenemhat III. By far the highest floods occurred under this king.

Opinions are divided on how to explain these records. According to one interpretation, the high water level was caused by a dam built between the two fortresses. Others argue that the water discharge from the Ethiopian highlands was exceptionally high in this period, leading to catastrophic floods that resulted in water levels over 5 m higher even than those documented in the late nineteenth century AD.[176] Both explanations suggest that Nile floods were of real concern in this period. Whatever the truth, these considerations suggest that the tradition about Amenemhat's irrigation works may contain more than a kernel of truth. However, the evidence available at that time may well document a crisis in the already established Nile water management at the Fayum, rather than its inception.

It is conceivable that these circumstances played a part in the momentous administrative innovations of the period. We have seen that, as early as the reign of Senusret III, nomarchal courts had begun to disappear in many parts of Egypt. This process reached its completion under Amenemhat III. In its place, a new system developed in which offices dependent on the royal palace played a major role. To this can be added evidence from a few Thirteenth Dynasty papyri, such as Papyrus Bulaq 18 and Papyrus Brooklyn 35.1446. These documents all seem to reflect a single administrative system, which differed from that of the earlier Twelfth Dynasty, but connected the late Twelfth Dynasty with the Thirteenth.[177]

---

175. Besides Tallet 2005: 98–108, see Siesse 2019: 277–278 for the administrative titles and Willems et al. 2017: 327–334 for the interpretation of the landscape.

176. For an overview of the evidence, see Seidlmayer 2001a: 73–80.

177. Quirke 1990; 2004; Siesse 2019.

These documents no longer explicitly refer to officials charged with the rule of nomes. On the local level, power seems to have been vested in people with combined titles like *hati-a imi-ra hemu-netjer*. These title strings as such were not new, but the disappearance of the nomarchal cemeteries with their huge tombs suggest that the status of their bearers had changed. Other local administrators were designated as "mayor of a town X" (*hati-a en* X).[178] Above these regional subdivisions largely based on (institutions in) towns, there was a regional subdivision designated as *Tep-resy* ("Head of the South"), clustering the southern part of Egypt around Thebes. In the process, Thebes developed into a sort of southern counterpart of Itj-tawy. Dozens of new titles emerged, and there is a strong increase in the number of scarabs in the archaeological record, suggesting the growing importance of administrative control over economic transactions.[179] Other documents concern the management of the royal palace, or of the "Enclosure of the Great One" (*kheneret wer*), a kind of work camp for corvée laborers.[180] Some of these sources already postdate the Twelfth Dynasty, but they reflect the same administrative system as the Lahun papyri.

The central administration consists of three branches: a sector dependent on the vizier, another dependent on the overseer of the seal (*imi-ra khetemet*), and the military. As regards the former, the texts make frequent references to the "vizier's office," which existed in different parts of Egypt, which the vizier could visit during tours through the country, and where his representative resided during his absence. This suggests that the administration had developed an entirely new system for monitoring affairs in the provinces.[181]

---

178. In cases where the title *hati-a* occurs alone or precedes the title "overseer of priests," Siesse 2019 assumes the same functional title is being referred to (translated by him as "governor"). This is unlikely, cf. Willems 2013: 360–381.

179. Quirke 2004.

180. Quirke 1990. The common translations as "Great Enclosure" or "Great Prison" are grammatically incorrect.

181. For the branches of the central administration, see Siesse 2019: 165–258.

This must be one of the explanations for the demise of the nomarchal cemeteries, which probably reflects a decline in the social standing of the regional administrators. Whether this means that the families that formerly held power were detached completely from the local administration is impossible to determine. In some cases, the regional administrators bore names that are identical to those of the nomarchs that preceded them. This could indicate that they belonged to the same families. It is, however, also possible that these were locally popular names. Since there is hardly any evidence of direct genealogical links, the question must, for the time being, remain open.

19.10.   The Thirteenth Dynasty

Reconstructing the Thirteenth Dynasty is much more challenging than the periods discussed so far. There are hardly any contemporary texts that clarify even basic issues, like which kings ruled, how the sequences of those kings should be ordered, and how long they reigned. The most important groups of contemporary written sources are scarab seals and funerary steles, but the latter only rarely provide biographical information. The desert in Saqqara South, Dahshur, and Mazghuna contains the remains of at least four Thirteenth Dynasty pyramids, two of which belonged to the kings Khendjer and Ameny-Qemau. They are surrounded by the tombs of the highest elite.[182] Unfortunately the restricted amount of epigraphic material from there is insufficient to allow historical interpretation.

Just east of the tomb complex of Senusret III at Abydos South, a royal cemetery of roughly the same date has recently been found. The area was reused during the Second Intermediate Period, but it is possible that Thirteenth Dynasty kings like Neferhotep I and Sobekhotep IV may also have been buried here. Several tombs here still await proper excavation, and their interpretation is still unclear.[183] Were some Thirteenth Dynasty

---

182. Schiestl 2015. The cemetery extends to the west into an area currently being excavated by a Japanese mission: Baba and Yazawa 2015.

183. E.g., Wegner 2017: 479–483.

kings buried at Dahshur and others in Abydos? Or do we have to assume that these kings, like Senusret III, had a cenotaph at Dahshur and a real tomb at Abydos? We do not know.

In addition to these contemporary sources there are king lists. The most important of these, the Turin Canon, is full of gaps, and the Karnak King List, while better preserved, frequently refers to different kings. The order in which they are arranged displays great inconsistencies. A further complication is that Egyptian kings had protocols of five different names. Because the king lists and the contemporary evidence from scarabs often mention only one or two of these, different names in these sources may often refer to one individual.

Until recently, the standard analytical method was to work from the king lists and fit the contemporary epigraphic evidence into the skeleton provided by these lists as best as possible. One of the most authoritative attempts in this tradition is Kim Ryholt's reconstruction.[184] Among other things, he argued that the numerous early Thirteenth Dynasty royal double names were "filiative nomina," meaning that the royals involved combined their names with those of their fathers ("X's son Y"). This would happen where the king's father had also been a king. Says Ryholt,

> This has the interesting implication that, within the relevant period, those kings who did not use filiative nomina would not have been of royal descent. The rapid succession of kings would have taken place in the context of elite families periodically sharing the monarchal office.[185]

Government responsibility had accordingly come to be vested in the highest administrators of the state, the viziers, who, functioning as kingmakers, pushed forward whomever they liked as figureheads. Similarly, Quirke has argued that the kings may not have been weak, but that

---

184. Ryholt 1997.

185. Ryholt 1997: 207–209. The idea goes back to Hayes 1955: 144–149.

there was a system of circulating succession: when a new king was to be appointed, he was drawn from one of the most influential families of the country, and was later replaced by a member of another such family.[186]

A recent re-evaluation of the evidence by Siesse offers a somewhat different approach to the evidence. Arguing that the king lists are contradictory and contain demonstrable errors, he no longer considers these secondary sources as a starting point,[187] but instead takes the contemporary written record as his point of departure. In his work, the typological development of scarab seals is crucial. Moreover, he rejects Ryholt's "filiative nomina," arguing convincingly that kings, like many non-royal contemporaries, had double names.[188] The result is an entirely different Thirteenth Dynasty. With about thirty kings, it has less than half the number of monarchs that had hitherto been attributed to the Thirteenth Dynasty, and the earliest kings, who all seem to allude to Amenemhat III with their own names, clearly attempted to position themselves in the Twelfth Dynasty tradition. Moreover, in a significant number of cases, the position of kings within the sequence has changed. For instance, Siesse situates Wegaf, who had been thought to be the first king of the dynasty, much later; the first king is now Sekhemra-khuytawy Amenemhat Sobekhotep.[189] He also offers convincing evidence that the residence was still at Itj-tawy after the end of the Thirteenth Dynasty.[190] In this way he discredits the traditional idea (already rejected by Ryholt) that the last kings of the Thirteenth Dynasty moved their capital to Thebes.

Another key issue in Ryholt's interpretation is that the Fourteenth Dynasty, thought to be a line of early Hyksos kings, had appeared as early as the late Twelfth Dynasty. This hypothesis was discredited within the

186. Quirke 1991: 123–139.

187. Siesse 2019: 23–37.

188. Siesse 2019: 55–67. For double names during the period, see Vernus 1986.

189. Siesse 2019: 23–125.

190. Siesse 2019: 110–112, building on Davies 2010.

two years following the publication of Ryholt's study.[191] It seems that, during most of the Thirteenth Dynasty, Egypt was still a united kingdom. According to Siesse, it is only after the Thirteenth Dynasty that the state structure of the country disintegrated; but this topic falls outside the scope of the present chapter.[192]

The fact remains that several Thirteenth Dynasty kings were not of royal descent. Royal succession along the paternal line was frequently replaced by a succession of brothers. Moreover, in many cases non-royals were crowned, and offspring of high officials frequently married members of the royal family. The family network thus established frequently led to a "non-royal" official (for instance, a soldier like Wegaf) succeeding a king. Such appointments must have been the outcome of a selection process, which is sometimes given ideological expression in temple texts suggesting a divine choice.[193]

Lineal succession from father to son (which certainly could still occur) increasingly interchanged with collateral forms of succession. Also, marital alliances were continuously being established between the families of high officials and the kings, implying that the whole idea of a "royal family" became blurred. Such marital policies led to the women involved gaining remarkably strong positions.

The principles observed here seem to have characterized not only the family network surrounding the king. This can be observed, for instance, in indications of filiation after a person's name. From the late Twelfth Dynasty onward, such filiations increasingly stress descent through the maternal line ("A, whom B [♀] has born"). Likewise, care for the dead is traditionally the responsibility of the eldest son, but texts from the late Middle Kingdom stress with growing frequency that it was the deceased's brother, rather than his son, who took the responsibility.[194]

---

191. With restrictions, the reconstruction of Ryholt 1997 was still accepted until recently, e.g., by Franke and Marée 2013: 7–10. For the debate on the Fourteenth Dynasty, see Siesse 2019: 112–117.

192. Siesse 2019: 108–123.

193. Siesse 2019: 127–160.

194. Nelson-Hurst 2010; 2011.

Summing up, society as a whole seems to have developed different kin-ship constellations, favoring the establishment of broad networks based on collaterality rather than patrilineality. In the highest circles, it must have been within such networks that the decision regarding who suc-ceeded the previous king was taken.

Siesse designated this as a "clientelist" system from which both the royal house and the families of the highest officials benefited.[195] This seems to be a misnomer. As we have seen earlier, a patron-client system is strictly hierarchical. The designations "royal house" and "officials" used by Siesse also imply such a hierarchy, but this is not the system he describes. He argues that the royal house and the administrative elite are, in fact, one and the same, based on strategic kinship alliances established through marital links. The highest elite constitutes one dynamic and very extended family network from which kings are recruited. I suggest that the political changes that began in the reign of Amenemhat III reflect a broader social change in which the age-old patron-client system (based primarily on estates being passed on by lineal descent) was replaced by a plutocratic (or even oligarchic) network shared by the most influential members of the administrative elite.

It is unlikely that the change from a clientelist system to this net-work system was sudden and exclusive. Power networks probably always existed, and patronage clearly survived in later phases of Egyptian his-tory as well. What we are witnessing is merely a tendency reflecting an increasing emphasis on broadening social networks.

This happened on other social levels as well. A crucial source of information is provided by the private steles that were erected in chapels along the processional roads at Abydos. In the late Middle Kingdom, the traditional focus on the deceased, his wife, and his children increas-ingly gave way to very extensive groups of people, which may include not only relatives, but colleagues and friends as well.[196] These groups are still firmly embedded in a clientelist framework: a chapel was built for a

---

195. Siesse 2019: 154.

196. Szafrański 1983.

leading individual (even perhaps an individual on an intermediate social level). However, other individuals are represented on his stele as well, a gesture which can be explained as a gesture of patronage. But people of low standing could also place steles in the chapels, and depict their own groups of friends and relatives. A famous case is the harpist Neferhotep from ANOC group 38. On the Stele Leiden V68, he is depicted rendering musical service to his master, the overseer of priests Iki. This represents a patron-client relationship. But the Stele Leiden V95, which undoubtedly also stood in Iki's chapel, was given to Neferhotep by two friends and colleagues: a scribal assistant and a "draftsman," who was probably responsible for making the stele. The group involved in this second case is not a family group, and it is not a group of clients, but a group of equals: friends and colleagues.[197]

Many late Middle Kingdom steles not only consist of depictions of large numbers of persons, but also include long written lists of people. In several cases, depictions of persons are dispensed with altogether. Instead, the documents only include offering formulae addressed to a multitude of people, designated in several cases as the stele owner's *semyt* or "desert." This term must refer to quarters in cemeteries on the desert fringe that belonged to larger social groups. In a recent study, Leire Olabarria was able to show that the members of these groups might not all be actually buried where they were commemorated in writing, and also that the groups could include kin on both the paternal and maternal sides, as well as friends and colleagues and other more distant categories of relations.[198]

These groups differ significantly from those alluded to in earlier funerary inscriptions, which generally are rooted in a world dominated by patrilineal patronage. In the late Middle Kingdom, more randomly organized and more wide-ranging social networks become prominent,

---

197. Ward 1977. I express my gratitude to Alexander Ilin-Tomich who, commenting on a version of this chapter, pointed out to me that Ward's interpretation of one of the titles as "bricklayer" is incorrect.

198. Olabarria 2018. An additional case of the *semyt*-formula occurs on Stele Brussels E. 5264.

and it is likely that this reflects wider sociological changes. With this, we are gradually shifting to the more complex, more "modern," and, for us, more easily understandable society of the New Kingdom.

REFERENCES

Adrom, F. 2006. *Die Lehre des Amenemhet*. Turnhout: Brepols.

Allen, J.P. 1996. Some Theban officials of the early Middle Kingdom. In Der Manuelian, P. (ed.), *Studies in honor of William Kelly Simpson, vol. I*. Boston: Museum of Fine Arts, 1–26.

Allen, J.P. 2002. *The Heqanakht papyri*. New York: Metropolitan Museum of Art.

Allen, J.P. 2003. The high officials of the early Middle Kingdom. In Strudwick, N., and Taylor, J.H. (eds.), *The Theban necropolis: past, present and future*. London: British Museum Press, 14–29.

Allen, J.P. 2009. L'inscription historique de Khnoumhotep à Dahchour. *Bulletin de la Société Française d'Égyptologie* 173: 13–31.

Altenmüller, H. 2015. *Zwei Annalenfragmente aus dem frühen Mittleren Reich*. Hamburg: Buske.

Arnold, Di. 1971. *Grabung im Asasif 1963–1970, vol. I: das Grab des Jnj-jtj.f: die Architektur*. Mainz: Zabern.

Arnold, Di. 1974. *Der Tempel des Königs Mentuhotep von Deir el-Bahari, vol. II: die Wandreliefs des Sanktuars*. Mainz: Zabern.

Arnold, Di. 1976. *Gräber des Alten und Mittleren Reiches in El-Tarif*. Mainz: Zabern.

Arnold, Di. 1979. *Der Tempel Qasr el-Sagha*. Mainz: Zabern.

Arnold, Di. 1987. *Der Pyramidenbezirk des Königs Amenemhet III. in Dahschur: die Pyramide*. Mainz: Zabern.

Arnold, Di. 1988. *The pyramid of Senusret I*. New York: Metropolitan Museum of Art.

Arnold, Di. 1992. *Die Tempel Ägyptens: Götterwohnungen, Kultstätten, Baudenkmäler*. Zürich: Artemis & Winkler.

Arnold, Di. 2002a. *The pyramid complex of Senwosret III at Dahshur: architectural studies*. New York: Metropolitan Museum of Art.

Arnold, Di. 2002b. Middle Kingdom mastabas at Dahshur. *EA* 21: 38–40.

Arnold, Di. 2007. *Middle Kingdom tomb architecture at Lisht*. New York: Metropolitan Museum of Art.

Arnold, Di. 2014. Ein zweiter Mentuhotep-Tempel? *Sokar* 28: 20–27.

Arnold, Di. 2015. *The pyramid complex of Amenemhat I at Lisht: the architecture*. New York: Metropolitan Museum of Art.

Arnold, Do. 1988. Pottery. In Arnold, Di., *The pyramid of Senusret I*. New York: Metropolitan Museum of Art, 106–146.

Arnold, Do. 1991. Amenemhat I and the early Twelfth Dynasty at Thebes. *Metropolitan Museum Journal* 26: 5–48.

Arnold, F. 1990. *The control notes and team marks*. New York: Metropolitan Museum of Art.

Assmann, J. 1990. *Ma'at: Gerechtigkeit und Unsterblichkeit im alten Ägypten*. Munich: Beck.

Baba, M., and Yazawa, K. 2015. Burial assemblages of the late Middle Kingdom: shaft-tombs in Dahshur-North. In Miniaci, G., and Grajetzki, W. (eds.), *The world of Middle Kingdom Egypt (2000–1550 BC): contributions on archaeology, art, religion and written sources, vol. I*. London: Golden House, 1–24.

Barbotin, C., and Clère, J.J. 1991. L'inscription de Sésostris Ier à Tôd. *BIFAO* 91: 1–32.

Bietak, M. 2010. From where came the Hyksos and where did they go? In Marée, M. (ed.), *The Second Intermediate Period (Thirteenth–Seventeenth Dynasties): current research, future prospects*. Leuven: Peeters, 139–181.

Blackman, A.M. 1914. *The rock tombs of Meir, vol. I*. London: Egypt Exploration Fund.

Blackman, A.M., and Apted, M.R. 1953. *The rock tombs of Meir, vol. VI: the tomb chapels of Okh-hotpe son of Iam (A, no. 3), Senbi son of Ukhhotpe son of Senbi (B, no. 3) and Ukhhotpe son of Heny-Hery-ib (C, no. 1)*. London: Egypt Exploration Society.

Blom-Böer, I. 2006. *Die Tempelanlage Amenemhets III. in Hawara: das Labyrinth. Bestandsaufnahme und Auswertung der Architektur- und Inventarfragmente*. Leiden: NINO.

Bourdieu, P. 1977. *Outline of a theory of practice*. Cambridge: Cambridge University Press.

Bourriau, J. 1991. Patterns of change in burial customs during the Middle Kingdom. In Quirke, S. (ed.), *Middle Kingdom studies*. New Malden: SIA Publishing, 3–20.

Bourriau, J. 2000. The Second Intermediate Period (c. 1650–1550 BC). In Shaw, I. (ed.), *The Oxford history of ancient Egypt*. Oxford: Oxford University Press, 184–217.

Brunton, G. 1920. *Lahun, vol. I: the treasure*. London: Quaritch.

Buchberger, H. 2006. Sesostris I. und die Inschrift von et-Tod? Eine philologische Anfrage. In Zibelius-Chen, K., and Fischer-Elfert, H.-W. (eds.), *'Von reichlich ägyptischem Verstande': Festschrift für Waltraud Guglielmi zum 65. Geburtstag*. Wiesbaden: Harrassowitz, 15–21.

Callender, G. 2000. The Middle Kingdom renaissance (c. 2055–1650 BC). In Shaw, I. (ed.), *The Oxford history of ancient Egypt*. Oxford: Oxford University Press, 148–183.

Couyat, J., and Montet, P. 1913. *Les inscription hiéroglyphiques et hiératiques du Ouâdi Hammâmât*. Cairo: Institut français d'archéologie orientale.

Czerny, E. 2015. *Tell el-Dab'a, XXII: 'Der Mund der beiden Wege': Die Siedlung und der Tempelbezirk des Mittleren Reiches von Ezbet Ruschdi*. Vienna: Verlag der Österreichischen Akademie der Wissenschaften.

Damarany, A., Abd el-Raziq, Y., Okasha, A., Wegner, J., Cahail, K., and Wegner, J. 2015. A new temple: the Mahat of Nebhepetre at Abydos. *EA* 46: 3–7.

Davies, W.V. 2010. Reniseneb and Sobeknakht of Elkab: the genealogical data. In Marée, M. (ed.), *The Second Intermediate Period (Thirteenth–Seventeenth Dynasties): current research, future prospects*. Leuven: Peeters, 223–240.

de Buck, A. 1938. The building inscription of the Berlin Leather Roll. In Blackman, A.M., and Stock, H. (eds.), *Studia Aegyptiaca, I*. Rome: Pontificium Institutum Biblicum, 48–57.

Dee, M.W. 2013. A radiocarbon-based chronology for the Middle Kingdom. In Shortland, A.J., and Bronk Ramsey, C. (eds.), *Radiocarbon and the chronologies of ancient Egypt*. Oxford: Oxbow, 174–181.

Delia, R.D. 1982. Doubts about double dates and coregencies. *Bulletin of the Egyptological Seminar* 4: 55–69.

Derchain, P. 1992. Les débuts de l'histoire: Rouleau de cuir Berlin 3029. *RdE* 43: 34–63.

Díaz Hernández, R. 2019. Der heliopolitanische Türpfosten mit der 2. Annaleninschrift Sesostris' I. *ZÄS* 146: 18–29.

Dorn, A. 2015. *Elephantine XXXI: Kisten und Schreine im Festzug: Hinweise auf postume Kulte für hohe Beamte aus einem Depot von Kult- und anderen Gegenständen des ausgehenden 3. Jahrtausends v. Chr.* Wiesbaden: Harrassowitz.

El-Enany, K. 2003. Le saint thébain Montouhotep-Nebhépetrê. *BIFAO* 103: 167–190.

El-Khadragy, M. 2012. The nomarchs of Asyut during the First Intermediate Period and the Middle Kingdom. In Kahl, J., El-Khadragy, M., Verhoeven, U., and Kilian, A. (eds.), *Seven seasons at Asyut: first results of the Egyptian-German cooperation in archaeological fieldwork.* Wiesbaden: Harrassowitz, 31–43.

Engelbach, R. 1923. *Harageh.* London: Quaritch.

Fiore Marochetti, E. 2010. *The reliefs of the chapel of Nebhepetra Mentuhotep at Gebelein (CGT 7003/I-277).* Leiden: Brill.

Franke, D. 1984. *Personendaten aus dem Mittleren Reich (20.–16. Jahrhundert v.Chr.): Dossiers 1-796.* Wiesbaden: Harrassowitz.

Franke, D. 1987. Zwischen Herakleopolis und Theben: Neues zu den Gräbern von Assiut. *SAK* 14: 49–60.

Franke, D. 1988. Zur Chronologie des Mittleren Reiches (12.–18. Dynastie), Teil 1: die 12. Dynastie. *Orientalia* 57: 113–138.

Franke, D. 1991. The career of Khnumhotep III of Beni Hasan and the so-called "decline of the nomarchs." In Quirke, S. (ed.), *Middle Kingdom studies.* New Malden: SIA, 51–67.

Franke, D. 1994. *Das Heiligtum des Heqaib auf Elephantine: Geschichte eines Provinzheiligtums im Mittleren Reich.* Heidelberg: Heidelberger Orientverlag.

Franke, D., and Marée, M. 2013. *Egyptian stelae in the British Museum from the 13th to 17th Dynasties, vol. I, fasc. 1: descriptions.* London: British Museum Press.

Gabolde, L. 2018. *Karnak, Amon-Rê: la genèse d'un temple, la naissance d'un dieu.* Cairo: Institut français d'archéologie orientale.

Gabra, G. 1976. Preliminary report on the stela of Ḥtpj from El-Kab from the time of Wahankh Inyôtef II. *MDAIK* 32: 45–56.

Gautschy, R. 2011. Lunar and Sothic data from the archive of el-Lahun revisited: chronology of the Middle Kingdom. In Horn, M., Kramer, J., Soliman, D., Staring, N., van den Hoven, C., and Weiss, L. (eds.), *Current research in Egyptology 2010.* Oxford: Oxbow, 53–61.

Gestermann, L. 1987. *Kontinuität und Wandel in Politik und Verwaltung des frühen Mittleren Reiches in Ägypten.* Wiesbaden: Harrassowitz.

Gestermann, L. 2008. Die Datierung der Nomarchen von Hermopolis aus dem frühen Mittleren Reich: eine Phantomdebatte? *ZÄS* 135: 1–15.

Gnirs, A.M. 2013a. Zum Verhältnis von Literatur und Geschichte in der 18. Dynastie. In Bickel, S. (ed.), *Vergangenheit und Zukunft: Studien zum historischen Bewusstsein in der Thutmosidenzeit*. Basel: Schwabe, 127–186.

Gnirs, A.M. 2013b. Geschichte und Literatur: wie 'historisch' sind ägyptische literarische Texte? In Moers, G., Widmaier, K., Giewekemeyer, A., Lümers, A., and Ernst R. (eds.), *Dating Egyptian literary texts*. Hamburg: Widmaier, 367–403.

Goedicke, H. 1994. The Berlin Leather Roll (P. Berlin 3029). In Müller, W. (ed.), *Festschrift zum 150-jährigen Bestehen des Berliner Ägyptischen Museums*. Berlin: Akademie-Verlag, 87–104.

Le Goff, J. 2014. *Faut-il vraiment découper l'histoir en tranches?* Paris: Éditions du Seuil.

Grajetzki, W. 2003. *Die höchsten Beamten der ägyptischen Zentralverwaltung zur Zeit des Mittleren Reiches: Prosopographie, Titel und Titelreihen*. Berlin: Achet Verlag.

Grajetzki, W. 2006. *The Middle Kingdom of ancient Egypt: history, archaeology and society*. London: Duckworth.

Griffith, F.L., and Newberry, P.E. 1895. *El Bersheh II*. London: Egypt Exploration Fund.

Habachi, L. 1940. The monument at Biyahmū. *ASAE* 40: 721–739.

Habachi, L. 1985a. Devotion of Tuthmosis III to his predecessors: à propos of a meeting of Sesostris I with his courtiers. In Posener-Kriéger, P. (ed.), *Mélanges Gamal Eddin Mokhtar I*. Cairo: Institut français d'archéologie orientale, 349–359.

Habachi, L. 1985b. *Elephantine IV: the sanctuary of Heqaib*. Mainz: Zabern.

Hayes, W.C. 1955. *A papyrus of the late Middle Kingdom in the Brooklyn Museum (Papyrus Brooklyn 35.1446)*. Brooklyn, NY: The Brooklyn Museum.

Ilin-Tomich, A. 2015. King Seankhibra and the Middle Kingdom appeal to the living. In Miniaci, G., and Grajetzki, W. (ed.), *The world of Middle Kingdom Egypt (2000–1550 BC): contributions on archaeology, art, religion and written sources, vol. I*. London: Golden House, 145–168.

Jánosi, P. 2016. *The pyramid complex of Amenemhat I at Lisht: the reliefs*. New York: Metropolitan Museum of Art.

Jansen-Winkeln, K. 1997. Zu den Koregenzen der 12. Dynastie. *SAK* 24: 115–135.

Jansen-Winkeln, K. 2017. Zur Datierung der mittelägyptischen Literatur. *Orientalia* 86: 107–134.

Kahl, J. 2016. *Ornamente in Bewegung: die Deckendekoration der großen Querhalle im Grab von Djefai-Hapi I. in Assiut.* Wiesbaden: Harrassowitz.

Kaiser, W. 1993. Die Entwicklung des Satettempels in der 11. Dynastie. *MDAIK* 49: 145–152.

Kanawati, N., and Evans, L. 2014. *Beni Hassan, vol. I: the tomb of Khnumhotep II.* Oxford: Aris & Phillips.

Kanawati, N., and Evans, L. 2016. *Beni Hassan, vol. III: the tomb of Amenemhat.* Oxford: Aris & Phillips.

Kemp, B. 2006. *Ancient Egypt: anatomy of a civilisation.* London and New York: Routledge. 2nd rev. ed.

Laboury, D. 2013. Citations et usages de l'art du Moyen Empire à l'époque thoutmoside. In Bickel, S. (ed.), *Vergangenheit und Zukunft. Studien zum historischen Bewusstsein in der Thutmosidenzeit.* Basel: Schwabe, 11–28.

Larché, F. 2018. Nouvelles données et interprétation des vestiges du temple de Sésostris Ier à Tôd. *Journal of Egyptian Architecture* 3: 100–139.

Lehner, M. 1997. *The complete pyramids.* Cairo: American University in Cairo Press.

Lehner, M. 2000. The fractal house of pharaoh: ancient Egypt as a complex adaptive system. In Kohler, T.A., and Gumerman, G.J. (eds.), *Dynamics in human and primate societies: agent-based modeling of social and spatial processes.* Oxford: Oxford University Press, 275–353.

Lepsius, R. 1853. *Über die zwölfte ägyptische Königsdynastie.* Berlin: Hertz.

Luft, U. 1992. *Die chronologische Fixierung des ägyptischen Mittleren Reichs nach dem Tempelarchiv von Illahun.* Vienna: Verlag der Österreichischen Akademie der Wissenschaften.

Marée, M. 2010. Foreword. In Marée, M. (ed.), *The Second Intermediate Period (Thirteenth–Seventeenth Dynasties): current research, future prospects.* Leuven: Peeters, xi–xv.

Moeller, N. 2015. *The archaeology of urbanism in ancient Egypt: from the Predynastic period to the end of the Middle Kingdom.* Cambridge: Cambridge University Press.

Mond, R. 1905. Report of work in the necropolis of Thebes during the winter of 1903–1904. *ASAE* 6: 65–96.

Montet, P. 1936. Les tombeaux de Siout et de Deir Rifeh. *Kêmi* 6: 131–163.

Morenz, L. 2010. *Die Zeit der Regionen im Spiegel der Gebelein-Region: kulturgeschichtliche Re-Konstruktionen.* Leiden: Brill.

Morfoisse, F., and Andreu-Lanoë, G. (ed.) 2014. *Sésostris III: pharaon de légende.* Ghent: Snoeck.

Murnane, W.J. 1977. *Ancient Egyptian coregencies.* Chicago: The Oriental Institute of the University of Chicago.

Nelson-Hurst, M.G. 2010. ". . . who causes his name to live": the vivification formula through the Second Intermediate Period. In Hawass, Z., and Wegner, J.H. (eds.), *Millions of jubilees? Studies in honor of David P. Silverman, vol. II.* Cairo: Supreme Council of Antiquities, 13–31.

Nelson-Hurst, M.G. 2011. The increasing emphasis on collateral and female kin in the late Middle Kingdom and Second Intermediate Period: the vivification formula as a case study. In Horn, M., Kramer, J., Soliman, D., Staring, N., van den Hoven, C. and Weiss, L. (eds.), *Current research in Egyptology, 2010.* Oxford: Oxbow, 116–123.

Newberry, P.E. 1893a. *Beni Hasan, vol. I.* London: Egypt Exploration Fund.

Newberry, P.E. 1893b. *Beni Hasan, vol. II.* London: Egypt Exploration Fund.

Nutz, R. 2014. *Ägyptens wirtschaftliche Grundlagen in der Mittleren Bronzezeit.* Oxford: Archaeopress.

Nyord, R. 2019. Introduction: Egyptian and Egyptological concepts. In Nyord, R. (ed.), *Concepts in Middle Kingdom funerary culture.* Leiden: Brill, 1–23.

Obsomer, C. 1993. La date de Nésou-Montou (Louvre C1). *RdE* 44: 103–140.

Obsomer, C. 1995. *Sésostris Ier: étude chronologique et historique du règne.* Brussels: Connaissance de l'Égypte ancienne.

Olabarria, L. 2018. Formulating relations: an approach to the *smyt*-formula. *ZÄS* 145: 57–70.

Parkinson, R.B. 1997. *The Tale of Sinuhe and other ancient Egyptian poems, 1940–1640 BC.* Oxford: Oxford University Press.

Parkinson, R.B. 2002. *Poetry and culture in Middle Kingdom Egypt: a dark side to perfection.* Oxford: Oxford University Press.

Petrie, W.M.F. 1889. *Hawara, Biahmu, and Arsinoe.* London: Field & Tuer.

Petrie, W.M.F. 1890. *Kahun, Gurob, and Hawara.* London: Kegan Paul, Trench, Trübner.

Petrie, W.M.F. 1891. *Illahun, Kahun and Gurob 1889–1890.* London: David Nutt.

Petrie, W.M.F., Brunton, G. and Murray, M.A. 1923. *Lahun, vol. II.* London: Quaritch.

Petrie, W.M.F., Wainwright, G.A. and Mackay, E. 1912. *The Labyrinth, Gerzeh, and Mazghuneh.* London: Quaritch.

Piccato, A. 1997. The Berlin Leather Roll and the Egyptian sense of history. *Lingua Aegyptia* 5: 137–159.

Pignattari, S. 2018. *Amenemhat IV and the end of the Twelfth Dynasty: between the end and the beginning.* Oxford: BAR.

Posener, G. 1956. *Littérature et politique dans l'Égypte de la XIIe Dynastie.* Paris: Champion.

Posener, G. 1988. Le vizir Antefoqer. In Baines, J., James, T.G.H., Leahy, A., and Shore, A.F. (eds.), *Pyramid studies and other essays presented to I.E.S. Edwards.* London: Egypt Exploration Society, 73–77.

Postel, L. 2004. *Protocole des souverains égyptiens et dogme monarchique au début du Moyen Empire.* Turnhout: Brepols.

Postel, L., and Régen, I. 2005. Annales héliopolitaines et fragments de Sésostris Ier réemployés dans la porte de Bâb el-Tawfiq au Caire. *BIFAO* 105: 229–293.

Quirke, S. 1990. *The administration of Egypt in the late Middle Kingdom: the hieratic documents.* New Malden: SIA.

Quirke, S. 1991. Royal power in the 13th Dynasty. In Quirke, S. (ed.), *Middle Kingdom studies.* New Malden: SIA, 123–139.

Quirke, S. 2004. *Titles and bureaux of Egypt, 1850–1700 BC.* London: Golden House.

Redford, D.B. 1986. *Pharaonic king-lists, annals and daybooks: a contribution to the study of the Egyptian sense of history.* Mississauga: Benben Publications.

Richards, J. 2005. *Society and death in ancient Egypt: mortuary landscapes of the Middle Kingdom.* Cambridge: Cambridge University Press.

Rummel, U. 2013. Gräber, Feste, Prozessionen: der Ritualraum Theben-West in der Ramessidenzeit. In Neunert, G., Gabler, K., and Verbovsek, A. (eds.), *Nekropolen: Grab—Bild—Ritual.* Wiesbaden: Harrassowitz, 207–232.

Ryholt, K. 1997. *The political situation in Egypt during the Second Intermediate Period, c. 1800–1550 BC.* Copenhagen: Museum Tusculanum Press.

Saadino Haney, L. 2018. A new look at the stela of Ameny (Cairo CG 20691) and the possible coregency of Senwosret III and Amenemhat III. *JARCE* 54: 85–91.

Schenkel, W. 1962. *Frühmittelägyptische Studien.* PhD dissertation, Rheinische Friedrich-Wilhelms-Universität Bonn.

Schenkel, W. 1975. Die Bauinschrift Sesostris' I. im Satet-Tempel von Elephantine. *MDAIK* 31: 109–125.

Schenkel, W. 1999. "Littérature et politique": Fragestellung oder Antwort? In Assmann, J., and Blumenthal, E. (eds.), *Literatur und Politik im pharaonischen und ptolemäischen Ägypten*. Cairo: Institut français d'archéologie orientale, 63–74.

Schiestl, R. 2015. Locating the cemeteries of the residential elite of the Thirteenth Dynasty at Dahshur. In Kousoulis, P., and Lazaridis, N. (eds.), *Proceedings of the tenth international congress of Egyptologists*. Leuven: Peeters, 429–442.

Schneider, T. 2003. *Ausländer in Ägypten während des Mittleren Reiches und der Hyksoszeit, vol. I: die ausländische Bevölkerung*. Wiesbaden: Harrassowitz.

Seidlmayer, S.J. 1987. Wirtschaftliche Situation und gesellschaftliche Entwicklung im Übergang vom Alten zum Mittleren Reich: ein Beitrag zur Archäologie der Gräberfelder der Region Qau-Matmar in der Ersten Zwischenzeit. In Assmann, J., Burkard, G., and Davies, W.V. (eds.), *Problems and priorities in Egyptian archaeology*. London and New York: Routledge, 175–217.

Seidlmayer, S.J. 1990. *Gräberfelder aus dem Übergang vom Alten zum Mittleren Reich: Studien zur Archäologie der Ersten Zwischenzeit*. Heidelberg: Heidelberger Orientverlag.

Seiler, A. 2012. Middle Kingdom pottery in the Theban necropolis. In Schiestl, R., and Seiler, A. (eds.), *Handbook of the pottery of the Egyptian Middle Kingdom, vol. II: the regional volume*. Vienna: Verlag der Österreichischen Akademie der Wissenschaften, 299–320.

Sethe, K. 1928. *Ägyptische Lesestücke zum Gebrauch im akademischen Unterricht*. Leipzig: Hinrichs.

Sethe, K. 1935. *Historisch-biographische Urkunden des Mittleren Reiches, vol. I*. Leipzig: Hinrichs.

Shaw, I. (ed.) 2002. *The Oxford history of ancient Egypt*. Oxford: Oxford University Press.

Siesse, J. 2019. *La XIIIe dynastie: histoire de la fin du Moyen Empire égyptien*. Paris: Presse de l'Université Paris-Sorbonne.

Simpson, W.K. 1963. Studies in the Twelfth Egyptian Dynasty, I: the residence of Itj-towy. *JARCE* 2: 53–59.

Simpson, W.K. 1974. *The terrace of the Great God at Abydos: the offering chapels of Dynasties 12 and 13*. Philadelphia: University of Pennsylvania Museum of Archaeology and Anthropology.

Simpson, W.K. 2001. Studies in the Twelfth Egyptian Dynasty, III: year 25 in the era of the Oryx nome and the famine years in early Dynasty 12. *JARCE* 38: 7–8.

Stauder, A. 2013. *Linguistic dating of Middle Egyptian literary texts*. Hamburg: Widmaier.

Stauder-Porchet, J. 2017. *Les autobiographies de l'Ancien Empire égyptien*. Leuven: Peeters.

Szafrański, Z.E. 1983. Some remarks about the process of democratization of the Egyptian religion in the Second Intermediate Period. *Études et Travaux* 12: 53–66.

Tallet, P. 2005. *Sésostris III et la fin de la XIIe dynastie*. Paris: Pygmalion.

Vernus, P. 1986. *Le surnom au Moyen Empire: répertoire, procédé d'expression et structures de la double identité du début de la XXIe dynastie à la fin de la XVIIIe dynastie*. Rome: Pontificium Institutum Biblicum.

Vogel, C. 2003. Fallen heroes? Winlock's 'slain soldiers' reconsidered. *JEA* 89: 239–245.

Vogt, K. 2019. *Meir, die Nekropole im Mittleren Reich: eine Archivgrabung*. PhD dissertation, University of Basel.

von Lieven, A. 2010. Zur Funktion der ägyptischen Autobiographie. *WdO* 40: 54–69.

Walsh, W.H. 1974. Colligatory concepts in history. In Gardiner, P.L. (ed.), *The philosophy of history*. Oxford: Oxford University Press, 127–144.

Ward, W.A. 1977. Neferhotep and his friends. *JEA* 63: 63–66.

Wegner, J.W. 1996. The nature and chronology of the Senwosret III–Amenemhat III regnal succession: some considerations based on new evidence from the mortuary temple of Senwosret III at Abydos. *JNES* 55: 249–268.

Wegner, J.W. 2001. The town of *Wah-sut* at South Abydos: 1999 excavations. *MDAIK* 57: 281–308.

Wegner, J.W. 2007. *The mortuary temple of Senwosret III at Abydos*. Philadelphia: University of Pennsylvania Museum of Archaeology and Anthropology.

Wegner, J.W. 2017. Raise yourself up: mortuary imagery in the tomb of Woseribre Seneb-kay. In Miniaci, G., Betrò, M., and Quirke, S. (eds.),

Company of images: modelling the imaginary world of Middle Kingdom Egypt. Leuven: Peeters, 479–511.

Wiedemann, A. 1884. *Ägyptische Geschichte.* Gotha: F.A. Perthes.

Willems, H. 1985. The nomarchs of the Hare nome and early Middle Kingdom history. *JEOL* 28: 80–102.

Willems, H. 1988. *Chests of life: a study of the typology and conceptual development of Middle Kingdom standard class coffins.* Leiden: Ex Oriente Lux.

Willems, H. 2007. *Deir el-Bersha, I: the rock tombs of Djehutinakht (No. 17K74/1), Khnumnakht (No. 17K74/2), and Iha (17K74/3), with an essay on the history and nature of nomarchal rule in the early Middle Kingdom.* Leuven: Peeters.

Willems, H. 2011. Review of Arnold 2007. *JEA* 97: 283–291.

Willems, H. 2013. Nomarchs and local potentates: the provincial administration in the Middle Kingdom. In Moreno Garcia, J.C. (ed.), *Ancient Egyptian administration.* Leiden: Brill, 341–392.

Willems, H. 2014. *Historical and archaeological aspects of Egyptian funerary culture: religious ideas and ritual practice in Middle Kingdom elite cemeteries.* Leiden: Brill.

Willems, H. 2015. Family life in the hereafter according to Coffin Texts spells 131–146: a study in the structure of ancient Egyptian domestic groups. In Nyord, R., and Ryholt, K. (eds.), *Lotus and laurel: studies on Egyptian language and religion in honour of Paul John Frandsen.* Copenhagen: Museum Tusculanum Press, 447–472.

Willems, H. 2017. Review of Altenmüller, Hartwig: Zwei Annalenfragmente aus dem frühen Mittleren Reich. *OLZ* 112: 1–6.

Willems, H. 2019. Who am I? An emic approach to the so-called "personal texts" in Egyptian "funerary literature." In Nyord, R. (ed.), *Concepts in Middle Kingdom funerary culture.* Leiden: Brill, 204–247.

Willems, H. 2020. Deir el-Bersha and Dayr al-Baḥrī: two ritual landscapes in the time of Mentuhotep II. In Geisen, C. (ed.), *Ritual landscape and performance.* New Haven, CT: Yale Egyptological Seminar, 25–46.

Willems, H., Creylman, H., De Laet, V., and Verstraeten, G. 2017. The analysis of historical maps as an avenue to the interpretation of pre-industrial irrigation practices in Egypt. In Willems, H., and Dahms, J. (eds.), *The Nile: natural and cultural landscape in Egypt.* Bielefeld: Transcript, 255–343.

Willems, H., De Meyer, M., Peeters, C., Vereecken, S., Depraetere, D., Dupras, T., Williams, L., Herbich, T., Verstraeten, G., van Loon, G., and Delattre,

A. 2009. Report of the 2004–2005 campaigns of the Belgian mission to Deir el-Bersha. *MDAIK* 65: 377–432.

Winlock, H.E. 1945. *The slain soldiers of Neb-Hepet-Re Mentu-Hotpe.* New York: Metropolitan Museum of Art.

Winlock, H.E. 1947. *The rise and fall of the Middle Kingdom in Thebes.* New York: Macmillan.

20

Middle Kingdom Egypt and Africa

Kathryn A. Bard

20.1. Introduction

Throughout pharaonic history, Egypt's most important southern contacts were with the lands of Nubia (see chapter 6 in volume 1), which the
ancient Egyptians sought to control directly, through conquest and (military) occupation, and later also through colonization.[1] Egyptian names
for some regions in Nubia changed through time, reflecting changing
Nubian polities and probably ethnic groups, but in the Middle Kingdom
(figure 20.1 a–c), Egyptian textual records and archaeological evidence
point to the identification of Lower Nubia as "Wawat," while Upper
Nubia was "Kush."[2] David O'Connor argued that while the polity of
Shaat, mentioned in so-called execration texts of the Twelfth Dynasty,[3]
had its own ruler (*heqa*), "Kush seems to be considered as having some
kind of domination over Shaat."[4]

---

1. We would like to thank Aaron De Souza (Austrian Academy of Sciences, Vienna)
for providing feedback and additional bibliographical suggestions.

2. O'Connor 1978: fig. 25; see also O'Connor 1986: 39–45.

3. For the "execration texts," see section 20.4 and also chapter 21 in this volume.

4. O'Connor 1991: 147.

Kathryn A. Bard, *Middle Kingdom Egypt and Africa* In: *The Oxford History of the Ancient Near East*. Edited
by: Karen Radner, Nadine Moeller, and D. T. Potts, Oxford University Press. © Oxford University Press 2022.
DOI: 10.1093/oso/9780190687571.003.0020

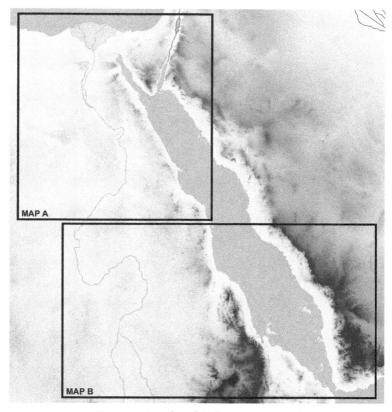

FIGURE 20.1A. Sites mentioned in this chapter. Prepared by Andrea Squitieri (LMU Munich).

There is evidence of Egyptians in Lower Nubia in the Old Kingdom,[5] but Egyptian occupation there ceased by late Old Kingdom times,[6] and the C-Group peoples (so called after the distinctive pottery) began to occupy the region. With a reunified state in the Middle Kingdom, however, Egypt once again sought to control Lower Nubia. Although the C-Group peoples were not chased out of Lower Nubia by military

5. See O'Connor 2014.

6. Trigger 1976: 48.

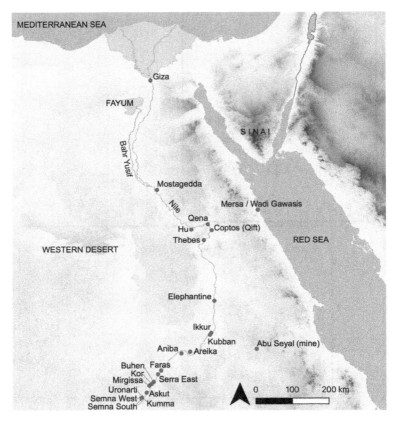

FIGURE 20.1B. Detail map A.

action, as might have happened with the earlier A-Group when the Early Dynastic state emerged in Egypt around 3000 BC,[7] the Egyptians built a series of large forts in Lower Nubia in the early Twelfth Dynasty, and later beyond the Second Cataract during the reign of Senusret III. Thus, in the Middle Kingdom there was a much greater Egyptian presence in Lower Nubia than in the Old Kingdom.

---

7. The recent fieldwork at Elephantine points to a more complex picture, with some underlying encounters and presence of Nubians in the Aswan region during the Second through Fifth Dynasties; see Raue 2008: 4–5.

FIGURE 20.1C. Detail map B.

The Middle Kingdom Egyptian forts in Nubia not only checked the activities of local peoples (C-Group and *Medjay*), but they also were the means by which the Egyptians controlled and maintained their interests in the region with the rise of a major new player in Upper Nubia—the Kerma kingdom, the second oldest state in Africa.[8] By Middle Kingdom times, Kerma became a powerful polity that would check Egypt's expansion and control of Nubia. Later in the Second Intermediate Period, the Kerma expansion in Nubia continued, when the polity controlled both Upper and Lower Nubia, and the Egyptian state was confined to a much smaller polity in southern Egypt centered at Thebes.[9]

Beyond Nubia, to the southeast in the northern Horn of Africa, was the land of Punt, known from ancient Egyptian texts.[10] Unlike Lower Nubia, Punt was too distant from Egypt to control, and there was no direct access to Punt from Egypt via the Nile. But with the rise of the Kerma kingdom in Middle Kingdom times, Egyptian access to the highly desired, exotic products of Punt—especially incense and ebony, but also elephant ivory, gold, obsidian, and exotic live animals—would have been controlled by Kerma. Thus, in the Twelfth Dynasty the Egyptians sent a number of seafaring expeditions to Punt's harbor(s) in the southern Red Sea region to bypass Kerma's control of Upper Nubia. This was a strategy first seen in the Fifth Dynasty during the reign of Sahura, which was considerably earlier than the rise of the Kerma state.

---

8. Emberling 2014 offers some good arguments for early Kush having been a "pastoral state."

9. There is now increasing evidence that the Kingdom of Kush ventured into Upper Egypt, at least for some raids, see Davies 2003. During the late Seventeenth–early Eighteenth Dynasty transition there might be an important development affecting the Egyptian-Nubian relations in Upper Egypt through the establishment of the office of viceroy of Kush; see De Souza 2020.

10. See, e.g., Breyer 2016; Diego Espinel 2011; Kitchen 1993; Meeks 2003; O'Connor 2003: 9–10.

20.2. Kush: the Kerma state in Upper Nubia

The most important factor for Egypt's actions in Africa to the south of
the First Cataract in Middle Kingdom times, especially Egypt's military occupation of Lower Nubia, was the rise of the Kerma kingdom,
the capital of which was located to the south of the Third Cataract in
Upper Nubia. In the early twentieth century, George Reisner excavated
at Kerma and thought that it was an Egyptian outpost in the Middle
Kingdom, controlled at one time by an Egyptian governor, Hepzefa
(Djefaihapy), "Prince of Asyut," whose fragmented statue had been
found, along with that of his wife, Sennuwy, in the very large tumulus K III.[11] But this tomb dates to a later period (Kerma *classique*, ca.
1750–1450 BC) than the Egyptian statues (Twelfth Dynasty), which had
probably been robbed from a tomb (or temple?) in Middle Egypt. We
now know, based on the long-term and ongoing excavations at Kerma by
Charles Bonnet, that by Kerma *moyen* times (ca. 2050–1750 BC) it was a
powerful independent state that arose in competition with Egypt.[12]

Beginning ca. 2300–2200 BC, a small settlement dating to the "Kerma
ancien" phase developed at Kerma with mainly mudbrick architecture.[13]
This settlement is different and later than the Pre-Kerma settlement excavated in the area of the Kerma Eastern Cemetery. But by Middle Kingdom
times ("Kerma *moyen*"), Kerma was the seat of a growing power in Upper
Nubia, identified as Kush in Egyptian texts. Kerma society had become
more complex by then, as evidenced in burials in the Eastern Cemetery.[14]
From the end of Kerma *ancien*, tumuli "appear as the most visible sign of
the occupant's social rank . . . as . . . some of them started to dominate others in size."[15] In the area of the cemetery dating to the beginning of Kerma
moyen there are concentrations of tumuli 20–30 m in diameter.[16] Some of

11. Reisner 1923: 85; and more recently Minor 2012.

12. For dating, see Bonnet 2014: 20.

13. Honegger 2004: 66.

14. Bonnet 1990: 77–83.

15. Geus 1991: 64.

16. Bonnet 2004a: 240.

the Kerma *moyen* tombs included chapels of mudbrick, and there was an increase in human sacrifices in burials of this period.[17] One tomb of a high-status male was associated with a crescent-shaped deposit of 4,351 cattle bucrania that had been placed in forty rows,[18] a practice that is seen on a much smaller scale, in some Pan-Grave cemetery deposits (see section 20.4).

The Kerma *moyen* town (figure 20.2) was located within a rectangular defensive wall (200 × 150 m), built of walls made of mud (*galous*) with round bastions.[19] Two Kerma *moyen* gateways were excavated near the southeast corner of the town.[20] The first royal complex also appeared in the town, from the end of Kerma *ancien* and beginning of Kerma *moyen*, in M36 and M37.[21] Dating to ca. 1900 BC, a secondary settlement, to the southwest of the main town and separated from the main town by a deep ditch, was also within an enclosure wall (70 × 30 m) with bastions.[22] Such defensive systems may well have been a response to the extensive Egyptian forts farther north, as well as to protect the raw materials that must have been coming to Kerma from regions to the south.

Reisner excavated a huge mudbrick structure at Kerma known as the Western Deffufa, which was preserved up to 20 m in height.[23] Initially Reisner[24] had thought that this structure was a fort, but more recently Bonnet's excavations have demonstrated that it was a temple of a very different design than those in Egypt but built in mudbrick, which was an Egyptian building material. With at least twelve building phases of construction and occupation levels from earlier phases, the Western Deffufa

17. Bonnet 1992: 622.

18. Bonnet 2004c: 75; Chaix 1996.

19. Bonnet 2004a: 237; 2004c: 79.

20. Bonnet 2004a: 238.

21. Bonnet and Valbelle 2014: 14.

22. Bonnet 2004a: 240.

23. Reisner 1923: 22.

24. Reisner 1923: 24.

FIGURE 20.2. Plan of the city of Kerma in the Kerma moyen period. Courtesy of Charles Bonnet.

was the center of a walled temple complex that included chapels and workshops such as furnaces for bronze production.[25] This was the main temple in the town—its monumental core—and it was in use through different time periods, when it was remodeled and expanded.

Considerable craft production, not only of bronze, was also associated with the Western Deffufa temple complex.[26] Raw materials for craft goods, including mica, copper oxide (for glazing), and bead materials (rock crystal, carnelian, ostrich eggshell), were found there by Reisner.[27] Faience vessels were also produced in this complex; this was a technology "borrowed" from Egypt, along with many borrowed stylistic motifs on artifacts made there.[28]

To the east of Kerma were desert tracks that were probably also under Kerma control in Middle Kingdom times, as suggested by the later evidence of a fortified site dating to the Kerma *classique* period, ca. 17 km to the east of Kerma.[29] The desert to the east of Upper Nubia may also have been dominated by nomadic peoples who posed a potential threat to Egyptian overland travel there.[30] Clearly the Nubians of both river and desert regions posed a military threat to the Egyptians.[31] This was the most important reason that seafaring expeditions to obtain the exotic raw materials of Punt were sent from the Egyptian harbor of Sauu on the Red Sea in the Twelfth Dynasty, in order to bypass Kerma's control of the Upper Nile and desert routes to the east.

25. Bonnet 1992: 613–614.

26. S.T. Smith 1996: 77.

27. Reisner 1923: 32, 39.

28. S.T. Smith 1996: 75. There has also been some new evidence that the Nubians had their own glazing tradition and produced faience locally; see Lacovara and Markowitz 2019: 54–54.

29. Bonnet and Reinold 1993: 32.

30. Bard and Fattovich 2013: 5.

31. O'Connor 1993: 26, 30–31.

By Kerma *classique* times, dating to the Second Intermediate Period in Egypt, a large fortified settlement existed at Kerma, and the southern part of the Eastern Cemetery contained huge tumuli of kings with many human and animal sacrifices, which were excavated by Reisner.[32] During Egypt's Second Intermediate Period, Kerma controlled much of Upper and Lower Nubia, and the Kushite state may have included regions as far south as the Fourth Cataract, where burials and grave goods correlate with three phases of Kerma culture: *moyen, classique,* and *terminal.*[33] Regarding the southern extent of the Kushite state, however, Geoffrey Emberling cautions that this state was a decentralized polity "in which the connections between center and periphery are extractive—tribute in gold reciprocated by gifts of relatively low value."[34]

20.3. *Egyptian forts in Nubia*

With Kerma's control of Upper Nubia in Middle Kingdom times, the Egyptians built forts along the Nile in Lower Nubia, but also above the Second Cataract at Semna. There were also a series of forts to the southeast of Aswan, including one that protected access to the amethyst mines,[35] and James Harrell and Robert Mittelstaedt have reported four more Middle Kingdom forts in this region along routes leading to ancient gold mines.[36] The great importance that the state placed on control of Lower Nubia during the Middle Kingdom is seen in this series of forts—and the organization required to man and supply them from Egypt in the Twelfth Dynasty through Egypt's bureaucracy of officials and the military.[37]

---

32. Reisner 1923.

33. Kołosowska, el-Tayeb, and Paner 2003: 25; see also Edwards 2004: fig. 76. More recently on this topic, see Emberling et al. 2014.

34. Emberling 2012: 74.

35. Shaw and Jameson 1993.

36. Harrell and Mittelstaedt 2015.

37. Bard 2015: 208.

Peoples known archaeologically as the C-Group first came into Lower Nubia in the late Old Kingdom when Egyptian control had waned there (phase Ia in the relative chronology of the C-Group[38]). However, recent archaeological evidence has demonstrated some small-scale but continuous presence of Nubians in the area around the First Cataract, which is not surprising.[39] The C-Group population lived in small, sedentary villages along the Nile in Lower Nubia, where they practiced agriculture in the most fertile areas, but archaeological evidence for those sites remains relatively sparse and pastoralism continued to play an important role.[40] Egyptian re-conquest of Lower Nubia, occupied by the C-Group,[41] may have begun under Mentuhotep II of the Eleventh Dynasty, when Egypt was once again a unified territorial state, and concluded early in the Twelfth Dynasty.[42] During the reign of Senusret I, a number of Egyptian forts were built throughout the region, and with Egyptian occupation of Lower Nubia, the Egyptians practiced a policy of "colonial exclusionism" among the local C-Group population.[43] Stuart Tyson Smith demonstrates this colonial policy of "separation" in his analysis of the pottery at the fort of Askut, where in the Middle Kingdom only 3.6 percent of the pottery was Nubian, which increased to 13.8 percent when Askut was under Kerma's control

---

38. Bietak 1968; see also Edwards 2004: 80–81, Table 4.1. There is now increasing evidence that the Kerma *ancien* phase might correspond to C-Group phase Ia; see Honegger 2018.

39. Raue 2018: 129–132.

40. Sadr 1991: 101; Trigger 1965: 151–152; Edwards 2004: 88. It has been a challenge to determine how sedentary these communities really were.

41. Edwards 2004: fig. 4.6.

42. Wegner 1995: 155.

43. S.T. Smith 1991. This has recently been also discussed by Ellen Morris, who proposes that there might have been "a conscious rejection of all things Egyptian and a refusal by the C-Group to act in partnership with those who occupied their land"; see Morris 2018: 84. Both models, "colonial exclusionism" and "conscious rejection," are not mutually exclusive and the reality might have been a mix of both.

during the Second Intermediate Period.[44] What this official rhetoric and policy consisted of is suggested in the fragmented texts known as the "Semna Dispatches," which report Nubians coming to the fortresses for purposes of trade (but not living there), as well as control of the movements of nomadic peoples of the Eastern Desert known as the *Medjay*.[45]

The forts were definitely large-scale works of Egyptian architecture in mudbrick.[46] They served multiple functions, not only military ones.[47] On opposite banks of the Nile, the forts at Ikkur and Kubban protected river access to the gold mines of the Wadi Allaqi.[48] At Kubban there is also evidence of slag from treating copper ore,[49] which may have come from a mine at Abu Seyal.[50] Aniba was located near an important C-Group settlement,[51] and Faras was in a major area of the C-group population.[52] Kor and Uronarti were administrative centers,[53] and Uronarti probably served as a local command center.[54] The fort of Serra East was named "Repelling the Medjay," and Bruce Williams suggests that the fort's rectangular, stone-lined basin, which had no opening to the river, was a "place of confinement for dangerous military prisoners."[55]

---

44. S.T. Smith 2003: 116.

45. Smither 1945.

46. Lawrence 1965: 69.

47. Lawrence 1965: 72–73; S.T. Smith 1991: fig. 12.

48. Trigger 1976: 67; Williams 1999: 442.

49. Ogden 2000: 150–151.

50. Lucas and Harris 1962: 205.

51. Williams 1999: 442–443.

52. Trigger 1965: 153.

53. Williams 1999: 447. For new fieldwork at Uronarti, see Bestock and Knoblauch 2014; Levine et al. 2019.

54. S.T. Smith 1991: 131.

55. Williams 1999: 448–449.

The large Twelfth Dynasty fort at Buhen was where a fort had first been built during the Old Kingdom. Buhen was strategically located on the west bank at the downstream end of the Second Cataract, and could control traffic coming north through the cataract region.[56] Buhen also would have been an important base for Egyptian military expeditions heading south, by ship or overland, and where returning expeditions could have been received along with any captives and plunder.[57]

The size and design of the Middle Kingdom fortress of Buhen reflects not only its strategic importance to the Egyptians in the southern end of Lower Nubia, but also the large scale of the state's operations there (figure 20.3). A thick outer defensive wall with a rock-cut moat and rampart spanned an area of ca. 450 × 200 m; it would have provided a first line of defense against a large-scale attack. The inner fort at Buhen formed a smaller rectangle, ca. 150 × 138 m.[58] The inner fort was built with a 5-m thick mudbrick wall with external towers and three gates, one on the west and two facing the river. At the base of the inner fort walls was a lower rampart, with slits for archers ("loophole system"). Below this was a dry moat, cut over 3 m deep into the bedrock, with a sloping glacis built up on its outer side. The fort was designed to be defended by archers, and the dry moat and glacis were to protect the walls from tunneling or being undermined by siege devices. Beneath the northeast gate was a stone-lined passage that provided access to river water if the fort was under siege.[59]

Inside Buhen's inner fort, rectangular buildings of the garrison were laid out in a grid along streets,[60] like a state-planned Egyptian town of the Middle Kingdom. In the northwest corner was the garrison head-quarters ("Block A"), built with pillared halls and a stairway to the top,[61]

---

56. O'Connor 2014: 327.

57. O'Connor 2014: 337.

58. Emery, H.S. Smith, and Millard 1979: pl. 14.

59. Emery, H.S. Smith, and Millard 1979: 27–42.

60. Emery, H.S. Smith, and Millard 1979: pl. 14.

61. Kemp 2006: 233.

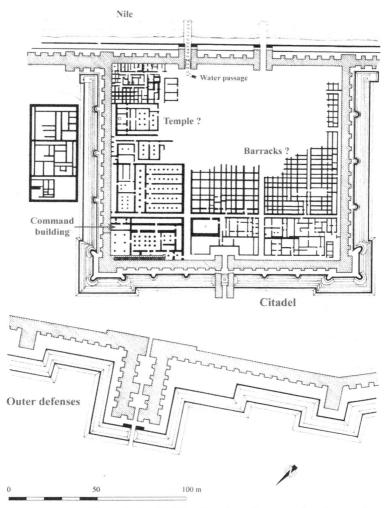

Nile

Water passage

Temple ?

Barracks ?

Command
building

Citadel

Outer defenses

0   50   100 m

FIGURE 20.3. Plan of the Middle Kingdom fortress of Buhen, Nubia. Reproduced from Moeller 2016: 299 fig. 8.34.

to the east of which were five long narrow galleries with columns in the center ("Block D"). The galleries are similar in size and design to what were possibly sleeping barracks in the Fourth Dynasty gallery complex that Lehner has excavated at Giza.[62] Buhen also had a temple,[63] and there would have been a number of granaries.

To the south of Buhen and located at the head of the Kabuka Rapids was Mirgissa, the largest of the Middle Kingdom forts in Nubia. This was the principal entrepôt for trade with Kush, which is reflected in its size, as well as the size of its enormous granary. The large rectangular fort was situated on high ground overlooking the Nile with a double retaining wall on the three landward sides. To the north was a partially fortified town along the river with a number of port facilities.[64] A mud-covered slipway of a length of 2 km was constructed to drag ships around the cataracts when the water level was low.[65]

The presence of the Kerma kingdom in Upper Nubia partly explains the impetus for constructing the southernmost Egyptian forts in Nubia later in the Twelfth Dynasty. Through military campaigns, Senusret III pushed Egyptian control south, and duplicate steles marking the permanent southern frontier were found at Uronarti and Semna.[66] The text on these steles also indicates that Mirgissa (Iqen) was designated as the major trade center.[67] Four forts were built to control the new frontier— in an area where the passage along the entire Nile was the most constricted.[68] But these later forts also served multiple functions. As Stuart Tyson Smith put it,

---

62. Lehner 2002.

63. Emery, H.S. Smith, and Millard 1979: pl. 14.

64. Trigger 1976: 72.

65. Vercoutter 1970: 13–15.

66. Lichtheim 1973: 130–132.

67. S.T. Smith 1990: 203.

68. Trigger 1976: 67.

The native population was carefully watched but otherwise left to themselves in a classic example of Equilibrium Imperialism. . . . the fortresses were designed to provide the infrastructure necessary to meet imperial economic and political goals, the extraction of local resources, maintenance and security of the trade in southern exotica, and the security of the Egyptian border.[69]

On the west bank were the forts of Semna West and Semna South, with the fort of Kumma on the east bank and Uronarti, on an island. The largest of these forts was Semna West, built on a rocky outcrop, with the much smaller fort of Kumma on an outcrop on the opposite side of the Nile. Semna South, a rectangular fortification, was located about 1 km south of Semna West. Trigger suggests that this fort was used for military expeditions and preparing trading convoys coming from the south for the overland trip to Mirgissa.[70] According to Stuart Tyson Smith, Semna South would have been a good staging area for Nubian caravans, or where Nubian goods could be transferred to Egyptian ships.[71]

The island fort of Askut, also built during the reign of Senusret III, was located about midway between Mirgissa and the cluster of southernmost forts in the region of the Semna Cataract. To the north of Askut on the west bank were a number of C-Group settlements and cemeteries, with more on the east bank to the south of Askut.[72] A gold mine was also located near Askut on the east bank to the south, and tools for processing gold ore were found in the fort.[73] None of the Second Cataract forts

---

69. S.T. Smith 1995: 50.

70. Trigger 1976: 72.

71. S.T. Smith 1991: 131.

72. S.T. Smith 1991: 109–111.

73. S.T. Smith 1991: 111.

had larger storage facilities than Askut,[74] and Barry Kemp has suggested that it was an important granary depot for supplying army needs during the military campaigns of the later Twelfth Dynasty.[75] Askut must have also played a role in controlling the river traffic from the south and regulating control of Nubians in the region.[76]

The cataract forts to the north of Shalfak were linked by a series of lookouts and signaling posts.[77] There also was a system of smaller forts, such as at Areika,[78] which was excavated in the early twentieth century and originally was thought to be the "castle" of a Nubian chief.[79] Josef Wegner's analysis of the Areika evidence, both artifactual and textual, however, points to the use of this site in the Twelfth Dynasty as a "fortified Egyptian center which maintained regional control."[80] According to Wegner, there are two possible interpretations of the Areika evidence. Possibly Nubian/C-Group persons, either soldiers cooperating with the Egyptians or captives, lived at the site together with the Egyptians in the Twelfth Dynasty.[81] Another possibility, however, is that Areika had two different occupational phases, with the Egyptian abandonment of the fort in the late Twelfth Dynasty, followed by an occupation and use of the site by local C-Group peoples.[82]

Pottery was essential for life in these forts, and marl wares from workshops in both Upper and Lower Egypt were shipped to the Nubian forts in large quantities.[83] Some of the marl wares were for shipping and storage

74. S.T. Smith 1991: 115.

75. Kemp 1986.

76. S.T. Smith 1991: 126.

77. Trigger 1976: 74. New fieldwork has resumed recently at Shalfak, see Näser et al. 2017.

78. Wegner 1995: 159.

79. Randall-MacIver and Woolley 1909.

80. Wegner 1995: 153.

81. Wegner 1995: 158.

82. Wegner 1995: 158–159.

83. S.T. Smith 2014: 103.

of materials, especially grain, going south from Egypt, but other forms of Egyptian pottery were also found at these forts, such as the "tableware" at Areika. Egyptian-style pottery in Nile Silt was also locally produced in large quantities at Mirgissa and Serra East, and Stuart Tyson Smith has identified a potter's wheelhead and other artifacts associated with a potter's workshop at Askut.[84]

An Egyptian practice that is well attested at Middle Kingdom settlements in Egypt, as well as in the Nubian forts, is that of sealing commodities and documents.[85] Administrative use of sealings was "strongly connected with control over commodities in containers and storehouses, especially in an official context"—such as the Nubian forts.[86] Sealings were attached to sacks, pegs from boxes, miscellaneous containers (e.g., baskets), bundles, and documents/letters—and doors, which left specific impressions on the backs of the sealings.[87] Imprinted on the front of these sealings were different types of seals: the shield-shaped seals for economic control of government departments, such as the treasury and the granary, in addition to scarab seals used by officials and private individuals or families.[88] Countersealing was a common practice, where the official stamps were countersealed with private seals, or with overstamps (decorative symbols and patterns).[89] The large number of seal impressions found in Middle Kingdom strata at the Nubian forts "attests to a high degree of hierarchical control down to the end of the Middle Kingdom," with the number of sealings dropping greatly in the Second Intermediate Period.[90]

84. S.T. Smith 2014: 103.

85. Reisner 1955; S.T. Smith 1990; 2018.

86. S.T. Smith 2018: 308.

87. S.T. Smith 1990: 199–201.

88. S.T. Smith 1990: 199.

89. S.T. Smith 1990: 200, 205.

90. S.T. Smith 2003: 113.

Through trade via the Second Cataract forts, Egyptian goods in sealed containers were also sent south to Kerma, where Egyptian jars have been found in the Kerma cemeteries (especially Kerma *moyen* graves[91]). Scarab sealings, typical of Egyptian officials of the late Twelfth through Thirteenth Dynasties and occurring in the Nubian forts, are also known from Kerma.[92]

In the late Middle Kingdom, the Egyptian sealing system spread to Kerma, and large deposits of sealings there date to the Second Intermediate Period.[93] Kerma did not have a written language, and the later seals of the Second Intermediate Period that were attached to containers had geometric patterns or were without patterns, while those with "heraldic designs or royal figures" had been used to seal doors of official buildings.[94]

Harry S. Smith has argued that at the end of the Twelfth Dynasty a system of rotating military units for the garrisons in the Nubian forts shifted to permanent settlers.[95] The archaeological record at Askut confirms this major change of organization, which helped to make the occupation of Lower Nubia more self-sufficient; this represents a fundamental change in the imperial Egyptian system, from "equilibrium imperialism" to "equilibrium colonialism".[96] Sealings of officials at Askut show that Lower Nubia remained under Egyptian control until the later Thirteenth Dynasty, and Egyptian pottery (in Marl A and Marl C) found in late Thirteenth Dynasty contexts there demonstrates that goods were still being shipped from both Upper and Lower Egypt.[97] At the end of the Thirteenth Dynasty, the descendants of the first Egyptian settlers in the Nubian forts remained there under the rule of the king of Kush.

---

91. Bourriau 2004: 6–10.

92. Gratien 1991; 1993; 2004: 77.

93. S.T. Smith 1996: 75–79; 2018: 308–309.

94. Gratien 2004: 80–81.

95. H.S. Smith 1976: 67–69.

96. S.T. Smith 1995: 51; Morris 2018: 89–92.

97. S.T. Smith 1995: 70, 80.

Thus, during the Middle Kingdom there were a number of major Egyptian fortresses located along a ca. 400-km stretch of the Nile, from the southern frontier of Egypt at Elephantine to Semna South, as well as smaller ones and numerous lookout points. Built for military control of local peoples and Egypt's frontier extending into Lower Nubia, the forts were a strong symbol of Egyptian authority to the Kerma kingdom farther upstream. The forts allowed trade goods—as well as administrative communications and diplomatic envoys—to flow north via the river to Egypt, and men, supplies, and information to move south through Lower Nubia.[98] Large amounts of the highly valued, exotic raw materials from regions to the south and southeast of Upper Nubia also must have been coming to Lower Nubia and then to Egypt through Kush, and the Egyptian forts in Lower Nubia played a major role in this traffic.

Like the state-founded towns at Lahun and South Abydos, the Nubian forts were pre-planned and designed on a model with an interior grid of mudbrick buildings and streets. These planned Egyptian forts/settlements also provide evidence of the huge state redistributive system, when the forts were supplied from Egypt, which reached its maximum during the reign of Senusret III.[99] Granaries have been found in many of the forts, and Kemp has estimated that the largest complex of granaries at Askut had a capacity of ca. 1,632 cubic meters, which could supply over 5,628 (minimum) annual ration units.[100] Calculating the number of persons at any fort based on food storage capacity, however, is problematic.

Maintaining these garrisons in Nubia would certainly have required a large, effective administrative system, both state and military, to acquire and/or manufacture, organize, transport, and redistribute food, goods, and materials, to areas with few local resources that were remote from Egypt but reachable via the river and valley. Thousands of men were needed to construct and then maintain the forts, and to serve as soldiers,

---

98. Bard 2015: 211; Kemp 2006: fig. 88.

99. Bard 2015: 211.

100. Kemp 2006: 241.

sailors, scribes, officials, workers, and other personnel—certainly a great administrative accomplishment.[101]

Further information about these forts is also provided by inscriptions relating to the military campaigns in Nubia of Twelfth Dynasty kings.[102] But even though an elaborate system of forts was put in place during the reign of Senusret III, control of the Nubian frontier then still required military intervention every three to four years.[103]

20.4. *Peoples of the Eastern Desert*

Beginning with the unification of the Early Dynastic state in Egypt, and throughout much of the third and second millennia BC in periods when there was a strong centralized state, Egypt sought to directly control Lower Nubia, for a number of reasons, as stated earlier. This meant the end of the A-Group culture in Lower Nubia in the early third millennium BC, and later much more extensive Egyptian occupation there in the Middle Kingdom when the region was occupied by C-Group peoples. But nomadic peoples moving in the Eastern Desert to the east of Nubia did not come under Egyptian control.

Problems for Egyptian overland trade going southward via the Nile and the Eastern Desert were apparent in the later Old Kingdom, when Sahura sent a seafaring expedition to Punt in the early Fifth Dynasty. In the Sixth Dynasty, Harkhuf, the nomarch of Aswan, led four overland expeditions to Yam (to obtain the products of Punt), as recorded in his tomb biography (see chapter 6 in volume 1).[104] During these expeditions he had to deal with different Nubian groups. Clearly there were issues of security for these expeditions, and on the third expedition Harkhuf was guarded by a strong contingent of "Yamite recruits" who were returning to Egypt with him.[105]

---

101. Bard 2015: 211.

102. Hamblin 2006: 397–411.

103. Hamblin 2006: 404.

104. Strudwick 2005: 328–333.

105. Trigger 1976: 56; Cooper 2012.

Security issues for Egyptians moving in the Eastern Desert must have continued in the Twelfth Dynasty, even when Lower Nubia was reoccupied by the Egyptian state and the impressive series of forts were constructed and manned there. Trigger states that between Semna and Kerma there were tribal groups along the Nile and adjacent regions of the Eastern Desert that moved in and out of these two zones—with the possibility of strong leaders who could have harassed traders and expeditions passing through these regions.[106] That the Medjay were moving between the Nile valley and the Eastern Desert is suggested in Semna Dispatch No. 3, from Iqen:

> It is a communication to your scribe, l.p.h., about the fact that those two guardsmen and seventy [?] Medjay-people who went following that track in month 4 of Proyet, day 4, came to report to me on this day at the time of evening, having brought three Medjay-men, . . . four . . . saying, "We found them on the south of the desert-edge . . . likewise three women [?] – so said they. Then I questioned these Medjay-people, saying, "Whence have you come?" Then they said, "We have come from the Well of Yebheyet."[107]

What this textual evidence about the Medjay in the Middle Kingdom suggests is that although the Egyptians controlled the Nile valley in Lower Nubia, there were probably large stretches of the Eastern Desert to the east of Lower Nubia in which nomadic peoples (Medjay and/or others?) moved who were not controlled by Egypt and whose activities were monitored by the Egyptians from their forts.[108] Hence in Nubia the Egyptians were dependent on the movement and acquisition of exotic goods and materials from regions to the southeast (Punt) to come

---

106. Trigger 1982: 4.

107. Smither 1945: 6–7.

108. For recent research on the Semna Dispatches and the Egyptian administration of Nubia, see Kraemer and Liszka 2016.

through Kush/Kerma, which may have also controlled the desert tracks
to the east of Upper Nubia.

The Medjay in ancient Egyptian texts frequently have been identified with the archaeological evidence of the Pan-Grave culture,
although there is some disagreement with this.[109] William Flinders
Petrie excavated what he called "Pan-Graves" when he was working at
Hu (Cemetery X).[110] Petrie called these burials "Pan-Grave" because
the burial pit was circular and shallow, resembling a frying pan.[111]
These burials were clearly distinguished from contemporary Egyptian
burials by a number of traits, especially types of grave goods (e.g.,
handmade ceramic bowls incised with cross-hatched decoration, and
bracelets of rectangular beads). In Cemetery X at Hu Petrie also found
a deposit (X 57) with the (partial) crania of 138 goats, five oxen, five
calves, and one sheep, stacked in rows with noses to the west and horns
to the east.[112]

Subsequent to Petrie's identification of Pan-Graves, these burials
(and associated deposits) have been identified at a number of sites in
Upper Egypt and Lower Nubia.[113] Pan-Grave pottery also has been
identified at several sites in Lower Egypt.[114] Pan-Grave burials often
included horns and frontal skull fragments of goats and sheep, and less
frequently cattle, placed around the burial pit or stone circle, which

---

109. See Liszka 2015, who questions this identification based on the existing evi-
    dence. However, there are also indications that at least some Pan-Grave people
    served in the military and might have fought alongside the Egyptians against
    the Hyksos; see De Souza 2019: 149–150.

110. Petrie 1901.

111. Petrie 1901: 45.

112. Petrie 1901: 46.

113. Bietak 1966: 64–70; Cooper and Barnard 2017; Näser 2012: 81–82; Sadr 1987;
    Säve-Söderbergh 1941: 136–137; Weschenfelder 2014. De Souza 2019 conve-
    niently lists and describes all known attestations of Pan-Grave material culture
    from the Nile delta to the Fourth Cataract and the surrounding deserts.

114. Weschenfelder 2014: 358.

sometimes surrounded the pit.[115] These animals must have been symbolically important for the Pan-Grave peoples—ideologically as well as economically.

Pan-Grave people have been characterized as semi-nomadic pastoral nomads practicing an economy of mixed animal husbandry (mainly goats and sheep, but also some cattle).[116] Hunting in the desert may have played a (small?) role in the Pan-Grave economy. Petrie found the (partial) crania with horns of two gazelles in Hu X 49, along with those of domesticated animals,[117] and at Mostagedda the horns of gazelles and ibex(?) were identified in deposits.[118] This was an economy that required access to agricultural produce in an exchange system in which nomadism and sedentism were "symbiotic" forms of life.[119] This exchange system would have involved Pan-Grave peoples with sedentary communities of Egyptians in Upper Egypt and in the forts in Lower Nubia, as well as with communities of C-Group peoples in Lower Nubia.

It has often been assumed that Pan-Grave groups provided a connection between the Red Sea and Nile valley, based on the presence of Red Sea shells and beads in Pan-Grave burials. Guy Brunton lists several species of Red Sea shells found in burials at Mostagedda, with *Nerita* the most common.[120]

Although absolute and relative dating of Pan-Grave sites in Egypt and Nubia is problematic, typical Pan-Grave ceramics are common in Middle Kingdom and Second Intermediate Period strata at Tell Edfu.[121]

---

115. Näser 2012: 82–83.

116. Näser 2012: 84–85; Liszka 2015: 46; De Souza 2019: 12–13.

117. Petrie 1901: 46. Interestingly, no gazelle crania were found in the Pan-Grave cemeteries excavated by the Scandinavian Joint Expedition to Sudanese Nubia (SJE concession); see Bangsgaard 2013.

118. Brunton 1937: 131.

119. Näser 2012: 84.

120. Brunton 1937: 126, 131–132.

121. Bietak 1987: 124; Ayers and Moeller 2012; De Souza 2020.

At Elephantine the range of pottery of the Pan-Grave culture is found in Stratum 13, which corresponds to the late Middle Kingdom (ca. 1850–1700 BC) and Pan-Grave sherds continue to appear until the early Eighteenth Dynasty,[122] thus offering a time frame for when the Pan-Grave movement into the Nile valley occurred.[123] When Pan-Grave sites appear in the Nile valley, they represent a "cultural transition in a hybrid situation," when Pan-Grave peoples were in the process of abandoning their traditional way of life and practicing new forms of interaction with their sedentary neighbors[124]—in Upper Egypt and Lower Nubia.

Based on a study of the ceramics, Sadr and more recently Manzo have pointed out the close relationship between the Pan-Grave culture of Egypt and Nubia and the Gebel Mokram Group of eastern Sudan (Kassala/Gash delta).[125] New dating of the earliest phase of the Gebel Mokram Group to ca. 1800 BC (and not ca. 1500 BC, as previously thought) now places this culture group as roughly contemporary with Pan-Grave sites in Egypt and Lower Nubia.[126] According to Manzo, the Gebel Mokram Group evidence, with "sudden quantitative abundance of the Pan-Grave traits" (ceramics as well as burial types) can be explained either by a migration ca. 1800 BC or a new pattern of "regular and repeated seasonal movements of mobile livestock herders"—and the increasing relevance of cattle.[127]

What the archaeological evidence in Upper Egypt, Lower Nubia, and eastern Sudan means is that around 1800 BC there was a change in the pattern of seasonal movements of Eastern Desert peoples. The migration and/or settlement in these regions (Upper Egypt, Lower Nubia, and

---

122. Raue 2002: 22; 2012; 2018: 200–207.

123. For the earliest Pan-Grave evidence in the Nile Valley, see Gatto 2014; at Hierakonpolis the earliest Pan-Grave contexts date to the late Twelfth–Thirteenth Dynasty; see De Souza 2019: 66–68.

124. Näser 2012: 89.

125. Sadr 1987; Manzo 2017b.

126. Manzo 2017b: 104, 108.

127. Manzo 2017a: 53; De Souza 2019.

eastern Sudan) of groups originating in the Eastern Desert seems to have occurred when something favored the presence of, and intense contacts with, groups from the Eastern Desert and regions around it.[128] Thus, there was a wider movement of groups of Eastern Desert peoples at this time—not only into the Nile valley, but also into eastern Sudan.

The usual suspects ("prime movers") probably played interrelated roles in the Pan-Grave culture change, which brought them into the Nile valley and Gash delta:[129]

(1) Sociopolitical change in Egypt and Nubia in the late Middle Kingdom, as the Egyptian state waned and Kerma became increasingly powerful and expansionary;

(2) A changing economy: changing subsistence practices by the Pan-Grave peoples, as well as changing patterns in the seasonal rounds. New exchanges among Pan-Grave groups and with the Nile valley also may have occurred. There were also new opportunities for Pan-Grave men to provide labor/service for the Egyptians, such as in Egyptian troops in Nubia;[130]

(3) Demography: increasing(?) populations of Pan-Grave (and other desert groups?);

(4) Climate: increasing(?) environmental stress in regions of the Eastern Desert.

Thus, in the late Middle Kingdom, the movements of Pan-Grave peoples would probably have been a concern not only for the Egyptians who occupied the forts in Lower Nubia, but also for communities in the Egyptian Nile valley itself.

More information regarding Egypt's problems with Nubians in the Middle Kingdom is provided by the "execration texts," a genre of texts which are known from most periods of ancient Egyptian history. These

---

128. Manzo 2017b: 108–109.

129. Manzo 2017a: 52–53; Näser 2012: 85–86.

130. See Smither 1945: 7: Semna Dispatch no. 3 from *Iqen*.

texts, which are inscribed on artifacts, relate to Egypt's (potential) enemies in Nubia, but also in the Near East and Libya, naming foreign chiefs/rulers, countries/regions, and ending in a "rebellion formula." According to Seidlmayer, these texts were formulated to forestall any potential threats from these peoples.[131]

An execration text on an alabaster (travertine) figurine, which has been dated to the early Twelfth Dynasty and is said to have come from Helwan, includes Nubian enemies as well as the Medjay, and Asiatics:

> And every rebel who plans to rebel
> in the entire land:
> all the Medjai of Webat-sepet
> all the Nubians of [the tribes of provinces of] Wawat, Kush,
> Shaat and Beqes,
> [their] heroes, [their] runners,
> all Egyptians who are with them,
> all the Nubians who are with them,
> all the Asiastics who are with them. . . ."[132]

Most relevant for Nubia in the Middle Kingdom are the execration texts found in a deposit outside the fortress of Mirgissa, which dates to the middle of the Twelfth Dynasty. In this pit were 197 inscribed pots that had been intentionally broken, as well as mud figurines of different animals and parts of human bodies.[133] Eleven meters from this deposit, inscribed figurines were buried: three bound prisoners and the head of a fourth. Four meters from the central pit was a human skull, minus a mandible, buried upside down on top of half of a broken cup, inscribed potsherds, and a flint blade. Nearby was a decapitated and disarticulated human skeleton. The human remains suggest a sacrificial victim, and the traces of red-colored beeswax found with the cranium were probably

---

131. Seidlmayer 2001: 488.

132. Parkinson 1991: 125–126.

133. Vila 1963.

the melted figurines of enemies, a practice known from Spell 37 of the "Coffin Texts."[134]

Although other execration texts found in Egypt from this period do not have a specific archaeological context, the Mirgissa execration texts, on both pots and figurines, which were associated with a human sacrifice (presumably a Nubian enemy), demonstrate the strong beliefs and rituals associated with these texts. Scholars have tried to locate the places and geography of enemies listed in these texts, but there is disagreement on specific locations in different times/periods.[135]

Thus, in the later Middle Kingdom, although the Egyptians built a very impressive series of fortresses in Lower Nubia up to the Semna region, they still had concerns about the potential threats of Nubians (both Upper and Lower Nubia), as well as desert peoples known as the Medjay, as reflected in the magical ritual practices of the execration texts. This was also at a time when increasing numbers of desert nomads, known from archaeological evidence of their burials and ceramics as the Pan-Grave peoples (probably in some cases to be associated with the Medjay in Egyptian texts), were moving into the Nile valley. It is also possible that there were different groups of (semi-)nomadic peoples moving in wide areas of the Eastern Desert at this time, not only Medjay groups, and the Egyptians lumped them together in their texts as "Medjay," as an expression of the potential threats of such peoples.

20.5. *Middle Kingdom ports on the Red Sea and the Punt expeditions*

Although the majority of exotic imported materials originating in Punt in Middle Kingdom times must have come to Egypt via the Kerma kingdom in Upper Nubia, and then through Egypt's forts in Lower Nubia, a more direct route to Punt was also taken via the Red Sea. The sea route

---

134. Ritner 2008: 163.

135. See, e.g., Posener 1940: 47–64; O'Connor 1986: 39–42.

was an attempt to bypass Kerma's control of the exotic products of Punt, as well as to avoid the potential threats of different desert groups in Nubia. But the daunting logistics of mounting these seafaring expeditions and then the risks of long voyages on the Red Sea (and back) made this second option much more complex and difficult than the transport of goods along the Nile.

Two Egyptian ports were located on the Red Sea in Middle Kingdom times: Ayn Sukhna on the Gulf of Suez, and Mersa Gawasis farther south. At Mersa/Wadi Gawasis there is unquestionable evidence (artifacts and inscriptions) of seafaring expeditions to Punt, but evidence of such long-distance seafaring at Ayn Sukhna is more equivocal.

The harbor at Ayn Sukhna, ca. 120 km from the Cairo region, was used during the Old and Middle Kingdoms. This was where boats crossed the Gulf of Suez for expeditions to the mines in southwestern Sinai. Evidence of facilities at the harbor site includes ten rock-cut galleries for storage, as well as numerous copper workshops, for reduction and smelting.[136]

Although inscriptions at Ayn Sukhna date from Old Kingdom to Coptic times, the main period of inscriptions there is the Middle Kingdom.[137] Expeditions recorded in these inscriptions include one from Year 1 of the reign of Mentuhotep IV, an expedition of 3,000 men concerned with bringing back turquoise, copper, and "all the good products of the desert."[138] Another inscription from the early Twelfth Dynasty records an expedition of 4,000 men during the reign of Amenemhat I.[139] Inscriptions of other expeditions from the Twelfth Dynasty include expeditions during the reigns of Senusret I (Year 9) and then only later during the reign of Amenemhat III.[140]

---

136. Abd el-Raziq et al. 2012: 5–8.

137. Abd el-Raziq et al. 2002.

138. Abd el-Raziq et al. 2002: 40–41.

139. Abd el-Raziq et al. 2002: 42.

140. Abd el-Raziq, Castel, and Tallet 2004: 11–12.

Pierre Tallet has suggested that Ayn Sukhna was used for Punt expeditions early in the Middle Kingdom but ceased to be used in the early Twelfth Dynasty, when there is evidence of the burning of two boats there, at which point Mersa/Wadi Gawasis, where the names of all Twelfth Dynasty kings beginning with Senusret I are found on artifacts, was used for the Punt expeditions.[141] This is a possibility, but one would expect to find inscriptional evidence at Ayn Sukna of expeditions to Punt—and the shorter seafaring route to Punt was definitely from Mersa/Wadi Gawasis.

Ancient Sauu, the modern site of Mersa/Wadi Gawasis, was located approximately 150 km from the closest point in the Nile at Coptos (Qift) or Qena, and all expedition supplies, from ceramics to food (as well as the dismantled ships, which were made in a shipbuilding yard at Coptos)[142] had to be brought by desert caravans to the Red Sea harbor via a system of wadis.[143]

Evidence at Mersa/Wadi Gawasis mainly represents the aftermath of seafaring expeditions: what was left at the site at the end of return voyages from Punt and/or Bia-Punt. Excavations at the site from 2001 to 2011 by Bard and Fattovich focused on shrine structures built along the seashore, and an inland area to the west where there is evidence of temporary shelters (tent circles and light structures with post-holes) on top and along the western edge of the fossil coral terrace. But the most important evidence of use in this sector of the site are eight rock-cut storerooms/man-made caves and galleries along the western slope of the terrace, overlooking what was once a large, sheltered harbor embayment. At the foot of this terrace was a large industrial area, where bread was baked in long, cylindrical ceramic bread molds. To the south of this is a beach area with evidence of two phases of camps. There is no evidence, however, of permanent architecture and full-time occupation at the harbor, and the site was only used for periodic seafaring expeditions.[144]

---

141. Tallet 2015: 64–66.

142. Sayed 1977: 169–170.

143. Bard, Fattovich, and Manzo 2013.

144. Bard and Fattovich 2018: 36–56.

Ships were reconstructed there for the voyage to Punt and then later disassembled, after the products of Punt had been unloaded and packed for transport by caravan to the Nile valley. Forty-three cargo boxes were unpacked in one area of the site, and two of these boxes were inscribed in hieroglyphic texts describing their contents as "the wonderful things of Punt," from an expedition of Year 8 of the reign of Amenemhat IV.[145]

Resources—food, fresh water, and all other necessities for daily life—were lacking at the harbor site, and emmer wheat and barley to make bread (and probably beer?) were brought from the Nile valley. Thus, many of the necessary resources were brought by caravan through wadis of the Eastern Desert, and such difficult logistics of supply would have discouraged more full-time occupation at the harbor. Since what is today the lower Wadi Gawasis was filled with saltwater 4,000 years ago, forming a natural lagoon/harbor,[146] fresh water had to be brought from a distance, probably from where there is evidence of a well—and Middle Kingdom pottery—ca. 9 km from the harbor site.[147]

Evidence at the site of ships used on the Punt voyages include many ship timbers, some of which still show evidence of their original tenon fastenings, secured in place by copper strips.[148] The large ship timbers were made of cedar imported from Lebanon.[149] Limestone anchors are also found scattered throughout the site.[150] The most remarkably preserved evidence consists of an estimated twenty-six coils of rope/ship riggings made of papyrus, placed in the rear of Cave 5.[151]

---

145. Bard and Fattovich 2018: 75, 96–98.

146. Hein et al. 2011.

147. Sayed 1977: 141–146.

148. Ward and Zazzaro 2007: 139–142.

149. Gerisch 2007: 185–188.

150. Zazzaro 2007.

151. Veldmeijer and Zazzaro 2008; Borojevic and Mountain 2011.

Commemorative steles that give information about these seafaring expeditions were first recorded at the harbor site by Abdel Monem Sayed in the 1970s. A major find of Sayed's was the stele of Intefiqer, vizier and nomarch under Senusret I.[152] This stele records an expedition of 3,756 men, and describes ships being built in the dockyards at Coptos, on the Nile in Upper Egypt. The ships then had to be disassembled and taken across the desert to the harbor site, from where the reassembled ships traveled to Bia-Punt "in peace" and returned "in peace."[153]

The shrine of Ankhu, a high official, also was recorded by Sayed.[154] The shrine consisted of three inscribed stone anchors arranged perpendicularly and placed upright on top of two horizontal stone anchors. The texts record an expedition sailing to Bia-Punt (the mine of Punt) and the tribute of "god's land," in Year 24 of Senusret I's reign.[155]

The best preserved of the steles from the later excavations at Mersa/Wadi Gawasis of Bard and Fattovich is about an expedition(s) to Punt and Bia-Punt during the reign of Amenemhat III (figure 20.4).[156] This text could either represent two different expeditions to Punt and Bia-Punt,[157] or one expedition that separated at some point on the voyage, going to different end locations.[158] Another partially preserved stele (Stele 29), dating to Year 2 of Senusret II, records an expedition directed by an official named Henenu to the mines (plural: *Biaw*) of Punt.[159]

152. Sayed 1977: 169–173.

153. Sayed 1977: 170.

154. Sayed 1977: 150.

155. Sayed 1977: 159–163.

156. Bard and Fattovich 2018: 64–65.

157. Pirelli 2007: 98.

158. Bard and Fattovich 2018: 65.

159. Mahfouz 2010: 23.

FIGURE 20.4. Stele 5 of Amenemhat III about his expedition(s) to Punt and Bia-Punt, excavated at Mersa/Wadi Gawasis. Photo by Kathryn A. Bard; drawing by Rosanna Pirelli.

Evidence at Mersa/Wadi Gawasis of materials obtained in Punt includes carbonized ebony and ebony charcoal, as well as several obsidian tools.[160] Potsherds excavated at the harbor site and identified by Andrea Manzo, of exotic wares from the southern Red Sea region, also demonstrate the wide-ranging contacts of these seafaring expeditions. These include ceramics from:

(1) Nubia and/or the Eastern Desert,
(2) the northern Horn of Africa, and
(3) coastal regions of Yemen.[161]

160. Bard and Fattovich 2018: 168.

161. Manzo 2007; 2010b; 2012a; 2012b; see also Bard and Fattovich 2018: 169.

Potsherds in a Nubian style are the majority of the exotic ceramics at Mersa/Wadi Gawasis. These sherds are related to Nubian cultures: C-Group, Pan-Grave (in Lower Nubia, Upper Egypt, and the Eastern Desert), and Kerma.[162] Most of these fragments also occur in the Gash Group and Gebel Mokram assemblages in the Sudanese-Eritrean lowlands.[163] Manzo has suggested that Nubians may have participated in the seafaring expeditions as soldiers, which is supported by the similarity of Nubian ceramics at Mersa/Wadi Gawasis and those from other Egyptian sites in Egypt and Nubia.[164] There is also the possibility that Eastern Desert peoples with ceramics similar to Middle Nubian ones interacted with the Egyptians directly at the harbor site.[165]

Potsherds at Mersa/Wadi Gawasis of Ancient Ona ware (Eritrean highlands) and early Adulis ware (coastal region of Eritrea) may be evidence of where the Egyptian ships were sailing to (a port along the northern Horn of Africa). Sabir ware (from coastal regions of the southwestern Arabian peninsula as far as Aden in southern Yemen), identified by Manzo at the harbor site, represents other means of contact with the southern Red Sea region.[166]

An estimated twelve to twenty expeditions were successfully sent to Punt from Sauu, based on archaeological and textual evidence there.[167] From textual evidence found at Mersa/Wadi Gawasis and nearby Wadi Gasus, we know that the seafaring expeditions date to the reigns of all Twelfth Dynasty kings beginning with Senusret I, with the most expeditions (probably three) during the reign of Amenemhat III.[168] Given a 200+ year time span, these expeditions were not frequent. The

---

162. Manzo 2018: 128.

163. Manzo 2012b; 2012c; 2018; see also Bard and Fattovich 2018: 169.

164. Manzo 2007: 133.

165. Manzo 2007: 134.

166. Bard and Fattovich 2018: 169–171.

167. Bard and Fattovich 2018: 192.

168. Bard and Fattovich 2018: 72.

complicated logistics and huge outlay of resources—both human and material—would have limited more frequent sea travel to Punt, and the potential risks of failure of the sea voyages are well known from the Middle Kingdom literary composition today known as "Shipwrecked Sailor."[169]

Seafaring expeditions to Punt/Bia-Punt from the harbor of Sauu ended in the late Twelfth Dynasty or early Thirteenth Dynasty, with the onset of increasing sociopolitical problems in Egypt.

20.6. The Gash delta and Punt

But where did the Egyptian ships sail in the southern Red Sea region, and where was Punt located? Punt could be reached from Egypt by both overland routes via the Upper Nile and Eastern Desert, as well as the much more difficult seafaring expeditions. Hatshepsut's expedition in the early New Kingdom definitely landed at a harbor somewhere along the seashore of Punt, but this was probably a gateway where the goods and materials were collected from hinterland regions. These hinterland regions probably included the Sudanese-Eritrean lowlands to the west where aromatic resins and ebony are found, as well as herds of elephants that provided ivory, and the baboons and large savannah animals depicted in the Hatshepsut reliefs.[170] Gold could have been obtained from deposits in the highlands of Eritrea and northern Ethiopia.[171]

Incense was one of the most prized commodities from Punt. Aromatic resins—especially myrrh (*Commiphora* spp., *Opobalsamum* spp.) and frankincense (*Boswellia* spp.)—occur along the western and eastern slopes of the Eritrean highlands, with a major production area between the Barka and Setit valleys in the western lowlands, as well as in the highlands in Tigray.[172] Southern Arabia has also been considered

---

169. Lichtheim 1973: 211–215.

170. Bard and Fattovich 2013.

171. Manzo 1999: 9.

172. Manzo 1999: 8.

a likely location of Punt because this region was the main supplier of frankincense and other aromatic resins to Mediterranean countries in the first millennium BC.[173] It is possible, however, that myrrh and frankincense from southern Arabia did not reach Egypt until the first millennium BC, or that in the second millennium BC these aromatics were transported to the African side of the southern Red Sea, where they could be traded with Egyptian seafaring expeditions there. Or possibly some of the Egyptian voyages in the Middle Kingdom continued from Punt on the African side to southern Yemen.

That Egyptian seafaring expeditions in the Middle Kingdom were connected to regions in the northern Horn of Africa is also demonstrated by the evidence of ebony at Mersa/Wadi Gawasis, as charcoal and fragmented sticks.[174] Obsidian, which is not found in Egypt, also has been identified at Mersa/Wadi Gawasis: the obsidian that Giulio Lucarini has analyzed comes from what is today Eritrea—as well as Yemen, but not from Ethiopia.[175]

Some of the exotic potsherds excavated at Mersa/Wadi Gawasis are also of cultures in regions in the southern Red Sea, including the Ancient Ona in the Eritrean highlands in the area of Asmara, and the earliest levels/culture at the site of Adulis from the coastal region of Eritrea—as well as the Sabir culture in the southern coastal regions of Yemen.[176]

Although some evidence of exotic ceramics at Mersa/Wadi Gawasis suggests that Punt could have been located on the African and/or Arabian side of the southern Red Sea, it is more likely that Punt was located on the African side, where all of the commodities of Punt could be found, especially in the region of Kassala in the Sudanese-Eritrean lowlands. This is where Manzo has found evidence of potsherds of Egyptian ware of the early Middle Kingdom and an Egyptian-style, round-topped stele at the site of Mahal Teglinos (K1) (Gash Group).[177] The Egyptian

173. Boivin and Fuller 2009: 140.

174. Gerisch 2010: 25–27.

175. Giulio Lucarini, personal communication (April 2018).

176. Manzo 2010a.

177. Manzo 2014.

potsherds are from Marl A3 jars dating to the First Intermediate Period/ early Middle Kingdom, which are rare at Kerma,[178] and thus probably did not get to Mahal Teglinos via Kush on the Upper Nile.

Also excavated at Mahal Teglinos in a Gash Group context are clay stamp seals with mushroom-shaped, rounded tops, with simple impressed designs on them (figure 20.5), and sealings,[179] which would have been useful for identifying and/or tracking container goods and some commodities for (long-distance?) trade and exchange. Clay tokens, also excavated in these contexts,[180] provide possible evidence of a simple accounting system that would have been useful for trade and exchange. But some commodities which were probably exported from the Gash delta, such as ebony logs and elephant ivory, would leave no evidence of such trade.[181] Although the expeditions to Punt from Mersa/Wadi Gawasis were via a sea route, the Mahal Teglinos Gash Group evidence also suggests that Egyptians in the early Middle Kingdom may have reached (a region of) Punt via an overland route—probably coming inland from an anchorage on the Red Sea.[182]

That Punt was most likely located in Africa is also suggested by a later (Second Intermediate Period, Seventeenth Dynasty) inscription from the tomb of governor Sobeknakht at Elkab, about a Kushite raid in Upper Egypt: "Kush came, roused along his length, he having stirred up the tribes of Wawat, the island-[dwellers?] of Khenthennefer [Upper Nubia], Punt and the Medjaw...."[183] The invaders consisted of a coalition of different Nubians as well as Puntites and Medjay: different African groups located to the south of Egypt.

Other later evidence also suggests that Punt was located in the northern Horn of Africa. Although the same species of baboon (*Papio hamadryas*) is found in both the northern Horn of Africa and southern

---

178. Manzo 2017a: 50.

179. Fattovich 1991.

180. Fattovich 1991: 70–71.

181. Manzo 2017a: 50.

182. Manzo 2017a: 50–51; Bard and Fattovich 2018: 189.

183. Davies 2003: 52.

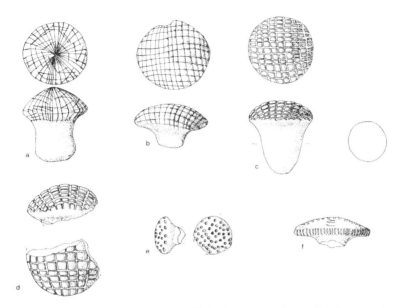

FIGURE 20.5. Stamp seals from the Gash Group sites of Mahal Teglinos (a–d) and Shurab el-Gash (e–f). Reproduced from Fattovich 1991: fig. 1. Courtesy of the Italian Archaeological Mission to the Sudan (Kassala).

Arabia, stable isotope analysis of two *Papio hamadryas* mummies from Twentieth Dynasty tombs in Egypt indicates a "high likelihood match with eastern Somalia and the Eritrea-Ethiopia corridor."[184]

Given the location of resources obtained in Punt by the Egyptians, and the evidence of exotic ceramics at Mersa/Wadi Gawasis, Rodolfo Fattovich has proposed this hypothesis for where the ships were sailing:

(1) Bia-Punt (or Bia-n-Punt, Biaw-Punt) corresponds to the gold-bearing regions of the Eastern Desert in the hinterland of Port Sudan and/or the Barka and Anseba valleys and northern highlands in Eritrea.

---

184. Dominy et al. 2015.

(2) Punt corresponds to the coastal plains (and immediate hinterland) of Eritrea, from Aqiq to Adulis, where Egyptian ships could meet both the nomads from the African hinterland and traders from the opposite side of the Red Sea in Yemen.[185]

Punt was too distant for the Egyptians to ever try to control directly, but its raw materials were so desirable that the Egyptians went to great lengths—and distances—to obtain them by trading expeditions, either by overland routes or the much more difficult and risky sea routes.

20.7. Conclusions

In the Middle Kingdom, Egypt had a new power to contend with on the Upper Nile: the Kerma kingdom. Kush/Kerma not only controlled the Upper Nile, but also controlled access to raw materials coming from southern regions—especially Punt—which were so highly desired by the Egyptians.

In Lower Nubia in the Middle Kingdom there were also concentrations of Nubians called the C-Group, who were not a threat to Egyptians there, but still had to be controlled. Textual evidence of desert peoples known as the Medjay point to other problems for Egyptian occupation in Lower Nubia, and by the later Middle Kingdom (ca. 1800 BC) peoples known from their burials as the Pan-Grave culture were moving into the Nile valley, both in Lower Nubia and Upper Egypt—as well as farther southeast into the Gash delta in eastern Sudan, where major resources that Punt was known for were located (ebony, aromatics, elephant ivory, gold).

The Egyptians took actions to control Lower Nubia directly, which also included access to gold mines, through the construction of a series of forts there, first built during the reign of Senusret I, and later during the reign of Senusret III farther upstream at Semna, where the passage along the Nile was most constricted. Constructing, manning, and

---

185. Bard and Fattovich 2018: 175.

maintaining these forts required an enormous economic outlay by the Egyptian state—of manpower (soldiers, officials and other personnel, and workers), as well as huge quantities of materials and food shipped southward from Egypt.

In the Twelfth Dynasty, the Egyptians sought to bypass Kerma's control of the Upper Nile and to reach Punt directly by seafaring expeditions from their harbor on the Red Sea at Mersa/Wadi Gawasis. Like the forts in Nubia, expeditions to Punt from this harbor required a great deal of state organization of resources and personnel, as well as logistical planning of the expeditions,[186] for risky sea voyages hundreds of kilometers to the south and back. Materials (ebony, obsidian) identified at Mersa/Wadi Gawasis, and exotic ceramics from cultures in the southern Red Sea region, provide evidence of where these seafaring expeditions were going, as well as texts at the harbor site relating to these expeditions.

The seafaring voyages to Punt only lasted until the early Thirteenth Dynasty at the latest, and Egyptian control of Lower Nubia ended by the Second Intermediate Period, when Egypt was divided between an Egyptian polity centered at Thebes in the south, and a Hyksos polity controlling northern Egypt—and Kush in control of both Upper and Lower Nubia (see chapters 23–25 in volume 3).

REFERENCES

Abd el-Raziq, M., Castel, G., and Tallet, P. 2004. Les mines de cuivre d'Ayn Soukhna. *Archéologia* 414: 10–21.
Abd el-Raziq, M., Castel, G., Tallet, P., and Ghica, V. 2002. *Les inscriptions d'Ayn Soukhna.* Cairo: Institut français d'archéologie orientale.
Abd el-Raziq, M., Castel, G., Tallet, P., and Marouard, G. 2012. The pharaonic site of Ayn Soukhna in the Gulf of Suez, 2001–2009 progress report. In Tallet, P., and Mahfouz, E. (eds.), *The Red Sea in pharaonic times: recent discoveries along the Red Sea coast.* Cairo: Institut français d'archéologie orientale, 3–20.

186. Bard and Fattovich 2018: 16.

Bangsgaard, P. 2013. Pan-Grave faunal practices: ritual deposits at five cemeteries in Lower Nubia. *Anthropozoologica* 48: 287–297.

Bard, K.A. 2015. *An introduction to the archaeology of ancient Egypt*. Malden, MA: Wiley-Blackwell.

Bard, K.A., and Fattovich, R. 2013. The land of Punt and recent archaeological and textual evidence from the pharaonic harbor at Mersa/Wadi Gawasis, Egypt. In Chrisomalis, S., and Costopoulos, A. (eds.), *Human expeditions, inspired by Bruce Trigger*. Toronto: University of Toronto Press, 3–11.

Bard, K.A., and Fattovich, R. 2018. *Seafaring expeditions to Punt in the Middle Kingdom: excavations at Mersa/Wadi Gawasis, Egypt*. Leiden: Brill.

Bard, K.A., Fattovich, R., and Manzo, A. 2013. The ancient harbor at Mersa/Wadi Gawasis and how to get there: new evidence of pharaonic seafaring expeditions in the Red Sea. In Förster, F., and Riemer, H. (eds.), *Desert road archaeology in ancient Egypt and beyond*. Cologne: Heinrich-Barth-Institut, 533–556.

Bestock, L., and Knoblauch, C. 2014. Revisiting Middle Kingdom interactions in Nubia: the Uronarti regional archaeological project. *JAEI* 6: 32–35.

Bietak, M. 1966. *Ausgrabungen in Sayala-Nubien, 1961–1965: Denkmäler der C-Gruppe und der Pan-Gräber-Kultur*. Vienna: Verlag der Österreichischen Akademie der Wissenschaften.

Bietak, M. 1968. *Studien zur Chronologie der nubischen C-Gruppe*. Vienna: Verlag der Österreichischen Akademie der Wissenschaften.

Bietak, M. 1987. The C-Group and the Pan-Grave culture in Nubia. In Hägg, T. (ed.), *Nubian culture past and present*. Stockholm: Almqvist & Wiksell International, 113–128.

Boivin, N., and Fuller, D.Q. 2009. Shell middens, ships and seeds: exploring coastal subsistence, maritime trade and the dispersal of domesticates in and around the ancient Arabian Peninsula. *JWP* 22: 113–180.

Bonnet, C. 1990. *Kerma, royaume de Nubie*. Geneva: Mission archéologique de l'Université de Genève au Soudan.

Bonnet, C. 1992. Excavations at the Nubian royal town of Kerma, 1975–91. *Antiquity* 66: 611–623.

Bonnet, C. 2004a. The archaeological excavations at Kerma (Northern State, Sudan): recent discoveries, 1996–1998. In Kendall, T. (ed.), *Nubian studies 1998: proceedings of the ninth conference of the international society of Nubian studies*. Boston, MA: Northeastern University, 237–246.

Bonnet, C. 2004b. Kerma. In Welsby, D.A., and Anderson, J.R. (eds.), *Sudan: ancient treasures*. London: British Museum Press, 78–90.

Bonnet, C. 2004c. The Kerma culture. In Welsby, D.A., and Anderson, J.R. (eds.), *Sudan: ancient treasures*. London: British Museum Press, 70–77.

Bonnet, C., and Reinold, J. 1993. Deux rapports de prospection dans le désert oriental. *Genava: Revue des Musées d'Art et d'Histoire de Genève* 41: 31–38.

Bonnet, C., and Valbelle, D. 2014. *La ville de Kerma: une capitale nubienne au sud de l'Égypte*. Lausanne: Favre.

Borojevic, K., and Mountain, R. 2011. The ropes of pharaohs: the source of cordage from "Rope Cave" at Mersa/Wadi Gawasis revisited. *JARCE* 47: 131–141.

Bourriau, J. 2004. Egyptian pottery found in Kerma *ancien*, Kerma *moyen* and Kerma *classique* graves at Kerma. In Kendall, T. (ed.), *Nubian studies 1998: proceedings of the ninth conference of the international society of Nubian studies*. Boston, MA: Northeastern University, 3–11.

Breyer, F. 2016. *Punt: die Suche nach dem "Gottesland."* Leiden: Brill.

Brunton, G. 1937. *Mostagedda and the Tasian culture*. London: Quaritch.

Chaix, L. 1996. Les boeufs à cornes parallèles: archéologie et ethnographie. *Sahara* 8: 95–97.

Cooper, J. 2012. Reconsidering the location of Yam. *JARCE* 48: 1–22.

Cooper, J., and Barnard, H. 2017. New insights on the inscription on a painted Pan-Grave bucranium, Grave 3252 at Cemetery 3100/3200, Mostagedda (Middle Egypt). *African Archaeological Review* 34: 363–376.

Davies, V. 2003. Kush in Egypt: a new historical inscription. *Sudan & Nubia* 7: 52–55.

De Souza, A. 2019. *New horizons: the Pan-Grave ceramic tradition in context*. London: Golden House.

De Souza, A. 2020. Nubians at Tell Edfu: reconciling the archaeological and historical records. *ÄL* 30: 313–342.

Diego Espinel, A. 2011. *Abriendo los caminos de Punt*. Barcelona: Bellaterra.

Dominy, N.J., Ikram, S., Moritz, G.L., Christensen, J.N., Wheatley, P.V., and Chipman, J.W. 2015. Mummified baboons clarify ancient Red Sea trade routes. *American Journal of Physical Anthropology* 156: 122–123.

Edwards, D.N. 2004. *The Nubian past: an archaeology of the Sudan*. London and New York: Routledge.

Emberling, G. 2012. Archaeological salvage in the Fourth Cataract, northern Sudan (1991–2008). In Fisher, M.M., Lacovara, P., Ikram, S., and D'Auria,

S. (eds.), *Ancient Nubia: African kingdoms on the Nile*. Cairo: American University in Cairo Press, 71–77.

Emberling, G. 2014. Pastoral states: toward a comparative archaeology of early Kush. *Origini* 36: 125–156.

Emberling, G., Williams, B.B., Ingvoldstad, M., and James, T.R. 2014. Peripheral vision: identity at the margins of the early kingdom of Kush. In Anderson, J.R., and Welsby, D.A. (eds.), *The Fourth Cataract and beyond*. Leuven: Peeters, 329–336.

Fattovich, R. 1991. Evidence of possible administrative devices in the Gash Delta. *Archéologie du Nil Moyen* 5: 65–78.

Gatto, M. 2014. Cultural entanglement at the dawn of the Egyptian history: a view from the Nile First Cataract region. *Origini* 36: 93–123.

Gerisch, R. 2007. Identification of charcoal and wood. In Bard, K.A., and Fattovich, R. (eds.), *Harbor of the pharaohs to the land of Punt: archaeological investigations at Mersa/Wadi Gawasis, Egypt, 2001–2005*. Naples: Universitá degli Studi di Napoli "L'Orientale," 170–188.

Gerisch, R. 2010. Charcoal and wood remains (pp. 25–27). In Bard, K.A., and Fattovich, R., Mersa/Wadi Gawasis 2009–2010. *Newsletter di Archeologia CISA* 1: 7–35.

Geus, F. 1991. Burial customs in the upper main Nile: an overview. In Davies, W.V. (ed.), *Egypt and Africa: Nubia from prehistory to Islam*. London: British Museum Press, 57–73.

Gratien, B. 1991. Empreintes de sceaux et administration à Kerma (Kerma *classique*). *Genava: Revue des Musées d'Art et d'Histoire de Genève* 39: 21–24.

Gratien, B. 1993. Nouvelles empreintes de sceaux à Kerma: aperçus sur l'administration de Kouch au milieu du 2e millénaire av. J.-C. *Genava: Revue des Musées d'Art et d'Histoire de Genève* 41: 39–44.

Gratien, B. 2004. From Egypt to Kush: administrative practices and movements of goods during the Middle Kingdom and Second Intermediate Period. In Kendall, T. (ed.), *Nubian studies 1998*. Boston: Northeastern University, 74–82.

Hamblin, W.J. 2006. *Warfare in the ancient Near East to 1600 BC: holy warriors at the dawn of history*. London and New York: Routledge.

Harrell, J.A., and Mittelstaedt, R.E. 2015. Newly discovered Middle Kingdom forts in Lower Nubia. *Sudan & Nubia* 19: 30–39.

Hein, C.J., FitzGerald, D.M., Milne, G.A., Bard, K.A., and Fattovich, R. 2011. Evolution of a pharaonic harbor on the Red Sea: implications for coastal response to changes in sea level and climate. *Geology* 39: 687–690.

Honegger, M. 2004. The pre-Kerma settlement at Kerma. In Welsby, D.A., and Anderson, J.R. (eds.), *Sudan: ancient treasures*. London: British Museum Press, 64–69.

Honegger, M. 2018. New data on the origins of Kerma. In Honegger, M. (ed.), *Nubian archaeology of the XXIst century*. Leuven: Peeters, 19–34.

Kemp, B.J. 1986. Large Middle Kingdom granary buildings (and the archaeology of administration). *ZÄS* 113: 120–136.

Kitchen, K.A. 1993. The land of Punt. In Shaw, T., Sinclair, P., Andah, B., and Okpoko, A. (eds.), *The archaeology of Africa: food, metals and towns*. London and New York: Routledge, 587–608.

Kołosowska, E., el-Tayeb, M., and Paner, H. 2003. Old Kush in the Fourth Cataract region. *Sudan & Nubia* 7: 21–25.

Kraemer, B., and Liszka, K. 2016. Evidence for administration of the Nubian fortresses in the late Middle Kingdom: the Semna Dispatches. *JEH* 9: 1–65.

Lacovara, P., and Markowitz, Y.J. 2019. *Nubian gold: ancient jewelry from Sudan and Egypt*. Cairo: American University in Cairo Press.

Lawrence, A.W. 1965. Ancient Egyptian fortifications. *JEA* 51: 69–94.

Lehner, M. 2002. The Pyramid Age settlement of the southern mount at Giza. *JARCE* 39: 27–74.

Levine, E.I, Rothenberg, M.A.W., Siegel, O., Knoblauch, C., Bestock, L., and Klein, L. 2019. The Uronarti regional archaeology project: Second Cataract fortresses and the Western Desert of Sudan. *Antiquity* 93: 1–8.

Lichtheim, M. 1973. *Ancient Egyptian literature, vol. 1: the Old and Middle Kingdoms*. Berkeley and Los Angeles: University of California Press.

Liszka, K. 2015. Are the bearers of the Pan-Grave archaeological culture identical to the Madjay-people in the Egyptian textual record? *JAEI* 7: 42–60.

Lucas, A., and Harris, J.R. 1962. *Ancient Egyptian materials and industries*. London: Arnold.

Mahfouz, E. 2010. Epigraphy (pp. 23–24). In Bard, K.A., and Fattovich, R., Mersa/Wadi Gawasis 2009–2010. *Newsletter di Archeologia CISA* 1: 7–35.

Manzo, A. 1999. *Échanges et contacts le long du Nil et de la Mer Rouge dans l'époque protohistorique (IIIe et IIe millénaires avant J.-C.): une synthèse préliminaire*. Oxford: Archaeopress.

Manzo, A. 2007. Exotic ceramics. In Bard, K.A., and Fattovich, R. (eds.), *Harbor of the pharaohs to the land of Punt: archaeological investigations at Mersa/Wadi Gawasis, Egypt, 2001–2005*. Naples: Universitá degli Studi di Napoli "L'Orientale," 126–134.

Manzo, A. 2010a. Commercio e potere nell'Africa nordorientale antica: una prospettiva nubiana. In Carioti, P., and Mazzei, F. (eds.), *Studi in onore di Adolfo Tamburello*. Naples: Universitá degli Studi di Napoli "L'Orientale," 1559–1573.

Manzo, A. 2010b. Exotic ceramic materials from Mersa Gawasis, Red Sea, Egypt. In Godlewski, W., and Łatjar, A. (eds.), *Between the cataracts*. Warsaw: Warsaw University Press, 439–453.

Manzo, A. 2012a. From the sea to the deserts and back: new research in eastern Sudan. *British Museum Studies in Ancient Egypt and Sudan* 18: 75–106.

Manzo, A. 2012b. Nubians and the others on the Red Sea: an update on the exotic ceramic materials from the Middle Kingdom harbour of Mersa/Wadi Gawasis, Red Sea, Egypt. In Agius, D.A., Cooper, J.P., Trakadas, A., and Zazzaro, C. (eds.), *Navigated spaces, connected places*. Oxford: Archaeopress, 49–58.

Manzo, A. 2014. Preliminary report of the 2013 field season of the Italian archaeological expedition to the eastern Sudan of the Università degli Studi di Napoli "L'Orientale." *Newsletter di Archeologia CISA* 5: 375–412.

Manzo, A. 2017a. *Eastern Sudan in its setting: the archaeology of a region far from the Nile valley*. Oxford: Archaeopress.

Manzo, A. 2017b. The territorial expanse of the Pan-Grave culture thirty years later. *Sudan & Nubia* 21: 98–112.

Manzo, A. 2018. Appendix 3: Nubian and southern Red Sea ceramics. In Wallace-Jones, S., *Egyptian and imported pottery from the Red Sea port of Mersa Gawasis, Egypt*. Oxford: Archaeopress, 128–135.

Meeks, D. 2003. Locating Punt. In O'Connor, D., and Quirke, S. (eds.), *Mysterious lands: encounters with ancient Egypt*. London: UCL Press, 53–80.

Minor, E. 2012. *The use of Egyptian and Egyptianizing material culture in Nubian burials of the Classic Kerma period*. PhD dissertation, University of California, Berkeley.

Moeller, N. 2016. *The archaeology of urbanism in ancient Egypt: from the Predynastic period to the end of the Middle Kingdom*. Cambridge: Cambridge University Press.

Morris, E. 2018. *Ancient Egyptian imperialism.* Hoboken, NJ: Wiley-Blackwell.

Näser, C. 2012. Nomads at the Nile: towards an archaeology of interaction. In Barnard, H., and Duistermaat, K. (eds.), *The history of the peoples of the Eastern Desert.* Los Angeles: Cotsen Institute of Archaeology, University of California, 81–89.

Näser, C., Kossatz, K., Grajetzki, W., Elawad Karrar, O.K., and Becker, O. 2017. Shalfak Archaeological Mission (SAM): the 2017 field season. *JEA* 103: 153–171.

O'Connor, D. 1978. Nubia before the New Kingdom. In Wenig, S. (ed.), *Africa in antiquity: the arts of ancient Nubia and the Sudan.* Brooklyn, NY: The Brooklyn Museum, 46–61.

O'Connor, D. 1986. The location of Yam and Kush and their historical implications. *JARCE* 23: 27–50.

O'Connor, D. 1991. Early states along the Nubian Nile. In Davies, W.V. (ed.), *Egypt and Africa: Nubia from prehistory to Islam.* London: British Museum Press, 145–165.

O'Connor, D. 1993. *Ancient Nubia: Egypt's rival in Africa.* Philadelphia: University of Pennsylvania Museum of Archaeology and Anthropology.

O'Connor, D. 2014. *The Old Kingdom town at Buhen.* London: Egypt Exploration Society.

O'Connor, D., and Quirke, S. 2003. Introduction: mapping the unknown in ancient Egypt. In O'Connor, D., and Quirke, S. (eds.), *Mysterious lands: encounters with ancient Egypt.* London: UCL Press, 1–21.

Ogden, J. 2000. Metals. In Nicholson, P.T., and Shaw, I. (eds.), *Ancient Egyptian materials and technology.* Cambridge: Cambridge University Press, 148–176.

Parkinson, R.B. 1991. *Voices from ancient Egypt: an anthology of Middle Kingdom writings.* London: British Museum Press.

Petrie, W.M.F. 1901. *Diospolis Parva: the cemeteries of Abadiyeh and Hu.* London: Egypt Exploration Fund.

Pirelli, R. 2007. Two new stelae from Mersa Gawasis. *RdE* 58: 87–110.

Posener, G. 1940. *Princes et pays d'Asie et de Nubie: textes hiératiques sur des figurines d'envoûtement du Moyen Empire.* Brussels: Fondation Égyptologique Reine Élisabeth.

Randall-MacIver, D., Woolley, L., and Griffith, F.L. 1909. *Areika.* Oxford: Oxford University Press.

Raue, D. 2002. Nubians on Elephantine Island. *Sudan & Nubia* 6: 20–24.

Raue, D. 2008. Who was who in Elephantine of the third millennium BC? *British Museum Studies in Ancient Egypt and Sudan* 9: 1–14.

Raue, D. 2012. Medja vs. Kerma at the First Cataract: terminological problems. In Forstner-Müller, I., and Rose, P. (eds.), *Nubian pottery from Egyptian cultural contexts of the Middle Kingdom and the early New Kingdom*. Vienna: Österreichisches Archäologisches Institut, 49–58.

Raue, D. 2018. *Elephantine und Nubien vom 4.-2. Jahrtausend v. Chr.* Berlin: De Gruyter.

Reisner, G.A. 1923. *Excavations at Kerma, parts I–III*. Cambridge, MA: Peabody Museum of Harvard University.

Reisner, G.A. 1955. Clay sealings of Dynasty XIII from Uronarti fort. *Kush* 3: 26–69.

Ritner, R.K. 2008. *The mechanics of ancient Egyptian magical practice*. Chicago: The Oriental Institute of the University of Chicago.

Sadr, K. 1987. The territorial expanse of the Pan-Grave culture. *Archéologie du Nil Moyen* 2: 265–291.

Sadr, K. 1991. *The development of nomadism in ancient northeast Africa*. Philadelphia: University of Pennsylvania Press.

Säve-Söderbergh, T. 1941. *Ägypten und Nubien: ein Beitrag zur Geschichte der altägyptischen Aussenpolitik*. Lund: Hǎkan Ohlssons Boktryckeri.

Sayed, A.M.A.H. 1977. Discovery of the site of the 12th Dynasty port at Wadi Gawasis on the Red Sea shore. *RdE* 29: 140–178.

Seidlmayer, S.J. 2001. Execration texts. In Redford, D.B. (ed.), *The Oxford encyclopedia of ancient Egypt, vol. 1*. Oxford: Oxford University Press, 487–489.

Shaw, I., and Jameson, R. 1993. Amethyst mining in the Eastern Desert: a preliminary survey at Wadi el-Hudi. *JEA* 79: 81–97.

Smith, H.S. 1976. *The fortress of Buhen: the inscriptions*. London: Egypt Exploration Society.

Smith, S.T. 1990. Administration at the Egyptian Middle Kingdom frontier: sealings from Uronarti and Askut. In Palaima, T.G. (ed.), *Aegean seals, sealings and administration*. Liège: Université de Liège, 197–219.

Smith, S.T. 1991. Askut and the role of the Second Cataract forts. *JARCE* 28: 107–132.

Smith, S.T. 1992. A model for imperialism in Nubia. *GM* 122: 91–92.

Smith, S.T. 1995. *Askut in Nubia: the economics and ideology of Egyptian imperialism in the second millennium BC*. London and New York: Kegan Paul International.

Smith, S.T. 1996. The transmission of an Egyptian administrative system in the second millennium BC: sealing practice in Lower Nubia and at Kerma. In Ferioli, P., Fiandra, E., and Fissore, G.G. (eds.), *Administration in ancient societies*. Turin: Centro Internazionale di Ricerche Archeologiche Antropologiche e Storiche, 67–86.

Smith, S.T. 2003. *Wretched Kush: ethnic identities and boundaries in Egypt's Nubian empire*. London and New York: Routledge.

Smith, S.T. 2014. A potter's wheelhead from Askut and the organization of the Egyptian ceramic industry in Nubia. *JARCE* 50: 108–121.

Smith, S.T. 2018. Middle and New Kingdom sealing practice in Egypt and Nubia: a comparison. In Ameri, M., Costello, S., Jamison, G., and Scott, S. (eds.), *Seals and sealing in the ancient world: case studies from the Near East, Egypt, the Aegean, and South Asia*. Cambridge: Cambridge University Press, 302–324.

Smither, P. 1945. The Semnah dispatches. *JEA* 31: 3–10.

Strudwick, N.C. 2005. *Texts from the Pyramid Age*. Atlanta, GA: Society of Biblical Literature.

Tallet, P. 2013. Deux notes sur les expéditions au pays de Pount à la lumière de nouvelles données archéologiques. *RdE* 64: 189–210.

Tallet, P. 2015. Les "ports intermittents" de la Mer Rouge à l'époque pharaonique: caractéristiques et chronologie. *Nehet* 3: 31–72.

Trigger, B.G. 1965. *History and settlement in Lower Nubia*. New Haven, CT: Yale University Publications in Anthropology.

Trigger, B.G. 1976. *Nubia under the pharaohs*. London: Thames & Hudson.

Trigger, B.G. 1982. The reasons for the construction of the Second Cataract forts. *Journal of the Society for the Study of Egyptian Antiquities* 12: 1–6.

Veldmeijer, A.J., and Zazzaro, C. 2008. The "Rope Cave" at Mersa/Wadi Gawasis. *JARCE* 44: 9–39.

Vercoutter, J. 1970. *Mirgissa, I*. Paris: Centre national de la Recherche scientifique.

Vila, A. 1963. Un dépôt de textes d'envoûtement au Moyen Empire. *Journal des Savants* 1963: 135–160.

Ward, C., and Zazzaro, C. 2007. Ship timbers: description and preliminary analysis. In Bard, K.A., and Fattovich, R. (eds.), *Harbor of the pharaohs to the land of Punt: archaeological investigations at Mersa/Wadi Gawasis, Egypt, 2001–2005*. Naples: Universitá degli Studi di Napoli "L'Orientale," 135–150.

Wegner, J. 1995. The function and history of the site of Areika. *JARCE* 32: 127–160.

Weschenfelder, P. 2014. Linking the Eastern Desert and the Nile valley: Pan-Grave people from the late Middle Kingdom to the early New Kingdom. In Anderson, J.R., and Welsby, D.A. (eds.), *The Fourth Cataract and beyond.* Leuven: Peeters, 357–366.

Williams, B.B. 1999. Serra East and the mission of Middle Kingdom fortresses in Nubia. In Teeter, E., and Larson, J.A. (eds.), *Gold of praise: studies on ancient Egypt in honor of Edward F. Wente.* Chicago: The Oriental Institute of the University of Chicago, 435–453.

Zazzaro, C. 2007. Stone anchors and pierced stones. In Bard, K.A., and Fattovich, R. (eds.), *Harbor of the pharaohs to the land of Punt: archaeological investigations at Mersa/Wadi Gawasis, Egypt, 2001–2005.* Naples: Universitá degli Studi di Napoli "L'Orientale," 153–163.

21

Middle Kingdom Egypt and the Eastern Mediterranean

Ezra S. Marcus

21.1. Introduction

The resumption of unified rule during the Middle Kingdom, which had its origin, heyday, and decline, respectively, in the Eleventh, Twelfth, and Thirteenth Dynasties, brought with it a revival of many social, religious, political, and economic patterns of the Old Kingdom, which were variously continued, reimagined, transformed, and expanded.[1] Among those that were destined to impact significantly on the history of Western Asia in the second millennium BC were Egypt's re-establishment of relations with its nearest neighbor, the Levant, and then with other regions of the Eastern Mediterranean, notably Cyprus and Crete (figure 21.1 a–c).

Sustained Egyptian contacts with the Levant can be traced back, at least, to the Predynastic period (cf. chapter 4 in volume 1),[2] and continued and intensified during the Old Kingdom (cf. chapter 6 in volume 1) until they apparently ceased with Egypt's collapse and the onset of the First Intermediate Period. These relations are generally perceived

---

1. Cf. Hayes 1971; 1973; Kemp 1983; Oppenheim 2015.

2. Van den Brink and Levy 2002; Marcus 2002a.

Ezra S. Marcus, *Middle Kingdom Egypt and the Eastern Mediterranean* In: *The Oxford History of the Ancient Near East*. Edited by: Karen Radner, Nadine Moeller, and D. T. Potts, Oxford University Press. © Oxford University Press 2022. DOI: 10.1093/oso/9780190687571.003.0021

as having been predicated on an Egyptian demand for a variety of Mediterranean arboreal and horticultural products, as well as for ores and minerals from the latter's immediate and more distant regions. Prior to the Middle Kingdom, many raw materials and finished products from the Levant had become widespread in Egyptian society, economy, and religion, where they were crucial for the construction of buildings and boats (conifers, especially cedar), for a wide range of elite social interactions, especially drinking and banqueting (e.g., wine, juices, spices), for ritual and funerary practices (e.g., conifers, resins, spices), and for the work of artisans (e.g., metals, bitumen, semi-precious stones). To maintain the supply of these important imports, Egypt's rulers employed a

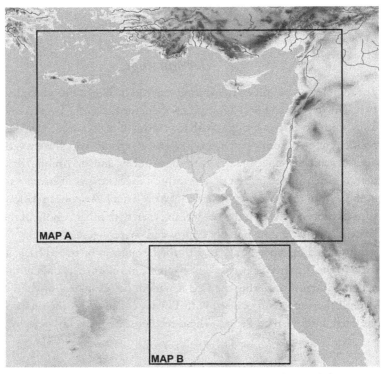

FIGURE 21.1A.   Sites mentioned in this chapter. Prepared by Andrea Squitieri (LMU Munich).

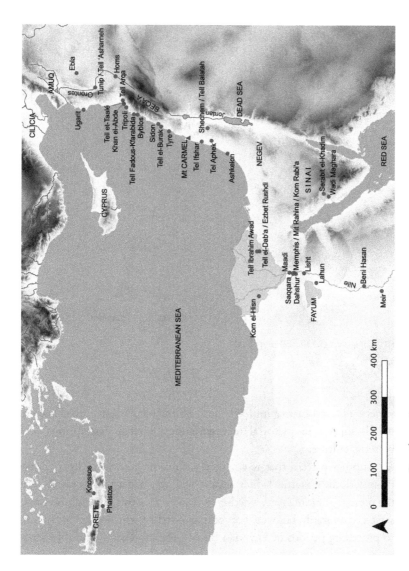

FIGURE 21.1B. Detail map A.

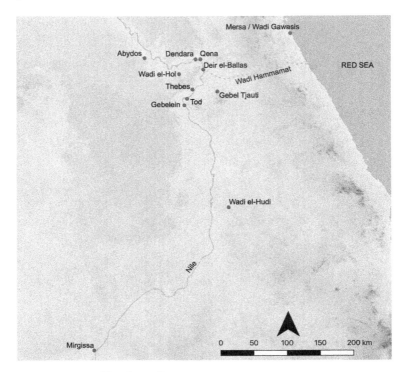

FIGURE 21.1C. Detail map B.

variety of diplomatic, military, and commercial means, evidence for which survive in pictorial representations, textual descriptions, and material culture.

Another pattern that re-emerged within the context of Egypt's relations with the eastern Mediterranean—if it ever had actually ceased—was the presence of foreigners, whether as visitors, residents, or sojourners who stayed temporarily, but were not seeking to settle permanently.[3] In contrast to preceding periods of Egyptian history, the professions and roles these

---

3. See the excellent and comprehensive survey and discussion in Mourad 2015: 19–130.

foreigners held in the Middle Kingdom became much more varied, numerous, and consequential. Indeed, by the late Middle Kingdom, their numbers had increased considerably, particularly in the delta, where at Tell el-Dabʿa, the demographic estimates (based on the extensively available material culture, including religious, domestic, and funerary architecture and finds) indicate substantial immigration. The size, diversity, and permanence of the foreign presence sets this period apart from previous periods[4] and establishes the template for one of the largest expatriate, cosmopolitan communities in Egypt in pre-Classical times: the Hyksos in Avaris (cf. chapter 23 in volume 3).

All of the preceding aspects were essential to the high degree to which Middle Kingdom Egypt appears to have been integrated into an increasingly larger maritime interaction zone that encompassed the Middle Bronze Age (MBA) Levant and the eastern Mediterranean, including Cyprus and the Aegean, and acted as a key catalyst within this zone. These relations decisively shaped contemporary and subsequent Egyptian and Mediterranean culture and history.

21.2. Approaches and methodological issues

Modern scholars' characterizations of the relations between Middle Kingdom Egypt and the Levant have been extremely diverse. They have ranged from arguing for direct Egyptian control over the Levant[5] to the assumption of asymmetrical political and economic relations[6] or to claiming the existence of a geographically restrictive relationship that would see only limited or no contact with the southern Levant, as Egypt would have negotiated its interests with the northern Levant, solely via the port of Byblos in Lebanon.[7] Until recently, all of these characterizations

---

4. Such as at Predynastic Maadi and Old Kingdom Tell Ibrahim Awad; cf. Bard 1994: 277–279; Bietak 2003.

5. Albright 1928; 1941; Maisler 1947: 34; Mazar 1968: 74; 1986: 8; Giveon 1967; 1987.

6. Cf. Ward 1961a; 1961b; Posener 1971: 547.

7. Weinstein 1975; D. Ben-Tor 1997; 2007: 117–119; 2011: 24–27; 2018: 337–338.

have relied on a very limited body of textual and pictorial records, or stratigraphically unreliable archaeological data. However, in the last few decades, new evidence has emerged. This includes two important texts (discussed in sections 21.4.2 and 21.4.4) that have radically transformed and enriched our understanding of Egyptian-Levantine relations; new, more reliably stratified archaeological data that have been excavated at a number of archaeological sites along the eastern Mediterranean littoral zone; and the re-evaluation of old finds and contexts—all adding new insights and stimulating the application of new approaches, such as "world systems" and "center-periphery" models[8] as well as maritime models for understanding the broader eastern Mediterranean interaction zone and the impact of "port power."[9]

In considering the processes affecting Egyptian–eastern Mediterranean relations within a chronological rather than a thematic framework, it is necessary to synchronize the astrochronologically anchored Egyptian chronology and its historical and archaeological records based on the reign of individual rulers with the relative archaeological sequences of the Levant and the eastern Mediterranean. Unfortunately, the relevant data for synchronizing these chronologies is based on a limited corpus of Egyptian textual references, some with toponyms and ethnonyms (or, better, exonyms) whose identification, respectively, with specific sites or groups, may be unknown, uncertain, or merely lacking in consensus.[10] Primarily, these synchronisms have been based on the very same material cultural evidence (e.g., ceramics, scarab seals, and sealings) that also contribute to characterizing these relations. In such an approach, the absence of synchronisms in any particular time span ostensibly renders mute any discussion of either

---

8. See reviews in Cohen 2002: 21–31; 2009; 2015b: 255–260; 2016: 42–48.

9. Marcus 1991; 1998; 2002b; 2007. For the concept of "port power," see Stager 2002; Cohen 2009.

10. Mourad 2015: 13–14 and *passim* reviews the various terms the Egyptians applied to those with whom they interacted in and from the Levant. For simplicity's sake, they are referred to here as Levantines or Asiatics.

issue—contemporaneity or contact—as well as negating any comparison or contrast between the relevant regions' social, political, economic,
or cultural developments. Recently, however, the increasing application
of radiocarbon analysis, especially to single-year growth samples (typically plant seeds) from archaeological sites in the eastern Mediterranean
region, has enabled previously held notions regarding the absolute or
calendrical chronology and material culture-based synchronisms to be
independently investigated, or, in the latter case, has helped overcome
the limits imposed by their absence.[11] Moreover, the integration of scientific and traditional archaeological data bodes well for the eventual construction of high-precision sub-century chronological schemes.[12] In this
chapter, that evidence will be considered as necessary.

21.3. Early Middle Kingdom relations with the Levant

Evidence for the resumption of contacts between Egypt and the Levant
begins to appear during the reign of Mentuhotep II Nebhepetra (2055–
2004 BC), probably following Egypt's reunification (ca. 2023 BC) under
this ruler, when the necessary investments in resources and manpower
(not easily available during internal conflict) could be allocated for commercial and military expeditions abroad.[13] The evidence from the last
three decades of Mentuhotep II's reign is scant: belligerency or outright
military activity toward Asiatics is limited to two pictorial depictions of

---

11. On the radiocarbon chronology of the Middle Kingdom, see Ramsey et al. 2010;
Dee 2013; and in particular Marcus et al. 2016 for the radiocarbon determina-
tions of Lahun Papyrus 10012B, which offers a *terminus post quem* of 1886 BC
for the earliest known astronomical datum in the reign of Senusret III. In this
volume, the chronology in *The Oxford History of Ancient Egypt* (Shaw 2004) is
used, which eschews co-regencies, but note also the "high chronology" for Egypt
used by Kitchen 2000: 46–47, 49, and the "low" alternative of Hornung, Krauss,
and Warburton 2006.

12. Cf. Marcus 2013; see also chapter 11 in this volume.

13. Ward 1971: 59; Redford 1992: 69. See also discussion in Marochetti 2010: 12–13.

the king "smiting" Asiatics on reliefs from Dendara and Gebelein, accompanied by textual references to their submission.[14] Explicit references to actual military actions that may have been directed against the Levant are relatively sparse. The available data include the text of a stele from the tomb of Khety at Thebes (TT 311) that mentions reprisals against Asiatics in "their countries" or "highlands" during a mining expedition to the Sinai;[15] a reference in the autobiographical tomb inscription of Henenu, the king's steward, at Thebes (TT 313) to his marshalling of 1,000 (?) men to exact tribute from the "sand [dwellers]";[16] and the graffito of the Nubian mercenary Tjemhemau, who commemorates his participation in a war against the Asiatics of Djaty.[17] These attestations are complemented by a number of army and siege scenes dating to either the late Eleventh or the early Twelfth Dynasty in the tombs at Beni Hasan of Baqet III (No. 15) and Khety (No. 17),[18] with individuals depicted as typical Asiatics shown both on the Egyptian and the enemy side.[19] In addition, the tomb of Intef at Thebes offers a rare depiction of the siege of a fortified Asiatic stronghold[20] and of a riverine battle engagement,[21] although it is impossible to identify either of the locations.

Non-military, commercial relations with the northern Levant might be reflected in the presumably seaborne expedition to the "cedar slopes" in

---

14. Ward 1971: 60–61; Cohen 2002: 34; Marochetti 2005: fig. 2.

15. Gardiner 1917: 35; Ward 1971: 59.

16. Hayes 1949: 46; Cohen 2002: 35–36. The often-cited reference in the Deir el-Ballas inscription to activity in Qedem (e.g., Redford 1992: 69; Cohen 2002: 34), interpreted as the eastern inland areas of the Levant, as initially read by H.G. Fischer, has been refuted on philological grounds by Darnell 2008: 94–95.

17. Ward 1971: 62; cf. Redford 1992: 70, who suggests an identification with Zarethan in the Jordan valley that is, however, unsupported by current archaeological evidence. See also the discussion in Marochetti 2010: 12 n. 95, 96.

18. Newberry 1894: pls. V, XV; Mourad 2015: 81–82, figs. 4.46, 4.47, 4.55.

19. Note the reservations articulated by Schulman 1982 regarding the historical context of these scenes.

20. Di. Arnold and Settgast 1965: pl. 2.

21. Settgast 1969.

order to cut wood, as described in the Henenu inscription.[22] The acquisition of "fresh" cedar for the construction of a coffin is mentioned in the funerary stele of Abkau at Abydos; this and other contemporary coniferous woods dated to this period occur in the form of coffins, boxes, or models.[23] Under Mentuhotep III Sankhkara (1992–1980 BC), an inscription of Henu incised on a rock cliff in the Wadi Hammamat, which connects the great bend in the Nile near Qena with the Red Sea, records the construction of a "Byblos ship" (*kebenet*) for an expedition to Punt (cf. chapter 20 in this volume),[24] probably indicating the import of coniferous wood (and possibly even cedar) from the Levant for the construction of seagoing vessels.[25] The reference to lapis lazuli brought to Egypt from Khety's Sinai expedition[26] indicates the resumed participation in a much larger trade network that ultimately includes the lapis sources in distant Afghanistan.

21.4. The Twelfth Dynasty and the Levant

21.4.1. Soldiers, servants, and travelers: Levantine relations under Amenemhat I and Senusret I

In the wake of internecine violence,[27] Amenemhat I (1985–1956 BC) founded the Twelfth Dynasty, which would eventually mark Middle Kingdom Egypt's political zenith and the heyday of its ever increasing, if seemingly contradictory, contacts with the Levant and with Levantines.[28]

---

22. Hayes 1949: 46, n. j, k; Ward 1971: 61–62; Redford 1992: 69; Cohen 2002: 35–36.

23. Ward 1971: 62; Lucas and Harris 1989: 430–432; Davies 1995: 146–147, n. 31, Table 1, pl. 10:1.

24. Breasted 1906: §§432–433; Säve-Söderbergh 1946: 48.

25. On the term *kebenet*, see Esposito 2019: 48, n. 76, 77.

26. Gardiner 1917: 36–37.

27. Cf. Redford 1992: 71–75.

28. See the comprehensively researched and authoritative review of the evidence in Mourad 2015, and especially her discussion of the ideological, religious, and theoretical aspects of the discordant Egyptian treatment of the "other" (Mourad 2015: 13–16, 189–193).

On the one hand, the Asiatics continue to be treated pejoratively through-out this period by this dynasty's rulers and aristocracy, in textual references that reflect real or rhetorical animus and occasional military intervention, as well as in pictorial depictions, some of which are highly detailed.[29] Yet while the ancient trope of the wretched Asiatic was routinely used, Egypt would seem to have maintained with the Levant what has been called an "entente cordiale,"[30] manifest in a variety of contexts: coopera-tion in the working of the Sinai mines; engaging in trade both abroad and, presumably, within Egypt; the respectful reception of delegations; the employment of Asiatics in a great range of professional roles within Egypt; and allowing, if not encouraging, the long-term, sometimes multi-generational, residency of foreigners in Egypt, as individuals and as com-munities, and often immersed in local culture as well as bringing their own cultural traditions.

In the twenty-fourth regnal year of Amenemhat I, his gen-eral Nesmontu attacked the fortresses of three different Asiatic population groups, located somewhere in the north and east.[31] Contemporary wall paintings in the tomb of the governor Khnumhotep I at Beni Hasan (No. 14) include scenes depicting foreign-ers, among them bearded Asiatic mercenaries brandishing character-istically Levantine weapons such as socketed fenestrated (or duckbill) axes and daggers, and a siege scene.[32] An incomplete inscription from

29. Schulman 1982: 167–168. The lack of such imagery may be a result of poor preservation of monuments in the area of the Middle Kingdom capital of Memphis, owing to the violent events at the beginning and the end of the Second Intermediate Period, or merely misfortune.

30. Vercoutter 1965: 365.

31. Breasted 1906: §§470–471; Ward 1961a: 38; Redford 1992: 77; Cohen 2002: 38; Mourad 2015: 100, 280, 286.

32. Newberry 1893: pl. XLVII; Rabehl 2006: 179; Mourad 2015: 83–84, figs. 4.48, 4.49, 4.55. The siege scene is discussed in Rabehl 2006: 179, but remains to be published in full.

his tomb records a naval expedition involving twenty cedar ships and attacks against Asiatic groups.[33]

By contrast, evidence for non-military interaction is scant. Amenemhat I's mortuary temple at Lisht may feature depictions of Asiatics arriving in a procession, as evinced by a fragment of a yellow-skinned child on its mother's back.[34] A tomb scene restored from fragments found in a pit near his pyramid complex, possibly belonging to the tomb of one of his high officials, shows Levantine ceramic imports,[35] namely large storage vessels with and without handles[36] being filled with wine and sealed. Unfortunately, no actual Levantine pottery from Egypt can be securely dated to this period.[37]

Senusret I (1956–1911 BC), who may have initially ruled as co-regent, including at the time of Nesmontu's attack, was referred to as one "who cuts the throats" of the Asiatics and who has "numerous emissaries in

---

33. Newberry 1893: 84–85, pl. XLIV; Breasted 1906: §§463–465; Ward 1961a: 38; Redford 1992: 74. Note that Mourad 2015: 84 considers this text to be the historical background for the wall paintings.

34. Mourad 2015: 72, fig. 4.39.

35. Di. Arnold 2008: 64, 66–67, 85; Mourad 2015: 73, fig. 4.40. For a photograph of the restored relief (Metropolitan Museum of Art 16.3.1) see https://www.metmuseum.org/art/collection/search/546715.

36. Both Mourad (2015: 73, n. 844) and Do. Arnold (cited by Di. Arnold 2008: 66, n. 124) reference two-handled storage jars as parallels for these vessels. However, if the proportions in the scene are consistent, their apertures greatly exceed that of those parallels. Only one parallel cited by Mourad (cf. Thalmann 2008: fig. 2:4.), a handled and wide-apertured foundation deposit jar in the Levantine Painted Ware tradition (Bagh 2013: 124), which was found in the Ba'alat Gebal Temple in Byblos and which may belong to an EB IV horizon, is comparable. As none of the depictions is complete, some of these vessels could be kraters (Thalmann 2006: pl. 93: 4). Handleless *pithoi* (large vessels not meant to be readily moved), similar to those in the scene, have a long history from EB IV Tell Arqa (Thalmann 2006: pls. 70–72; 2008: fig. 2: 16–17) through MB IIB Kinet Höyük (Gates 2000: fig. 5), but are under-represented in the published literature as they are rarely preserved whole and fragmentary sherds are often misidentified.

37. Do. Arnold et al. 1995: 16–17, fig. 6:1 reported what could have been the earliest Canaanite import, an S-profiled (or carinated) bowl with a twin rope decoration; but it was found in a later robbers' tunnel of the pyramid of Amenemhat I at Lisht.

every land, the couriers do what he has willed."[38] His vizier Mentuhotep is said to be "one who pacifies the sand dwellers," an epithet referring perhaps to the vanquished Asiatics depicted on a block from his king's funerary temple at Lisht,[39] while a stele from Abydos describes him as one who "puts his oppression/terror into the foreigner . . . pacifies the *Heriu-sha* . . . the *Setje(t)iu*."[40] The temple of Montu, the god of war, at Tod bears an undated inscription probably belonging to this Senusret,[41] whose tone is belligerent toward Asiatics and others. It details endowments of foreign materials such as silver, bronze, lapis lazuli, and possibly imported copper, all of which parallels his successor Amenemhat II's similar offerings to Montu (see section 21.4.2).

In the tomb of Amenemhat in Beni Hasan (No. 2), dated to Year 43, Asiatic soldiers wearing tricolor kilts and carrying Levantine fenestrated axes and javelins are depicted near the siege of a fortified city that may have been defended by Egyptians.[42] In addition, fair-skinned individuals populate other scenes in the tomb as hunters, as dancers or performers, as bakers and brewers, and even as the supervisor (or scribe) overseeing the filling of jars; based on the indication of their skin tones, these people have been interpreted as (possibly second-generation) Asiatics or the children of Egyptian-Asiatic intermarriage.[43] As part of a pot-making scene, foreign ceramic shapes are depicted, indicating at the least local Egyptian awareness of these shapes[44] and possibly hinting at attempts

---

38. Rowe 1939: 188–191; Posener 1971: 538, 540; Mourad 2015: 144.

39. Posener 1971: 538; Mourad 2015: 73–74, figs. 4.41–4.43.

40. Mourad 2015: 280 (CG 20539).

41. Redford 1987: 42; Barbotin and Clère 1991: 9; Mourad 2015: 113–114.

42. Newberry 1893: 24, 32–33; Schulman 1982: 176–178; Mourad 2015: 84–85, figs. 4.50, 4.55.

43. Newberry 1893: pl. 12; Mourad 2015: 84–85.

44. Newberry 1893: pl. 11; Mourad 2015: 85, figs. 4.51. While drawing on parallels from the EB IV/MB I Levant might make sense, given the chronological horizon and some of the idiosyncrasies of the shapes, Mourad's parallels in the Levant and the dates given are far from convincing. Numerous comparable parallels for the flat-based jug occur also in MB II Tell Arqa (Phase N: Thalmann 2006: pls.

to copy them. In the tomb of the nomarch Ukhhotep at Meir, a possible female Levantine slave is shown attending to the deceased's wife.[45] A wooden statue found in Beni Hasan Shaft Tomb 181 depicts an Asiatic woman who carries a child on her back and is dated to sometime between the reigns of Senusret I and his predecessor.[46]

The Levant and Asiatics also played a role in Middle Kingdom literary works that were either produced or set in this period, the most notable being the "Story of Sinuhe." The earliest extant manuscript of what was probably one of the most popular works of Middle Kingdom literature (judging from the thirty-two papyrus copies that have survived from antiquity) dates to the reign of Amenemhat III (1831–1786 BC), but was composed shortly after the reign of Senusret I.[47] This work belongs to a long-lived narrative genre that includes, e.g., the "Shipwrecked Sailor" and the "Story of Wenamun," wherein an Egyptian who had traveled abroad recounted in first person his trials and tribulations in foreign lands until he finally succeeded in returning home. In this story,[48] Sinuhe had fled Egypt following the suspicious death of Amenemhat I and, fearing for his life should he return, he headed northward, eschewing Byblos, and reached Qedem ("Story of Sinuhe" B29),[49] where he dwelled among the Asiatics (*aamu*) in a land called Iaa (B81).[50] There he rose to great status and wealth under a ruler named Amunenshi (B76–B77), marrying

84–85) and her comparisons for the "bi-handled" storage jar from Byblos, quoted as an EB IV parallel, is in fact an MB form (Thalmann 2008: fig. 3).

45. Mourad 2015: 94–95, fig. 4.56.

46. Do. Arnold 2010; Mourad 2015: 91.

47. Parkinson 1991: 36; 1997: 21–26.

48. Numerous translations exist, e.g., Breasted 1906: §§486–497; Wilson 1950a:18–22; Simpson 1973; Lichtheim 1973: 222–235; and Parkinson 1997: 21–53, which was used for this chapter, together with the treatment of Mourad 2013: 301–304.

49. Possibly to be read as Qatna: Schneider 2002: 261.

50. See Gubel and Loffet 2011–2012 and Mourad 2013 for the most recent discussions of where these toponyms are located: the Akkar plain or the Beqaa valley.

his daughter (B78), fathering his grandchildren (B92), becoming a commander in his army (B100), and defeating an enemy warrior in man-to-man combat (B109–B143)—all until, ostensibly utterly Levantinized (B265), he is summoned home by Senusret I (B175–B188).

Sinuhe's description of his sojourn in the Levant has attracted much scholarly attention and stimulated debate, not the least because he seemingly was an eyewitness whose testimony could shed light on the social, political, and economic conditions in the Levant, and its relations with Egypt in this period.[51] While no consensus exists regarding the narrative's reliability as a historical document, its success with ancient audiences would have certainly relied on "embedded factual elements"[52] in the form of plausible descriptions of the geography, the people, their titles, and their behavior, as well as the historical circumstances; anything less, and this tale might never had achieved the popularity and longevity it enjoyed, particularly given the increasing familiarity and interaction between Egypt and the Levant and Levantines, which characterized the remainder of the second millennium BC.[53] In addition to the aforementioned and additional toponyms and Semitic names,[54] the "Story of Sinuhe" provides insights into the regular movement of Egyptians within the Levant (B94–B95), some of whom appear to be residents there (B34); bilingualism among Levantines and Egyptians (B31), perhaps partly facilitated by instances of exogamy (B78); two-way communication and news of Egypt circulating in the Levant (B31–B36); diplomatic gift-giving (B175); the existence of settled communities in the Levant, some living in cities with walls and gates (B116);[55] and the lifestyles of communities that pursue a combination of agriculture,

---

51. Cf. Rainey 1972; 2006; Baines 1982; Green 1983; Goedicke 1992; Redford 1992: 82–87; Cohen 2002: 38–41; Gubel and Loffet 2011–2012; Mourad 2015: 120–123.

52. Mourad 2013: 72; 2015: 122.

53. Note that extracts of this story are known on over thirty New Kingdom ostraca (Mourad 2015: 120), which suggests its wide distribution.

54. Mourad 2013: 71.

55. Mourad 2015: 303.

horticulture, apiculture (bee-keeping), and pastoralism, as well as hunting and fowling (B81–B85, B89–B91).

Although clearly biased in its presentation of Egypt's status and its relations with the Levant, this literary work offers a multifaceted portrait of interaction in the latter half of the twentieth century BC that would have been familiar to contemporary and later Egyptian audiences accustomed to their countrymen being abroad, as well as to the arrival of foreigners in Egypt. By land, that movement would have been controlled by the so-called Walls of the Ruler (B16), a fortress or border system constructed apparently in the time of Amenemhat I. Other literary works, too, mention or allude to this fortification, such as the "Prophecy of Neferti" and the "Teaching for King Merykara," which were probably composed in the late Middle Kingdom, if not later,[56] but are set in the maelstrom of the Herakleopolitan period (ca. 2160–2025 BC). There, reference is made to the receipt of imported woods like cypress (*meru*) and juniper (*wan*) and to Asiatic robbers inhabiting the eastern delta, against whom fortifications should be erected.[57] This description probably best reflects the earlier period, while serving as a justification for contemporary policies.

Apart from the allusions to possible non-military commercial interaction in literary texts, as with his predecessor, relevant textual and archaeological evidence from the reign of Senusret I is scant,[58] and whatever evidence exists could have equally derived from booty or tribute. This includes the depictions of possible carob pods depicted as offerings

---

56. Parkinson 1997: 131–133, 212–215. Lichtheim (1973: 97, 139) dates the former to the first ruler of the Twelfth Dynasty and the latter to the Ninth–Tenth Dynasties. Redford (1992: 66) concurs with her regarding the former (cf. chapter 19 in this volume). See also Gnirs 2006; 2013.

57. Ward 1971: 22–36; Lichtheim 1973: 97–109; Redford 1992: 67–68; Parkinson 1997: 222–224.

58. A number of long-lived Egyptian forms, which initially appeared in Senusret I's reign, occur in the Levant at Tel Ifshar and Sidon Level 1, but these contexts' stratigraphic horizon and accompanying Levantine forms (e.g., bichrome Levantine Painted Ware; see later discussion) preclude such an early date (see later discussion). See, e.g., Bader et al. 2009: fig. 1; Marcus et al. 2008b: 209, fig. 3:1; Schiestl and Seiler 2012: 396–397, I.A.7.b: 4, 5.

in the tomb of Amenemhat at Beni Hasan (No. 2),[59] and some of the cedar and other coniferous woods found in Middle Kingdom contexts in Egypt without specific dating.[60]

21.4.2. The resumption of Mediterranean maritime trade during of Amenemhat II

Amenemhat II's reign (1911–1877 BC) was once considered one of the most poorly documented periods of the Twelfth Dynasty,[61] particularly considering its length. The discovery of a single royal inscription has ameliorated this deficiency, and his reign now stands out as the one with the most detailed information available regarding Egypt's military and commercial relations with the Levant. That inscription (figure 21.2) is incised on a wall fragment, apparently from the temple of Ptah in Memphis (Mit Rahina), which was reused as a plinth for a statue of the New Kingdom pharaoh Rameses II. This ancient repurposing preserved more than a year of entries from the daybook of the royal court, spanning the very end of Amenemhat II's co-regency with his father and part of his first year as sole regent. Now known as the Mit Rahina inscription (or the Annals of Amenemhat II), the text continues to stimulate discussion.[62]

The Mit Rahina inscription describes a sequence of actions, decisions, and events that took place in the royal court of Memphis. While those descriptions are succinct, detailed attention is paid to locations, to

---

59. Mourad 2015: 85.

60. Willems 1988: 51; Lucas and Harris 1989: 430; Davies 1995.

61. Fay 1996: 7; Simpson 2001: 455.

62. For the inscription with collations, transliterations, translations, and interpretations, see Farag 1980; Altenmüller and Moussa 1991; Malek and Quirke 1992; Obsomer 1995: 595–606; Dantong 1998; 1999; Cohen 2002; Marcus 2007; Mourad 2015: 78–79, 275–277; Altenmüller 2015. In this chapter, Altenmüller and Moussa's translation is generally followed. "M" numbers refer to the inscription's column.

FIGURE 21.2. The Mit Rahina inscription. The upper photograph shows the block in situ, nestled between two walls being examined and, to the left, the inscribed base with the feet of a colossal statue of Rameses II, which had covered and preserved the inscription. The lower photograph shows a close-up of the inscribed block. Reproduced, respectively, from Malek 1992: 18 and Malek and Quirke 1992: pl. II; © Norbert Böer (Cologne).

functionaries and groups of foreigners, to materials and objects, and for these to the precise quantities, weights, and volumes (often to the fraction). Entries directly relating to Egypt's involvement with the Levant include commercial, military, and mining expeditions; the arrival of Asiatic dignitaries with tribute; and endowments, distributions, and rewards of foreign products.

In the late winter or early spring of 1908 BC,[63] an expedition was dispatched by sea to Khenti-she (M7),[64] a generic geographical term for the northern Levant. Afterward, following a gap in the text in which the levying of recruits must have been described, a military expedition is dispatched by sea, led by a general,[65] in order to destroy the Asiatics (*setjet*) of Iua (M8), a toponym that has been variously identified as "Old Tyre" in Lebanon,[66] Ura in Cilicia,[67] or the land of Iaa.[68] The next entry records endowments to the god Montu (following his father's example: see section 21.4.1), including imported silver and Asiatic copper vessels (M9–M10), perhaps to elicit the god's support for the military venture. Sometime in late spring or early summer, another expedition (for which no prior entry regarding its dispatch is preserved in the extant text) returns from the "Turquoise Terraces," presumably in the western Sinai Peninsula, bringing back turquoise and other minerals as well as wild animals and their skins, along with other organic products, aromatics,

---

63. See Altenmüller and Moussa 1991: 26–27, 38 for the date and internal chronology and Marcus 2007: 143, 145–146 for the actual seasons in which these events occurred, which are consistent with those of traditional sailing and military campaigns. Note that the text's only firm date is based on the mention of the Sokar festival held sometime in late February (M4: "[IV] *akhet* 25–26"; see especially Obsomer 1995: 595).

64. Marcus 2007: 143–144.

65. Ward 1982: 28, no. 194; Mourad 2015: 275, n. 35.

66. Goedicke 1991: 93, n. 32.

67. Helck 1989; Redford 1992: 79, n. 47; Eder 1995: 191; Quack 1996. Note the reading of Kizzuwatna (that is, Cilicia) in Sinuhe by Schneider 2002: 265–266.

68. Gubel and Loffet 2011–2012: 82.

silver, and cattle (M13–M14); the latter four materials probably originated from exchange with Levantine groups.

In late summer or autumn, after destroying the two fortified cities Iua and Iasy, an army returned on foot with 1,554 captives, a variety of finished products (e.g., weapons, tools, jewelry, household vessels) as well as raw and scrap materials of bronze, copper, silver, lead, and wood, tallied by either quantity, mass, or volume and totaling at least 100 kilograms (M16–M18).[69] Clearly, the principal goal of this expedition was military and punitive, with the captives being the main commodity returned to Egypt. Some scholars have identified the second town as Alašiya (Cyprus), but for a number of reasons that seems unlikely.[70] More recently, an identification with Ullaza has been suggested,[71] a Levantine port which subsequently plays an important role in Egypt's cedar trade under Senusret III (see section 21.4.4).[72]

The next entry (M18–M21) records the return of the Khenti-she expedition in two transport ships (*depet*),[73] followed by a long list of cargo, including sixty-five Asiatics; finished products such as weapons and personal items; raw metals such as silver, gold, bronze, copper, white lead; minerals such as marble, emery, grinding stones, and polishing sand; organic materials such as resins, spices, herbs, aromatics, fruits, seeds, plants, and trees; and as the final entry, 231 units of cedar (presumably trunks or planks). As in the previous entry of the inscription, each item is tallied either by quantity, mass, or volume, making this detailed list the earliest ship's manifest known from the Mediterranean. Not counting the cedar and those items for which only their quantity is noted, the two ships carried at least 28 tons of cargo. However, an estimate based

---

69. Marcus 2007: 150, Table 1. This crude minimum includes an arbitrary kilogram for each of the 54 *henu* vessels.

70. Marcus 2007: 146–148.

71. Gubel and Loffet 2011–2012: 82.

72. It might seem that this identification would presuppose a return by sea, given the coastal topography (Mourad 2013: 81). However, note the difficulty or even impossibility of transporting so many captives by ship; see Marcus 2007: 157.

73. Jones 1988: 150.

on possible cedar measurements, both for cut boards and trunks, would add cargo between 8 tons (based on two-meter long boards, the minimum length required for the construction of a Middle Kingdom coffin) to a least 460 tons (for a reasonable minimum size trunk with a length of 2 m and a diameter of 1.5 m).[74] Given the evidence for the large scale of cedar wood being imported during the Middle Kingdom, both for Nilotic funerary boat construction and for vessels for the Red Sea maritime expeditions out of the port of Wadi Gawasis (cf. chapter 20 in this volume) and given the fact that the very absence of any measurements presupposes a known size or common unit, it is much more likely that whole trunks were listed, thus indicating a larger cargo volume and mass and hence the use of larger ships. The fact that the timber was mentioned last may have been intended to emphasize this commodity's great importance and suggest that it was the main objective and cargo of this expedition.

In between the dispatch and return of the aforementioned expeditions, the royal court received tribute-bearing foreign delegations, including the Asiatics (*setjet*) who brought silver, gold (?), cattle and other small domestic animals, 1,002 Asiatics, lead and white lead (M12–M13), and obeisant bearers of lead from Tjemepau (M15),[75] which has been identified as Tunip (Tell Asharneh in Syria).[76] Following the arrival of the last expedition of the year, (additional?) tribute is recorded from Retenu and Khenti-she, and various goods were brought to the palace (M21–M23), from whence they were redistributed to soldiers and officials for services rendered to the crown, including the successful destruction of Iua and Iasy (M25–M26).

Despite its various lacunae and lack of clarity on some issues, the Mit Rahina inscription offers important insights into Egyptian-Levantine relations from the vantage point of the royal court, documenting a year's worth of selected interaction. Clearly, a distinction is made between

---

74. Marcus 2007: 150–154, Table 2.

75. Alternatively, *kheru* "nomads" from *Tjemepau*: Altenmüller and Moussa 1991: 12.

76. Goedicke 1991: 90–93; Eder 1995: 188–189; Gubel and Loffet 2011–2012: 82.

military and commercial activity, with tributary payments perhaps augmenting both.[77] While military action was directed against a specific target in this particular text, the commercial expedition refers only to a general region, wherein Egyptian ships could make land in multiple ports of call and trade for a variety of goods, even if the principal objective was clearly to procure cedar wood. The range of goods brought back to Egypt illustrates not only the great variety of goods available in the Levant, but also the local capability to supply them, which presumes a high level of complexity and organization in cultivation, production, packaging, and storage of local commodities, as well those that originated in the immediate hinterland or even further afield.

The text also hints at some of the means by which Asiatics might arrive in Egypt: as coerced or captured prisoners, cargo, or tribute. Contemporary evidence for such mobility and possible acculturation may be seen in the burial of an Egyptian official whose mother was an Asiatic woman, uncovered near the pyramid of Amenemhat II in Dahshur, or in the depiction of two Asiatics with Egyptian names in the tomb of Ukhhotep, son of Ukhhotep, in Meir.[78]

Communication was conducted both on land and maritime routes, with the latter enabling the speedy transport of large quantities and bulk items that could not have been conveyed by land. The increased pace of movement was crucial to the completion of an expedition within a single sailing season, as the majority of the time abroad would have been spent ashore: trading, waiting for goods, unloading, loading, and stowage of cargo, the last of which was critical to the ship's stability at sea. Once back in Egypt, the cargo (including any booty and tribute) was apparently channeled through the royal court to various state institutions and functionaries and members of the elite, contributing to further economic, social, religious, and funerary activities. Such control of the flow and distribution of goods was a source and demonstration of the ruler's

77. Mourad 2015: 79 suggests that the tribute offered by the Asiatics was an attempt to end the military campaign against Iua and Iasy.

78. Mourad 2015: 62, 95.

status, particularly in the year following his father's death, and accrued obligations from the beneficiaries whose support enabled the outfitting and manning of future expeditions, both in the Mediterranean and the Red Sea.[79]

This extraordinary textual evidence for relations between Egypt and the eastern Mediterranean is complemented by contemporary archaeological finds, of which the most notable and lavish is the so-called Tod Treasure (figure 21.3). Similarities between the offerings to the temple of Montu at Tod according to the Mit Rahina inscription (M9–M10), the products brought back from Khenti-she, and the contents of the four copper chests bearing Amenemhat II's name found under this temple's floor are compelling.[80] The chests contain a panoply of Near Eastern and eastern Mediterranean raw materials and finished products: gold, silver bowls, electrum, lapis lazuli, semi-precious stones, and obsidian, as well as stamp and cylinders seals—most of which find some correspondence with the data offered by the Mit Rahina inscription either in material, form, or quantity.[81]

Moreover, although stylistic, metrological, and lead isotope analyses as well as the general craftsmanship of the treasure's principal component—silver cups and bowls—suggest a metal source in the Aegean region or Taurus Mountains and subsequent manufacture somewhere in Anatolia or the northern Levant,[82] the locations of their acquisition are unknown, with numerous possible candidates.

---

79. Regarding the latter, a stele found in Wadi Gasus (Birch 1880: 267–268, pl. III; Breasted 1906: 275, §§604–605), which is dated to Year 28, states that the nobleman Khentkhetwer and his *hau* ships returned safely from Punt to the port of Sauu, the ancient name for Mersa/Wadi Gawasis: see chapter 20 in this volume.

80. Lilyquist 1993: 35–36; Pierrat 1994: 23–24; 2008; Marcus 2007: 158–160; Mourad 2015: 114–115. For the discovery and formal publication, see Bisson de la Roque 1937; 1950; Bisson de la Roque, Contenau and Chapouthier 1953.

81. Marcus 2007: 158–160.

82. Walberg 1984; Warren and Hankey 1989: 131–134; Laffineur 1988; Lilyquist 1993: 35–37; Pierrat 1994: 24–25; 2008; Menu 1994; Aruz 1995: 33–35; Maxwell-Hyslop 1995; MacGillivray 1998: 103–104.

FIGURE 21.3. Two of the four copper chests from the treasure buried in the temple of Montu at Tod, including a selection of their contents: silver cups; silver tablet, rod (?), and chain ingots; a gold floret; lapis lazuli chunks, blanks, and various finished objects (including beads, cylinder, and scarab seals); and copper nails found around the chests. © 2013 Musée du Louvre, dist. RMN-Grand Palais/Christian Décamps.

Although the precise entrepôts in Khenti-she that supplied Amenemhat II's ships with cargo and the specific port(s) of export for the contents of the Tod Treasure may never be identified beyond doubt, it is likely that Ezbet Rushdi, the precursor of the settlement that would subsequently become Tell el-Dabʿa (Avaris) was one of the Middle Kingdom ports in the delta region, through which such foreign goods entered the Nile valley—and, quite possibly, this site was even Egypt's principal port. It was founded at least by the reign of Amenemhat II (Ezbet Rushdi Phases e/4 to e/1), and excavations there have produced the earliest reliable evidence for contacts with the Levant and Crete.[83] Levantine imports include painted wares, a red-polished jug, and storage jars (amphorae).[84] While comparative analysis of the monochrome red Levantine Painted Ware jugs and juglets (which occur in all four of these sub-phases) shows the best parallels with examples from Byblos, petrographical analysis allows only to place the origin of the two sampled jugs as very generally in the northern Levant, somewhere in the region from the Galilee coast to the Akkar Plain.[85] In contrast, analyzed amphora sherds come from multiple sources, including at least the aforementioned area, as well as locales in the northwestern Negev, the southern coastal plain of Israel, the Carmel coastal plain, and the northern Syrian coast stretching from Ugarit to Cilicia; the red polished jug comes from the northwestern Negev or Shephelah.[86] This geographical distribution may suggest either multiple ports of call or intra-Levantine cabotage to more restricted points of export. Moreover, the Egyptian pottery from Ezbet Rushdi (Phases e/4 to e/1) correlates well with the material from Lisht North Tomb 756,[87] allowing a better refinement for the date of the

---

83. Bagh 2013: 40–45; Czerny 2015: 470–471.

84. Czerny 2015: 360, figs. T118: 1, 2, T119, T121: K7972.

85. Cohen-Weinberger and Goren 2004: Table 1a: 1, 2; Bagh 2013: 43–45, 159–161, figs. 6, 15a–c, e–f, h, q; pl. 2g–i, q; Czerny 2015: 357–359, 471, figs. T113: 1–10, T114, T115.

86. Cohen-Weinberger and Goren 2004: Table 1a: 4–8; Bagh 2013: 45; Czerny 2015: 359–361, 471 n. 913.

87. Schiestl and Seiler 2012: 646–647, II.H.2:1; Czerny 2015: 359.

latter context, which also produced monochrome red Levantine Painted Ware juglets and a red burnished jug.[88] This correspondence lends credence to a similarly early arrival for other poorly dated Levantine Painted Ware imports in the delta region, such as at Kom el-Hisn.[89] Dating Lisht North Tomb 756 to the reign of Amenemhat II would add an additional Levantine import to the list: bitumen, presumably from the Dead Sea, which was found in this burial.[90]

Regarding the Levantine side of this interaction, it is worth noting that the earliest well-stratified and securely dated Egyptian pottery occurs at Tel Ifshar (Phase A "late"; figure 21.4: 3) and is dated to no earlier than the beginning of Amenemhat II's reign.[91] Thus, a synchronism may be posited between the late twentieth to early nineteenth centuries BC Egypt and the early archaeological phases of the Middle Bronze sequence of the Levant. Additionally, petrographic analysis points to established communities in areas for which contemporary archaeological evidence is still lacking.[92]

In contrast to the presence of Levantine pottery in Egypt (which is hardly unexpected given the textual and pictorial evidence), the discovery of pottery from Crete at Ezbet Rushdi, namely fragments of Middle Minoan (MM) IIA "oval-mouthed" amphorae, could not have been anticipated.[93] While these vessels are well known from Minoan palaces on the island of Crete, such as Knossos and Phaistos, the ten pieces assigned stratigraphically to Ezbet Rushdi Phase e/1 represent some three to five complete vessels[94] that are so far the only documented occurrence of

---

88. Cf. Do. Arnold, F. Arnold, and Allen 1995: 17–18, fig. 2; Bagh 2013: 62, fig. 30: b–d.

89. Bagh 2013: 61–62, fig. 30a; Czerny 2015: 358–359.

90. Merrillees 1973: 55.

91. Marcus et al. 2008b: 207, fig. 2: 2; Schiestl and Seiler 2012: 408.

92. Marcus 2007: 165.

93. Marcus 2007:162–163; Czerny 2015: 363–366, 471, figs. T122–T124. Their identification was the result of the serendipitous presence of Minoan pottery specialist Peter Warren at the Tell el-Dab'a excavation house, when these sherds were being studied: Czerny 2015: 445 n. 1225, 471 n. 5.

94. Czerny 2015: 363–364.

FIGURE 21.4. Middle Kingdom pottery from Tel Ifshar, Israel (cf. Marcus et al. 2008b). 1: Marl A3 bottle (Phase C); 2: fragments of a Dan E3 globular jar (Phase B); 3: Marl A4 bottle (Phase A "late"); 4: Marl C1 *zir* (Phase A "late"); 5: Marl C1 medium bag-shaped jar; 6: Marl C1 *zir* (Phase B); 7: small marl C2 globular jar (Phase B); 8: Marl C1 *zir* (Phase B); 9: small Marl C2 globular jar (Phase A "late"). Photo by Yoram Porath; graphics by S. Haad.

these ceramic transport containers outside the Aegean region.[95] Clearly, these utilitarian forms pale in comparison to the fancy, polychromatic Middle Minoan ceramic forms from other, probably later, Twelfth Dynasty tombs and sites, but owing to their well-stratified context, they remain the best securely dated and earliest Aegean imports anywhere in Egypt or the Levant.[96] In addition, they potentially demonstrate that Egypt expanded its scope of interaction beyond the Levant to a much broader eastern Mediterranean zone, thus reviving yet another feature that had ended with the collapse of the Old Kingdom. At the very least, the imports found at Ezbet Rushdi offer a potential stratigraphically based synchronism for the beginning of the Middle Minoan IIA period;

---

95. Cf. Marcus 2007: 162; Knapp and Demesticha 2017: 75–79.

96. Marcus 2007: 163.

in doing so, they complement the purported attestation of Aegean silver in the Tod Treasure and of early Middle Kingdom Egyptian scarabs in Early Minoan III and Middle Minoan II tombs on Crete.[97]

21.4.3. The procession of the Asiatics in the tomb of Khnumhotep II at Beni Hasan

Presumably, the foreign interactions that preceded Senusret II (1877–1870 BC) continued during his brief reign, although there is no evidence for the crown's direct involvement. On the other hand, the tomb of one of his nobles, the governor Khnumhotep II, features the only known Middle Kingdom depiction inside a private tomb of the arrival of foreigners (Beni Hasan No. 3: figure 21.5; see also figure 22.3 in chapter 22: upper register of the line drawing and the same detail in the photograph).[98] This procession of fifteen Asiatic men, women, and children is led by a man identified by the name Ibesha (certainly Northwest Semitic, either representing Abishai ["My father is a nobleman"] or Abishar ["My father is king"]) and with the Egyptian title *heqa khaset* ("ruler of a foreign land") (the earliest Middle Kingdom attestation of that historically significant denomination; cf. chapter 23 in volume 3).[99] These foreigners are led by two Egyptians: the tomb owner's son, Khnumhotep III, and a scribe holding a docket that declares in Regnal Year 6, thirty-seven Asiatics (*aamu*) of the *Shu*(*t*) were brought on account of "black eye paint" (*mesedjemet*).[100] The depicted Asiatics carry a lyre, various bags, and weapons, including socketed spears, a duckbill axe, and a bow and quiver. They accompany animals, both domesticated (donkeys) and wild (Nubian ibex and Dorcas gazelle), the latter possibly offerings.

---

97. D. Ben-Tor 2006; Höflmayer 2007.

98. Newberry 1893:69, pls. XXVIII, XXX–XXXI; Gaballa 1976: 40. For the most recent discussions and extensive literature, see Saretta 1997: 110–133; 2016: 87–108; Cohen 2015a; Mourad 2015: 86–93.

99. Mourad 2015: 86–87; Candelora 2017: 213, Table 1:8.

100. Saretta 1997: 112; 2016; Mourad 2015: 87.

FIGURE 21.5. Khnumhotep II's tomb at Beni Hasan (Tomb 3). Detail of the Asiatic procession showing Ibesha (right) and a member of his entourage presenting, respectively, a Nubian ibex and a Dorcas gazelle. Reproduced from the facsimile painted by Norman de Garis Davies in 1931. Tempera on paper, MMA Rogers Fund 33.8.17. Courtesy of the Metropolitan Museum of Art (https://www.metmuseum.org/art/collection/search/544548).

While the delegation's precise geographical origin and identity are unclear,[101] the ceremonial character of their reception (be that for the Egyptian New Year's celebration or for tribute-giving) stands in stark contrast to the previously discussed martial scenes in the earlier tombs at Beni Hasan (see section 21.4.1). The individuals' appearance (hairstyle, skin tone, clothing, and accessories) and weapons clearly place them both within Middle Kingdom Egyptian pictorial conventions for Asiatics and the realia of contemporary Middle Bronze Age Levantine

---

101. Among the suggested locations of *Shu(t)* are the arid zones of Sinai or Transjordan, and other settled areas of the latter; cf. Cohen 2015a: 23–24; Mourad 2015: 86 n. 1028.

lifestyle and material culture. While previous scholarly characterizations of this group as nomads or pastoralists may have been biased, more recent approaches emphasize their clear association with the contemporary sedentary population, living either as part of it or adjacent to it. This assessment is based on the depicted lifestyle, material culture, as well as possibly the manner in which affluence and social status are displayed and differentiated: silver headbands on the women; a toggle pin on the leader's garment and a staff in his hand; the different weapons in the hands of the men and the older children; the presence of donkeys as riding animals; the garments worn,[102] all of which would have reflected their "holiday best." Saretta has stressed the social and economic significance of the multicolored dyed wool garments depicted, which clearly impressed the Egyptian artists who portrayed them in vivid detail.[103] Such details demonstrate shared motifs and color schemes between these garments and the elegant Levantine Painted Ware, which presumably served as high-status drinking vessels for the Levantine elites of the early Middle Bronze Age.[104]

Although to date no earlier such scenes (royal or private) are known from the reign of Amenemhat II, the Khnumhotep II procession may depict tribute bearers like the ones described in the Mit Rahina inscription (see section 21.4.2). Importantly, this scene offers two potential chronological synchronisms for Levantine material culture: a *terminus post quem* for the duckbill axe,[105] and for the appearance of the color scheme and motifs that characterize the bichrome Levantine Painted

---

102. Mourad 2015: 87–88.

103. Saretta 2016.

104. The monochrome red or a bichrome red and blue-black color scheme on a white background appears on both garments and actual ceramics. Most of the motifs displayed on the garments (wavy, oblique, and chevron-like patterns, as well as tassel fringes) are well documented in the early Middle Bronze Age painted tradition (Bagh 2013); other motifs, such as the crenellation and true-chevrons, appear on later Tell el-Yahudiya Ware (cf. Stager and Voss 2018b: figs. 8.1, 8.9: 46, 47, 49).

105. Shaheen 1990; Bietak 1997: 125. The positive identification of the duckbill axe has been reconfirmed personally by Mourad 2015: 87 n. 1067.

Ware, the latter of which first occurs at Tel Ifshar (Phase A "late"),[106] along with a sherd of a Middle Kingdom–type of a large aperture vessel (figure 21.4: 4; a shape dubbed *zir* after the modern Egyptian water jugs that it resembles) made of Marl C fabric (a characteristic type of Egyptian clay found along the desert skirting the Nile valley) that might have appeared as early as the reign of Senusret II.[107]

Khnumhotep II's tomb features further evidence for the presence of Asiatics in Upper Egypt. At least three fair-skinned men, albeit with Egyptian names, function as overseers of, respectively, the sealers, the treasury, and the inner chamber/chamberlain, and another one is depicted, seemingly in an official capacity, overseeing the construction of a boat.[108] Asiatic material culture includes the depictions of a vessel either with a Levantine or possibly hybrid Egypto-Levantine ceramic form[109] and of black pods of carob, acacia, or tamarind, as well as the reference to the tomb owner building doors from cedar wood brought from Lebanon (Negau).[110]

As it so happens, the acquisition of cedar timber would have consequences for the activities of Khnumhotep's son, the vizier Khnumhotep III, who was later drawn into events that would embroil Egypt in a war in the Levant under Senusret III (see section 21.4.4). On the other hand, trade in ceramics was still rare during this time and can only be reliably documented at Tell el-Dab'a (Ezbet Rushdi Phase d), beneath a temple assigned to Senusret III's Year 5 (and thus, some of the pottery might also date to the following reign).[111] Here, Levantine imports included

---

106. Marcus et al. 2008a: fig. 9: 6–9; Marcus 2013: 185.

107. Marcus et al. 2008b: fig. 2.1; Schiestl and Seiler 2012: 602–603. However, this type of pottery is much better documented in the later Middle Kingdom.

108. Mourad 2015: 89–90.

109. Cf. Mourad 2015: 90, Fig. 4.53 for a more accurate rendition of a vessel cited by Do. Arnold et al. 1995: 18, 20 n. 36 and Cohen Weinberger and Goren 2004: 82 from Newberry 1893: pl. XXIX (left, reg. 2).

110. Mourad 2015: 90–91, fig. 4.54.

111. Bietak and Dorner 1998; Czerny 2015.

a monochrome Levantine Painted Ware jug or juglet and three storage jars, one of which came from the Akkar Plain in the north of modern Lebanon.[112]

21.4.4. Senusret III's "Cedar Trade War" and Egyptian relations with Byblos

Later historians (e.g., Herodotus 2.102–110) extolled the reign and the vast eastern Mediterranean conquests of "Sesostris,"[113] which was apparently the Hellenized form of Senusret III (1870–1831 BC).[114] However, until recently, contemporary textual sources for this ruler's activities in the Levant have been limited to a single laconic reference in the autobiographical inscription on the stele of the soldier Khusobek that mentions a military engagement in the area of Shechem (discussed below). His relations with the Levant are further illustrated by depictions of a possible diplomatic visit by Asiatics bearing tribute to his palace and of their subjugation,[115] as well as other idiomatic expressions of belligerency and dominance.[116]

These sources, however, are overshadowed in importance for our subject by the recently published inscription on the burial monument (mastaba) of the vizier Khnumhotep III, the son of the local governor Khnumhotep II, whose tomb at Beni Hasan (No. 3) was discussed earlier (section 21.4.3). Together with the Mit Rahina inscription, this is the second of the two "new" Middle Kingdom texts that have transformed our characterization of Egypt's interactions with the Levant (see section

---

112. Cohen-Weinberger and Goren 2004: Table 1a: 9; Bagh 2013: 181, figs. 6, 15: g; Czerny 2015: 234, 357, 361, figs. T113: 11, T119.

113. Liotsakis 2014.

114. Note the discussion of the length of this king's reign in Wegner 1996.

115. Mourad 2015: 110.

116. See, e.g., Montuemhat's stele from Semna: Delia 1980: 81–85, 122; or various examples from the Lahun Papyri: Mourad 2015: 71, 269–270 (UC32157), fig. 7.3.

21.2). This text clearly confirms that Senusret III, like his grandfather, Amenemhat II, was involved in broad commercial and military activities by land and sea in the northern parts of the eastern Mediterranean.

The first fragments of the inscription were discovered during excavations at Dahshur in the nineteenth century AD, which identified Khnumhotep III as the mastaba's owner; but renewed fieldwork of a Metropolitan Museum of Art team produced additional inscribed architectural remains and enabled the reconstruction of the monument's superstructure.[117] This reconstructed plan enabled the partial reassembly of a three-dimensional epigraphic puzzle of inscribed fragments of horizontal and vertical sections, whose correct placement permits some 40 percent of the inscription to be read in its proper order and provides a generally coherent narrative.[118] Owing to this important accomplishment, we now know that sometime during the reign of Senusret III, Khnumhotep III led an expedition of sailors in ships (*deput*) to Retenu to bring cedar from the harbor of Ullaza.[119] En route, for reasons not preserved (possible options include unfavorable winds, a navigational lapse, a need for provisions or repairs, or merely a courtesy call), his expedition made port at Byblos, where Khnumhotep III was received by the *malku*, a Semitic term for a high-ranking ruler ("king") that is accompanied throughout this text by the kneeling, bound Asiatic determinative, indicating an adversarial relationship with Egypt.[120] Such poor rapport is in accordance with the Byblian ruler's emphatic demand to know whether the Egyptian's destination was Ullaza and, if so, why he had come to Byblos. Khnumhotep III

---

117. Allen 2008: 29–30.

118. Allen 2008: 31–32. See also Mourad 2015: 62–63, 267–269.

119. Allen 2008: 32–33. The precise location of this port is unknown, but it is probably located near the mouth of the Nahr al-Bared at the southern end of the Akkar plain, where a number of sites are known around a possible silted-up palaeo-embayment: Tell et-Taalé, Site 28 and Khan el-Abde; see Gestoso Singer 2008: 188; Gubel 2009; Thalmann 2000: fig. 1; Gubel and Loffet 2011–2012: 86; Ahrens 2015: 144. Another suggested location is near Tripoli; Forstner-Müller and Kopetzky 2009: 144.

120. Allen 2008: 33.

responded by citing the age-old relationship between Egypt and all foreign lands, and an apparent long-standing permission to moor in this harbor. Although the sense of the following passage is unclear, as is an ambiguous reference to the *Mentiu* (Asiatic bedouins), what transpired was probably unanticipated by Khnumhotep III: the *malku* dispatched his son with an army of 100 Asiatics to Ullaza, and Egyptian speakers (perhaps Egyptian expatriates or intermediaries) were sent in their ships to speak with the ruler (*heqa*) of Ullaza, whose message refers to a previously unknown "people of Habilaya"[121] and the demand that the ships not return to Byblos.[122] This apparent diplomatic exercise was subsequently revealed to have been a ruse, as the *malku* and his son prepared for a land-sea pincer assault on Ullaza, while also exchanging letters with Senusret III regarding the apparent dispute between the two ports and the disposition of Khnumhotep's expedition.[123] The result was clearly not favorable to the *malku*, as the Egyptian king marshaled an army that set forth toward Lebanon to Ullaza, perhaps to relieve a siege. A further text fragment, which is positioned near the end of the inscription, apparently refers to the return home of the ships of this expedition, followed by another departure: this time to Byblos.[124]

The implications of this inscription are profound. In addition to the previously undocumented military activities of Senusret III in the eastern Mediterranean (which might have been the source of his renown in later times), it completely changes our understanding of

---

121. Allen 2008: 35 places this toponym in the area of Ullaza, while Mourad 2015: 268 n. 5 notes modern locales with similar names in the Byblos region.

122. Allen 2008: 34–35. While he suggests that these ships are from Khnumhotep's expedition, there is no indication that he succeeded in departing from Byblos. Mourad 2015: 63 suggests that this last passage be read that the ships should not return empty.

123. Allen 2008: 35–36.

124. Allen 2008: 37 suggests that this marks a resumption of trade with Byblos, while Mourad 2015: 63 considers the possibility that they sought Byblos' aid in re-establishing relations with Ullaza.

Egypt's relationship with its traditional partner in the Levant: the port Byblos.[125] This relationship was clearly far from exclusive in the period prior to and during the events recounted in Khnumhotep III's Dahshur inscription. That lack of exclusivity is underscored by the total absence of any mention of Byblos anywhere in the earlier Mit Rahina inscription (see section 21.4.2),[126] neither in the entries recording the dispatch of the various Egyptian expeditions to the Levant nor in the return reports.[127] Such an omission strengthens the impression that the re-emergence of eastern Mediterranean maritime relations during the first half of the Twelfth Dynasty cannot be described as simply a resumption of the Old Kingdom modus operandi.[128] While this observation does not preclude some commercial relations between Egypt and Byblos (as is implied by the initial exchange between the *malku* of Byblos and Khnumhotep III), the animosity and belligerency between the two parties is unprecedented and must be taken into account when considering all aspects of the relationship between Egypt and Byblos in this period.

Even before the Mit Rahina inscription and Khnumhotep III's mastaba inscription were known, it was notable that beyond an early attestation to a "Byblos ship" (*kebenet*) on the Red Sea coast (section 21.3), the mention of Byblos as a geographical reference point in the "Story of Sinuhe" (section 21.4.1), and some comparisons in ceramic typology, neither written nor pictorial sources nor archaeological finds from secure contexts supported a close link between Egypt and Byblos.[129] Also, both documented maritime expeditions of Middle Kingdom Egypt to the

---

125. Ward 1961b; Posener 1971: 545; Weinstein 1975; Ryholt 1997: 86–90; D. Ben-Tor 1997; 2007: 117–119; 2011: 24–27; 2018: 337–338.

126. Contra Cohen 2000: 95, 2002: 44.

127. The lack of any lacunae at these junctures of the text reinforces the validity of this absence.

128. Note that even in the Old Kingdom, any notion of complete exclusivity has now been undermined if not refuted by the Sixth Dynasty autobiography of Iny; Marcolin and Espinel 2011.

129. All three groups of Execration Texts (see later discussion), which probably do not precede Senusret III's reign, refer solely to the "tribes of Byblos," rather than the city of Byblos or its ruler; Rainey 1972: 382; Koenig 1990: 102, 111; Redford 1992: 91.

Mediterranean made use of an Egyptian type of transport ship (*depet*) rather than the "Byblos ship" that had featured so prominently in Old Kingdom, and later, seafaring.[130]

There are numerous Middle Kingdom Egyptian artifacts that have been found at Byblos, many featuring royal names (beginning with Senusret I).[131] However, their relevance for the period in question must be reconsidered, as most lack secure archaeological contexts. The earliest well-stratified Middle Kingdom Egyptian finds at Byblos are the ninety scarab seals of the so-called Early Egyptian Scarab Series from the celebrated "Montet Jar" (so named after its excavator), a sealed votive deposit containing a wide variety of prestige objects, which was found in the "Syrian Temple" dedicated to Ba'alat Gebal, the "Lady of Byblos."[132] Unfortunately, these scarabs can only be dated very broadly, ranging from the late Eleventh to the mid-Twelfth Dynasties, i.e., before the beginning of mass production of scarabs during the reign of Senusret III or his successor.[133] Nevertheless, the chronological range of this deposit can be further refined. First, one must take into account the vessel itself, which belongs to the monochrome red Levantine Painted Ware family that can be dated in Egypt, at present, no earlier than the period of Amenemhat II.[134] Second, apart from the scarabs, there are other chronologically significant objects in the hoard: most importantly, one of three cylinder seals in the Montet Jar has long been dated, based on stylistic parallels, to Kültepe Level II (ca. 1925–1840 BC;

---

130. Sowada 2009: 7–10; Esposito 2019: 48 n. 76, 77. As, clearly, the Egyptians had an ample supply of cedar during this period and were sailing at sea to the northern Levant, this distinction raises anew the question of whether "Byblos ships" refer to the raw material used in their construction, the location of construction, their destination, or some other undocumented distinguishing physical characteristic (e.g., appearance of the prow, shape of the hull, etc.).

131. Ward 1971: 68 n. 272.

132. Tufnell and Ward 1966; D. Ben-Tor 1998; 2003: 240.

133. D. Ben-Tor 2003: 240.

134. Bagh 2013: 43–45, 122–125, fig. 6. At present in the Levant, only Tel Ifshar (Phase A "early") offers a mid-twentieth century BC *terminus post quem* for its limited monochrome red painted pottery based on a single radiocarbon determination; Marcus 2013: 185, Table 15.3 (1930 BC).

cf. chapter 17 in this volume),[135] while two metal objects have parallel forms in stone and metal at Ebla in inland Syria, where they have been dated to the latter part of that century and are, therefore, consistent with the date of cylinder seal.[136] Thus, the Montet Jar and its contents would appear to have been sealed no earlier than the very late twentieth or early nineteenth century BC and, in the absence of any scarabs from the late Middle Kingdom series, seemingly no later than the reign of Senusret III. Given the lack of prior evidence for contacts with Byblos and the aforementioned tumultuous events, it is possible that this hoard is in some way connected to their resolution or aftermath.[137]

Further implications of the Dahshur inscription must be considered from both the Egyptian and the Byblian perspective. The Egyptian political terminology used to describe the ruler of Byblos with the Semitic word *malku*, combined with a kneeling, bound Asiatic as the determinative—rather than the term *heqa*, with a seated, bearded man displaying a mushroom hairdo and holding a round-bladed axe, or the term *hati-a* (for a high official or governor),[138] which purportedly first appears in Amenemhat III's reign (see section 21.4.6)[139]—not only reflects animosity, but indicates that Byblian rule was not inspired, dependent, or enabled by Egypt. As Allen has stressed,[140] this revelation may be the most important information provided by the Dahshur text, with the events therein recorded providing a possible explanation.

135. Porada 1966: 246, no. 81; Porter 2001: 52–56.

136. Nigro 2009: 162–166.

137. Note that, this late date only refers to this deposit and does not preclude the earlier, but unproven, arrival of such scarabs at Byblos or their distribution further west; D. Ben-Tor 2006; Höflmayer 2007. However, this and the other evidence discussed herein weaken any argument that scarabs from the early series reached Crete via Byblian intermediaries.

138. Allen 2008: 33–34.

139. Redford 1992: 97; Ryholt 1997: 86–90; Allen 2008: 34.

140. Allen 2008: 33–34.

This conflict, which should be dubbed the "cedar trade war," may have been a watershed event that led to a profound change in the relationship between Egypt and Byblos and likely had direct political consequences for Byblos, perhaps a regime change or occupation.[141] This war's exceptional repercussions might also help explain the prominent location of Khnumhotep III's tomb monument near the pyramid of Senusret III, where the publicly displayed inscription could be read by or for all,[142] thus serving to glorify the king and Egypt.[143]

Khnumhotep had been raised in the palace of Amenemhat II and subsequently spent some thirty years in the service of the crown, from the reign of Senusret II to that of Amenemhat III, during which he represented Egyptian interests abroad both in the Red Sea and the eastern Mediterranean regions.[144] And yet, for his tomb inscription it was the events of the "cedar trade war" that were selected as particularly worthy of commemoration. This choice seems to attest to their exceptional nature not only for modern scholarship, but also and especially in contemporary Egyptian political and economic affairs. Allen further suggested that the events described in the funerary stele of the soldier Khusobek, which mentions a military engagement in the district (*sepat*) of Shechem (*Sekemem*) that fell along with miserable Retenu, might have been part of the same expedition.[145] Khusobek's inscription describes an attack against the Asiatics (*mentiu setjet*) in that region during which he fought valiantly, and in return the king rewarded him with an electrum staff as well as a dagger and sheath decorated with electrum.[146] Any Egyptian army heading to the northern Levant would have certainly marched through the inner corridor of the Sharon coastal plain, situated to the

---

141. Allen 2008: 37.

142. Allen 2008: 37.

143. Mourad 2015: 62.

144. Allen 2008: 29–31, 38.

145. Allen 2008: 37.

146. Manchester 3306 has been widely discussed (Breasted 1906: §676–§687; Wilson 1950a: 230; Delia 1980: 115–120; Baines 1987), and most recently by Mourad 2015: 100–101, 281 with further references.

west of the main highland center of Tell Balatah (Shechem/Nablus), where raiders could have harassed them.[147]

Lastly, while typically the Egyptian textual, pictorial, and material cultural records provide insights into at least some of the Levantine products the Egyptians sought to procure, no indication is ever given as to what was offered in return. In the absence of any surviving contemporary written records from the Levant, only material evidence may be identified, and that is largely limited to prestige items in Egyptian style or the remains of ceramic containers whose former contents are presently unknown. The Khnumhotep III inscription, like the Mit Rahina inscription before it, offers no direct indication of what the inhabitants of the Levant wanted in return for the products Egypt desired. However, in their attempt to interfere in the affairs of Egypt and their rival port of Ullaza and prevent the two from trading, the presumption is that Byblos itself was keen to fill, or control, that role. The *malku* of Byblos challenged Egypt's representatives and therefore the crown itself, risking and, in this instance, realizing a confrontation with the sole superpower in the eastern Mediterranean. This bold act seems to indicate that, from his perspective, the benefits outweighed the risk, and suggests that Egypt practiced true trade, in the sense of exchange for mutual material gain, in addition to extracting tribute, plundering, and participating in elite gift-giving. The implication is that coercion was not the sole apparatus in Egypt's relations with the Levant, a topic that will be further considered in the conclusion (section 21.6).

Imports that can be associated specifically with Senusret III's reign include, not surprisingly, cedar, with the most impressive examples being

---

147. Traditionally, during certain periods of highland settlement, lowland areas to the north and west of the central hills have been affected if not controlled by highland centers, e.g., during the Amarna period (Rainey and Notely 2006: 82–85) or during Ottoman times, when Nablus (i.e., Neapolis, Shechem's name in the Classical period) was the capital of the Sharon coastal plain. The present author is currently studying the pottery from the limited exposure of MB IIa remains at that site.

the five or six funerary boats from his pyramid complex at Dahshur.[148] Another funerary boat, although poorly preserved, was probably also made of cedar and was found near his tomb at South Abydos; it was buried in a mudbrick building whose plastered interior walls were decorated with depictions of more than 120 incised watercraft.[149] On the other hand, an often-cited mention of Asiatic cattle in Egypt[150] lacks the appropriate determinative for the foreign land Retenu and should therefore no longer be used as evidence for Levantine imports.[151]

When Senusret III's treasurer Iykhernofret embellished the shrine of Osiris at Abydos, the materials used included lapis lazuli, *meru* wood (perhaps pine), and silver,[152] which were sourced from or via locations in the eastern Mediterranean. The port of entry in the Nile delta was still likely Ezbet Rushdi, which seems to have gained in importance, as evidenced by a temple that was built there during the reign of Senusret III (Ezbet Rushdi Phase c).[153] Absolute numbers of Levantine ceramic imports overall, and amphorae in particular, reached their peak at the site during this time.[154] One amphora originated in the northeastern part of the Mediterranean: somewhere in northwestern Syria (Ugarit,

---

148. Haldane 1997: 176; Ward 2000: 83–85. Strontium isotope analysis indicates that the Dahshur boat at the Carnegie Museum was made from Lebanese cedar: Rich et al. 2016: 516–517. My thanks to Karin Kopetzky for this reference.

149. Wegner 2016. Given this unparalleled tableau of boats, organized in no coherent decorative scheme, by multiple hands, possibly at different times, it is tempting to view this symbolic activity as having been performed by nautically oriented individuals and perhaps even related to this ruler's waterborne commercial and military activities.

150. Blackman 1915; Posener 1971: 542; Delia 1980: 124; Cohen 2002: 47 n. 60.

151. Wilson 1950a: 230, n. 11; Mourad 2015: 93.

152. Delia 1980: 124.

153. Bietak and Dorner 1998; Czerny 2015.

154. N = 37 and N = 23, respectively, with the former representing 28 percent of the total assemblage and the amphorae being 62 percent of those imports; Czerny 2015: 359–361, fig. T119.

Amuq), on the Cilician coast or Cyprus.[155] Five monochrome red Levantine Painted Ware jugs date to this phase, one of which originated somewhere in the northern Levant, in the region between the Galilee coast to the Akkar plain in northern Lebanon.[156]

The only corresponding Egyptian ceramic exports that begin in this period are an example attested in Sidon (Level 2),[157] but it could also have arrived later during the co-regency with Amenemhat III. In addition, it is possible that some long-lived ceramic forms, whose production ceased in this period, had arrived in the Levant by this time.[158]

Although the Levantine ceramic imports are limited to closed vessels (which could be inferred as indicators for trade), the period of Senusret III otherwise clearly marks the beginning of an increase in the evidence for an Asiatic presence in Egypt. This impression is owed to the Lahun Papyri, the steles from Abydos, and other inscriptions and representations that attest to the visibility and incorporation of Asiatics in a variety of roles throughout Egypt.[159] The earliest Lahun Papyri date to the reign

---

155. Cohen-Weinberger and Goren 2004: Table 1a: 10. The analysis was performed on a body sherd from an unreliable context (Czerny 2015: n. 113), and the one published rim sherd was not sufficiently preserved to be indicative; Czerny 2015: fig. T118: 3.

156. Cohen-Weinberger and Goren 2004: Table 1a: 3; Bagh 2013: 43–45, figs. 6, 15: d, i–l; Czerny 2015: 357–359, figs. T113: 12–16, T116.

157. Bader et al. 2009: fig. 1; Schiestl and Seiler 2012: 592, 594, II.E.13.d: 7.

158. The globular jars from Ifshar (Phase B) and Sidon (Phase 2) are possible examples, although in both cases they occur with bichrome Levantine Painted Ware, which postdates the Rushdi Phase c at Tell el-Dab'a: Bagh 2013: 43–56; Marcus et al. 2008b: fig. 3.1; Schiestl and Seiler 2012: 396–397, I.A.7.b: 4, 5 (here: figure 21.4: 2). However, the bichrome stage may well have appeared in the Levant somewhat earlier than in Egypt (i.e., at Tell el-Dab'a, Stratum H). Supporting evidence for that may be found in the scarab seals (no. 1808–1810) associated with Sidon Level 1, Burial 12, which are dated to the first half of the Twelfth Dynasty (Mlinar 2004b: 63; Taylor 2004: 157) and belong to the Early Scarab Series (Mourad 2015: 176), but occur in a context with complete examples of bichrome Levantine Painted Ware; Doumet-Serhal 2004: Table 3, fig. 14: S1814.

159. Mourad 2015: 69–72.

of Senusret III, although their volume increases markedly under his co-regent and successor Amenemhat III. They mention Asiatic men and women with their names and occupations, both inside and outside the temple of Senusret II in Lahun (also known as Kahun) near the entrance to the Fayum, and attest to dancers at local, regional, and national religious festivals and temple servants such as a butcher and a door-keeper (with the name Senusret).[160] Asiatics mentioned in the funerary steles at Abydos include a brewer, an overseer of a storehouse, and a hall-keeper;[161] an Asiatic steward of storehouses and controller of works is mentioned in an inscription at Wadi Hammamat;[162] and an inscription at Wadi el-Hudi extols the virtues of an Asiatic butler, who shares the Egyptian name of his master.[163] In Meir, the depictions in the tomb of (yet another) Ukhhotep show a procession of women of possible Levantine or mixed ancestry, bearing deltaic and perhaps Near Eastern items.[164]

Finally, although only one Asiatic is mentioned in an inscription from this period at Serabit el-Khadim in Sinai, this text marks the resumption of the exploitation of this area for turquoise (and perhaps also copper) in cooperation with various functionaries of Asiatic origin and heritage and members of their elite.[165] This enterprise and its implications would expand significantly under Amenemhat III (see section 21.4.6).

21.4.5 The Execration Texts

Three groups of hieratic inscriptions are known collectively as the "Execration Texts" and contain the names of Asiatic rulers, various social

---

160. Mourad 2015: 70–71, 126, 208, 269, fig. 7.10, Appendix B.2 (Papyrus Berlin 10050).

161. Mourad 2015: 100, 280 (CG 20296).

162. Mourad 2015: 143.

163. Mourad 2015: 100, 280 (CG 20296).

164. Mourad 2015: 95–97. This tomb might also belong to the reign of Amenemhat III.

165. Mourad 2015: 135, 305, 309, B.12: 81, fig. B.3: 81.

groups, and settlements. Individually, they are known as the Berlin, Mirgissa, and Brussels groups.[166] The texts of the Berlin and Mirgissa groups were written on ceramic bowls, and the texts of the Brussels group on anthropomorphic figurines that were often shaped in order to evoke an Asiatic phenotype, with the characteristic hairstyle and beard.[167] The Execration Texts list enemies of Egypt in neighboring regions, and the figurines and bowls on which they were inscribed were broken and buried in rituals that were intended to affect the peoples and places named. As the richest source of onomastic and toponymic evidence for the Levant, the Execration Texts have long been the focus of extensive debates regarding the social, ethnic, and political makeup of the Levant during the Middle Kingdom.[168]

However, open questions regarding their provenance and dating remain obstacles to a full understanding of their significance. The bowls of the Berlin group and the figurines of the Brussels group were acquired in Thebes and Saqqara, respectively, and only the archaeological context of the bowls of the Mirgissa group is known.[169] Based on orthography, a date in the first half of the Twelfth Dynasty is preferred for this last group;[170] however, most of the shorter-lived complete pottery shapes

166. Sethe 1926; Posener 1940; 1966; Koenig 1990; Mourad 2015: 80, 115–116.

167. Mourad 2015: 80. A multispectral study of these artifacts is currently underway and may reveal further decorative and inscriptional details; Van der Perre et al. 2016.

168. Redford 1992: 87–93; 1996; Rainey 1972; 1994; Cohen 2002; A. Ben-Tor 2006; Streit 2017. Interpretations for these incantations include sympathetic magic associated with Egyptian rule (Albright 1928: 223), the protection of commercial interests (Ward 1961a: 142), or a symbolic rite against perceived enemies (Redford 1992: 87; Ritner 1993). Ritner 1993: 136–180 has provided by far the most holistic, detailed and nuanced discussion of the significance of this phenomenon, based on the only properly excavated and documented context. For the toponymic and onomastic readings, see Wilson 1950b: 328–329; Rainey 1972; 1994; 2006: 52–53, 58; Ahituv 1984.

169. Koenig 1990: 101–102; Ritter 1993: 153–180. The Brussels figurines come both from the antiquities market and from a deposit buried along the north wall of Teti's Old Kingdom Pyramid at Saqqara (Mourad 2015: 80; Streit 2017: 59), but no accompanying datable material was reported.

170. Posener 1966; Koenig 1990; Redford 1992: 88.

found in the Mirgissa deposit provide a fairly consistent *terminus post quem* from Senusret III onward.[171] Kopetzky, however, notes the presence in this deposit of a Type 3 zir fragment, which would indicate a date no earlier than the reign of Amenemhet III.[172] The texts of the Mirgissa and Berlin groups are quite similar and presumably contemporaneous, while those of the Brussels group are considered to date somewhat later.[173] The dating of the Execration Texts of the Berlin group to the time of Senusret III and/or the early reign of Amenemhat III[174] is consistent with the tentative mid-Twelfth Dynasty forms of the ceramic bowls on which they were written.[175] Thus, at present, these texts should be treated as dating to the mid-Twelfth to Thirteenth Dynasties.[176]

The geographical scope covered by these texts is broad and includes identifiable toponyms from the southern Levant to coastal Syria, and possibly even the arid zones east of the Jordan river. Rulers of these locales, both as individuals and groups, are identified with thoroughly

---

171. Schiestl and Seiler 2012: 80, 82, Type I.A.8.c: 6; 325, Type I.G.4.b: 9 (albeit with a *floruit post* Amenemhat III); 936–937, Type IV.2.1: 6; 1034–1035, Type IV.2.F.2.a: 1; 1036–1037, Type IV.2.F.2.b: 5; 1046–1047, Type IV.2.G.1.a: 2, Type IV.2.G.1.b: 1. This would accord with Redford's lower limit (1992: 88 n. 98) in the early years of Senusret III.

172. Kopetzky 2010: 164–165.

173. Note that if the genealogy of the Nubian rulers in the Berlin and Brussels groups is properly understood, then they are probably separated by only a generation or two; Ward 1987: 528 n. 87.

174. Koenig 1990: 102; Redford 1992: 88; Streit 2017: 59.

175. Do. Arnold, quoted as personal communication received by Rainey 1994: 83, contra the secondhand personal communication from L. Bell quoted by Cohen 2002: n. 14. The lack of systematic morphological and fabric analyses or even line drawings of the Berlin bowls by any Middle Kingdom ceramic specialist is a singular lacuna in research on this topic.

176. Redford 1992: 87–88; Rainey 2006: 52; Mourad 2015: 80, 115–116. Even A. Ben-Tor 2006: 65, 81–82 supports this date, although he argues, based on the southern Levantine archaeological data and some archaisms, that these texts are copies of Old Kingdom originals. Stefan Wimmer (quoted by Sass 1989: 45) suggests that the archaic grammar is an intentional characteristic of this genre and that all other attributes indicate a late Twelfth–early Thirteenth Dynasty date for all three groups.

Northwest Semitic ("Amorite") names[177] and various Egyptian terms for collective groups, which reflect identity, social class, and function. One such example is a reference to all the Asiatics of the *demitiu*, i.e., the "harbor people,"[178] which corresponds to the generally good representation of coastal towns and regions among the attested toponyms.[179]

Many attempts have been made to reconstruct the sociopolitical landscape of the Levant based on the relative increase in the number of settlements and the numbers of rulers per settlement[180] from the earlier to the later groups of Execration Texts, generally assuming a rather dubious "evolutionary" trajectory from semi-nomadic/pastoral to urban society.[181] The texts themselves provide no indication of whether they are meant to be a comprehensive gazetteer of all the settlements and population groups or a subjective selection, perhaps further distorted by unknown criteria related to the ritual act of the execration itself or by chance preservation and acquisition. However, given the unclear provenance of most of the evidence, the lack of any possibility of assessing how representative the data may be for the period's settlement system, and finally the lack of any contemporary evidence that could corroborate or falsify the suggested identifications, the presence or absence of any particular toponym among the available Execration Texts may be quite arbitrary.

For present purposes, what matters most is the range of detailed knowledge concerning the settlements in the Levant and its social and political makeup that Egyptians possessed during the reigns of Senusret III, Amenemhat III, and well into the Thirteenth Dynasty. The data in

---

177. Rainey 2006: 52.

178. Rainey 1972: 387; 2006: 53.

179. Redford (1992: 90–91) notes the use of a particular prefix, the morpheme *iye* (Semitic "island" or "coast"), which may reflect either a geographical distinction or importance ascribed by the Egyptians.

180. Cf. Ward 1987: n. 88; Rainey 1994: 83; 2006: 52.

181. Redford 1992: 90–93; Cohen 2002: 16–17; both with references. A discussion of the problems with this approach in detail is beyond the scope of this chapter.

the Execration Texts are clearly the minimum preserved byproduct of Egypt's interactions with the wider world, including the Levant.

21.4.6. Amenemhat III and the zenith of the Middle Kingdom

The reign of Amenemhat III (1831–1786 BC) was the longest of any of the rulers of the Twelfth Dynasty and is generally viewed as the zenith of the Middle Kingdom.[182] But unlike his father Senusret III, with whom he may have enjoyed a long co-regency,[183] no records of any military or commercial activities in the Levant or of any receipt of tribute from the region have been identified. Nevertheless, the Execration Texts, some of which certainly date to his reign, clearly reflect detailed informed knowledge of the Levant. Other evidence suggests the continuation of preexisting patterns of interaction with the Levant and its inhabitants: the familiar trope of the Egyptian ruler "smiting" the Asiatics; the collaboration of Asiatics in Egyptian expeditions to the Sinai mines; contacts with the port of Byblos; the presence of imports from the eastern Mediterranean in Egypt; and the increased presence of Asiatics in Egypt, especially in Tell el-Dabʿa, and their integration and acculturation into many aspects of Egyptian society.

Two pectorals from the Tomb of Mereret, the sister of Amenemhat III, depict the only scenes of the smiting king attested for her brother's reign: one shows the Egyptian ruler striking kneeling Asiatics and the other armed Asiatics.[184] Inscriptions from Wadi Hammamat also declare his crushing supremacy over the Asiatics (*aamu*).[185] However, these seemingly disparaging representations do not match the reality of close Asiatic involvement in Egyptian activities in the arid zones during this period. For example, individual Asiatics serve as "overseer of the infantry,

---

182. Hayes 1971: 509.

183. Wegner 1996.

184. Mourad 2015: 63–64.

185. Mourad 2015: 143.

inspector of retainers" and "retainer of the ruler of the first battalion" during Egyptian-led expeditions, according to other texts from Wadi Hammamat,[186] while in the inscriptions at the mines at Wadi Maghara on the Sinai peninsula, a "remover of scorpions" and an "interpreter" are identified as Asiatics.[187]

The most extensive evidence for Egyptian-Asiatic collaboration comes from Serabit el-Khadim in the Sinai. The majority of inscriptions and depictions, primarily from the Hathor Temple, are attributed to Amenemhat III and date to various points in time from his fourth regnal year to his penultimate year on the throne.[188] These sources provide names of Asiatics and individuals with Asiatic connections, the latter distinguished by their names and physiognomy, and identify their roles and titles, such as "donkey driver," "hall-keeper," "deputy of the chief steward," and "major-domo."[189]

Some individuals are mentioned multiple times in these texts, yielding detailed information on the often complex biographies. One Khebeded(em), "brother of the *heqa* of *Retenu*," appears four times, including as a donkey-rider accompanied by an entourage, possibly his personal guard—all indicative of his elite status and role in the joint mining enterprise at Serabit el-Khadim.[190] While Khebeded(em) is connected to the land of Retenu (a geographical term that occurs in multiple inscriptions, including general tallies of expedition members), this does not necessarily mean that he arrived directly from the Levant during all of his multiple visits, which cover at least twenty years.[191] Khebeded(em) may have arrived at the mines from Egypt, perhaps his (occasional?) place of residence;[192] if he voyaged by sea to and from Egypt, this would

---

186. Mourad 2015: 143.

187. Mourad 2015: 134–135.

188. Mourad 2015: 135–142, Appendix B.12, fig. B.3.

189. Mourad 2015: 135–136, Appendix B.12, fig. B.3.

190. Mourad 2015: 136–138, Appendix B.12, fig. B.3.

191. Mourad 2015: 137–139.

192. Mourad 2015: 137.

have greatly shortened his travel time and that of the materials and other Asiatics accompanying him. Another man, depicted with the pointy beard typical for Asiatics in Egyptian art, is called Imenyseshenen, whose name appears thirteen times in the inscriptions.[193] He was the son of a first- or second-generation immigrant Asiatic mother and a foster child of the king, upon whose daughter's statue at the Hathor Temple his name was inscribed. He rose to the lofty position of "sealer of the king of Lower Egypt." Ptahwer is mentioned four times and is identified as "Asiatic" (*aam*) in one text, despite his Egyptian name.[194] He was "chief chamberlain of the treasury" and is explicitly stated to have been involved in expeditions to foreign lands.

Today, the commercial and cultural contacts of the joint Egyptian-Asiatic exploitation of the Sinai mines are widely seen as the nexus that enabled the development of a Proto-Alphabetic script,[195] the earliest known form of alphabetic writing and clearly influenced by familiarity with the Egyptian hieroglyphic script. At Serabit el-Khadim, this alphabet is attested for recording a Northwest Semitic language in the form of dedicatory inscriptions at the Hathor Temple, albeit in an iconoclastic manner that sees the writing nonchalantly incised on existing, and presumably revered, Egyptian statuary.

Back in Egypt proper, Asiatics can be shown to have continued to fill niche roles and to have climbed the social ladder from menial to more prominent professions during the reign of Amenemhat III. While only two of the very many dedicatory steles at the Osiris Temple of Abydos may be assigned to his reign (mentioning a butler and an Asiatic named Senusret, son of Ibener), many other steles from the Twelfth and Thirteenth Dynasties show Asiatics in a wide range of positions in Egyptian households and institutions.[196] In the Lahun Papyri, the frequency of Asiatic names increases, some with

---

193. Mourad 2015: 135.

194. Mourad 2015: 135.

195. Most recently discussed by Mourad 2015: 139–141 (with extensive references).

196. Mourad 2015: 99–100.

Egyptian names or nicknames. Among the temple roles filled by Asiatics are singers and dancers (at court and for festivals); retainers; door-keepers; priests and other temple functionaries, such as couriers, attendants, and bookkeepers. Outside the temple, attested occupations include butchers, workmen, domestic servants, and stone carters. Some servants worked through multiple generations of the same household, while other households had servants whose progeny continued to serve them. Asiatic soldiers are recorded as being led by an "overseer of the expedition of Asiatics (*aamu*)," a title also held by the Asiatic Bebi in an inscription at the Wadi el-Hol near Thebes.[197] Lastly, a scribe servicing his fellow Asiatics is recorded,[198] which may hint at a level of literacy beyond the sphere of record-keeping and other writing necessary for dealing with various Egyptian institutions. Beyond the testimony of the texts, the material finds from the Lahun excavations, while not reliably assigned to specific periods, include many Levantine, Cypriot, and Minoan ceramics, jewelry, evidence for weaving, as well as organic remains of imported materials[199] that suggest the kind of mixed Egyptian-Asiatic milieu that we know from the contemporary settlement of Tell el-Dabʿa (whose wet environment in the Nile delta has not allowed the preservation of papyri, unlike at desert-bound Lahun).

Indeed, that cosmopolitan port city had its real start during the latter part of Amenemhat III's reign, when Tell el-Dabʿa's future main settlement experienced a major influx of Asiatic culture and population. In Area F/I (Stratum d/2), that phenomenon is reflected in a settlement that comprises Near Eastern architecture of large elite and more modest domestic buildings, as well as a nearby and intramural cemetery with tombs displaying both Middle Kingdom Egyptian architecture and Levantine funerary traditions, with a mix of Egyptian and Levantine

---

197. Mourad 2015: 71, 108.

198. Mourad 2015: 71.

199. Mourad 2015: 69–72.

offerings.[200] In contrast, the contemporaneous Stratum H horizon in Area A/II features flimsily constructed and poorly preserved one-room houses.[201] Although the material culture of this settlement is predominately Egyptian, 12.6 percent of the total assemblage (comprising jars, drinking and domestic wares) are clearly of Levantine origin, of which 92.9 percent can be identified as imported vessels.[202] Petrographic analysis of a sample of twenty-one pieces comprised primarily of Levantine Painted Ware and amphorae demonstrated that for these, 90 percent of the identifiable sources of clay are situated in the northern Levant, with one amphora from the southern Levantine coast and a possible cooking pot reported from the Mount Carmel region.[203] Macroscopic fabric analysis of the amphorae sherds confirms this preponderance of imports from the northern Levant.[204]

Outside of the Nile delta region, Levantine imports from the reign of Amenemhat III are rare in reliable contexts and may include sherds of three Levantine storage jars and a burnished jug from Amenemhat III's pyramid complex in Dahshur.[205] The intact burial of Lady Sitweret in the mastaba of Horkherti at Dahshur produced a cedar coffin and an Egyptian Marl C jar with the label *irep en Ketj* "wine of Ketj," a region near Homs on the Orontes river in northwestern Syria.[206]

Egyptian exports to the Levant attributable to no earlier than this reign include at least three ceramic examples from the destruction horizons of Tel Ifshar (Phases B and C: figure 21.4: 5, 7, 8)[207] and three

---

200. Bietak 1996: 10–14.

201. Bader 2018: 111.

202. Kopetzky 2010: fig. 52.

203. Cohen-Weinberger and Goren 2004: Table 1b. The presence of this imported cooking pot is not reported in any of the publications of pottery from the site.

204. Kopetzky 2010: fig. 66.

205. Di. Arnold 1982: 41–42, fig. 13: 1–4.

206. Di. Arnold 2004; Allen 2009: 327, fig. 1: 11; Mourad 2015: 64.

207. Marcus et al. 2008b: figs. 3: 2, 3, 4: 1 (?); Schiestl and Seiler 2012: 384, 386, II.A.3.b.2: 5, 573. Both phases have additional Middle Kingdom imports, but

examples from Sidon (Phase 2), but at the latter site, only a complete
zir vessel was found in situ, used as burial container.[208]

These finds, however, pale in comparison to those from Byblos, at
least in size and quantity, albeit not necessarily in the quality of their
stratigraphic context and chronological precision. While it is not known
when (or even if) Egypt's relations with Byblos were (re-)established following Senusret III's "cedar trade war," the Egyptian finds from Byblos
have long been interpreted as indicating the existence a close relationship
during the reign of his successor Amenemhat III.[209] However, beyond
the finds from the jar and other closed deposits in sacred areas or from
architectural complexes such as the Temple of the Obelisks, the Syrian
Temple, and the so-called Royal Tombs, this assumption has largely been
based on non-contextualized finds.[210] The first of these buildings owes
its modern designation to its twenty-six obelisks, including one with an
Egyptian hieroglyphic inscription mentioning a ruler with the Egyptian
title *hati-a*, and obviously featuring strong Egyptian influences; both
structures have relevant and datable finds.[211] This temple was built on
top of a burned third millennium BC temple, from which some of the

those lack the same chronological precision. See also the *zir* mentioned in section 21.4.3.

208. Bader et al. 2009; Forstner-Müller et al. 2006: figs. 2 (9586/299), 3; Schiestl and
Seiler 2012: 418, II.B.1: 3, 592, II.E.13.d: 7, 614–615. The other fragmentary long-
lived examples are from a later Phase 4 settlement horizon, where they could be
residual.

209. E.g., Redford 1992: 97; Flammini 1998; 2010; Mourad 2015: 165–171 (with copi-
ous references).

210. For the stratigraphic relationship between the deposits and the different areas
and complexes, see Negbi and Moskowitz 1966. For the identification of various jars as Levantine Painted Ware, see Bagh 2013: 124, fig. 76 and Tufnell and
Ward 1966: 171 n. 1, 172 n. 6. Unfortunately, no royal inscriptions or scarabs
with royal names are known from this site: Mourad 2015: 170–171. Apart from
those in the Montet Jar, few of the hundreds of scarabs are well stratified and
most can only be dated stylistically; Ward 1978: 11.

211. Flammini 1998; Mourad 2015: 166–167.

obelisks possibly originate.[212] At present it is not possible to date its construction with any precision,[213] but the temple contains a deposit (F, nos. 15121–15567) of Egyptian faience figurines that demonstrates its use at least by ca. 1850/1800 BC.[214] A bas-relief fragment from the temple, also featuring the Egyptian title *ḥati-a*, attests to the building's continued use at least into the Thirteenth Dynasty.[215] The re-dating of the Montet Jar (see section 21.4.4), which was found below the Syrian Temple's floor, results either in a *terminus post quem* from the time of his predecessor or in it being contemporaneous with Amenemhat III's reign. Finally, the highest-profile Egyptian finds at Byblos, with seemingly secure dates based on two of this king's cartouches, are found among the burial goods in the earliest of the three so-called royal tombs of Byblos. However, its dating, as well as the assignment of Tomb II to the time of Amenemhat IV and Tomb III to the Thirteenth Dynasty, is no longer tenable. In a detailed study based on the tombs' Egyptian and Levantine pottery and other finds,[216] Karin Kopetzky has convincingly demonstrated that these tombs date to later periods: Tomb I to the late Thirteenth Dynasty or early Second Intermediate Period; Tomb II slightly later in the Second Intermediate Period; and Tomb III to the Hyksos Period. Thus, the ornate Egyptian finds from the Byblos tombs are best interpreted within the general pattern of looting and exporting Egyptian "antiques" (including stone vessels and statuary), as attested throughout the eastern Mediterranean.[217] These new insights and datings must be considered

---

212. Miniaci 2018: 379. On the continuity between these temples, see Bietak 2019.

213. Other than a crude late third millennium *terminus post quem* (ca. 2100 BC) based on a Mesopotamian cylinder seal of the Ur III period; Miniaci 2018: 382.

214. Miniaci 2018: 384–389. As some of the figurines have dates no earlier than 1800 BC, the lower date should probably serve as the *terminus post quem* of the deposit.

215. Mourad 2015: 166. Kilani 2016: 80 (citing Boschloos 2011: BYB 556) notes a jar deposit near the southern wall of the temple courtyard that contains a late Middle Kingdom scarab.

216. Kopetzky 2018 (with references).

217. Weinstein 1975; Ahrens 2016 (with references); Kopetzky 2018: 313–315;

when characterizing and dating the political relations between Egypt and Byblos, the nature of the assimilation and appropriation of Egyptian practices at Byblos, and the use of the Egyptian title (*hati-a*) for the local ruler.[218]

21.5. Interaction with the Levant during the late Twelfth and the early Thirteenth Dynasties

If the long reign of Amenemhat III constituted its zenith, the short reigns of his two successors (of whom the second marked the end of the dynasty), as well as of the plethora of rulers that characterize the Thirteenth Dynasty,[219] appear to set the path of the Middle Kingdom to its nadir. However, despite the political turmoil of this age, which would culminate with the onset of the Second Intermediate Period and the rise of the Hyksos (cf. chapter 23 in volume 3), relations with the eastern Mediterranean appear to have initially increased along with the Asiatic presence in Egypt. Unfortunately, the lack of a coherent regnal sequence precludes the type of diachronic discussion maintained thus far in this chapter. Instead, the following can only present the evidence and sketch general trends.

No more royal expeditions to the Levant are documented. However, imported coniferous wood (probably cedar) was probably used as timber to construct the seagoing ships for the last recorded successful expedition from Wadi Gawasis on the Red Sea to Punt (cf. chapter 20 in this volume) in Year 8 of Amenemhat IV, the final ruler of the Twelfth Dynasty.[220] Later in the Thirteenth Dynasty, a stele of Sobekhotep IV at Karnak references *ash* wood brought from Khenti-she for building doors (one specifically stated to be ten cubits high) in the Temple of

218. Flammini 1998; 2010; Mourad 2015: 166–171.

219. Ryholt 1997: 69–75.

220. Bard and Fattovich 2018: 45, 86, 98.

Amun, which clearly demonstrates access to northern Levantine materials,[221] although there is no indication as to whether these were acquired through direct or indirect contacts.

Ceramic imports from the Levant are documented at Thirteenth Dynasty Kom Rabiʾa (Level VII) in the Memphis region,[222] at Lisht, and at Dahshur,[223] while the quantities and range of Levantine forms occurring at and imported to Tell el-Dabʿa rise considerably.[224] Again, both petrography and macroscopic fabric analyses demonstrate that the majority of the imports come from the northern Levant.[225] These ceramic developments accompany Tell el-Dabʿa's significant growth in size and importance, as evidenced by palatial, administrative, and religious structures and the increasing evidence for the presence of Asiatics who practiced their rituals, funerary traditions, and crafts.[226] Among the other evidence available at Tell el-Dabʿa for contacts with the eastern Mediterranean are the earliest imported jars from Tell Arqa in northern Lebanon (Stratum G/4), followed later by a cooking pot (Stratum F);[227] some reliably dated Middle Cypriot imports (Stratum G/1–3), as well as locally produced examples of hybrid Tell el-Yahudiya ware (including a piece with a Cypriot potter's thrust-through handle);[228] and in Stratum

---

221. Mourad 2015: 109.

222. Ownby 2010; 2012: 24–26 (with references).

223. Do. Arnold et al. 1995.

224. Kopetzky 2010: 175–268; fig. 52: while the frequency of Levantine forms in Stratum G/4, G/1–3 and F increase (16.2 percent, 20.6 percent and 39.2 percent, respectively), imports of those forms actually decline from 98.8 percent to 73.2 percent, as local production increases—a trend that will continue into the Hyksos Period; fig. 67: imported amphorae rise from 14.4 percent (Stratum G/4) to 17.3 percent (Stratum G/1–3) to a peak of 24.1 percent (Stratum F) of the ceramic assemblage, and then decline as well.

225. Cohen-Weinberger and Goren 2004: Table 1c–1d; Kopetzky 2010: fig. 66; cf. Ownby 2010: Tables 4.1, 4.2, 5.9 (Samples 3, 10, 12, 15, 21 and 22).

226. Bietak 1996: 21–49.

227. Kopetzky 2007/8.

228. Maguire 2009: 21–23, 40, fig. 3, Table 2.

G/4, the first securely dated imported Aegean pottery since the time of Amenemhat II.[229]

Elsewhere in Egypt during this period, Asiatics continue to feature prominently in a variety of written sources. Rock graffiti at Gebel Tjauti mentions an Asiatic police officer, an attendant, and an overseer of metalworkers.[230] Papyrus Brooklyn provides a long list of Asiatic men, women, and children, with their familial relations and their occupations (primarily domestic).[231] Papyrus Bulaq offers information about workers on an estate near Thebes.[232] A stele from Abydos (if it is not to be dated earlier) mentions five generations of Asiatics in a single household, whose names underscore their gradual acculturation.[233] Finally, the mention of a "senior chief lector priest" in Memphis is the most lofty and senior position recorded for a man described as an Asiatic.[234]

During the reign of Amenemhat IV, Egyptian-Levantine collaboration continued in the Sinai mines. However, a general decrease in activity is apparent during and especially after the Thirteenth Dynasty.[235]

In the southern Levant, the port of Ashkelon demonstrates contacts with Egypt from the beginning of its Middle Bronze Age sequence (Late MB IIa). Evidence includes forty-four mud sealings stamped with Thirteenth Dynasty scarab seals and five unstamped mud sealings, found both in the lining of the city's moat (Phase 14) and recycled as part of the construction of the later Phase 13 street that covered the moat.[236] These

---

229. Walberg 1991; Bietak 1996: 29, pl. IA. Note that while some examples of Middle Minoan Kamares Ware were found in earlier Middle Kingdom contexts throughout Egypt, these are generally not thought to be reliable or precisely dated.

230. Mourad 2015: 144.

231. Mourad 2015: 116–117.

232. Mourad 2015: 104.

233. Mourad 2015: 100, 282–283 (ÄS 160).

234. Mourad 2015: 136, 307, Appendix B.12: no. 123.

235. Mourad 2015: 146.

236. Mlinar 2004a: n. 15–16; D. Ben-Tor and Bell 2018.

include sealings used to secure door locks, a silo opening, boxes of various sizes, baskets, and various types of ceramic vessels.[237] Petrographic analysis of the clay of the sealings and the Levantine shapes of the sealed vessels indicate the local presence of an Egyptian administration.[238] The lining of the moat also contained two Egyptian alabaster vessels and Thirteenth Dynasty pottery (a *zir*, a storage jar, and a stand), the latter of which increases in quantity in subsequent phases.[239] At Ashkelon,[240] and also elsewhere in this region, the earliest imports of Middle Kingdom Egyptian scarabs are attested (e.g., at Tel Aphek) as well as the beginning of a local production (dubbed the "Early Palestinian Scarab Series").[241]

In the northern Levant, Egyptian exports are more plentiful. There is late Middle Kingdom pottery at Sidon, which continues to receive increasing amounts (reaching fifty-one sherds in Level 4),[242] as well as scarabs.[243] A Middle Kingdom carinated bowl, cooking pot, and *zir*s were found at Tell Fadous-Kfarabida,[244] as well as Middle Kingdom pottery at Tell Arqa.[245] The aforementioned material at Byblos, now re-dated to the Thirteenth Dynasty (see section 21.4.6), is complimented by similarly assigned objects and influences that reached inland Syria at Ebla and Tell Sakka, where fragments of wall paintings with Egyptian decorative elements are attested.[246]

---

237. D. Ben-Tor and Bell 2018; Brandl 2018.

238. D. Ben-Tor and Bell 2018: 337–339; Brandl 2018: 390. Although Ben-Tor and Bell note the lack of any indication of sealed documents, Brandl notes that the repetitive sealing of identical boxes supports the notion that papyri were stored in them.

239. Voss and Stager 2018: 31–33; Stager and Voss 2018a: 237–238.

240. Keel and Ben-Tor 2018: 325, 327, no. 3.

241. D. Ben-Tor 2007: 117–121.

242. Doumet-Serhal 2006: 39.

243. Mlinar 2004b: 62; Taylor 2004: 157.

244. Genz 2010/11: 118.

245. Charaf 2009: 295–297, fig. 2:5–7.

246. Mourad 2015: 171–173, 175.

In that respect, the wall paintings discovered at the "palace/strong-hold" of Tell el-Burak, south of Sidon on the coast of southern Lebanon, with their obvious Middle Kingdom influences deserve particular mention.[247] The depictions include hunting scenes with dogs, a rearing caprid in a tree, a procession (figure 21.6)—motifs and color schemes that seem to have been inspired by examples from the Beni Hasan and Meir tombs, as well as from artistic traditions attested elsewhere in the eastern Mediterranean and the Middle East.[248]

Unfortunately, no Egyptian pottery was identified in the excavation, but a single late Middle Kingdom scarab, probably from the Thirteenth Dynasty, was found on the floor of the building,[249] suggesting that this structure was still in use at that time. This date is supported by the remains of approximately ten "ridge-necked pithoi" on a floor in a room adjoining the wall paintings, as well as two other examples in basal and other deposits.[250] The only other known occurrences of this ceramic type are in the Thirteenth Dynasty Ashkelon Moat lining and the subsequent fill,[251] and later in Tell el-Dab'a Stratum G/1-3.[252] This evidence clearly does not correlate with the radiocarbon-based date in the early nineteenth century suggested for the Tell el-Burak building,[253] which relies

247. Sader and Kamlah 2010; 2019a.

248. Sader and Kamlah 2010: 137–138; Bertsch 2018; 2019; van Ess 2019.

249. Kamlah and Sader 2019b: 334–335, fig. 10.23:2. The cited parallels derive from Thirteenth Dynasty contexts (e.g., Tell el-Dab'a Stratum G/4), or later, as does a further parallel from the Ashkelon Moat Deposit; Ben-Tor and Bell 2018: 352.

250. Kamlah and Michelau 2019: 184–185, fig. 7.83:19; Badreshany 2019: 288–290 n. 12, fig. 10.2. The group of vessels is touted as one of the site's few in situ assemblages: Badreshany 2019: 288.

251. Stager et al. 2018: 184–185, fig. 4.83.

252. Bietak et al. 2008: 52, fig. 2: 6; Stager and Voss 2018: fig. 3.2: 6. Note that neither article is updated to reflect the important stratigraphic and chronological revision, which interprets the "Moat deposit" as a protective lining, and thus assigns it to the incipient Phase 14 Gate 1, both of which then date to the Thirteenth Dynasty (Stager 2018: 10–12, fig. 1.3; Voss and Stager 2018: 27–33).

253. Badreshany and Kamlah 2010–2011: 81–83 n. 4; Höflmayer et al. 2016.

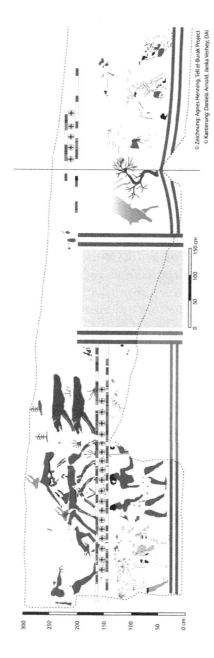

© Zeichnung: Agnes Henning, Tell el-Burak Project
© Kartierung: Daniela Arnold, Janka Verhey, DAI

150 cm 100 50 0

300 250 200 150 100 50 0 cm

FIGURE 21.6. Middle Bronze Age wall painting from Tell el-Burak, Lebanon, exhibiting Middle Kingdom influences. Drawing by A. Henning, D. Arnold and J. Verhey. © The Tel Burak Excavation Project; courtesy Jens Kamlah and Hélène Sader.

on single-year cultigens and charcoal from constructional fills and not from occupational accumulation. Their calibrated date ranges, like much of the ceramic assemblage, have broad chronological ranges and should be considered residual, like their accompanying third millennium BC radiocarbon measurements;[254] thus, they were probably brought with quarried soil and debris of earlier contexts from elsewhere at the site before being poured into the building for construction. This chronological issue notwithstanding, the painted scenes presuppose very close relations between Egypt and Tell el-Burak sometime in the late Middle Kingdom/Middle Bronze Age IIA, although these relations are otherwise poorly reflected in the other aspects of the site's material culture.

The terminal phase of the Middle Kingdom is characterized by the extreme brevity of most rulers' reigns, and this "staccato" succession might not seem to have lent itself to the planning and execution of expeditions overseas. However, some relations and commercial activity were clearly maintained, and there was an increase in the visibility of Asiatics in Egypt in various roles. These are well attested at Tell el-Dabʿa, which would take on an increasingly prominent role in relations with the eastern Mediterranean as the political cohesion of the central authority continued to decline.

21.6. In conclusion: Egypt, the Mediterranean world, and beyond

While the preceding presentation and discussion have sought to present a diachronic history based on the most reliably dated and attributable written and material data, a much more extensive body of data can be subsumed under a broad Twelfth Dynasty or Middle Kingdom designation, sometimes accorded relative headings like early, middle, and late.[255] These Middle Kingdom imports support and magnify the overall picture, but do not change its implications: Egypt during this period both

---

254. Badreshany and Kamlah 2010–2011: n. 4; Höflmayer et al. 2016: fig. 8.

255. Mourad 2015.

continued to venture increasingly into the greater eastern Mediterranean world and, at the same time, opened its own door, the delta (literally, the Semitic word for "door"),[256] and the entire Nile valley and its arid periphery to foreign peoples, most importantly the "Asiatics." Given its geographical location and its importance for riverine movement and transport, the eastern delta and in particular the area of Tell el-Dabʿa (situated in an area called the "door/mouth of the two ways/roads")[257] was the principal gateway for the movement of goods and people into Egypt, about which the long-term excavations there provide an important source of data.

The textual record both before and during the period under consideration in this chapter suggests a priori that the procurement of foreign materials was due to royal initiative, with the successful completion of such ventures and the goods gained in this way worthy of being celebrated in texts and in some extant pictorial depictions. The royal commemoration and consumption of foreign goods notwithstanding, many of these procurement enterprises were carried out through agents who were members of the Egyptian elite, and they would have been well compensated for the risks involved in such ventures. Status would therefore have been shared top-down, as many of the imported materials circulated widely within Egypt. Thus, a reciprocal relationship would have existed between the perceived power of the king to reach foreign lands and the actual objects thus acquired and supplied to his supporters and the priesthood, who were thereby further encouraged to support the king's rule and his endeavors.

An important byproduct and economic multiplier of the royal maritime ventures in the Mediterranean Sea would have been the supply, via the Nile river and overland via Wadi Hammamat, of coniferous longwoods, especially cedar, to the shipyards on the Red Sea in order to construct the boats dispatched in expeditions to eastern Africa (especially Punt) for the acquisition of spices and other products (cf. chapter 20 in

256. For the history of this geographical term and its origin as a proper name adopted from Ionian Greeks, see Celoria 1966.

257. Adam 1959: 17; Bietak 1991: 28; 1996: 7.

this volume).[258] Inscriptional evidence from Mersa Gawasis on the Red Sea indicates that these expeditions took place throughout most of the Twelfth Dynasty, and only ceased with its final ruler Amenemhat IV.[259] The result of this long-distance exchange was the integration of two maritime interaction zones, with Egypt as the nexus.

The Egyptians' tolerance, if not encouragement, of Asiatics in their midst and their acceptance, socially, economically, and familiarly, is previously unparalleled in both scope and numbers. We cannot supply an explanation for this tolerance, or for the possible needs that led to the demand for skilled and unskilled labor. In any case, this growing integrated population surely served as a demographic and political foundation for what would be known as the Fourteenth Dynasty under the so-called Hyksos (cf. chapter 23 in volume 3). Despite the perceived ignominy of foreign rule, the presence of non-Egyptians in the Nile valley would continue in the New Kingdom and after, particularly in the delta.

Finally, in the absence of written records, it remains very unclear how important relations with Egypt were for eastern Mediterranean polities. Nevertheless, the diverse evidence discussed in this chapter clearly indicates that Egypt fulfilled a role that went beyond simply being the regional superpower, with which a relationship was unavoidable. One possible explanation for the Levantine interest in its southwestern neighbor may have been Egypt's surplus agricultural production, which relied on the monsoon-fed water source of the annual Nile flood. The possibility of importing grain from Egypt may well have been a key component in the risk-abatement strategies practiced in the eastern Mediterranean in the face of the unpredictability of the local climate.[260] Although there is no concrete evidence for Egypt exporting grain prior to the Late Bronze Age,[261] the data presented in this chapter have made it abundantly clear that the requisite maritime transport capability was available already at

---

258. Bard and Fattovich 2018.

259. Bard and Fattovich 2018: 9, 32.

260. Marcus 2019: 158–160.

261. Monroe 2007.

the time of the Middle Kingdom (if not earlier). Further exploration of this and other issues of the relations between Egypt and the eastern Mediterranean must continue to be a research priority, and its results are likely to challenge the current state of our knowledge, as sketched in this chapter.

REFERENCES

Adam, S. 1959. Report on the excavations of the Department of Antiquities. *ASAE* 56: 207–226.

Ahrens, A. 2015. Objects from afar: the distribution of Egyptian imports in the northern Levant: parameters for ascertaining the character of diplomatic contacts between Egypt and the Levant during the Bronze Age? In Pruzsinszky, R., and Eder, B. (eds.), *Policies of exchange: political systems and modes of interaction in the Aegean and the Near East in the 2nd millennium BCE*. Vienna: Verlag der Österreichischen Akademie der Wissenschaften, 141–156.

Ahrens, A. 2016. Remarks on the dispatch of Egyptian Middle Kingdom objects to the Levant during the Second Intermediate Period: an addendum to the Egyptian statues from Tell Hizzin (Lebanon). *GM* 250: 21–24.

Albright, W.F. 1928. The Egyptian empire in Asia in the twenty-first century BC. *Journal of the Palestine Oriental Society* 8: 223–256.

Albright, W.F. 1941. New Egyptian data on Palestine in the Patriarchal Age. *BASOR* 81: 16–21.

Allen, J.P. 2008. The historical inscription of Khnumhotep at Dahshur: preliminary report. *BASOR* 352: 29–39.

Allen, S.J. 2009. Funerary pottery in the Middle Kingdom: archaism or revival? In Silverman, D.P., Simpson, W.K., and Wegner, J. (eds.), *Archaism and innovation: studies in the culture of Middle Kingdom Egypt*. New Haven, CT: Yale University Press, 319–339.

Altenmüller, H. 2015. *Zwei Annalenfragmente aus dem frühen Mittleren Reich*. Hamburg: Buske.

Altenmüller, H., and Moussa, A.M. 1991. Die Inschrift Amenemhets II. aus dem Ptah-Tempel von Memphis: ein Vorbericht. *SAK* 18: 1–48.

Arnold, Di. 1982. Keramikbearbeitung in Dahschur 1976–1981. *MDAIK* 38: 25–65.

Arnold, Di. 2004. The pyramid complex of Senwosret III, Dahshur: private tombs to the north. In Heilbrunn Timeline of Art History. New York: The Metropolitan Museum of Art, 2000–. Retrieved from https://www.metmuseum.org/toah/hd/dapt/hd_dapt.htm (last accessed February 2020).

Arnold, Di. 2008. *Middle Kingdom tomb architecture at Lisht*. New Haven, CT: Yale University Press.

Arnold, Di., and Settgast, J. 1965. Erster Vorbericht über die vom Deutschen Archäologischen Institut Kairo im Asasif unternommenen Arbeiten. *MDAIK*: 47–61.

Arnold, Do. 2010. Foreign and female. In D'Auria, S. (ed.), *Offerings to the discerning eye: an Egyptological medley in honor of Jack A. Josephson*. Leiden: Brill, 17–31.

Arnold, Do., Arnold, F., and Allen, S. 1995. Canaanite imports at Lisht, the Middle Kingdom capital of Egypt. *ÄL* 5: 13–32.

Aruz, J. 1995. Imagery and interconnections. *ÄL* 5: 33–48.

Bader, B. 2018. On simple house architecture at Tell el-Dabʿa and its parallels in the late Middle Kingdom. *ÄL* 28: 107–142.

Bader, B., Forstner-Müller, I., Kopetzky, K., and Doumet-Serhal, C. 2009. An Egyptian jar from Sidon in its Egyptian context: some fresh evidence. *Archaeology and History in Lebanon* 29: 79–83.

Badreshany, K. 2019. The Middle Bronze Age pottery from Areas 1 and 2. In Kamlah, J., and Sader, H. (eds.), *Tell el-Burak I: the Middle Bronze Age, with chapters related to the site and to the Mamluk-Ottoman periods*. Wiesbaden: Harrassowitz, 283–316.

Badreshany, K., and Kamlah, J. 2010–2011. Middle Bronze Age pottery of Tell el-Burak, Lebanon. *Berytus* 53–54: 81–113.

Bagh, T. 2013. *Tell el-Dabʿa XXII: Levantine painted ware from Egypt and the Levant*. Vienna: Verlag der Österreichischen Akademie der Wissenschaften.

Baines, J. 1982. Interpreting Sinuhe. *JEA* 68: 31–44.

Baines, J. 1987. The stela of Khusobek: private and royal military narrative and values. In Osing, J., and Dreyer, G. (eds.), *Form und Maß: Beiträge zur Literatur, Sprache und Kunst des alten Ägypten (Festschrift für Gerhard Fecht)*. Wiesbaden: Harrassowitz, 43–61.

Barbotin, C., and Clère, J.-J. 1991. L'inscription de Sésostris Iᵉʳ à Tôd. *BIFAO* 91: 1–32.

Bard, K.A. 1994. The Egyptian Predynastic: a review of the evidence. *Journal of Field Archaeology* 21: 265–288.

Bard, K.A., and Fattovich, R. 2018. *Seafaring expeditions to Punt in the Middle Kingdom: excavations at Mersa/Wadi Gawasis, Egypt*. Leiden: Brill.

Ben-Tor, A. 2006. Do the execration texts reflect an accurate picture of the contemporary settlement map of Palestine? In Amit, Y., Ben Zvi, E., Finkelstein, I., and Lipschits, O. (eds.), *Essays on ancient Israel in its Near Eastern context: a tribute to Nadav Na'aman*. Winona Lake, IN: Eisenbrauns, 63–87.

Ben-Tor, D. 1997. The relations between Egypt and Palestine in the Middle Kingdom as reflected by contemporary Canaanite scarabs. *IEJ* 47: 162–189.

Ben-Tor, D. 1998. The absolute date of the Montet Jar scarabs. In Lesko, L.H. (ed.), *Ancient Egyptian and Mediterranean studies in memory of William A. Ward*. Providence, RI: Brown University, 1–17.

Ben-Tor, D. 2003. Egyptian-Levantine relations and chronology in the Middle Bronze Age: scarab research. In Bietak, M. (ed.), *The synchronisation of civilizations in the Eastern Mediterranean in the second millennium BC, vol. II*. Vienna: Verlag der Österreichischen Akademie der Wissenschaften, 239–248.

Ben-Tor, D. 2006. Chronological and historical implications of the early Egyptian scarabs on Crete. In Czerny, E., Hein, I., Hunger, H., Melman, D., and Schwab, A. (eds.), *Timelines: studies in honour of Manfred Bietak, vol. II*. Leuven: Peeters, 77–86.

Ben-Tor, D. 2007. *Scarabs, chronology, and interconnections: Egypt and Palestine in the Second Intermediate Period*. Fribourg: Academic Press.

Ben-Tor, D. 2011. Egyptian-Canaanite relations in the Middle and Late Bronze Ages as reflected by scarabs. In Bar, S., Kahn, D., and Shirley, J. (eds.), *Egypt, Canaan and Israel: history, imperialism, ideology and literature*. Leiden: Brill, 23–43.

Ben-Tor, D., and Bell, L. 2018. Clay sealings from the moat deposit. In Stager, L.E., Schloen, J.D., and Voss, R.J. (eds.), *Ashkelon 6: the Middle Bronze Age ramparts and gates of the north slope and later fortifications*. University Park, PA: Eisenbrauns, 337–381.

Bertsch, J. 2018. Preliminary remarks on the technical and iconographical aspects of the Middle Bronze Age wall paintings from Tell el-Burak (Lebanon) in relation to the Aegean and Egypt. In Becker, J., Jungfleisch, J., and von Rüden, C. (eds.), *Tracing technoscapes: the production of Bronze Age wall paintings in the Eastern Mediterranean*. Leiden: Sidestone, 85–100.

Bertsch, J. 2019. Preliminary report on the wall paintings of Tell el-Burak: iconography. In Kamlah, J., and Sader, H. (eds.), *Tell el-Burak I: the Middle Bronze Age, with chapters related to the site and to the Mamluk-Ottoman periods*. Wiesbaden: Harrassowitz, 385–400.

Bietak, M. 1991. Egypt and Canaan during the Middle Bronze Age. *BASOR* 281: 27–72.

Bietak, M. 1996. *Avaris, the capital of the Hyksos: recent excavations at Tell el-Dabʿa*. London: British Museum Press.

Bietak, M. 1997. The center of Hyksos rule: Avaris (Tell el-Dabʿa). In Oren, E.D. (ed.), *The Hyksos: new historical and archaeological perspectives*. Philadelphia: University of Pennsylvania Museum of Archaeology and Anthropology, 87–139.

Bietak, M. 2003. Two ancient Near Eastern temples with bent axis in the eastern Nile delta. *ÄL* 13: 13–38.

Bietak, M. 2019. The Obelisk Temple in Byblos and its predecessors. In Pieńkowska, A., Szeląg, D., and Zych, I. (eds.), *Stories told around the fountain: papers offered to Piotr Bieliński on the occasion of his 70th birthday*. Warsaw: University of Warsaw Press, 165–186.

Bietak, M., and Dorner, J. 1998. Der Tempel und die Siedlung des Mittleren Reiches bei ʿEzbet Rushdi. *ÄL* 8: 9–40.

Birch, S. 1880. *Catalogue of the collection of Egyptian antiquities at Alnwick Castle*. London: Clay, Sons, and Taylor.

Bisson de la Roque, F. 1937. *Tôd, 1934 à 1936*. Cairo: Institut français d'archéologie orientale.

Bisson de la Roque, F. 1950. *Le Trésor de Tôd: catalogue générale des antiquités égyptiennes du Musée du Caire, nos. 70501–70754*. Cairo: Institut français d'archéologie orientale.

Bisson de la Roque, F., Contenau, G., and Chapouthier, F. 1953. *Le trésor de Tôd*. Cairo: Institut français d'archéologie orientale.

Blackman, A.M. 1915. An indirect reference to Sesostris III's Syrian campaign in the tomb-chapel of *Ḏḥwty-Ḥtp* at El-Bersheh. *JEA* 2: 13–14.

Boschloos, V. 2011. *The geo-chronological distribution of Egyptian scarab-shaped seals in the Northern Levant (Syria and Lebanon) from the late 3rd millennium to the Late Iron Age*. PhD dissertation, Vrije Universiteit Brussel.

Brandl, B. 2018. Morphology and function of the sealings from the Moat Deposit. In Stager, L.E., Schloen, J.D., and Voss, R.J. (eds.), *Ashkelon 6: the*

Middle Bronze Age ramparts and gates of the north slope and later fortifications. University Park, PA: Eisenbrauns, 383–426.

Breasted, J.H. 1906. *Ancient records of Egypt: historical documents from the earliest times to the Persian conquest, vol. 1.* Chicago: University of Chicago.

Candelora, D. 2017. Defining the Hyksos: a reevaluation of the title ḥḳȝ ḫȝswt and its implications for Hyksos identity. *JARCE* 53: 203–221.

Celoria, F. 1966. Delta as a geographical concept in Greek literature. *Isis* 57: 385–388.

Charaf, H. 2009. Arqa and its regional connections redux. In Maila-Afeiche, A.-M. (ed.), *Interconnections in the Eastern Mediterranean: Lebanon in the Bronze and Iron Ages.* Beirut: Minstère de la Culture, Direction Générale des Antiquités, 295–309.

Cohen, S.L. 2002. *Canaanites, chronologies, and connections: the relationship of Middle Bronze IIA Canaan to Middle Kingdom Egypt.* Winona Lake, IN: Eisenbrauns.

Cohen, S.L. 2009. Cores, peripheries, and ports of power: theories of Canaanite development in the early second millennium BCE. In Schloen, J.D. (ed.), *Exploring the Longue Durée: essays in honor of Lawrence E. Stager.* Winona Lake, IN: Eisenbrauns, 69–75.

Cohen, S.L. 2015a. Interpretative uses and abuses of the Beni Hasan tomb painting. *JNES* 74: 19–38.

Cohen, S.L. 2015b. Periphery and core: the relationship between the southern Levant and Egypt in the early Middle Bronze Age (MB I). In Mynářová, J., Onderka, P., and Pavúk, P. (eds.), *There and back again: the crossroads, II.* Prague: Charles University, 245–263.

Cohen, S.L. 2016. *Peripheral concerns: urban development in the Bronze Age southern Levant.* Sheffield, UK: Equinox.

Cohen-Weinberger, A., and Goren, Y. 2004. Levantine-Egyptian interactions during the 12th to 15th Dynasties based on the petrography of the Canaanite pottery from Tell el-Dabʿa. *ÄL* 14: 69–100.

Czerny, E. 2015. *Tell el-Dabʿa XXII: 'Der Mund der beiden Wege': die Siedlung und der Tempelbezirk des frühen Mittleren Reiches von ʿEzbet Ruschdi.* Vienna: Verlag der Österreichischen Akademie der Wissenschaften.

Dantong, G. 1998. The relationship of Egypt and the Western Asia during the Middle Kingdom reflected in the inscription of Amenemhet II from Memphis. *Journal of Ancient Civilizations* 13: 83–90.

Dantong, G. 1999. The inscription of Amenemhet II from Memphis: transliteration, translation and commentary. *Journal of Ancient Civilizations* 14: 45–66.

Darnell, J.C. 2008. The Eleventh Dynasty royal inscription from Deir el-Ballas. *RdE* 59: 81–110.

Davies, W.V. 1995. Ancient Egyptian timber imports: an analysis of wooden coffins in the British Museum. In Davies, W.V., and Schofield, L. (eds.), *Egypt, the Aegean and the Levant: interconnections in the second millennium BC*. London: British Museum Press, 146–156.

Dee, M.W. 2013. A radiocarbon-based chronology for the Middle Kingdom. In Shortland, A.J., and Bronk Ramsey, C. (eds.), *Radiocarbon and the chronologies of ancient Egypt*. Oxford: Oxbow, 174–181.

Delia, R.D. 1980. *A study of the reign of Senwosret III*. PhD dissertation, Columbia University, New York.

Doumet-Serhal, C. 2004. Sidon (Lebanon): twenty Middle Bronze Age burials from the 2001 season of excavation. *Levant* 36: 89–154.

Doumet-Serhal, C. 2006. Sidon: mediterranean contacts in the Early and Middle Bronze Age, preliminary report. *Archaeology and History in Lebanon* 24: 34–47.

Eder, C. 1995. *Die ägyptischen Motive in der Glyptik des östlichen Mittelmeerraumes zu Anfang des 2. Jts. v. Chr.* Leuven: Peeters.

Esposito, S. 2019. Riverboats and seagoing ships: lexicographical analysis of nautical terms from the sources of the Old Kingdom. In Manzo, A., Zazzaro, C., and de Falco, D.J. (eds.), *Stories of globalisation: the Red Sea and the Persian Gulf from late prehistory to early modernity*. Leiden: Brill, 30–52.

Farag, S. 1980. Une inscription Memphite de la XIIe dynastie. *RdE* 32: 75–82.

Fay, B. 1996. *The Louvre Sphinx and royal sculpture from the reign of Amenemhat II*. Mainz: Zabern.

Flammini, R. 1998. The ḫȝtyw-ʿ from Byblos in the early second millennium BC. *GM* 164: 41–61.

Flammini, R. 2010. Elite emulation and patronage relationships in the Middle Bronze: the Egyptianized dynasty of Byblos. *Tel Aviv* 37: 154–168.

Forstner-Müller, I., and Kopetzky, K. 2006. An Upper Egyptian import at Sidon. *Archaeology and History in Lebanon* 24: 60–62.

Gaballa, G. 1976. *Narrative in Egyptian art*. Mainz: Zabern.

Gardiner, A.H. 1917. The tomb of a much-travelled Theban official. *JEA* 4: 28–38.

Gates, M.-H. 2000. Kinet Höyük (Hatay, Turkey) and MB Levantine chronology. *Akkadica* 119/120: 77–101.

Genz, H. 2010–2011. Middle Bronze Age pottery from Tell Fadous - Kfarabida, Lebanon. *Berytus* 53/54: 115–132.

Gestoso Singer, G. 2008. *El intercambio de bienes entre Egipto y Asia Anterior desde el reinado de Tuthmosis III hasta el de Akhenaton.* Buenos Aires: Centro de Estudios de Historia del Antiguo Oriente, Universidad Católica Argentina.

Giveon, R. 1967. Royal seals of the XIIth dynasty from Western Asia. *RdE* 19: 29–37.

Giveon, R. 1987. The impact of Egypt on Canaan in the Middle Bronze Age. In Rainey, A. (ed.), *Egypt, Israel, Sinai: archaeological and historical relationships in the Biblical Period.* Tel Aviv: Tel Aviv University, 23–40.

Gnirs, A.M. 2006. Das Motiv des Bürgerkriegs in Merikare und Neferti: zur Literatur der 18. Dynastie. In Moers, G., Behlmer, H., Demuß, K., and Widmaier, K. (eds.), *Jn.t dr.w: Festschrift für Friedrich Junge.* Göttingen: Seminar für Ägyptologie und Koptologie, 207–265.

Gnirs, A.M. 2013. Geschichte und Literatur: wie "historisch" sind ägyptische literarische Texte? In Moers, G., Widmaier, K., Giewekemeyer, A., Lümers, A., and Ernst, R. (eds.), *Dating Egyptian literary texts.* Hamburg: Widmaier, 367–403.

Goedicke, H. 1991. Egyptian military actions in "Asia" in the Middle Kingdom. *RdE* 42: 89–94.

Goedicke, H. 1992. Where did Sinuhe stay in "Asia"? (Sinuhe B29–31). *Chronique d'Égypte* 67: 28–40.

Green, M. 1983. The Syrian and Lebanese topographical data in the story of Sinuhe. *Chronique d'Égypte* 58: 38–59.

Gubel, E. 2009. Ibirta et le "Nahr el-Bared": notes de toponymie historique akkariote, I. *Syria* 86: 221–232.

Gubel, E., and Loffet, H. 2011–2012. Sidon, Qedem and the land of Iay. *Archaeology and History in Lebanon* 34/35: 79–92.

Haldane, C. 1997. Review of Davies, W.V., and Schofield, L. (eds.), Egypt, the Aegean and the Levant: interconnections in the second millennium BC. *International Journal of Nautical Archaeology* 26: 175–176.

Hayes, W.C. 1949. Career of the great steward Henenu under Nebhepetre Mentuhotep. *JEA* 35: 43–49.

Hayes, W.C. 1971. The Middle Kingdom in Egypt: internal history from the rise of the Heracleopolitans to the death of Ammenemes III. In Edwards, I.E.S., Gadd, C.J., and Hammond, N.G.L. (eds.), *The Cambridge ancient history, vol. I, part 2: early history of the Middle East*. Cambridge: Cambridge University Press, 464–531.

Hayes, W.C. 1973. Egypt: from the death of Ammenemes III to Seqenenre II. In Edwards, I.E.S., Gadd, C.J., Hammond, N.G.L., and Sollberger, E. (eds.), *The Cambridge ancient History, vol. II, part 1: history of the Middle East and the Aegean region c. 1800-1380 B.C.* Cambridge: Cambridge University Press, 42–76.

Helck, W. 1989. Ein Ausgreifen des Mittleren Reiches in den zypriotischen Raum? *GM* 109: 27–30.

Höflmayer, F. 2007. Ägyptische Skarabäen auf Kreta und ihre Bedeutung für die absolute Chronologie der minoischen Altpalastzeit (MM IB–MM IIB). *ÄL* 17: 107–125.

Höflmayer, F., Kamlah, J., Sader, H., Dee, M.W., Kutschera, W., Wild, E.M., and Riehl, S. 2016. New evidence for Middle Bronze Age chronology and synchronisms in the Levant: radiocarbon dates from Tell el-Burak, Tell el-Dabʿa, and Tel Ifshar compared. *BASOR* 375: 53–76.

Hornung, E., Krauss, R., and Warburton, D.A. (eds.) 2006. *Ancient Egyptian chronology*. Leiden: Brill.

Jones, D. 1988. *A glossary of ancient Egyptian nautical titles and terms*. London and New York: Kegan Paul International.

Kamlah, J., and Michelau, H. 2019. Excavations on the northern slope, close to the northern corner of the monumental building. In Kamlah, J., and Sader, H. (eds.), *Tell el-Burak I: the Middle Bronze Age, with chapters related to the site and to the late medieval period*. Wiesbaden: Harrassowitz, 171–188.

Kamlah, J., and Sader, H. 2010. Deutsch-libanesische Ausgrabungen auf Tell el-Burak südlich von Sidon: Vorbericht nach Abschluss der siebten Kampagne 2010. *Zeitschrift des Deutschen Palästina-Vereins* 126: 93–115.

Kamlah, J., and Sader, H. (eds.) 2019a. *Tell el-Burak I: the Middle Bronze Age, with chapters related to the site and to the Mamluk-Ottoman periods*. Wiesbaden: Harrassowitz.

Kamlah, J., and Sader, H. 2019b. Two scarabs from the Middle Bronze Age and the Late Bronze Age. In Kamlah, J., and Sader, H. (eds.), *Tell el-Burak I: the Middle Bronze Age, with chapters related to the site and to the Mamluk-Ottoman periods*. Wiesbaden: Harrassowitz, 332–335.

Keel, O., and Ben-Tor, D. 2018. Scarabs found on the north slope of Ashkelon. In Stager, L.E., Schloen, J.D., and Voss, R.J. (eds.), *Ashkelon 6: the Middle Bronze Age ramparts and gates of the north slope and later fortifications*. University Park, PA: Eisenbrauns, 325–336.

Kemp, B.J. 1983. Old Kingdom, Middle Kingdom and the Second Intermediate Period, c. 2686–1552 BC. In Trigger, B., Kemp, B.J., O'Connor, D., and Lloyd, A. (eds.), *Ancient Egypt: a social history*. Cambridge: Cambridge University Press, 71–182.

Kilani, M. 2016. *Byblos in the Late Bronze Age: interactions between the Levantine and Egyptian worlds*. PhD dissertation, University of Oxford.

Kitchen, K.A. 2000. Regnal and genealogical data of ancient Egypt (absolute chronology I): the historic chronology of ancient Egypt, a current assessment. In Bietak, M. (ed.), *The synchronisation of civilizations in the Eastern Mediterranean in the second millennium BC, vol. I*. Vienna: Verlag der Österreichischen Akademie der Wissenschaften, 39–52.

Knapp, A.B., and Demesticha, S. 2017. *Mediterranean connections: maritime transport containers and seaborne trade in the Bronze and Iron Ages*. London and New York: Routledge.

Koenig, Y. 1990. Les textes d'envoûtement de Mirgissa. *RdE* 41: 101–125.

Kopetzky, K. 2007–2008. Pottery from Tell Arqa found in Egypt and its chronological contexts. *Archaeology and History in Lebanon* 26/27: 17–58.

Kopetzky, K. 2010. *Tell el-Dabʿa XX: die Chronologie der Siedlungskeramik der Zweiten Zwischenzeit aus Tell el-Dabʿa*. Vienna: Verlag der Österreichischen Akademie der Wissenschaften.

Kopetzky, K. 2018. Tell el-Dabʿa and Byblos: new chronological evidence. *ÄL* 28: 309–358.

Laffineur, R. 1988. Réflexions sur le trésor de Tôd. *Aegaeum: Annales d'archéologie égéenne de l'Université de Liège* 2: 17–30.

Lichtheim, M. 1973. *Ancient Egyptian literature, vol. 1: the Old and Middle Kingdoms*. Berkeley and Los Angeles: University of California Press.

Lilyquist, C. 1993. Granulation and glass: chronological and stylistic investigations at selected sites, ca. 2500–1400 BCE. *BASOR* 290/291: 29–94.

Liotsakis, V. 2014. Notes on Herodotus' Sesostris (Hdt. II 102–110). *Maia* 66: 500–517.

Lucas, A., and Harris, J. 1989. *Ancient Egyptian materials and industries*. London: Histories and Mysteries of Man. 4th ed.

MacGillivray, J. 1998. *Knossos: pottery groups of the Old Palace Period*. London: British School at Athens.

Maguire, L.C. 2009. *Tell el-Dab'a XXI: the Cypriot pottery and its circulation in the Levant*. Vienna: Verlag der Österreichischen Akademie der Wissenschaften.

Maisler, B. 1947. Palestine at the time of the Middle Kingdom in Egypt. *Revue de l'histoire juive en Égypte* 1: 3–68.

Malek, J. 1992. The Annals of Amenemhet II. *EA* 2: 18.

Malek, J., and Quirke, S. 1992. Memphis, 1991: epigraphy. *JEA* 78: 13–18.

Marcolin, M., and Espinel, A.D. 2011. The Sixth Dynasty biographic inscriptions of Iny: more pieces to the puzzle. In Bárta, M., Coppens, F., and Krejčí, J. (eds.), *Abusir and Saqqara in the year 2010*. Prague: Charles University, 570–615.

Marcus, E.S. 1991. *Tel Nami: a study of a Middle Bronze IIA period coastal settlement*. MA thesis, University of Haifa.

Marcus, E.S. 1998. *Maritime trade in the southern Levant from earliest times through the MB IIa period*. PhD dissertation, University of Oxford.

Marcus, E.S. 2002a. Early seafaring and maritime activity in the southern Levant from prehistory through the third millennium BCE. In van den Brink, E.C., and Levy, T.E. (eds.), *Egypt and the Levant: interrelations from the 4th through the 3rd millennia BCE*. London: Leicester University Press, 403–417.

Marcus, E.S. 2002b. The southern Levant and maritime trade during the Middle Bronze IIa period. In Oren, E.D., and Aḥituv, S. (eds.), *Aharon Kempinski memorial volume: studies in archaeology and related disciplines*. Beer Sheva: Ben-Gurion University of the Negev Press, 241–263.

Marcus, E.S. 2007. Amenemhet II and the sea: maritime aspects of the Mit Rahina (Memphis) inscription. *ÄL* 17: 137–190.

Marcus, E.S. 2013. Correlating and combining Egyptian historical and southern Levantine radiocarbon chronologies at Middle Bronze Age IIa Tel Ifshar, Israel. In Shortland, A.J., and Bronk Ramsey, C. (eds.), *Radiocarbon and the chronologies of ancient Egypt*. Oxford: Oxbow, 182–208.

Marcus, E.S. 2019. A maritime approach to exploring the Hyksos phenomenon. In Bietak, M., and Prell, S. (eds.), *The enigma of the Hyksos, vol I*. Wiesbaden: Harrassowitz, 149–164.

Marcus, E.S., Dee, M.W., Bronk Ramsey, C., Higham, T.F., and Shortland, A.J. 2016. Radiocarbon verification of the earliest astro-chronological datum. *Radiocarbon* 58: 735–739.

Marcus, E.S., Porath, Y., and Paley, S.M. 2008a. The early Middle Bronze Age IIa phases at Tel Ifshar and their external relations. *ÄL* 18: 221–244.

Marcus, E.S., Porath, Y., Schiestl, R., Seiler, A., and Paley, S.M. 2008b. The Middle Kingdom Egyptian Pottery from Middle Bronze Age IIa Tel Ifshar. *ÄL* 18: 203–219.

Marochetti, E.F. 2005. The temple of Nebhepetre Mentuhotep at Gebelein: preliminary report. In Pantalacci, L., and Berger-El-Naggar, C. (eds.), *Des Néferkarê aux Montouhotep: travaux archéologiques en cours sur la fin de la VIe dynastie et la Première Période Intermédiaire.* Lyon: Maison de l'Orient et de la Méditerranée, 145–163.

Marochetti, E.F. 2010. *The reliefs of the chapel of Nebhepetra Mentuhotep at Gebelein (CGT 7003/1–277).* Leiden: Brill.

Maxwell-Hyslop, K. 1995. A note on the Anatolia connections of the Tôd Treasure. *AnSt* 45: 243–250.

Mazar, B. 1968. The Middle Bronze Age in Palestine. *IEJ* 18: 65–97.

Mazar, B. 1986. The Middle Bronze Age in Canaan. In Mazar, B. (ed.), *The early Biblical Period: historical studies.* Jerusalem: Israel Exploration Society, 1–34.

Menu, M. 1994. Analyse du Trésor de Tôd. *Bulletin de la Société Française d'Égyptologie* 130: 29–45.

Merrillees, R.S. 1973. Syrian pottery from Middle Kingdom Egypt. *Australian Journal of Biblical Archaeology* 2: 51–59.

Miniaci, G. 2018. Deposit F (nos. 15121–15567) in the Obelisk Temple at Byblos: artefact mobility in the Middle Bronze Age I–II (1850–1650 BC) between Egypt and the Levant. *ÄL* 28: 379–408.

Mlinar, C. 2004a. The scarab workshops of Tell el-Dabʿa. In Bietak, M., and Czerny, E. (eds.), *Scarabs of the second millennium BC from Egypt, Nubia, Crete and the Levant: chronological and historical implications.* Vienna: Verlag der Österreichischen Akademie der Wissenschaften, 107–140.

Mlinar, C. 2004b. Sidon: scarabs from the 2001 season of excavation, additional notes. *Archaeology and History in Lebanon* 20: 61–64.

Mourad, A.-L. 2013. Remarks on Sinuhe's Qedem and Yaa. *GM* 238: 69–84.

Mourad, A.-L. 2015. *Rise of the* Hyksos: Egypt *and the Levant from the Middle Kingdom to the early Second Intermediate Period.* Oxford: Archaeopress.

Negbi, O., and Moskowitz, S. 1966. The "Foundation Deposits" or "Offering Deposits" of Byblos. *BASOR* 184: 21–26.

Newberry, P.E. 1893. *Beni Hasan, vol. I.* London: Egyptian Exploration Fund.

Newberry, P.E. 1894. *Beni Hasan, vol. II.* London: Egyptian Exploration Fund.

Nigro, L. 2009. The eighteenth-century BC princes of Byblos and Ebla and the chronology of the Middle Bronze Age. In Maila-Afeiche, A.-M. (ed.), *Interconnections in the Eastern Mediterranean: Lebanon in the Bronze and Iron Ages.* Beirut: Minstère de la Culture, Direction Générale des Antiquités, 159–175.

Obsomer, C. 1995. *Sésostris Ier: étude chronologique et historique du règne.* Brussels: Connaissance de l'Egypte ancienne.

Oppenheim, A. 2015. Introduction: what was the Middle Kingdom? In Oppenheim, A., Arnold, Di., Arnold, Do., and Yamamoto, K. (eds.), *Ancient Egypt transformed: the Middle Kingdom.* New York: Metropolitan Museum of Art, 1–8.

Ownby, M.F. 2010. *Canaanite jars from Memphis as evidence for trade and political relationships in the Middle Bronze Age.* PhD dissertation, University of Cambridge.

Ownby, M.F. 2012. The importance of imports: petrographic analysis of pottery jars in Egypt. *JAEI* 4: 23–29.

Parkinson, R.B. 1991. *Voices from ancient Egypt: an anthology of Middle Kingdom writings.* London: British Museum Press.

Parkinson, R.B. 1997. *The Tale of Sinuhe and other ancient Egyptian poems, 1940–1640 BC.* Oxford: Oxford University Press.

Pierrat, G. 1994. À propos de la date et de l'origine du Trésor de Tôd. *Bulletin de la Société Française d'Égyptologie* 130: 18–27.

Pierrat-Bonnefois, G. 2008. The Tôd Treasure. In Aruz, J., Benzel, K., and Evans, J.M. (eds.), *Beyond Babylon: art, trade, and diplomacy in the second millennium BC.* New York: Metropolitan Museum of Art, 65–67.

Porada, E. 1966. Les cylindres de la jarre Montet. *Syria* 43: 243–258.

Porter, B. 2001. *Old Syrian popular style cylinder seals.* PhD dissertation, Columbia University, New York.

Posener, G. 1940. *Princes et pays d'Asie et de Nubie: textes hiératiques sur des figurines d'envoûtement du Moyen Empire.* Brussels: Fondation Égyptologique Reine Élisabeth.

Posener, G. 1966. Les textes d'envoûtement de Mirgissa. *Syria* 43: 277–287.

Posener, G. 1971. Syria and Palestine: relations with Egypt. In Edwards, I.E.S., Gadd, C.J., and Hammond, N.G.L. (eds.), *The Cambridge ancient history, vol. I, part 2: early history of the Middle East.* Cambridge: Cambridge University Press, 532–558.

Quack, J.F. 1996. *Kftȝw* and *iȝśy. ÄL* 6: 75–81.

Rabehl, S.M. 2006. Das Grab des Amenemhet (*Jmnjj*) in Beni Hassan oder der Versuch einer Symbiose. PhD dissertation, Ludwig-Maximilians-Universität Munich.

Rainey, A.F. 1972. The world of Sinuhe. *Israel Oriental Studies* 2: 369–408.

Rainey, A.F. 1994. Remarks on Donald Redford's Egypt, Canaan, and Israel in ancient times. *BASOR* 295: 81–85.

Rainey, A.F. 2006. Sinuhe's world. In Maier, A.M., and de Miroschedji, P. (eds.), *"I will speak the riddles of ancient times": archaeological and historical studies in honor of Amihai Mazar.* Winona Lake, IN: Eisenbrauns, 277–299.

Rainey, A.F., and Notley, R.S. 2006. *The sacred bridge: Carta's atlas of the Biblical World.* Jerusalem: Carta.

Ramsey, C.B., Dee, M.W., Rowland, J.M., Higham, T.F.G., Harris, S.A., Brock, F., Quiles, A., Wild, E.M., Marcus, E.S., and Shortland, A.J. 2010. Radiocarbon-based chronology for Dynastic Egypt. *Science* 328: 1554–1557.

Redford, D.B. 1987. The Tod inscription of Senwosret I and early 12th Dynasty involvement in Nubia and the South. *Journal of the Society for the Study of Egyptian Antiquities* 17: 36–55.

Redford, D.B. 1992. *Egypt, Canaan and Israel in ancient times.* Princeton, NJ: Princeton University Press.

Redford, D.B. 1996. A response to Anson Rainey's Remarks on Donald Redford's Egypt, Canaan, and Israel in Ancient Times. *BASOR* 301: 77–81.

Rich, S., Manning, S.W., Degryse, P., Vanhaecke, F., Latruwe, K., and Van Leberghe, K. 2016. To put a cedar ship in a bottle: dendroprovenancing three ancient East Mediterranean watercraft with the 87Sr/86Sr isotope ratio. *Journal of Archaeological Science: Reports* 9: 514–521.

Ritner, R.K. 1993. *The mechanics of ancient Egyptian magical practice.* Chicago: The Oriental Institute of the University of Chicago.

Rowe, A. 1939. Three new stelae from the South-Eastern Desert. *ASAE* 39: 187–194.

Ryholt, K. 1997. *The political situation in Egypt during the Second Intermediate Period, c. 1800–1550 BC.* Copenhagen: Museum Tusculanum Press.

Sader, H., and Kamlah, J. 2010. Tell el-Burak: a new Middle Bronze Age site from Lebanon. *NEA* 73: 130–141.

Saretta, P. 1997. *Egyptian perceptions of West Semites in art and literature during the Middle Kingdom: an archaeological, art historical and textual survey.* PhD dissertation, New York University.

Saretta, P. 2016. *Asiatics in Middle Kingdom Egypt: perceptions and reality.* London: Bloomsbury.

Sass, B. 1989. The Egyptian Middle Kingdom system for writing foreign names and the beginning of the West-Semitic alphabet. In Ben-Tor, A., Greenfield, J.C., and Malamat, A. (eds.), *Eretz Israel 20: Yadin memorial volume.* Jerusalem: Israel Exploration Society, 44–50 (Hebrew), 195* (English summary).

Säve-Söderbergh, T. 1946. *The navy of the Eighteenth Egyptian Dynasty.* Uppsala: Lundequistska Bokhandeln.

Schiestl, R., and Seiler, A. 2012. *Handbook of the pottery of the Egyptian Middle Kingdom.* Vienna: Verlag der Österreichischen Akademie der Wissenschaften.

Schneider, T. 2002. Sinuhes Notiz über die Könige: syrisch-anatolische Herrschertitel in ägyptischer Überlieferung. *ÄL* 12: 257–272.

Schulman, A.R. 1982. The battle scenes of the Middle Kingdom. *Journal of the Society for the Study of Egyptian Antiquities* 12: 165–183.

Sethe, K. 1926. *Die Ächtung feindlicher Fürsten, Völker und Dinge auf altägyptischen Tongefäßscherben des Mittleren Reiches.* Berlin: Verlag der Akademie der Wissenschaften.

Settgast, J. 1969. Zu ungewöhnlichen Darstellungen von Bogenschützen. *MDAIK* 25: 136–138.

Shaheen, A.M. 1990. EB III–MB I axe in the Egyptian private Middle Kingdom tombs: an assessment. *GM* 117/8: 203–217.

Shaw, I. 2004. *The Oxford history of ancient Egypt.* Oxford: Oxford University Press. Rev. ed.

Simpson, W.K. 1973. The story of Sinuhe. In Simpson, W.K. (ed.), *The literature of ancient Egypt: an anthology of stories, instructions, and poetry.* New Haven, CT: Yale University Press, 57–74. Rev. ed.

Simpson, W.K. 2001. Twelfth Dynasty. In Redford, D.B. (ed.), *The Oxford encyclopedia of ancient Egypt, vol. 3.* Oxford: Oxford University Press, 453–457.

Sowada, K.N. 2009. *Egypt in the Eastern Mediterranean during the Old Kingdom: an archaeological perspective.* Fribourg: Academic Press; Göttingen: Vandenhoeck & Ruprecht.

Stager, L.E. 2002. The MB IIA ceramic sequence at Tel Ashkelon and its implications for the "port power" model of trade. In Bietak, M. (ed.), *The Middle Bronze Age in the Levant.* Vienna: Verlag der Österreichischen Akademie der Wissenschaften, 353–362.

Stager, L.E. 2018. Introduction: Ashkelon in the Middle Bronze Age. In Stager, L.E., Schloen, J.D., and Voss, R.J. (eds.), *Ashkelon 6: the Middle Bronze Age ramparts and gates of the north slope and later fortifications.* University Park, PA: Eisenbrauns, 3–23.

Stager, L.E., and Voss, R.J. 2018a. Egyptian pottery found in Middle Bronze Age Ashkelon. In Stager, L.E., Schloen, J.D., and Voss, R.J. (eds.), *Ashkelon 6: the Middle Bronze Age ramparts and gates of the north slope and later fortifications.* University Park, PA: Eisenbrauns, 237–243.

Stager, L.E., and Voss, R.J. 2018b. Special ceramic wares found in Middle Bronze Age Ashkelon. In Stager, L.E., Schloen, J.D., and Voss, R J. (eds.), *Ashkelon 6: the Middle Bronze Age ramparts and gates of the north slope and later fortifications.* University Park, PA: Eisenbrauns, 267–298.

Stager, L.E., Voss, R.J., Herrmann, V.R., Johnston, P.J., and Walton, J.T. 2018. The Middle Bronze Age pottery of Ashkelon. In Stager, L.E., Schloen, J.D., and Voss, R J. (eds.), *Ashkelon 6: the Middle Bronze Age ramparts and gates of the north slope and later fortifications.* University Park, PA: Eisenbrauns, 117–207.

Streit, K. 2017. A maximalist interpretation of the Execration Texts: archaeological and historical implications of a high chronology. *JAEI* 13: 59–69.

Taylor, J.H. 2004. Scarabs from the Bronze Age tombs at Sidon (Lebanon). *Levant* 36: 155–158.

Thalmann, J.-P. 2000. Le peuplement de la plaine du Akkar à l'âge du Bronze. In Matthiae, P., Enea, A., Peyronel, L., and Pinnock, F. (eds.), *Proceedings of the first international congress on the archaeology of the ancient Near East, vol. 2.* Rome: Università degli studi di Roma "La Sapienza," 1615–1632.

Thalmann, J.-P. 2006. *Tell Arqa, I.* Beirut: Presses de l'IFPO.

Thalmann, J.-P. 2008. Tell Arqa et Byblos: essai de corrélation. In Bietak, M., and Czerny, E. (eds.), *The Bronze Age in the Lebanon: studies on the archaeology and chronology of Lebanon, Syria and Egypt.* Vienna: Verlag der Österreichischen Akademie der Wissenschaften, 61–78.

Tufnell, O., and Ward, W.A. 1966. Relations between Byblos, Egypt and Mesopotamia at the end of the third millennium BC. *Syria* 43: 165–241.

van den Brink, E.C., and Levy, T.E. (eds.) 2002. *Egypt and the Levant: interrelations from the fourth through the third millennia BCE.* London: Leicester University Press.

van der Perre, A., Hameeuw, H., Boschloos, V., Delvaux, L., Proesmans, M., Vandermeulen, B., and Watteeuw, L. 2016. Towards a combined use of IR, UV and 3D-imaging for the study of small decorated and inscribed artefacts. In Homem, P.M. (ed.), *Lights on . . . cultural heritage and museums!* Porto: University of Porto, 163–192.

van Ess, M. 2019. The Middle Bronze Age wall paintings at Tell el-Burak. In Kamlah, J., and Sader, H. (eds.), *Tell el-Burak I: the Middle Bronze Age, with chapters related to the site and to the Mamluk-Ottoman periods.* Wiesbaden: Harrassowitz, 381–384.

Vercoutter, J. 1965. Egypt in the Middle Kingdom. In Bottéro, J., Cassin, E., and Vercoutter, J. (eds.), *The Near East: the early civilizations.* London: Weidenfeld and Nicolson, 347–382.

Walberg, G. 1984. The Tod Treasure and Middle Minoan absolute chronology. *Opuscula Atheniensia* 15: 173–177.

Walberg, G. 1991. The finds at Tell el-Dabʿa and Middle Minoan chronology. *ÄL* 2: 115–120.

Ward, C.A. 2000. *Sacred and secular: ancient Egyptian ships and boats.* Philadelphia: University of Pennsylvania Museum of Archaeology and Anthropology.

Ward, W.A. 1961a. Egypt and the East Mediterranean in the early second millennium BC. *Orientalia* 30: 22–45.

Ward, W.A. 1961b. Egypt and the East Mediterranean in the early second millennium BC (concluded). *Orientalia* 30: 129–155.

Ward, W.A. 1971. *Egypt and the East Mediterranean world, 2200–1900 BC: studies in Egyptian foreign relations during the First Intermediate Period.* Beirut: American University of Beirut.

Ward, W.A. 1978. *Studies on scarab seals, I: pre-12th Dynasty scarab amulets.* Warminster: Aris and Phillips.

Ward, W.A. 1982. *Index of Egyptian administrative and religious titles of the Middle Kingdom*. Beirut: American University of Beirut.

Ward, W.A. 1987. Scarab typology and archaeological context. *AJA* 91: 507–532.

Warren, P., and Hankey, V. 1989. *Aegean Bronze Age chronology*. Bristol: Bristol Classical Press.

Wegner, J. 1996. The nature and chronology of the Senwosret III–Amenemhat III regnal succession: some considerations based on new evidence from the mortuary temple of Senwosret III at Abydos. *JNES* 55: 249–279.

Wegner, J. 2016. A royal boat burial and watercraft tableau of Egypt's 12th Dynasty (c. 1850 BCE) at South Abydos. *International Journal of Nautical Archaeology* 46: 5–30.

Weinstein, J.M. 1975. Egyptian relations with Palestine in the Middle Kingdom. *BASOR* 217: 1–16.

Willems, H. 1988. *Chests of life: a study of the typology and conceptual development of Middle Kingdom standard class coffins*. Leiden: Ex Oriente Lux.

Wilson, J.A. 1950a. Egyptian historical texts. In Pritchard, J.B. (ed.), *Ancient Near Eastern texts relating to the Old Testament*. Princeton, NJ: Princeton University Press, 227–264.

Wilson, J.A. 1950b. Egyptian rituals and incantations. In Pritchard, J.B. (ed.), *Ancient Near Eastern texts relating to the Old Testament*. Princeton, NJ: Princeton University Press, 325–330.

22

Egypt's Middle Kingdom

PERSPECTIVES ON CULTURE AND SOCIETY

Wolfram Grajetzki

22.1. Introduction

In terms of literature and material culture, the ancient Egyptians came
to regard the Middle Kingdom as the "classical" period of their own history.[1] The language of that period continued to be used until the late
first millennium BC when Egypt was ruled by the Ptolemaic Dynasty,
and its sculpture achieved new levels of innovation and techniques that
were copied in the later periods. This chapter focuses on the culture and
society of Middle Kingdom Egypt (figure 22.1).

The Middle Kingdom period is often divided into an early and a late
phase. The early phase was characterized politically by decentralization,
which enabled local governors, especially in Middle Egypt, to build monumental rock-cut tombs for themselves. Otherwise, the Old Kingdom
traditions in art and in craft production remained strong, and the first
two kings of the Twelfth Dynasty were buried in Old Kingdom–style
pyramids. Senusret I started a process of re-centralization of the country, which reached its peak under Senusret III, and his reign is therefore

---

1. This chapter was language-edited by Denise Bolton and Karen Radner.

Wolfram Grajetzki, *Egypt's Middle Kingdom* In: *The Oxford History of the Ancient Near East.* Edited
by: Karen Radner, Nadine Moeller, and D. T. Potts, Oxford University Press. © Oxford University Press 2022.
DOI: 10.1093/oso/9780190687571.003.0022

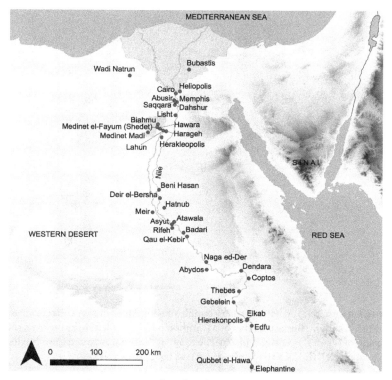

FIGURE 22.1. Sites mentioned in this chapter. Prepared by Andrea Squitieri (LMU Munich).

typically seen as the beginning of the Middle Kingdom's late phase. The governors now lost control over the local resources and could no longer support the construction of monumental tombs for themselves. The country's resources were concentrated at royally controlled centers in the Memphis region, at Abydos and at Thebes, and Egypt's administration became heavily centralized, with the state's desire for unified control manifesting itself at every level of society. For example, the practice of using double names became common, which served to identify people more precisely, and scarab seals identifying their owners by name were used to manage the flow of commodities by sealing goods (cf. sections 22.4 and 22.7).

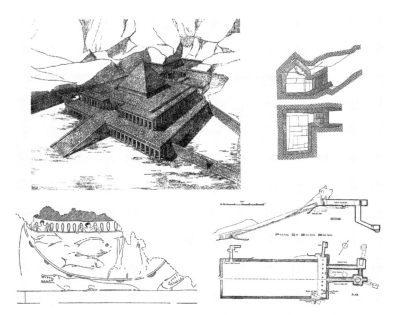

FIGURE 22.2. Top left: mortuary temple of King Mentuhotep II (reconstruction). Top right: burial chamber of Mentuhotep II. Lower left: painting from the tomb of Djari. Lower right: plan of the tomb of Meketra. Adapted from Naville 1907: pls. XXII, XXXIII; Winlock 1941: 18 fig. 2, 205 fig. 11.

22.2. Mentuhotep II's mortuary complex at Thebes as a window on his royal court

In culture and the arts, the beginning of a new era is not always easy to pinpoint, as they often have their own pace of development, not necessarily directly related to political events even in periods of major change and transformation. Nevertheless, an exceptional monument was built at the beginning of the Middle Kingdom that clearly marked the dawn of a new era. The funerary complex of Mentuhotep II (figure 22.2) was built by the king who united the country after a long period of political fragmentation (see chapter 19 in this volume). Our survey of the cultural and social history of the Middle Kingdom will therefore begin with a discussion of this monumental royal building complex, the first to be constructed since the end of the Old Kingdom.[2]

King Mentuhotep II's funerary complex at Deir el-Bahri at Thebes was built close to the high, rocky desert mountains on the western bank of the Nile. Its key features are platforms that were adorned all around with rectangular pillars. While rock-cut tombs with a façade of pillars (so-called *saff* tombs, from the Arabic word *saff* for "row") were popular for the ruling class of Thebes during the First Intermediate Period and also were used for the royal family, the combination of such pillar façades with platforms is new in Mentuhotep's funerary complex, making it a unique creation. The complex has a causeway that is 40 m wide and over 1,000 m long, which starts near the Nile at the edge of the cultivation zone. At the other end of the causeway, in front of the funerary complex, was a wide courtyard with planted trees and statues of the king, which perhaps symbolized the grove of the underworld god Osiris. This courtyard also housed the entrance to a burial chamber that was accessed through a long underground corridor. The chamber was found undisturbed and contained a simple wooden coffin with an impressive statue depicting King Mentuhotep II. The function of this dummy burial is today not clearly understood; perhaps it symbolized the burial of Osiris.[3]

The main building of the funerary complex consists of two rectangular platforms that were constructed at different levels. The front of the lower, larger platform was adorned with a double row of square sandstone pillars while the upper, smaller platform was surrounded by a forest of octagonal pillars. The purpose of the second platform is debated. The first excavator Eduard Naville reconstructed a pyramid on top of it,[4] but Dieter Arnold, who re-excavated part of the complex, instead suggested that the platform held only a simple block-like structure as he could not find any stone elements that would support the idea of a

2. Although the First Intermediate Period Theban predecessors of Mentuhotep II were buried in large-scale funerary complexes, there is only a limited decoration program and far fewer architectural extras; see Di. Arnold 1976.

3. Di. Arnold 1974a: 51–53.

4. Naville 1910: pls. XXXIII–XXXIV.

pyramid.[5] At the rear of the structure, carved into the cliffs, is a second courtyard as well as a second large hall supported by a forest of columns. At the very back, partly cut into the natural rocks, was a sanctuary for Amun-Ra, the main deity of Thebes. At the western end of this hall were at least two false doors, one most likely for the king, the other perhaps for his wife Tem, who was also buried in the temple complex. This was the primary location for the mortuary cult of the king.[6] The entrance to the king's actual underground tomb, carved deep into the bedrock, is located here. The chamber lies at the end of a 150-m-long corridor. Fully paved with red granite, it contains a unique alabaster shrine that is not attested for any other known royal burial.[7] The chamber was found looted, but fragments of wooden figures and boats—typical burial goods during this time—have been found there during excavations. The figures appear rather roughly sculpted, indicating that they are the work of various locally sourced craftsmen rather than artisans attached to the court.[8]

The entire funerary complex was once richly decorated with reliefs, but the state of preservation of the building makes it hard to obtain a clear idea of the decoration program. While the detailed function of the Amun-Ra chapel is not clear, it seems certain that the confirmation of the king's status as a god was the central message, as he is prominently depicted as a god in the company of other deities.[9] The chapel contained scenes of the king being led by Horus and Seth,[10] the two main deities connected with kingship, and also shows the ruler guiding the barque of Amun[11] and participating in temple-founding ceremonies.[12]

------

5. Compare Di. Arnold 1974a: 28–32; Kemp 2006: 157, fig. 57.

6. Di. Arnold 1974a: 59–60.

7. Di. Arnold 1974a: 44–51, pls. 34–40.

8. Di. Arnold 1981: 11–48; Do. Arnold 1991: 25.

9. Di. Arnold 1974b: 30–31.

10. Di. Arnold 1974b: 24, pl. 14.

11. Di. Arnold 1974b: 26–27, pl. 22.

12. Di. Arnold 1974b: 24, pl. 15.

Other parts of the mortuary temple contained images of a wide variety of subjects, including scenes of battle and hunting, as well as depictions of officials and bearers of offerings. The reliefs are well executed, but in a style that differs markedly from the many other reliefs produced in Mentuhotep II's reign. They follow the classic traditions established in earlier Egyptian formal art and are very similar to Old Kingdom reliefs from the Memphis region. Constructing such a large building created a high demand for artists and craftsmen, and it seems certain that specialists from the Memphite region were brought to the south to participate in the work.[13]

The funerary complex also included six mortuary chapels for royal women, which were integrated into the back wall of the second platform already at an early building stage. Each consists of a cube-shaped chapel and a burial shaft. The chapels each housed a small chamber that likely contained a statue, while the chapel exteriors were decorated with reliefs portraying the royal women, most of whom bore the titles "king's wife" and "priestess of Hathor." The women are depicted with the king, but also on their own with servants bringing offerings.[14] The style of these reliefs is very bold and markedly different from those of the funerary temple itself. The reliefs are executed in the highest quality, even better than those of the king's mortuary temple, and depict figures and objects in rich detail. The style is very close to reliefs at Thebes created during the early Eleventh Dynasty, before the conquest of Memphis,[15] and it seems likely that they were created by artists other than those who were responsible for the reliefs of the mortuary temple itself. Most of the royal women's burial chambers were found looted, but they still contained some objects. The burial chambers of Kemsit, Ashait, and Kawit held limestone sarcophagi whose reliefs are executed in a style similar to the reliefs on the chapels. Unusually, these sarcophagi show objects in interaction with people and so-called daily life scenes, while most coffins of

13. Fischer 1959: 252.

14. Naville 1907: pls. XVII–XV; 1910: pls. XI–XX.

15. Naville 1907: pls. XXII–XXIII.

the period depict only the objects. Hence, while the seven "sacred oils" are being brought by supplicants (differing from the usual depiction on coffins, which typically shows only the vessels without bearers), the royal women are portrayed at the offering table, having their hair arranged by a servant.[16] A granary, too, is shown with a complement of workers, while typical depictions of granaries on coffins of this period rarely include people. Artistically, the funerary complex of Mentuhotep II therefore merges different traditions. While the reliefs of the main temple are heavily influenced by an Old Kingdom style familiar from Memphis, the reliefs of the queen's chapels are executed in the local Theban style of the First Intermediate Period, although at its highest level.

Mentuhotep II's unique monument and its surrounding mortuary landscape communicate prominently that the king was the center of Egyptian society. The presence of mortuary priests at the temple is well attested throughout the Middle Kingdom, and the building clearly served the king's mortuary cult as well as that of the royal women. It was also a place of worship: Mentuhotep II was venerated here as a god, and so was Amun-Ra, most likely as the deity who confirmed the divine status of the king.[17] The king's status as a god on earth was expressed in many different ways. Images show him in the company of gods. His name, too, announces his divine status, as he is called "son of (the sun god) Ra," while the other names of his titulary underline his extraordinary social status: for example, for his Horus name, the king's name is written within a hieroglyphic sign that symbolizes a palace, topped by the falcon god Horus.

In death as in life, the king was surrounded by his family and his court. The most important royal woman at Mentuhotep II's court was the king's mother, Iah, wife of Intef III (the king's father and predecessor). Her high status is well expressed by a rock inscription at Shatt el-Rigal, where she is depicted as the only woman behind King Mentuhotep II.[18] Her burial place is unknown, but she was most likely buried within the funerary complex of her husband, and not at her son's

---

16. Naville 1907: pls. XX (Kawit); Winlock 1921: 47, fig. 22 (Ashait).

17. Di. Arnold 1974b: 72–75.

18. Petrie 1888: pl. XVI (489).

funerary complex. Mentuhotep II was married to his sister Neferu, who had a well-equipped tomb not far away from the king's funerary complex. The woman who gave birth to Mentuhotep's successor, Sankhkara Mentuhotep (III), was the "king's wife" Tem, who was buried within the king's funerary complex. Tem does not bear the title "king's daughter," suggesting that she did not come from the royal family. This evidence indicates that the Middle Kingdom ruler could marry his sisters, but also women coming from other social backgrounds. The latter is also confirmed by the examination of the skeletons of two queens buried in the pyramid of Amenemhat III at Dahshur whose results show that these women were not related: one of them may have belonged to the royal family, while the other most likely had a different background.[19] As the mortuary temple of Mentuhotep II contained the burial of Tem and also, as we have discussed, of six other royal women, some with the title "king's wife," the king's female relatives clearly played an important role within Mentuhotep's concept of kingship. This importance is also apparent in the pyramid complex of Senusret I at Lisht, where nine smaller pyramids are placed around the king's.[20] A similar arrangement is evident in the pyramid complex of Senusret III at Dahshur.[21] But beyond such evidence from the funerary landscape, little is known of any political function held by the royal women during their lifetimes. They clearly had important ideological and religious roles: not only providing an heir for the king, but also promoting fertility more generally and, in a broader sense, securing the rebirth of the king in the underworld (at least within the king's funerary complex). To this end, the royal women were identified with goddesses and further confirmed the king's divine status.[22] On the other hand, while wives, sisters, and daughters are prominent, the king's sons are almost invisible in the available sources, as they are

19. Strouhal and Klír 2006.

20. Di. Arnold 1992: 19–40.

21. Di. Arnold 2002b: 58–87.

22. Troy 1986; Grajetzki 2014b: 180–188.

generally not buried within the pyramid complex and the title "king's son" is rarely attested in the Middle Kingdom documentation.[23]

At the royal court, the king was surrounded by the officials running the palace and its estates. The main task of these officials was to secure the supply of commodities for the king, his court, and his building projects, and there was little yet of what one might term a national administration. The duties of the officials are often clear from their titles, although there is much flexibility to these offices and their associated duties. The king could appoint any official to any given task when it needed to be done. Directly under the king was a man with a title traditionally translated as "vizier" (although "prime minister" would also be a suitable translation). He was in charge of the palace, of the scribal offices, and of the provinces. The "treasurer" (*imi-ra khetemet*) was in charge of the economic parts of the palace, including the "treasury" (*per-hedj*). The "high steward" was mainly in charge of the estates which supplied the palace with food and other commodities. These highest officials are known from a wide range of sources, such as statues, tombs, steles, and rock inscriptions. Their titles include "member of the elite," "foremost of action," "royal sealer," and "sole friend,"[24] highly exclusive designations reserved only for a small, select group of people. The original background of these highest officials is often unclear. It seems likely that they came from influential families, but hard evidence for this is missing. Importantly, there is no indication that any high official was the son of his predecessor or another high official. It would seem that the king appointed these men from a wider pool of officials at the royal court.[25]

These high officials accompanied the king also in death, as they had large tombs cut into the cliffs of Deir el-Bahri around the king's mortuary complex. The architecture of these tombs is still very much in the tradition of the First Intermediate Period; many of them are *saff* tombs. The façade adorns a row of pillars with a cult chapel behind it, followed by a

23. Grajetzki 2006: 162.

24. Grajetzki 2009: 15–100.

25. Grajetzki 2009: 140–144.

long corridor to an inner cult chapel. The ground plan is therefore almost T-shaped. The burial chamber proper was carved into the rocks underneath the cult chapels. The decorations of these chapels are often badly destroyed, and therefore it is difficult to analyze the style and specifics of their decoration. But a wide range of styles are apparent in their reliefs and paintings, and it seems yet again that there were not yet enough well-trained craftsmen and artists available locally.[26] A good example is the tomb of the "overseer of the compound" Djari, whose paintings show two very different styles. Some scenes are still in the tradition of the First Intermediate Period, with parts of the figures' bodies often slightly out of proportion, which Herbert Winlock, the original excavator, declared a "monstrous ugliness."[27] More conventionally executed depictions include an offering scene with Djari receiving offerings from another man.[28] It is evident that artists of different abilities and trained in different traditions worked side by side on the decoration of Djari's tomb. On the other hand, the tomb of the "high steward" and "treasurer" Meketra, who was in office from the reign of Mentuhotep II until the beginning of the Twelfth Dynasty, was abused as a limestone quarry in antiquity, but the few preserved fragments of its painted relief decoration demonstrate that this later monument had included work of superb quality.[29]

Next in the hierarchy came the middle-ranking administrators serving the royal palace, many of them most likely serving as part of the high officials' staff. These men are typically known only from a limited number of objects, as they could not afford to have as many artifacts made as their higher-ranking colleagues. One example is the "store overseer" Wah, who is known from his undisturbed burial in front of the much bigger tomb of the "high steward" Meketra. Wah was a member of Meketra's staff, which is also reflected in being buried next to his master. For his modest burial, his body was wrapped in many layers of linen and

26. Jaroš-Deckert 1984: 102–138.

27. Roehrig 1995: 262.

28. Roehrig 1995: 265.

29. Fischer 1975: 300, pl. XXVI; Do. Arnold 1991: 22–23.

placed in a coffin whose exterior was decorated with offering formulas. He had a mummy mask and his body was adorned with an array of personal items, most importantly a silver scarab inscribed with the names of both Meketra and Wah:[30] presumably a present from the higher official to his loyal minion. Beyond that relationship to his superior, nothing is known about Wah, neither about his social background nor his family. Another rare example of a lower-ranking official serving at the royal court is the *ka*-priest Heqanakht, who is known from a number of letters that accidentally survived in a tomb; part of a correspondence with his family about managing his estate, they mention working family members as well as servants and show that the family's fields were situated in different parts of the country.[31] Otherwise, lower-ranking officials serving the Eleventh and early Twelfth Dynasties at the royal residence are largely invisible in the available archaeological and textual records.

22.3. At the royal residence: the burial practices of the Twelfth Dynasty rulers and their court

Unlike Mentuhotep II, the kings of the early Twelfth Dynasty were again buried in pyramids, following the Old Kingdom model (cf. chapter 5 in volume 1). The remains of the pyramid complexes of Amenemhat I and Senusret I have been excavated at Lisht. While Amenemhat I's complex is heavily destroyed,[32] Senusret I's is the best-preserved and documented example of a Middle Kingdom pyramid complex. The pyramid itself was once 105 m wide at the base, equaling 200 ancient Egyptian cubits. It was the largest pyramid constructed in Egypt since the Fifth Dynasty king Neferirkara.[33] It is built of limestone, although only the casing was

---

30. Roehrig 2003.

31. Allen 2002. Agatha Christie based her novel *Death Comes as the End* (first published in 1944) on these papyri.

32. Di. Arnold 2015.

33. Di. Arnold 1988: 64.

made of properly hewn blocks, while the inner part consisted mainly of roughly prepared rocks that formed a kind of rubble core. The three foundation deposits that were found at the corners of the pyramid indicate that rituals were performed when the construction of the building began, and such founding rituals are indeed well attested in texts and depictions during this period. The deposits contained pottery, entire skeletons of birds and bones of bulls, evidently from food offerings. They also contained mudbricks with plaques made of different materials, such as alabaster, faience, metal, and wood, which provide us with the pyramid's name: "Senusret is Viewing the Two Lands."[34] Around the king's pyramid are the smaller pyramids of the royal women, all found heavily disturbed; only a few revealed the names of the owners.

On the east side of Senusret I's pyramid complex, facing the river Nile, was the mortuary temple, which consisted of a large open courtyard with pillars, five chapels, and a large number of magazine rooms and closely corresponded to the model of a Sixth Dynasty mortuary temple.[35] It was once richly adorned with statues. Ten limestone statues were found, buried already in ancient times under the mortuary temple. The almost identical statues show the king seated and adorned with a *nemes* headdress, with his hands on his lap. While the faces are finely carved, they appear somehow lifeless, almost as if a puppet is depicted rather than a human.[36] The whole pyramid complex was surrounded by a wall, decorated with a continuous series of depictions of the king's Horus name.[37]

In contrast to the king's pyramid, the funerary chapels of the highest state officials did not follow Old Kingdom models, as they were now built as temple-like structures. In the Old Kingdom, the main overground structures for the funerary cult of private individuals were so-called mastabas, solid buildings with just a few rooms. Instead, the early

---

34. Di. Arnold 1988: 87–91.

35. Di. Arnold 1988: 56–57.

36. Saleh and Sourouzian 1987: no. 87; Wildung 1984: 80–81; Di. Arnold 1988: 56.

37. Di. Arnold 1988: 58–63.

Twelfth Dynasty cult chapels in the Memphis region resemble small temples. In comparison to the nearby Old Kingdom mastabas, the chapels of Hetep and Ihy at Saqqara are small in size.[38] Their stone superstructure encloses a courtyard adorned with pillars and three chapels at the back, where statues of the tomb owners were placed, as well as a false door. The walls are decorated with reliefs. In Ihy's tomb, only some of the reliefs are well preserved: next to the gigantic false door at the back wall, Ihy is shown on a side wall to be seated in front of an offering table, with servants bringing offerings. In their plan, these chapels are almost identical to contemporary temples, especially with regard to their axial layout with the three rear chapels and the columned hall in front of them.

Similar structures were found at Lisht but are less well preserved, and it is often impossible to reconstruct the ground plan.[39] One of the better-preserved examples at Lisht is the tomb chapel of the "hall keeper" Djehuti.[40] Its mudbrick enclosure measured about 21.8 × 25 m, with a wall of 1.6–1.8 m. Within the walled area stood the main tomb chapel of 14.3 × 12.8 m, also built of mudbricks. The overall plan is of a T-shape and therefore similar to Theban tomb chapels. At its entrance were four columns, and a short corridor led into a wide hall with a niche for a false door at the back, in the main axis of the building. The inside of the chapel was decorated with reliefs, of which little survives. In the late Twelfth Dynasty, similar tomb chapels are attested at Abydos and at Thebes.[41]

Their false doors are the main focus of all these chapels, which corresponds to the architecture of Middle Kingdom and also New Kingdom tomb chapels, but differs from the previous Old Kingdom mastabas, whose false doors were rarely located along the main axis of the buildings. However, it is hard to tell whether this new type of mortuary architecture indicates that the religious beliefs underpinning cult practices also had changed. The decoration program of these chapels seems greatly

---

38. Firth and Gunn 1926: 61–65, 273–288.

39. Di. Arnold 2008: 55–56, fig. 13, pl. 62, 147.

40. Di. Arnold 2008: 52–54, pls. 96–101.

41. Nelson and Kalos 2000: 133 fig. 2; 135 fig. 4.

reduced in comparison to both the Old Kingdom mastabas and the rock-cut chapels in Middle and Upper Egypt.

On the other hand, mastabas following the Old Kingdom model were still being built, and are particularly well known from Lahun and Dahshur. These mastabas were now constructed as solid buildings with the decoration placed on the exterior. The burial chambers are entered through shafts whose entrance was positioned next to the mastaba,[42] whereas the access shafts of Old Kingdom mastabas had been located inside the building. The decoration was now even more reduced and mainly showed the tomb owner, his family, and the bearers of offerings. Some of these mastabas were decorated all around with a palace façade motif in the shape of a recessed pattern with niches imitating the palace walls,[43] and here again it seems that Old Kingdom models were copied. Only occasionally were longer biographical inscriptions included, for example on the mastaba of the "high steward" and vizier Khnumhotep at Dahshur.[44]

The sources for our understanding of the Middle Kingdom officials as a social group increased during the Twelfth Dynasty as officials now placed steles and statues at sacred places throughout Egypt. On these monuments or cenotaphs, they are commemorated by name and title, and sometimes even short biographical inscriptions are added. Most Twelfth Dynasty steles have been found at Abydos, where the underworld god Osiris was worshipped and where rich offerings to the god were made. One of the royal tombs of the First Dynasty kings, namely that of Djer (cf. chapter 4 in volume 1), was regarded as the burial place of Osiris, and the processional road to this tomb was seen as especially holy. The sides of this sacred road were lined with a large number of steles that the worshippers erected there, showing the owner of the stele (usually an official), members of their families, and occasionally even people

---

42. de Morgan 1895: figs. 18–20, 39; Petrie, Brunton, and Murray 1923: pl. xxxivA.

43. Di. Arnold 2008: 16–18, pls. 2–6; Petrie, Brunton, and Murray 1923: pl. xxxivA (Mastaba 609).

44. Allen 2008.

who belonged to the owner's staff. Also small commemorative chapels were erected along the processional way or else in other parts of the cemeteries of Abydos. These chapels often housed several steles and statues commissioned by one and the same official, with each monument showing him and/or a different group of dependents from his social circle. A good example is the group of steles of the "high steward" Hor, who held his office under Senusret I.[45] The first stele portrays him alone with an inscription consisting of a long list of his titles, a second depicts him in front of family members, and a third shows various people working on Hor's estate. Another good example is a group of steles belonging to the "treasurer" Iykhernofret, whose main stele shows him with family members and features a long biographical inscription that provides useful information about the Osiris procession.[46]

22.4. Away from the royal residence: the changing burial practices in the provinces

In the early Middle Kingdom, Egypt was divided into administrative units consisting of distinct regions along the Nile valley and delta whose creation goes back to the beginning of the Old Kingdom and that modern scholars call provinces or nomes (from the Greek term *nomos* for "administrative unit"; cf. chapter 19 in this volume). Especially in the Twelfth Dynasty, the governors of some of these nomes were able to build large rock-cut tombs. These governors' tombs at Asyut, Meir, Deir el-Bersha, and Beni Hasan (just to mention the best preserved) are typically fully decorated with reliefs or paintings that provide rich information on life in Middle Kingdom Egypt. Several tombs at Beni Hasan,[47] Qubbet el-Hawa, Deir el-Bersha,[48] and Asyut have longer biographical inscriptions, and the texts in the tombs at Beni Hasan make it particularly clear that

---

45. Simpson 1974: 19, 23, pls. 44–45 (ANOC 29.1–3).

46. Simpson 1974: 17, 22–23, pls. 1–4 (ANOC 1).

47. Newberry 1893a: pls. VIII, XXV–XXVI, XLIV.

48. Newberry 1895: pl. XIV.

these governors belonged to one family that ruled over their province as a powerful local dynasty, connected to some neighboring nomes by marriage. The inscriptions and especially the titles allow the reconstruction of these governors' rights and duties to a certain degree: they collected dues, protected the nome's border, were responsible for internal security, and acted as the nome's highest judicial authority,[49] while the king was able to send them on missions on his behalf.[50] They also oversaw significant building projects, as chapels and sanctuaries were constructed and adorned by officials and local governors, contributing to the sacred landscape of towns and cemeteries. This is best described by the governor Khnumhotep II in his tomb at Beni Hasan: "Within my city did I make my memorial, having (re)constructed a columned hall which I found in ruins and having it supported with columns of granite...."[51]

The Heqaib sanctuary on Elephantine Island is among the best-known chapels that received the patronage of local governors.[52] Heqaib (cf. chapter 7 in volume 1) had been a local Old Kingdom official whose achievements resulted in his worship as a saint by the local population after his death, and also by state officials passing through during their expeditions.[53] His sanctuary was most likely built at the end of the Old Kingdom, renovated in the Eleventh Dynasty,[54] and adorned over the years with shrines, statues, and steles, most of them dating to the Twelfth Dynasty. Most of the larger monuments placed there were commissioned by local governors, although there are also statues of high state officials, such as the "overseer of the gateway" Ipy, who most likely was on a mission in the region when he decided to donate a statue to the sanctuary.[55]

---

49. Favry 2004: 340–374.

50. Favry 2004: 336–338.

51. Lloyd 1992: 24; Newberry 1893a: 65–66; Kanawati, Evans, and Mourad 2014: 35 (lines 192–200).

52. Franke 1994.

53. Franke 1994: 131–146.

54. Franke 1994: 30–31.

55. Franke 1994: 55–56; for the person, compare Grajetzki 2009: 94–95.

Such worship and care for ancestors and great men of the past are also
attested at cemeteries, for example at Meir, where later governors renovated the tombs of their predecessors.[56]

The style and motifs of the decorations for the local governors' tombs
vary considerably from place to place, which suggests the existence of
different local workshops. Alternatively, specialists may also have
come from the royal residence, as in the case of the tomb of Sarenput
I, governor of Elephantine during the reign of Senusret I, who claims
in his tomb inscriptions that artists and craftsmen from the royal residence were involved in building his tomb at Qubbet el-Hawa.[57] The
decoration of the rock-cut tomb is only partly preserved, complicat-
ing any judgment of its style, but its façade is decorated in sunk relief
of the highest quality that indeed suggests the work of royal artists.
The same can be argued for the tombs of the local governors at Meir,
whose relief style is close to examples from Old Kingdom Memphis.[58]
While several early Twelfth Dynasty tomb chapels are decorated with
fine reliefs, the Eleventh Dynasty tomb paintings at Beni Hasan look
rather provincial in contrast: the figures are not well proportioned, and
even the base lines are often not straight. In general, these tombs feature images of the governor and his wife; hunting scenes with mythological animals depicted in desert settings; fortress siege scenes; and
large-scale compositions with numerous pairs of wrestlers.[59] Several
Twelfth Dynasty chapels at Beni Hasan (figure 22.3)[60] and Deir el-
Bersha[61] depict long rows of officials and some Eleventh and Twelfth
Dynasty tombs at Asyut, Qubbet el-Hawa, Beni Hasan,[62] and Deir el-

---

56. Blackman and Apted 1953: 1–2, pl. V; Willems 1988: 85.

57. Franke 1994: 193.

58. For the style, compare Blackman 1914: 16–17; Smith 1981: 192; Willems 1988: 85.

59. Newberry 1893a: pl. XIV; Newberry 1893b: pls. V, XV.

60. Newberry 1893a: pls. XIII, XXX.

61. Newberry 1895: pl. XXVII.

62. Newberry 1893a: pls. VIII, XXV–XXVI, XLIV.

FIGURE 22.3. Khnumhotep II and his local court. Detail from his tomb at Beni Hasan. Photo by Karen Radner; line drawing adapted from Newberry 1893a: pl. XXX.

Bersha[63] have longer, sometimes biographical inscriptions—two features that are not attested at Meir.

In proximity to the monumental tombs of the local governors, lesser officials were buried, often in simple shaft tombs, and these same lower officials are frequently also depicted in the governors' tombs.[64] From the titles given, the entourage of the governors appears to copy the royal court. There was a "steward," a "treasurer," an "overseer of the troops," and an "overseer of the sealers," just to mention a few of the subordinate

---

63. Newberry 1895: pl. XIV.

64. Newberry 1895: pl. XX.

officials.[65] These were the people managing the province for the local governors. Interestingly, certain titles attested at the royal court were not used in the provincial administration under the governors: most importantly, there was no "vizier," but there was also no "overseer of the marshland dwellers."[66] Our main sources of information about these lower-ranking officials are their own burials and their depictions in the tombs of the governors mentioning their names and titles. None of these sources provides much evidence about their family and social background, which therefore remain relatively unclear. But at least in some cases, there is evidence that these men could be related to the governor's families, as one governor buried at Meir was the son of an "overseer of fields,"[67] while a governor buried at Qau el-Kebir was the son of an "overseer of the *meret*-people."[68]

The best-known burials for such lower-ranking officials close to the governors' tombs are known from Middle Egypt, where many of these were found intact at the beginning of the twentieth century AD. In general, these burials seem quite standardized. However, the relatively poor recording techniques employed by these early excavations make it difficult for us to reconstruct the complete burial assemblage of particular tombs.[69]

The burials of these lower-ranking officials have provided us with a large number of rectangular, decorated wooden coffins. They were often inscribed on the inside with long religious texts (the "Coffin Texts"; see figure 22.4), along with offering lists and depictions of offerings and objects that represent those used in rituals of burial and mummification, with the actual versions of many of these items also found in the tombs. The "Coffin Texts" show that the afterlife was understood to be a continuation of life on earth: communal scenes with the deceased person's

---

65. Seidlmayer 2007.

66. Grajetzki 2017b: 155–156.

67. Willems 1988: 87.

68. D'Amicone 1988: 118, fig. 159.

69. The best overviews are those offered by Garstang 1907 and Schäfer 1908: 15–110.

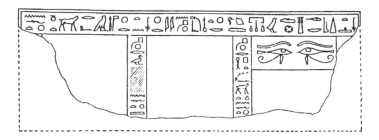

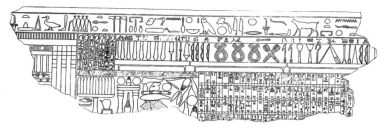

FIGURE 22.4. A typical Middle Kingdom coffin, front outside and front inside with the frieze of objects and coffin texts. Adapted from Gautier and Jéquier 1902: 82, fig. 101; pl. XXVII.

family, social life in general, and the nourishment of the deceased were important subjects, while there was little interaction between the deceased and any deity.

Early Middle Kingdom coffin styles varied from region to region, making it easy to distinguish coffins from different places and to identify local styles. For example, those at Asyut have double or triple textlines on the outside, while those at Gebelein show human figures. The latter appear on coffins from Asyut, too, but are not attested on those from Beni Hasan or Meir.[70] All this provides evidence for the existence of regional traditions. However, in the course of the Twelfth Dynasty, coffin styles became more standardized throughout Egypt, and under

70. Willems 1988: 58–117.

Senusret III, coffins decorated on all sides with a palace façade were common.[71]

Deposited inside the coffin, the deceased was displayed as a god-like being. The head was covered by a mummy mask[72] and the body decorated with a broad collar, armlets, and anklets: these are "divine jewelry,"[73] adornments worn by deities and also depicted in art. A head rest, wooden sandals, and wooden models were usually placed in or on the coffin, typically made especially for the tomb. Further wooden models showing scenes of daily life, such as servants producing food, weavers, scribes, and even soldiers were frequently placed next to the coffin,[74] with at least one figure in these groups depicting the tomb owner. Other common burial goods consisted of pottery vessels, cosmetics containers, and personal adornments that the deceased had also worn in life. Otherwise, objects used in life are not common in this type of burial, although the generally high looting activity makes it hard to reconstruct a typical and complete example of a burial for this period. Some burials exhibit special features, demonstrating that individual choices were made concerning the rituals and objects deposited during a burial: for example, two early Middle Kingdom tomb chambers at Abusir were filled with grain,[75] presumably evoking fertility and rebirth. Very importantly and in contrast to the graves of the highest ruling class, canopic jars and boxes containing the entrails that were removed from the deceased's body during mummification are very rare in the lower-ranking officials' tombs. This suggests that although their bodies were generally carefully wrapped in linen, proper mummification was not commonly practiced.

It is not always clear how the shafts of the burials of the lower officials were marked on the surface. In Lisht, many such burial shafts have been identified close to the chapels of high officials, and it is therefore possible

---

71. Willems 1988: 163–164; Bourriau 1991: 9–10.

72. Caisino 2017: 59–61.

73. Craig Patch 2005: 192.

74. Eschenbrenner-Diemer 2017.

75. Schäfer 1908: 99–100.

that these chapels were the cult place not only for the chapel owner, but also for his wider family and dependents. The same holds for the rock-cut tomb chapels of local governors, whose tomb decorations often mention dependent officials that were buried close by. It is also possible that their mortuary rituals were generally performed in the governor's chapel, especially as such practices are mentioned in the biographical tomb inscription of Khnumhotep II at Beni Hasan.[76]

The burials of the majority of the population are significantly simpler and often do not contain much, apart from some pottery vessels, with the coffins resembling undecorated wooden boxes. However, typical burial goods for (young) women that are attested in the graves of the poor, as well as in those of the daughters of queens and kings, were cosmetics such as oil and eye paint (kohl), sometimes placed in special containers, and personal adornments once worn close to the body, including protective amulets.[77] The early Middle Kingdom tomb 2076 at Badari is a good example: although this surface burial of a woman was found disturbed, numerous amulets of blue faience were recovered and include the stylized figures of a human, a lion, and a dog, a hand, a fist, and two scarabs with hieroglyphs and floral and geometric patterns on their undersides.[78]

Most likely, many of these burials were originally marked in some way on the surface. At sites such as Rifeh, crude clay models of houses and offering trays have been found that were once placed above burials. These trays take the form of an offering table, with offerings modeled in clay placed on top. The house models show the most important part of the house, the garden, and the portico in front of the main rooms. These items are called "soul houses" by modern scholars, and some examples have also been found in settlement contexts,[79] indicating that they were used in the ancestor cult performed at home.[80]

76. Lloyd 1992: 21–122; Kanawati, Evans, and Mourad 2014: 31, pl. 7 (lines 4–13).

77. Dubiel 2008.

78. Brunton 1928: pl. LXVI (tomb inventory); Seidlmayer 1990: 134, 395 (dating).

79. Petrie 1891: pl. IV: 20, 22; Müller and Forstner-Müller 2015.

80. Salvador 2015.

Analyzing the personal jewelry found in poorer Middle Kingdom burials offers another glimpse at the growing centralization and standardization of Middle Kingdom culture. At the end of the First Intermediate Period and in the early Middle Kingdom, two main traditions are visible in the archaeological record, particularly in burials. At the royal residence and in burials of the ruling class throughout Egypt, personal adornment seems to have been quite formalized as deceased men and women were equipped with broad collars, armlets, and anklets.[81] In contrast to such formalized jewelry sets, provincial burials contained a wide range of personal adornment, including many types of amulets. Some of these amulets depict parts of human bodies (such as legs, hands, and faces) but also a wide range of animals (including jackals, hippopotami, frogs, or flies). Many amulets are made of carnelian, but other materials such as faience appear, too. Other amulets take the form of so-called button seals. These are small and often round, with carvings of figures or geometric or floral patterns on the underside that often differ greatly from canonical Egyptian art. The seals' backs, too, feature a wide range of decorations, including animal figures. While such button seals were mainly found in burials, there is good evidence that they were also used for sealing commodities, based on the discovery of many broken clay sealings that show impressions made with button seals from administrative contexts.[82]

However, during the early Middle Kingdom period, such amulets disappeared from burials and other contexts,[83] and were replaced during the time of the Twelfth Dynasty by other types of personal jewelry and amulets that match the repertoire of adornment found at the royal residence.[84] The button seals were almost entirely replaced by the much more standardized scarab seals. These always show a beetle on top, with carvings of floral or geometric decorations and/or hieroglyphs on the

---

81. Yamazaki 2008: 443–444.

82. Pantalacci 1996.

83. Dubiel 2008.

84. Grajetzki 2017a: 197–209.

underside. While amulets are still known from the late Middle Kingdom, the repertoire is much more limited. One of the few surviving types are small falcon figures, which were common in the early Middle Kingdom and continued to be used into the late Middle Kingdom. The falcon represented the god Horus, who was the king on earth, and evidently the amulets' connection with kingship ensured that they remained important. Similarly, fish amulets, as common in the early Middle Kingdom, were still found later. While fish amulets from late Middle Kingdom burials vary widely in quality,[85] there are some very finely crafted examples made in gold dating to the late Middle Kingdom period, with one piece from Harageh that was most likely produced in a palace workshop.[86] This difference in quality is typical: the burials of poorer people no longer contained different types of objects, but items similar to those found in the burials of the ruling class, executed in lesser materials and quality of craftsmanship. Evidently, the craft production at the royal palace was now the prototype for the entire country, and the local traditions that had been so prominent in the preceding First Intermediate Period or early Middle Kingdom faded away.

22.5. The temples of the early Middle Kingdom

The founder of the Middle Kingdom, Mentuhotep II, started a substantial temple-building program in Upper Egypt and had many existing temples rebuilt or renovated. Old mudbrick structures were replaced with stone buildings, and consequently, stone blocks inscribed with the king's name have been found at many Upper Egyptian sites. One small chapel at Dendara survived almost intact until today, providing a clear picture of the decoration program, with its reliefs concentrating on depictions of the king and several deities, overloaded with symbolism. The scene on the rear wall, for example, shows the king in the pose of

---

85. Andrews 1981: 91–92.

86. Engelbach 1923: 15, pl. X.14; Aldred 1971: 213, pl. 78; Stünkel 2015.

smiting an enemy, an image used since the time of Egyptian state formation (cf. chapter 4 in volume 1, with figure 4.3). However, in this particular depiction, the king is not smiting a human enemy but two plants, the lotus and the papyrus, as the emblems of Upper and Lower Egypt, in a scene that celebrates the reunification of the country.[87] Another small chapel of Mentuhotep II was found at Abydos in 2014.[88] Both these buildings appear small, especially in comparison to the monumentality of later New Kingdom and Ptolemaic temples.

Mentuhotep II's successor continued his temple-building program,[89] and Senusret I went one step further by systematically renovating temples not only in Upper Egypt, but throughout the country: stone blocks with the name of this king are attested from many sites, and substantial remains of a decorated gateway were found at Coptos. The remains of a barque shrine at Karnak in Thebes are sufficient to fully reconstruct it, while the remains of Karnak's Amun-Ra temple allow us at least to visualize that enormous building. The substantial structure had a façade of pillars and was adorned with an array of private and royal statues. About a dozen of these statues belong to the "treasurer" Mentuhotep, who also bears the title "overseer of all royal works" on several statues. It seems likely that he was the main official in charge of the temple's construction under Senusret I.

Another important temple-building project of Senusret I was at Heliopolis, where the king erected an obelisk, the oldest example still standing in its original place. Remains of temple annals that record events dated yearly under Senusret I presumably come from his temple at Heliopolis, as the text includes lists of temple offerings.[90] A building inscription from Senusret I's Heliopolis temple that survived as a New Kingdom copy on a leather scroll[91] provides evidence that temples could

---

87. Habachi 1963: 21.

88. Damarant et al. 2015.

89. Gestermann 1987: 116–120.

90. Postel and Regen 2005.

91. Parkinson 1991: 40–43. However, the Middle Kingdom dating is debated; cf. Stauder 2013: 249–257.

be decorated with long historical texts. Similar texts were also found at the Satet temple on Elephantine Island[92] and at the Montu temple at Tod.[93]

The custom of inscribing longer texts on temples is also attested in the later Middle Kingdom, although it is not always clear where these inscriptions were originally placed. Hence, the remnants of a substantial inscription with annals of Amenemhat II that were found on granite blocks at Memphis (cf. chapter 19 in this volume) may have originally been part of the Ptah temple in Memphis,[94] but the king's funerary temple in Dahshur is another option.[95] In the Fayum, a long religious text was found that deals with the accession of King Amenemhat III, and it is unknown whether the text once adorned the local Sobek temple at Shedet (modern Medinet el-Fayum) or the king's funerary temple at Hawara.[96]

Senusret I's temple building program was perhaps not only motivated by piety, as there are clear indications that Egypt was heavily reorganized and centralized at the beginning of the Twelfth Dynasty. This included matters of cultic importance, which previously, in the First Intermediate Period and the time of the early Middle Kingdom, had been very much local concerns, at least at places far from royal power. With the new program of temple-building that the central government realized throughout the country, the cults of the provinces came under state control.[97]

92. Schenkel 1975.

93. Barbotin and Clère 1991.

94. Altenmüller 2015.

95. Altenmüller 2015: 281–283.

96. Generalverwaltung der Königlichen Museen zu Berlin 1913: 138–139; Ma. Müller 2013.

97. Bussmann 2010: 512–513.

22.6. Lahun: a window on urban life in the later Twelfth Dynasty

The Middle Kingdom saw the height of ancient Egyptian town-planning. Several such settlements, dating mainly to the Twelfth Dynasty, have been excavated, including two sites at Tell el-Dabʿa in the eastern Nile delta and Wah-sut, a town close to Abydos. All these places are laid out on a grid pattern,[98] as is also Hetep-Senusret, which will serve as the central case study in this section, allowing us some rare insights into Middle Kingdom urban life, literature, and material culture.

22.6.1. The planned settlement of Hetep-Senusret (Lahun)

Hetep-Senusret, the ancient name of modern Lahun (also Illahun or—erroneously—Kahun; figure 22.5: a), is the largest known of the planned Middle Kingdom settlements. Lahun was discovered in the late nineteenth century AD, and the recording of its architecture and small finds in the subsequent excavations under the British archaeologist William Flinders Petrie, although pioneering for its time, is unfortunately insufficient by modern standards. The Middle Kingdom town was founded at the entrance to the Fayum, near the modern village of Lahun, and adjacent to the huge valley temple belonging to the pyramid complex of Senusret II. Although part of the town's population evidently worked for the king's cult, it seems unlikely that Hetep-Senusret was founded solely as a local center for the royal cult as, for example, the office of a vizier was located there (figure 22.5: g).[99]

The walled town of Hetep-Senusret is laid out in an orthogonal pattern. One-quarter encompassed about ten huge building complexes belonging to members of the ruling class, and the other sections contained many more and much smaller houses for inhabitants with fewer resources, probably dependents of the owners of the large estates.[100]

---

98. Moeller 2016: 252–262, 290–296.

99. Collier and Quirke 2006: 110–111, 238–239.

100. Kemp 2006: 216.

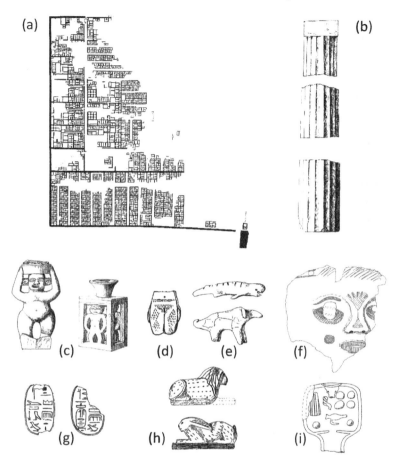

FIGURE 22.5. Lahun and some finds from the excavations there. (a) Plan of Lahun (north is on the left); (b) a column; (c) two lamps; (d) a fragmentary faience figure of a naked woman; (e) two clay animal figures; (f) a mask; (g) two seal impressions naming a vizier's office; (h) two faience animal figures; (i) a clay offering table. Adapted from Petrie 1890: pl. VIII, XIII; 1891: pls. VI, IX, XIII–XIV.

Hetep-Senusret had an external fortification wall constructed from mudbricks. Within the settlement, there was another wall separating the quarters with large and middle-sized estates from the section with smaller houses that were arranged in several rows. Archaeological and architectural investigations have shown that this dividing wall was the original town wall and that the settlement part on the western side was a later addition to the town.[101] This addition with the smaller houses was called Sekhem-Senusret.[102]

The large estates in the original portion of the settlement consisted of a main building with a reception hall, the owner's bedroom, and living quarters, and a small courtyard in front, perhaps also used as a garden. The most important rooms of the main building had painted walls,[103] and its façade was adorned with a row of columns, mainly made of wood, although some stone examples have also been found (figure 22.5: b).[104] The rest of the estate was occupied by granaries as well as smaller building units, perhaps reserved for the owner's wife and his key staff.

The most important public building of the entire settlement was certainly the stone-built funerary temple for the king, whose stone parts had already been dismantled in antiquity by looters. A structure of unknown function in the middle of the town in front of one of the large estates may also have been a temple,[105] while the badly preserved remains of a larger building to its south, including a hall with ten columns, may have functioned as an administrative building.[106]

Several cemeteries for the people of Hetep-Senusret are known, including one in the immediate proximity to the town. Cemetery 900 lies a mere 200 m northwest of the town and consists of a central mastaba with several shaft tombs arranged around it. On some of the stone

---

101. Moeller 2016: 273.

102. Horváth 2009.

103. Petrie 1890: 24; 1891: 6.

104. Petrie 1891: 6.

105. Moeller 2016: 281.

106. Moeller 2016: 283–285.

fragments, the name Senusret has survived. It is possible that this single mastaba also served as the funerary chapel and main cult place for all of the tombs surrounding it.[107] Another cemetery was excavated 3.5 km southeast of Hetep-Senusret at Harageh[108] and consisted of about 300 late Middle Kingdom tombs.[109] Furthermore, many burials of newborn and young children were discovered inside the houses of the settlement itself, often placed in small wooden boxes that had not originally been intended as coffins and buried underneath the floors.[110]

The analysis of the remains of the houses at Hetep-Senusret bring the social divisions in Middle Kingdom Egypt into sharp focus, as the relative size of the houses clearly expresses great social inequality. But who exactly lived in the big estates, and who in the smaller houses? It has been suggested that one particular mansion, built on the higher elevation of a natural stone outcrop, belonged to the governor of the town,[111] and the people occupying the other grand estates may have shared this elevated social level. One wonders whether the royal court of Senusret II, or parts of it, were ever based here. The number of the great estates of the secluded settlement quarter correspond well to the number of the highest state officials, so could these officials have resided here under Senusret II?[112] A tempting assumption, although hard evidence is missing. The identity of the residents who lived there following Senusret II's reign remains just as elusive, and it is possible that some of the original large estates were divided into smaller units at a later time.[113]

107. Petrie, Brunton, and Murray 1923: 30, pls. XIII, XXXVI.

108. Engelbach 1923; Grajetzki 2004; Richards 2005: 90–97.

109. Richards 2005: 93; Quirke 2005: 102.

110. Petrie 1890: 24.

111. Quirke 2005: 55; Moeller 2016: 278.

112. Quirke 2005: 69–73.

113. Petrie 1891: 7.

22.6.2. Middle Kingdom literature

The finds from Lahun provide a good idea of urban life in the late Middle Kingdom, also because many fragmentary papyri have been found due to the generally good conditions of preservation. Most of these texts are accounts, and one of them mentions a leading state official who is well known from other sources: the "treasurer" Senebsumai,[114] who was in office in the middle of the Thirteenth Dynasty, when the town was clearly still flourishing. The papyri found at Lahun provide evidence that many officials of medium rank were based at the settlement of Hetep-Senusret, such as the "funerary priests" (*hem-ka*) for the highest state officials that were buried around the pyramid of Senusret II.[115] Some officials of medium rank were subordinate to the local governor, but others were working for state-run projects that were organized from Lahun, such as the building of a pyramid at Hawara under King Amenemhat III.[116] While the "steward" Horemsaf, for example, was clearly working locally for the mortuary temple of Senusret II,[117] it remains unclear whether many of the officials mentioned in the Lahun papyri operated on a local level or whether they were palace staff dispatched to the region on a mission; an example is a "store overseer" mentioned in a badly preserved papyrus fragment.[118]

The papyri also include many letters, of which a large number belong to the archive of the mortuary temple of Senusret II and date to the reign of Amenemhat III, with the "steward" Horemsaf as the main correspondent. The letters provide details about the economic organization of the mortuary temple and about Middle Kingdom labor organization more generally. Other fragmentary papyri include the "Story of Sinuhe"[119]

---

114. Collier and Quirke 2006: 162–163, 170–171.

115. Collier and Quirke 2006: 48–49.

116. Kemp 2006: 211; Grajetzki 2009b.

117. Luft 1982: 119–123; 1992; 2006: 75–81, 101–107, 119–128.

118. Collier and Quirke 2006: 266–267.

119. Collier and Quirke 2004: 34–35.

and part of the "Story of Horus and Seth," with a homosexual encounter between the two deities as a key element in the fight between the two gods.[120] An example for a well-preserved papyri is a hymn to King Senusret III.[121] Other remarkable text finds include several medical papyri, one of which deals with veterinary matters[122] and another with gynecological concerns.[123] Fragments of many other texts, often religious in content, and of stories without known parallels, further emphasize the wide use of writing at Hetep-Senusret.

The Middle Kingdom is the period of Egyptian history that is credited with the appearance of literature (cf. chapter 19 in this volume), as only longer texts from tombs are preserved from the Old Kingdom, including biographical inscriptions and relatively short offering formulae. The longest compositions of this period are the "Pyramid Texts" that were inscribed on the walls of the pyramid chambers of kings and queens, mostly religious liturgies. From the Middle Kingdom, however, several works survive that might be called literature in a narrower sense.[124] These include stories, teachings, and laments. The most famous composition is arguably the "Story of Sinuhe." Its protagonist is a high court official who fled Egypt after King Amenemhat I had died, for fear of being accused of involvement in the king's death, and who came to Palestine, where he had several adventures and founded a family. However, still longing for Egypt, he eventually received a letter from King Senusret I summoning him home, and he was welcomed back to the royal court in Egypt. The story is a parable of the significance of being Egyptian and was already widely read in the Middle Kingdom, as indicated by the widespread copies of the story, including the fragment from Lahun, while later

---

120. Collier and Quirke 2004: 20–21.

121. Collier and Quirke 2006: 16–19.

122. Collier and Quirke 2006: 54–57.

123. Collier and Quirke 2006: 58–64.

124. An excellent overview of Middle Kingdom literature is Parkinson 2002.

copies from the New Kingdom attest to the ongoing popularity of the composition.[125]

So-called "teachings" were a very popular text genre of the Middle Kingdom, providing guidance in social behavior for the sons of the ruling class. The most famous composition is the "Teaching of Ptahhotep," of which several Middle Kingdom copies are known.[126] While Ptahhotep was an Old Kingdom vizier of the late Fifth Dynasty, there is little doubt that the composition was created only in the Middle Kingdom, dated back in time to give it more authority. Pessimistic works of literature were also popular. An example is the "Dialogue of a Man with his Soul," which expresses negative thoughts about the world and human existence.[127]

It is not easy to fathom the cultural context of all these compositions. Recently it has been suggested that they were not (only) read privately but were performed aloud (see also chapter 19 in this volume).[128] A depiction of Queen Ashait, wife of Mentuhotep II, on the inside of her sarcophagus, may provide an idea of how Egyptian literature was consumed in the Middle Kingdom. She is shown in front of the "scribe of the god's book" Intef, who is sitting on a chair with a book roll in his hands, most likely reciting a liturgy.

22.6.3. Egyptian faience

A high percentage of the objects found at Lahun can be called "religious," but due to insufficient recording of the exact find spots it is often hard to put the objects found during William Flinders Petrie's excavations in a clear context. Nevertheless, many are likely connected to rituals linked to female fertility and childbirth as well as the protection for mother and child in general. An exceptional find is a mask of linen with leonine features painted on it (figure 22.5: f). Lion figures are often depicted in

---

125. Parkinson 2009: 280–295.

126. Hagen 2012.

127. Parkinson 2009: 315–322.

128. Parkinson 2009: *passim*, but especially 3–19; 2015: 182–183, fig. 86.

connection with birth rituals,[129] and one wonders whether the mask was worn during such rituals at childbirth.[130] Crude clay figures depicting animals or highly stylized naked women and faience figures of naked women shown without legs (figure 22.5: d–e) seem to attest to religious practices in domestic contexts,[131] with the female figures most likely connected to fertility and related rituals. In addition, there are faience figures of animals, as attested also at other sites and burials dating to the late Middle Kingdom.[132] Examples of roughly hewn stone lamps and statues in the shape of naked women or dwarves are less common, but again are known from other late Middle Kingdom sites (figure 22.5: c).[133] They almost look un-Egyptian based on the iconography and workmanship, and their exact meaning remains enigmatic.

The widespread use of Egyptian faience, that is, sintered-quartz ceramics displaying surface vitrification that creates bright colors, most commonly green-blue, is a highly distinctive feature of the material culture of the late Middle Kingdom.[134] Popular faience shapes include small figures of animals or women, vessels, inscribed tiles, and items of jewelry. Among the animal figures, hippopotami are most common, but there are also dogs, cats, hedgehogs, and jerboas (cf. the examples in figure 22.5: h). Numerous examples were found in burials, but they might have been made originally for use in daily life, as the evidence from Lahun and other settlements indicates, where they were recovered in both domestic and sacred contexts. The female figures are often naked, without lower legs, and with tattoos covering parts of the body, wearing distinctive types of jewelry such as body chains, a girdle, armlets, and a necklace with a shell pendant.[135]

129. Quirke 2016: 335–344.

130. Quirke 2016: 83–83.

131. Quirke 2005: 98.

132. Miniaci 2017: 247–248 on the figures from Lahun.

133. Quirke 2015a; 2015b.

134. Miniaci 2017.

135. Grajetzki 2014b: 115–116, 130.

Intriguingly, many of these faience figurines have prototypes dating to the Early Dynastic period (cf. chapter 4 in volume 1), and even earlier. It is not clear whether old objects were found and copied, using an improved technology and a more refined style, or whether their production was an ongoing and evolving tradition. The Early Dynastic objects are often found in temple deposits, while the Middle Kingdom figures typically come from tombs. As these types of objects were not placed in tombs during the Old Kingdom and First Intermediate Period, they may have remained invisible in the archaeological record.[136] Other typical Middle Kingdom faience objects, although far less common, include a series of tiles with royal names recovered from Lisht,[137] and inscribed vessels, some decorated with floral patterns and some naming kings or officials.[138]

22.6.4   Sculpture

From the papyrus archive of the mortuary temple of Senusret II at Lahun, several fragments of lists naming statues are preserved, which demonstrate that the sanctuary was richly equipped with statues made of different materials. One such list records several statues of high officials, including two of viziers, while another text refers to statues of members of the royal family.[139] Middle Kingdom sculpture could serve different functions. As in previous periods, larger statues were often erected in the chapels of monumental tombs, whereas smaller examples, often made of wood, were placed in the burial chamber next to the coffin. However, the installation of royal and private statues in temples is a new feature of the Middle Kingdom, with royal statues sometimes having been executed in monumental scale. Statues depicting officials are now often donated to

---

136. Morris 2017: 323–330.

137. Di. Arnold 2015: 59, pl. 93.

138. Petrie 1890: pl. X.72 (naming the Thirteenth Dynasty king Wahibra); Bourriau 1988: 128–132; Quirke 2003.

139. Borchardt 1899: 96–97.

temples as well as to important chapels of local "saints," such as Heqaib at Elephantine (see section 22.4).[140]

Middle Kingdom statues are made of a wide range of materials: stone and wood are very common, and small statues made of bronze, most often depicting officials, are also typical, although they had been relatively rare during the Old Kingdom.[141] Eleventh and early Twelfth Dynasty sculpture generally appears plain and not very refined. The figures look robust, with little modeling of facial features. A well-known example is the statue of the "overseer of troops" Intef under Mentuhotep II (Egyptian Museum Cairo, JE 91169 and 89858), who is shown with an unmodeled face, a short wig, a short neck, as well as a square and robust chest.[142] Contemporary royal sculpture shows similar features. The statue of King Mentuhotep II that was found in the dummy burial of the king's funerary complex at Deir el-Bahri (see section 22.2) depicts the king sitting on a block-like throne, with his arms crossed over the chest (Egyptian Museum Cairo, JE 36195; figure 22.6).[143] Mentuhotep wears the red crown of Lower Egypt and his skin is painted black, perhaps to link him to the underworld god Osiris, who is also sometimes shown black. The whole figure appears robust and somehow archaic. The broad facial features might also reflect the African roots of the king and of Egyptian culture in general.[144]

As Middle Kingdom sculpture underwent a rapid stylistic development, it is often possible to date works of royal sculpture and those of the highest officials to specific reigns within the Twelfth Dynasty.[145] It seems that such objects were created by artists attached to the royal residence, although they were not necessarily produced at the residence; alternative options include workshops at the building site where the statues were intended to be put on display[146] or the quarries where the stone was

---

140. Habachi 1985.

141. Smith 1981: 183; Delange 1987: 211–213.

142. Saleh and Sourouzian 1987: no. 70.

143. Smith 1981: 160; Saleh and Sourouzian 1987: no. 67; Russmann 1989: 49–52.

144. Wildung 2018: 327–328.

145. Fay 1996: 53; Connor 2018: 14.

146. Oppenheim 2015a: 26.

FIGURE 22.6. The statue of King Mentuhotep II from Deir el-Bahri. Egyptian Museum Cairo, JE 36195. Photo by Djehouty, via Wikimedia Commons (https://commons.wikimedia.org/wiki/File:Ägyptisches_Museum_Kairo_ 2016-03-29_Mentuhotep_02.jpg). Creative Commons Attribution Share Alike 4.0 (CC-BY-SA-4.0) license. Adapted by Karen Radner.

FIGURE 22.7. Left: head of King Senusret III; Ägyptisches Museum, Berlin (accession number ÄM 20175). Right: head of King Amenemhat III; Palazzo Altemps, Rome (accession number 8607). Reproduced from Fechheimer 1922: pls. 54, 59.

cut.[147] Under Senusret I and Amenemhat II, Middle Kingdom sculpture reached a first artistic peak. The statues of the local governor Ibu, most likely dating to the reign of Amenemhat II, from Qau el-Kebir belong to the best works of Egyptian art,[148] as does the head of a queen or princess, now kept in the Brooklyn Museum (New York).[149]

A second peak was reached under Senusret III and Amenemhat III (figure 22.7). The royal face is now portrayed radically different in comparison to works depicting the early Middle Kingdom kings. Senusret III is no longer shown as youthful, but as a mature man with a certain harshness in his expression. The images of Amenemhat III are similar in style, but his facial features are so clearly different from those of Senusret

147. Connor 2018: 21–24.

148. Fay 1988: 53, pl. 67a; Do. Arnold 2015b.

149. Fay 1988: 53, 28–30, pls. 55–57; Freed 2015.

III that these may be actual portraits, designed to resemble the likeness of the living person.[150] These changes in royal representation are so radical that one wonders whether they also reflect a change in the concept of kingship.[151] The images of these kings had a clear impact on private sculpture, as many officials of the late Middle Kingdom are depicted as elderly, mature men. However, in addition to these seemingly realistic depictions, there is also a series of sculptures that show Amenemhat III as an eternally youthful ruler,[152] and there are also statues that show officials as young men.[153]

Middle Kingdom reliefs arguably reached their artistic peak under Senusret III. Both the reliefs from the king's pyramid complex at Dahshur and the accompanying mastabas of the king's officials are of high quality, albeit typically very fragmentarily preserved. An outstanding example are the reliefs of Saiset, a "treasurer" and vizier, who is depicted on four panels as sitting in front of an offering table. He is shown as a middle-aged man with an almost bald head and a characteristic face which might have been an actual portrait, presumably influenced by the contemporary royal depictions.[154] Even the hieroglyphic signs used in the inscriptions, such as those on the exterior facade of the mastaba of the vizier Nebit, are works of art of the highest quality, carved in bold relief with many details.[155]

The royal sculpture of the early Thirteenth Dynasty is still very much in the tradition of the late Twelfth Dynasty. The most famous example is the statue of King Sekhemkara Amenemhat V from Elephantine, an

150. Freed 2010: 903.

151. Oppenheim 2015b.

152. Connor 2015b: 58–63.

153. Connor 2015b: 64–67.

154. de Morgan 1903: pl. xiv; Fischer 1975: 302, no. 276; Simpson 1988; El-Husseiny and Okasha Khafagy 2010.

155. Di. Arnold 2002a: 622–623, figs. 3–4; Oppenheim 2006.

almost life-sized schist figure showing the king sitting on a throne,[156] a work of art of the highest technical standard. While the face resembles that of Amenemhat III, Amenemhat V is shown smiling, in contrast to the earlier king. A short time later, the preserved statues of King Neferhotep I depict him as a youthful king, with features generally resembling late Twelfth Dynasty royal sculpture,[157] and the wooden statue of King Awibra Hor from his burial at Dahshur also has a youthful face.[158]

As in the Twelfth Dynasty, it seems that the statues of highest court officials and those of the king and of members of the royal family were produced by the same artists and workshops.[159] Perhaps the best-known work of non-royal sculpture is the almost life-size (1.50 m high) granodiorite statue of Sobekemsaf, the "reporter of Thebes," who is shown as a bald, overweight man of middle age, wearing a long kilt.[160] A comparable sculpture of equally flawless execution is the almost life-size (1.48 m high) statue of the vizier Neferkara Iymeru from Thebes, which can be dated to the reign of King Khaneferra Sobekhotep IV and shows the vizier in a long garment with a string around his neck, as is typical for a vizier's attire.[161] The many smaller statuettes that can be dated to the late Middle Kingdom rarely reach the quality of the larger statues of kings and high officials, and it seems that many of them were produced in local workshops by less well-trained artists.[162]

Judging from the few surviving pieces of royal reliefs commissioned under the Thirteenth Dynasty, it seems that their craftsmanship did not reach the same high standards of contemporary sculpture. At Abydos,

---

156. Habachi 1985: 113–114, pl. 198c–200. Its missing head was identified as a piece that had been kept in Vienna since 1821: Fay 1988.

157. Connor 2015a: 90, no. 32.

158. de Morgan 1896: pl. XXXV.

159. Connor 2018: 14–15.

160. Do. Arnold 2015a.

161. Delange 1987: 66–68.

162. Connor 2018: 16–18.

small relief fragments have been recovered of the false door of a ruler named Sobekhotep (most likely Khaneferra Sobekhotep IV), which was decorated in sunken relief.[163] The style is similar to reliefs of King Sekhemra-khuytawy Amenemhat Sobekhotep on the gateway of the Montu temple at Medamud, whose decoration mirrors closely a gateway set up at the same place by Senusret III:[164] the Thirteenth Dynasty gateway reliefs do not match the level of quality of the Twelfth Dynasty examples, as the cutting of the stone is sloppy and the figures are not as well proportioned. A relief block from Atawala in Middle Egypt shows King Hetepibra Aamusahornedjitef before the local deity Nemty, executed in a style that seems similar to the reliefs of King Sekhemra-khuytawy Amenemhat Sobekhotep at Medamud.[165] From the Memphis region, so few examples of royal reliefs are known that our understanding of the stylistic developments there is severely limited; there are some fragments from the pyramid of King Khendjer, but these have only been published in drawings.[166]

22.7. Aspects of late Middle Kingdom society and administration

As we have discussed, the late Middle Kingdom saw major changes in many aspects of state administration and also material culture. There was now a concentration of royal resources in the Fayum-Memphis region, at Abydos, at Thebes, and perhaps also at Tell el-Dabʿa (ancient Avaris) in the eastern Nile delta. The administration became much more focused and precise, and scarab seals with not only decorative motifs but also private names and titles are in wide use (see already section 22.4).

---

163. Wegner and Cahail 2015: figs. 15–17.

164. Bisson de la Roque 1931: pl. VIII (Senusret III gate); pl. X (Sobekhotep gate); Bisson de la Roque and Clère 1929: 59–60, figs. 48–49 (Sobekhotep gate); Fischer 1975: 303, pl. 278; Wildung 1984: 225, figs. 195–196.

165. Habachi 1952: 61, pls. X–XIA.

166. Jéquier 1933: figs. 1–5, 14–15.

The sealing and checking of goods, commodities, and documents evidently acquired a new prominence in management procedures, and at most late Middle Kingdom settlement sites, including the fortresses in Lower Nubia (cf. chapter 20 in this volume), huge deposits of broken clay sealings bearing seal impressions have been found during excavations. Double naming also became very important in the late Middle Kingdom, with individuals habitually bearing two names both in official documents and on monuments. As many of the Egyptian personal names were very common, double naming would have reduced the likelihood of confusing individuals, and the practice clearly indicates a desire to achieve administrative precision.[167]

It is relatively easy to track these changes in the material culture and in the administrative documentation, where many new titles for officials appear. But the underlying forces behind these transformations are harder to identify. From the reigns of Senusret III and Amenemhat III onward, the large, decorated rock-cut tombs of the provincial governors in Middle Egypt disappear. While governors are still well attested in the following period, they no longer had such tombs constructed for themselves and are instead known to us from steles, statues, and other object types.[168] It had been argued that the sons of the governors were brought to the royal residence to embark on a career there, leaving the local succession open. The king may well have promoted such a policy in order to weaken the local governors.[169] However, it seems more likely that other forces were at work in this regard. The reorganization in the provincial administration may have left the governors with fewer resources, and unable to afford decorated tombs or even local courts at the same level as before. As a result, there were no more rich provincial cemeteries, which is particularly noticeable in Middle Egypt. On top of that, burial customs saw some profound changes over time as well. Decorated coffins became rarer, and the previously popular wooden models disappeared

---

167. Vernus 1986.

168. Franke 1994: 40–49; Grajetzki 1997: 61–62.

169. Franke 1991: 63–65.

from the tombs. However, the late Middle Kingdom provincial cemeteries are not as well researched as one would hope, as the prospect of excavating poorly equipped tombs that contain only few funerary objects, and even fewer inscribed ones, has not been overly attractive to modern Egyptologists.

In many ways, Egypt in the late Middle Kingdom appears to us as a country with one culture.[170] In the early Middle Kingdom period, we have seen many local styles flourishing, clearly visible in material culture from personal adornments to pottery styles and coffin decoration. In the late Middle Kingdom, these differences in style seem to have become rather minor and the biggest differences are now in regard to the objects' quality. The art production at Egypt's centers was of a high standard, whereas the products of the provinces seem often rather poor in quality while copying models from the centers with little creative input.

The overall impact of the reorganization of the country on Egyptian society is hard to judge. Evidently, as the local governors lost resources, the provincial courts gradually decreased in size, but the organizational structures might not have changed much. In the overall state administration, new positions began to emerge, such as "commander of the ruler's crew" (*atju en tjet heqa*), a military title that became very common in the Thirteenth Dynasty and Second Intermediate Period.[171] A considerable number of steles naming high officials and their families are known from the late Middle Kingdom and in these, social relationships are much more explicit and emphasized than before: as a result, the administration of the late Middle Kingdom is also perhaps the most thoroughly researched in all of Egyptian history.[172]

There has been some discussion about whether there was a "middle class" in Middle Kingdom Egypt, a social group that did not receive its income from the state or the royal administration but from running an

---

170. Bourriau 1988.

171. For a list of title holders, see Stefanović 2006: 72–94.

172. Quirke 2004.

enterprise.[173] The idea is not new, but has become more influential in the last decades with the rise of neoliberal ideas according to which purely state-run economies are seen as unworkable.[174] In this context, Janet Richards noted the wide spread of wealth in Middle Kingdom burials, which seems to attest to a complex society where there were not just rich and poor people.[175]

One possible example of a "middle class" individual is Senusretankh, who is known from his tomb at Harageh, dating to the late Twelfth Dynasty. This tomb is situated slightly apart from the main cemeteries and may once perhaps have overlooked fields. Senusretankh does not bear any administrative titles on the inscriptions of his coffin and his canopic box, the only two inscribed objects in the tomb.[176] Was he a wealthy landowner who was able to afford a substantial burial with fitting equipment, despite the fact that he seems to not have had any administrative titles?[177] However, Senusretankh may also have been a member of the local administration who simply did not think it necessary to include his titles on his coffin. Another example, again open to different interpretations, is provided by a letter from Lahun. It was written, or at least commissioned, by the "lady of the house" Ir.[178] The letter is partly destroyed, but the main concern seems to be female weavers who were not able to work. In the letter, Ir does not bear any titles relating to weaving or weavers. Perhaps she was running a small weaving business, but other interpretations are possible, as the weavers may have worked for a local institution or she may have managed the enterprise for somebody else.

There may well have been independent craftsmen, traders, and farmers in Middle Kingdom Egypt. However, it has been argued that

173. Richards 2005: 173–180; Mi. Müller 2015a; 2015b.

174. Harvey 2005: 5.

175. Richards 2005.

176. Engelbach 1923: 23, 26, pl. LIX (tomb inventory).

177. Grajetzki 2006: 150.

178. Collier and Quirke 2002: 114–115.

independent craftsmen or traders would always run the risk of not get-
ting enough customers, which could become critical in economically or
politically unstable times, whereas working for an institution or an official would provide a more stable and guaranteed income.[179] But there
are arguably further options beyond the stark opposites of being entirely
independent or permanently working for a large estate: some craftsmen
at least seem to have been mobile and traveled around the country as
parts of bigger projects.[180] Farmers and craftsmen working for an estate
could evidently also produce commodities and sell them privately on a
local market while also paying dues to their institutions.

The bulk of the population of Middle Kingdom Egypt consisted
most likely of farmers, and to a much lesser degree of craftsmen. Oleg
Berlev proposed that most of them held a legal status that was comparable to that of medieval serfs, and that in Egyptian texts, such people
were called "king's servant"[181] and "female servant"[182] (there was no
designation "king's female servant") and, as a group, "*meret*-people."[183]
During the Middle Kingdom, there is also an increase in the appearance
of "Asiatic" people (*aamu*)[184] who originally came from the lands of the
Levant (cf. chapter 19 in this volume); although they are never additionally called "king's servants," these people seem to have held a similar legal
status. Even if we attribute a serf-like status to many or perhaps even
most Egyptians, this does not mean that they could not run their own
businesses or buy or sell goods, including houses. Modern commentators often display too narrow a view when they automatically assume that
the status of a "serf" (or even "slave") would have precluded individuals
from owning property or means of production. But the reality was more

179. Bernbeck 1994: 63.

180. Oppenheim 2015a: 24.

181. Berlev 1972: 7–27; cf. English summary in Grajetzki 2006: 147–148.

182. Berlev 1972: 45–73.

183. Berlev 1972: 128–146.

184. Berlev 1972: 74–95.

complex, and most individuals who could be described as constituting the elusive "middle class" would have belonged to these "serfs."

The papyri found at Lahun mention "king's servants" several times. According to one letter, the "king's servant" Sobekemhab has fled from the pyramid-building site at Hawara and has consequently been put in some kind of prison; it seems that the writer of the letter was very concerned that he might die there.[185] It is impossible to decide whether the case of Sobekemhab was exceptional or not, but it seems most likely that the incident happened while Sobekemhab was doing corvée work at Hawara. There is good evidence for a corvée work system in the Middle Kingdom, which meant that most people, including those in higher positions, had to work at least some time per year on state projects. It seems that this work load was perceived quite negatively, as many references concern the evasion from such work. Corvée work was organized by an institution called the "Great Compound," whose main officials were the "great overseer of the Compound," the "overseer of the Compound," and the "scribe of the Great Compound,"[186] but it has been impossible to identify such structures archaeologically so far.

22.7.1. Commemorative steles

Many Abydos steles (cf. also section 22.3) are known from the reign of Senusret III, but they are of much lesser quality than the reliefs from his reign found at Dahshur (see section 22.6.4). The reliefs on these steles are often rather rudimentarily carved, even though some of them belong to the highest state officials; evidently, different artists were at work here and at the tombs near the royal residence. The set of Abydos steles of the "treasurer" Iykhernofret, one of the highest state officials under Senusret III, are a good example. Although finely carved monuments, the steles

185. Collier and Quirke 2002: 128–129.

186. Di Teodoro 2018.

are no match for both the earlier Twelfth Dynasty Abydos steles and the contemporary reliefs from Dahshur.[187]

The late Middle Kingdom period saw a great increase in the production of steles, at Abydos and elsewhere, with a high proportion of the known Middle Kingdom steles belonging to this period. Steles that just show one or two people are relatively rare. Most of these are presumably burial steles, such as the stele of Nehri from Beni Hasan,[188] the stele of "the great one of the tens of Upper Egypt" Iayseneb from Thebes,[189] or the stele of the "lady of the house" Iytenhab from Harageh,[190] which were all found in tombs. A more common type of stele of the late Middle Kingdom, known from many different sites, shows the owner of the stele with his family, mainly with his wife and children, but occasionally also with his mother, father, or wetnurse. Many of these steles can be interpreted as commemorative steles or cenotaphs that were erected at or near a sacred place so that the family was symbolically present there and could take part in related festivals and rituals that were regularly performed there.[191] A third type of stele depicts its owner with colleagues at their workplace, typically the royal palace. These examples are very useful for reconstructing work relationships at the palace and an important source for insights into social hierarchies. Several such steles were commissioned by officials in honor of their superiors and depict the stele's owner with his family, while the higher-ranking official holds the most important position in the scene, usually in the top left part of the stele, but is depicted without his family.[192]

For the first time, deities are now being included on steles of non-royal individuals. In the earliest examples, the deities are shown on their own in the upper part of the steles, while some Thirteenth Dynasty steles

---

187. Simpson 1974: pls. 1–4.

188. Garstang 1907: 187–188, fig. 195; Grajetzki 2009: 139, fig. 57.

189. Franke 2003b.

190. Engelbach 1923: pl. LXXIII.

191. Ilin-Tomich 2017: 1–2.

192. Leprohon 1978; Grajetzki 2009: 125–129.

depict the donor standing in front of the deity; such steles typically have an inscription with a hymn to Osiris, but also to the god Wepwawet, shown with a dog or jackal's head, or the fertility god Min-Hornakht.[193] That these steles depict deities in interaction with the human owners of the monuments is a radical innovation of this time. On occasion, the inscriptions on other steles also include biographical information.[194]

The quality of the late Middle Kingdom steles' relief carvings varies greatly, but on the whole, they never reached the high standard of the early and mid-Twelfth Dynasty steles. While many are poorly executed, indicative perhaps of a kind of mass production that did not see a high standard of craftsmanship as overly important, there are also some well-crafted steles, in particular dating to the later Thirteenth Dynasty. One such example is the limestone stele of the "treasurer" Senebi, carved in sunken relief and possibly the product of a royal workshop. It shows Senebi seated on a chair at the top of a stele, and the well-proportioned figures are depicted in great detail, for example with curly hairstyles.[195] Another fine example with figures carved in raised relief is a stele from Thebes that names King Wahibra Ibiau and the "overseer of the compound" Ibiau and shows the stele's owner Sihathor and his wife Senebsen in the bottom left part of the stele.[196]

Recently, there have been several studies attempting to identify late Middle Kingdom sculpture workshops.[197] For some places, the existence of such workshops seems plausible: the steles from Elephantine, for example, exhibit clear common features that indicate a local production tradition.[198] Elsewhere, such identifications are more problematic, and instead of assuming the existence of one workshop at one given place, it is more likely that individual artisans or groups of craftsmen traveled

193. Franke 2003a.

194. Kubisch 2011.

195. Grajetzki 2001: 61, pl. 4.

196. Bourriau 1988: 57–59, no. 45.

197. Cf. Ilin-Tomich 2017.

198. Franke 1994: 105–117.

around the country and worked together for a time, resulting in different styles of steles.[199]

22.7.2. Funerary practices at the royal residence and the role of the god Osiris

In the following, we will focus on the changing religious beliefs that appeared during the late Middle Kingdom period, as seen through the lens of the funerary practices of the ruling class,[200] and in particular with regard to the role of the underworld god Osiris.

The tomb of Ukhhotep at Meir is an exceptional monument from the reign of Senusret III that clearly reflects the changes shaping religious beliefs in the mid-Twelfth Dynasty. Ukhhotep was the last of the local governors at Qusae to have constructed a decorated rock-cut tomb there.[201] The tomb chapel is relatively small, but fully painted with scenes and symbols otherwise known exclusively from royal contexts, with many additional and unique features. Most remarkably, Ukhhotep is the only man depicted in the main chapel, while otherwise only women are shown. On its south wall, women are shown working in the marshes, catching birds, and operating papyrus boats, while on the north wall, there are rows of female bearers of offerings, bringing cattle, birds, and plates with vegetables and meat. A religious festival for Hathor is depicted on the south wall, with Ukhhotep shown together with two women of his family, facing female singers and musicians. There is a similar scene on the north wall which shows Ukhhotep sitting on a chair beside two rows of female musicians, playing the harp and the flute, clapping and singing. Behind them sit female members of Ukhhotep's family. Other men are only shown in the much smaller inner chapel, where they are depicted performing funerary rituals, which evidently could

---

199. Cf. Oppenheim 2014b.

200. Cf. also Bourriau 1988.

201. The tomb of Ukhhotep at Meir was fully published by Blackman and Apted 1953.

only be carried out by men. This inner chapel is overloaded with royal symbolism. The lower part of its walls is decorated with a palace façade, above which a row of figures linked to fertility is depicted: almost naked women and corpulent men who bear offerings. Previously, such processions are only attested in royal mortuary temples. In the register above are men performing rituals. A caption reads:

> A king's offering may be given to the mayor and overseer of priests, Ukhhotep, may he appear as king of Upper Egypt; a king's offering may be given to the mayor and overseer of priests, Ukhhotep, may he appear as king of Lower Egypt.[202]

Early commentators assumed that Ukhhotep had claimed royal privileges, which contributed to the eventual elimination of the local governors.[203] However, the use of such symbolism in word and image that was previously reserved for royalty is widely attested in the funerary sphere of this period. Although its decoration is badly destroyed, the tomb of Wahka II at Qau el-Kebir, which dates to the same period, had a comparable decorative scheme, as its paintings also show fertility figures and women catching birds.[204] While the religious concepts underpinning such scenes are not fully understood, better-known examples of royal symbolism are attested in contemporary burials from many other sites. Perhaps the most striking is the mummy mask of the "steward" Khnumhotep found at Meir, which is adorned with a gilded uraeus snake, the symbol of Wadjet, one of the Egyptian crown goddesses.[205] Many coffins dating to the mid-Twelfth Dynasty, too, show a wide range of royal symbols.[206]

---

202. Blackman and Apted 1953: 35, pl. XVII.

203. Blackman and Apted 1953: 31.

204. Petrie 1930: pls. xxiii–xxviii; compare the comments of Franke 1991: 54.

205. Hayes 1953: 310, fig. 201.

206. Willems 1997.

Therefore, rather than appropriating royal privileges, the use of such symbols of kingship by Ukhhotep and others likely relates to the god Osiris, ruler of the underworld. In order to guarantee a smooth transition into the afterlife, the deceased identified himself with Osiris and was equipped in death as if he were Osiris, and since Osiris had once been the king on earth and only later became the king of the underworld, this included depicting the royal insignia. Moreover, the use of royal symbols may relate to the performance of royal rituals during the embalming ceremony.

In general, the underworld god Osiris rose to further prominence in the late Middle Kingdom. With Abydos being the principal cult center for Osiris in Egypt (cf. section 22.3), it is not a coincidence that Senusret III built a monumental tomb complex at Abydos.[207] Moreover, at least two Thirteenth Dynasty kings were buried there.[208] Osiris now also became an increasingly prominent deity within the context of the burials of the ruling class. The burial customs of the late Middle Kingdom differed from those of the early Middle Kingdom, as decorated coffins are now much rarer, most often only bearing some short texts on the exterior faces. Only at places closely connected to the royal court, longer religious texts are still occasionally found on the exterior faces of coffins, and these prominently indicate new religious beliefs about the afterlife, with the focus of these texts now on the underworld and the interaction between the deceased and the underworld deities. With the burial now primarily concerned with the transformation of the deceased from one world to another, the wooden models that were so typical for the burials of the early Middle Kingdom (see section 22.4) gradually disappear.

In the late Middle Kingdom cemeteries of members of the royal court, there appears a distinctive new type of burial, often of royal women but also of other high-status individuals, that has recently been dubbed "Osirification burial."[209] One example is the tomb of the "king's

---

207. Wegner 2009.

208. Wegner and Cahail 2015.

209. Miniaci and Quirke 2009: 358. In earlier works, these burials are called "court-type burials."

daughter" Neferuptah at Hawara, which was found undisturbed by looting but heavily damaged by inundation water.[210] The "king's daughter"
was placed within a set of three coffins. The outer one is a sarcophagus of
red granite, adorned in the lower part all around with the palace façade
motif, which in this case most likely emulates the façade of the Third
Dynasty pyramid complex of King Djoser at Saqqara (cf. chapter 5 in volume 1).[211] Within this sarcophagus was placed a rectangular coffin that
was decorated with inscriptions in gold foil, badly preserved but mostly
relating to rituals performed in the embalming chamber: such texts are
also known from the royal sarcophagi of the Eighteenth Dynasty of the
New Kingdom, about 500 years later. Within this coffin rested a third,
badly preserved mummy-shaped coffin containing the body of the princess with weapons and royal insignia, of which a mace head, beads from
a flail, and the remains of a *was*-scepter were recovered.[212]

These royal insignia can be connected to the underworld god Osiris,
as the burial seemingly sought to recreate the embalming of Osiris. In
the Egyptian myth, after Osiris had been killed by his brother Seth, he
was embalmed and mummified and as a consequence came alive again
to become the ruler of the underworld. To secure her rebirth in the
underworld, the deceased princess Neferuptah was ritually identified
with Osiris in the embalming chamber.[213] In the comparable burials of
the royal women Nubheteptikhered[214] and Senebtisi,[215] the royal insignia and weapons were found not only in the coffin next to the mummy,
but also in a separate box within the tomb. It seems possible that during the mummification of these high-status individuals, the rituals of the
hour vigil of Osiris were performed, which see different deities approach
Osiris in the twelve hours of the day and the twelve hours of the night, in

---

210. Farag and Iskander 1971.

211. Di. Arnold 1987: 32–35.

212. Farag and Iskander 1971: 81–89.

213. Grajetzki 2014b: 150–153.

214. de Morgan 1895: 107, fig. 250, 109, fig. 253.

215. Mace and Winlock 1916: 77.

order to say spells over the mummy and perhaps also to help in the process of mummification. The rituals of the hour vigil go back to the Old Kingdom and were originally reserved exclusively for royalty, with lists of the required ritual objects (weapons and insignia) forming part of the Old Kingdom pyramid texts.

In the late Middle Kingdom, these ritual objects have only been found in the tombs of a highly select group of individuals, possibly because only they could afford to have the full hour vigil conducted for their burials. However, depictions of these royal objects are found on many coffins of the mid-Twelfth Dynasty,[216] and although the knowledge of the Osiris rituals was therefore more widespread, one can still argue that such knowledge was restricted to a limited number of people close to the royal court. In the late Middle Kingdom, the "Coffin Texts" (cf. section 22.4) are much more rarely inscribed on coffins, and this too may be linked to a restriction of relevant knowledge to a small group at the top of society.

Other known rich burials of the late Middle Kingdom contain a wide variety of objects and it is hard to find any consistent patterns. Such burials still use decorated coffins (although their designs are much simpler than before) but sometimes already include mummy masks or anthropoid coffins. In some cases, the burial equipment used appears simple in comparison to the burials of the early Middle Kingdom. To give some examples, the only objects in the burial of the "general" Senu at Dahshur were the decorated coffin, the mask covering the head of the mummy, and a single pottery bowl,[217] while the burial of the "steward" Khnumhotep at Rifeh contained four sets of coffins for four people, with one of the coffins partly covered with silver foil, just a few personal adornments, and two pottery vessels.[218] Such burials seem to indicate that elaborate burial goods were no longer seen as essential.

---

216. Willems 1997: 357–359.

217. Baba and Yazaha 2015: 12–14, pls. VIII–IX.

218. Grajetzki 2014a.

But more richly equipped burials are also attested, typically the graves of women with a high number of personal adornments, including amulets in the form of faience figures of animals or naked women or of golden fish (cf. section 22.4).[219] A typical burial good of the time is the so-called birth wand.[220] These objects are made of the curved, long sections of hippopotamus tusks, incised on one or both sides with an array of animal figures, deities, and demons, and sometimes inscriptions. Some of these objects show evidence of actual use (such as repair holes and worn edges) and therefore they evidently were not created primarily as burial goods but originally for the world of the living. It is certain that such birth wands were used in rituals connected to childbirth, conducted to protect mother and child. Why they were placed in burials is unclear. Were the wands meant to guarantee the rebirth of the deceased as they were used in life for birth and protection rituals? Or were the figures incised on the wands, generally seen as helpful and protective, meant to protect the deceased against any evil spirits in the underworld? Only the (typically unknown) details of the deceased's personal biography may explain why the wands are only found in some individuals' burials.

One of the highlights of late Middle Kingdom art and craft production is arguably the jewelry found in the "Osirification burials" of the royal women around the pyramids of Amenemhat II, Senusret II, and Senusret III at Lahun and Dahshur. In particular, the craftsmanship of the goldsmiths exhibited in these works belongs to the best ever created in Egypt. The burial of the "king's daughter" Khnumet (perhaps a daughter of Amenemhat II) at Dahshur contained several outstanding pieces, including two crowns.[221] One of these is made of gold wire decorated with flowers that are inlaid with carnelian, lapis lazuli, and turquoise to imitate water-weeds wound around the head. The flowers were created in the cloisonné technique whereby small cells of gold were formed and filled with different materials, typically semi-precious stones. The crown's

---

219. Grajetzki 2014a: 94–113.

220. Quirke 2016.

221. de Morgan 1903: 55–68.

centerpiece is made of carnelian and consists of six Maltese crosses connected with each other by ten gold wires that are decorated with flowers
consisting of five petals, each filled with turquoise.[222]

The cloisonné technique can be seen to have reached perfection in five
pectorals from the burials of three Twelfth Dynasty "king's daughters."
Two of these pieces come from the burial of Sithathoriunet at Lahun,[223]
and the other three from two burials discovered at Dahshur, next to the
pyramid of Senusret III: one from the jewelry box of Sithathor[224] and
another two from the jewelry box of Mereret.[225] The two pectorals of
Sithathoriunet show two falcons framing the names of Kings Senusret II
and Amenemhat III, respectively, with a sun disc crowning the head of
each falcon, the hieroglyphic sign for "one million years" placed underneath the cartouche of the royal names, and the entire scene resting on
a long rectangular box filled with the hieroglyphic sign for "water." The
pectoral with the name of Amenemhat III, while identical in design to
the one with Senusret II's name, is of lesser workmanship.[226] Sithathor's
pectoral from Dahshur was praised as "the acme of the jeweler's art in
ancient Egypt" by Cyril Aldred.[227] Its centerpiece shows the Golden
Horus and the throne name of Senusret II, which is flanked by two
falcons sitting on the hieroglyphic sign for "gold." The falcons wear
the double crown of Upper and Lower Egypt and are placed within a
naos. The two pectorals found in the jewelry box from Mereret's tomb at
Dahshur are similarly framed by a naos. The first piece shows the throne
name of Senusret III, flanked by two griffins trampling enemies.[228] The
scene is topped by a falcon that spreads its wings over the scene. The

---

222. de Morgan 1903: 61, pl. IX; Aldred 1971: 186, pl. 28.

223. Brunton 1920: 28–29, pls. I, VI, XI.

224. de Morgan 1895: pls. XV.1, XVI, XXI.

225. de Morgan 1895: pls. XIX–XXI.

226. Brunton 1920: 29.

227. Aldred 1971: 192.

228. de Morgan 1895: pls. XIX.1, XXI.

second pectoral shows a similar falcon; underneath it, King Amenemhat III is twice depicted smiting an enemy.[229] The scene is filled with hiero-glyphs, which creates an overcrowded impression, and the quality of craftsmanship no longer reaches the high standard of the pectorals pro-duced under Senusret II.[230]

In comparison to the pieces discussed, the jewelry found in the unlooted burial of the "king's daughter" Neferuptah, a daughter of Amenemhat III, is much plainer.[231] As no pieces of royal jewelry can be safely attributed to the time of the Thirteenth Dynasty, it is impossible to trace the further development of personal adornment at the royal court during this period.

22.7.3. The age of the god Sobek

In many ways, the late Middle Kingdom period can be considered the age of Sobek, as this crocodile god became the principal deity associated with kingship, especially under Amenemhat III and perhaps in connec-tion with the focus of this king's activities in the Fayum.

Amenemhat III's main building project was the construction of his funerary complex at Hawara.[232] The king had first started building a pyramid at Dahshur, but there were problems with the construction site, and the complex was never used for burying the king.[233] Around Year 20 of his reign, the king instead started a new funerary complex at Hawara at the entrance to the Fayum, not far from Lahun, which became the headquarters for managing the building process.[234] In Greco-Roman times, a huge temple connected to the Hawara pyramid complex became

---

229. de Morgan 1895: pls. XX.2, XXI.

230. Cf. Aldred 1971: 194: "The workmanship is inferior to earlier pectorals of the Twelfth Dynasty."

231. Grajetzki 2014b: 70–71.

232. Blom-Böer 2006.

233. Di. Arnold 1987: 83–84, 93.

234. Quirke 1990: 170–173; Kemp 2006: 211; Grajetzki 2009b.

famous as the "labyrinth"; today, this temple is heavily destroyed and it is hard to get a clear picture of its original appearance.[235] The entire pyramid complex seems to have been inspired by Djoser's mortuary complex at Saqqara which dates to the Third Dynasty of the Old Kingdom (see chapter 5 in volume 1),[236] attesting to the deep interest in the past that is so noticeable throughout the Middle Kingdom. Judging from the preserved remains and ancient descriptions, Amenemhat III's Hawara complex was richly adorned with reliefs and statues.[237] The statuary is especially remarkable for the many new types introduced, often referring back to forms of the Early Dynastic period.[238] For instance, several monumental sphinxes of the king show a human head wearing an impressive lion mane,[239] whereas most Old and Middle Kingdom royal sphinxes have a human head with the royal *nemes* headdress, but not a lion's mane.

Also other monuments of King Amenemhat III in the Fayum demonstrate his special focus on this region. At Biahmu, close to the Fayum Lake, two colossal statues were erected that once looked across the lake. At Medinet Madi, the king had a small chapel built for Sobek and the goddess Renenutet. It later formed the core of a Ptolemaic temple that incorporated the older temple structure, which caused the original Middle Kingdom structure to be still well-preserved. A further, considerably larger temple was built, or at least extended, at Shedet, the main town in the Fayum region whose principal deity was Sobek.[240]

However, in the sources of the late Middle Kingdom, Sobek was often mentioned as "lord of Sumenu," a town in Upper Egypt, indicating that the god was not restricted to the Fayum region. It was indeed Sobek of Shedet who was also the main deity invoked in the texts preserved within the king's funerary complex at Hawara. The general importance

235. Uphill 2000.

236. Freed 2010: 905.

237. Blom-Böer 2006: 40–43, 139–191.

238. Freed 2010: 905.

239. Fay 1996: pls. 90–92.

240. Zecchi 2010: 38–39.

of the god Sobek is also seen in the royal names of the period. While Queen Sobekneferu is the first member of the ruling family to invoke Sobek in her name, several kings of the Thirteenth Dynasty are called Sobekhotep, a name that had already been very popular in the Old Kingdom. In the temple dedicated to Sobek and the goddess Renenutet at Medinet Madi in the Fayum, the depictions clearly convey that the god gave Amenemhat III the power to be king of Egypt, and Amenemhat III is even called the "son of Sobek." Half of the roughly twenty known Thirteenth Dynasty royal cylinder seals and beads inscribed with a king's name and that of a deity mention Sobek.[241]

The most remarkable testimony of Sobek's importance to Middle Kingdom kingship is a papyrus scroll from a Theban tomb with two hymns to Sobek,[242] who appears as an all-powerful god, with a long list of the places over which he presides, including Sumenu and the major cities of Thebes and Heliopolis. He is described as "ruler of the foreign lands" and "ruler of the rivers" and as the one "at whom the two lands yell for fear of him," with powerful sexual qualities ascribed to him as the "ejaculating bull" and the "bull of the Hathors." In the second hymn, Sobek is identified with Horus in the Osiris myth and therefore given a prominent funerary role, as it is Horus who brings his dead father Osiris back to life.[243] A further hymn to the diadem of Sobek is known from a papyrus dating to the Second Intermediate Period, which was most likely composed in the Middle Kingdom.[244] Many of the phrases and epithets used in these hymns for describing the god Sobek were adapted for other deities in later periods.

241. Ryholt 1997: 336–357.

242. Gardiner 1957.

243. Zecchi 2010: 95–101.

244. Lichtheim 1975: 201–202.

22.8. In conclusion

Although it was seemingly easy to mark, for the purpose of this chapter, the beginning of the Middle Kingdom and its specific culture with the creation of one outstanding architectural monument, the mortuary complex of Mentuhotep II at Deir el-Bahri in Thebes (see section 22.2), it is not possible to demarcate the end of Middle Kingdom culture as precisely. Similarly to their predecessors, the kings of the Thirteenth Dynasty were still buried in pyramids and continued to build temples and to erect statues, albeit on a more modest scale. Even the beginning of Middle Kingdom culture was clearly observable only at the centers of royal power, but with difficulties elsewhere in the country. While pottery and other materials can be organized in distinct phases, these do not easily correlate with our customary historical divisions into dynasties. Material culture develops at its own speed, not always in sync with political history, and many of the aspects discussed in this chapter therefore feature also in the Second Intermediate Period (chapters 23 and 24 in volume 3).

REFERENCES

Aldred, C. 1971. *Jewels of the pharaohs: Egyptian jewellery of the Dynastic period.* London: Thames & Hudson.

Allen, J.P. 2002. *The Heqanakht papyri.* New York: Metropolitan Museum of Art.

Allen, J.P. 2008. The historical inscription of Khnumhotep at Dahshur: preliminary report. *BASOR* 352: 29–39.

Altenmüller, H. 2015. *Zwei Annalenfragmente aus dem frühen Mittleren Reich.* Hamburg: Buske.

Andrews, C.A.R. 1981. *Catalogue of Egyptian antiquities in the British Museum: jewellery, vol. I.* London: British Museum Press.

Arnold, Di. 1974a. *Der Tempel des Königs Mentuhotep von Deir el-Bahari, vol. I: Architektur und Deutung.* Mainz: Zabern.

Arnold, Di. 1974b. *Der Tempel des Königs Mentuhotep von Deir el-Bahari, vol. II: die Wandreliefs des Sanktuares.* Mainz: Zabern.

Arnold, Di. 1976. *Gräber des Alten und Mittleren Reiches in El-Tarif.* Mainz: Zabern.

Arnold, Di. 1981. *Der Tempel des Königs Mentuhotep von Deir el-Bahari, vol. III: die königlichen Beigaben.* Mainz: Zabern.

Arnold, Di. 1987. *Der Pyramidenbezirk des Königs Amenemhet III. in Dahschur, vol. I: Pyramide.* Mainz: Zabern.

Arnold, Di. 1988. *The pyramid complex of Senwosret I: the south cemeteries of Lisht, vol. I.* New York: Metropolitan Museum of Art.

Arnold, Di. 1992. *The pyramid complex of Senwosret I: the south cemeteries of Lisht, vol. III.* New York: Metropolitan Museum of Art.

Arnold, Di. 2002a. Die letzte Ruhestätte ägyptischer Beamter. *Antike Welt* 2002, no. 6: 621–629.

Arnold, Di. 2002b. *The pyramid complex of Senwosret III at Dahshur: architectural studies.* New York: Metropolitan Museum of Art.

Arnold, Di. 2008. *Middle Kingdom tomb architecture at Lisht.* New York: Metropolitan Museum of Art.

Arnold, Di. 2015. *The pyramid complex of Amenemhat I at Lisht.* New York: Metropolitan Museum of Art.

Arnold, Do. 1991. Amenemhat I and the early Twelfth Dynasty at Thebes. *Metropolitan Museum Journal* 26: 5–48.

Arnold, Do. 2015a. Statue of the reporter in Thebes, Sebekemsaf. In Oppenheim, A., Arnold, Do., Arnold, Di., and Yamamoto, K. (eds.), *Ancient Egypt transformed: the Middle Kingdom.* New York: Metropolitan Museum of Art, 135–137 (no. 67).

Arnold, Do. 2015b. Statue head of a normarch, possibly Ibu. In Oppenheim, A., Arnold, Do., Arnold, Di., and Yamamoto, K. (eds.), *Ancient Egypt transformed: the Middle Kingdom.* New York: Metropolitan Museum of Art, 127 (no. 61).

Bernbeck, R. 1994. *Die Auflösung der häuslichen Produktionsweise.* Berlin: Reimer.

Baba, M., and Yazaha, K. 2015. Burial assemblages of the late Middle Kingdom: shaft-tombs in Dahshur North. In Miniaci, G., and Grajetzki, W. (eds.), *The world of Middle Kingdom Egypt (2000–1550): contributions on archaeology, art, religion, and written sources, vol. I.* London: Golden House, 1–24.

Barbotin, C., and Clère, J.J. 1991. L'inscription de Sésostris Ier à Tôd. *BIFAO* 91: 1–32.

Berlev, O. 1972. *Трудовое население Египта в эпоху Среднего царства.* Moscow: Nauka.

Bisson de la Roque, F. 1931. *Médamoud: fouilles de l'Institut Français d'Archéologie Orientale du Caire (année 1930)*. Cairo: Institut français d'archéologie orientale.

Bisson de la Roque, F., and Clère, J.J. 1929. *Médamoud: fouilles de l'Institut Français d'Archéologie Orientale du Caire (année 1928)*. Cairo: Institut français d'archéologie orientale.

Blackman, A.M. 1914. *The rock tombs of Meir, part 1: the tomb-chapel of Ukhḥotp's son Senbi*. London: Egypt Exploration Society.

Blackman, A.M., and Apted, M.R. 1953. *The rock tombs of Meir, part 5: the tomb-chapels of Ukhhotpe son of Iam (A, no. 3), Senbi son of Ukhhotpe son of Senbi (B, no. 3), and Ukhhotpe son of Ukhhotpe and Heny-Hery-Ib (C, no. 1)*. London: Egypt Exploration Society.

Blom-Böer, I. 2006. *Die Tempelanlage Amenemhets III. in Hawara: das Labyrinth, Bestandsaufnahme und Auswertung der Architektur- und Inventarfragmente*. Leiden: NINO.

Borchardt, L. 1899. Der zweite Papyrusfund von Kahun und die zeitliche Festlegung des Mittleren Reiches der ägyptischen Geschichte. *ZÄS* 37: 89–103.

Bourriau, J. 1988. *Pharaohs and mortals: Egyptian art in the Middle Kingdom*. Cambridge: Cambridge University Press.

Bourriau, J. 1991. Patterns of change in burial customs. In Quirke, S. (ed.), *Middle Kingdom studies*. New Malden: SIA, 3–20.

Brunton, G. 1920. *Lahun I: the treasure*. London: Quaritch.

Brunton, G. 1927. *Qau and Badari I*. London: Quaritch.

Brunton, G. 1928. *Qau and Badari II*. London: Quaritch.

Bussmann, R. 2010. *Die Provinztempel Ägyptens von der 0. bis zur 11. Dynastie: Archäologie und Geschichte einer gesellschaftlichen Institution zwischen Residenz und Provinz*. Leiden: Brill.

Caisino, E. 2017. Remarks on ancient Egyptian cartonnage mummy masks from the late Old Kingdom to the end of the New Kingdom. In Chyla, J.M., Dębowska-Ludwin, J., Rosińska-Balik, K., and Walsh, C. (eds.), *Current research in Egyptology 2016: proceedings of the seventeenth annual symposium*. Oxford: Oxbow, 56–73.

Collier, M., and Quirke, S. 2002. *The UCL Lahun papyri: letters*. Oxford: Archaeopress.

Collier, M., and Quirke, S. 2004. *The UCL Lahun papyri: religious, literary, legal, mathematical and medical*. Oxford: Archaeopress.

Collier, M., and Quirke, S. 2006. *The UCL Lahun papyri: accounts*. Oxford: Archaeopress.

Connor, S. 2015a. Upper part of a statue of a Thirteenth Dynasty king seated. In Oppenheim, A., Arnold, Do., Arnold, Di., and Yamamoto, K. (eds.), *Ancient Egypt transformed: the Middle Kingdom*. New York: Metropolitan Museum of Art, 90 (no. 32).

Connor, S. 2015b. The statue of the steward Nemtyhotep (Berlin ÄM 157000) and some considerations about royal and private portrait under Amenemhat III. In Miniaci, G., and Grajetzki, W. (eds.), *The world of Middle Kingdom Egypt (2000–1550 BC): contributions on archaeology, art, religion, and written sources, vol. I*. London: Golden House, 57–79.

Connor, S. 2018. Sculpture workshops: who, where and for whom. In Miniaci, G., Moreno Garcia, J.C., Quirke, S., and Stauder, A. (eds.), *The arts of making in ancient Egypt: voices, images and objects of material producers, 2000–1550 BC*. Leiden: Sidestone, 11–30.

Craig Patch, D. 2005. Jewelry in the early Eighteenth Dynasty. In Roehrig, C.H. (ed.), *Hatshepsut: from queen to pharaoh*. New York: Metropolitan Museum of Art, 191–195.

Damarant, A., Abd el-Raziq, Y., Okasha, A., Wegner, J., Cahail, K., and Wegner, J. 2015. A new temple: the *mahat* of Nebhepetre at Abydos. *EA* 46: 3–7.

D'Amicone, E. 1988. Le tombe rupestri dei governatori di Gau el Kebir: Uahka I, Uahka II e Ibu. In Donadori Roveri, A.M. (ed.), *Le credenze religiose*. Milan: Mondadori Electa, 114–127.

Delange, E. 1987. *Catalogue des statues égyptiennes du Moyen Empire, 2060–1560 J.-C.* Paris: Éditions de la réunion des musées nationaux.

de Morgan, J. 1895. *Fouilles a Dahchour, Mars–Juin 1894*. Vienna: Holzhausen.

de Morgan, J. 1903. *Fouilles a Dahchour, 1894–1895*. Vienna: Holzhausen.

Di Teodoro, M. 2018. *Labour organisations in Middle Kingdom Egypt*. London: Golden House.

Dubiel, U. 2008. *Amulette, Siegel und Perlen: Studien zu Typologie und Tragesitte im Alten und Mittleren Reich*. Fribourg: Academic Press; Göttingen: Vandenhoeck & Ruprecht.

El-Husseiny, S., and Okasha Khafagy, A. 2010. The Dahshur tomb of the vizier Siese rediscovered. *EA* 36: 21–24.

Engelbach, R. 1923. *Harageh*. London: Quaritch.

Eschenbrenner-Diemer, G. 2017. From the workshop to the grave: the case of wooden funerary models. In Miniaci, G., Betrò, M., and Quirke, S. (eds.), *Company of images: modelling the imaginary world of Middle Kingdom Egypt (2000–1500 BC)*. Leuven: Peeters, 133–191.

Farag, N., and Iskander, Z. 1971. *The discovery of Neferwptah*. Cairo: General Organisation for Government Printing Offices.

Favry, N. 2004. *Le normarque sous le règne de Sésostris Ier*. Paris: Presse de l'Université Paris-Sorbonne.

Fay, B. 1988. Amenemhat V - Vienna/Aswan. *MDAIK* 44: 67–77.

Fay, B. 1996. *The Louvre Sphinx and royal sculpture from the reign of Amenemhat II*. Mainz: Zabern.

Fechheimer, H. 1922. *Die Plastik der Ägypter*. Berlin: Bruno Cassirer Verlag.

Firth, C.M., and Gunn, B. 1926. *Excavations at Saqqara: Teti pyramid cemeteries*. Cairo: Institut français d'archéologie orientale.

Fischer, H.G. 1959. An example of Memphite influence in a Theban stela of the Eleventh Dynasty. *Artibus Asiae* 22: 240–252.

Fischer, H.G. 1975. Flachbildkunst des Mittleren Reiches. In Vandersleyen, C. (ed.), *Das Alte Ägypten*. Berlin: Propyläen-Verlag, 292–304.

Franke, D. 1991. The career of Khnumhotep III of Beni Hasan and the so-called "decline of the nomarchs." In Quirke, S. (ed.), *Middle Kingdom studies*. New Malden: SIA, 51–67.

Franke, D. 1994. *Das Heiligtum des Heqaib auf Elephantine*. Heidelberg: Heidelberger Orientverlag.

Franke, D. 2003a. Middle Kingdom hymns and other sundry religious texts: an inventory. In Meyer, S. (ed.), *Egypt, temple of the whole world: studies in honour of Jan Assman*. Leiden: Brill, 95–135.

Franke, D. 2003b. Die Stele Jayseneb aus der Schachtanlage K01.12. In Polz, D., and Seiler, A. (eds.), *Die Pyramidenanlage des Königs Nub-Cheper-Re Intef in Dra' Abu el-Naga*. Mainz: Zabern, 73–83.

Freed, R.E. 1996. Stela workshops of early Dynasty 12. In Der Manuelian, P. (ed.), *Studies in honor of William Kelly Simpson, vol. I*. Boston: Museum of Fine Arts, 297–336.

Freed, R.E. 2010. Sculpture of the Middle Kingdom. In Lloyd, A.B. (ed.), *A companion to ancient Egypt*. Malden, MA: Wiley-Blackwell, 882–912.

Freed, R.E. 2015. Head of a statue of a queen or princess as a Sphinx. In Oppenheim, A., Arnold, Do., Arnold, Di., and Yamamoto, K. (eds.),

Ancient Egypt transformed: the Middle Kingdom. New York: Metropolitan Museum of Art, 107–108 (no. 49).

Gardiner, A.H. 1957. Hymns to Sobk in a Ramesseum papyrus. *RdE* 11: 41–56.

Garstang, J. 1907. *The burial customs of ancient Egypt, as illustrated by tombs of the Middle Kingdom, being a report of excavations made in the necropolis of Beni Hassan 1902-3-4.* London: Archibald Constable.

Gautier, J.-E., and Jéquier, G. 1902. *Mémoire sur les fouilles de Licht.* Cairo: Institut français d'archéologie orientale.

Generalverwaltung der Königlichen Museen zu Berlin (ed.) 1913. *Aegyptische Inschriften aus den königlichen Museen zu Berlin III: Inschriften des Mittleren Reiches, erster Teil.* Leipzig: Hinrichs.

Gestermann, L. 1987. *Kontinuität und Wandel in Politik und Verwaltung des frühen Mittleren Reiches in Ägypten* Wiesbaden: Harrassowitz.

Grajetzki, W. 1997. Bemerkungen zu den Bürgermeistern (*ḥȝtj*ˁ) von Qaw el-Kebir im Mittleren Reich. *GM* 156: 55–62.

Grajetzki, W. 2001. *Two treasurers of the late Middle Kingdom.* Oxford: Archaeopress.

Grajetzki, W. 2004. *Harageh: an Egyptian burial ground for the rich around 1800 BC.* London: Golden House.

Grajetzki, W. 2006. *The Middle Kingdom of ancient Egypt: history, archaeology and society.* London: Duckworth.

Grajetzki, W. 2009a. *Court officials of the Egyptian Middle Kingdom.* London: Duckworth.

Grajetzki, W. 2009b. Urkunden aus einem Pyramidenbaubüro des Mittleren Reiches. *Sokar* 19: 46–51.

Grajetzki, W. 2014a. The tomb of Khnumhotep at Rifeh. In Dodson, A.M., Johnston, J.J., and Monkhouse, W. (eds.), *A good scribe and exceedingly wise man: studies in honour of W.J. Tait.* London: Golden House, 99–111.

Grajetzki, W. 2014b. *Tomb treasures of the late Middle Kingdom: the archaeology of female burials.* Philadelphia: University of Pennsylvania Press.

Grajetzki, W. 2017a. A zoo *en miniature*: the impact of the central government on the rise and fall of animal/zoomorphic amulets' production during the First Intermediate Period and Middle Kingdom. In Miniaci, G., Betrò, M., and Quirke, S. (eds.), *Company of images: modelling the imaginary world of Middle Kingdom Egypt (2000–1500 BC).* Leuven: Peeters, 193–212.

Grajetzki, W. 2017b. Sinuhe, Senusret I and the centralisation of Egypt. In Feder, F., Spereslage, G., and Steinborn, F. (eds.), *Ägypten begreifen: Erika Endesfelder in memoriam*. London: Golden House, 155–162.

Habachi, L. 1952. Khatâʿna-Qantîr: importance. *ASAE* 52: 443–479.

Habachi, L. 1963. King Nebhetepre Mentuhotp: his monuments, place in history, deification and unusual representations in the form of gods. *MDAIK* 19: 16–52.

Habachi, L. 1985. *Elephantine IV: the sanctuary of Heqaib*. Mainz: Zabern.

Hagen, F. 2012. *An ancient Egyptian literary text in context: the instruction of Ptahhotep*. Leuven: Peeters.

Harvey, D. 2005 *A brief history of neoliberalism*. Oxford: Oxford University Press.

Hayes, W.C. 1953. *The scepter of Egypt, vol. I*. New York: Metropolitan Museum of Art.

Horváth, Z. 2009. Temple(s) and town at El-Lahun: a study of ancient toponyms in the el-Lahun papyri. In Silverman, D.P., Simpson, W.K., and Wegner, J. (eds.), *Archaism and innovation: studies in the culture of Middle Kingdom Egypt*. New Haven, CT: Yale Egyptological Seminar, 171–203.

Ilin-Tomich, A. 2017. *From workshop to sanctuary: the production of Middle Kingdom memorial stelae*. London: Golden House.

Jaroš-Deckert, B. 1984. *Das Grab des Jnj-jtj.f: die Wandmalereien der XI. Dynastie* (Grabung im Asasif 1963–1970, vol. V). Mainz: Zabern.

Jéquier, G. 1933. *Deux pyramides du moyen empire*. Cairo: Institut français d'archéologie orientale.

Kanawati, N., Evans, L., and Mourad, A.-L. 2014. *Beni Hassan, vol. I: the tomb of Khnumhotep II*. Oxford: Oxbow.

Kemp, B. 2006. *Ancient Egypt: anatomy of a civilization*. London and New York: Routledge. 2nd rev. ed.

Kubisch, S. 2011. *Lebensbilder der 2. Zwischenzeit: biographische Inschriften der 13.-17. Dynastie*. Berlin: De Gruyter.

Leprohon, R.J. 1978. The personnel of the Middle Kingdom funerary stelae. *JARCE* 15: 33–33.

Lichtheim, M. 1975. *Ancient Egyptian Literature, vol. I: the Old and Middle Kingdoms*. Berkeley and Los Angeles: University of California Press.

Lloyd, A.B. 1992. The great inscription of Khnumhotep II at Beni Hasan. In Lloyd, A.B. (ed.), *Studies in pharaonic religion and society in honour of J. Gwyn Griffiths*. London: Egypt Exploration Society, 21–36.

Luft, U. 1982. Illahunstudien, I: zu der Chronologie und den Beamten in den Briefen aus Illahun. *Oikumene* 3: 101–156.

Luft, U. 1992. *Das Archiv von* Illahun: Briefe *1*. Berlin: Akademie-Verlag.

Luft, U. 2006. *Urkunden zur Chronologie der späten 12. Dynastie: Briefe aus Lahun.* Vienna: Verlag der Österreichischen Akademie der Wissenschaften.

Mace, A.C., and Winlock, H.E. 1916. *The Tomb of Senebtisi at Lisht.* New York: Metropolitan Museum of Art.

Miniaci, G. 2017. Unbroken stories: Middle Kingdom faience figurines in their archaeological context. In Miniaci, G., Betrò, M., and Quirke, S. (eds.), *Company of images: modelling the imaginary world of Middle Kingdom Egypt (2000–1500 BC).* Leuven: Peeters, 235–284.

Miniaci, G., and Quirke, S. 2009. Reconceiving the tomb in the late Middle Kingdom: the burial of the accountant of the main enclosure Neferhotep at Dra Abu al-Naga. *BIFAO* 109: 339–383.

Moeller, N. 2016. *The archaeology of urbanism in ancient Egypt from the Predynastic period to the end of the Middle Kingdom.* Cambridge: Cambridge University Press.

Morris, E. 2017. Middle Kingdom clappers, dancers, birth magic and the reinvention of ritual. In Miniaci, G., Betrò, M., and Quirke, S. (eds.), *Company of images: modelling the imaginary world of Middle Kingdom Egypt (2000–1500 BC).* Leuven: Peeters, 285–335.

Müller, Ma. 2013. Hatschepsut und der Umgang mit der Vergangenheit. In Bickel, S. (ed.), *Vergangenheit und Zukunft: Studien zum historischen Bewußtsein in der Thutmosidenzeit.* Basel: Schwabe, 187–202.

Müller, Mi. 2015a. New approaches to the study of households in Middle Kingdom and Second Intermediate Period Egypt. In Miniaci, G., and Grajetzki, W. (eds.), *The world of Middle Kingdom Egypt (2000–1550 BC): contributions on archaeology, art, religion, and written sources, vol. I.* London: Golden House, 237–255.

Müller, Mi. 2015b. Late Middle Kingdom neighborhood of Tell el-Dabʿa/Avaris. In Müller, Mi. (ed.), *Household studies in complex societies.* Chicago: The Oriental Institute of the University of Chicago, 339–370.

Müller, W., and Forstner-Müller, I. 2015. A newly discovered "Soul House" in Assuan. In Jiménez-Serrano, A., and von Pilgrim, C. (eds.), *From the Delta to the Cataract: studies dedicated to Mohamed el-Bialy.* Leiden: Brill, 189–201.

Naville, E. 1907. *The XIth Dynasty temple at Deir el-Bahari I*. London: Egypt Exploration Fund.

Naville, E. 1910. *The XIth Dynasty temple at Deir el-Bahari II*. London: Egypt Exploration Fund.

Nelson, M., and Kalos, K. 2000. Concessions du Moyen Empire découvertes au nord-ouest du Ramesseum. *Memnonia* 11: 131–152.

Newberry, P. 1893a. *Beni Hasan I*. London: Egypt Exploration Society.

Newberry, P. 1893b. *Beni Hasan II*. London: Egypt Exploration Society.

Newberry, P. 1895. *El Bersheh: the tomb of Tehuti-Hetep*. London: Egypt Exploration Society.

Oppenheim, A. 2006. Identifying artists in the time of Senusret III: the mastaba of the vizier Nebit (North Mastaba 18) at Dahshur. In Bárta, M., Coppens, F., and Krejčí, J. (eds.), *Abusir and Saqqara in the year 2005*. Prague: Czech Institute of Egyptology, 116–132.

Oppenheim, A. 2015a. Artist and workshops: the complexity of creation. In Oppenheim, A., Arnold, Do., Arnold, Di., and Yamamoto, K. (eds.), *Ancient Egypt transformed: the Middle Kingdom*. New York: Metropolitan Museum of Art, 23–27.

Oppenheim, A. 2015b. Sculptures of Senwosret III. In Oppenheim, A., Arnold, Do., Arnold, Di., and Yamamoto, K. (eds.), *Ancient Egypt transformed: the Middle Kingdom*. New York: Metropolitan Museum of Art, 78–83.

Pantalacci, L. 1996. Fonctionnaires et analphabètes: sur quelques pratiques administratives observées à Balat. *BIFAO* 96: 359–367.

Parkinson, R.B. 1991. *Voices from ancient Egypt: an anthology of Middle Kingdom writings*. London: British Museum Press.

Parkinson, R.B. 2002. *Poetry and culture in Middle Kingdom Egypt: a dark side to perfection*. London: Continuum.

Parkinson, R.B. 2009. *Reading ancient Egyptian poetry: among other histories*. Malden, MA: Wiley-Blackwell.

Parkinson, R.B. 2015. The impact of Middle Kingdom literature: ancient and modern. In Oppenheim, A., Arnold, Do., Arnold, Di., and Yamamoto, K. (eds.), *Ancient Egypt transformed: the Middle Kingdom*. New York: Metropolitan Museum of Art, 180–183.

Petrie, W.M.F. 1888. *A season in Egypt 1987*. London: Field & Tuer.

Petrie, W.M.F. 1890. *Kahun, Gurob and Hawara*. London and New York: Kegan Paul International.

Petrie, W.M.F. 1891. *Illahun, Kahun and Gurob*. London: David Nutt.

Petrie, W.M.F. 1930. *Antaeopolis: the tombs of Qau.* London: Quaritch.

Petrie, W.M.F., Brunton, G., and Murray, M.A. 1923. *Lahun, II.* London: Quaritch.

Postel, L., and Regen, I. 2005. Annales héliopolitaines et fragments de Sésostris Ier réemployés dans la porte de Bâb al-Tawfiq au Caire. *BIFAO* 105: 229–293.

Quirke, S. 1990. *The administration of Egypt in the late Middle Kingdom.* New Malden: SIA Publishing.

Quirke, S. 2003. "Art" and "the Artist" in late Middle Kingdom administration. In Quirke, S. (ed.), *Discovering Egypt from the Neva: the Egyptological legacy of Oleg D. Berlev.* Berlin: Achet Verlag, 85–105.

Quirke, S. 2004. *Titles and bureaux of Egypt, 1850–1700 BC.* London: Golden House.

Quirke, S. 2005. *Lahun: a town in Egypt, 1800 BC, and the history of its landscape.* London: Golden House.

Quirke, S. 2015a. Stand in the shape of a male dwarf. In Oppenheim, A., Arnold, Do., Arnold, Di., and Yamamoto, K. (eds.), *Ancient Egypt transformed: the Middle Kingdom.* New York: Metropolitan Museum of Art, 205 (no. 139).

Quirke, S. 2015b. Stand in the shape of a woman. In Oppenheim, A., Arnold, Do., Arnold, Di., and Yamamoto, K. (eds.), *Ancient Egypt transformed: the Middle Kingdom.* New York: Metropolitan Museum of Art, 205–206 (no. 140).

Quirke, S. 2016. *Birth tusks: the armoury of health in context, Egypt 1800 BC.* London: Golden House.

Richards, J. 2005. *Society and death in ancient Egypt: mortuary landscapes of the Middle Kingdom.* Cambridge: Cambridge University Press.

Roehrig, C.H. 1995. The early Middle Kingdom cemeteries at Thebes and the tomb of Djari. In Assmann, J., Dziobek, E., Guksch, H., and Kampp, F. (eds.), *Thebanische Beamtennekropolen: neue Perspektiven archäologischer Forschung.* Heidelberg: Heidelberger Orientverlag, 255–269.

Roehrig, C.H. 2003. The Middle Kingdom tomb of Wah at Thebes. In Strudwick, N., and Taylor, J.H. (eds.), *The Theban necropolis: past, present and future.* London: British Museum Press, 11–13.

Russmann, E.D. 1989. *Egyptian sculpture: Cairo and Luxor.* Austin: University of Texas Press.

Ryholt, K. 1997. *The political situation in Egypt during the Second Intermediate Period, c. 1800–1550 BC.* Copenhagen: Museum Tusculanum Press.

Saleh, M., and Sourouzian, H. 1987. *The Egyptian Museum, Cairo: official catalogue.* Mainz: Zabern.

Salvador, C. 2015. Modello di casa o "casa dell'anima." In Giovetti, P., and Picchi, D. (eds.), *Egitto: splendore millenario: la collezione di Leiden a Bologna.* Milan: Skira, 519–529.

Schäfer, H. 1908. *Priestergräber und andere Grabfunde vom Ende des Alten Reiches bis zur griechischen Zeit vom Totentempel de Ne-user-rê.* Leipzig: Hinrichs.

Schenkel, W. 1975. Die Bauinschrift Sesostris' I. im Satet-Tempel von Elephantine. *MDAIK* 31: 109–125.

Seidlmayer, S.J. 1990. *Gräberfelder aus dem Übergang vom Alten zum Mittleren Reich.* Heidelberg: Heidelberger Orientverlag.

Seidlmayer, S.J. 2007. People at Beni Hassan: contributions to a model of ancient Egyptian rural society. In Hawass, Z.A., and Richards, J. (eds.), *The archaeology and art of ancient Egypt: essays in honor of David B. O'Connor, vol. 2.* Cairo: Supreme Council of Antiquities, 351–368.

Shedid, A.G. 1994. *Die Felsgräber von Beni Hassan in Mittelägypten.* Mainz: Zabern.

Simpson, W.K. 1974. *The terrace of the Great God at Abydos: the offering chapels of Dynasties 12 and 13.* Warminster: Aris & Phillips.

Simpson, W.K. 1988. Lepsius Pyramid LV at Dahshur: the mastaba of Si-Ese, vizier of Amenemhet II. In Baines, J. (ed.), *Pyramid studies and other essays presented to I.E.S. Edwards.* London: Egypt Exploration Society, 57–60.

Smith, W.S. 1981. *The art and architecture of ancient Egypt.* Harmondsworth, UK: Penguin. 2nd rev. ed.

Stauder, A. 2013. *Linguistic dating of Middle Egyptian literary texts.* Hamburg: Widmaier.

Stefanović, D. 2006. *The holders of regular military titles in the period of the Middle Kingdom: dossiers.* London: Golden House.

Strouhal, E., and Klír, P. 2006. The anthropological examination of two queens from the pyramid of Amenemhat III at Dahshur. In Bárta, M., Coppens, F., and Krejći, J. (eds.), *Abusir and Saqqara in the year 2005.* Prague: Czech Institute of Egyptology, 133–146.

Stünkel, I. 2015. Fish pendant. In Oppenheim, A., Arnold, Do., Arnold, Di., and Yamamoto, K. (eds.), *Ancient Egypt transformed: the Middle Kingdom*. New York: Metropolitan Museum of Art, 203–204 (no. 137).

Troy, L. 1986. *Patterns of queenship in ancient Egyptian myth and history*. Stockholm: Almqvist & Wiksell International.

Uphill, E. 2000. *Pharoah's gateway to eternity: the Hawara labyrinth of king Amenemhat III*. London and New York: Kegan Paul International.

Vernus, P. 1986. *Le surnom au Moyen Empire*. Rome: Pontificium Institutum Biblicum.

Wegner, J. 2009. The tomb of Senwosret III at Abydos: considerations on the origins and development of the royal *amduat-* tomb. In Silverman, D.P., Simpson, W.K., and Wegner, J. (eds.), *Archaism and innovation: studies in the culture of Middle Kingdom Egypt*. New Haven, CT: Yale Egyptological Seminar, 103–169.

Wegner, J., and Cahail, K. 2015. Royal funerary equipment of a king Sobekhotep at South Abydos: evidence for the tombs of Sobekhotep IV and Neferhotep I? *JARCE* 51: 123–164.

Wildung, D. 1984. *Sesostris und Amenemhet: Ägypten im Mittleren Reich*. Munich: Hirmer.

Wildung, D. 2018. Afrikanisches in der ägyptischen Kunst? In Pischikova, E., Budka, J., and Griffin, K. (eds.), *Thebes in the first millennium BC: art and archaeology of the Kushite period and beyond*. London: Golden House, 323–331.

Willems, H. 1988. *Chests of life: a study of the typology and conceptual development of Middle Kingdom standard class coffins*. Leiden: Ex Oriente Lux.

Willems, H. 1997. The embalmer embalmed: remarks on the meaning of the decoration of some Middle Kingdom coffins. In van Dijk, J.J. (ed.), *Essays on ancient Egypt in honour of Herman te Velde*. Groningen: Styx, 343–372.

Winlock, H.E. 1921. The Egyptian Expedition 1920–1921, III: excavations at Thebes. *Metropolitan Museum of Art Bulletin* 16, no. 11/II: 29–53.

Winlock, H.E. 1942. *Excavations at Deir el-Baḥri, 1911–1931*. New York: Macmillan.

Yamazaki, S. 2008. Archaeological and iconographic analysis of the use of funerary personal adornments in the Middle Kingdom of ancient Egypt. *Sociology and Anthropology* 6: 433–446.

Zecchi, M. 2010. *Sobek of Shedet: the crocodile god in the Fayyum in the Dynastic period*. Todi: Tau Editrice.

Index

Abattum, 260, 349, 364
Abba-El, 389
Abba-El II, 389
Abda-el, 415, 417, 418n50
Abdi-Erah, 420
Abgig, 701, 707
Abi-ešuh, 430, 471–72, 478, 571, 578,
    625–32
Abi-sare, 203, 230n140, 234–36, 244,
    246, 273
Abihu, 82
Abilulu, 410n10
Abishai, 704, 803
Abkau, 785
Abu Ghalib, 68
Abu Seyal, 739
Abu-šalim, 423
Abusir, 58, 874
Abydos, 68, 75, 86, 89, 92, 94, 98–99,
    682–83, 698, 702–3, 710–11,
    714, 747, 815–17, 823, 830, 855,
    866–68, 878, 880, 893–94,
    899–900, 904
Acemhöyük, 33–35, 327, 507, 519
Adab, 135, 224, 281, 599n157
Adad, 242n200, 251, 282, 370, 372, 435

Adal-šenni, 444
AdamDUN, 445
Adhaim River, 331
Adulis, 761, 763, 766
Aegean Sea, 4, 26, 56, 64, 91, 104,
    425, 781, 798, 802–3, 830
Agum
    II, 571
    III, 571, 643–44
Agum-kakrime, 639
Ah-Purattim, 332
Ahanakht I, 94, 106, 683, 688
Ahazum, 358
Ahmose, 16, 26, 676
Ahu-ṭab, 257
Ahuna, 364
Ahušina, 430, 630n304
Akhmim, 48, 81
Akkad, 55–57, 122, 125–26, 127n8,
    132–36, 139, 140n33, 142, 161,
    166, 217–18, 220–21, 231, 262–63,
    293, 351, 421, 508, 548n217, 567,
    595–96, 599, 618–19, 637, 644
Akkar Plain, 800, 807, 808n119, 816
Akko, 315
Akšak, 242n200

Aktuppitum, 285
Akusum, 237
al-'Usiya, 380
Al-Damiq-ilišu, 284–85
Al-Kapim, 319n33, 325–26, 332, 380, 423. *See also* Tell Shishin
Alahtum, 332, 342–43. *See also* Alalakh; Tell Atchana
Alahzina, 545
Alalakh, 314, 332, 342–43, 381n279, 388–90. *See also* Alahtum; Tell Atchana
Alašiya, 322, 795
Aleppo, 202, 310, 316, 323, 328, 332, 363–64, 370, 384, 389–90, 469, 594, 595n134, 622, 630. *See also* Halab
Alexandria, 64
Alila-hadum, 243–44, 262
Alilanum, 384
Ališar, 506, 529
Allahad, 367
Ama-gula, 195n7, 284n410
Amanus, 349
Amar-Sin, 140, 149, 155–56, 164, 177–78, 222, 229, 445
Amaz, 372
Amenemhat
    of Beni Hasan, 699, 788, 792
    of Deir el-Bersha, 697n128
    I, 8, 25, 96, 106, 661, 665, 667–69, 683n72, 684n77, 685–86, 688–97, 756, 785–87, 789, 791, 864, 885
    II, 8, 700, 704, 707, 788, 792, 797–98, 800–1, 805, 808, 811, 813, 830, 879, 891, 907

    III, 8, 702–8, 712, 714, 756, 759–61, 789, 812–13, 816–17, 819–28, 861, 879, 884, 891–93, 895, 908–911
    IV, 8, 705–6, 758, 827–28, 830, 836
Ameny-Qemau, 710
Aminum, 318n27, 356, 422
Amkuwa, 543–44, 546
Amma-haštuk, 461n301
Ammi-ditana, 383, 386, 479, 571, 578, 629, 630n305, 631–33
Ammi-madar, 381
Ammi-ṣaduqa, 9, 11, 383, 473–74, 479, 571, 573, 580, 606, 629, 632–36
Amnan-Yahrur, 265, 573
Amnanum, 202, 259–60, 263–64, 573
Amud-pi-El, 346
Amun, 100–1, 672, 682, 684, 690, 829
Amun-Ra, 101, 858, 860, 878
Amunenshi, 789
Amuq Plain, 499, 816
Amurru (god), 292
Amurru(m), 166, 333, 339–40
Amut-pi-El, 296
An, 121, 206, 211, 213, 220, 233, 265, 283, 285, 288, 293, 601, 637
ANam (or Dingiram), 194, 264–65, 283, 573n16, 587–88
Anat. *See* Hanat
Andarig, 324n55, 332, 342, 356, 362, 366–69, 371, 375–77, 383–85, 468, 597
Aniba, 65, 739
Anih-Šušim, 474, 478–79
Anitta, 537–38, 544, 548
Ankhi, 77–78
Ankhtifi, 76, 80–82, 85, 89

Ankhu, 759

Anna, 529n134, 536–37

ANnubanini (or ᵈNubanini),
433n146, 434, 437, 440–42, 476

Annunitum, 242

Anšan, 56, 139, 161, 167, 214, 231, 322,
417–18, 445, 447–48, 450–53,
455, 457, 463–67, 475. *See also*
Tell-i Malyan

Anseba valley, 765

Anum-Hirbi, 327, 548n217

ANzabazuna (or ᵈZabazuna), 432–33,
435–37, 476

Aphroditopolis, 98

Apiak, 209

Apil-Sin, 286, 431n138, 478, 571, 578,
585, 587–88, 589n98

Apišal, 350

Aplahanda, 377

Apum, 332–33, 366, 383, 515, 622

Aqaba, Gulf of, 58

Aqba-Hammu, 598

Aqiq, 766

Aradmu, 149, 154, 171

Arbela, 331, 358. *See also* Urbilum

Areika, 744–45

Arku-atal, 511n60

Armamana, 533n149

Armi, 499

Arraphe, 319, 331, 358, 422. *See also*
Kirkuk

Arslantepe, 498

Asalluhi, 253

Ashait, 103, 859, 886

Ashkelon, 26, 315, 830–32

Ashurbanipal, 210, 223, 253, 472

Ašiši, 453

Aškašepa, 539

Askut, 738, 743–47

Ašlakka, 332, 363, 367–68, 372–73,
377, 444

Ašnakkum, 320n36, 324, 332, 360, 372,
375, 424. *See also* Chagar Bazar

Asqudum, 361

Ašratum, 292

Assur (city), 10, 270n331, 312, 314,
317–18, 320, 325–26, 328, 331,
333, 335–36, 342, 351, 353, 367,
380, 384–85, 387, 415n22, 422,
428, 501, 507–8, 510, 512n64,
515, 521, 526n123, 533n147, 539,
547, 549, 589, 599n157. *See also*
Qalat Sherqat

Aššur (god), 317, 352, 353, 415n22

Aššur-imitti, 443n193

Aššur-nada, 542

Aššur-re'i, 540–41

Assyria, 10, 210, 223–24, 253, 331, 353,
387, 549

Aštamar-Addu, 365

Aswan, 679, 697, 700, 730n7, 737, 748

Asyut, 63–65, 67, 68–70, 81, 86–89,
93–94, 97, 99, 106, 682–83, 696,
703, 733, 868, 870, 873

Atamrum, 345–46, 371, 373, 374n249,
375–77, 467–68, 470, 597

Atawala, 894

Atta-hušu, 453–54, 457n283,
464n321, 476

Atta-mera-halki, 473, 478

Atta-puni, 456n272

Attaya, 414n15

Atum, 700
Aurnahuš, 435
Avaris, 16, 92, 781, 800, 894. *See also*
  Tell el-Dabʻa
Awan, 445, 446n213
Awibra Hor, 893
Ayadaragalama, 571, 578, 639,
  641–44
Ayalatum, 583
Ayalum, 260
Ayn Asil. *See* Balat
Ayn Sukhna, 59, 102, 756–57
Azuzum, 419, 476

Baʻalat Gebal, 787n36, 811
Babylon, 9–11, 122, 172, 182, 191, 197,
  202, 227, 232n153, 236, 240,
  243–44, 250–51, 253, 255, 257–
  59, 264–66, 281–83, 286–87,
  293–96, 320, 323, 327, 345–46,
  348, 354–55, 359, 361, 365, 367,
  369, 371, 373, 375–81, 383–84,
  387–88, 391, 423–24, 428–31,
  463–73, 476, 506, 510, 566–67,
  570–71, 573–78, 580–85, 587–
  601, 613, 617–18, 620–21, 623–
  27, 629n294, 631–34, 636–40,
  643–44
Babylonia, 122, 132, 135–36, 140,
  143, 168–69, 245, 273, 281, 318,
  334n102, 371, 374, 376, 379–80,
  428, 430, 467, 472, 476, 483,
  508, 531, 567, 573, 576, 579–81,
  583, 608, 618–21, 624–27, 634,
  636–37, 639–44
Bad-tibira, 281, 616
Badari, 72, 875

Badna, 526n123
Baganna, 628
Baghdad, 122, 567
Bahariya oasis, 91
Bahlu-kullim, 260
Bahr Yusuf, 90, 707
Bahrain, 56, 168, 593, 643
Balat, 58. *See also* Ayn Asil
Bali-Erah, 344
Balikh River, 332, 350, 364
Balmunamhe, 291–92
Baneh, 438
Baniharzum, 543
Bannum, 361, 364
Banum, 236
Baqet III, 784
Bard-i Sanjian, 435
Barka valley, 762, 765
Barnugi, 63, 68, 90
Bassetki, 262n300, 314n10, 331. *See
  also* Mardaman
Bawu, 211
Bebi, 824
Bel, 434
Belakum, 420–21, 477
Belet-ekallim, 288. *See also* Ningal
Beli-ay-annadi, 237–38
Beltani, 288
Beni Hasan, 17, 63, 86, 93, 95–96,
  104, 106, 683, 691–92, 697, 699,
  703–4, 784, 786, 788–89, 792,
  803–4, 807, 832, 868–71, 873,
  875, 900
Bensimʻalites, 572. *See also* Simʻalite
Benyaminites, 572. *See also*
  Yaminite
Beqaa valley, 333, 357, 789n50

Beranan range, 438

Bia-Punt, 757, 759–60, 762, 765. *See also* Punt

Biahmu, 706, 910

Bilalama, 415–18, 432n144, 437, 450, 476

Binzird range, 438

Bismil, 388

Bit-Šu-Sin, 266, 283

Bitwata, 409, 432, 434–35

Boğazköy, 506, 530, 548n217

Borsippa, 208–9, 583n76, 599n157

Bosporus, 497

Buhen, 58, 697, 740–42

Bunu-Ištar, 358

Bur-Sin, 198, 213, 236, 239–40, 244

Burna-Buriaš, 571

Burullum, 331

Burundum, 332, 358n204, 362–63, 378, 444

Buzazu, 542

Byblos, 57–59, 65, 313, 315–16, 328, 333–34, 371, 391, 704–5, 781, 785, 787n36, 789, 800, 807–14, 821, 826–28, 831

Cambyses, 6

Cappadocia, 471, 504

Carchemish, 332, 363–64, 366, 377. *See also* Jarablus

Carmel
    Mount, 825
    Plain, 800

Caspian Sea, 445

Caucasus, 497–99

Chagar Bazar, 324, 332. *See also* Ašnakkum

Choga Gavaneh, 441n187

Cilicia, 499, 794, 800. *See also* Kizzuwatna

Coptos, 58–59, 64, 75–80, 82, 84–85, 757, 759, 878

Crete, 56, 64, 322, 777, 800–1, 803, 812

Cutha, 255n265, 582, 583n76, 599n157

Cyprus, 4, 16–17, 56, 64, 91, 322, 425, 704, 777, 781, 795, 816

Cythera, 425

Dada, 287

Daduša, 357–58, 423n91, 424n99, 425–27, 478, 592

Dagan, 212, 215, 273, 361, 374

Dagi, 102

Dahshur, 673, 675, 700, 702–4, 706, 710–11, 797, 808, 810, 812–13, 815, 825, 829, 861, 867, 879, 892–93, 899–900, 906–9

Dakhla, 58, 102

Dalaš, 535

Damascus, 333, 357

Damiq-ilišu of Isin, 198, 213, 285–86

Damiq-ilišu/Dam(i)q-ilišu of Sealand, 286, 633, 571

Damrum, 583n76

Damu, 212

Dannum-tahaz, 425, 478

Dara, 87

Darband-i Gawr, 432

Darband-i Khan, 432, 438

Deffufa, Western, 734, 736

Deir el-Bahri, 684–87, 699, 857, 862, 889–90, 912

Deir el-Ballas, 784n16

Deir el-Bersha, 63, 68, 75, 86, 93–94, 106, 683, 697, 703, 868, 870

Deir el-Gebrawi, 80

Dendara, 60, 64, 66, 68–70, 81–85, 89, 96, 98, 784, 877

Der, 232n153, 250–51, 415n22, 417–18, 450

Dilbat, 473–74, 583n76, 599n157, 637

Dilmun, Dilmunite, 56, 168, 208, 322, 359, 593, 643

Diqdiqqah, 195n6

DIŠ+U-EN?, 571

Diyala River, 140, 142, 154, 157, 168, 177, 215n70, 252, 278n374, 318–19, 333, 409–10, 421, 423, 426–27, 429–31, 438–39, 574, 580, 589, 599, 610, 620–22, 625, 634

Djari, 95, 856, 863

Djaty, 784

Djau, 80

Djaushemay, 80

Djefaihapy I, 733

Djehuti, 866

Djehutinakht, 94

Djehutinakht VI, 697n128

Djemi, 90, 99

Djer, 867

Djoser, 702, 905, 910

Drehem, 150, 204. *See also* Puzriš-Dagan

Dublamah, 214

Dugurasu, 57

Dumuzi, 146n43, 282

Dumuzi-gamil, 257

Dunnum, 222, 284

Dur-Abi-ešuh, 627–33, 635

Dur-Ammi-ditana, 631

Dur-Enlile, 644

Dur-Sin-muballiṭ, 628

Dur-Yahdun-Lim, 354n186

Dur-Yasmah-Addu, 354n186, 360

Duruduruwa, 533n149

Durum, 209, 217

E'urgira, 271

Ea, 601n166. *See also* Enki

Ea-gamil, 571, 578, 643

Eanna, 259, 265

Eastern Desert, 65, 79, 103, 739, 748–49, 752–53, 755, 758, 760–62, 765

Ebabbar, 226, 229, 247, 249, 254, 268, 277–78, 600, 619

Ebarat

  I, 445–47, 449, 450n247, 452, 476

  II, 448–49, 451–55, 476

Ebi-unni, 440n181

Ebla, 57–59, 166, 208, 313–14, 316, 318, 328, 390–91, 444, 499, 812, 831

Edana, 216, 221

Edaštušu, 638

Edfu, 68, 81–82, 87, 751

Edimgalana, 239, 271n339

Egalbara, 279–80

Egipar, 275. *See also* Gipar

Ekallatum, 18, 273, 320, 323, 331, 353–54, 357–58, 362, 367, 374–76, 378, 387, 424, 428, 439, 443, 468, 589, 593, 598

Ekišnugal, 234, 275

Ekitušbidu, 285

Ekur, 209n55, 224n111, 225, 601,
    629, 632
Ekurduana, 571
el-Hagarsa, 77, 81–82
el-Tarif, 680–82, 684
Elali, 511n60
Elam, 56–57, 121, 136, 139, 159, 167,
    180, 209, 231n145, 274, 293–94,
    318, 322, 346, 370–71, 373–74,
    378, 416–18, 422, 428–29,
    448–53, 455–57, 459, 461n303,
    463–71, 473–74, 481–82, 591,
    594, 616, 630, 638–39, 642–43
Elephantine, 58, 60, 65, 67–68, 77,
    80–81, 85, 88, 91, 95, 97, 101,
    104, 666, 669–70, 672, 675,
    683, 697, 730n7, 747, 752,
    869–70, 879, 889, 892, 901
Elkab, 71–72, 81, 85, 681, 764
Eluhut, 331, 358n204, 377, 384, 444
Emar, 253n253, 332, 342, 354n183,
    364, 380, 388, 392. *See also* Tell
    Meskene
Emṣium, 227, 229. *See also* Yamṣium
Emutbal(um), 202–3, 273–74, 278,
    293, 458–59, 617, 619n248, 620.
    See also Yamutbal
Enanatuma, 218–19, 231
Enanedu, 275, 458n292
Enninsunzi, 222, 231
Enamtila, 634
Eninnu, 139
Enišra, 534
Enki, 121, 211, 213, 225, 242n200, 246,
    282–83, 285, 601. *See also* Ea
Enki-Nirah, 234

Enkidu, 171
Enlil, 121, 135, 139, 158, 205–6, 208–9,
    211, 213, 215–20, 223, 225, 233,
    239–40, 242n201, 262, 270n331,
    272, 283, 285, 293, 351, 585, 600–
    1, 629, 634, 637, 644
Enlil-bani, 198, 203, 213–14, 217, 239,
    241, 244, 270–72, 286n420
Enlil-ibni, 209. *See also* Sidu
Enlil-mansum, 629
Ennam-Aššur, 541
Ennedi, 101
er-Rizeiqat, 88
Erciyes, Mount, 539
Ereš, 587
Ereškigal, 586
Erib-eli, 442
Eriba-Sin, 286
Eridu, 137, 209, 217, 239, 247, 270,
    281, 599n157
Erra-bani, 236, 419
Erra-imitti, 198, 199n16, 203, 236–38,
    240–41, 243–44, 270
Esagil, 575, 589, 639
Esikil, 416
Ešnunna, 149, 154, 159n71, 172, 182,
    250–52, 296, 319–20, 323–24, 327,
    334n102, 346, 350, 353–54, 357,
    359, 361, 363–64, 366–72, 375–76,
    378, 379n263, 409–411, 414–31,
    437, 441–43, 450, 457–59, 462–
    63, 466–70, 476–78, 584–85,
    589, 591–94, 596–98, 599n157,
    616n230, 617, 620–21, 630
Ešumeša, 240
Etemenniguru, 256

Euphrates River, 9, 18, 122, 132, 157, 166, 242n198, 247, 293, 314, 316, 318–19, 332, 338, 341, 349–54, 356–57, 359, 362–64, 366, 368, 374, 378, 380–84, 386, 423–24, 428, 443, 466, 498, 501, 509, 526n123, 547, 567, 572, 574, 577, 583, 589, 594, 598–99, 619, 622–23, 628n291, 635, 639, 642

Eusebius of Caesarea, 5

Ezbet Rushdi, 92, 693, 800–2, 806, 815

Fara, 240, 271n339. *See also* Šuruppak

Faras, 739

Fayum, 63, 68, 74, 90–92, 701, 703, 706–8, 817, 879–80, 894, 909–11

Flavius Josephus, 5

Ga'eš, 254n260

Ga'eš-rabi, 254

Gagiššua, 225

Galilee, 30, 800, 816

Galulu, 535

Garšana, 154

Gash delta, 65, 752–53, 762–66. *See also* Kassala

Gasur, 319, 326, 331, 333n98, 422. *See also* Nuzi; Yorghan Tepe

Gebel Abusir, 707

Gebel Mokram, 752, 761

Gebel Tingar, 65n44

Gebel Tjauti, 830

Gebel Uweinat, 101

Gebel Zeit, 104

Gebelein, 81–82, 88, 96, 683, 784, 873

Georgios Syncellus, 5

Gezer, 12

Gilgamesh, 127, 142, 147, 170–71, 265, 614–15, 641

Gipar (or Gipar-ku), 219, 222, 246, 261, 265, 275. *See also* Egipar

Girsu, 125, 129, 149, 151, 159n71, 163–65, 201, 204, 229–30, 237, 281, 287, 599n157

Giza, 742

Gol-e Zard, 502n24

Great Khorasan Road, 442

Gudea, 136–40, 142, 169n90

Gula, 191. *See also* Nin-Isina

Gulkišar, 571, 637, 640–41

Gungunum, 216, 219–22, 224, 226–27, 230–35, 241, 244, 256n275, 267, 269–70

Habannum, 288

Habilaya, 809

Haburatum, 331, 353n182

Hadni-Addu, 360

Hadudu, 533n149

Hahhum, 332, 380, 391, 444, 509, 515, 520–21

Halab, 332. *See also* Aleppo

Halabit, 364

Halman, 428, 434, 441

Halu-rabi, 438

Halun-pi-umu, 582

Hammurabi of Babylon, 9–11, 21, 34–35, 138n27, 143, 191, 197, 200n19, 203, 220–21, 227, 250, 287, 293–96, 323, 345–46, 348, 354–55, 365, 369, 375–81, 386–87, 429–30, 463–64, 466–70, 478, 506, 510, 566–67, 571, 574, 577n40, 584, 587, 589–606, 615–16, 623n264, 628, 644

Hammurabi of Yamhad
  I, 389, 622
  II, 389
Hana, 337–40, 348–49, 363, 369, 373,
  381–83, 386, 572, 623–24
Hanat, 332, 368
Hanigalbat, 638
Hanzat, 332, 362. *See also*
  Šubat-Šamaš
Hapuahšušar, 511n60
Hapuwaššu, 533n149
Harageh, 707, 877, 883, 897, 900
Harappa, 56
Harbe, 428
Harihari, 536–37
Harkhuf, 60, 748
Harkiuna, 545
Harradum, 332, 382, 386, 623,
  631n305, 634. *See also* Khirbet
  ed-Diniyeh
Harran, 332
Harsamna, 545
Hasi, 96
Haššum, 327, 332, 380, 391, 544,
  548n217
Haṣura, 333. *See also* Hazor
Hathor, 69, 86, 684, 822–23, 859,
  902, 911
Hatnub, 60, 70, 96, 691–92
Hatti, 528, 549
Hattuš, 511, 527, 530–31, 543–48. *See
  also* Hattusa
Hattusa, 322, 388, 392, 511, 527n128, 545
Hattusili I, 388, 391, 510, 521, 545,
  548n218
Hawara, 706–7, 879, 884, 899, 905,
  909–10

Haya, 233
Haya-Sumu, 370
Hazor, 14, 18, 21, 35, 322, 325–26, 333,
  367. *See also* Haṣura
Heliopolis, 92, 666, 672, 675, 692,
  695, 700, 878, 911
Helwan, 92, 754
Henenu, 90, 759, 784–85
Henu, 785
Hepzefa, 733. *See also* Djefaihapy
Heqaib
  of Elephantine, 85, 97, 697,
  869, 889
  of Thebes, 71
Heqanakht, 686, 689n98, 864
Herakleopolis, 55, 63–66, 68, 85,
  90–96, 101, 105–6, 676
Herodotus, 807
Hetep, 87, 866
Hetep-Senusret, 880, 882–85. *See
  also* Lahun
Hetepeni, 78
Hetepi, 82, 85, 681
Hetepibra Aamusahornedjitef, 894
Hetepwadjet, 64
Hierakonpolis, 752n123
Higiša, 536
Hiritum, 235, 374–75, 470
Hit, 332, 359, 378, 423, 593
Hor, 868
Horemsaf, 884
Horkherti, 825
Horus, 98, 690, 692, 858, 860, 865,
  877, 885, 908, 911
Hu, 79–80, 750–51
Huba-simti, 208
Huharimataku, 526n123

Huhnuri, 445. *See also* Tepe Bormi
Hulana River, 544
Humban, 440n182
Hurama, 526n124, 545–46
Hurma, 527
Hurra, 373, 375
Huršitum, 367
Hušla, 370
Hute-kazan, 456n279
Hutran-tem/pti, 448
Huzziya, 527n128, 545–47

Iaa, 789, 794
Iah, 860
Iasy, 704, 795–96, 797n77. *See also*
    Cyprus
Iayseneb, 900
Ibal-Addu, 363, 367, 377, 444
Ibal-El, 293
Ibal-pi-El
    I, 251, 260, 421–22, 477, 585
    II, 215n70, 296, 323, 346, 364,
        368–69, 426, 428, 478
Ibarum, 242n200
Ibbi-Sin
    of Ešnunna, 425, 478
    of Ur, 121–22, 130, 140, 149, 152,
        156, 159–61, 178–79, 190–91,
        203–6, 214, 227–28, 229n134,
        409–11, 414, 415n21, 433n145,
        442, 444–47, 450n246, 476,
        483
Ibbiṭ-Lim, 317n19
Ibener, 823
Ibesha, 803–4
Ibhat, 103
Ibhatit, 103

Ibiau, 901
Ibni-Dagan, 236
Ibni-Erra, 425
Ibni-šadum, 242–43
Ibrat, 250
Ibu, 891
Idamaraṣ, 332, 339, 350, 362, 364–65,
    367–68, 370–71, 373, 380, 421,
    468–70, 617, 638
Idattu
    I, 417, 446–52, 476
    II, 448–50, 451n251, 452
Idattu-Inšušinak, 451
Idattu-napir, 451
Idattu-temti, 451
Iddi(n)-Sin, 432–37, 441–42, 476
Iddin-Dagan, 198, 211, 214–17, 231,
    244, 272
Iddin-Enlil, 256n275
Iddin-Ilum, 242
Igmil-Sin, 459n293
Ihy, 866
Ikarum, 533n149
Iki, 715
Ikkur, 739
Ikun-pi-Sin, 235–36
Ikun-pi-Sin (king of Nerebtum),
    251–52
Ikun-pîša, 579n49
Ikuppiya, 426
Ila-kabkabu, 318–19, 321
Ilaliyanda, 536
Ilan-šemea, 264–65
Ilanṣura, 332, 334n102, 366,
    370–71, 384
Ili-babum, 229n134
Ili-iddinam, 194

Ili-ma-ilu, 571, 578, 624–25, 630–32
Ili-Samas, 385
Ili-wedaku, 542
Illahun, 880. *See also* Kahun; Lahun
Iltani, 356n193, 385, 598
Ilum-bani, 208n49
Ilum-gamil, 264
Ilum-muttabbil, 417–18, 450
Iluni, 430, 478, 616n230, 620–21
Ilurugu, 253
Imazu, 447
Imenyseshenen, 823
Imgur-Gibil, 266, 283
Imgur-Sin, 224, 232n152
Imhotep (king), 87
Inana, 146n43, 211–13, 216–17, 219,
     220n88, 233, 237, 239, 246, 263,
     265, 272, 282, 288, 417n39
Inana-of-Zabalam, 272
Inar, 511n60
Indi, 86
Inganum, 438
Ini (of Gebelein), 88
Inšušinak, 447n222, 451n251, 453
Intef
     overseer of troops, 84, 95, 104,
          784, 889
     scribe of the god's book, 886
     son of Ka, 97
     son of Myt, 71
     the Great, 80–81, 84–85, 95
     II, 85, 97–101, 681
     III, 97, 99, 860
Intefiqer, 98, 699, 759
Iny, 57, 62, 810n128
Ipi, 686, 689
Ipiq-Adad

I, 419–20, 477
II, 319, 421–23, 425, 458, 477
III, 319nn32–33
Ipqu-Erra, 292
Ipy, 869
Iqen, 742, 749. *See also* Mirgissa
Iqiš-Tišpak, 425, 478
Ique(r), 70
Ir, 897
Iri-Sagrig, 125n4, 130, 142, 155, 177
Irišum I, 318
Irkabtum, 389
IRnene (or Irdanene or Urdunene),
     263–66, 282
Irqata, 315. *See also* Tell Arqa
Irtjet, 55
Išar-kitti-Aššur, 542
Išar-ramašu, 418
Išbi-Erra, 160–61, 198–99, 202,
     204–6, 208–211, 244, 254n258,
     414–17, 418n50, 436–37, 442,
     447–48, 476
Išhara, 251
Išhi-Addu, 357
Ishkaft mountains, 332
Iṣi-Sumu-abum, 381–82, 386
Isin, 160, 182, 191, 195–211, 214, 217–22,
     224–27, 230–32, 235–37, 239–41,
     243–44, 257–58, 260–61, 266,
     270–73, 280–90, 296, 414–18,
     434, 436–37, 442, 447–48, 476,
     508, 570, 578–79, 587, 589, 592,
     599n157, 603n172, 617, 619, 625
Iškibal, 571
Iškur, 198, 213, 233, 252, 264, 281, 637
Išme-Addu, 375
Išme-bala, 420

Išme-Dagan, 198–200, 211–13, 216–19, 231, 238, 244, 260–61, 273, 338, 354–55, 358, 361–62, 364, 367, 374–76, 378, 387, 443, 589–90, 593, 597

Išme-karab, 461

Ištar, 352, 357, 435, 439, 441, 637

Ištar-of-Uruk, 626

Ištaran, 250, 415n22

Isu, 87

Išur, 251, 420

Itapalhum, 340

Iter-piša, 198, 272

Iti
    of Gebelein, 96
    king, 87

Iti-ibi, 67

Itj-tawy, 661, 686, 690, 693, 709, 712

Itti-ili-nibi, 571, 631

Itu. *See* Hit

Itur-Asdu, 296

Itur-Šamaš, 241–42, 260

Ituriya, 410, 414, 476

Iua, 704, 794–96, 797n77

Iyibkhentra, 87, 692

Iykhernofret, 702–3, 815, 868, 899

Iytenhab, 900

Jarablus, 332. *See also* Carchemish

Jebel Hamrin, 229

Jebel Sinjar, 597

Jeita Cave, 502n24

Jericho, 12, 26, 31–32, 57

Jerusalem, 12, 313, 434–35

Jezirah, 314, 319, 328–29, 331, 335, 337–42, 346, 350–51, 354–55, 360, 362–63, 366–71, 373–75, 379–80, 383–84, 415, 512

Jordan River, 819

Kabta, 215

Kabuka Rapids, 742

Kahat, 332, 362, 364–65, 384. *See also* Tell Barri

Kahun, 817, 880. *See also* Illahun; Lahun

Kakara-Iny, 87

Kakkulatum, 215, 424

Kakmum, 340

Kalhu, 331. *See also* Nimrud

Kaman Kalehöyük, 506–7, 529

Kamose, 16

Kaneš, 104, 316, 502, 504–7, 509–12, 515, 518–24, 525n120, 526n123, 527–29, 531–39, 543–49. *See also* Kültepe

Kanisura, 264n307

Kapitra, 543

Kar-Šamaš, 278

Karaca Dağ, 332

Karana, 332, 356, 368, 375–76, 384–85

Karhar, 127n6

Karkara, 599n157

Karnak, 101, 669, 672, 675, 682, 684, 695, 711, 828, 878

Karzida, 254n260

Kassala, 752, 763. *See also* Gash delta

Kaštiliaš
    of Terqa, 381
    III, 571

Kawit, 859

Kay, 688–89

Kayalıpınar, 507

Kayseri, 504

Kazallu, 160, 205, 209, 237, 243, 255, 277–78, 459, 582–83, 617

Kazane Höyük, 325, 332
Kelar, 431
Kemsit, 859
Kerma, 56, 101, 704, 732–38, 742,
    746–47, 749–50, 753, 755–56,
    761, 764, 766–67. *See also*
    Kush
Keš, 296, 599n157
Ketj, 825
Khabur, Lesser, 331
Khabur River, 320n36, 332, 339, 349–50,
    359, 362–64, 367–68, 370, 373,
    377, 382–84, 424, 468, 589, 594,
    598–99, 622–23, 625
Khafajah, 621
Khan el-Abde, 808n119
Khanaqin, 441
Khaneferra Sobekhotep IV, 893–94
Khebeded(em), 822
Khemenu, 692
Khendjer, 710, 894
Khenti-she, 794–96, 798, 800, 828
Khentkhetwer, 798n79
Khety
    of Beni Hasan, 784
    Heliopolis/Wadi Tumilat
        official, 92
    king, 61, 92, 94–95, 785
    official, 71, 103, 106
    overseer of priests at Naqada, 96
    overseer of the two treasuries, 102
    of Thebes, 784
Khirbet al-Batrawy, 57
Khirbet ed-Diniyeh, 332. *See also*
    Harradum
Khnumet, 907
Khnumhotep

steward, Meir, 903
steward, Rifeh, 906
I (of Beni Hasan), 96, 691–92, 786
II (of Beni Hasan), 17, 104, 691,
    704, 803–7, 869, 871, 875
III (of Dahshur), 673, 675, 696,
    703–5, 803, 806–10, 813–14, 867
Khui, 87
Khusobek, 705, 807, 813
Khuu, 82, 87
Khuzestan, 167, 445nn212–213
Khyan, 7, 25, 36
Kikalla, 616
Kindattu, 445–48, 449, 450n247,
    454, 476
Kinet Höyük, 787n36
Kirikiri, 415–16, 437, 450n246, 476
Kiritab, 255, 285
Kirkuk, 331. *See also* Arraphe
Kiš, 208, 220, 255, 284, 472, 582,
    583n76, 587, 599n157, 610, 616,
    620, 626, 637
Kisig, 229. *See also* Tell al-Laḥm
Kisurra, 191, 193n4, 196, 224, 238,
    241–43, 259, 261–63, 266, 270,
    283, 287, 580, 619
Kiten-rakittapi, 449
Kizzuwatna, 794n67. *See also* Cilicia
Kırşehir, 508
Kızılırmak River, 539, 541, 543. *See
    also* Marassanta
Knossos, 801
Kom el-Hisn, 63, 68, 90–91, 801
Kom el-Khalwa, 703
Kom Rabi'a, 829
Konya Karahöyük, 506n30
Konya Plain, 498

Kor, 739

Kubaba(t), 536

Kubban, 739

Kudu-zuluš

    I, 460, 462–64, 466–67,
       471–72, 478

    II, 473–75, 479–80

Kudur-mabuk, 202–3, 257, 273–82,
    458–59

Kudur-Nanhundi, 471

Kuk-kirwa, 454n266, 456–57

Kuk-Nahhunte, 456–57

Kuk-našur

    I, 456–57, 477

    II, 460, 471, 473–74, 475n375,
       478, 480

    III, 474, 475n375, 479, 480–82

    IV, 474, 480–81

Kuk-sanit, 455, 456n272, 464n321

Kuk-šigat, 459n293

Kukka-ᵈnašer, 474

Kuku, 543

Kulia, 533n148

Kuliya, 543

Kültepe, 33–35, 104, 313, 326–27, 502,
    505–6, 508–10, 513–14, 517, 519,
    527, 534–35, 537, 542–48, 550,
    812. *See also* Kaneš

Kulun(n)um, 435

Kumma, 708, 743

Kumme, 322

Kun(n)am(an), 468, 470

Kunsat, 534

Kurda, 332, 350, 355, 365–68, 375,
    384, 428

Kurigugu, 481

Kush, 56, 95, 101–2, 105, 699, 701, 728,
    732n9, 733, 737, 742, 746–47,
    750, 754, 764, 766–67. *See also*
    Kerma

Kuššara, 520, 531, 543–46, 548n218

Kutalla, 256, 276, 281, 287, 616, 618

Kuter-Nahhunte, 460–61, 471–72,
    474–75, 478

Kuter-Šilhaha, 472, 474–75, 478, 480

Kuwari, 443

Kuyunjik, 331. *See also* Nineveh

La'um, 260

Labarna, 545

Lagaba, 585n76, 625

Lagaš, 136–40, 142, 168–69, 235, 248,
    256, 276, 283n403, 599n157, 616

Lahun, 664, 678, 680, 700, 702,
    707, 709, 747, 816–17, 823–24,
    867, 880–81, 884–88, 897, 899,
    907–9. *See also* Illahun; Kahun

Lake Qarun, 706–7

Lake Urmia, 438, 445

Lakimišša, 544, 546

Lamassatum, 220n88

Lamma, 215, 482n390

Lankuku, 456

Larsa, 182, 191, 193n4, 195–98, 200–3,
    209–10, 219–20, 222, 224, 226–38,
    240–58, 260–61, 263, 266–70,
    272–74, 276–82, 284–87, 289–96,
    346, 373, 376, 378, 421, 434, 457–
    59, 469, 476, 508, 570, 578, 583–85,
    587–89, 592, 595–96, 599–601,
    605, 608, 616–18, 620, 626, 633,
    636, 639. *See also* Tell Senkereh

Lazapatum, 443n193
Lebanon, 27, 29, 315, 317, 333, 758, 781,
    794, 806–7, 809, 816, 829, 832–33
Lebanon mountains, 349, 704
Libur-beli, 208
Libur-ni'aš, 208
Lidar Höyük, 332, 380
Lila-irtaš, 461, 473
Lipit-Enlil, 198, 236, 240, 244
Lipit-Eštar, 198, 213, 215, 217, 220–
    24, 226, 230, 232, 239, 244, 603
Liriš-gamlum, 288
Lisht, 673, 686, 690, 693, 695, 699,
    703, 787–88, 829, 861, 864, 866,
    874, 888
Lisht North, 800–1
Lower Egypt, 59, 84, 92, 99, 106,
    688, 692, 744, 746, 750, 823,
    878, 889, 903, 908
Lu-igisa, 199n16, 235–36
Lu-Ninšubur, 208
Lu-Ninurta, 292
Lu-Utu, 164–65
Lugal-gudua, 598n153
Lugalbanda, 261
Lugalirra, 209, 261
Lugalkiduna, 256n275
Luhuzattiya, 520, 543, 546
Lullu(m), 340, 438, 443n193
Lullubum, 409–10, 433, 437–42, 476

Maadi, 781n4
Madawada, 534
Magan. *See* Makkan
Mahal Teglinos, 65, 763–65
Makkan, 56, 144n37, 168–69
Mala'a Basin, 707

Malgium, 232, 250–51, 278, 359, 378,
    592–93, 598, 599n157. *See also*
    Tell Yassir
Mamma, 327, 526n124, 529, 531, 544
Manetho, 5–6, 676
Mankisum, 354, 357, 429, 467–69,
    592, 594, 598
Manna-balti-El, 242–43
Mannum-kima-Sin, 292
Manzi-wartaš, 458
Marad, 209, 582–83, 587
Marassanta River, 539. *See also*
    Kızılırmak
Mardaman, 331. *See also* Bassetki
Mardin, 326, 426
Marduk, 589, 600–601, 636, 638–40
Marhaši, 56, 167
Mari, 10, 14, 18, 21, 35, 59, 154, 165–67,
    202, 205–6, 208–9, 215n70,
    242n198, 260, 273, 280, 293–94,
    296, 312–14, 316–24, 327–34,
    336–38, 340–57, 360–71, 373,
    375–79, 381–91, 410, 421–22,
    424, 426, 428, 429n129, 433,
    437–39, 442–44, 456–57, 460,
    463–66, 468–70, 483, 506, 572,
    577, 589–94, 596–99, 607, 622–
    23. *See also* Tell Hariri
Mariwan, 438
Martu, 229, 285, 572, 612n214
Maškan-šapir, 229–30, 232n153, 246,
    273–74, 278–79, 281, 284, 459,
    583, 596, 599n157, 619
Mašparum, 420
Matum-niatum, 214
Mavri Trypa cave, 502n24
Mazghuna, 710

Me-Kubi, 417, 450

Me-Turan, 424, 426–27, 429, 431n138

Medamud, 894

Medinet el-Fayum, 706, 879. *See also* Shedet

Medinet Madi, 706, 910–11

Mediterranean Sea, 4–5, 16, 27, 35, 56–57, 59, 63, 65, 68, 88, 91, 101–2, 134, 166, 169, 315, 317, 322, 349, 392, 497–98, 763, 777–78, 780–83, 792, 795, 798, 807–11, 813–15, 821, 827–29, 832, 834–37

Medjay, 103, 732, 739, 749–50, 754–55, 764, 766

Megiddo, 27, 57

Meir, 64, 75, 683, 697, 703, 789, 797, 817, 832, 868, 870–73, 902–3

Meketra, 61, 684–86, 688, 856, 863–64

Melamkura, 571

Meluhha, 168

Memphis, 75, 77, 80, 93, 664, 786n29, 792, 829–30, 855, 859–60, 866, 870, 879, 894. *See also* Mit Rahina

Menat-Khufu, 691

Menirum, 294n460

Mentuhotep
    treasurer and overseer of all works, 878
    vizier, 788
    I, 80–81
    II Nebhepetra, 71, 88–89, 94–97, 101–6, 661, 676, 682–88, 697, 738, 783, 856–57, 859–60, 863–64, 877–78, 886, 889–90, 912

III Sankhkara, 102, 684–88, 693, 785, 861

IV, 102, 686, 688–89, 756

Merenra, 57

Mereret, 821, 908

Mereri, 89, 98

Mersa/Wadi Gawasis, 58–59, 79, 756–61, 763–65, 767, 796, 798n79, 828, 836. *See also* Sauu

Meryaa, 77

Merykara, 66, 70, 86, 90, 93–94, 791

Meslamta'ea, 209, 260–61

Min, 75, 78–79

Min-Hornakht, 901

Mirgissa (Iqen), 742–43, 745, 754–55, 818–19

Mišlan, 316, 363

Mit Rahina, 792–93, 796, 798, 805, 807, 810, 814. *See also* Memphis

Moalla, 76, 80–81, 85, 88–89, 106

Montu, 100, 669, 671, 699, 788, 794, 798–99, 879, 894

Montuuser, 674

Mostagedda, 751

Mount Batir, 433, 439

Mubalsaga, 356

Mukannišum, 344

Mursili I, 391, 545, 637–39

Murub, 250

Murum, 283, 587

Mut-Aškur, 387

Muti-abal, 278, 573n13

Mutiya, 383

Mutmuti, 86

Myt, 71

Nabada, 316
Nabi-ilišu, 266
Nablus, 814. *See also* Shechem; Tell
  Balatah
Nabonidus, 275–76, 599
Naduhtum, 526n123
Naga ed-Der, 81, 86
Naga el-Shebaykah, 87
Nagar, 350
Nahr al-Bared, 808n119
Nahur, 370
Nanaya, 211, 237, 239, 263, 272, 282,
  293
Nanna, 121, 144n37, 159, 172, 178,
  195n6, 212, 218, 219n83, 231n147,
  233, 242n200, 246, 249–50,
  254n260, 257, 275, 278–79,
  458n292
Nanna-ki'ag, 215, 221–22
Nanna-manšum, 233
Nanše, 230
Napiriša, 455n271
Naplanum, 227–29, 244
Naqada, 96
Nar Lake, 502n24
Naram-Sin
  of Akkad, 127, 166, 262, 548n217
  of Ešnunna, 320, 423–25, 478
  of Uruk, 244, 262–63, 267, 269
Naṣarum, 255, 266, 283
Naznannum, 218
Neapolis, 814n147. *See also* Nablus;
  Shechem
Nebit, 892
Neferet, 689
Neferhotep, 715
Neferhotep I, 710, 893

Neferirkara, 864
Neferiu, 70
Neferkara Iymeru, 893
Neferu, 861
Neferukayet, 97
Neferuptah, 905, 909
Negev Desert, 58, 91, 800
Nehri
  of Beni Hasan, 900
  I, 688, 691–92
  II, 697n128
Nemtiui, 48
Nemty, 894
Nenu, 77
Nepaš, 536–37
Nerebtum, 251, 260, 420, 422–23,
  426–27, 429
  Nergal, 211–12, 264–65,
  278n371, 282
Neša, 505
Nesmontu, 786–87
Nesutnefer, 98
Nihriya, 325, 332, 444
Nihru, 438
Nile River, 58, 62, 66, 68, 90, 92, 96,
  101–2, 105, 329, 682, 708, 732,
  736–39, 742–43, 747–49, 756–57,
  759, 762, 764, 766–67, 785,
  835–36, 857, 865
  Cataract, Second, 56, 101, 730, 737,
  740, 743, 746
  Cataract, Third, 56, 733
  Cataract, Fourth, 56, 737, 750n113
  delta, 16, 57, 63–64, 68, 90–92,
  693, 701, 705, 750n113, 781, 791,
  800–1, 815, 824–25, 835–36,
  868, 880, 894

Nile River (*cont.*)
  valley, 49, 55–56, 61, 64–65, 68,
    74, 95, 105, 691, 707, 747, 749,
    751–53, 755, 758, 766, 800, 806,
    835–36, 868
Nimrud, 331. *See also* Kalhu
Nin-egal, 288. *See also* Belet-ekallim
Nineveh, 224, 253, 316, 326, 331,
    359, 380, 387, 599n157. *See also*
    Kuyunjik
Ningal, 195n6, 219, 232, 250, 275,
    279n377
Ningirsu, 137–39
Ningišzida, 255
Ningublaga, 211, 216, 222, 231
Ninhursag, 121, 435
Ninibgal, 271
Nin-Isina, 191, 201, 211, 213, 233, 237,
    239, 253, 271, 277. *See also* Gula
Ninki, 221
Ninlil, 158, 209, 211, 214, 219, 225,
    274n357
Ninšatapada, 233, 260–61, 292
Ninsianna, 433, 435
Nin-Šubur, 211
Nintinuga, 271
Ninurta, 212–13, 219, 225, 240, 272,
    285n415
Nippi, 459n293
Nippur, 125n4, 140, 142, 149n49,
    150–52, 155, 158–60, 200, 204–
    5, 208–10, 212, 214, 216–18,
    220–21, 224–26, 229, 238–40,
    252–56, 270–73, 274n357, 279,
    281–83, 285, 287, 290–91, 567,
    580, 585, 587, 599n157, 600–1,
    610–13, 616, 618–19, 624–25,
    627–30, 632, 635, 640–41

Niqmi-epuh, 389
Niqqum, 441
Nisaba, 211, 217, 223
Nišba, 433–35
Niši-inišu, 261
Nkiliet, 533n149
Nubheteptikhered, 905
Nubia, 54–55, 58–59, 63, 65, 80–81,
    87–90, 95, 99, 102, 692, 697,
    699, 701, 704, 728–30, 732–33,
    736–38, 740–42, 746–56,
    760–61, 764, 766–67, 895
Nukar, 628
Numhâ, 332, 337, 365, 380, 572–73
Numhium, 421
Numušda, 233, 255–56
Nunamnir, 220
Nur-Adad, 195n7, 201, 203, 238,
    243–49, 257, 267–70
Nur-ahum, 415, 416n27, 437, 442,
    476
Nur-Sin, 236
Nurrugum, 331, 359
Nusaybin, 326
Nuska, 212
Nuṭuptum, 285
Nuzi, 331. *See also* Gasur; Yorghan
    Tepe

Oman, 56, 144n37, 168
Onuris, 70
Onurisnakht, 82
Opis, 429, 594. *See also* Upi
Orontes River, 18, 825
Osiris, 86, 97, 682–83, 698, 702–3,
    815, 823, 857, 867–68, 889, 901–2,
    904–6, 911
Oylum Höyük, 380

Pahatima, 526n123

Pala-iššan, 452–56, 457n284, 477

Palmyra, 333. *See also* Tadmur

Pan-Grave, 734, 750–53, 755, 761, 766

Parka, 536–37

Pašime, 231. *See also* Tell Abu Sheeja

Pelkiša (or Welkiša), 461

Pepy
  I, 57
  II, 57

Persian Gulf, 122, 168–69, 208, 224, 281, 283n403, 286, 289, 322, 359, 567, 593, 636, 642–43

Peruwa, 535–36, 538

Pešgaldarameš, 578, 639

Phaistos, 801

Pi-naratim, 242, 255, 266, 283

Pira Magrun range, 432, 434

Pišenden, 437

Pithana, 385, 544, 546

Ptah, 792, 879

Ptahhotep, 886

Ptahwer, 823

Pududu (or Pundudu), 449n237

Pungla River, 431

Punt, 58–59, 65, 79, 102, 732, 736, 748–49, 755–67, 785, 798n79, 828, 835

Purušhaddum, 520, 526n124, 540–42, 544–45

Puzriš-Dagan, 129n11, 130, 150–52, 157, 174, 177, 227. *See also* Drehem

Puzur-Aššur, 542

Puzur-Inšušinak, 132, 139, 142, 168

Puzur-Numušda, 415n21

Puzur-Sin, 387

Puzurran, 332, 364n219, 424

Qabra, 331, 358, 426

Qakara-In(tef), 692

Qal'at al-Hadi, 380

Qal'at al-Bahrain, 643

Qal'at Sherqat, 331. *See also* Assur (city)

Qal'at Širwana (or Qalay Širwana), 431

Qara Dagh, 432, 438

Qasr el-Sagha, 707

Qatna, 18, 296, 315–16, 329, 333, 339, 346–47, 356–57, 366, 373, 594, 630n305, 789n49. *See also* Tell al-Mishrifeh

Qaṭṭara, 323–24, 328, 332, 356n193, 367, 375, 385, 428, 433, 437–39, 443, 598. *See also* Tell al-Rimah

Qattunan, 332, 363

Qau el-Kebir, 72, 101, 703, 872, 891, 903

Qau-Matmar, 679

Qedem, 102, 784n16, 789

Qedes, 88

Qena, 678, 757, 785

Qubbet el-Hawa, 104, 697, 868, 870

Qusae, 902

Ra, 99, 690, 860

Rabbûm, 260, 573

Rajasthan, 56

Ram Hormuz, 445n212

Rameses II, 792–93

Ramesseum, 676

Raniya Plain, 432, 434, 435n156

Rapiqum, 266, 282, 332, 354, 364, 369, 423, 428, 593

Ras Shamra, 332–33. *See also* Ugarit

Razama, 324, 326, 369, 371, 373, 375, 384, 428, 468. *See also* Tell al-Hawa

Razama-in-Yamutbal, 332, 375

Razama-in-Yussan, 332, 366

Red Sea, 58–59, 65, 79–80, 88, 101–2, 104, 732, 736, 751, 755–57, 760–64, 766–67, 785, 796, 798, 810, 813, 828, 835–36

Rediukhnum
of Beni Hasan, 96
of Dendara, 83

Renenutet, 910–11

Retenu, 75, 796, 808, 813, 815, 822

Rifeh, 696, 703, 875, 906

Rim-Anum, 296, 616–18

Rim-Sin
I, 191, 195n7, 200n19, 201, 203, 227, 232–33, 257, 261, 266, 270, 273, 275, 279–96, 346, 459, 469, 478, 587–89, 595–96, 599
II, 296, 616, 617n234, 619–20, 621n253, 636

Rim-Sin-Šala-baštašu, 285, 288

Sabbuganni, 372

Sabini, 440n181

Sabium, 251–53, 255, 260, 477, 571, 575, 578, 584–85, 587–89, 599

Sabum, 619

Šaduppûm, 423

Saggar, Mount, 367. *See also* Jebel Sinjar

Saggaratum, 332, 360, 363, 383n287, 624

Sahura, 732, 748

Saiset, 892

Šakdunuwa, 535

Šalatiwara, 544. *See also* Šalatuwar

Šalatuwar, 521–22, 540–42, 544. *See also* Šalatiwara

Šalil-la-miklum, 417

Šalim-Aššur, 541–42

Šallum, 242

Šallurtum, 193n4, 260, 583

Samanum, 260, 349

Šamaš, 242, 254, 279, 372, 583, 600–1, 603, 605, 620

Šamaš-hazir, 608

Šamiran, 432

Samium, 227, 229–30, 244

Sammetar, 372

Samsi-Addu (also Šamši-Adad I), 10–11, 34, 270n331, 273, 318–21, 322–30, 333–34, 338, 345n153, 348, 350–62, 364, 366–67, 374, 379, 387, 424, 426, 428, 439, 443, 456n275, 458, 462n308, 477, 506, 589, 592–93, 622

Samsi-Erah, 372

Samsu-ditana, 383, 479, 571, 628, 636–38, 640

Samsu-iluna, 227, 295–96, 381–84, 386, 389, 430, 478, 566–67, 571, 578, 580n54, 596n140, 605, 610, 615–26, 621, 625, 628

Samu-Addu, 356n193

Šamuha, 520

Šanahwitta, 545, 548n218. *See also* Šinahuttum

Sankhibra, 692

Sankhkara Mentuhotep (III), 861

Santorini, 4, 31–33

Sapiratum, 332, 364n219

Saqqara, 94, 686, 818, 866, 905, 910

Saqqara South, 710

Sar-i Pol-i Zohab, 432

Šar-kali-šarri, 135

Šarapunuwa, 535
Ṣarbat, 443
Sarenput I, 67, 697, 870
Sargon, 127, 132–33, 139, 166, 218,
    548n217
Sarikaya Palace, 34
Šarriya, 420, 477
Šarrum-Adad, 458
Šarrum-andulli, 293
Šašim, 459n293
Šat-Sin
    daughter of Sumu-El, 243
    wife of Sumu-El, 193n4
Satet, 669–70, 683, 879
Satuni, 440n181
Sauu, 736, 757, 761–62, 798n79. *See*
    also Mersa/Wadi Gawasis
Šayana, 237
Sea of Marmara, 497
Sealand, 286, 570–71, 573, 575–78,
    618, 624–26, 630–33, 636–44
Segerseni, 87
Šehna, 324, 332, 333n98, 351, 383–85,
    388–89, 428, 433, 437–38, 471,
    622–23. *See also* Šubat-Enlil;
    Tell Leilan
Sekhem-Senusret, 882. *See also*
    Lahun
Sekhemkara Amenemhat V, 892–93
Sekhemra-khuytawy Amenemhat
    Sobekhotep, 712, 894
Semin, 83
Semna, 708, 737, 742–43, 749, 755, 766
Semna Dispatches, 739, 749
Semna South, 743, 747
Semna West, 743
Šemti-šilhaki, 459n294

Senebi, 901
Senebsen, 901
Senebsumai, 884
Senebtisi, 905
Seneni, 60
Seniiqer, 79
Sennedjesu, 64
Sennuwy, 733
Senu, 906
Senusret
    butcher, 817
    doorkeeper, 817
    father of Amenemhat I, 689
    son of Ibener, 823
    I, 8, 98, 106, 665–67, 669–73, 675,
        686, 693–701, 707, 738, 756–57,
        759, 761, 766, 787–91, 811, 854,
        861, 864–65, 868, 870, 878–79,
        885, 891
    II, 8, 17, 678, 700–1, 704, 707, 759,
        803, 806, 813, 817, 880, 883–84,
        888, 907–9
    III, 8, 664–65, 693, 701–5, 708,
        710–11, 730, 742–43, 747–48,
        766, 795, 806–17, 819–21, 826,
        854, 861, 874, 885, 891–92,
        894–95, 899, 902, 904, 907–8
Senusretankh, 897
Šeplarpak, 463
Šepratu, 437
Serabit el-Khadim, 104, 817, 822–23
Serra East, 739, 745
Seth, 858, 885, 905
Setjau, 55
Setka, 65, 85, 88, 91, 95, 101
Sety I, 669n32
Sextus Julius Africanus, 5

Shaat, 728, 754

Shahrizor Plain, 432, 438–39

Shalfak, 744

Sharon Plain, 28, 814

Shatt el-Rigal, 87, 860

Shechem, 807, 813–14. *See also*
    Nablus; Tell Balatah

Shedet, 706–7, 879, 910. *See also*
    Medinet el-Fayum

Sheikh Farag, 92

Shephelah, 800

Shurab el-Gash, 765

Shushtar, 445n213

Ṣibat, 357n199. *See also* Zobah

Sidon, 791n58, 816, 826, 831–32

Sidu, 209–10. *See also* Enlil-bani

Sihathor, 901

Šihišnuman, 533n148

Šikšabbum, 358

Šilha, 414n15

Šilhaha, 452–57, 461n301, 462, 474,
    476, 481–82

Šilhak-Inšušinak, 447n222, 448,
    450n247, 452, 454, 456, 462,
    481–82

Ṣilli-Adad, 245, 256–57, 276, 278,
    459, 477

Ṣilli-Eštar, 274

Ṣilli-ibri, 436–37

Ṣilli-Sin, 429, 431, 478, 596–97

Sim'alite, 202, 273, 337, 339–41, 349,
    360–61, 363, 365, 366, 373–74,
    573, 593

Simah-ilane, 365–66

Šimalā, 547

Simanum, 158, 167, 175

Šimaški, 56, 121, 157 –58, 161, 417–18,
    444–57, 465, 474, 481–82

Simat-Eštar, 288

Simat-Ištaran, 154

Simbar-Šipak, 286

Simti-Šilhak, 274, 277, 458

Simurrum (or Šimurrum), 127n6, 152,
    159, 175–76, 409–10, 430–38,
    441–42, 476

Simut-wartaš, 460

Sin, 201, 251

Sin-gamil, 263–65

Sin-iddinam, 201n22, 233, 238, 245–54,
    257, 260, 268–70, 280, 282,
    422n81, 459, 477, 585, 608

Sin-iqišam, 233, 255–57, 272, 458–59, 477

Sin-iribam, 254–55, 257, 263–65,
    278n371

Sin-kašid, 193n4, 202, 244, 251–52,
    257, 259–67, 269, 292, 583, 585

Sin-magir, 198, 284–85, 289

Sin-muballiṭ, 264, 283, 348, 478, 571,
    578, 587–88, 589n98, 619, 628

Sin-talu, 236

Sin-tillati, 215

Šinah, 375

Šinahuttum, 543, 545. *See also*
    Šanahwitta

Sinai, 57, 59, 91, 102–4, 701, 756,
    784–86, 794, 804n101, 817,
    821–23, 830

Šinamum, 331

Sinjar, 332, 350–51, 356, 361–62,
    367–69, 371, 373, 375, 384–85,
    428, 443. *See also* Jebel Sinjar;
    Saggar, Mount

Sinuhe, 662, 665, 668, 673–75,
  692–93, 696, 789–90, 810,
  884–85
Sippar, 220, 230, 253n253, 271, 316,
  389, 423n87, 425n108, 431n138,
  472, 576, 582–84, 588, 589n98,
  592, 599n157, 600, 605, 608,
  610, 613, 619, 625, 637
Sippar-Amnanum, 420n66, 423,
  573, 635
Sippar-Yahrurum, 470, 573, 635
Šiqlanum, 420
Širtuh, 475, 479–80
Širuktuh, 422, 454n266, 456n275,
  458, 460–63, 465, 472, 477, 481
Sirwan River, 431–32, 434
Širwun, 331, 385
Sithathor, 908
Sithathoriunet, 908
Šitullum, 357, 361
Sitweret, 825
Ṣiwe-palar-huppak, 454n266, 460–67,
  470–73, 478
Sneferu, 665
Sobek, 706, 879, 909–11
Sobekemhab, 899
Sobekemsaf, 893
Sobekhotep IV, 710, 828. *See also*
  Khaneferra Sobekhotep IV
Sobeknakht
  of Dendara, 81
  of Elkab, 764
Sobekneferu, 8, 705, 911
Sothis (Sirius), 7, 664
Šu-ilišu, 198, 206, 210–11, 214, 244,
  416–18, 476

Šu-iliya, 414–15, 416n27, 422, 476
Šu-Ištar, 512n62
Šu-Kabta, 154
Šu-Ninkarrak, 208
Šu-Sin, 140, 156–59, 175, 177–79,
  203, 229, 409–11, 414–16, 437,
  445–46, 476
Subartu, 331–32, 337, 367, 378, 470
Subarum (or Šubarum), 512n62. *See
  also* Subartu
Šubat-Enlil, 273, 323–24, 328, 332,
  348, 350–51, 354, 362, 366,
  368–69, 371–72, 374–75, 383,
  428, 433, 437–38, 443n193,
  468, 470–71, 589, 622. *See also*
  Šehna; Tell Leilan
Šubat-Šamaš, 332. *See also* Hanzat
Šubram, 372
Ṣubutu. *See* Ṣibat
Sud, 213, 239, 242n200, 271
Šuda, 332
Suez, Gulf of, 756
Suhum, 332, 350, 354–55, 359, 361,
  364, 366, 368–69, 378, 382–83,
  386, 424, 426, 428, 466, 589,
  593, 623, 634
Šulgi, 126–27, 130–31, 134, 140, 142n34,
  143, 148–52, 154–55, 171, 173, 175–
  78, 180–81, 219, 223, 229, 265, 408
Šulgi-dan, 236
Šulgi-simti, 154–55
Sumenu, 910–11
Sumer, 121–22, 126, 133, 136, 138–40,
  142, 147, 171–72, 204–6, 217,
  220–21, 225, 231, 293, 567, 585,
  595, 599, 601, 618–19

Sumu-abum, 193n4, 196, 236, 243–44, 579–82, 585
Sumu-binasa (or Sumu-kanasa), 243–44, 262
Sumu-El, 193n4, 199n16, 201, 203, 235–38, 240, 242–44, 270
Sumu-epuh, 389n307
Sumu-la-El, 236, 240, 244, 253, 260, 477, 571, 578–84, 588, 589n98, 601, 619, 627, 632, 644
Sumu-Yamam, 321, 349–51, 360
Šunuhru-Ammu, 381
Šuppi-ibra, 535
Ṣuprum, 319, 349, 351n172, 360
Šurnat, 380
Šuruhtuh, 437
Šuruppak, 239–40. *See also* Fara
Šuruš-kin, 208
Susa, 122, 139, 149, 159, 161, 167–68, 231n145, 409–10, 416–17, 419, 444–46, 449–53, 455–57, 459, 461, 463–67, 471n355, 473–83, 601–2, 642
Šušarra, 324, 331, 358–59, 433, 437, 442–43. *See also* Tell Shemshara
Susiana Plain, 139, 167–68, 409–10, 445, 452
Šušši, 571
Sutium, 266, 282
Šutruk-Nahhunte, 419

Ṭabatum, 332, 382. *See also* Tell Ṭaban
Tadmur, 333. *See also* Palmyra
Tahišra, 533n148
Talhayum, 332, 372
Talia, 533n148
Talwahšušara, 535

Talyahum, 444
Tan-Ruhurater, 416–17, 446–50, 452, 454, 476
Tan-uli, 474, 479–82
Tar-dunni, 440
Tarnip, 424
Tatta, 473, 478
Taurus Mountains, 331, 391, 539, 544, 798
Tawananna, 527
Tawiniya, 526n124, 543
Tebadda, 453
Tefreret, 103
Teheš-atal, 436
Tel Aphek, 831
Tel Ifshar, 27–28, 791n58, 801–2, 806, 811n134, 816n158, 825
Tel Kabri, 27, 29–30
Tel Lachish, 26, 31–33
Tel Nami, 27
Telepinu, 638
Tell al-Hawa, 326
Tell al-Laḥm, 229n134. *See also* Kisig
Tell al-Mishrifeh, 333. *See also* Qatna
Tell al-Munbaqa, 332. *See also* Yakaltum
Tell al-Rimah, 324, 332, 433, 437, 443, 598. *See also* Qaṭṭara
Tell Abu Sheeja, 231. *See also* Pašime
Tell Arbid, 326, 333n98
Tell Arqa, 315, 787n36, 788n44, 829, 831. *See also* Irqata
Tell Ashara, 325, 332. *See also* Terqa
Tell Asharneh, 796. *See also* Tjemepau; Tunip
Tell Atchana, 332. *See also* Alahtum; Alalakh

Tell Balatah, 814. *See also* Nablus; Shechem
Tell Barri, 332. *See also* Kahat
Tell Beit Mirsim, 12
Tell Bi'a, 325, 332. *See also* Tuttul
Tell Brusti, 409
Tell ed-Der, 579
Tell el-Ajjul, 26, 31
Tell el-Burak, 27–29, 328, 832–34
Tell el-Dab'a, 16–19, 21–22, 26–29, 31, 33, 35, 66, 92, 781, 800, 806, 816n158, 821, 824, 829, 832, 834–35, 880, 894. *See also* Avaris
Tell el-Hayyat, 26, 28–32
Tell el-Hesi, 12
Tell el-Yahudiya, 805n104, 829
Tell et-Taalé, 808n119
Tell Fadous-Kfarabida, 831
Tell Hammam et-Turkman, 326
Tell Hariri, 320. *See also* Mari
Tell Ibrahim Awad, 59, 781n4
Tell-i Malyan, 445. *See also* Anšan
Tell Jokha, 204. *See also* Umma
Tell Khaiber, 639, 641n351
Tell Kunara, 442
Tell Leilan, 273, 324, 332, 369, 433, 437–38, 622. *See also* Šehna; Šubat-Enlil
Tell Meskene, 332. *See also* Emar
Tell Muhammad, 577n40, 634
Tell Sakka, 328, 380, 381n280, 831
Tell Senkereh, 226. *See also* Larsa
Tell Shemshara, 324, 331, 409, 426, 433, 437, 439, 442–43, 458, 460, 462, 483. *See also* Šušarra
Tell Shishin, 332, 422n82, 423. *See also* Al-Kapim

Tell Ṭaban, 332. *See also* Ṭabatum
Tell Taya, 325, 351n169
Tell Yassir, 592n114. *See also* Malgium
Tem, 858, 861
Tem-sanit, 456
Temti-Agun
    I, 452–55, 457, 464n321, 477
    II, 460–61, 471–74, 478, 480n381
Temti-halki, 474, 479–82
Temti-hiša-haneš, 461
Temti-Rappa, 482n390
Temti-raptaš, 474–75, 479–80
Tepe Bormi, 445. *See also* Huhnuri
Tepe Surkhegan, 445n213
Terqa, 313n6, 316, 323, 325, 332–33, 349, 360–61, 363, 381–83, 386, 430, 622–23, 634. *See also* Tell Ashara
Tetep'-mada, 453n263
Teti, 818n169
Thebes, 55, 58–59, 61, 66, 71, 75–76, 79–81, 83–85, 87–88, 92, 94–97, 99, 101, 106, 682–83, 686, 688, 693, 699, 709, 712, 732, 767, 784, 818, 824, 830, 855–59, 866, 878, 893–94, 900–1, 911–12
Thinis, 76, 86, 89–90, 97–98
Tiburziya, 526n123
Tidnum, 156, 178
Tigris River, 9, 122, 132, 229, 247, 249, 268, 274, 278n374, 284n406, 314, 318–19, 324, 327, 331, 333, 335, 340, 346, 350–51, 353–54, 356–59, 367, 371, 374, 379, 385, 388, 410, 424, 428–30, 444, 462, 466–70, 472, 483, 567, 587, 589, 592, 594, 597–99, 628–32, 641–42

Tigunanum, 331, 350, 353n182, 388, 439

Till-abnu, 383, 438

Tilmen Höyük, 332

Timna, 58

Tirigan, 140

Tišpak, 251, 414–16, 419, 429n123, 467

Tjauty
of Coptos, 80, 84
of Hu, 80

Tjemepau, 796. *See also* Tell Asharneh; Tunip

Tjemerery, 89

Tjemhemau, 784

Tjetji, 99–100

Tod, 666, 669, 671–72, 675, 698–99, 788, 798–800, 803, 879

Transjordan, 804n101

Tuba, 389

Tuhtuhan(n)um, 536–37

Tulul Khatab, 429

Tumliya, 533

Tunib-Teššub, 388

Tunip, 796. *See also* Tell Asharneh; Tjemepau

Tur Abdin, 331, 444

Turam-ili, 164n82

Tuttul, 260, 313n6, 314, 316, 325, 332–34, 338, 342, 349, 351n172, 354n186, 360, 364, 381, 599n157. *See also* Tell Bi'a

Tutub, 420

Tuz Khurmatu, 326

Tyre, 794

Ubar-Adad, 264

Ubaya, 242

Ubrabium, 260

Udannu, 633, 636

Ugarit, 315–17, 332, 371, 388, 392, 800, 815. *See also* Ras Shamra

Uhna, 538, 543

Ukal, 455

Ukhhotep, 789, 797, 902–4

Ulam-Buriaš, 571, 643

Ulama, 540, 542

Ullaza, 704, 795, 808–9, 814

Umm al-Wawiya, 230n143, 232, 260

Umma, 125, 129, 154, 159n71, 163, 204. *See also* Tell Jokha

Upi, 429, 467, 469, 594. *See also* Opis

Upper Egypt, 62, 64, 71, 75–76, 79–81, 84, 88–90, 93, 97, 99, 676, 678, 732n9, 750–52, 759, 761, 764, 766, 806, 867, 877–78, 900, 903, 910

Uprapûm, 573

Ur, 56, 121–22, 125–36, 138, 140–80, 182, 190–91, 195–99, 201–6, 208–10, 214, 217–22, 224, 226, 228–32, 234, 236–37, 240, 245–50, 252n2, 254–57, 268, 270–71, 275–76, 281, 287, 289, 292, 295, 310, 317, 321, 351, 408–10, 414, 416, 431, 433, 442, 444–48, 451, 476, 483, 508, 510, 566–67, 578, 595–96, 599, 610–13, 615–16, 618, 639, 641, 644

Ur-dukuga, 272–73

Ur-Ninurta, 198, 213, 224–26, 230, 239, 241, 244

Ur-Utu, 608, 635

Ura, 704, 794

Urbilum, 331, 358. *See also* Arbela
Urdukuga, 198
Ur-Namma, 122, 127, 131, 136, 138n27,
    140–49, 155, 166, 171, 175, 220,
    265, 444, 595n137, 603
Ur-Ningišzida, 419–20, 477
Ur-Ninmarki, 416n30, 419–20, 476
Uronarti, 739, 742–43
Uršu, 544, 548n217
Ursum, 332, 354n183, 391
Uruk, 127, 135–36, 139, 142, 159,
    170–71, 191, 193n4, 202–3, 209,
    214, 217, 220, 224–26, 237, 239,
    243–44, 251, 257–67, 269–70,
    278n371, 281–83, 287, 296, 421,
    458n292, 583, 585, 587–88, 592,
    599n157, 616–18, 626, 628, 633,
    641
Urukug, 640
Uṣarpara, 237, 264, 266, 283
Ušašum, 415–18
Usumu, 536
Uṣur-awassu, 417n33, 418–19, 476
Uṣur-ša-Ištar, 541–42
Utu, 172, 191, 195n7, 228, 232n154,
    233, 235n161, 245–47, 249, 253,
    268, 276n368, 278, 279n377, 637
Utu-hegal, 139–40

Waburtum, 409
Wadi Allaqi, 739
Wadi el-Hol, 824
Wadi el-Hudi, 817
Wadi Faynan, 57
Wadi Gasus, 761, 798n79
Wadi Hammamat, 87, 689, 785, 817,
    821–22, 835

Wadi Maghara, 822
Wadi Tumilat, 92
Wadjet, 903
Wah, 863–64
Wah-sut, 702, 880
Wahibra Ibiau, 901
Wahka II, 903
Wahšušana, 520, 526n124, 540–43
Walls of the Ruler, 692, 791
Wanuzal, 533n148
Warad-Nanna, 288n429
Warad-Sin, 195n6, 201, 203, 233,
    256n275, 263, 272–81, 284 289,
    291, 459, 477
Warassa, 250–51, 420, 477
Waršama Palace, 33–34, 519, 529, 546
Warûm, 414
Wašhaniya, 526n124, 529n134, 543
Wawat, 90, 99, 728, 754, 764
Webat-sepet, 754
Wegaf, 25, 712–13
Welkiša (or Pelkiša), 461
Wenamun, 789
Weni, 62, 75–76
Wepwawet, 901
Western Desert, 65, 79–80, 89, 92,
    97–99, 101–2
Wiyušti, 546
Wušunalam, 541

Yabliya, 319, 332, 364n219, 423n87, 428
Yadih-abum, 381–83, 624
Yagid-Lim, 319, 349
Yahdun-Lim, 260, 319–21, 325, 327,
    333–34, 340–41, 349–51, 354–55,
    360–61, 363–66, 382, 424
Yahrurum, 573

Yakaltum, 332, 356, 380. *See also* Tell
  al-Munbaqa
Yakun-Ašar, 384, 622n262
Yam, 55, 65, 102, 748
Yamhad, 296, 329, 332, 339, 342–43,
  346–47, 350, 353, 357, 359–60,
  363–64, 367, 370–71, 373, 379,
  381n219, 384, 388–89, 391,
  594, 622
Yaminite, 202, 242n198, 259, 264,
  337–39, 341, 349, 359, 362, 366,
  368–69, 373–74, 573, 581n60
Yamṣium, 227, 244. *See also* Emṣium
Yamutbal, 202, 273, 332, 337, 380,
  421, 572. *See also* Emutbal
Yapa-šemu-abi, 315
Yapah-Sumu-abum, 381
Yapṭurum, 332, 350
Yarîh, 573
Yarim-Addu, 293
Yarim-Lim
  of Alalakh, 389
  I, 296, 323, 346, 370, 389n307
  II, 389
  III, 389
Yasim-Addu, 293
Yasmah-Addu, 273, 320n39, 325, 338,
  347, 350, 354–57, 360–61, 363,
  443, 589
Yassıhöyük, 508
Yawi-ila, 372
Yeškit-El, 293
Yorghan Tepe, 331. *See also* Gasur;
  Nuzi
Yussan (or Yassan), 332, 368–70,
  384

Zab River, 358
  Lower, 358–59, 439
Zab(b)an, 430–31, 433n144
Zabalam, 224
Zabaya, 220, 227, 229–30, 232,
  244–46
Zabšali, 157, 445
Zagros Mountains, 133, 135, 146, 155,
  157–58, 167, 179, 310, 322, 331,
  333, 340, 358–59, 391, 409–10,
  430–31, 435, 438, 444, 450,
  462, 466, 470, 483, 570, 573,
  621
Zalmaqum, 332, 350, 359, 362, 366,
  373, 378, 444
Zalpa, 326, 548n217
Zalpuwa, 537–38, 543–45
Zalwar, 327, 332, 356, 391, 544
Zambiya, 198, 272
Zarethan, 784n17
Zaziya, 438
Zazum, 438
Zewiya valley, 432
Zibnatum, 266, 283
Zidanum, 450
Zikru, 242
Zimri-Addu, 293–94
Zimri-Lim, 261n294, 280, 293–94,
  312n2, 320n39, 321–27, 331,
  334, 338–46, 349n164, 353,
  355, 360–73, 375–79, 381–87,
  428–29, 438–39, 444, 456n275,
  463–64, 466–70, 478, 506, 591,
  593–95, 597–98
Zobah, 357n199. *See also* Ṣibat
Zuzu, 545